THE YEAR'S WORK IN
MODERN LANGUAGE
STUDIES

THE
YEAR'S WORK IN
MODERN LANGUAGE
STUDIES

GENERAL EDITOR
STEPHEN PARKINSON

SECTION EDITORS

LATIN, ROMANCE LINGUISTICS,
FRENCH, OCCITAN
BRIAN J. LEVY, M.A., PH.D.
Reader in French,
University of Hull

SPANISH, CATALAN, PORTUGUESE,
GALICIAN, LATIN AMERICAN
STEPHEN PARKINSON, M.A., PH.D.
Lecturer in
Portuguese Language and Linguistics,
University of Oxford

ITALIAN, ROMANIAN, RHETO-ROMANCE
JOHN M. A. LINDON, M.A.
Professor of Italian Studies,
University College London

CELTIC
DAVID A. THORNE, M.A., PH.D.
Reader in Welsh,
University of Wales, Lampeter

GERMANIC
DAVID A. WELLS, M.A., PH.D.
Professor of German,
Birkbeck College, University of London

SLAVONIC
PETER J. MAYO, M.A., PH.D.
Formerly Senior Lecturer in
Russian and Slavonic Studies,
University of Sheffield

VOLUME 59
1997

Published by
W. S. MANEY & SON LTD
for the
MODERN HUMANITIES RESEARCH ASSOCIATION
1998

The Year's Work in Modern Language Studies may be ordered from the Hon. Treasurer, MHRA, King's College London, Strand, London WC2R 2LS, England.

ISBN 0 901286 94 X

ISSN 0084-4152

Printed in Great Britain by
W. S. MANEY & SON LIMITED
HUDSON ROAD   LEEDS LS9 7DL

CONTENTS

PREFACE

This volume surveys work, published in 1997, unless otherwise stated, in the fields of Romance, Celtic, Germanic, and Slavonic languages and literatures. This is the first volume to be edited by Stephen Parkinson, who continues in his role as editor of the Spanish, Catalan, Portuguese, Galician, and Latin American sections. Up-to-date information on *YWMLS*, including current contributors and abbreviations lists, is now available on the MHRA's WWW site (http://www.MHRA.org.uk/YWMLS/).

The attention of users is drawn to the lists of abbreviations at the end of the volume. An asterisk before a title indicates that the item in question has not been seen by the contributor.

Many authors, editors, and publishers supply review copies and offprints of their publications. To these we and our contributors are grateful and we invite others to follow their example, especially in the case of work issuing from an unusual or unexpected source of publication. We would ask that, whenever possible, items for review be sent directly to the appropriate contributor rather than to one of the editors. However, items relating to a number of fields are best sent to one of the editors who will then take appropriate steps.

The compilation of a contribution to the volume, especially in the field of the major languages and periods of literature, is a substantial research task requiring wide-ranging and specialized knowledge of the subject besides a huge reading effort accompanied by the constant exercise of critical judgement. Our thanks are due both to the authors and to the many other individuals and institutions who have contributed in one way or another to the making of this volume. They include the various institutions that have made research grants to contributors, the compiler of the name index, Peter Mayo, Mrs Lan Ngoc Nguyen for her secretarial services, and our printers, W. S. Maney & Son Ltd, amongst whose staff we would single out Michael Gallico, Julia Silk, and Liz Rosindale with whom, as ever, it has been a pleasure to collaborate.

5 December 1998   S.R.P., B.J.L., J.M.A.L., D.A.T., D.A.W., P.J.M.

1

LATIN

I. MEDIEVAL LATIN

By C. J. McDonough,
Professor of Classics, University of Toronto

1. General

Richard Sharpe, *A Handlist of the Latin Writers of Great Britain and Ireland before 1540*, Turnhout, Brepols, xxxvii + 912 pp., offers an indispensable record of works by more than two thousand authors from the 5th to the 16th century. Peter Dronke, *Sources of Inspiration. Studies in Literary Transformations, 400–1500*, Rome, Edizioni di storia e letteratura, 401 pp., includes three new items: 'The Return of Eurydice' (281–92), presents a critique of scholarship on the poem *Parce continuis*; 'Gli dei pagani nella poesia latina medievale' (243–62), discusses the treatment of pagan gods by Hildebert, Bernardus Silvestris and Peter of Blois; 'Amour sacré et amour profane au moyen âge latin: témoignages lyriques et dramatiques' (375–93), reviews poems from the 10th to the 12th cs, including *O admirabile Veneris idolum* and *Febus abierat*. P.-A. Deproost, 'L'épopée biblique en langue latine. Essai de définition d'un genre littéraire', *Latomus*, 56:14–39, reviews the state of the question with attention to late antique authors, before he suggests directions for further research. D. R. Bradley, 'Some textual problems in the "Getica" of Jordanes', *Hermes*, 125:215–30, revisits ten passages. A. Keely, 'Arians and Jews in the *Histories* of Gregory of Tours', *JMH*, 23:103–15, shows how prejudicial imagery and conversion accounts concerning minority groups helped to create a sharper sense of self identity for Catholics. T. O'Loughlin, 'Adomnán and Arculf: the case of an expert witness', *JMLat*, 7:127–46, reassesses information from Adomnán and Bede to illuminate the role of Arculf in the narrative and structure of the *De locis sanctis* Book 1. A. Peyronie, 'Le mythe de Thésée pendant le moyen âge latin', *Médiévales*, 32:119–33, finds the episode of the labyrinth dominant in glosses on Latin poetry, in the *Mythographi Vaticani*, in illustrations and in church wall paintings. B. Obrist, 'Wind diagrams and medieval cosmology', *Speculum*, 72:33–84, includes selected poetic texts to illuminate conceptions concerning the corporeal world's structure and the role of the winds in relation to God. *Media Latinitas. A Collection of Essays to Mark the Occasion of the Retirement of L. J. Engels*, ed. R. A. I.

Nip, H. van Dijk, E. M. C. van Houts et al. (Instrumenta Patristica, 28), Turnhout, Brepols, 1996, xii + 408 pp., includes many relevant pieces: L. J. Engels, 'Van den vos Reynaerde and *Reynardus vulpes*: A Middle Dutch source text and its Latin version, and vice versa' (1–28), studies the vernacular source texts of the Latin translation; H. van Dijk, 'Jacob van Maerlant and the Latinitas' (51–58), examines the poet's appropriation of Alexander the Great, Arthur, and Charlemagne from various Latin texts; E. van Houts, 'Medieval Latin and historical narrative' (75–87), looks at historical writing that issued from a collective, not from just one individual; C. H. Kneepkens, 'There is more in a biblical quotation than meets the eye: on Peter the Venerable's letter of consolation to Heloise' (89–100), investigates the exegesis of several scriptural quotations to unearth a subtext on the topic of the humility of the Christian scholar; D. Luscombe, 'Peter Abelard and the arts of language' (101–16), shows how Abelard's preference for the plain style when teaching is linked with his theory of signification in his teaching of logic; G. Orlandi, 'Some afterthoughts on the *Carmen de Hastingae Proelio*' (117–27), reassesses his previous textual emendations and offers some new ones; P. G. Schmidt, 'Zur Geschichte der mittellateinischen Philologie' (147–57), surveys the scholarship from the 15th to the 18th c. that concentrated on works written in the 13th and 14th; P. Binkley, '*Tractatus novarum decretalium*; verses on the *Liber Extra*' (187–91), edits a satire on the venality of the Papal court; B. Ebels-Hoving, 'William of Tyre and his patria' (211–16), examines William's *Chronicle* to understand his distinctive concept of *patria*; W. P. Gerritsen, 'Exculpating Æneas. An Ovidian argument in Maerlant's *History van Troyen*' (217–21), notes Maerlant's paraphrase of the story about Theseus taken from Ovid's *Metamorphoses* and the alterations he made to the original; A. Hilhorst, 'The Escorial fragment on the Heavenly Jerusalem' (223–28), offers a new edition and discussion of a work cast in question and answer form on biblical subject matter; M. de Jong, 'The emperor Lothar and his *bibliotheca historiarum*' (229–35), analyses the use of the word *historia* in the correspondence between Hrabanus Maurus and Lothar I to show that the phrase referred to his collection of commentaries on the books of the Old Testament; F. A. van Liere, 'Andrew of St Victor and the Gloss on Samuel and Kings' (249–53), cites evidence to show that Andrew used the *Glossa ordinaria* extensively and that therefore the latter must have been composed before 1147; C. A. A. Linssen, 'Latinitas Limburgensis, a triptych' (255–62), assembles data on Latin schools and Latin instructors in Limburg up to the reformation; L. M. de Ruiter, 'An indispensable manuscript for the reconstruction of the textual tradition of Hugh of Fleury's *Historia ecclesiastica*: MS

Vat. Reg. lat 545' (329–33), studies Hugh's working manuscript, the author's second draft and the only one that preserves the complete letters to Ivo of Chartres and Adela of Blois; J. B. Voorbu and M. M. Woesthuis, 'Editing the "Chronicon" of Helinand of Froidmont: the use of textual witnesses' (345–54), illustrate the difficulties in applying the principles of textual criticism in a way that does not obscure preceding or later textual traditions; and W. C. M. Wüstefeld, 'A medieval combination: an unpublished fragment of the *Geta* by Vitalis of Blois and Maximian's *Elegies* and its place in the text tradition (Utrecht, Museum Catharijneconvent, ms. BMH Warm h fragm 234G10)' (365–74), explains the presence of the two texts in a single manuscript before he edits the verses, M. Gorman, 'A critique of Bischoff's theory of Irish exegesis. The commentary on Genesis in Munich Clm 6302 (Wendepunkte 2)', *JMLat*, 7:178–233, contests the hypothesis that many biblical commentaries in 9th-c. MSS were composed in Ireland or in Irish institutions on the Continent between 600–800, before he presents an edition of a commentary on Genesis. Vittore da Tunnuna, *Chronica. Chiesa e Impero nell' età di Giustiniano*, ed. Antonio Placanica, Florence, SISMEL, lxiv + 142 pp., has a full introduction with emphasis on the manuscript tradition and previous editions. A. Putter, 'Sources and backgrounds for descriptions of the Flood in medieval and renaissance literature', *SP*, 94:137–59, lists the literary motifs of a tradition that goes back to Ovid's *Metamorphoses* and Avitus, *De spiritalis historiae gestis* Book 4. P. M. Bertrand, 'La Fortune mi-partie: un exemple de la symbolique de la droite et de la gauche au moyen âge', *CCMe*, 40:373–79, draws on literary and iconographic material to illustrate the theme.

2. ANGLO-SAXON

M. McKie, 'The origins and early development of rhyme in English verse', *MLR*, 92:817–31, argues that Christian and Hiberno-Latin transmitted rhyme to OE and to other vernacular literatures, before considering the factors that led to its emergence in Latin hymns and sequences. T. D. Hill, 'The *Liber Eliensis* "Historical Selections" and the Old English *Battle of Maldon*', *JEGP*, 96:1–12, concludes that the *Liber Elienses* provides an independent account of the battle that confirms the broad outlines of the OE narrative, while P. Pulsiano, '"Danish men's words are worse than murder": Viking guile and *The Battle of Maldon*', *ib.*, 13–25, draws upon Sven Aggesen's *Brevis historia regum Dacie* and the 14th-c. chronicle *Flores Historiarum* to suggest that a tradition of Danish verbal manipulation may stand behind the word *lytegian*. S. Gwara, 'Further Old English scratched glosses and merographs from Corpus Christi College, Cambridge MS 326

(Aldhelm's *Prosa de Virginitate*)', *ESt*, 78 : 201–36, edits dry-point glosses that shed light on the grammatical and semantic interests of native readers, before he analyses their transmission in Brussels, Bibliothèque royale, MS 1650 and Oxford, Bodleian Library, MS Digby 146. M. J. Toswell, 'The relationship of the metrical Psalter to the Old English glossed psalters', *ib.*, 297–315, finds the influence of the latter on the vocabulary of the former to be much less than expected, given the great number of MSS available to the translator. C. Fee, '*Judith* and the rhetoric of heroism in Anglo-Saxon England', *ib.*, 401–06, argues that the alteration of events in the vernacular work from those depicted in the Vulgate, especially the appropriation of female heroism by man, reflects specific cultural ideals. P. R. Kitson, 'Old English bird-names (1)', *ib.*, 481–505, cites literary works among the other records consulted for studying native and foreign bird fauna. J. F. Nieus, 'La passion de S. Géréon de Cologne (*BHL* 3446). Une composition d'époque ottonienne', *AB*, 115:5–38, sketches a chronology for the Latin literature of Cologne in attempting to locate the work among those written for patrons of the city's monasteries or for its bishops. P. Bertrand, 'La vie de Sainte Madelberte de Maubeuge. Édition du texte (*BHL* 5129) et traduction française', *ib*, 39–76, dates the hagiography between the 9th and 11th c., identifies sources, and constructs a stemma for the nine MSS. A. Corrêa, 'St Austraberta of Pavilly in the Anglo-Saxon liturgy', *ib.*, 77–112, analyses a blessing in two benedictionals from Christ Church, Canterbury, and traces the saint's cult in France before examining Anglo-Saxon liturgical collections in order to understand the development of her cult in England. C. E. Newlands, 'Bede and images of Saint Cuthbert', *Traditio*, 52:73–109, explores the role of Bede's prose *vita* in promoting Cuthbert's cult and in shaping his identity as a figure of unity and leadership within the English church. G. Wieland, '*Aures lectoris*: orality and literacy in Felix's *Vita Sancti Guthlaci*', *JMLat*, 7:168–77, detects signs that OE orality influenced Latin literacy and examines the techniques that privileged the former over the latter. *Anglo-Saxon Conversations. The Colloquies of Ælfric Bata*, ed. Scott Gwara, trans. David W. Porter, Woodbridge, The Boydell Press, 209 pp., contains 42 Latin texts about life within and outside the classroom; while D. W. Porter, 'Anglo-Saxon colloquies: Ælfric, Ælfric Bata and *De raris fabulis retractata*', *Neophilologus*, 81:467–80, claims that Oxford, St John's College, MS 154, represents a collection of school texts compiled by Ælfric Bata. G. R. Isaac, 'The date and origin of "Cædmon's Hymn"', *NMi*, 98:217–28, argues that the Northumbrian version of the hymn is a translation from Bede's *Historia ecclesiastica* 4. 24.

3. CAROLINGIAN

D. W. Lumsden, '"Touch no unclean thing": apocalyptic expressions of ascetic spirituality in the early Middle Ages', *Church History*, 66:240–51, classifies Haimo of Auxerre's commentary among works that developed an apocalyptic justification for the spiritual life of ascetics. M. Gorman, 'The commentary on Genesis of Claudius of Turin and biblical studies under Louis the Pious', *Speculum*, 72:279–329, shows how the aims and interpretive methods of Claudius differed from those of Wigbod, especially in departing from the practice of linking excerpts without regard for the Scriptural text itself. Id., 'The commentary on Kings of Claudius of Turin and its two printed editions (Basel, 1531; Bologna, 1755)', *FilM*, 4:99–131, surveys evidence from seven manuscripts to provide a clearer picture of the commentary's textual history. T. Head, 'Letaldus of Micy and the hagiographic traditions of the abbey of Nouaillé. The context of the *Delatio corporis S. Juniani*', *AB*, 115:253–67, argues that a monk, Constantine, instigated the writing of the *Delatio* in 994 to remind Poitevin ecclesiastical and secular magnates of the Council of Charroux. Teodulo, *Ecloga. Il canto della verità e della menzogna*, ed. Francesco Mosetti Casaretto, Florence, SISMEL, cxxviii + 61 pp., presents a full introduction that places the poem in its cultural and literary context, and a text with a facing Italian translation. J.-Y. Tilliette, 'Le retour du grand Pan. Remarques sur une adaptation en vers des "Mitologiae" de Fulgence à la fin du XIᵉ siècle (Baudri de Bourgueil, c. 154)', *SM*, 37, 1996:65–93, examines the poet's fidelity to and departures from his source to show how the discourse of myth served to express knowledge about the physical or moral worlds. F. M. Biggs, 'Unidentified citations of Augustine in Anglo-Saxon writers', *NQ*, 242:154–60, tracks down quotations by Bede and uses citations from Boniface and Alcuin to show that works by other authors circulated under Augustine's name. A. Galli, 'La fortuna di un traduttore sconosciuto: la versione della *Vita Basilii* ad opera di Eufemio e le leggende dello schiavo di Proterio e della morte di Giuliano l'apostata', *FilM*, 4:69–97, offers some philological considerations of Euphemius's translation (*BHL* 1023) and an analysis of its *Fortleben* with regard to two miracles, the first of which forms the plot of Hrotswitha's *Basilius* and is also elaborated in *Carmina Cantabrigiensia* 30a. L. G. G. Ricci, 'A proposito della paternità attoniana del *Polipticum*', *ib.*, 133–52, advances an interpretation that shows Atto to be the author of both the prefatory letter and of the work itself. J. Glenn, 'The lost works of Richer. The *Gesta Adalberonis* et *Vita Gerberti*', *ib.*, 319–24, uncovers the remnants of two works that antedate Richer's history from a codicological examination of the fifth quire of

Bamberg, Hist. 5. M. Innes, 'The classical tradition in the Carolingian renaissance: ninth-century encounters with Suetonius', *International Journal of the Classical Tradition*, 3:265–82, documents Einhard's linguistic and literary debts to Suetonius in constructing a new biography and shows the broader impact of the *Vita Caroli* upon contemporary intellectuals.

4. THE ELEVENTH CENTURY

A. B. Tscherniak, 'Flüchtige Bemerkungen zum "Carmen Harleianum"', *MJ*, 32:19–22, offers some textual and exegetical notes on a love poem. C. J. McDonough, 'Warner of Rouen and the monk from Mont Saint-Michel', *ib*., 23–51, identifies the Benedictine attacked by Warner as a certain Fromond and offers a new edition of the dialogue poem. A. Zissos, 'Marriage in the "Ruodlieb"', *ib*., 53–78, analyses three types of marriage, ranging from the good to the bad, all presented with didactic intent. M. Lapidge and P. S. Baker, 'More acrostic verse by Abbo of Fleury', *JMLat*, 7:1–27, discuss and edit four poems found in scientific MSS associated with Abbo, three of which are printed for the first time. J. Howe, 'La *Vita Leopardini* (*BHL* 4882), source pour la Paix de Dieu', *CCMe*, 40:175–80, examines the biography as a source for the life of the activist Aymo of Bourges. Sunhee Kim Gertz, *Poetic Prologues. Medieval Conversations with the Literary Past*, Frankfurt am Main, Klostermann, 282 pp., includes Hildegard of Bingen's *Scivias* and Alain of Lille's *De planctu naturae* to show how authors initiated conversations about their art by means of the prologue. M. Frassetto, 'Reaction and reform: reception of heresy in Arras and Aquitaine in the early eleventh century', *The Catholic Historical Review*, 83:385–400, examines the *Acta synodi Atrebatensis in Manicheos* of Gerard of Arras-Cambrai and the history and unedited sermons of Adémar of Chabannes for insights into the nature of religious dissent and orthodox beliefs. L. Violette, 'Le problème de l'attribution d'un texte rouennais du XIe siècle: les *Acta archiepiscoporum Rothomagensium*', *AB*, 115:113–29, infers from sources and chronological error that the records were produced by the clerks of the Cathedral and not by the monks of Saint Ouen. J. Cooke, 'Problems of method in early English lexicography: the case of the Harley Glossary', *NMi*, 98:241–51, uses London, BL, MS Harley 3376 to show the presence of alphabetical and other organizational features that are usually attributed to dictionaries of the 15th and 16th centuries. J. Demetracopoulos, 'The monk Gaunilo of Marmoutier: inventor of a philosophical example or latent user of an ancient tradition?', *SM*, 37, 1996:329–37, links the illustration of 'the lost island', used to contest Anselm's famous proof for the existence of

God, to an ancient tradition of Atlantis and favours Pliny's *Natural History* as the source. In two notes, R. Beare, 'Earl Godwin's son as a barnacle goose', *NQ*, 242:4–6, and 'Gerald of Wales on the barnacle goose', *ib.*, 459–62, explains a puzzling passage in a verse life by suggesting that Godwin's children are compared to birds. M. Staunton, 'Eadmer's *Vita Anselmi*: a reinterpretation', *JMH*, 23:1–14, analyses the themes of exile and Anselm's reluctant response to high office to argue that church tradition played a more important part in shaping a biography than previously acknowledged.

5. TWELFTH CENTURY

S. F. Kruger, 'Medieval Christian (dis)identifications: Muslims and Jews in Guibert of Nogent', *NLH*, 28:185–203, investigates three texts, the *Tractatus de incarnatione*, *Gesta Dei per Francos* and *De vita sua*, to show that the rejection of Muslim and Jewish bodies served to promote a sense of Christian cultural, social, and political unity. J. W. Baldwin, 'The image of the jongleur in Northern France around 1200', *Speculum*, 72:635–63, includes Peter the Chanter and Philippe the Chancellor as he explores how far minstrels in fictional works can illuminate the historical reality behind the term *ioculatores*. C. Burnett, 'The works of Petrus Alfonsi: questions of authenticity', *MAe*, 66:42–79, first establishes that the works generally attributed to Peter are the work of a single author, before he examines other texts linked to Peter to determine the extent of Peter's involvement in their production; two appendices catalogue the works and present an edition and translation of the prologue to the astrological tables. R. Jakobi, 'Die *recusatio* des Thiodamas', *Philologus*, 141:159–60, uncovers an idea concerning imperial panegyric in Sigbert of Gembloux's *Vita Lamberti* that derives from Statius *Theb.* 8. 285. Sarah Spence, *Texts and the Self in the Twelfth Century*, CUP, 1996, xi + 167 pp., examines the interrelationship of body, language and space in Abbot Suger's *De administratione* and in the autobiographical works of Guibert of Nogent and Abelard. M. Calabrese, 'Ovid and the female voice in the *De amore* and the *Letters* of Abelard and Heloise', *MP*, 95:1–26, detects in the work of Andreas Capellanus and in the correspondence a narrative pattern that reflects a movement from Ovid's *Ars amatoria* to the *Remedia amoris*, and suggests that both medieval authors drew upon Ovidian conventions to project the female voice; while E. Freeman, 'The public and private functions of Heloise's letters', *JMH*, 23:15–28, demonstrates how the spheres of autobiographical and rhetorical interests intersect to show that the boundaries of social categorization are not fixed. K. Reindel, 'Petrus Damiani bei Helinand von Froidmont und

Alberich von Troisfontaines', *DAEM*, 53:205–24, documents the presence of Peter's works in two authors. G. A. Zinn, Jr, 'Hugh of St. Victor's *De scripturis et scriptoribus sacris* as an *accessus* treatise for the study of the Bible', *Traditio*, 52:111–34, proposes that the work was a practical book designed to introduce students to the interpretive techniques, information, and resources needed for exegesis. A. Speer, 'The discovery of nature: the contributions of the Chartrians to twelfth-century attempts to found a *scientia naturalis*', *ib.*, 135–51, investigates Thierry of Chartres's *Tractatus de sex dierum operibus*, Adelard of Bath's *Quæstiones naturales* and the work of William of Conches to conclude that the intellectual motives for interest in the translation and reception of Aristotle's works lie in the 12th century. M. Okubo, 'La licorne et les prophètes: la cathédrale de Laon et la *Nativité Jhesu Crist* en prose', *Reinardus*, 10:125–36, suggests that the sculptures on the western façade of the cathedral and their literary representation in the prose work were inspired not by the *Speculum ecclesiae* of Honorius Augustodunensis, but by the *Physiologus* and the pseudo-Augustinian *Sermo contra Judæos, paganos et Arianos*.

6. Thirteeth Century

M. Reeve, 'Dating *Three Girls*', *FilM*, 4:319–24, finds on the basis of a palæographical inquiry into the history of capital ampersands that the work was probably composed in the 13th century. E. Feistner, '*Manlîchiu wîp, wîplîche man*. Zum Kleidertausch in der Literatur des Mittelalters', *BGDSL*, 119:235–60, examines the motif of cross-dressing in courtly narratives and in Latin literature from the perspective of gender theory and cultural anthropology. C. Brinker-von der Heyde, '*ez ist ein rehtez wîphere*. Amazonen in mittelalterliche Dichtung', *ib.*, 399–424, investigates Amazon lore in the chronicles of Adam of Bremen and Otto of Freising before she discusses the assimilation of Penthesilea, Camilla, and Thalistria into a new cultural context. G. Dinkova-Bruun, '*De virtutibus imitandis*: an anonymous Latin poem on the cardinal virtues', *JMLat*, 7:28–41, offers a first edition of a versification of Martin of Braga's prose treatise *Formula vitae honestae*, based on London, BL, MS Cotton Julius D. iii, together with a discussion of authorship and sources. G. Dona-vin, '"De sermone sermonem fecimus": Alexander of Ashby's *De artificioso modo predicandi*', *Rhetorica*, 15:279–96, underscores Alexan-der's application of classical rhetorical terms to preaching, before she examines how the treatise's awareness of the intended audience determined the form, aims, and proof of the sermon. *The Fables of 'Walter of England'. Edited from Wolfenbüttel, Herzog August Bibliothek, Codex Guelferbytanus 185 Helmstadiensis*, ed. Aaron E. Wright, Toronto,

PIMS, viii + 168 pp., edits 60 poems accompanied by interlinear glosses and prose commentaries. M. Brossard, 'Les pseudo-apôtres de Gérard Ségalelli, dans la *Chronique* de Salimbene de Adam: mise en scène d'une déviance', *Actes* (Montpellier), 51–63, analyses the organization of the discourse, arguments, and stylistic procedures used to create a deviant image of a religious movement. T. Haye, 'Das "Novale" des William Pore: ein Beitrag zur mittellateinischen Reisedichtung', *SM*, 37, 1996:387–442, offers a first edition of a hexameter poem uniquely transmitted in Cambridge, Corpus Christi College, MS 150.

7.   THE FOURTEENTH AND FIFTEENTH CENTURIES

M. Burns, 'Classicizing and medievalizing Chaucer: the sources for Pyramus' death-throes in the *Legend of Good Women*', *Neophilologus*, 81:637–47, claims that Chaucer drew, not on Geoffrey of Monmouth's *Historia regum Britanniae*, but on Ovid's *Metamorphoses*, *Ovide moralisé*, and *Waltharius*, among others. A. Galloway, 'Private selves and the intellectual marketplace in late fourteenth-century England: the case of the two Usks', *NLH*, 28:291–318, finds in the narrative writing of both men *apologiae* for their political and professional identities. M. O'Rourke Boyle, 'Chaff: Thomas Aquinas's repudiation of his *Opera omnia*', *ib.*, 383–99, sets Aquinas's withdrawal from work on his *Summa theologiae* in the context of epideictic rhetoric, in which St Nicholas's episcopal charity was figured as grain and Aquinas's theology as chaff. M. Okubo, 'Encore la licorne', *Actes* (Keio), 255–63, discovers that the attribution of small stature to the fabled creature played an essential part in Christological symbolism. L. Olson, 'Reading Augustine's *Confessiones* in 14th-c. England: John de Grandisson's fashioning of text and self', *Traditio*, 52:201–57, transcribes and examines interlinear and marginal annotations in Lambeth Palace MS 203, a 12th-c. copy of the *Confessions*, to reveal how the autobiography helped to transform the Englishman into an ideal spiritual guide and Christian bishop. C. A. Márquez, 'Un manuscrito de Beda, propiedad de Coluccio Salutati (ms. 56–1–26 de la Biblioteca Capitular y Colombina de Sevilla)', *BHR*, 59:613–20, describes a codex that includes Bede's exegetical works and sermons. K. Busby, 'Hagiography at the confluence of epic, lyric, and romance: Raimon Feraut's *La Vida de Sant Honorat*', *ZRP*, 113:51–64, demonstrates how the crossing of genres influenced the vernacular life, itself an adaptation of an anonymous Latin prose *Vita sancti Honorati*. P. Murgatroyd, 'The similes at Tito Strozzi *Erotica* 1. 3. 1ff.', *BHR*, 59:57–62, connects three similes applied to Anthia to images used by Propertius of his own mistress, Cynthia. Id., 'Landino, *Xandra* 2. 20: a

Renaissance paraclausithyron', *ib.*, 105–09, tracks the variations of classical models and the new directions taken by the poet to complain about his lover's infidelity. Id., 'Landino's *Xandra* 3. 3 and its ancient Latin models', *RenS*, 11:57–60, shows how Roman poetical texts were used to enhance the standing of Florence and the Medici. E. Beltran, 'Un panégyrique de saint Bernard par l'humaniste méconnu Charles le Sac', *BHR*, 59:67–85, edits from Paris, BN lat. MS 14117 a *Collatio in laudem Bernardi* that is based on the first three biographies of the saint and is full of models of classical Latinity. E. Rummel, 'Marineo Sículo: a protagonist of humanism in Spain', *RQ*, 50:701–22, documents one attempt to promote classical Latin in Spain and sketches Marineo's professional life as a university teacher and his relationships with fellow humanists. J. S. Pujalte, 'El hexámetro del *Aeneidos Liber XIII* de Maffeo Vegio y sus modelos clásicos (1)', *Latomus*, 56:382–95, establishes the close relationship of the supplement with the *Aeneid* on the basis of two metrical criteria.

II. NEO-LATIN

By C. A. Upton, *University of Birmingham*

1. General

Two bibliographies of Catholic books from the Renaissance period will prove invaluable. *English Catholic Books 1641–1700. A Bibliography*, ed. Thomas H. Clancy, Aldershot, Scolar Press, 1996, xviii + 215 pp., is a revised update of this work, with a useful index of dedicatees, as well as of authors and printers. The steadily growing study of emblem literature will be aided by *Corpus Librorum Emblematum. The Jesuit Series: Part One (A–D*, ed. Peter M. Daly and G. Richard Dimler, Montreal, McGill–Queen's U.P., lx + 229 pp., being the first vol. of a series that will ultimately contain 1,600 items in total, itself a testimony to the importance and popularity of emblem books in Catholic Europe. The rival claims of a number of textbooks of Latin grammar (not only those of Antonio de Nebrija) are considered by L. A. Hernández Miguel, 'La gramática Latina en Alcalá de Henares en el siglo XVI', *HL*, 45:319–47. Martine Furno, *Le Cornu Copiae de Niccolò Perotti*, Geneva, Droz, 1995, 251 pp., is an analysis of the lexicographical commentary on Martial (though much wider in its range of reference than this) begun by P. in the 1450s but not completed. Sadly, P.'s tireless classical scholarship was destined for almost immediate redundancy. The relationship between a printer and his author is the subject of J. de Landtsheer, 'The correspondence of Thomas Stapleton and Johannes Moretus: a critical and annotated edition', *HL*, 45:430–503, printing for the first time the 30 extant letters between the two men in the archives of the Plantin Moretus Museum in Antwerp, covering eight years in all. Much of the correspondence concerns the two *Promptuaria* (1589–91) of this English Catholic at the University of Louvain. *Reformation and Latin Literature in Northern Europe*, ed. Inger Ekrem et al., Oslo, Scandinavian U.P., 1996, 254 pp., is an offshoot of a longer term project to uncover the Latin literature of Scandinavia and relate it to the general European tradition. Many of the papers relate to the teaching of Latin at schools and universities, but there is some analysis of a number of prose and verse works from Norway and Sweden. There has hitherto been too little scholarly attention to the Latinity and use of language by neo-Latin writers. Two welcome articles attempt to reverse this trend. G. Tournoy and T. O. Tunberg, 'On the margins of Latinity? Neo-Latin and the vernacular languages', *HL*, 45:134–75, present a convincing argument that the classical Latin employed by Renaissance humanists stretches considerably wider than the narrow limitations of 'Ciceronian'. The authors illustrate the point with a number of appearances of later Latin vocabulary and usage by writers ranging across the 'republic of letters' from Lorenzo Valla to Charles de Bovelles. Even medievalisms are not uncommon. T. O. Tunberg, 'Ciceronian Latin: Longolius and others', *ib.*, 41:13–61, extends this study to examine the use of the language by so-called Ciceronians, in the light of Erasmus's condemnation of such slavish imitation. Even Christophorus Longolius (1488–1522), believed to have been the model for *Ciceronianus*, is found to be far from purely Ciceronian either in his syntax or vocabulary. It is argued here that only when the language ceased to be a developing and working tool for scholars did Latin become 'frozen' in terms of its models and usage. The challenges and difficulties of editorial work in this field are outlined by E. Rabbie, 'Editing neo-Latin texts', *Editio*, 10:25–48, and in *Editing Texts from the Age of Erasmus*, ed. Erika Rummel, Toronto U.P., 1996, xviii + 102 pp., a collection of six papers delivered at the annual conference on editorial problems at Toronto. It focuses on a number of the great editorial enterprises of recent years: the new editions of Erasmus, Thomas More, and Peter Martyr Vermigli.

2. DRAMA AND POETRY

Ijsewijn Vol. is a well-deserved Festschrift for the leading scholar in the field and the pioneer of neo-Latin studies. In effect this is an intercalatory issue of *HL*, with a number of important articles. Those dealing with the poetic tradition are singled out here. P. G. Schmidt (53–86) prints a Christian epic poem of some 1,000 lines on the Last Judgement, from the late 15th century; F. J. Nichols (152–70) examines the verse of two Greek exiles in Naples, Michael Marullus and Manilius Rhallus, and places them in the context of other exile verse from the Renaissance; C. Fantazzi (230–48) discusses the interrelation of Christian and classical themes in the *De Partu Virginis* of Jacobo Sannazzaro and its (acknowledged) debt to Giles of Viterbo, drawing on the writer's extensive work on the genesis and MS transmission of the poem; G. H. Tucker (264–91) provides the cultural and political background to a set of Virgilian *centos* by Lelio Capilupi of Mantua (1497–1560), and discusses contemporary reaction to a genre that could easily be dismissed as mere plagiarism. J. Binns (292–304) introduces us to the *Regina Literata* (1565) of Abraham Hartwell, a narrative account of Queen Elizabeth's visit to Cambridge University in the previous year. I. D. McFarlane (305–308) argues that much is yet to be done on the MSS and printed versions of George Buchanan's secular verse before an authoritative edition can be produced; finally, F. Rädle (309–23) examines the use of comedy in a number of 16th-c. academic plays in Germany, mostly from Jesuit colleges, where Latin drama continued to flourish. Marc Bizer, *La Poésie au Miroir. Imitation et Conscience de soi dans la Poésie Latine de la Renaissance*, Paris, Champion, 1995, 229 pp., may serve as an admirable introduction to the intertextuality of neo-Latin verse, concentrating on the works of the Pléïade, but ranging confidently over the whole field of classical and Renaissance texts. The practice of Renaissance verse-writing is also related to its theoretical background. J. Leonhardt, 'Classical metrics in Medieval and Renaissance poetry: some practical considerations', *CM*, 47:305–23, is a rare example of metrical analysis in the study of post-classical poetry. Issues of gender and the condition of women have come to dominate Renaissance studies in recent years, particularly in America. The field has included both the rediscovery of forgotten female writers and humanist views on women. Both are represented in *Sex and Gender in Medieval and Renaissance Texts: The Latin Tradition*, ed. Barbara K. Gold et al., Albany, NY State U.P., viii + 330 pp. This interesting collection of essays includes a study of the depiction of women in the English university drama in the age of Elizabeth and a comparison of the Greek and Latin verse of five Italian women humanists, as well as a discussion of the gendered writings of Cornelius Agrippa and the Scot, George Buchanan. There is some work elsewhere on the interrelations between English and Continental writers. N. J. Kinnamon, 'God's "scholer": the Countess of Pembroke's *Psalmes* and Beza's *Psalmorum Davidis ... Libri Quinque*', *NQ*, 242:85–88, argues that Mary Sidney Herbert used both the Latin and the English translation of the psalm paraphrases of Théodore de Bèze in creating her own version. The argument has implications for our assessment of the Countess of Pembroke's education. L. Bryan and R. C. Evans, 'Jonson's response to Lipsius' *On the Happy Life*', *ib.*, 241:181–82, follows up earlier work on Ben Jonson's reading of the works of Justus Lipsius. This study is based upon a set of L.'s works in Emmanuel College, Cambridge, which include J.'s MS annotations; a lyric entitled *Laus et Votum Vitae Beatae* seems to have struck a particular chord in the mind of the ageing playwright. *Unpublished Works by William Alabaster (1568–1640)*, ed. Dana F. Sutton (Salzburg Studies in English Literature: Elizabethan and Renaissance Studies, 126), Salzburg U.P., xxx + 178 pp, contains 50 previously unknown poems by the Elizabethan neo-Latin poet William Alabaster, from commonplace books and unpublished MSS. D. R. Carlson, 'Three Tudor epigrams', *HL*, 45:189–200, continues his work on the Latin verse of the early Tudor period with three uncollected examples of occasional verse: one is a lament on the poor quality of English printing by

Robert Whittinton (1534), the other two being by resident Italians, Andreas Ammonius and Giovanni Gigli. John Milton's Latin verse continues to attract attention. J. Shub, 'Argument and form in Milton's *First Prolusion*', *PQ*, 75:287–309, examines one of his earliest Latin poems; whilst E. Haan, 'John Milton among the neo-Latinists: three notes on *Mansus*', *NQ*, 242:173–76, finds in M.'s verse epistle to Giovanni Battista Manso verbal echoes from the poetry of John Leland, Angelo Poliziano's *Sylvae* and Petrarch's *Epistola ad Amicum Transalpinum*. Id., 'Milton and two Italian humanists: some hitherto unnoticed neo-Latin echoes in *In Obitum Procancelarii Medici* and *In Obitum Praesulis Eliensis*', *ib*., 176–81, goes on to detect further resemblances to elegies by Politian and another Italian humanist, Hieronymo Aleander; not an easy task, given the time-honoured imagery of such a genre. Id., 'Two neo-Latin elegists: Milton and Buchanan', *HL*, 46:266–78, finds further close parallels between the subject matter of M.'s elegies and those of George Buchanan, as well as specific verbal echoes. The reception of Politian's *Sylvae* is also the subject of L. M. Jerez, 'Las *Sylvae* de Poliziano comentadas por El Brocense', *ib*., 45:406–29, an examination of the commentary by Francisco Sánchez de las Brozas (called El Brocense) published in 1554. The commentary tells us much about the influence of Politian at the University of Salamanca by the middle of the 16th century. M. Steggle, 'A new Marprelate allusion', *NQ*, 242: 34–36, uncovers a previously overlooked reference to the controversial and widely reviled writings of the so-called 'Martin Marprelate' in a Cambridge University Library MS. The verses were produced by an unknown graduand in *c*.1590. The poetry of the Scottish proto-humanist Florence Wilson is discussed in *Stewart Style 1513–1542*, ed. Janet Hadley Williams, Tuckwell, East Linton, 1996, xvii + 323 pp. *Sir Francis Kynastons Übersetzung von Chaucers Troilus and Criseyde: Interpretation, Edition und Kommentar*, ed. Helmut Wolf (Bibliotheca Humanistica, 6), Berne–Frankfurt, Lang, 1996, 493 pp., is an edition of K.'s Latin verse translation of the medieval epic from the published text of 1635 and the more complete MS in the Bodleian Library, Oxford. It provides interesting evidence of the reception of Chaucer's poem in the 17th c. and the changes in the English language that had made a Latin version necessary. *Phineas Fletcher. Locustae vel Pietas Iesuitica*, ed. Estelle Haan (Supplementa *HL*, 9), Leuven U.P., 1996, lxxx + 151 pp., in addition to publishing F.'s 800 line poem, provides a useful synthesis of parallel poetry on the failed Gunpowder Plot of 1605, including the contributions of Thomas Campion, Michael Wallace and, of course, John Milton. A welcome development of recent years has been the reappearance of more familiar works in new editions. David Price, *Janus Secundus* (MRTS, 143), Tempe,

Arizona, 1996, x + 118 pp., returns to print one of the most read and influential lyric writers of the Dutch Renaissance. Likewise, *Le Zodiaque de la Vie (Zodiacus Vitae). XII Livres*, ed. Jacques Chomarat (THR, 307), 1996, 531 pp., is a new edition of the immensely popular and influential poem by Palingenius (Marzello Palingenio Stellato). The text in French and Latin is accompanied by a collection of contemporary commentaries and judgements on P. from the 16th to the 18th century. Study of the poetry of Battista Spagnuoli (called Mantuan) is generally limited to his pastoral verse or *Adulescentia*. It is therefore pleasing to find M. M. Castro, 'Baptistae Mantuani Contra Poetas Impudice Loquentes', *HL*, 45:93–133, containing the text of the elegaic poem first published in 1489, together with the informative commentary of his German contemporary, Sebastianus Murrho. *The Erotopaegnion: A Trifling Book of Love of Girolamo Angeriano*, ed. Allan M. Wilson, Nieuwkoop, De Graaf, 1995, 465 pp., is a new edition of the collection of some 200 love poems first published in 1512. They are not particularly original, or very interesting, but the frequent appearance of A. in anthologies attests to his popularity, and useful comparisons are made here with the verse of Secundus, Piccolomini and others. *HL* continues to make available previously unpublished or rare Latin works. I. Reineke, 'C. Silvani Germanici *In Pontificem Clementis Septimi Pont. Opt. Max. Panegyris Prima. In Leonis Decimi Pont. Max. Statuam Sylva*. Text mit Einleitung', *HL*, 45:245–318, presents, with introduction and commentary, two substantial hexameter panegyrics by S. on Pope Clement VII and Leo X. E. O'Connor, 'Panormita's reply to his critics: the *Hermaphroditus* and the literary defense', *RQ*, 50:985–1010, examines the use of an apologetic topos dating back to the verse of Catullus in defence of scurrilous or obscene poetry, called here the *pagina lasciva, vita proba* defence. Antonio Beccadelli of Palermo (commonly known as Panormita) discovered that such a defence was not sufficient protection in the light of the criticism he received. A curious, though far from uncommon, subject for Latin verse was disease, as is illustrated by D. Sacré, 'An imitator of Fracastorius's *Syphilis*: Gadso Coopermans (1746–1810) and his *Varis*', *HL*, 45:520–38. This didactic poem on smallpox was delivered at Franeker University in 1783 at the time when C. relinquished his rectorship, and shows a considerable and understandable debt, outlined here, to the most famous medical poem of them all. There is a useful discussion of this unusual sub-genre of Latin verse composition. The continued use of Latin into the modern era is illustrated by D. Velghe, 'Domien Cracco: an introduction to a nineteenth-century Latin poet', *ib.*, 46:363–80, presenting two poems by this priest and teacher from 1844. Both first appeared, surprisingly, in a newspaper, the *Journal des Flandres*.

Two studies highlight the use of drama as aspects of the ceremonies surrounding Renaissance court weddings. Mara R. Wade, *Triumphus Nuptialis Danicus. German Court Culture and Denmark: The Great Wedding of 1634* (WAB, 27), 1996, 444 pp., gives a complete account of the entertainments, both literary and musical, provided for the marriage of Prince Christian and Princess Magdalena Sibylle at Copenhagen in 1634, including the plays of Johann Lauremberg (1590–1658). M. Licht, 'Elysium: a prelude to Renaissance theater', *RQ*, 49: 1–29, similarly examines the literature that emerged from the wedding of Eleonora of Aragon and Ercole d'Este in Rome in 1473. L. uncovers the nature of the nuptial entertainments via the poems of Porcellio Pandonis and Emilio Boccabella, and sees the allegorical setting as leading to the full adoption of classical, humanist drama in the Rome of Paul II. *Pompeii Exitus Variazioni sul Tema dall'Antiquità alla Controriforma*, ed. Giorgia Brugnoli and Fabio Stok, Pisa, Ets, 1996, 259 pp., studies the 17th-c. drama *Pompeius* by Ludovico Aureli, together with other Italian Renaissance readings of the life of the Roman general. J. Devereux, 'Dromo: a minor dramatic character adapted for Protestant propaganda', *NQ*, 242: 27–29, shows a continuity in stock characterization in Protestant literature of the 1540s from the Latin plays of Nicholas Grimald and John Foxe (*Christus Redivivus* to *Christus Triumphans*) to Luke Shepherd's vernacular verse satire. *Een Theatergeschiedenis der Nederlanden. Tien Eeuwen Drama en Theater in Nederland en Vlaanderen*, ed. R. L. Erenstein, Amsterdam U.P., 1996, 276 pp., includes two essays of interest: K. Porteman (170–77) examines the use of neo-Latin drama by the Jesuits; and J. R. de Vroomen (80–85) discusses the *Grisellis* by Eligius Houcharius, performed at Ghent in 1512. L. Poelchau, 'Johannes Sommer (1542–1574)', *HL*, 46: 182–239, edits verse by the Transylvanian writer, including his *Colicae et Podagrae Tyrannis* of 1569, together with a German translation; the latter more of an essay in lyric metres than a piece of genuine theatre.

3. PROSE

There seems little doubt that the works of Erasmus still receive more attention than any Renaissance writer, whether for critical or textual study. The monumental *Opera Omnia Desiderii Erasmi* continues with vol. VII, 6, *Paraphrasis in omnes epistolas apostolicas: pars tertia*, ed. John J. Bateman, 330 pp., which includes Paul's Letter to the Hebrews, and two further letters by Peter and John; and vol. IX, 3, *Apologia ad Iacobum Fabrum Stapulensem*, ed. Andrea W. Steenbeek, Amsterdam, Elsevier, 1996, xxv + 250 pp., with an appendix covering further disputes with Jacques Lefèvre d'Étaples up to 1518. I. Bejczy,

'Erasmus becomes a Netherlander', *SCJ*, 28:387–99, looks at the evidence (particularly in the correspondence) for E.'s perception of his nationality, and decides that E. makes an increasing distinction between Netherlandish and German. The *Collected Works of Erasmus* project continues to produce important offshoots. *Erasmus on Women*, ed. Erika Rummel, Toronto U.P., 1996, viii + 251 pp., collects together a variety of Erasmian texts, though relying principally on the Colloquies, in their new CWE translations, organized under the traditional stereotypical headings of virgin, wife, and widow. The extracts illustrate not only E.'s views of women, but also general opinions in the Renaissance. There are many other studies of specific aspects of E.'s life and work, of which the following is only a brief selection. Cornelis Augustun, *Erasmus. Der Humanist als Theologe und Kirchenreformer*, Leiden, Brill, 1996, x + 376 pp., provides an introduction to E. in a series of articles, some of which have been published earlier. M. Verweu, 'Remarks on some so-called Erasmian correspondence', *HL*, 46:114–26, argues that in our readings of E.'s letters we should take more account of E.'s attitude towards the publication of such material. Comparison between original letters and those which E. had reworked for publication show important differences, additions and interpolations. In correspondence, as in poetry, authorial intention has a significant effect upon our interpretation. More theological concerns are reflected in Hilmar M. Pabel, *Conversing with God: Prayer in Erasmus' Pastoral Writing* (Erasmus Studies, 13), Toronto U.P., 264 pp. L. A. Homza, 'Erasmus as hero, or heretic? Spanish humanism and the Valladolid Assembly of 1527', *RQ*, 50: 78–118, discusses the examination of Erasmian texts by the Spanish Inquisition at Valladolid and finds a less clear-cut division between anti- and pro-Erasmian arguments, with implications for our assessment of E.'s influence in this country. A similar ambiguity is outlined by L. J. Taylor, 'The influence of humanism on pre-reformation Catholic preachers in France', *ib.*,119–35, which seeks to show the uncertain balance of theology and humanism in France at the close of the 15th century. The writings of Robert Gaguin receive some overdue attention by Sylvie Charrier, *Recherches sur l'œuvre latine en prose de Robert Gaguin (1433–1501)* (BLR, 35), 1996, 576 pp. A number of long-term projects have advanced this year. *Ioannis Calvini Opera Omnia* progresses, with two new editions of C.'s New Testament commentaries: vol. 19, *Commentarii in Epistolam ad Hebræos*, ed. T. H. L. Parker, 1996, xlvi + 272 pp., and *Commentarii in Evangelium Joannis. Prima Pars*, ed. Helmut Feld, Geneva, Droz, 416 pp. The huge undertaking to collect, edit and translate the letters (in Latin and vernacular languages) of the 16th-c. Dutch scholar Marnix van Sint-Aldegonde is attested by *Marnixi Epistolae: Die Briefwisseling van Marnix van Sint-Aldegonde. Een Kritische Uitgave*, ed. Aloïs Gerlo and Rudolf de Smut, Brussels U.P., 1996, 3 vols, 329 pp., covering the correspondence of 1558–81. The entire collection will run to five vols. A parallel project progresses with the *Correspondance de Théodore de Bèze: Tome 19 (1578)*, ed. Hippolyte Aubert et al. (THR, 304), 1996, xxxi + 280 pp., a collection of 46 further letters by the leading Huguenot writer of his age. The letters of a humanist at the court of Ferdinand and Isabella are the subject of E. Rummel, 'Marineo Siculo: a protagonist of humanism in Spain', *RQ*, 50: 701–22. M. was born in Sicily, but came to Salamanca in 1484 to promote humanist practice and a return to classicism at a time when Spain lagged far behind Italy. The letters illustrate M.'s teaching methods as well as his circle of friends. M. V. Ronnick, *NQ*, 241: 273–74, explores the reasons behind John Milton's hellenistically derived coinage, 'thaumasious', in his *Pro Populo Anglicano Defensio*. Id., 'Mugiles and Raphani: Milton's Pro Populo Anglicano Defensio Secunda, 142.11–13 and Catullus, 1.15.19.', *ib.*, 242: 181–82, finds an echo of the Roman poet in M.'s vitriolic denunciation of Thomas More.

Scholarly attention to Renaissance philosophy continues to grow. This is particularly evident in the need for the *Cambridge Translations of Renaissance Philosophical Texts*, ed. Jill Kraye, 2 vols, CUP, xiv + 281, xii + 315 pp., companions to the earlier *Cambridge History of Renaissance Philosophy*. They contain new translations and introductions to key texts by familiar figures like Poggio Bracciolini, Marsilio Ficino, and Juan Luis Vives, as well as to less well-known writers such as John Chase. Ficino is also covered by Maria Grazia Pernis, *Le Platonisme de Marsile Ficin et la Cour d'Urbin* (Études et Essais sur la Renaissance, 17), Paris, Champion, 261 pp. Kees Meerhoff and Jean-Claude Moisan, *Autour de Ramus: Texte. Théorie, Commentaire*, Cap-Saint-Ignace, Quebec, Nuit Blanche, 412 pp., consider this important linguist both in relation to his classical models such as Quintilian as well as to contemporaries like Rudolf Agricola and Nicolas Bérauld. The latter's discussions of the Roman historian Suetonius can be usefully compared with those of Politian in P. Galand-Hallyn, 'La Præelectio in Suetonium de Nicolas Bérauld (1515)', *HL*, 46: 62–93, reproducing B.'s text with French translation. There are a number of important essays in *Juste Lipse (1547–1606) en son Temps: Actes du Colloque de Strasbourg, 1994*, ed. Christian Mouchel (Colloques, Congrès et Conférences sur la Renaissance, 6), Paris, Champion, 1996, 534 pp., including a discussion of L.'s pronunciation of Latin and his use of Cicero. *Lipsius en Leuven*, ed. G. Tournoy et al. (Supplementa *HL*, 13), Leuven U.P., xiv + 387 pp., is principally a catalogue of the 1997 exhibition held at the Centrale Bibliotheek in Leuven to commemorate the 450th anniversary of his birth, although the extensiveness of the catalogue provides a more than adequate introduction to the scholar's work and influence. Work on the German Renaissance is increasingly evident. John L. Flood and David J. Shaw, *Johannes Sinapius (1505–1560): Hellenist and Physician in Germany and Italy* (THR, 311), x + 304 pp., show the important link between medicine and the study of Greek. Kurt Stadtwald, *Roman Popes and German Patriots: Antipapalism in the Politics of the German Humanist Movement from Gregor Heimburg to Martin Luther* (THR, 299), 1996, 237 pp., covers a range of antipapal literature, from theological work to pasquil, with useful analysis of the views of the Humanist circle surrounding Conrad Celtis. The links between humanism and politics are further explored by Thomas A. Brady Jr, *The Politics of the Renaissance in Germany: Jacob Sturm (1489–1553) of Strasbourg*, Atlantic Highlands, NJ, Humanities Press International, xiii + 280 pp., continuing his examination of the life and influence of perhaps the most important educationalist to emerge from Germany at this time. The interconnection between theological and humanist thought is explored by Lewis W. Spitz, *Luther and German Humanism*, Brookfield, VT, Variorum, 1996, x + 350 pp., a collection of essays, some previously published, on the growth and dissemination of humanism in Martin Luther's Germany. Evidence of less amicable relations between humanism and theology are found in *Johannes Cochlæus. Philippicae I–VIII*, ed. Ralph Keen (Bibliotheca Humanistica & Reformatica, 54), Nieuwkoop, De Graff, 1995, 2 vols, xxiii + 375, 297 pp., the first new edition of the work of this leading Catholic controversialist's attack on Philip Melanchthon since C.'s death in 1552. Athina Lexutt, *Rechtfertigung im Gespräch: Das Rechtfertigungsverständnis in den Religionsgesprächen von Hagenau, Worms und Regensburg 1540–41*, Göttingen, Vandenhoeck & Ruprecht, 1996, 299 pp., is an examination of the three colloquies in Germany, principally for the light they shed on contemporary arguments over the key issue of justification. S. Pearce, 'Nature and supernature in the dialogues of Girolamo Fracastoro', *SCJ*, 27:111–32, examines the three extant dialogues — *Turrius, Fracastorius*, and a third uncompleted work — and uncovers that synthesis of Aristotelian philosophy and scholastic theology so typical of Florentine Neoplatonism. Gerard B. Wegemer, *Thomas More on Statesmanship*, Washington DC, Catholic U. of America P., 1996, 262 pp., traces M.'s thought back to its Greek and Roman origins and finds more coherence and interconnectedness than modern scholars are inclined to admit. *Europäische Sozietätsbewegung und Demokratische Tradition*, ed. Klaus Garber and Heinz Wismann (Frühe Neuzeit, 26–27), Tübingen, Niemeyer, 1996, 2 vols, xviii + 947 pp., is a massive collection of essays on the official and unofficial 'academy' in early modern Europe, an institution that stretches educationally from high school and university to poetic circle, and geographically from Spain to Russia. The education of women, generally beyond the scope of any kind of academy, is discussed in *De Institutione Feminae Christianae: Liber Primus*, ed. C. Fantazzi and C. Matheeussen, Leiden, Brill, 1996, xxviii + 218 pp., a new edition (with new Latin text and English translation) of Vives's important and influential tract of 1523, written for the education of the English Princess, Mary Tudor. Similar interests are served by the *Declamation on the Nobility and Preeminence of the Female Sex*, ed. Albert Rabil, Chicago U.P., 1996, xxxii + 109 pp., presenting the Latin treatise by Cornelius Agrippa in a new translation with commentary, and arguing for its reassessment as an early attempt to challenge the prevailing orthodoxy of misogyny. Rebecca W. Bushell, *A Culture of Teaching: Early Modern Humanism in Theory and Practice*, Ithaca, Cornell U.P., 1996, xiii + 210 pp., examines the writings of a number of educational theorists, including Erasmus, Vives and Buchanan, and finds (not surprisingly) considerable slippage between theory and practice. The vast range of Francis Bacon's scientific and philosophical studies is reflected in a sympathetic and readable collection of newly commissioned essays: *The Cambridge Companion to Bacon*, ed. Markku Peltonen, CUP, 1996, xv + 372 pp., rounds up the usual experts in the field. *Francis Bacon. Philosophical Studies c.1611–1619*, ed. Graham Rees, OUP, 1996, cxvi + 503 pp., offers editions and translations of six of B.'s philosophical works in Latin; these include *De Viis Mortis, De Fluxu et Refluxu Maris* and *Descriptio Globi Intellectualis*. There is, of course, much work on the Italian Renaissance. K. Gouwens, 'Discourses of vulnerability: Pietro Alcionio's orations on the Sack of Rome', *RQ*, 50:38–77, examines the reactions of one humanist to that significant event in May 1527 in the light of his four contemporary orations. A. pessimistically seeks to relocate his city's destiny within a more modestly civic and less imperial tradition. Id., 'Life-writing and the theme of cultural decline in Valeriano's *De Litterarum Infelicitate*', *SCJ*, 27:87–96, examines the impact of the same event in Pierio Valeriano's more famous dialogue. It is argued here that the oft-quoted lament for the end of humanism has been taken out of its context, and that V. shows the possibility of continued scholarly endeavour through the narrative of his own experience. Matters of rhetorical style and register are to the fore in Francesco Bausi, *Nec Rhetor Neque Philosophus: Fonti, Lingua e Stile nelle Prime Opere Latine di Giovanni Pico della Mirandola (1484–87)*, (Studi Pichiani, 3), Florence, Olschki, 1996, 213 pp. *Vita Viri Clarissimi et Famosissimi Kyriaci Anconitani*, ed. Charles Mitchell and Edward W. Bodnar (TAPS, 86), Philadelphia, American Philosophical Society, 1996, vii + 246 pp., presents the life of the traveller Ciriaco de Filippo de' Pizzicolli, composed by his close friend, Scalamonti, newly edited from the original MS, along with C.'s correspondence with Leonardo Bruni and Francesco Filelfo. M. H. Keefer, 'The dreamer's path: Descartes and the sixteenth century', *RQ*, 49:30–76, takes as its starting point Derrida's examination of the metaphor of 'path or journey' in philosophical discovery, relating Descartes' espousal of it to the earlier 'journeys' of his 16th-c. predecessors, Jean Calvin and Cornelius Agrippa. Marc van der Poel, *Cornelius Agrippa: The Humanist Theologian and his Declamations*, Leiden, Brill, 1996, xiv + 303 pp., concentrates on A.'s position within a rhetorical tradition, showing his debt to Erasmus. There is a useful chapter on declamation in the humanist period. *The Bondage and Liberation of the Will: A Defence of the Orthodox Doctrine of Human Choice against Pighius*, ed. A. N. S. Lane (Texts & Studies in Reformation & Post-Reformation Thought, 2), Grand Rapids, MN, Baker Books, 1996, xxxix + 264 pp., is a first English translation of the 1543 response of John Calvin to the attack by the Dutch Catholic, Albert Pighius, on Calvinist doctrines of predestination and free will. P. R. Sellin, 'The reference to John Milton's *Tetrachordon* in *De Doctrina Christiana*', *SEL*, 37:137–49, argues that what appears to be a cross-reference in *De Doctrina* to the earlier work does not conclusively prove M.'s authorship of this work. Barbara Correll, *The End of Conduct: 'Grobianus' and the Renaissance Text of the Subject*, Ithaca, Cornell U.P., 1996, xv + 225 pp., is a serious consideration of a less than serious text, Friedrich Dedekind's *Grobianus de Morum Simplicitate* (1549). This popular work, later translated into German and English, is a spoof on the genre of conduct manuals, advocating instead offensive behaviour in public, such as self-exposure and spitting. There is discussion of the issue of gender (a later edition included a 'Grobiana' for a female readership) and the implications of the act of translating the text for a new audience. D. Shuger, 'Irishmen, aristocrats, and other white barbarians', *RQ*, 50:494–525, is an interesting synthesis of descriptions of those societies seen to be 'outside the civilized world' by writers such as Bodin and Sir Thomas Smith. Issues of ethnic tolerance are also examined in Z. V. David, 'Hájek, Dubravius and the Jews: a contrast in sixteenth-century Czech historiography', *SCJ*, 27:997–1013. The *Historia Regni Boiemiae* of Jan Dubravius (1552) shows considerably more tolerance and enlightenment than is to be found in the vernacular chronicle of his contemporary, Václav Hájek.

Work on scientific texts in the Renaissance continues to progress. A useful collection of recent work on, amongst others, Copernicus, Tycho Brahe and the Melanchthon circle, can be found in *The Scientific Enterprise in Early Modern Europe: Readings from Isis*, ed. Peter Dear, Chicago U.P., 337 pp. N. G. Siraisi, 'Vesalius and the reading of Galen's teleology', *RQ*, 50: 1–37, discusses the distance between a 16th-c. medical theorist and his Greek master, and the delicate balance between teleological presupposition and empirical theory. The analysis concentrates on the *Fabrica* of 1543. S. J. Rabin, 'Kepler's attitude towards Pico and the anti-astrology polemic', *ib*.:750–70, argues that Johannes Kepler modified his belief in astrological determinism in the light of his research in astronomy, rather than from his reading of Pico's *Disputationes*. The new edition of the works of Battista della Porta advances with *Cœlestis Physiognomonia*, ed. Alfonso Paolella (Edizione Nazionale delle Opere di Giovan Battista della Porta, 8), Naples, ESI, 1996, xxxi + 353 pp. Della Porta's work of 1604 explores the links between astrology and human physiognomy. Heinrich C. Kuhn, *Venetischer Aristotelismus im Ende der Aristotelischen Welt: Aspekte der Welt und des Denkens des Cesare Cremonini (1550–1631)*, Berne-Frankfurt, Lang, 1996, 864 pp., chronicles the work of this natural philosopher at the University of Padua over the full range of his scientific and philosophical work, and shows the continued influence of Aristotle even in the universities of Italy and Germany in the 18th century. In the same series there is also *Ars Reminiscendi*, ed. Raffaele Sirri, Berne-Frankfurt, Lang, 1996, xxxi + 106 pp., with a useful bibliography of related texts on the art of memory. Latin also remained the vehicle for mathematical work in the 16th century. *Pedro Nunes (1502–1578). His Lost Algebra and Other Discoveries*, ed. J. R. C. Martyn, NY-Berne-Frankfurt, Lang, 1996, collects a number of Portuguese commentaries on the work in verse and prose. On the same theme, A. Meskens, 'The Jesuit mathematics school in Antwerp in the early seventeenth century', *SCen*, 12: 11–22, illustrates a flourishing tradition that overlapped into the fields of physics and geography; of special importance are the *Opticorum Libri Sex* of Franciscus de Aguilon (1613) and the work of Gregorius a Sancto Vicentio, much of it still in MS. Harold Samuel Stone, *Vico's Cultural History: The Production and Transmission of Ideas in Naples, 1685–1750*, Leiden, Brill, xxiv + 328 pp., places V.'s life and work in its cultural, social and academic context. Although concentrating on *The New Science* there is much information too on contemporary methods of book production and on the Neapolitan scene in the early 18th century.

2

ROMANCE LANGUAGES

I. ROMANCE LINGUISTICS

By JOHN N. GREEN, *University of Bradford*

1. ACTA, FESTSCHRIFTEN

The protracted publication of *Actas* (Santiago de Compostela), ends with volumes VIII and I (in that order) together with a handy fascicule of contents and indexes; the dated air of some shorter monolingual items is the regrettable price to be paid for the undeniable symbolic value of the comprehensive record. *Konvergenz und Divergenz in den romanischen Sprachen*, ed. Wolfgang Dahmen et al. (TBL, 396), 1995, xviii + 400 pp., assembles 18 papers from the eighth annual *Romanistisches Kolloquium*, including three interesting reflections on theory and methodology: W. Oesterreicher, 'Die Architektur romanischer Sprachen im Vergleich' (3–21); W. Schweickard, 'Teleologie und Methodik des Vergleichens' (22–46); and P. Stein, 'Quantitative Aspekte des Sprachvergleichs' (47–62). Papers from the ninth and tenth meetings appear respectively as: Dahmen, *Romanischen Sprachen* and Dahmen, *Sprache und Geschlecht*. The proceedings of a further regular colloquium, *Studien zum romanisch-deutschen und innerromanischen Sprachvergleich*, ed. Gerd Wotjak, Frankfurt, Lang, xiv + 630 pp., concentrate on morphosyntax, lexis and discourse, with special reference to the Spanish-German pair.

Tributes pullulate. The three imposing tomes of *Fest. Pfister* contain a bibliography of P.'s writings compiled by D. Schlupp and G. Tancke (ix–xl) and numerous contributions, mostly monolingual and some very short, on many sub-areas of Romance and general linguistics. Also conceived on the heroic scale, the two volumes of *Fest. Fisiak* concentrate respectively on historical linguistics and modelling, with Romance under-represented among its 135 contributions. *Fest. Figge* and *Fest. Kontzi* are substantial undertakings but narrower in scope, focusing respectively on semiotic processes and Arabic influences on Romance. More modest but no less noteworthy are: *Martin Vol.*, *Mańczak Vol.*, and *Rothwell Vol.*, some of whose papers are discussed below. *La Corónica* 26.1, ed. F. Marcos Marín, dedicated to the memory of 'Joan Coromines i Vigneaux, 1905–1997', combines a bibliography of C.'s writings compiled by D. M. Rogers (9–24) with 11 contributions on Hispanic lexicography. *RRL*, 40.1–3, 1995

[1997], ed. Emanuel Vasiliu, dedicated 'A la mémoire de Alexandru Rosetti (1895–1990) à l'occasion du centenaire de sa naissance', celebrates R.'s vision in founding the Romanian Institute of Phonetics and Dialectology, with its journal *FD* relaunched in 1991 after a fifteen-year lull.

2. GENERAL ROMANCE AND LATIN

Romanists have gained a brilliant reference work in Barbara Frank and Jörg Hartmann's *Inventaire systématique des premiers documents des langues romanes*, 5 vols, Tübingen, Narr, 394, 387, 389, 523 and 531 pp. After an introduction and extensive bibliography, there are four volumes of listings, ranging in size from fragments to complete charters and grouped by theme and geography, each document described in terms of appearance, medium, content, provenance, MS date and location, together with a short excerpt usually consisting of the opening and closing sequences; the standard box layout greatly facilitates look-up and comparison. Continuing his dissection of overlapping phases of early Romance (*YWMLS*, 58 : 16), R. de Dardel contributes: 'La référence locale avec prépositions IN et AD en protoroman', *Mańczak Vol.*, 29–37, showing syncretism of movement and location (STO/VADO IN) giving way to differentiation (STO IN versus VADO AD) and returning to syncretism (STO/VADO AD); 'Trois normes latines relatives aux complétives assertives', *CFS*, 49, 1995–96 [1997]: 165–70, proposing earlier dates for J. Herman's reconstruction of the loss of Acc + Inf in favour of finite complementation; and 'Les bases positionnelles protoromanes', *VR*, 56 : 10–23, postulating three basic word orders, chronologically VSO > OVS > SVO, while admitting that the descent cannot have been direct but mediated by variant forms. W. Mańczak retaliates to sundry attacks with the hopeful title 'La question de l'origine des langues romanes est-elle un faux problème?', *RRL*, 41, 1996 [1997]: 3–9, only to disappoint by repeating well-known diagrams and diatribes. A clever reconstruction by F. Fanciullo of 'Anticipazioni romanze nel latino pompeiano', *AGI*, 82 : 186–98, makes sense of a misspelled non-scanning couplet if the writer was representing *rafforzamento sintattico*, a mere hair's breadth from the familiar *raddoppiamento*.

Gualtiero Calboli, *Über das Lateinische. Vom Indogermanischen zu den romanischen Sprachen*, Tübingen, Niemeyer, xxiv + 387 pp., brings together 18 of C.'s papers, some new and others reworked, examining passives, reflexives, complementation and the emergence of articles, generally within a Montague framework. The themes overlap two more specialized works: Marie-Dominique Joffre, **Le Verbe latin: voix et diathèse*, Louvain-Paris, Peeters, 1995, 486 pp. (well reviewed by

J. M. Baños, *Emérita*, 45:134–36), and Roland Hoffmann, *Lateinische Verbalperiphrasen vom Typ* amans sum *und* amatus fui: *Valenz und Grammatikalisierung*, Frankfurt, Lang, xvi + 465 pp., which attempts to pinpoint the reanalysis from verbal complex to copula plus predicative adjective. According to M.-D. Joffre, 'Sens et emplois de *iste* à la fin de l'époque républicaine', *REL*, 74:145–54, ISTE was highly expressive and used to attract attention, but it was not necessarily linked to the second person, was certainly not an equal partner of HIC and ILLE, and no one could have foretold its later success. B. M. L. Bauer, 'Residues of non-nominative syntax in Latin', *HSp*, 109:241–56, regards impersonals and gerunds as archaic and ripe for replacement by transitive structures. S. Luraghi, 'Omission of the direct object in Latin', *IF*, 102:239–57, finds that omission was common in classical authors, especially with whole-sentence antecedents, and may even have been obligatory in some types of co-ordination. Lastly, H. Krenn, '"*m* obscurum in extremit-ate dictionum sonat" (Priscian)', *Fest. Figge*, 347–65, seeks out the ramifications of a well-known loss: there are implications across the case system, for locatives, adverbs, prepositions, and conjunctions, and many important linking words in -*m* (ADMODUM, ADVERSUM, TOTIDEM, etc.) are lost; could it be a case of post-*m* lassitude and homonymy?

Trudel Meisenburg, *Romanische Schriftsysteme im Vergleich. Eine diach-rone Studie*, Tübingen, Narr, 1996, xii + 437 pp., well documented and comprehensive in coverage, distributes Romance varieties along two clines, simple versus complex systems, and continuous versus interrupted transmission. Investigating attitudes to language and the fixing of scribal practice, N. Andrieux-Reix and S. Monsonégo, 'Écrire des phrases au Moyen Age', *Romania*, 115:289–336, point out that while Old French was never written in continuous script, diplomatic editions of Carolingian documents reveal that the white spaces do not always match what we would now identify as graphical words. Weighing the benefits and disadvantages of 'Linguistic standardization in the Middle Ages', *Rothwell Vol.*, 261–75, R. Wright concludes that the Carolingian reforms were, on the whole, a Bad Thing. W. also reflects on the possibility of 'Translation between Latin and Romance in the Early Middle Ages', Beer, *Translation Theory*, 7–32, concluding that it would be inappropriate to speak of 'translation', with its implication of hardened language boundaries, before the 12th-c. renaissance. Commenting on W.'s earlier work, L. Williams, 'The act of reading: how straightforward is it?', *BHS(L)*, 74:265–74, points to the internal tensions of mixed phonographic and logographic systems: the pressure for reform need not have been imported. Perfection remains elusive: R. Pellen, 'Le CD-ROM: un nouvel âge pour la recherche?', *RLiR*, 61:89–131, reviewing a series of computerized corpora of medieval Spanish, alternately thrills to the analytical possibilities and excoriates the editors for gross errors, noting ruefully, as 2000 approaches, that once you get bugs into a database, you can't get them out.

3. HISTORY OF ROMANCE LINGUISTICS

Learned, prolific, and honoured above any of his contemporaries, Varro remains one of the best sources on Imperial usage, now made accessible in a new critical text, translation, and commentary by Daniel J. Taylor: *Varro. De lingua latina X*, Amsterdam, Benjamins, 1996, x + 205 pp. H. Aschenberg, 'Zwischen *ars* und *usus*. Zur Metasprache in den ersten Grammatiken des Spanischen', *RF*, 109:187–220, traces the tension in early grammars between reliance on (simplified) analytic frameworks derived directly from Greek and Latin, and the wish for linguistic emancipation, recognizing the new prestige of the Romance languages; Nebrija is seen as pivotal in anticipating Enlightenment thought. But in a complex diasystem such as obtained in the 16th and 17th centuries, usage will be affected by the mere attempt at codification, whether or not the purpose was normative; so argues J. L. Girón Alconchel, 'Las gramáticas del español y el español de la gramáticas en el Siglo de Oro', *BRAE*, 76, 1996:285–308, and 'La doctrina y el uso de los futuros en las gramáticas renacentistas', *HistL*, 24:15–28. The themes recur in W. Ayres-Bennett, ' "Tres-estrange et tres-François" ', *Actas* (Santiago de Compostela), VIII, 81–90, where Vaugelas's use of *français* as a term of both approval and rebuke is related to his not wholly successful attempts to shake off the yoke of Latin tradition.

Courting hubris, G. Holtus, 'Romanistik einst und jetzt', *Fest. Pfister*, III, 371–89, contrasts the 27 contributions that Gröber deemed adequate to cover the entire field in his 1888 *Grundriß* with the hundreds still spilling forth from the *Lexikon der romanistischen Linguistik* (*YWMLS*, 50:16, 51:20, 52:18, 53:12, 54:17, 56:33, 57:22, 58:16). Elusive and at times unproductive, the relations between Romance and general linguistics are probed by contributors to a Round Table reported in *Actas* (Santiago de Compostela), VIII: R. Posner, 'La linguistique romane au début du XIXe siècle' (161–67), wonders whether Romanists from Diez onwards have always been out on a limb, overshadowed by the theoretical high-fliers; more assured, P. Swiggers, 'Linguistique romane et linguistique générale' (347–69), locates the distinctiveness of Romance in diachronic studies, dialectology and sociolinguistics; while B. Schlieben-Lange, 'Les études romanes avant Raynouard et Diez' (371–77), finds abundant debate on matters Romance before 1800, but within the traditions of rhetoric and philosophy, while general linguistics was reserved for the domain of logic. Under the general title 'De François Raynouard à Auguste Brun', *Lengas*, 42, ed. D. Baggioni and P. Martel, seeks to reclaim history for the South, trumpeting the achievements of Occitan Romanists given scant credit in manuals published in the North. In 'Daniel Matras: sein Beitrag zur romanischen Grammatiko- und Lexiko-graphie', *ZRP*, 113: 190–207, K.-H. Röntgen profiles another neglected southerner, an itinerant scholar/teacher born in Vendôme in 1598, who became adviser to Christian IV of Denmark, compiled a pioneering multilingual dictionary, and wrote extensively on the description and teaching of foreign languages. In a long and complex review article on *Ernst Robert Curtius et l'idée d'Europe*, ed. Jeanne Bem and André Guyaux, Paris, Champion, 1995, 396 pp., M. Nerlich, 'Curtius trahi par les siens', *RF*, 109: 436–74, chastises the editors for including poor quality papers to rebalance a colloquium whose outcome had fallen short of hagiography: in N.'s contention, Curtius was an important figure, and certainly anti-Nazi, but also pro-fascist, anti-Semitic, undemocratic and (coincidentally, as it were) unconvinced by Enlightenment ideals. To end with a lighter footnote, E. Radtke, 'Leo Spitzer als Soziolinguist?', *ASNS*, 234: 97–98, does not seek to portray S. as the founder of the modern discipline, but does note him using the term around 1950, some years before the alleged first attestation.

4. PHONOLOGY

Kenneth J. Wireback, *The Role of Phonological Structure in Sound Change from Latin to Spanish and Portuguese*, Frankfurt, Lang, 152 pp., and its companion piece 'On the palatalization of /kt/, /ks/, /k'l/, g'l/, and /gn/ in Western Romance', *RPh*, 50: 276–94, deal with interlinked processes of palatalization and lenition that resulted in altered syllabic structure and a new obstruent strength scale; incidentally, traditional Ibero-Romance 'yod-inversion' is dismissed as spurious (because there was no off-glide to invert) and unpacked into three semi-autonomous changes. Meanwhile, J. Gulsoy, 'Castellano *viejo*, portugués *velho*, catalán *vell*', *La Corónica*, 26: 67–86, attributes the irregular diphthongization before a palatal cluster in *viejo* to the pull of *viedro*, its regular doublet, which survived to the 13th century; and I. Roca, 'There are no "glides", at least in Spanish', *Probus*, 9: 233–65, offers selective enrichment of high vowels with lexical nuclearity as an alternative to the feature [±syllabic], so demonstrating the superiority of optimality theory over old-style generative phonology. Using similar data for different ends, M. Iliescu, 'Les groupes consonantiques et la classification des langues romanes', *Mańczak Vol.*, 87–91, contrasts Romanian faithfulness to Latin clusters with near-uniform assimilation in Italian, and three-way dismantling to increase sonority in Spanish, while French meanders towards outcomes often mirroring Spanish. Widely divergent explanations for phonetic irregularity are offered by W. Mańczak, 'Double évolution phonétique de certains mots latins en français', *RLaR*, 101:29–36, who tests the effects of frequency on doublets, averring that his explanation applies as well to bound morphs as to free lexemes; by F. Jensen, 'On syntactic phonetics in Romance', *Romania*, 115:541–47, who attributes some anomalies to 'regular' changes hopping over word boundaries when aided by phrasal stress or other syntactic prominence; and by A. Christol, 'Le rhotacisme', *Latomus*, 55, 1996:806–14, who favours sociolinguistic factors to account for doublets like the non-rhotic high-register QUAESO alongside everyday QUAERO. Elucidating 'On the Romance inflectional endings -*i* and -*e*', *RPh*, 50, 1996:147–82, leads M. Maiden to conclude that eastern vocalic endings are better explained by phonology (perhaps abetted by morphology) than by morphology alone; conversely, however, in 'La dissimilation à la lumière des pronoms clitiques en roman', *ZRP*, 113:531–62, M. accepts that morphology can tip the balance in wavering dissimilatory processes — a fascinating area of research, unjustly neglected of late.

5. MORPHOSYNTAX AND TYPOLOGY

John Hewson and Vit Bubenik, *Tense and Aspect in Indo-European Languages. Theory, Typology, Diachrony*, Amsterdam, Benjamins, xii + 403 pp., contains Guillaume-inspired chapters by H. on 'The Latin verbal system' (189–208), classified as a ternary system with retrospective:imperfective:prospective values; and 'From Latin to Modern Romance' (314–30), claiming that Romance is unusual in having two immanent aspects, a performative related to ascending time and an imperfective related to descending time. Bernd Kortmann, *Adverbial Subordination*, Berlin, Mouton de Gruyter, xxiv + 425 pp., is a typological investigation of the subordinators *when, if, because, although*, etc. and their equivalents in all European languages, concluding that all vo languages use such subordinators clause-initially and that Romance languages are prototypical, with Ibero-Romance and Italian sharing all 17 of his putative core 'Euroversals'. G. Altman and K.-H. Best, 'Wortlänge in romanischen Sprachen', *Fest. Figge*, 1–13, use diversification modelling to show evolution away from Latin word length: Italian remains the closest, French and Spanish the furthest removed, though for different reasons. Quantitative analysis of a corpus of translations enables Peter Stein, *Untersuchungen zur Verbalsyntax der Liviusübersetzungen in die romanischen Sprachen*, Tübingen, Niemeyer, xiv + 604 pp., to investigate relative frequency in syntax, especially preferences for finite and non-finite structures. Using a similar corpus, D. Varga, 'Classification des langues romanes selon des critères syntaxiques', *RLaR*, 101 : 5–27, identifies a highest common factor for renderings of indirect speech, finding to his surprise that Sardinian closely matches the norm, followed by Catalan, Occitan and Italian, while Engadinish is by some way the most remote. Coincidentally, neighbouring Surselvan is the variety selected by J. S. Turley as the best example of 'The renovation of Romance reflexives', *RPh*, 51 : 15–34, which provides a sensible taxonomy and applies S. Kemmer's marking conventions (*me* is 'heavy' while /-r/ is 'light') en route to a theory of cyclic renewal.

Actas (Santiago de Compostela), VIII, opens with a plenary by A. Varvaro, 'État actuel et perspectives de la linguistique romane' (15–26) cautiously welcoming cross-fertilization and methodological renewal, while strongly advocating continued concentration on empirical data and comparative analysis. The advice is heeded at the round table on Romance word order led by L. Renzi, *ib.*, 1 (1039–47), with contributions by J. Herman on Vulgar Latin (1049–60), P. Benincà on medieval Romance (1061–73), G. Salvi on Gallego-Portuguese (1075–88), E. Blasco Ferrer on Catalan (1089–1106), G. Cinque on Italian (1107–14), B. Combettes on French (1115–22), and C. Dobrovie-Sorin on Romanian (1123–34). J. Niemeyer and H. Krenn, 'Zur Stellung des attributiven Adjektivs im Lateinischen und in den romanischen Sprachen', *Fest. Figge*, 411–23, tell a tale of rigidification: between Latin and Romance over 90% of freely floating adjectives became fixed in postnominal position, the few prenominals could only be contiguous, even fewer of them could be qualified, and splitting of co-ordinates ceased. M. Gawełko, 'Sur la place des adjectifs de couleur dans les langues romanes', *Mańczak Vol.*, 55–59, investigates eight possible patternings of colour terms, other adjectives, nouns and conjunctions, finding the most frequent orders to be Adj + Noun + Colour and Colour + Noun. In a detailed and well exemplified account, J. Aguirre, '"*Cujum pecus*" anne *Latinum*? Inestabilidad de los relativos posesivos', *Tesserae*, 3 : 43–87, studies the evolution of *cuyo* 'whose' from Latin to modern Spanish, concluding that it has always been anomalous among its rivals in not extending to interrogatives and that it is gradually being replaced by analytic forms through attrition of its favoured contexts; with the elimination of the aberrant *cuyo* (and its attendant problems of ambiguity, agreement and word order), Spanish will have reinvented the Latin system and the WH- will have come full circle.

6. Syntactic Theory and Semantics

Comparative syntax is the study of syntactic variation that crosses groups of languages but stops short of universality. So says R. S. Kayne in his preface to *Microparametric Syntax and Dialect Variation*, ed. James R. Black and Virginia Motapanyane, Amsterdam, Benjamins, 1996, xviii + 269 pp., a collection of 11 papers from a 1994 colloquium, including J.-M. Authier and L. Reed, 'Une analyse microparamétrique des moyens dans les langues romanes' (1–23), which explains variation in Romance middle constructions by appeal to base generation of *se*, parameter setting, and role absorption. A companion volume, *Clitics, Pronouns and Movement*, ed. B. and M., *ib.*, 375 pp., and introduced by A. Holmberg, 'Some reflections on movement' (9–22), contains a further 12 papers, many illustrated from lesser-studied varieties of Romance. A complementary minimalist account of *se* impersonals is provided by J. Guéron, 'Qu'est-ce qu'une phrase impersonnelle?', *RLVin*, 25, 1996:53–82. Anna-Maria Di Sciullo, *Projections and Interface Conditions*, OUP, 272 pp., offers case studies on modularity illustrated from French and Italian. Alex Alsina, *The Role of Argument Structure in Grammar: Evidence from Romance*, Stanford, CSLI Publications, 1996, xi + 306 pp., elevates argument structure above other forms of representation, adducing evidence from voice relations, case marking, and causatives. Kemenade, *Parameters*, brings together 18 papers on diachronic aspects of argument structure, clitics, V_2 phenomena, and scrambling, including N. Vincent, 'The emergence of the D-system in Romance' (149–69), on the convergent grammaticalization of ILLE and IPSE, brought about by parametric shift, analogy, and exaptation. *Negation and Polarity; Syntax and Semantics*, ed. Danielle Forget et al., Amsterdam, Benjamins, viii + 365 pp., assembles contributions centred on French from a panoply of distinguished names, including P. Rowlett, 'Jespersen, negative concord and A'-binding' (323–40), which flatteringly reformulates J.'s intuitions within the NegP hypothesis of J.-Y. Pollock and weakens Specifier-Head constraints from congruity to mere compatibility. An illuminating monograph by Raffaella Zanuttini, *Negation and Clausal Structure. A Comparative Study of the Romance Languages*, OUP, xiv + 201 pp., explicates the different syntactic properties of preverbal and postverbal negative markers by projections to head position, or by adjunctions when the preferred path is blocked or results in faulty scope relations.

Franco Benucci, *Destrutturazione due*, Padua, Unipress, 105 pp., studies Romance factitive, perceptual, and causative constructions, concluding that the original two clauses have melded into a single phrasal projection capable of preventing clitic extraction, following diachronic collapse of the intermediate structure. (Similar conclusions are reached, less theoretically, by D. Cerbasi, 'Las construcciones causativas del tipo *hacer*+infinitivo en español, portugués e italiano', *LEA*, 19:155–71.) In 'Restructuring, head movement, and locality', *LI*, 28:423–60, I. Roberts ingeniously retains the benefits of the incorporation analysis by postulating that infinitives can carry the results of complex restructuring which itself is incapable of morphological realization. H. Campos, 'On subject extraction and the anti-agreement effect in Romance', *ib.*, 92–119, is a detailed rebuttal of proposals by J. Ouhalla, arguing instead that subject extraction always proceeds from postverbal position and that divergent results arise from differences in the licensing of expletive subjects. A novel analysis by C. Donati of 'Comparative clauses as free relatives', *Probus*, 9:145–66, proposes that comparatives, which involve head-movement to C^0 and are selected by *più*, are two-place predicates where both terms of comparison are quantifier phrases. In 'Demonstratives and reinforcers in Romance and Germanic languages', *Lingua*, 102:87–113, J. B. Bernstein argues that the deictic bivalency of demonstratives and the unexpected postnominal position of reinforcers in Romance involve base generation of both terms allied to movement of a phrasal category to the left of the functional projection [effectively, *livre* hops over -*là* to form *ce livre-là*]. S. Carmack, 'Object-participle argeement with complex controllers', *Probus*, 9:33–77, traces patterns of agreement in Old Spanish, Catalan, and Aragonese, uncovering a hierarchy of preferences starting — unsurprisingly — with the closest conjunct; while M.-A. Friedeman and T. Siloni, 'Agr$_{object}$ is not Agr$_{participle}$', *LRev*, 14:69–96, resort to the complexities of minimality theory to rediscover the valency of the past participle; and A. Bartra and A. Suñer, 'Inert agreement projection and the syntax of bare adjectives', *Probus*, 9:1–31, develop the idea that the adverbials in structures like *había llovido duro y seguido* might be morphologically impoverished adjectives. Whatever next?

7. DISCOURSE AND PRAGMATICS

Constructions like *l'hai preso*, *il giornale*/ *tu l'as pris*, *le journal*, according to R. Simone, 'Une interprétation diachronique de la "dislocation à droite" dans les langues romanes', *LaF*, 115:48–61, cannot be treated merely as mirror images of more familiar left dislocation; they have become base structures in Romance and are controlled by pragmatic factors in spoken registers. J. C. Smith, 'Types and tokens in language change', *Fest. Fisiak*, 1099–1111, refines his own previous account of the loss of past participle agreement, appealing to 'hyperanalysis' on the part of hearers as they factor out opaque and non-functional agreements. P. Ramat, 'Why *veruno* means "nobody"', *RPh*, 51 : 1–14, draws on a substantial body of comparative data to validate a historical pathway familiar in French but uncommon in Italian: the etymon VERE + UNU was not originally negative, but the emphasizer *vere* gradually became a marker of negative focalization. M. Tuțescu, 'Du modalisateur épistémique au connecteur discursif', *Martin Vol.*, 387–96, applies concepts developed by the dedicatee to the connector *après tout* and its Romanian equivalent *la urma urmelor*: it is an argumentative discourse marker not a modalizer — modalizers can evolve into discourse markers but not vice versa. In 'La pragma-sémantique de l'identité', De Mulder, *Relations Anaphoriques*, 201–20, M. Manoliu-Manea distinguishes comparative, particularizing, and argumentative functions of *même* in addition to the assertion of identity; in contrast, Romanian has a three-way distinction *chiar/ însuși/ singur* which is not a perfect match for the pragmatics, but does come closer.

8. LEXIS

Two dissertations deal with lexical innovation in Romance: Andreas Blank, *Prinzipien des lexikalischen Bedeutungswandels am Beispiel der romanischen Sprachen*, Tübingen, Niemeyer, xiv + 533 pp., focuses on the key notions of similarity, contrast, and contiguity; while Franz-Josef Klein, *Bedeutungswandel und Sprachendifferenzierung*, *ib.*, xii + 360 pp., models the distintegration of common Romance through the history of 32 verbs, finding that Romanian and Ibero-Romance are often more innovative than the conservative central zone (a conclusion disputed — needless to add — in W. Mańczak's review, *RPh*, 51 : 215–19). Most welcome is James H. Dee's *Lexicon of Latin Derivatives in Italian, Spanish, French and English*, 2 vols, Hildesheim, Olms-Weidmann, lvi + 1083 pp., a parallel-column glossary of all items directly inherited or subsequently borrowed from Latin, in all some 10,000 ancestor words and 75,000 reflexes. Prompted by a faulty dictionary dating to investigate 'L'asterisco nella linguistica italiana, francese e spagnola', *Fest. Pfister*, III, 441–47, S. C. Sgroi finds the sense 'undocumented form' attested in Ascoli (1873) and Brunot (1887) if not, indeed, in Aristarch's use of ἀστερίκος in classical antiquity. Drawing out common patterns of innovation and register differentiation in 'Grec populaire et latin vulgaire', *RLiR*, 61 : 5–40, W. Dietrich notes striking similarities: compare EQUU/CABALLU with classical ἵππος 'horse', supplanted in everyday speech by medieval ἄλογο 'wordless, dumb [beast]', and now surviving only in the technical meaning 'steam-horse' or in derivatives like ἱππόδρομος 'race-track'.

Toponomastics with an ulterior motive, Maria Besse's *Die Namen-paare im Bereich der germanisch-romanischen Sprachgrenze*, Tübingen, Niemeyer, 950 pp., investigates placename doublets right along the Romance-German linguistic frontier, ingeniously uncovering the chronology and directionality of phonological change (on which, see also R. Posner, 'Romance Germanic contact and the peripheral vowel feature', *Fest. Fisiak*, 1039–54). Even more ambitious, T. Vennemann gen. Nierfeld, 'Der Kastalische Quell, die Gastein und das Rätische', *Fest. Bergmann*, 479–503, links the Catalan small town *Castalla* not with 'castle' but with Greek κασταλία 'spring' (a truth already spied by a well-known Spanish publisher), finding apparent cognates in Basque and a Tyrolean inscription, and speculating on whether this much travelled root is pre-Indo-European and may betoken a distant relationship between Basque and Rhaetic. J.-P. Chambon, 'A propos du "troisième point de vue" en anthroponymie', *Fest. Pfister*, III, 149–68, examines the widespread progeny of DENTE, BUCCA and VISU in Romance surnames, arguing that etymologists must now contend with motivation and information content as well as derivational morphology. D. Pharies, 'Adverbial expressions signifying bodily movements and postures', *HR*, 65:391–414, devises a common template for 358 Hispano-Romance expressions like *a gatas*, *de puntillas*; while E. Marques Ranchhod and M. de Gioia, 'Frozen adverbs in Italian and Portuguese', *LInv*, 20, 1996 [1997]:33–85, find that success as a fixed simile brings severe syntactic restrictions in its wake. M. Fanfani, 'La terminologia linguistica di Bruno Migliorini', *LN*, 57, 1996:117–24 and its sequel 'Onomaturgia miglioriniana', *ib.*, 58:12–29, highlighting social values, traces M.'s preference for native roots (*unicismo* not *hapax*), metaphors (*coagulazione* 'coalescence'), and derivational suffixes, of which *-oid* (first appearing in *prefissoide*, *suffissoide*) was his most successful export. Derivational productivity is also illuminated by M. M. T. Watmough, 'The suffix *-tor*-: agent-noun formation in Latin and the other Italic languages', *Glotta*, 73, 1995–96 [1997]:80–115; and by S. C. Albert, 'Gebrauch und Funktion der femininen Nomina agentis im Lateinischen', Dahmen, *Sprache und Geschlecht*, 1–13, on the use of *-TRIX*, not only to denote the woman performing the task, but also as an appositional or metaphorical adjunct to any word that happens to be feminine, as in PESTIS NECATRIX.

9. SOCIOLINGUISTICS AND DIALECTOLOGY

Two general works have much to interest Romanists: *Kontaktlinguistik. Ein internationales Handbuch*, ed. Hans Goebl et al., 2 vols, Berlin, de Gruyter, xxxix + 936, xxv + 1,235 pp., the second claiming blanket coverage of all language pairs in contact throughout Europe; and *Contrastive Sociolinguistics*, ed. Marlis Hellinger and Ulrich Ammon, *ib.*, 1996, viii + 504 pp., specializing in bilingualism, language planning, and glottopolitics, and including G. Lüdi, 'Multilingual through migration' (103–33) and G. Held, 'Two polite speech acts in contrastive view' (363–84), on whimperatives, hedges, and formal rhetoric in French and Italian. The conflictual/phenomenological view of sociolinguistics is deftly sketched by H. Boyer, 'Configurations et traitements des conflits de langues intra et intercommunautaires', *Lengas*, 41:95–102. In less committed vein, A. Ganzoni, 'Problems da codificaziun d'üna lingua pitschna', *ASR*, 109, 1996:49–59, contrasts Corsican with Rhaeto-Romance, which share distanciation from Italian but differ in their willingness to embrace 'light' standardization. A recent Swiss referendum showed strong support for four official languages and the will to devote federal funds to the teaching of Romansh, but C. Pitsch, 'Perspectivas da la politica da linguas da la Confederaziun', *ib.*, 110:53–60, nonetheless reports anxieties over its future. According to R. Cathomas, 'Survesta dellas cundiziuns da basa per il svilup della cumpetenza linguistica tier minoritads', *ib.*, 110:7–51, it must satisfy three sets of conditions: intrinsic value, a cultural matrix, and sound pedagogical support.

E. Radtke discovers and documents 'Tortorella — eine bislang unbekannte galloitalienische Sprachkolonie im Cilento', *ZRP*, 113:82–108, where lenition, final vowel reduction and rhotacism of -t-, as in ['foɣo] 'fire', [sa've] 'know' and [ma'rirə] 'husband', make speakers sound rather different from their neighbours. *FM*, 65.1, ed. J. Chaurand, is devoted to 'La dialectologie aujourd'hui', surveying with pride the 70 volumes of dialect atlases published in France and the steady progress towards the computerization of data, but also warning of the probable loss of the CNRS subvention at the end of the present phase. Other sensitivities are identified in a thoughtful piece by W. Strauss, 'Wie genau können Sprachkarten sein?', *Fest. Figge*, 531–47, which, in a five-stage zoom from the whole of Romania down to Huesca province, graphically illustrates its point that juxtaposing maps of differing scale and detail, and above all different political information, creates perceptions and prejudices that could be all too intentional.

II. FRENCH STUDIES*

LANGUAGE

By GLANVILLE PRICE, *University of Wales Aberystwyth*

1. GENERAL AND BIBLIOGRAPHICAL

P. Desmet, L. Melis, and P. Swiggers, 'Chronique de la linguistique générale et française (VIII)', *TrL*, 33:133–78 (see *YWMLS*, 58:34), is devoted to the 'Histoire de la linguistique (française) aux temps modernes'.

R. Anthony Lodge et al., *Exploring the French Language*, London, Arnold, vii + 216 pp., is a carefully devised and clearly presented introduction to the language for advanced learners and others with a serious interest in the structure and use of French; there are chapters on varieties (social as well as geographical) of French, word formation and etymology, meaning, two on pronunciation, morphology, syntax, pragmatics ('Doing things with French'), and discourse analysis. *Dictionnaire encyclopédique de la langue française: le Maxidico*, Éds de la Connaissance, 1996, x + 1718 pp.

Ada Giusti, *La Langue française*, Flammarion, 128 pp. Henri Meschonnic, *De la langue française: essai sur une clarté obscure*, Hachette, 356 pp. Claire Blanche-Benveniste, *Approches de la langue parlée en français*, Gap, Ophrys, 164 pp. Catherine Fuchs, *Les Ambiguïtés du français*, Gap, Ophrys, 1996, 184 pp. Horst Geckeler and Wolf Dietrich, *Einführung in die französische Sprachwissenschaft*, 2nd rev. edn, Berlin, Schmidt, 247 pp.

RFP, 14, mainly devoted (but see also p. 45 below) to the theme of 'la transcription et [...] l'utilisation des données', includes: D. Willems, 'Histoire, linguistique et sources orales' (11–20); R. Coppetiers, 'Quelques réflexions sur la question des données: corpus et institutions' (21–41); G. Tuaillon, 'Les calembours en toponymie dans le domaine francoprovençal' (43–56); M. Bilger et al., 'Transcription de l'oral et interprétation; illustration de quelques difficultés' (57–86); C. Blanche-Benveniste, 'Transcriptions et technologies' (87–99); S. Branca, 'Transcription et édition de manuscrits. Quelques problèmes autour de la "représentation" des textes' (101–15); and P. Cappeau, 'Données erronées: quelles erreurs commettent les transcripteurs?' (117–26).

* The place of publication of books is Paris unless otherwise stated.

Dennis Ager, *Language Policy in Britain and France: The Processes of Policy*, London, Cassell, 1996, xiii + 226 pp., ranges over a number of different fields, concentrating on policy towards the English and French languages respectively but covering also policy towards regional languages and immigrant communities and the teaching of foreign languages; as far as French goes, there is informed treatment of such topics as movements, organizations, and institutions directly concerned with the fostering of the language, legislation, and spelling reform.

Haut Conseil de la francophonie, **État de la francophonie dans le monde: données 1995–1996*, Documentation française, 629 pp. **Regards sur la francophonie*, ed. Marc Gontard and Maryse Bray, Rennes U.P., 322 pp. **Francophonie: mythes, masques et réalités: enjeux politiques et culturels*, ed. B. Jones, A. Miguet, and P. Corcoran, Publisud, 1996, 319 pp. Charles Durand, **La Langue française: atout ou obstacle?. Réalisme économique, communication et francophonie au XXIe siècle*, Le Mirail-Toulouse U.P., 447 pp.

2. HISTORY OF GRAMMAR AND OF LINGUISTIC THEORY

Although much of it falls outside the scope of *YWMLS*, Pierre Swiggers, *Histoire de la pensée linguistique*, PUF, vii + 312 pp., deserves mention here for the attention it devotes to the evolution of French linguistic thought and to attitudes to the French language and the teaching of it, particularly from the 16th to the 18th century. *Les 'Remarques' de l'Académie française sur le 'Quinte-Curce' de Vaugelas*, ed. Wendy Ayres-Bennett and Philippe Caron, Presses de l'École normale supérieure, 1996 [1997], 426 pp., is a handsomely produced volume providing us with the complete text of the Academy's hitherto unpublished *Remarques*, the manuscript of which survives in the archives of the Institut de France; the editors have adopted the excellent principle of providing a facsimile reprint of the French and Latin texts of the 1709 edition of Vaugelas's text (the one used by the Academy for its *Remarques* which date from 1719–20), with the remarks themselves set out as footnotes and commented on in an introductory section on the 'Typologie générale des *Remarques*'. E. Werner discusses 'Das Syntaxkonzept von Gabrile Girard in den *Vrais Principes de la langue françoise* (1747)', *VR*, 56: 146–78. G. Antoine, 'De F. Brunot à E. Littré en passant par F. de Saussure', *Martin Vol.*, 31–40, seeks to establish the credentials of Littré (who has been dismissed as 'antilinguistic') as a 'linguist' — more of one, indeed, than Brunot. P. Swiggers discusses 'Signe, signification et sens chez les grammairiens de l'*Encyclopédie*', *ib.*, 377–85. A. Joly, 'Autour du concept d'"opération" chez Gustave Guillaume', *ib.*, 203–18, identifies and arranges in chronological order all instances of the term 'opération' in G.'s writings and concludes that his linguistics is 'de toute évidence, une *linguistique opérative*'.

CFS, 49, 1995–96 [1997] includes three important documentary contributions: an annotated edition by A.-M. Frýba-Reber and J.-P. Chambon of letters from Jules Ronjat to Ch. Bally (9–63); M. Linda, 'Kommentiertes Verzeichnis der Vorlesungen F. de Saussures an der Universität Genf (1891–1913)' (65–84); H. Parret, 'Réflexions saussuriennes sur le Temps et le Moi' (85–110), drawing on manuscripts and books kept at the Houghton Library at Harvard; and three other articles of relevance to this section of *YWMLS*: A.-M. Frýba-Reber, 'Charles-Albert Sechehaye, un linguiste engagé' (123–37); L. de Saussure, 'Le temps chez Beauzée: algorithmes de repérage, comparaison avec Reichenbach et problèmes théoriques' (171–95); and B. Turpin, 'Discours, langue et parole dans les cours et les notes de linguistique générale de F. de Saussure' (251–66). *TrL*, 31, is a thematic issue, 'Vers une terminologie grammaticale européenne? Nécessité et obstacles', ed. Sonia Branca, Alicia Piquer and Dominique Willems; inevitably, a number of the contributions are either not language-specific or else relate to languages other than French, but the following are relevant to this section of *YWMLS*: J. Deulofeu, 'Le dilemme de la "modernisation des terminologies" en linguistique' (25–45); S. Branca-Rosoff, 'La subordination et la "grammatisation" du français. Deux étapes dans la définition d'une catégorie normative' (47–62); J. Goes, 'De la linguistique à la grammaire (scolaire): l'adjectif de relation' (63–78); G. Engwall, 'Les formes verbales en suédois et en français: définitions et terminologies' (119–30); R. Tomassone, 'Quelques remarques sur l'usage et le non-usage de la terminologie grammaticale en France' (131–44). *TrL*, 33, another thematic issue, 'Langue et linguistique. Mouvements croisés et alternés (1790–1860)', ed. Jacques-Philippe Saint-Gérand, includes: J. Guilhaumou, 'Sieyès et le "monde lingual" (1773–1803)' (9–28); É. Martin, 'Observation de l'usage dans les grands corpus textuels (exemples choisis entre 1790 et 1840)' (29–38); B. Combettes, 'Grammaire de phrase et cohérence textuelle: le traitement des constructions détachées' (39–49); H. Weiss, 'Les traditions et leurs destins: contribution à la recherche sur les relations franco-allemandes' (51–67); P. Swiggers, 'L'éviction de la grammaire générale par la philologie comparée: relations intercontinentales, sédimentations mouvantes, et rôle du français et des Français' (69–90); J.-P. Saint-Gérand, 'L'exemple d'une revue: le *Journal grammatical et didactique de la langue française* [1826–1840]' (91–114); and B. Nehrlich,

'Un chaînon manquant entre rhétorique et sémantique: l'œuvre d'Auguste de Chevallet' (115–31).

3. HISTORY OF THE LANGUAGE

The title of the opening chapter, 'Why another history of French?', makes clear by implication what is not perhaps immediately evident from the title itself of Rebecca Posner, *Linguistic Change in French*, Oxford, Clarendon Press, xxi + 509 pp., namely that this *is* 'another history of French' — but a very welcome one, probing as it does into the nature and possible causes of linguistic change. Part I, 'Language change', defines the domain of 'French' ('What is French?'), covering *inter alia* such disparate topics as language standardization and French creoles, and offers a sociolinguistic history of the language. Part II, 'Linguistic change', has an introductory chapter on 'Processes of linguistic change', followed by others on lexical, semantic, phonological, morphological and syntactic change. There is an impressive and useful bibliography of about 1,000 items. There is no evidence in T. Arnavielle, 'Pour construire une grammaire historique du français', *RLaR*, 101:91–120, that he is familiar with any of the vast amount of relevant work published in German, English or various other languages. Maxim W. Sergijewskij, **Einführung in das ältere Französisch* (ed. Uwe Petersen et al.), Tübingen, Narr, xiv + 146 pp.

W. Mańczak reiterates his view that frequency of use is a conditioning factor of allegedly irregular sound change with 'Double évolution phonétique de certains mots latins en français', *RLaR*, 101:29–36. P. van Reenen discusses 'Contractions of preposition and plural article without *s* (e.g. *a + les > au*) in Old French, a completely overlooked problem of paradigm formation with implications for the theory of language change', Fisiak, *Dialectology*, 175–215. G.-M. Noumssi, 'Le relatif en Moyen Français: XIVe-XVIe siècle', *RLaR*, 101:63–89, is inspired by Guillaumian principles.

The bibliography to G. Siouffi, 'Vaugelas et la notion de variation', *ib.*, 121–43, is lamentably inadequate.

4. TEXTS

O. Nandeau offers 'Observations sur la langue de *Aïgar et Maurin*', *Romania*, 115:337–67. *Martin Vol.* includes: A. Henry, '*La huese, la bot(t)e* et le *DMF*' (181–84), a reflection on the meaning of *huese* ('botte' or 'tonneau'?) in a passage of the *Roman du comte d'Anjou*; N. Andrieux-Reix, 'Sur des vers anciens faire du nouveau. Aspects du vocabulaire des chansons de geste tardives' (21–40), looking at the coexistence in late *chansons de geste* of older (possibly somewhat archaic) words and expressions and of more newly created ones; G. Hasenohr, 'Un exemple d'accommodation linguistique au début du XVIᵉ siècle' (167–74), comparing a mid-14th-c. French translation of the Rule of St Benedict with an early-16th-c. revision of it and examining what the revision reveals of 'ce qui de la graphie et de la langue du XIVᵉ siècle était admis ou admissible au début du XVIᵉ siècle et mieux encore ce qui ne pouvait plus être accepté'; and P. Rézeau, '"Tire toy la, Colin Greguille". Richessess lexicales d'un noël poitevin du XVIᵉ siècle' (343–54).

5. PHONETICS AND PHONOLOGY

Léon Warnant, *Orthographe et prononciation en français*, avec la collaboration scientifique de Louis Chalon, Louvain-la-Neuve, Duculot, 1996, 238 pp., lists, with a substantial introduction, 'Particularités phonétiques du français', twelve thousand words 'qui ne se prononcent pas comme ils s'écrivent'; though deriving primarily from W.'s *Dictionnaire de la prononciation française* (1962, last edn, under the expanded title *Dictionnaire de la prononciation française dans sa norme actuelle*, 1987 — see *YWMLS*, 49:28), this new work adopts a somewhat less conservative position, acknowledging in particular the pronunciation [a] as well as [ɑ] (the only one recognized in 1987) in words such as *pas*, *pâte* ('on peut considérer [...] qu'il est aujourd'hui d'un bon usage aussi de ne connaître qu'un seul timbre pour *a*); as for [œ̃] however, the authors are prepared to go no further than to say that 'une articulation en [ɛ̃], qui n'est pas majoritaire, peut sans doute être tolérée, sans que nous l'estimions recommandable'. Pierre Martin, **Éléments de phonétique avec application au français*, Quebec, Laval U. P., 1996, 253 pp.

6. ORTHOGRAPHY

B. Cerquiglini, 'Un âge d'or de l'écriture? En relisant Charles Beaulieux', *Martin Vol.*, 59–65, argues that B. had an unduly rosy view of medieval French orthography.

7. GRAMMAR

OLD AND MIDDLE FRENCH

Gaston Zink, *Morphosyntaxe du pronom personnel (non réfléchi) en moyen français (XIVᵉ–XVᵉ siècles)* (PRF, 218), 425 pp., is a revised version of a 1981 Paris doctoral thesis — one can only regret that it took so long to see the light of day as it is a major contribution, and will doubtless prove to be an enduring one, to our understanding of Middle French syntax. It is characterized by an impressive mastery of detail and an admirable familiarity with earlier work (including considerably earlier but still valid items, many of them in English or German) in the field.

Actes (Nancy), being the *Actes* of the 1994 colloquium on Middle French, contains the following items of primarily linguistic interest: (A) under 'Éditions — philologie — morphologie': Y.-C. Mourin and M. Bonin, 'La formation des -*s* analogiques des 1sg en français à la lumière de la *Bible* de Macé de La Charité' (101–29); W. Müller, 'Sur la morphologie de l'ancien fribourgeois (14e siècle)' (131–41); E. Suomela-Härmä, 'Considérations linguistiques sur la mise en prose de *Renart le Nouvel*' (151–61); W. Zwanenburg, 'Le développement du suffixe dérivationnel -*e* en moyen français: la polyfonctionnalité et le blocage' (181–91); (B) under 'Lexique — discours': F. Möhren, 'Bilan sur les travaux lexicologiques en moyen français, avec un développement sur la définition' (195–210); A. Attali and S. Monsonégo, 'L'emploi des adjectifs dans *Le Mesnagier de Paris* (1394) — les adjectifs de couleur' (211–32); T. Kähärä, 'Nom d'adresse "sire" en moyen français' (281–95); R. Martin, 'Les "normes" du *DMF* (*Dictionnaire du moyen français*)' (297–305); H. Naïs, 'Vocabulaire technique et traduction: le cas particulier de l'agriculture' (307–18); C. Buridant, 'La phrase des chroniqueurs en moyen français: l'exemple de [J.] Monstrelet-Le Fèvre' (319–38); E. Sakari, 'Observations sur quelques adverbes de temps (*or, lors, alors*) en moyen français' (369–68); (C) under 'Syntaxe': B. Combettes, 'Bilan sur les études en syntaxe' (395–413); C. Brucker, 'La relative dans la phrase des traducteurs du XIVe siècle' (415–30); P. Demarolle, 'A propos de la syntaxe de *plus … que* chez Villon: méthodes de description' (431–41); R. van Deyck, 'La conjonction de coordination à l'initiale de propositions indépendantes dans les *Testaments* de F. Villon' (443–61); F. Dupuis and M. Dufresne, 'Les pronoms personnels français: un cas de réanalyse structurale' (463–81); P. Hirschbühler and M. Labelle, 'La syntaxe de position dans les infinitivales négatives en moyen français' (483–506); U. Jokinen, 'Le syntagme nominal non-déterminé et indéfini pendant la période 1430–1530 du moyen français' (507–15); P. Kunstmann, 'Relatif et liaison: le cas du relatif dit "de liaison"' (517–27); M. Lemieux and C. Marchello-Nizia, 'L'analyse quantitative en diachronie: l'évolution de l'ordre des mots' (529–39); F. Martineau, 'Évolution de l'alternance infinitif/subjonctif dans les compléments de verbes de volonté' (541–61); E. Oppermann, 'Les emplois injonctifs du futur en moyen français: une approche transphrastique' (563–71); G. Parussa, '*Rimoier* et *exposer*: quelques remarques sur la syntaxe de Christine de Pizan' (573–93); P. van Reenen and L. Schøsler, 'La déclinaison en ancien et en moyen français: deux tendances contraires' (595–612); and A. Valli, 'Étude des modalités d'introduction des régimes directs des verbes *avoir*, *donner* et *faire* en moyen français' (613–25).

O. Soutet, 'Épistémologie et linguistique diachronique: l'exemple des démonstratifs dans l'histoire du français', *Martin Vol.*, 367–76, argues that the forms in *i-* disappeared because the prefix 'n'était porteur d'aucune signification strictement identifiable et comme telle discursivement rentable' but otherwise has little new to say. C. Buridant, 'La place de l'adjectif épithèthe en ancien français: esquisse de bilan et perspectives', *VR*, 56: 109–40, is a useful overview.

Annie Bertin, *L'Expression de la cause en ancien français* (PRF, 219), Geneva, Droz, 207 pp., is a fine piece of research, well documented and well argued; a chapter devoted to the prepositions (*por, de, par*) entering into causal constructions is followed by others analysing the values and functions of 'les connecteurs principaux' (*car, que, por ce que, puisque*) and of 'des outils auxiliaires' (*quant, comme, qui, de ce que, a ce que*, parataxis), and a final chapter on 'prolongements stylistiques'. Th. Ponchon, 'L'alternance modale dans les complétives objects en ancien français', *TrL*, 32 : 73–110, draws its inspiration from the work of G. Guillaume.

In a perceptive and methodologically rigorous article, P. van Reenen and L. Schøsler, 'The thematic structure of the main clause in Old French: *or* versus *si*', *Papers* (ICHL 11), 401–19, demonstrate convincingly that OF thematic *si* 'tends to connect two clauses having the same implicit subject' whereas preverbal *or* 'tends to connect two clauses having different implicit subjects'. P. Kunstmann, '*Faire que sage(s)/faire que fol(s)*: prudence!', *Martin Vol.*, 233–40, is well documented but inconclusive. P. Ménard offers 'Remarques sur certains emplois de *com(me)* en ancien français', *ib.*, 257–67.

MODERN FRENCH

The title of Alain Fournier, *La Grammaire du français*, Belin, 751 pp., is carefully chosen (it is not *Grammaire française*), for, while serving as a well documented French grammar, it is also a book *about* French grammar. Pointing out that grammatical treatises are often 'faits pour être consultés', F. tells us that his aim was to write a book that could be read 'non comme un catalogue de paradigmes, de règles et d'exceptions, mais comme un livre'. And he has indeed succeeded in writing an eminently readable book, in which grammatical comment is illustrated by authentic examples ranging from 17th-c. literature to contemporary journalese and colloquial usage as represented in writing. Roger Hawkins, Marie-Noëlle Lamy, and Richard Towell, *Practising French Grammar*, London, Arnold, xii + 256 pp., is a workbook to accompany Hawkins and Towell's *French Grammar and Usage* (see *YWMLS*, 58 : 33).

P. H. Miller, G. K. Pullum, and A. M. Zwicky, 'The principle of phonology-free syntax: four apparent counter examples in French', *JL*, 33 : 67–90, conclude that their apparent counter examples 'are in fact spurious'.

D. Gaatone, 'Les clitiques et les règles: quelques jalons', *Martin Vol.*, 135–44, argues (on the basis of French examples) that clitics are to be regarded as words and not as affixes or bound morphemes.

M. Braud, 'L'attribut ethnique: adjectif ou nom?', *RRL*, 40, 1995 [1997]: 263–70, concludes that it constitutes 'une catégorie lexicale moyenne' on the border-line between 'adjectif qualificatif' and 'adjectif relationnel'. J. Goes, 'L'attribut: *objet* de *être*?', *TrL*, 34 : 49–64, suggests that '*objet* et *attribut* font partie d'une ressemblance de famille, tout en restant des fonctions différentes'.

De Mulder, *Relations anaphoriques*, includes, in addition to two items not specifically or exclusively on French (but mentioned here for completeness): an introductory essay by the editors (i–ix); G. Kleiber, 'Anaphore pronominale et référents évolutifs ou Comment faire recette avec un pronom' (1–29); M.-J. Reichler-Béguelin, 'Anaphores pronominales en contexte d'hétérogénéité énonciative: effets d'(in)cohérence' (31–54); H. Nølke, 'Anaphoricité et focalisation: le cas du pronom personnel disjoint' (55–67); B. Gaiffe, A. Reboul and L. Romary, 'Les SN définis: anaphore, anaphore associative et cohérence' (69–97); C. Schnedecker, 'A quelles conditions l'anaphore associative peut-elle être transitive? Quelques suggestions ...' (99–112); L. Lundquist and R. J. Jarvella, 'Anaphores et échelles. Comment les inférences scalaires contribuent à la désambiguïsation référentielle' (117–34); J.-M. Marandin, 'Une autre perspective sur la dépendance contextuelle des GN sans nom du français' (135–57); D. Apothéloz and C. Chanet, 'Défini et démonstratif dans les nominalisations' (159–86); M. Van Peteghem, 'Mécanismes anaphoriques sous-jacents aux "indéfinis" *autre* et *même*' (187–200); M. Manoliu-Manea, 'La pragma-sémantique de l'identité' (201–20), on French and Romanian; M. Riegel, '*Tel* adjectif anaphorique: variable de caractérisation et opérateur d'abstraction' (221–40); A. Rousseau, 'L'anaphorique en indo-européen: faits, réflexions et hypothèses' (241–64); Z. Guentcheva, 'Le phénomène de "redoublement clitique" est-il l'expression d'anaphore?' (265–76); F. Corblin, 'L'anaphore en subordination modale' (277–95); and A. Reboul, '(In)cohérence et anaphore: mythes et réalité' (297–314).

W. De Mulder, 'Le pronom *il* véhicule-t-il un sens référentiel?', *TrL*, 34 : 91–106, inspired by the work of G. Kleiber and F. Corblin, argues that one must not overlook the non-referential uses of *il*. R. Veland follows up his earlier work on the demonstratives (see in particular *YWMLS*, 58 : 35) with 'Cet adjectif qui ne simule pas: le problème de la détermination du pronom *celui*, *FM*, 65:169–83. Marie-Odile Junker, *Syntaxe et sémantique des quantifieurs flottants 'tous' et 'chacun': distributivité en sémantique conceptuelle* (Langue et Cultures, 28), Geneva, Droz, 1995, 183 pp., though a rigorous and demanding work of Chomskyan inspiration (and also acknowledging a debt to, *inter alia*, R. Jackendoff's cognitive semantics), is, unlike too many other works of that school, likely to prove largely accessible to scholars of other theoretical persuasions.

John Hewson, *The Cognitive System of the French Verb*, Amsterdam, Benjamins, xii + 187 pp., is a welcome volume inspired by and seeking to interpret the teachings of Gustave Guillaume. Referring to the extensive corpus of G.'s work now available in print, the author comments, doubtless correctly, that 'there exists no single comprehensive volume, in either French or English that presents a coherent overview of this material', a lack that his own book goes a long way towards making good. Three chapters devoted to more general concepts (including the very specifically Guillaumean one of chronogenesis) are a prelude to a wide-ranging discussion of aspect, voice, tense, and mood, which constitute the core of the volume and are followed by chapters on 'Present and present perfect', semiology, and verbal paradigms. Though the primary focus of atttention is French, there is also consideration of English and other languages.

I have not infrequently drawn attention in these surveys to the excellence of theses emanating from one or other of the Nordic countries, and here comes another, this time from Finland, characterized like many (not all ...) others from Denmark, Norway or Sweden by thorough documentation and rigorous and clear presentation; Eva Havu, *De l'emploi du subjonctif passé* (*AASF*, Ser. Humaniora), Helsinki, Suomalainen Tiedeakatemia, 1996, 240 pp., analyses the circumstances in which the perfect subjunctive has taken over the functions of the imperfect subjunctive. A.-M. Berthonneau and G. Kleiber discuss 'Subordination et temps grammaticaux: l'imparfait en discours indirect', *FM*, 66:113–41. J. Carruthers, 'The *passé surcomposé général*: on the relationship between a rare tense and discourse organization', *RPh*, 50:183–200, concludes that 'internal factors relat[ing] directly to the discourse organization and the patterns of temporal sequencing found in spoken French' contribute to the rarity of the form in question. R. Veland, 'Maigret et le subjonctif paradigmatique', *TrL*, 32:111–37, shows that *la subordonnée complétive* accounts for more than half of the morphologically identifiable subjunctives in his corpus of a dozen Simenon novels. Angela Schrott, **Futurität im Französischen der Gegenwart: Semantik und Pragmatik der Tempora der Zukunft*, Tübingen, Narr, 431 pp. *Martin Vol.* includes: F. J. Hausmann, 'L'imparfait avec et sans mystère' (175–80), which has some well-chosen examples of what he terms 'l'imparfait narratif' (as in: il y a cinq ans, le mur de Berlin s'ouvrait); C. Muller's reflexions, 'A propos de quelques impératifs' (275–80); and Co Vet, 'Modalités grammaticalisée et non-grammaticalisée' (405–12). B. Peeters offers a GB interpretation of 'L'accord du participe passé et la notion d'objet affecté', *FM*, 65;143–68. Teddy Arnavielle, *Le Morphème -ant: unité et diversité. Étude historique et théorique*, Louvain – Paris, Peeters, 374 pp., is a carefully planned, thoroughly documented and eminently useful presentation, covering the whole period from the *Eulalia* and the Jonah fragment to the early 17th c. All facets of the subject seem to be covered, with an introductory survey of the views of grammarians from the 16th to the 20th c., and two main sections: 'L'incidence médiate ou les constructions prépositionnelles' (*en* + *ant*, other prepositions + *-ant*), and 'L'incidence immédiate ou les constructions non-prépositionnelles', which includes *inter alia multa* a wide range of verbal constructions (*être, aller* + *-ant*), *-ant* as an attribute of the object, 'les constructions épithétiques' (types *vaillant chevalier, l'empereur oyant ceste clameur*), absolute constructions, detached constructions (type *Aigres dit à Milie, moult tendrement plourant*), substantivization (*le demourant de sa vie*). All in all, this is a fine work and a major contribution to our understanding of the evolution of French syntax.

Claude Guimier, **Les Adverbes du français: le cas des adverbes en* -ment, Gap, Ophrys, 170 pp. M. Blasco, 'Pour une approche syntaxique des dislocations', *JFLS*, 7 : 1–21, is clear and useful. K. Watson, 'French complement clitic sequences: a template approach', *ib.*, 69–89, argues that 'the constraints operating within complement clitic sequences [...] result from the interaction of two features — [+Accusative] and [−Individuation]'.

James Grieve, **A Dictionary of French Connectors*, London, Routledge, 1996, 544 pp.

La Place du sujet en français contemporain, ed. Catherine Fuchs, Louvain-la-Neuve, Duculot, 217 pp., provides a comprehensive coverage of the field, with contributions by: P. Le Goffic, 'Forme et place du sujet dans l'interrogation partielle' (15–42); C. Guimier, 'La place du sujet clitique dans les énoncés avec adverbe initial' (43–96); N. Fournier, 'La place du sujet nominal dans les phrases à complément prépositionnel initial' (97–132); C. Fuchs, 'La place du sujet nominal dans les relatives' (135–78); and N. Le Querler, 'La place du sujet nominal dans les subordonnées percontatives [= interrrogatives indirectes]' (179–203). In two studies of the *syntagme nominal* in contemporary French, M. H. Larsen, 'L'emploi des prépositions concrètes dans les syntagmes nominaux en français', *RevR*, 32 : 5–26, looks at the use of prepositions such as *avec, envers, sans, entre, dans, contre, pour, sur, dans, par*; while L. Stage, 'La transposition des actants dans le syntagme nominal', *ib.*, 51–86, is concerned only with 'la préposition la plus "vide" de sens', namely *de*. P. Cadiot, 'Intension vs. extension: clé de l'alternance des prépositions *à* et *de* en contexte binomial', *TrL*, 32:33–72, argues that the opposition intension vs extension underlies previous suggested oppositions (container vs content, quality vs quantity, abstract vs concrete, etc.).

M. Forsgren, 'Un classique revisité: la place de l'adjectif épithèthe', *Martin Vol.*, 115–26, includes a critical survey of recent work on the subject; while M. Riegel, 'Il est gentil de nous avoir aidés ou: à propos de compléments de l'adjectif qui n'en sont pas vraiment', *ib.*, 355–65, makes what seems the fairly obvious point that, in constructions of the kind in question, 'l'élargissement infinitif n'est pas un complément de l'adjectif'. H. Nølke, 'Note sur la dislocation du sujet: thématisation ou focalisation?', *ib.*, 281–94, is inspired by the ideas of Robert Martin. M.-N. Roubaud, 'Le sujet dans les énoncés pseudo-clivés', *RFP*, 14:147–71, studies pseudo-cleft sentences of the type '*Ce qui* [...], *c'est*'. M. Wilmet, 'L'apposition: une fonction à réestimer', *Martin Vol.*, 413–22, is characteristically shrewd.

H. Ossipov, 'A tale of two corpora of French dislocations', *Word*, 48:195–205, is based, for Canada, on N. Beauchemin and P. Martel, *Recherches sociolinguistiques dans la région de Sherbrooke: échantillon de textes libres*, III (1977), and, for France, on Betsy Barnes, *The Pragmatics of Left Detachment in Spoken Standard French* (Amsterdam, Benjamins, 1995). Elisabeth Stark, **Voranstellungsstrukturen und 'topic'-Markierung im Französischen*, Tübingen, Narr, x + 356 pp. M.-N. Roubaud, 'Les énoncés pseudo-clivés en: *le plus/le moins*', *JFLS*, 7:181–93, argues that constructions in spoken French of the type *le plus qui me plaît c'est*... are not just variations on the construction *ce qui me plaît le plus c'est*... A. Coveney continues his work on interrogative constructions with 'L'approche variationniste et la description de la grammaire du français: le cas des interrogatives', *LaF*, 115:88–100. Arguing that the grammar of spoken French has still not been adequately analysed, C. Blanche-Benveniste, 'A propos de *Qu'est-ce que c'est* et *C'est quoi*', *RFP*, 14:126–46, proposes 'une justification grammaticale et non stylistique des formes interrogatives'. L. Bouchard, L. Emrikanian and M. Labelle, 'Traitement de l'ellipse du verbe dans les coordonnées en Grammaire Syntagmatique Généralisée', *TrL*, 32:7–32, specifically on French, are inspired by G. Gazdar et al., *Generalized Phrase Structure Grammar*, 1985).

Though of general relevance, I. Évrard, 'La phrase au-delà du texte: décrire pour diviser ou diviser pour décrire? Linguistique textuelle et niveaux de description', *TrL*, 34:121–33, relies entirely on French examples.

8. LEXICOGRAPHY

The *FEW* has reached fasc. 154, 1996, 120 pp. Eva Büchi, *Les Structures du 'Französisches etymologisches Wörterbuch': recherches métalexicographiques et métalexicologiques*, *ZRP*, Beiheft 268, 1996, xiii + 593 pp., is an impressively thorough and shrewd critique of its monumental subject; characterizing the *FEW* as 'un trésor d'une richesse prodigieuse' whose structure however is 'extrêmement touffue', B. concludes that 'la combinaison de ces deux caractéristiques génère une situation quelque peu paradoxale, car à l'abondance matérielle (documentation et analyses) s'oppose l'insuffisance des voies d'accès (incohérence du programme lexicographique)'. Kurt Baldinger, *Dictionnaire étymologique de l'ancien français*, Tübingen, Niemeyer, reaches the beginning of the letter H with fasc. H1, 104 pp.; and is now supplemented by Martina Fietz-Beck, **Index G*, Tübingen, Niemeyer, ix + 237 pp.

The latest fascicule of the *Dictionnaire de l'Académie française*, 9th edn, covers HACHURE-HOMÉRIDE. *Les Préfaces du Dictionnaire de l'Académie française, 1694–1992*, ed. Bernard Quemada, Champion, xi + 564 pp., is the kind of book that makes one wonder why no one had thought of doing it before. We have here scholarly editions of the preface to each of the nine editions of the Academy's dictionary and of accompanying texts (*épîtres*, *privilèges*, *discours préliminaires*, etc.), with introductions and notes providing a wealth of information on the background to each edition and on the theoretical and methodological considerations that govern its content and shape; this is an important contribution to the history of French lexicography. Jacques Damade, **Petite archéologie des dictionnaires: Richelet, Furetière, Littré*, Éds de la Bibliothèque, 139 pp. Dorothea Behnke, **Furetière und Trévoux: Eine Untersuchung zum Verhältnis der beiden Wörterbuchserien*, Tübingen, Niemeyer , 1996, vi + 271 pp. H. Thomassen, 'Zur Behandlung der Datierung im *Dictionnaire historique de la langue française*', *ZRP*, 113:39–50, on the 1992 Robert publication (see *YWMLS*, 54:37–38), is critical.

Bernard Luce, **Dictionnaire gastronomique français-anglais*, Maison du Dictionnaire, 500 pp.

9. LEXICOLOGY

Hilary Wise, *The Vocabulary of Modern French: Origins, Structure and Function*, London, Routledge, xiii + 256 pp., is an admirably comprehensive and user-friendly survey of the fields referred to in the subtitle, with 'function' covering, *inter alia multa*, such topics as the *féminisation des noms de métier*, euphemism and taboo, register, argot, and

'Codification, control and linguistic mythology' (including dictionary-making, the myth of *la clarté française*, and the 'defence' of the French language).

Aïno Niklas-Salminen, *La Lexicologie*, Armand Colin, 192 pp. *TeN*, 15 (June and Dec. 1996), publishes the proceedings of the 'Table ronde sur les banques de terminologie' held at Quebec in January 1996. With an extensive list of sources ranging from the *Châtelaine de Vergi* to the 1995 film *Le Plus Bel Âge*, Marie Treps, *Le Dico des mots-caresses*, Seuil, 350 pp., provides, with an erudite and entertaining commentary and a wealth of literary examples, a classified survey of some nine hundred affective and erotic terms: a book to be read for edification and with pleasure — could one ask for more? The idea of an entire dictionary devoted to spoonerisms may be surprising, but Joël Martin's *Dico de la contrepèterie*, Seuil, 541 pp., in the same series, is just that; an alphabetical listing of some hundreds of *mots contrepétogènes*, with examples (usually several) based on each, is complemented by a key based on the use of bold type (*Les* **châ**tains n'ont pas droit au **pu**pitre); the great majority of the examples are onomasiologically comparable with Rabelais's *A Beau***m**ont-le-Vi**c**omte. Claude Lecouteux, *Charmes, conjurations et bénédictions*, Champion, 1996, 141 pp., a work that appears to have no close parallel in French, is both a collection with commentary of (mainly but by no means exclusively medieval) magical and cabbalistic terms and formulae, names of good and evil entities invoked in charms, and so on, and an encyclopedia of related notions (*croix, exorcisme, runes, tetragrammaton*, etc.). Michel Martins-Baltar and Geneviève Calbris, *Le Corps dans la langue. Esquisse d'un dictionnaire onomasiologique. Notions et expressions dans le champ de 'dent' et de 'manger'*, Tübingen, Niemeyer, xxi + 203 pp. *Dictionnaire étymologique des mots inventés*, ed. Jean-Louis Mathieu, Saint-Maximin (Gard), Théétète, 92 pp. A.Bollée discusses 'Das *Dictionnaire des termes officiels* und die Europäisierung des Französischen', *Fest. Bergmann*, 383–91.

A. Henry discusses (inconclusively) the origin and meaning of '*Ester(c)*: un adjectif méconnu de l'ancien français', *Romania*, 115:536–40. T. Vennemann, *NOWELE*, 31–32:439–62, proposes a Basque origin for Eng. *knife*, Fr. *canif*, and related words in other languages. U. Jokinen, 'Observations sur les locutions verbales en moyen français', *Martin Vol.*, 195–202, inclines one to think that she could develop this into a much fuller study. Henriette Walter, *L'Aventure des mots français venus d'ailleurs*, Robert Laffont, 345 pp. Nicolas Cazelles, *Les Comparaisons du français*, Belin, 235 pp. *La Mesure des mots: cinq études d'implantation terminologique*, ed. Loïs Depecker, Rouen U.P., 528 pp.

Martin Vol. includes: C. Fuchs, 'L'interprétation des polysèmes grammaticaux en contexte' (127–33) (taking French illustrations); G. Gorcy, 'À propos des mots-valises: de la fantaisie verbale à la néologie raisonnée' (145–48), considering some recent examples; and S. Mejri, 'Binarisme, dualité et séquences figées' (249–56). J.-J. Franckel, 'Approche de l'identité d'un préverbe à travers l'analyse des variations sémantiques des unités préverbales', *JFLS*, 7 : 47–68, is an ingenious but not wholly convincing attempt at 'une caractérisation unitaire du préverbe *RE-*'. D. Corbin, 'Décrire un affixe dans un dictionnaire', *Martin Vol*, 79–94, looks at the way affixes are treated in a number of dictionaries and has her own proposals for how it should be done. J. Danell, **Le Phénomène de concurrence en français moderne. Réflexions à partir de "an--année, jour--journée, paraître-apparaître" et d'autres*, Umeå U.P., 1995, 128 pp. H. Huot, 'À propos des nominalisations en *-ion*: mots-thèmes et lacunes dans les séries dérivationnelles du français', *TrL*, 34: 5–19, considers possible and impossible unattested derivatives, and stresses the importance of the learned element in the derivational morphology not only of French but of the Romance languages generally and indeed of certain others, particularly English. S. Feigenbaum, 'Le mot composé [Sans + SN]', *ib.*, 21–47, seeks, with considerable success, to 'établir une typologie des mots composés à SANS sur la base de leur structure syntaxique, sémantique et morphologique'.

J. Picoche, 'Le vocabulaire de la douleur en français. Recherche de quelques primitifs sémantiques', *Martin Vol.*, 311–19, reflects on the semantics of *souffrir/souffrance, douleur, faire mal*, and the interjection *aïe!*. J. E. Médélice discusses 'Les désignations du rouge-gorge en gallo-roman de France', *Géolinguistique*, 7 : 59–75; and J. R. Ferraris traces 'Une évolution sémantique longue et intéressante: les mots de la famille de *lourd* en gallo-roman', *ib.*, 77–91. H. Lagerqvist, 'Langue et société: l'exemple de *entor* en ancien français', *RLiR*, 61 : 41–78, seeks to demonstrate that 'même un mot grammatical peut subir l'influence des mœurs et du milieu où l'on s'en sert'. G. Lavis devotes a major and impressive article to 'La synonymie verbale en ancien français: le concept "frapper"', *RLiR*, 61 : 133–211.

Gorgette Dal, **Grammaire du suffixe -et(t)e*, Didier-Érudition, 270 pp. M. Plénat offers an 'Analyse morpho-phonologique d'un corpus d'adjectifs dérivés en *-esque*', *JFLS*, 7 : 163–78. Starting from the problems presented by the translation of the term '[Government and] Binding' into French, B. Defrancq, 'Entre *la liaison* et *le liage*. Étude morphologique', *TrL*, 32 : 139–54, seeks to show that 'la dérivation est une opération linguistique complexe dont les aspects morphologiques et syntaxiques sont étroitement liés'. W. Zwanenburg, 'Les noms d'action de forme participiale passée en français', *RLFRU*,

16:53–61, argues, taking Turkish as a basis of comparison, that nouns such as *entrée* and the corresponding participles, which in OF could be analysed as instances of polysemy, should be interpreted in modern French as homonyms.

10. SEMANTICS

The series 'Langue et Cultures' (Paris – Geneva, Droz) has established itself as an outlet for major dissertations on, *inter alia*, the linguistic study of modern French. The latest (no. 31) in the series, Anne Theissen, *Le Choix du nom en discours*, 486 pp., is no exception. Inspired by E. Rosch's work on psycholinguistics, it takes up the problem posed by R. Brown's 1958 article, 'How shall a thing be called?' (*Psychological Review*, 65.1, 14–21), namely that of the choice between hypernyms and hyponyms: what, in a given context, determines the choice of, say, *chien*, rather than that of one of its possible hypernyms (e.g. *quadrupède*, *animal*) or a hyponym such as *caniche*? Organized in two main sections, on respectively first mention (type *un N*) and second mention (*le N*, *ce N*), this thorough and penetrating book ranges widely and deeply into discourse analysis, psycholinguistics, semantics, and syntax. The corpus consists mainly of 19th- and 20th-c. French literary texts but also includes translations (the brothers Grimm, Graham Greene, Thomas Mann, Turgeniev, among others) and recent journalism.

G. Kleiber, 'Cognition, sémantique et facettes: une "histoire" de livres et de ... romans', *Martin Vol.*, 219–31, takes up views expressed by A. Cruse in *Lexical Semantics* (1986). P. Cadiot and F. Nemo take French examples as the basis of their discussion of 'Propriétés extrinsèques en sémantique lexicale', *JFLS*, 7:127–46.

11. DIALECTS AND REGIONAL FRENCH

FM, 65.1, is largely devoted to dialects and regional French and includes: J. Le Dû, 'La disparition du groupe des atlas et l'avenir de la géographie linguistique' (6–12); J.-P. Chauveau, 'L'indexation des atlas linguistiques par régions' (13–14); W. Bal, 'La dialectologie en Wallonie' (15–19); X. Ravier, 'Des choses aux mots, des mots au discours: pour une utilisation maximale des données des atlas linguistiques et ethnographiques' (20–34); J.-C. Bouvier, 'État actuel des travaux sur les ethnotextes' (35–44); N. Gueunier, 'Questions sur le genre ethnotexte' (44–53); and J.-B. Martin, 'Le français régional.. La variation diatopique du français de France' (55–69). J.-L. Fossat, 'Néologie dialectale et implantation en socioterminologie spatiale utile', *TeN*, 16:7–32, is a key-note address given to the March 1985 *journées d'étude,* 'Vers une convergence des méthodologies en mesure de l'implanation terminologique', held at Toulouse. Manfred Höfler and Pierre Rézeau, **Variétés géographiques du français: matériaux pour le vocabulaire de l'art culinaire,* Klincksieck, 233 pp.

Le français en Belgique: une langue, une communauté, ed. Daniel Blampain et al ., Louvain-la-Neuve, Duculot, xvii + 530 pp., is a very welcome volume, superbly produced with a wealth of illustrations, by a team of thirty-two scholars, offering and indeed providing 'un exposé complet sur la langue française en Belgique'; in twenty-seven chapters it covers *inter alia,* in masterly fashion, the history of the language in Belgium, dialectology, phonetics and phonology, morphology and syntax, the lexicon, onomastics, the role of French in the linguistically diverse regions of Belgium and in former Belgian territories in Africa, attitudes to and the use of the language, linguistic legislation, and 'La promotion du français en Communauté française de Belgique'. P. V. Cassano has two articles in *Orbis,* 36, 1991–93[n.d.] on 'An introduction to the influence of Flemish on the French of Brussels', one on phonology (136–61), the other on morphology and syntax (162–202). B. Van Gysel reports on an 'Enquête sur les particularités du français de Belgique dans les langues de spécialité', *TeN,* 16:63–73. J. Kruijsen, 'Débordements de la Romania: adaptation et permanence à la frontière linguistique en Belgique', *Géolinguistique,* 7:43–57, considers possible Dutch phonetic, grammatical and lexical influence on the Walloon of the Hesbaye/Haspengouw area.

   Jean-Michel Eloy, *La Constitution du picard: une approche de la notion de langue,* Louvain-la-Neuve, Peeters, 259 pp., takes an informed and informative look at the linguistic status of Picard (language or dialect?), and does so within the framework of a wide-ranging and fruitful general discussion of the concepts of *langue, dialecte* and *patois* with, specifically on Picard, a historical survey ('Pour une histoire du fait picard', 45–85) and a morphological description (129–207), devoted principally to the verb; the answer to the question 'Qu'est-ce que le picard?', which is addressed not merely by the conclusion under that title but by the book as a whole, is that '"le picard" est potentiellement une vraie langue, qui a déjà construit et fixé une autonomie linguistique réelle'. Patrick Brasseur, **Atlas linguistique et ethnographique de la Normandie,* vol. 3, CNRS, 240 pp., completes the atlas of Normandy. **Mots et expressions des patois angevins: petit dictionnaire,* ed. Gérard Cherbonnier, Brissac, Petit pavé, 74 pp. Edgar Chaigne, **Trésors du parler des parlers de l'Ouest: Poitou, Charente, Vendée,* Bordeaux, Aubéron, 256 pp.

   P. Singy, 'Les francophones de péripherie face à leur langue: étude de cas en Suisse romande', *CFS,* 49, 1995–96 [1997]:213–35, reports on a questionnaire-based investigation of the linguistic insecurity felt by speakers of the Vaudois 'régiolecte'.

12. Anglo-Norman

P. Damian-Grint,'*Estoire* as a word and genre: meaning and literary usage in the twelfth century', *MAe*, 66:189–206, is based on Anglo-Norman sources. L. Jefferson and W. Rothwell, 'Society and lexis: a study of the Anglo-French vocabulary in the fifteenth-century accounts of the Merchant Taylors' Company', *ZFSL*, 107:273–301, demonstrate and illustrate with nearly 40 examples the lexicological importance for both English and French of the wealth of material to be found in these accounts and call for a rigorous policy of investigating other such non-literary documents. W. Rothwell, 'The Anglo-French register of late Middle English',*NMi*, 97, 1996:423–36, argues that the usual conduit for the introduction of French terminology into late Middle English and 'its consequential transformation of the English lexicon' was Anglo-French rather than, as has often been supposed, 'the continental variety'. L. Iglesias-Rábade, 'Non-"technical" Anglo-Norman lexicon in Early Middle English texts: a sociolinguistic interpretation', *Orbis*, 36, 1991–93[n.d.]:81–103, fails to mention either the *Anglo-Norman Dictionary* or any of Rothwell's articles.

13. French in Canada

Les Origines du français québécois, ed. Raymond Mougeon et Édouard Beniak, Quebec, Laval U.P., 1994[1995], x + 332 pp., is an informative and interesting volume, with an extensive 'Présentation' by the editors (1–55). There are five papers on 'Perspective externe': H. Charbonneau and A. Guillemette, 'Les pionniers du Canada au XVIIᵉ siècle' (59–78); P. Barbaud, 'Des patois au français: la catastrophe linguistique de la Nouvelle-France' (79–99); C. Asselin and A. McLaughlin, 'Les immigrants en Nouvelle-France au XVIIᵉ siècle parlaient-ils français?' (101–30); P. Laurendeau, 'Le concept de *patois* avant 1790, *vel vernacula lingua*' (131–66); and R. Chaudenson, 'Français d'Amérique du Nord et créoles français: le français parlé par les immigrants au XVIIᵉ siècle' (167–80). Four papers are on 'Perspective interne': A. Hull, 'Des origines du français dans le Nouveau Monde' (183–98); Y.-Ch. Morin, 'Les sources historiques de la prononciation du français du Québec' (199–236); C. Poirier, 'La langue parlée en Nouvelle-France: vers une convergence des explications' (237–73); and K. Flikeid, 'Origines et évolution du français acadien à la lumière de la diversité contemporaine'

(275–326); and there is a brief 'Postface' by L. Wolf (327–32). Taken together, the lists of references to the various papers constitute a good source of bibliographical documentation. Pierre Martel and Hélène Cajolet-Laganière, *Le Français québécois: usages, standard et aménagement*, Quebec, Laval U.P., 1996, 143 pp. A. Martin discusses 'Quelques aspects d'une problématique de l'implantation terminologique: le cas de la terminologie officielle de l'éducation au Québec', *T&N*, 16:86–94.

14. FRENCH IN AFRICA

Le Français au Maghreb: actes du colloque d'Aix-en-Provence, septembre, 1994, ed. A. Queffélec, F. Benzakour, and Y. Cherrad-Benchefra, Aix-en-Provence, Univ. de Provence, 1995, 272 pp.

15. CREOLES

Guy Hazaël-Massieux, *Les Créoles: problèmes de genèse et de description*, Aix-en-Provence, Univ. of Provence, 1996, 374 pp. *Créoles de la Caraïbe*, ed. Alain Yacou, Karthala, 1996, 222 pp., publishes the papers given at a conference in Point-à-Pitre in March, 1995. *Matériaux pour l'étude des classes grammaticales dans les langues créoles*, ed. Daniel Véronique, Aix-en-Provence, Univ. of Provence, 1996, 306 pp. Pravina Nallatamby, *Mille mots du français mauricien: réalités lexicales et francophonie à l'Île Maurice*, CILF, 1995, 299 pp.

16. SOCIOLINGUISTICS

Though described as a 'workbook' (and it does indeed present an ample selection of well-devised exercises), Rodney Ball, *The French-Speaking World: A Practical Introduction to Sociolinguistic Issues*, London, Routledge, xvi + 228 pp., is helpfully informative on a wide range of topics, including among others *le monde francophone*, multilingualism in Switzerland, Belgium and Canada, languages other than French in France, regional varieties of French, creoles, and situational and social variation. *Französische Sprache in Deutschland im Zeitalter der Französischen Revolution*, ed. Bernd Spillner, Bern, Lang, 257 pp.

17. SPECIAL REGISTERS

I. Villebrun studies the 'Genèse d'une terminologie au XVIIIᵉ siècle: l'exemple des forges à la Catalane', *T&N*, 16:55–62. Adrian C. Ritchie, *Media French: A Guide to Contemporary French Idiom*, Cardiff, Univ. of Wales Press, ix + 268 pp. D. M. Engel, 'The recipe for success', *JFLS*, 7 : 195–207, examines 'some syntactic features in the discourse of food, and in particular recipes and cookery pieces published in the French press'. Jean-Pierre Goudailler, **Comment tu tchatches! Dictionnaire du français contemporain des cités*, Maisonneuve et Larose, 192 pp. David Burke, *Street French Slang Dictionary and Thesaurus*, New York — Chichester, John Wiley, ix + 323 pp., consists mainly of a dictionary of 'popular French terms' (giving both definitions or equivalents and literal translations) aand a two-part 'Street French thesaurus', starting from English, with in addition brief sections on 'Popular French gestures' and 'English words used in French' (with no indication, however, of the different meanings some of these have in French).

18. DISCOURSE ANALYSIS

G. Dostie and J.-M. Léard offer a penetrating analysis of 'Les marqueurs discursifs en lexicographie. Le cas de *tiens*', *Martin Vol.*, 95–114; while M. Hug provides a thorough-going study of 'Emplois de *donc*. Remarques sur mille cinq cents emplois relevés dans *FRANTEXT* ', *ib.*, 185–94. S. Porhiel studies 'Le marqueur de catégorisation *point de vue*', *FM*, 65 : 184–200. Y. Ellis, 'Laughing together: laughter as a feature of affiliation in French conversation', *JFLS*, 7 : 147–61, proposes to 'show how the analysis of episodes of laughter in French interaction can be approached from the theoretical perspective of Conversation Analysis'.

19. CONTRASTIVE STUDIES

The stated aim of Chantal Dupas, *Perception et langage: étude linguistique du fonctionnement des verbes de perception auditive et visuelle en anglais et en français*, Louvain, Peeters, 351 pp., is to 'apporter un éclairage nouveau sur les verbes de perception et d'ouvrir des perspectives extra-linguistiques relatives à la relation de l'homme avec le monde', within the framework of *la linguistique énonciative*, whose principal theoretician is A. Culioli. G. Gréciano, 'La variance du figement', *Martin Vol.*, 149–56, is a contrastive study of French and German, as is P. Valentin, 'Les épithèthes en français et en allemand', *ib.*, 397–404.

EARLY MEDIEVAL LITERATURE

By A. E. COBBY, *University of Cambridge*, and FINN E. SINCLAIR

1. GENERAL

Alain Corbellari, *Joseph Bédier: écrivain et philologue* (PRF, 220), xxv + 765 pp., is a monumental assessment of the life, works and influence of the great philologist. It includes a *bibliographie raisonnée* of B.'s writings and of their reviews, his genealogy, and a number of unpublished texts and fragments, mostly critical but including a three-act play, 'La Légende des Aliscamps'. Pierre Jonin, *L'Europe en vers au moyen âge: essai de thématique* (Nouvelle Bibliothèque du Moyen Age, 35), Champion, 1996, 845 pp., is an anthology of some 500 thematically arranged excerpts from medieval verse literature in many languages, French being the most heavily represented. Its purpose is to facilitate cross-cultural comparison, and several 20th-c. poems are included to this end. Each of the 71 themes is discussed in an introductory 'Thématique' section, which is followed by the textual section in which short (one-page or less) extracts are presented in modern French, together with contextual summaries. There are several indices. Dietmar Rieger, *Chanter et dire: études sur la littérature du moyen âge*, Champion, 297 pp., reprints 14 articles on a wide range of subjects published from 1979 to 1995, some originally in German but all now translated. Rossi, *Jongleurs*, includes: M. Zink, 'Contorsions jongleresques' (5–8), an attempt to rehabilitate the *jongleur*; L. Rossi, 'Jean Bodel: des *flabiaus* à la chanson de geste' (9–42), which probes Bodel's understanding of the genres to which he was adding and his self-presentation as a *jongleur*, viewing his whole work as a representation of *jongleurs*; C. Jacob-Hugon, 'Pour une lecture "jongleresque" de la *Chanson des Saisnes*' (43–57), a reading which reveals at the same time an experienced epic *jongleur*, a master of the oral style, and an intellectual with a critical attitude to his sources; and R. E. F. Straub, 'Un amusement jongleresque: le *Débat du Cul et du Con*' (59–72), who sees this text as a *summa* of erotic metaphors and motifs found also in romance and fabliaux. J. W. Baldwin, 'The image of the jongleur in northern France around 1200', *Speculum*, 72:635–63, uses Latin and French texts (the latter by Jean Renart, Gerbert de Montreuil and Gace Brulé), to trace the various functions of the *jongleur* (performative, musical, literary), the centrality of music and, behind the literary references, the historical reality. The clarity of the French image contrasts with the shadowy figure found in contemporary Latin chronicles. B. concludes that the romance portrayal of the *jongleur* is historically accurate. *Cahiers de Recherches Médiévales (XIIIe-XVe s.)*, 2,

1996, entitled *Regards sur le Moyen Age*, has several articles on modern interpretations of the Middle Ages: S. Baudelle-Michels, 'Une relecture de *Renaut de Montauban*: le *Jeu des Quatre Fils Aymon* (1941)' (25–35), on a play by Herman Closson performed in occupied Brussels; W. Lucas, 'Réception de la littérature médiévale à travers le médium cinématographique' (149–53), a brief piece mostly on the US commercial film; F. Amy de la Bretèque, 'Présence de la littérature française du moyen âge dans le cinéma français' (155–65), a more penetrating study of early 20th-c. French exploitation of the Middle Ages as a cultural intertext; and C. Ridoux, 'La nouvelle école de philologie romane et sa perception de la littérature médiévale' (187–98), on the attitudes of the 19th-c. philologists to various texts and on the two tendencies in their work, pure philology and literary history.

J. E. Burns et al., 'Feminism and the discipline of Old French Studies: "Une bele disjointure" ', Bloch, *Medievalism*, 225–66, point to the ambiguous position of the feminist medievalist, caught between the shifting subjectivities of the present and the elusiveness of textuality and identity in the past. Emphasis is placed on the complex interrelation between feminine representation and female identity in the context of epic and lyric texts. Theorizing a new reading of 'woman' challenges medievalists to look beyond the traditional analytical categories of the discipline. Chance, *Gender*, is, despite its title, a collection of articles on a range of selected women authors, from the 8th to the 15th c., including the *trobairitz* and women mystics as well as Marie de France and Christine de Pizan. These authors wrote either in Latin or in the vernacular, in various European countries. The themes of the sections hold the work together, essays being divided into three: 'M/F: Authority, Domination, Misogyny', 'Autohagiography and Self-Mimesis: The Construction of Female Subjectivity' and 'Speaking the Body: Transhumanization and Subversion'. *Bakhtin and Medieval Voices*, ed. Thomas J. Farrell, Gainesville, Florida U.P., 1996, 240 pp., addresses theory as much as Medieval Studies, relating the flexibility of Bakhtin's terminology to the unclassifiable nature of medieval texts in regard to genre. A range of essays fall into three sections: 'Carnival Voices in Medieval Texts', 'Multiple Voices in Medieval Texts', and 'Dissenting Voices with Bakhtin'. Sun Hee Kim Gertz, **Poetic Prologues: Medieval Conversations with the Literary Past*, Frankfurt am Main, Klostermann, 1996. S. G. Nichols, 'Modernism and the politics of medieval studies', Bloch, *Medievalism*, 25–56, views modernism as the 'hidden agenda' of medieval studies in the late 19th century. The new role played by philology and the emphasis on 'le dit' (the said) instead of on 'le dire' (the performative act and contexts of speaking) are related to nationalism and the primacy of French as a historical and literary language; the 19th c. is seen as constructing a modernist canon in a medieval setting, with an alterity proper to modernism itself. Helen Solterer, *The Master and Minerva: Disputing Women in French Medieval Culture*, Berkeley, California U.P., 1995, xii + 301 pp., considers the relationship between women and the domain of the written text. The work is presented as a diptych: Part 1 traces the ritual practices of the clerical world of learning as it appears in medieval French narrative, focusing on the symbolic domination of women. Part 2 investigates how the woman respondent came to dispute this dominant masculine discourse on women, and draws a connection between the critique of feminine representation internal to this discourse and the critique coming from without.

Two articles in *Agriculture in the Middle Ages: Technology, Practice, and Representation*, ed. Del Sweeney, Philadelphia, Pennsylvania U.P., 1995, xiii + 371 pp., rely on literary sources: H. Braet, 'A thing most brutish: the image of the rustic in Old French literature' (191–204), uses many examples, mostly from the fabliaux, to give an overview of the social and psychological characteristics of the peasant and to show how authors reveal the outlook of their upper-class patrons; and J. B. Dozer-Rabedeau, '*Rusticus*: folk-hero of thirteenth-century Picard drama' (205–26), finds this hero in ribald tavern scenes, the tavern being a comic space in which the rustic can function, free of the tyranny of a church-dominated society. F. Möhren, 'Edition et lexicographie', Glessgen, *Philologie*, 153–66, advocates a thorough philological approach as a prerequisite for lasting works, and makes a plea for good, complete glossaries, based on firm knowledge of the MSS, as a foundation for lexicographical work. G. Roques, 'La critique des éditions de textes', *ib.*, 145–51, draws conclusions from personal experience and much reviewing, concerning desiderata for editions and dictionaries, and tasks not worth undertaking. The editor's role is to give the texts their meaning and to make it accessible to others. G. Bianciotto, 'Des souris et des hommes', *Actes* (Keio), 41–72, examines the history and literature of the mouse and the rat, through encyclopedias, fables, fabliaux, and *Renart* literature. He finds little symbolic value and no clear implication of evil. S. G. Nichols, 'Aux frontières du rire médiéval', *Poirion Vol.*, 315–44, considers medieval attitudes to laughter from various sources before focusing on Jean Bodel's *Les Sohais desvez* and *Pathelin*. Important themes are laughter as the defining characteristic of the human, and the link between genitals and laughter.

2. EPIC

GENERAL.   Valérie Galent-Fasseur, *L'Epopée des pèlerins: motifs eschatologiques et mutations dans la chanson de geste*, PUF, 254 pp., uses the figure of the pilgrim as a guide to the essence and development of the genre, from the earliest to the last poems. The changing role and character of the epic pilgrim crystallize the evolution both of the *chanson de geste* and of the individual's relationship with God. H. Akkari, 'La déclaration amoureuse de l'héroïne dans la chanson de geste, ou pour une autre poétique amoureuse', *BDBA*, 15:7–18, studies the words and gestures used by women to express love, and finds a new form of courtesy in which the woman makes the knight her lord by offering the service of her body. A. Labbé, 'La poétique des ruines dans quelques chansons de geste', *Littératures*, 36:5–32, 37:237–59, reflects upon the use of ruined buildings in a wide range of *chansons de geste*, and finds that the Middle Ages does not know the power of evocation of tragic grandeur attributed to them by the Romantics. Ruins of contemporary buildings are a sign of desolation, since a property-owning society sees the ruin of buildings as indicative of the destruction of civilization and of the symbols of its power; but ancient ruins have the potential for recivilization through recolonization.

ROLAND AND CHARLEMAGNE.   *Il testo assonanzato franco-italiano della 'Chanson de Roland': cod. Marciano fr. IV (= 225)*, ed. Carlo Beretta, Università di Pavia, 1995, lxiii + 692 pp., offers a solid edition with many textual notes and, for the first time for a Franco-Italian text, a complete glossary to aid lexical study. M. Ailes, 'From epic to chronicle and back: the *Pseudo-Turpin Chronicle* and the *chanson de geste Fierabras*', pp. 17–24 of *Thirty Years of Medieval Studies at the University of Reading, 1965–1995: A Celebration*, ed. Anne E. Curry, University of Reading, 1996, 99 pp., shows through close textual analysis the indebtedness of the *Pseudo-Turpin* to *La Chanson de Roland* and that of *Fierabras* to the *Pseudo-Turpin*, concentrating on the episode of the fight between Roland and Ferragut. D. Kahn, 'La *Chanson de Roland* dans le décor des églises du XIIe siècle', *CCMe*, 40:337–72, uses many architectural examples in France and elsewhere to examine how, through oral transmission, legendary characters (those of *La Chanson de Roland*, but also Arthurian and Norse heroes) were translated into religious imagery.

GUILLAUME D'ORANGE AND THE GARIN CYCLE.   The year sees two new textual editions. *La Chevalerie Vivien: édition critique des Mss S, D, C*, ed. from materials left by Duncan McMillan by Jean-Charles Herbin, Jean-Pierre Martin and François Suard, 2 vols (Senefiance, 39–40), Aix-en-Provence, CUER MA, 414, 415–748 pp., gives a critical edition of MS *S* (Oxford Bodleian French e. 32), related to the *AB* redaction, with critical texts of *D*, facing, and *C*, as an appendix. *Les Enfances Vivien*, ed. Magali Rouquier (TLF, 478), xliii + 226 pp., the first new edition of this text since 1895, uses redaction *a* and thus completes the series of texts published from this family of MSS. The edition is based on MS *A²* (B. N. f. fr. 1449), with lacunae supplied from other MSS of the *a* group, and includes comprehensive variants from groups *a* and *b*. *MedRom*, 21.2–3, a special issue entitled *La chanson de geste e il ciclo di Guglielmo d'Orange: atti del Convegno di Bologna, 7–9 ottobre 1996*, includes many articles on William texts, early and late. M. Tyssens, 'Aspects de l'intertextualité dans la geste des Narbonnais' (163–83), shows how authors of *chansons de geste* use echoes to elaborate their individual narratives, while *remanieurs* use them to set up intertextual links between members of the cycle. A. Vàrvaro, 'La *Chanson de Guillaume* et l'histoire littéraire du XIIe siècle' (184–207), reviews critically opinions on the dating and composition of *La Chanson de Guillaume*. F. Suard, 'Héros et action héroïque, des batailles de Larchamp au *Moniage Guillaume*' (208–40), looks at the tension between the constant undermining of heroism implicit in the slaughter of the French armies and their heroes, and the assertion of heroism encapsulated in the couple Guillaume-Guibourc, and also in Rainouart. B. Guidot, 'La fantaisie souriante dans le cycle d'Aymeri' (241–75), argues that the portrait of the court has a satirical bite not present in the portrayal of pagan religion. The satire nonetheless reveals a good humour and self-critical attitude which do not fundamentally undermine the stability of the community celebrated in the poetry. J.-C. Herbin, 'Guichardet/Begonnet: une rencontre entre le cycle de Guillaume et la geste des Loherains?' (276–95), compares the armings of Guiot in *La Chanson de Guillaume*, Guichardet in *La Chevalerie Vivien*, and Garin and Begonnet in *Hervis de Metz*. While they could be simply variations on a motif, with no clear indication of which text may have influenced which other, H. tentatively concludes that the last two may borrow from a lost version of *La Chanson de Guillaume*. P. E. Bennett, 'Des jongleurs et des rois: réflexions sur le "prologue" du *Couronnement de Louis*' (296–312), is a close reading of the opening *laisses* of the *Couronnement* compared with the 'prologues' offered by characters in *Huon de Bordeaux* and Chrétien's *Yvain*, to show how the author of the *Couronnement* establishes his text as didactic discourse. J. Subrenat, 'Vivien a-t-il respecté son vœu?' (313–32), considers the evolution of Vivien's vow from *La Chanson de Guillaume* to *Les Enfances Vivien*, in the light of changing juridical and theological expectations, to show how poets' attitude to Vivien evolved between *c.* 1150 and *c.* 1220. J.-P. Martin, 'Le motif de l'adoubement dans le cycle de Guillaume' (333–61), compares arming scenes in songs of the cycle from a stylistic viewpoint and finds variations on several themes. The motif seems to appear earlier in literary sources than in non-literary ones, so it cannot inform us on contemporary social reality, but it does reveal an awareness, at an early date, of the ritual character of the scene: the arming of Girard in *La Chanson de Guillaume* may be a parodic reference to an already existing norm. N. Andrieux-Reix, 'Le jardin saccagé: une leçon du *Moniage Guillaume*' (362–81), analyses the symbolic and allegorical import of Guillaume's destruction of the garden in his hermitage, particularly tracing the way the episode changes from redaction to redaction. A. Fassò, 'Le petit cycle de Guillaume et les trois péchés du guerrier' (421–40), finds the archetypal three faults of the warrior from Dumézilian trifunctional analysis in the career of Guillaume d'Orange. J. H. Grisward, 'La naissance du couple littéraire Vivien et Rainouart' (441–56), argues that Vivien represents the outwards, centrifugal force of the warrior expanding his world and is a spiritual, magician, Odin-figure, while Rainouart is a consolidator, representing the interior of the kingdom, a Thor-figure. Far from being the result of a chance meeting between a memory of Roland and a folklore type, they thus form a balanced pair incarnating the two aspects of the warrior function. A. Barbero, 'Les chansons de geste et la mutation féodale de l'an mil' (457–75), finds traces of the pre-feudal 9th and 10th c. in the earliest William songs, specifically a coherent noble hierarchy, the city as the seat of power, and Vikings in the guise of Saracens. J. Flori, 'L'idée de croisade dans quelques chansons de geste du cycle de Guillaume d'Orange' (476–95), reviews five central aspects of the crusade preached by Urban II and their manifestations in *Le Couronnement de Louis*, *Le Charroi de Nîmes* and *La Chanson de Guillaume*. He concludes that the texts present less the idea of crusade preached at Clermont than that of the Spanish Reconquista, or even of the Carolingian conquest and extension of the Christian empire. J. E. Ruiz-Domènec, 'La *Chanson de Guillaume*: relato de frontera' (496–506), analyses *La Chanson de Guillaume* to show how Guillaume exists on a psychological, socio-political and geographical boundary, allowing an imaginative escape for warriors more and more constrained by the limitations of feudal society. D. Boutet, 'La pusillanimité de Louis dans *Aliscans*: idéologie ou *topos* de cycle? Topique, structure et historicité', *MA*, 103:275–92, studies the scenes, found in almost all the 12th-c. William songs, in which Guillaume opposes Louis in full court, and finds three realizations of the type of the pusillanimous king: the childish king, the foolish king, and the ungrateful king. These types, which may contaminate each other, are not a narrative sequence but an ideological structure. B. Guidot, 'Aélis et Rainouart dans la *Chanson des Aliscans*: un renouveau oblique de la famille de Narbonne', *TLit*,

9, 1996:21–35, which starts from the same court scene as the previous item, finds in Aélis and Rainouart a paradoxical couple, a picture of harmony whose unity cannot last, so that Rainouart, like Christ, remains terribly alone. P. Haugeard, 'L'avenir des fils dans la chanson des *Narbonnais*: héritage indo-européen, histoire féodale et crise des relations familiales', *Romania*, 115:406–33, challenges Grisward's view that Aymeri's giving land to his youngest son is an expression of the myth of the first king. The poet seems not to understand the myth, but the gift can be made coherent in terms of 12th to 13th-c. society, and of Aymeri's ambiguous status as part of a split father-figure. *Les Narbonnais* is an atypical *chanson de geste* which gives a glimpse of the disruptive effect of primogeniture. M. Okada, '*Se laissed* au vers 632 de la *Chanson de Guillaume*: un emploi pronominal inconnu ou mal connu du verbe *laissier* et de son équivalent occitan *laissar*', *ELLF*, 70:3–15, shows by comparison with other *chansons de geste*, romances, and Occitan texts, that *soi laissier* and *soi lancier* are found as variants of *soi eslaissier*, *soi eslancier* and should therefore be left unemended.

OTHER EPICS. *Garin le Loherenc*, ed. Anne Iker-Gittleman, 3 vols (CFMA, 117–19), Champion, 1996–97, 264, 265–523, 525–856 pp., is the first edition of MS *F* (B.N. f. fr. 1582), considered the closest to the 'original'. A. Brasseur, 'Les manuscrits de la *Chanson des Saisnes*', *Olifant*, 19, 1994–95[1997]:57–99, is a codicological study of the three extant MSS containing *La Chanson des Saisnes* and the lost Turin MS. M. Burrell, 'The specular heroine: self-deception versus silence in *Le Pèlerinage de Charlemagne* and *Erec et Enide*', *Parergon*, 15.1:83–99, argues that, like Enide, the queen in the *Pèlerinage* forgets her true role, that of reflecting back to her husband the image he wishes to have, and that both are punished for ceasing to be specular objects. K. A. Campbell, 'Commemorative formulae in the *Geste des Loherens*', *Olifant*, 19, 1994–95[1997]:101–12, explores intertextual formulae referring to people or events across the cycle to show how a framework of repetition actualized in such formulae creates an illusion of permanence and so enables the community to manage change. E. J. Mickel, 'The manuscripts of the *Enfances Godefroi*', *Romania*, 115:434–50, is a comparative study of episodes in the various MSS, which are analysed for evidence of adaptation and growth.

3. ROMANCE

GENERAL. J. M. Ganim, 'The myth of medieval romance', Bloch, *Medievalism*, 148–66, sees the invention of Medieval Studies in the 19th c. as a form of sentimentalized escapism, which turned the

medieval romance into a myth. The study of the romance now
provides a focus for tracing the politics of medievalism, while its
disenchantment forms part of a larger questioning of the concept of
literacy. D. F. Hult, 'Gaston Paris and the invention of courtly love',
ib., 192–224, questions the implications of the term 'courtly love',
relating it to the specific circumstances leading to Paris's formulation
of the concept, including national identity and cultural heritage.
Courtly love is seen to be rooted in a homosocial professional
discourse which privileges the masculine through an emblematic
appropriation of the feminine. D. James-Raoul, 'Le chevalier démuni
ou la non-declaration amoureuse', *BDBA*, 15:131–44, examines
romances and *lais* from the 12th and 13th centuries which reveal the
male ineptitude to declare love. Declarations are either elided,
refused, or exhorted by women, illustrating an imbalance between
the sexes in regard to the art of speech. M. Mikhaïlova, 'De la
différence aux ressemblances: du lai de "Fresne" au roman de
Galeran', *PRIS-MA*, 13:199–207, compares the binary nature of
resemblance in the *lai* with the profusion of its representation in the
romance, which reinterprets the story of 'Fresne'. Difference,
opposition and reflection are emphasized as the original of the image
is mirrored by copies, which it in turn echoes and mimics. This is
related to the medieval author and his copyist, the nostalgia for the
original being the only generator of writing. *The Honeysuckle and the
Hazel Tree: Medieval Stories of Men and Women*, trans. Patricia Terry,
Berkeley, California U.P., 1995, x + 218 pp., is a translation into
English with a critical introduction discussing the nature of love as
revealed through the selected poems. These are: Chrétien de Troyes,
Philomena; several *lais* by Marie de France; Jean Renart's *Le Lai de
l'ombre*; and *La Chasteleine de Vergi*. The translation is not intended to
be literal, but to 'capture the experience' of the poems. It could
possibly be of use to undergraduate students studying medieval
literature in translation.

CHRÉTIEN DE TROYES. C. Alvarez and A. Diogo, 'La demande de
l'amour dans *Cligès* de Chrétien de Troyes', *BDBA*, 15:109–17
consider the ambiguous and problematic nature of the courtly
declaration of love, simultaneously constructed as a demand and a
gift. Drawing on Derrida and Lacan, the article posits the body as the
site of the gift which is 'impossible à dire'. The heart replaces the
body as its supplement, becoming the gift of love. Since the
declaration of love is, however, incapable of stating its true desire, it
can never obtain its object. N. Cobyn, 'Irony and gender performance
in *Le Chevalier de la Charrette*', *ArLit*, 15:37–54, argues that Lancelot is
such an enduring object of debate because he represents subjectivity
in crisis and a crisis of subjectivity. The theories of Judith Butler and

Eve Sedgwick provide a basis for the argument that what is at stake in the debate over Lancelot is the naturalization of the performative subject and the harmonization of the dissonances inherent in subjectivity. R. Corradetti, 'L'abbigliamento del cavaliere nei romanzi di Chrétien de Troyes', *QFLR*, 11:33–94, provides an alphabetical list of all items of clothing referred to in Chrétien's romances. Textual extracts are analysed and interpreted to produce a definition of the exact garment in question. *L'Estoire del saint Graal*, II, ed. Jean-Paul Ponceau (CFMA, 121), Champion, 279–677 pp., contains the edition of the text from section 445 to the end, this covering 'Le déluge' to 'Miracle de sa tombe'. Variations are contained in footnotes, while endnotes contain all textual notes to both volumes, the Index of Names, and a glossary. M. Guerét-Laferté, 'De Philomèle à Philomena', *BDBA*, 15:45–56, supports the argument that Chrétien's *Philomena* had Ovid's *Metamorphoses* as its source. An important innovation, however, is the courtly framing of the declaration of love. This adds a certain psychological and narrative incoherence to the tale, but also lends a greater degree of equality to the depiction of the male and female protagonists. S. Kay, 'Who was Chrétien de Troyes?', *ArLit*, 15:1–35, casts doubt on the integrity and reliability of the literary portrayal of Chrétien as author. K. argues that the name 'Chrétien' is a common noun with a particular importance and resonance for the medieval audience. Rather than as a pseudonym, it can be read as an anonym, dispensing the author from responsibility, while invoking a notion of Christianity which could serve as a cover for many different types of religious ideas. J-M. Pastré, 'L'oubli des armes, l'oubli des femmes et l'oubli de Dieu: le péché du guerrier dans trois romans médiévaux', *Actes* (Montpellier): 287–301, refers to *Erec et Enide*, the *Chevalier au Lion* and the *Conte du Graal*, all of which deal with the harmony of three elements: the warrior ideal, the conjugal link, and the sacred. The motif of 'l'oubli' is pursued through a gradation of these elements in the three romances, culminating in 'l'oubli de Dieu' of the *Conte du Graal*. B. N. Sargent-Baur, 'Alexander and the *Conte du Graal*', *ArLit*, 15:1–18, examines the changing perception and portrayal of Alexander from his depiction as worthy in *Erec* and *Cligès* to his denunciation in the preface of the *Conte du Graal*. This is seen as motivated by the desire to impress a patron, Count Philip of Flanders, whose generosity is morally superior to that of Alexander. The Prologue is thus connected with the underlying theme of charity and its lack which runs through the *Conte*. P. Walter, 'Mélancoliques solitudes: le roi Pêcheur (Chrétien de Troyes) et Amfortas (Wolfram von Eschenbach)', Siganos, *Solitudes*, 21–29, suggests that the critical debates on the Grail romances have not taken enough account of the medieval medical and astrological theories which point to the humours as dictators of human character. Both the 'Roi Pêcheur' and Amfortas manifest the typical melancholic traits of solitude and introspection, but these are perceived as positive, melancholy being the catalyst for the quest for knowledge for both authors.

OTHER ARTHURIAN. R. Baudry, 'Ou l'amour ou le Graal! Déclarations et disqualifications amoureuses dans *L'Enchanteur* de René Barjavel', *BDBA*, 15:157–66, examines the opposition of love and the quest for the grail in Barjavel's romance. New elements of fantasy are introduced, but the author remains faithful to Arthurian tradition, as only Galahad is proved pure enough to undertake the quest. F. Bogdanow, 'Robert de Boron's vision of Arthurian history', *ArLit*, 14:19–52, points to the important influence of Robert de Boron on the subsequent development of Arthurian romance. Written 1191–1212, *Le Roman de l'estoire du graal* and the *Estoire de Merlin* gave a 'historical' context to the story of the Grail, integrating it into the wider scheme of the fall and redemption of man and the history of Arthur's kingdom. L. Jefferson, 'A new fragment of the *First Continuation* of the *Perceval* (London, PRO, E122/100/13B)', *ib.*, 15:55–76, reports the identification of a bifolium containing two sections of the *First Continuation*, often referred to as the *Continuation-Gauvain*. Given the great similarity between this fragment and MSS *T* and *V* of the text, it is suggested that it was transcribed during the same period (1250–1300), in the same workshop or scriptorium, and by the same scribe as MS *T*. A description and edition of the fragment are given. L. D. Stephens, 'Gerbert and Manessier: the case for a connection', *ib.*, 14:53–68, posits that these two early 13th-c. authors of separate continuations to Chrétien de Troyes's *Conte du Graal* were connected. It is suggested that Gerbert knew Manessier's work, composing his own continuation as an deliberate interpolation designed to fit immediately before Manessier's in the logic of the texts. N. Thomas, 'Gauvain's guilt in *L'Atre périlleux*: the subtext of sexual abuse', *RMS*, 23:107–19, links the ethos of the text with the earlier romances by Chrétien de Troyes, rather than with those of its own generation (*c.* 1230–50). It is the presentation of Gauvain as flawed hero which provides this connection, but here the hero has an evil double on to whom his own deviances are projected. The unsparing analysis of the militant masculine ethic which dominates the text is read as a continuation of Chrétien's own exploration of the tensions present in the masculine value system of chivalric society.

TRISTAN AND ISEUT. P. E. Bennett, 'Tristan à la Joyeuse Garde: transmission et réception de la matière tristanienne aux XIIe et XIIIe siécles', pp. 25–35 of *Tristan-Tristrant, Mélanges en l'honneur de Danielle Buschinger à l'occasion de son 60ème anniversaire*, ed. André Crépin and

Wolfgang Spiewok (Wodan, 66), Greifswald, Reineke Vlg, 1996, xxxiv + 555 pp., examines the motif of the heroine enclosed in a tower which appears in the 'Joyeuse Garde' episode of *Tristan*. This appears in oriental texts, often held to be the source for the Tristan legend, but the significance which it holds here has been lost from the Tristan tales of Béroul and of Thomas. The *Prose Tristan* sees a denial of the archetype and a return to the primitive forms of the legend. A. Berthelot, 'Dynadam, le chevalier non-conformiste', *Actes* (Montpellier): 34–41, traces the development of the character of Dynadam from a banal to a non-conformist knight, through whom the principles of chivalry are denounced. The Arthurian romance is, however, perceived as absorbing those elements which at first sight would most appear to menace it and the threat which Dynadam poses to the chivalric ideal is defused.

LAIS.   F. Bonifazi, 'Per un edizione del lai di "Equitan"', *QFLR*, 12: 141–62, describes the two MSS in which the *lai* is found, *H* and *S*. The present edition is based on *H* and is given in full, including notes. G. S. Burgess, 'The lay of *Trot*: a tale of two sittings', *FSB*, 66: 1–4, announces a new edition of this *lai*, to be made available on the Internet. Hitherto somewhat neglected, the *lai* is claimed to be worthy of closer study, owing to its close thematic structure, which features neat thematic and linguistic parallels. R. T. Pickens, 'Marie de France and the body poetic', Chance, *Gender*, 135–71, examines the nature of M.'s poetics in the light of her preoccupation with the generation, transmission, and reception of discourse. The focus lies on the human body as the site of meaningful discourse, and on the social and poetic function of violence as a form of 'male' poetics. The female poet and her writing allegedly become sexually ambiguous, owing to her necessary appropriation of this' male' poetic form.

ROMANS D'ANTIQUITÉ.   C. Abril, 'Les enfances d'Alexandre: essai de comparaison entre le *Roman d'Alexandre* et le *Libro de Alexandre*', *PRIS-MA*, 13: 1–12, points to the difference in tone between these two texts, the one romantic, the other didactic, while a further dichotomy revolves around the role played by fate. In spite of this, there are similarities between the texts, as in both the construction of the hero is drawn from earlier works and historic references. The episodes relating to Alexander's childhood are compared, drawing out these connections.

OTHER ROMANCES.   M.-M. Castellani, 'Stratégies amoureuses dans *Athis et Prophilias*', *BDBA*, 15: 119–30, points to the evolution of the motif of the declaration of love between the two parts of this romance. From an initial emphasis on the homosocial bond between two friends, where the woman acts as potential obstacle, the tale shifts to become a humorous *récit* in which women play a more substantial role. J. Gilbert, 'Boys will be ... what? Gender, sexuality and childhood in *Floire et Blancheflor* and *Floris and Lyriope*', *Exemplaria*, 9:39–61, focuses on the sexuality of the boy heroes of these two romances to examine whether the boy is regarded as distinct from the man, and to explore the meanings given by the individual texts to the similarities and differences thus uncovered. G. concludes that while *Floire et Blancheflor* brings its audience to interrogate assumptions about the roles of sexuality and childhood in the construction of the social order, the later *Floris and Lyriope* sets up a hierarchical distinction between sex and gender in which reproduction provides the narrative's sole signifying structure. Herbert, *Le Roman de Dolopathos*, ed. Jean-Luc Leclanche, 3 vols, Champion, 668 pp., is an edition of the 13th-c. MS H 436, of the Bibliothèque de l'Ecole de Médicine at Montpellier (*M*), perhaps the oldest of all the extant MSS of this romance based on the oral tradition of the *Sept Sages de Rome*. The edition provides a full introduction, with information on language, syntax, and morphology. In addition, Herbert's romance is compared to that of Jean de Haute-Seille, whose 12th-c. prose romance in Latin provided the source for the present work. Sarah Kay, *The Romance of the Rose*, CGFT, 1995, 125 pp., provides an analysis of the romance, covering various themes including 'Text and continuation', 'Allegory and irony', and 'Voice and writing', and giving a short *résumé* of the work. E. Langille, '"Mençunge ou folie?"': commentaire sur la mise en "romanz" de Wace', *DFS*, 39:19–32, places Wace's romances in the context of the later 12th-c. move to translate literary works from Latin to French in the Anglo-Norman area of Western France. The notion of translation as a form of referring back to a historical truth is seen to affect Wace's perception of his literary role. Instead of taking on the affirmative role of writer, he avoided the implications of a medium which was inevitably linked with untruth, preferring the truth' of history and of translation. B. Sargent-Baur, 'Dating the romances of Philippe de Rémi: between an improbable source and a dubious adaptation', *RPh*, 50:257–75, concentrates on the dating of *La Manekine* and *Jehan et Blonde*, and examines the case for claiming that Rudolf von Ems borrowed from Philippe for his romance *Willehalm von Orlens* (1230–40), concluding that this is not proven. The *terminus ad quem* of 1242 for *Jehan et Blonde* can therefore be abandoned. The internal chronology of the romances, as well as codicological indications, do, however, point to the earlier 13th c. for a date of composition. G. S. Williams, 'Konstruirte Männlichkeit: Genealogie, Geschlecht und ein Briefwechsel in Heldris von Cornwalls *Roman de Silence*', Wenzel, *Gespräche*, 193–211, reiterates the point that the sex-gender conflict of Heldris's romance exemplifies the cultural construction of gender identity.

4. RELIGIOUS WRITINGS

J.-L. Benoît, 'L'Amplificatio narrative dans les *Miracles de Notre Dame* de Gautier de Coinci', *PRIS-MA*, 13:124–35, concentrates on the narrative miracles, rather than on the lyric works. Although Gautier claims to follow an earlier Latin version of the *Miracles*, he does introduce significant differences into his text, producing a work which is an *amplificatio*, instead of a direct translation. M. Camille, 'Philological iconoclasm: edition and image in the *Vie de Saint Alexis*', Bloch, *Medievalism*, 371–401, examines the split between *Literaturwissenschaft* and *Kunstwissenschaft* in MS *L* of this *Vie*, a rupture which has divided this text since the 19th century. C. argues for a reconciliation between the two, and points to the fact that both word and image ultimately refer back to the primacy of the voice.

5. OTHER GENRES

LYRIC. Blondel de Nesle, *L'Oeuvre lyrique de Blondel de Nesle: mélodies*, ed. Avner Bahat and Gérard Le Vot (Nouvelle Bibliothèque du Moyen Age, 24), Champion, 1996, 272 pp., accompanies Lepage's edition (*YWMLS*, 56, 1994:77) in the same series. A detailed introduction on B. de N. and his work is followed by a table of MSS and editions, a glossary of musical terms which will be generally useful for the medieval literary scholar, a bibliography, and a synoptic edition of the melodies in a version of ancient notation. *Chansons des trouvères: chanter m'estuet*, ed. Samuel N. Rosenberg and Hans Tischler (Lettres gothiques), Livre de Poche, 1995, 1,090 pp., is an updated adaptation into French of the editors' *Chanter m'estuet: Songs of the Trouvères* (*YWMLS*, 43, 1981:66), with facing translations of the texts. R. Crespo, 'La quinta strofa di R. 1088 (Guiot de Dijon)', *Neophilologus*, 80, 1996:25–28, points out that the stanza is transmitted in three *chansonniers* including the hitherto unnoticed B. A. V. Reg. lat. 1490, and corrects the reading of the *incipit*. M.-G. Grossel, 'La déclaration amoureuse dans la chanson de trouvère', *BDBA*, 15:57–69, finds a wealth of variation in the works of the *trouvères*, in registers ranging from the shepherdess song to the *grand chant courtois*. T. Städtler, 'Für eine philologische Interpretation altfranzösischer Motettentexte', Glessgen, *Philologie*, 189–200, makes a plea for a new edition of OF motets based on all the extant MSS, according to the criteria of critical philology and through collaboration between philologists and musicologists, as the foundation for future linguistic, literary and musicological advances.

HISTORICAL. P. E. Bennett, 'La Chronique de Jordan Fantosme: épique et public lettré au XIIe siècle', *CCMe*, 40:37–56, examines the extent of the epic's contribution to the composition of Jordan's chronicle, and finds that its formulaic expression is supported by a scholastic rhetoric, indicating that it was composed by a literate clerk for a literate king, to be sung or read aloud at court or at pilgrimage sites, possibly to counter the pro-Capetian propaganda of the *chanson de geste*. K. M. Broadhurst, 'Henry II of England and Eleanor of Aquitaine: patrons of literature in French?', *Viator*, 27:53–84, searches many texts which have been linked with the royal couple for clear evidence of their patronage, and concludes that only Wace's *Roman de Rou* and Benoit's *Chronique des Ducs de Normandie* can confidently be connected with Henry, while for Eleanor there is no evidence to prove any influence at all on vernacular literature. C. Croizy-Naquet, 'Un modèle de transposition: l'imaginaire oriental dans les *Faits des Romains*', *PRIS-MA*, 13:157–67, points to the double alterity of time and space in this early prose text. The perspective of the Orient as 'other', as ambivalent and disquieting, marks the author's fidelity to his Latin sources. Its representation has, nonetheless, been recomposed to produce an image more readily in tune with the medieval Christian imagination.

MORAL, DIDACTIC, AND ALLEGORICAL WORKS. M. Amri, 'Symbolisme animal et souvenir amoureux dans le *Bestiaire* de Richard de Fournival', *BDBA*, 15:31–43, points to the unique nature of the text, whose declaration of love is hidden by its animal allegory. This is expressed through the double solicitation of memory, in the book and in love, as themes of the traditional courtly lyric are interwoven with the bestiary's allegorical format. G. S. Burgess, 'The fables of Marie de France: some recent scholarship', *FSB*, 61:8–13, lists and gives substantial descriptions of many recent studies of the *Fables*, including editions and theses. Tony Hunt, *Anglo-Norman Medicine*, II: *Shorter Treatises*, Cambridge, Brewer, 1997, 284 pp., completes the edition of the vernacular medical texts contained in MS Cambridge, Trinity College, O.1.20. To these are added the two most extensive medical compendia in French extant in the U.K., the *Euperiston* and the Trinity *Practica*. Full notes and glossaries are provided. H. R. Runte, 'Marie de France's *Fables* as trilingual palimpsest', *DFS*, 38:17–24, contests the notion that M. translated her fables from English to French; the syntax of the *Fables* reflects differences between the 'Latin', 'French', and 'English' tales, in which the general trend is towards a diminishing syntactic flexibility. The English material is, however, cast in a Franco-Latin syntactic mould, possibly to cater for the tastes and expectations of an aristocratic audience. F. E. Sinclair, 'Defending the castle: didactic literature and the containment of female sexuality', *RMS*, 22:5–19, examines three 13th-c. texts: Robert de Blois, *Le Chastoiement des Dames*, Philippe de Novarre, *Les Quatre Ages de l'homme*, and Ramon Llull, *Doctrina pueril*. All present a codification of female duty and comportment which appears to be designed to control women's behaviour in social and moral terms. S. argues that all the texts are aimed at an essentially male audience and that their ultimate aim is the containment of female sexuality and its expression.

ROMAN DE RENART. R. Bellon, 'Les Enfances Renart', *PRIS-MA*, 13:23–31, analyses the *enfances* section found in MSS *C* and *M*, arguing that it is not an independent branch but a well-integrated episode placed to fill a gap. G. Bianciotto, 'Y a-t-il un "sens" à une *dégradation?* A propos de *Boivin de Provins*', *Reinardus*, 10:17–43, disagrees with the accepted view that *P* is a rewriting of *A*: *P* shows greater coherence, both in detail and on the level of narrative structure, and though less brilliant, may well be the older. A. Kuyum-cuyan, 'Le dialogue renardien: propositions d'analyse', *Actes* (Keio), 135–57, applies the techniques of discourse analysis to two episodes, 'Le Moniage' and 'Le Puits', showing how variants modify the dialogue and change our view of Renart's discursive strategy. H. Matsubara, '*Esopo-no-Fabulas* et le *Roman de Renart*', *ib.*, 179–95, wonders if the 1593 Jesuit translation of Aesop into Japanese may have been influenced by a Renart tradition. E. Nieboer, 'Classes et familles à la lumière de la branche IV: "Le Puits"', *ib.*, 239–54, illustrates her views on the classification of Renart MSS by the example of branch IV. Classes of MSS and families of texts are not necessarily co-extensive. Y. Takana, 'Le discours sur l'adultère dans *Le Roman de Renart*: avant et après le serment ambigu', *ELLF*, 70:16–26, explains the insignificant presence of Renart's adultery in the branches written immediately after VI-Va by its link with the ambiguous oath, which makes the adultery a central motif through its ironic and parodic function. C. Zemmour, 'Les hommes du *Roman de Renart* ont-ils un corps? Appréhension lexicologique et symbolique d'un phénomène existentiel', *Actes* (Keio), 343–62, is a study of the semantics and symbolism of the words *cors* and *charpent*, used of men and of beasts.

FABLIAUX. J. Berlioz, 'Résumé et amplification: une fausse notion? Le premier témoignage du fabliau *Du prestre qui fu mis au lardier* chez Étienne de Bourbon', *PRIS-MA*, 13:137–45, compares the fabliau and the earlier *exemplum*, relates them both to a folklore motif, and concludes that the two versions are variants within one genre. F. Berriot, 'Les fabliaux de Gautier le Leu', *Actes* (Montpellier), 23–32, brings out G.'s dark view of society and of contemporary religious practice. R. Pearcy, 'A neglected Anglo-Norman version of *Le Cuvier* (London, British Library Harley 527)', *MedS*, 58,

1996:243–72, edits the version in a 13th-c. MS of the *Disciplina Clericalis*, discusses the possible origins of the story, and gives an 'actantial analysis', revising M. J. S. Schenck's functional study.

LATE MEDIEVAL LITERATURE

By ROSALIND BROWN-GRANT, *University of Leeds*

1. NARRATIVE GENRES

EPIC. B. Guidot, 'Le *Siège de Barbastre* dans le *Guillaume d'Orange en prose*: l'originalité dans l'écart', *Actes* (Montpellier), 171–89, emphasizes that, in comparison with the verse treatment of this passage, the author of the prose version evokes a courtly and elegant atmosphere in which the theme of refined love is paramount. Id., 'La géographie de l'imaginaire dans *Renaut de Montauban*', *MA*, 103: 507–26, argues that the hero's displacements in the course of his adventures are motivated by symbolic concerns rather than by any attempt on the author's part to evoke real places. G. J. Brault, 'The FitzEdmund arms (Herald's Roll 586–89) and the French epic *Renaud de Montauban*', *The Coat of Arms*, 177: 2–6, comments that the names given for four unidentified coats of arms are those of the four sons of Aymon, and wonders whether other unidentified coats next to them might not also be of literary origin. L. Jefferson, 'Fragments of a French prose version of Gautier de Châtillon's *Alexandreis*', *Romania*, 115: 90–117, reproduces the text preserved in some previously unknown fragments and argues that the language of this version may have been derived from the glosses of MSS of the original verse text which use a macaronic mixture of French and Latin. M.-J. Pinvidic, 'La tradition en prose de *Doon de Maience*, chanson de geste. Inventaire des éditions des XVIe et XVIIe siècles', *ib.*, 115: 207–46, provides detailed descriptions of these later versions and suggests that study of the full MS tradition will shed further light on how the text is transformed when reworked from verse into prose. D. Régnier-Bohler, 'Arthur en enfances (*Le Chevalier au Papegau*)', *PRIS-MA*, 13: 91–106, examines how, in taking the unusual step of depicting the life of the young king Arthur, this late 14th/early 15th-c. text adopts a lighter tone than that generally employed in the Arthurian tradition, using the humorous device of the talking parrot as the king's companion and removing any hint of forthcoming tragedy or any enigma about the hero's identity from the series of adventures which it recounts. M. G. Capusso, 'Le jeune Roland dans la "Geste Francor" (Cod. Marc. fr. XIII de Venise)', *ib.*, 41–58, emphasizes the unusually naturalistic and sympathetic representation of childhood in the treatment of the young Roland in this Franco-Italian text. *Hugues Capet. Chanson de geste du XIVe siècle*, ed. Noëlle Laborderie, Champion, 464 pp., is a new critical edition of this late work affiliated to the Guillaume and

Charlemagne cycles, complete with a useful introduction and glossary.

ROMANCE. J.-L. Picherit, 'Le "Miroir aux dames"', *ZRP*, 113:26–29, analyses the use of the metaphor of the mirror to refer to a character's exemplary conduct and argues that in *Tristan de Nanteuil* and *Bauduin de Sebourc*, where the male protagonist is described as a 'miroir à dames', this metaphor is in fact pejorative, implying that the protagonist is acting like a base seducer. *Arthuriana*, 7.2, an uneven collection of studies devoted entirely to Heldris de Cornuälles's *Roman de Silence*, includes: L. Kochanske Stock, 'The importance of being gender "stable": masculinity and feminine empowerment in *Le Roman de Silence*' (7–34), which examines how H. represents the gender construction of male and female characters and concludes that the text ultimately rejects the reliability of any stable system of gender identification; E. A. Waters, 'The third path: alternative sex, alternative gender in *Le Roman de Silence*' (35–46), which uses queer theory to examine how the text explores the performative aspect of Silence's cross-dressing which is reinforced by her sense of shame at being revealed for what she really is; K. M. Blumreich, 'Lesbian desire in the Old French *Roman de Silence*' (47–62), which examines the text's binary opposition between the normative heterosexuality of Eufemie and the covert homosexuality of Eufeme, who is punished in the narrative for her transgressive sexual desires towards Silence; E. F. Labbie, 'The specular image of the gender-neutral name: naming Silence in *Le Roman de Silence*' (63–77), who uses feminist and psychoanalytical theories in order to examine the significance of naming as part of the construction of the heroine's identity; F. R. Psaki, 'The modern editor and medieval "misogyny": text editing and *Le Roman de Silence*' (78–86), which suggests that modern editing practices, largely established by 19th-c. medieval scholars, may have promoted a view of the Middle Ages as more misogynistic than the texts of the period themselves would support; C. A. Jewers, 'The non-existent knight: adventure in *Le Roman de Silence*' (87–110), which compares H.'s text with Marie de France's *Lais* to show how the two different authors attempt to feminize and thus re-evaluate the nature of the *aventure* in romance narratives; and G. Thomas Gilmore, '*Le Roman de Silence*: allegory in ruin or womb of irony?' (111–23), which offers a somewhat impenetrable analysis of the text's use of allegory in terms of both personification theory and linguistic troping. C. J. Harvey, 'From incest to redemption in *La Manekine*', *RoQ*, 44:3–11, suggests that this text is multi-layered in incorporating elements of courtly and pious discourse, Greek mythology and Christian martyrology; whilst K. Gravdal, 'Confessing incests: legal erasures and literary celebrations in medieval France', *CLS*, 32, 1995:280–95, analyses a range of 13th-c. romances, including *La Manekine*, for the way in which they inscribe anxieties about incest in this period. B. N. Sargent-Baur, 'Dating the romances of Philippe de Remi: between an improbable source and a dubious adaptation', *RPh*, 50:257–75, reassesses the literary and historical evidence for dating P.'s works and concludes that *La Manekine* was conceived if not completed in the late 1220s and that *Jehan et Blonde* belongs to the second quarter of the 13th century. A. Tarnowski, '*Jehan et Blonde* and the exemplary hero', *CLS*, 32, 1995:263–79, shows how the author highlights the process of writing in this text and recasts canonical elements of romance in his depiction of an unlikely hero. F. Guichard-Tesson, 'Jeux de l'amour et jeux du langage', *MoyFr*, 38:21–44, argues that courtly games such as chess and the linguistic game 'le jeu du Roi qui ne ment' depicted in the *Vœux du Paon* function in the text as a means of exploring the sexual and amorous tensions between characters; whilst M. Felberg-Levitt, 'Jouer aux "Demandes d'amour"', *ib.*, 93–124, examines the influence these collections of questions and answers on love had on medieval game-playing in general as represented in later courtly narratives. *The Prophet of Islam in Old French: The Romance of Muhammad (1258) and the Book of Muhammad's Ladder (1264)*, ed. Reginald Hyatte (Brill's Studies in Intellectual History, 75), Amsterdam, Brill, 208 pp., is an English translation of Alexandre du Pont's *Li romans de Mahon* and the anonymous *Livre de l'eschiele Mahomet*. E. Languille, 'Le "courtois Saladin"', *DFS*, 38:25–30, examines how two 15th-c. Burgundian romances attribute a French origin to the figure of Saladin and rework him into a symbol of chivalric and amorous prowess as part of their propaganda effort to legitimate the political and dynastic ambitions of the Dukes of Burgundy. N. Black, 'The politics of romance in Jean Maillart's *Roman du Comte d'Anjou*', *FS*, 51:129–37, shows how M., a chancery poet at the court of Philippe le Bel, uses the medium of romance to support the moral and political ideology of his royal patron. C. Azuela, 'L'activité orale dans la nouvelle médiévale: les *Cent Nouvelles Nouvelles*, le *Décaméron* et les *Contes de Canterbury*', *Romania*, 115:519–35, argues that all three texts question their own status as fictions by exploring the issue of the fundamental unreliability of language as a vehicle for truth-telling. M. Jeay, 'Le travail du récit à la cour de Bourgogne: Les *Évangiles des Quenouilles*, Les *Cent Nouvelles Nouvelles* et *Saintré*', *LR*, special issue, 71–86, reaches similar conclusions to those of Azuela in her analysis of these Burgundian works which she characterizes as privileging discursive heterogeneity, ambiguity and irony. G. R. Mermier, '*Jehan de Saintré* ne serait-il donc qu'un roman médiéval?', *Actes* (Montpellier), 253–60, asserts that this text should be seen as being very much of its own time in lacking thematic and didactic coherence rather than as a formalistic experiment which anticipates the modern novel. L. Doyle Gates, 'Distaff and pen: producing the *Evangiles des Quenouilles*', *Neophilologus*, 81:13–20, puts forward a pluralistic reading of this work, claiming that the oral authority of the women in the sewing circle is challenged but not wholly undermined by the written authority of the male clerk whom they have asked to record their nightly conversations. S. Schwam-Baird, 'Sweet dreams: the pursuit of youthful love in Jean Froissart's *Joli Buisson de Jonece* and René d'Anjou's *Livre du Cuer d'Amours Espris*', *MoyFr*, 38:45–60, compares and contrasts the way in which the middle-aged narrators of these two texts treat the theme of love, arguing that the former turns away without regret from youthful passion and towards religious devotion, whilst the latter adopts a more bitter attitude in choosing to abandon love altogether. B. Ribémont, 'Les procédés d'insertion lyrique chez Froissart: conformité et déviance dans l'*Espinette amoureuse*', *Actes* (Montpellier), 303–17, analyses how F. distinguishes himself from his model, Machaut, in using the techniques of both collage and montage to incorporate lyric poems into his verse narrative in order to explore different psychological aspects of the lover's amorous state. Laurence de Looze, *Pseudo-Autobiography in the Fourteenth Century: Juan Ruiz, Guillaume de Machaut, Jean Froissart, and Geoffrey Chaucer*, Gainesville, Florida U.P., xi + 211 pp., devotes chapters to M.'s *Voir-Dit* and F.'s *Espinette amoureuse* and *Prison amoureuse* in this study of how medieval pseudo-autobiographies explore the issues of the representation of lived experience, the rhetoric of sincerity, writerly self-consciousness, the link between erotic and poetic activity and the role played by the reader in the construction of the text. M. Colombo Timelli, 'Entre *histoire* et *compte*: de l'*Erec* de Chrétien de Troyes à la prose du XVe siècle', *LR*, special issue, 23–30, shows how the anonymous author of a 15th-c. reworking of C.'s text adopts a deferential attitude towards the authority of his source, which he refers to as an 'histoire', and self-effacingly denigrates his own work as simply a 'compte'. J. H. M. Taylor, 'Perceval/Perceforest: naming as hermeneutic in the *Roman de Perceforest*', *RoQ*, 44:201–14, argues that whereas Chrétien uses the naming motif in order to explore the issue of an individual's lost identity, the author of this later text employs it as an indicator of the hero's successful completion of his public and collective mission to rid the country of its enemies. A. Berthelot, 'Zéphyr, épigone "rétroactif" de Merlin, dans le *Roman de Perceforest*', *MoyFr*, 38:7–20, is a comparative study of these two figures in terms of their trick-playing and comical interventions in the narrative. *Le Roman de Ponthus et Sidoine*, ed. Marie-Claude de Crécy, Geneva, Droz, clvii + 458 pp., is the first modern critical edition of this anonymous late 14th-/early 15th-c. prose reworking of the Anglo-Norman *Romance of Horn* which also contains didactic elements more typical of the 'mirror for princes' genre. The scholarly apparatus includes a detailed study of the MS tradition, an analysis of the themes and language of the text, full variants, textual notes, a glossary and a table of proper names.

2. POETRY

F. Wolfzettel, 'Au carrefour des discours lyriques: le trouvère Richard de Fournival', *Romania*, 115:50–68, argues that, as a lyric poet, R. distinguishes himself from his contemporaries by his subjectivity, his erudite and satirical self-consciousness and his critique of the language of courtly eroticism. M. Gally, 'Accords et dissonances du Grand Chant. Les poésies de Richard de Fournival et d'Adam de la Halle', *Actes* (Montpellier), 115–28, shows how these two authors develop key topics of the lyric tradition, innovate by introducing into their verse non-canonical elements such as images from everyday life, and ultimately reject the idea of a love whose effects are wholly destructive. C. J. Harvey, 'L'amant éploré de la lyrique anglo-normande', *MoyFr*, 38:35–43, examines a corpus of six poems in a 14th-c. English MS for the way in which they offer insular variations on the well-worked continental courtly theme of the unhappy lover. D. Hüe, 'Le Chant Royal: le pur et le patois, *Actes* (Montpellier), 191–206, recounts how poets working within this strict five-stanza plus refrain form gradually incorporated dialectal elements and images from pastoral activities into their poems in praise of the Virgin. *Eustache Deschamps en son temps*, ed. Jean-Patrice Boudet and Hélène Millet, Publications de la Sorbonne, 314 pp., is a handsomely-produced anthology of 70 poems, each accompanied by a short introduction and detailed literary commentary, which offers an in-depth contextualization of D.'s poetic response to the key social, religious and political issues of his day. J.-F. Kosta-Théfaine, 'L'*Epistre a Eustace Morel* de Christine de Pizan', *MoyFr*, 38:79–91, provides a new transcription of the text of BL, MS Harley 4431, and emphasizes the important role played by C. in the development of the verse epistle, particularly in her use of 'rimes léonines' and treatment of the theme of contemporary decline. S. Thonon, 'Le *Purgatoire d'Amours* et la *Bataille des deux deesses*: l'envers de la tapisserie', *LR*, special issue, 219–31, compares the use made in these two late 15th-c. poems of motifs from classical mythology, and deduces that their sources were both textual and visual, the latter being provided either by a *tableau vivant* or a tapestry. A. Armstrong, 'Pattern and disruption in formalist poetry: the example of Jean Molinet', *NMi*, 98:209–15, uses R. Pensom's method for studying accentual distribution in French texts in order to argue that there is a creative tension in *rhétoriqueur* poetry, such as that of M., between its formal rigidity and rhythmic fluidity. Id., 'The practice of textual transmission: Jean Molinet's *Ressource du Petit Peuple*', *FMLS*, 33:270–82, examines a variety of MSS in which this political allegory is preserved and shows that each version reveals a different reception of the text according to the precise historical and political circumstances in which it was produced. T. Van Hemelryck, 'Jean Molinet ou de l'autre côté du *Miroir*. Etude des rapports entre le *Miroir de Mort* et le *Miroir de Vie*', *LR*, special issue, 233–51, argues that M.'s *MV* is a response to and not simply a continuation of George Chastelain's *MM*, in using octosyllables rather than decasyllables and in emphasizing life after death rather than the process of dying itself. E. Rassart-Eeckhout, 'La mécanique proverbiale: l'épiphonème dans le *Passe temps* de Michault Taillevent', *ib.*, 147–61, argues that T.'s insertion of a proverb into each stanza of his poem enhances the didactic authority and thematic coherence of the text; whilst T. Van Hemelryck, 'Le viel homme et la Mort: observations sur le *Passe temps* de Michault Taillevent', *LR*, 51:19–34, suggests that the work serves as a kind of exorcism for the author's anxieties about his impoverished condition. E. Devriendt, 'Eléments pour la définition d'une prose poétique: à propos de l'*Archiloge Sophie* de Jacques Legrand', *RHLF*, 97:963–85, evaluates the significance of this work as a theoretical discussion of the interplay between rhetoric and poetics in edifying prose discourse of the late Middle Ages. J.-P. Chambon, 'Les *Complaintes et epitaphes du Roy de la Bazoche* d'Andrieu de la Vigne: un songe après boire?', *MoyFr*, 38:139–44, rejects the traditional view that the Pierre de Baugé referred to in this text is a real historical character, and argues instead that the work is a subversive pastiche of the funeral lament, being a dream-vision inspired by a hangover. R. Crespo, 'I *Vers d'Amours* di Guillaume d'Amiens', *CN*, 57:55–101, reproduces the 14 stanzas of this poem, with variants, as preserved in Vat. Reg. lat. 1490, which thus corrects the version published by Alfred Jeanroy in 1893. J.-F. Kosta-Théfaine, 'Charles d'Orléans: bibliographie récente', *MoyFr*, 38:145–50, is a list (culled from the I.R.H.T. database in Paris) of recent publications on the prince-poet which supplements Deborah Hubbard Nelson, *Charles d'Orléans: An Analytic Bibliography*, London, Grant and Cutler, 1990 (see *YWMLS*, 52:65). The first part of V. Beltran, 'El cancionero de Charles d'Orléans y *Dregz de Natura* de M. Ermengau', *Romania*, 115:193–206, explains how the medieval copyists of BN f. fr. 25458, a collection of C.'s verse, accidentally turned a double folio of this manuscript inside-out and thus inverted the order of his poems. A. E. B. Coldiron, '*Translatio*, translation and Charles d'Orléans' *paroled* poetics', *Exemplaria*, 8, 1996:169–92, argues that the discontinuities between the French and English versions of C.'s poems reveal the author's desire to experiment rather than simply find equivalent forms of lyric expression in the language of his captors. C. Martineau-Génieys, 'L'homosexualité dans le *Lais* et le *Testament* de François Villon', *Actes* (Montpellier), 235–51, suggests that the author's vitriolic portraits of homosexuals are in fact an attempt to 'out' his gay contemporaries and that the anagrams concealing the names of his lovers actually conceal the identity of a man — Ythier Merchant — whom V. vilifies for abandoning him for another male lover.

3. DRAMA

J. Koopmans and P. Verhuyck, 'Jean Molinet et ses *Pronostications Joyeuses*', *LR*, special issue, 117–36, provides a preliminary key to the interpretation of this series of semi-dramatic monologues parodying the astrological predictions peddled by almanac sellers. Jelle Koopmans is also the editor of *Le Mystère de Saint Remi*, Geneva, Droz, 824 pp., a previously unedited poem of the early 16th c. which puts hagiography to the service of local propaganda glorifying the Bishop of Rheims. The edition includes an introduction to the MS, synopsis of the text, and suggestions as to how it might have been staged. R. L. A. Clark and C. Sponsler, 'Queer play: the cultural work of crossdressing in medieval drama', *NLH*, 28:319–44, claim that transvestite characters in plays such as the *Miracles de Nostre Dame par personnages* momentarily expose the arbitrariness of fixed gender categories, even if the texts themselves ultimately reassert heterosexuality as the prescribed sexual norm. G. A. Runnalls, 'Sponsorship and control in medieval French religious drama: 1402–1548', *FS*, 51:257–66, examines the impact of the edicts granting and repealing permission to perform religious plays in the Paris area in the late Middle Ages, and concludes that their effect was, in reality, quite limited. E. Caron, 'Les *Passions* du bas moyen âge français, ou la prise en charge bourgeoise de l'imaginaire chrétien populaire', *MoyFr*, 38:125–37, shows how the Passion plays prior to 1440 use elements of farce and the grotesque in order to put forward their anti-semitic and often virulently anti-feminist messages. K. Becker, 'La mentalité juridique dans la littérature française (XIIIe-XVe siècles)', *MA*, 103:309–27, argues that the quasi-dramatic *Arrêts d'Amour* uses juridical language in its satire of contemporary lovers whose behaviour falls short of the courtly ideal. O. A. Dull, 'Le rire de la sottie: mises en scène du jeu de mots', *MoyFr*, 37:7–20, examines how, in the *sottie*, the figure of the fool conveys moral messages to the audience by acting out verbal puns. C. Kent, 'L'équivoque verbale de la farce: son comique et son sérieux', *ib.*, 65–76, discusses the serious side of farce in a corpus of six texts from 1450–1550 which use trickery and verbal ambiguity as a means of exploring confrontation between characters of different social classes. *Recueil de farces (1450–1550)*, ed. André Tissier, Geneva, Droz, 385 pp., is the eleventh volume in the series and contains six works, each preceded by a brief introduction and study of its themes and versification, which also includes an extensive glossary for the volume as a whole.

4. HISTORICAL LITERATURE

J.-C. Faucon, 'Rumeur et ouï-dire chez Joinville', *Littératures*, 37:5–20, analyses how J. uses aural testimony in order to authenticate his account of Saint Louis's crusade. C. Croizy-Naquet, 'La description de Jérusalem dans la *Chronique d'Ernoul*', *Romania*, 115:69–89, contrasts the author's extreme sobriety and attention to factual detail in his account of the Holy City as a place of pilgrimage with the tendency of romance authors to emphasize the exotic in their topographical descriptions. B. J. Levy, 'Un bestiaire oriental? Le monde animal dans *Le Devisament dou monde* de Marco Polo', *Actes* (Keio), 159–77, argues that M.'s observations on animals in this work are at once more 'scientific' than those found in medieval encyclopedias such as bestiaries and yet more hyperbolic than those found in contemporary travel texts. Two articles by N. Chareyron are 'De l'histoire à la chanson. Les fiançailles rompues de Louis de Male', *MA*, 103:545–59, which notes how 14th-c. chroniclers such as Jean le Bel and Froissart represent the circumstances surrounding the broken engagement between Louis de Male, Count of Flanders, and Isabelle, daughter of Edward III of England; and 'Les nouveaux justes de 1349. Regards de chroniqueurs sur les flagellants', *Actes* (Montpellier), 99–113, which examines the account given by these same chroniclers of the flagellant movement before the church took its eventual decision to proscribe it. J. Devaux, 'Le *Saint Voyage de Turquie*: croisade et propagande à la cour de Philippe le Bon (1463–1464)', *LR*, special issue, 53–70, shows how three different historical works of this period serve to legitimate the Duke's religious and political ambitions for a new crusade. G. Palumbo, 'Le *Livre et histoire royal* (ou *Livre des trois fils de roys*): politique, histoire et fiction à la cour de Bourgogne', *ib.*, 137–45, similarly demonstrates that this prose text about three princes who deliver Naples from the Saracens is part of the same pro-crusading propaganda effort by writers under the Duke's patronage. Graeme Small, *George Chastelain and the Shaping of Valois Burgundy: Political and Historical Culture at Court in the Fifteenth Century*, Woodbridge, The Boydell Press, 302 pp., examines C.'s career, his position at the Burgundian court as chronicler and *indiciaire*, and the impact of his ideas on his contemporary audience, concluding that he played a central role in the historical culture of his time. A. C. de Nève de Roden, 'Les *Mémoires* de Jean de Haynin: des "mémoires", un livre', *LR*, special issue, 31–52, re-evaluates the literary qualities of this Burgundian text and argues that the author should be properly considered as a 'mémorialiste' in terms of his principles of composition and historiographical agenda. C. Thiry, '"Que mes maistres soient contens": Jean Regnier, prisonnier, au carrefour de Bourgogne et de France', *ib.*, 183–205, examines R.'s *Livre de la Prison* for the way in which he discusses his kidnapping of 1432 and his subsequent appeal to his benefactor, Philippe le Bon, to help negotiate his release. Christine de Pizan, *Le Livre des Faits et Bonnes Moeurs du roi Charles V le Sage*, trans. Eric Hicks and Thérèse Moreau, Stock, 371 pp., is an elegant Modern French translation of Suzanne Solente's edition of 1936–40 which also provides an insightful analysis of C.'s political and historical works and an up-to-date chronology of her complete *œuvre*.

5. Religious, Moral and Didactic Literature

G. Hasenohr, '*Lacrimae pondera vocis habent*. Typologie des larmes dans la littérature de spiritualité française des XIIIe-XVe siècles', *MoyFr*, 37:45–63, argues that pious texts destined for a lay audience use the same classification of terms for weeping as that developed in asceticism, yet maintain a distinction between these two forms of piety by emphasizing for the layperson the link between tears and charity towards others rather than the strict identification between the ascetic and Christ's Passion. S. Huot, 'Popular piety and devotional literature. An Old French rhyme about the Passion and its textual history', *Romania*, 115:451–94, shows how the interpolation of this short verse work into successive literary works is an example of the interaction between popular and learned traditions. G. Mombello, 'Les noëls de Jehan Tisserant', *SFr*, 61:20–54, reproduces in full and analyses the MS tradition of the 5 *noëls* or short verse sermons on the Nativity written by this Franciscan friar of the late 15th century. E. Dupras, 'La joye de men cueur est faillie, men chant est tourné en plour', *MoyFr*, 37:21–34, examines how different 14th-c. and 15th-c. prose versions of *La Vision de Tondale* represent the protagonist, an Irish knight, as he learns to reject laughter as identified with sin and worldliness in favour of joy as associated with salvation and the end of purgatory. M. J. Raby, 'Le péché "contre nature" dans la littérature médiévale: deux cas', *RoQ*, 44:215–23, compares the way in which late medieval penitential manuals and literary texts such as *Bérinus* and *Tristan de Nanteuil* discuss the sexual sins of masturbation and homosexuality. E. Gaucher, '*Pour abregier…Robert le Diable*: du roman au dit', *Pris-MA*, 13:169–79, argues that the writer of an early 14th-c. *dit* which reworks this romance treats the tale as an *exemplum* about the need for penitence and thus subordinates all aspects of the original story to his desired moral message. P. Ménard, 'Une nouvelle version du dit *Des putains et des lecheors*', *ZRP*, 113:30–38, suggests that the text is an example of a *dit*, not a *fabliau*, and reproduces it in its entirety from a hitherto little-known MS, Nottingham University Mi. L. M. 6, ff.349–350. M.-G. Grossel, 'L'*Amplificatio* (et l'*abreviatio*) dans les versions en vers de la *Vie de Saint Eustache*', *Pris-MA*, 13:181–97, is a comparative study of the way poets from different literary and social milieux — religious, courtly or theatrical — embellish or reduce their versions of this story according to their precise rhetorical, didactic and æsthetic aims. M. Thiry-Stassin, 'Les "nourritures terrestres" dans la vie de sainte Colette de Corbie', *LR*, special issue, 207–18, analyses the complex attitude towards food depicted in the life of this late 15th-c. Flemish saint. Jacques de Voragine, *La Légende dorée*, ed. Brenda Dunn-Lardeau, Champion, 1563 pp. + vii, is a new critical edition of Jean Batallier's important late 15th-c. revision of the French translation of the *Legenda aurea* by Jean de Vignay, complete with a brief introduction and an extensive glossary. J. E. Merceron, 'Prélude aux Sermons joyeux. L'équivoque hagiographique et la sanctification facétieuse au XIIIe et XVe siècle', *MA*, 103:527–44, examines this genre of hagiographical parody which specializes in puns linking saints' names with particular curative powers and in spurious stories of saints who are associated with specific bodily functions. K. V. Sinclair, 'Le "Dit des paternostres" de Gieffroy: parodie d'un thème pieux', *ib.*, 561–70, discusses this early 14th-c. liturgical-poetical hybrid which uses the Lord's prayer as a framing device for an estates-satire. M.-R. Jung, '*Ovide Metamorphose* en prose (Bruges, vers 1475)', *LR*, special issue, 99–115, shows how a late 15th-c. prose version of the *Ovide Moralisé* abandons the type of religious allegories previously included in this work, thus marking the beginning of a literary tendency in the late Middle Ages to return to the original Ovidian text. R. E. F. Straub, 'Les manuscrits du *Livre des bonnes meurs* conservés à la Biblioteca Apostolica Vaticana', *ib.*, 163–81, supplements Evencio Beltran's 1986 edition of Jacques Legrand's *LBM*, which is based on BN f. fr. 1023, by examining how the different lessons in the Vatican MSS shed light on the author's reworking of his text. P. Walter, 'Les *tripes* de Saint-Marcel (*Roman de la Rose*, v.5023)', *RF*, 109:427–35, refutes the traditional interpretation of the line 'Et vont a Saint Marcel as tripes' as referring to eating offal, arguing instead that it means frequenting a tavern where boisterous dancing takes place; *tripe* being derived from the verb *triper* or *treper* (to dance), and the feast day of

Saint Marcel being an occasion for such dancing. S. Kay, 'The birth of Venus in the *Roman de la Rose*', *Exemplaria*, 9:7–37, shows how Jean de Meun's version of the story of Venus functions as a myth through which he explores the ambiguous significance of sexuality as a transgressive force in civilized society. G. Berger, '*Mouvance, variance* und die Folgen: Griselda und ihre "Nachkommen"', Glessgen, *Philologie*, 255–65, is a survey of printed reworkings of the French translation of the Griselda story up to 1800 which argues that each version should be treated as a text in its own right. J. B. Williamson, 'Philippe de Mézières' menagerie for monarchs', *Actes* (Keio), 325–41, analyses a range of P.'s texts for the way in which he uses traditional animal symbolism and popular animal proverbs in order to deliver lessons in political and moral conduct to his aristocratic audience. J. Batany, 'Du dépeçage du cerf à l'Aigle d'Occident: chasse et idéologie sociale dans *Modus et Ratio*', *Reinardus*, 10:3–16, examines this two-part work, which is both an allegorized hunting treatise and a dream-vision containing a political prophecy, and argues that the rituals of hunting and the hierarchy of the animal world are assimilated here to a critique of the three estates in contemporary society. K. Sullivan, 'The inquisitorial origins of literary debate', *RR*, 88:27–51, claims that the models for Christine de Pizan's famous quarrel over the *Romance of the Rose* with leading intellectual figures of her day were provided by the judicial disputes between clergy and heretics in the 12th c. and the inquisitorial rhetoric of the later Middle Ages; whereas D. F. Hult, 'Words and deeds: Jean de Meun's *Romance of the Rose* and the hermeneutics of censorship', *NLH*, 28:345–66, argues that C. was not so much attacking the use of obscene words or anti-feminist *topoi* in the *Rose* as condemning its lack of clear authorial intention and moral direction for the reader. J.-F. Kosta-Théfaine, 'Les *Proverbes moraulx* de Christine de Pizan', *MoyFr*, 38:61–77, offers a new transcription of this work, based on BL MS Harley 4431, and stresses the importance of C.'s use of proverbs for didactic purposes. Christine de Pizan, *La Città delle dame*, ed. Earl Jeffrey Richards and Patrizia Caraffi, Milan, Luni Editrice, 526 pp., is an edition of *La Cité des Dames* based on the same MS, with a facing-page translation into Modern Italian, short introduction in Italian on C.'s life and works and a useful bibliography of recent studies of the text. C. Hall, 'The genealogy of an idea: from *La Cité des Dames* to *Le Fort inexpugnable de l'honneur du sexe femenin*', *FCS*, 22, 1995:109–18, contrasts C.'s and François de Billon's use of the allegory of the fortified city in their respective works as determined by the specific agenda and writing strategy of each author. R. L. Krueger, '*Chascune selon son estat*: Women's education and social class in the conduct books of Christine de Pizan and Anne de France', *PFSCL*, 24:19–34, is a comparative

study of C.'s *Livre des Trois Vertus* and A.'s *Enseignements* which claims
that whilst both authors support social and gender hierarchies in their
respective texts, C.'s analysis of the breakdown of the sartorial and
behavioural codes of contemporary society may unwittingly have
suggested to her bourgois readers that women can achieve upward
social mobility.

6. MISCELLANEOUS

E. Birge Vitz, 'Rereading rape in medieval literature: literary,
historical, and theoretical reflections', *RR*, 88: 1–26, offers scholars a
timely warning against imposing late 20th-c. sensibilities and standards of realism on to medieval works depicting scenes of sexual
violence. J. H. M. Taylor, '*Le Roman de la Dame à la lycorne et du biau
chevalier du lion*: text, image, rubric', *FS*, 51: 1–18, argues that detailed
analysis of the stages involved in producing MSS such as BN f. fr.
12562, which preserves this particular text, reveals the different roles
played by the *chef d'atelier*, artist and rubricator in creating a set of
rubrics and miniatures which help explicate the work for the reader.
B. Laurioux, *Le Règne de Taillevent: Livres et pratiques culinaires à la fin du
Moyen Age*, Publications de la Sorbonne, 424 pp., is a study of the
early 14th-c. *Viandier* of Taillevent and its place in the history of
medieval cookery in both France and Europe.

THE SIXTEENTH CENTURY

By SARAH ALYN-STACEY, *Trinity College, Dublin*

1. GENERAL

Brucker, *Traduction*, offers important perspectives on a variety of aspects of translation, and is divided into 5 sections: 'Théorie, méthode d'approche et langage technique' (15–104); 'Traduction, histoire des idées et esthétique littéraire' (105–58); 'Présence du monde antique et italien' (159–204); 'Traduction, pédagogie et histoire de la langue' (205–80); 'Une nouvelle ère de la traduction: le XVIe siècle' (281–387). Papers on specific authors will be found under the heading appropriate to them, and we shall mention here only those of a more general nature and which concern the period 1450 onwards. C. Brucker, 'Avant-propos' (7–14), offers a survey of the aims of the conference and the subjects covered. B. Vewiebe, 'La vie sociale dans les premières traductions des *Annales* de Tacite' (177–86), focuses on what she sees as two conflicting translation criteria: responsibility to the original text versus responsibility to the target society. Through a close comparative analysis of various sections of the *Annales* with their translations by La Planche and Fauchet, V. demonstrates how this conflict leads to a reworking of the text which reflects greater respect for the norms of the target society. W. Berschin, 'Plutarque en France: XIVe-XVIe siècle' (295–98), states nothing new in a very summary paper which argues that P. was well known in the Middle Ages, and that his success was assured by Amyot's translation. A.-M. Chabrolle, 'L'idée d'une spécificité linguistique et culturelle au XVIe siècle et sa manifestation dans l'activité traduisante' (319–24), considers the link between language and culture, and after a brief survey of the views of Dolet and Seyssel, concludes that the Renaissance translator had to decide between a 'semantic translation' oriented towards the original text, and a 'communicative translation' oriented towards the target culture. O. Millet, 'Les préfaces aux traductions françaises de la Bible (1523–1588): la question de la langue' (373–87), examines the translators' attitudes towards biblical language (as expressed in their prefaces) in relation to the general promotion of the vernacular and the question of fidelity to the source language, asking whether a new language emerged from these numerous translations; the failure of any one edition to impose itself as the definitive version exegetically and linguisitically leads M. to conclude that these diverse translations represent a failed project. Dealing less extensively with the same subject but also worthy of note is Beer, *Translation*, which includes the following: J. Beer, 'Patronage and the translator: Raoul de Presle's *La Cité de Dieu* and Calvin's *Institution de la religion chrestienne* and *Institutio religionis christianae*' (91–142); M. van der Poel, 'The French translation of Agrippa von Nettesheim's *Declamatio de incertitudine et vanitate scientiarum et artium*: *Declamatio* as paradox' (305–29); and V. Worth-Stylianou, 'Reading monolingual and bilingual editions of translations in Renaissance France' (331–58). Two articles in *Actes* (Nice) also deal with language: M. Jacquemier, 'Du désordre babélien à la conscience de l'altérité' (123–38), considers the dual significance of the myth of Babylon, a symbol of theological, political and linguistic order and disorder; and C. Demaizière, 'Un besoin naturel: ordonner le langage', (139–47), may not offer any new insights, but does provide a useful survey of the confused state of the French language at the beginning of the 16th c., and of the efforts made to establish a coherent, unified language, largely as a result of the edict of Villers-Cotterêts.

Actes (Rheims) offers a collection of articles of a consistently high standard. It is divided into six sections: 'Les Princes lorrains' (21–112); 'Le "beau XVIe siècle" et son crépuscule autour de Claude de Lorraine, premier duc de Guise' (113–74); 'Françoise de Guise et le début des Guerres de Religion' (175–292); 'Le Cardinal Charles de Lorraine' (293–494); 'Henri de Guise et la Ligue' (495–610); and 'La Fin des Guises' (611–50). Articles on specific authors will be found in the appropriate section, mention being made here only to those of a more general nature. Y. Bellenger, 'Avant-propos' (7–10), highlights the hitherto lack of a detailed interdisciplinary study of the Guise family which played such a key role in so many areas of 16th-c. life; J.-P. Babelon, 'Conférence inaugurale' (11–20), briefly considers the far-ranging patronage offered by the Guises from the Middle Ages to the 17th century; A. Jouanna, 'Les Guises et le sang de France' (23–38), focuses on the conflict for rulership between the Guises and the Bourbons following the death of Henri II, highlighting the political vulnerability of the Guises, sketching out their strategies (celebration of their lineage, etc.) up to the Treaty of Joinville (1584), and arguing that their desire to rule persisted well into the 17th century; M. M. Fontaine, 'Dédicaces lyonnaises aux Guises-Lorraines (1517–1570)' (39–79), reveals the far-reaching consequences in Lyons of the patronage of Jean de Lorraine and Charles III, Duke of Lorraine, giving rise as it did to works of art, and the publication of religious, legal, medical, literary, military and political texts; L. Bouquin, 'Les fidèles des Guises parmi les chevaliers de l'ordre de Saint-Michel sous les derniers Valois' (95–112), examines the political consequences of belonging to the royal order, offering important profiles of the knights linked to the Guises 1559–88, and showing how, ironically, the monarchy had great difficulty in acquiring their allegiance; R. Cooper, 'Le rêve italien des premiers Guises' (115–41), offers a detailed survey of the considerable political and dynastic ambitions of the Guises in Italy; J. Barbier, 'La musique au temps de Claude de Lorraine, premier duc de Guise' (143–59), considers how music served as a propaganda tool to celebrate the Guises, focusing particularly on its use by composers such as Janequin, Costeley, Le Fèvre, Caietain, to celebrate the military victories and heroism of Claude and his son François; R. Freedman, 'Le Cardinal Jean de Lorraine: un prélat de la Renaissance mécène de la musique' (161–73), offers insights into the little-documented musical patronage of the cardinal; J. McClelland, 'Le Tournoi de juin 1559 et les deux François de Guise' (177–85), is interesting but rather speculative, reconstructing as it does the political considerations governing how François, chevalier de Guise, and his older brother, François de Guise, would joust with Henri II in the 1559 tournament which led to the king's death, and attributing the fatal event in part to these considerations; J. Brooks, 'Les Guises et l'air de cour: images musicales du prince guerrier' (187–210), examines the musical patronage of the Guises in the latter half of the 16th c., showing how composers (usefully listed in an appendix) produced *airs de cour* which fused the image of the cultivated courtier with that of the warrior to produce an heroic ideal; F. Lestringant, 'André Thevet et les Guises' (211–31), reviews the minor patronage which this cosmograher received, showing how T. contributed to the history of the family; I. Wardropper, 'Un projet de monument aux cœurs de François de Lorraine et d'Anne d'Este' (279–91), examines the literary and artistic attitudes expressed towards F.'s heart (seen as a protective charm, discouraging enemies of Paris, France and Catholicism), and argues (rather speculatively) that although no monument was erected to it, a study attributed to the School of Fontainebleau and now in the Louvre is almost certainly a proposed monument, possibly commissioned by Anne d'Este and destined for Joinville but never executed; J. Boucher, 'Le Cardinal de Lorraine, premier ministre de fait ou d'ambition (1559–1574)' (295–310), retraces the cardinal's subtle but vain political manœuvres to become prime minister again following his dismissal from the post in 1560; M. Venard, 'Le Cardinal de Lorraine dans l'église de France (1564–1574)' (311–29), examines the cardinal's very active and influential ecclesiastical career, focusing on his introduction into France of the reforms proposed by the Council of Trent, his political role at the head of the Church in France, and his intellectual patronage; A. Tallon, 'Le Cardinal de Lorraine au Concile de Trent' (331–43), offers an explanation for the

cardinal's apparent volte-face whereby he renounced all the objectives he was to propose to the Council, attributing this to reduced
influence and support, and to his encounter with other strands of
catholicism; F. Giacone, 'Les Lorraine et le psautier de David'
(345–63), argues that the Huguenot psalter represented a 'terrain
d'entente' between Papists and Huguenots, being used by both
factions, and that, contrary to popular belief, the cardinal de
Lorraine, despite being one of the most active Inquisitors, played an
important role in this attempt at conciliation; C. Demaizière, 'Le
Cardinal de Lorraine protecteur de Ramus' (365–80), offers a very
clear analysis of the protection which R. enjoyed from the cardinal,
discussing its origins, duration, and why it stopped (when R. was
suspected of Lutherism); I. Balsamo, 'Le Cardinal de Lorraine et ses
commandes artistiques pour Reims' (443–67), focuses on the cardinal's commissions while he was archbishop in Rheims (1545–74),
and particularly the work he had done on the cathedral, concluding
that they reflect his desire for the spiritual renewal of France; J.-M.
Constant, 'La culture politique d'Henri de Guise vue à travers son
comportement' (497–508), offers a rather speculative political profile
of H., concluding that his behaviour may largely be explained by a
desire to resemble his father and by the norms of the time; J.-L.
Bourgeon, 'Les Guises valets de l'étranger ou trente ans de collaboration avec l'ennemi (1568–1598)' (509–22), suggests that despite their
various alliances with the French kingdom, at various times during
the Wars of Religion the Guises (especially Charles) seemed on the
verge of collaborating with the Spanish; L. Willett, 'Anomalies
picturales dans la représentation d'Henri de Guise' (523–46), offers
an interesting chronological survey of the portraits done of H.,
arguing that the duke used them to promote a certain image
appropriate to his political and social ambitions; V. Larcade, 'Le Duc
d'Épernon et les Guises' (547–55), retraces the conflict between Jean-
Louis de La Valette, Henri III's 'archi-mignon', and the Guises who
regarded him as a threat. Paradoxically, despite this antagonism, the
Guises became a political model to imitate; L.Zilli, 'Le meurtre des
Guises et la littérature pamphlétaire de 1589' (581–93), examines the
language, rhetoric, structure and ideas of four Catholic pamplets
drawn up 1588–89 in the aftermath of the murders of the duke and
cardinal de Guise, concluding that pamphleteer literature of 1589
marks a turning point in the political reflections of the Ligue which
now turns to writing to protest against a tyrannical king; Y.-M. Bercé,
'Les échos du drame de Blois' (595–610), makes an important point
about the partiality of Renaissance chronicles, focusing on the
allegedly widespread shock and revulsion felt on the death of the two
Guise brothers, which, B. claims, was not as general and immediate

as some historians of the time would have us believe; and Y. Bellenger, 'Pour conclure...' (639–50), usefully retraces the history of the Guises, concluding that their influence has often been severely underestimated.

J.-C. Arnould, 'Canards criminels des XVIe et XVIIe siècles: le fait divers et l'ordre du monde (1570–1630)', Arnould, *Touments*, 149–61, analyses a selection of texts relating criminal deeds 1574–1628, discerning a visible formal homogeneity which reflects a desire to impose order on the world. P. Matarasso, 'Seen through a squint: the letters of Jacques de Beaune to Michelle de Saubonne, June to September 1505', *RenS*, 11:343–57, draws attention to a relatively neglected archival collection comprising 23 letters written to Anne of Brittany's wardrobe mistress, which M. sets in the context of the unstable political climate of the time. M. Konnert, 'Civic rivalry and the boundaries of civic identity in the French Wars of Religion: Châlons-sur-Marne and the towns of Champagne', *RenR*, 21:19–33, challenges Bernard Chevalier's view of the *bonne ville* collapsing through religious division and bourgeois treason, arguing that a civic agenda united institutional and occupational lines. I. Paresys, 'Aux marges du royaume: les contemporains picards de Lefèvre d'Étaples sous François Ier', *Actes* (Étaples), 141–54, is useful for 16th-c. social history; P. analyses the repercussions on the Picardy population of their geographical position at the frontier between the Netherlands and France, of the wars, and of the pardons granted by François I; and concludes that a distinctive mentality evolved which was more aggressive and focused on local rather than national identity. L. F. Parmelee, *Good Newes from Fraunce: French Anti-League Propaganda in Late Elizabethan England*, NY, Rochester U.P., 1996, vii + 204 pp., is a clear and interesting examination of the influence of French ideas on late Elizabethan political thought, arguing that they were instrumental in the establishment of Stuart absolutism. H. Viallat, 'Le clergé du diocèse de Genève-Annecy d'après le dénombrement de la gabelle du sel de 1561', *Mélanges Devos*, 325–58, uses the salt registers of 1561 to offer insights into the distribution of the clergy in the Geneva-Annecy diocese, so highlighting the importance of this kind of document in historical research. A. Mansau, 'Marguerite de Savoie, duchesse de Mantoue et vice-reine du Portugal (1589–1655) à travers ses lettres familières', *ib.*, 359–64, establishes a profile of the duchess, but is principally of interest because it draws attention to the rich holdings of the Turin archives. M.-T. Bouquet-Boyer, 'Étude comparative des chapelles musicales de Chambéry, Turin et Genève de 1440 à 1535', *ib.*, 427–33, offers important insights into the musical activities of these three centres.

M. Grandjean, 'Apports de la Renaissance italienne dans l'architecture régionale avant la réforme (des nouveautés décoratives aux œuvres monumentales de Montluel et d'Annecy)', *ib.*, 435–56, assesses the impact of Italian architecture on Savoy in the 16th c., arguing that it is greater than is generally thought. D. Sadler, 'The vision of the Renaissance during the reign of Marguerite de Navarre', Reynolds-Cornell, *Marguerite de Navarre*, 5–14, examines the affinities between the late medieval sensibility in France and the Italian Mannerist style of the 1520s, which shortly afterwards arrived at the French court thanks to the patronage of François I. R. Cooper, 'Le miroir du désordre: Lafréry, Du Cerceau et le ruinisme en France sous Henri II', *Actes* (Nice), 203–19, examines the King's Mannerist taste for ruins, and the 'culte de la décadence' to which this gave rise, largely, it is argued, because of the French community in Rome, and the publication of engravings by L. and Du C. Id., *Litterae in tempore belli: études sur les relations littéraires italo-françaises pendant les guerres d'Italie* (THR, 308), xx + 414 pp., is a very clear, well-documented, and scholarly study which considers literary links between France and Italy from a variety of angles: the French presence in Savoy and Piedmont, contacts between the intellectual milieux of France and Italy, rivalries between French and Italian humanists, French relations with the Vatican. L. Binz, 'Les débuts de la chasse aux sorcières dans le diocèse de Genève', *BHR*, 59:561–581, offers an interesting survey of witch hunts in the 16th c. in and around Geneva. P. Béhar, *Les Langues occultes de la Renaissance: essai sur la crise intellectuelle de l'Europe au XVIe siècle*, Desjonquères, 1996, 348 pp., offers two chapters of relevance to the 16th c.: 'Le talisman de Catherine de Médicis', pp. 63–89; and 'L'occultisme divinatoire et les prophéties de Nostradamus', pp. 121–61. E. Bury, *Littérature et politesse: l'invention de l'honnête homme 1580–1750*, PUF, 1996, 268 pp., examines the notion of *paideia* in relation to Man's cultural conditioning, looking particularly at the links between 'politesse' (defined in the broader sense of civilization and culture) and literature. The first two chapters are particularly relevant to the Renaissance, dealing with the place of literature and philosophy in the educational programme and theories of the day. N. Kuperty-Tsur, *Se dire à la Renaissance: les mémoires au XVIe siècle* (Collection de Pétrarque à Descartes, 65), Vrin, 223 pp. is an interesting and detailed analysis of 16th-c. memoire writing, highlighting the hybrid and subjective nature of these texts which are, it is argued, usually intended to reconstruct the past to dilute the repercussions of a personal disgrace suffered by the author. F. Goyet, *Le sublime du 'lieu commun': l'invention rhétorique dans l'Antiquité et à la Renaissance*, Champion, 785 pp., is a very scholarly work which defines the *lieu commun* and its role in Renaissance rhetoric, tracing its use back to antiquity when it had an essentially political function, and highlighting Cicero's influence on major figures of the Renaissance (notably Melanchthon, Erasmus, Ramus and Montaigne), when the figure had a broader application. M. Bideaux, 'Un motif narratif: la statue de chair', *Hommage Baril*, 119–32, adopts a Greimasian perspective to trace the evolution of this motif which was so popular in medieval and Renaissance narrative. C. Martin-Ulrich, 'Humble mais reine: la reine et la vierge', *ib.*, 245–54, analyses the complementary relationship between the figure of the queen and the Virgin Mary, arguing that they are both representatives of celestial compassion and royal power. C. Bouzy, 'Crime et châtiment dans les livres d'emblèmes français et espagnols aux XVIe et XVIIe siècles', *RLC*, 281:5–23, draws attention to the emphasis put on crime and punishment by French and Spanish emblemists 1539–1610. A. Saunders, 'Expanding the emblematic canon: how many emblems did Gilles Corrozet actually produce?', *RenS*, 11:89–107, reviews the long publishing career of C., arguing that many of the illustrated and even unillustrated works he produced reflect an almost obsessively emblematic way of thinking. On C.'s own emblem book, *L'Hecatongraphie*, see POETRY: PRE-PLÉIADE below. J.-C. Moisan, 'La notion d'ordre dans les commentaires des *Métamorphoses* d'Ovide', *Actes* (Nice), 249–60, considers the disruptive nature of the commentaries accompanying the numerous Latin and French editions of this work. H. Campagne, '*Arrest memorable contre Gilles Garnier pour avoir en forme de loup-garou dévoré plusieurs enfants et commis autres crimes*: métamorphoses et commentaire dans une lettre de Daniel d'Auge', *NRSS*, 15:343–57, is interesting, drawing attention to the importance attached to the werewolf in a wide range of Renaissance writings (literary, theological, legal, scientific, medical texts). J. Céard, '"Mirabilis facta est scientia tua, i tui, ex me". De l'apologétique à la morale', *Hommage Baril*, 187–201, seeks to demonstrate that 16th-c. apologetic texts are essentially anthropocentric, even though they are ontologically theocentric in their reflections.

BIBLIOGRAPHICAL

Cinq années de bibliographie érasmienne (1971–1975), ed. J.-C. Margolin (Collection de Pétrarque à Descartes, 64), Vrin, 632 pp., provides an essential critical bibliography. M. Magnien, *Étienne de la Boétie* (Collection Bibliographie des Écrivains français, 7), Memini, 200 pp., is a very comprehensive research tool. J. M. de Bujanda, **Index des livres interdits. Tome X: Thesaurus de la littérature interdite au XVIe siècle. Auteurs, ouvrages, éditions*, Geneva, Droz, 1996, 840 pp., is enlightening. S. von Gültingen, **Répertoire bibliographique des livres imprimés en France* *au seizième siècle*, fasc. Hors série. *Bibliographie des livres imprimés à Lyon au seizième siècle: Sébastien Gryphius*, vol. v (Bibliotheca Bibliographica Aureliana, 160), Baden-Baden-Bouxwiller, Koerner, 237 pp., will prove very useful. A. Ravier, 'Roger Devos et l'édition des *Entretiens spirituels* de saint François de Sales', *Mélanges Devos*, 19–22, retraces the history of the various editions of this work from its first publication in 1625 up to the Pléiade edition of 1969 on which D. collaborated. J. Veyrin-Forrer, 'Le *Tiers Livre* toulousain de 1546', *BHR*, 59:321–23, is important because it argues that two of the three 1546 editions of the *Tiers Livre* were probably published by the Lyons publisher Jacques Fournier, despite the fact that Paris and Toulouse are indicated on their title-pages. K. Csürös and D. Bjaï, 'Le long poème narratif à la Renaissance: tableau chronologique', *NRSS*, 15:185–214, provide a useful catalogue of long narrative poems. A. Cœurdevey, 'Une nouvelle bibliographie des poésies de Marot mises en musique', *Actes* (Cahors), 503–11, draws attention to the minimal bibliographical resources available on *chanson* musical settings, and explains the criteria underpinning her own forthcoming catalogue of musical sources for M.'s profane poetry. G. Banderier, 'Notes nouvelles sur la bibliothèque d'Honoré d'Urfé', *BHR*, 59:325–33, signals five philosophical books (including three commentaries on Aristotle) acquired by d'U. 1600–1603. Id., 'Du Bellay et Tabourot', *ib.*, 335, draws attention to a copy of Du B.'s *Poematum libri quatuor* (1558) which belonged to T.

HUMANISM, THOUGHT

Centuriae latinae: cent une figures humanistes de la Renaissance aux Lumières offertes à Jacques Chomarat, ed. C. Nativel (THR, 314), 832 pp., is an excellent reference work, providing bio-bibliographical entries for a range of humanists. J. Chomarat, 'Faut-il donner un sens philosophique au mot humanisme?', *RenR*, 21:49–64, challenges the view that humanism was synonymous with atheism just because it placed man at the centre of the universe; C. argues that humanism viewed pagans as deserving of salvation as they had lived in accordance with many of the same moral principles which define Christianity. G. Gadoffre, *La Révolution culturelle dans la France des humanistes: Guillaume Budé et François Ier*, Geneva, Droz, 349 pp., is well-documented, and presents a clear survey of the role played by B. and the king in promoting humanism in every cultural sphere.

On Renaissance philosophy, Pinchard, *Fine Folie*, offers the following: B. Pinchard, 'Transcendantal humaniste ou "fine folie"' (11–31), begins by outlining the problems facing a study of Renaissance philosophy, arguing that either a historical or a philosophical approach is possible, and then defining transendentalism (in the Aristotelian sense); J.-L. Solère, 'Une passion de l'être: les discussions sur le bien transcendantal dans les commentaires de la "somme théologique" — 1a p., q.5, a.1 — à la Renaissance' (33–52), examines Aquinas's views on desirability and goodness, and the debate it provoked; C. Trottmann, 'Des transcendantaux à la vision de Dieu: renversements cusains' (53–83), analyses the theological ideas of Nicolas de Cues, notably his vision of God and Man's dignity, and highlights the originality of his views which stand at the crossroads of the Middle Ages and the Renaissance; E. Faye, 'Le symbole de Prométhée dans la philosophie de Bovelle et en son temps' (115–38), offers an analysis of this myth, a symbol of philosophical quest, as it emerges in the work of B., comparing it to other contemporary or near-contemporary treatments of it; and A. Robinet, 'La critique des transcendentaux de La Ramée à Descartes' (253–63), argues that, in many respects, Cartesian thought regarding the dialectic of transcendentalism has its origins in the work of La Ramée, which reflects a conflict between Platonism and Aristotelianism. The following also deal with philosophy: C. Bené, 'Une polémique réactivée au XVIIIe siècle: le mensonge est-il parfois légitime?', *Hommage Baril*, 269–81, examines what Marullus states on lying in his *Institutio* (sometimes it is justified) and what is said on the subject by his first French translators; and M. Marin, 'Le stoïcisme de Juste Lipse et de Guillaume du Vair', 397–412 of *Juste Lipse (1547–1606). Actes du colloque de Strasbourg 1994*, ed. C. Mouchel (Collection Colloques, congrès et conférences sur la Renaissance, 6), Champion, 1996, 542 pp., compares the metaphysical and stoical views of the two men, concluding that they both exercised considerable influence on the philosophy of the time, preparing the way for Descartes's rigorous rationalization and Pascal's profound fideism.

Actes (Nice) also offers a number of insights into various spheres of Renaissance thought, and is divided as follows: section one, 'Ordre des choses, ordre de Dieu' (13–148), sub-divided into 'Le Corps humain' (13–48), 'La Société' (49–84), 'La Religion' (85–120), and 'Le Langage' (121–47); section two, 'L'Écrivain entre ordre et désordre' (149–344), subdivided into 'L'Italie' (151–220), 'Poésie française' (221–94), and 'Prose française' (295–344). Papers on specific authors will be found under the appropriate headings, and we will mention here only those of a more general nature. G. A. Pérouse, 'Avant-propos' (5–7), offers a brief overview of the subjects dealt with; E. Berriot-Salvadore, 'La médecine restauratrice de l'ordre universel' (13–24), focuses particularly on the works of Jean Fernel to show how medicine was considered a reflection of order in the world, but gradually, towards the last quarter of the 16th c., it became associated with conflict, change and diversity; M.-L. Demonet, 'Le lieu où l'on pense, ou le désordre des facultés' (25–47), is a very interesting article which deals with Renaissance writings on the faculties, highlighting how, because of its ventricles, the brain was seen as a microcosm reflecting order in the world; however, the dissension over the number of ventricles, together with, amongst other factors, progress in anatomy, caused the man-cosmos parallel to become a mere rhetorical figure; A. Jouanna, 'Un idéal d'ordre politique en France au XVIe siècle: la monarchie mixte' (51–63), examines the revived popularity of the antique ideal of a combined monarchy, aristocracy, and democracy, which was not, however, put into practice, so that the power of absolute monarchy prevailed; M. Soulié, 'Ordre et désordre dans la pensée de Jean Calvin' (97–107), offers a very clear study of the new 'order' which C. and the Reformers proposed, and the opposition with which it met; H. Weber, 'Ordre et désordre pendant les débuts de la réforme en France' (109–19), attempts to answer two questions: how could men of order such as Briçonnet and Lefèvre d'Étaples be the cause of what the authorities termed 'les désordres de Meaux'? Does a correlation exist between the explosion of economic discord and the strength of the Reform in Lyons and Saintonge? W. concludes that the uneducated pro-Reform people brought about the disorder, and that the economic relief proposed by the Reformers was undoubtedly a cause of the movement's success.

Actes (Étaples) offers many insights into the leading humanist Jacques Lefèvre d'Étaples. G. Bedouelle, 'Lefèvre d'Étaples et Erasme: une amitié critique' (23–49), examines the links between these two men, focusing particularly on the polemic which divided them up until *c.* 1526, following L.d'É's commentary to St Paul's *Letter to the Hebrews*; B. Roussel, 'Jacques Lefèvre d'Étaples et ses "retours aux écritures"' (43–54), argues that an understanding of L.d'É.'s writings on the Bible permit a better understanding of 16th-c. Christianity, and considers three areas of his career: editing, translation, preaching; M. Engammare, 'Pierre Caroli, véritable disciple de Lefèvre d'Étaples?' (55–79), offers a new analysis of the cause of the polemic between L.d'É.'s followers and C., highlighting the differences between C.'s theological views and those of L.d'É.; S. Baddeley, 'Le choix des langues: Lefèvre d'Étaples et les questions linguistiques au début du XVIe siècle' (81–95), examines L.d'É's position in the debate on the publication in the vernacular of sacred texts; a brief analysis of his 1523 vernacular edition of the Bible (the punctuation is exceptional for the time), leads B. to conclude that he was a courageous innovator whose sensitivity to regional linguistic difference may probably be attributed to his Picard origins; J. Veyrin-Forrer, 'Simon de Colines, imprimeur de Lefèvre d'Étaples' (97–117), offers an enlightening profile of C., the principle person responsible for the diffusion of L.d'É.'s works, and also provides interesting details about the censorship imposed by the Sorbonne; M. Veissière, 'Lefèvre d'Étaples et Guillaume Briçonnet' (119–23), is a brief historical review of the links between these two friends, V. arguing (but not always convincingly) that they influenced each other's humanist views; a detailed comparative analysis of their respective views would have better proved the point; J.-M. Legall, 'Les moines au temps de Lefèvre d'Étaples et Guillaume Briçonnet à Saint-Germain-des-Prés' (125–40), is an interesting article which draws attention to the tensions between pro-Reformist and anti-Reformist monks; L. argues that B. was in charge of the Abbey not in order to promote the Reform, but as a result of a family strategy to preserve benefices, and his decision to reform it suggests the influence of L.d'É. who stayed there; and T. Wanegffellen, 'Lefèvre nicodémite? Qu'est-ce que le nicodémisme?' (155–80), examines Calvin's term *nicodémite* (someone intrinsically Protestant who accommodates him/herself to Catholicism), and sketches out the faith of such people (notably Erasmus and L.d'É.).

P. Chiron, 'Pierre de Chastel et la Faculté de Théologie de Paris: règlement de compte autour de la mort du roi François', *BHR*, 59:29–39, looks at the controversy arising from C.'s funeral sermon in which he decreed that François I went to Paradise, the Sorbonne recognizing this as Reformist in tone. C. Demaizière, 'Le projet de Ramus pour moraliser les pratiques de l'Université de Paris', *Hommage Baril*, 177–86, examines how and why R. attempted to reform the University, focusing on two of his works: *Oratio de legatione* (1557) and *Advertissement sur la Réformation de l'Université de Paris* (1562). J. K. Farge, 'Marguerite de Navarre, her circle, and the Censors of Paris', Reynolds-Cornell, *Marguerite de Navarre*, 15–28, argues that censorship should not be considered just from the point of view of the Reformists (the popular approach) but also from the perspective of the censoring body, the Faculty of Theology and the Paris *Parlement*; F. provides a well-documented survey of the censorship employed both against and on behalf of M. de N. and her circle (Clément Marot, Lefèvre d'Étaples, etc.) from the 1520s up to 1549. R. E. Hallmark, 'Defenders of the faith: the case of Nicole Grenier', *RenS*, 11:123–40, draws attention to this little-known figure, 'the first serious, committed Catholic apologist in French', offering a profile of his works and highlighting the need for further research on him. C. Randall, 'Shouting down Abraham: how sixteenth-century Huguenot women found their voice', *RQ*, 50:411–42, focuses on the minority of 16th-c.

Huguenot women writers, examining the particular case of Charlotte de Mornay, and offering some suggestions as to how, in France and Switzerland, they circumvented obstacles to their expression. L. Taylor, 'The Good Shepherd: François LePicart (1504–56) and preaching reform from within', *SCES*, 28:793–810, reviews the life and sermons of L., arguing that far from being a Catholic prophet of doom, he was optimistic that if the Reform could be accomplished, the religious conflicts would end. F. Lestringant, *Une Sainte Horreur ou le voyage en eucharistie: XVIe–XVIIIe siècle*, PUF, 1996, 358 pp., is a useful survey (relying upon literary rather than archival sources) of the conflict between Catholics and Protestants world-wide over the question of the Eucharist. I. Hentz-Dubail, 'Dispute et civilité dans la concorde religieuse (1560–1610)', *Hommage Baril*, 255–68, examines the various oral forms in which the religious conflict manifested itself, ranging from the university *disputatio* to the informal dialogue. *Discours merveilleux de la vie, actions et déportements de Catherine de Médicis, Royne-mère*, ed. N. Cazauran (Les Classiques de la Pensée Politique, 15), Geneva, Droz, 1995, 355 pp., is a welcome publication because of the insights this anonymous work provides into the political climate immediately following the Saint-Barthélemy, and the attitudes of the opposing faction towards Catherine de Médicis; C. provides the 1575 text with all known variants, and a scholarly introduction which situates the work clearly in its context.

INDIVIDUAL WORKS OR WRITERS

A number of forgotten figures have been the focus of scholarly attention. *Bernard Palissy: Œuvres Complètes*, ed. K. Cameron et al., 2 vols, Éditions Interuniversitaires, 1996, 228, 462 pp., is divided as follows: vol. 1: *Architecture et ordonnance de la grotte rustique de Monseigneur le duc de Montmorancy, pair, & connestable de France (1563)* (1–38); *Recepte veritable (1563)* (39–226); vol. 2: *Discours admirables[. . .] (1580)* (5–398)'. The introduction is very detailed and useful, but the omission of a glossary is unfortunate. *Recette véritable (1563)*, ed. F. Lestringant and C. Barataud, Macula, 1996, 319 pp., acknowledges the forementioned edition which it draws upon, and which it does not perhaps equal for the following reasons: the orthography of L.'s edition has been over-modernized (eg. 'voudroyent' has been replaced by 'voudraient'; 'estoit' by 'était'); there are no line numbers to facilitate reference; illustrations by various contemporaries make the work a little cumbersome. However, what might constitute defects for a specialist undoubtedly serve to make this work more accessible to students and newcomers to the 16th century. S. Charrier, *Recherches sur l'œuvre latine en prose de Robert Gaguin (1433–1501)* (BLR, 35), 1996, 578 pp., offers a detailed analysis of G.'s *Epistolae et orationes* and *Compendium de origine et gestis Francorum*, providing thereby important insights into the historical and intellectual developments of the end of the 15th century. *Jean Thenaud: Le Triumphe des vertuz. Premier traité. Le Triumphe de prudence (ms. Ars. 3358, ff. 1–148)*, ed. T. J. Schuurs-Janssen and R. E. V. Stuip (TLF, 489), clxviii + 423 pp., provides the first published edition of the first of four pedagogical treatises written for François d'Angoulême by this obscure ecclesiast. It is particularly useful because of the insights it gives into the court of Louise de Savoie and the influences nurturing the future king. Complementing this is *Wit and Proverbial Wisdom: an Illustrated Moral Compendium for François I, Facsimilé of a Dismembered Manuscript with Introduction and Description*, ed. J.-M. Massing (Studies of the Warburg Institute, 43), London, Warburg Institute, 1995, 135 pp., which usefully reproduces and annotates the anonymous drawings which were, M. believed, intended for the moral education of the young François. R. Bourgeois, 'L'énigme de Nicolas Barnaud', *Hommage Baril*, 231–44, first considers B.'s alchemical interpretation of the Bologna Stone, then offers a profile of his life and works. *Anthoine Vérard, Parisian Publisher 1485–1512: Prologues, Poems, and Presentations*, ed. M.B. Winn (THR, 313), 600 pp., presents an enlightening study of this neglected yet important figure. The first four chapters preceding the texts are particularly interesting, reconstructing as they do his personal and professional activities, and his links with other writers of the time and his various patrons. One quibble: there is no glossary. *Mistere de l'institucion de l'Ordre des freres prescheurs. Texte de l'édition de Jehan Trepperel (1504–1512?)*, ed. S. de Reyff et al. (TLF, 473), 446 pp., is the first critical edition of this relatively unknown text which relates the founding of the Dominican order; the introduction is particularly clear and useful. C. Skenazi, 'Marie Dentière et la prédication des femmes', *RenR*, 21:5–18, focuses on the obscure author of the *Epistre très utile* (1539) which, using Farel's model of predication, defended the right of women to preach in public. E. Beltrane, 'Un panégyrique de Saint Bernard par l'humaniste méconnu Charles Le Sac', *BHR*, 59:67–85, reproduces the MS *Collatio in laudem Bernardi* (1470), composed by this Rector of the Sorbonne, and bearing strong humanist imprints. C. Magnien, 'Jean Du Sin, ou Achille de Harlay, d'Aubigné, Aristote et l'apothicaire de La Rochelle', *ib.*, 241–62, considers Du Sin and his *Lettres et Occupation* (1602).

J.-C.Ternaux, 'Les excès de la maison de Lorraine dans l'épître et la satire du *Tigre* (1560–1561)', *Actes* (Reims), 381–403, examines Hotman's exploitation of antique models (Juvenal and Cicero particularly) to produce a satire of the cardinal of Lorraine, his brothers and uncle, the anonymous 1561 adaptation of the work into verse, and the counter current it provoked of encomiastic literature which either developed the arguments of the *Tigre* or violently opposed it. Three articles have appeared on the Estiennes: U. Langer, 'Désordre du monde, ordre du proverbe chez Henri Estienne: "l'homme propose et dieu dispose" (*Les Premices*)', *Actes* (Nice), 87–96, draws attention to the importance which E. accords to this proverb, highlighting how it may signify either order or disorder depending upon how it is contextualized; K. Lloyd-Jones, '"La grécité de notre idiome": *correctio, translatio,* and *interpretatio* in the theoretical writings of Henri Estienne', Beer, *Translation,* 259–304, is thorough; and T. R. Wooldridge, 'Vitruve latin et français dans les dictionnaires de Robert Estienne', Brucker, *Traduction,* 261–80, analyses the presence of V. in E.'s dictionaries, pointing to the influence of Guillaume Budé and Jean Martin's 1547 translation of V.'s *De architectura.* The following are on Etienne Pasquier: *Etienne Pasquier, Pourparlers,* ed. B. Sayhi-Périgot (Textes de la Renaissance, 7), Champion, 1995, 619 pp.; *Les Recherches de la France,* ed. M.-M. Fragonard and F. Roudaut, 3 vols (Textes de la Renaissance, 11), Champion, 1996, 2,277 pp.; and C. Moins, 'La nouveauté dans la littérature des troubles. Autour d'une lettre d'Etienne Pasquier (X, 6)', Arnould, *Tourments,* 119–28, who draws attention to the frequency with which the novelty topos appears in late 16th-c. literature, taking this letter as an example. P. Demarolle, 'Tourments et inquiétudes dans le dernier livre de la *Chronique* de Philippe de Vigneulles (1500–1526)', *ib.,* 21–30, considers the theme of torment in this work of *c.*1520, arguing that despite fears of war, illness, natural disasters, the main causes of worry at the time were to do with belief and insecurity. B. Biot, *Barthélemy Aneau, régent de la Renaissance lyonnaise* (BLR, 33), 1996, 532 pp., is a very scholarly and important study which adds to the growing number of recent studies on this key figure, and which corrects many popular, largely negative views about him. Divided into three, the first section comprises a detailed and well-documented biographical study, and the second and third parts provide an analysis of his works. E. Kotler, 'La sexualité et ses désordres dans la *Confession du sieur de Sancy* d'Agrippa d'Aubigné', *Actes* (Nice), 329–44, argues that perverse sexuality is an implicit but prevalent concern in this negative portrayal of Catholics and traitors to the Reform. B. Grosperrin, 'La leçon d'histoire de René de Lucinge', *Mélanges Devos,* 467–71, examines L.'s diverse views on history as expressed in *La Manière de lire l'histoire* (1614). C. A. Mayer and D. Bentley-Cranch, 'François Robertet: French sixteenth-century civil servant, poet and artist', *RenS,* 11:208–22, offer a detailed profile of R., highlighting his poetical and artistic output, and raising questions about his authorship of a number of drawings. Y. Le Hir, 'Béroalde de Verville:

Hérodias', *Hommage Baril*, 169–75, considers this relatively neglected narrative and its moral message. G.-A. Pérouse, 'Symétries narratives et désordres conjugaux dans *Le Printemps* de Jacques Yver (1572)', *Actes* (Nice), 321–28, is a clear examination of the order/disorder dichotomy which characterizes this work at a thematic and structural level, and draws attention to the need for a new critical edition. *Correspondance de Théodore de Bèze*, vol. 19, ed. A. Dufour et al. (THR, 304), Geneva, Droz, 1996, xxxi + 280 pp., covers the year 1578. *La Popelinière. Les Trois Mondes de la Popelinière*, ed. A.-M. Beaulieu (THR, 310), 536 pp., reproduces the 1582 edition of this text which offers useful insights into the geographical knowledge of the time.

On female writers, *Marie de Gournay. Le Promenoir de monsieur de Montaigne. Texte de 1641, avec les variantes des éditions de 1594, 1595, 1598, 1599, 1607, 1623, 1626, 1627, 1634*, ed. J.-C. Arnould (Études Montaignistes, 26), Champion, 1996, 220 pp., is a welcome publication in anticipation of the forthcoming complete works of de G.; however, the criteria for punctuating the text are inconsistent: A. argues for maintaining the original punctuation (p. 30), but modifies it. Also on de G. are the following, in Tetel, *Montaigne*: G. Dotoli, 'Montaigne et les libertins via Mlle de Gournay' (105–41), is interesting because it argues that de G.'s works should be analysed in the light of her strong affinities with the libertines which, incidentally, compromised Montaigne; P. F. Cholakian, 'The economics of friendship: Gournay's *Apologie pour celle qui escrit*' (143–58), analyses de G.'s essay on false friendship, arguing that it must be seen both as a personal text and also as a defence of all women writers; L. D. Kritzman, 'Of ashes born: Montaigne's surrogate daughter' (159–76), argues that de G. was the victim of a literary seduction which left her imprisoned in an unproductive passion, although there is a partially realized autonomy in her discourse; J. Balsamo, 'Marie de Gournay et la famille de Montaigne: les poèmes du *Proumenoir* et l'édition des *Essais* (1594–1599)' (177–94), focuses on the textual divergence between the three editions of the *Proumenoir*, notably regarding what she says about M.'s family; G. Mathieu-Castellani, 'La Quenouille ou la lyre: Marie de Gournay et la cause des femmes' (195–216), is an interesting, close analysis of how de G. continues the feminist tradition, but is innovative in her use of rhetoric; D. De Courcelles, 'Le rire de Marie de Gournay, fille d'alliance de Montaigne' (217–34), demonstrates how de G.'s irony and elegant derision were a response to the hostility she met with from 1610 onwards, and may be seen as a perpetuation of the *serio ludere* characteristic of M.; C.-G. Dubois, 'Autour de l' *Adieu de l'âme du roy Henry de France* (1610) de Marie de Gournay' (235–50), offers an interesting analysis of this work; C. Bauschatz, 'Marie de Gournay's gendered images for language and poetry' (251–67), is a very lucid article which focuses on de G.'s interest in language, notably her personifications of poetry and language as female figures, arguing that these are attempts to represent and to exteriorize herself as an ideal feminine force. Helisenne de Crenne is the subject of the following: J. C. Nash, 'Renaissance mysogyny, biblical feminism, and Helisenne de Crenne's *Epistres familières et invectives*', *RQ*, 50:379–410, is a very clear examination of how de C. counters misogyny (she exploits the same sources often used to denigrate women), pointing to affinities (a common "biblical feminism") with Christine de Pisan; and *Les Angoysses douloureuses qui procedent d'amours*, ed. C. de Buzon (Textes de la Renaissance, 13), Champion, 729 pp., reproduces the 1538 edition of this work, accompanied by a fine scholarly apparatus.

A number of interesting articles on translators have appeared, notably in Brucker, *Traduction*. G. Mombello, 'Du doute à la conscience du succès: le cas de Claude de Seyssel (1504–1514)' (17–34), is a very scholarly analysis of this Savoyard's translation of Greek texts into French via Latin; M. shows that although his translations were not always faithful, S. played a significant role in promoting knowledge of Greek texts in francophone countries. R. Trachsler, 'Jean de Beauvau, traducteur de François Philelphe' (47–61), examines B.'s translation into French of P.'s translation into Latin of Dion's *Chrysostome*, concluding that national prestige, not fidelity to the original, is a priority. S. Bazin-Tacchella, 'Traduction, adaptation et vulgarisation chirurgicale: le cas de la *Chirurgia parva* de Guy de Chauliac' (91–104), looks at how the numerous translations of C.'s work (1363) brought about many modifications to the original text especially during the 15th century. G. Bianciotto, 'La cour de René d'Anjou et les premières traductions d'oeuvres italiennes en France' (187–203), offers an interesting comparative analysis of the translation into French of the *Filostrato* by Louis de Beauvais and of the *Teseida* by an anonymous translator. P. Demarolle, 'John Palsgrave et les problèmes pratiques de la traduction' (249–59), considers P.'s *Éclaircissement de la langue française* (1530), and concludes that, despite its apparent aims, it is not oriented towards a comprehension of French. C. Demaizière, 'Michel de Castelnau, traducteur de Ramus' (283–93), offers a profile of C., analysing his translation of R.'s *De moribus veterum Gallorum* (1559), and arguing that his decision to put it into French reflects a conscious revolt against the monopoly of Greek and Latin culture. M. Colombo-Timelli, 'La première édition bilingue de l'histoire d'Aurelio et d'Isabel (Gilles Corrozet, Paris, 1546) — ou: quelques problèmes de traduction d'italien en français au XVIe siècle' (299–317), examines the first bilingual (French-Italian) edition of this popular Spanish text. As well as offering an interesting comparative analysis of the two texts (by Corrozet?), C.-T. highlights an important *lacuna* in Renaissance studies: scholars tend to focus on translation from Latin and Greek and neglect the translation of Italian texts. J.-C. Arnould, 'Jean Martin dans ses préfaces: un traducteur à la Renaissance' (335–44), challenges those who accuse M. of a lack of originality; emphasizing his importance for the diffusion in France of Italian texts, A. analyses his translation methodology which reveals a desire for fidelity to the text but also a sensitivity for the French language. G. Luciani, 'A propos d'une des premières versions françaises du *Prince* de Machiavel', *Hommage Baril*, 213–30, analyses Gaspard d'Auverge's 1571 translation, drawing attention to style and divergence from the original. On the anonymous *Violier*, the following have appeared: J. Chocheyras, 'Le *Violier des Histoires romaines* (1521), traduction-adaptation des *gesta romanorum*', Brucker, *Traduction*, 133–39, considers this anonymous translation (commissioned by Louise de Savoie?), then proceeds to a a brief survey of the original text's themes (family and social relationships), drawing attention to the syncretism which characterizes it and the need for further research on it; a useful bibliography is appended with this in mind. Id., 'Le masculin et le féminin dans un recueil de *moralia*, *Le Violier des histoires romaines* (1521), *Hommage Baril*, 151–55, provides a clear survey of the moral issues (usually problems between couples) raised in this anonymous translation of the *Gesta romanorum*. G. R. Hope, 'Tales of literacy and authority in the *Violier* (1521): the French *gesta romanorum*', *BHR*, 59:353–63, also examines the nature of these tales, and the text's accessibility to a broad public.

Also worthy of mention are B. Combettes, 'Évolution des outils linguistiques de l'argumentation; la topicalisation de la subordonnée chez Saint François de Sales', Arnould, *Tourments*, 129–36; and F. Roudaut, 'Nouvelles annotations de Guillaume Postel', *NRSS*, 15:215–33.

MULTIPLE WORKS OR WRITERS

B. Sayhi-Périgot, 'Ordre et désordre dans les théories politiques du XVIe siècle: Seyssel, Machiavel, Pasquier', *Actes* (Nice) (65–74), compares and contrasts the political theories of these three men, notably what they say on keeping order in society, and the debt their ideas owe to myth and to history. M. Randall, 'Un roi, deux portraits, et trois freins: "L'Apparition du mareschal sans reproche, feu messire Jacques de Chabannes" de Guillaume Cretin et *La Monarchie de France* de Claude de Seyssel', *Actes* (Baltimore),131–53, draws attention to a paradoxical representation of the king in a double portrait: on the one hand he is subject to the political system's laws, on the other, because of his royal status, he is beyond the law; through reference to

C. and C.'s poetry and Claude de Seyssel's *Monarchie* (1519), R. demonstrates that this view was far from unusual. G. Polizzi, '*Le Songe de Poliphile* ou l'invention du désordre', *ib.*, 177–202, seeks to demonstrate that Francesco Colonna's *Hypnerotomachia Poliphili* (1499) is a paradigm of disorder, and that his utopic discourse informs Rabelais's description of the Île des Macréons in the *Quart Livre* and Verville's *Voyage des princes fortunez*. J.-C. Arnould, 'Ordre et désordre dans quelques recueils narratifs de la seconde moitié du seizième siècle (Boaistuau, Belleforest, Yver, Poissenot, Habanc)', *ib.*, 309–20, argues that although narrative texts are discreet on the subject of order, the order/disorder dichotomy is their key concern. G. Defaux, '"Inter otia animorum et spes inanes": Quintilien, La Boétie, Montaigne', *BHR*, 59:513–35, is a useful analysis of the links between the *Essais* and Q.'s *Institution oratoire*. D. M. Marchi, 'Virginia Woolf crossing the borders of history, culture, and gender: the case of Montaigne, Pater and Gournay', *CLS*, 34:1–30, is an interesting study of M.'s influence on W., mediated through Walter Pater and Marie de Gournay both directly and indirectly.

2. RABELAIS AND THE CONTEURS

M. Gauna, *The Rabelaisian Mythologies*, Madison Teaneck, Fairleagh Dickinson U.P. — London, Associated University Presses, 1996, 293 pp., is a challenging and stimulating work which examines major aspects of *Pantagruel*, *Gargantua*, *Tiers Livre*, and the *Quart Livre* in the light of scholarly criticism to date and modern theory, especially Post-Modernism and Deconstructionism. G. Defaux, *Rabelais Agonistes: du rieur au prophète. Études sur Pantagruel, Gargantua, Le Quart Livre* (THR, 309), 630 pp., comprises a useful distillation of articles (previously published 1971–96, but revised), covering a broad range of aspects. A number of studies on the individual texts have also appeared. J. C. Persels, 'Bragueta humanistica, or humanism's codpiece', *SCES*, 28:79–99, is particularly interesting; after setting the references to codpieces in *Pantagruel* in the context of 16th-c. fashion, P. draws a parallel between this accessory, an obvious symbol of virility, and humanism, 'a moral program presented in and through the male body'. A. Presti Russell, 'Epic *agon* and the strategy of reform in Folengo and Rabelais', *CL*, 34:119–48, draws attention to R.'s debt to F.'s *Baldus*, focusing particularly on how this text informs *Pantagruel*, and on the seriousness of its frequently overlooked Reformist polemic. S. Goffard, 'Fonctions et valeurs des listes dans le *Gargantua* et le *Pantagruel*', *Actes* (Nice), 297–308, argues that R. subtly subverts the usual function of a list (ie. to create order), in order to introduce an implicit disorder: his lists serve to make his radical ideological views more palatable. On the *Tiers Livre*, Dauphiné, *Tiers Livre*, offers the following: M. Jacquemier, 'Le babélisme dans le *Tiers Livre* de Rabelais' (9–20) questions whether R. wanted to insert his writing into a mythical framework , or whether the text situates itself in a political, theological, and literary reality transcending the myth; E. Berriot-Salvadore, 'La question du scepticisme scientifique dans le *Tiers Livre* et le *Quart Livre*' (21–30), argues that in the interval which lapsed between the writing of these two works, R.'s views on a number of philosophical subjects were modified, and, like many of his contemporaries, he became increasingly sceptical; R. Crescenzo, 'Les controverses interprétatives de Pantagruel et Panurge dans le *Tiers Livre*: étude des stratégies rhétoriques et argumentatives' (31–43), focuses on the question of interpretation which is at the heart of this work, looking particularly at how, paradoxically, the techniques employed in the quest for answers serve only to obscure the truth: *logos* engenders *alogia*; P. Ménard, 'Survivances de l'antiféminisme mediéval dans le *Tiers Livre* de Rabelais' (45–59), says nothing new, namely that we must not underestimate the influence of medieval texts on R.; C.-G. Dubois, 'L'enveloppe économique à la substantifique moelle: réflexions sur la dynamique de composition du *Tiers Livre*' (61–70), presents the interesting argument that the text's dynamism derives from the fact that its structure is founded not on the image of a circle, but on all possible extensions and transformations of a circle; M. Léonard, 'Anecdotes, exemples et récits secondaires dans le *Tiers Livre*: du procédé de style à l'émergence d'un sens' (71–91), demonstrates very convincingly how anecdotes, far from undermining the unity of the main story, reinforce it; J.-C. Margolin, 'La présence d'Erasme dans le *Tiers Livre* de Rabelais' (93–112), is important because it highlights the influence of E. but argues that, contrary to what M. Screech maintains, Pantagruelism and Christianity are not synonymous; M. argues that Pantagruelism reflects R.'s distinctive Epicurism, and it is this which distinguishes him from Erasmus; M. Pintaric, 'Panurge ou la satire de l'identité' (113–19), is an interesting analysis of Panurge, who appears incapable of promoting his own identity, because of his inability to make a decision and to act; E. Kotler, 'La parenthèse dans le *Tiers Livre*' (121–34), is also of interest because it argues that, given the frequency with which they occur and their systematic use, the parentheses probably reflect R.'s desires, not those of the printer; through an analysis of the text's parenthical statements, K. demonstrates clearly their importance to the fantasy/reality dichotomy, and to R.'s style; J. Dauphiné, 'Le théâtre des conclusions ou la vérité du *Tiers Livre*' (135–37), elaborates on J. Céard's view that 'la vérité du *Tiers Livre* est celle du théâtre'. Also on the *Tiers Livre*, see J. Veyrin-Forrer, *supra*,

GENERAL: BIBLIOGRAPHICAL. The following deal specifically with the *Quart Livre*: C. Bené, 'Mythes humanistes et désordre politique. L'*Oncle Maroje* et Marin Drzic', *Actes* (Nice), 75–84, draws attention to comparisons between the prologue of this Slav work and the *Quart Livre*; M. B. Harp, *The Portrayal of Community in Rabelais's Quart Livre*, Berne, Lang, 130 pp., is a stimulating and clear survey of all the episodes in the text, which argues convincingly that it is the theme of community (a leitmotif intrinsic to Pantagruelism) which confers unity on what appears, at first glance, to be a largely incoherent text. Also on the *Quart Livre*, see G. Polizzi, *supra*, MULTIPLE WORKS OR WRITERS. Also worthy of mention is F. M. Weinberg, 'Fischart's Rabelais', Beer, *Translation*, 227–57, which examines J. Fischart's 1575–1590 translations of *Gargantua*. A number of new editions have appeared, among which the following two edited by F. Gray: *Gargantua* (Textes de la Renaissance, 2), Champion, 1995, 317 pp., which reproduces the François Juste edition (Lyon, 1542), without modernization of the original spelling and punctuation; although the critical apparatus is rather summary, the introduction provides a useful review of R.'s biography in the light of recent scholarship; and *Pantagruel* (Textes de la Renaissance, 12), Champion, 268 pp., which also reproduces the François Juste 1542 text without modernization. Although this method permits a (still partial) insight into how the text appeared in R.'s day, it is questionable whether it makes the work more accessible.

On Marguerite de Navarre, Reynolds-Cornell, *Marguerite de Navarre*, offers the following on her prose: N. Clerici-Balmas, 'Le langage érotique de l'*Heptaméron*, situations et formes' (29–36), is an interesting analysis of the portrayal of the erotic in this work, demonstrating how M. de N. has a predilection for implication rather than explicit denotation. C.-B. attributes this to her religious sensibility, and her optimism regarding Man: an explicit evocation of the sexual would debase him. F. Ellsworth Peterson, 'Italian music in French Renaissance courts: a hint from the *Heptaméron*' (37–44), draws attention to Story 19 in which the song addressed to Poline has been identified as a *frottola* published in Andrea Antico's *Canzoni, sonetti, strambotti et frottoli libro III* (1513), and concludes (what is already generally acknowledged) that French musicians borrowed more from the Italians than they readily admitted. S. L. F. Richards, 'La poésie dans la prose: les épîtres de l'*Heptaméron*' (45–51), demonstrates how the particular contextualization of *épîtres* in stories 13, 24, 54 subverts the clichés of courtly love, and accentuates the theme of perfect, divine love versus fallible, human love. M.-T. Noiset, 'Marguerite de Navarre et les règles du jeu' (63–70), is an interesting analysis of the voice of convention in the *Heptaméron*, showing how it unites the other voices in the narrative, underpins the divergent concepts of male and female honour, and reveals much about 16th-c. society. D. A. Beecher, 'Marguerite de Navarre's *Heptaméron* and the received idea: the problematics of lovesickness' (71–78), considers M. de N.'s depiction of lovesickness, asking to what extent a knowledge of the medical condition assists the study of the literary expression of the illness. C. H. Winn, '"Trop en corps": figures du corps transgressif dans l'œuvre de Marguerite de Navarre' (93–109), is a worthy analysis of a central dichotomy in the *Heptaméron*: on the one hand M. de N. states that the body must be rejected, on the other she views it in a neo-Platonic light as the visual stimulus for love and therefore a return to God; the failure to resolve the dichotomy leads W. to conclude that M. de N. is resigned to the ontological duality of Man. C. Brucker, 'Inquiétude et quiétude dans l'œuvre de Marguerite de Navarre: évolution ou permanence', Arnould, *Tourments*, 43–56, argues that, as in medieval texts, anxiety permeates M. de N.'s work, revealing itself in her preoccupation with world order, Man's destiny, the soul's well-being etc.; however, what distinguishes her from her predecessors is the personalization of these anxieties. N. Cazauran, 'Des devisants *peu* ou *prou* "mortifiés"? Note en marge du prologue de l'*Heptaméron*', *BHR*, 59:7–12, explains the subtle, spiritual significance of the MS variant 'mortiffiez'.The following focus on particular stories of the *Heptaméron*: F. Goyet, 'Rhétorique et "vérité": la première nouvelle de l'*Heptaméron*', *Hommage Baril*, 157–68, considers the divergence between M. de N.'s text and the real events which inspired it; and N. Virtue, '"Le Sainct Esperit ... parlast par sa bouche": Marguerite de Navarre's evangelical revision of the *Chastelaine de Vergi*', *SCES*, 28:811–24, offers an interesting intertextual reading of story 70 of the *Heptaméron*, arguing that it strongly reflects M. de N.'s evangelical spirituality.

J.-P. Aubrit, *Le Conte et la nouvelle*, Armand Colin, 191 pp., is a useful work, aimed primarily at undergraduates; it reviews the development of the *conte* and the *nouvelle* from the *lais* of Marie de France up to the 20th c., with pp. 14–25 dealing with the Renaissance.

3.　Poetry

S. Perrier offers two enlightening articles: 'Jeux de l'ordre et du désordre: l'adynaton dans la poésie lyrique et la tragédie du XVIe siècle', *Actes* (Nice), 223–37, which takes examples from a number of poets to demonstrate the duality of this rhetorical device: on the one hand it reflects admiration for the cosmos, on the other it betrays a fascination with the possibility of destroying this order; and '"Sous les dernières loys ou du vray ou du faux": les vers gnomiques dans l'épopée au XVIe siècle', *Hommage Baril*, 75–88, which analyses the use and effects of gnomic verse in epic poetry, making reference to a variety of Renaissance poets. P. Galand-Hallyn, 'Des "vers échoï-ques" ou comment rendre une âme à Echo', *NRSS*, 15:253–76, traces the parallel evolution of *versus echoici* and *rime couronnée* from Antiquity to the Renaissance, arguing that the former was probably imported into France largely thanks to Poliziano's *Miscellanea* and Erasmus's *Iuuenis et Echo*; G.-H. evaluates the esteem in which the figure was held, reflecting the concern at the time with mimesis and synesthetic representation. P. Debailly, 'Le miel et le fiel: *laus* et *vituperatio* dans la satire classsique en vers', *Hommage Baril*, 101–17, explores the rhetorical link between encomiastic poetry and satirical poetry. P. Desan and K. Van Orden, 'De la chanson à l'ode: musique et poésie sous le mécénat du cardinal Charles de Lorraine', *Actes* (Reims), 469–94, draw attention to the cardinal's court as an important centre for the development of poetry and music, particu-larly that composed by the little-known Jacques Arcadelt; less original is the section which reviews in relation to the Pléiade's theories the status of the ode and the *chanson*, and the relationship between music and poetry. On long narrative poetry, the following are of interest: D. Bjaï, 'Le long poème narratif à la Renaissance: essai de présenta-tion', *NRSS*, 15:7–25, offers a very detailed definition of this genre which became so popular 1594–95; S. Himmelsbach, '"Long poëme" et "grand genre": l'élaboration de formes narratives longues au début du XVIe siècle', *ib.*, 27–40, examines long narrative historical poems published *c.* 1500 which conform more or less to the epic genre and the *grand genre* of the Rhétoriqueur; and K. Csürös, 'La fonction de l'*ekphrasis* dans les longs poèmes', *ib.*, 169–83, is a well-illustrated and interesting survey. H. Fernandez, 'Une paix suspecte: la célébration littéraire de la paix du Cateau-Cambrésis', *ib.*, 325–41, considers (rather summarily) how the poetry written to commemorate the treaty articulates themes of the Golden Age, unanimity, harmony, and unity, and has a relatively muted celebratory tone. J. Miernowski, *Signes dissimilaires: la quête des noms divins dans la poésie française de la Renaissance* (THR, 312), 304 pp., is a scholarly survey of the multipli-city of names by which God is referred to in Renaissance poetry. S. Alyn-Stacey, 'L'intertextualité translinguistique: réécritures franco-phones de sources italiennes à la Renaissance', Le Calvez, *Texte(s) et Intertexte(s)*, 97–112, examines the mechanisms governing poetical translinguistic transposition, arguing that they are the same in any period (linguistic, thematic, formal), and attempting to demonstrate this through an analysis of three rewritings in French (by Baïf, Magny, Buttet) of an Italian poet (Sannazaro).

PRE-PLÉIADE

Three sets of conference papers have appeared commemorating the birth of Clément Marot in 1496. *Actes* (Cahors) is the most important of these and commendably comprehensive. The collection is divided as follows: 'L'Héritage gréco-latin: Virgile, Ovide, les traductions' (21–140); 'Le Legs du Moyen Age: *Le Roman de la Rose*, Villon, Jean Lemaire de Belges et la "grande rhétorique' (141–212); '"La Court du roy, ma maistres d'escolle ...": le poète et le prince, Pétrarque, l'exil et l'Italie' (213–378); 'Marot "balladin": le pastoreau, la syrinx et la harpe' (379–512); 'Poésie scientifique et persona: du profane au sacré' (513–680); 'Les Fortunes Marot: XVIe et XVIIe siècles' (681–814). G. Defaux and M. Simonin, 'Préface' (7–20), deplore the neglect of M. and his father (no modern edition); G. Demerson, 'Marot mythographe' (23–47), considers in detail M.'s judicious and innovative use of myth, setting it in the context of the time; F. Preisig, 'Marot et la traduction de la première églogue' (49–56), situates M.'s translation of Virgil in the context of early 16th-c. translation tendencies, and highlights humanist influences apparent in the text (notably that of Jodocus Badius Ascensius); C. Skenazi, 'De Virgile à Marot: l'"églogue au roy, soubs les noms de Pan & Robin"' (57–66), presents an intertextual reading between M.'s text and its source, comparing his concept of imitation with that of Erasmus in the *Ciceronianus* (1528); G. Luck, 'Tenerorum lusor amorum: Marot disciple d'Ovide' (67–76), offers little critical analysis of O.'s influence on M., only pointing to possible sources; P. Maréchaux, 'L'Arrière-Fable: la préface de Marot à la *Métamorphose* et les commentaires latins d'Ovide' (77–92),considers M.'s considerable debt to neo-Latin commentators of O., notably Raffaële Regio; J.-C. Moisan and M.-C. Malenfant, 'D'Ovide à Marot: l'évolution des programmes narratifs dans les *Métamorphoses*' (93–105), offer a very interesting study of the transformational operations occuring between the source text and the target text, drawing attention to the influence of neo-Latin commentaries; J. Céard, 'Marot, traducteur d'Érasme' (107–20), focuses on M.'s translation of E.'s *Colloques*, particularly the *Abbatis et eruditae*; J.-E. Girot, 'Clément Marot traducteur de Musée' (121–39), analyses M.'s translation of Musæus's Hero and Leander, drawing attention to his moralising interpretation and general amplification; D. Hult, 'La Fortune du *Roman de la Rose* à l'époque de Clément Marot' (143–56), is an interesting survey of the diverse attitudes towards the allegorical interpretation of this text; J. Cerquiglini-Toulet, 'Clément Marot et la critique littéraire et textuelle: du bien renommé au mal imprimé Villon' (157–64), considers M.'s 1533 edition of V.'s works, arguing that, paradoxically, the æsthetic underlying it seems diametrically opposed to that of Villon; F. Cornilliat, 'La Complainte de Guilliaume Preudhomme ou l'adieu de Marot à la "Grande rhétorique"' (165–83), sees this work as a hommage to the *Rhétoriqueur* tradition; F. Rigolot, '"De peu assez": Clément Marot et Jean Lemaire de Belges' (185–200), convincingly overturns a popular misconception by demonstrating that M.'s apparently flattering references to L.deB. are not sincere but ironic; A. Williams, 'Clément Marot, "le cler soleil": intertexte médiéval de l'épigramme amoureuse' (201–12), focuses on M.'s use of the epigram, a genre at the crossroads between the Middle Ages and the Renaissance; M. Gutwirth, 'Molière redevable à Marot, ou comment remercier un roi?' (215–23), considers similarities between the two men's attitudes to kingship, but is rather inconclusive about sources; S. Bamforth, 'Clément Marot, François Ier et les Muses' (225–35), is an interesting analysis of M.'s very personal relationship with the king, as manifested in what B. recognizes as sincerely admiring poetry; T. Hampton, 'Vergers des lettres: allégorie politique et morale dans *L'Enfer*' (237–48), argues that in this text M. successfully resolves the tension common at the time between political and moral allegory; R. La Charité, '"Couraige et invention": Marot et le cycle carcéral' (249–68), offers an interesting examination of the highly personal poems in which M. evokes his experiences of prison; U. Langer, 'L'éthique de la louange chez Marot: la ballade "de paix, & de victoire"' (269–81), focuses on the theme of the poet who reminds the prince of his obligations to his subjects; particularly interesting is the analysis of the obligations of both parties, and the rhetorical strategies which are defined; O. Rosenthal, 'Clément Marot: une poétique de la requête' (283–99), is an interesting attempt to define the *épîtres de requête* as a specific genre, arguing that they are not merely autobiographical, circumstancial, or commemorative; R. Cooper, 'Marot et Ovide: un nouveau manuscrit à peinture du premier livre des *Metamorphoses* traduit par Marot' (301–21), is an important article which examines a neglected MS of *c.* 1530 [Bodleian: MS Douce 117] which comprises an illustrated copy of M.'s translation; J. Balsamo, 'Marot et les origines du pétrarquisme français (1530–1540)' (323–38), returns to the debate as to who wrote the first French sonnet, but the real merit of this article is that it draws attention to M.'s little-known publication, *Six sonnets de Pétrarque* (1539), which further testifies to M. importance in popularizing the genre in France, although B. claims that he saw himself not so much as a French Petrarch as a French Ovid or David; R. Gorris, '"Un franzese nominato Clemente": Marot à Ferrare' (339–64), offers few new insights, although providing useful archival references; F. Tinguely, 'Marot et le miroir vénitien' (365–77), presents a very full analysis of M.'s *épître* to Renée de France, highlighting its rich symbolism, decoding problems, and M.'s originality: contrary to tradition, and paradoxically as the city welcomed him during his exile, he does not praise Venice; J. Dellaneva, 'A propos de "folle amour"; Marot, Pétrarque et la Pléiade' (381–89), looks at the figure of *folle amour* in relation to M.'s rewritings of P.'s text, making comparisons with Ronsard which suggest his debt to Marot; D. Ménager, 'La syrinx et le pastoureau' (391–403), is an interesting examination of M.'s pastoral poetry, highlighting the evolution from pagan to spiritual text; F. Higman, 'La "Complainte d'ung pastoureau chrestien" et "le riche en pauvreté" dans leur contexte: vrai ou faux Marot?' (404–16), considers the question of the authorship of these two works, indicating that, contrary to what is generally thought, they were not first published in 1588 but first appeared in 1545; H. concludes that the 'Complainte' is probably by M., whilst the other is undoubtedly by Matthieu Malingre; D. Vinay, 'Clément Marot, Martin Luther et Pierre Caroli: aux sources des *Trente Premiers Psalmes*' (417–34), examines the influence (no doubt promoted by C.) of Luther on M.'s psalms, and argues that M.'s imitation is not servile, as is attested by his depiction of David; B. Roussel, 'Les Psaumes: le texte massorétique, les vers de Clément Marot' (435–53), argues and attempts to demonstrate that M.'s versification of the psalms owes much to his reading of renditions of the *veritas hebraica*; G. Morisse, 'Les Psaumes de Marot chez les Huguenots: le texte' (455–61), examines the appropriation of M.'s psalms by the Huguenots, highlighting the modifications which the text underwent in Protestant hands; O. Millet, 'Marot et Calvin: chanter les psaumes' (463–76), traces the historical background to the singing of psalms, and focusing on M.'s two prefaces to his *Pseaumes*, draws attention to what he says on the subject; J. D. Candaux, 'Les Psaumes de Marot chez les Huguenots: la musique' (477–81), offers a useful survey of what is known to date on the music of the Huguenot psalter 1539–62, ie. before it became fixed, and concludes that three different composers (Guillaume Franc, Loys Bourgeois, the third unknown) are responsible for putting M.'s psalms to music during this period; F. Dobbins, 'Les premières mises en musique des chansons, des épigrammes et des rondeaux de Marot' (483–502), focuses on Copenhagen MS Ny kgl. Samling 1848 2°, which contains the first texts and musical settings of seven of M.'s *chansons*, therefore predating the *Chansons nouvelles* (1528), and already attesting M.'s popularity with contemporary musicians as well as his own musical sensitivity; D. emphasises the importance of these settings for the reader as much as for the musician: they contain earlier versions of the published text; R. Mélançon, 'La Personne de Marot' (514–29), argues that M.'s works read as autobiographical, or more precisely as 'une variété morale de prosopographie'; J. Miernowski, 'Le Pas chancelant de la fiction marotique' (531–43), offers an analysis of some of M.'s poems to support his view that doubts and hesitations are manifested in his poetical fiction; J.-M. Collard, 'Marot: une parole de proximité' (545–57), is a clear and interesting analysis of the dual theme of proximity and distance in M.'s poetry; E. M. Duval, 'Marot, Marguerite, et le chant du cœur: formes lyriques et formes d'intériorité' (559–71), traces the evolution of the theme of the heart in three of M.'s poems written 1514–43, and also in Marguerite de Navarre's *L'Inquisiteur*, on which, D. argues, M. undoubtedly collaborated; F. Rouget, 'Marot poète lyrique' (573–91), presents a synthesis of M.'s lyrical rhymes and strophic systems, concluding that he is at the crossroads of tradition and innovation; F. Goyet, 'Sur l'ordre de *L'Adolescence clémentine*' (593–613), is an interesting analysis of the modified order in which the poems of this work appear in 1532 and 1538, and draws attention to the links between the first five *épîtres*; M. B. Mckinley, 'Marot, Marguerite de Navarre et "L'Epistre du despourveu"' (615–26), presents a sound reading of this poem, arguing that it is undeserving of the generally negative criticism it has provoked, reflecting as it does M.'s mastery of the *récit spéculaire*; J. Berchtold, 'L'Enfer: les enjeux d'une transposition mythique' (627–43) considers M.'s use of mythology, notably his exploitation of the motif of the descent to Hell, and its propagandist function; L. K. Donaldson-Evans, 'Le blason du beau tetin: une relecture' (645–55), highlights the frequently overlooked serious intent of this blason; in a close textual reading, D.-E. reveals how the iconography associated with the Virgin Mary implies the worthy and divine nature of marriage, so uniting Eros and *ferme amour*, and going counter to the Catholic Church which asserted the superiority of celibacy over marriage; S. G. Nichols, 'Ut epigramma poesis: tableaux de la poésie dans les épigrammes de Marot' (657–67), considers the relationship between the epigramme and the image in M.'s poetry, making extensive reference to Martial, his major model; G. Mallary Masters, 'L'Eros marotique: du profane au sacré' (669–79), is a very clear and interesting analysis of three poems exemplifying M.'s generally polyvalent use of myth; P. Desan, '"Profit du libraire" et "honneur de l'auteur": Marot face à ses lecteurs' (683–97), is an interesting article which examines the relationship between the writer, text, and the reader; D. examines the role of M.'s liminary poems and the material presentation of his works, indicating that through the editor's intervention, the text acquires an identity/existence independent of its author; G. Mathieu-Castellani, 'Les enfants de Marot' (713–34), offers a clear, intertextual survey showing how M.'s texts inform the works of Du Guillet, Scève, Du Bellay, d'Aubigné; J. O'Brien, 'Chanter marotiquement: survie et contestation' (735–46), considers the continued popularity M.'s poems enjoyed with musicians well after his death, situating him in the context of later 16th-c. developments, notably those of the Pléiade; C. Pascolo, 'Présence de Marot et du marotisme dans les recueils collectifs de chansons et de poésies de *La Fleur de poésie françoyse* (1542) *au Courtisan amoureux* (1582)' (747–58), looks at the sustained popularity of Marot and the Marotic tradition as attested by these two anthologies; M. Simonin, 'De Marot à Ronsard: Les *Traductions de latin an françois* (1550 et 1554)' (759–82), considers M.'s position in the editions of these works; B. Beugnot, '"L'Inspiration à rênes courtes": Marot chez les classiques' (783–97), examines M.'s status and influence in the 17th c., arguing that he was an intermediary betweeen Antiquity and 'la gaieté lafontainienne'; P. J. Smith, 'Clément Marot aux Pays-Bas: présence de Marot dans les bibliothèques privées des Hollandais au XVIIe siècle' (799–813), draws attention to the popularity of M. in the 17th-c. Netherlands, manifested essentially in the various re-editions of his psalms and translations, and in imitations by Marotic disciples. 'Appendice: Lettre de Boyssonné à Jacques Delexi (1er mars 1547 [N.S.?])' (819–24), offers a useful transcription of the letter in which appears the famous sentence "Marotus latine nescivit".

Dauphiné, *Marot*, offers the following, all concerned with the *Adolescence clémentine*: M. F. Notz, 'Ballades et rondeaux dans *L'Adolescence clémentine*: au confluent de la tradition et de l'invention' (7–18), is a rather vague and summary analysis of M.'s use of the *ballade* and *rondeau* in this work; M. Leonard, 'Une tournure médiévale: l'emploi de *si* adverbe de phrase dans *L'Adolescence clémentine*' (19–40), examines M.'s frequent use of this relatively archaic adverbial phrase; A. Bertin, 'Les couleurs dans *L'Adolescence clémentine*' (41–55), argues that at times M. subverts the tradition of colour symbolism, and points out a gradual movement in his works from bright to dark colours, attributing this to religious and philosophical factors, and also to the æsthetic values of the *Grands Rhétoriqueurs*; P. Chiron, 'Le Jugement de Momus' (57–66), draws a comparison between Marot and this mythological figure: both are exiled, judged and escape judgement; it is this deliberately elusive quality of M.'s poetry which forms the focus of this interesting paper; J. Dauphiné, 'Marot, traducteur de *La Canzone delle visioni* de Pétrarque' (67–72), presents a brief analysis of M.'s translation, arguing that far from being a mere paraphrase of P.'s text, it reveals a very personal style, notably a predilection for emblematic representation; R. Crescenzo, 'L'antique, l'ancien et le nouveau dans le *Temple de Cupido*' (73–87), sees this work as reflective of M.'s hesitation between old and new tendencies, and offers an interesting analysis of the various sources it relies upon; C. argues that this early work already contains the themes which M. would develop at greater length later (notably *ferme amour*); E. Berriot-Salvadore, 'La mutation de fortune de Clément Marot' (89–101), shows that M.'s presentation of fortune has affinities with the very personalized and original portrayal it receives at the hands of Christine de Pizan; F. Lestringant, 'Variations volatiles sur le Christ-Pélican. A propos de la Ballade XIII de *L'Adolescence clémentine*' (103–19), retraces very clearly the symbolic value of the pelican in literature from Antiquity to M.'s day, and then situates M. within the context of this tradition by analysing his (very traditional) use of the bird; M. Pintaric, 'Clément Marot, la *personne rimante*' (121–31), seeks rather narrowly to define M.'s poetic identity through an analysis of his attitudes towards poetry, woman, and God; J.-C. Margolin, 'Féminisme et évangélisme chez Erasme et Marot d'après le colloque *Abbatis et Eruditae* et sa traduction par le poète français' (13–67), focuses on M.'s translations on three of E.'s *colloques*, most of the article being dedicated to an enlightening commentary on the first one; and J. Dauphiné, 'Marot libertaire' (169–71), offers some brief comments on the essentially personal tone of M.'s poetry, arguing that '[a]vec lui naît le mythe de l'intellectuel moderne, engagé et libertaire'.

Actes (Baltimore) considers the influence of Marot, and is divided as follows: 'Clément Marot "Guide et porte-enseigne/De tous rimeurs..."' (19–190); 'La Génération Marot: domaines français et néo-latin' (191–346); '"Treschiers Freres" et autres "enfans d'Apollo"' (347–525). G. Defaux, 'Préface' (7–18) signals that this conference is intended to complement the one held at Cahors (see *supra*, p.104), and aims essentially to focus on some relatively forgotten poets; he presents a useful survey of research to date on Marot and the Rhétoriqueurs. Interestingly, D. criticizes the partisan attitudes of some critics, and invites a return to a focus on the text. F. Rigolot, 'Clément Marot et l'émergence de la conscience littéraire à la Renaissance' (21–34), evaluates M.'s considerable contribution to the evolution of literary consciousness in the 16th c., arguing that it is reflected in his works, which display a gradual departure from both reverence to his masters and exposure of his weaknesses, and a greater confidence in himself and in his role of author. C. Brown, 'Les *Abus du monde* de Pierre Gringore: de l'imprimé au manuscrit?' (35–58), draws attention to certain similarities between the works of M. and G., arguing that, although it is difficult to ascertain what, if any, direct links they had with each other, G.'s influence on M. is even greater than that of Jean Marot; B. then proceeds to examine the place of the MS in the evolution of G.'s works, focusing particularly on the *Abus du monde* in its MS and printed form. F. Cornilliat, 'Rhétorique, *poésie*, guérison: de Jean à Clément Marot' (59–80), examines the differences between the two men as manifested in the way they fuse rhetoric and poetry, taking the particular example of the father's *Prières sur la restauration de la sancté de Madame Anne de Bretagne, royne de France* (1512) and the son's *Cantique de la royne, sur la maladie, & convalescence du roy* (1539). G. Defaux, '"Effacer Jean, & escrire Clement": une douloureuse (et double) affaire de succession' (81–112), emphasizes the personal motivation of the son's poetry, and highlights the importance of his relationship with his father; D. also appeals for a re-evaluation of the period 1514–19, and the alleged date when the father died. S. Bamforth, 'Clément Marot et le projet de paix universelle de 1518: poésie et propagande' (113–29), is an interesting examination of M.'s links with humanism during the period 1518–20, making particular reference to the project for universal peace and the treaty signed with England; B. offers a summary analysis of *ballades* 7 and 8, and *rondeaux* 23 and 26, highlighting their propagandist references, and situating M. in the context of general propagandist trends. M. Clément, 'Marot politique dans *L'Adolescence clémentine* et dans *La Suite*' (155–67), draws attention to affinities between M.'s views on kingship and those of some of the major 16th-c. theorists, eg. Machiavelli, Erasmus, Budé, More (a possible influence?), arguing that M. was not afraid to criticize the monarchy, reflecting thereby his dislike of absolutism. J. McClelland, 'Marot et ses compositeurs: coïncidences et interférences des langages poétique et musical' (169–89), examines those poems which M. set to music before they were published in purely literary form, and focuses particularly on three chansons in the *Adolescence clémentine* (nos 34, 35, 36) written 1532–38; McC. concludes that their largely rhetorical nature goes counter to the musical tendencies of the time, and this would explain why his epigrams were preferred by musicians. C. Scollen-Jimack, 'Vers une typologie marotique: Eustorg de Beaulieu, Victor Brodeau, Charles de Sainte-Marthe' (193–209), proposes some criteria by which to define followers of Marot, then offers a brief profile of three 'marotiques possibles'. More detailed textual analysis would have been welcome. P. Galand-Hallyn, 'Marot, Macrin, Bourbon: "Muse naïve" et "tendre style"' (211–40), is a dense, scholarly article divided into three parts, analysing rhetoric, paratextual elements, and the *topos* of the poet-shepherd. J. Balsamo, 'Trois "poëtes renommez de ce tems"', Claude Chappuys, Antoine Héroët, Mellin de Saint-Gelais et la *Fable de Cupido et Psyché*' (241–59), examines this work commissioned by François I from C., H., and S.-G., revealing the accompanying production constraints. M. Magnien, 'Marot et l'humanisme (suite): Jean de Boyssoné et le

Maro Gallicus' (261–79), enlightens us on the undeniable influence of M. on Boysonné. T. Conley, 'Le Poème-monde: Oronce Finé et Clément Marot' (281–97), is an interesting discussion of the geometrical affinities between a *rondeau* by F. and M.'s *Adolescence clémentine*, exposing a cosmic crisis expressed in the text; A. Tomarken, '"Icy dessoubz": la rhétorique de l'épitaphe dans la génération Marot' (299–313), considers a selection of verse epitaphes composed by M. and other contemporaries, demonstrating how they renew old *topoi*; J. E. Girot, 'La poétique du coq-à-l'âne: autour d'une version inédite du "grup" de Clément Marot (?)' (315–46), does not say anything that C. Mayer has not already said on this genre in 'Coq à l'âne; définition, invention, attributions', *FS*, 16:1–13; P. Desan, 'Le feuilleton illustré Marot-Sagon' (348–80) argues that the cause of the quarrel between M. and S. was not just literary and theological, but largely inspired by rivalry for public position; T. Mantovani, 'La querelle de Marot et de Sagon: essai de mise au point' (381–404), offers a useful survey of the quarrel, revealing how at times the exchanges were quite friendly; M. Simonin, 'A chacun son fréron: Jean Le Blond, adversaire (?) de Clément Marot' (405–24), is a detailed profile of L. B., highlighting his contribution to the quarrel; J. Britnell, 'Le dernier triomphe de Jean Bouchet: les *Triomphes du Roy de France* (1550)' (425–43), presents an interesting and detailed analysis of this work, focusing particularly on B.'s use of myth; R. Cooper, 'Michel d'Amboise, poète maudit?' (445–470), calls for further research into A., arguing that he is undeserving of his reputation as a mediocre translator; F. Tinguely, 'Eros géographe: Bertrand de la Borderie et *Le Discours du voyage de Constantinoble*' (471–86), draws attention to this largely unknown work by B., claiming that its originality lies in its curious fusion of amatory and travel language; R. Cottrell, 'Rhétorique et foi dans *Le Temple de vertu* de François Habert' (487–99), is a stimulating analysis of the literary links between H. and Marot, focusing particularly on his notion of virtue which is more explicitly oriented towards religious orthodoxy, scholastic thought, and Aristotelian ethics than M.'s.; H. Glidden, 'Hugues Salel, Dame, poésie, et la traduction d'Homère' (501–11) examines S.'s 1542–45 French translation of the *Iliad*, the first in French verse, arguing that it influenced Marot; F. Rouget, 'Marot, Magny, et les raisons d'un silence' (513–25), is an interesting survey of Magny's debt to Marot.

The following are also on M.: *Cinquante pseaumes de David mis en françoys selon la vérité hébraïque. Édition critique sur le texte de l'édition publiée en 1543 à Genève par Jean Gérard*, ed. G. Defaux (Textes de la Renaissance, 1), Champion, 1995, 345 pp.; despite its merits (the introduction offers a very clear analysis of the psalms), the 'Bibliographie chronologique et critique' is rather summary, and there are glaring omissions, as well as what some might view as peevish, unjustified criticism of previous critics. Id., *Le Poète en son jardin: étude sur Clément Marot et 'L'Adolescence clémentine'*, Champion, 1996, 283 pp., proposes a useful 'bilan de connaissances actuelles' on M.; the biographical section (ch. 1–3) is particularly interesting. Treading in the steps of C. Mayer and P. M. Smith, D. draws attention to M.'s frequently overlooked originality. See also H. H. Glidden, 'Marot's *Le Roman de la Rose* and evangelical poetics', Beer, *Translation*, 143–74.

On the poetry of Marguerite de Navarre, the following are worthy of mention: M. Morris, 'Diotima Liberata', Reynolds-Cornell, *Marguerite de Navarre*, 53–61, offers a brief but clear and useful analysis of *Les Prisons*, drawing attention to M. de N.'s close adherence to the spiritual ideals outlined by Diotima in the *Symposium*, and to the prevalent influence of Ficino's commentaries; G. Mallary Masters, 'La Libération des prisons structurées: les prisons de Marguerite de Navarre', *ib.*, 111–22, focuses on the images in the last section of the third 'Prison', arguing that they hold the key to the text, and insisting upon the Platonic-Christian syncretism underpinning M.de N.'s concept of spiritual liberty; K. Kupisz, 'Ordre et désordre dans *La Navire* de Marguerite de Navarre', *Actes* (Nice), 261–70, challenges P. Jourda's view that this work lacks 'une composition savante et régulière'; S. Snyder, 'Guilty sisters: Marguerite de Navarre, Elizabeth of England, and the *Miroir de l'âme pécheresse*', *RQ*, 50:443–58, is rather speculative, arguing that the Miriam-Moses relationship depicted by M. de N. corresponds to a true resentment she felt towards her own brother, and that the future Elizabeth I perceived an affinity with this (given her relative inferiority to her brother Edward VI), hence her translation of this work; and *Marguerite de Navarre. Poésies chrétiennes*, ed. N. Cazauran, Cerf, 1996, 352 pp., aimed primarily at undergraduates, offers a selection of M. de N.'s poetry.

On the Lyons poets, the following have appeared: *Maurice Scève. Délie*, ed. F. Joukovsky, Dunod, 1996, lxxi + 446, reproduces the 1544 edition and emblems, with only very discreet editing and very efficent elucidation of the text's meaning. N. Fournier, 'Plurivocité, ambiguïté, ambivalence dans la *Délie* de Maurice Scève', *Hommage Baril*, 9–30, considers the *Délie*'s intrinsic ambiguity from a linguistic perspective. J. Helgeson, '"Chantant Orphée": lyrisme et orphisme dans la *Délie* de Maurice Scève', *BHR*, 59:13–28, examines the figure of Orpheus in the *Délie* in the broader context of the lyrical issues he represents. The following are on Louis Labé: D. Lesko Baker, *The Subject of Desire. Petrarchan Poetics and the Female Voice in Louise Labé*, West Lafayette, Purdue U.P., 1996, 240 pp., is a dense and scholarly analysis of L.'s 1550 *Œuvres*, examining the question of artistic and erotic desire, and perceiving an energetic, distinctly female voice which transcends male Petrarchan poetics; the close textual readings are particularly good. F. Rigolot, *Louise Labé lyonnaise, ou: la Renaissance au féminin* (Études et essais sur la Renaissance, 15), Champion, 347 pp., is to be highly recommended; R. offers a clear and comprehensive study of L.'s poetical practice (imitation, use of myth, themes etc.), demonstrating her originality and importance to 16th-c. literary developments. C. Scott, 'Engendering the Sonnet, loving to write/writing to love: Louise Labé's 'tout aussi tot que je commence à prendre''', *MLR*, 92:842–50, offers a close reading of this sonnet, examining it in relation to L.'s general writing ethos.

A number of editions have appeared: G. Corrozet, *L'Hecatongraphie (1544) & les emblemes du tableau de Cebes (1543) reproduits en facsimilé avec une étude critique*, ed. A. Adams (TLF, 480), [variable pagination], usefully reproduces one of the masterpieces of French Renaissance, although the notes accompanying each emblem could have been more extensive, and a critical bibliography would have been an asset. *Jean Lemaire de Belges. Traicté de la différence des schismes et des conciles de l'Église avec l'histoire du Prince Sophy et autres Œuvres*, ed. J. Britnell (TLF, 484), 354 pp. , is a useful scholarly edition of this 1511 text, which offers insights into the religious conflicts of the time, and L.deB.'s role in diffusing royalist anti-Papal propaganda. *Bertrand de La Borderie. L'Amie de court (1542)*, ed. D. Trudeau (Textes de la Renaissance, 16), Champion, xxxvii + 161 pp., is an important publication, as it offers the first of the four texts involved in the 'Querelle des Amyes' (1542–54).

Mention should also be made of the following: P. Ford, 'Jean Salmon Macrin's *Epithalamiorum Liber* and the joys of conjugal love', Smet, *Eros et Priapus*, 65–84, is an interesting examination of the understated eroticism of M.'s poems to his wife; T. Van Hemelryck, 'Note sur la postérité du *Miroir de mort*, Olivier de La Marche et une prétendue traduction bretonne', *BHR*, 59:337–52, reviews the erroneous attribution to L.M. of George Chastellain's *Miroir de mort*, and the equally erroneous view that it was translated into Breton *c.*1530 and 1570; P. Demarolle, 'Autour de la Guerre des Paysans (1525): matière et registres de l'épopée chez Nicolas Volcyr', *NRSS*, 15:41–53.

RONSARD AND THE PLÉIADE

PLÉIADE GENERAL.   M. Bizer, *La Poésie au miroir: imitation et conscience de soi dans la poésie latine de la Pléiade* (Études et essais sur la Renaissance, 8), Champion, 1995, 233 pp., offers a very clear intertextual study, focusing particularly on the Latin poetry of Du Bellay, Belleau, and Baïf, and highlighting the fine line between imitation and translation.

RONSARD. A.-M. Lebersorger-Gauthier, *Les Voix du mythe dans les sonnets pour Hélène de Pierre de Ronsard*, Klagenfurt, Die Blaue Eule, 1995, 232 pp., presents a useful survey of the use of myth in the Hélène cycle, offering some sensitive, close readings. Y. Bellenger, *Lisez la Cassandre de Ronsard: étude sur les Amours (1553)*, Champion, 187 pp., is a comprehensive overview of this collection, aimed primarily at undergraduates. *Ronsard. Les Amours de Cassandre*, ed. M. Simonin, Klincksieck, 196 pp., is a useful distillation of articles, only two of which have not been published before: D. Lesko Baker, 'Poetic beginnings and subjectivity in the *Amours* of Ronsard' (145–49), a psychoanalytical analysis of the liminary 'Vœu', which L. B. considers to be a fundamental marker of individual poetic voices and subjectivities; and F. Vuilleumier, 'Les *Amours* de Pierre de Ronsard: sources ou modèles d'invention?' (150–70), a clear and interesting analysis of some of R.'s Italian and Antique sources, which makes useful comparative reference to R.'s contemporaries. P. Ford, *Ronsard's Hymnes: A Literary and Iconographical Study* (MRTS, 157), xi + 339 pp., is a very clear, scholarly analysis of both the literary aspects of the *Hymnes*, and the parallels between R.'s writing and the plastic arts; the first two chapters offer a particularly useful survey of the theoretical background informing R.'s poetry and the visual arts. M. Quainton, 'Ronsard et la "libre contrainte"', *Actes* (Nice), 271–84, focuses on the *discordia concors* complex which characterizes both R.'s concept of the universe and his poetic æsthetic. H. Lindner, 'Rhétorique, poésie, mécénat: le procès de Ronsard contre le cardinal de Lorraine', *Actes* (Reims), 404–23, presents an analysis of R.'s poem "Le Proces", in order to demonstrate the complex dialectic between litterature and patronage after 1560. N. Dauvois-Lavialle, 'Ordre et désordre dans les odes de Ronsard, l'élan et la règle', *Actes* (Nice), 285–94, offers an interesting analysis of some of R.'s Pindaric odes, positing that in terms of its rythmn, apostrophes, themes etc., the ode is both an expression of order and disorder. M. Bizer, 'Ronsard the poet, Belleau the translator; the difficulties of writing in the Laureate's shadow', Beer, *Translation*, 175–226, argues that B. was intimidated by R., but gradually, by translating his own poems into Latin, he became more confident. D. Bjaï, 'De l'épopée nationale à l'histoire auvergnate: Ronsard et Jean de Boyssières', *NRSS*, 15:55–71, draws attention to R.'s praise of B.'s skill as an epic poet, then proceeds to review B.'s epic poetry.

DU BELLAY. G. H. Tucker, 'Le "cry non entendu" du poète: relecture intertextuelle de *L'Olive* XLV [XLI, 1549] de Du Bellay', Le Calvez, *Texte(s) et Intertexte(s)*, 55–70, offers a close reading of this sonnet, arguing that imitation constitutes both reinterpretation and appropriation (through a rewriting) of a chosen model. J.-C. Monferran and O. Rosenthal, 'A quoi sert de nommer? Politique du nom dans *Les Regrets* de Du Bellay', *NRSS*, 15:301–23, offer an interesting, dense analysis of the political ideology informing the names in this text. F. Roudaut, 'Le Cardinal de Lorraine, François de Guise et Joachim Du Bellay', *Actes* (Reims), 425–42, argues that in Du B.'s poetry the figures of these two Guises permit a *reductio ad unum* of past and present history, so that they surpass mythical history and heroes.

DORAT. E. Karagiannis, 'Procès et éloge d'un fripon modèle: le discours ΕΙΣ ΕΡΜΗΝ de Jean Dorat', *BHR*, 59:87–103, reproduces D.'s Greek poem and its Latin translation, accompanied by a dense, critical analysis. H. Demay, *Jean Dorat (1508–1588): 'l'Homère du Limousin', âme de la Pléiade, et poète des rois*, L'Harmattan, 1996, 157 pp., is also useful. On Baïf, an important publication is J. Vignes, *Mots dorés pour un siècle de fer. Les Mimes, enseignements et proverbes de Jean-Antoine Baïf: texte, contexte, intertexte* (BLR, 37), 680 + xiv pp., which provides a multi-faceted, scholarly analysis of this long neglected work. E.Vinestock, 'Quelques procédés de traduction et d'adaptation dans les poèmes de Jean-Antoine de Baïf', Brucker, *Traduction*, 325–34, is an interesting, very clear analysis of the processes of translation and adaptation in a number of B.'s poems. Y. Roberts, 'Jean-Antoine de Baïf and the Saint-Barthélemy', *BHR*, 59:607–11, challenges the view that in his eighth book of *Poèmes* B. expresses full support for the Saint-Barthélemy. On Belleau, J. Braybrook, 'Joinville, les Guises, et l'œuvre de Rémy Belleau', *Actes* (Reims), 233–49, considers B.'s links with the Guises, notably the transformation (attributable to the changing political climate) which his depiction of them underwent in the *Bergerie* 1565–72. Complementing this is J. Rieu, '*La Bergerie* de Remy Belleau: une "fête" à la gloire des Guises', *ib.*, 251–78, which examines the allegorical significance of the *Bergerie*, which R. sees in terms of a festival celebrating the Guises. On Jodelle, E. Buron, 'Le cosmos et la vicissitude: néoplatonisme et parole poétique dans quelques sonnets à Diane des *Amours* d'Estienne Jodelle', *Actes* (Nice) 239–48, argues that J. espouses Platonism only to contest it. On Tyard, F. Rouget, 'La poétique de Pontus de Tyard dans les *vers lyriques* (1555) et les *nouvell' œuvres poétiques* (1573): de la célébration lyrique aux adieux à la poésie', *NRSS*, 15:277–99, offers a general analysis of these two relatively neglected works. On Magny, see F. Rouget, *supra*, PRE-PLÉIADE. On Magny, Baïf, and Buttet, see S. Alyn-Stacey, *supra*, POETRY.

ASSOCIATES OF THE PLÉIADE. *Peletier du Mans. L'Amour des amours*, ed. J.-C. Monferran (STFM, 208), 1996, lxxvii + 312 pp. , is a welcome publication. M. Clément, 'La morale et le coq-à-l'âne dans

La Gélodacrye de Jacques Grévin', *Hommage Baril*, 45–57, argues that this genre reflects G.'s Reformist views and an evolution in his poetical practice. L. Terreaux, 'Marc-Claude de Buttet entre la Savoie et la France', *Mélanges Devos*, 457–65, relies heavily upon S. Alyn-Stacey's biographical research (and acknowledges this), to present a profile of the Savoyard poet. G.-A. Pérouse offers 'Un pétrarquisme bourgeois. *Les Erotasmes de Phidie et Gelasine* de Philibert Bugnyon', *Hommage Baril*, 31–43, which demonstrates how B. transposes provincial and bourgeois morals onto the *canzoniere* schema.

M. Clément, *Une politique de crise: poètes baroques et mystiques (1570–1660)* (BLR, 34), 1996, 434 pp., redefines the concept of the baroque, taking into account the importance of mystic writings, a selection of which are analysed. On Pierre Poupo, two items have appeared: *Pierre Poupo. La Muse chrestienne*, ed. A. Mantero (STFM, 210), lxvii + 581 pp., a welcome publication, with an enlightening introduction, relating the biography of this relatively obscure Protestant poet; and Y. Quenot, 'Bible, poésie et pédagogie dans les sonnets sur la création de Pierre Poupo', *Hommages Baril*, 59–73, examining P.'s eight sonnets (1590). *Jean de Sponde. Meditations sur les Pseaumes*, ed. S. Lardon (Textes de la Renaissance, 9), Champion, 1996, 515 pp., offers the 1588 text; the introduction deals essentially with the rediscovery of the text, but regrettably there is little (if any) critical comment on the poems themselves. C. Deloince-Louette, 'Morale antique et calvinisme chez Jean de Sponde: fonction de la sentence', *Hommage Baril*, 89–100, analyses S.'s syncretism in the *Commentaire d'Homère* and the *Prolégomènes* (1583), focusing particularly on his use of the moral sentence. On d'Aubigné, *Agrippa d'Aubigné. La Responce de Michau l'aveugle, suivi de La Replique de Michau l'aveugle: deux pamplets thélogiques anonymes publiés avec les pièces catholiques de la controverse*, ed. J.-R. Fanlo (Textes de la Renaissance, 10), Champion, 1996, xxxiii + 241 pp., is important because it deepens our insight into d'A.'s political views and his role in the religious polemic. A. Thierry, 'La Maison de Guise dans l'œuvre d'Agrippa d'Aubigné: exécration et estime', *Actes* (Reims), 81–94, is an interesting analysis of the paradoxical portrait d'A. offers of the Duke de Guise, attributing this to political events. G. Schrenck, *La Réception d'Agrippa d'Aubigné (XVIe-XXe siècles). Contribution à l'étude du mythe personnel* (Études et essais sur la Renaissance, 4), Champion, 1995, 83 pp., sets d'A. in his historical context. M.-H. Prat, *Les Mots du corps. Un imaginaire lexical dans "Les Tragiques" d'Agrippa d'Aubigné* (THR, 303), 1996, 398 pp., is a detailed analysis of d'A's corporeal

references, and what they reveal about his writing processes. J. Dauphiné, 'Le "chevalier" Du Bartas: lettre inédite de Jacques VI
d'Écosse', *BHR*, 59:63–66, reproduces a hitherto unpublished letter
from James VI of Scotland which reflects the esteem in which he held
Du Bartas. Y. Bellenger, 'Rupture dans la poésie française de la fin du
XVIe siècle: l'exemple de Desportes', Arnould, *Tourments*, 95–105,
argues that D.'s innovations (reworking of old clichés, etc.) amount to
a rupture in Renaissance poetry. *Anne de Marquets. Sonets spirituels*, ed.
G. Ferguson (TLF, 481), 425 pp., offers the 1605 edition of this work
which will broaden awareness of the role played by women in the
Counter-Reformation movement. R. Gorris, 'Sous le signe des deux
Amédée: l'*Amedeide* d'Alphonse Delbene et le poème dynastique à la
cour de Savoie sous Charles Emmanuel I', *NRSS*, 15:73–105,
examines the use of the heroico-dynastic poem to celebrate the Dukes
of Savoy, and offers interesting insights into the cultural climate at
the Savoy court. J.-C. Ternaux, 'Les *Trois visions de Childéric* de Pierre
Boton: les mémorables faits à venir', *ib.*, 107–18, analyses this
relatively neglected work. H. Charpentier, 'Jean Le Blanc: de la
Henriade et de quelques autres *Poèmes*', *ib.*, 119–33, also focuses on a
forgotten text. Y. Bellenger, 'Une chronique versifiée: l'*Enlèvement
innocent* de Claude-Enoch Virey', *ib.*, 137–51, offers an interesting
analysis of this MS account of how Henri de Condé kidnapped his
wife to 'protect' her from Henri IV. M.-M. Fragonard, 'Pierre de
Deimier, *L'Austriade*, la *Nereide* et le goût littéraire', *ib.*, 153–68,
analyses these two neglected texts. *Clovis Hesteau de Nuysement. Œuvres
poétiques. Livre III et dernier*, ed. R. Guillot (TLF, 464), 232 pp.,
completes the publication of all his poetry. A. R. Larsen, 'Paradox
and the praise of women: from Ortensio Lando and Charles Estienne
to Marie de Romieu', *SCES*, 28:759–74, challenges the view that de
R.'s *Brief discours, que l'excellence de la femme surpasse celle de l'homme* (1581)
is a mere translation of E.'s rewriting of L.'s *Paradossi*, and argues that
it ultimately reflects her refusal of the conventional role assigned to
women.

4. DRAMA

Recueil de farces (1450–1550), vol. XI, ed. A. Tissier (TLF, 482), 388 pp.,
offers the texts of the following six plays: *La Résurrection de Jenin Landore*
(19–58); *George le veau* (59–?); *Les Trois Amoureux de la croix* (115–81); *Le
Poulier* (183–234); *L'Abbese et sœur fessue* (235–89); *L'Aveugle et le boiteux*
(291–342). Despite the commendably detailed critical apparatus, one
major problem: pp. 108–29 are missing.

Turning to tragedy, J. Rohou, *La Tragédie classique (1550–1793)*,
SEDES, 1996, 418 pp., has a useful general section on the subject

(pp. 51–94). A. Howe, 'La place de la tragédie dans le répertoire des comédies françaises à la fin du XVIe et au début du XVIIe siècle', *BHR*, 59:283–303, refers to the repertories of professional actors to challenge the traditional view that between the end of the 16th c. and 1625 tragedy began to regain its hegemony. O. Millet, 'L'ombre dans la tragédie française (1550–1640), ou l'enfer sur la terre', Arnould, *Tourments*, 163–77, argues that the frequent appearance of the shade in Renaissance and baroque tragedy is a symptom of the civil conflict. D. Stone, 'Le Duc de Guise: personnage littéraire', *Actes* (Reims), 557–65, focuses on the contradictory figure of Henri de Lorraine as portrayed in two plays: Pierre Matthieu's *La Guisade* (1589) and Christopher Marlowe's *Massacre in Paris* (1592), the first depicting him as a paragon fighting for religious and public wellbeing, the second revealing him as power-hungry, exploiting the religious wars for personal ambition. Also on Matthieu is G. Ernst, 'Senèque et Matthieu dans *Clytemnestre* (1589)', Brucker, *Traduction*, 345–58, which is an interesting intertextual analysis of M.'s debt to Seneca L. Lobbes, 'L'exécution des Guises prétexte à tragédie', *Actes* (Reims), 567–79, briefly considers two tragedies on the Religious Wars, Simon Belyard's *Le Guysien ou perfidie tyrannique* (1592) and Pierre Matthieu's *La Guisade* (1589). *Antigone ou la piété tragedie*, ed. J.-D. Beaudin (Textes de la Renaissance, 17), Champion, 288 pp., offers the 1588 text; the introduction comprises a useful literary study. M. Roig Miranda, 'Une traduction française de *La Célestine*', Brucker, *Traduction*, 359–71, analyses Jacques de Lavardin's 1578 French translation of this Spanish tragi-comedy; unfortunately, the comparison between translation and original is impeded by R. M.'s decision to translate the Spanish text into French.

On the theatre of Marguerite de Navarre, R. Reynolds-Cornell, 'Waiting in the wings: the characters in Marguerite de Navarre's *Théâtre profane*', Reynolds-Cornell, *Marguerite de Navarre*, 79–91, demonstrates that in many respects this work anticipates a number of characters and themes dealt with in the *Heptaméron*. R. Aulotte, 'Sur l'expérience religieuse de Marguerite de Navarre dans le T*héâtre profane*', *ib.*, 123–30, is a useful examination of M. de N.'s religious views as they emerge in this text.

E. Forsyth, 'Le Théâtre français de la Renaissance: a question of method', *AJFS*, 34:239–52, is a largely negative critique of the editorial criteria used in the series 'Le Théâtre français de la Renaissance', directed by E. Balmas and M. Dassonville. G. A. Runnalls, 'Sponsorship and control in medieval French religious drama: 1402–1548', *FS*, 51:257–66, is very interesting, showing that, paradoxically, patronage was often synonymous with censure.

5. MONTAIGNE

Blum, *Montaigne*, is divided as follows: 'La Fabrique du texte' (21–132); 'Éditer les essais' (133–226). C. Blum, 'Ouverture: l'édition des *Essais* à travers les ages: histoire d'un sinistre' (3–19), is an interesting survey of the complex editorial history of the *Essais*, arguing that only very partial perceptions of the text are generally given; J. Veyrin-Forrer, 'La composition par formes et les essais de 1580' (23–44), offers a useful analysis of Simon Millanges's use of this 16th-c. printing practice, whereby the text was not printed in its normal *seriatim* order; P. Desan, 'Numérotation et ordre des chapitres et des pages dans les cinq premières éditions des *Essais*' (45–77), is very important because it argues (quite convincingly) that, contrary to the general view, M. did not order his *essais* carefully; C. Blum, 'Dans l'atelier de Millanges: les conditions de fabrication des éditions bordelaises des *Essais* (1580, 1582)' (79–97), posits the interesting argument that M.'s decision to publish his 1580 edition in Bordeaux was politically motivated; G. Hoffman, 'Le monopole Montaigne' (99–132), examines the motivation behind M.'s corrections; the insights into the publisher's legal position, notably the role of the privilege, are useful; N. Catach, 'L'orthographe de Montaigne et sa ponctuation, d'après l'exemplaire de Bordeaux' (136–72), argues that modern editions should respect as far as possible the original punctuation and orthography; A. Tournon, 'La segmentation du texte: usages et singularités' (173–95), analyses 'Du parler prompte ou tardif' to highlight the originality of M.'s segmentation. B. Croquette, 'Faut-il (re)découper les *Essais*?' (197–201), raises an important editorial issue: the organization of the text into paragraphs (C. argues against departure from the original structure). J. McClelland, 'La tradition de l'édition critique face au texte des *Essais*' (203–26), provides a useful review of the editorial practice employed in the various editions , then offers his own curious suggestion: each chapter should be delegated to an individual editor. The fact that this could lead to inconsistencies (eg. variable base text) seems to have been overlooked, and the causality individually edited chapter = 'lecture plus assise, plus éclairée, plus provocatrice' is hardly clear.

Tetel, *Montaigne*, comprises the following: M. Simonin, 'Aux origines de l'édition de 1595' (7–51), is dense and rather long-winded, but usefully retraces the history of the base text, arguing that, despite the popularity of the Bordeaux copy, the 1595 edition is a better reflection of M.'s final wishes; A. Compagnon, 'Les repentirs de Fortunat Strowski' (53–77), reviews how the 1595 edition was eclipsed as base text in the 19th and 20th c. by the Bordeaux copy, but concludes (like Simonin) that it should not be dismissed; P. Desan,

'Marie de Gournay et le travail éditorial des *Essais* entre 1595 et 1635: idéologie et stratégies textuelles' (79–103), highlights a conflict in de G.'s editorial practice: on the one hand, a desire to be faithful to the 1595 text, and on the other, a desire to make the text more accessible; and N. Clerici-Balmas, 'Les courtisanes de Montaigne' (271–81), considers what M.'s *Journal de voyage* reveals about Italian courtesans.

D. G. Coleman, *Montaigne, quelques anciens et l'écriture des Essais* (Études Montaignistes, 20), Champion, 1995, 158 pp., is an enlightening collection of articles on M.'s sources and influences. P. Hendrick, *Montaigne et Sebond: l'art de la traduction* (Études Montaignistes, 27), Champion, 1996, 252 pp., is a detailed, well-written work, shedding new light on this largely neglected work. N. Dauvois, *Prose et poésie dans les Essais de Montaigne* (Études Montaignistes, 31), Champion, 213 pp., is a very thorough examination of the interaction of prose and poetry in the *Essais*, demonstrating how the two genres complement each other. P. Statius, *Le Réel et la joie: essai sur l'œuvre de Montaigne*, Kimé, 392 pp., is dense but very readable, examining M. from a philosophical rather than a literary perspective, and engaging in a dialogue with M.'s views which emphasizes the topicality of the *Essais*. E. Baillon, 'Le corps de l'être', Pinchard, *Fine Folie*, 201–20, examines Montaigne's links with transcendentalism, and presents a particularly interesting analysis of *De la vanité*. P. Magnard, 'Montaigne ou le singulier universel', *ib.*, 221–37, focuses on how M. approaches the question of Man's essence under two opposing influences: Occamism and ontology. N. Panichi, 'La "place marchande" della libertà. Ancora su Montaigne e la storia', *BHR*, 59:537–59, discusses the theme of freedom in the *Essais*. R. M. Mésavage, 'Montaigne, entre l'amitié et l'amour', *Hommage Baril*, 203–11, reviews what the *Essais* reveal about M.'s links with La Boétie. M. O'Rourke Boyle, 'Montaigne's consubstantial book', *RQ*, 50:723–49, focuses on M.'s assertion that his book is 'consubstantiel à son autheur', drawing attention to the misinterpretation of this adjective (it is not Trinitarian but Christological), and assessing the *Essais* in this light. G. Defaux, '"Inter otia animorum et spes inanes": Quintilien, La Boétie, Montaigne', *BHR*, 59:513–35, is a good analysis of the links between the *Essais* and Q.'s *Institution oratoire*. A.Marcetteau-Paul, '*Montaigne propriétaire foncier. Inventaire raisonné du Terrier de Montaigne conservé à la Bibliothèque municipale de Bordeaux* (Études Montaignistes, 24), Champion, 1995, 152 pp., usefully reproduces 97 notary acts drawn up 1527–58, giving important insights not just into M.'s family, but into 16th-c. social history. B. Schneider, *Nature und

Art in Montaignes Essais, Paris–Seattle–Tübingen, PFSCL, 1996, 337 pp. Also on M., see the items by G. Defaux and by D. M. Marchi, *supra*, MULTIPLE WORKS OR WRITERS.

THE SEVENTEENTH CENTURY

By ELFRIEDA DUBOIS, *sometime Reader in French,
University of Newcastle upon Tyne*

1. GENERAL

LitC, 29, 'La Fontaine, Adonis, Le Songe de Vaux, Les Amours de
Psyché. Actes de Marseille, 1996'. J.-P. Chauveau, 'L'ambition du
poète: La Fontaine et la transgression des genres' (17–30), points to
the preference for a variety of genres and styles; M. Fumaroli, 'De
Vaux à Versailles: politique de la poésie' (31–45), examines the
change from 'néo-épicurianisme' to the 'religion royale'; A. Génetiot,
'Un art poétique galant: *Adonis, Le Songe de Vaux, Les Amours de Psyché*'
(47–66), examines the meanings of 'galanterie' with a historical
perspective; B. Donné, 'Adonis et Psyché: deux approches d'une
sagesse des passions?' (67–92), contrasts the 'passion fatale' with the
'passion regulée', with references to Senault and Descartes; G. Polizzi,
'Psyché dans les jardins de Poliphile: La Fontaine et l'intertexte
colonnien' (93–110), discusses the relation to Colonna (1499), and to
Martin (1546), and La Fontaine's borrowings in 'Psyché'; A. Tournon,
'L'ironie poétique: désirs et mirages dans *Les Amours de Psyché*'
(111–22), traces, from two different lines in Plato, paradoxical
conceptions of the 'mystère du désir'; R. Démoris, 'Le monstre et la
monstre' (123–36), refers to Saint-Réal's *De l'usage de l'histoire* and to
Mme de Villedieu's Annales galantes in self reflection; R. Zuber, 'La
qualité du regard dans *Les Amours de Psyché*' (137–44), using the term
'ekphrasis', discusses different ways of looking, with a reference to
Poussin's use of 'regardant'; D. Delenda-Denis, 'Les voix de La
Fontaine: vers une lecture sémio-stylistique d'*Adonis, Le Songe de Vaux
et Les Amours de Psyché*' (145–79), examines the variety of voices and
styles; P. Dandrey, 'Les temples de Volupté Régime de l'image et de
la signification dans *Adonis, Le Songe de Vaux, et Les Amours de Psyche*'
(181–210), traces an æsthetics of 'volupté' with its allegories, and
refers to its ornamental function; and Id., 'Choix bibliographique'
(211–21).

LitC, 30, is devoted to 'L'Histoire au XVIIe siècle'. S. Guellouz,
'Avant-propos' (5–7); B. Chédozeau, 'Les jésuites et l'histoire au
XVIIe siècle' (9–19), analyses the development of historical writing
(Petau, Labbe, Briet) and the awareness and introduction of the new
world of science; J.-L. Quantin, 'Port-Royal et l'histoire' (21–32),
points to the hagiographical purpose of their writing, while insisting
on consulting original documents; D.-O. Hurel, 'Les Bénédictins de
Saint-Maur et l'histoire au XVIIe siècle' (33–50), accounts for the

Order's great historians, Achery, Mabillon, Montfaucon, Ruinart et al, and points to the *Annales ordinis Sancti Benedicti* as the impetus for their historical writing; S. Mazauric, 'L'histoire, le roman et la fable: le statut épistémologique de l'histoire dans les Conférences du Bureau d'Adresse' (51–62), analyses the relationship between the genres, and examines the questions treated in the Conférences (5 vols, 1634–55); A. Niderst, 'L'ère du soupçon: à la recherche de l'histoire de Montaigne à Bayle' (63–72), points to pedagogical aspect of history, the search for historical truth; P. Hourcade, 'Problématique de l'anecdote dans l'historiographie à l'âge classique' (75–82), shows that the introduction of anecdotes is related to the 'sociabilité mondaine' with their 'curiosité potinière'; C. Poulouin, 'Le recours aux origines ou la neutralisation de la chronologie' (83–94), investigates the origin of myths, with reference to S. Bochart, *Geographia sacra* (1646) and the search for their origin; A. Mansau, 'Alliance de la France et de la Savoie: trois conceptions historiques, Pierre Mathieu, Samuel Guichernon, Samuel Chapuzeau' (95–104), discusses the divergent views of three historians on the tensions between the two countries; M.-G. Lallemand, 'Les ornements rhétoriques des récits historiques: l'exemple du portrait' (105–19), looks at 'harangues' and portraits as rhetorical figures in historical writing by Mézeray and Varillas; E. Bury, 'Le "Père de l'Histoire de France": André Duchesne (1584–1640)' (121–31), examines the *Historia Francorum*, as the first scholarly edition of medieval texts; Y. Coirault, 'Vérité et valeurs chez Jean le Laboureur' (133–43), discusses this political historian and places him between the humanists and Mabillon; D. Riou, 'Charles Sorel historien et historiographe de France' (145–57), examines his methods as historiographer and his intention of writing for 'honnêtes gens'; P. Gouhier, 'Culture classique et histoire locale: l'apport de N.-J. Foucault à la recherche historique' (159–72), presents the Caen-based local historian at the turn of the century, and his *Mémoires sur la généralité de Caen*; D. Lopez, 'Discours pour le prince: Bossuet et l'histoire' (173–86), recalls the purpose of teaching political history to the dauphin, based on a religious point of view; F. Briot, 'Gabriel Naudé, ou l'histoire développée' (187–95), shows N.'s interest in political history (*Considérations politiques sur les coups d'état*; M.-C. Ganova-Green, 'Le héros et le solitaire ou les deux figures de la magnanimité dans l'*Histoire de la vie du duc d'Épernon*' (197–207), analyses the panegyric, written by G. Girard, of a hero's rise and fall; E. Flamarion et C. Volpilhac-Auger, 'La collection *Ad usum Delphini* et l'histoire' (209–19), examines the texts published between 1674 and 1691, under the editorship of the Daciers, with examples positive and negative; S. Guellouz, 'Figures d'Auguste de Coëffeteau à Morvan de Bellegarde' (223–38), discusses the historical sources and the changing presentations of Augustus related to the changing conceptions of the monarchy; F. Pelisson-Karro, 'Sources théâtrales, sources historiques: l'apprentissage de l'histoire de l'Orient sur la scène jésuite' (239–53), reviews subjects from extant texts and programme notes, including jesuit missionary experiences; S. Guellouz, 'Eléments de bibliographie' (255–58).

LitC, 31, 'Les "minores" ', ed. P. Hourcade. G. Polizzi, 'Le Moyen de (ne pas) parvenir: Béroalde de Verville, auteur mineur?' (27–38), attempts a rehabilitation of the author; N. Oddo, 'Antoine de Nervèze: pieux Protée ou caméléon mondain?' (39–62), examines his writings, some devout, others mundane, with a bibliography; C. Rizza, 'Autour des Grotesques' (63–79), reviews critical accounts of early 17th-c. writers, beginning with Gautier, and their rehabilitation, down to our times; B. Louvat, 'De quelques créateurs mineurs: l'opéra français avant Lully' (81–97), discusses some minor composers, Perrin and Cambert with his successful *Pomone* of 1671; M. Bombart, 'La production d'une légitimité littéraire: Classements et hiéarchisation des auteurs dans la fiction allégorique critique (*La Nouvelle allégorique* d'Antoine Furetière' (99–114), analyses the classification in a critical work for the general public; A. Viala, ' "Qui t'as fait minor?" Galanterie et classicisme' (115–34), reviews the term with examples (mostly from Molière); J.-M. Goulemot, 'Minores et livres de second rayon du XVIIIe siècle' (135–44), discusses the ambiguous situation of pornographic writings; J. Cormier, 'Robert Challe, ou des dangers de l'anonymat' (145–53), points to the posthumous rehabilitation of a work criticized at the time; E. Rufi, 'Le Nouveau Spectateur de Le Fuel de Méricourt: une entreprise très mercierienne' (155–64), indicates Mercier's influence and the New Spectator as model in other journals; C. Piau-Gillot, 'Comment s'échapper du second rayon? ou le parcours littéraire de Marie-Jeanne Riccoboni' (165–76), discusses the successful 18th-c. woman writer; E. Petifier, 'La question des auteurs et des œuvres dramatiques qu'on ne joue plus' (177–82), points to the task of the 'metteur en scène'; P. Jourda, 'Le fantastique de l'œuvre mineure à la fin du dix-neuvième siècle (183–202); L. Campa, 'Sous le signe d'Aphrodite et d'Athena: Guillaume Apollinaire et l'œuvre libertine des poètes du dix-neuvième siècle' (203–16); S. Audaguy, 'Queneau et les fous littéraires: le fils, le père et la littérature' (217–22); P. Casanova, 'Nouvelles considérations sur les litteratures dites *minores*' (233–47); and P. Hourcade, 'Bibliographie succincte' (249–50). *SCFS*, 19, includes: W. Ayres-Bennett, 'From Malherbe to the French Academy on Quinte-Curce: the role of obervations, translations, and commentaries in French linguistic thought' (1–9), discusses Malherbe's and Vaugelas's contributions, as well as the Academy's commentaries, but there was no direct linguistic work; E. Dubois, 'The value of human relationships: the correspondence of Jeanne Françoise de Chantal' (11–23), looks at personal and family relationships and her leadership of the Visitation Order of which she was co-foundress; M. Bannister, 'Vanini and the development of seventeenth-century thought' (25–36), assesses him as a rationalist who, from his 16th-c. background, tries to come to terms with the seventeenth; P. Bayley 'Accommodating rhetoric' (37–47), investigates pulpit rhetoric and Counter-Reformation theology; A. Erskine, 'Combien est grande la foiblesse humaine: Pierre Charron's view of the human condition' (49–59), sees him as a humanist with an Augustinian bias, but not as a libertine; W. Dickson, 'Descartes: language and method' (61–72), discusses the use of imagery and metaphor as techniques in argument; E. James, 'La Bruyère on values in practice' (73–82), stresses the relevance of personal circumstances and judgements related to them; C. Keaveney, 'La Bruyère and the civilizing process' (83–94), discusses interpretations of civilization, with particular reference to Elias; G. Rowlands, 'The ethos of blood and changing values? *Robe, épée* and the French armies, 1661 to 1715' (95–108), in reply to other studies, shows the growing status of the *robe*, even though the *épée* retains its superiority; H. T. Barnwell, 'Il faut que je vous conte . . .': fact into fiction in the letters of Madame de Sévigné' (109–24), analyses the function of both as interrelated; J. Charnley, 'Béat-Louis de Muralt: some thoughts on the France of Louis XIV' (125–34), examines the Swiss writer's views, in his *Lettres*, as an outsider; M. Bertaud, 'Deux *Ariane* au XVIIe siècle: Alexandre Hardy et Thomas Corneille' (135–48), compares the two versions; C. Gossip, '*Cinna* and the Marais Company in 1642–43' (149–59), comments on the relations between author and actors; J. Emelina, 'La mer dans la tragédie classique' (161–74), examines the poetic use of 'la mer', but never a technical one; M. Gutleben, 'Scène, cercles et seuils: les lieux de l'effroi dans quelques pièces du Grand Siècle (175–84), discusses settings, in space and time, to convey fear; S. Johnson, 'André Mareschal's *La Chrysolite*: from preface to text' (185–97), analyses this 1626 novel; P. Chaplin, 'Changing colours, changing times' (199–209), examines the symbolism of colours and the manufacturing process. *TLit*, 10, contains the following, relevant to the 17th c.: P. Rossetto, 'La rêverie aquatique dans *L'Astrée*' (101–17), examines imagery connected with water and its importance in the novel, such as the Lignon; M. Debaisieux, '*La Pourmenade de l'âme dévote* de Jean Auvray, du "triomphe de la croix" au triomphe de l'écrivain' (119–33), discusses religious poetry at the turn of the century and analyses the parts of Aubray's poem, more oriented to the poet than the religious topics; J.-P. Landry, '*Bérénice*: travail de deuil et rite de sacrifice' (135–47), examines the role of death in tragedy, and follows the theme of sacrifice in the play, with a comparison to Abraham's; E. Keller, 'Mort et *mimesis*, le corps à l'épreuve de la description dans le roman classique' (149–61), looks at the descriptions of the dying, from a physical and emotional angle, both 'classically' controlled; J. Caplan, 'Un sujet post-absolutiste: Saint-Simon at la politique de l'invisible' (163–74), examines the Regence, where law triumphs over 'blood', and explains Saint-Simon's personal satisfaction.

DSS, 196, contains: F. Lemerle, 'Fréart de Chambray ou les enjeux du *Parallèle*' (419–53), who in an illustrated article examines the architectural trends, between ancient models and modern developments; J.-L. Suberchicot, 'Contrainte sanitaire et grandes escadres: la flotte de Tourville à Béveziers' (455–78), who investigates health conditions among navy personnel of all ranks, with details on the battle of Béveziers (1689/90); P. Legros, 'Approche iconologique de l'oraison dédicatoire du *Traité de l'amour de Dieu* de François de Sales' (479–93), who dissects the Preface into elements of space, time, light and its sources; R. Briand, 'Le Nouveau Testament "de Mons": une entreprise de subversion?' (495–518), recalls the controversies around de Sacy's translation; V. Grégoire, 'Les "réductions" de Nouvelle France: une illustration de la pratique missionnaire jésuite' (519–29), discusses the residences, in particular St Joseph de Sillery, for the purpose of settling nomadic tribes and converting them; J. Zufferey, 'Entre littérature profane et exercice spirituel: J.-P. Camus, *L'amant sacrilège*' (531–45), shows the epidictic character of novels and short stories, and the cross-influence between sermon and fiction; A. Duc, 'Résistance d'une figure: le monstre au dix-septième siècle' (549–65), looks at natural and moral deformity, as invoked in literature; E. Safty, 'La déchéance physique et la perspective de la mort dans la poésie de l'âge baroque' (567–89), discusses, with examples, the themes of old age, concrete evocations of imminent death, repentance, and retreat; T. Malachy, 'L'*Athalie* de Racine: au croisement des traditions' (591–96), examines *Athalie* as standing between the Biblical text and the Greek conception of tragedy, 'un christianisme hellénisé'; *DSS*, 197, 'Les Italie', is introduced by D. Dalla Valle. M. L. Doglio, 'Charles-Emmanuel Ier de Savoie, Honoré Laugier de Porchères et Isabella Andreini entre poèmes d'amour, devises et théâtre encomiastique (avec un sonnet inédit de Charles-Emmanuel Ier)' (647–57), accounts for the literary work and gives the text and French translation of the sonnet; G. Berberi Squarotti, 'Le silence de la tragédie: *Adone*, V' (659–76), shows Part V of *Adone* to be a tragedy, as its title indicates; C. Sensi, 'La poésie lyrique: état des lieux, I: Marino le premier astucieux' (677–713), in a revisionist article, looking at recent critical judgements, examines M.'s variety of poetical devices; M. Guglielminetti, 'Giacomo Lubrano poète baroque' (715–25), presents the Neapolitan poet of the late 17th c.; C. Sensi, 'La poésie lyrique: état des lieux, II: Constellations' (727–52), presents further critical investigations of the poetry in its time, with emphasis on Italian baroque; F. Vazzoler, 'Le spectacle baroque: tendances et orientations des études en Italie' (1968–94)' (753–66), presents a critical account of writings on the theatre; D. Dalla Valle, 'la dernière étape de l'italianisme ; Les traductions françaises du roman italien' (767–74), establishes a list of 17th-c. Italian novels, translated into French and assesses the versions.

PFSCL, supp. 100, 'Et in Arcadia ego, Actes du XXVIIe Congrès Annuel de la North American Society for XVIIth-Century French Literature', has an initial section devoted to Poussin, ed. A. Soare, J.-F. de Raymond, ' "Ego cogito": Le mémorial de Descartes' (19–24), describes the monument in Stockholm of 1781 as a Northern Arcadia; A. Mérot, 'Des patries à la terre: pour un portrait-paysage de Nicolas Poussin' (25–37), investigates the use of classical mythology and poetic fiction, and relates them to Poussin's 'two homes'; R. Morel, *Et in pictura ego* ou le tombeau de Poussin' (39–52), examines paintings related to death; P.-J. Salazar, 'Poussin ou peindre la littérature' (53–63), comments on historical paintings, as an 'Arcadie littéraire'; and A. Albert-Galtier, 'Trois regards contemporains sur Poussin' (65–76), sets Yourcenar's literary comment against Bonnefoy's historical and R. Camus's poetical. P. Dandrey, there is a section on La Fontaine: 'La Fontaine, poète arcadien' (77–97), comments on Arcadian themes in his poetic work, mythological, bucolic, and nostalgic; D. Maher, 'La Fontaine et l'Orient: point de repère ou fausse piste?' (99–106), looks at fables borrowed from Pilpay and their adaptation; M. Slater, 'La Fontaine fabuliste et les contes d'enfant' (107–16), explains the change from an early liking for fairy tales to a hardening attitude to children; J. Grimm, ' "Proprement toute notre vie . . ." Evasion utopique, "rentrer en soi" et fol emportement dans les *Fables*' (117–23), looks at utopic dream and travel as complementary themes; A. Szogyi, 'Les méditations de La Fontaine: l'intervention de l'auteur dans sa propre narration' (125–32), argues that introducing oneself is a pre-Romantic trait; A. G. Wood, 'L'Inde fabuleuse et La Fontaine' (133–35), is a critical reply to Maher's paper; S. Akerman, 'De *l'Ecole des femmes* à "La Laitière et le pot au lait" '; (137–39), points to the dramatic side of the poem; C. Grisé, 'Pouvoir et pièges: La Fontaine et "Le Pouvoir des Fables" ' (141–42), is a reply to Slater's paper; M. Gutwirth, 'La Fontaine poète de la mort en Arcadie' (143–59), discusses the various treatments of death in the fables; M. Pereszlenyi-Pinter, 'Boccace, La Fontaine et les Contes: avoir 'moralement raison, mais esthétiquement tort" ' (161–67), discusses La F.'s rewriting of Boccacio; F. Assai, ' "Joconde": texte, contexte, pré-texte?' (169–78), compares Ariosto's original text with La F.'s adaptation; T. Meding, 'Fleurs et pleurs: mythe de l'Arcadie, mythe de la féminité dans *Les Amours de Psyché et de Cupidon*' (179–85), comments on the significance of the two tombs of the happy and unhappy *bergères*; D. Lafon, 'Le théâtre de La Fontaine: la mise en pièces du conteur' (187–97), comments on La F.'s unsuccessful attempts in the genre; and P. Dostic and H. Sanko offer brief critical comments on earlier papers (199–205).

The third section deals with 'Le mythe arcadien et la pastorale'. E. Bury, 'Le mythe arcadien' (207–23), presents Arcadia, historically from classical origins to the 17th c.; R. Zaiser, 'le mythe arcadien menacé: la présence de la mort dans *La Silvanire* de Jean Mairet' (225–32), relates the *memento mori* theme in *La Silvanire* to a Poussin painting; J.-P. Raffinot, 'Une innocence de la dualité: les femmes travesties dans les pastorales de Rotrou' (233–40), recognizes 'traves-tissement' as 'un jeu', hence innocent; B. Bolduc, 'Les lieux de la pastorale dramatique: L'Arcadie à Suresne et au Forez' (241–54), describes the *locus amœnis* as the proper lieu' for the 'pastorale'; C. Carlin, 'La menace du baroque' (255–58), is a 'critical review of other papers'; G. Spielmann, 'Le mythe de l'Arcadie dans le texte du pouvoir royal: sémiotique et ésoterisme' (259–75), examines the theme of the Sun King in a semiotic interpretation and Versailles as reconstructed nature; P. Gethner, 'Les imperfections de l'Arcadie dans les pastorales de Hardy' (277–83), presents Hardy's as the first pastoral play into which are introduced comic and tragic elements; J. F. Gaines, 'La relation de l'"Isle imaginaire": variations burlesques sur le mythe arcadien' (285–92), discusses Arcadian elements in travel accounts; L. Plazenet, 'Utopie et parodie arcadiennes chez Hardy et chez Segrais' (293–99), is a critical assessment of earlier papers; P. Sellier, 'Les rayons et les ombres (1654–79)' (301–14), presents a bibliographical assessment of critical works (within the French speaking area); F. Charbonneau,' 'Portrait du mémorialiste en bière' (315–23), discusses the official and private treatment of death; F. Lagarde, ''Critique savante et critique littéraire au XVIIe siècle' (325–35), examines two forms of critical writing, with refer-ences to modern scholarship; C. McCall, 'Les études dix-septiémistes se portent bien' (337–39), offers a brief critical assessment.

PFSCL, supp. 101: 'L'esprit en France au XVIIe siècle. Actes du 28e congrès annuel de la North American Society for Seventeenth-Century French Literature', ed. François Lagarde. P.-J. Salazar, '*Philia*: connaissance et amitié' (11–27), analyses relationships among scholars, from the intellectual to the sexual; H. Merlin, 'L'esprit de la langue' (29–51), comments on Bouhours's *Entretiens* (II); A. Viala, 'L'esprit galant', (53–74), lists definitions from various sources: dictionaries, Bouhours, Callières, and shows changing attitudes; A. Niderst, 'Le bel esprit' (75–84), complements the previous paper from similar sources stressing the literary aspect; E. Bury, 'Les lieux de l'esprit mondain' (85–93), discusses the 'topography', 'cabinet' or 'salon', as well as the topics, in their ingenuity and inventiveness; A. Aciman, '*L'esprit de pénétration*: Psyché and insight' (95–111), analyses the attempts at insight, shown in the frequent use of 'sonder, pénétrer, discerner', to uncover the hidden personality; F. Jacouën, 'Pascal et l'esprit de la géométrie' (113–27), comments upon and distinguishes the scientific from the rhetorical aspects; R. Zaiser, 'L'esprit de géométrie et l'esprit de finesse: le Mémorial de Pascal entre épiphanie de Dieu et création littéraire' (129–36), analyses the *Mémorial* and shows its Augustinian and biblical influences; G. Declercq, '*Bon Sens et Bel Esprit*: L'esprit de curiosité entre science et politesse' (137–59), using various sources (Lamy, Descartes, Bouhours), concludes on some convergence between the two; R. G. Hodgson, 'De "l'esprit fin" à "l'esprit faux": la différence des esprits chez La Rochefoucauld' (161–67), investigates the two forms of 'esprit', with reference to *Réflexions XIII* and *XVI*; M. Ricord, '*Les Caractères* de La Bruyère ou les exercices de l'esprit' (169–78)', examines in particular 'Des ouvrages de l'esprit', the 'moraliste' guiding the reader; M. Cohen, 'Tout l'esprit d'un auteur: the Role of esprit in the opening sections of La Bruyère's *Caractères*' (179–85), is centred on 'Des Ouvrages de l'esprit', and with reference to Theophrastus, concludes that La B. addresses himself to the 'honnête' readership; L. Leibacher-Ouvrard, 'Femmes d'esprit ou substance étendue? *L'Ecole des filles ou la Philosophie des dames* (1655)' (186–96), examines this first pornographic work in French; S. C. Toczyski, 'Ce dont l'esprit est capable: beauty and truth in *Les femmes illustres*' (197–205), examines the Scudéry *Harangues* of 1642 on the relation between 'beauté' and 'esprit'; J. Emelina, 'Les comiques de l'esprit dans les comédies de Molière' (207–23), points to the variety of meanings, with its great comic principle of the *monde renversé*. P. Gethner, 'Playful wit in salon games: the Comedy-Proverbs of Catherine Durand' (225–30), discusses these short plays of the late 17th c., in a feminist spirit; D. Steinberger, 'Wit and wisdom in Françoise Pascal's *Le Commerce du Parnasse*' (231–38), examines this text of 1668–69 as a reply to the *Lettres Portugaises* and Mme de Villedieu's *Lettres et billets galants*, with the triumph of virtue; B. Norman, 'The best way to skin a cat: thought and expression, words and music in Quinault and Lully' (239–47), bases his comparison on Cerf de la Viéville's *Comparaison de la musique italienne et de la musique française*

(1705–06); A. Bontea, 'L'esprit par excellence' (249–60), bases her analysis on Corneille's *Préfaces and Examens* and Descartes's *Les passions de l'âme*; A. Soare, ' "L'instant tragique dans *Polyeucte*' (261–72), in a careful 'explication de texte', shows Polyeucte's supreme sacrifice, 'de l'extrême amoureux à l'extrême religieux'; E. Forman, 'Spirit, will and autonomy in Racine's later tragedies' (273–81), with examples, comments on English renderings of èsprit, and their different attitudes, and concludes on the relevance of the notions of individuality, responsibility and freedom; P. Laude, 'Malaval et la vision de l'esprit' (283–90), discusses this Marseille lay 'mystic' and his writings on contemplation; M. Rowan, 'Manifestations of mind as wit and intellect: Marie Eléanore de Rohan and Jacqueline Bouette de Blémur' (291–98), compares the writings of two benedictine nuns, one mainly in aphorisms, the other in 'annales'; M. F. Hilgar, 'Fondation de la Congrégation des Filles du Saint-Esprit de la paroisse de Plérin' (299–305), relates the foundation of this teaching order by a widow (Marie Balavoine), in the diocese of Saint-Brieux in the very early 18th century. Cecilia Rizza, *Libertinage et littérature*, Nizet, 1996, 245 pp., a collection of reprinted articles, some translated from Italian, one new: 'Cyrano lecteur de Montaigne dans "L'autre monde" ' (185–203), which emphasizes Montaigne's influence in the 17th century. Roger Zuber, *Les émerveillements de la raison, Classicismes littéraires au XVIIe siècle français*, Klincksieck, 326 pp., is a series of reprinted articles, linked by themes, with additional notes. Nicholas Hammond, *Creative Tensions, An Introduction to Seventeenth-century French Literature*, Duckworth, 160 pp., deals, in turn, with literary terms, drawing examples from dramatists, religious movements, etc.; the field is somewhat restricted to Jansenist-Jesuit controversies, but notes the varieties of literary genres, and the tensions arising.

PFSCL, supp. 102, 'Car demeure l'amitié. Mélanges offerts à Claude Abraham', ed. Francis Assaf. M. Bertaud, ' "Jamais un tendre amour n'expose ce qu'il aime": sur quelques héroines de Corneille' (1–13), examines the development of love themes, and sees C. as a 'chantre de l'amour'; M. Gutwirth, 'De *Pertharite* à *Andromaque*: ou les aléas de l'invraisemblance' (15–24), presents a comparative study, in particular of Rosalinde and Andromaque; J. Grimm, ' "On ne vit onc si cruelle aventure." A propos du Conte d'un paysan qui avait offensé son seigneur' (25–37), interprets the story in the light of social reality; S. Ackerman, 'Les Comédies sans comique mais avec des ballets' (39–49), discusses comédies-ballets, together with other critical articles, and lists Molière's roles; S. H. Fleck, 'The play of illusion in *Monsieur de Pourceaugnac*' (51–61), provides a reassessment of a play infrequently considered. M. F. Hilgar, 'L'ombre de Molière dans le théâtre de Dancourt' (63–73), offers a comparative study;

F. Nies, 'Alceste soixante-huitard ou Prolegomènes à un Molière allemand' (75–86), accounts for translations, performances, the teaching of Molière in German, all very different from the French; M.-O. Sweetser, 'Naissance fortuite et fortune d'un nouveau genre: *Les Fâcheux*' (87–98), reassesses the hastily prepared 'divertissement' with its music and ballet; R. W. Tobin, 'Pascal and the Jews' (111–18), examines Pascal's attitude to Muslims and Jews, 'juifs charnels' who have put themselves outside redemption; J. Dubu, 'Faut-il marier Antiochus avec l'Infante du *Cid*?' (119–24), takes an anecdotal remark by the Grand Condé to develop the theatrical possibility; B. Norman, 'Taking things into your own hands: *Phèdre* on the eighteenth-century operatic stage' (125–37), discusses mainly the Pellegrini-Rameau version of 1733; A. Carriat, 'A la découverte de Tristan: les devanciers creusois de Bernardin' (139–44), notes the early discoveries of Tristan L'Hermite as a writer, by a mason and a printer, before Bernardin de Saint-Pierre and later theses; M. J. Muratore, 'The gender of truth: rhetorical privilege in Tristan L'Hermite's *Mariane*' (145–53), examines the moral and dramatic importance of Mariane over Hérode; D. Dalla Valle, 'Une relecture d'*Osman*' (145–53), discusses Tristan's last tragedy in the light of its Italian model; G. Saba, '*Pyrame et Thisbé* de Théophile de Viau au XVIIe siècle' (171–82), recalls the critical reception of the play, including Boileau's 'éreintement'.

DSS, 195, is devoted to 'La littérature pamphlétaire à l'époque classique'. C. Jouhaud, 'Les libelles en France dans le premier XVIIe siècle: lecteurs, auteurs, commanditaires, historiens' (203–17), assesses the role of the pamphlets in their political and literary function. A. Goosens, 'Le pamphlet des "Douze Articles" (Bruxelles 1568) et la répression religieuse dans les Pays-Bas méridionaux' (219–31), describes the pamphlet concerning the Inquisition and political issues; T. Verbeek, 'La philosophie cartésienne à travers la littérature pamphlétaire' (233–41), deals with pamphlets published in the Netherlands throughout the 17th and into the 18th c., more intended as hostile propaganda than actual knowledge; A. McKenna, 'Des pamphlets philosophiques clandestins' (243–52), discusses the variety of pamphlets in their political, religious, and philosophical impact on public opinion; J. Israel, 'Les controverses pamphlétaires dans la vie intellectuelle hollandaise et allemande à l'époque de Bekker et Van Leenhof' (253–64), stresses the importance of pamph-lets for the intellectual movements in modern Europe, on the eve of the Enlightenment; C. Secretan, 'L'urgence et la raison: la généalogie des concepts dans les pamphlets politiques néerlandais à la fin du XVIe et au XVIIe siècles' (265–79), is concerned with political issues in the Netherlands; C. Gheeraert-Graffeuille, 'Satire et diffusion des

idées dans la littérature 'a l'aube de la guerre civile anglaise
1640–1642' (281–96), argues for the important role of the pamphlets
prior to the civil war; H. Carrier, 'Le pamphlet et la vulgarisation de
la culture au XVIIe siècle. L'exemple des Mazarinades' (297–303),
looks at their informative and propaganda purpose, to reach a wide
public.

2. POETRY

Emmanuel Bury, *L'Esthétique de La Fontaine*, SEDES, 1996, 219 pp.,
deals in its first part with La F. and the poetry of his time, his
humanism, the variety of his writings, and the fables as such; then
provides an anthology illustrating the previous chapters, and a
detailed bibliography covering all aspects of La F.'s work. *CRIN*, 31,
1996, is entitled 'Fabuleux La Fontaine', ed. Kees Meerhoff and
Paul J. Smith. P. Pelckmans, 'Permettez qu'en forme commune la
parole m'expédie . . .' (13–27), investigates the theme of death in its
different presentations; M. Slater, 'La Fontaine et les dieux' (29–37),
assesses the role of pagan gods and their transformation in the fables;
J.-P. Collinet, 'Chimères et chimériques: un motif majeur de La
Fontaine dans ses *Fables*' (39–48), shows the discreet, but not
infrequent use of 'chimères', and their poetic quality; D. Russell, 'Le
relais de l'illustration dans les *Fables* de Gilles Corrozet et de La
Fontaine' (51–61), presents a comparative study of illustrations for
the 16th-c. *fabuliste* and the Chauveau work for La F., discussing the
use of emblems; L. Grove, 'Les *Fables* et les emblèmes, l'influence de
Guillaume Gueroult' (65–71), discusses G.'s *Premier livre des emblèmes*
(1550) and its influence on La Fontaine; S. Houppermans, 'L'autre
La Fontaine sur le conte *Les Lunettes* (75–85), reassesses the 'conte' in
its ironic treatment; P. J. Smith, 'Autour d'un inédit: La Fontaine a-t-
il traduit *Gallus* de Commire?' (87–109), comments on the political
fable, in Latin of 1672–73, and prints the translation together with
Commire's text; G. Parussa, 'Les fables de Pierre de Saint-Glas, ou
comment "porter la chose plus loin?" ' (113–26), presents S.-G.'s
work, with numerous traces of la Fontaine's influence; K. Meerhoff,
'Une pédagogie pour enfants ou pour adultes? La réception des *Fables*
au dix-huitième siècle' (129–53), details the pedagogic use of the
Fables, and presents Marmontel's view that the fable is aimed at
adults. Marc Fumaroli, *Le Poète et le Roi. Jean de La Fontaine en son siècle*,
Fallois, 511 pp., is an historical-political study, discussing the *Contes*
and the *Fables*, and containing chapters on La F.'s relations with
Foucquet and with Colbert's cultural policy, as he moved from his
province to Paris, on social life in the capital, on La F.'s travels, and
on the end of his life and his final conversion. *Le Fablier*, 8, 1996, is

devoted to 'La Fontaine, 1695–1995. Colloque du Tricentenaire', ed. P. Dandrey, 220 pp. Introductions (9–20); R. Duchêne, 'La Fontaine devant la vie' (23–30), gives biographical details; J.-P. Collinet, 'La Fontaine devant la mort' (31–42), presents his meditation and state of mind; J. Truchet, 'La Fontaine devant Dieu' (43–48), discusses La F.'s ambivalent attitudes; M.-O. Sweetser, 'Les esthétiques de La Fontaine' (49–57), reviews critical articles; B. Bray, 'Art narratif, art poétique dans les œuvres galantes de La Fontaine' (59–66), examines the 'narrateur(s)' as a 'personnage' or rather a 'marionette'; J. Mesnard, 'Le jeu sur le merveilleux dans les *Fables* de La Fontaine' (67–74), examines the rhetoric of the 'merveilleux naturel'; R. Zuber, 'Le goût de La Fontaine' (75–77); J. Grimm, ' "Qui t'engage à cette entreprise?" Les engagements de la Fontaine' (79–89), discusses his commitment, as coming from others and from himself; J. Dagen, 'La Fontaine et les modernes' (91–99), discusses, as 'modern', La Motte and Perrault; E. Bury, ' "*Fable*" et science de l'homme: la Paradoxale Paideia d'un moderne' (103–09), examines La F.'s ideas of culture, in a humanist tradition with modern tendencies; A. Genétiot, ' "Que de grâces bons dieux! Tout rit dans Luxembourg": La Fontaine et le badinage galant' (111–19), looks at the 'poète galant' and his language; F. Nepote-Desmarres, 'Au terme d'une lecture des *Fables*: l'image du roi et du poète' (121–28), analyses poetic images of the king and political implications; M. Slater, 'La Fontaine imitateur de lui-même: les dernières fables' (129–36), discusses La F.'s 'auto-imitatisme' in Book XII; S. Schoettke, 'La Fontaine et la poétique de l'amour' (137–43), analyses the badinage and eroticism in the *Contes*; J.-Ch. Darmon, 'La Fontaine et le plaisir' (145–59), notes the theme of pleasure in its different forms; P. Dandrey, 'La féerie d'Hortésie, éthique, esthétique et poétique du jardin dans l'œuvre de La Fontaine' (161–70), discusses the garden in its literary aspects; L. van Delft, 'La scène de l'univers: théâtre du monde et théâtre de la mémoire chez La Fontaine' (171–80), bases his comments on the line from *Le Bûcheron* '. . . une ample comédie . . .'; M. Fumaroli, 'La Fontaine et l'Académie française' (185–90), recalls La F.'s regular attendance at the sessions. *La Fontaine, Oeuvres 'galantes'. Adonis, Le Songe de Vaux, Les Amours de Psyché et de Cupidon*, ed. Patrick Dandrey, Klincksieck, 1996, 218 pp. Introduction; R. J. Kohn, 'Réflexions sur l'*Adonis* de La Fontaine' (35–44), is a reprint from *RR*, 47, 1956; J. Brody, 'D'Ovide à La Fontaine: en lisant l'*Adonis*' (45–63), M. Fumaroli, 'Politique et poétique de Vénus: L'*Adonis* de Marino et l'*Adonis* de La Fontaine' (64–74), is reprinted from *Le Fablier*, 5, 1993; J. D. Hubert, 'La Fontaine et Pellisson ou le mystère de deux Acante' (77–90), is a reprint from *RHLF*, 1966; F. Dumora, 'Le Songe de Vaux "Paragone" de La Fontaine' (91–111): reprinted from *DSS*, 175, 1992; B. Donne,

'Le parnasse de Vaux et son Apollon, ou la clé du songe?' (112–32), J. Demeure, 'Les quatre amis de Psyché' (135–57), reprint from *MF*, 1928; M. Raymond, '*Psyché* et l'art de La Fontaine' (158–72): reprinted from *Cahiers du Rhône*, 4, 1942; B. Beugnot, 'L'idée de retraite dans l'œuvre de La Fontaine' (173–80): reprinted from *CAIEF*, 26, 1974; J. Rousset, 'Psyché ou le génie de l'artificiel' (181–88): reprinted from *Renaissance, maniérisme, baroque*, Vrin, 1972; Y. Giraud, 'Un mythe lafontainien: *Psyché*' (189–201): reprinted from *SLF*, 1990; M. Jeanneret, '*Psyché* de La Fontaine: la recherche d'un équilibre romanesque' (202–15), is reprinted from *FFM*, 36, 1982.

Présence de La Fontaine, Actes de la Journée La Fontaine, ed. J.-P. Landry, CEDIC, Montrouge, 1996, 127 pp. T. Lassalle, 'Discours pluriel, voix singulière, l'éternel féminin dans quelques *Fables* de La Fontaine' (9–21), discusses the variety of views on women; I. Morlin, ' "Désormais je ne bouge". Du voyageur malgré lui aux voyageurs repartis' (23–44), studies the recurrent theme of travel; J.-P. Landry, 'La retraite dans les fables. Variations sur la retraite dans les *Fables* de La Fontaine' (45–58), discusses the search for the *locus amoenis*. O. Leplatre, 'Du temps que les bêtes parlaient" ' (59–73), examines the voices and their significance, man and animal; S. Gruffat, 'De la moralité du récit ou comment se jouer des lois du genre' (75–83), asserts that moral issues are built in; P. Michel, 'Le Renard, le puits et l'horloge' (85–93), presents a textual analysis with reference to other fables; S. Claudier, 'Discours et conflit dans les *Fables* de La Fontaine' (95–106), examines the fables from a cultural angle; J.-Y. Debreuille, 'Le rêveur définitif' (107–15), underlines the dreamer hiding behind ambiguous language; A. Sancier-Chateau, 'Modernité de La Fontaine' (117–26), comments on La F.'s 'voix narrative', later used in novels.

PFSCL, 44, *La Fontaine, Colloque de Londres, 1996*, ed. M. Slater. J. Brody, 'Lire La Fontaine: la méthode de Leo Spitzer' (15–21), refers to Spitzer's art de transition', and leads on to the real quality of the fables, their language; M. Slater, 'Reading La Fontaine's titles' (23–33), points to the frequent double titles which lead to a more interesting reading and deeper understanding, if one looks at all the characters; M. Vincent, 'Myth/Tragedy/Fable' (35–46), looks, comparatively, at La F. and Lucretius, concludes on 'les jugements de cour', as 'cour de justice' or 'royal'; A. L. Birberick, 'L'écriture circulaire: La Fontaine and the sovereign reader' (47–56), looks, in Book II, at five fables about the 'roi-lion', and four on Jupiter, which show mercy against the lion's wrath; R. Duchêne, 'Un exemple de lettres galantes: la *Relation d'un voyage de Paris en Limousin* de La Fontaine' (57–71), examines the stages of the journey and the account as a 'galanterie littéraire'; P. Dandrey, 'Le cordeau et le hasard:

réflexions sur l'agencement du recueil des *Fables*' (73–85), reviews critical approaches and suggests an architectural structure; D. L. Rubin, '[Dis]solving double irony: La Fontaine, Marianne Moore and Ulysse's companions' (67–94), investigates English versions and their interpretations; M.-O. Sweetser, 'Conseils d'un vieux Chat à une jeune Souris: les leçons du livre XII' (95–103), underlines the character of the 'moraliste' in this collection; T. Allott, 'John Ogilvy, the British Fabulist — A precursor of La Fontaine . . . and his model?' (105–14), discusses O.'s fables, the reputation, and suggests that La Fontaine may have been made aware through links between the two countries; A. L. Becher, 'Un de ces grands hommes — Phaedrus, a precursor of La Fontaine' (115–22), discusses P.'s verse rendering of Aesop, revealing the political aspect, not unlike La Fontaine's, who was inspired by him; J. Dubu, 'La Fontaine mélode ou narration et prosodie d'*Adonis* aux *Contes*' (123–33), explores the development of the poetic-musical quality of his verse; A. Soare, 'Lasse! Cigale hélas! Fourmi: chant et cri dans la premiere fable de La Fontaine' (135–46), closely examines the sound qualities in the expression of the two animals; C. Grisé, 'The horns of dilemma: the world of cuckoldry in La Fontaine's *Contes*' (147–57), discusses the cuckold as comic figure and points to the ambiguity of knowledge between characters on one hand, and the narrator-reader on the other; J. Grimm, ' "Comment on traite les pervers": la satire anticléricale dans les *Contes*' (159–72), examines three *Contes*: *Les frères de Catalogne*, *L'Hermite*, *Mazet de Lampotechio*, which reveal a deliberate denunciation of hypocrisy; J.-P. Collinet, 'Un peu d'aconit sur la langue: ou La Fontaine et la tentation du suicide' (173–87), explores the theme in La Fontaine's writings, together with attitudes towards death.

Alain Genetiot, *Poétique du loisir mondain, de Voiture à La Fontaine*, Champion, 614 pp., begins with an historical outline from Hellenistic antiquity and its transformation in 17th-c. France. Burlesque, heroic and comic strands in poetry are included; the 'esthétique galante', linked to the evolving social order — serious and flattering in some ways — turns into a 'galanterie de jeu et de badinage'. G. recalls the Latin distinction between *otium* and *negotium*, and describes the poets' evocation as an '*otium* littéraire', set in an Arcadian *locus amoenis*, the apogee of which is to be found in *L'Astrée*. There is a survey of the poets studied: Voiture, Benserade, Sarasin, Pellison, and La Fontaine.

Renate Kroll, *Femme Poète: Madeleine de Scudéry und die 'Poésie précieuse'*, Tübingen, Niemeyer, 1996, 499 pp., is a study of *précieux* poetry in its diverse forms, assimilated into the context of the position of women at the time. K. deals with aspects of *galanterie* in personal experience and in poetry, and concludes on the changing role of women in their bourgeois status.

Guido Saba, *Fortunes et infortunes de Théophile de Viau. Histoire de la critique, suivie d'une bibliographie*, Klincksieck, 389 pp., contains, in chronological order, the reception and criticism of T.'s writings, from the 17th c. to the 20th. Boileau's ironic criticism survived up to Gautier's *Les Grotesques* (1844), with a subsequent gradual rehabilitation, partly through the Baroque phase of critical works, and then completely in the view of T. as a 'poète libertin'. Attention is also given to A. Adam's 1935 thesis, the critical accounts by A. Boase et al., J. Streicher's 1951–58 critical edition, and the success of *Pyrame et Thisbé*. S. concludes on T.'s status as poet and within the 'pensée libertine'.

3. DRAMA

Daniela Mauri, *Voyage en Arcadie. Sur les origines italiennes du théâtre pastoral français à l'âge baroque*, Champion — Fiesole, Edizioni Caomo, 1996, 350 pp., includes translations and adaptations from the late 16th c., studies R. Brisset, translator of some obscure and some better-known Italian plays, and compares the style and verse of the originals and of the French renderings.

BENSERADE. *Benserade. Ballets pour Louis XIV*, ed. Marie-Claude Canova-Green, 2 vols, Toulouse, Société de littératures classiques, 431, 437–923 pp., is an edition of original 'livrets', together with a study of the genre and its development. Its elements, grotesque or serious, were eventually to become the 'ballet de cour', many of which were danced by the young king. The first vol. contains the early ballets from 1651–58; the second vol. covers 1659–69 (mostly taking place during the carnaval), with a last one from 1681.

CORNEILLE. Juanita Villena-Alvarez, *The Allegory of Literary Representation as Hybrid in Corneille's 'L'Illusion comique', Diderot's 'Le Neveu de Rameau', and Arrabal's 'La Nuit est aussi un soleil'*, Berne–Frankfurt, Lang, 220 pp., notes (5–79) how *L'Illusion comique* starts from 'un étrange monstre', and comments on the play, an 'anachronistic text', along deconstructivist lines, looking at director, narrator, and audience. R. L. Barnett, 'Sirens of the void: configurations of absence in Corneille's *Horace*', *DFS*, 39–40:33–43, argues for an anti-presence of real drama, and concludes that non-events are set against the text, a mere pretence. D. Maskell, 'Corneille's "examens" examined: the case of *Horace*', *FS*, 51:266–80, looks at the *Discours* of 1660 as multivoiced, concerning the unity of place (with an indirect dialogue with D'Aubignac), and examines the two Horaces, father and son: there is a questionable patriotism covering other motives. Play and *Examen* are seen in dialogue, with Horace as a new dramatic departure.

MOLIÈRE. S. C. Bold, ' "Ce noeud subtil": Molière's invention of comedy from *L'Étourdi* to *Les Fourberies de Scapin*', *RR*, 88:67–88, studies the two plays in their inventiveness, both linguistic and rhetorical, allowing the actors the possibility of improvization. Marie-France Hilgar, *Onze Mises en scène parisiennes du théâtre de Molière, 1989–97*, (*PFSCL*, supp. 107), 112 pp., discusses the productions and reviews of *L'Avare, Le Misanthrope, Le Médecin malgré lui, Le Malade imaginaire, Dom Juan, La Comtesse d'Escarbagnas, Georges Dandin, Les Précieuses ridicules*, and *Les Fourberies de Scapin*. Constant Venesoen, *Quand Jean-Baptiste joue du Molière. Essai* (*PFSCL*, supp. 94), 1996, 222 pp., dissociating himself from C. Mauron's psychocritical method, examines the plays through M.'s personal experiences and those of his career as actor-playwright, his relationship with the public and in the King's service. Beginning with the strolling players, and the playwright learning his métier, V. suggests that in *Les Précieuses* M. warns his future wife not to be one, moves on to married life in *L'École des femmes* (and its *Critique*), considers that after the humiliating failure of *Tartuffe* M. was set on vengeance with *Dom Juan* and *Le Misanthrope*. Then comes court entertainment in the form of ballets, and the new *Tartuffe*, which encourages M. in his later plays: *Le Bourgeois gentilhomme*, seen as the actor's play; *Les Femmes savantes*, expressing his increasingly aggressive attitude towards women; and the final *Malade imaginaire*, and his ultimate personal involvement.

RACINE. Jean-Claude Joye, *Méditations raciniennes. Seize ouvertures en forme d'oratorio intérieur*, Berne–Frankfurt, Lang, 1996, 315 pp., are 'meditations' based on short quotations from plays, with the titles as themes. The emphasis, through the 16 chapters, is on 'regard': in fact, 'le degré zéro du regard'.

TRISTAN L'HERMITE. C. Guillot, 'Image et représentation théâ-trale: le frontispice d'A. Bosse pour la *Marianne* de Tristan l'Hermite', *RHT*, 151–62, discusses the Bosse illustration for the 1637 edition as a document for theatre history, links such frontispieces to stage sets, and suggests their usefulness in understanding plays.

4. PROSE

English Showalter, 'The debate in the classical era between "roman" and "nouvelle" ', Nisbet, *Criticism*, 210–17, discusses critical attitudes to the genre in the 17th c.: Huet's *Lettre-traité sur l'origine des romans*, 1670; Valincour's *Lettres sur la Princesse de Clèves*, 1679; Charnes's *Conversations sur la critique de la Princesse de Clèves*, 1679; and Du Plaisir's *Sentiments sur l'histoire*, 1683. *Nouvelles du XVIIe siècle*, ed. J. Lafond et al., Gallimard, lxxxix + 1810 pp. Presenting 'Histoires comiques et tragiques', and 'Nouvelles espagnoles et françaises', these are critical, annotated editions of what in the preface is called 'l'art du bref', by the following authors: Du Souhait, Rosset, Camus, Bassompierre, Sorel, Scarron, Segrais, Mme de Lafayette, Donneau de Visé, Fléchier, Saint-Réal, Mme de Villedieu, Courtiz de Sandrar; Prechac; Mourette, Poisson, Catherine Bernard, Saint-Évremond, the abbé de Choisy, Le Noble, and short stories in *Le Mercure Galant*.

PFSCL, supp. 105 : 101–383, is devoted to *Les voyages en France au XVIIe siècle*. R. Duchêne, 'En voyage avec Mme de Sevigné' (101–11), recalls her travels; S. Requemora, 'Un seul genre de "Voyage en France": entre modèle réel et reécriture fictionnelle, l'espace du voyage' (113–34), discusses real travelogues and fictitious journeys: bucolic, 'galants', imaginary-satirical; C. Liaroutzos, 'Savoir et pouvoir dans les guides routiers français du XVIIe siècle' (135–48), discusses guidebooks: C. Etienne, *Le Guide des chemins de France* (1553); Coulon, *Les fidèles conducteurs pour le voyage de France* (1654); and Du Verdier, *Le Voyage de France dressé pour la commodité des Français et des étrangers*, 1662 (3rd ed); J.-C. Dubé, 'De France en Italie, Les voyages d'un noble dauphinois au début du XVIIe siècle' (149–59), relates, from a B.N. MS, two journeys to Rome and Loretto 1608 and 1610; L. Mongâ, 'Trois versions du *Viaggio di Francia* de S. Locatelli (1666–93): du journal de voyage au voyage initiatique' (161–72), recounts the 'Grand Tour' of two young noblemen, under the guidance of a priest, to Lyon and Paris, C. Mazel, 'Un récit à deux voix: *Le Journal de Voyage du Cavalier Bernin en France de Paul Fréart de Chantelou*' (173–84), analyses the account in its two voices, of Bernini and his companion; S. J. Linon-Chipon, 'L'épisode du voyage en France dans le voyage maritime aux Indes orientales, Carprau de Saussay et Luillier-Legaudier, le long de la Loire' (185–205), recalls the accounts of journeys to various parts of France; P.-F. Burger, 'Les voyages littéraires du mauriste Jacques Boyer (1710–14)' (207–27), alongside Mabillon's *Iter gallicum*, comments on the search in abbeys for original documents; R. Duchêne, 'En Province et à Monaco: un voyage imaginaire de Mme de Sévigné' (229–44), quotes from letters as she follows her daughter's travels; E. Mathé, 'Le voyage à Arles au XVIIe siècle, ou l'invention de l'Arlésie' (245–55), discusses this politico-geographical folkloric invention; C. Magrini, 'Madame de Sévigné et les voyageurs sur le Rhône au dix-septième siècle' (257–72), on 'prendre le Rhône' as a convenient way of travelling; P. Boucquei, '*Les Lettres d'Uzès* de Racine: les lettres d'un voyageur?' (273–89), assesses the letters as a literary rather than a travel document; G. Polizzi, '*Le Voyage* de Du Mont en Provence, ou la part de la fiction: remarques méthodologiques' (291–313), establishes a methodology for distinguishing authentic accounts from fictitious ones; E. Desiles, 'Les pérégrinations du *Gascon extravagant* d'Onésime

Sommain de Claireville' (315–32), compares the 'vagabondage' to picaresque novels; D. Bertrand, 'Les aventures de Dassoucy en France: une odyssée burlesque' (333–45), comments on the wanderings and 'fugues' around France; I. Sokologorsky, 'Le voyage de Simplicius à Paris' (347–67), based on Grimmelshausen, comments on the misfortunes of travel; N. Doiron, 'Le voyage burlesque: théorie d'un genre' (369–78), establishes it as an epic genre; and P. Ronzeaud, 'Conclusion du colloque' (379–83).

MADAME D'AULNOY. *Contes, édition du tricentenaire: I. Les Contes des Fées*, ed. J. Barahilon and P. Hourcade, STFM, lvci + 604 pp., gives a detailed biography and a critical account of fairytales, their style, with some feminist references.

BERGERAC. J. McCabe, 'Cyrano de Bergerac en Angleterre. Réception outre-Manche de l'œuvre et de la pensée de l'écrivain français' *RLC*, 71 : 31–58, reviews English translations and their reception.

FURETIÈRE. Grazia Maria Tordi, *La Nascita della borghesia Antoine Furetière e le roman bourgeois*, Florence, Atheneum, 1996, 105 pp., is a monograph divided into two parts: the life and writing of Furetière; and an analysis of the novel, with a critical, but unoriginal comment on its bourgeois aspect.

LA BRUYÈRE. Bernard Roukhomosky, *L'Esthétique de La Bruyère*, SEDES, 170 pp., analyses several æsthetic aspects: the salon badinage, a burlesque yet moralizing element, theatrical elements and a comparison with Molière, followed by an anthology of accompanying quotations from *Les Caractères*, and paratextes (préfaces, discours), bibliography.

LA FAYETTE. Anne Green, *Privileged Anonymity. The Writings of Madame de Lafayette* (Legenda Research Monographs in French Studies, 1), Oxford, EHRC, 1996, 93 pp., goes chronologically through the writings, mostly published anonymously, or under another name, in the first instance, and discusses the reasons for it, against the historical background. Notes themes of reticence as well as of revelation.

DE GOURNAY. *Les Advis ou les presens de la Demoiselle de Gournay, 1641*, 1, ed. J.-P. Beaulieu, H. Fournier et al., Amsterdam, Rodopi, 262 pp., is the first of three planned volumes to publish her writings; it contains some 20 texts on a variety of subjects, literary, linguistic moral and religious, and contemporary references. Since Mlle de G. revised her texts, this first modern edition of her work has entailed substantial annotation, and also a glossary and bibliography.

LA ROCHEFOUCAULD. Charlotte Schapira, *La Maxime et le Discours d'Autorité*, SEDES, 178 pp., investigates the 'maxime' in its various definitions, alongside similar forms, proverbs and clichés, according to subjects, descriptive, cognitive, moralizing in character, and assesses their stylistic and linguistic forms. Commented quotations come from La Rochefoucauld, and others.

SAINT-SIMON. Emmanuel Le Roy Ladurie and Jean-François Fitou, *Saint-Simon ou le système de la Cour*, Fayard, 636 pp., is a largely sociological study in two parts, covering the period 1690–1715, and then the Regency. It discusses the hierarchical structure in its principles, extended from the profane to the sacred, including an extensive discussion on 'bâtardise' (and 'légitimation'), the court 'cabales' and their political implications, and on demographic issues and the 'retraite' with Jansenist links. The Regency is covered in two chapters: 'la Régence libérale, 1715–18', when Saint-Simon was politically active without quite understanding government policies (the Jansenist issue is discussed) and 'La Régence autoritaire, 1718–23': the Regent asserting his power against parliament, the 'robins', his anglophile foreign policy, the Law debacle, colonial losses, and Saint-Simon's embassy in Spain. In conclusion, the monograph considers Saint-Simon's 'conception petit-ducale': where the regency would be centre-left, Saint-Simon was on the far right. There is also a Bibliography.

SCHOMBERG. Jeanne de Schomberg. *Règlement donné par une dame de haute qualité à M*** sa petite-fille, pour sa conduite, et pour celle de sa maison: avec un autre règlement que cette dame avoit dressé pour elle-même*, ed. Colette H. Win, Champion, 226 pp., is an educational treatise first published posthumously in 1698 (by the abbé) J.-J. Boileau, which follows the then traditional ideas of a girl's education with emphasis on religious practice of a strict kind, it suggests a careful timetable, as is also found in her own 'Reglement'; a document of social history. There is a bibliography and a list of educational writings from the 12th to the 18th century.

SÉVIGNÉ. *Mme de Sévigné*, Musée Carnavalet, 192 pp., is an exhibition catalogue. Anne Bernet, *Madame de Sévigné. Mère passion*, Perrin, 1996, 395 pp.: the first chapters give the historical background and biographical details; from chapter 8, the mother-daughter relationship is presented for a general reading public, with some questionable statements. *Autour de Madame de Sévigné. Deux colloques pour un tricentenaire*, (*PFSCL*, supp. 105 : 1–99), ed. Roger Duchene and Pierre Ronzeaud, offers the following: M. Lazard, 'Les Dames des Roches: une dévotion réciproque et passionnée' (9–18), accounts for two 16th-c. learned women; M. Bernos, 'Mères et filles à l'époque classique' (19–39), discusses mothers as educators; R. Duchene, 'Mère-fille au XVIIe siècle: le mariage de la princesse de Clèves' (41–50), compares the marriage in the novel to that of Mme de Grignan and the respective mothers' attitudes: J. Duchêne, ' "Mes petites entrailles'', ou l'art d'être grandmère de Mme de Sévigné' (51–60), follows Mme de S.'s relations with her grandchildren; M.-C. Grassi, 'Mère et fille au miroir de leurs lettres' (61–72), investigates later correspondence between parents and children; I. Vissière, 'Belle (Madame de Charrière) et Manon (Madame Roland) parlent de leur mère' (73–80), discusses the correspondence of two 18th-c. intellectual women; Y. Knibiehler, 'Mères et filles depuis la Révolution' (81–95), discusses girls' education from the early 19th c. to 1970; J.-L. Vissière, 'Une mère très douce. La relation de Simone de Beauvoir avec sa mère' (97–99), is based on her memoirs.

SOREL. E. Desilles, 'Les avatars de l'Histoire comique de *Francion*' *SFr*, 120, 1996:501–16, examines the changes in the three editions, 1623, 1626 and 1633, the first of which the most 'libertin' is transformed to a near moral character.

D'URFÉ. James M. Hembrée, *Subjectivity and the Signs of Love Discourse. Desire and the Emergence of Modernity in Honoré d'Urfé*, Berne, Lang, 236 pp., in the first part examines the subjective consciousness with parallels in Don Quixote, Hamlet, and Othello and sees the narrative as a quest for meaning; the second part looks at levels of subjectivity in an idealistic dialectic, an attempt to explain relationships in abstract terms.

VAUGELAS. *Les Remarques de l'Académie française sur le Quinte Curce de Vaugelas*, 1719–20, ed. W. Ayres-Bennett and P. Caron, Presses de l'Ecole Normale Supérieure, 1996, 427 pp., contains *La Vie D'Alexandre de Quinte Curce* and the two volumes of *Remarques*.

5. THOUGHT

Geneviève Rodis-Lewis, *Les Développements de la Pensée de Descartes*, Vrin, 224 pp., presents a carefully built-up study (based on papers 1985–1995) on the development of Descartes's thought, from mathematics at school, through religious topics, attitudes towards Montaigne, Charron, his positions on metaphysics, and surrounding problems relating to *La Naissance de la paix*, attributed to him. Jean Lafond, *L'Homme et son image. Morales et littérature de Montaigne à Mandeville*, Champion, 1996, 474 pp., reprints articles, with a large section on La Rochefoucauld; one 'inédit': 'Madame de Sablé, La Rochefoucauld, Jacques Esprit: un fonds commun, trois œuvres' (115–39), which discusses from letters and mutual criticism an earlier common ground, but one that led to different works. Louis Marin, *Pascal et Port-Royal*, ed. Alain Cantillon et al., PUF, 424 pp., is a collection of M.'s articles, written between 1976 and 1993, in sections: 'La Force du discours', 'La Critique de la représentation', 'La Question du portrait', 'Dans un indiscernable retrait', and 'Des

Fondements de Port-Royal', all emphasizing rhetorical, semantic, and linguistic topics. Simone Mazauric, *Savoirs et Philosophie à Paris dans la première moitié du XVIIe siècle. Les conférences du bureau d'adresse de Théophraste Renaudot (1633–1642)*, Sorbonne U.P., 393 pp. The first part deals with the intellectual *mouvements* of the early century, the establishment of the conferences from 1632, at regular Monday afternoon sessions, open to the public; the second part analyses the five volumes of 'Centuries des questions traitées ez Conférences du Bureau d'Adresse', published in 1634, 1636, 1639, 1641, 1655, the variety of topics, modern in the use of French, but traditional philosophically, with a final part on the crisis of scientific developments, a pre-history of modern rationality.

DSS, 194, *La Bible au XVIIe siècle*: B. Chédozeau, 'La lecture de la Bible chez et par les catholiques' (9–17), points to the two strands of tradition, oral and biblical, the opposition between the Tridentine cleric and the now learned laity; the Sacy translation of both Testaments is intended for spiritual reading; J. Lebrun, 'Exégèse herméneutique et logique au XVIIe siècle' (19–30), traces the history of hermeneutic interpretation to Lutheran scholars, and to some points in Spinoza's system; F. Laplanche, 'Le sens mystique des Ecritures' (31–41), argues that, towards the end of the century, a mystical interpretation was faced with a new exegesis, literal, historical and philological, the end of the century witnessing a crisis in theological thought; H. Ostrowiecki, 'La Bible des libertins' (43–55), discusses the reading attitudes of various *libertins*, not hostile to the text and its implicit authority, but refusing imposed interpretations by human authorities; P. N. Miller, 'Aux origines de la *Polyglotte* parisienne: *philologia sacra*, Contre-Réforme et Raison d'Etat' (57–66), discusses the Polyglot Bible as an encyclopaedic work, linked to historical and intellectual circumstances, patronage and developments in oriental studies and printing technics; V. Selbach, 'La Bible illustrée' (67–92), shows, alongside reproductions, allegorical cover pictures on Vulgate editions; J.-R. Armogathe, 'Les interprètations catholiques de l'*Apocalypse*' (93–103), points to the century as being especially biblical, and to the controversial variety of interpretation of Revelations, eschatological, historical, favoured by Bossuet.

THE EIGHTEENTH CENTURY

By J. E. FOWLER, *Dept of French, University of Kent, Canterbury*, and D. A. DESSERUD, *Associate Professor of Politics, University of New Brunswick at Saint John*

1. GENERAL

CULTURE AND THOUGHT. T. C. Jacques, 'From savages and barbarians to primitives: Africa, social typologies, and history in eighteenth-century French Philosophy', *HTh*, 36: 190–215, describes itself as an 'archæological investigation of knowledge' about Africa in 18th-c. France. P. Haudrère, 'Jean-Baptiste d'Après de Mannevillette et les progrès de la connaissance de l'Océan Indien au XVIIIe siècle, d'après les routiers et les cartes françaises', *RFHL*, 94–95:53–62. Arnoux Straudo, *La Fortune de Pascal en France au dix-huitième siècle* (*StV*, 351), Oxford, Voltaire Foundation, vii + 524 pp.

X. Salmon, 'La *Chasse Chinoise* de Jean-Baptiste Pater demeura-t-elle après 1739 dans la galerie des *Chasses en pays étrangers* au château de Versailles?', *GBA*, 129: 101–08. D. Lardy, 'La sculpture monumentale de Guillaume Boichot (1735–1814) dans les années 1770 en Bourgogne', *ib.*, 130:81–96. *Intimate Encounters: Love and Domesticity in Eighteenth-Century France*, ed. Richard Rand, Princeton U.P., xii + 220 pp., includes: R. Rand, 'Love, domesticity, and the evolution of genre painting in eighteenth-century France' (3–20); V. E. Swain, 'Hidden from view: French women authors and the language of rights, 1727–1792' (21–38); S. Maza, 'The "bourgeois" family revisited: sentimentalism and social class in pre-Revolutionary French culture' (39–48); M. Ledbury, 'Intimate dramas: genre painting and new theatre in eighteenth-century France' (49–69); and A. L. Schroder, 'Genre prints in eighteenth-century France: production, market, and audience' (69–86). N. Mirzoeff, 'Revolution, representation, equality: gender, genre and emulation in the Académie Royale de Peinture et Sculpture, 1785–93', *ECS*, 31: 153–74. R. Benhamou, 'Fashion in the *Mercure*: from human foible to female failing' *ib.*, 27–43. The *Mercure*, published between 1672 and 1791 and better known for its coverage of social and literary events, provides some surprisingly revealing fashion information, reflecting a shift in attitudes towards women. M. L. Bellhouse, 'Erotic "remedy" prints and the fall of the aristocracy in eighteenth-century France', *Political Theory*, 25:680–715, provides an examination of sexually-coded engravings portraying remedies for specific bodily complaints, which reveals the decline of the aristocracy and the rise of bourgeois prudery towards bodily functions; particularly interesting in the context of Rousseau's *Confessions*, discussed at some length. M. Fumaroli, 'Une amitié paradoxale:Antoine Watteau et le comte de Caylus (1712–1719)', *Revue de l'art*, 114, 1996:34–47. J. Hervier, 'Jünger, Rousseau, Voltaire, Sade et quelques autres', *RLC*, 71:463–78.

D. J. Siddle, 'Migration as a strategy of accumulation: social and economic change in eighteenth-century Savoy', *Economic History Review*, 50:1–20, notes how the 'mountain economies' of Savoy laid the basis for kinship networks that eventually spread into wider France and helped establish the economic infrastructure of the industrial revolution. D. M. Hafter, 'Female masters in the Ribbon-making Guild of eighteenth-century Rouen', *FHS*, 20:1–14, shows that the last of a long tradition of female guildmasters were found in the ribbonmaking industries in 18th-c. Rouen. Exceptional for their time, these women enjoyed legal rights including policing powers over their profession. M. Vergé-Franceschi, 'Un tricentenaire: 1693–1993. M. de La Galissonnière (1693–1756) le vainqueur de Minorque (1756)', *HES*, 16:99–116. P. Haudrère, 'Les officiers des vaisseaux de la compagnie des Indes. Un corps d'élite dans la Marine française du XVIIIe siècle', *ib.*, 117–49. C. M. Desbarats, 'France in North America: the net burden of empire during the first half of the eighteenth century', *French History*, 11:1–28. Between the capitulation of Montreal to the British in 1760 and the treaty of Paris in 1763, France defaulted on 40 per cent of its Canadian debt, and saw about 50 colonial officials charged with conspiracy to defraud the crown; did such mismanagement occur in isolation, or were the foundations laid over the previous fifty years? D. argues that historians have been too quick to assume that 18th-c. French Canada was a 'white elephant', without first looking for verification in government accounts. S. Maza, 'Luxury, morality, and social change: why there was no middle-class consciousness in pre-Revolutionary France', *JModH*, 69:199–229. The concept of the middle-class is a relativistic one: the members can only be identified by showing why they were neither aristocrats nor peasants. While each of these had some form of class identity, by being so defined in opposition to other classes, the middle class did not. One should hardly be surprised that such an abstractly defined group would fail to attract the attention of 18th-c. French writers; yet M. wonders why no 'French writers of the later eighteenth century . . . single[d] out a middle class either as a problem or as a solution — indeed, they almost never identified such a class at all'. Nevertheless, at least one writer in the first half of the 18th c. did: Montesquieu's writings discuss the increasing importance of the merchant class, the 'gens médiocres'. This is a puzzling article that appears to be arguing against something few would suspect in the first place. Surely a middle-class as Maza defines it would have been anachronistic in pre-Revolutionary, and for that matter, pre-industrial revolutionary France? L. N. Rosenband, 'Jean-Baptiste Réveillon: a man on the make in Old Regime France', *FHS*, 20:481–510, after a magnificent opening, tells a fascinating and intertwined tale revealing much of the complexity of Ancien Régime French bourgeoisie. P. Benedict, 'More than market and manufactory: the cities of early modern France', *ib.*, 511–38, looks at the growth and development of urban economics in 18th-c. France, and calls for a new look at the 'full range of economic functions and contributions of the country's cities'. P. Roux, 'Le recrutement de la milice royale au XVIIIe siècle: l'exemple du bataillon d'Albi (1740–1771)', *AMid*, 108, 1996:461–78, shows how the recruitment of the royal militia constituted an early draft of a 'national service', bringing civil society and military society together. In so doing, historians are provided with a rare means of understanding the individual and unconscious collective of 18th-c. French population. A. M. Azcona Guerra, 'Une entreprise navarraise dans le réseau commercial de la France méridionale: Les Vidarte (1754–1823)', *ib.*, 479–504.

P. Guignet, 'Lille, Valenciennes et les autres au miroir des courbes paroissiales longues (1715–1789). "Temps des baisses" ou âge des croissances ralenties?', *Revue du Nord*, 320–21:331–56. G. Garner, 'L'enquête Orry de 1745 et les villes de la France septentrionale: valeur et finalité d'une statistique administrative', *ib.*, 357–80. H. Knop-Vandambosse, 'Distribution spatiale et mobilité résidentielle de la bourgeoisie lilloise au XVIIIe siècle', *ib.*, 429–46. C. Engrand, 'Pôle urbain et circulation des hommes à la fin de l'Ancien Régime, l'exemple de la Picardie', *ib.*, 447–62. C. Bruneel and L. Delporte, 'Approche socio-professionelle de la population bruxelloise en 1783', *ib.*, 463–94. F. Bliaux, 'Les Saintes-Claires d'Amiens au XVIIIe siècle', *ib.*, 319:101–18. M.-L. Legay, 'Les Etats provinciaux face à leurs administrés: du dialogue à la censure (Artois, Cambrésis, 1680–1789)', *ib.*, 69–92. R. Grevet, 'L'absolutisme en province: l'intendant Caumartin en Artois (1759–1773)', *RHMC*, 44:213–27. Id., 'La réforme des études en France au siècle des Lumières', *RHis*, 601:85–124. F. Di Donato, 'Constitutionnalisme et idéologie de robe. L'évolution de la théorie juridico-politique de Murard et Le Paige à Chanlaire et Mably', *AHSS*, 52:821–52. T. E. Kaiser, 'The drama of Charles Edward Stuart, Jacobite propaganda, and French political protest, 1745–1750', *ECS*, 30:365–81, argues that, while a familiar story, the Parisian arrest of the Bonnie Prince has yet to be seen in the 'political context of Louis XV's monarchy'. The affair was partly responsible for 'an acute crisis of legitimation', perhaps the crucial moment when public opinion turned decisively against the French king: this was the first display of contempt for the public which would be replayed many times. J. Vinatier, 'La géométrie variable de la diplomatie européenne 1713–1763', *Revue d'histoire diplomatique*, 1996:25–46. P.-Y. Beaurepaire, 'Fraternité universelle et pratiques discriminatoires dans la Franc-Maçonnerie des Lumières', *RHMC*, 44:195–212. C. Bergé, 'Identification d'une femme. Les écritures de l'Agent inconnu et la franc-maçonnerie ésotérique au XVIIIe siècle', *L'Homme*, 144:105–30.

P. Jarnoux, 'Mortagne-au-Perche au XVIIIe siècle: zones d'influences et espaces relationnels d'une petite ville', *AnN*, 46, 1996:709–22. J. Boyer, 'Une loge maçonnique aixoise de la fin du XVIIIe siècle: l'harmonie des amis libris', *PrH*, 47:71–82. R. Chambordedon, 'Le négociant-hôte: une forme diffuse de sociabilité au XVIIIe siècle', *ib.*, 201–14. C. Gigan, 'Faïenceries rouennaises au XVIIIe siècle', *ib.*, 227–43.

Eighteenth-Century Life, 21 (May), is devoted to monstrosity in the 18th century. The study of deviant births provided the *philosophes* with an excellent means for reorienting man's understanding of nature's order, away from the domain of metaphysical speculation. Of interest to readers of the French 18th c. are: A. Curran and P. Graille, 'Exhibiting the monster: Nicolas-François and Geneviève Regnault's *Les Escarts de la Nature*' (16–22); A. C. Kors, 'Monsters and the problems of naturalism in French thought' (23–47); A. Curran, 'Monsters and the self in the *Rêve de d'Alembert*' (48–69); P. Graille, 'Portrait scientifique et littéraire de l'hybride au siècle des Lumières' (70–88); A. Richardot, '*Thérèse philosophe*: les charmes de l'impénétrable' (89–99); J.-M. Kehrès, 'Libertine anatomies: figures of monstrosity in Sade's *Justine ou les malheurs de la vertu*' (100–14); S. Rosenfeld, 'Deaf men on trial: language and deviancy in late eighteenth-century France' (157–75); and A. de Baecque, 'Robespierre, monstre-cadavre du discours thermidorien' (203–21).

Mary Seidman Trouille, *Sexual Politics in the Enlightenment: Women Writers Read Rousseau*, NY State U.P., ix + 411 pp., provides a detailed introductory chapter on R.'s views of women, then examines the female response, beginning with Henriette, and continuing through Madames d'Epinay, Roland, Staël, Wollstonecraft, de Genlis and de Gouges. R.'s views on women have been the subject to much discussion by contemporary scholars, but T. wants to know what women of R.'s time thought. This book reveals much, and is a refreshing take on what has become a well-worn subject.

M.-Fr. Piguet, 'L'émergence de la famille de *produire* dans les écrits des économistes du XVIIIe siècle', *CLe*, 68, 1996:5–23, examines the neologisms of the Physiocrats to reveal the foundations of economic terminology. Quesnay's writings show the integration of the word 'produire,' hence: 'produit,' 'production,' 'productif' and 'reproduction.'

LITERARY HISTORY, PUBLISHING AND JOURNALISM. L. Velay, 'Une famille d'imprimeurs à Montpellier au XVIIIe siècle: les Rochard', *AMid*, 109:5–32. K. Yamazaki, 'La bibliothèque d'un érudit toulousain du XVIIIe siècle, l'abbé Magi', *ib.*, 33–51.

2. NON-FICTION

INDIVIDUAL AUTHORS

BABEUF. I. H. Birchall, 'Babeuf and the oppression of women', *BJECS*, 20:63–75, is a reconsideration of B.'s attitudes towards women, placing it in the context of his 'commitment to the political, economic and social equality of all human beings'. Although B. is included in the pantheon of late 18th-c. writers who accepted the inferiority of women, he also writes about the sufferings of rural women, advocates equality in marriage and divorce, and argues against the notion that physical strength of men should translate into social superiority.

CONDORCET. D. Winch, 'Malthus versus Condorcet revisited', *The European Journal of the History of Economic Thought*, 3, 1996:21–43.

DORTOUS DE MAIRAN. Ellen McNiven Hine, *Jean-Jacques Dortous de Mairan and the Geneva Connection: Scientific Networking in the Eighteenth Century* (*StV*, 340), 1996, Oxford, Voltaire Foundation, viii + 196 pp. Voltaire described de M. as one of the five most outstanding scientists of his century: indeed, it was from de M. that Voltaire learnt about Newton. Yet he is often portrayed as a die-hard Cartesian; this has unjustly damaged his reputation and coloured modern historians' assessment of his influence.

LESPINASSE. François Bott, *La demoiselle des lumières*, Gallimard, 125 pp.

LEVIER. É. Wenzel, 'Une hagiographie janséniste au 18e siècle: petite vie d'Alexandre Levier, prêtre parisien (1677–1733)', *RHE*, 92:499–505.

MABLY. Johnson Kent Wright, *A Classical Republican in Eighteenth-Century France: The Political Thought of Mably*, Stanford U.P., vii + 261 pp. Famous in his own lifetime, Mably is one of those familiar figures, the 'unjustly neglected' thinker. Yet M. authored 'perhaps the most extensive and important body of republican thought to be produced in eighteenth-century France'. Beginning his career as a royalist, he 'joined the intellectual method of Montesquieu to the political values of Voltaire' (199). By mid-century he had become a classical republican, a French heir to Machiavelli and Harrington.

QUESNAY. W. Eltis, 'The *Grand Tableau* of François Quesnay's economics', *The European Journal of the History of Economic Thought*, 3, 1996:21–43.

DIDEROT AND THE ENCYCLOPÉDIE

THOUGHT, INFLUENCE, INTELLECTUAL RELATIONSHIPS. Eric-Emmanuel Schmitt, *Diderot ou la philosophie de la séduction*, Albin Michel, 334 pp., revisits many topics familiar to specialists, yet manages to achieve an admirably lucid reappraisal which argues that D.'s practice as a philosopher is characterized by the critical distance which he maintains from his own writing. Raymond Trousson, *Images de Diderot en France 1784–1913*, Paris, Champion — Geneva, Slatkine, 393 pp., is a fascinating exploration of reactions to D. which traces in all their complexity successive repudiations and appropriations founded on literary, political and ideological grounds. G. Goggi, 'Diderot et le concept de civilisation', *DhS*, 29:353–73, examines D.'s *Sur la Russie*, one of 16 *fragments politiques* written in 1772 and later incorporated in the *Histoire des deux Indes*. D. is shown to hesitate between two visions of how the process of civilizing Russia might be accelerated, envisaging on the one hand a stage-by-stage political project to be imposed from above, and on the other a slow process of social evolution reminiscent of Voltaire's thoughts on the same topic.

THOUGHT AND PROSE FICTION. Nicolas Rousseau, *Diderot: L'écriture romanesque à l'épreuve du sensible*, Paris, Champion — Geneva, Slatkine, 260 pp., is an intricate and scholarly study of the importance in D.'s writing of the *sensible*, a term which, we are reminded, can be divided into two interrelated concepts: the observable world which the artist aims to represent, and the literary and cultural phenomenon of *sensibilité*. This perspective leads to a stimulating reappraisal of D.'s major novels which manages never to lose his philosophy from sight. J. E. Fowler, 'Diderot's family romance: *Les Bijoux indiscrets* reappraised', *RR*, 88:89–102, argues that in D.'s first novel the sultan's fascination with the shifting nature of desire is underpinned by a longing for a dyadic union protected from change, and that the text's apparent misogyny is connected with a tendency to idealize the object of love. A. Kotin Mortimer, 'Naive and devious: *La Religieuse*', *ib.*, 241–50, revisits the contradictions of D.'s novel, viewing them not in terms of a blemished mimesis but according to the role they assign to the reader.

ÆSTHETICS. J.-C. Rebejkow, 'La musique dans les *Salons* de Diderot', *RevR*, 32:131–47, analyses D.'s evolving view of the

relations between painting, music and poetry in the *Salons*, showing
that an initial presentation of painting as a superior method of
representation yields to an interest in the suggestive possibilities of
the sketch and so by extension of artistic forms which set the
imagination in motion rather than striving for mimesis.

ENCYCLOPÉDIE. *RDE*, 20, 1996, contains a wide range of articles
on topics from D.'s correspondence to aspects of the *Encyclopédie*. *Ib.*,
21, 1996:69–178, presents seven discussions of D'Alembert's contribution to the *Encyclopédie* which were originally presented at the Ninth
International Congress on the Enlightenment held at Münster in
1995. These cover areas such as physics, musicography, and the
analysis of probability. C. A. Porter, 'Voltaire, Diderot, Rousseau and
the *Encyclopédie*', Nisbet, *Criticism*, 489–521, offers an admirably lucid
account of the theories of the major *philosophes* set against the generally
more mundane theories expressed by Encyclopædists such as
D'Alembert, Saint-Lambert, Marmontel and the Chevalier de
Jaucourt, along with the offerings of journalists and critics. The
comparison founds the persuasive argument that 'with a few rare
exceptions [...], French critical thought of this period appears to be
caught in the dilemma of holding on to what all were still convinced
was a tradition of incomparable perfection, while struggling at the
same time with the desire to bring "progress" and at least a measure
of cosmopolitanism to the literary arts as well as to the rest of
society'.

MONTESQUIEU

François Cadilhon, *Montesquieu ou l'ingrate réalité du quotidien bordelais*,
Mont-de-marsan, Editions Interuniversitaires, 1996, 122 pp. W. R. E.
Velema, 'Republican readings on Montesquieu: *The Spirit of the Laws*
in the Dutch Republic', *HPT*, 18:43–63. M. was one of the most
widely-quoted foreign philosophers in the second half of the 18th c.
in the Dutch Republic, but assessing his impact is not easy. Since
Amsterdam was widely used as a safe place in which to publish
controversial works, the fact that at least six editions of the *SL* were
published proves little; besides, given that most literate Dutch read
French, determining the number of translations does not provide
much further help. By examining the Patriot versus anti-Patriot
debate that raged in this country towards the end of the century, and
the ease at which M. was employed by both sides, we get a better idea
of his influence. Panajotis Kondylis, *Montesquieu und der Geist der Gesetze*,
Berlin, Akademie Verlag, 1996, 105 pp. C. Nyland, 'Biology and
environment: Montesquieu's relativist analysis of gender behaviour',
History of Political Economy, 29:391–412, notes that M. pioneered

'economics of gender' through his relativistic claim that both biology and environment shaped gender behaviour; economic historians, however, have tended to ignore this aspect of his work. Celine Spector, *Montesquieu, les 'Lettres persanes': de l'anthropologie à la politique*, PUF, 120 pp.

ROUSSEAU

CORRESPONDENCE, WORKS, BIOGRAPHY. Maurice W. Cranston, *The Solitary Self: Jean-Jacques Rousseau in Exile and Adversity*, Chicago U.P., xii + 247 pp., is the awaited third volume in his biography of R. (the first appeared in 1983, the second in 1991). In this volume, C. describes the last years of R.'s life, hounded and harassed, eventually installed on the Isle des Peupliers. More important, he discusses how R., who spent so much of his life seeking solitude, became after his death a most public symbol for revolutionary politics. Helena Rosenblatt, *Rousseau and Geneva: From the First Discourse to the Social Contract, 1749–1762*, CUP, xiii + 298 pp. M. O'Dea, 'Correspondance et autobiographie: le cas des *Rêveries du promeneur solitaire*', *RHLF*, 97:550–58. *Les Confessions de Jean-Jacques Rousseau*, ed. Jean-François Perrin, Gallimard, 233 pp.

THOUGHT AND INTELLECTUAL RELATIONSHIPS. B. Waggaman, 'Imaginaire rousseauiste, utopie tahitienne et réalité révolutionnaire', *RHLF*, 97:219–31. R's noble savage and Bougainville's exploration of Tahiti combine to create a utopian vision of uncorrupted mankind, which in turn informed the principles and ideals of French revolutionary texts. N. Fermon, 'The female fulcrum: Rousseau and the birth of nationalism', *The Philosophical Forum*, 28:21–41, deconstructs and elaborates R.'s metaphor of the body politic; worth reading just for the section on the politics of indigestion. Id., *Domesticating Passions: Rousseau, Woman, and Nation*, Hanover, Wesleyan U.P., xiii + 231 pp. G. Gaus, 'Does democracy reveal the voice of the people? Four takes on Rousseau', *Australian Journal of Philosophy*, 75:141–62, admits, somewhat ingenuously, that it is not always clear what Rousseau was saying; and nowhere is this more apparent than when we try to puzzle through what R. meant by the 'general will'. G. examines four contemporary theories of popular democracy in the wake of R.'s political theory. A. Kaufman, 'Reason, self-legislation and legitimacy: conceptions of freedom in the political thought of Rousseau and Kant', *The Review of Politics*, 59:25–52, notes that while both K. and R. employ contractarian theories of justice, each understands political reasoning quite differently. R. anticipates post-modernism, while K. was prescient of those 'contemporary accounts of justice' which reject skepticism. Mira Morgenstern, *Rousseau and the Politics of Ambiguity: Self, Culture, and Society*, Pennsylvania State U.P., xviii + 270 pp.

Jean-Jacques Rousseau and the Sources of the Self, ed. Timothy O'Hagan, Aldershot, Ashgate, viii + 121 pp., includes: D. Gauthier, 'Making Jean-Jacques' (1–15); H. Caygill, 'The master and the magician' (16–24); N. Dent, '"An integral part of his species ..."?' (25–36); J. H. Mason, 'Originality: moral good, private vice, or self-enchantment' (37–55); M. Hollis, '"A remarkable change in man"' (56–65); T. O'Hagan 'Amour-propre' (66–84); Z. Trachtenberg, 'Subject and citizen: Hobbes and Rousseau on sovereignty and the self' (85–105); and R. Wokler, 'Deconstructing the self on the wild side' (106–19). L. Luporini, "Rousseau e un nuovo Enrico IV', *RivF*, 87, 1996:497–502.

The eighth volume of the *Études Jean-Jacques Rousseau* is titled *Rêver Rousseau* and contains papers by: L. Viglieno, 'Rousseau et l'inteprétation des rêves' (9–24); F. Bocquentin, 'L'écriture secrète de Rousseau' (25–50); M.-P. Brunet-Rancœur, 'La gaieté de Rousseau' (51–66); R. Galliani, 'Rousseau, utopiste ou réaliste?' (67–72); R. Trousson, 'Sophie Cottin, disciple indocile de J.-J. Rousseau' (73–88)' D. Marie, 'Le rêve aristocratique: L.-E. de Wurtemberg, correspondant de Rousseau' (89–120); R. Bonnel, 'Lezay-Marnésia, seigneur, poète et paysan, "lit" Clarens' (121–42); S. Faessel, 'Entre l'état de nature et la civilisation: le mythe de Tahiti' (143–60); and T. L'Aminot, 'Rousseau et le rêve naturien' (161–204). Other articles include: J.-P. Marcos, 'De l'aporie du *Contrat social*' (205–24); and H. Yamazaki-Jamin, 'Rousseau et l'Hôtel Lambert' (225–35). Y. Etane, 'Rousseau: le contrat social en question', *Philosopher*, 19, 1996:23–42. Francis Imbert, *Contradiction et altération chez J.-J. Rousseau*, L'Harmattan, 333 pp. Paul Audi, *Rousseau, éthique et passion*, PUF, 417 pp. Armand Farrachi, *Rousseau, ou L'Etat sauvage*, PUF, 125 pp. Frederick W. Dame, **Jean-Jacques Rousseau on Adult Education and Revolution: Paradigms of Radical, Pedagogical Thought*, NY, Lang, 236 pp. Id., **Jean-Jacques Rousseau and Political Literature in Colonial America*, Lewiston, NY, Mellen, 1996, ix + 127 pp.

LITERARY. Three articles in *Esprit*, 235, on R.'s *Emile* and *La Nouvelle Héloïse*, are part of a forum entitled 'Les modernes en mal d'amour': P. Manent, 'Variations sur l'amour et l'amitié. Rousseau, Shakespeare et Platon lus par Allan Bloom' (19–32); P. Hochart, '"Le plus libre et le plus doux de tous les actes." Lecture du livre V de l'*Émile*' (61–76); and C. Habib, 'Les lois de l'idylle. Amour, sexe et nature' (77–91). N. B. Rogers, 'De l'*Émile* à *Émile et Sophie*: les malheurs du récit', *FrF*, 22:41–58. Guillemette Johnston, *Lectures poétiques: La Représentation poétique du discours théorique chez Jean-Jacques*

Rousseau, Birmingham, AL, Summa, 1996, ix + 231 pp. Philippe Lefebvre, **L'esthétique de Rousseau*, SEDES, 219 pp.

VOLTAIRE

WORKS. The new critical edition of V.'s works continues with *Anti-Machiavel* (Œuvres complètes de Voltaire, 19), ed. Werner Bahner and Helga Bergmann, Oxford, Voltaire Foundation, 1996, xxiii + 523 pp.. The inclusion in the series of this work by Frederick the Great is justified by the fact that V. not only encouraged the initial project and went to considerable lengths in order to organize the anonymous publication of the finished work, but also persuaded Frederick to allow him to edit it. This meticulous scholarly edition includes an introduction which brings out the full significance of V.'s involvement.

THOUGHT AND INFLUENCE. *Voltaire et ses combats*, ed. Ulla Kölving and Christiane Mervaud, 2 vols, Oxford, Voltaire Foundation, x + 758, 759–1610 pp., contains some 140 talks which bear witness to the current strength of research in the field; a number of the contributions are of especial interest to the literary scholar. B. Didier, 'Le paradoxe de la "Raison par alphabet"' (351–64), is a rich and stimulating exploration of the tensions which arise as V. turns to the supremely irrational order of the alphabet as a means of structuring the *Dictionnaire philosophique*, which aims to be an instrument of reason. The conclusion reached is that, in spite of the paradoxical nature of the project, the *Dictionnaire* becomes under V.'s pen a form which invites the reader to play an active role, 'de découvrir le vrai sens des mots, de l'Histoire et finalement du Livre, et de faire triompher la Raison'. Other contributions are also devoted to the *Dictionnaire philosophique*: M.-H. Cotoni, 'Les clausules des articles du *Dictionnaire philosophique*' (365–76), examines the art which V. applies to bringing many entries to a close in a strikingly effective manner'; while S. Werner, 'Philosophie et comédie par alphabet: le *Dictionnaire philosophique*' (377–84), examines the literary as well as the polemical qualities of the work. V.'s attitude towards atheism provides another important theme. P. Casini, 'Voltaire, la lumière et la théorie de la connaissance' (39–45), argues that in *Éléments de la philosophie de Newton* V. hovers between mathematical epistemology and idealist metaphysics, an attitude which can be connected with his uneasy opposition to atheistic materialism as represented by d'Holbach and his allies. R. Mortier, 'Ce maudit *Système de la nature*' (697–704), reconstructs from V.'s correspondence his complex, ambivalent and increasingly bitter attitude to d'Holbach's atheist-materialist thesis and the new generation of thinkers associated with it. The reaction of various writers to V. constitutes another area of interest. Jean Ehrard, 'Voltaire vu par Montesquieu' (939–51), brings out nuances in Montesquieu's criticism of V. as poet, historian and *conteur* which are absent from those of his more intransigent commentators. M. Cook, 'Bernardin de Saint-Pierre, lecteur de Voltaire' (1079–84), is an interesting discussion which serves to relativize the widespread view of B. as entirely a disciple of Rousseau, since here the later writer's practice as an author of *contes* is shown to be influenced by V.'s example. M. Delon, 'Sade et la réécriture des *Questions de Zapata*' (1129–35), shows how in *La Nouvelle Justine* Sade both plagiarizes and distorts V.'s *Questions* in order to cast the great *philosophe* in the role of champion of the atheist cause. Contributions devoted to V.'s theatre include the following: P. Weller, 'Voltaire's intervention in the stage practice of his time: encounters with stage declamation in *tragédie* and *tragédie en musique*' (1457–69), who reads V.'s nostalgia for the *Grand Siècle* into his combative defence of stylized declamation; and R. Niklaus, 'La diversité des conflits présentés dans *Les Scythes*' (1493–99), who adds nuance to previous discussions of V.'s play by reexamining the questions of the play's effectiveness as propanda and its significance for future developments in French drama. Nor are the *contes* neglected. W. F. Edmiston, 'Making connections: sexuality as satire in Voltaire's philosophical tales' (189–97), is a rich discussion which opens by drawing a distinction between 'preterition, the comic and the satiric', and by setting up a contrast between, on the one hand, traditions which represent women's sexuality as comical and/or regenerative, and, on the other, the ascetic tendency of medieval Christianity. This permits the argument that V. uses 'this ancient and negative image of female lust, to call into question the very theological system that affirmed and perpetuated such views'. R. Pearson, 'Conter contre; ordre et désordre dans *L'Homme aux quarante écus*' (199–207), exposes a principle of order in V.'s polyphonic *conte*. It is argued that, in responding to La Rivière's *L'Ordre naturel et essentiel des sociétés politiques*, V. does not oppose physiocracy as such but rather the extremist fiscal and political prescriptions which La Rivière founds upon the theory, and so, more generally, the false order which is imposed by any explanatory system which ignores the individual and arbitrary aspects of human experience. Two contributions focus on the relatively neglected topic of V.'s activity as autobiographer, and point the way towards further research: A. Owen Aldridge, 'The art of autobiography in Voltaire's *Mémoires*' (319–27); and J. Hellegouarc'h, 'Finalité des *Mémoires pour servir à la vie de M. de Voltaire*: règlement de compte ou mise au point?' (329–37). Finally, N. Cronk, 'Translation and imitation in the *Lettres anglaises*' (99–124), probes the function in the *Lettres anglaises* (i.e. the *Letters concerning the English nation*, the

Lettres écrites de Londres sur les Anglois, and the *Lettres philosophiques*) of V.'s various translations and commentaries on English literature, showing that he offers them within and against the English tradition of Imitation (a form of Augustan poetry whose effect depends in part on the reader's knowledge of the original). This approach serves to assimilate the passages discussed to V.'s satirical project in striking new ways, and we are also usefully reminded that 'the two French versions of the text presuppose a reader-response quite distinct from that of the English'. V.'s activity as a translator is also analysed in A. Billaz, 'Voltaire traducteur de Shakespeare et de la Bible: philosophie implicite d'une pratique traductrice', *RHLF*, 97 : 372–80, which revisits V.'s French versions of Hamlet's soliloquy and the Song of Songs in order to draw out his implicit conception of the translator as an imitator who freely adapts the original to the expectations of the target culture. From this it emerges that whilst V. uses Shakespeare in order to serve his campaign against 'l'Infâme', when it comes to translating the Bible passage his classical French restraint leads him to compromise his own satirical intent. D. Morgan, 'Sources of Enlightenment: the idealizing of China in the Jesuits' *Lettres édifiantes* and Voltaire's *Siècle de Louis XIV*', *RoN*, 37 : 263–72, uses V.'s case to suggest that by representing the Chinese as a reasonable and enlightened people ripe for conversion, the Jesuits 'incidentally furnished the *philosophes* with precisely the sort of model they wished to set before the European public'.

LITERARY. (See also, *supra*, THOUGHT AND INFLUENCE.) Interest in the *contes* continues. David Williams, *Voltaire: Candide* (CGFT, 117), 104 pp., exposes with commendable clarity the themes and techniques of V.'s most famous *conte* whilst adding new insights. Particularly interesting is the treatment of the structural and thematic significance of the Eldorado episode (53–61). R. Howells, 'Pleasure principles: tales, infantile naming, and Voltaire', *MLR*, 92 : 295–307, combines psychoanalytic and literary-historical perspectives in order to suggest that V.'s *contes* exemplify the sway of a 'pleasure principle' operating in literary production from late Classicism into the Enlightenment, so that V.'s use of allegory and naming can be read as being related to a 'regression to the pleasures of babble'. M. Sandhu, 'Le théâtre de Voltaire: tragédie ou drame?' *DFS*, 38 : 77–84, provides further support for the view that whilst in his dramas V. seeks in many respects to prolong the æsthetics of Classicism, he nevertheless manages to renew the tired conventions of French theatre, especially in terms of pathos, spectacle and technique, and so prepares the way for the revolution of Romantic drama.

3. PROSE FICTION

GENERAL

Jean Ehrard, *L'Invention littéraire au XVIIIe siècle: fictions, idées, société*, PUF, 287 pp., includes stimulating discussions of Montesquieu, Prévost, Marivaux, Rousseau, Diderot, Rétif de la Bretonne, Laclos, Bernardin de Saint-Pierre, Volney, Sade, and a comparison of Crébillon *fils* with Constant. Although the volume gathers together pieces previously published between 1970 and 1992, they are all worth rereading, and their juxtaposition allows an interesting overview of the 18th-c. novel to be sketched in the Introduction. Here the relationship of narrative form to philosophy and ideology is presented as a testing, indeed subversive one, a position which permits the pregnant assertion 'quand le roman n'est pas ce qu'il devient avec Diderot, la conscience critique du siècle, il est du moins sa mauvaise conscience'. John C. O'Neal, *The Authority of Experience: Sensationist Theory in the French Enlightenment*, Penn State U.P., 284 pp., is an ambitious and on the whole persuasive study which examines the influence of sensationist theory in æsthetics, the novel, and the political realm. An opening section analyses the thinking of Condillac, Bonnet and Helvétius, whose echo is subsequently held to be detectable in the fiction of Graffigny, Laclos and Sade. Whilst we might occasionally question whether characters' responses as general as curiosity and surprise necessarily owe as much as suggested to (for instance) Condillac's statue-man, the consistency of the approach leads to interesting new perspectives on the fiction discussed. Ahmad Gunny, *Images of Islam in Eighteenth-Century Writings*, London, Grey Seal, 1996, vii + 212 pp.. E. Showalter, 'Prose fiction: France', Nisbet, *Criticism*, 210–37, briefly but impressively traces the evolution of theories of literary criticism from 1640 to 1800. After an opening survey of criticism in Lafayette's time, the novel's rising popularity in the 18th c. is placed in relation to an increase of adverse criticism based on considerations of morality. In this context, even the novel's defenders are shown to have recourse to justifications based on the genre's moral potential, and Sade is presented as a conventional novelist with an unconventional, indeed surprisingly modern, theory of the novel.

INDIVIDUAL AUTHORS

CHARRIÈRE. Jacqueline Letzter, *Intellectual Tacking: Questions of Education in the Works of Isabelle de Charrière*, Amsterdam-Atlanta, GA, Rodopi, 217 pp., is a clear and interesting study which discusses the importance of education and related themes in C.'s life and works.

The difficulties which meet C.'s attempt to achieve recognition as a writer and thinker in a traditionally male domain provide a major strand of the argument.

GRAFFIGNY. Three interesting articles reexamine the *Lettres d'une Péruvienne*. M. Dobie, 'The subject of writing: language, epistemology and identity in the *Lettres d'une Péruvienne*', *ECent*, 38:99–117, draws on Lacan, feminist theory and deconstruction in order to argue that the narrator's constitution of her subjecthood in writing and, more generally, in a patriarchal symbolic order, involves an act of radical self-alienation. A. Wolfgang, 'Intertextual conversations: the love-letter and the footnote in Mme de Graffigny's *Lettres d'une Péruvienne*', *ECentF*, 10:15–28, suggests that the 'masculine' voice of philosophical reason which is generated by G.'s footnotes enters into a relation of opposition with the 'feminine' voice of sensibility which speaks in the main text (this opposition being at the same time present within the love-letters themselves). This interpretation is related to the wider issue of 'the contradictory attitude of French Society towards educated women'. L. Mall, 'Traduction et original dans les *Lettres d'une Péruvienne* de Graffigny', *RoQ*, 44:13–23, explores the novel's 'réseau métaphorique, si heureusement unifié, entre texte et lecture, traduction et voyage, écriture et exil', and in particular the way in which Zilia, as an exotic figure who supposedly translates the Peruvian part of her own text into French, implies the possibility of 'un texte premier, propre, proprement sien'.

LESAGE. *Lesage, Écrivain (1695–1735)*, ed. Jacques Wagner, Amsterdam-Atlanta, GA, Rodopi, 370 pp., makes available the acts of an international conference held in 1995 in Sarzeau and offers a wide range of useful articles. H. Coulet, 'Lesage romancier et le roman de son temps' (47–66), traces L.'s evolution against the background of a post-classical 'crise du genre romanesque' which is followed by the discovery of new directions for the novel. R. Howells, 'Lecture bakhtinienne de *Gil Blas*' (231–48), only partially assimilates L.'s novel to Bakhtin's concept of the carnivalesque, arguing, for instance, that whilst there is a representation of social diversity in *Gil Blas* the body is allocated a limited role. J. Wagner, 'Les gaîtés de Gil Blas, ou les vigilances du mémorialiste' (249–78), examines three types of *gaîté* in *Gil Blas*, gaiety overall being represented as strategy adopted by the work's narrator and hero as an alternative to gloomier post-Classical attitudes such as 'l'esprit sombre de la fatalité' or 'les inquiétudes de la raison' . F. Deloffre, 'Lesage et la Nouvelle-France' (305–23), explores L.'s interest in Canada, especially as it is reflected in *Les Aventures de M. Robert Chevalier, dit de Beauchesne, capitaine des flibustiers dans la Nouvelle France* (1732), of which L. claimed merely to be the editor. Here it is argued that whilst an authentic document was at L.'s disposal, he elaborated on it considerably and in doing so made his contribution to the *topos* of the *bon sauvage*. R. Runte, 'Le rôle du théâtre dans *Gil Blas*', *DFS*, 38:57–67, is an interesting reading which makes two major claims: first, that a new perspective on L.'s novel is opened up when we attend to the network of allusions to theatricality which it contains, including the adoption of roles by various characters; and second, that L. 'enters' the text through his discussion of actors and playwrights in order to effect a personal commentary on the theatre.

MARIVAUX. Elena Russo, 'The self, real and imaginary: social sentiment in Marivaux and Hume', *YFS*, 92:126–48, argues that in contrast to some of his classically-influenced predecessors and contemporaries, M. shows in his novels 'that *amour-propre* can be seen as a positive force, the basis of morality and a source of social cohesion', a position which echoes Hume's thinking.

PRÉVOST. *Histoire d'une Grecque moderne*, ed. Raymond Trousson, Paris-Geneva, Slatkine, 369 pp., is an affordable edition whose preface makes out a convincing case for reassessing one of P.'s relatively neglected novels. E. Leborgne, 'L'Orient vu par Prévost dans l'*Histoire d'une Grecque moderne*: l'ambassadeur et l'eunuque', *DhS*, 29:449–464, is an excellent piece which draws on psychoanalytic theory in order to examine the problematic nature of the narrator's 'libertinage éclairé'. G. Ansart, 'L'imaginaire politique de l'abbé Prévost: de *Cleveland* aux *Mémoires de Malte*', *ECentF*,10:29–42, analyses the utopian passages of *Cleveland* (which, it is stressed, can also be seen as dystopias) in order to argue that the passages in question represent a coherent vision of political power, and that this vision is reflected in the subsequent *Mémoires de Malte*. From this comparison it emerges that the *Cleveland* 'utopias' do not form a contemplation of a possible alterity but a reflection on the origin, essence and function of political power as it operates everywhere in the real world. S. Charles, 'Un "avis" enigmatique: l'"Avis de l'auteur des *Mémoires d'un homme de qualité*"', *RTr*, 53:95–112, methodically analyses the preamble in question in terms of a tension between two voices (that of *auteur* and that of *éditeur*) in order to demonstrate the complexity of the *Avis*'s relationship both to *Manon Lescaut* and the *Mémoires* as a whole.

SADE. Philippe Mengue, *L'Ordre sadien: loi et narration dans la philosophie de Sade*, Kimé, 285 pp., adopts as its point of departure the idea that S. is constrained to express his philosophy, which is not without its peculiar rigour and coherence, in narrative form. Reading S.'s novels above all as the expression of a philosophy yields points of comparison and contrast with Kant: both writers, it is argued, 'mènent en parallèle une déconstruction du concept de "loi naturelle", quoique selon des directions et intentions nettement différentes' (267). Lucienne Frappier-Mazur, *Writing the Orgy: Power and Parody in Sade*, trans. Gillian C. Gill, Philadelphia, Pennsylvania U.P., 1996, 245 pp., adopts a psychoanalytic approach to examine not only the text, but also the author, and above all that phase of his life marked by imprisonment and the Revolution. An analysis of the dual structure of orgy and dissertation founds the argument that the *Histoire de Juliette*, more than previous narratives by S., establishes a symbolic link between the sexual and the political.

4. THEATRE

GENERAL

Emmet Kennedy et al., *Theatre, Opera, and Audiences in Revolutionary Paris: Analysis and Repertory*, Westport, Connecticut-London, Greenwood Press, 1996, 412 pp., is an immensely useful volume which devotes 90 pages to discussions by the four co-authors of topics such as 'The most performed plays of the decade' (21–34), 'Old Regime tragedy and the Terror' (51–58), and 'Theatres and their directors' (65–74). The remainder of the volume is devoted to a repertory of French Revolutionary Theatre arranged by author followed by a repertory of anonymous and unattributed plays, indices of titles, authors, and composers, a list of operas, and a statistical overview with tables. R. Tarin, 'L'éducation par le théâtre sous la Révolution', *DhS*, 29, 495–504, examines in what ways Revolutionary theatre was used in order to inculcate bourgeois morality and the values of a new social pact.

INDIVIDUAL AUTHORS

BEAUMARCHAIS. Two articles present previously unpublished material which throws light on the context of B.'s activities as a man of letters. G. S. Brown and D. C. Spinelli, 'The Société des auteurs dramatiques, Beaumarchais, and the "Mémoire sur la 'Préface' de *Nadir*"', *RoN*, 37:239–49, reassesses the function of the Society co-founded in 1777 by B., showing that in addition to defending the proper remuneration of playwrights the individuals involved were 'highly concerned not to oppose but to gain acceptance into the highest ranks of the Old Regime élite'. The *Mémoire* in which B. undertakes to defend the Society against the attack penned by Paul-Ulrich Du Buisson in a Preface to his own play *Nadir* is published here for the first time. R. Pomeau, 'Beaumarchais et les lendemains du 14 juillet 1789: une lettre inédite', *RHLF*, 97:1024–30, makes available the text of a letter written by B. at the beginning of the Revolution which reflects the precariousness of his situation at the time.

DORAT. *Les deux 'Régulus' de Dorat*, ed. Jean-Noël Pascal, Perpignan U.P., 1996, 210 pp., presents two distinct versions of D.'s tragedy *Régulus*, that of 1765, ostensibly intended to be read rather than performed, and that of 1773. The editor argues that D.'s second version, which reflects his anxiety concerning new audience expectations, vitiates the neo-classical linearity of the earlier version.

GENLIS. Marie-Emmanuelle Plagnol-Diéval, *Madame de Genlis et le théâtre d'éducation au XVIIIe siècle* (*StV*, 350), Oxford, Voltaire Foundation, 440 pp., is a scholarly examination of a previously neglected topic. Whilst the main body of the study is devoted to G.'s rich experimentation with the possibilities of the *théâtre d'éducation*, a broad perspective is achieved by relating her plays to the writing of her precursor Mme de Maintenon, and also to the work of lesser-known contemporaries.

PALISSOT DE MONTENOY. C. Bonfils, 'Charles Palissot et la tradition moliéresque: l'homme dangereux', *RHLF*, 97 : 1008–23, is a very interesting piece which examines the ambiguity of P.'s play *L'Homme dangereux*, composed in order to trick the *philosophes* into believing it to be an attack on P. himself so that they might be ridiculed when its authorship became known. This bizarre project is shown to place severe constraints on the representation of the central character, a satirized satirist who must be initially recognizable as P. yet somehow turn out to be distinguishable from him once the secret is out.

PIRON. See *infra*, POETRY.

LA TOUCHE. R. Bonnel, 'L'*Iphigénie en Tauride* de Guimond de la Touche: l'herméneutique d'un mythe grec au temps des Lumières', *DFS*, 38 : 69–75, argues that La T.'s play of 1757 serves as an example of Enlightenment appropriation of Antiquity; for instance, Iphigénie learns to embrace natural religion, with the result that 'le devoir d'humanité s'est substitué au devoir religieux'. Moreover, the play's rationalism and eschewal of recourse to a love-story are held to form part of a more general reaction against the rise of *sensibilité* in the period.

5. POETRY

Pascale Verèb, *Alexis Piron, poète (1689–1773) ou la difficile condition d'auteur sous Louis XV* (*StV*, 349), Oxford, Voltaire Foundation, 683 pp., is a meticulous and scholarly study which opens with a biography based on new data, followed by an examination of P.'s works. The latter includes a discussion of P.'s activity as a poet (331–94) which situates him in relation to the *Querelle des Anciens et des Modernes* and brings out the variety of his experimentation in various forms and registers. There is also an important discussion of P.'s drama in two parts: first, the *œuvre foraine* (422–508), then the comedies and the tragedies (510–85). The study benefits from the genre-based approach, combined with a stress on thematic continuities wherever possible. C. Seth, 'La cave des poètes: poétique des vins, imaginaire de l'ivresse', *DhS*, 29:269–80, shows how the fact that 18th-c. poets begin to name specific wines is emblematic of a number of trends in Enlightenment thought, from the desire to classify phenomena in general to a turning-away from classical poetic periphrasis towards a more direct representation of reality.

THE ROMANTIC ERA

By JOHN WHITTAKER, *University of Southampton*

1. GENERAL

S. Thorel-Cailleteau, 'Dandys et orgies', *Romantisme*, 96:71–81, compares descriptions of orgies in Gautier's *Histoire du Romantisme* and in Rémy de Gourmont's *Promenades littéraires*, reaching the conclusion that, despite differences in the Romantic and the Naturalist way of life, their orgies were mainly literary affairs, and that literature tends to produce clichés. Allan H. Pasco, *Sick Heroes: French Society and Literature in the Romantic Age, 1750–1850*, Exeter U.P., 250 pp., extends the Romantic era to cover the second half of the 18th c. and attempts a new definition of the movement. Bringing together methodologies of sociology, psychology, history, and literary criticism, P. presents Romanticism as the product of social change and a new mass market for novels, poems and plays which polarizes attitudes and behaviour. Individual chapters examine the topics of migration, maternal deprivation, paternal deprivation, and absence of authority, writers seeking a new order, incest and suicide. The essence of Romanticism is identified as helplessness and insecurity. On occasion, this leads to a somewhat negative perspective: 'Romantics told their story many, many times, and with minor variations, it was always the same'.

2. CONSULATE WRITERS

CHATEAUBRIAND. C. Bailey, 'Beneath the surface of *Atala*: "Le Crocodile au fond du bassin"', *FS*, 51:138–54, suggests a reading of *Atala* as an artfully duplicitous, multilayered narrative which explains the foundations of the masculine erotic and portrays its repression by Christianity as a monstrous mutilation. Chactas's crocodile becomes a key image, evoking the fear of destruction and castration which satisfaction of both infantile and œdipal impulses towards the mother would entail. P. Guinet, 'De Sade à Chateaubriand, Delphine, Comtesse de Clermont-Tonnerre, Marquise de Talaru', *RHLF*, 97:673–81, introduces a lady who was related both to Sade and to C., referring to the former as her uncle and the latter as her cousin. Though C. met her in 1802, it seems that none of the three was affected by the connection. Philippe Antoine, *Les Récits de voyage de Chateaubriand: Contribution à l'étude d'un genre*, Champion, 328 pp., shows that C. changed the status of travel writing, by taking it beyond factual accounts and into a truly creative sphere, where it can develop a new unity and identity through the use of language. Fabienne

Bercegol, *La Poétique de Chateaubriand: Le Portrait dans les 'Mémoires d'Outre-Tombe'* Champion — Geneva, Slatkine, 564 pp. *Chateaubriand inconnu*, ed. Bruno Chaouat, Villeneuve d'Ascq, Revue des Sciences Humaines, 209 pp. Philippe Le Guillou, *Chateaubriand*, Saint-Cyr-sur-Loire, C. Pirot, 148 pp., is from a series which focuses on the places where great works have been written. This is not the case with Combourg, though it is nevertheless a place in which C.'s ideas were formed. Though mainly for the literary tourist, it is also a guide to the importance of his early experiences in Combourg as a background to C.'s later development as a writer.

CONSTANT.   K. Kloocke, 'Editionstheorie und Editionspraxis bei französischen Texten der Neuzeit', Glessgen, *Philologie*, 283–94, gives an account of the publication of successive editions of C.'s works and finds in them evidence of a significant cultural change. Tzvetan Todorov, *Benjamin Constant: la passion démocratique*, Hachette, 214 pp., examines not only the essence of C.'s position as one of the main theoreticians of French Liberalism, but also his distinctive views on love and on religion. T. demonstrates that these views lie behind a political stance which is intended to preserve the dignity of the individual, while maintaining social structures.

MME DE STAËL.   Virginie Wortmann-Lacouronne, *Germaine de Staël und George Sand*, St Ingbert, Röhrig Universitätsverlag, 352 pp., considers the direct and the indirect influence of S. upon the German novel. A comparison is made between the reception of *Delphine* and *Corinne* in France and in Germany, before moving on to the way in which the former provided an important model for Madame de Krüdener, and the latter for the Countess Ida Hahn-Hahn and Fanny Lewald. George Sand sought to emulate S., and she in turn was emulated by Hahn-Hahn, Lewald, Louise Aston and Luise Mühlbach.

3.   POETRY

HUGO.   J. C. Ireson, *Victor Hugo: A Companion to his Poetry*, OUP, 519 pp., lays claim to being the first detailed study to deal with the whole range of H.'s poetry. As such, it undertakes a formidable task, carefully and economically guiding the reader from the *Cahiers de vers français* all the way to the lines from *Océan* which are identified as probably the last which H. wrote. There is enough biographical background to explain strategic considerations relating to particular collections, though H.'s development as a poet remains the essential focus throughout. This would be a good introduction for students, but there are also new ideas and perspectives which will encourage those who know H. well to re-read certain poems. Graham Robb,

Victor Hugo, London, Picador, xix + 682 pp., is an accessible biography aimed at the general reader. It addresses a target audience whose knowledge of French may be limited and, though it tells the story of H.'s life accurately and energetically, it does not really consider his writing closely. Agnès Spiquel, *La Déesse cachée: Isis dans l'œuvre de Victor Hugo*, Champion, 204 pp., shows that, in H.'s poetry, the veiled goddess Isis may be variously taken to represent nature, woman, the soul or poetry. She represents a means of access from the mythical to the mystical and is crucially important in *La Fin de Satan*. H. identifies her as one of the daughters of Satan and an embodiment of Fatality and Liberty. Isis is associated with images of self-effacement, but not self-negation, along with openness to holiness and the presence of the holy. As such, she becomes a fundamental figure of the Hugolian æsthetic: 'La poésie est sœur d'Isis'. Pierre Laforgue, *Victor Hugo et 'La Légende des Siècles'*, Orléans, Paradigme, 426 pp.

LAMARTINE. Jean-Pierre Reynaud, *Un Ange passe: Lamartine et le féminin*, Klincksieck, 242 pp., explores the distinctive personal mythology behind L.'s portrayal of women. On more than one level, his particular concept of the feminine may be considered an integral part of his poetic inspiration. *Répertoire de la correspondance de Lamartine (1807-29)*, ed. Christian Croisille, Clermont-Ferrand, Centre de recherches révolutionnaires et romantiques de l'université Blaise-Pascal (Clermont 1), 206 pp.

MUSSET. B. Leuilliot, 'Situation de "Namouna"', *RHLF*, 97:232-43, considers the changing fortunes of M.'s poetry in the 140 years since his death, suggesting that he has now become 'invisible', and calls for vital editorial and biographical work which has not so far been carried out. With the avowed intention of making M. more visible, the article draws attention to one of the poems mentioned in Rimbaud's letter to Paul Demeny, identifying the possible influence of Sand's *Indiana* in the poem's dénouement and showing how this is symptomatic of the poet's view of the perils of the modern world. Françoise Zamour, *Musset*, Nathan, 1996, 128 pp., is a revision guide for pupils in secondary schools.

NERVAL. J. Strauss, 'Nerval's "Le Christ aux Oliviers": the subject writes after its own death', *RR*, 88:103-29, compares the poem with a letter to Jules Janin and fragments from N.'s notebook in order to clarify the identity of the subject. N. is shown to identify with a written subject that has no non-written original, the poem's identification of an onto-epistemological status inverting the Romantic sublime by reasserting the dominance of the individual over his linguistic annihilation. Pierangela Adinolfi, *Le Illusioni di Gérard de*

Nerval, Champion, 136 pp., gives a systematic account and classification of terms relating to illusion and chimera in N.'s writing. In so doing, the evolution of N.'s particular conception of the dream is clearly charted. Michel Brix, *Les Déesses absentes: Vérité et simulacre dans l'œuvre de Gérard de Nerval*, Klincksieck, 282 pp., attempts to clarify the nature and the causes of N.'s scepticism. We are led towards a fuller appreciation of the relationship between intangible truths, the absent goddesses of the title and the absent mother figure. Michel Brix, *Manuel bibiographique des œuvres de Gérard de Nerval*, Namur U.P., 506 pp., undertakes the difficult task of identifying manuscript sources and successive editions of each of N.'s works. We are given guidance in our approach to the question of the definitive text, and of the comparative faithfulness of the different editions available. Gabrielle Chamarat, *Nerval, réalisme et invention*, Orléans, Paradigme, 186 pp., is a collection of 14 previously-published articles. *Nerval*, ed. Loïc Chotard et al., Paris-Sorbonne U.P., 260 pp., brings together articles on N. by Dumas, Baudelaire, Proust and other, lesser-known writers. *Nerval*, ed. André Guyaux, Paris-Sorbonne U.P., 203 pp., contains the proceedings of a conference held at the Sorbonne on the 15 November 1996, and marks the return of N. to the Agrégation syllabus after an absence of 11 years. It includes: F.P. Bowman, 'Les *Filles du Feu*: Genèse et intertextualité' (7–21), on how scenes and anecdotes reappear in several of N.'s texts; M.S. Moretti, 'Réflexions sur un faux titre, *Les Filles du Feu*'(23–39), on the various titles considered by N. during composition, generally based on *Love's Labour's Lost*; F. Endô-Satô, 'Sur l'unité du recueil *Les Filles du Feu*' (41–67), a detailed examination of the structure and the relationship between the prose, often written some years before and for other works, and the sonnets written in the year before publication; H. Bonnet, 'Le mythe arcadien dans *Sylvie*' (69–87), suggesting that N. revived the myth in order to revive a certain style of writing; P. Jourde, 'Les Chimères: la voix du neutre' (89–110), on the motif of fragmentation of identity which can be found in certain poems; J. Bony, 'Du *Contrabandista* au *Desdichado*: Hugo, Nerval et Manuel Garcia' (111–16), on possible sources of a scene from *Leo Burckart* and certain images in 'El Desdichado'; B. Marchal, '*Les Chimères* de Nerval' (117–27), on reasons for the choice of the collective title and the titles of the individual sonnets; M. Marchetti, '*Pandora* ou la crise du récit' (129–39), on a narrative which reflects the difficulties associated with its composition; M. Brix, 'Nerval et le thème de la "prison heureuse"' (141–51), a theme which probably derived from N.'s many periods of detention in mental hospitals but which is also a literary metaphor serving as the key to the romantic æsthetic; P. Campion, 'L'écriture de la désignation dans *Aurélia*' (153–64), on the nature of the language used, for example the prevalence of shifters; J. Huré, 'La mémoire d'Orient et le discours sur la "maladie" de l'esprit dans *Aurélia*' (165–75), showing how the text presents the Orient as a potential remedy, recovery from illness being associated with harmony between East and West; M. Jeanneret, 'Dieu en morceaux: avatars de la figure divine dans *Aurélia*' (177–90), on the importance and the significance of the many images of the deity which are found therein. Christian Leroy, *'Les Filles du feu', 'Les Chimères' et 'Aurélia' de Gérard de Nerval ou La Poésie est-elle tombée dans la prose?*, Champion, 200 pp., identifies the tension between poetry and prose as being the key to many 19th-c. works. N. is shown to have 'fallen' from the one to the other on many occasions, to the extent that the inspiration for his prose could be said to be fundamentally poetic.

PORCHAT. V. Pott-Rovera, 'Trois fables inédites de Jean-Jacques Porchat, fabuliste suisse du 19e siècle', *Reinardus*, 10 : 137–51, draws attention to a Swiss writer who followed in the tradition of La Fontaine and whose fables enjoyed some success during his residence in Paris in the years 1845–57. Three hitherto unpublished fables are presented: 'L'Aristarque de Collège', 'Les Rats d'église et les Rats de grenier' and 'La Futaie et le Taillis'.

VIGNY. M. Cambien, 'Entre la satire et le poème philosophique: le discours polémique dans *Les Destinées*', *NCFS*, 25 : 320–34, suggests that the initial inspiration of each of the poems is essentially satirical, yet that it is the way that they are organized within the collection that gives them a status as 'poèmes philosophiques' and enables them finally to constitute a new poetic genre. Gonzague Saint-Bris, *Alfred de Vigny ou La Volupté et l'honneur*, Grasset, 316 pp., is a biography which focuses on the erotic and the political, yet which extends our perspective of the poet, not least in an appreciation of his debt to the writers of the previous century.

4. THE NOVEL

Richard Bales, *Persuasion in the French Personal Novel*, Birmingham, Alabama, Summa, 155 pp., includes essays on Chateaubriand's *René*, Constant's *Adolphe*, Balzac's *Le Lys dans la vallée*, Nerval's *Sylvie* and Fromentin's *Dominique*. In each of these texts, the hero displays characteristics of a kind which require an unusual amount of self-justification. In consequence, techniques of persuasion are ubiquitously deployed, to the extent that they inform the substance of the novel.

BALZAC

ABa, n.s., 18, 511 pp., includes: A. Michel, 'Balzac d'hier et d'aujourd-'hui: Alain lecteur de Balzac' (7–31), which shows that the philosopher shared with B. a way of thinking based on experience, a strong belief in moral freedom and a profound respect for love; Y. Loskoutoff, 'L'héraldique d'Honoré de Balzac' (33–69), on the importance of heraldry in *La Comédie humaine*; J. Martineau, 'La physiologie musicale balzacienne' (71–90), on the link between music and sexuality in a number of descriptions which may have been influenced by medical theories; A.-M. Lefebvre, 'Fleurs du mal balzaciennes' (91–132), showing that B.'s awareness of pathology influenced the structure of the 'Scènes de la vie de campagne'; C. Dédéyan, 'Balzac et La Bruyère' (133–43), demonstrating the influence of *Les Caractères* on Balzac; S. Menant, 'Note sur la culture poétique du jeune Balzac et le dix-huitième siècle' (147–58), showing how Voltaire and Jean-Baptiste Rousseau, in particular, as well as a number of other poets influenced B.'s development as an author; R.-A. Courteix, 'Les philosophes et la Révolution française dans l'œuvre de Balzac' (159–70), demonstrating that B.'s view of society was essentially shaped by 18th-c. ideas; M.-C. Aubin, 'Le système d'alimentation de Balzac: de quelques influences du siècle précédent' (171–91), analysing the complex nature of B.'s references to food, and tracing a network of influences on his description including Brillat-Savarin and Rousseau; A.-M. Lefebvre, 'Balzac et les médecins du dix-huitième siècle' (193–219), indicating B.'s interest in the medical theories of the previous century, from which he derived a surprisingly modern concept of the living organism; D. Dupuis, 'Du *Neveu de Rameau* à *La Maison Nucingen*' (221–34), showing that Diderot's work was a vital model; M. Labouret, 'Pavane pour une marquise défunte' (235–50), on B.'s various portraits of dowagers; D. Dupuis, 'Le pathétique balzacien ou l'héritage du dix-huitième siècle' (251–73), examining the 'Scènes de la vie de province' and showing that B.'s appeal to the reader's emotions updates an 18th-c. technique; C. Dédéyan, 'Balzac et Alexandre de Humboldt' (277–88), considering the occasions when the two met, and what B. may have gained from the experience; T. Bodin, 'Autour d'une critique de *La Peau de chagrin*' (289–92), comparing Désiré Nisard's anonymous review in the *Journal des Débats* with the more favourable account by Philarète Chasles, and identifying a letter which suggests that B. may have contributed to the latter; P.-Y. Balut, 'Modeste Mignon à Potsdam' (303–10), on a possible model for the Château de Rosembray; A. Brudo, 'Langage et représentation dans *Vautrin*' (311–24), on the play which was first performed in 1840; and M. Andreoli, 'La troisième mort d'Hyacinthe

Chabert' (325–57), stressing the importance of the colonel's final self-sacrifice as an element which is unchanged by successive reinterpretations. There follow three papers from a conference on B.'s early novels, held at the Maison de Balzac in May: A.-M. Baron, 'Romans de jeunesse, genèse du roman' (361–74), on *La Dernière Fée*; L. Besson, 'La figure du père dans les œuvres de jeunesse de Balzac' (375–92), showing that Bernard-François B. was a significant model; E. Bordas, 'Ecriture frénétique, écriture drolatique dans *L'Héritière de Birague*' (393–410), analysing the evolution of the two styles of writing which coexist in the novel. W. Johnson, 'That sudden shrinking feeling: exchange in *La Peau de chagrin*', *FR*, 70:543–53, contrasts the speech of the antiquarian proposing the pact inscribed on the skin with that of Planchette, on the nature of the universe as movement, demonstrating that the novel operates within constraints which resemble those governing exchange systems. C. Testa, 'The sins of Utopia: Balzac's *Le Médecin de campagne*', *NCFS*, 25:280–92, takes the explanation of the melancholic vision of Utopia in the novel beyond the debate on the ambiguities of B.'s politics and into a broader consideration of Western philosophical dualism. O. Heathcote, 'Balzac's purloined postcards: *mises en abyme* and the poetics of death in *Albert Savarus*', *ib.*, 26:66–79, considers the points of tension between real and metaphorical death in the novel and asks whether it is suggested that death is so common that it passes unnoticed. A. Lorant, '*L'Héritière de Birague*, d'H. de Balzac, sous les pseudonymes de A. de Viellerglé et Lord R'Hoone: une parodie du roman terrifiant', Mildonian, *Parodia*, 151–61, shows that, in this early novel, B. made use of procedures which he acquired from the gothic novel, not only in order to exploit a fashionable genre, but also to profit from the opportunity for parody in a work whose main purpose was to amuse. I. Weill, 'Balzac auteur médiéval satirique dans *Les Paysans*', *Reinardus*, 10:181–95, suggests that in this novel, the first with a realistic rural setting, B. revived a mediæval satirical tradition which had last been observed in the *Roman de Renart*. He may have been influenced by the *Fabliaux* in his description of disorder becoming almost normal in an unjust society which has abandoned traditional values. T. E. Peterson, '"Le Dernier Coup de pinceau": perception and generality in *Le chef d'œuvre inconnu*', *RR*, 88:385–407, concludes that B.'s implicit opposition to Rubens and Titian in favour of Poussin advances a 19th-c. Classicism and a stable if melancholy myth of harmony between visual and literary arts, set amidst the turbulence of the Romantic movement. M. Lantelme, 'Anticipation et fiction: *La Peau de chagrin*', *Romantisme*, 95:29–38, shows that B. is inclined to reduce suspense in the novel by describing events before they happen, and that this makes a fundamental change to the relationship between the crucial terms:

'Vouloir' and 'Savoir'. Eric Bordas, *Balzac, discours et détours: Pour une stylistique de l'énonciation romanesque*, Le Mirail-Toulouse U.P., 367 pp., suggests that all B.'s work derives from a single manner of writing. It nevertheless imposes considerable stylistic complexity, by requiring a multiplicity of perspectives and voices, and this is the true sign of B.'s modernity. Philippe Bruneau, *Guide Balzac*, F. Hazan, 192 pp., is partly a guide for the literary tourist and partly an introduction to the main characters of *La Comédie humaine*. René-Alexandre Courteix, *Balzac et la Révolution française*, PUF, 480 pp., sets out to explain the importance of the Revolution for B., both in a historical and in a personal perspective. For a writer who sought to portray the whole of a society in the first half of the 19th c., the Revolution was a recent key event in the history of humanity, and he could not remain indifferent to its ideological significance. Gérard Pouchain, *Balzac en Normandie*, Condé-sur-Noireau, C. Corlet, 170 pp., is entirely for the literary tourist, if not the most obvious place to find him. Marie-Caroline Vanbremeersch, *Sociologie d'une représentation romanesque: Les Paysans dans cinq romans balzaciens*, L'Harmattan, 298 pp., is specifically concerned with *Les Chouans*, *Le Médecin de campagne*, *Le Lys dans la vallée*, *Le Curé de campagne* and *Les Paysans*. The society portrayed in these novels is shown to be one which reflects the fundamental social changes taking place at the time when B. wrote.

EDITIONS. *Le Père Goriot*, ed. Marie-Hélène Robinot-Bichet, Hachette Education, 351 pp.

STENDHAL

D. F. Bell, 'Stendhal's legacy: Jean Baudrillard on seduction', Fisher, *Difference*, 18–33, suggests that Baudrillard's *De la séduction is*, at least partially, a rewriting of *De l'amour* and that *Le Rouge et le Noir*, *La Chartreuse de Parme* and *Lucien Leuwen*, as treatises on male/female relationships, may also have served as significant models. S.'s analysis of love, eschewing relations of pure desire, domination, power and production in favour of ritualized yet 'natural' confrontations, was of interest to Freudian psychologists at the end of the century. Baudrillard's attempt to shortcircuit Freudianism and Freudo-Marxism implied reference to this tradition of seductive confrontations. E. Bruschini and A. Amoia, 'Stendhal's *Promenades dans Rome*: an archæological and historical perspective', *NCFS*, 26: 24–52, identify the monuments described by S., not only in relation to possible influences on their description found in ancient and contemporary sources, but also in the light of their subsequent history. Robert André, *Écriture et pulsions dans le roman stendhalien*, Champion, 267 pp., takes a psychoanalytical approach to S.'s novels, and in particular to

La Chartreuse de Parme. A justification for this approach is found in the manner in which the novel was composed. Rapid dictation of the draft of a work of some 800 pages over a period of three weeks may have allowed more opportunities for the subconscious to surface than would otherwise have been the case. In any event, S.'s writing tended towards spontaneity, and he declared a disinclination to start with a plan. As a result, his writing tended to be governed and directed by impulses. *La Chartreuse* presents a number of themes that appear to derive from an Œdipus complex, among others the difficult relationship with the father, the search for maternal substitutes, the regression to childhood when in prison. André suggests that the complex lies at the core of S.'s imagination, and that its origins may be found in Henri Beyle's early childhood. Although he readily admits the limitations of the psychoanalytical approach, it presents a number of useful insights as to how and why Beyle became S. the novelist. Philippe Berthier, *Espaces stendhaliens*, PUF, 343 pp., is a guide to S.'s universe, leading the reader through eight places and spaces with a particular significance in his life, and eight from his novels. Most of the chapters are revised versions of previously published articles. There are also new essays on S.'s view of Europe, on Octave Malivert's Paris, on the seminary in *Le Rouge et le Noir* and a comparison of the ball in that novel with the Princesse de Parme's 'grand gala'. All combine to provide a clear, accessible, informative and challenging perspective of the writer and his work. Georges Blin, *Stendhal et les problèmes de la personnalité*, José Corti, 608 pp., is a revised edition of the essay which first appeared in 1958. Nicolas Broussard, *Stendhal, campagne de Russie 1812: Le Blanc, le gris et le rouge*, Kimé, 160 pp., is concerned with the influence of the Napoleonic era on French Romanticism in general and on S. in particular. C. W. Thompson, *'Lamiel', fille du feu: Essai sur Stendhal et l'énergie*, L'Harmattan, 159 pp., compares the two main versions of the unfinished novel and examines the the evolution of S.'s thinking on energy, the body and the soul. The conclusion notes that, despite the striking portrayal of symbolic vitality in the character of Lamiel, S.'s thinking remained uncertain, though time may have turned his heroine into an archetype of women's emancipation.

EDITIONS. *Correspondance générale (1800–09)*, ed. Victor Del Litto, Champion, 952 pp., is the first volume of a new edition of S.'s letters. The term 'générale' in the title reflects the intention to avoid arbitrary separation of official from personal letters, and to seek a coherent chronological organization. The resulting juxtaposition of different types of material helps to give a clearer perspective of S.'s distinctive style. *Promenades dans Rome*, ed. Id., Gallimard, 868 pp. *Vie de Henry Brulard écrite par lui-même*, ed. Gérald Rannaud, Klincksieck, xlix + 907 pp., is a new transcription of the Bibliothèque de Grenoble manuscript.

DUMAS PÈRE. C.J. Beaudan, 'La fascination du bourreau chez Alexandre Dumas', *NCFS*, 25 : 293–301, considers the literary motivation for description of executions in the four novels written in 1844–45: *Les Trois Mousquetaires, Vingt ans après, La Reine Margot*, and *Le Comte de Monte-Cristo*. Yves-Marie Lucot, *Dumas, père et fils*, Woignarue, Vague Verte, 167 pp., gives an account of the relationship between the father and his natural son. Their views on life and on literature were very different, and the links between the two are quite as difficult to explain as their consanguinity. *Le Grand Livre de Dumas*, Les Belles Lettres, 272 pp., as one might gather from the Dumas crossword by Michel Laclos attached to the cover, is addressed to the general reader. A book generally produced by writers rather than scholars, it is accessible and informative, containing: F. Taillandier, 'Les héros: drôles d'amis' (9–17); S. Jay, 'Les amis: l'ami du genre imprimé' (19–27); J. Leroy, 'Les héroïnes: Alexandre et Donatien ou comment sortir de l'enfance' (28–37); J. M. Monod, 'Les femmes: un goût décidé pour les femmes mariées' (38–49); C. Dantzig, 'Postérité: le véritable fils d'Alexandre Dumas Père' (50–55); P. de Saint Robert, 'L'histoire: ce sont les poètes qui font l'histoire' (56–66); J. Tulard, 'Napoléon: le Mahomet de l'Occident' (67–74); S. Jay, 'Les hommes d'état: galerie des grands hommes' (75–82); J.-B. Baronian, 'Fantastique: or j'aime les fantômes' (83–89); D. Zimmerman, 'L'argent: je vous défends de me ruiner' (90–100); J. Effel, 'La cuisine: on mange bien quand on travaille bien' (101–09); G. Brochard, 'Dumas en France: la caravane Dumas' (110–24); G. Poisson, 'Paris: le principal était d'être à Paris' (125–36); J. de Langlade, 'Les voyages: j'ai fait en six mois trois mille lieues' (137–49); J. Leroy, 'L'Italie: six siècles de genèse' (150–58); D. Zimmerman, 'La peinture: les peintres sont frères' (159–68); J. Roy, 'La musique: Dumas emmène Dantès à l'opéra' (169–83); E.-E. Schmitt, 'Théâtre: lorsque Dumas inventait le cinéma' (186–95); F. Beigbeder, 'Le cinéma: deux cents ans après' (196–201). The volume ends with an extract from the scenario of *La Fille de d'Artagnan*, a filmography and a chronology. Claude Schopp, *Alexandre Dumas: Le génie de la vie*, Fayard, 550 pp., is a biography which shows how D., by his intellectual strength and his energy, managed to become a tremendously popular writer whose work was appreciated throughout Europe.

GAUTIER. Peter John Whyte, **Théophile Gautier, conteur fantastique et merveilleux*, Durham U.P., 1996, viii + 166 pp.

HUGO. P. Gaitet, 'Hybrid creatures, hybrid politics, in Hugo's *Bug Jargal* and *Le Dernier Jour d'un Condamné*', *NCFS*, 25:251–65, examines the covert political contradictions and ambiguities in these two works of 1826, conveyed through hybrid constructions in language and character. P. Mines, 'The role of the Marquis de Sade in the late novels of Victor Hugo', *NFS*, 36.2:10–23, calls for further research to explain H.'s interest in Sade. Not least because Sade called into question the fallibility of human cognition, H. was drawn in the latter years of exile to favour the harsh reality of the Marquis's perception of the universe. D. Denby, 'Civil war, Revolution and justice in Hugo's *Quatrevingt-treize*', *RoS*, 30:7–17, situates the novel within a widespread process of reflection, as the century progressed, on the Revolution as an event which commenced the modern age and which enabled particular visions of the future. H.'s view of the revolution is shown to be fundamentally sentimentalist and, like others, he has some difficulty in reconciling the Utopian and the historicist versions of history. Claude Gély, *'Les Misérables' de Hugo: Étude de l'œuvre*, Hachette Education, 95 pp., is an introductory guide for students.

LAMARTINE. J. Gleize, 'Graziella, une socio-physiologie de la lecture naïve', *Romantisme*, 95:51–60, sets the story within the context of the popular literature of the years 1844–49 and suggests that L. envisaged a new genre of prose fiction which would compete with serial publications.

MÉRIMÉE. P. W. M. Cogman, 'Cheating at narrating: back to Mérimée's "La Partie de trictrac"', *NCFS*, 26:80–90, focuses on the tension between the psychological content and the narrative technique, and suggests it can be resolved by the identification of two centres to the story: on the one hand, there is the actual moment of cheating, on the other, there is its motivation. The ellipsis of the former and the continuing interest of the latter enable M. to return repeatedly to the key moment while maintaining the reader's interest in the eventual outcome. P. Michelucci, 'Prétérition et ambiguïté énonciative: les doubles sens de "Lokis" de Prosper Mérimée', *ib.*, 91–103, notes that this is a text which has given rise to very different interpretations, not least because it interrogates the conception of the unitary self, the fallacy of civilized behaviour and also the nature-culture dichotomy, by presenting binary oppositions at various semantic levels. This strategy is shown to be reinforced by the frequent use of paraleipsis. Pierre H. Dubé, *Bibliographie de la critique sur Prosper Mérimée 1825–1993*, Geneva, Droz, 399 pp., reminds us, at a time when bibliographical research tends to be done by electronic means, of the value of such a volume. On-line and CD-Rom sources can give direct answers to particular keywords, but it is not easy to browse through them and notice the unexpected, nor to gain a full perspective of all the work done on a particular subject or author. Of course, the problem with the compilation of a printed bibliography is knowing when to stop. This is produced in anticipation of the bicentenary of M.'s birth, and it should prove a valuable tool for scholars. Nearly all entries provide a summary of the content. Although they are arranged alphabetically by author, indexes of subjects and of proper names permit the reader rapidly to search for material by topic.

NERVAL. M. Brix, 'Nerval et le recueil de *La Bohème galante*', *RHLF*, 97 : 312–16, compares the version of the story in *L'Artiste* of 1852 with the posthumous version published for Théophile Gautier and Arsène Houssaye by Michel Lévy in 1855, alludes to the debate as to how far N. was involved in the later edition, and concludes that it is difficult to determine from documentary evidence what material he might have chosen to include. S. Iankova, '*Aurélia* lue par son rêve inaugural', *ib.*, 57–70, compares the handling of perceptions of reality in the dream from the second chapter of the first part, the dream at the end of the first part, the similar description in the second part, and variants in the manuscript and the *Revue de Paris* edition. Johannes Baptist Antonius van Haperen, *Le Langage d'Œdipe dans 'Aurélia' de Gérard de Nerval*, Utrecht U.P., 296 pp., suggests that the structure of the work is fundamentally governed by the Œdipan drama, and all themes and motifs are connected with it. Particular attention is given to the dominant position of Aurélia as the only named character, her ambivalent relationship with the narrator, the narrator's nocturnal walks when he is subject to visions and discovers secret desires, his anxiety and guilt, the way in which the Œdipan triangle stifles the narrator's feelings and the appearance of the double as a sign of imminent death.

SAND. N. Harkness, 'Writing under the sign of difference: the conclusion of *Indiana*', *FMLS*, 33 : 115–28, continues the debate on the ending, which for 19th-c. critics was problematic on account of its stylistic difference whereas more recent commentaries have stressed the novel's unity. Harkness suggests that we should concentrate on its otherness and its refusal of patriarchal models for, by freeing the conclusion from the unity/difference dichotomy, a new and more positive interpretation becomes possible. D. L. Terzian, 'Feminism and family dysfunction in Sand's *Valentine*', *NCFS*, 25 : 266–79, proposes a reading of S.'s second novel as an exemplary fiction of female development which, though firmly grounded in the literary traditions of its time and a pre-œdipally organized narrative, opens up new opportunities for a story with a feminist perspective. J.-M. Bailbé, 'George Sand et la Normandie: *Mademoiselle Merquem*',

RHLF, 97:559–70, is concerned with the importance of a visit to the Normany coast at the time when S. was beginning to write the novel. Anne-Marie de Brem, *George Sand: Un diable de femme*, Gallimard — Paris Musées, 112 pp., is a thorough and concise introduction for students. The many colour illustrations help to bring alive the world in which S. wrote. The section 'Témoignages et documents' includes appreciations of S. from Théophile Gautier to Françoise Sagan, as well as an interview with Georges Lubin, editor of the *Correspondance*, on her distinctive epistolary style and status. *George Sand: L'Ecriture du roman*, ed. Jeanne Goldin, Montreal, Paragraphes, 1996, 447 pp. Nicole Mozet, *George Sand, écrivain de romans*, Saint-Cyr-sur-Loire, C. Pirot, 250 pp., seeks to discover within S.'s novels the basis of her originality. M. considers the influence of particular sources, but also presents a new perspective of S.'s Romantic imagination.

TRISTAN. K. Hart, 'An I for an Eye: Flora Tristan and female visual allegory', *NCFS*, 26:52–65, proposes a parallel reading of the novel *Méphis ou le prolétaire* and of the travel narrative *Les Pérégrinations d'une paria*, both published in 1838. In both, the visual image of an emancipated woman guiding humanity, drawn from the allegorical representations of the time, is intended to inspire and to support courageous women.

5. DRAMA

L. Ashdown-Lecointre, 'Bouffon sublime, bouffon grotesque: chute de l'acteur romantique', *EFL*, 34:23–36, is concerned with the changing status of the actor during the Romantic period, the increasing demands of audiences and the resulting transient popularity of certain performers. Sand's *La Marquise* and Dumas's *Kean* provide very different examples of actors, yet they both share a pessimistic view of the actor's role which is typical of the time. F. W. J. Hemmings, 'The voice on the page and the voice from the stage: contemporary dramatic adaptations of the works of Balzac and George Sand', *Minogue Vol.*, 58–77, gives a number of examples of the relative freedom with which playwrights, during the first half of the 19th c., were able to adapt successful novels for the stage without seeking the approval of the author. Balzac complained that he received no payment for stage adaptations, and he probably resented even more strongly the changes that were made. In some cases, adaptation took the form of parody; in others, scenes which were acceptable in a novel were judged to be potentially offensive to the sensibilities of the theatre audiences of the time, and radical revision was considered necessary. Adaptations of Sand's novels were sometimes wrongly attributed to her. The greatest success was achieved where novelists made their own adaptation, as was the case for Dumas Fils and *La Dame aux camélias*.

HUGO. Bernard Savoy, *'Hernani' de Victor Hugo*, Nathan, 1996, 128 pp., is an introductory guide aimed at secondary schools. **Ruy Blas*, ed. Patrick Berthier, Gallimard, 288 pp.

MUSSET. G. Piacentini, 'Le débat sur la vertu entre Pierre Corneille et Alfred de Musset', *RHT*, 335–44, considers the extent to which *Lorenzaccio* was written as a response to *Cinna*. Whereas Corneille proposed the potential harmony of a world based on reason, M. emphasized the irrational and portrayed human liberty as the freedom to do evil.

6. WRITERS IN OTHER GENRES

J.-P. Saint-Gérand, 'Métaphores correspondancielles dans quelques écrits sur la musique du début du dix-neuvième siècle', *NCFS*, 26:1–23, is concerned with the use of metaphors in French art criticism during the first half of the 19th c. and the way that, at the same time, they observe particular rules applied to this kind of writing while remaining open to the internal impulse of poetry. Patrick Berthier, *La Presse littéraire et dramatique au début de la monarchie de Juillet (1830–1836)*, 4 vols, Villeneuve-d'Ascq, Septentrion U.P., xviii + 2187 pp., presents a vast panorama of all kinds of literary journals, more than 400 of them published in Paris at the time. After an introduction to the historical background, B. starts with the debate between Classicism and Romanticism, before proceeding with a detailed survey of journalistic activity involving criticism of prose, poetry and the theatre. It is a thorough account, with many valuable insights. Wendelin Guentner, *Esquisses littéraires: Rhétorique du spontané et récit de voyage au XIXe siècle*, Saint-Genouph, Nizet, 316 pp., has two chapters devoted to Chateaubriand and to Hugo. In the 18th c., travel writing had striven for simplicity. Chateaubriand claimed that his *Itinéraire de Paris à Jérusalem* was merely the diary of his journey, yet the *Voyage en Italie* made a distinctive contribution to the style of the genre. G. gives particular attention to 'Tivoli et la Villa Adriana' and 'Promenades dans Rome au clair de lune'. These demonstrate Chateaubriand's awareness of a stylistic hiatus. The text becomes an example of the link between textuality and metonymy. The *Voyage* remains incomplete, both in a semantic and in a structural sense. As such it constitutes no more than a 'literary sketch' though, by means of its stylistic innovation, it prepares the way for other 19th-c. writers. Hugo turned the letter written during a journey into a distinct literary form. He was probably guided by the Voyage en Italie when he wrote *Le Rhin, lettres d'un ami*, though he developed the letter as a vehicle for spontaneous rhetoric. The letter became a means of recording personal experience, though the fidelity of its message was eventually subsumed by literary convention. A comparison between the notes which Hugo made during the journey and the final published version of the letters shows a general move towards stylistic complexity.

GUÉRIN. Mary Summers, *Eugénie de Guérin: A Life of Reaction*, Lewiston–Queenston–Lampeter, Mellen, 338 pp, is concerned less with reaction in the political sense than with her manner of living which was driven by the love she felt for other human beings, and particularly for her brother Maurice. The areas covered include her family life, literary development, the origins of the *Journal*, the two visits to Paris and meetings with Barbey d'Aurevilly, the feelings of rejection and disappointment in her later years, and the critical reception of the *Journal* since its publication. S. ends by observing that there has been a renewed interest in G.'s life and work during the last few years.

NERVAL. Françoise Sylvos, *Nerval ou l'antimonde: Discours et figures de l'utopie, 1826–55*, L'Harmattan, 220 pp., shows that N. was initially hesitant in his contribution to the Utopian tradition, preferring to maintain an ironic approach to the genre. It was only when he had become disillusioned with the stagnation of social and political progress, following the revolutions of 1830 and 1848, that he returned to this literary and philosophical tradition as a means of escape from reality.

THE NINETEENTH CENTURY
(POST-ROMANTIC)

By EMILY SALINES, *Middlesex University*

1. GENERAL

M. Ambrière, **Dictionnaire du XIXe siècle européen*, PUF, 1376 pp. P. Aubin, **L'État québécois et les manuels scolaires au XIXe siècle*, Sherbrooke, Ex Libris, 1996, 119 pp. *La Belgique artistique et littéraire, une anthologie de langue française, 1848–1914*, ed. J. Aron et al., Brussels, Complexe, 700 pp. **Les 'Remarques' de l'Académie française sur le 'Quinte-Curce' de Vaugelas, 1719–1920: Contribution à une histoire de la norme grammaticale & rhétorique en France*, ed. W. Ayres-Bennett and P. Caron, Presses de l'École Normale Supérieure, 1996, 417 pp. E. Behler, *Ironie et modernité, De Schlegel à Nietzsche*, trans. from the Ger. by O. Manoni, PUF, 416 pp., in fact includes thinkers from antiquity to contemporary American authors; for the 19th c., Hegel, Marx, Kierkegaard, Nietzsche. P. Blanckart, *Une histoire de la ville. Pour repenser la société*, La Découverte, 194 pp., has a chapter on the 19th c.: 'Ville industrielle, thermodynamique et lutte des classes'. J. Birkett and J. Kearns, **A Guide to French Literature: From Early Modern to Postmodern*, Basingstoke-London, Macmillan, x + 298 pp. *The Play of Terror in 19th-Century France*, London, Associated University Presses (Delaware U.P.), 280 pp., ed. J. T. Booker and A. H. Pasco, presents the 17 papers from the 1993 19th-Century French Studies Colloquium at the University of Kansas. B. C. Bowles, 'Alfred Delvau's dictionaries: vehicles of linguistic and socio-cultural change in Second Empire France', *FR*, 71:213–24, explores the socio-cultural significance of Delvau's *Dictionnaire érotique moderne* (1864) and *Dictionnaire de la langue verte: argots parisiens comparés* (1866). P. Brunel, *Les Arpèges recomposés, Musique et Littérature*, Klincksieck, 302 pp., looks (for the 19th c.) at Nietzsche, Fauré, and Debussy, among others. S. Callens, *Les Maîtres de l'erreur. Mesure et probabilité au XIXe siècle*, PUF, 576 pp. *Repression and Expression: Literary and Social Coding in Nineteenth-Century France*, ed. C. F. Coates, NY–Berne–Paris, Lang, 1996, xv + 342 pp., has 27 papers from the 18th 19th-Century French Studies Colloquium (1992). *Moving Forward, Holding Fast. The Dynamics of 19th-Century French Culture*, ed. B. T. Cooper and M. Donaldson-Evans, Amsterdam-Atlanta, Rodopi, 239 pp. J. DeJean, **Ancients against Moderns: Culture Wars and the Making of a Fin de Siècle*, Chicago U.P., xix + 216 pp. *Genèses des fins: De Balzac à Beckett, de Michelet à Ponge*, ed. C. Duchet and I. Tournier, Saint-Denis, Vincennes U.P., 1996, 235 pp. H. Dufour, *'Portraits en* *phrases', Les recueils de portraits littéraires au XIXe siècle*, PUF, 320 pp. *La Belgique fin de siècle. Romans, Nouvelles, Théâtre*, ed. P. Gorceix, Brussels, Complexe, 1,170 pp. E. Duperray, *L'Or des mots, une lecture de Pétrarque et du mythe littéraire de Vaucluse des origines à l'orée du XXe siècle. Histoire du Pétrarquisme en France*, Sorbonne U.P., 366 pp. S. Fiette, *La Noblesse française des Lumières à la Belle Époque. Psychologies d'une adaptation*, Perrin, 346 pp. W. Guentner, *Esquisses littéraires: rhétorique du spontané et récit de voyage au XIXe siècle*, Saint-Genouph, Nizet, 315 pp., explores the poetics of the fragment and its links with travel narrative; it charts the origins of the genre (from the 16th to the 18th c.) before turning to specific authors, including Chateaubriand, Hugo, Flaubert, Fromentin and the Goncourt brothers; the last section concentrates on the 20th century. D. Houk, 'Self construction and sexual identity in nineteenth-century French dandyism', *FrF*, 22:59–73, adopts a Lacanian approach to the play on identity achieved by dandyism, looking at representations of the dandy in Balzac, Baudelaire, Huysmans and Rachilde. H. Hermans et al., **1894, European Theatre in Turmoil, Meaning and Significance of the Theatre a Hundred Years Ago*, Amsterdam-Atlanta, Rodopi, 1996, 147 pp.. C. Lamiot, **Eau sur eau: Les dictionnaires de Mallarmé, Flaubert, Bataille, Michaux, Leiris et Ponge*, (Chiasma, 4), Amsterdam-Atlanta, Rodopi, 174 pp. C. Millet, *Le Légendaire au XIXe siècle: Poésie, mythe et vérité*, PUF, 280 pp., includes, for the post-romantic period, studies of Flaubert, Leconte de Lisle, Renan, and Zola. C. Montalbetti, *Le Voyage, le monde et la bibliothèque*, PUF, 260 pp. *French Literature in/and the City*, ed. B. Norman, Amsterdam-Atlanta, Rodopi, xi + 234 pp., includes articles on the 19th Century. **Le Même et l'Autre. Regards européens*, ed. A. Montandon, Association des Publications de la Faculté des Lettres et Sciences humaines de Clermont-Ferrand, 'Littératures', x + 276 pp., adopts a comparative approach and concentrates on texts from the late 18th c. to the end of the 19th. *La Censure en France à l'ère démocratique (1848...)*, ed. P. Ory, Brussels, Complexe, 350 pp. J. Prungnaud, *Gothique et décadence. Recherches sur la continuité d'un mythe et d'un genre au XIXe siècle en Grande-Bretagne et en France*, Champion, 498 pp., explores the two great moments of Gothicism (1820 and 1880), looking, for the *fin de siècle*, at Amanda Ros, Marie Corelli, Jane de la Vaudère, and distinguishing three archetypal Gothic characters — the scientist, the ghost, and the vampire. A. Rauch, *Vacances en France de 1830 à nos jours*, Hachette, 1996, 279 pp. *Romantisme*, 96, is a special issue on 'le nouveau savoir-vivre' and has the following articles: A. Motandon, 'Le nouveau savoir-vivre' (7–16), which explores the new panorama of social interaction and its causes; M.-C. Grassi, 'Autour de la notion de manuel' (17–30), about the history of the word; C.-I. Brelot,

'Savoir-vivre, savoir-être: attitudes et pratiques de la noblesse française au XIXe siècle' (31–40); R. Fisher, 'La pédagogie de la politesse dans l'école laïque de la Troisième République' (41–50), which looks at the importance of *politesse* in the pedagogy and curriculum of the public primary school, which is linked to the egalitarian, republican and nationalist ideals of the Third Republic; J.-L. Guerena, 'La transmission des codes sociaux dans l'espace scolaire en Espagne au XIXe siècle' (51–58); S. Zenkine, 'Etre poli avec l'au-delà' (59–70), which looks at the role played by the code of politeness as a mediation between the earthly and the infernal worlds; and S. Thorel-Cailleteau, 'Dandys et orgies' (71–83). *Romantisme*, 98, is entitled 'Influences' and includes the following: J.-L. Diaz, 'Un siècle sous influence' (11–32), about the notion of influence as 'opérateur de scientificité' but also as a means to create new social space in which the power of ideas is asserted; A. Vaillant, 'Conversations sous influence — Balzac, Baudelaire, Flaubert, Mallarmé' (97–110), on the transformation of the notion of influence, from textual to conversational (see also BAUDELAIRE); and F. Gaillard, 'L'homme-foule' (111–20). Fromentin, Gourmont. E. Roy-Reverzi, *La Mort d'Eros. Mésalliance dans le roman du second XIXe siècle*, SEDES, 367 pp. *Le Théâtre en France des origines à nos jours*, ed. A. Viala, PUF, 503 pp.

2 POETRY

La Conscience de soi de la poésie: Poésie et rhétorique. Colloque de la fondation Hugot au Collège de France, ed. O. Bombarde, Pleine Marge, 298 pp. E. Ravoux Rallo, 'Les poètes du spleen, "Valse mélancolique et langoureux vertige"', *Littératures*, 37: 209–20, on the relationship between spleen and music in Baudelaire, Leopardi and Pessoa. J. Thélot, *La Poésie précaire*, PUF, 150 pp., includes studies of Baudelaire and Rimbaud.

BANVILLE. E. F. Dalmolin, 'Modernity revisited: past and present female figures in the poetry of Banville and Baudelaire', *NCFS*, 25 : 78–91, explores the de-idealization of classical female beauty into modern urban women, and the interaction between ideal and modern beauty. S. Hartung, *Parnasse und Moderne. Theodore de Banvilles Odes funambulesques (1857) Parisdichtung als Ästhetik des Heterogenen*, Stuttgart, Franz Steiner, ix + 285 pp. E. Souffrin-Le Breton, 'Banville and the first edition of *Les Fleurs du mal* (with unpublished letters to Poulet-Malassis', *FSB*, 64: 7–9.

BAUDELAIRE. See also BANVILLE. *L'Année Baudelaire*, 2, 1996, is entitled 'Baudelaire. Figures de la mort, Figures de l'éternité', and has the following articles: M. Milner, 'Le Paradis se gagne-t-il?'

(11–24); M. Edwards, 'Magie, prosodie, mystère' (25–44); J. E. Jackson, 'Vers un nouveau berceau? Le rêve de palingénésie chez Baudelaire' (45–62); A. Compagnon, 'Le rire énorme de la mer' (63–74); M. Vibe Skagen, 'Pour s'exercer à mourir. Ennui et mélancolie dans *Le Tir et le Cimetière* de Baudelaire' (75–106); and D. Wiser, 'Les *ekphraseis* de la mort dans *Les Fleurs du Mal*' (107–32). E. Barón, 'Baudelaire en Cernuda', *RLit*, 59:67–88. *Buba*, 32, has: C. Pichois, '1871: *Les Fleurs du mal* sous haute surveillance' (45); M. Brix, 'Mademoiselle Person et La Béatrice' (46–47); J. Deprun, 'Glanes Baudelairiennes, I et II' (48–52); J.-C. Susini, 'Liszt/ Analyste: dimension rhétorique du jeu de mots dans *Le Thyrse*' (53–62); C. Delon, 'Du parfait fléau à l'ami dévoué: Narcisse Ancelle' (63–72); C. Pichois, 'Baudelaire et A. de La Guéronnière' (73–74). N. Babuts, 'Baudelaire's "Le Voyage": the dimension of myth', *NCFS*, 25:348–59, looks at the links between B.'s poem and the classical epic as embodied by the *Odyssey*. E. S. Burt, '"An immoderate taste for truth", censoring history in Baudelaire's "Les Bijoux"', *Diacritics*, 27.2:19–43. E. Cohen, 'Mud into gold: Baudelaire and the alchemy of public hygiene', *RR*, 87 (1996):239–55, looks at the ways in which B.'s discourse converges with or diverges from the common hygienic discourses of his days. J. R. Barberet, 'Baudelaire: homoérotismes', Fisher, *Difference*, 52–63; and D. D. Fisher, 'The silent erotic/rhetoric of Baudelaire's mirrors', *ib.*, 34–51, both explore homoeroticism in Baudelaire. D. Carrier, 'High Art: *Les Paradis artificiels* and the origin of modernism', *19th-Century Contexts*, 20:215–38. *Baudelaire in English*, ed. C. Clark and R. Sykes, Hardmondsworth, Penguin, lv + 267 pp., gives a selection of translations from *Les Fleurs du Mal* and some of the *Petits Poèmes*. There is an general introduction, which outlines B.'s biography and the reception of his works in the English-speaking world (and details of the history of the translation of his works). There are sometimes several versions of the same poems, and introductions about the translators, which makes the book a good tool for translation studies. It is unfortunate, however, that the presence of the source text should seem haphazard, sometimes there and sometimes not. S. Hartung, 'Victor Cousins ästhetische Theorie. Eine nur relative Autonomie des Schönen une ihre Rezeption durch Baudelaire', *ZFSL*, 107:173–213. F. G. Henry, 'Gautier/Baudelaire: *homo ludens* versus *homo duplex*', *NCFS* 25:60–77, reassesses Gautier's importance in literary history through a fascinating analysis of ludism in his works as opposed to B.'s satanism. J. Hiddleston, 'Baudelaire, Delacroix and religious painting', *MLR*, 92:864–76, is an in-depth analysis of B.'s perception of the religious in Delacroix, perceived by B. as his painterly counterpart. C. Jaurès Noland, 'The performance of solitude: Baudelaire, Rimbaud and the Resistance poetry of René

Char', *FR*, 70:562–74, outlines B.'s and R.'s poetics of solitude and show their impact on and transformation in Char's works. P. Laforgue, 'Naïveté, modèle et idéal dans le *Salon de 1846* de Baudelaire', *Romantisme*, 98:65–74, looks at B.'s creation of a second Romanticism. R. N. Lowe, *The Fictional Female: Sacrificial Rituals and Spectacles of Writing in Baudelaire, Zola, and Cocteau*, NY-Berne, Lang, xii + 239 pp. M. Lowrie, '*Spleen* and the monumentum: Mmmory in Horace and Baudelaire', *CL*, 49:42–58, is a fascinating comparison of *Spleen* ('J'ai plus de souvenirs . . .') and Horace's Ode 3.30 which emphasizes B.'s reversal of Horace's thematics and his hidden memory of the ode. A. E. E. Mensah, 'Vers l'ontologie de la "Dédicace" des *Fleurs du mal*', *FR*, 71:237–50, emphasizes the phrasing of B.'s initial dedication, 'Au magicien ès langue française', as closer to his true opinion of Gautier, rather than the later, better known 'Au magicien ès lettres françaises'. C. Milat, 'Baudelaire, ou la dualité de l'artiste à la poursuite de l'unité primordiale', *RHLF*, 571–88, explores B.'s alchemical quest for unity, through art and love. E. Salines, 'The figure of the innocent prostitute in two French versions of Thomas De Quincey's *Confessions of an English Opium Eater*', *WIFS*, 5:205–14, looks at translation as appropriation in A. de Musset's *L'Anglais mangeur d'opium* and Baudelaire's *Un Mangeur d'opium*. **Understanding 'Les Fleurs du Mal': Critical Readings*, ed. W. J. Thompson, introd. Claude Pichois, Nashville-London, Vanderbilt U.P., xi + 241 pp. S. Walton, ***'Baudelaire and the roots of "négritude"', *DFS*, 39–40:77–88. A. Wanner, 'Cutting Baudelaire's rope: Ivan Turgenev's re-writing of "La Corde"', *CLS*, 34:31–40, is a fascinating reading of two prose poems by T. as conservative appropriations of B.'s text. J. Wilner, 'Drinking rules! Byron and Baudelaire', *Diacritics*, 27.3:34–48, explores the theme of intoxication, exposing the literary resonance with Byron in 'Enivrez-vous'. N. Wing, 'Baudelaire's *frisson fraternel*, horror and enchantment in "Les Tableaux parisiens"', *Neophilologus*, 81:21–33, concentrates on 'les sept vieillards', 'les petites vieilles', 'les aveugles', showing that in the encounters central to these poems the indistinguishability of life and death brings on the return of 'repressed, primitive fears'.

LAFORGUE. *Les Complaintes*, ed. J.-P. Bertrand, Flammarion, 184 pp. Id., *Les Complaintes de Jules Laforgue, Ironie et désenchantement*, Klincksieck, 404 pp. C. Brown, 'Laforgue in *The Sacred Fount*', *English Language Notes*, 34.3:39–42, looks at the figure of the pierrot in Henry James' text. S. Larnaudie, 'Romantisme et modernité chez Jules Laforgue', *TLit*, 9, 1996:325–30.

MALLARMÉ. See also GENERAL. P. Audi, **La Tentative de Mallarmé*, PUF, v + 95 pp. C. Chadwick, 'Mallarmé's capital letters', *FSB*, 64:14, answers A. Holmes' 'Mallarmé's first and second thoughts', *ib.*, 63:6–8. J. R. Lawler, 'Mallarmé and latency: the case of 'Triptyque', *FS*, 51:412–21, looks at 'Triptyque' as 'an uniquely subtle evocation of the idea of the poem conceived in the face of antagonistic forces', and as a proposal of poetry as redemption. J. Chatlos, 'Loss of self and coming to voice in *Les Noces d'Hérodiade'*, *RR*, 87, 1996:257–70, explores the crisis of the speaking subject. R. Killick, 'Mallarmé's rooms: the poet's place in *La Musique et les Lettres'*, *FS*, 51:155–68. M. L. W. Marvick, 'Mallarmé and Wagner on rhythm', *RLMC*, 50:43–50. S. Meitinger, 'Une définition de la poésie ou Mallarmé Philosophe', *NCFS*, 26:161–81, shows how Mallarmé's 1886 definition of poetry announces 20th-c. philosophy trends, and how the poem is at the origin of theory rather than its result. R. Saunders, 'The syntactic panopticon and Mallarmean resistance', *RR*, 87 (1996):363–75, argues that M.'s poetic language constitutes a resistance to disciplinary power (structured like a language) and the knowledge disciplinary relations of power produce, through a dismantling of syntax. D. Streifford Reisinger, 'Le retour au rien: la circulation mallarméenne à travers *Sonnet en -yx* et *salut'*, *RoN*, 37:273–80, expores the circularity of both poems. A. Vaillant, 'Verba Hermetica, Mallarmé, Rimbaud, Hugo', *Romantisme*, 95:81–98. G. Zachmann, 'Developing movements: Mallarmé, Manet, the "Photo" and the "Graphic" ', *FrF*, 22:81–202.

MONTESQUIOU. A. Bertrand, *Les Curiosités esthétiques de Robert de Montesquiou*, Geneva, Droz, 1996, 2 vols, 936 pp., is an in-depth presentation of M. and an evaluation of his impact on writers of his and later generations.

RIMBAUD. See also *supra*, BAUDELAIRE, and MALLARMÉ. J. T. Argote , 'Colliding fragments: the *Illuminations* as collage', *RoN*, 37:199–206. M. Arouimi, 'Les lettres d'Afrique de Rimbaud dans *Le pain dur'*, *Claudel Studies*, 24:73–86 looks at the Rimbaldian echoes in Claudel. D. Berry, 'Thematics of hunger and thirst in Rimbaud's poetry', *RoS*, 30:85–95, is a fascinating study of 'Comédie de la soif' and 'Fêtes de la faim'. J. W. Brown, *'"Voix et voyance" in Rimbaud's "Départ"'*, *DFS*, 38:95–102. G. M. Macklin, 'Prayer and parody in Rimbaud's "Dévotion"', *FS*, 51:281–92, studies R.'s reinventing and subverting of the litany form. A. M. Paliyenko, 'Re-reading *la femme poète:* Rimbaud and Louisa Siefert', *NCFS*, 26:146–60, explores R.'s ambivalence towards the creativity of women, celebrated in the *lettre du voyant* but seen from a phallocratic point of view in his reading of Louisa Siefert.

SIEFERT. See *supra*, RIMBAUD.

VERHAEREN. H. Peters, *'"De part en part, mordent les vers des maladies"*: analyse métrique d'un poème de Verhaeren, *EtF*, 12.2:113–26. *Emile Verhaeren, un musée imaginaire*, ed. M. Quaghebeur,

Éditions de la Réunion des musées nationaux, 200 pp. E. Van Balberghe, *'*Voici quelqu'un': Emile Verhaeren critique de Léon Bloy. Avec le relevé des articles de et sur Léon Bloy parus dans* L'Art moderne *[1884–1895]*, Brussels, Les Libraries momentanément réunis, 99 pp.

VERLAINE. *Paul Verlaine*, ed. O. Bivort, Paris-Sorbonne U.P., 506 pp. C. D. Minahen, 'Homosexual erotic scripting in Verlaine's *Hombres'*, Fisher, *Difference*, 119–35.

3. FICTION

Antimimesis. Tendenze antirealiste nel romanzo francese di fine Ottocento, ed. G. Bogliolo and P. Toffano, Fasano di Brindisi, Schena, 304 pp. M. Coen, 'Women and fiction in the nineteenth century', Unwin, *French Novel*, 54–72, outlines the evolution of the place of women writers in the corpus of 19th-c. fiction, emphasizing a lack of contribution on their part between 1850 and 1880 and a resurgence after 1880, concentrating, for that period, on Gyp, Rachilde, Jean Bertheroy (Berthe LeBariller) and Marcelle Tinayre. C. also provides a bibliography. D. Coward , 'Popular Fiction in the nineteenth century', *ib.*, 73–92, traces the evolution of the genre throughout the century, presenting a clear and lively picture of the market for popular fiction and its significance; there is also a useful bibliography. I. Daunais 'La réversibilité des arts: littérature et peinture au confluent de la critique (Zola, Huysmans)', *EF*, 33.1:95–108. A. Finch, 'Reality and its representation in the nineteenth-century novel', Unwin, *French Novel*, 36–53, explores the reasons for the æsthetic success of Stendhal, Balzac, Hugo, Flaubert, and Zola, and the tensions between reality and representation in their novels. R. Innerhofer, *Deutschsprachige Science Fiction 1870–1914. Rekonstruktion und Analyse der Anfänge einer Gattung*, Vienna, Völhan Verlag, 1996, 508 pp. S. Mombert, 'Les frères ennemis du roman historique: sur quelques romans du XIXe et XXe siècles consacrés aux guerres de religion', *TLit*, 10:281–93, shows the evolution of the genre and its increasing autonomy from history or adventure novels. C. Pierre-Gnassounou, 'Séquestrations et quarantaines: aux frontières des Rougon-Macquart', *Romantisme*, 95:3–16, looks at the secondary characters, who are at the confines of the novelistic framework and curb the naturalist 'tell it all' principle, and are therefore quarantined. G. Ponnau, *La Folie dans la littérature fantastique*, PUF, xv + 355 pp. L. M. Porter, 'Decadence and the *fin-de-siècle* novel', Unwin, *French Novel*, 93–110, provides a clear presentation of decadence in its historical and cultural contexts; aspects focused on include *À Rebours* as a model, the misogynist portrayal of women, the decadent author's ambivalent attitude to contemporary society, the *acte gratuit*, general æsthetics, and Rachilde, and concludes on the idea of the 'asocial' dimension of the decadent novel; there is also a good bibliography. *Narrative Ironies*, ed. R. A. Prier and G. Gillespie, Amsterdam-Atlanta, Rodopi, 304 pp., includes, with a comparative approach, studies of Huysmans and Maupassant. V. A. Rosario, 'Histoires d'inversion: novelizing homosexuality at the Fin de Siècle', Fisher, *Difference*, 100–18, explores the roles of the *belle-lettristes* in shaping the medical discourse of medical science about homosexuality. *Ile des merveilles. Mirage, miroir, mythes*, ed. D. Reig, L'Harmattan, 298 pp., is based on papers of a Cerisy colloquium concentrating on the fantastic and the *merveilleux*. E. Roy-Reverzy, **La Mort d'Eros: La mésalliance dans le roman du second XIXe siècle*, SEDES, 367 pp. M. Watroba, '*Thérèse Raquin:* le naturalisme entre mensonge et vérité', *Romantisme*, 95 : 17–28, explores the relations between truth and falsity, sex and death.

BARBEY D'AUREVILLY. P. Auraix-Jonchière, *L'Unité impossible. Essai sur la mythologie de Barbey d'Aurevilly*, Saint-Genouph, Nizet, 425 pp., analyses the place of myth in Barbey's writing, with chapters on 'Barbey démiurge', 'Barbey héros', 'Barbey archange et titan'. P. Cogman, 'Criminal conversation: telling and knowing in Barbey's "La Vengeance d'une femme', *FS*, 51 : 30–42.

CÉARD. J.-M. Céard, 'Écriture et négativité dans *Une belle Journée* d'Henri Céard', *CNat*, 71 : 221–35.

DUMAS *fils*. L. Auchincloss, 'Dumas "fils"', *New Criterion*, 15.3 (1996): 73–77.

FLAUBERT. See also GENERAL. *Selected Letters*, trans. and introd. Geoffrey Wall, Hardmondsworth, Penguin, 430 pp., has an introduction which outlines F.'s biography and reflects on a poetics of the letter; there is also a chronology and details about 'the Flaubert circle', with succinct presentations of F.'s correspondents. N. Buchet Rogers, 'Adultère, arsenic ou crème à la vanille?: Écrire le scandale dans *Madame Bovary*', *NCFS*, 26 : 119–32, is 'a study of textual proliferation and perversion surrounding the inscription of scandal in *Madame Bovary*.' I. Daunais, 'La frontière du récit dans *Le Voyage en Orient* de Flaubert', *RR*, 87 (1996): 69–81. A.-C. Dobbs, 'Le dépoussiérage de *Madame Bovary*', *ib.*, 481–91, analyses the motif of dust in the novel, and its functions (descriptive, metaphoric and structural), showing it to symbolize the precarity of the imaginary. L. Fournier, 'Flaubert nihiliste: une idée reçue?', *LR*, 51 : 53–74, provides the basis for a reconsideration of F.'s so-called nihilism, with special mention of *La Tentation de Saint Antoine*. E. J. Gallagher, 'Last (w)rites: extreme unction and Flaubert's *Madame Bovary*', *FSB*, 63 : 8–10. **Le Dictionnaire des Idées Reçues' suivi du 'Catalogue des idées chic'*, ed. A. Herschberg Pierrot, Librairie Générale Française, 255 pp. J. Kupper, 'Erwägungen zu *Salammbô*', *ZFSL*, 24 : 269–310. E. F. Lacoste, '*Bouvard et*

Pécuchet ou *Quatre vingt-treize* "en farce"', *Romantisme*, 95:99–112, studies the parodic dimension of F.'s novel with relation to Hugo. E. Le Calvez, 'Description et psychologie: génétique et poétique de l'indice dans *L'Éducation sentimentale*', *Minogue Vol.*, 113–42, is a fascinating and detailed analysis of *description indicielle* and its function. B. Le Juez, 'Représentations de femmes d'intérieur dans *Un Cœur Simple* de Gustave Flaubert', *WIFS*, 5:19–25, explores the use of artistic references to orientalist themes to express the exclusion and reclusion of occidental women. K. Ley, **Flauberts Salammbô in Musik, Maleri, Literatur und Film*, Tübingen, Narr, 450 pp. P. A. McEachern, 'True lies: fasting for force or fashion in *Madame Bovary*?', *RoN*, 37:289–98, analyses how Emma Bovary attempts to gain control of her life by manipulating her body. B. Nelson, 'Flaubert and semanalysis: rereading *L'Éducation sentimentale*', *Minogue Vol.*, 101–11, applies Julia Kristeva's theories of the symbolic and the semiotic for an integrated reading of the novel. D. Philippot, **Vérité des choses, mensonge de l'homme dans 'Madame Bovary' de Flaubert: De la nature au Narcisse*, Champion, 466 pp. A. Raitt, 'The date of the projected epilogue to *Madame Bovary*', *FSB*, 62:7–10. C. Rigelj, *'"Ces tableaux du monde": keepsakes in *Madame Bovary*', *NCFS*, 25:360–85. M. A. Schmid, 'Reading it right: transparency and opacity in the *avant-texte* and the published text of Flaubert's *L'Éducation sentimentale*', *ib.*, 26:119–32, analyses F.'s systematic elimination from the published version of factual explanations or psychological motivations present in the *avant-texte* of *l'Education sentimentale*, and opposes views that the obscuring of the text such elimination produces is conscious choice — instead, it is the unavoidable result of textual dislocation of relevant story material. N. Segal, '"Voilà le poëte hystérique": Flaubert, Frédéric and Emma', *Minogue Vol.*, 79–100, explores the genealogical relation in art-for-art's sake writers and realism, and looks at the author-character relation as one 'that fantasizes a loss of the body, a kind of paternity fraught by the wish to be a father without having a child, and is most clearly represented in the motif of gender ambiguity'. G. Séginger, **Naissance et métamorphoses d'un écrivain: Flaubert et 'Les Tentations de saint Antoine'*, Champion, 442 pp. Id., 'Fiction et transgression épistémologique: le mythe de l'origine dans *La Tentation de Saint Antoine*', *RR*, 88:131–44, is on the relationship between documentation and fiction, showing how fiction questions and transforms documents and scientific knowledge. A. Weber-Caflish, 'A propos de *Salammbô*: enjeux du "roman archéologique"', *TLit*, 10:253–79, looks at F.'s reaction to Guillaume Froehner's 1862 article on *roman archéologique*. N. White, 'Dying for Flaubert: two naturalist versions of the death of the subject', *NZJFS*, 18.1:20–29, considers Zola's *Le Docteur Pascal* and Armand Charpentier's *La Folie*

Claustrophobique (both of 1893) to have been composed largely in response to Flaubertian models.

FOURNIER. S. Naliwajek, *Alain Fournier romancier. Le Grand Meaulnes,* pref. Pierre Brunel, Orléans, Paradigme, 314 pp., explores the genesis of the novel from 1896 and its links with symbolism (H. de Régnier, Maeterlinck, Francis Jammes, Laforgue, Rimbaud, Mallarmé).

FROMENTIN. See also GENERAL, under Guentner. P. Petitier, 'L'influence ou la relation du regard dans *Les Maîtres d'autrefois',* *Romantisme,* 98: 75–85, explores F.'s two conceptions of influence — part of both comparative and contextual appreciation.

GEFFROY. J.-L. Cabanès, 'Gustave Geffroy et l'apprentissage du fait divers', *Romantisme,* 97: 59–68, looks at *L'Apprentie,* in which G. distinguishes himself from other naturalist writers, inserting a selection of desriptions from *faits divers,* bringing on discords and genetic conflicts, and announcing 20th-century collages.

HENNIQUE. *CNat,* 71: 7–150, constitutes a *dossier* on H., edited by J. de Palacio. It includes a chronology, presentations of H. as novelist, playright, poet, as well as unpublished letters, an unpublished play (*Simplicité*) and unpublished letters from Alexandrine Zola to the Hennique family edited by R. Rheault (127–48).

HUYSMANS. P. Genova, 'Japonisme and Decadence: painting the prose of *A Rebours',* *RR,* 88: 267–90, explores attempts to integrate fundamental Japanese æsthetic theories into Decadent poetics, using *A Rebours* for the centrality of the dynamics of painting to the themes of the novel. J.-M. Seillan, 'Huysmans, un antisémite fin de siècle', *Romantisme,* 95: 113–26.

LAUTRÉAMONT. P. Dayan, **Lautréamont et Sand,* Amsterdam-Atlanta, GA, Rodopi, 178 pp. J. Stuffs, 'Surrealism's *Book of Revelation:* Isidore Ducasse's *Poésies, détournement* and *automatic writing',* *RR,* 87, 1996: 493–509.

LORRAIN. P. Winn, **Sexualités décadentes chez Jean Lorrain: le héros fin de sexe,* Amsterdam-Atlanta, GA, Rodopi, 303 pp. M. Dottin Orsini, 'Problèmes littéraire et iconographiques du Mythe de Salomé: le cas de Jean Lorrain', *Littératures,* 34, 1996: 85–100, sees L. as emblematic of banalization of myth through the systematic use of pictoral quotation.

LOTI. *Cette éternelle nostalgie. Journal intime (1878–1911),* ed. B. Vercier et al, La Table Ronde, 588 pp. Y. Y. Hsieh, **From Occupation to Revolution: China through the Eyes of Loti, Claudel, Segalen, and Malraux (1895–1933),* Birmingham, AL, Summa, 1996, *ix* + 202 *pp.*

MAETERLINCK. B. Dieterle, 'L'Abyme du rêve: à propos d'*Onirologie* de Maurice Maeterlinck', *TLit,* 10: 295–309, shows the blend of narrative and essay in this text.

MAUPASSANT. N. Benhamou, 'De l'influence du fait divers, les chroniques et contes de Maupassant', *Romantisme*, 97 : 47–58, explores the use made by M. of *faits divers* as source, and their effect on his stories, timeless, universal and at the same time very much of their time. P. W. M. Cogman, 'Maupassant's inhibited narrators', *Neophilologus*, 81 : 35–47, looks at M.'s exploitation in his *chroniques* of the humorous possibilities offered by euphemism and ellipsis, developing simple anecdotes into complex verbal and narrative play. C. Giacchetti, 'La "bosse au flanc": Maupassant et l'obstétrique, *ib.*, 355–63, looks at the womb as threat to manhood, women being both perpetrators and victims of obstetrical terrorism. *'Yvette' et autres nouvelles*, ed. L. Forestier, Gallimard, 265 pp. R. Lefèbre, 'Le ridicule raisonnement de *Fort comme la mort*', *Romantisme*, 95 : 69–80, sees resemblance as central to the novel. M. Picchi, *'Quel picchio di legno dietro Leopardi e Maupassant', *Belfagor*, 54 : 466–72.

MIRBEAU. *Cahiers Octave Mirbeau*, 4, 416 pp., contains the papers from the international colloquium held May 1996 at the University of Caen.

RACHILDE. R. Ziegler, 'Interpretation as mirage in Rachilde's "Le Château hermétique"', *NCFS*, 26 : 283–92, sees this particular text as acting out the difficulties of interpreting R.'s stories, turning the reader's own attempts at analysis into acts of self-narration.

RENARD. H. Laroche, 'Le renard et la bécasse', *Romantisme*, 95 : 61–68, relates the different stages which lead 'Poil de carotte' to the status of an adult author, concentrating on the figure of the hunter.

RICHEPIN. V. Zarini, 'D'une lettre de Symmaque à un conte de Richepin, ou d'une 'décadence' à une autre', *TLit*, 9, 1996 : 199–216, looks at the Latin source of R.'s "Les Trente braves" in *Contes de la décadence romaine*.

SAND. M. Lecarpentier, *Les Ailes de courage [1872]*, Flammarion, 160 pp.

SÉGUR. V. C. Lastinger, 'Le sang des cerises: l'écriture de la féminité chez Sophie de Ségur', *NCFS*, 26 : 133–45, considers the image of menstruation as central to Ségur's novels, and for her the very core of the writing act.

VERNE. C. Mortelier, 'La source immédiate de *L'Ile mystérieuse* de Jules Verne', *RHLF*, 97 : 589–98. identifies François Raynal's *Les Naufragés ou vingt mois dans les Iles Auckland* (1863–65) as the source to V.'s novel, also present in *Une Ville flottante* and *Deux Ans de vacances*. B. Taves, 'Jules Verne's *Paris in the Twentieth Century*, *SFS*, 24.1 : 133–38, presents the recently translated novel.

VILLIERS DE L'ISLE-ADAM. *Jeering Dreamers: Villiers de L'Isle-Adam's 'L'Eve Future' at our Fin de Siècle*, ed. J. Anzalone, Amsterdam-Atlanta,

Rodopi, 1996, 210 pp, offers 13 essays on Villiers. M. Blain Pinel, 'Edison créateur, profanateur ou redempteur? À propos de *L'Eve Future* de Villiers de l'Isle-Adam', *RHLF*, 97: 599–621, sees Edison as a Christ figure saving creation from God's desertion. M. Lathers, **The Æsthetics of Artifice: Villiers's 'L'Eve future'*, Chapel Hill, North Carolina U.P., 1996, 148 pp. A. Le Feuvre, 'Le récitant et son double: Villiers de l'Isle-Adam et R. Wagner', *RLC*, 71: 293–306, explores V.' device of 'recitation' for stereotypes and sacred discourse, and studies this identification and agreement with Wagnerian æsthetics.

ZOLA. See also *infra*, DREYFUS. M.-S. Armstrong, 'Une lecture "Hugo-centrique" de *La Fortune des Rougon*', *RR*, 87, 1996: 271–83, shows, through an intertextual reading of the character of Miette, the importance of Hugo's influence on the novel, and through a metatextual reading explores the link between Zolian and Hugolian writing, arguing that *La Fortune des Rougon* is the key to the relationship between the two authors throughout the *Rougon Macquart*. M.-S. Armstrong, 'Où le petit Zola tire parti de Hugo le Grand ... et du dilemme qui en résulte', *FrF*, 22: 165–80, centres around Chapter 6 of *Germinal,* exploring the ambivalence of the relationship with the literary precursor. L.-M. Badsu-Cosmas, **Parler ou ne pas parler: la prise de parole comme faire-part identitaire dans *Germinal* d'Emile Zola', *DFS*, 39–40: 111–26. K. Basilio, 'Les mystères de Virginie', *CNat*, 71: 151–56, explores the presentation of Virginie in the first chapter of *L'Assommoir*. L. Bilodeau, '*Le Rêve:* des *Rougon Macquart* à la scène lyrique', *ib.*, 239–59. J. Breines, '"Submerging and drowning" the characters: Zola's wet determinism', *RR*, 87, 1996: 511–29, looks at the link between the theory and the practice of naturalism, showing how Zola provides indications that his novels have been written with some distance from theory, 'wet determinism' being the link between determinist theories and artistic freedom. J. J. Duffy Jr. 'Blood and money: symbolic economies in *La Bête humaine*', *RoQ,* 44: 143–58, studies the relationship between murder, monetary economy and process of marginalization, and brings to the forefront the political and economic content of the novel. S. Guermès, '"Une épopée burlesque et triste"': lecture des *Repoussoirs, CNat*, 71: 191–202. S. Harrow, 'Dressed/undressed: objects of visual Ffcination in Zola's *L'Assommoir*', *Minogue Vol.*, 143–63, explores the hidden narrative of the dressed/undressed body and its links with questions of identity and the construction of self and other. J.-P. Leduc-Adine, **L'Assommoir' d'Émile Zola*, Gallimard, 224 pp. Y. Mortazavi, 'Toulouse, Zola et Poincaré: génie volontaire / génie-aptitude', *CNat*, 71: 281–91. E. Notinger, 'Les chambres de Nana', *ib.*, 157–73, looks at the structural function of Nana's bedrooms. N. Rennie, **Benjamin and Zola: narrative, the individual, and crowds in an age of mass production', *CLS*, 33 (1996): 396–413. A. Riboud, 'Le Zola du pauvre (Zola et San Antonio', *CNat*, 71 : 271–79, explores the references to Zola in Frédéric Dard. F. Robert, 'Zola en chansons: Jules Jouy et *La Terre*', *ib.*, 261–69. E. Roy-Reverzy, 'Les perversions de la pastorale: *La Faute de l'abbé mouret* et *Le Jardin des supplices*', *Littératures*, 36 : 81–95, explores the challenge to genre and tradition achieved by naturalism through a study of the *pastorale*, highlighting the fundamental decadence of the naturalist text, first and foremost parodic. C. Saminadayar, '*La Débâcle*, roman épique?', *CNat*, 71 : 203–19. *La Bête humaine*, ed. G. Séginger, Livre de Poche, 510 pp., includes, in the commentary section, 'La genèse', 'De la représentation du réel au vertige de l'inconnu', 'Un roman impressionniste', together with biographical details and bibliography. P. Solda, 'Émile Zola et le parti pris du nauséabond', *CNat*, 71 : 75–202, is based on *L'Assommoir*, *Nana* and *Pot-Bouille*. R. M. Viti has three articles: '(Self-) portrait of the artist in middle age: time in Zola's *L'Œuvre* and "Madame Sourdis"', *RoQ*, 44 : 159–64, which takes the two texts as providing clues to a Zolian concept of successful artistic productions, and a depiction of the artist which serves as a self -defense of Zola's artistic presence against critics; 'Time, art and heredity in Zola's *L'Œuvre*', *ib.*, 53–60; and *Mobility, immobility and descent (dissent): on the edge in Zola's Rougon-Macquart, *DFS*, 39–40: 27–35. N. White, 'Reconstructing the city in Zola's *Paris*', *Neophilologus*, 81 : 201–14, studies the novel 'as a crisis in the Naturalist plot's powers of assimilation', showing this text as putting to the test the anti-taboo ideals of Naturalist writing.

4. NON-FICTIONAL PROSE

I. Daunais, 'Les récits de la critique d'art, entre naturalisme and modernisme', *Littérature*, 107 : 20–34, looks at the links between the arts as perceived by the *fin de siècle* and their effects on art criticism. *Ecriture du chemin de fer*, ed. F. Moureau and M.-F. Polino, Klincksieck, 160 pp. *Romantisme*, 97, is a special issue on the *fait divers*, with articles including the following (see also MAUPASSANT, FÉNÉON, and GEFFROY: V. Gramfort, 'Les crimes de Pantin: quand Troppmann défrayait la chronique' (17–30), which shows the impact of this *fait divers* on the press and writers (including Flaubert, Du Camp, Marmier, Turgenev, Lautréamont, Rimbaud), seeing it as the crime of the 19th century; P. Désormaux, 'Les assassins de Pierre Larousse: encyclopédisme et fait divers' (31–46), which explains the important place given to murderers and *faits divers* in Larousse's *Dictionnaire Universel* by the educational and civic role taken on by the encyclopedia; D. Compère, 'Faits divers et vulgarisation scientifique (69–76), which is based on the study of 178 'Nouvelles scientifiques et faits divers' published in 1890 in *La Science illustrée*, arguing that these are structured as *faits divers*, while playing the role of scientific popularization; A.-C. Ambroise-Rendu, 'Le suicide ou les silences de la chronique des faits divers' (77–88), showing the refusal to consider suicide as a social phenomenon common to most *faits divers*, a point which is symptomatic of the newspapers of the time, unable to treat social matters; and D. Kalifa, 'Faits divers en guerre (1870–1914)' (89–102), looking at the presentation of war, quickly reduced to a recital mode obeying the canons of a new item. A. Smith, 'Le soleil et le prisme: ambiguïtés de l'anticolonialisme au dix-neuvième siècle. Le cas Gasparin.', *NCFS*, 26: 193–203.

ALLAIS. *Alphonse Allais, écrivain, actes du premier colloque international Alphonse Allais, Université de Liège, Wégimont, 9–11 sept 1996*, ed. J.-M. Degays and L. Rosier, Saint-Genouph, Nizet, 308 pp.

BARRÈS. *Ego scriptor: Maurice Barrès et l'écriture de soi*, ed. E. Godo, Kimé, 204 pp.

BLOY. D. Millet-Gérard, 'L'envers et l'effigie: écriture de l'analogie spéculaire chez Leon Bloy', *TLit*, 10: 311–34.

DREYFUS. *Émile Zola: The Dreyfus Affair. 'J'accuse' and Other Writings*, ed. A. Pagès, and trans. Eleanor Levieux, New Haven–London, Yale U.P., 1996, xxxvi + 208 pp.

FÉNÉON. J.-P. Bernard, 'Par fil spécial: à propos de Félix Fénéon', *Romantisme*, 97: 103–12, on the compromise between reality and fiction in the *Nouvelles en trois lignes*.

GONCOURT. W. Guentler, 'La poétique de l'esquisse littéraire: *L'Italie d'hier* des Frères Goncourt', *NCFS*, 26: 204–219, explores Edmond de G.'s æsthetics of the fragment. E. Heil, *The Conflicting Discourses of the Drawing Room: Anthony Trollope and Edmond and Jules de Goncourt*, NY, Lang, x + 204 pp. See also GENERAL, under W. Guentner.

GOURMONT. M.-F. Melmoux-Montaubin, 'La décadence, une histoire d'influences', *Romantisme*, 98: 85–96, is based on G.'s 'Stéphane Mallarmé et l'idée de décadence'.

RENAN. J. Landrin, 'Le romantisme de Renan', *TLit*, 10: 231–62, explores the coexistence of the opposed tendencies of romanticism and classicism in R.'s writing, and reacts against the critical clichés about R. as being first and foremost a positivist and scientist.

VALLÈS. *Les Amis de Jules Vallès: revue de lectures et d'études vallésiennes*, 24. S. Disegni, 'Vallès et la censure', *RLMC*, 50: 421–38.

THE TWENTIETH CENTURY, 1900–1945

By ANGELA M. KIMYONGÜR, *Lecturer in French, University of Hull*

I. ESSAYS AND STUDIES

Questions of gender and literature are explored in a number of volumes. Jennifer E. Milligan, *The Forgotten Generation. French Women Writers of the Inter-War Period*, Oxford–NY, Berg, ix + 236 pp. is an invaluable contribution to the study of women's writing in France in its belated recognition of the literary achievements of this 'forgotten generation' of women writers. It takes a polemical standpoint in asserting that the oblivion into which these writers fell was no reflection on their calibre as writers. As M. reminds us, 'when women writers were lost, *someone lost them*'. The responsibility for their loss is placed squarely on the shoulders of those who form the canon, and of those critics, including women, who dismissed and marginalized women writers at this time. The study is divided into three parts which consider respectively the critical and social context within which women writers operated in the early 20th c; the genres of autobiography and of popular romantic fiction. The second of these sections casts new light on the traditional association between autobiography and women writers, while the final chapters consider both the ways in which female writers have perpetuated traditional patterns of male dominance and female subservience, but also looks at those writers who succeeded in subverting and reappropriating romance through a feminist and/or lesbian voice. M.'s initial hypotheses are, to a large extent, confirmed by Robinson, *Women*, in that from a four-volume compendium of women writers, there are only four entries for French women writers from this period, and of these only Colette and, arguably, Simone Weil are well known. The other two writers, Catherine Pozzi and Anna de Noailles are only known to a very limited readership. Entries take not the usual format of an authored presentation of the writers, but a collection (necessarily brief for the latter two) of critical views of each writer. Catherine O'Brien, *Women's Fictional Responses to the First World War. A Comparative Study of Selected Texts by French and German Writers* (Studies in Modern German Literature), NY–Berne, Lang, xi + 204 pp., attempts a similar task to that of Milligan. Taking as her starting point the traditional appropriation of war narratives by men, O'B. shows how the canon excluded voices which could have provided a counterbalance to the predominantly male voice of World War I literature. This study also represents an attempt to rediscover female voices, voices which had been lost, not entirely by accident. A useful historical and literary overview is followed by analysis firstly of war narratives which promote traditional views of gender roles, the binary divide which associates man with war and woman with peace, while later chapters focus on ways in which this order is subverted in some narratives, a subversion which acts as a useful corrective and also completes a partial view of the war experience. The author shows control and clarity in constantly shifting between German and French narratives in a way which demonstrates the amount of common ground between two nations at war. *EsC*, 37.4, a number on 'Women of the *Belle Epoque*', includes a number of articles on this period. M. Antle, 'Mythologie de la femme à la *Belle Epoque* (8–16), presents the period as a time of contradictions for women; apparent signs of progress and liberation coexisting with a political and economic reality which ensured that little changed in women's lives; J. M. Rogers, 'Women at work: the Femme Nouvelle in *Belle Epoque* fiction' (17–28), examines novels which provide contrasting representations of working women; D. Brahimi writes on 'Exotisme, nationalisme, socialisme chez trois écrivaines de la *Belle Epoque*' (29–45); D. D. Fisher, 'Du corps travesti à l'enveloppe transparente: *Monsieur Venus* ou la politique du leurre' (46–57), explores the issue of cross-dressing in Rachilde's novel; M. C. Hawthorne, '"Du Du that voodoo": M. Venus and M. Butterfly' (58–66), discusses questions of gender role confusion; L. Constable, 'Being under the influence: Catulle Mendès and *Les Morphinées* or decadence and drugs' (67–81), looks at the 'ideological recycling' of Baudelairean themes; L. R. Schehr, '*Rachel, quand du Seigneur*' (83–93) discusses representations of female Jewish identity in Proust's *A la recherche du temps perdu*; C. Perry, 'In the wake of decadence: Anna de Noailles' revaluation of nature and the feminine' (94–105), demonstrates how N. attempted to overcome the traditional polarities associating masculinity with intellect and femininity with nature; and E. Cardonne-Arlyot, '"Un néant follement attifé": modernité de Renée Vivien et Catherine Pozzi' (106–24), explores questions of dress, femininity and modernity. Fisher, *Difference*, is a collection of essays on various aspects of the 'representation, theories and problematics of homosexuality'. The introduction charts the development and the politics of this area of gender studies in both the French and Anglo-American contexts; G. H. Bauer, 'Gay incipit: botanical connections, nosegays and bouquets' (64–82), examines the use of the language of flowers in the representation of homosexuality, concentrating in particular on Balzac, Proust, and Gide; M. Hawthorne, 'The seduction of terror: Annehine's annihilation in Liane de Pougy's *Idylle Sapphique*' (136–54), proposes an autobiographical reading of *Idylle Sapphique*; and G. R. Heysel, 'René Crevel's body algebra' (155–66), attempts to counter the neglect of C.'s work through an exploration of questions of desire and the body in *Mon corps et moi*. Publications on surrealism and the *avant-garde* continue to be well represented. Marie-Paule Berranger, *Panorama de la littérature française. Le surréalisme* (Les Fondamentaux, 82), Hachette Education, 160 pp., is a manual aimed at undergraduates and provides a useful, succinct overview of the movement, looking at its origins, development and preoccupations, together with a brief analysis of two surrealist texts (*Le Paysan de Paris* and *L'Amour fou*). *The Cubist Poets in Paris. An Anthology*, ed. L. C. Breunig, Lincoln, Nebraska U.P., 1995, xxviii + 326 pp., is, in appropriately cubic format, a bilingual anthology of the poetry associated with Cubism in Paris, concentrating particularly on the close collaboration between artists and poets. The introduction highlights these associations, which are also echoed in the text through the carefully chosen illustrations accompanying the poems. Apart from brief biographical introductions to each poet, critical material is kept to a minimum to enhance the impact of the works themselves. *Surrealism. Surrealist Visuality*, ed. Silvano Levy, Keele U.P., 1996, 173 pp., is a collection of essays which contribute to an analysis of the visual imagery associated with surrealism. Its particular frame of reference is film and painting, though it does contain an essay which discusses Breton's 'poèmes-objets' (57–77). P. Ffrench, '*Tel Quel* and surrealism: a re-evaluation. Has the avant-garde become a theory?', *RR*, 88:189–96, poses a number of questions about the notion of the *avant-garde* in culture. The questions are explored in the framework of a discussion of the relations between surrealism and its apparent successor *Tel Quel*. F. reaches the conclusion that theory, which represents closure, has no place in the *avant-garde*, which should open up creative practice rather than close it. Vincent Kaufmann, *Poétique des groupes littéraires (Avant-gardes 1920–1970)*, PUF, 200 pp., defines the 20th c. as 'le siècle des avant-gardes', movements which are literary communities rather than groups of individuals. K. sets out to identify the poetics of the *avant-garde*, a poetics which is historically determined, since the notion of community on which they are based is itself in crisis in the wake of the collapse of communism. The study is organized by theme rather than by individual groups, in order to concentrate on common elements rather than on what divides the different movements. *'Cultures, contre-cultures', *Mélusine*, 16, ed. Henri Béhar, Lausanne, Age d'homme, 431 pp. *'Chassé-croisé Tzara-Breton: actes du colloque international', Paris, Sorbonne, 23–25 mai 1996', *Mélusine*, 17, ed. Id., Lausanne, Age d'homme, 347 pp. Gérard Durozoi, **Histoire du mouvment surréaliste*, F. Hazan, 816 pp. Aude Préa de Beaufort, *Le surréalisme, Ellipses-Marketing, 120 pp. Georges Sebbag, **Le point sublime: André Breton, Arthur Rimbaud, Nelly Kaplan*, J.-M. Place,

245 pp. D. Brewer, 'The French intellectual, history and the reproduction of culture', *EsC*, 37.2 : 16–33, reflects on the changing role of
the intellectuals in contemporary France, and questions whether or
not the intellectual can any longer play a role in political matters, a
question posed in the wake of the erosion of the intellectuals' image,
not merely through the decline of communism, but also through the
undermining of that image in relation to the activities of intellectuals
during the Occupation. M. Cornick, 'Living memory. French intellectuals and the experience of phoney war, 1939–1940', *JES*,
27 : 261–80, is an interesting study of an aspect of the culture of World
War II which has received little attention: the reaction of the
intellectuals to the phoney war. Sources studied include war journals
and contemporary reviews, and these reveal a tendency to express
experiences of the phoney war through the optic of memories of the
First World War. Michel Winock, *Le siècle des intellectuels*, Seuil,
695 pp. *Elisabeth Rechniewski, *Suarès, Malraux, Sartre: antécédents
littéraires de l'existentialisme* (Situations, 49), Lettres Modernes, 1996,
148 pp. Tom Bishop, *From the Left Bank: Reflections on the Modern French
Theatre and Novel*, New York U.P., x + 298 pp. Unwin, *French Novel*, is
one of two general survey works to appear and includes chapters on
broad tendencies and sub-genres of the novel. The volume is a
thorough and readable account which provides a useful overview of
the novel of the 19th and 20th centuries. Chapters of relevance to this
period include: C. McDonald, 'The Proustian revolution' (111–25)
which traces the overarching principles of P.'s literary project and
briefly indicates trends in P. criticism; D. H. Walker, 'Formal
experiment and innovation' (126–44), who gives a lucid insight into
the development of the questioning of and experimentation into the
novel from Gide to Perec; S. Ungar, 'Existentialism, engagement,
ideology' (145–60), who identifies the thematics of choice and identity
over and above purely ideological questions as being the unifying
features of the work of authors such as Sartre, Camus, Malraux,
Nizan in the period 1930–60; and D. Boak, 'War and the Holocaust'
(161–78), who considers the novels to have come out of the significant
conflicts of the 20th. century: World War I, the Spanish Civil War,
World War II and the associated subgroups of novels of resistance,
occupation, deportation, and concentration camps. Birkett, *French
Literature*, has a more explicitly pedagogical aim than Unwin: 'to
orientate the reader confronted with a continuum of cultural
discourses'. It is also more ambitious in the scope of its coverage, with
a starting point of 1515. Driven by historical chronology and genre
rather than by themes or movements, and necessarily covering more
ground than Unwin, it does provide the orientation it promised with
a good sense of the continuum of French literature. The years of

interest to this section are covered in 'The first interwar years 1871–1914' (158–82), and 'Changing forms and subjects' (200–75). Luc Rasson, *Ecrire contre la guerre: littérature et pacifismes 1916–1938*, L'Harmattan, 185 pp. Limore Yagil, *'L'Homme nouveau' et la révolution nationale de Vichy (1940–1944)*, Villeneuve d'Ascq, Septentrion U.P., 382 pp. C. Shorley, 'The war between the wars in the French novel', *FrCS*, 8 : 241–56, argues that the novel came to be the primary genre in the depiction of war in France, over and above the genres of poetry, drama and painting which failed to get to grips with the subject. S. traces the evolution of war fiction from the early 'témoignages' to the later novels, where the changing literary and political perspective of the 1930s had a profound impact on the representation of the Great War. Michel Mopin, *Littérature et politique. Deux siècles de vie politique à travers les œuvres littéraires*, La Documentation française, 342 pp. M. J. Green, 'Gender, fascism and the *Croix de Feu*: the women's pages of *Le Flambeau*', *FrCS*, 8 : 229–29, provides fascinating insights into the role women were encouraged to play within the *Croix de feu* by its newspaper *Le Flambeau*. Within the context of a post-war hostility to women's emancipation and the pressure on them to return to the home, *Le Flambeau* appeared to be promoting contradictory messages for women: on the one hand pressure to conform to marriage and motherhood, but on the other, a promotion of women's equality with men. The contradiction is explained in the way in which only unmarried women were considered to be fit for political involvement. *Le roman populaire en question(s). Actes du colloque international de mai 1995 à Limoges*, ed. Jacques Magozzi, Limoges U.P., 613 pp., is a substantial collection of papers on this topic, covering both 19th. and 20th. cs, and dealing with such topics as Poulaille and proletarian literature, Simenon, *roman sentimental* or *roman d'amour*, stereotype in science fiction and the place of the popular novel in cultural studies. The range of contributions bears witness to the vitality of research in the previously neglected area. Brunel, *Transparences*, ranges widely and with assurance across ten examples of the modern European novel in order to uncover the meaning of the notion of 'transparence' in the novel and its relation with the role of the novelist, who represents not himself but a double of himself. Authors covered who are relevant to this period are Proust and Char. Olivier Rony, *Les années roman, 1919–1939: anthologie de la critique romanesque dans l'entre-deux-guerres*, Flammarion, 702 pp. Suzanne Guerlac, *Literary Polemics: Bataille, Sartre, Valéry, Breton*, Stanford U.P., 294 pp., is a detailed and sophisticated analysis which traces the origins of *Tel Quel* back to show that, far from representing a complete break with the intellectual past, the work of the journal in fact draws significantly on the thought of writers such as Valéry, Breton and Sartre, as well as on that of

Hegel and Bergson. Notions of *engagement*, pure art, automatism and transgression are analysed in order to show the place of such ideas in the emergence of critical theory and, in so doing, to 'remap the modern'. Carol Mann, *Paris: Artistic Life in the Twenties and Thirties*, London, Lawrence King, 1996, 208 pp., is a beautifully illustrated volume which vividly communicates through the text, but particularly through the photographs, the excitement and dynamism of artistic life in Paris at this time. Photographs include portraits of artists, writers, fashion shots, cafe interiors, public buildings, shops and street scenes. The final section, on the 'Portentous Thirties' contains photographs of street scenes taken during the *Front Populaire* period, of the preparations for war and one of the *exode*. Marie-Claire Banquart, **Paris Belle Epoque par ses écrivains*, Biro, 192 pp. Ungar, *Identity*, sets out to analyse the often problematic links between notions of identity, Frenchness and citizenship in a nation where one may well be French without necessarily participating in established notions of Frenchness of French culture. The study is divided into four sections focusing on the interwar years, colonialism, Vichy and memory, and covers a wide variety of cultural forms, in particular cinema. Contributions of relevance to this section include: S. Peer, 'Peasants in Paris: representation of rural France in the 1937 International Exposition' (19–49), which shows how the image of the French peasant was recast in order to encourage a new, modern attitude to farming; P. H. Solomon, 'Céline on the 1937 Paris Exposition Universelle as Jewish conspiracy' (66–87), who explores *Bagatelles pour un massacre* as an anti-Semitic response to perceived Jewish domination in France, characterized for C. by the exhibition, and makes out a powerful case for not relegating C.'s pamphlets to the sidelines as mere aberrations and forgiving their content on the grounds of stylistic innovation, but rather remembering his attempts to undermine Jewish integration; and L. A. Higgins, 'Pagnol and the paradoxes of Frenchness', attempting to account for the perennial popularity of P.'s novels and their cinematic interpretations, and finding in them reflections of questions of national and regional identity which still have resonance today. Fréderic Lefèvre, **Une heure avec M. Barrès, J. Cocteau, G. Courteline, R. Dorgelès ... 2*, Laval, Siloë, 416 pp.

2   POETRY

Michel Collot, *La matière emotion* (Ecriture), PUF, 334 pp., is an attempt to accord emotion its full place in poetry. C. feels that its importance has been underestimated in modern poetry and criticism. He sees emotion as very much at the centre of poetic creativity, even for those poets who are not traditionally associated with lyricism, and sets out to establish this through precise analysis of language and of the construction of the subject and the world in a number of works and their *avant-textes*. Poets referred to include Ponge, Supervielle, Michaux, Reverdy and others. Laurent Fourcaut, *Lectures de la poésie moderne et contemporaine*, Nathan, 128 pp., approaches its subject not as a general survey, but as a series of detailed 'lectures' of extracts from the works of seven poets (Henri Michaux, René Char, Jacques Prévert, Yves Bonnefoy, Philippe Jaccottet, Claude Royet-Journoud and Esther Tellerman), in an attempt to analyse the notion of 'poéticité'. **Trois poètes face à la crise de l'histoire. André Breton, Saint-John Perse, René Char: actes du colloque de Montpellier III 22–23 mars 1996*, ed. Paule Plouvier et al., L'Harmattan, 270 pp.

3. AUTHORS

ALAIN-FOURNIER.   Zbigniew Naliwajek, *Alain-Fournier romancier. Le Grand Meaulnes*, Orléans, Paradigme, 318 pp., proposes a detailed reading of the novel in order to account for its perennial appeal. The overall approach is somewhat mechanical, analysing the development of critical opinion, the genesis of the novel and tracing the representation of character, time and space, but the insights drawn from this analysis are often sensitive. Z. concludes that the novel offers a new combination of symbolist influence and 'roman d'aventure', a reworking of the novel form which appeared at a moment of crisis for the novel. E. Ford, 'The Primitivist structure of Alain-Fournier's *Le Grand Meaulnes*', *RoQ*, 44: 165–71, also sees the novel as incorporating two different modes of narrative, describing it as 'part of a Primitivist movement to break away from Symbolism' in which elements of symbolism still persist.

APOLLINAIRE.   Willard Bohn, *Apollinaire and the International Avant-Garde*, Albany, NY State U.P., xi + 369 pp., is a scholarly and wide-ranging investigation of the initial critical reactions to A.'s work by the *avant-garde* outside France: in Britain, North America, Germany, Spain and parts of South America. B. analyses the ways in which A. provided a source of inspiration, both direct and indirect, for the international *avant-garde,* and uncovers a number of new documents as yet unpublished. The volume ends in a curiously abrupt fashion, with no conclusion. Pierre Brunel, *Apollinaire entre deux mondes. Le contrepoint mythique dans Alcools (Mythocritique II)* (Ecriture), PUF, 221 pp., is a detailed exploration of A.'s place between the two worlds of antiquity and modernity, with specific reference to *Alcools*. Taking as his starting point the opening lines of 'Zone', B. identifies poetic versions of the musical techniques of fugue and counterpoint, whereby the *fuite*/fugue from the ancient world is counterbalanced by a contrapuntal relationship between the ancient and modern, a balance which encapsulates A.'s sense of being 'entre-deux-mondes'. Hubert de Phalèse, *Quintessence d'Alcools. Le recueil d'Apollinaire à travers les nouvelles technologies* (Cap'Agreg, 8) La Riche, Nizet, 1996, 162 pp., is the latest in this collection of computer-based analyses of literary texts. Apollinaire, 'ouvert à la modernité', is considered as being a particularly apt choice for this treatment. The study is divided into three parts: the first section deals with A.'s historical and literary context, the second is a lexical study and the third is organised thematically. It is a useful pedagogical tool and reference work. M. Aquien, 'La voix d'Apollinaire', *Poétique*, 111:289–306, takes as its starting point the essentially individual nature of the human voice and proceeds to an analysis of a A.'s 1913 recording of three of his poems ('Le pont Mirabeau', 'Marie' and 'Le Voyageur'), detecting in the reading 'une nostalgie du chant derrière le poème'. Wilhelm Woltermann, **Guillaume Apollinaire und die Stadt*, (EH, 13, Französische Sprache und Literatur, 218), xv + 293 pp. Michel Decaudin, 'Léger, Apollinaire et les futuristes', *Europe*, 818–19:97–104. Marie-Louise Lentengre, **Apollinaire, le nouveau lyrisme*, J.-M. Place, 1996, 234 pp.

ARAGON.   The centenary of A.'s birth has seen a flurry of critical activity with a large number of publications. *Œuvres romanesques complètes*, I, ed. Daniel Bougnoux and Philippe Forest (Bibliothèque de la Pléiade), Gallimard, lxvi + 1317 pp., is perhaps the most important for the scholar as the first step in the publication of A.'s complete works in an accessible form. Olivier Barbarant, *Aragon, la mémoire et l'excès* (Champ Poétique), Seyssel, Champ Vallon, 256 pp., reminds the reader that, paradoxically for a writer whose popular reputation is as a poet, few studies of A.'s work focus exclusively on his poetry. B. maintains that this is because the collective memory is a selective one, remembering certain poems, certain aspects of his poetic career at the expense of others, a partial view which reflects A.'s tendency to provoke extreme reactions of dislike or admiration. B.'s aim is to reconstitute a whole image of A. as poet and to fill in the gaps in the collective memory, a task which he achieves admirably, touching not only on the successes but also on the failures of A.'s poetic career. Nathalie Piégay-Gros, *L'Esthétique d'Aragon*, SEDES, 283 pp., follows the usual format of this collection, comprising an extended analysis of the writer followed by an anthology of extracts from A.'s critical works. The analytical section acknowledges the difficulty in writing of the æsthetics of an author who has himself written at length on his own literary and critical practice. P.-G. sets herself the substantial task of getting to grips with the contradictions inherent in A.'s work while avoiding over-simplification. The complex question of identity is used as a critical focus, his writing seen as a means of attempting to define identity. The important relationship between writing and history forms a second branch of this rigorous yet elegantly written study. Raphaël Lafhail-Molino, *Paysages urbains dans Les Beaux Quartiers* (PUE, ser. 13, Langue et Littérature Françaises, 224), NY–Berne–Frankfurt, Lang, 531 pp., is an ambitious and scholarly study which sets itself a dual objective: to contribute to the ongoing elaboration of theories of description in the novel, and to explore A.'s use of description in greater detail. By means of detailed analysis of passages from *Les Beaux Quartiers*, L.-M. highlights the continuity between A. the surrealist, with his interest in urban description and the poetic dimension of 'le réel', and A. the socialist realist, revisiting a 19th-c. model of realism. This is a welcome contribution to A. studies, all the more so since (with the exception of *Aurélien*) it is rare for a full-length study to be given over to one novel. Carine Trévisan, *Aurélien d'Aragon: un nouveau mal du siècle* (ALUB, 611), Les Belles Lettres, 1996, 283 pp., does just that in this meticulously researched study of *Aurélien* which views the novel throught the optic of Arland's notion of the 'nouveau mal du siècle'. Analysis centres on the impact of World War I upon the disfunctional central character, making particular use of the psychological notion of 'dépersonnalis-ation' in Aurélien's alienation from self and society. T. sees in A.'s representation of a problematic subjectivity a foreshadowing of the novels of his 'troisième carrière'. *Louis Aragon. Du surréalisme au réalisme socialiste, du Libertinage au Mentir vrai, des Incipit à la postériorité*, ed. Gavin Bowd and Jeremy Stubbs, Manchester–Huddersfield, AURA, 1997, iv + 136 pp., contains papers from a centenary conference on Aragon at the University of Manchester in May 1997, together with a number of other documents. Contributions include: A. Jouffroy, 'Un Aragon, des Aragon' (1–12), a very personal evocation of Aragon; J. Ristat, 'Lettre du Cap Brun' (13–15), an open letter to A. previously published in *Les Lettres Françaises*; R. Short, on 'A fertile figure: the Paris peasant' (16–21); J. H. B. Bennett on 'Aragon et les surréalistes de Londres et...d'ailleurs pendant la Deuxième Guerre Mondiale' (22–33); H. Cornford, 'Aragon translated by Frances Cornford' (34–43), containing a number of English translations of poems by Aragon; J. O'Reilly on 'Le groupe Manouchian et le manuscrit du *Roman inachevé*' (44–63) ; A. Kimyongür on '"La femme des temps modernes"? The representation of women in Louis Aragon's *Le Monde reel*' (64–76); M. Hilsum on 'Le roman de Catherine ou la "grande songerie"' (77–93); M. Wetherill on '*La Semaine sainte*: thématique du voyage' (94–99); P. Forest on 'Aragon et l'avant-garde romanesque des annees 60' (100–12); V. Staraselski on 'L'imaginaire dans les romans post-réalistes ou l'invention contre l'utopie' (113–19);

and D. Lagorgette on 'Elsa Triolet, épouse Aragon' (120–36). *Digraphe*, 'Aragon lisant', nos. 82–83, contains the same papers with a number of additional contributions for this special centenary edition. *Au miroir de l'autre. Les Lieux de l'hétérogénéité dans Le Fou d'Elsa*, ed. Hervé Bismuth and Suzanne Ravis, Aix-en-Provence, Provence U.P., 129 pp., comprises a series of papers from the Centre Aixois de Recherches sur Aragon on the subject of the representation of the other in A.'s poem *Le Fou d'Elsa*. N. Shahnaei, 'Une voix sans regard psalmodiant des mots de Perse' (9–16), explores the influence of Iranian Islam in the Granada of *Le Fou d'Elsa*; H. Bismuth, 'L'Autre du roman historique: *Le Fou d'Elsa* au miroir de l'écriture historienne' (17–38), considers the more literary aspects of 'altérité' through the appropriation of one genre (the historical document) by another (fiction); N. Ramzi, 'Alhambra/al-Kassaba: les coulisses d'un palais' (39–47), analyses the closed spaces of the Alhambra palace and its prison al-Kassaba as depicted in *Le Fou d'Elsa;* H. Bismuth, 'Discours poétique et discours des philosophes: une lecture des "falâssifa" dans *Le Fou d'Elsa'* (49–65, is an analysis of a specific sequence of the poem and the 'double dialogue philosophique' which takes place within it; E. Burle, 'Une mise en scène théâtrale du "je lyrique" entre fiction et réalité: la "Parabole du montreur de ballet" dans *Le Fou d'Elsa'* (67–79), also focuses on a specific interlude in the poem, a reworking of a real event into a poetic dialogue; F. Gulkasehian, 'Les "Chants du Medjnoûn": le camouflage révélé d'un rendez-vous manqué' (81–97), is on the presentation of the couple in the poem; L. G. Elduayen, '"Le Démon d'analogie" ou le langage de la "semblance"' (99–116), considers the structures of analogy used in the poem; and S. Ravis, 'L'autre du manuscrit. Bifurcations génétiques et reformulations des figures de l'auteur' (117–27), studies the manuscript of the poem in order to analyse manipulations of the figures of the author. François Taillandier, *Aragon 1897–1982: quel est celui qu'on prend pour moi?*, Fayard, 175 pp., is in many ways an exasperating book: allusive, lacking in clear construction and even in clear purpose. Yet it contains a number of perceptive insights and is marked by enormous sympathy and compassion for A.; if there is a certain lack of direction, perhaps it is because the author is trying to get to grips with the haunting question of his subtitle, in other words attempting to identify the real A. beneath the mythology. Frédéric Ferney, *Aragon, la seule façon d'exister*, Grasset, 195 pp., is an essay in a similar vein to Taillandier's, described as an 'éloge impitoyable et fraternel'. Concerned very little with Aragon's writing — F. confesses that he is not 'un spécialiste' — he focuses particularly on the figure and myth of A. the man. Valère Staraselski, *Aragon l'inclassable. Essai littéraire: lire Aragon à partir de La Mise à mort et de Théâtre-Roman*, L'Harmattan, 367 pp. Dominique

Desanti, *Les Aragonautes. Les Cercles du poéte disparu*, Calmann-Lévy, 323 pp., is an intellectual biography of A. structured around the rather spurious conceit of the 'Aragonautes', deemed to be A.'s literary and political contemporaries. His career is traced through the six 'navires' of which D. sees him as being captain. As in D.'s other biographical studies of A. there is a mixture of personal recollection and anecdotal, and some insights. Much of the information is already in the public domain. Confidence in the rest is not inspired by a lack of critical apparatus, and a number of inaccuracies of spelling. Pierre Hulin, *Elsa et Aragon, souvenirs croisés*, Ramsay, 237 pp., is another biography, this time written by one of A.'s younger collaborators on *Les Lettres Françaises*, of which A. was editor from 1953 until 1972, and not until his death, as is claimed on the back cover. In many respects similar to Desanti's work, it is a very personal series of memories and anecdotes. Although providing some insights into significant events such as the fateful affair of the Stalin portrait, it is limited in scope to the daily routine of the paper and is as much about the author as about Aragon. *Aragon, anti-portrait: dessins et textes inedits de Louis Aragon*, ed. Hamid Fouladvind, Maisonneuve et Larose, 128 pp., contains a collection of hitherto unpublished drawings and texts completed by A. between 1979 and 1982, brought together to celebrate the centenary. Philippe Olivera, *Louis Aragon*, Publications ADPF, 75 pp., is a short volume written to accompany the Aragon exhibition put on by the ADPF. While too general to be of interest to the specialist, it forms a well written introductory guide for those unfamiliar with his work and provides a number of insights along the way. Jean Ristat, *Aragon: commencez par me* lire, Gallimard, 128 pp., is one in a series of introductory guides, and provides a well-illustrated summary of A.'s life and career. Illustrations include more than the usual run of photographs of the author, with a range of paintings reflecting A.'s interest in the visual arts. Monique Dupont-Sagorin and Jean D'Ormesson, **Aragon parmi nous*, Cercle d'Art, 150 pp. Nedim Gürsel, **Le mouvement perpetuel d'Aragon: de la révolte dadaïste au monde réel*, L'Harmattan, 195 pp. A. Kimyongür, '*Nouvelle occupation, nouvelle résistance*: Aragon, poetry and the Cold War', *FrCS*, 8:93–102, included in a special number on France and the Cold War, examines A.'s role in the campaign to promote 'poésie nationale' in the context of cold-war anti-Americanism. J.-P. Chimot, 'Léger/Aragon', *Europe*, 818–19:177–85, traces A.'s interest in Léger.

ARTAUD.   Catherine Bouthors-Paillart, **Antonin Artaud: l'énonciation ou l'épreuve de la cruauté* (HICL, 357), 1996, xii + 231 pp. M. De Julio, 'Nancy Spero's *Codex Artaud*', *DFS*, 39–40:137–50, analyses a series of scrolls produced by the artist Nancy Spero which juxtapose A.'s surrealist poetry with her own images and symbols. The discussion focuses on the relationship between A.'s text and S.'s images. H. Casanova, *'Autofiction et création dans *Héloïse et Abelard* d'Antonin Artaud', *RoN*, 37 : 139–46. A. and O. Virmaux, *'Dieu merci, Artaud n'est plus à la mode', *Europe*, 813–14 : 207–11.

BARRÈS. *Ego scriptor: Maurice Barrès et l'écriture de soi*, ed. Emmanuel Godo, Kimé, 204 pp., is a collection of papers from a conference on B. in 1996 which sets out to identify both the modernity of B. in opposition to the usual critical tendency to represent him as a traditionalist, and also the underlying unity of his work seen in the writing of the self. Papers include: J. Foyard, 'Petite rhétorique barrésienne: de l'image profonde au symbole ou de l'écriture comme garde-fou' (15–28), presenting B. as a writer for whom the act of writing has a therapeutic value; T. H. Ton-That on 'Proust et Barrès: l'écriture de soi et les masques de la fiction romanesque (1888–1902)' (29–42); P. Bernard, *'Le Secret de Tolède* ou le voyage égotiste' (43–48), on B.'s travels in Spain and his interest in El Greco; *écriture de soi* is traced through a number of papers on *Mes Cahiers*; C. Bompaire-Evesque, 'La réception du premier volume des *Cahiers* de Barrès. Y a-t-il une lecture spécifique des écrits intimes?' (49–67); T. Clerc, 'L'écriture des *Cahiers*' (69–81); M. Bouvier, 'Barrès et Pascal ou Comment Barrès s'engendre par Pascal' (83–98); V. Rambaud, 'Ecriture de soi et culture du Moi dans *Mes Cahiers*' (99–111); M.-O. Germain, *'Les Mémoires* ou l'autobiographie inachevée' (113–125), on another autobiographical project; C. Mignot-Ogliastri, 'Poursuite amoureuse et création de soi chez Barrès d'après la correspondance Noailles-Barrès' (127–41); E. Godo, on 'Maurice Barrès et la connaissance par les gouffres' (143–58); J.-M. Domenach, 'Maurice Barrès ou l'accomplissment du romantisme' (159–63), on B. as a post-romantic; M.-A. Kirscher, on 'Le paradoxe de Narcisse, Barrés et l'invention d'une écriture' (165–84); and E. Godo on 'De l'individualisme au nationalisme, réflexions sur la cohérence de l'œuvre de Maurice Barrès' (185–200). Emmanuel Godo, *La légende de Venise. Barrès et la tentation de l'écriture*, Villeneuve d'Ascq, Septentrion U.P., 300 pp.

BERNANOS. Malcolm Scott, *Bernanos: Journal d'un curé de campagne* (CGFT, 116), 82 pp., is a sensitive study of the novel, its themes, form and language which makes out a convincing case for it to be considered not as a work only of interest for Christians or Catholics, but as an accessible and universal study of human suffering and belief. Thomas Molnar, *Bernanos. His Political Thought and Prophecy*, New Brunswick–London, Transaction, xxxvii + 202 pp., is a new edition of M.'s 1960 work on B. with a substantial new introduction by the author which brings to bear the insights of the late 20th c. on B. and on his own insights into the writer as a significant political and literary figure. M. gives particular weight to the importance of B. as a prophetic figure in terms of his grasp of totalitarianism.

BRASILLACH. P. Mazgaj, '"Ce mal du siècle": the romantic fascism of Robert Brasillach', *Historical Reflexions*, 23:49–72, is a well-documented and persuasive re-evaluation of the place of B. in right-wing politics and culture. M. maintains that the label of 'romantic fascist' has been responsible for a certain amount of misunderstanding of B.'s significance. It has enabled critics to minimize his importance as a fascist, to dismiss him as a politically naïve and uniquely literary figure, and therefore sideline him or rehabilitate him as a writer without having to condone his political views. Both tendencies, M. argues, have underestimated the nature of his fascism. He challenges the dichotomy between the political and the cultural fascist, demonstrating the B. was both a literary figure and politically engaged, and therefore more powerful as a figure in French fascism than critics have hitherto accepted.

CÉLINE. *Actes du colloque international de Paris (1994)*, ed. André Derval, Société d'études céliniennes – Tusson, Du Lérot, 1996, 260 pp., brings together the work of a number of established C. scholars and includes: I. Blondiaux, 'Le vocabulaire de l'hystérie dans *Féerie pour une autre fois* et les versions préliminaires' (9–19); J.-L. Cornille, 'La dédicace effacée (De Céline à Proust)' (21–29), on the insistent presence of Proust in C.'s work; A. Cresciucci, 'Mon oncle. Le personnage de l'oncle Edouard dans *Mort à Crédit*' (31–39); N. Debrie le Goullon, 'Le lyrisme de Céline ou la quête du poétique dans le prosaïque' (41–54); P. Destruel, 'Silence de Céline' (55–69), who explores the role of silence in *Mort à Crédit;* M. Donley, 'Céline musicien' (71–79), on the importance of music as symbolic of movement and life in C.'s work; V. Flambard-Weisbart, 'Ressentiment pour une autre fois' (81–93), exploring C.'s minority voice; A. Henry, 'Céline et l'histoire: le ratage volontaire de *Féerie pour une autre fois*' (95–103), judging *Féerie* to be an æsthetic failure, symptomatic of a creative crisis; P. A. Ifri, 'Une reconsidération de la crise de la petite bourgeoisie dans *Mort à Crédit*' (105–12), taking issue with Hewitt's interpretation of the novel as a historically accurate representation, and arguing that C.'s depiction is an exaggeration of historical reality; J. Karafiath, 'La vie et l'œuvre d'*Ignace* Philippe Semmelweiss (1818–1865) (113–124), comparing C.'s representation of Semmelweiss with the historical reality; A. Loselle, 'La traduction musicale de *Voyage au bout de la nuit*: "Journey to the End of Night" de Morton Feldman' (125–136); V. Maurice, 'Une "silencieuse persistance poétique des choses": instruments de musique et tableaux comme décodeurs du texte célinien' (139–69); I. Milkoff, 'L'énumération à trois termes dans *Féerie*' (171–82); P. M. Miroux, 'S'éclater la tête' (183–88), on C.'s interest in the head, specifically injuries to the head; Y. Pagès, 'Les crises d'identité du racisme célinien (II). Entre arguments du ballet et arguments de pamphlet' (189–199), on the historical origins of C.'s racism; J. Steel, 'Le vertige identitaire de la France dans *Féerie pour une autre fois*' (201–12), who explores C.'s tendency in his later fiction to look back on World War I and the *poilus* as representative of a better and more heroic age, inscribing this in a tradition of other texts which at times of crisis and uncertainty hark back to a time when French identity was less problematical; R. Tettamanzi, 'L'iconographie célinienne des pamphlets' (213–21); T. Tinsley, 'Des flammes naît une femme: l'identité et le désir féminins dans *Féerie pour une autre fois* et *Normance*' (223–34), on positive images of women in these novels; P. Watts, 'Les mémoires de Céline' (235–43); and S. Zymla, 'Une représentation fantastique de la mort chez Céline: le personnage mythique de "Caron"' (245–52). Jean-Pierre Martin, *Contre Céline*, Corti, 192 pp., is a polemical study which, like that of Mazgaj above (see BRASILLACH), casts doubt on the rehabilitation of problematic literary figures, by questioning a tendency in C. criticism to examine language and style in isolation from the content, as though it were intellectually acceptable to turn a blind eye to the content of the pamphlets and the later novels. For M., C. is a monster who represents not the future of literature through his modernity, but rather 'une défaite de la litterature' in his insistent racism, and he calls on the reader to resist C.'s spell. Hanns-Erich Kaminski, *Céline en chemise brune*, Mille et une nuits, 94 pp., is a new edition of a contemporary analysis of C., an analysis which in 1938 saw beyond the recent success of *Voyage au bout de la nuit* and *Mort à Crédit* to the dangerous nature of C.'s anti-Semitic pamphlets. The value of this contemporary view is underlined in the *Postface* which challenges the tendency to forgive C. everything because he was such a great writer, and argues for a redressing of the critical balance. *Exil (H)*. Dominique de Roux, *Louis-Ferdinand Celine*, Charleville-Mézières, Au Signe de la Licorne, 53 pp., contains a series of documents, letters and texts on Dominique de Roux, editor of the *Cahiers de l'Herne*, and his role in C. studies.

CENDRARS. A. Leaman, 'Simultaneity and gender in the *Premier livre simultané*', *Symposium*, 51:158–71, explores questions of gender and the search for poetic and sexual identity as elaborated in the joint project between C. and Sonia Delaunay, in which his poem 'La Prose du Transsibérien et de la petite Jehanne de France' is reproduced in a folding book two metres high in which it is placed next to a painting by Delaunay. The project is seen as a representation of the 'movement of life's journey transposed into a kaleidoscopic profusion of colors, shapes, and sensations'. A. Bouillaguet, 'Cendrars, lecteur de lui-même. Un fait d'autotextualité', *Poétique*, 112:409–21, is a closely argues analysis of 'autonutrition', in other words C.'s reworking of one of his early works to create a work of his maturity. 'La Prose du Transsibérien et de la petite Jehanne de France', written when he was 26, is analysed as the *avant-texte* of 'Lotissement du ciel', his 'testament poétique' written at the age of 62. C. Noland, 'Poetry at stake: Blaise Cendrars, cultural studies and the future of poetry in the literature classroom', *PMLA*, 112:40–55, is included in a special number on 'The teaching of literature' and explores the reasons for the decline of teaching poetry. 'Dix-neuf poèmes élastiques' is used to demonstrate how it can be read as 'one set of possible responses to a competitive cultural market controlled increasingly by commercial and popular form', thus highlighting ways in which the study of poetry can be reconciled with the teaching of cultural studies. C. Leroy, 'Les trois rencontres de Léger avec Cendrars', *Europe*, 818–19:105–15, discusses the artistic dialogue between the poet and the artist.

CHAR. Jean-Dominique Poli, *Pour René Char. La place de l'origine*, La Rochelle, Rumeur des Ages, 254 pp., comprises a very full analysis of C.'s poetry, focusing on the question of origins from its first tentative appearances in the early poems to the post-war period, where it became a central element of his writing. The problematic of origins is placed in an autobiographical context, presenting C.'s family background as being the driving force behind this preoccupation. L. Fourcaut, 'L'Eden est après: paradis du poème pulvérisé. Une lecture de "Evadné" de René Char', *RR*, 88:173–87, proposes a detailed reading of the poem in question, discovering contradictions and ambivalences which achieve a creative tension. M. Viegnes, 'Origine, nostalgie et sens de l'histoire dans l'œuvre de René Char, *Neophilologus*, 81:529–37, identifies a central paradox in C.'s poetry, in that while it is characterized by a nostalgia for the past expressed through a utopian dream of a return to a time when man and nature were in harmony, there is also a sense in which his poetry looks ahead to 'ce horizon futur fécondé par la révolte, et une restauration de l'innocence'. C. A. Hackett, 'Correspondance with René Char', *FS*, 51:183–87, reflects on the author's correspondance with the poet over 39 years. C. J. Noland, *'The performace of solitude: Baudelaire, Rimbaud and the resistance poetry of René Char', *FR*, 70:562–74.

CLAUDEL. Pascale Alexandre, *Traduction et création chez Paul Claudel. L'Orestie*, Champion 263 pp, is a scholarly study which firmly places C.'s translation of *L'Orestie* at the heart of C.'s spiritual and literary development. The translation is seen as a formal apprenticeship which will develop ideas for later use. A. points out that it is not simply a question of evaluating the faithfulness of the translation, but also of the evolution of a modern poetics. Dominique Millet-Gérard, *Formes baroques dans Le Soulier de satin. Etude d'esthétique spirituelle* (Unichamp, 68), Champion, 220 pp., attributes the appearance of baroque forms in *Le Soulier de satin* to C.'s time in Brazil, where the spontaneity of baroque, both architectural and spiritual, suited him much better than the narrow spirituality of France. M.-G. argues that C.'s espousal of baroque allowed him to elaborate a new Christian æsthetic. *Paul Claudel et Jacques Madaule. Connaissance et reconnaissance: correspondance 1929–1954*, ed. Andrée Hirschi and Pierre Madaule, Desclée de Brouwer, 1996, 433 pp., contains the previously unpublished correspondence between C. and Madaule, with a substantial introduction and notes. The letters are grouped into three periods: the first from 1929–33, characterized as a dialogue between Christians; the second from 1934–37, focusing on C.'s relations with others, in particular his hostile relationship with the university establishment and, more positively, with other Christian intellectuals; the third from 1943–54, marking the resumption of the correspondence after a break caused by a political disagreement over the Spanish Civil War. The volume provides insights into the intellectual, social, political and religious debates of the time. D. Millet-Gérard, 'L'impossible dialogue d'André Rouveyre et Paul Claudel: "Exaltations éperdues" ou "testament intelligible"?', *RHLF*, 97:71–101, on the difficult relationship between the two men. *Paul Claudel, ed. Pierre Brunel, Cahiers de l'Herne*, 70, 424 pp. Francois Angelier, *Claudel ou la conversion sauvage*, Turnhout, Brepols, 256 pp. Gérard Antoine, *Paul Claudel, Partage de midi: un drame revisité (1948–49)* (Collection du centre Jacques Petit), Lausanne, Age d'homme, 96 pp. *Ecritures claudéliennes: actes du colloque de Besançon 27–28 mai 1994*, Lausanne, Age d'homme, 375 pp. *Claudel et l'Europe: actes du colloque de la Sorbonne, 2 décembre 1995*, Lausanne, Age d'Homme, 153 pp. Ruth Reichelberg, *L'aventure baroque chez Claudel et Calderon* (ALUB, 609), Les Belles Lettres, 1996, 81 pp. *Supplément aux œuvres completes, 4* (Publication Centre Jacques-Petit de l'Université de Besançon), Lausanne, Age d'homme, 237 pp.

COLETTE. Dana Strand, *Colette: A Study of the Short Fiction*, NY, Twayne–London, Prentice-Hall, 1995, xvii + 182 pp., is the first full-length study of C.'s short fiction. The main section contains a detailed analysis, thematically organized, of the short stories which demonstrates the difficulty of categorizing C.'s writing, but also the way in which the stories fit into contemporary notions of feminist writing with their problematizing of gender roles and sexual identity. Less successful are the subsequent sections; the second is a very brief chapter on C. and writing and, even less successful, a final section which simply reproduces articles and chapters by other critics, rather than incorporating other such views into the critical analysis itself. Nicole Ferrier-Caverivière, *Colette L'authentique* (Ecrivains), PUF, 256 pp., attempts to capture 'la vraie Colette', a figure distinct from that of the legend. F.-C. sees in C.'s writing a constant searching for self, a progression towards self-knowledge. A biographical rather than a literary study, this volume progresses not in a chronological fashion, but rather on a thematic basis. 'Colette 1935–54. Colloque de Saint-Sauveur-en-Puisaye, 30–31 mai 1997', *Cahiers Colette*, 19, contains a number of papers on C.'s later writings. The papers are divided into four sections on: 'L'Imaginaire', Le récit et ses techniques', 'Le nouvel ordre de l'écriture' and 'Voix croisées'. Fernande Gontier, Claude Francis, **Colette*, Perrin, 439 pp. Régine Detambel, *Colette, comme une Flore, comme un zoo*, Stock, 280 pp. *Colette: Claudine à l'école et Gigi*, ed. Michèle Hecquet, *Roman 20–50*, no.23, 197 pp.

DESNOS. Y. Seïté, 'Robert Desnos "critique de disques"', *Europe*, 820–21: 62–7, traces D.'s interest in jazz through his musical columns in a number of newspapers.

DRIEU LA ROCHELLE. C. Trévisan, 'Jazz martial. Note sur un poème de Drieu la Rochelle', *Europe*, 820–21: 58–61, sees in D.'s poem 'Jazz' an unexpected association with war with Jazz seen as a type of military music. More predictable is the link with natural energy perceived in the primitive rhythms of jazz.

DUHAMEL. C. Todd, 'Georges Duhamel: enemy-cum-friend of the radio', *MLQ*, 92: 48–59, explores D.'s ambivalent relationship with the radio. Although in charge of programming on French radio from 1939 to 1940, D. was critical of it and what he saw as its negative impact on culture. For him radio discouraged the kind of individual effort and reflection required for reading, which remained for him the channel for true culture. The author clearly has sympathies with D.'s views and sees in them an important message for today's media culture.

FARGUE. Jean-Pierre Goujon, **Leon-Paul Fargue: poète et piéton de Paris* (NRF Biographies), Gallimard, 311 pp.

FONDANE. Benjamin Fondane, *L'Ecrivain devant la révolution*, ed. Louis Janover, Paris-Méditerranée, 119 pp., contains the text of a speech written for, but not presented to the Paris Writers' Congress of 1935, in which F. is critical of the way in which writers are prevented from speaking freely and of the way in which the pressing problems of the 1930s have been evaded. A long introduction places the speech in its historical and political context, and is critical of those who followed the Communist Party line in literary questions, while praising F. whose speech is seen as 'un acte de résistance, la réaffirmation [...] des droits imprescriptibles de l'expérience politique.'

GIDE. Hilary Hutchinson, *Théories et pratique de l'influence dans la vie et l'œuvre immoraliste de Gide* (La Thésothèque, 31), Fleury-sur-Orne, Minard, 355 pp., is a reworked version of a thesis on the question of influences in G.'s writing. Not satisfied simply with identifying influences on G., Hutchinson analyses G.'s theory of influence. She identifies four different types of influence elaborated by Gide; 'influence par rétroaction, influence par ressemblance, influence par autorisation, influence par protestation', and in the light of these theories explores how G.'s writing is in practice infused by influences, both on the biographical and literary levels. An analysis of three of G.'s works within this framework forms the concluding section. Russell West, *Conrad and Gide: Translation, Transference and Intertextuality* (Internationale Forschungen zur allgemeinen und vergleichenden Literaturwissenshaft), Amsterdam–Atlanta, Rodopi, 1996, 187 pp., tackles another aspect of the same topic. This is a well-written and persuasive account of G.'s literary debt to Joseph Conrad, a debt which began with G.'s reading of C.'s fiction, progressed into translation, an important part of his activity and one which is associated for G. with detailed reflection on a text, and culminated in his gradual distancing from C. as he matured as an artist. The analysis looks in particular at the influence of *Lord Jim* on *Les Caves du Vatican*, on G.'s translation of *Typhoon*, and, as G. gradually asserted his own identity as a writer, the relationship between *Under Western Eyes* and *Les Faux-Monnayeurs* and between *Heart of Darkness* and *Voyage au Congo*. In broader critical terms, the relationship between the two writers is placed at a crucial moment in the development of modernism, with G. going beyond C.'s response in order to find a way out of the dilemmas of modernism. Claude Foucart, *Le temps de la "gadouille" ou Le dernier rendez-vous d'André Gide avec l'Allemagne (1933–1951)* (Ser. II, Gallo-Germanica, 21), NY–Berne–Frankfurt, Lang, 220 pp., traces G.'s complex relationship with Germany in these years, contrasting it with his earlier literary and political attitude to the country in the wake of World War I and his commitment to communism. He demonstrates how G.'s attitude to the country is ambivalent: on the one hand he sees in Germany a utopian vision of how Europe could develop, yet he also perceives Germany as a threat. Jean-Michel Wittmann, *Symboliste et déserteur. Les œuvres fin-de-siècle' d'André Gide* (Romantisme et modernités, 13), Champion, 408 pp., is a detailed and scholarly analysis of G.'s reaction against the symbolism of his early 'fin-de-siècle' works, and demonstrates how this reaction led him not only towards a new form of satirical and parodic writing which developed into the *sotie*, but also led him to a new conception of the artist. Yaffa Wolfman, *Engagement et écriture chez Andre Gide*, La

Riche, Nizet, 404 pp., is a wide-ranging study of G.'s fiction, non-fiction, journals and correspondence within the framework of *engagement*. Anxious to dispell the image of G. as an æsthete unconcerned by the outside world, W. sets out to identify the ways in which he expressed views on war, colonialism and totalitarianism. Since W. concentrates very much on the techniques used to elaborate these issues, it is surprising that such a slippery term as *engagement* is not defined in more detail and in relation to other committed writers. While a sustained attempt is made to incorporate G.'s fiction into the analysis, W is forced to admit, albeit implicitly, that *engagement* is not easily detected in these works, despite the sociological themes which she has identified in them. Pierre Lepape, **Andre Gide: le messager*, Seuil, 512 pp. J.-M. Wittmann, 'Responsabilité de l'écrivain et légitimité de l'écriture dans *L'Immoraliste*', *LR*, 51 : 75–83, explores the tension involved in G.'s attempts to reconcile the notion of the responsibility of the writer and his faithfulness to the more abstract ideal of the work of art, an ideal which has its origins in his *fin-de-siècle* works. P. W. Lasowski, 'Gidean nights', *RSH*, 248 : 207–20, in a special number on 'La Nuit', explores 'l'ecriture de la nuit' in G.'s writings. R. La Capra, *'Rencontre avec André Gide', *Positif*, 433 : 56–57. E. Marty, *'La politique de l'écrivain — Pierre Herbart et André Gide', *NRF*, 529 : 41–57.

GIONO. W. D. Redfern, *Giono. Le Hussard sur le toit* (GIGFL, 40), 64 pp., provides a lively introduction to G.'s novel, placing it as one in a tradition of novels about plagues. Arguing that to read the novel, as to read *La Peste*, as an allegory of World War II is a reductive approach, R. elaborates on its *démesure*, its insistence on finding life in death and sets it in the lineage of the literature of extreme situations. A final chapter charts the difficulty of transferring *Le Hussard* to film. Dismissing psychoanalytical approaches to the novel, R. extols G.'s skill as a story-teller. Véronique Anglard, *Les romans de Giono* (Mémo, 62), Seuil, 64 pp. *Giono autrement: l'apocalyptique, le panique, le dionysiaque*, ed. Béatrice Bonhomme, Aix-en-Provence, Provence U.P., 1996, 119 pp. M. Bertoncini, 'Petit précis de décomposition du roman réaliste: le début du *Hussard sur le toit*', *Littératures*, 37 : 111–33, is a long and complicated analysis of the opening of this novel which pays particular attention to the musical motifs underlying its structure, making comparisons with *Madame Bovary* on the fictional level and with expressionism in the visual domain.

GIRAUDOUX. Elisabeth Scheele, *Le 'Discours aux morts' de Jean Giraudoux* (PUE, ser. 13, Langue et Littérature françaises, 214), NY–Berne–Frankfurt, Lang, 292 pp., is a very full analysis of this famous speech from *La Guerre de Troie n'aura pas lieu*. While the focus might seem from the title of the work to be excessively narrow, in fact the analysis is very wide-ranging and places the *Discours aux morts* in the context of other such speeches from Greek, German and French classical drama. The study is organized thematically and ends on a very personal note of appeal for literary and media representations of war to play their part not in the promotion of war, but in the promotion of peace. **Electre de Jean Giraudoux: regards croisés*, ed. Jacques Body and Pierre Brunel, Klincksieck, 201 pp. 'La Folle de Chaillot 1945–1995. Lectures et métamorphoses', ed. Guy Teissier and Pierre d'Almeida, *CJG*, 25, is the second volume celebrating the fiftieth anniversary (in 1995) of the first performance of *La Folle de Chaillot* and contains a number of articles and notes on various aspects of the play. V. B. Korzeniowska, 'Elementary ecofeminism or patriarchal paradigm. Giraudoux's *Suzanne et le Pacifique* and *Supplément au Voyage de Cook*', *NFS*, 36:57–70, sees in G. 'a precursor of the modern ecofeminist movement' in his advocacy of the restoration of man's close association with nature, a restoration which can only be accomplished by women. G.'s credentials as an ecofeminist are measured against these two texts, and the limitations of his position explored.

GRACQ. **Julien Gracq*, ed. Jean-Louis Leutrat (Cahiers de l'Herne), Fayard. 405 pp. Alain Coelho, **Julien Gracq, appareillage: suivi d'un entretien avec Julien Gracq*, Nantes, Joseph K., 87 pp.

GREEN. Michael O'Dwyer, *Julien Green: a Critical Study*, Dublin, Four Courts Press, 165 pp. is a sympathetic and sensitive survey of G.'s prolific writing career. O'D. provides lucid insights into all aspects of G.'s writing: the *nouvelles*, the novels, autobiographical writing, his journal and other miscellaneous writings. Although dealing with a vast amount of material. O'D. succeeds in presenting a succinct synthesis which yet avoids superficiality, highlighting recurrent themes and issues as well as identifying a progression through the years of writing.

GUILLOUX. Jean-Claude Bourlès, *Louis Guilloux: les maisons d'encre* (Maisons d'écrivain), Saint-Cyr-sur-Loire, C. Pirot, 143 pp., is a series of reflections, rather than a straightforward biography, on the life of G., particularly in relation to Saint-Brieuc and the house in which he lived there. It is a sympathetic and very readable account, which evokes very well the life of this largely neglected author.

JACOB. Arlette Albert-Birot, *Max Jacob et la création: colloque d'Orléans* (Surfaces), J.-M. Place, 256 pp.

LEROUX. E. M. Knutson, 'Le fantôme de l'Opéra: le charme de la supercherie', *FR*, 70:416–26, attributes the appeal of L.'s famous novel to the ludic nature of the text and its constant alternation between the evocation of the fantastic, the story of the phantom, and the voice of rational discourse attempting to explain the apparently supernatural.

MALRAUX. Patrick Dambon. *André Malraux ou l'anti-destin*, Woignarue, Vague Verte, 1996, 40 pp., sees a unity of thought in M.'s writing career, so often divided by critics into two distinct halves. For D. the 'fil conducteur' of M.'s work is the struggle against destiny, with art an 'anti-destin', that which gives meaning to the human condition. Mireille Cornud-Peyron, *La Condition humaine de Malraux* (Repères Hachette, 26), Hachette, 1996, 96 pp., and Marc Bochet, *L'Espoir de Malraux* (Repères Hachette, 27), Hachette, 1996, 96 pp., are both succinct and practical introductions to the two novels, oriented towards student readers. Following the same format, the studies contain commentaries on the text, analyses of the major characters and the principle themes, together with a series of critical judgements on the novels. Pol Vandromme, **Malraux: du farfelu au mirobolant*, Lausanne, Age d'homme, 73 pp. Robert Grossmann, **Le choix de Malraux: l'Alsace une seconde patrie*, Strasbourg, Nuée Bleue, 160 pp. **André Malraux: actes du colloque de Nice du 15 mars 1996*, ed. Béatrice Bonhomme, Sophia Antipolis, Nice U.P., 1996, 88 pp. Komnen Becirovic, **André Malraux, chantre de la grandeur humaine*, Lausanne, Age d'homme, 1997, 80 pp. G. Harris, 'Malraux, myth, political commitment and the Spanish Civil War', *Modern and Contemporary France*, 5:319–228, attempts to disentangle myth and reality in M.'s political commitment as represented in *L'Espoir*. H. argues that the novel is politically committed only insofar as it is anti-fascist and that it is by no means a pro-communist novel. This distinction is made in order to account for M.'s subsequent development towards Gaullism which is not therefore the betrayal of communism it has frequently been seen as. M.-P. Ha, 'The cultural other in Malraux's Asian novels', *FR*, 71:33–43, is an interesting discussion of the problematic nature of M.'s representation of the 'cultural other'. H. argues that despite his fascination with oriental culture, his representation of East–West relations is marred by the unequal power relationship between colonizer and colonized. This ambivalence is most marked in M.'s drawing of hybrid characters who, far from representing a union of two cultures, are anxious to reject their Asian culture. C. Moatti, '"Lunes en papier" signé Léger et Malraux', *Europe*, 818–19, 122–35, presents a brief analysis of *Lunes en papier*, an early work by M., illustrated by Léger, and seen as an early indication of the artistic direction M. was to take. C. Moatti, 'Malraux vingt ans plus tard', *ib.*, 815:209–16, is a presentation of recent M. criticism on the twentieth anniversary of his death, an occasion which marked 'un regain exceptionnel d'attention pour l'homme et son œuvre'. L. Fraisse, 'Le portrait dérobé dans *La*

Condition humaine', *Poétique*, 113:83–96, explores the function of M.'s representation of his fictional characters, defined through action rather than detailed portraits, looking in particular at 'les conséquences pratiques de cet engagement de la description dans l'action'.

MAURIAC.   Pierre Mauriac, *François Mauriac, mon frère. Correspondance Pierre et François Mauriac* (Malagar), Le Bouscat, L'Esprit du temps, 111 pp., contains a previously unpublished correspondence between the two brothers, primarily letters from Pierre to François. The text linking them was written in the late 1940s, although there was at the time no intention to publish. The letters demonstrate movingly the affectionate relationship between the brothers which persisted despite their political differences. *Mauriac Malagar*, ed. Centre François Mauriac de Malagar, Bordeaux, Confluences, 283 pp., is a lavishly illustrated volume published to commemorate the opening in July 1997 of the Centre François Mauriac at Malagar, M.'s property, which was handed over to the Conseil Régional d'Aquitaine and has been restored to create a 'centre de documentation' for both public and researchers. The volume includes numerous photographs of M., his family and the property itself from the family archives. as well as texts by Philippe Sollers, Claude Roy, Jean Mauriac and others on the importance of Malagar in M.'s life and work.

MICHAUX.   Anne le Bouteiller, **Michaux, les voix de l'être exilé*, L'Harmattan, 383 pp.

MILLE.   Yaël Schlick, 'The "French Kipling": Pierre Mille's popular colonial fiction', *CLS*, 34:226–41, demonstrates that while M. saw the function of 'littérature coloniale', unlike earlier exotic colonial fiction by writers like Loti, as the transmission of a realistic depiction of colonial life for the French public, his fiction is by no means an objective or neutral representation of this reality, but is imbued with a colonialist ideology which sought to engender support at home in France for the nation's colonizing mission.

NIZAN.   Geoffrey T. Harris, *Antoine Bloyé and La Nausée. A Neglected Intertextuality*, Salford, European Studies Research Unit Working Papers in Literary and Cultural Studies, 22 pp., argues persuasively that it is *Antoine Bloyé* rather than *La Nausée* which should be considered as the prototype of the existentialist novel. In support of his argument, H. adduces a significant number of parallels between the two novels. On the general level there is the proto-existentialist discourse and the critique of bourgeois values, while on a more specific level, H. cites the similar treatment of female characters, the importance of railways and the notions of nausea and contingency.

PAULHAN.   Frédéric Badré, *Paulhan le juste*, Grasset, 1996, 330 pp., is a very detailed, but always readable biography of P. which will be of use not only to scholars of Paulhan and the NRF but also to those with an interest in the intellectual and cultural currents of the 20th c., which are evoked through the figure of P., who, throughout much of his career was at the centre of French literary and intellectual life as editor of the NRF.

PÉGUY. Françoise Gerbod and Françoise Mélino, *L'Egalité au tournant du siècle. Péguy et ses contemporains* (Varia, 13), Champion, 1997, 296 pp. H. Douillet, 'De la suite du *Mystère de la Charité* au *Porche du mystère de la deuxième vertu* de Charles Péguy: nationalisme ou patriotisme', *LR*, 51:85–93, defends P. from the charge of nationalism, seeing him instead as a patriot. C. Daudin, 'Péguy et le dépassement de la littérature polémique', *RHLF*, 97:274–88, demonstrates that while P.'s writing is in a sense polemical, it is distinguished from the usual run of polemical texts by its tendency to persuade and to touch the reader rather than seeking confrontation through 'une écriture neuve qui s'efforce de supprimer l'obstacle entre l'auteur et le lecteur'.

PERSE. Andrew Small, '"Oiseaux" de Saint-John Perse: un art poétique', *FrF*, 22:279–302, presents 'Oiseaux' as a poem which is both an exposition of the author's poetics, 'un traité de l'esthétique persienne', and an attempt to put them into practice.

PONGE. Annick Fritz-Smead, *Francis Ponge de l'écriture à l'œuvre* (Currents in Comparative Romance Languages and Literatures, 47), NY–Berne–Frankfurt, Lang, x + 150 pp., is a sensitive analysis of P.'s attempts to translate faithfully into poetry the reality of objects. F.-S. show how P., suspicious of language and its ability to give an objective account of things, challenges accepted views of poetic language, the role of the poet and genre definition in an attempt to convey the specificity and solidity of objects, 'traduire la matière des choses par la matière du langage'. P. is seen as a visionary in this respect, his approach to everyday objects heralding a new respect between the poet and his world. Jean-Charles Gateau, *Le parti-pris des choses de Francis Ponge* (Foliothèque), Gallimard, 224 pp. D. E. Sears, '"La loi et les prophètes": Ponge, the Bible and the *Proême*', *FrF*, 22:303–17, explores P.'s ambivalent ('love-hate') relationship with the Bible, tracing intertextual references and biblical parodies, illustrated with particular reference to *Proêmes*.

PRÉVERT. Jean-Claude Lamy, *Prévert, les frères amis*, Robert Laffont, 350 pp., is an informative and sympathetic biography of the Prévert brothers. While Pierre was largely hidden in his brother's shadow, L. shows with affection their joint career, not wishing to separate 'les frères amis'. The volume is also a record of the cultural history of the 1920s to the 1970s, tracing in particular the involvement of the brothers with the surrealists and with the cinema of the 1930s and 1940s, when they collaborated with Marcel Carné, Jean Vigo and Jean Renoir. Bernard Chardère, **Jacques Prévert: inventaire d'une vie* (Jeunesse), Gallimard, 128 pp.

PROUST. Luc Fraisse, *Proust au miroir de sa correspondance* (Les livres et les hommes), SEDES, 1996, 514 pp. is a substantial, scholarly yet very accessible analysis of P.'s correspondence, a corpus of some 5,000 letters. The work is divided into three sections, concentrating in turn on 'Une personnalité d'écrivain', 'L'écrivain public' and 'L'écrivain au travail'. The first section uses the correspondence to elaborate on P.'s family, illness and preoccupation with death; the second considers his homosexuality and his representation of his time, while the third explores P.'s way of writing as well as his perception of his artistic vocation. This will be an essential reference work for the P. scholar, but also contains much of interest to the non-specialist. Patrick Brunel, *Le rire de Proust* (Littératures de notre siècle, 5), Champion, 272 pp., proposes a detailed, lucid analysis of *A la recherche* as a comic novel, maintaining that while P. himself recognized the comic element in his work, little critical attention has been paid to it. Judiciously ruling out a general analysis of *le comique*, B. concentrates instead on the text and its characters, looking in turn at the ludic nature of character representation and of the narrative, and at the figure of the narrator, concluding that far from having a purely decorative function, the comic is very much part of P.'s view of the world and of humanity. Catherine Bidou-Zachariasen, *Proust sociologue. De la maison aristocratique au salon bourgeois*, Descartes et Cie, 212 pp., sees *A la recherche* not as a novel which reflects on a certain sociological reality but rather as a sociological work in its own right, offering a model for the understanding of the society of the time. Concentrating on the 'scènes et espaces mondaines, B.-Z. presents a synchronic and diachronic analysis of the relationship between the aristocracy in decline and the rising bourgeoisie, finding in these scenes a crucial cultural battleground between the classes which came ever closer together in the transition to modernity. Luc Fraisse, *Proust et le japonisme*, Strasbourg U.P., 112 pp., investigates the influence of *japonisme*, much in vogue at the time of the writing *of A la recherche* on Proust. F. shows that it was not merely a case of using the trend as a decorative background for his works, but a means of reviving the tradition through his projected novel, and looks at the way in which *japonisme* infuses the work. *Le Jaloux: lecteur de signes, Proust, Svevo, Tolstoï* (Cahiers de littérature générale et comparée), SEDES, 1996, 81 pp., contains articles on works by these three authors where the figure of the 'jaloux' is always a man, reflecting on the unfaithful woman, on his rival and on himself, and constantly on the lookout for signs to interpret. This activity is seen as a metaphor for the act of reading. P. E. Robert, 'le jaloux, archétype proustien' (61–70) studies the function of signs and their interpretation by 'le jaloux' in *Un amour de Swann*, before looking at jealousy in the context of the whole of P.'s work. Both P. Chardin, 'La jalousie ou la fureur de lire' (11–29), and D. Lévy-Bertherat, 'De la lecture à l'invention des signes: la jalousie chez Tolstoï, Svevo et Proust' (71–79), look at the question of reading signs in a more general framework. Juliette Frølich, *Des hommes, des femmes et des choses. Langages de l'Objet dans le roman de Balzac à Proust*, Saint-Denis, Vincennes U.P., 171 pp., proposes a detailed reading of the role of the object in Balzac, Flaubert and P. where it is not simply an element of decor but central to the reader's interpretation of character and period. Taking as examples the 'romans parisiens' of the three writers, she distinguishes the unique way in which each author used objects: B. as social historian, F. as 'moraliste' and P. as 'mémorialiste'. The two chapters on P. focus on 'Proust paysagiste de Paris' in an analysis of the spaces inhabited by Mme Swann and on 'L'écriture nature morte' in which P. attempts to emulate in writing Chardin's visual perception of the reality of everyday objects. Bal Mieke, *Images litteraires ou Comment lire Proust visuellement*, Toulouse–Le Mirail U.P., 230 pp. Jacques Dubois, *Pour Albertine: Proust et le sens du social*, Seuil, 182 pp. Annick Bouillaguet, *Proust et les Goncourt; suivi de Le Pastiche du Journal dans Le temps retrouvé* (*ALM*), Lettres Modernes, 112 pp. Philip Bailey, *Proust's Self Reader: the Pursuit of Literature as Privileged Communication*, Birmingham, AL, Summa, 182 pp. Martine Blanche, *Poétique des tableaux chez Proust et Matisse*, Birmingham, AL, Summa, 1996, 206 pp. M. Bowie, 'Proust and politics', *Minogue Vol.*, 183–213, is a stimulating analysis of *A la recherche* as a profoundly political novel. While clearly the novel is not political on a document-ary level, B. demonstrates the complex political strands of the work, concluding that P.'s political vision is an intensely pessimistic one. F. Letoublon and L. Fraisse, 'Proust et la descente aux enfers: les souvenirs symboliques de la Nekuia d'Homère dans *A la recherche du temps perdu*', *RHLF*, 97:1058–85, points out that while P. is acknow-ledged as a 'phare de la modernité', he none the less makes extensive use of his knowledge of antiquity. The motif of Homer's Nekuia is recalled and is seen to be symbolic of P.'s perception of the act of creation, the vocation of the writer. R. MacKenzie, 'Hitting the mine: modulations in narrative voice in Proust's *A la recherche*', *Minogue Vol.*, 165–82, is a close reading of a passage from *La Prisonnière* which explores questions of narrative identity and authority through the shifts in the narrative voice, shifts identified with different types of memory, voluntary, involuntary and associative. P. M. Wetherill, 'Flânes proustiennes', *SFr*, 60, 1996:529–45, places *A la recherche* in the context of growing 19th-c. interest in *flânerie*, travel and tourism.

Discussion of Baudelaire and Flaubert paves the way for an illustration of the specific function of travel and movement in P. which W. sees as intimately bound up with the experience of involuntary memory. The nature of his interest is therefore radically different from his predecessors. M. R. Finn, 'Neurasthenia, hysteria, androgyny: the Goncourts and Marcel Proust', *FS*, 51:293–304, explores the influence on P. of his reading of the Goncourts, in particular the way in which P. derived inspiration from the Goncourts' interest in nervous diseases. This influence is traced through a series of parallels between *Germinie Lacerteux* and *A la recherche*. R. M. J. Mackenzie, 'Marcel aux enfers', *AJFS*, 34:202–15, is an analysis of the relationship between myth and irony with particular reference to the 'mythème' of the descent to the Underworld in *A la recherche*. L. Cairns, 'Homosexuality and lesbianism in Proust's *Sodome et Gomorrhe*', *FS*, 51:43–57, demonstrates that alongside the explicit negative presentation of homosexuality there is a 'contestatory subtext' which shows it in a much more favourable light. This is in striking opposition to the unremittingly negative representation of lesbianism which, C. argues is filtered through Marcel's fear of it. While acknowledging that this difference of presentation may have its roots in greater social antagonism to lesbianism or in P.'s own rejection of the feminine side of himself which accounted for his own homosexuality, C. chooses to see this disparity in terms of the demands of the narrative, which require that Marcel resents the lesbian power which takes Albertine from him. D. Cohn, 'L'ambiguïté générique de Proust', *Poétique*, 109:105–23, is a closely argued discussion of the ambiguities surrounding questions of genre in *A la recherche*: is the work a novel, an autobiography or both at the same time? The discussion is placed in the context of Lejeune's definition of autobiography and of a whole range of critical interpretations of this problem. The analysis ends not with a resolution but with a series of new questions. G. Henrot, 'Le fléau de la balance. Poétique de la réminiscence', *Poétique*, 113:61–82, explores the possibility of a fruitful interaction between the separate approaches of structuralism and genetic criticism in P. criticism and applies it to an analysis of involuntary memory.

QUENEAU. Jean Helion, **Lettres d'Amerique. Correspondance avec Raymond Queneau 1934–1967*, IMEC, 184 pp. **Raymond Queneau. Journaux 1914–1965*, ed. Anne Isabelle Queneau, Gallimard, 1996, 1,242 pp.

REVERDY. E.-A Hubert, 'Envergure de Léger selon Reverdy, *Europe*, 818–19:116–21, discusses the relationship between R. and L., the use made by R. of L.'s work in *Nord-Sud* and his particular interest in L. as painter of the city.

ROLLAND. Pierre Sipriot, *Guerre et paix autour de Romain Rolland. Le désastre de l'Europe 1914–1918*, Bartillat, 430 pp., closely based upon R.'s *Journal des années de guerre*, traces R.'s sustained opposition to war. While never politically engaged, R. did not remain on the sidelines but worked tirelessly for peace. S.'s book is a substantial work not just on R. but also on the European experience of the Great War. Maria Hülle-Keeding, **Romain Rollands visionäres Beethovenbild im Jean-Christophe* (Studien zur Französische Literatur, 7), NY–Berne–Frankfurt, Lang, 224 pp.

ROUSSEL. François Caradec, **Raymond Roussel*, Fayard, 455 pp.

ROMAINS. Dirck Degraeve, *La Part du mal: essai sur l'imaginaire de Jules Romains dans Les Hommes de bonne volonté* (HICL, 360), 311 pp., is a lucid and meticulous analysis of the role of evil in *Les Hommes de bonne volonté*. D. explores some of the ambiguities implicit in the work: the inadequacy of good will in the historical framework of the novel set against the overriding presence of evil. Evil proliferates throughout the novel on both the individual and collective level and it seems to be oriented much more towards evil than its title would suggest. Parallels are drawn between family life, social groups and the war — all characterized by evil. The only possible solution is seen in art, but the momentous historical framework of the novel means that this is only a very partial solution to the enormity of evil.

SACHS. B. Acinas, 'Entre l'autobiographie et le picaresque: Maurice Sachs', *LR*, 51:95–105, argues that S.'s life tended to dominate critical perceptions of his writing. She proposes an analysis of *Histoire de John Cooper* as a picaresque novel and, placing his choice of genre in the context of his own life, explores the links between fiction and autobiography.

SAINT-EXUPÉRY. Walter Wagner, *La Conception de l'amour-amitié dans l'œuvre de Saint-Exupéry* (PUE, Série 13, Langue et littérature françaises, 212), NY–Berne–Frankfurt, Lang, 1996, 234 pp., is a very sympathetic and readable study which considers the theme of *amour-amitié* in the novels in an attempt to complete the picture of S. which he feels has been distorted by the popularity of *Le Petit Prince*. W. attempts to define this dual concept in order to ascertain what it meant to S. He places the notion of friendship in its historical context to distinguish *amour-amitié* from *amour-passion* and this is then explored through the fiction. D. Boissier, 'Saint-Exupéry et Tristan Derème: l'origine du *Petit Prince*', *RHLF*, 97:622–48, proposes a source for *Le Petit Prince* in Derème's *Patachou, petit garçon*, published 14 years before the more famous novel. This assertion is supported by a series of lexical and thematic parallels between the two works and by a reminder of S.'s need to write a work which had been requested by his publishers, at a time of moral crisis for the writer, a pressure which led to his use of the source book. Léon Werth, *Saint-Exupéry tel que je l'ai connu*, V. Hamy, 160 pp.

SOUPAULT. S. is another writer who has benefited from increased critical interest in the centenary year of his birth. Myriam Boucharenc, *L'Echec et son double. Philippe Soupault romancier* (Littératures de notre siècle, 1), Champion, 406 pp., proposes a sustained and detailed analysis of S.'s novelistic output, an analysis which takes as its starting point the relative neglect of the author's work, in particular his novels. She accounts for such neglect by evoking the difficulty of achieving a global view of such a substantial œuvre as well as S.'s own ambivalent relationship to the novel. Such critical failure is matched by S.'s own sense of failure which permeates his writing and which B. sees as an integral part of S.'s æsthetics. She explores a number of questions arising from this perspective, attempting to tease out the relationship of cause and effect between failure and creation. These questions are elegantly elaborated in a work which makes a substantial contribution to setting right critical neglect of Soupault. *Portrait(s) de Philippe Soupault*, ed. Mauricette Berne and Jacqueline Chénieux-Gendron, Bibliothèque Nationale de France, 182 pp., is a volume published to accompany a centenary exhibition on S. It contains a selection of illustrations: photographs, letters and a number of accompanying texts. Some of the latter are by friends of the author, others are more scholarly and include: M.-C. Bancquart, '"Balayeur inspiré": Philippe Soupault et Paris' (109–17); D. Lefort, 'Cette voix qui répète mon nom' (119–29), on the search for the self; I. Cantaloube-Ferrieu, 'Airs' (130–42), on S.'s *chansons*; and H. Meschannic, 'Le rythme de Philippe Soupault' (143–63). It also contains an autobiographical account and a bibliography. Lydie Lachenal, *Philippe Soupault. Sa vie, son œuvre, chronologie*, Lachenal et Ritter, 199 pp., is a useful reference work for the reader interested in S. or in surrealism. Like the preceding volume it contains a chronology of the author's life, but the major part of the text is taken up with an extensive chronological bibliography of S.'s works classed by genre. Sylvie Cassayre, **Poétique de l'espace et imaginaire dans l'oeuvre de Philippe Soupault* (Bibliothèque des Lettres Modernes, 40), Lettres Modernes, 379 pp.

TARDIEU. Jean-Louis Cottet-Ernard, **Jean Tardieu, un passant, un passeur*, Charlieu, La Bartavelle, 100 pp.

VALÉRY. William Kluback, *Paul Valéry. The Continuous Search for Reality* (AUS, Series II: Romance Languages and Literature, 219), NY–Berne–Frankfurt, Lang, xii + 173 pp., is the fourth volume in a series of critical essays on V., part of the author's continued reflections on the man whom he sees as 'one of the great Europeans'. K. focuses on V.'s aphorisms and explores the major themes of history and mortality, with particular reference to *M. Teste* and *Mon Faust*. While lacking in the usual scholarly apparatus of biliography and footnotes, it is nonetheless a very scholarly study in its range of reference and perception. Christina Vogel, *Les Cahiers de Paul Valéry: 'To go to the last point': celui au-delà duquel tout sera changé*, L'Harmattan, 284 pp. Serge Bourjéa, *Paul Valéry: le sujet et l'écriture*, L'Harmattan, 381 pp. M. Jarrety, 'Valéry: Faust écrit', *Europe*, 813–14: 117–23, contains a brief analysis of V.'s *Mon Faust* in a special number on Faust. S. Bourjéa, 'Paul Valéry: "un certain regard"', *Poétique*, 113: 29–44, explores the nature of V.'s *regard*, acknowledging that his work is characterized by 'une multiplicité de visages qui semblent s'exclure l'un l'autre'.

WEIL. Rachel Feldhay Brenner, *Writing as Resistance. Four Women Confronting the Holocaust: Edith Stein, Simone Weil, Anne Frank and Etty Hillesum*, University Park, Pennsylvania State U.P., 224 pp., is a persuasive and rigorous analysis of the response of these four women to the Holocaust. W. emerges as an intensely problematic figure in terms of her resistance to human suffering which coexisted with sustained silence on the subject of the Holocaust. The author focuses particularly on the complex nature of W.'s extreme self-sacrifice as a means of resistance and of her rejection of her Jewishness at a time when it could have been construed as a form of escapism. The four writers are systematically compared and contrasted, and this comparative approach provides valuable insights into W. and her work. R. Chenavier, 'Simone Weil, "la haine juive de soi"', *Historical Reflexions*, 23: 73–103, is another interesting study of W.'s problematic relationship with her Jewishness. Thomas Stokes, *Audience, Intention and Rhetoric in Pascal and Simone Weil* (Currents in Comparative Romance Languages and Literatures, 22), NY–Berne–Frankfurt, Lang, 1996, viii + 170 pp., sees numerous parallels between W. and Pascal in their respective search for God. These parallels are elaborated before setting out to analyse them in terms of the audiences the two writers were writing for, the purpose of their writing and the devices and language used to achieve these aims. The work is organized thematically, rather than by writer, and S. carries off this approach, successfully casting light on both writers.

THE TWENTIETH CENTURY SINCE 1945

By H. G. McIntyre, *Lecturer in French at the University of Strathclyde*

1. GENERAL

Robinson, *Women*, I–IV, is a substantial four-volume reference work containing entries on a wide selection of women writers, both well-known and less familiar. While undoubtedly an impressive undertaking and a useful reference point, it differs from the norm in that each entry is composed of a selection of extracts from other critics and sources. It is arguable that this policy always results in a representative overview of the writer concerned, especially in the shorter entries. Bell, *Aphorism*, claims to be breaking new ground, since there is to date no substantial study of this phenomenon in the novel. This study is limited, however, to seven specific novels, even if they do represent a wide spectrum of modern Francophone writing, including Canada, Switzerland and the Caribbean. The Hexagon is represented by Saint-Exupéry, *Terre des Hommes*, and Simon, *La Route des Flandres*. An introductory chapter draws on a wide variety of theorists to define the nature and narrative function of aphorism, establishing an analytical schema which is applied rigorously to each individual text. Discussion is nothing if not methodical and well-signposted throughout. M. Antle, 'The frame of desire in the novel of the 1980s and 1990s', Fisher, *Differences*, 189–95, ponders the use of photographic and filmic images in the contemporary novel, in particular how seeing the action through various kinds of frame (doors, windows) distances the viewing subject from the object of his carnal desire. Despite the ambitious title, however, the article concentrates on Duras, *Blue Eyes, Black Hair* and Guibert, *L'Homme au chapeau rouge*. P. Horn, *Modern Jewish Writers of France*, NY, Mellen, 176 pp., deliberately selects writers who are self-consciously Jewish and deal mostly or solely with Jewish themes. This inevitably excludes a number of famous names, e.g. Maurois or Sarraute, but these are well catered for elsewhere. The book is a mixture of general background chapters surveying topics such as the literature of the Holocaust or particular groups of writers, e.g. Ashkenazi and Sephardic writers, and specific chapters on individual writers, e.g. Gary and Albert Cohen. The analysis tends to be more descriptive than critical, but the application of Jewishness as a criterion has the advantage of bringing a number of lesser-known figures to our attention. T. Freeman, 'Minor plays, major polemics: Korean War crossfire in the French theatre 1951–52', *FrCS*, 8: 81–92, turns his back on the recognized canon of Fourth Republic theatre (Sartre, Camus etc.), and considers 'a substantial corpus' of other successful plays dealing with political issues which made the Parisian theatre an ideological battlefield at the peak of the Cold War. Dramatists like Arout, Raphael-Leygues, Soria, Claude Martin and Henri Dumas rate a mention, but there is more detailed consideration of two diametrically opposed responses to the climate of fear engendered by the McCarthyite anti-communist witch hunts: Marcel, *Rome n'est plus dans Rome*, and Vailland, *Le Colonel Foster plaidera coupable*. L. Enjolras, 'Gomorrah and the word; but where are they?', Fisher, *Differences*, 215–25, surveys and laments the dearth of lesbian writing today and the lack of academic recognition, before turning to an analysis of Hélène de Monferrand's first novel, *Les Amies d'Héloise* (1990), awarded the Goncourt ironically not for its specifically Lesbian content but its general literary merits. M. Sirvent, 'Reader-investigators in the post-*Nouveau Roman*: Lahougue, Peeters and Perec', *RR*, 88:315–33, argues that a new hybrid, narrative form is emerging, sharing characteristics of the mystery story and the early *nouveau roman*. The distinguishing characteristic of the new genre seems to be the crucial pro-active role of the reader participating in an intrigue which they are expected to complete. The three novels chosen as representative are Peeters, *La Bibliothèque de Villers*, Lahougue, *Comptine des Height* and Perec, '*53 jours*'. There is interesting discussion of the debt of all three to Agatha Christie and of Lahougue's debt to Simenon. P. Mesnard, 'Terreur ou fiction chez les écrivains français de l'après-guerre', *RLC*, 71:151–64, looks at how postwar intellectuals came to terms with the terror they had experienced during the war and in particular the revealed horror of the concentration camps. Paulhan, Sartre, Duras, Bataille and Blanchot are mentioned, among others. N. Elia, 'In the making: Beur fiction and identity construction', *WLT*, 71:47–54, surveys a number of examples of contemporary Beur fiction in France (Kalouaz, Yacine, Tadjar, but mainly Mehdi Charef, *Le thé au harem d'Archi Ahmed*), to illustrate the social and racial problems faced by this substantial ethnic minority. M. Sorrell, 'Irony and the female self: Claude de Burine, Andrée Chedid and Jo-Ann Léon', *AJFS*, 34:313–20, considers the use of irony by three women poets all linked by the 'structural irony' of trying to express and protect female identity in a language which is 'the hunting ground of the predatory male'. The subsequent analysis identities fairly straightforwardly some examples and expressions of irony in each author in turn. J. M. Maulpoix, 'Existe-t-il en France un nouveau lyrisme?' *ib.*, 259–69, seems to offer something of a judgement of Solomon in answer to the question posed. On the one hand, he subscribes to a renaissance of lyricism in the eighties but, on the other hand, despite dividing lyricism into several sub-categories, deems it to be part of a 'permanence et reviviscence du lyrisme' which is a perennial expression of human experience. The article does, however, contain a good roll-call of contemporary poets. M. Bishop, 'Pinson, Tellermann, Leclair, Zins: shifting modes of figurative being', *ib.*, 283–97, offers a few pages of general comment on each of the poets named. The discussion focuses mainly on Pinson, *J'habite ici* and *Laius au bord de l'eau*, Tellermann, *Trois plans inhumains*, and Leclair, *L'Or du commun*. Each author is treated separately, however, with no attempt at synthesis or comparison. P. Broome, 'Flames of Flammarion: Moses, Bénézet, Auxeméry', *ib.*, 402–24, records the reading public's debt to Flammarion's poetry series under the direction of Yves di Manno. Choosing recent collections by Emmanuel Moses, Mathieu Bénézet and Jean-Paul Auxeméry, the article manages by a mixture of insightful comment and generous apposite quotation to give a very good flavour within the limits available of these poets and, implicitly, of the value of the Flammarion enterprise. Unwin, *French Novel*, contains a number of chapters relevant to the postwar period: S. Ungar, 'Existentialism, existence, ideology' (145–60), traces the shift toward commitment in the novel from the thirties to the sixties in an æsthetic as well as an ideological perspective. *La Nausée* figures prominently, of course, but *La Condition humaine, Antoine Bloyé* and *La Chute* are also discussed; D. Boak, 'War and the Holocaust', (161–78), despite his title, devotes a good deal of space to First World War and pre-Second World War fiction — Barbusse, Dorgelès, Genevoix, Malraux (*L'Espoir*) et al. — thereby setting his topic against a broad background. He also chooses to include concentration camp and deportation narratives. Noting the failure of the Great War and interwar generations to digest and transpose the debacle of the forties, he considers the echoes of these events in Tournier, *Le Roi des Aulnes*, Simon, *La Route des Flandres*, and Gracq, *Un balcon en forêt*; S. F. Noreiko, 'From serious to popular fiction' (179–93), sets out successfully to blur the distinction between the two in modern France and, in the process, acquaints us with an impressively broad spectrum of authors and titles, not all necessarily familiar to the 'academic' critic. One might well take to heart his moral that judgement and labels matter less than a greater awareness of the whole literary corpus and its interactions; J. Winston, 'Gender and sexual identity in the modern French novel' (223–41), starts out from Simone de Beauvoir's destruction of patriarchal thinking to survey a wide spectrum of women's writing, from the 'realist pulp' of Sagan, Mallet-Joris and d'Eaubonne to Rochefort, Duras and many other — pace Noreiko — 'serious' figures. Like the previous contribution, it is characterized by a wide range of references and would be a useful first point of contact for anyone wanting to explore the field further; J. Gratton, 'Postmodern French fiction: practice and theory' (242–60), takes as its premise the existence of an identifiable and definable postmodern sensibility and outlines some of the broad background cultural developments necessary to understanding this phenomenon in a specifically French context, e.g. the *retour du sujet*, the waning of Marxism and structuralism. Barthes, Tournier, Perec and Duras are drawn into the discussion which retains throughout a clarity and readability not always associated with the area of (post)modern theory and practice.

2. AUTHORS

ANOUILH. J. Plainemaison, 'Jean Anouilh et le mythe d'Antigone', *RHT*:37–54, revisits familiar territory by comparing Sophocles and A., concluding, unsurprisingly, that both plays are a reflection of their time and that A.'s modern dramatization, or better 'subversion', of the myth makes it an authentic expression of contemporary absurdist revolt. J .E. Mwantuali, 'Anouilh et l'humanité: *Pauvre Bitos* ou le miroir des siècles', *ib.*, 55–68, offers a structural analysis of A.'s use of theatre-in-the-theatre in *Pauvre Bitos*, arguing, with the help of diagrams and schemas, that the complex juxtaposition and superimposition of play and play-within-the-play serves only to demonstrate society's inability to look at itself in the mirror of history and learn from the experience. E. Knight, 'Contributions à l'étude du théâtre de Jean Anouilh: I. Jean Cocteau dans le thèâtre de Jean Anouilh. II. Revues et journaux dans le théâtre de Jean Anouilh', *ib.*, 69–78, proffers some reflections on the formative influence of Cocteau on A., as well as drawing our attention to the increasing number of references to newspapers and magazines in his plays over the years. C. P. Marie, 'L'Honneur de Dieu ou la tentation de l'absolu dans *Beckett* de Jean Anouilh', *ib.*, 79–93, adopts an oneiric approach, inspired by Bachelard and by Bergson's theories of *perception pure* and *mémoire pure*, with a view to assessing the role of reverie and the characters' imaginations in moving forward the action of the play. L. J. Poulosky, 'Représentations du couple tragique dans le théâtre français du 20e siècle: Ondine et Hans, Inès et Pedro, Antigone et Hémon', *ib.*, 293–316, contains some discussion, *passim*, of A.'s *Antigone* in comparison with Giraudoux's and Sartre's plays.

ARAGON. A. Kimyongür, 'Nouvelle occupation, nouvelle résistance: Aragon, poetry and the Cold War', *FrCS*, 8: 98–102, examines the influence of A.'s *poésie nationale* campaign on other poets of the Cold War years. A survey of the poetry of the period would obviously be beyond the scope of the paper, but the discussion, interesting and informative, concentrates on A.'s motives, his troubles with the

Communist Party hierarchy and his eventual reinstatement as a Communist intellectual.

ARTAUD.   H. Finter, 'Antonin Artaud and the impossible theatre: the legacy of the theatre of cruelty', *DR*, 41 : 15–40, as its title suggests, takes A. as a starting point and ranges widely across English and European theatrical practice. There is a good deal of reference to A., however, and other French figures, e.g. Mnouchkine, are mentioned in passing. C. Ho, 'Antonin Artaud: from centre to periphery, from periphery to centre', *Performing Arts Journal*, 19.2:6–22, adopts a psychoanalytical approach to A., with due acknowledgement to Freud's *Beyond the Pleasure Principle* and *Moses and Monotheism*. H. considers A.'s mental problems against the background of a wide-ranging review of his career and paints a picture of A. as a traumatized neurotic, paralysed by the internal disorder of his own mind.

BATAILLE.   See CAMUS.

BEAUVOIR.   N. S. Hellerstein, 'Food and the female existentialist body in Simone de Beauvoir's *L'Invitée*', *FF*, 22:203–16, prompted by growing critical interest in the 'semiotic and cultural dimensions of the theme of food', studies the link between food symbolism and human relations in *L'Invitée*, showing how various kinds of food act as metaphors for relationships between characters in the book. The alimentary theme in de B. is a reflection of her specifically female experience of the body. Eating is a form of self-perception and food is an inseparable part of the (female) phenomenological condition. T. Keefe, 'Rites of passage, revelation and release: drink in the fiction of Simone de Beauvoir', *RoS*, 29:35–46, constructs a chronology of imbibing in de B. through *Quand prime le spirituel*, *L'Invitée*, *Les Mandarins* and *La Femme rompue*, finding that drink in her early work is associated with excitement and discovery — especially sexual — whereas, in the later books, it is a more sombre compensation for life's disappoint-ments in maturity. Id., 'Commitment, re-commitment and puzzle-ment: aspects of the Cold War in the fiction of Simone de Beauvoir', *FrCS*, 8:127–36, deals in fact mainly with *Les Mandarins*, where it seeks echoes of the Cold War. Despite bracketing *Les Mandarins* between *Le Sang des autres* and *Les Belles Images*, none of these mainstream texts yields much in the way of evidence. The strongest political references are in a discarded *inédit* from 1966, *Malentendu à Moscou*, which is set entirely in the Soviet Union of that year. See also Robinson, *Women*, I, 243–251.

BECKETT.   L. Hill, 'Up the Republic! Beckett, writing, politics', *MLN*, 112:909–28, reopens the debate about B. as a political writer, in particular his relationship to Irish cultural politics. From some imaginative analysis of Malone's cry of "Up the Republic!", it broadens its scope to encompass *L'Innommable* and concludes that any politics of textuality in B. can only be a politics beyond representation. J. R. Malkin, 'Matters of memory in *Krapp's Last Tape* and *Not I*', *Journal of Dramatic Theory and Criticism*, 11:25–40, deals with the familiar area of dislocated memory in B., comparing two attempts to objectify memory by means of two very different 'organs of remembrance' — Krapp's tape recorder and the disembodied mouth — and reaffirming the shift from mimetic theatre to postmodernist dissolution, ontological dispersal and centreless being. L. J. Jenkins, 'Le tourment qui est un rire: Maurice Blanchot with Beckett', *RR*, 88:145–62, is principally concerned with highlighting 'a certain laughter if not comedy' underlying Blanchot by juxtaposing him with B., but there is enough discussion of B., especially the trilogy, to make it worthwhile, and the juxtaposition is interesting in itself. K. Schoell, 'Beckett et le théâtre abstrait', *RHT*:111–24, begins by asking if B. has created an abstract theatre and, after some general considerations on abstraction in literature and the avant-garde, answers in the affirmative by tracing B.'s move away from mimetism towards the minimalism of the later dramaticules.

BONNEFOY. M. Brophy, 'Le récit et la figuration du rêve dans l'œuvre d'Yves Bonnefoy', *FR*, 70:687–97, considers the importance of B.'s prose writing beside that of his poetry. Discussion focuses on a number of parallels between *Ce qui fut sans lumière* and *Récits en rêve*, with a detailed examination of the constituent texts of *Récits en rêve* serving to highlight the theme of the 'revalorisation du rêve'.

CAMUS. *MLN*, 112.4, is a special 'Camus 2000' issue. The two opening contributors deal with C.'s complex relationship with his native Algeria: E. Apter, 'Out of character: Camus' French Algerian subjects' (499–516), adduces critical assessments of this relationship by such as Conor Cruise O Brien and Edward Said to demonstrate a dichotomy between C.'s 'political curriculum vitae' and the 'never-never land of French Algeria' we find in his creative writing, and which she judges to be an impossible political artefact; and D. Carroll, 'Camus' Algeria: birthright, colonial injustice and the fiction of a French-Algerian people' (517–49), covers much of the same ground, especially Conor Cruise O Brien's analysis, and supports the view of C.'s Algeria as an imaginary place, owing more to C.'s emotional and imaginative needs than to his sense of history or politics. L. D. Kritzman, 'Camus's curious humanism or the intellectual in exile' (550–75), is a wide-ranging tripartite study. It deals firstly with C.'s critique of Marxism in *L'Homme révolté*, the famous querelle and his deteriorating relationship with Sartre, before exploring the applications of the epistemological and political issues inherent in C.'s critique to the Algerian situation, and finishes by analysing two stories — 'La femme adultère ' and 'L'hôte' — from *L'Exil et le*

Royaume. R. S. Salgado, 'Memoir at Saint-Brieuc' (576–94), offers a detailed, if personal, reading of, or reaction to, *Le Premier Homme*, based on her own preoccupation with memory and death. She sees the book as the expression of a conflict between the unsystematic and random nature of memory and the natural human need to impose (narrative) order on experience. C. Imbert, 'De *L'Etranger* à *L'Homme révolté*' (595–99), and S. Debout, 'Sartre et Camus, témoins de la liberté' (600–07), provide two short but overlapping contributions. Imbert sees in the contrasting reactions of S. and C. to the Hiroshima bomb in 1945 the seeds of their future estrangenent during the *L'Homme révolté* affair while Debout chronicles it in more detail, with particular reference to C.'s journalistic writing in *Combat*. D. Reid, 'The rains of empire: Camus in New York' (608–24), ranges more widely than its title suggests. It describes C. as a poor, unhappy, and unwilling traveller in general and relates life to writing, as well as providing details of his three-month stay in the USA in 1946 and his visit to Amsterdam in 1954. There is also some discussion of ground already covered by other contributors: C.'s relationship to French Algeria. J. I. Abecassis, 'Camus' pulp fiction' (625–40), starts from the premise that the second part of *L'Etranger* 'simply does not work'. Descartes and Pascal are drawn into the controversy, as is *Le Premier Homme*, to support a ludic approach to language and convention which makes *L'Etranger* 'the *Pulp Fiction* of metaphysics'. E. L. Constable, 'Shame' (641–65), identifies shame as one of the 'principal affective responses' in C.'s work. The ethics of shame are traced retrospectively from *Le Premier Homme*, via *La Chute* and *Chroniques algériennes*, back to the post-war essays of *Combat*, and the article argues for a rapprochement between C.'s exploration of a man with no past and his own failure to come to terms with the realities of Algerian politics. M. Blanchard, 'Before ethics: Camus' *Pudeur*' (666–82), insists on the importance of the *Carnets* for a proper understanding of Camus. Approaching the *Carnets* from different perspectives, he argues in favour of a collective significance for these insignificant bits and pieces, despite C.'s own low estimation of their importance. A. Aciman, 'From Alexandria' (683–97), does not seem to have any particular axe to grind but offers a number of relaxed observations on *Le Premier Homme* from an autobiographical point of view. C. Davis, 'Altericide: Camus, encounters, reading', *FMLS*, 33 : 129–41, looks at 'the urge to eliminate the Other', represented in this instance ultimately by the reader, in *L'Etranger* and *La Chute*. Some of the ground may seem familiar but the analysis is clear and thoughtful throughout. V. Howells, '*Le Rénégat*: an ironic re-enactment of Camus' Djihad?', *Minogue Vol.*, 215–37, argues, in a close, extended analysis of this enigmatic tale, that the key to understanding it lies in the close relationship of form and content and that the confusion in the protagonist's mind is a reflection of the moral tensions or ambiguities in C.'s response to the Algerian War. D. H. Walker, 'In and out of history: Albert Camus', *FrCS*, 8: 103–15, places C.'s Cold War writings in a chronological framework and political context, to test the hypothesis that C. had already defined his position on Cold War issues well in advance of the debates of those years. The detailed and well-documented analysis is persuasive. L. A. Boldt-Irons, 'The fall from and into grace: Camus and Bataille on happiness and guilt', *NFS*, 36:45–56, explores not the affinities but the profound opposition between C. and Bataille, based on differing attitudes to happiness, misfortune, guilt and innocence. The study relies principally on a comparison of *La Chute* and Bataille's novel *L'Abbé* written six years before. G. F. Montgomery, 'Œdipe mal entendu: langage et reconnaissance dans *Le Malentendu* de Camus', *FR*,70:427–38, illustrates C.'s own analysis of how a failure of communication and understanding leads to the tragedy of the play, while emphasizing the Œdipal nature of the dramatic situation. Y. Ansell, *La Chute (dossier)*, Collection Folio Plus, Gallimard, 188 pp.

CHAR. C. A. Hackett, 'Correspondence with René Char', *FS*, 51: 83–87, offers us an all-too-brief glimpse at his correspondence with C. over a period of some forty years from 1949 to 1988. This touches on a variety of topics such as C.'s estimation of some of his contemporaries (Grosjean, Bonnefoy, Boissonnas, du Bouchet), his anti-nuclear protests and his reactions to H.'s criticism of his work. C. J. Noland, 'The perfection of solitude: Baudelaire, Rimbaud and the Resistance poetry of René Char', *FR*, 70:562–74, suggests that C. explores in his poetry of the thirties and forties the political implication, applications and limits of an aesthetic model of nonconformity based on a poetics of solitude which may be compared to the similarly non-conformist stance of Baudelaire and Rimbaud. L. Fourcaud, 'L'eden est après: paradis du poème pulvérisé. Une lecture de *Evadné* de René Char', *RoR*, 88: 173–87, is what its title suggests: a well-organized and presented study which, despite delving into the minutiae of text and metrics, does not lose sight of broader issues and sets the poem clearly in the context of C.'s work as a whole.

CIXOUS. B. Fort, 'Theatre, history, ethics: an interview with Hélène Cixous on *The Perjured City or The Awakening of the Furies*', *NLH*, 28:425–56, turns out to be an in-depth and interesting interview providing not just useful background insights into *The Perjured City* but a number of quotable comments from C. on her writing in general and on a range of other incidental topics, such as the relationship of history and politics to theatre, the profound influence of Shakespeare on her sensibilities, and her relationship with Mnouchkine. See also Robinson, *Women*, I, 555–62.

CLUNY. C. Andrews, 'Claude-Michel Cluny's travelling theatre', *AJFS*, 34:361–68, tries to account for the critical neglect and ignorance of C. and his absence from the canonical anthologies of contemporary poetry, despite the fact that he is the author of seven major collections and a recipient of the *Grand Prix de Poésie de l'Académie Française*. The explanation may be that C.'s practice is antithetical to the 'three conditions of contemporary canonicity' which A. identifies: representing a movement or trend, being innovative, and 'presenting itself urgently'. Since C. is an individualist with an unhurried approach to publication, he seems destined to be relegated to the sidelines by those compiling the modern canon; unjustly so, to judge by the glimpse into his work in this article.

COHEN. P. Horn, 'Albert Cohen: between laughter and despair' pp. 101–24 of *Modern Jewish Writers of France* (see *supra*, GENERAL), describes C.'s four-novel saga of the life of a Sephardic family, *Solal* (1930), *Mangeclous* (1938), *Belle du Seigneur* (1968) and *Les Valeureux* (1969), introducing us to a multi-faceted figure: poet, novelist, dramatist, diplomat, and 'unquestionably the greatest Jewish writer in the French language'.

DESBIOLLES. J. Rancourt, 'Maryline Desbiolles: la traversée du paysage', *AJFS*, 34:298–312, provides a very useful and informative overview, with a generous helping of quotation, of D.'s writing, including her poetry, two novels and a collection of short stories. The approach is unpartisan and intended to provide the reader with access to a poet who is herself accessible, using everyday language, concrete vocabulary and taking her inspiration from the 'saveur de l'instant' rather than retreating into 'le jeu des phantasmes'.

DURAS. C. Rodgers, 'Le *je* durassien féminin: un miroir aux alouettes?'', *Minogue Vol.*, 239–58, charts D.'s search for an 'énonciation au féminin', citing a good selection of novels and films in the process. But what if, ironically, this *je* becomes increasingly dominant and sadistic i.e. phallocratic, reinforcing the Lacanian contention, acknowledged at the outset, that any 'énonciation au féminin' is by definition impossible? The answer may lie in D.'s adoption of a multiplicity of subjective positions, a multiplicity which can be considered feminine. M. Sankey, 'The Duras phenomenon', *AJFS*, 34:60–76, is prompted by D.'s death in 1996 to take a retrospective look at her relationship with her reading public. The article surveys the various obituaries at the time, but is more concerned with how D.'s growing media profile may have contributed to her estrangement from the Left and her 'recuperation' by the Right. T. Selous, 'Imaginary pictures in *Le Vice-consul* and *India Song*', *ib.*, 77–87, highlights the paradox of D.'s use of images in her films in contrast to their growing prominence in her writing. The article is, in fact, broader in scope than its title suggests, embracing a range of references to D.'s cinematic activities in particular. M. Royer, 'Produire l'œuvre au-dehors: l'écriture durassienne face au regard de l'autre', *ib.*, 88–99, deals basically with D.'s anxious and conflictual relations with her readership, and how the cinema eventually becomes a 'lieu de résolution' where this fear of the 'regard de l'autre' is resolved or dissipated. Principal reference is to *L'Amant de la Chine du Nord* and *L'Homme atlantique*. S. Williams, 'Silent spaces: places for storytelling in the works of M. Duras', *ib.*, 115–32, indicates how various types of stylized patterning and references aid storytelling in D., despite the apparently fragmented nature of her narrative: e.g. geographical and geometric circles in *India Song*, or musical references and patterns of sound and silence which create rhythms and patterns of movement within the text. J. Solomon, '"J'ai un visage détruit": pleasures of self-portraiture in M. Duras' *L'Amant*', *ib.*, 100–14, discusses the scopophiliac tendencies in D.'s implicitly autobiographical novel *L'Amant*. R. K. Gunther, 'Liquid passions: Marguérite Duras', *RoS*, 29:21–34, is a revealing analysis of the centrality of alcohol to both D.'s life and work. The presence of drinking in a number of novels is related directly to D.'s own increasing reliance on alcohol as a palliative for the loneliness of the writing process. G. Jacobs, 'Spectres of remorse: Duras' war-time autobiography', *ib.*, 30:47–58, examines in some detail the first four texts of *La Douleur*, initially casting doubt on their reliability as autobiographical accounts but commending in the end the honesty of D.'s self-analysis in them and the sincere admission and expiation of guilt for past actions. F. Maury, *Un barrage contre le Pacifique (dossier)*, Collection Folio Plus, Gallimard, 392 pp. M. Borgomano, *Marguerite Duras: Le Ravissement de Lol V. Stein*, Collection Foliothèque, Gallimard, 214 pp. See also Robinson, *Women*, I, 767–76.

ETCHERELLI. S. McIlvanney, 'Feminist *Bildung* in the novels of Claire Etcherelli, *MLR*, 92:60–69, views three novels (*Elise, A propos de Clémence* and *Un arbre voyageur*) in a feminist optic. While initial indications are not promising, the case for a feminist E. is strengthened by construing the novels as *Bildungsromane*. However, even if E. assimilates some of the characteristics of the genre, in the end her female protagonists assert their increasing self-possession and independence, thereby subverting the narrative pattern of the traditional, i.e. male-centred, *Bildungsroman*. See also Robinson, *Women*, I, 831–35.

GENET. A. Lingis, 'Love song', Fisher, *Difference*, 167–84, starts from the assertion that G.'s five novels are nothing if not love songs, and proceeds to comb them for expressions of love in its various manifestations and consequences: love of murder and murderers, the abject lover, loving betrayal etc.; not for the squeamish or the prudish. C. Lane, 'The voided role: on Genet', *MLN*, 112:876–908, chooses to run counter to the prevailing tide of criticism which emphasizes 'transgression' between G.'s life and work. He ponders G.'s own view of *Les Bonnes* as a failure and, reassessing G.'s declared interest in character, argues that G.'s view of this play affects how we read his other works. There is detailed discussion of the play and Leo Bersani's study of it. Y. Morali, 'Genet et Sartre; le dialogue des œuvres à partir des deux premiers textes théoriques de Jean Genet', *RHT*:102–12, is based on two texts by G. — *Jean Cocteau* and *Lettre à Léonor Fini* — neither of which is included in G.'s *Œuvres complètes* and which are compared to Sartre's *Saint Genet*. Moraly finds in Sartre echoes of ideas in the G. essays. which constitute a 'prodigieux dialogue d'œuvres' between the two writers, but this is more taken for granted than demonstrated. G. Child-Olmstead, 'Transfiguration of the mother in G.'s *Journal du voleur* and *Un Captif amoureux*', *FR*, 71:44–54, shows how abiding was G.'s obsession with the mother figure by comparing and contrasting two episodes in these early and late autobiographical texts, and how the ambiguity of the mother figure — both idealized and reviled — is fundamental to an understanding of G.'s search for meaning and identity.

IONESCO.   N. Macé-Barbier, 'Onirisme et dramaturgie chez Ionesco', *RHT*:649–67, concentrates on two late plays: *L'Homme aux valises* and *Voyages chez les morts*, which are autobiographical in nature. It is a clear and readable discussion of how I. manages to dramatize his 'thème obsédant du langage' and of a number of language-related problems, such as the difficulty of human communication, in an oneiric fashion and in an original and poignant way.

KOLTÈS.   *Europe*, 823–24, devotes half of its pages to Koltès. It reprints a number of texts by K. himself — a letter from Africa to Hubert Gignoux, some extracts from his first original play *L'héritage* and an interview with J.-P. Han — as well as *témoignages* from those who knew him or who worked with him , such as his brother François and Bruno Boeglin.Too many of the critical pieces are unfortunately too short. Among the more substantial and interesting is J.-Y. Coquelin, 'Point de fuite à l'horizon' (52–73), which guides us around K,'s work in general, providing valid insights into various aspects of it. Others, although shorter, contain some useful comments as a starting point for further thought: A. Hakim, 'L'argent comme purgatoire' (74–79), on *Quai Ouest*; D. Lemahieu, 'Climats d'une écriture' (89–96), on *Le Retour au désert*; and J.-M. Lanteri, 'Babylone de tous les martyrs' (106–17), on *Prologues*. Despite the unevenness of the individual contributions, taken as a whole they constitute none the less a welcome addition to an as yet thin body of criticism on Koltès.

LECLERC. M.-A. Hutton, 'Seeing but not believing: Annie Leclerc's *Exercices de mémoire*', *FS*, 51:432–46, examines L.'s text against the background of current theoretical arguments about Holocaust writing and L.'s reactions to Lanzmann's film *Shoah*, in an attempt to assess to what extent L. manages to avoid the pitfalls — reductionism, trivialization, mystification — associated with this 'notoriously problematic' genre. The discussion is detailed and interesting, and broadens out in the last pages to consider L.'s move away from a strictly feminist agenda.

LE CLÉZIO. *WLT*, 71, is devoted in part to Le Clézio. It contains three texts by him, a good bibliography and a number of critical assessments of his work. W. Motte, 'Writing away' (689–94), concentrates on what he regards as Le C.'s most exotic recent novel, *Onitshu*, in order to illustrate his distinctive gift for creating exotic, narrative 'elsewheres'. A. Anderson, 'Translating Jean-Marie Gustave Le Clézio' (695–702), reveals that translating Le C. comes naturally to her, and shares some of the rewards and exhilaration of the process by reference to *Onitshu* and *La quarantaine*, as well as being disarmingly honest about her difficulties and mistakes. B. L. Knapp, 'Jean-Marie Le Clézio's *Désert*: the myth of transparency' (703–08), focuses mainly on the first two sections of the novel, describing the unrestricted oneness with nature and freedom of worship of his archetypal, quasi-mythical Berber nomads, and the symbolic significance of Lalla, his child of nature. W. Thompson, 'Voyage and immobility in Jean-Marie Le Clézio's *Désert* and *La quarantaine* (709–16), considers the complex interrelationship between the two ideas in an attempt to resolve some of the contradictions or tensions between the attractions of movement and stasis in Le C.'s creative imagination. J.-X. Ridon, 'Between here and there: a displacement in memory' (717–22), also addresses the origins of multiple forms of movement in Le C., instancing travel to Mauritius as the doorway to escape for Léon in *La quarantaine*, which is also a journey back through memory to retrace the history of his ancestors. B. Thibault, 'Awaité Pawana: Jean-Marie Le Clezio.'s vision of the sacred' (723–29), describes a long short story by Le C., set in 1856 at a time of imminent domestication of the North American continent by man and the exploitation and destruction of its natural resources, a story which seems to exemplify all the great themes of Le C.'s writing in the 70s and 80s. J. L. Brown, 'A new book of flights: immigration and displacement in Jean-Marie Le Clézio's *Poisson d'or*' (731–34), illustrates Le C.'s concern with the plight of the immigrant through the story of *Poisson d'or* and the tribulations of its young black African eponymous heroine. S. Jollin, 'From the Renaudot Prize to the Puterbaugh conference: the reception of Jean-Marie Le Clézio' (735–40), provides an informative resume of Le C.'s career to date; while W. Putnam, 'Jean-Marie Le Clézio and the questions of culture (741–44), reproduces Le C.'s answers to a questionnaire, also put apparently to J. Conrad at one time, which duplicates several questions in the celebrated Proust questionnaire.

LE GROS. R. Smith, 'Shellfish treasure trove — new writing by Marc Le Gros', *AJFS*, 34:369–77, reveals Le G.'s preoccupation with shellfish, to be specific a particular kind of clam (*tapes decussatus*), and explores in *Eloge de la Palourde* (1996), a sequence of prose paragraphs, the parallels which Le G. makes explicit elsewhere between the pursuits of writing and clam-gathering.

MAULPOIX. R. Pickering, '"Parler juste dans l'incertain": l'univers poétique de Jean-Michel Maulpoix', *AJFS*, 34:270–82, rests on a comparison of his 1994 series of reflections on the vocation and work of the poet, *L'Ecrivain imaginaire*, and the later *Une histoire de bleu*, the collection which seems best to exemplify the ideas in the earlier work. This rapprochement succeeds in conveying a good overall impression of the aims and objectives of a writer who is 'aux antipodes de tout credo prétentieux du moi'.

MURAIL. L. M. Porter, 'Beyond feminism: Elvire Murail's *Escalier C*', Fisher, *Difference*, 196–214, describes the various relationships, principally sexual, of the denizens of Staircase C, arguing that M. transcends a gender-based narrative viewpoint and presents both homosexual and heterosexual relations sympathetically and without preference as points on a spectrum of sexual behaviour.

PERSE. A. Small, '*Oiseaux* de Saint John Perse: un art poétique', *FF*, 22:279–302, emphasizes the dual nature of this poem as at once an *ars poetica* and a working demonstration or application of its own principles; a veritable 'traité de l'esthétique persienne'. There is some detailed treatment of metrics but the article concerns itself for the most part with the generalities of Perse's æsthetics: understandable, but a bit more quotation would help those less familiar with the text.

PEY. C. Debon, 'Serge Pey et la poésie orale d'action', *AJFS*, 34:332–39, chooses to concentrate on P.'s 1993 collection *Dieu est un chien dans les arbres* which is, we are assured, the most accessible collection by this author of, among other things, a massive five-volume doctorate on *oralité* in modern poetry. P. is a somewhat unconventional practitioner of the art, given to inscribing his poems on sticks and branches, for example, when not indulging in trances and 'neo-shamanism'. Undeterred, D. rises to the challenge, and manages to produce some straightforward literary criticism of P.'s main ideas.

PLANTIER. V. A. La Charité, 'Thérèse Plantier; a feminist poesis', *AJFS*, 34:321–31, explains P.'s rejection of traditional *écriture féminine* as phallocentric in favour of her own brand of militant *féminisme*, the determination to subvert or eliminate male literary models, suggesting that P. has been almost totally ignored because of this, and because of her generally anti-(theoretical) establishment stance and rejection of traditional poetic form and content. The analysis might benefit from less description and more direct illustration of P.'s 'feminine anti-text', which would allow the reader to form a better first-hand judgement of P.s merits.

PONGE. D. E. Sears, '"La loi et les prophètes": Ponge, the Bible and the Proême', explores P.'s love-hate relationship with the Bible as evidenced, for example, by his irreverent and ironic intertextual references or by the allegorical significance he attaches to certain Biblical episodes. In a close scrutiny of 'La Loi et les prophètes', many interesting biblical parallels are identified. *Francis Ponge: Le parti pris des choses, suivi de Proêmes*, ed. J.-C. Gateau (Foliothèque), Gallimard, 208 pp.

SALLENAVE. B. Thibault, 'Danièle Sallenave et le thème de la vie séparée', *FF*, 22:75–92, settles down, after an introductory section on S.'s criticisms of Bourdieu's views on culture and some comment on her reservations about the *nouveau roman*, to a clear and interesting examination of S.'s collection of short stories, *Un printemps froid*, choosing examples to illustrate S.'s theoretical convictions and her creative predilection for portraying the difficulties and problems of ordinary lives in real contemporary settings, and the stresses and strains of coping with modern living.

SARRAUTE. S. M. Bell, 'Orchestrated voices: selves and others in Nathalie Sarraute's *Tu ne t'aimes pas*', *Minogue Vol.*, 13–35, explores, in the context of S.'s preoccupation with the *for intérieur*, the complex interrelationships between the plural self/selves and others in *Tu ne t'aimes pas*, finding that the use of plural, indeed rival, voices in S.'s dialogue to express these relationships makes for a very flexible narrative, highly sensitive to shifts of tone and feeling. Robinson, *Women*, IV, 31–45, offers a selection of critical extracts on S. from 1958 to1993 . While these extracts are brief, the entry itself is substantial enough to provide a reasonable overview of S.'s work and main themes.

SARTRE. D. Nott, 'Sartre and his childhood: the inconsolable in pursuit of the irretrievable?', *RoS*, 29:97–108, traces S.'s difficulties, as evidenced in the inconsistencies of recollection in *Les Mots*, with his autobiographical project, in an effort to assess how uncertainties of introspection may have affected or undermined the therapeutic value of the autobiographical exercise, influencing S.'s own self-perception and his relationships with others in the process. R. Pickering, '*Témoignage* and *engagement* in Sartre's war-time writings', *MLR*, 92:308–23, focuses on S.'s creative and journalistic writings during and after the war, to demonstrate the extent to which the Resistance concept of *témoignage* is a determining factor in S.'s advocacy of commitment and authenticity in post-Liberation France. M. Scriven, 'Cold War polarization and cultural productivity in the work of Sartre', *FrCS*, 8:117–26, is a well-structured and clearly presented discussion of S.'s ideological and cultural evolution in the immediate post-war decade, in response to developing Cold War tensions. Two stages are identified in this evolution: 1946–50 and 1950–56. This effort to adapt to a changing situation may help explain the richness and diversity of his 'Herculean productivity' in these years. H. Davies, 'Sartre and the mobilization of Lévy-Bruhl', *FS*, 51:422–31, measures the influence of L.-B.'s anthropological theory of the pre-logical mentality on S., particularly as manifested in his first *carnet de la drôle de guerre*. There is no analysis of S.'s creative writing as such, but since S. drew on L.-B. for his own phenomenological psychology, the article may provide some interesting background material for the literary inquirer. W. Redfern, 'Praxis and parapraxis; Sartre's *Le Mur*', *RoR*, 88:163–72, offers a readable and thoughtful consideration of *Le Mur*, not from any one narrow theoretical slant, but covering various aspects of the work, although returning inevitably to the theme of impending death. (See also *supra*, GENET.)

SCHMITT. A special Modern Theatre issue of *NRF*, 534–535, contains a lengthy interview by J.-C. and S.-J. Lieber, 'L'art du mystère' (76–96), which will serve as an introduction to a new contemporary playwright who, despite five successful productions in the 90s, is not widely known as yet. There is some interesting biographical information to hand, as well as comment on his main creative themes and preoccupations.

SIMON. M. Bell, '*La Route des Flandres*', Bell, *Aphorism*, 79–92, takes issue with the prevailing critical view that it is fruitless to try to deduce any kind of meaning from the novel's narrative sequences, arguing that analysis of the narrative structure can in fact be particularly productive. The ensuing examination of aphoristic discourse aims to affirm the coherence of the narrative and leads us from the particular, e.g. the frequency of demonstrative adjectives in the text, to more general considerations of how the use of aphorisms supports conclusions, metaphysical or epistemological in nature, reached by other methods. M. Borrut, '*Le Sacre du Printemps* et les origines de l'Espagne romanesque chez Claude Simon', *RLC*, 283:323–40, traces the recurring importance of Spain in S.'s work, back to *Le Sacre du Printemps* written in 1954 and subjected to a detailed analysis. M.

Thouillot, 'Guerres et écriture chez Claude Simon', *Poétique*, 109:65–82, reviews the nexus of tensions on various levels or 'paliers hiérarchisés' by the treatment of war in Simon. The discussion, which is informed and well-structured, recognises in this treatment and these tensions a familiar need or search for equilibrium and the reconciliation of opposites which is to be found elsewhere in Simon. F. Dupont, 'Lecture d'un extrait des *Géorgiques* de Claude Simon', *IL*, 49.4:20–24, is a highly methodical examination of a three-page extract, sequence by sequence, to reinforce the point, if need be, that this apparently historical novel is in fact much more of an 'épopée problématique'.

STEINMETZ. R. Lloyd, 'Jean-Luc Steinmetz: celui qui frapperait l'huis d'un nom', *AJFS*, 34:350–58, brings to our attention a poet who, born in 1940 and with seven collections to his credit, is only now beginning to attract critical attention. She sees his poetry as driven by two things: a 'lyrisme démocritéen', an atomistic concept of the universe founded on oneness rather than a hierarchy of being, and a 'côté agonistique', a secular combat between the individual and the world, between *variances* and *permanences*. The ensuing discussion of S.'s inspiration and themes provides a clear, informative overview which suggests he has indeed been unjustly neglected.

TOURNIER. J. Krell, 'Tournier féministe? Histoires d'Eve', *RR*, 88:453–70, conducts a spirited and creditable defence of T. against the charges of phallocracy and misogyny frequently levelled at him. He reconsiders the feminine ideal/ideal female, insisting that, while T.'s work can be read as a celebration of the androgynous, his 'new Eve' is a significant feminization of the androgynous, and that T., 'abatteur de la virilité', emphasizes the positive nature of female sexuality.

VEGLIANTE. P. Broome, '*Forme et informe*: the poetry of Jean-Charles Vegliante', *AJFS*, 34:339–49, looks at V.'s exclusive use of the sonnet form in his first major collection, *Sonnets du petit pays entraîné vers le nord*, and the serial quatrains of his latest collection, *Les Oublies*, in the light of V.'s declaration: 'sans forme, qui nous consolera'. This reliance on form as a compensation for or counterweight to 'abandonment and dispersion into the void' is contrasted with the *informe*, the various forces of disorder and undoing which threaten to destabilize and deconstruct the poetic fabric from within.

VELTER. J. Birnberg, 'André Velter: fulgurances oraculaires. Le poète des deux versants des ténèbres et de la lumière', *AJFS*, 34:379–401, exceeds his brief by dealing with many matters: V.'s long friendship with Serge Sautrean, their creative collaboration on *Aisha*, the influence of René Char and V.'s extensive travels in Asia. He identifies two stages in V.'s work: his early collections of the 70s, written before his expeditions to Afghanistan, Kashmir and the Himalayas, and those of the later 80s inspired by his exotic travels. The article as a whole succeeds in conveying a good overall impression of V. and of his later work in particular.

VINAVER. G. Lester, 'Industrial art: the theatre of Michel Vinaver', *Theater*, 28.1:69–73, is a brief but none the less objective and useful survey of V.'s achievement, emphasiszng his originality in subject-matter and dramatic technique. It is accompanied by an excerpt in translation from *Mémoire sur mes travaux* and the script of *The Interview*.

FRENCH CANADIAN LITERATURE

By CHRISTOPHER ROLFE, *Senior Lecturer in French, University of Leicester*

1. ESSAYS, GENERAL STUDIES, ANTHOLOGIES

Laurent Mailhot, *La Littérature québécoise depuis ses origines*, Montreal, Typo, 450 pp., greatly expands and brings up to date his 1974 *La Littérature québécoise* (Que sais-je?), which is no longer in print. Although it shares many of the weaknesses endemic to literary histories, this wide-ranging study is never less than competent and is frequently very stimulating. Guy Frégault, *Histoire de la littérature canadienne-française. Seconde moitié du XIXe siècle*, ed. Réginald Hamel, Montreal, Guérin, 1996, vi + 626 pp. This volume, prepared by H., from F.'s lecture-notes, covers the period 1860–1920 and analyses the work of 30 or so writers. Although the study has been superseded in certain respects by more recent research, it is in no sense redundant. *Panorama de la littérature québécoise contemporaine*, ed. Bernard Andrès and Réginald Hamel, Montreal, Guerin, ix + 822 pp.

Écrire la pauvreté. Actes du VIe colloque international de sociocritique. Université de Montréal, septembre 1993, ed. Michel Biron and Pierre Popovic, Toronto, Editions du Gref, 1996, 389 pp., has a section on 'Le pauvre du nouveau monde'. This includes papers by: M. Cambron, 'Pauvreté et utopie: l'accommodement poétique selon le petit Gazetier du journal *Le Canadien*' (301–17); R. Major, 'Instruit, mais pauvre' (310–31), which has some interesting comments on Pierre-Joseph-Olivier Chauvreau's *Charles Guérin* and Antoine Gérin-Lajoie's *Jean Rivard*; F. Roy, 'La pauvreté et l'écriture dans *Au pied de la pente douce* de Roger Lemelin' (357–66); and M. Biron, 'La pauvreté Anthropos' (367–75), whose subject is Gaston Miron. Bell, *Aphorism*, has chapters on Gabrielle Roy's *Alexandre Chenevert* and Hubert Aquin's *Neige noire*. Roy, B. argues, uses aphorism ironically 'to criticize prevalent attitudes and to demonstrate [. . .] the incongruity of her lofty ideals with the onerous reality of the quotidian'. Aquin, on the other hand, uses it 'to involve the reader in his discourse and to goad us into some kind of response.' Aurélien Boivin, *Pour une lecture du roman québécois. De 'Maria Chapdelaine' à 'Volkswagen Blues'*, Quebec, Nuit blanche, 1996, 369 pp., is aimed at the general public. This is not to say it is facile or light-weight. In fact, it offers solid, thoughtful readings of, in addition to the two mentioned in the title, the following 'key' texts (the choice is certainly somewhat contentious): *Menaud, maître-draveur, Le Survenant, Bonheur d'occasion, Le Temps des hommes, Agaguk, Le Libraire, Une Saison dans la vie d'Emmanuel, Salut Galarneau!, La Guerre, yes sir!, Un Dieu chasseur, L'Emmitouflé, Thérèse et Pierrette à l'école des Saints-Anges*, and *Les Fous de Bassan*. Id. has also edited *Les Meilleurs nouvelles québécoises du XIXe siècle*, Montreal, Fides, 1996, 450 pp. This is an important anthology of short stories by 25 authors, including those such as Louis Fréchette, Honoré Beaugrand and Pamphile Lemay, whose respective collected works have been published, and others such as Eugène l'Ecuyer and Charles Leclère, whose work has been confined to newspapers and journals. Georges Desmeules, *La Littérature fantastique et le spectre de l'humour*, Quebec, L'instant même, 209 pp., discusses a wide range of authors who have drawn inspiration from the seemingly paradoxical association of the fantastic and the humorous. 'Le diable à ressort: "Le livre de Mafteh Haller" de Marie José Thériault' (77–86), 'La victime comme bouc émissaire: "L'objection" de Jacques Brossard' (86–100), 'La revanche du condamné: "Le pendu" de Michel Tremblay (117–24), and 'Le fantôme qui s'ignore: "La fin" de Roch Carrier' (161–66) will be of particular interest to Quebec specialists.

Questions d'histoire littéraire. Mélanges offerts à Maurice Lemire, ed. Aurélien Boivin, Gilles Dorion, and Kenneth Landry, Quebec, Nuit blanche, 1996, 302 pp., presents 21 essays on different aspects of Quebec literature from its beginnings early in the 19th c. to the present. There are pieces on, amongst others, Edmond de Nevers, Emile Nelligan, Louis Hémon, Félix-Antoine Savard, Yves Thériault, Anne Hébert, and Jacques Ferron. A particularly interesting contribution by Alonzo Le Blanc discusses 'Les boucs-émissaires dans le théâtre québécois' (267–79). Rainier Grutman, *Des Langues qui résonnent. L'hétérolinguisme au XIXe siècle québécois*, Montreal, Fides, 224 pp., confronts the important but hitherto rather neglected issue of textual plurilinguism. Georges-André Vachon, *Une Tradition à inventer*, Montreal, Boréal, 228 pp., is a collection of a number of influential essays published over the years by V. (who died in 1994) and brought together by Lise Gauvin and Patrick Poirier. The volume is divided into three main parts: 'Une tradition à inventer', which maps out the landmarks in Quebec literature, followed by 'L'espace politique et social', and 'Des mots se suivent', which concentrates on poetry. *Imaginaire et représentations du monde. Romantisme, réalisme et naturalisme, symbolisme et fantastique dans la littérature française et québécoise*, ed. Vital Gadbois et al, Sainte-Foy, Le Griffon d'argile, 356 pp., is a superbly produced *manuel d'étudiant* that would undoubtedly serve as a valuable reference tool, especially for those interested in the links between the two literatures. Gontard, *Francophonie*, has a section on Quebec which includes a number of insightful articles on literary topics: G. Dorion, 'Le face-à-face canadien dans le roman québécois' (284–91); R. Chapman, 'La ville comme territoire chez Anne Hébert et France Théoret' (293–99); C. D. Rolfe, 'Réévaluer *Les Vendeurs du temple* d'Yves Thériault' (301–06), J. K. Sanaker, 'La francophonie et l'entre-deux-langues: cinéma et littérature' (307–14); M. Gontard, 'Littérature et altérité dans *Kamouraska* d'Anne Hébert et *Volkswagen blues* de Jacques Poulin' (315–22). Axel Maugey, *Propos sur le Québec et la francophonie*, Montreal, Humanitas, 1996, 154 pp., is a collection of short essays that have appeared in newspapers such as *Le Devoir* and reviews such as *Vie des Arts*. Sections entitled 'A propos du Québec poétique' and 'A propos du Québec romanesque' have most to offer the Quebec specialist.

Postcolonial Subjects: Francophone Women Writers, ed. Mary Jean Green, Karen Gould et al, Minneapolis, Minnesota U.P., 1996, xxii + 359 pp., is a collection of 19 critical essays that explore gender, race, and cultural identity; it contains pieces on established French Canadian women writers such as Antonine Maillet, Marie Laberge, Anne Hébert and on the less well known Nicole Houde, Louise Bouchard, and Francine Noël. M. B. Velloso Porto, 'Aprendizagem e cultura no plural: pedagogia e feminino na literatura canadense de língua francesa', Lavallée, *Brasil–Canadá*, 163–74, is an interesting discussion of the symbolical figure of the school-mistress in Quebec literature. *Anthologie 'Arcade' 1981–1996: 80 voix au féminin*, ed. Claudine Bertrand and Louise Cotnoir, Montreal, *Arcade*, 35–36, 1996, 279 pp. is a special volume of the revue presenting an anthology of women writers, both established figures and relative unknowns. Robinson, *Women*, has entries that usefully reproduce key pieces of critical comment on Marie-Claire Blais, Monique Bosco, Denise Boucher, Nicole Brossard, Henriette Dessaulles, Anne Hébert, Françoise Loranger, Gabrielle Poulin, and Gabrielle Roy. *VI*, 22.1, has a dossier on 'Effets autobiographiques au féminin'. Typical of the pieces on offer are: P. Smart, 'Mémoires d'une jeune fille qui refuse de se ranger: *Une Mémoire déchirée* de Thérèse Renaud' (10–21); and B. Havercroft, 'Hétérogénéité énonciative et renouvellement du genre: le *Journal intime* de Nicole Brossard' (22–37), which situates B.'s generally neglected text at the crossroads of feminism and postmodernism. J.-M. Moura, 'Francophonie et critique postcoloniale', *RLC*, 71:59–87, usefully situates Quebec literature within the broader historical, political, and cultural context.

D. Boak, 'The French-Canadian novel', Unwin, *French Novel*, 214–22, offers — unsurprisingly perhaps given the limitations of the *Companion* genre — a very distorted view. Indeed, a contribution that fails even to mention the likes of Carrier, Blais, Thériault, Aquin, Poulin, is ultimately misleading. The comments on *joual* are flawed. Jacques Allard, *Le Roman mauve. Microlectures de la fiction récente au Québec*, Montréal, Québec/Amérique, 393 pp., is a collection of A.'s weekly reviews that appeared in *Le Devoir* from 1992 to 1996, and constitutes an extremely valuable overview of a prolific fictional output. (The mysterious title was prompted by Ozias Leduc's painting *L'Heure mauve*. Apparently, A. made an immediate mental association between this title and the sort of novel that has made most impact over the last few years.) Lucie-Marie Magnan and Christian Morin, *Lectures du postmodernisme dans le roman québécois*, Quebec, Nuit blanche, 219 pp., offer an essay defining postmodernism and then analyse 30 texts, including works by Hubert Aquin, Réjean Ducharme, Jacques Godbout, Anne Hébert, and Jacques Poulin, according to the proposed schema. Really rather useful.

Lettres des années trente, ed. Michel Biron and Benoît Melançon, Ottawa, Le Nordir, 1996, 141 pp., includes a number of essays of interest to Quebec specialists: J. Everett, 'Cher Monseigneur: appels, salutations et signatures épistolaires dans la correspondance de Camille Roy' (51–68); M.-A. Beaudet, 'Voix et jeux de coulisses: la correspondance Simone Routier — Louis Dantin' (69–83); R. Giguère, 'Les années de la Crise dans la correspondance Simone Routier — Louis Dantin' (85–107); M. Biron, 'Configurations épistolaires et champ littéraire: le cas d'Alfred DesRochers et de Saint-Denys Garneau' (109–24); E. Kushner, 'Saint-Denys Garneau épistolier: monologue ou dialogue?' (125–39). *The Drama of Our Past. Major Plays from Nineteenth-Century Quebec*, trans. and ed. Leonard E. Doucette, Toronto U.P., 327 pp., offers translations of five plays and five 'playlets' which it is claimed, are representative of the range of plays written in French in 19th-c. Quebec. Whilst the rationale for presenting these plays solely in English is dubious, D.'s introduction to each is a model of economy, scholarship, and readability. *Cahiers de Théâtre Jeu*, 78, 1996, has four articles on recent Quebec drama, notably: D. Godin, 'La laideur, le bruit et la fureur' (73–78), which looks at the work of Anne-Marie Cadieux, Yvan Bienvenue and François Archambault, all of whom 'ont la particularité de faire du théâtre plus vrai que nature'; and J. C. Godin, 'Qu'est-ce qu'un *Dragonfly*?' (90–95), a sprightly discussion of why Larry Tremblay chose to write *The Dragonfly of Chicoutimi* in English. Claude Beausoleil, *Le Motif de l'identité dans la poésie québécoise*, Montreal, *Revue Estuaire*, 83–84, 1996, 262 pp., ultimately disappoints since it largely reduces this significant issue to poetry that evokes Montreal, and also tends to perpetuate an outdated formalism. Y. Resch, 'La dimension américaine de la poésie québécoise', *ECan*, 43:75–83, discusses how Québécois poetry has been influenced by the underground culture of the 70s and, in the 80s, the widely embraced concept of 'américanité'. Catherine Pomeyrols, *Les Intellectuels québécois: formation et engagements 1919–1939*, Paris, L'Harmattan, 1996, 537 pp., seeks to present a detailed description of the education that a generation of Quebec intellectuals received and the extent to which this influenced their subsequent nationalism. A comparison is also drawn with what was happening in France. Although interesting, the study is based on faulty premisses and uncertain methodology.

François Paré, *Exiguity. Reflections on the Margins of Literature*, Waterloo, Wilfrid Laurier U.P., 183 pp., is a translation (by Lin Burman) of P.'s 1993 *Les Littératures de l'exiguïté*. Critical musings on so-called marginal literature(s) including Quebec, Franco-Ontarian and Acadian literatures. Excellent, stimulating stuff. *La Littérature franco-ontarienne: enjeux esthétiques. Actes du colloque tenu à l'Université McGill le 17 mai 1996*, ed. Lucie Hotte and François Ouellet, Ottawa, Le Nordir, 1996, 139 pp., is a collection of seven essays which resolutely address æsthetic issues rather than questions of identity within the given context. An essay by Hotte, 'L'inscription du littéraire dans *La Bagarre* et *Le Semestre* de Gérard Bessette' (43–51), probably has the most to offer. *Nuit blanche*, 62, 1996, has a useful dossier on 'Littérature franco-ontarienne' (40–71), including short pieces on Daniel Poliquin, Patrice Desbiens, poetry and theatre. *Mélanges Marguerite Maillet, Recueil de textes de création et d'articles sur la littérature, la langue et l'ethnologie acadiennes en hommage à Marguerite Maillet*, ed. Raoul Boudreau et al., Moncton, Editions d'Acadie, 1996, 579 pp., is dominated, unsurprisingly, by essays on Antonine Maillet: D. Bourque, 'Une Renaissance au pays du rire: *Cent ans dans les bois* d'Antonine Maillet et le carnavalesque' (83–95); E. A. Brière, 'Antonine Maillet et la construction d'une identité acadienne' (97–109); U.C. Lange, 'Femme au volant: les héroïnes nautiques d'Antonine Maillet' (225–35); R. LeBlanc, 'La musique et l'identité acadienne dans l'œuvre d'Antonine Maillet' (237–48); R. Mane, 'De Longfellow à la bande dessinée en passant par Antonine Maillet' (249–58); L. Petroni, 'Paysage et paysage-état d'âme dans *Pélagie-la-Charrette* d'Antonine Maillet' (303–11); and E. Voldeng, '*Pélagie-la-Charrette* et le folklore de la France de l'ouest' (511–18).

2. INDIVIDUAL AUTHORS

AQUIN. Hubert Aquin, *Prochain épisode*, ed. Jacques Allard, Montreal, Bibliothèque québécoise, 1996, 384 pp., is an excellent critical edition.

ASSELIN. Hélène Pelletier-Baillargeon, *Olivar Asselin et son temps*, Montreal, Fides, 1996, 780 pp. This splendid biography, as informative about the period as it is about A., takes the reader from 1874 to 1916, the year of the polemicist's momentous 'Pourquoi je m'enrôle'. Olivar Asselin, *Liberté de pensée. Choix de textes politiques et littéraires*, ed. Robert Lahaise, Montreal, Typo, 153 pp., makes readily available 12 of A.'s pieces, including 'Pourquoi je m'enrôle' and his preface to Jules Fournier's 1920 *Anthologie des poètes canadiens*.

BEAULIEU. Jacques Pelletier, *L'Ecriture mythologique: essai sur l'œuvre de Victor-Lévy Beaulieu*, Quebec, Nuit blanche, 1996, 281 pp., sets out to assess B.'s massive corpus in the light of his stated objective of effecting 'la récréation mythologique des pays québécois'. Although written with insight and clarity, the essay is profoundly dull and rarely succeeds in convincing one that, as P. extravagantly claims, 'nous sommes en présence d'une création majeure, sans doute la plus complexe et la plus riche de toute la production contemporaine au Québec'.

BESSETTE. Danila Donnarumma, **Un caso di narrativa post-moderna del Quebec: Gérard Bessette*, Istituto universitario orientale Napoli, 1996, 235 pp.

BORDUAS. Gilles Lapointe, *L'Envol des signes. Borduas et ses lettres*, Montreal, Fides, 1996, 275 pp., is a study of B.'s correspondence between 1923 and 1960 that sheds light on his intellectual development, his relationship with Robert Elie and Claude Gauvreau, and the intellectual exchanges and conflicts in the Quebec of the 1940s and 1950s. See also P. Smart, 'La biographie comme approche de l'histoire culturelle: les femmes du *Refus global*', Dvorak, *Création*, 153–60. This seminal essay provides a portrait of the women who belonged to the group of automatist artists and reveals unexpected facets of the period.

BRAULT. *Cahiers d' 'Agonie'. Essais sur un récit de Jacques Brault*, ed. Robert Dion, Quebec, Nuit blanche, 210 pp., presents eleven essays — five of which, it might be noted, have already appeared elsewhere — on B.'s celebrated work. Jacques Paquin, *L'Ecriture de Jacques Brault. De la coexistence des contraires à la pluralité des voix*, Sainte-Foy, Laval U.P., 260 pp., is an important monograph. P. concludes that B.'s æsthetic 'privilégie le passager, l'égarement et l'inachevé et [. . .] se traduit formellement par le recours à la fragmentation'.

BROUILLET. *Lettres québécoises*, 86, includes a brief, useful dossier on B.

CASGRAIN. *VI*, 22.2, has a dossier on C. Of particular interest perhaps are: M. Brunet, 'Henri-Raymond Casgrain et la paternité d'une littérature nationale' (205–24); M. Lord, 'Pour une relecture des *Légendes canadiennes* de Casgrain' (240–60); and M. Lemire, 'Henri-Raymond Casgrain, historien' (261–75).

DUCHARME. Maryel Archambault, *Une Etude de 'L'Avalée des avalés' de Réjean Ducharme*, Montreal, Boréal, 85 pp., is a perfectly competent *manuel d'étudiant* that would certainly help the undergraduate to come to terms with this daunting text.

FERRON.   G. Michaud, 'Expérience du ressouvenir et écriture palimpseste: le conte perdu de Jacques Ferron', *VI*, 22:309–33, is a detailed comparison of 'Une fâcheuse compagnie' and 'Les têtes de morues'.

GARNEAU.   *Mémorial. Inédits de Saint-Denys Garneau*, ed. Giselle Huot and Benoît Lacroix, Saint-Hippolyte, Le Noroît, 1996, 118 pp., is a slight collection of miscellaneous letters and personal papers written by friends and relatives of the poet. Three pieces by Robert Elie are alone in rising above pious platitudes. However, the volume does include one hitherto unpublished poem, entitled 'Le Cimetière', by G.

GAUVIN.   A. de Vaucher, '*Lettres persanes/Lettres d'une autre*. Un essai/fiction de Lise Gauvin', Mildonian, *Parodia*, 331–40, examines the links between G.'s text (dubbed a Genettian 'parodie sérieuse') and Montesquieu's famous epistolary novel.

GAUVREAU.   Serge Provost and Lorraine Pintal, *La Création de l'inimitable. Composition et mise en scène de l'opéra 'Le Vampire et la nymphomane' sur un livret de Claude Gauvreau*, Montreal, Chants Libres, 1996, 64 pp. The composer Provost and the director Pintal discourse on their response to G.'s libretto and in so doing illuminate both it and its metamorphosis into the opera eventually presented some 40 years after its creation. (*Cahiers de Théâtre Jeu*, 81, 1996, has short articles by A. Lazaridès and M. Vaïs on this production of *Le Vampire et la nymphomane*.)

GODBOUT.   Josias Semujanga, *Configuration de l'énonciation interculturelle dans le roman francophone. Eléments de méthode comparative*, Quebec, Nuit blanche, 1996, 147 pp., seeks to 'tenter une interprétation des images de "soi" et de l' "Autre" et d'en proposer une méthode de lecture dans les textes francophones modernes' based on G.'s *Les Têtes à Papineau* and Valentin-Yves Mudimbe's *L'Ecart*. Unremittingly rebarbative.

GODIN.   Gérald Godin, **Tendres et emportés: récit et nouvelles*, ed. André Gervais, Outremont, Lanctôt, 131 pp., is a welcome critical edition of seven of G.'s pieces.

GRANDBOIS.   *Nuit blanche*, 65, has a brief dossier on G. by J.-G. Hudon (36–40).

GROULX.   Réal Bertrand, *Lionel Groulx*, Montreal, Lidec, 61 pp., provides a basic biography of G.

GUÈVREMONT.   Jean-Jacques Lachapelle, '*Le Survenant*' *et son temps*, Centre d'interprétation du patrimoine de Sorel, 30 pp., is a slim volume published to mark the exhibition of the same name held in Sorel in 1997. Really quite useful. Alain Charbonneau, '*Le Survenant*' *de Germaine Guèvremont*, Montreal, Hurtubise HMH, 96 pp. *EF*, 33.3, is given over to six essays that tackle *de concert* Germaine Guèvremont's

Le Survenant and Gabrielle Roy's *Bonheur d'occasion*, two novels which, although published in the same year, are usually assumed to belong to different worlds. The essays not only shed light on the two texts but also on current critical trends. The volume also includes four previously unpublished letters written by R. to her husband and a brief essay on these by S. Marcotte (93–102).

HÉBERT. *Anne Hébert, parcours d'une œuvre. Colloque de Paris III et Paris IV — Sorbonne mai, 1996*, ed. Madeleine Ducrocq-Poirier et al., Montreal, L'Hexagone, 454 pp., presents some 34 essays by the likes of: N. Bishop, 'Guerre, errances et exils dans l'œuvre d'Anne Hébert' (163–74); J. M. Paterson, 'Figures de l'Autre dans *Kamouraska*' (243–50); and I. Oore, 'Le silence dans *L'Enfant chargé de songes* d'Anne Hébert' (383–95). The majority of the essays are devoted to themes and narrative technique, but H.'s poetry is not neglected. Two enterprising pieces are given over to cinematographic response to H.'s novels. Essential reading. Constantina Thalia Mitchell and Paul Raymond Côté, *Shaping the Novel: Textual Interplay in the Fiction of Malraux, Hébert and Modiano*, Providence–Oxford, Berghahn Books, 1996, 224 pp., offer self-contained readings that seek to promote comparison and contrast of works by, on the face of it, a somewhat eclectic group of writers. H.'s 1992 *L'Enfant chargé de songes* is thus contextualized in a modern/post-modern current of self-conscious writing that explores social dislocation and crisis. Astute and stimulating. A. de Vries, 'Anne Hébert et la quête identitaire de ses personnages', *RHFB*, 66, 1996:41–48, concludes that 'l'écriture d'Anne Hébert est essentiellement pré-œdipale, cherchant la vie de rêve'. L. Guillemette, 'Pour une nouvelle lecture des *Fous de Bassan* d'Anne Hébert: l'Amérique et ses parcours discursifs', *VI*, 22:334–54, proposes a far from convincing rereading that revolves around the supposed meaning that can be given to the presence of the USA in H.'s novel.

HÉMON. Louis Hémon, *Maria Chapdelaine. Récit du Canada français*, ed. Dominique Cyr, Anjou, CEC, 304 pp., is yet another edition that first-year undergraduates in particular would find useful, including as it does exercises and spirited essays on stylistic and thematic issues ('Le roman paysan' for example). Nicole Bourdeau, *Une Etude de 'Maria Chapdelaine'*, Montreal, Boréal, 111 pp., is a *manuel d'étudiant* that does not merely spoonfeed. G. Chovrelat, 'Louis Hémon: d'un manifeste aux masques de l'écriture', Dvorak, *Création*, 169–78, discusses H.'s largely neglected short story *Jérôme*, published in the sports paper *Le Vélo* in 1904. D. L. Parris, 'Québec — two views from the outside: Louis Hémon and J. E. Le Rossignol', *BJCS*, 12:41–47, is an engaging and stimulating comparison of *Maria Chapdelaine* with a little-known English-language novel, Le R.'s *Jean-Baptiste — A Story of French Canada.*

LABERGE. *Lettres québécoises*, 81, 1996, has a section (10–15) devoted to L. with brief pieces by L. Lapierre, M. J. Green, and J. De Decker.

LAFERRIÈRE. A. Lamontagne, ' "On ne naît pas Nègre, on le devient": la représentation de l'autre dans *Comment faire l'amour avec un Nègre sans se fatiguer* de Dany Laferrière', *QuS*, 23 : 29–42, undertakes a detailed study of alterity in L.'s first novel. G. Moreau, 'L'inscription des valeurs dans *L'Odeur du café* de Dany Laferrière', *QuF*, 105 : 66–69, is part of a dossier on 'La nouvelle littérature québécoise' that also includes H.-J. Greif, 'La littérature allophone au Québec. Ecrire en terre d'accueil', 61–65. This piece offers a brief survey of such writers as Naïm Kattan, Mona Latif Ghattas and Marco Micone as well as L.

LALONDE. J. Demers, 'Autour de la question linguistique. Le manifeste québécois des années '60–'70', *CanL*, 152–53 : 17–35, has some interesting comments on L.'s 'Speak White' and other linguistic manifestos.

LANGEVIN, A. Martin Doré, **'Poussière sur la ville' d'André Langevin*, Montreal, Hurtubise HMH, 90 pp.

LANGEVIN, G. Gilbert Langevin, *PoéVie*, ed. Normand Baillargeon, Montreal Typo, 268 pp., is an anthology of L.'s poems, songs, pieces of prose, and aphorisms that would serve as a good introduction to him. **VI*, 23.3, has a dossier on L.

LA ROCQUE. K. Meadwell, 'Temporalisation et altérité chez Gilbert La Rocque', Dvorak, *Creation*, 187–94, is a brief but useful discussion of *Serge d'entre les morts*, *Les Masques*, and *Le Passager*.

LAURENDEAU. Félix Bouvier, *André Laurendeau*, Montreal, Lidec, 1996, 62 pp., is a straightforward biography with a pronounced nationalist bias.

LECLERC. Félix Leclerc, *Tout Félix en chansons*, ed. Roger Chamberland, Quebec, Nuit blanche, 1996, 287 pp., brings together all L.'s songs. The volume includes a short but insightful introduction by A. Gaulin, and a valuable discography and bibliography by A. Boivin.

LOZEAU. M. Lemaire, 'Le rythme dans la poésie d'Albert Lozeau. Contribution à l'étude du vers régulier symboliste', *VI*, 22 : 355–75, is a close analysis of L.'s development of a personal mode of versification that led to poetry 'remarquable par sa fluidité, son expressivité et sa douceur murmurée.'

MARCOTTE. Pierre Popovic, *Entretiens avec Gilles Marcotte. De la littérature avant toute chose*, Montreal, Liber, 1996, 195 pp., presents a readable but somewhat superficial series of conversations between P. and M. Some insight is offered into M.'s thoughts on literature and on those literary figures who inspired him, notably in the second section entitled 'Texte et vérités probables' (95–143).

MIRON. **Les Adieux du Quebec à Gaston Miron*, ed. Simone Bussières, Montreal, Guérin, 220 pp. J. Royer, 'L'Orpailleur Miron', *Les Ecrits*, 89:5–20, consists of R.'s personal memories of and reflections on the poet.

MONETTE. G. Adamson, 'Autogénération du langage, mode d'emploi de l'écriture narrative de Madeleine Monette', *QuS*, 23:54–61, discusses textual self-generation in *Le Double suspect* and 'L'Américain et la jarretière'.

NELLIGAN. André Vanassé, *Emile Nelligan: le spasme de vivre*, Montreal, XYZ, 1996, 201 pp., is one of a series of so-called *biographies romancées* and consequently, although not without interest, must be taken with a big pinch of salt. Louis Dantin, *Emile Nelligan et son œuvre*, ed. Réjean Robidoux, Montreal U.P., 293 pp., is an exemplary critical edition of Dantin's 1904 presentation of N.'s work — a landmark in the history of Quebec literature — which does justice to both the unjustly vilified D. and the poet he championed.

OLLIVIER. E. Brière, '*Mère solitude* d'Emile Ollivier: apport migratoire à la société québécoise', *IJCS*, 13, 1996:61–70, shows how the exiled Haitian not only influenced native Quebec writers but also helped to establish an allophone variant of Quebec literature centred on the experience of migrant peoples. An important contribution to an important debate.

OUELLETTE. Fernand Ouellette, *En forme de trajet: essais*, Montreal, Editions du Noroît, 1996, 197 pp., is a collection of essays by the poet. It includes a section entitled 'Spirales' (119–71) that reveals something of his personal poetics.

POTIER. Robert Toupin, *Les Ecrits de Pierre Potier*, Ottawa U.P., 1996, 1,329 pp. This massive compendium presents all the writings, hitherto scattered in various libraries and archives, of the Belgian Jesuit who was a missionary to the Hurons from 1744 to 1781, and constitutes a quite superb reference work. Of particular value perhaps is P.'s lexicon of 'façons de parler' in New France.

POULIN. *Lettres québécoises*, 83, 1996, has several useful pages devoted to Poulin J. Lintvelt, 'La dualité identitaire dans l'œuvre de Jacques Poulin', *RHFB*, 64, 1996:23–30, is a useful, lucid reading, as is H. van's Land, 'La *Kérouacquisition* du territoire américain: Poulin, Godbout, et LaRue comme représentants du discours littéraire québécois des années 80', *ib.*, 31–40.

ROY. Linda M. Clemente and William A. Clemente, *Gabrielle Roy. Creation and Memory*, Toronto, ECW Press, 202 pp., draws on scholarship, R.'s autobiography and correspondence, and published interviews to explore those aspects of her life that account for the scope of her writing and to examine the roots of her major themes. Worthy but unoriginal and not very challenging or stimulating. M. E. Chaves de Mello, '*Bonheur d'occasion*: a ficção às margens da história', Lavallée, *Brasil–Canadá*, 175–83.

SAVARD. Jean de Gaguiers, *Monseigneur de Charlevoix. Félix-Antoine Savard*, Montreal, Fides, 1996, 278 pp., is, in the author's own words, 'un modeste ouvrage [qui] n'a rien d'une étude savante'. Within its unambitious parameters the book's attempts to trace S.'s biography and to comment on aspects of his art and thought are successful enough. *Fraternellement . . . Félix-Antoine Savard. Lettres de Menaud à André Major 1965–1971*, ed. André Major, Montreal, Leméac, 117 pp., is a collection of letters that sheds some light on the literary world in Quebec at a time when the Quiet Revolution was coming to an end, and on S. himself.

TOUGAS. P. R. Côté, '*La Mauvaise foi* de Gérald Tougas: masques, miroirs et production textuelle', *QuS*, 23:62–72, examines how the triple retelling of the same tale creates allegorical implications for Quebec's linguistic and cultural situation.

TREMBLAY. Jean-Marc Barrette, *L'Univers de Michel Tremblay. Dictionnaire des personnages*, Montreal U.P., 1996, 544 pp. T.'s dramatic world does indeed teem with so many characters that, as the blurb has it, 'même le plus passionné des lecteurs peut y perdre son latin'. Obviously, then, a dictionary such as this — it actually lists and describes some 2,170 characters, fictional and real — is going to come in useful. Somehow, however, it does seem a vaguely fatuous undertaking . . . M. Boucher-Marchand, 'Michel Tremblay et l'auto-biographie du "Nous"', Dvorak, *Création*, 195–201, argues that 'l'autobiographie de Tremblay sème la confusion sur la distance minime qui sépare l'œuvre romanesque du récit de vie'.

CARIBBEAN LITERATURE

By MARY GALLAGHER, *University College Dublin*

I. GENERAL

Rinne, *Antilles*, most notably offers contributions on forgotten women writers such as Virgile Valcin and Annie Desroy, the first Haitian women to write of the American occupation. Also of interest are articles on new writers, both better-known, such as Suzanne Dracius (Martinique) or Gisèle Pineau (Guadeloupe), and less well known, for example, Ina and Michèle Césaire (Martinique), Gerty Dambury (Guadeloupe) or Yanick Lahens, Lilas Desquiron and Jan J. Dominique (Haiti). The articles all focus on a single author; there are no comparative studies and no general consideration of the theoretical issues raised by 'women writing'. Arnold, *History*, III, is devoted to Cross-Cultural Studies, examining discursive intersections between Europe, the Caribbean, Africa and the American continent from the 15th c. to the present. Although it does include essays of considerable general interest, such as the contributions on the comparative history of Caribbean literatures in Creole or on the oral tradition in Caribbean poetry, an opportunity has perhaps been lost to consider the question of (cross-cultural) intertextuality in Caribbean literature. Three articles directly and substantively address French Caribbean writing, of which two are on Edouard Glissant. The third, K. Balutansky, 'Anglophone and Francophone fiction by Caribbean women: redefining "female identity"' (267–82), suggests that, from the early 1970s, rather than mirroring social realities, novels by women challenge traditional definitions of Caribbean women's identity. A number of studies, distributed over at least three volumes, focus on the language question in Francophone Caribbean literature. M.-C. Hazaël-Massieux, 'Du français, du créole et de quelques situations plurilingues: données linguistiques et sociolinguistiques', Jones, *Francophonie*, 127–58, is a clear and lively article with an explicit bearing on the literary use of French and Creole. J. Bernabé, 'Conflit, complémentarité des langues et élimination des barrières linguistiques dans la Caraïbe', Gontard, *Francophonie*, 193–200, calls for a more lucid approach to the interrelations of various languages in the Caribbean, outlining, for example, some of the (nefarious) implications of what is euphemistically termed 'l'élimination des barrières linguistiques'. H. A. Murdoch's essay, 'Dédoublement créolisé et performance narrative: le discours post-colonial des Antilles francophones', *ib.*, 211–216, relates the theory of writers such as Homi Bhabha and Edouard Glissant to Maryse Condé's *En attendant le bonheur*, while M. Gallagher, 'La littérature de la créolité: traduire le créole, est-ce le trahir?', *ib.*, 201–10, examines the meaning of translation (from Creole into French) within contemporary French Caribbean literary texts. D. Delas, 'Introduction à une poétique des écritures métissées', *ASCALFY*, 2:8–17, relates the writing of Patrick Chamoiseau and other contemporary Caribbean authors to the æsthetics of Yves Bonnefoy, Gilles Deleuze, and Henri Meschonnic.

2. DRAMA

Bridget Jones and Sita E. Dickson Littlewood, *Paradoxes of French Caribbean Theatre: An Annotated Checklist of Dramatic Works from Guadeloupe, Guyane and Martinique from 1900*, London, Roehampton Institute Department of Modern Languages, 125 pp., is prefaced by an informative introduction on the institutional past and present of theatre in the French Caribbean. About 400 works are listed, and the database is all the more useful as such a negligable proportion of the repertoire (especially in Creole) is available in written form. B. Jones, 'Quelques choix de langue dans le théâtre antillais (1970–1995)', Little, *Black Accents*, 17–29, relates the evolution of language choice (between Creole and French) to the divergent and evolving socio-cultural and political contexts of the French Caribbean, charting the transition from a clear, politically-aligned polarization to a more subtle interplay of codes; while the second part of C.-A. Upton, 'Words in space: filling the empty space in Francophone theatre', *ib.*, 253–76, studies the theatrical language of the French Caribbean in relation to Francophone Africa in particular, commenting on the art of Aimé Césaire, Daniel Boukman, and Simone Schwarz-Bart. E. Stephenson, 'Théâtre et francophonie en Guyane française', Jones, *Francophonie*, 251–60, outlines the evolution of Guyanese theatre since the 1970s, blaming its currently bleak state in part on the unresolved relation of Creole to French.

3. INDIVIDUAL AUTHORS

CAPÉCIA. T. Denean Sharpley-Whiting, 'Sexist, mysogynist or anti-racist humanist? Frantz Fanon and Mayotte Capécia', in the new *IJFS* 1:19–32, highlights the blind spots both in F.'s criticism of C., and in 'Euro-American lit-crit femininists'' gendered criticisms of Fanon'. E. A. Hurley, 'Intersections of female identity or writing the woman in two novels by Capécia and Marie-Magdeleine Carbet', *FR*, 70:575–86, outlines textual convergences between the two novels which are both presented as transgressive.

CÉSAIRE. A. Chambers, 'Universal and culturally specific images in the poetry of Aimé Césaire', Little, *Black Accents*, 31–46, considers the evolution of C.'s poetics through the gradual incorporation of the specific within the universal.

CHAMOISEAU. M. McCusker, 'Intersections of gender, space and language in Chamoiseau's autobiographies', *ASCALFB*, 15 : 3–13, is a short but persuasive analysis of the polarization of feminine and masculine space.

CONDÉ. An important contribution to C. criticism, *L'Œuvre de Maryse Condé*, L'Harmattan, 1996, 268 pp., is a collection of papers delivered at a conference in Pointe-à-Pitre in 1995, with one section on literary criticism and another on translation. The former emphasizes C.'s reluctance to conform to various orthodoxies, from African-American or American feminist versions of political correctness, to the tenets of *Négritude*, *Antillanité* or *Créolité*. M.-D. Le Rumeur, 'À la recherche de ... la quête de Condé', Little, *Black Accents*, 47–57, argues that C.'s concerns have shifted from the Old World to the New, from genealogy and the past to existential questions pertinent to the present and future. See also Id., 'L'anglophilie condéenne; une francophonie "blackboulée"', Gontard, *Francophonie*, 217–22, on C's alleged anglo- (or americano-) centric evolution. M. Rosello, '*Les Derniers Rois mages* et *La Traversée de la mangrove*: insularité ou insularisation?', Rinne, *Antilles*, 175–192, is original in approach, questioning the near-standard critical interpretations of C.'s fiction in relation to the author's geographical trajectory. R. Erlam, 'Tentative de communication dans *Traversée de la Mangrove* de Maryse Condé', *NZJFS*, 18.2 : 29–38, highlights the reflexive nature of C.'s novel, which explores difficulties in communication through its representation of silence, speech and writing.

DAMBURY. A thoughtful interview with S. Houyoux, Rinnes, *Antilles*, 267–76.

GLISSANT. Arnold, *History*, III, includes: K. A. Sprouse, 'Chaos and Rhizome: introduction to a Caribbean poetics' (79–86), and R. de la Campa, 'Resistance and Globalization in Caribbean Discourse: Antonio Benítez-Rojo and Edouard Glissant', (87–116). Both articles are comparative studies of the complexities and possibilities of the Cuban's and the Martinican's theorization of Caribbeanness.

SCHWARZ-BART. Kathleen Gyssels, *Filles de Solitude. Essai sur l'identité antillaise dans les (auto-)biographies fictives de Simone et André Schwarz-Bart*, L'Harmattan, 1996, 464 pp., is a wide-ranging and exhaustively well-researched study of the problematic of Caribbean and/or Creole identity as constructed in this literary corpus. Not only are interesting comparisons persuasively drawn between the latter and the literary traditions of the Anglophone Caribbean and of African America, but it is argued that the æsthetic and political dimensions of these texts are more in line with those of the *créolité* movement, than with the tenets of *négritude* or *antillanité*. The critical perspective is enhanced by its consideration of the S.-B. couple's literary collaboration. K. Smyley Wallace, 'Créolité and the feminine text in Schwarz-Bart', *FR*, 70:554–61, argues that language fusion in S.-B.'s *Pluie et vent sur Télumée Miracle* actualizes simultaneously the æsthetic of 'écriture féminine' and that of the 'créolité' movement. N. Aas-Rouxparis, Espace antillais au féminin: présence, absence' *ib.*, 854–64, traces the gradual transformation, from S.-B.'s *Pluie et vent sur Télumée Miracle*, through Maryse Condé's *La Vie Scélérate* to S.-B.'s *Ton beau capitaine*, of similar images of absence and alienation into images of presence and integration.

MAXIMIN. E. Sellin, Intertextual dynamics of identity retrieval and creation in Francophone literature', *IJFS*, 1 : 3–10, is more convincing on intertextuality in M.'s *L'Isolé Soleil* than on Maryse Condé's use of this device in *Moi, Tituba sorcière . . . Noire de Salem*.

WARNER-VIEYRA. P. J. Proulx, 'Inscriptions of silence and violence in the Antillean text: reading Warner-Vieyra's *Juletane* and "Sidonie"', *FR*, 70:698–709, studies how these texts link oppression with repression and voicelessness with violence.

AFRICAN AND MAGHREB LITERATURE

By HÉLÈNE GILL, DEBRA KELLY, ETHEL TOLANSKY, *University of Westminster*, and MARGARET MAJUMDAR, *University of Glamorgan*

1. FRANCOPHONE MAGHREB: GENERAL

The general work on francophone African issues confirms the shift observed in 1996, away from the immediate coverage of the increasingly tragic events in Algeria and towards two major preoccupations: a renewed interest in colonialism and in the Algerian war of liberation; and interest in *francophonie* per se, especially against the challenge of globalization. Contributions to the analysis of the current Algerian crisis have included articles in various issues of *Esprit*: O. Mongin, 'Le sale avenir de la guerre civile en Algérie', 230–231:16–26; F. Gèze, 'Algérie, pourquoi le silence?', 235:189–92; L. Provost, 'Algérie entre l'oubli et le rejet', 228:74–81; B. Stora and F. Oussedik, 'Ce que disent les cadavres en Algérie', 237:5–12; and B. Stora, 'L'onde de choc des années algériennes en France', *ib.*,13–28. Books have included: Martin Stone, *The Agony of Algeria*, London, Hurst, 274 pp.; and Slimane Medhar, *La Violence sociale en Algérie*, Algiers, Thala, 267 pp. However, many authors sought for the root causes in the colonial and pre-colonial period, as in: Joseph Jurt, *Algérie — France — Islam*, L'Harmattan, 254 pp.; *Imperialism and Colonialism*, ed. H. L. Wesseling, London, Greenwood Press, 241 pp.; Laroussi Amri, *La Tribu au Maghreb médiéval*, Tunis I U.P., 310 pp.; A. Lounis, 'Alger. Une ville et ses discours', *BFA*, 10:35–51; *Essai historique sur l'intérêt général (Europe, islam, Afrique coloniale)*, ed. Sophia Mappa, Karthala, 200 pp.; Henri Bangou, *Aliénation et désaliénation dans les sociétés post-esclavagistes*, L'Harmattan, 164 pp.; and a special issue of *Confluences Méditerranées*, no.22, 'La France et le monde arabe. Au-delà des fantasmes', ed. Abderrahim Lamchichi and Jean-Christophe Ploquin, 184 pp. A particular focus has been the Algerian war of liberation. *La Guerre d'Algérie et les Algériens*, ed. Charles-Robert Agéron, Armand Colin, 340 pp. includes an Algerian perspective with contributions by Omar Carlier, Mohammed Harbi, and others. Further contributions to the debate include: H. Roberts, 'The politics of *The Battle of Algiers*', *JAS*, 2:90–99; Id., 'Ernest Gellner and the Algerian army', *ib.*, 27–42; Benjamin Stora, *Imaginaires de guerre*, La Découverte, 250 pp.; Id., *Appelés en guerre d'Algérie*, Gallimard, 128 pp.; Alain-Gérard Slama, *La Guerre d'Algérie, histoire d'une déchirure*, Gallimard, 176 pp.; Martin Evans, *The Memory of Resistance. French Opposition to the Algerian War, 1954–62*, Oxford, Berg, 250 pp.; and *Les Accords d'Evian, en conjoncture et en longue durée*, ed. René Galissot, Karthala — Institut Maghreb-Europe, 265 pp. Perceptions of the other are further investigated in *Une Altérité questionnée*, ed. François Devalière, L'Harmattan, 334 pp. Issues of modernity and ideological influences upon the Maghreb are treated by: Juliette Bessis, *Maghreb: la traversée du siècle*, L'Harmattan, 538 pp.; Abdallah Laroui, *Islamisme, modernisme, libéralisme: esquisses critiques*, Centre Culturel Arabe, 239 pp.; Ramdane Hakem, *Islamisme et barbarie*, L'Harmattan, 170 pp.; Jacques Locquin, *L'Intégrisme islamique: mythe ou réalité?* L'Harmattan, 190 pp.; Hélé Béji, *L'Imposture culturelle*, Stock, 165 pp.; A. Bouabaci, 'Entre la reconnaissance par le clan et l'adhésion aux valeurs de l'universalité', *BFA*, 10: 1–14; and Abdou Filali-Ansary, *L'Islam est-il hostile à la laïcité?*, Casablanca, Le Fennec, 160 pp. Issues specific to particular countries of the Maghreb are explored in: Abdallah Hammoudi, *Master and Disciple. The Cultural Foundations of Moroccan Authoritarianism*, Chicago U.P., 194 pp.; *Maghreb-Machrek*, no.157, a special issue entitled *Tunisie: dix ans déjà*, ed. Michel Camau and Vincent Geisser, 214 pp; *Tunisie. Mouvements sociaux et modernité*, ed. Mahmoud Ben Ramdhane, Karthala, 268 pp.; and *Ifriquiya*, no.1, 176 pp., a new review of Tunisian writing and criticism. The review of specific issues within the broader context of the francophone world is covered by: Agence de la Francophonie, *Quelle Francophonie pour le XXIème siècle?*, ed. Jean-Louis Roy, Karthala, 290 pp.; *Political Reform in Francophone Africa*, ed. John Clark and David Gardinier, Oxford, Westview, xviii + 318 pp.; *Regards russes sur les littératures francophones*, ed. Robert Jouanny, Irène Nikiforova and Svetlana Projoghina, L'Harmattan, 476 pp.; *Littérature maghrébine et littérature mondiale*, ed. C. Bonn and A. Rothe, Würzburg, Koenigshausen and Neumann, 1995, 196 pp; and Peter Hawkins, 'Homo Authénegrafricanicus? Applying Bourdieu to African literature in French', *ASCALFB*, 15:28–35. Bernard Botiveau and Jocelyne Césari, *Géopolitique des islams*, Economica, 110 pp., discuss the relationship with global issues. J. Samuel, 'Euro-Mediterranean partnership: the case of Tunisia', *BFA*, 10:26–34, examines Euro-Maghrebian relations, as do M. Blunden, 'Euro-Mediterranean relations: the conditions for partnership in the Maghreb', *ib.*, 15–25; and *Le Partenariat euro-méditerranéen*, ed. Bichara Khader, L'Harmattan, 230 pp. Conversely, the African diaspora in Europe is the subject of: *Post-Colonial Cultures in France*, ed. Alec G. Hargreaves and Mark McKiney, London, Routledge, 299 pp.; and *HM*, no.1207, special issue, 'Imaginaire colonial, figures de l'immigré'. Jocelyne Césari offers two studies: *Faut-il avoir peur de l'islam?*, Presses de Sciences Po, 132 pp. and *Etre Musulman en France*, Hachette, 238 pp. Others in this field include: Yamina Benguigui, *Mémoires d'immigrés: l'héritage maghrébin*, Canal + Editions, 210 pp.; and Lucienne Martini, *Racines de papier: essai sur l'expression littéraire pied-noire,* Publisud, 294 pp. *Sociétés Africaines et Diasporas,* no.4, 206 pp., is a special issue entitled 'L'immigration dans "tous" ses états', with articles by C. Quiminal, M. Timera, and S. Yatera. S. Nini writes on 'L'Entre-deux Cultures', *BFA,* 11:1–7. Two companion-pieces are: A. Hargreaves, 'Ni Beurs, ni immigrés, ni jeunes issus de l'immigration', *ib.,* 8–12; and Y. Rocheron, ' Ni bizarre ni banal: le couple franco-étranger', *ib.,* 13–28. *PAf,* no. 67, is a special issue, 'La France et les migrants africains',160 pp. Gender issues figure prominently in *ib.,* no. 65, a special issue, 'L'Afrique des femmes', 165 pp. H. Gill, 'From veils to dual identities', *BFA,* 11:32–41; and Andrée Dore-Audibert and Annie Morzelle, *Vivre en Algérie. Des Françaises parlent,* Karthala, 216 pp. The following are particularly concerned with women in literature: Marta Segarra, *Leur Pesant de poudre: romancières francophones du Maghreb,* L'Harmattan, 238 pp.; Obiama Nnaemeka, *The Politics of (M)Othering: Womanhood, Identity and Resistance in African Literature,* London–NY, Routledge, 230 pp.; and N. Hitchcott, '"She's not a feminist, but . . ." Francophone African women's writing and feminist ideology', *ASCALFB,* 15:18–27. The debate around language continues with: J. Lavoie, 'Le Français créolisé comme option de traduction du vernaculaire noir américain', *La Censure,* 51:116–38. *Algérie-Littérature-Action,* no.9:105–116, has an interview with Jacques Derrida about his 1996 book, *Le Monolinguisme de l'autre,* Galilée, 140 pp. A new review, *IJFS,* 1.1, includes: F. Aitsiselmi, 'Langue et identité beur dans l'*Hexagone*' (41–52); and E. Sellin 'Intertextual dynamics of identity retrieval and creation in Francophone literature' (3–10). The æsthetics of orientalism are illustrated by: Jean-Charles Humbert, *La Découverte du Sahara en 1900,* L'Harmattan, 296 pp.; Guy Barthélémy, *Fromentin et l'écriture du désert,* L'Harmattan, 146 pp.; Rachid Boudjedra, *Peindre l'Orient,* Zulma, 1996, 77 pp.; and Alain Fleig, *Rêves de papier. La photographie orientaliste, 1860–1914,* Ides et Calendes, 160 pp. Other æsthetic issues are debated by: H. Abdel-Jaouad, 'Le Surréalisme et la question coloniale', *BFA,* 10:60–73; V. Holman, 'Fine Arts or fetishes? Paris re-presents Africa', *ib.,* 11:102–112; and *Algérie-Littérature/Action,* 15–16, a special issue on 'Peinture: Baya parmi nous', ed. A. Breton et al., 343 pp.

2. FRANCOPHONE MAGHREB LITERATURE

Although established writers, especially Djebar and Ben Jelloun, continue to dominate the literary scene, lesser-known writers also attract critical attention. The year has seen the publication of a number of conference proceedings which either analyse the place of and the contribution made by Francophone writing, or affirm the identity of particular Maghreb countries. In recent years Djebar has been the focus of numerous articles and university dissertations, and a new book by Jeanne Marie Clerc, *Ecrire, Transgresser, Résister,* L'Harmattan, 173 pp., reflects on the tension between the individualistic trajectories of D.'s heroines striving to widen the boundaries of emancipation, and the pull of the traditional society in which they live. This book also underlines the inseparable link between the æsthetic quest and the quest for identity in D.'s writing. D.'s contribution to film-making is also touched on, and is further developed in *Littérature et cinéma en Afrique francophone. Ousmane Sembène et Assia Djebar,* ed. S. Niang, L'Harmattan, 254 pp. Articles on D. include: S. A. Khodja, 'Assia Djebar. La parole obstinée', *Le Jardin d'Essais,* 7:8–12, a piece in a new Paris literary review; S. A. Rosenblum, 'M'introduire dans ton histoire: entrée des narrateurs dans *L'Amour, la fantasia* d'Assia Djebar', *EtF,* 12.2:67–80; and D. Brahimi, 'Assia Djebar ou la hantise de la disparition', *Algérie-Littérature/Action,* 12–13:137–46. D. is also included in Marta Segarra, *Leur pesant de poudre: romancières francophones du Maghreb,* L'Harmattan, 237 pp., which focuses on her narrative and style, particularly in *Loin de Médine.* This book also includes a chapter on Hélé Béji's *L'Œil du jour,* on the themes of identity, space and the problems of memory. This confirms B.'s emerging importance as both writer and critic, as evidenced in her own long article, 'Equivalence des cultures et tyrannie des identités', *Esprit,* January, 107–18. Among other writers beginning to attract critical attention are Malika Mokeddem, in C. Chaulet-Achour and L. Kenfa, 'Ecriture et implication', *Algérie-Littérature/Action* 14:185–99, who give an overview of her four novels to date; and Fatima Gallaire, in E. Liso, 'Ecriture et mémoire dans les nouvelles de Fatima Gallaire. Une lecture critique', *BFA,* 10:52–57, the first article devoted to G.'s short stories as opposed to her theatre. The re-publication of works by Marguerite and Taos Amrouche has led to renewed interest in them, including D. Foster, 'La tension entre l'affirmation et l'effacement du moi dans *L'Histoire de ma vie*', *PF,* 50:67–88. This focus on Maghrebian women's writing is continued by the inclusion in Robinson, *Women,* of Assia Djebar (I, 702–708), and Leila Sebbar (IV, 91–95). Articles on Ben Jelloun include: L. Ibnlfassi, 'Tahar Ben Jelloun's formation of the self in *L'Enfant de sable* and *La Nuit sacrée*', *ASCALFY,* 2:36–44; A. Hafez-Engaut, 'L'espace dans trois romans de Tahar Ben Jelloun', *PF,* 50:113–33; R. Elbaz and R. Amar, 'De l'oralité dans le récit Benjellounien', *MaL,* 1.1:35–53, focusing on form rather than content; and A. Attafi, 'L'identité fragmentée dans *La Prière de l'absent*', *EtF* 12.1:75–82. Other Moroccan writers receiving attention are: Mohammed Khaïr-Eddine, in R. Saïgh-Bousta, 'Une vie, un rêve, un homme toujours errant ...', *MaL*, 1:17–33; and Abdelkébir Khatibi, in M. Benalil, 'Tatouer ou écrire la décolonisation: *La Mémoire tatouée*', *ib.*,71–89, and in V. Orlando, 'Defining a new North African identity. Abdelkébir Khatibi's *Amour bilingue*', *IJFS*, 1.1:33–40. There are two new books on the Tunisian writer Hédi Bouraoui: *Hédi Bouraoui. La Transpoésie*, ed. Mansour M'Henni, Tunis, L'Or du Temps, 160 pp., which deals both with his poetry and his novels or 'romanpoèmes'; and *Hédi Bouraoui: Iconoclaste et chantre du transculturel*, ed. Jacques Cotnam, Toronto, Le Nordir, 290 pp., providing an overview of B. as writer, poet, novelist and translator. The Algerian writer Tahar Djaout features in three articles: I. Djaout, 'Le roman moderne et le roman du passé dans *L'Invention du désert* de Tahar Djaout', *EtF*, 12.2:39–54; S. A. Khodja, 'Tahar Djaout ou la parole pérenne', *Algérie-Littérature/Action*, 12–13:213–17; and M.-G. Bernard, 'L'invention du regard. Tahar Djaout et la peinture algérienne contemporaine', *ib.*, 223–34. The first complete bibliographical study devoted to the Algerian Kateb Yacine, *Bibliographie Kateb Yacine*, ed. Charles Bonn, L'Harmattan, 184 pp., covers Y.'s works, interviews, translations, and prefaces, as well as criticisms, theses, and articles. Bonn, *Littérature francophone*, devotes pp.179–241 to the Maghreb, focusing essentially on Yacine's *Nedjma*, the contribution of the Moroccan literary and political review *Souffles*, and Albert Memmi. F. Lionnet, 'The colonial and postcolonial francophone novel', Unwin, *French Novel*, 194–213, includes not only Africa and North Africa, but also Lebanon. Other general surveys give an overview of literary production and its preoccupations, as in *Ecrire le Maghreb*, ed. H. Salha and C. Bonn, Cérès, Tunis, 274 pp.; *Les racines du texte maghrébin*, ed. H. Salha and H. Hemaidi, Cérès, Tunis, 235 pp; T. Michel-Mansour, 'L'enjeu de l'espace dans le roman maghrébin', *EtF* 12.1:83–95; and Najib Redouane, 'Littérature du Maghreb: une mouvance plurielle', *MaL*, 1:1–15. Gontard, *Francophonie*, devotes its second part to 'Pratiques littéraires', with a section on the Maghreb, pp. 223–82. A striking trend this year is the focus on Tunisia, as shown by *Tunisie plurielle*, ed. H. Bouraoui, Tunis, L'Or du Temps, 334 pp., which shows the large range of different types of writing in French by Tunisian writers such as Memmi, Meddeb, Hélé Béji, and Emna Bel Hadj Yahia, and analyses such elements as the Jewish contribution to this writing. Articles on Tunisia include Mahfoudh Ahmed, 'La quête de l'espace originel dans le roman tunisien des années 90', *Ibla*, 180:153–61, concentrating on the novels of Hédi Bouraoui, Magid El Houssi, E. B. H. Yahia, and their concern with the crisis of identity as Tunisia modernizes itself. The literary review

Le Jardin d'Essais, 4:48–63, gives an overview of various contemporary Moroccan writers. As for Algeria, C. Bonn and C. Chaulet-Achour have produced a 'Panorama littéraire', *Algérie-Littérature/Action*, 7–8:201–210. A further new focus is on immigration writing, with *L'Ecriture décentrée. La langue de l'autre dans le roman contemporain*, ed. M. Laronde, L'Harmattan, 211 pp. Beur writing continues to attract attention with an updated edition of Alec Hargreaves, *Immigration and Identity in Beur Fiction*, Berg, 197 pp. Also in this field are: S. Ménager, 'Sur la forme du roman de Leila Sebbar', *EtF*, 12.2:55–66; and D. Fisher, 'Rue du Phantasme: paroles et regards inter-dits de *La Voyeuse interdite* de Nina Bouraoui', *PF*, 50:45–65.

3. FRANCOPHONE SUB-SAHARAN AFRICA
POSTPONED

III. OCCITAN STUDIES

LANGUAGE

By KATHRYN KLINGEBIEL, *Associate Professor of French,*
University of Hawaii at Mānoa

This chapter essentially covers 1996 publications, postponed from
YWMLS, 58; in *YWMLS*, 60, both years 1997 and 1998 will be covered.

I. BIBLIOGRAPHICAL AND GENERAL

C. Bonnet, 'Occitan Language', *MLAIntBibl,* 3,1995[1996]: 168–71,
is also available on CD-ROM. In two ongoing series, K. Klingebiel
provides 1994 and 1995 listings for Occitan linguistics: 'Recent
studies in Occitan linguistics', *CRLN,* 44, 1995:27–33; 'Current
studies in Occitan linguistics, 1995', *ib.,* 45, 1996:13–22; 'Bibliography of Occitan linguistics for 1994', *Tenso,* 11, 1995–96:93–122;
and 'Occitan linguistic bibliography for 1995', *ib.,* 12, 1996:36–76.
Jean Fourié has published the fourth and fifth in his series: *Bibliographie
des ouvrages, œuvres, études et articles en langue d'oc ou intéressant la langue et la
littérature d'oc, publiés en 1995 (Lou Félibrige,* no. 220, supp.), 56 pp.; and
*Bibliographie des ouvrages, œuvres, études et articles en langue d'oc ou intéressant
la langue et la littérature d'oc, publiés en 1996 (Lou Félibrige,* no. 224, supp.),
61 pp. (see *YWMLS* 55:291, 56:271, and 57:242). From May 1997,
this bibliography is also available on the Internet, at http//www.
felibrige.com. J. Wüest, 'Bibliographie des enquêtes sociolinguistiques
en domaine occitan', *Lengas,* Montpellier, 40, 1996:149–53, finds
only 47 items to report from the years 1957–94. P. Berengier,
'Thesaurus occitan', *PrA,* 105, 1996:13, reviews electronic sources
for Occitan, with brief summaries of round table presentations at the
fifth AIEO congress (Toulouse, August 1996): troubadour texts (G.
Gonfroy); the Concordance de l'Occitan Médiéval (P. Ricketts);
modern dialects (J.-P. Dalbera); texts for pedagogical applications
(J.-L. Fossat); the GIDILOc (P. Sauzet). All participants described
their legal problems with editors as being potentially more trouble-
some than the work of adapting to data base format. See also J.-P.
Dalbera, 'La Base de données dialectales du "Thesaurus Occitan"',
BALI, 3rd ser., 20, 1996:187–201. Id., *Aspects heuristiques: strates
et représentations dans une base de données dialectales', *Actes* (Corte),
103–16.
　For Occitan listings on the Worldwide Web up to July 1997, see
'Adreças Occitanas sus Internet', *EOc,* 21:51–52. *List-oc,* the e-mail
talksite run by the Coumita Culturau Oucitan in collaboration with
the University of Toulouse, remains lively (see *YWMLS,* 57:242).

Attention has been paid to ensuring user access to the WWW. M. van Den Bossche, J.-J. Maureta, C. Stecòli, and T. Merger, 'En occitan sul Net, o la nòstra lenga se reviscòla sus Internet', *GS*, 461, 1996:183–88, have been tireless in their efforts. J.-F. Blanc, 'Sus Internet se charro en lengo nostro', *PrA* 99, 1996:13, presents the young team (see preceding item) who created a WWW page for "óucitan vo lengo d'O vo prouvençau". Anon., 'La lengo d'oc sus lou resau Internet', *ib.*, 97, 1996:5.

Y. Gourgaud, 'La pensée normative de Patric Sauzet', *CEPONB*, 1.1, 1996:1–8, reviews Sauzet's 18 norms for Occitan, with emphasis on the 18th: 'la langue normée, employée en littérature, redonne à tout lecteur le vrai contact avec l'œuvre en la rendant linguistiquement accessible. Le dialectalisme condamne tout auteur à être d'abord jugé sur la forme [...]'. In conclusion, these norms provide a theoretical and practical framework, beyond Occitan itself, for any of the minority Romance languages currently undergoing normalization. B. Schlieben-Lange, 'Les études romanes avant Raynouard et Diez', *Actas* (Santiago de Compostela), VIII, 371–77, outlines four early hypotheses concerning the genesis and filiation of the Romance languages, from authors of the Midi: Cary (1746), Papon (1777–86, *Histoire générale de Provence*), Achard (1785, *Dictionnaire de la Provence et du comtat Venaissin*), and Bouche. Rather than choosing to follow Achard's view of Provençal as an intermediary stage between Latin and all of Romance, Raynouard would have done better to heed Papon, for whom the Romance languages descended from Vulgar Latin. H. Morimoto, 'Les estudis occitans al Japon', *L'Occitan*, 124, 1996:5, succinctly describes Japanese publications since 1914 on medieval and modern Occitan literature and linguistics, translations into Japanese of Mistral's *La Granouio de Narbouno*, collections of troubadour poems, and grammars of modern Occitan and Gascon. M. Chapduèlh, 'La latinitat granda de l'occitan', *Lo Convise*, 13, 1996:11, reminds his general readers that 'l'occitan es benleu un marrit latin e pas un marrit francés'. Pierre Bec, *La Langue occitane* (Que Sais-Je? 1059), PUF, 1995, is in its sixth edition since 1963.

2. Medieval Period (To 1500)

GENERAL. Cantalausa (alias Louis Combes), 'Aux racines de notre langue', *RRou*, 45, 1996:125–30, reviews uses of the vernacular from AD 400 and key texts in the early history of Occitan, concluding that during the period 480–780, differences in vocabulary and intonation between the dialects of northern and southern Gaul were probably no greater than they are today. M. Banniard, 'Latin tardif et langue d'oc: de quelques témoignages sociolinguistiques', pp. 33–46 of *PerM*, no. 22, supp., 'Actes du colloque "Languedoc et langue d'oc" (Toulouse, janvier 1996)', ed. Groupe de Recherches 'Lectures médiévales', Toulouse II, concludes that 'la prise de conscience d'une différence de nature entre la langue traditionnelle et la langue populaire ne date que du 9e s. en terres d'oïl [...] mais il faudra attendre le 10e s. pour que la latinité du Sud change', due to a dearth of monasteries in the Midi, with its less sharply delineated split between spelling and pronunciation. P. Ménard, *'Rotiers, soldadiers, mainadiers, faidits, arlots*. Réflections sur les diverses sortes de combattants dans la *Chanson de la croisade albigeoise*', *ib.*, 155–79, studies vocabulary for simple soldiers and mercenaries in several texts: *Chanson de la croisade albigeoise, Historia albigensis* (Pierre de Vaux-de-Cernay, 1213), and the *Chronique* of Guillaune de Puylaurens (completed 1273–76). Terms include: O Occ. *rôtier, soldadier, mainadier* 'mercenary'; *faidit* 'exile'; *ribaud* (cf. *truan, gartz*) 'goujat'; mysterious *tafur*, perhaps of Arabic or Armenian origin; and thoroughly pejorative *[h]arlot*. X. Ravier, 'Images d'un milieu de vie médiévale', *ib.*, 181–96, lists, inter alia, *casaux* (lists from *c.*1163 and *c.*1250) and *maisons* (list from 1250–72), found in the *censiers* of Lourdes (from the *Cartulaire de Bigorre*, which R. is currently editing). R. cites the work of Benoît Cursente, **Du casal à l'oustau. Habitat, société, pouvoirs, dans la Gascogne médiévale*, 2 vols, 1995, 605 pp., who has concluded that Gascon society of the 11th to the 13th c. was *casalière* rather than feudal.

PHONETICS AND PHONOLOGY. J.-P. Chambon, 'Pour l'étude linguistique des troubadours: traits amphizoniques dans la langue de Peire Cardenal', *RLiR*, 60, 1996:73–94, maps pp. 95–109, judges the dialectalisms in the poems of Peire Cardenal to be typical of the Velay amphizone east of Le Puy; he distinguishes: *amphizone vellave* (Le Puy and environs), *amphizone vivaro-vellave* (west of the Rhône), and *Velay provençal* (outside the amphizone).

LEXIS AND LEXICOLOGY. Fascicles of a major new dictionary have begun to appear, *Dictionnaire de l'occitan médiéval (DOM)*, Fasc. 1, a-*acceptar*, Tübingen, Niemeyer, 1996, ix + 80 pp., and *Supplément*, Fasc. 1, viii + 157 pp. Originally planned by Helmut Stimm, *DOM* is now being carried forward by Wolf-Dieter Stempel, with the collaboration of Claudia Kraus, Renate Peter, and Monika Tausend; a publication rate of one or two fascicles per year is announced. B. Henschel, 'L'Occitan à Heidelberg', *Occitans!*, 73, 1996:8, briefly reviews the progress of two of the dictionary projects headed by Kurt Baldinger, *Dictionnaire onomasiologique de l'ancien occitan (DAO)* and *Dictionnaire onomasiologique de l'ancien gascon (DAG)*. H. collaborated from 1957 to 1962 on both *DAO* and *DAG* in Berlin, before materials were transferred to Heidelberg. Meanwhile, additional fascicles of both

DAO and *DAO Supplément* are now available: *DAO*, Fasc. 7. (1000 *orchis*-1233 *Les excréments*), Tübingen, Niemeyer, 1996, pp. 481–560; and *DAO, Supplément*, Fasc. 6 (945 *campêche*-1233 *Les excréments*), Tübingen, Niemeyer, pp. 401–80. Cantalausa has published *Du gallo-roman parlé du VIIIe siècle au gallo-roman écrit du Xe siècle. Glossaires historique et étymologique*, Le Monastère-sous-Rodez, Éditions Culture d'Oc, 1996, 200 pp. (2nd edn, 1997), a historical and etymological dictionary with some 1,500 entries culled from the Reichenau and Cassel glossaries and the *Passion de Clermont d'Auvergne*. O. Naudeau, 'OF *de tel aigroi*, O Pr. *de tal agrei*', *Romania*, 114, 1996:517–21, discusses the five known examples, and cites phonetic evolution in arguing for a northern origin for *agrei* 'tel poids', quasi-adverbial *per agrey de* 'effet subi de ce qui pèse, de ce qui accable', 'sous le poids accablant, en en subissant l'effet accablant' (deverbal from OF *agregier* 'rendre lourd, pesant'). See also Id., 'Observations sur la langue de *Aigar et Maurin*', *ib.*, 115:337–67. G. Colón Doménech, 'El fantasmagórico *amainar* de Guillem de Berguedà', *RFE*, 76, 1996:155–60, studies the verb *amainar* (variants *amagar* 'to hide', *lamagar, amainiar*), found in *Eu non cuidava chantar*, verse 8 (PC 210,11). For C. D., Coromines's *Diccionari Etimologic e Complementari de la Llengua Catalana* wrongly cites Guillem de Berguedan in its article on *amainar*, since the Spanish verb is attested only from the mid-15th century. R. Sindou studies 'Ancien provençal *pozaranca* et ses variantes', *TLP*, 33–34, 1995–96:491–97, 'puits, fossé' (cf. *pozaraca*), in the context of suffixal Latin -*aca* and Gaulish -*āco*. A. Soutou, 'Le leudaire de Balaruc-le-Vieux au XIVe s.', *AMid*, 106, 1996:247–49, lists 247 more-or-less latinized dialect terms for objects subjected to the *leuda* 'tax' imposed on visiting traders in the fortified village of Balaruc, e.g. *bredola, calpol, cabotos, mujolos, saumada* 'charge d'une bête de somme'; S.'s source is the 1292 *Cartulaire de Maguelonne* (Archives départementales de l'Hérault, MS G1124, fol. 2ʳ).

ONOMASTICS. J. Vesòla, 'Les noms de baptisme a l'Atge-mejan (XIV–XV sègle)', *Lo Convise*, 13, 1996:19–20, reviews late medieval Christian names for girls, e.g. Alys, Astruga, Fina, Flor, Gaudeta, Girmana, Helis, Marina, Saura; and boys, e.g. Amalric, Arnal, Bodon, Danis, Folca, Gisbèrt. J.-C. Hélas, *'Prenoms en Gévaudan au début du XIVe s. d'après les *Feuda Gabalorum*', *Fossier Vol.*, 341–53. P.-H. Billy, *'Nommer à Toulouse aux XIe–XIVe siècles', *Actes* (GREHAM 3), 171–89. [P.L.], 'Los noms los mes ancians coneishuts a Bayoune', *PGA*, 49, 1996:19–23, concludes that Bayonne has had a primarily Gascon-speaking population since at least the 10th century. R. Cierbide Martinena, *'Onomástica personal de los habitantes de Pamplona (ss. XII–XIV)', *NRO*, 27–28, 1996:87–96.

DIALECTS: GASCON. B. Cursente, *'Pouvoir des noms et pouvoir de nommer dans une seigneurie ecclésiastique gasconne du XIe siècle', *Duby Vol.*, 109–17. *Notaire de Prince. Regíster de Bernat de Luntz, notaire de Béarn sous Gaston Fébus*, ed. Pierre Tucoo-Chala and Jacques Staes, Pau, Covedi–Pau U.P., 1996, 198 pp., publish 229 acts dating from 1371–76; S. is curator of the Archives départementales des Pyrénées-Atlantiques.

HISTORICAL SOCIOLINGUISTICS. L. Stouff, *'Identité de la Provence médiévale', Carozzi, *Peuples*, 145–68. *L'abbé Henri Grégoire, 'Rapport sur la nécessité et les moyens d'anéantir les patois, d'universaliser l'usage de la langue française...'. Suivi d'un Essai historique et patriotique sur les arbres de la liberté*, (re)ed. Philippe Gardy and Jean-Claude Richard, Le Pouget, Arts et traditions populaires, 1995, 16 + 19 + 67 pp.

TEXTS. Gérard Zuchetto, *Terre des troubadours XIIe-XIIIe siècles. Anthologie commentée*, pref. Max Rouquette, Les Éditions de Paris, 455 pp., is accompanied by a CD of selected materials sung by Zuchetto. Part I, 'Troubadours et *trobar*', includes 'La langue des troubadours' (42–44), a bibliography (433–43), and a lexicon of *trobar* (444–51). Other CD recordings of troubadour song and verse: Jean-Marie Carlotti and Michel Marre, *Trobar 1*, Silex, 1995; La Compagnie Médiévale, *Jaufre Rudel*, Aniane, 1995; and Gérard Zuchetto, *Troubadours d'Italie*, Aliénor, Harmonia Mundi, 1996. Constanzo Di Girolamo and Charmaine Lee, **Avviamento alla filologia provenzale*, Rome, Nuova Italia Scientifica, 271 pp., offer an Old Provençal grammar, a 90-page anthology, and a glossary. L. Borghi Cedrini, *'Schede per il *joc grosser* di Guglielmo IX (*BdT* 183.2 v.45) e altri *jocs* occitanici', *ST*, 4, 1996:167–99. S. Guida, 'Il minirepertorio provenzale tràdito dal MS *H*.', Guida, *Uc de Saint Circ*, 171–213, presents a mid-13th-c. index intended to facilitate the consultation of troubadour manuscript *H*. *Grand Cartulaire de La Sauve-Majeur*, ed. Charles Higounet and Arlette Higounet-Nadal, with the collaboration of Nicole de Peña (Études et documents d'Aquitaine), 2 vols, Bordeaux, Fédération historique du Sud-Ouest, 1996, 1,072 pp., provides the text of the *Silve majoris abbatie chartularium majus*, *c.*1190–1250, Bibliothèque Municipale de Bordeaux, MS 769. **Le Cartulaire du chapitre cathédral de Saint-Etienne d'Agde*, ed. Raymonde Foreville (Documents, études et répertoires), CNRS, 1995, 583 pp. **Documentación medieval del monasterio de Santa Clara de Estella (ss. XIII–XVI)*, ed. Ricardo Cierbide Martinena and Emiliana Ramos Remedios, San Sebastián, Eusko Ikaskuntza, 1996, x + 317 pp. J. Clémens, M. Bochaca and F. Mouthon, 'Testaments bordelais de la fin du moyen âge', *Garona*, 13, 1996:77–94, note the structure and dispositions of late 15th-c. wills from Bordeaux, with examples from 1462, 1473, 1490, and 1495. J. Lafita has published the 'Carta de

Herrèra (1278)', *LDGM*, 7, 1996:5–8, one of the oldest extant Bearnese texts, discovered in 1976. Id., 'Las purmèras cartas de Comenges (s. XIIau)', *LDGM*, 8, 1996:4–11, provides a facsimile of 11 charters predating 1200 from the Comminges, previously published in the 1950s by Clovis Hughes. L. also publishes a study of two versions of the *Coutumes de Montsaunèrs* (*c.* 1300 and *c.* 1500), *LDGM*, 8, 1996:12–17. R. Teulat has been working on a critical edition of the first 18 sermons of St. Martial of Limoges (Paris, BN lat. 3548 B, *c.* 1120), known as the *sermons limousins*; in a series of issues of *Lo Convise*, he publishes a diplomatic version directly from the MS, with a modernized version from critical editions by C. Chabaneau (1880–83) and Frederick A. Heilbronn (1884): 'Sermons de Sant-Marçal (1, 2)', *Lo Convise*, 9, 1995:2–5; '3, 4, 5', *ib.*, 10, 1995:2–5; '6, 7, 8', *ib.*, 11, 1995:2–4; '9, 10, 11', *ib.*, 13, 1996:2–5; '12, 13, 14, 15', *ib.*, 15, 1996:2–6; and '16, 17, 18', *ib.*, 17:6–11.

3.　Post-Medieval Period

GENERAL.　M. Chapduèlh, 'Lo Lemosin e lo "recentratge" d'Occitania', *Forra Borra*, 106, 1995:1–2, is the complete version of a paper part-published in *Occitans!*, 65, 1995:33 for the 50th anniversary of the IEO (see *YWMLS*, 57:251); C. fears that modification of the map of Occitania would result in loss of cultural and linguistic identity for Limousin. C.'s wake-up call is timed to 'arriba[r] a bon ponch', according to R. Lafont, 'Multi-Occitània', *Forra Borra*, 108, 1995:2–3. J.-F. Blanc, 'En occitan, tota la setmana!', *ib.*, 108, 1995:1. **Actes de l'Université d'été, 1994; Universitat occitana d'estiu*, ed. Jòrgi Peladan, Nîmes, MARPOC-IEO, 1995, 172 pp.; see below for *Actes de l'Université d'été, 1995*.

ORTHOGRAPHY.　J. Chirio, 'Réflexions à propos du "t" muet (deuxième partie)', *LSPS*, 120:44–45, proposes the addition of an etymological 't' to certain words, in keeping with medieval usage, e.g. *doucument, ensegnament*; see also *ib.*, 119, 1995. C. Laus, 'L'escritura dels noms geografics formats de mai d'un element', *Occitans!*, 74, 1996:8, proposes, in the absence of any fixed usage in Occitan, (i) for Noun + Adjective, either a single unit for historically known forms like Vilafranca (exception *Nòva Iòrc*) or else two capitalized elements, e.g. *Auvèrnha Bassa*; (ii) for juxtaposed Noun + Noun or for *départements*, elements joined by a hyphen; (iii) use of article, or lack thereof, before names of countries.

MORPHOSYNTAX.　C. Rapin, 'Nostra lenga: *Un + de + Nom*', *Lo Lugarn*, 57, 1996:22, looks at expressive syntax, e.g. *Lo Marcèl, n'a un d'aparelh de fòto que fonciona practicament tot sol*. Id., '*Un, una*', *ib.*, 58, 1996:23, reviews uses of indefinite *un(a)*.

LEXIS AND LEXICOLOGY. Joan de Cantalausa, *Comment le dire en occitan? Petit glossaire étymologique de la langue parlée*, Le-Monastère-sous-Rodez, Cultura d'Oc, 1995, 64 pp., lists some 3000 Occitan spoken terms for frequently-used French items, e.g. 74 entries for 'ravin', identifying etyma, regional variants and occasionally date of earliest attestation. Jean Journot, *Les Mots occitans: occitan-français, français-occitan* (Collection Colporteur), Nîmes, Lacour, 1995, 101 pp. C. Rapin, 'Nostra lenga: *totis tan coma son* (fem. *totas tantas coma son*) "tous tant qu'ils sont"', *Lo Lugarn*, 55, 1996:23, reviews expressions for 'every one of them', including O Occ. *totis quantis son*. Id., 'Occitan contemporanèu', *Occitans!*, 73, 1996:19, prefers *contemporanèu* to *contemporan*, following Alibert's recommendations on reflexes of -AUS, -EUS. P. Grover, 'Los mots occitans en anglés', *PN*, 74, 1996:15–20 (trans J. Roux from the English), summarizes (i) words that passed through French (food, flora, fauna, wine, war, clothing); (ii) vocabulary for dance, song, poetry, and theatre; (iii) miscellaneous items; and (iv) suffixal -*ade*.

PARTICULAR SEMANTIC FIELDS. Y. Gorgaud, 'De l'usança del mot "occitan"', *Occitans!*, 74, 1996:6–7, reminding readers that 'le Felibrige faguèt jamai la guèrra al mot *occitan*', cites an early 16th-c. phrase, *pays de la langue occitane*, from the work of Esteve Metge (1475–1565), a bourgeois from Le Puy-en-Velay. E. Roux, '*Occitan* dempuei quoras?', *PN*, 73, 1996:16–17, gently corrects G.'s dating of *Occitan* by some two centuries: *en toute la langue Occitane* occurs in a text dated 26 October 1356, which was published in *Recueil sommaire des titres qui établissent l'antiquité et l'authenticité des immunités dont jouissent les Citoyens, Bourgeois et Habitants de Perigueux ...*, Périgueux, 1770. P. A. Clément, 'L'origine du mot *draille*', *LiCC*, 104, 1996:1, hypothesizes a common origin for Hindi *dagra* 'crible à riz', Celtic *draga*, Lat. *tragulum*, Occ. *drai* 'grand crible en peau de porc à gros trous que les paysans provençaux pendaient à un chevalet pour séparer le grain de la balle après piquâge', and *drail* 'crible en éclisses de châtaignier qui servait au calibrage des châtaignes sèches'. Id., 'Le *Cami Ferrat* est bien le chemin muletier', *ib.*, 106, 1996:1–2, finds the key to *cami ferrat* in Isidore of Seville < VIA FERRRARIA, cf. FERRARUM 'bête ferré (mule, mulet)' and 17th-c. Andalusia *caminos de herradura* 'chemins de bêtes ferrées'. J. Eygun, 'Nommer les fruits de la terre: de quelques glossaires botaniques occitans (XVIe–XXe s.), *Lengas*, Montpellier, 40, 1996:7–33, describes a rich but fairly inaccessible source for specialized lexicon. Felip Carbona, *Camparòls-Ensag de nomenclatura* (*GS*, special issue), Auréville, 1996, 108 pp., proposes semi-learned botanical names for 114 species of mushrooms, with the stated purpose of eliminating some of the confusion among multiple popular names. This is C.'s 'Occitan solution', based on Latin rather than the

vernacular, e.g. (Lactarius >) *Lactaris* as against **laitièr*. Id., 'Camparòls', *GS*, 461, 1996:237–40, presents the German approach to
botanical naming, namely, to translate the first element of a learned
name, e.g. *Rohr* 'tube'. E. Ros and M. Chapduèlh, 'En segre los
champanhòus-camparòls', *PN*, 74, 1996:11–14, detail the principles
of classification for mushrooms: each species is identified by Latin
name, reference name, and popular name(s). R. summarizes the
problems of nomenclature; C. provides supplementary information
and recipes. J. Roux, 'Camparòls, Champanhòus, Botareus, Godar-
èls', *ib.*, 73, 1996:22–23, describes a new version of the French card
game *jeu des sept familles*, using two sets of mushroom names from
northern and southern Occitan.

ONOMASTICS.   A. Lieutard, *Prénoms occitans (Auvergne, Dauphiné,
Gascogne, Guyenne, Languedoc, Limousin et Provence)*, Belin-Beliet, Princi
Negre, 1996, 124 pp., lists Languedocien and French versions. J.-P.
Chambon, 'Note sur les noms de famille méridionaux *Chab(b)ert,
Chabbal, Chabaud, Chatard, Xatart, Xammar* et quelques autres (domaines
occitan, francoprovençal et catalan)', *TLP*, 33–34, 1995–96:81–108.
M. Mulon, 'La descendance de *Berengarius/Bernegarius*', *Mélanges Roux*,
275–81, traces this name on French soil in both its full and contracted
forms, e.g. Rouergue *Bringuier*. R. Aymard, **Les Pyrénées au miroir de
leur toponymie*. 1, *Toponymes pyrénéens. Noms importants, controversés, insolites
des montagnes Pyrénées'*, Uzès, p.p., 1995, 198 pp. Id., **Les Pyrénées au
miroir de leur toponymie*, 2, *Atlas toponymique*, Uzès, p.p., 1996, 226 pp.
Id., **Les Pyrénées au miroir de leur toponymie*, 3, *Pyrénées sacrées*, Uzès, p.p.,
183 pp. Id., **Les Pyrénées au miroir de leur toponymie*, 4, *Peuples des Pyrénées*,
Uzès, p.p., 1996, 122 pp. J. Roux, 'Toponimia: Leymarie,
Leygonie...Lozeille', *PN*, 73, 1996:24, traces the phonetic development of toponyms composed of article + name of house + suffix *-ía*,
noting that stress is no longer consistent: e.g. *Leymarie* = *L'Aimaria* (<
Aimar); *Leygonie* = *L'Eigonia* < **L'Igonia* < *Uc, Hugo*.

SOCIOLINGUISTICS.   In a review of *Euromosaïc, production et reproduction des groupes linguistiques minoritaires au sein de l'Union européenne*,
Brussels-Luxembourg, Commission européenne, 1996, P. Blanchet,
FL 123, 1996:104–12, argues for use of *sociolinguistiques* in the plural
and reiterates his refusal to group Provençal with Occitan. Id., 'Le
mythe de la pureté dialectale en langue et culture régionales', *AsP*,
31, 1996:89–96, again argues against any simple reduction of the
langues d'oc to a singular *Occitan*, favouring instead 'une conception
complexe de l'*unitas multiplex*'. J. Wüest, 'Attitudes et représentations',
Lengas, Montpellier, 40, 1996:139–48, notes the 'quasi-inexistence
d'une identité (pan)occitane' as he studies the ways in which his own
informants evaluate the competence of other Occitan speakers. The
reality of minority status for modern Occitan is clear to P. Berengier

as she reports on the June 1996 convention in Barcelona that yielded the 'Declaracioun Universalo di Dre Linguisti', *PrA*, 102, 1996:2; two of the 52 articles are given in B.'s Provençal translation. G. Kremnitz, 'Situationen sprachlicher Dominanz in der Romania', Dahmen, *Romanischen Sprachen*, 171–83, discusses the fate of modern Occitan. A. Viaut, 'Gérer le plurilinguisme. Regards croisés sur des réponses (France-Espagne)', *Lengas*, Montpellier, 39, 1996:7–35, suggests that a look at multi-lingual Spain may yield useful parameters for Occitan. Id., 'Normalisation linguistique et patrimoine', Viaut, *Langues d'Aquitaine*, 41–70, suggests that the concept of *patrimoine*, collective and hereditary, can play a role in the resolution of a(n unstable) diglossic situation, encouraging normalization in its wider sense as language planning rather than language substitution and eventual disappearance. M. Martin, 'Le statut juridique des langues régionales en France', *ib.*, 71–86, has little change to report as regards the obstructionist attitude of the French state toward minority languages; the best cause for hope comes from the economic sphere and the opening of frontiers with Italy, Spain, and Germany. G. Mercadier, 'Quel partenariat institutionnel pour soutenir l'enseignement de l'occitan? L'exemple de l'Académie de Toulouse', *ib.*, 171–96, emphasizes the importance of support from the Ministère de l'Éducation nationale, foremost among all institutional partners involved with the Academy of Toulouse in the teaching of Occitan; in conclusion, the teaching of the language remains in a precarious state. P. Gardy, 'La télévision régionale en occitan (Aquitaine, Midi-Pyrénées, Languedoc-Roussillon, Val d'Aran): des sujets à la langue', *ib.*, 267–86, sees an Occitan television that exhibits the language without allowing it to function, as if Occitan were the subject rather than the vehicle of communication. C. Lagarda, 'Un possible dialòg sus la lenga?', *GS*, 461, 1996:278–82, reminds Enric Gogaud and others that in matters of diglossia 'crear, criticar *en* occitan val mai que *sus* l'occitan' . L.'s interviews with Gogaud have elicited further discussion, including F. Bardou, *'Responsa a l'Enric Gogaud', *ib.*, 462, 1996:242–45. A. Viaut, 'La Langue minoritaire comme nouveau patrimoine', pp. 197–213 of *L'Alchimie du patrimoine: discours et politiques*, ed. Yvon Lamy, Bordeaux, Maison des Sciences de l'Homme d'Aquitaine, 1996, 532 pp. J. Marty-Bazalgues, 'Compliments et monologues pour mariage en situation de diglossie', *Lengas*, Montpellier, 39, 1996:71–98, presents texts from the region of Figeac, 1918–41. J.-F. Blanc, 'Discors, paraula, lenga?', *Forra Borra*, 114, 1996:3–5, refutes any call for an Occitanism that reduces the language to a pedagogical tool; cf. E. Fraj's summation of modern-day Occitanism in *Lo Leberaubre* 21 (1995), with another response from M. Maratuech, *'Prètzfaches occitans', *Forra Borra*, 115,

1996:3–4. M. Audoièr, 'Escasuda de la normalisacion, *L'Occitan*, 122, 1996:9, regrets that so much of the 'bad' Occitan appearing in print lately is Languedocien being written by school-learned people who lack contact with the popular spoken language; the most artificial normalization of Occitan appears to A. to be that of the central dialect. Id., 'L'Occitan general', *ib.*, 124, 1996:6, argues further that among the effects of the choice of Languedocien as normalized Occitan, the negative outweigh the positive; A. calls for a *lenga comuna*, even as he clearly lists the drawbacks: many pedagogical materials would be rendered obsolete, just as the resulting language might well prove incomprehensible as well as artificial.

TEXTS. B. Manciet, 'Ua "costuma" disputada: Milhan sober Garone', *Oc*, Nice, 321, 1996:29–40, edits a document from Bazas, *c.* 1300–10, also known as 'Aso toqua lo senhor e las gents de Milhan' (Vieux Inventaire Taillebourg ... De la cotte D), Archives départementales des Pyrénées-Atlantiques, MS E 190 IA/194. P. Gardy, 'La Leçon de Nérac (1578)', *Lengas*, Montpellier, 39, 1996:53–70, carries the subtitle 'Le *Poème dressé par G. de Saluste, Seigneur du Bartas, pour l'accueil de la Royne de Navarre* ...', matrice sociolinguistique et modèle poétique pour les écrivains occitans des XVIe et XVIIe s.'

PAREMIOLOGY. M. Chapduèlh, 'Biais de dire', *PN*, 74, 1996:21–22: sayings and aphorisms in Occitan, with good-natured corrections, e.g. 'fau pas dire: "Un cop fai pas costuma", mas "Un còp fai pas puta"'.

GASCON AND BÉARNAIS

GENERAL. J. Lafitte, *Lenga d'òc. Ont èm? que har?*, 2nd ed. (*LDGM*, special no., 3), 1996, 28 pp., continues to argue for Gascon as a fully fledged language, beyond the boundaries of a unitary Occitan. Id., *Le Gascon, langue à part entière, et le béarnais, âme du gascon, suivi de la Lettre aux Gascons d'Yves Gourgaud* (*ib.*, special no., 4), 1996, 44 pp. In general, L. proposes to distinguish *occitan* from *lenga d'òc*: the former should be used only for northern and southern dialects, excluding Gascon and Catalan, never to designate a single dialect, notably Lang.; *occitano-romanic* should be used to designate the ensemble of Occitan, Gascon and Catalan; *lenga d'òc* should be avoided in academic texts. In a multi-pronged response to L.'s theories, J. Sibille wonders: '*Lo Gascon dialècte o lenga a part entièra? Es que la question a un sens?*', *EOc*, 20, 1996:38–40, and points out the lack of historical support for such attempts to differentiate *Occitan* from *lenga d'òc*. J.-F. Blanc, 'L'Institut d'Estudis Occitans de París e lo projècte de Diccionari deu Gascon Modèrn (DiGaM)', *Forra Borra*, 123, 1996:3–6, is able to endorse the DiGaM as a language-related project, while otherwise calling for the national IEO to remain the sole arbiter of norms for Occitan linguistic research. Some of the readers of *Forra Borra*, as well, hope to see an end to one-man reform movements. B. reports additional reader responses in 'En seguida de l'article "L'IEO París e lo projècte DiGaM"', *ib.*, 124, 1996:3–6.

ORTHOGRAPHY. P. Bec, 'A prepaus de la grafia deu gascon', *LDGM*, 7, 1996:33, reviews and corrects several reports of his own work on Occitan spelling that have been published in the pages of this journal J. Lafitte, *'Punts divèrs de grafia', *ib.*, 7, 1996:44–47, meanwhile publishes his own views, including *inter alia* comparison of rules for spelling [dj] in Gascon and in Languedocien; and 'Grafia: escríver -[r] en gascon: *goalhard, part, pitarr, torr, esquèrr', ib.*, 8, 1996:32–35. Id., *'Grafia: E podem goardar lo *punt interior?*', *ib.*, 8, 1996:44–46, suggests further spelling modifications made necessary by computer constraints. Id. calls doubly for a *lenga populària*, based on spoken rather than learned forms, in *ib.*, 21–26, as well as under the rubric 'Proposicions' in *Oc*, Nice, 319, 1996:34–43. P. Bec and R. Lafont, 'Per una lenga populara/ària', *ib.*, 321, 1996:44–46, quickly rebutt, arguing against the devisive results of periodic reforms of any norm, and concluding that the time has come to view Occitan within its Romance context, not as a language atypical of its Latin base or afflicted with a derivative pathology. The final word is reserved for himself by J. Lafitte, *LDGM*, 8, 1996:26–31.

MORPHOSYNTAX. G. Narioò studies 'L'auxiliar *aver* a la forma impersonal', *PG*, 175, 1996:15, as found in *que'm demandè çò que m'avè arribat* 'ce qui m'était arrivé'. Id., 'Plaça deu pronom complement de un grop verbau', *ib,,* 177, 1996:12. J. Lafita returns to 'Enclisi e proclisi deus pronoms', *LDGM*, 7, 1996:37–43 as he reviews positions taken by various Gasc. grammarians.

LEXIS AND LEXICOLOGY. M. Belly, 'Fortunes et infortunes d'une recherche en lexicographie: Le Dictionnaire de Simin Palay', *Garona*, 13, 1996:95–117, recaps his iconoclastic examination of P.'s monumental dictionary. J. Eygun, 'La Lenga deus ausèths: quauques mimologismes de Gasconha', *RBG*, 1–3, 1996:49–54, reviews birds by species, with illustrations and literary quotations; among his sources is F. Beigbeder, *Les Noms gascons des oiseaux sauvages*, Orthez, Per Noste et Nosauts de Bigòrra, 1986, 160 pp. Continuing his single-handed quest for reform in Gascon, J. Lafitte, *LDGM*, 7, 1996:27–32, decries various lexical items used by Occitanists, e.g. *discutida, espepissar, soscar, capitar, compausaicion, difusir, situir, lo liber tot* and calls for spelling reform of *image* and *privilège*. Id., *'De Wasconia: tuta, tutar', ib.*, 8, 1996:25. Id., *'Vocabulari: *ignoble, ignorar, hantauma, prefàcia, sistèrna/sistèmi', ib.*, 32–35.

PARTICULAR SEMANTIC FIELDS.   G. Nariòo, 'B'ac sabem', *PG*, 170,
1996:12, studies intensifying values of *be* 'bien'. Id., 'Ací qu'avetz
pomas', *ib*., 174, 1996:17, reviews uses of *ací, aquí*. M. Grosclaude,
'*Só/sorelh*', *ib*., 177, 1996:13, compares and contrasts etyma, arguing
that (SOLEM >) *sór* should rightfully be written *só*.

ONOMASTICS.   B.   Boyrie-Fénié,   'La   Carte   archéologique   des
Landes', *Garona*, 13, 1996:49–56. B. Lesfargues, 'Entau s'apelen
nòstras comunas', *BP*, no. 2, 1996:20–22 (Hautefort, Montagrier,
Montpon-Ménéstérol, Mussidan). M. Prim, 'Recherche et locali-
sation des patronymes liés au problème des Cagots', *BSAHLSG*,
1996:223–37, uses the Minitel to study proper names relating to the
cagots and equivalents (*capot, mesté, crestia, cougot, gézites*); according to
his findings, all terms can be linked in some way to the Goths, through
the intermediary of, e.g. *cans de Goths, chiens de Goths*, and the like.
Robert Aymard, **Dictionnaire des noms de lieux des Hautes-Pyrénées*, Uzès,
p.p., 1996, 151 pp.

SUB-DIALECTS.   The group Aci Gasconha (M. Dicharry et al.) has
brought out a bilingual guide, with index, to the Gascon of Bayonne:
*Que parlam: guide de la conversation français-gascon (gascon maritime ou 'de
Bayonne')*, Bayonne, Jakin, 1996, 280 pp., in *graphie normalisée* and
noting local pronunciations. Excerpts and background are presented
by Id., 'Apprendre et parler le gascon de Bayonne: *Parlam* Guide de
conversation', *PGA*, 46, 1996:15–24; *ib*., 47, 1996:28–30; *ib*., 48,
1996:21–26. This same dialect figures in Pierre Rectoran, *Le Gascon
maritime de Bayonne et du val d'Adour*, Bayonne, Harriet, 1996, 300 pp.,
which contains sections on phonetics, parts of speech, an alphabetized
glossary, proverbs, and short literary passages. H. Lartiga, 'Lo gascon
negue, parlar de la mar', *LDGM*, 7, 1996:19–20, presents the very
particular phonology of *gascon 'noir'*.

SOCIOLINGUISTICS.   P. Heiniger, 'L'Institut Culturau de Gasconha: un essai manqué?', Viaut, *Langues d'Aquitaine*, 113–24, pinpoints marginalization, lack of government funding, and outright
intra-regional disapproval, even hostility, as causes of the Institut's
all-too-short active life (1980–86). A. Surre-Garcia, 'Bilan d'une
politique culturelle du Conseil Régional de Midi-Pyrénées en matière
de langue et de culture occitanes: 1989–95', *ib*., 125–32, paints a
cautiously optimistic picture. J.-M. Sarpoulet, 'Configuration et
perspective de l'enseignement du basque et de l'occitan dans
l'Académie de Bordeaux', *ib*., 147–62, tables 163–69, sees four steps
necessary to safeguard the future of regional languages: training
teachers; finding jobs for them; making teaching materials available
to them; and informing parents, students, and interested parties of
the inherent interest of these languages. A. Viaut and J.-J. Cheval,
'L'Occitan gascon à la radio et à la télévision dans le Val d'Aran', *ib*.,

259–63, note that a majority of the 6,000 inhabitants of this Pyrenean valley know and use their Gascon-Commingeois *aranais*; interestingly, the effort to prevent an influx of catalanisms and castillanisms into *aranais* as heard on radio and television comes, not from within the Val d'Aran itself, but from the Catalan quarter. J. Allières, 'Occità, català i gascó: punts de contacte', *PdO*, 1996:7–17, reviews the relationship of Gascon with the south Pyrenean area. R. Martí, 'Un Iamassocrò, salsa biarnesa', *Occitans!* 73 (1996):3, calls for support of Occitan language, without which Pau, with its new Centre Occitan, will come to resemble Iamassocrò, the new capital city of Ivory Coast, which is a ghost town without a past. J.-M. Sarpoulet, *inspecteur en langues régionales* for the Academy of Bordeaux, returns to 'L'ensenhament de l'occitan dens l'Acadèmia de Bordèu', *RBG*, 4–6, 1995:53–57. M. Pujol assures his readers that 'Eth occitan que n'ei pas ua lenga estrangèra', *ib.*, 7–9, 1995:130–31.

TEXTS. J. Eygun describes the 'Lo libe deus pariatges de la Comunautat de Beòst-Bagès', *RBG*, 8, 1996:41–43, printed late 17th or early 18th century. Its language is typical of 16th-c. notarial documents in *gascon béarnais*. This hitherto unknown book sheds new light on the use of Occitan in local communities of the Béarn for administrative and juridical purposes before the Revolution. Bernard Manciet has been the subject of concentrated interest recently, viz. a CD-ROM of the poet-novelist reading his own works, Montpellier, Aura (Trésors d'Occitanie, 2), in addition to monographs and individual papers. *Colloque Manciet* includes: a bibliography of M.'s work (203–26); A. Surre-Garcia, **Sur la traduction du Gojat de novémer* (189–91); G. Kremnitz, 'Les versions françaises du *Goujat de novémer*, première approche' (193–202), reviews the three French translations of M.'s novel, noting that he has chosen not to normalize or regularize the language in which he writes; and K. Mok, 'La prose de Bernard Manciet: aspects linguistiques' (171–79), addresses the alternance of first-person plural atonic personal and relative pronouns, so-called enunciatives, the junction between principal and subordinate clauses, and the overall construction of sentences, concluding that M. has chosen to free his style from certain syntactic constraints in order fully to benefit from the poetic resources of his *parler*. Philippe Gardy, *L'Écriture occitane contemporaine: une quête de mots* (Sociolinguistique), L'Harmattan, 1996, 290 pp., has, as a final chapter, 'Les écrivains d'expression occitane de la seconde moitié du XXe s. écrivent-ils en occitan? L'exemple de Bernard Manciet', and answers his own question in the affirmative: M.'s writing unfolds as a zigzag between two systems of linguistic usage, the Occitan and the French. Id., 'Bernard Manciet: la parole et ses doubles', *La Lettre d'Atlantique*, Bordeaux, January, 1996:14–16.

PAREMIOLOGY. Two more magnificent volumes have appeared in the *Œuvres complètes* of Félix Arnaudin: II, *Proverbes de la Grande-Lande*, ed. the late Jacques Boisgontier, Bordeaux, Confluences, 1996, 580 pp.; and IV, *Chants populaires de la Grande-Lande*, vol. 2, ed. Jacques Boisgontier and Lothaire Mabru, xiv + 837 pp., which is a revised edition of the *inedita* originally published in 1970; it concludes the series of dance and other songs, and includes a glossary of selected Gascon terms (813–24); see *YWMLS*, 58:269, for vols I, III. All songs are translated; melodies are included where originally noted by Arnaudin.

SOUTHERN OCCITAN

LANGUEDOCIEN

GENERAL. P. Cousinié, 'Utilisacion de l'occitan dins la vida vidanta' (in Occitan), *Occitans!*, 74, 1996:4–5, advocates greater use of Occitan in everyday life, e.g. on commercial food labels, as he interprets results of a survey taken among some 200 attendees of a conference on 'Comèdia d'Occitania' in Montpellier, 4–5 May 1996; a Provençal version of the above appeared, Id., 'Nosto lengo dins la vido vidanto', *PrA*, 107, 1996:7. See also *YWMLS*, 57:260 for discussion of the CEEPOC-Lengadòc (Cramba Economica Europenca dels Països Occitans; in Pr., Cambro Ecounoumico Euroupenco di Païs d'O). Adelin Moulis, **La Langue d'oc: Défense de la vraie langue d'Oc; Notre vraie langue d'oc*, Nîmes, Lacour, 1995, 51 pp.: two short 1977 works (both originally published separately by the author) are now available together in a new printing. R. Chatbèrt continues his series devoted to 'Questions de lenga' , *Oc*, Nice, 318, 1996:42–44 (see *YWMLS*, 54:258, 262; 56:285, and 57:270): 'D'un e de l'autre: *inedich o inedit?* ('qui n'a pas été publié'), *mannat* ('gentil' > 'magnifique'?, 'parfait'), *una filha panadoira/un temps getador, barra la mecanica* 'mets le frein', *escampar d'aiga/pausar las cauças, gran pena!* 'certainement pas'/*gran pena que* 'il est peu probable que'. Id., 'Datius etics', *ib.*, 319, 1996:31–33. Id., 'Addenda: *Renat e cambalarg*; emplecs de *entre*; a propaus de *s'estepar*', *ib.*, 319 [320], 1996:38–30. Id., 'Sintaxi expressiva e sintaxi cambarivada', *ib.*, 321, 1996:41–43, is devoted to literary turns of phrase also found in the spoken language: repetition of various parts of speech, inversion of verb + subject, object + verb (e.g. *Flamenca* v.1152 'qui dòmna garda, temps i pèrd'), attribute + verb ('Paure soi coma un rat', Auger Galhard).

ORTHOGRAPHY. J. Taupiac continues his series 'L'Occitan blos' (see *YWMLS*, 57:270). 'La quantitat', *L'Occitan*, 120, 1996:12, discusses André Martinet's proposed reform of French spelling, termed *alfonic*, according to which a given phoneme is always represented by the same grapheme. 'La *patz. Son arribats.* La *pensada.* La *premsa*', *ib.*, 121, 1996:8, reviews plurals in 'ts', as against word-final 'tz', and the two spellings for [ns]: 'ns', 'ms'. '*Téner* e *prene*', *ib.*, 122, 1996:12, admits that variant spellings are sometimes allowed, for reasons of etymology and Alibertian normalization, e.g. O Occ. *prener*, Occ. béarnais *préner*, but Occ. languedocien *prene.* '*Maria* e *Cecília*', *ib.*, 123, 1996:8, compares spellings for the varying stresses on final *-ia*: e.g. It. *filosofia-provincia*; Sp. *filisofía-provincia*; Ptg.-Cat.-Occ. (Alibertian) *filosofia-província.* 'Lo ròtle jogat per aquela fèsta', *L'Occitan*, 124, 1996:12, illustrates the phonological oppositions conveyed by graphies 'é', 'è', and 'o', admitting as exceptions certain traditional spellings, e.g. 'ròtle' (rather than *'lo ròlle'). '*Transferir* e *trasplantar*', *ib.*, 125, 1996:8, proposes *transferir* for Alibert's *trasferir* ('tras', 'tres' being better reserved for popular words). L. Delhostal, 'Graphie et orthographe de la langue d'Oc, II ', *Lou Païs*, 336, 1996:14–15, is mildly critical of the general lack of interest in spelling matters shown by Olivier Alle, founder of *Lou Païs*, by certain authors, and by the Escolo Gabalo itself, which more or less champions the *graphie gévaudanaise-phonétique.* C. Camproux, 'Graphie et orthographe de la langue d'Oc, III', *ib.*, 15–17, reiterates Alibert's spelling rules, after a review of Occitan spelling reforms set in motion by Mistral, Perbosc and Estieu. É. Tichet, 'Graphie et orthographe de la langue d'Oc (suite): Lettre du capiscol', *ib.*, 337, 1996:40–41, would like to 'faire part égale entre les deux graphies (classique-étymologique et gévaudanaise-phonétique)'. R. Buchon, 'Réflexion sur l'orientation de l'École Gabale', *ib.*, 339, 1996:100–02, argues for what he calls a living orthography rather than *graphie normalisée.*

MORPHOSYNTAX. In his series 'La vida de la lenga', C. Laus reports 16th-c. attestations of *-ificar* in support of the forms '*Acidificar, liqueficar*', *L'Occitan*, 123, 1996:9, while reviewing the treatment of neologisms by Patrick Sauzet and Josiane Ubaud, *Lo vèrb occitan* (see *YWMLS*, 57:270–71), which is also reviewed by C. Rapin, 'Conjugui, conjugas', *Occitans!*, 72, 1996:21.

LEXIS AND LEXICOLOGY. Cantalausa has published a fourth edition (1st edn, Toulouse, IEO-CREO, 1979) of his *Diccionari fondamental occitan illustrat (lengadocian)*, Le Monastère-sous-Rodez, Cultura d'Oc, 1995, 344 pp., with 15000 words and some 1550 images. André Lagarde, *Dictionnaire occitan-français, français-occitan 'La Palanqueta'* (Pédagogie en classe de langues), Toulouse, CRDP Midi-Pyrénées, 421 pp., bills itself as the first bilingual dictionary for high-school and university students. For this new dictionary, L. relied on a Québecquoise linguist to alphabetize his onomasiological *Vocabulaire occitan par centres d'intérêt*, 1971, 2d edn, 1990. S. Granier's review of the '*Palanqueta*' in *Occitans!* 74, 1996:16, while acknowledging it as the first effort of its kind, finds its lack of notation for vowel quality of [e] and [o] nothing less than disastrous. Mireille Braç et al., *Lexique élémentaire occitan-français, français-occitan selon les parlers languedociens*, [Toulouse], IEO, 1996, 321 pp. Pierre Mazodier, *Lexique du francitan de la région alésienne. Paroles d'ici*, Montpellier, Espace Sud, 1996, 200 pp., includes many items of *occitan naturalisat francés*. P. Sauzet, 'La Lenga foncciona', *Occitans!* 73, 1996:18, assures his readers that the handful of spellings specific to the GIDILOc, e.g. *co(h)erent, co(n/s)sí, utili(s/z)ar*, constitute no threat to the *unitat grafica* sought by the IEO. Apropos of the GIDILOc, Sauzet and J. Ubaud have also published two descriptive pieces: *'Données lexicales de l'occitan: déconstruction ou construction? Présentation de la base de données lexicales occitanes du GIDILOc (Montpellier)', *Actes* (Corte), 137–51; and *'Lo vèrb occitan et lo GIDILOc', pp. 40–55 of *Actes de l'Université d'été, 1995*, ed. Jòrgi Peladan, Nîmes, MARPOC-IEO, 1996, 214 pp. M. Tarbouriech, 'A prepaus de: Simon-Jude Honnorat', *AqAq*, 101, 1996:6–7, traces the genesis of Honnorat's *Vocabulaire français-provençal, Dictionnaire de la langue d'oc ancienne et moderne*, Digne, Repos, 1846–48, most recently reprinted Digne, Les Petites Affiches, 1996. Abbé Léger Gary, *Dictionnaire patois-français du département du Tarn* (Rediviva), Nîmes, Lacour, 1996, fac. repr., xxii + 396 pp., originally Castres, Pujol, 1845. G. Bazalgues, 'Inventaire lexical de quelques constructions de pierre sèche sur le causse de Gramat', *QR*, 85, 1996:54–64. The vocabulary of the Garonne bargemen (13th–19th c.) is the object of Z. Bòsc, 'En Valòia d'Olt: Los Gabarrièrs. Ensag de vocabulari', *Canta-Grelh*, 29, 1996:6–16; items fall into three main categories: the *mairan transportat* 'merrain' or 'stave-wood', the barge itself (*gabarra*), and navigation terminology. J. Taupiac, 'Nòstra lenga: l'occitan blos', *La setmanada, lo setmanièr, lo setmanari, una emission de television setmanala; oblidar. GS*, 461, 1996:194–96. C. Laux, 'Los mots perduts', *L'Occitan*, 125, 1996:7, sollicits additional details from his readers about *pompil* mod. 'mollet', with older acception 'étalage'.

SUB-DIALECTS. Cristian Lagarda, *Le Parler 'melandjao' des immigrés de langue espagnole en Roussillon* (Collection Études), Perpignan U.P., 1996, 367 + xi pp., has reworked his 1993 Perpignan *thèse d'État* describing the hybrid language used by Spanish immigrant workers struggling among three cultures in Roussillon.

SOCIOLINGUISTICS. Cristian Lagarda has published his habilitation thesis as *Conflits de langues. Conflits de groupes* (Sémantiques), L'Harmattan, 1996, 318 pp. M.-J. Verny, *chargée de cours* in Montpellier, details 'Una experiéncia d'ensenhament de l'occitan dens l'academia de Montpelhier', *RBG*, 4–6, 1995:71–76. The Service de la Langue Occitane, jointly supported by the Région Languedoc-Roussillon and the Université Paul Valéry in Montpellier, created in early 1996 and directed by J.-F. Courouau, offers help to all with questions about Occitan language use or to those interested in communicating through the medium of Occitan, e.g. place names, botanical names, menus, pronunciation, advertising texts. E. Claret, 'L'Occitan, notre langue vivante', *OS*, 1996:22–23, describes this new service as an interesting initiative that could well benefit from the experience of Québec and its linguistic policy. P. Sauzet, 'Vers un service de la Langue Occitane en Languedoc-Roussillon', Viaut, *Langues d'Aquitaine*, 133–46, insists on accessibility as the keystone of a coherent language policy, in order to ensure the pertinence of Occitan in today's world. 'Il faut définir une langue accessible et ses outils' (139–40); among these tools, the GIDILOc is now joined by this new Service. C. Laux, 'Un pas cap a una politica linguistica', *L'Occitan*, 121, 1996:3, further explains that the Service is modeled on prototypes in Catalonia and in Brittany. Id., 'La Mediatèca occitana inaugurada a Còrdas (Tarn)', *ib.*, 120, 1996:8, announces a new home in the medieval quarter of Cordes for the GEMP La Talvèra, in a 14th-c. building which will also house the new CORDAE mediatheque. Id., 'Nòstra cultura, una font pels creators', *ib.*, 123, 1996:4. An interview with Daniel Loddo, director of the CORDAE, who expresses the hope that the traditional cultures of France will provide the best tool for resisting invasion by other powerful cultures in the world.

TEXTS. Occitan was used into the mid-16th c. for notarial acts and registers. C. Laux, 'Trilinguisme latin-occitan-francés cò dels notaris d'Albigés', *Lengas*, Montpellier, 39, 1996:37–52, edits the registers of Albigeois (Tarn) notaries Antòni de Rippis, André Correg, Laurent Malapelli, and Guilhem Delacumba. Id., '(Archius) L'Occitan langue des notaires au XVIe siècle: *Compra de Peyre Bru per Johan Duraul*', *RT*, 3rd ser., 158, 1995: 338–40, provides diplomatic version, vocabulary, and translation of a text by Laurent Malapelli (or Malapel or Malapeau) documenting the purchase of property on 1 April 1540 from the *seigneurie* of Puybegon (Archives départementales du Tarn, MS 3 E 28 (61), fol. 1ᵛ. Id., '(Archius) L'Occitan langue des notaires au XVIe siècle: *La Vente à crédit, Deute de Peyre Laval*', *RT*, 3rd ser., 159, 1995: 551–55; diplomatic version, with vocabulary, notes and French translation, of a *reconnaissance de dette* registered on 24 March 1561 by Guilhaume Bartha (Archives départementales du Tarn, MS 6 E 13–427, fol. IIIC LXXVIIᵛ., with notes on "Les Monnaies", pp. 554–55). In a completely different vein, Id. studies 'La lenga de Calelhon', *Canta-Grelh*, 26, 1995:8–16, as found in the texts of *Contes del Papanon, Nanet del Rampalm*, and *Al Fial de las Sazons*.

PAREMIOLOGY. Daniel Loddo, *Al país de Boneta, canton de Carlus (Tarn-et-Garonne)*, La Talvèra, Còrdas, CORDAE, 1996, 250 pp., presents the locality's archæology, place names, everyday life, and oral literature, with accompanying audio cassette (for a partial listing of earlier GEMP recordings and publications, see *YWMLS*, 55:302–03, 56:289, and 57:277–79). Id., **Al païs del Lop Garon, canton de Salvagnac (Tarn)*, Gaillac, GEMP/La Talvèra, 1995. P. Rambier, 'Lou biais nostre de parlar', *Lou Païs*, 341, 1996:160, lists and translates into French a number of expressions dealing with his *terroir* and with general Occitan culture, all offered in the two spellings adapted by the Escolo Gabalo.

PROVENÇAL

GENERAL. B. Giély, 'Centre International de l'Écrit en Langue d'Oc', *PrA*, 102, 1996:16. The director of the CIEL d'Òc explains the choice of using information-science technology to safeguard the entirety of Occitan/Provençal literary production by making it available on diskette or CD-ROM. The CIEL d'Òc is planned as the complement of a museum of art and tradition, the joint goal being 'promoure la lengo e la cultuo [sic] prouvençalo'. CIEL d'Òc is welcomed by two short articles: 'Libres electronics', *L'Occitan*, 124, 1996:4; and J. de Marmont, 'La "Blibioutèco d'Óucitanìo" de Bèrra', *ib.*, 12. In 1996 the following became available, on 3.5″ diskette MAC/PC, with printed book: Mistral's *Lou pouèmo dòu Rose* and *Lis oulivado*; *Clouvis Hughes, fiéu de Menerbo, enfant terriblo de Marsilho* ed. Tricìo Dupuy; Batisto Bonnet's *Lou Carpan*; Marius Jouveau's *Pontgibous*; and René Jouveau's *La Bello Nuie*. A CD of **André Chiron canto Brassens en Prouvençau*, containing 15 songs, is now available; other volumes are promised. C. Rostaing continues his commentaries on Mistral's *Calendau* (1867): 'Calendau (29). Lis endrè. A. Cassis (c. III, v. 295–350)', *RPC*, 78–78 bis, 1996:6–8; and 'Calendau (30). Lis endrè. B. La Prouvènço d'enfre Terro (c. III, v. 36–56)', *ib.*, 80, 1996:2–4 (see *YWMLS*, 55:303, 56:290 and 57:280). These historical, ethnographic, and linguistic comments, which are pedagogical rather than analytic, have been collected by Id., **Commentaires de l'œuvre de Frédéric Mistral 'Calendau'*, Marseille, Prouvènço d'Aro, 1996, 164 pp. They cover: characters and background, the life of the people, folklore and legends, popular art, history of Provence, and literature.

ORTHOGRAPHY. P. Blanchet finds much that is worthwhile in 'Le système graphique du dictionnaire provençal-français de J. T. Avril (1840)', *Mélanges Roux*, 29–44. R. Toscano, 'Question de lenga: L'Invasion dau "a"', *AqAq*, 103, 1996:9, discusses the tendency toward overuse of the letter a' in Provençal and Nissart, where it represents not only /a/ but also /e/, /o/, /u/.

MORPHOSYNTAX. P. Vouland, 'Pèr leis aprendis', *AVEPB*, 77, 1996:8–9, contrasts Latin and Provençal demonstrative systems.

LEXIS AND LEXICOLOGY. Florian Vernet, *Petit lexique du provençal à l'époque baroque*, Nice, Institut d'Études Niçoises, Centre d'Études Occitanes, 1996, n.p., is based on a corpus encompassing most extant Provençal texts from the Baroque period, ranging from *Chansons au Carrateyron* (*c.* 1530) to Jean Sicard's *Paraphraso* (1673). Glaudi Barsòtti, *Le Bouil et le Tian, la cuisine du terroir provençal*, Aix-en-Provence, Édisud, 1996, 223 pp., is reported to include a list of ichthyonyms with equivalents in Provençal, as well as a Provençal-*francitan*-French lexicon. Jean-Claude Rey, *Érotisme et sexualité en Provence: les mots et la chose* (Temps choc), Marseille, Autres Temps, 1996, 199 pp., has produced a serious collection of some 3000 words and expressions classified by subject. A. Compan, 'Étude sur quelques mots provençaux et niçois', *L'Astrado*, 31, 1996:158–85, studies: *tros* 'morceau'; nic. *piech/pitre* 'poitrine'; *ferpa* 'peluche, frange'; *ceguinola* 'qui a la forme d'un cou de cigogne'; *trepadou* 'promenoir, trottoir; *ensouble* 'déchargeoir de métier à tisser' (terme technique de broderie); *bouiroun* 'amas de vers réunis pour pêcher l'anguille ou le poulpe', 'furoncle'; *galejado* 'plaisanterie'; *maluc/malu* 'hanche, tête du fémur; *tousello* 'froment sans barbe'; *magau/bêchard* 'houe, pioche'; niç. *chautroun* 'guenipe, souillon'.

PARTICULAR SEMANTIC FIELDS. L. Coulier continues the illus-trated series 'Lis flour dóu nouestre' (see *YWMLS*, 55:304, 56:290, and 57:280) with: 'L'erbo-de-la-roumpeduro', *JEA*, 82, 1995:10–11; 'La coulemelle o coucoumello', *ib.*, 83:12–13; 'L'esclop de Venus', *ib.*, 84, 1996:12–13; 'Lou pastel, *Isatis tinctoria*', *ib.*, 85:12–13; 'L'île de Santo Catarino', *ib.*, 86:10–11; and 'L'épicea (sapin de nouvè)', *ib.*, 87:8–9. V. Ferrat, 'A propos de quelques dénominations provençales du *ver luisant*. Étude géolexicale', *TCLN*, 17, 1995:127–38, is a comparison of Mistral's and Alibert's dictionaries with *ALP* 1028 'ver luisant', yielding 13 major types for this one insect. O. Ovchinnikova, 'Les désignations provençales de la *bugrane*. Notes sur la carte 252 de l'*ALP*', *ib.*, 138–48. finds multiple referents per species. J.-P. Dalbera, *A propos de quelques ichtyonymes dialectaux. Notes lexicologiques, étymologiques et géolinguistiques', *Actes* (Monaco), 97–110. M. Firpo, 'A Casa mentounasca', *OPM*, 80, 1996:7–8, presents vocabulary pertaining to farmers' and fishermen's houses in Menton. R. Gibelli, 'L'histoire des mots: *tian* et *triaca*', *ib.*, 78, 1996:27, studies *tian* 'poêle' in the dialects of the Italian Riviera, and *triaca* 'thériaque' (a foul-tasting mixture reputed to cure every ailment), which the author remembers from his youth as a term for 'rotgut'. Jacky Granier and Henri Charmasson, *Les Poissons du sud-est* *de la France. Catalogue des espèces et de leur nom vernaculaire*, Avignon, Société d'Étude des Sciences Naturelles de Vaucluse, 1996, 241 pp.

ONOMASTICS. C. Rostaing, 'Étude sur les noms d'Endoume, Malmousque, Séon, quartiers de Marseille', *Mélanges Roux*, 289–98, reviews problematic names for three Marseillais neighbourhoods. He revises his 1950 derivation of *Endoume* from Lat. DUMUS 'buisson', seeing now a Galloroman compound meaning 'cap rocheux' (289–92); *Malmousque*, attested as early as 1286 (*Lumena moscas*), is traced to pre-Latin **mus-k* 'roche' (292–94); underlying *la vallée de Séon* (294–96), R. sees prototypical *sed-oniu*, from a Ligurian root **sed*. André Compan, *Étude sur l'origine des noms des communes dans les Alpes-Maritimes*, 2nd ed., Nice, CRDP, 1995, 103 pp. Pau Nougier, *Coume te dison? Coume as noum? Li Sant benurous, venerable e pichot noum ounoura vo couneigu dins li païs d'oc*, Marseilles, p.p., 1995, 96 pp., presents a list of more than 1000 saints' names found in the pays d'Oc.

SUB-DIALECTS. René Toscano, **Conjugar en niçard*, Nice, Auba Nouvella, 1996, 48 pp. J. Chirio, 'Une famille de verbes irréguliers', *LSPS*, 120, 1996:44–45, studies *veni, parti, veure, deure, dire, esta/estaire, faire, teni, vale, voule, vieure, cale, ploure*. A. Viani, 'Li neoulougisme en nissart', *PrA*, 94, 1995:15, reviews learned words, borrowings from Greek, Arabic, Piemontese and other sources. W. Forner, 'La position linguistique du Mentonnais', *OPM*, 79, 1996:25–26, identifies Mentonnais (Menton, Sospel) as a transitional dialect between Nissart and Royasque, rather than between Nissart and Ligurien, as had been thought. J.-L. Caserio, 'A propos de chauve-souris: *ratapignata* ou *rata-penata*?', *ib.*, 77, 1996:26, argues against the choice of *ratapignata* as it appears in *Vocabulaire du parler Mentonnais*, Fasc. 3 (*c*), 1991, and in favour of *rata-penata*, attested as early as 1234, and which was also the choice of James Bruyn Andrews in his *Vocabulaire français-mentonnais*, Nice, Impr. Niçoise, 1875.

SOCIOLINGUISTICS. U. Brummert, 'Jean Jaurès et la langue occitane', *RT*, 3rd ser., 160, 1996:737–49, concludes her study of Jaurès's appreciation of Occitan as a great historical language (see *YWMLS* 57:274). For René Merle, *Les Varois, la presse varoise et le provençal (1859–1910)*, La Sanha/La Seyne, Société d'Études historiques du texte dialectal, 1996, 420 pp., Provençal was never used in the pre-WWI press of the Var as a political weapon, although it did occasionally serve to appeal to the masses. J.-M. Marconot, 'Patois et occitan: Le cas des quartiers de Nîmes', *Lo Lugarn*, 55, 1996:8–10, reports that in certain working-class quarters of Nîmes, the *langue d'oc* is spoken by a quarter to half of the population; yet these very people often feel estranged from the Felibrige or the Occitanist movement, which appears to M. to be spinning its wheels in intellectual circles. Gilles Rebull, 'Nationalité et régionalisme en Provence de 1859 à

1893. 1', *Lou Felibrige*, 22, 1996, 48 pp., compares mid-19th-c. Provence with Catalonia.

NORTHERN OCCITAN

LIMOUSIN

LEXIS AND LEXICOLOGY. **Les Mots en limousin: Dictionnaire français-limousin, Parlers, limousinismes et traditions*, Limoges, SELM, 1996. Yves Lavalade, **Dictionnaire français-occitan (dialecte limousin). Limousin-Marche-Périgord*, 2 vols, Limoges U.P., 1996[1997], 550 pp.

ONOMASTICS. Jacques Duguet, *Noms de lieux des Charentes*, Bonneton, 1995, 232 pp. Yves Lavalade, *Règne animal et toponymie limousine* (*ClL*, special no., 114), 1996, 40 pp., reviews mammals, insects, fish and shellfish, worms, amphibians, and reptiles, in the Haute-Vienne (1–31), Corrèze (32–36), and Creuse (37–39). Jean Roux, **Espingue-lebre et autres lieux ... éléments de géographie linguistique et d'onomastique du Périgord*, Périgueux, IEO-Périgord/Novelum, 1995. É. Théron continues his series, 'L'Histoire de Tulle à travers ses fontaines', *Lemouzi* 138, 1996:97–107 (Font de la Basiouge, Tour-de-Maysse); and *ib.*, 139, 1996:119–27 (Fontaine du Touron [ou de Lausanne]).

SUBDIALECTS. Nicolas Quint, **Grammaire du parler nord-occitan marchois de Gartempe et de St-Sylvain-Montaigut (Creuse)*, Limoges, Clau Lemosina, 1996, 230 pp. Robert Joudoux, 'Fables, contes et "gnorles"' (*parler* of Argentat), *Lemouzi* 140, 1996, 129 pp., edits the work of Marcellin Caze, with translation by André Lanly.

SOCIOLINGUISTICS. Jean-François Ratonnat, **La Vie d'autrefois en Périgord*, Bordeaux, Sud-Ouest, 1995, 190 pp.

PAREMIOLOGY. Ives Lavalada, *Nuveus Proverbis lemosins* (*ClL*, special no., 111), 1996, 67 pp.

AUVERGNAT

LEXIS AND LEXICOLOGY. J. Vesòla, 'Quauquas bèstias sauvatjas d'aici. 4, Las emplumadas', *Lo Convise*, 12, 1995:18–20, arranges names for wild birds into six columns: French, general Occitan, southwest Cantal (Aurillac and Castagnau), the Auvergnat zone (represented by Mauriac), and the Margeride (Planesa).

ONOMASTICS. J.-P. Chambon, **'Méthodes en anthroponymie historique: cinq noms de famille bas-auvergnats (Chassa[i]gnon, Vorilhon, Torrilhon, Fayon, Chandezon)', RIOn, 2, 1996:263–85. P.-H. Billy, **'Toponymie et archéologie: essai méthodologique sur la Basse-Auvergne', NRO, 27–28, 1996:147–68. J. Vesole, 'Vièlhs noms de las carrièras d'Orlhac', *Lou Convise*, 10, 1995:10–11.

TEXTS. L. Gerbeau, 'Per la religion de Sant Joan', *Lo Convise*, 12, 1995:9–11, presents in diplomatic version an Auvergnat document dated 26 May 1453 (Archives communales d'Aurillac, MS CC 34 P 16), with modern version by Joan Vesòla, relating the opening of a chest full of money destined for the Espitalièrs de Sant-Joan de Jerusalem, today known as the Ordre sobeiran de Malta. J. Boyer, 'La téulisso de l'Abadié de Séuvo-Cano', *NP*, 48, 1996:46–47, offers a diplomatic transcription of a 1505 Occitan text, Archives départementales des Bouches-du-Rhône, MS 309 E 274, fol. 620, dealing with change of tiles on the roof of the Cistercian abbey of Silvacane; as the editor notes, the orthography of this text is already virtually that of the Felibrige.

PROVENÇAL ALPIN

LEXIS AND LEXICOLOGY. Claudette Germi, *Mots du Champsaur, Hautes-Alpes*, Grenoble, ELLUG, 1996, 270 pp. J.-M. Effantin, 'Essai d'analyse quantitative des relevés de l'*Atlas linguistique de la Provence* en Briançonnais', *EOc*, 19, 1996:34–47. In its treatment of Oisans, Briançonnais cisalpin, Embrunais, and Queyras (little-known *parlers* of the region of Briançon), *ALP* compares unfavourably with *Atlas ethnographique du Jura et des Alpes du Nord*, ed. J. B. Martin and G. Tuaillon, CNRS, 1972, 1975, 1978, 1982. *ALP* fails to capture either the lexical richness of this otherwise undocumented region of the Hautes-Alpes, or the accurate locations of its lexical variants.

SUB-DIALECTS. W. Forner, 'La fumée et le feu. A propos des tentatives de délimitation de l'aire occitane sud-orientale. Première partie: De 1850 à 1950', *Mélanges Roux*, 155–80, with very complete bibliography, pp. 177–80. Tracing the tumultuous history of linguistic studies of Royasque through 1950, F. concludes: 'le Royasque s'oppose aux dialectes liguriens de la côte intémélienne'. J.-P. Dalbera, 'Polymorphisme et innovation dans l'aire occitane alpine. Le parler de Ste Agnès (Alpes-Maritimes)', *TCLN*, 17, 1995:3–35, studies features of a dialect which has remained far removed from channels of communication and exchange: apocope (Tende *l'ubu*, Ste Agnès *l'owp*); nasal vowels; and rising diphthongs. M. Olivieri, 'Aperçu sur le système verbal du parler de Sainte-Agnès (Alpes-Maritimes)', *ib.*, 37–64, notes how this community shows unusual albeit superficial evidence of phonetic evolution, as well as considerable polymorphism. J.-C. Ranucci, 'Etude de microtoponymie. La commune de Sainte-Agnès (Alpes-Maritimes)', *ib.*, 65–87. A. Samouillan, 'Las valadas occitanas d'Italia', *BP*, 1, 1996:36–37, outlines characteristics *a nosto modo* of the local varieties of Occitan in the Italian valleys, e.g. pronunciation of [v], final -[s]; definite articles include *lo, li*; intervocalic [d], [l], [s] are represented by [h]. J.-P.

Hilaire, '"Valades Ousitanes"', *Lo Lugarn*, 58, 1996:18, reviews a documentary film by Diego Anghilante and Fredo Valla on Occitan speakers in Italy, painting a comprehensive picture of Italy's most forgotten linguistic minority. The Trobaires de Comboscura have produced a CD of 12 Occitan songs, *A toun soulei*, featuring the language of the Occitan-speaking valleys.

SOCIOLINGUISTICS.   F. Calvetti, 'Una ricerca sulla situazione linguistica nelle valli Chisone e Germanasca', *La Beidana* 26, 1996:22–29, reports on the results of two surveys, 1992 and 1993, undertaken by Marina Gardiol of the Ufficio Cultura della Comunità Montana di Perosa Argentina (Val Chisone): among children, 17% say their first language is *patouà*; 60% of the parents and 71% of the grandparents claim to be dialect speakers.

ONOMASTICS.   O. Coïsson surveys the *'Toponomastica delle valli del Pinerolese (Valli Pellice, Germanasca, Chisone)', *BSSPin*, 11.1–2, 1994:70–71. M. Bruno, *'Il mistero di un nome: Bric, caire, truc, montagne, cime, alture delle Alpi occidentali', *Coumboscuro*, 280–281, 1995:4–5.

TEXTS.   E. Martin, 'Il *Codice Gouthier*', *BSSPin*, 11.1–2, 1994:72–97, describes and transcribes a MS, also known as 'Anciennes ordonnances de la Communauté de Mentolles', which was brought back to Villaretto in 1947, remained almost unknown to scholars until 1970, and has now disappeared again. The MS was drawn up by two different notaries between 1515 and 1549; with pages in *dialetto provenzale alpino*, Latin, and French, it must be considered a fundamental document for the study of linguistic uses and graphies in Val Chisone. A. Genre, O. Mula, and D. Tron, 'Chantoummo ën patouà: Salmi e inni nel dialetto della val Germanasca', *La Beidana* 26, 1996:30–54, give 12 psalms and hymns, with melodies by various 16th-c. composers. Most of these psalms were originally the work of Clément Marot (1542); the remainder are due to Calvin's colleague, Théodore de Bèze (*c.* 1562).

LITERATURE

By CATHERINE LÉGLU, *Lecturer in French, University of Bristol*

I. MEDIEVAL PERIOD

Stefano Asperti, *Carlo I d'Angiò e i trovatori: componenti provenzali e angioine nella tradizione manoscritta della lirica trobadorica* (Memoria del tempo, 3), Ravenna, Longo, 1995, 270 pp., offers a detailed examination of the multilingual poetic activity around Charles I of Anjou, focusing on Paris BN fr.12472 (Chansonnier Giraud), Paris BN fr.12474, and Vat. lat. 3207. Charles's patronage of composition in French, Occitan, and Tuscan, and links with the courts of Aragon, Sicily, and Northern Italy, are viewed in terms of the decline of the troubadour tradition in this period. Elizabeth Aubrey, *The Music of the Troubadours (Music: Scholarship and Performance)*, Bloomington, Indiana U.P., 1996, xxi + 326 pp., examines the many issues attached to the understanding and performance of troubadour songs with melodies. Combining medieval music scholarship with an awareness of the needs of the modern performer, A. examines transmission, poetics, genre, form and style, and addresses such issues as repetitive structures and through-composition. Wendy Pfeffer, *Proverbs in Medieval Occitan Literature*, Gainesville, Florida U.P., x + 155 pp., analyses the use of proverbial material by troubadours, especially in terms of the light this sheds on the training and education of poets and audiences in medieval Occitania. She suggests that literacy in Occitania was greater than has been supposed, and that the *Salutz d'Amors* genre points to a literate general audience. The book examines the uses made of proverbs by Guilhem IX, Marcabru (34–42), Folquet de Marselha, Bertran de Born, Peire Vidal (49–62), Amanieu de Sescars, Cerveri de Girona and Guillem de l'Olivier (86–91). These studies, along with a section on proverbial phrases in the *Canso de la Crozada*, establish that the use of proverbs in poetry is a matter of individual choice. *Une Belle au Bois Dormant médiévale: 'Frayre de joy et sor de plaser': nouvelle d'oc du XIVe siècle*, ed. Suzanne Thiolier-Méjean (Collections du CEROC, 8), Paris–Sorbonne U.P., 1996, 236 pp., is an edition with notes and a study of the language and themes of this *nova*, which was previously thought to be in Catalan. The text is included among five other *novas* in *Nouvelles courtoises occitanes et françaises* ed. Suzanne Thiolier-Méjean and Marie-Françoise Notz-Grob (Collection Lettres Gothiques, Le Livre de Poche, 4548), Librairie Générale Française, 704 pp. *Le Rosier alchimique de Montpellier. Lo Rosari. Textes, traductions, notes et commentaires*, ed. Antoine Calvet (Collections du CEROC, 9), Paris–Sorbonne U.P., xci + 134 pp., attributes the Latin text of this treatise to Arnaud de Villeneuve and dates it *c.* 1370–1410. The anonymous Occitan translation is edited with a study of the language, glossary and translation into French. *Les poesies del trobador Guillem de Berguedà*, ed. Martín de Riquer (Serie Gran, 18) Barcelona, Quaderns Crema, 1996, 428 pp., is a re-edition in one volume, translated into Catalan, of his definitive edition of 1971. *The Song of the Cathar Wars: A History of the Albigensian Crusade*, trans. Janet Shirley, Aldershot, Scolar Press, 1996, xiv + 210 pp., is a translation into English of the *Canso de la Crotzada*, based on the Martin-Chabot edition. S.'s translation aims to provide an accessible student text. The dissemination of the troubadour lyric and its influence on other languages is examined in *Actes* (AIEO 1995). For the role of literary courts in the Iberian peninsula, see: C. Alvar, 'Alfonso X, poeta profano. Temas poéticos. La corte poética del Rey' (3–17); V. Beltran, 'Tipos y temas trovadorescos. XIV. Alfonso X, Raimon de Castelnou y la corte literaria de Rodez' (19–39); A. Resende de Oliveira, 'Le surgissement de la culture troubadouresque dans l'occident de la Péninsula Ibérique, I: Compositeurs et cours' (85–95). J. C. Ribeiro Miranda gives Part II of this paper, 'Les genres, les thèmes et les formes' (97–105). Comparative studies of the presence of Occitan lyric songs in other lyric poetry are: V. Bertolucci Pizzorusso, 'La funzione encomiastica nei trovatori provenzali e galego-portoghesi' (41–49); M. Winter-Housman, 'Domna et dame, images différentes?' (255–83); A. Touber, 'Les sens occitans, cachés dans la poésie des Minnesänger' (285–96); and N. Unlandt, 'Le vocabulaire religieux des premiers troubadours et minnesinger: comparaison des champs sémantiques *dieus* et *got*' (297–311). There are two studies of *contrafacta*: D. Billy, 'Contrafactures de modèles troubadouresques dans la poésie catalane, XIVe siècle' (51–74); and V. Mertens, 'Kontrafaktur als intertextuelles Spiel. Aspekte der Adaptation von Troubadour-Melodien im deutschen Minnesang' (269–83). Broader comparative treatments are found in: L. Formisano, 'Troubadours, trouvères, Siciliens' (109–24); C. Dijkstra, 'Troubadours, trouvères and Crusade lyrics' (173–84); and A. Rieger, 'Relations interculturelles entre troubadours, trouvères et Minnesänger au temps des croisades' (201–25). R. Lafont, '*Sai* et *lai*. Le concept d'Espagne chez Marcabru' (75–83). A. Tavera, 'A propos des "petits troubadours" qui allèrent en Italie' (143–59). Intertextual studies between the Old French and Occitan lyric: P. Bec, 'Bernard de Ventadour et Thibaut de Champagne. Essai de bilan comparatif' (163–71); and R. Rosenstein, 'La douce voix de châtelain. Le Châtelain de Coucy et les troubadours. Vingt ans après (227–53). E. B. Hayes, 'Arnaut Daniel et Danté (125–32), studies the links between later Italian literature and the troubadours. Those between Occitan and Hebrew poetry are examined by A. Schippers, 'Les troubadours et la tradition poétique hébraïque en Italie et en Provence: les cas de Abraham ha-Bedarshi et Immanuel ha-Rami' (133–42). Maurizio Perugi, *Saggi di linguistica trovadorica: saggi su "Girart de Roussillon", Marcabruno, Bernart de Ventadorn, Raimbaut d'Aurenga, Arnaut Daniel e sull' uso letterario di oc e oïl nel trecento italiano* (Romanica et Comparatistica, 21), Tübingen, Stauffenberg, 1995, 197 pp., is reviewed in great detail by G.-B. Speroni, 'Questioni di filologia provenzale', *RPh*, 50:315–28. S. Guida, 'Uc de Saint Circ e la crociata contro gli Albigesi', *CN*, 57:1–36, suggests that Uc went to Treviso as an economic migrant, not a heretic, and traces his political position through *vidas* and *razos*. C. Léglu, 'A reading of troubadour insult songs: the *Comunals* Cycle', *RMS*, 22, 1996[1997]:63–83, is an analysis of the songs of Garin d'Apchier and Torcafol, proposing an æsthetic rather than historical reading of the cycle. Also by L, 'Defamation in the troubadour *sirventes*', *MAe*, 46:28–41, examines songs found in legal cases brought for defamation in the early 14th century. Also by L., 'Negative self-promotion: the troubadour *Sirventes Joglaresc*', *Papers* (ICLS 8), 47–55, presents a reassessment of this corpus as a form of self-advertising, and self-definition in reverse. M. Rolland Quintanilla, 'Parodia de lo cortés en la poesía medieval', Mildonian, *Parodia*, 45–55, is an analysis of the parodic strategies of a set of poems, from Guilhem IX to Peire Cardenal, which she suggests are intertextually related. C. Jewers, 'The name of the ruse and the Round Table: Occitan Romance and the case for cultural resistance', *Neophilologus*, 81:187–200, reads *Jaufre* as an instance of Occitan resistance, via parody and systematic deflation, to French Arthurian material, especially through naming. K. Busby, 'Hagiography at the confluence of epic, lyric and romance: Raimon Feraut's *Vida de Saint Honorat*', *ZRP*, 113:51–64, examines the text's combination of several genres, in the light of its generic indeterminacy as a narrative text in the Occitan language. A. A. MacDonald, 'The Catalan–Occitan Easter Play', *Romania*, 115:495–518, examines the 14th-c. Easter play known as the Didot Passion, and compares it to a Catalan Passion play, now in Vic. M. concludes that the Occitan text was probably first composed in Catalonia, in the region of Vic or Ripoll, and reflects a Catalan–Occitan cultural and literary network. S. Marnette, 'L'expression féminine dans la poésie lyrique occitane', *RPh*, 51:170–93, is a reading using linguistic and sociolinguistic criteria, which concludes that the *trobairitz* did not merely reproduce the template of the male-voiced lyric, but evolved an enunciation of their own. P. Onesta, '*L'Amor de lonh* di Jaufre Rudel e il *Longinquus Amor* di Properzio', *QFLR*, 12:89–109, rejects any parallel between the terms, interpreting Propertius's adjective as a temporal, not a spatial reference. A. Rossell, 'La música de los trovadores', *Música*, 8, 1996:53–100, is a general presentation of the main aspects of study of music in the troubadour corpus, with a discography. R. Moscatelli, 'La musica dei trovatori: indagine su aspetti melodico — ritmici ed esecutivi', *QFLR*, 12:111–39, examines the question of rhythm in non-mensural notation, and emphasizes the importance of performance in assessing specific melodies, with reference to Old French romances. J. Haines, 'Vers une distinction *leu/ clus* dans l'art musico-poétique des troubadours', *Neophilologus*, 81:341–47, divides the corpus, on the basis of a 20 per cent sample of the extant melodies, into *clus* (through-composed) and *leu* (repetition) forms, and traces their stylistic evolution. M. Stanesco, 'La fleur inverse et la "belle folie" de Raimbaut d'Orange', *CCMe*, 40:233–52, after redefining the 'flor enversa' of Raimbaut d'Aurenga in terms of the lily and the platonic image of the human body as *arbor inversa*, reads it as an *adynaton*, and applies it to Raimbaut d'Aurenga's poetics. F. Benozzo, 'Guglielmo IX e le fate. Il "vers de dreit nien" e gli archetipi celtici della poesia dei trovatori', *MedRom*, 21.1:69–87, identifies the enchantment on a mountain with a *topos* in Celtic (mostly Irish) literature. E. W. Poe, '*E potz seguir las rimas contrasemblantz*: imitators of the Master Troubadour Giraut de Bornelh', *Procs* (Madison), 279–97, is an enlivening article, proposing a reconsideration of the *contrafactum* technique, examining the dialogue between source and rewritten texts, through the use made by Peire de Bussignac, Raimbaut de Vaqueiras, Raimon de Miraval and others of the songs of Giraut de Bornelh. The second half of the paper examines the differing perceptions of plagiarism presented by Bertran de Born and Giraut de Bornelh (PC 242, 67 and 80, 44). S. Melani, 'Intorno al "vers del lavador". Marcabruno e la riconquista ispanica', *MedRom*, 21. 1:88–106, explains Marcabru's song in terms of the political context of 1144–45, and suggests it may be read as a sermon. R. Lafont, 'La Voix des dames', *RLaR*, 101.2:185–205, is a companion article to Pierre Bec, *Chants d'amour des femmes-troubadours*, Stock, 1995, 264 pp., attacking recent work on the *trobairitz* as too influenced by 19th-c. positivism. This polemical, but stimulating, paper hesitates between dismissing the *trobairitz* corpus as a heterosexual limitation of the troubadour love lyric, and making claims for a revolutionary role, strictly with relevance to masculine desire. C. Hershon, 'The Jews of mediæval Languedoc: the interplay of literature', *Tenso*, 12:89–111, addresses a number of questions about the literary contacts between Jews and Christians in Languedoc, citing Isaac Ha-Gorni, Abraham Bedersi, Guiraut Riquier and Matfre Ermengaud. H. suggests that Bonfilh (PC 199, 1) may be a fictional character, not Bedersi. *PerM*, suppl. to vol. 22, 1996, 'Actes du Colloque "Languedoc et Langue d'Oc" (Toulouse, janvier 1996)', includes: C. Alvar, 'N' At de Mons de Tolosa et Alphonse X de Castille' (21–32), which identifies the letter-debate on astronomy between At and the king as a quodlibetical disputation; P. Bec, 'Les deux sonnets occitans de Dante da Maiano (XIIIe siècle)' (47–57), who sets this minor poet (PC 121) in context, and gives a normalized Occitan version of both sonnets, with French translation; M.-H. Fernandez, 'Une bourrée rouergate à Paris au XIIIe siècle' (95–103), who analyses a motet from the Montpellier MS, which features a pastiche of Occitan, and suggests that 13th-c. Parisians already perceived Occitan culture as regional folklore; and G. Gouiran, 'Le regard sur l'autochtone: Sainte Enimie en Gévaudan' (105–17), who examines the *vida* of Sainte Enimie, in terms of Bertrand de Marseille's depiction of the Gévaudan people as primitives civilized by Parisian saints. M. Taylor, 'Addenda to "An Etat présent of Occitan Lyric" ', *Tenso*, 12:81–88, updates M. Routledge's article of 1993.

2. FROM 1500 ONWARDS

André Du Pré, *Pouesies Gascoues (1620)*, ed. Joan-Frances Courouau, Montpellier, Section Française de l'AIEO, 1996, 136 pp., is an Occitan-language edition, with a study of language and an analysis of style. F. Pic, 'Contribution bibliographique à l'étude de la posterité des troubadours: *Les Vies des plus célèbres et anciens poètes provençaux . . .* , de Jean de Nostredame (1575), leur diffusion depuis le XVIe siècle, leurs possesseurs et leurs lecteurs', *Actes* (AIEO 1995), 185–200. *Actes* (Villeneuve-lès-Avignon) includes critical studies: R. Pécout, 'L'écrivain et ses doubles: les différents plans d'écriture et de lecture du *Pouèmo dóu Rose*' (13–26); M.-F. Notz, 'La poétique du fleuve' (57–64); J.-F. Courouau, '*Lou Pouèmo dóu Rose*: entre romantisme alemand e fantastic occitan' (197–216); M. Blaise, ' "Une illusion sur l'eau glissante", le réalisme au fil du réel dans *Lou Pouèmo dóu Rose*' (217–40); F.-P. Kirsch, 'Aspects post-modernes de Mistral: *Lou Pouèmo dóu Rose*' (255–70); P. Martel, 'L'accueil du *Pouèmo dóu Rose*' (159–74); G. Latry, 'Le cours du *Rhône*: lectures et évaluations (1896–1954)' (175–88); and M. Boussy, '1897, *Lou Pouèmo dóu Rose*: conjoncture et conjectures' (189–96). Thematic studies: J.-Y. Casanova, 'La nature et l'homme dans le *Pouèmo dóu Rose*' (83–98); J.-C. Bouvier, 'Ethnographie et invention épique dans *Lou Pouèmo dóu Rose*' (99–108); C. Mauron, 'Lou maridage dins *Lou Pouèmo dóu Rose*' (117–26); and A. Krispin, 'Mistral et le mythe des mères: l'or des Vénitiennes' (127–34). The development of Occitan literature and identity in the Romantic era is examined in *Actes* (Pau), which includes F.-M. Castan, 'Précocité et longévité du romantisme occitan' (253–43); H. Jeanjean, 'Romantisme et nationalisme' (255–64); J. Gourc, 'Rochegude et l''

"Occitanie retrouvée" ' (15–23); J.-M. Auzias, 'Un précurseur de la renaissance des lettres d'Oc, Claude Fauriel' (25–35); P. Gardy, 'L'œuvre poétique d'Antoine Fabre d'Olivet: sujet littéraire et sujet linguistique' (55–68); F.-P. Kirsch, 'Aspects romantiques de Mistral' (327–39); R. Lafont, 'L'authentification du roman troubadour, ou l'autre littérature' (69–75); and K. Maurin, 'Mythe cathare, mythe romantique?' (77–86). The use of folklore is examined by: P. Martel, ' "La poésie populaire d'oc" à l'époque romantique: une découverte?' (265–84); C. Torreilles, 'Muse patoise et muse romantique: l'exemple de La Fare Alais' (307–25); and E. Gauzit, 'La chanson occitane pyrénéenne et le romantisme' (285–306). Philippe Gardy, *L'Ecriture occitane contemporaine. Une quête des mots*, L'Harmattan, 1996, 290 pp., is an overview of recently published work in Occitan, which examines the problem of Occitan literary identity, with close readings of Max Rouquette, Bernard Manciet and Robert Lafont.

IV. SPANISH STUDIES

LANGUAGE

POSTPONED

MEDIEVAL LITERATURE

By JANE E. CONNOLLY, *University of Miami*, MARÍA MORRÁS, *Universitat Pompeu Fabra*, and M. DOLORES PELÁEZ BENÍTEZ, *Simmons College*

1. GENERAL

Michael McGaha, *Coat of Many Cultures: The Story of Joseph in Spanish Literature 1200–1492*, Philadelphia, The Jewish Publication Society, xviii + 459 pp., translates with brief introductions three *aljamiado* texts, Rabbi Moses Arragel's translation and commentary of Genesis 37–50, *Historia de Josep* by Joan Roiç de Corella, *Book of Heroes*, and books 8–9 of the *General Estoria*. *Medieval Iberia: Readings from Christian, Muslim, and Jewish Sources*, ed. Olivia Remie Constable, UPP, 426 pp., is an anthology of mostly historical texts from the 6th to the 15th c. translated into English from Latin and the vernacular languages of medieval Iberia. L. P. Harvey, 'The arms of Madrid and the Warwick arms: some reflexions on the bear and ragged staff', *Deyermond Vol.*, 177–87, suggests that the Madrid and Warwick coats of arms may share a common pagan origin associated with the cult of the divinities called *Matronae*. D. Hook, 'The legend of the thirty pieces of silver', *ib.*, 205–21, enumerates the Iberian versions of the legend and traces their place within the European tradition. J. Rubio Tovar, 'Algunas características de las traducciones medievales', *RLMed*, 9: 197–243, surveys general aspects of medieval translation and includes a very useful bibliography. W. C. Stalls, 'Custom, authority and community in the Middle Ages: Aragon and Navarre in the twelfth century', Kagay, *Iberia*, 27–41, studies the customary practices of the *infanzones* and free peasantry through the analysis of 12th-c. charters recording land transfers, to show the customary authority on local communities. T. M. Vann, 'The town Council of Toledo during the minority of Alfonso VIII (1158–1169)', *ib.*, 43–60, presents the legal traditions of Toledo and studies the composition of the municipal council in 1155 and 1166, suggesting that with the reinstatement of the Laras in Toledo after 1166, the Castilians who had supported the Castros lost power while the Mozarabs gained a strong position. D. J. Kagay, 'The clash of royal and papal law: the resolution of lay murder of high clergy in the twelfth-century crown of Aragon', *ib.*, 61–75, investigates the legal interaction between ecclesiastical and lay principals through two historical cases: the murders of Ug de Cervelló, Archbishop of Tarragona, in 1171, and of Archbishop Ramón de Vilademuls in 1194. J. Sanz Hermida, '"Perdimos Príncipe en quien dos cosas juntas añaden nuestro quebranto: su terneza de años y vejez de consejos"': el tópico del *puer senex* como señal de una temprana muerte', *Procs* (MHRS 8), 119–26, explains the medical theory behind the association of the *puer senex* with premature death. D. Hook, 'Method in the margins: an archaeology of annotation', *ib.*, 135–44, outlines a method for the important task of establishing the chronology of textual annotations and the identification of the annotators. A. M. Beresford, '"Ençendida del ardor de la luxuria": prostitution and promiscuity in the legend of Saint Mary of Egypt', *Deyermond Vol.* (QMW), 45–56, offers a detailed analysis of the portrayal of Mary of Egypt in the three principle versions, showing that her personality differs radically from other prostitute saints, for she is both harlot and nymphomaniac. C. Marimón Llorca, 'Del orador cristiano al productor letrado: algo más sobre la retórica en la Edad Media castellana', *ib.*, 67–76, reviews the manifestation of the rhetorical 'I' in early Castilian literature, primarily the *cuaderna vía*. T. M. Capuano, 'The agricultural texts appended to the fourteenth-century Iberian translations of Palladius', *Manuscripta*, 38:253–63, presents the hypothesis that the miscellany of agricultural texts appended to the Aragonese and Catalan translations of Palladius are of Spanish origin and represent the first vernacular compositions (not translations) of the Valencian *huerta*. H. Goldberg, 'Cannibalism in Iberian narrative: the dark side of gastronomy', *BHS(G)*, 74:107–22, considers the types and function of cannibalism, primarily in ballads and sentimental romance, and finds that production of laughter is the key purpose and that children are frequently the cannibalized objects, perhaps because they are less human than adults and certainly because they are less powerful. B. Taylor, '"Dicta, scripta et facta": las inscripciones en la literatura sapiencial', *Diablotexto*, 3, 1996[1997]:199–244, deals with inscriptions and their central position in some titles from the 13th to the 15th centuries. P. Sánchez-Prieto Borja, 'Problemas lingüísticos en la edición de textos medievales (sobre la relación entre crítica textual e historia de la lengua)', *Incipit*, 16:19–54, poses the problematic nature of graphematic simplification current in so-called critical editions. C. Alvar, 'Manuscritos y tradición textual. Desde los orígenes hasta c. 1350', *RFE*, 77:33–68, is a compilation of information on manuscripts and editions of Spanish medieval texts. E. Blanco, 'Artes de bien morir: para vivir mejor', *Actas* (AHLM 6), 1, 297–305, comments on *artes moriendi.* D. Hook, 'Esbozo de un catálogo cumulativo de los nombres artúricos peninsulares anteriores a 1300', *Atalaya*, 7, 1996[1997]: 135–52.

2. The Early Reconquest and Hispano-Latin Literature

C. García Turza and J. García Turza, 'Siglo x: balbuceos de la lengua castellana (El manuscrito 46 de la Real Academia de la Historia: aspectos históricos y filológicos)', *Ínsula*, 607:1, 3–7, highlight inconsistencies in the claims for a later dating of the *Glosas Emilianenses*, arguing for a multidisciplinary (historic, linguistic, philological) approach to the subject, and offer a detailed description of MS 46, whose colophon indicates it was copied at San Millán in 964 and thus would precede *GE* were the recent dating accepted. C. Burnett, 'The works of Petrus Alfonsi: questions of authenticity', *MAe*, 66:42–79, isolates stylistic and doctrinal elements common to the works generally attributed to A. in order to evaluate the extent to which he contributed to other texts associated with him. The article includes an edition and translation of A.'s prologue to his astrological tables. G. West, 'The destiny of nations: treatment of legendary material in Rodrigo de Toledo's *De rebus Hispaniae*', *Deyermond Vol.*, 517–33, is an excellent study of Rodrigo Ximénez de Rada's critical approach to the sources of four legends in *De rebus* (the account of the origins of the Goths, the story of Wittiza, the legend of Bernardo el Carpio, and, briefly, the legend of Mainete), concluding that legend, like historical documentation, was manipulated to suit his aims. J. DuQuesnay, 'The political grammar of early Hispano-Gothic historians', Kagay, *Iberia*, 1–25, studies the use of 'populus' in Isidore of Seville, Apringius, John of Biclar, and Braulius. J. M. Díaz de Bustamante, 'Tendencias de investigación en literatura latina medieval', *Actas* (AHLM 6), 1, 73–86, is an annotated bibliography of the most important research on literary medieval Latin in the last decade.

3. Early Lyric Poetry, Epic, Ballads
KHARJAS, LYRIC POETRY

Otto Zwartjes, *Love Songs from Al-Andalus: History, Structure and Meaning of the Kharja*, NY, Brill, 385 pp., represents an important contribution to *kharja* studies. Employing a supra-national perspective of Andalusian strophic poetry in general and the *kharja* in particular, Z. discusses the most important theories on the use of bilingualism in al-Andalus; provides a survey of the evolution from *qasīd* to *muwaššah* and *zajal*, describes the literary sources of Hispano-Arabic and Hispano-Hebrew *muwaššaḥāt* and their development according to medieval Arabic and modern theory, and examines the relations with Western medieval literary traditions. Id., 'Algunas observaciones sobre elementos extra-andalusíes en las jarŷa-s romances y bilingües: la cuestión de la rima', *Actas* (AHLM 6), II, 1599–1618, describes and analyses the rhyme of the romance *jarŷas* in Arabic and Hebrew poems. F. Marcos Marín, 'Lecturas y lección de la jarcha VII', *Incipit*, 16:164–74, discusses its reading and interpretation. F. Corriente, 'Nuevas notas a las xara-t con texto romance en la serie árabe', *RFE*, 77:119–27, makes some lexical points on transliterating and reading the texts. L. Haywood, 'Lyric in medieval secular narrative', *Procs* (MHRS 8), 61–73, based on an examination of O.Sp. and Middle English texts, proposes a model for the study of the use of lyric in medieval secular narrative. L. Simó, 'Acerca del verso "El vino so el agua frida" y su relación con el poema *Razón de Amor*', *La corónica*, 25.2:115–22, examines the validity of various readings of line 6 of *villancico* 116 from the *Cancionero musical de Palacio* ('el vino / él vino / el pino / esspino so el agua frida') without reaching a firm conclusion. J. M. Pedrosa, '*La flor en la cama*: simbolismo y ritual de un epitalamio sefardí de Marruecos', *Deyermond Vol.* (QMW), 379–86, discusses the ritual significance of magical blossoming in Iberia. M. Masera, 'El simbolismo en la lírica tradicional hispánica: un recurso poético', *ib.*, 387–97, classifies traditional symbols according to their stability (i.e., symbols unchanged through time, those that are modernized, those that pertain solely to old lyric or to modern lyric), and shows that their meaning also depends on the poetic voice (masculine or feminine). M. L. Cuesta Torre, 'Tristán en la poesía medieval peninsular', *RLMed*, 9:121–43, is a survey of allusions to Tristán in Catalan and Provenzal lyric, Galician-Portuguese *cantigas*, the '*lais de Bretanha*', and Castilian ballads. P. Botta, '*Noche escura* y la canción de mujer', *Actas* (AHLM 6), I, 343–55, in a most interesting and convincing exposition, traces the debt of San Juan's 'Noche oscura' to traditional female poetry.

EPIC

V. Castro Lingl, 'The two wives of Count Garçi Fernández: assertive women in *La condesa traidora*', *Deyermond Vol.* (QMW), 9–21, based on an analysis of Sancha and Argentina, two powerful and essential characters for plot development, contests the classification of the epic as misogynist. X. Sanmateu, '*El Cid*, un ejemplo de épica cinematográfica: notas sobre el uso del espectáculo', *ib.*, 23–34, discusses the use of spectacle in the 1961 film, especially as it relates to episodes of a religious nature or involving weaponry. I. Zaderenko, 'Acerca de la fecha de composición del *Cantar de los siete infantes de Lara*', *La corónica*, 26.1 : 247–55, supports C. Smith's 13th-c. dating of the poem, citing cultural practices, legal references, religious attitudes, and chivalresque virtues characteristic of that period. F. Gómez Redondo, 'La otra épica', *Actas* (AHLM 6), I, 701–19, assesses the content and intentionality of lost texts, not necessarily *cantares de gesta*, from the 10th to the 12th centuries. P. Gracia, 'La leyenda de la Condesa traidora: observaciones sobre su estructura y significación', *ib.*, 720–28, remarks that Sancha's disgrace echoes her mother's history. M. Vaquero, 'El episodio del cohombro de los *Siete Infantes de Lara* en el marco de la épica española', *ib.*, II, 1543–53, presents a coherent interpretation of the *cohombro* episode as a war rather than a sexual motif, and shows how *SIL* and *Sancho* II share two epic motifs also present in the *Nibelungenlied* linking both Spanish texts to a common European epic tradition.

POEMA DE MIO CID

S. B. Raulston, 'Poetic craft and dramatic tension: the climax of the *Poema de mio Cid*', *La corónica*, 26.1 : 203–23, argues that the legal content of the *cortes* episode creates a dramatic tension resolved only in the final heroic combat, the poem's true climax, and argues that the poet and his audience shared a knowledge of customary law. C. Smith, 'Cardeña, last bastion of medieval myth and legend', *Deyermond Vol.*, 425–44, traces the fabrication of Cidian myth associated with the monastery at San Pedro de Cardeña. M. Harney, 'Social stratification and class ideology in the *Poema de Mio Cid* and the *Chanson de Roland*', Kagay, *Iberia*, 77–102, is a comparative social study showing that in social terms the *PMC* represents a more primitive stage than the one portrayed in the French poem. C. Marimón Llorca, 'Palabra de Rey: los actos de habla de Alfonso VI y el desarrollo estructural del *Cantar de Mio Cid*', *Actas* (AHLM 6), II, 967–75, analyses Alfonso VI's speeches in light of J. Austin's theory of speech acts.

BALLADS

H. Pomeroy, 'Love and barter in the Spanish ballad: Rosaflorida's offer to Montesinos', *Procs* (MHRS 8), 127–34, finds in Rosaflorida's offers to Montesinos a reflection of the economic situation of the Middle Ages. In '*Don Bueso y su hermana*: the survival of *Kudrun* in the *Romancero*', *Deyermond Vol.* (QMW), 353–60, the same author shows that there is a 'genetic connection' between the Austrian epic and the Sephardic ballad. L. González Fernández, 'An Asturian version of *Don Bueso y su hermana* and the popular tradition', *ib.*, 361–68, concludes that the sexual imagery in an Asturian version of *Don Bueso* collected in 1995 is more explicit than in other versions. S. Shakir-Khalil, 'Crossing the frontier: mixed-race characters in medieval Spanish ballads', *ib.*, 369–77, shows that the interpretation of Abenámar and Mudarra, figures who represent both Christian and Moorish societies, varies widely from one ballad version to another. D. E. Sieber, 'The frontier ballad and Spanish Golden Age historiography: recontextualizing the *Guerras Civiles de Granada*', *HR*, 65:291–306, analyses the use of ballads in G. Pérez de Hita's *GCG* as documentary evidence and re-evaluates the text as a work of history rather than fiction. V. Atero Burgos and N. Vázquez Recio, 'Hacia una tipología del romancero milagroso en un corpus del sur', *Actas* (AHLM 6), i, 191–200, propose a classification of the religious *romancero* collected in Cádiz. C. Tato, 'Algunas precisiones sobre el romance *Retrayda estava la reyna*', *ib.*, ii, 1479–89, concludes that this ballad attributed to Carvajal was probably written at the end of 1457 or beginning of 1458 as part of a cycle about Alfonso V and his wife María de Castilla.

4. THIRTEENTH AND FOURTEENTH CENTURIES

POETRY

CUADERNA VÍA VERSE.   T. H. E. White, 'The taboo of Antioch: incest and its consequences in the *Libro de Apolonio*', *Deyermond Vol.* (QMW), 57–66, finds that *Apolonio* is essentially a tale about incest and its negative impact on society. J. Weiss, 'Apolonio's mercantile morality and the ideology of courtliness', *Deyermond Vol.*, 501–16, focuses on social and economic exchange in *Apolonio*. M. L. Cuesta, 'Uso del poder y amor paternal en el *Libro de Apolonio*', *Actas* (AHLM 6), i, 551–60, finds a correspondence between the private and the public spheres of power: the good father is a good king and the bad father is also a bad king.

LIBRO DE ALEXANDRE.   E. Franchini, 'El iv Concilio de Letrán, la apócope extrema y la fecha de composición del *Libro de Alexandre*', *La Corónica*, 25.2:31–74, adds support to I. Uría Maqua's dating of the poem between 1220 and 1225. G. Hilty, 'La fecha del *Libro de Alexandre*', *ZRP*, 113:563–67, rejects F. Marcos Marín's analysis of strophe 1799 and thus his early dating of the text, and reasserts his own dating (1223). Id., 'Fecha y autor del *Libro de Alexandre*', *Actas* (AHLM 6), ii, 813–20, provides a detailed analysis of 1799cd to argue that the text was written in a period of ten years during the 1220s by a group of scholars under the direction of a teacher at the University of Palencia. A. Arizaleta, 'La jerarquía de las fuentes del *Libro de Alexandre*', *ib.*, 1, 183–89, maintains that the unknown author did not choose his sources at random, but rather considered how they completed each other, and in 'El exordio del *Libro de Alexandre*', *RLMed*, 9:47–60, develops the hypothesis that the *accessus ad auctores* technique is the model followed by the anonymous author in the *exordio*, which suggests that he had a high intellectual consciousness of his work. I. Michael, 'Automata in the *Alexandre*: pneumatic birds in Porus's palace', *Deyermond Vol.*, 275–88, proposes that both Lamprecht and the *Alexandre* poet drew on a similar source, possibly an illumination, for their descriptions of mechanical birds in golden boughs.

BERCEO. Gonzalo de Berceo, *Milagros de Nuestra Señora*, ed. Fernando Baños Vallejo, introd. Isabel Uría Maqua, B, Crítica, xlii + 117 pp., contains an excellent study and notes on sources and literary aspects. A. M. Beresford, 'The figure of the martyr in Gonzalo de Berceo's *Martirio de San Lorenzo*', *Procs* (MHRS 8), 107–18, finds that martyrdom is represented as a self-perpetuating, communal experience. J. W. Marchand, 'Putting the bite on hell: a reference in Berceo's *Duelo*', *La corónica*, 25.2:91–102, clarifies the meaning of quatrain 96 showing that Berceo, far from being a simple country poet, was well-versed in patristic exegesis. F. Baños Vallejo, ' "Teófilo" y "La iglesia robada" (¿o a la inversa?). El final de los *Milagros de Nuestra Señora* de Gonzalo de Berceo', *Actas* (AHLM 6), 1, 243–55, argues well that 'La iglesia robada' is the last miracle of Berceo's *Milagros de Nuestra Señora*, added after 'Teófilo' was already written as the closing story. A. Montaner Frutos, 'Un posible eco del *Cantar de Mio Cid* en Gonzalo de Berceo', *ib.*, 11, 1057–67, argues that Berceo modified his Latin source and used the Castejón de Henares attack in the *CMC* to compose the incursion of Guadalajara in one of the *post mortem* miracles in his *Vida de Santo Domingo*.

LIBRO DE BUEN AMOR. J. Lawrance, 'The rubrics in MS *S* of the *Libro de buen amor*', *Deyermond Vol.*, 223–52, is an important study for our understanding not only of the *LBA* but of textual (re)production and reception in oral/aural and reading cultures; citing textual, historical, and cultural evidence, L. demonstrates clearly that the rubrication in *S* is the product not of the poet but of Alfonso de Paradinas. N. Round, 'Juan Ruiz and some versions of *Nummus*', *ib.*, 381–400, connects the tirade on the properties of money to the goliardic *Nummus* poem, arguing that this seemingly outdated poem would be relevant in Juan Ruiz's day because of a transitional economic situation (from kind to coin), ecclesiastic concerns, and the medieval system of beliefs. J. Sánchez Montes, 'Lo grotesco en el *Libro de buen amor*: una aproximación bajtiniana', *Deyermond Vol.*

(QMW), 77–83, argues that viewing the *LBA* primarily as a manifestation of the grotesque would make the various debates about the
purpose of the poem (e.g., didactic, parodic) compatible. T. R. Hart,
'Exemplary storytellers: Trotaconventos and Doña Garoça', *Deyermond Vol.*, 165–75, classifies Trotaconventos and Doña Garoça as
intradiegetic and heterodiegetic narrators, examines their discourse
according to Aristotle's definition of rhetoric (*ethos, pathos, logos*), and
concludes that Doña Garoça wins the debate. J. Dagenais, ' "*Il nostro
maggior Musa*": Juan Ruiz and the medieval Virgil', Kagay, *Iberia*,
143–57, suggests that the legend of 'Virgil in the basket' introduced
in the *LBA* may have existed independently in an early text, and
explains its relevance to the work through two different and
interesting readings of the episode, one tropological and another
proto-Freudian. S. Kantor, 'Tiempo, espacio y espacio textual en la
tienda de Don Amor', *Actas* (AHLM 6), II, 857–66, concludes that
Don Amor's tent in the *LBA* does not provide a cosmological vision.

OTHER POETRY. J. Zemke, 'Shem Tov de Carrión's *Proverbios
morales*: a sermon addressed', *RPh*, 51:195–210, reviews general
features of the medieval sermon, studies the pronouns of address in
the *Proverbios* and presents the hypothesis that it is a medieval Jewish
sermon composed for recitation to an addressee of equal or inferior
status. M. Amasuno, 'La medicina y el físico en la *Dança General de la
Muerte*', *HR*, 65:1–24, studies the presence of the Black Death in the
DGM and analyses the author's denunciation of the *scientia medica*. Id.,
'La concepción de la enfermedad y el *Regimen sanitatis* en la *Dança
General de la Muerte*', *Actas* (AHLM 6), I, 151–67, is a more detailed
analysis of the *regimen sanitatis* in the *DGM*. R. C. Ryan, '*Disputa del
ánima y del cuerpo* and the rhetoric of culpability', *La Chispa '97*, 365–73,
is a close reading of the *Disputa* as a text where the poet adapts
traditional legal argumentation with rhetorical figures to argue the
culpability of both parties.

PROSE

ALFONSO X EL SABIO.   Leonardo Funes, *El modelo historiográfico alfonsí:
una caracterización* (PMHRS 6), 86 pp., deals primarily with the *Estoria
de España*. F. offers general observations related to the Alfonsine
historiographic enterprise, and then analyses the narrative process:
the spacial-temporal organization of the narrative; the use of historical
figures for exemplary purposes; the structure of historic events; the
incorporation of Latin verse and epic poetry. Charles F. Fraker, *The
Scope of History: Studies in the Historiography of Alfonso el Sabio*, Ann Arbor,
Michigan U.P., 235 pp., unites eight previously published articles on
Alfonsine historiography, dividing them into three groups according

to theme: Sancho II, the Alfonsine conception of Rome, philosophy and culture in the *General Estoria*. The volume includes a general introduction as well as a preface for each section intended to provide a guide for those unfamiliar with the subject. *Lapidary of King Alfonso X the Learned*, trans. Ingrid Bahler and Katherine Gyékényesi Gatto, New Orleans, U.P. of the South, xix + 330 pp., is an accessible translation of the *Lapidario* accompanied by a lengthy essay (223–322) by Jeffrey La Favre identifying the stars mentioned in the treatise. L. Rich, 'Kings and counts: pragmatics and the *Poema de Fernán González* in the *Primera Crónica General*', *La corónica*, 25.2 : 103–13, finds that in prosifying the *PFG*, the compilers of the *Estoria de España* used various techniques to attenuate the regal figure of the Count in order to assert the superiority of the monarchy. M. G. Campos Souto, 'Bases para una edición de la versión gallega de la *General estoria*: estudio codicológico del manuscrito O.I.1 del Monasterio de San Lorenzo del Escorial', *Deyermond Vol.* (QMW), 119–26, offers a detailed description of the Escorial MS. R. J. González Casanovas, 'Courtly rhetoric as a political and social code in Alfonso X: the prologues to the *Espéculo* and the *Siete Partidas*', Kagay, *Iberia*, 129–41, is a close reading of the two legal prologues as rhetorical code of authority. G. D. Greenia, 'University book production and courtly patronage in thirteenth-century France and Spain', Kagay, *Iberia*, 103–28, compares the patronage of Louis IX of France and Alfonso X to underscore the unique personal role of the latter in promoting a book market in Spain, as well as creating a monumental manuscript illumination industry that disappeared with his death in 1284. R. J. González Casanovas, 'La *historiografía* alfonsí: estado actual de las investigaciones', *Actas* (AHLM 6), I, 87–110. J. M. Cacho Blecua, 'La vergüenza en el discurso del poder laico desde Alfonso X a Don Juan Manuel', *ib.*, 393–411, studies the influence of Vegetius's and Aristotle's concept of *vergüenza* in Alfonso X's *Partidas* to establish and consolidate the power of the monarchy and the subordination of the community. P. Sánchez-Prieto Borja, 'Fuentes de la tercera parte de la *General Estoria*: la vida de Salomón', *ib.*, II, 1401–17, studies two sources for this episode, the *Vulgata* and Godfrey of Viterbo's *Pantheon*, and gives a detailed analysis of their differences in the translation. A. J. Cárdenas, 'The myth of Hercules in the works of Alfonso X: narration in the *Estoria de España* and in the *General estoria*', *BHS(G)*, 74 : 5–20, finds narration in the *GE* to be more self-conscious and subtle than in the *EE*. A. García Avilés, 'Alfonso X y el *Liber Razielis*: imágenes de la magia astral judía en el *scriptorium* alfonsí', *ib.*, 21–39, reviews Alfonsine works related to the *Liber Razielis*. **Text and Concordance of the Siete Partidas, October 25, 1491*, Hispanic Society of America, ed. Ivy A. Corfis, Madison, HSMS, 5 pp. + 14 microfiches.

JUAN FERNÁNDEZ DE HEREDIA. J. M. Cacho Blecua, *El gran maestre Juan Fernández de Heredia*, Saragossa, Caja de Ahorros de la Inmaculada, 214 pp., is the most complete and innovative overview on the life and work of Heredia. *Juan Fernández de Heredia y su época. IV curso sobre lengua y literatura en Aragón*, ed. A. Egido and J. M. Enguita, Saragossa, Institución Fernando el Católico, 369 pp. includes: J. M. Cacho Blecua, 'El prólogo del *Rams de flores*' (69–110), a brilliant and erudite study that reveals the prologue's textual debt to John of Salisbury's *Policraticus*; A.-G. Hauff i Valls, 'Texto y contexto de la *Flor de las historias de Oriente*: un programa de colaboración cristiano-mongólica' (111–54), which deals extensively with the historical context of the French source and makes some brief remarks on the Aragonese text and its likely relation to the Catalan version; R. af Geijerstam, 'La *Grant Crónica de Espanya*: problemas de su edición y estudio' (155–70), drawing on her years of study of the work to conclude that language varies in the text according to the translations used as source; M. C. Marín Pina and A. Montaner Frutos, 'Estado actual de los estudios sobre la vida y la obra de Juan Fernández de Heredia' (217–84), a complete and clear *status questionis*, which also includes some innovative insights, especially new information on F. de H.'s *scriptorium*. A. Montaner Frutos, 'La *Grant corónica de los conquiridores* de Juan Fernández de Heredia: problemas codicológicos y ecdóticos', *Deyermond Vol.*, 275–316, analyses three incomplete manuscripts of the *Primera Partida* of the *Corónica* with a meticulous description of C.

DIDACTIC LITERATURE. A. Arizaleta, 'De la fisiognomía: *Calila e Dimna*, cap. 4', *Procs* (MHRS 8), 31–38, finds that the opposition of physiognomy and free will in chapter 4 is a product of the encounter of Islamic and Christian traditions and reflects a polemic new in the 13th century. M. Haro Cortés, 'El *Calila e Dimna* y el *Sendebar*: ¿prosa sapiencial o de recreación? Reflexiones sobre su recepción en la Castilla del siglo XIII', *Deyermond Vol.* (QMW), 85–96, contests J. Keller's claim that *Sendebar* was principally intended for entertainment, showing that both it and *Calila e Dimna* belong to the category of wisdom literature destined for a royal reader. A. Arizaleta, 'El corazón y otros frutos amargos: notas acerca de un motivo literario medieval', *ib.*, 97–107, analyses chapter 7 of *Calila e Dimna*, focusing on its reception by a courtly audience. G. Cándano, 'Convergencias de la misoginia pre-cristiana y la misoginia de las colecciones de *exempla*', *ib.*, 109–18, finds that the misogynist concepts found in early eastern texts reverberate in 13th-c. Castilian translations. M. J. Lacarra, 'Hacia un *Thesaurus Exemplorum hispanicorum* (con especial referencia a las aportaciones de la crítica en los últimos diez años [1985–1995]', *Actas* (AHLM 6), I, 111–32, proposes that the *Thesaurus*, a project currently underway by a research team at the University of Zaragoza, should include all short didactic narrative that circulated in the Peninsula regardless of tradition, genre or mode of diffusion. M. J. Díez Garretas, 'El *Libro de los* gatos: fragmento de un nuevo manuscrito', *ib.*, 571–80, gives notice of two *exempla* from the *Libro de los gatos* found in an MS fragment from the Archivo de la Real Chancillería de Valladolid (Pleitos Civiles Moreno 940–1, Fenecidos c-940/2). M. Haro, 'Prólogos e introducciones de la prosa didáctica del XIII: estudio y función', *ib.*, 769–87. The same author, 'Consideraciones en torno al estudio de la prosa sapiencial medieval: el caso de las colecciones de sentencias', *Diablotexto*, 3, 1996[1997]:125–72, after some general remarks on their importance, underlines textual relationships between some works (*Flores de filosofía*, *Bocados de oro*, *Libros de dichos de sabios e filósofos*). M. Zugasti, 'La fábula del león y el chacal religioso (*Calila e Dimna*, cap. XIV) y su origen en la cuentística hindú', *RLit.*, 58:361–72, highlights an unknown source, *Mahabarata*, song XII.iv. H. A. Bizarri, 'La idea de la reconquista en el *Libro de los Doze sabios*', *RFE*, 76, 1996:5–29, distinguishes two parts: chapters 1–20, of later composition, which constitute a *speculum principis*, and chapters 21–65, which are a military treatise encouraging the undertaking of the Reconquest. The latter is the real nucleus of the work to which the first part and a praise in honour of Fernando III were added.

OTHER PROSE WRITERS. F. Rico, 'Entre el códice y el libro (Notas sobre los paradigmas misceláneos y la literatura del siglo XIV)', *RPh*, 51:151–69, presents the hypothesis that the codex miscellany with disparate but related texts may be the origin of certain books composed by the juxtaposition of different traditions, like *El caballero Zifar*. Carmen Hernández Valcárcel, *El cuento medieval español*, Murcia, U.P., 282 pp., includes selections from the 13th to the 14th c. for scholarly purposes. G. Orduna, 'La ejemplaridad como recurso narrativo en las *Crónicas* del Canciller Ayala', *Diablotexto*, 3, 1996[1997]:187–98, comments on how history becomes *exemplum*, thus becoming devoid of its (dangerous) political significance and acquiring a new universal and moral value. Id., 'La crítica textual ante la documentación histórica (los últimos años de la *Crónica de Enrique II*)', *Incipit*, 16:1–18, attributes chronological mistakes to a defective mansucript tradition. F. Gómez Redondo, 'La crónica real: "exemplos" y sentencias', *Diablotexto*, 3, 1996[1997]:95–124, after some general considerations of the importance and meaning of the *Crónica de tres reyes* by Ferrán Sánchez de Valladolid (14th c.), analyses in detail the construction of several narrations inserted in the *crónica* with different exemplary purposes.

5. THE FIFTEENTH CENTURY

GENERAL, BIBLIOGRAPHY, EARLY PRINTING

Michael Solomon, *The Literature of Misogyny in Medieval Spain: the Arcipreste de Talavera and the Spill*, NY–Cambridge, CUP, vii + 221 pp., first discusses contemporary concepts of disease, theories regarding sexual practices and their consequences, and the treatment of lovesickness, arguing that out of the latter grew the misogynist bent of medical theory. S. then contends that Alfonso Martínez de Toledo and Jacme Roig, intending to ameliorate the spiritual and physical health of men, shifted 'the focus of disease from a physiological imbalance in the male body' to the centre of contagion: women. G. Serés, *La traducción en Italia y España durante el siglo XV. La 'Ilíada en romance' y su contexto cultural*, Salamanca U.P., 313 pp., contains a documented study on translation theories and on the circumstances involved in the reception of the *Iliad* in Spain. J. Fradejas Lebrero, 'Notas sobre Fray Hernando de Talavera', *Deyermond Vol.*, 127–38, analyses sources, symbols and political content in two works composed by Fray Hernando at the request of Queen Isabel: la *Collation* (1475?) and *Tratado de los loores de San Juan Evangelista*, both preserved in MS 332 of Museo Lázaro Galdiano. J. M. Fradejas Rueda, 'Manuscritos y ediciones de las *Virtuosas e claras mugeres* de don Álvaro de Luna', *ib.*, 139–52, describes five manuscripts (Salamanca MS 207, MS 2200, MS 2654; Biblioteca Nacional de Madrid MS 19165; Biblioteca Menéndez Pelayo MS 76) and three editions (Marcelino Menéndez Pelayo, Manuel Castillo, José Fradejas Lebrero) of *Virtuosas e claras mugeres*. J. Guadalajara Medina, 'El retrato del anticristo en los textos castellanos medievales', *Actas* (AHLM 6), I, 729–36, draws a portrait of the Antichrist according to late medieval Castilian texts. C. Faulhaber, 'Sobre la cultura ibérica medieval: las lenguas vernáculas y la traducción', *ib.*, 587–97, gives some statistical data on languages and the content of sources of vernacular translations. G. Avenoza, 'Datos para la identificación del traductor y del dedicatario de la traducción castellana de los *Factorum et dictorum memorabilium* de Valerio Máximo', *ib.*, 200–24. P. M. Cátedra, 'Modos de consolar por carta', *ib.*, 469–87, offers a new instalment on the 'consolatorio' with the edition and study of two unpublished texts. V. Campo, 'Algunas consideraciones sobre la traducción castellana del *Contra hipócritas* de Leonardo Bruni', *ib.*, 413–22, describes the translation. F. Crosas López, 'Sobre los primeros mitógrafos españoles: El Tostado y Pérez de Moya', *ib.*, 543–50, identifies Alonso Fernández de Madrigal *el Tostado* as the source of much mythographical information in *Philosophia secreta* by Juan Pérez de Moya (1513–96). J. D. Rodríguez Velasco, 'Para una periodización de las ideas sobre la caballería en Castilla', *ib.*, II, 1335–46, divides chivalric ideas into three periods: definition (1250–1350), restriction (1330–1407) and expansion (1390–1492). M. L. Simó Goberna, 'Mitología e historia en los tratados de heráldica del siglo xv', *ib.*, 1427–37, studies the mythological, historical, and biblical origins of heraldry. C. Heusch, 'El Renacimiento del aristotelismo dentro del humanismo español, siglos xv y xvi', *Atalaya*, 7, 1996[1997]: 11–40, is an important and detailed study that treats the role of Aristotelianism in 15th-c. culture.

POETRY

CANCIONEROS. M. J. Duffell, ' "Come back, Dorothy Clarke, all is forgiven!": the scansional adequacy of medieval texts', *Deyermond Vol.*, 109–25, examines 300 lines of *Laberinto de Fortuna* from four 'critically adequate' editions in order to demonstrate that, while Clarke's *Morphology of Fifteenth Century Verse* has been considered unsatisfactory for its reliance on 'critically inadequate editions', her conclusions are sound and her work should be 'recognized as the most detailed and reliable analysis of the *verso de arte mayor* currently available'. J. Gornall, 'Two authors or one?: *romances* and their *desfechas* in the *Cancionero general* of 1511', *ib.*, 153–63, believes that Hernando del Castillo viewed the indication of authorship in the rubric to a *romance* as encompassing its *desfecha* as well. I. Macpherson, 'Text, context, and subtext: five *invenciones* of the *Cancionero general* and the Ponferrada affair of 1485', *ib.*, 259–74, dates and provides a revealing explanation of five *invenciones* by Rodrigo Alonso Pimentel, 4th Count of Benavente, his two sons, and Rodrigo Enríquez Osorio, Count of Lemos, as the literary counterpart of a famous litigation between two of the most powerful families in Spain. J. Whetnall, 'Mayor Arias's poem and the early Spanish *contrafactum*', *ib.*, 535–52, examines 'Ay mar braba' within the context of traditional verse and finds in it a paradigm for the identification and analysis of other 15th-c. *contrafacta*. A. Chas Aguión, ' "Pues no es yerro preguntar [. . .]": notas para la revaloración de una modalidad poética cuatrocentista olvidada, las preguntas y respuestas', *Procs* (MHRS 8), 85–93, isolates certain defining characteristics for the 'preguntas-respuestas', and thus justifies their consideration as an independent poetic group. M. I. Toro Pascua, 'Las dos ediciones del *Cancionero* de Pedro Manuel Ximénez de Urrea', *ib.*, 95–105, compares the 1513 and 1516 editions of the *Cancionero* and discusses X.'s active intervention in the publication of at least the second. A. Chas Aguión, 'A propósito de categorías discutidas: algunas consideraciones en torno a los *procesos* en el cancionero cuatrocentista castellano', *Deyermond Vol.* (QMW), 287–98, rejects the classification of the *proceso* as an autonomous literary category. C. Tato, 'Cronología de una serie poética en elogio de Alfonso V incluida en el *Cancionero de Palacio* (SA7)', *ib.*, 299–308, affirms that the sequential order of several poems in *Palacio* reflects their order of composition. R. Recio, 'La poética petrarquista en los cancioneros: las composiciones atribuidas a Álvar Gómez', *ib.*, 309–18, highlights Petrarchan imitation in several poems in *Gallardo* and concludes that Gómez, whose translation of P.'s *Triunfi* precedes them, may well be their author. A. Chas Aguión, 'La pregunta disyuntiva como vehículo de cuestiones de amor en la poesía cancioneril castellana', *Actas* (AHLM 6), I, 501–10, studies poetic debates on love of the *partimen* type in general

SANTILLANA. R. Beltrán, 'Lectura y adaptación de las glosas del Marqués de Santillana a sus *Proverbios* en la *Suma de virtuoso deseo*', *Procs* (MHRS 8), 49–60, believes that the *Proverbios*, and not Valerius Maximus's *Factorum et dictorum*, served as a direct source for the *Suma*. C. X. Ardavín, 'La ambigüedad temática de la *Comedieta de Ponza*', *Hispanófila*, 119:1–8, finds that while the poem has a didactic-moral function, it is best read from a socio-political perspective. J. Gutiérrez Carou, 'La visión alegórica de tres damas en la obra de Dante, Villasandino y el Marqués de Santillana', *Actas* (AHLM 6), I, 737–46, compares S.'s *Visión* to 'La noche terçera de la Redempçión' by Villasandino (num. 34, *Cancionero de Baena*) and to 'Tre donne intorno al cor mi son venute', concluding that S. had read Dante and was influenced by him, although he did not use his poem as a source.

JORGE MANRIQUE. V. de Lama and G. Fernández, 'Fortuna musical de las *Coplas* de Jorge Manrique en los Siglos de Oro', *Actas* (AHLM 6), II, 867–878, review the preserved musical versions of the *Coplas*.

JUAN DEL ENCINA. M. Kidd, 'Myth, desire, and the play of inversion: the fourteenth Eclogue of Juan del Encina', *HR*, 65:217–36, establishes the connection between E.'s *Égloga de Plácida y Vitoriano* and Ovid's tale of Pyramus and Thisbe through a detailed analysis of iconographic, narrative and structural similarities. C. Salinas Espinosa, 'Sueños y alegoría en el *Triunfo de Amor* de Juan del Encina', *Deyermond Vol.* (QMW), 319–29, situates *Triunfo* within the tradition of the allegorical voyage, concluding that it represents a new direction for the tradition.

OTHER POETS. M. B. Campos Souto, 'Problemas ecdóticos y de edición en la obra poética de Rodrigo Manrique', *Procs* (MHRS 8), 75–84, outlines the multiple obstacles faced by an editor of the poems attributed to M., ranging from the question of authorship to dubious readings, and proposes the formation of research teams for individual poets to tackle these problems. The same author, 'Núcleos temáticos en la poesía de Rodrigo Manrique', *Actas* (AHLM 6), I, 431–39, gives an introduction to M.'s poetry. A. Chas Guión, 'Las "otras preguntas" de temática amorosa en el corpus poético de Gómez Manrique', *RLMed*, 9:97–119, establishes the criteria (formal, functional and thematic) to identify the poetic genre of *preguntas y respuestas* in M.'s sentimental *corpus*, and increases the number of *preguntas* in the Dutton anthology by three, editing them with their respective *respuestas*. A. M. Beresford, 'Antonio López de Mata's *Tractado del cuerpo e de la ánima* and the Hispanic body-and-soul tradition', *BHS(L)*, 74:139–50, considers the significance of the poem within the body-soul tradition as well as how it functions as a debate, examining its problematic characteristics and deficiencies while highlighting its innovations. J. C. Conde and V. Infantes, 'Antes de partir: un poema taurino antijudaico en el Toledo medieval (1489?)', *Deyermond Vol.*, 91–108, study and edit an unpublished anonymous satirical *villancico* found in the 1489 testament of Vasco Ramírez de Ribera, Bishop of Coria and *Inquisidor Mayor* of Castile and Aragon, preserved in British Library Eg.482. B. Taylor, 'Cota, poet of the desert: hermits and scorpions in the *Diálogo entre el Amor y un viejo*', *ib.*, 457–68, convincingly argues that C.'s *Diálogo* could be read as a secularized version of a hermit tale, like the Temptation of St Anthony, and dicusses in an appendix '*Blanda cara de alacrán*', the animal image used by the Old Man to insult Love. I. Macpherson, 'Fray Íñigo de Mendoza, Francisco Delicado y dos enigmas salomónicos', *Actas* (AHLM 6), I, 39–56, ingeniously resolves two enigmas: he first deciphers the meaning of the word *sino* in one of the *invenciones* attributed to Fray Íñigo as a word game based on the two syllables *si no* and the polysemic meaning of *sino* in medieval Spanish as *signo* and *destino*, referring to the courtly lover's destiny (i.e., to be (*si*) or not to be (*no*) corresponded); then he gives a coherent and unambiguous interpretation of the *ñudo de Salomón* in *La Lozana Andaluza* in a magisterial gloss of its symbolism within the religious, literary and historical context of the 15th century. J. C. López Nieto, 'La glosa de *Canción agena* de Gómez Manrique y otras cuestiones conexas', *ib.*, II, 895–905, reproduces the text of *canción agena* with its *glosa* and analyses the peculiarities of the latter with respect to its genre. J. Whetnall, 'Unmasking the devout lover: Hugo de Urríes in the *Cancionero de Herberay*', *BHS(L)*, 74:275–98, presents convincing evidence to support C. Aubrun's identification of U. as the author of several poems in *Herberay* while rejecting his claim that U. was the compiler, proposing instead U.'s wife as the 'original owner, or proto-compiler'.

PROSE

CHIVALRESQUE AND SENTIMENTAL FICTION. *Chrónica del rey Guillermo de Inglaterra*, ed. N. Baranda, Frankfurt am Main, Vervuert-Iberoamericana, 212 pp., edits one of the two Spanish versions derived from the well-known legend of St Eustaquius, probably translated from a lost French text, according to the editor, 'Argumentos para una versión desconocida de la historia del Rey Guillermo', *Actas* (AHLM 6), I, 257–64. *La Poncella de Francia*, ed. V. Campo and V. Infantes, Frankfurt am Main, Vervuert-Iberoamericana, 288 pp. A. Contreras and Z. Jiménez Mola, *Actas* (AHLM 6), I, 523–32, a detailed comparison between the weapons listed in the Meleagant episode in *Lanzarote del Lago* (ms 9611 BN Madrid) and those in the various French copies of the original, allows the authors to locate the French text closest to the Castilian (MS 751 BN Paris). L. Haywood, 'Female voices in Spanish sentimental romances', *JIRS*, 4, 1996:17–35, offers a feminist reading of several romances. R. Ramos, '*Tirante el Blanco* y el *Libro del caballero Zifar* a la zaga de *Amadís de Gaula*', *Deyermond Vol.* (QMW), 207–25, shows through an examination of frontispieces that Pero Pérez's assertion in *Quijote* that *Amadís* was the first chivalresque romance printed in Spain is, in effect, correct, for it exerted an influence on the subsequent editions of *Tirant* and *Zifar*. H. Aled Lewis, 'The *Vision of the knight Túngano* in the literatures of the Iberian peninsula', *Speculum*, 72.1:85–99, examines the similarities between Túngano's vision and the structure of marvellous tales, the pagan images of Hell, and how the vision was made more suitable for a Hispanic audience. R. Beltrán, 'Urganda, Morgana y Sibila: el espectáculo de la nave profética en la literatura de caballerías', *Deyermond Vol.*, 21–47, studies the reciprocal influence between historical spectacle and literary text by analyzing in *Amadís de Gaula*, *Tirant lo Blanc* and *La corónica de Adramón* the motif of the prophetic ship, a medieval theatrical performance documented in urban festivities from the 13th to the 16th centuries. A. Deyermond, 'En la frontera de la ficción sentimental', *Actas* (AHLM 6), I, 13–37, establishes the connection of various works (Abelard's *Historia Calamitatum*, *Letters of Heloise*, Boccaccio's *Elegia di madonna Fiammetta*, Christine de Pizan's *Cent ballades d'amant et de dame*, the anonymous *Stòria de l'amat Frondino e de Brisona*) to Ovid's *Heroides*, and examines the relationship between Dante's *Vita Nuova*, King James I of Scotland's *The Kingis Quair*, and the Marqués de Santillana's *Triunphete de Amor/Sueño* and *Infierno de los enamorados* as part of the same literary tradition of the allegorical vision, in order to underscore the common denominator that places these works 'on the frontier of sentimental romance', the title of his book in progress. G. P. Andrachuk, 'The confrontation between reality and fiction in *Qüestión de amor'*, Gwara, *Studies*, 55–72, explores the question of the sentimental genre in *Qüestión*. I. A. Corfis, 'Sentimental lore and irony in the fifteenth-century romances and *Celestina*', *ib.*, 153–71, surveys proper names in nine sentimental romances, traces a network of intertextual references that shows the classical and biblical culture of the authors and their familiarity with each other's works, and underscores the importance of *Celestina* in this tradition of intertextuality. L. Haywood, 'Lyric and other verse insertions in sentimental romances', *ib.*, 191–206, argues that the appearance of verse in sentimental romances serves various purposes, from formal (hierarchical or structural) functions, as in *Grimalte y Gradissa* and *Siervo libre de amor*, to informal (descriptive, thematic, narrative) functions. V. Blay Manzanera, 'Las cualidades dramáticas de *Triste deleytaçión*: su relación con *Celestina* y con las llamadas "Artes de Amores"', *RLMed*, 9:61–96, studies dramatic components such as dialogues, transvestism, etc., to underscore the hybrid condition of the sentimental genre. In 'Espectáculos cortesanos y parateatralidad en la ficción sentimental', *BHS(G)*, 74:61–91, the same author considers theatrical manifestations, including *autos de amores* and *fiestas*, in sentimental fiction, principally *Triste deleytaçión*. M. F. Aybar Ramírez, 'Falsas imágenes en el modelo de realidad representado en la ficción sentimental', *Actas* (AHLM 6), I, 225–32, discloses the rigidity and irreality of the world constructed in sentimental fiction. V. Blay Manzanera, 'Anotaciones sobre la filosofía moral en *Triste Deleytaçión*: sus conexiones con la *Ética* del Príncipe de Viana y con la *Visión Deleytable*', *ib.*, 324–42, posits that *Triste deleytaçión* is the vehicle for a message of moral philosophy related to the *Ética* by Don Carlos, prince of Viana, and *Visión deleytable* by Alfonso de la Torre. K. Whinnom†, 'Cardona, the crucifixion, and Leriano's last drink', ed. Alan Deyermond, Gwara, *Studies*, 207–15, is an edition of two incomplete versions of one of W.'s last articles, probably from 1982, in which he suggests that the parallelism between Christ's death and Cristerno's in Juan de Cardona's *Tratado notable de amor* was inspired by Leriano's last drink, and analyses the reminiscence of this episode with the Crucifixion and other biblical sources. Deyermond offers a brief introductory summary of the cannibalistic critical interpretations of Leriano's last drink. *Historia delos nobles caballeros Oliueros de Castilla y Artus d'Algarve*, ed. Ivy Corfis, Madison, HSMS, 279 pp. *Texto y Concordancias de La ystoria del noble cauallero Paris & dela muy hermosa donzella Uiana. Burgos, 1524. British Library C.7.a.17*, ed. Cristina González, Madison, HSMS, 9 pp. + microfiches.

TRISTÁN DE LEONÍS. M. L. Cuesta Torre, 'Unos folios recuperados de una edición perdida del *Tristán de Leonís*', *ib.*, 227–36, believes that folios extraneous to the 1511 and 1528 editions bound with the 1528 copy held at the Pierpoint Morgan Library suggest the existence of other editions between 1501 and 1511. A. Campos García Rojas, 'Florisdelfa: un episodio insular en *Tristán de Leonís* desde una interpretación de sus elementos geográficos y la magia', *ib.*, 237–45, shows that geography and magic make an island of Florisdelfa, which then serves as a test for Tristán. M. C. Gates, 'El humor como privilegio y el humor como estigma en *Tristán el Joven*', *Hispanófila*, 120:1–14, discerns two types of humour in *Tristán*: a good-hearted form meant to unite characters representative of socially acceptable attitudes, and a deprecating mode intended benignly to mark the 'Other' such as the socially inept, or malevolently to isolate the them for their social or ideological values.

JUAN RODRÍGUEZ DEL PADRÓN. E. S. Dolz i Ferrer, '*Siervo libre de amor*: entre la alegoría y la anagogía', *Deyermond Vol.* (QMW), 247–57, examines *Siervo* within the exegetical tradition, proposing that it is 'un texto de aliento místico'. M. Pampín Barral, '"La excellençia de las dones sobre los onbres manifiesta ser te demostraré": el parlamento de la ninfa Cardiana en el *Triunfo de la donas* de Juan Rodríguez del Padrón', *ib.*, 259–68, finds in Cardiana's defence of women both traditional and modern, 'progressive' views of women. E. M. Gerli, 'The Old French source of *Siervo Libre de Amor*: Guillaume de Deguileville's *Le Rommant des trois pèlerinages*', Gwara, *Studies*, 3–19, pursues M. R. Lida's clues on the French sources of *Siervo*'s allegory and imagery, and discovers a direct O.Fr. antecedent used by Rodríguez del Padrón as the main allegorical and structural model of *Siervo*: the trilogy known as *Le Rommant des trois pèlerinages*, derived from a visionary allegorical tradition independent of Dante.

DIEGO DE SAN PEDRO. L. Voigt, 'La alegoría de la lectura en *Cárcel de amor*', *La Corónica*, 25.2:123–33, argues that metafiction in *Cárcel* not only blurs the line between reality and fiction, but causes readers to participate in the text and to bring it into their lived praxis. F. Martín Polo, 'La ficción del *yo* en Diego de San Pedro', *Deyermond Vol.* (QMW), 269–75, considers *Cárcel* from the perspective of autobiography claiming that the 'I' wears three masks: *Auctor*-omniscient narrator, *Auctor*-participant, and Leriano. M. M. Fernández Vuelta, 'La exploración de la subjetividad en la obra de Diego de San Pedro: la *Cárcel de amor* y el uso de la alegoría', *Actas* (AHLM 6), I, 599–609, defines *Cárcel de amor* as a fictional memoir within an allegorical frame. O. T. Impey, 'Apuntes sobre la onomástica de la *Cárcel de Amor*', *ib.*, II, 829–37, analyses the meaning of proper names and offers a revealing interpretation of *Laureola* (derived from *áurea*, associated with golden crown and a superior moral and social position) and of *Leriano* (associated with ivy, bronze, and a lower social position), arguing that it is L.'s secret intention to climb the political and social ladder. D. S. Severin, 'Diego de San Pedro's *Arnalte y Lucenda*: subtext for the Cardenio episode of *Don Quijote*', Gwara, *Studies*, 145–50, suggests that Cervantes adapts the *Tractado de amores de Arnalte y Lucenda* in the Cardenio episode of *Don Quijote*. D. M. Wright, '*Amor Hereos* and rhetorical invention in *Arnalte y Lucenda*', *La Chispa* '97, 431–37, shows how in *Arnalte y Lucenda* passionate love and desire generate rhetorical creativity, both oral and written.

JUAN DE FLORES. L. M. Haywood, 'The princess and the unicorn: Arthur, Prince of Wales, and Catherine of Aragon?', *Deyermond Vol.*, 189–204, re-examines questions of dating and authorship; dismissing *Gracisla* as a full *roman à clef*, H. suggests that it was composed probably between 1502 and 1503 as a fictional defence of Catherine of Aragon's virginity, and attributes elements of Flores's style to an anonymous imitator who also was familiar with court celebrations and imagery associated with virginity and marriage. J. J. Gwara, 'Another work by Juan de Flores: *La coronación de la señora Gracisla*', Gwara, *Studies*, 75–110, accepting *Gracisla*'s attribution to Juan de Flores, concludes that it was written no later than 1500, that its plot recalls Henry VII's abortive attempt to marry Juana de Aragón, and that it was probably based on an engagement or wedding among members of the Osorio or Álvarez de Toledo families. C. Parrilla García, 'La *Derrota de Amor* de Juan de Flores', *ib.*, 111–24, reviews the behaviour of the *dios Amor* in his relationship with the humans in *Triunfo de Amor* and provides clues for its interpretation. R. Rohland de Langbehn, 'Un mundo al revés: la mujer en las obras de ficción de Juan de Flores', *ib.*, 125–43, expands Weissberger's 'role-reversal' reinterpretation of *Grisel y Mirabella* and *Triunfo de Amor*, including *Grimalte y Gradissa*. B. F. Weissberger, 'Resisting readers and writers in the sentimental romances and the problem of female literacy', *ib.*, 173–90, illustrates the concept of the resisting reader, who resists the forced identification against herself required by the male author, with the analysis of three fictional readers: Braçayda in *Grisel y Mirabella*, Gradissa in *Grimalte y Gradissa*, and the 'Señora' of Segura's *Processo*.

ALONSO DE CARTAGENA. M. Campos Souto, 'Aproximación a las fuentes y al uso de autoridades en el *Memorial de virtudes* de Alonso de Cartagena', *Procs* (MHRS 8), 39–47, weighs C.'s use of his sources, principally Aristotle's *Nichomachean Ethics*; and in 'La Biblia en el *Memorial de virtudes* de Alonso de Cartagena', *Deyermond Vol.* (QMW), 127–34, illustrates the indebtedness of the work to the Bible. M. Morrás, 'Una cuestión disputada: Viejas y nuevas formas en el siglo XV', *Atalaya*, 7, 1996[1997]:63–102, edits a Latin *quaestio* written by Rodrigo Sánchez de Arévalo and Alonso de Cartagena.

M. Campos Souto, 'El *Memorial de virtudes* de Alonso de Cartagena', *Actas* (AHLM 6), I, 423–30, summarizes the content of the work. OTHER PROSE WRITERS.A. Cortijo Ocaña, 'La *Crónica del Moro Rasis* y la *Crónica Sarracina*: dos testimonios desconocidos (University of California at Berkeley, Bancroft Library, MS UCB 143, Vo. 124)', *La Corónica*, 25.2:5–30, gives a detailed description of the MS and general observations regarding authorship, and edits as an appendix the chapter rubrics of *Moro Rasis* and the first two chapters of *Sarracina*. M. I. Hernández González, 'El texto de *Claros varones de Castilla*', *Deyermond Vol.*, 135–47, outlines the transmission of *Claros varones* and an edition of a *semblanza* by Juan Pacheco, held in Escorial Y-I-9. C. García, 'Los tratados de Teresa de Cartagena dentro de la evolución de la epístola', *Deyermond Vol.* (QMW), 149–57, finds that C.'s treatises meet epistolary requirements. J. D. Rodríguez Velasco, 'Coordenadas y texto de una carta para regimiento del rey', *ib.*, 159–68, describes and edits an anonymous letter of instruction (*c.* 1455–60) to an unidentified king, held in BNM 1159. G. Montiel Roig, 'Los móviles de la redacción de la *Crónica de don Álvaro de Luna*', *RLMed*, 9:173–195, presents the hypothesis that the *Crónica* may be interpreted as a long *amplificatio* of a defensive bill in favor of the Condestable. J. R. Rank, 'Urban writing in the fifteenth century: on whose authority?', Kagay, *Iberia*, 159–69, argues that a philosophical view of the city introduced by F. Eiximenis in *Lo Crestià* probably serves as a subtext in Martínez de Toledo's *Corbacho*, where the urban discourse becomes an authority inherited and developed in *Celestina*. R. Beltrán, 'La justificación de la escritura en las biografías de Alonso Carrillo y Alonso de Monroy', *Actas* (AHLM 6), I, 265–77, explores the origins of biography. J. C. Conde, 'Una lanza por la existencia de una historiografía petrista sojuzgada: ecos y rastros en la historiografía del cuatrocientos castellano', *ib.*, 511–22, offers conjectures regarding the existence of a lost *Crónica verdadera* by Juan de Castro with a positive view on Pedro I's reign. S. M. Carrizo Rueda, 'Pero Tafur, un autor-personaje cuestionado desde su propio discurso', *ib.*, 461–67, finds four points of view in Pero Tafur's *Andanças e viajes* that she attributes to various versions or authors. M. Á. Pérez-Priego, 'Noticias sobre Alonso Martínez de Villaescusa, su *Espejo de Corregidores* y el *Directorio de Príncipes*', *ib.*, II, 1169–77, introduces the unknown and neglected *Espejo de Corregidores y de jueces* by Villaescusa, and states that the alleged anonymous *Directorio de Príncipes* edited by R. Tate is in fact part of the *Espejo*. *Text and Concordance of the Crónica particular del Cid (1512), based on the Huntington facsimile (1903) of the copy at the Hispanic Society of America*, ed. Matt Mayers et al., Madison, HSMS, 7 pp. + 4 microfiches.

THEATRE. *Teatro medieval. 1. Drama litúrgico*, ed. Eva Castro, B, Crítica, 318 pp., is a most useful anthology of Latin texts with translations and extensive notes. *Teatro Medieval, 2. Castilla*, ed. Miguel Ángel Pérez Priego, B, Crítica, 274 pp., includes the most important works, from the *Auto* to the end of the 15th c., accompanied by a useful collection of documents, legal and historical, concerning the existence of medieval theatre in Castile and its regulation. A. Beresford, 'Sobre la repetición léxica en el *Auto de los Reyes Magos*', *Incipit*, 16: 145–63, finds the structual and thematic lines by concentrating on the repetition and distribution of eight lexical units (*rey, criador, estrella, verdad, ver, saber, ir, adorar*).

ALJAMIADO LITERATURE

By CONSUELO LÓPEZ-MORILLAS, *Professor of Spanish,*
and MIGUEL ÁNGEL VÁZQUEZ, *Indiana University*

(This survey covers the years 1995–97)

L. F. Bernabé Pons, *El evangelio de San Bernabé: un evangelio islámico español,* Alicante U.P., 1995, 260 pp., is an analysis of the only extant apocryphal gospel written in Spanish. The fascinating text proposes a rectification of Jesus's message from a Muslim standpoint: Jesus came to the world to announce the coming of the seal of the prophets, Muḥammad. The discussion places the text within the history, religion, and culture that surrounded the creation of the gospel: Morisco Spain. B. concludes that the *Evangelio* represents the latest and most elaborate of a series of apocryphal texts written by crypto-Muslims who attempted to convince Christendom that syncretism between Christianity and Islam was possible. Y. Cardaillac-Hermosilla, **La magie en Espagne: morisques et vieux chrétiennes au XVIe et XVIIe siècles,* Zaghouan, FTERSI, 1996, 334 pp. A. Galmés de Fuentes, *Los moriscos (desde su misma orilla),* M, Instituto Egipcio de Estudios Islámicos, 1993, 136 pp., answers F. Márquez Villanueva's *El problema morisco (desde otras laderas),* and argues that among the Moriscos a cultured and bourgeois minority emerged that advanced the development of Aljamiado literature and the preservation of Islamic culture.

F. Guillén Robles, *Leyendas Moriscas,* 3 vols, introd. M. Paz Torres, Granada U.P., 1994, cxvii + 381 pp., 388 pp., 388 pp., is a facsimile edition of the 1885–86 classic collection of Morisco 'legends' transcribed from various Aljamiado manuscripts. The edition is not an attempt at a scientific transcription of the originals, but a modernizing one aimed at a large readership.

L. López-Baralt presents a shorter version of her 1992 extensive study and edition of a Morisco MS with *Un Kāma Sūtra español. El primer tratado erótico de nuestra lengua (MSS.S-2 Brah Madrid y Palacio 1767),* M, Prodhufi, 1995, 176 pp. (see *YWMLS,* 56:337). L.-B. adds a chapter at the beginning of this edition with the news of yet another copy of S-2, dated as late as the 18th c.; see below on *ShAn,* 12. The book has also appeared in a French version: *Ars amandi d'un morisque de Tunis. Texte établi par Luce López-Baralt,* Zaghouan, FTERSI, 1995, 144 pp. Since the 1992 book, L.-B. has published other articles on the same topic: 'España y Oriente. Un *Kāma Sūtra* español, como primer tratado erótico de nuestra lengua', pp. 171–97 of *Tierras lejanas, voces cercanas. Estudios sobre el acercamiento indio-ibero-americano,* ed. Shyama Prasad Ganguly, New Delhi, Indian Council for Cultural Relations,

1995, xx + 674 pp. Also 'Un místico de Fez, experto en amores: el modelo principal del *Kāma Sūtra español*', pp. 219–57 of *Erotismo en las letras hispánicas. Aspectos, modos y fronteras*, ed. L. López-Baralt and Francisco Márquez Villanueva, México, Colegio de México, 1995, 527 pp., in which she discusses how the author of the *Kāma Sūtra español* made use of his many Muslim erotological sources as well as other Spanish ones. Unlike most Morisco authors, this one did not limit himself to copying the sources, but made 'editorial' decisions on what to include in his treatise.

Abdeljelil Temimi, *Bibliographie générale d'études morisques*, Zaghouan, FTERSI, 1995, 331 + 51 Ar. pp., though a commendable effort, is not a reliable and rigorously written bibliography. Although the bibliography references more than 3,577 items there are abundant spelling errors and at times the authors are indexed under the wrong letter. Moreover, some entries are of conference papers that were never published.

Mélanges Cardaillac, the volume in honour of the French *moriscólogo* L. Cardaillac, M. S. Abdel Latif, 'Influencias del árabe en un texto morisco inédito' (21–48), identifies lexical, semantic, syntactic, and stylistic Arabisms from MS BNM 5354. With 'Le héros, maître du pouvoir magique: Salomon' (145–59), Y. Cardaillac-Hermosilla examines the figure of King Solomon, his magical powers, and why he appears so popular among the Morisco minority: Solomon represents the textual/mythic exteriorization of an internal desire for Islam's triumph over Christianity. L. López-Baralt, 'El conjuro mágico de Salomón a la Alhabiba' (431–47), presents an Aljamiado story in which King Solomon provides a magic spell to protect a child against a female demon who preys on newborns. Finally, R. Mami, 'Los milagros del profeta Mahoma en algunos manuscritos moriscos' (457–64), catalogues several of Muḥammad's miracles according to some Aljamiado manuscripts.

In *Fest. Kontzi*, the 'Iberische Halbinsel' section offers several pieces on Aljamiado and Moriscos. A. Labarta and C. Barceló, 'Latín y romance en oraciones cristianas halladas a moriscos valencianos' (315–24), analyse prayers written by Moriscos in a mixture of Castilian, Catalan, and Latin in Arabic letters, from Inquisition documents of 1573. O. Hegyi, 'Sprache im Grenzgebiet zwischen Islam und Christentum: Die Aljamiadoliteratur' (325–33), notes parallels between Spanish Aljamiado and other languages (such as Kapmalaien, Afrikaans written in Arabic script), particularly in their handling of specialized religious vocabulary: these languages restructure their lexicon, creating new semantic fields and systems of contrast that constitute a systematic Islamization. L. P. Harvey was offered a brief pre-sale peep at 'Magic and popular medicine in an *aljamiado* manuscript, possibly of Tunisian provenance, sold in London in 1993' (335–44): the text in question, unusual in being written in Aljamiado apparently after the Expulsion, may descend from the same original as J22 (see *YWMLS*, 56: 337). A. Vespertino Rodríguez investigates 'Fuentes y análisis estructural de un cuento morisco' (345–59), a case of a false accusation of bestiality against a chaste woman: the sources are the Bible, the Koran, and Islamic tradition, and the structural analysis (à la Todorov) is not very illuminating. L. López-Baralt takes a journey 'En busca de un profeta perdido: el viaje maravilloso de Buluquía a los confines del universo en una leyenda aljamiada del siglo XVI' (361–86, repeated in *Actes* (SIEM 6), 145–59): of its sources, *1,001 Nights* and *Qiṣaṣ al-Anabiyā* [Stories of the prophets], the latter is more fully exploited, and this tale of the fantastic acquires special overtones when seen against the background of the Moriscos' situation. R. Mami, 'Otra leyenda morisca' (387–403), an edition of a chapter of ʿĪsā ibn Jābir's *Breviario Çunni* from the Latin-letter MS BNM 6016, is as uninteresting as its title. Y. Cardaillac-Hermosilla offers an incoherent and disorganized recording of Christian and Muslim names for the devil: 'Les noms du diable: portée et mythe dans les textes espagnols des XVIème et XVIIème siècles' (419–32). T. Raczek, '*Gabañar(se)*–Beispiel einer lexicalischen Innovation in Aljamiadotexten' (447–53) clarifies the etymology of *gabañar* and its derivatives.

From *Actes* (SIEM 6), L. Cardaillac, 'Pour une bibliographie générale des morisques' (53–63), presents, in a bibliography of bibliographies, an insightful reflection on the state of the art of Morisco studies, its recent trends and future directions. The article ends with a list of compiled bibliographies on Morisco studies. Y. Cardaillac-Hermosilla, 'Evolution de l'idée de magie: morisques et chrétiens, aux XVIe et XVIIe siècles, d'après la documentation inquisitoriale, la littérature aljamiada et la litterature des vieux chrétiens' (65–84), explores attitudes toward magic from the Christian and Muslim points of view. M. J. Cervera Fras, 'Las adoas de Morata de Jalón' (85–95), reports the discovery in 1993 of two short Aljamiado MSS and provides detailed physical descriptions and pictures as well as a full transcription of one of them. A. López, 'Gonzalo de Berceo y un morisco aljamiado nos hablan del fin del mundo: acerca de los signos que aparecerán antes del juicio y el manuscrito aljamiado T-17 de la Biblioteca del la Real Academia de la Historia de Madrid' (135–43), compares Berceo's poem on the 15 signs announcing the Day of Judgement to an Aljamiado MS on the same subject. M. L. Lugo Acevedo, '*Kitāb al-anwār:* El copista ante su texto' (161–71), continues her studies on al-Bakrī's famous *Book of Lights*, on Muḥammad's genealogy, comparing three prose versions

in order to begin to determine the trajectory of the text from Arabic
to Aljamiado. T. Morales Arteaga, 'Dos profetas regatean por un
pueblo: Abraham y Mahoma' (219–26), compares the two dialogues
that Abraham and Muḥammad had with God as each prophet
attempts to convince God not to destroy Sodom and Gomorrah. Of
note is M. T. Narváez's 'Conocimientos místicos de los moriscos:
puesta al día de una confusión' (227–38): with concrete examples and
exploring all sides of the issue, she considers the possibility that the
Moriscos had knowledge of Sufi mysticism. Were they the bridge
between Arabic mysticism and Christian mystics like San Juan de la
Cruz and Santa Teresa? She concludes that the evidence is not strong
enough to claim any kind of deep mystical knowledge and practice
on the part of the Moriscos.

ACTES (SIEM 7) focuses on the Morisco family. Y. Cardaillac-
Hermosilla's 'Les livrets aljamiados de magie: une littérature à l'usage
des familles' (49–67), and B. Cruz Sotomayor's 'La reconstrucción
de una villa cripto-musulmana en Medinaceli a partir del libro de
cuentas de un comerciante morisco (Junta xxxvii de Madrid)'
(91–102), will be of interest. E. González Carmona reports on 'La
figura de Jesús vista por un polemista anónimo morisco (ms. 5302
BNM)' (131–44), providing a detailed discussion of the arguments
presented in an anti-Judeo-Christian polemic text. R. Iversen looks
into the religious practices of the Moriscos in 'En busca de una
alfombra de oración: una carta desesperada de un moriso de Tórtoles'
(167–75), presenting a content analysis within a Morisco cultural
context of a short letter written by a Morisco to a friend, urgently
requesting a small rug to perform his ritual prayers. M. L. Lugo, 'Las
sorpresas de la literatura morisca: un nuevo códice de Mahomet
Rabadán perteneciente al siglo xviii español (ms. 1767 de la
Biblioteca del Palacio Real de Madrid)' (186–93), describes another
MS written with Latin characters that shows that Morisco literature
extended up to the 18th century.

ShAn, 12, 1995, announces the journal's new orientation toward
'Estudios mudéjares y moriscos', with a 'Textos y contextos' section
of particular relevance for Aljamiado literature. In M. de Epalza, 'La
voz oficial de los musulmanes hispanos, mudéjares y moriscos, a sus
autoridades cristianas: cuatro textos, en árabe, en castellano y en
catalán valenciano' (279–97), the texts in question are the *Breviario
sunní*, the *Llibre de la çuna e xara*, the *fatwā* of al-Maghrāwī, and
Francisco Núñez Muley's *Memorial*. L. Bernabé Pons, 'Nueva hipótesis
sobre la personalidad de Baray de Reminŷo' (299–314), suggests that
'Baray' is a Navarrese form of 'Ibrāhīm', and that identifying this co-
author of the *Breve Compendio* as Navarrese permits a new dating of the
text to *c.* 1523 and casts new light on how the preservation of Islamic

doctrine in Spanish shifted from Castile to Aragon at this period. Taking advantage of Bernabé Pons's new chronology, M. J. Rubiera Mata offers, tentatively, a new theory of her own in 'Nuevas hipótesis sobre el Mancebo de Arévalo' (315–23): that the Mancebo's mother, a Christian for 25 years, was a convert from Judaism, not Islam; with interesting observations about this author's unique language of spirituality. S. A. Haggar studies 'Al-ǧihād, según el manuscrito aljamiado de *Al-tafrīʿ* de Ibn al-Ǧallāb' (325–38), and speculates on what meaning the *jihād* might still have held for Mudejars and Moriscos. M. Sánchez Alvarez reaches no firm conclusions in making her 'Observaciones sobre el arcaísmo lingüístico de los textos aljamiado-moriscos' (339–48), except to warn that Spanish was in flux and that older and newer usages competed in the works of Christian as well as Muslim writers. P. Valero Cuadra traces the Islamization by the Moriscos of a well-known folktale in 'La leyenda de la doncella Carcayona' (349–61). J. Zanón concentrates on the often-neglected Arabic MSS from Almonacid in 'Los estudios de lengua árabe entre los moriscos aragoneses a través de los manuscritos de la Junta' (363–74): among these are rapid, practical aids for learning the Arabic language. A Mudejar's pilgrimage to the East, described in Arabic, is the subject of F. Franco Sánchez's 'Los mudéjares, según la *Riḥla* de Ibn Aṣ-Ṣabbāḥ (m. después 895/1490)' (375–91). Shiite texts were rare in Islamic Spain, but J. F. Cutillas Ferrer finds one read by the Moriscos exiled to Tunis: 'Un texto chií en castellano, del s. xvii, en el universo cultural islámico de los moriscos expulsados' (393–400). A handful of Moriscos wrote in Arabic, not Spanish, in North Africa, as explained by A.-H. G. Slama in 'Aproximación al estudio de los textos en árabe de los morisco-andalusíes en Tunisia' (413–27). A. Stoll, 'Avatares de un cuento del Renacimiento. El *Abencerraje*, releído a la luz de su contexto literario-cultural y discursivo' (429–60), a wide-ranging study of the novella's reception, suggests in passing that the Mancebo de Arévalo was 'un modelo o, por lo menos, un análogo' of its anonymous author. L. López-Baralt announces 'Noticia de un nuevo hallazgo: un códice adicional del *Kāma Sūtra español* en la Biblioteca de Palacio de Madrid (ms. 1767)' (549–59): it is a late-18th-c. copy of BRAH S-2, which formed the basis for her 1992 book (*YWMLS*, 56:337). And L. P. Harvey finds 'Una referencia explícita a la legalidad de la práctica de la *taqīya* por los moriscos' (561–63) in the Mancebo de Arévalo's coinage of the Aljamiado expressions *amonestança* and *buena disimulança*; also in *Aljamía* 8, 1996:40–43.

L. López-Baralt, in three articles, describes the essential strangeness of Aljamiado literature in the Golden-Age context: 'Spanish Renaissance *à l'envers*: the secret literature of the last Muslims of Spain',

Friedman, *Brave New Words*, 79–89, 'The secret literature of the last
Muslims of Spain', *IsS*, 36:21–38, and 'La literatura secreta de los
últimos musulmanes de España', *Notas*, 7, 1996:18–31. A. Montaner
Frutos provides in 'Concordancias del *Recontamiento de Almiqdād y
Almayāça* (I)', *AFA*, 51, 1995:389–455, the concordance he did not
include in his 1988 edition (*YWMLS*, 50:302), up to the letter C (with
the rest of the alphabet to follow); but glosses are lacking, and the
calculation of relative frequencies adds little of use. G. Wiegers,
'Muḥammad as the Messiah: a comparison of the polemical works of
Juan Alonso with the *Gospel of Barnabas*', *BO*, 52, 1995, cols 245–91,
concerns itself chiefly with a source for the *Evangelio de Bernabé* not
previously noted by L. Bernabé Pons (see *El evangelio*, above), i.e. MS
BNM 9655 by Juan Alonso Aragonés; an illuminating account of the
history both of that false gospel and of the identification of the
Prophet with the Messiah.

L. Minervini presents 'Una versión aljamiada del Orlando furioso
de Ludovico Ariosto', pp. 295–98 of *Los judaizantes en Europa y la
literatura del Siglo de Oro*, Madrid, Letrúmero, 1994, 387 pp., about a
Hebrew-letter Aljamiado MS that contains a fragment of the famous
chivalric romance. A. Carmona González, 'El autor de las *Leyes de
moros*', *Homenaje Fórneas Besteiro*, II, 957–62 identifies the work for the
first time as a partial Spanish translation of Ibn al Jallāb's *Kitāb al-
tafri'* (see above, Haggar in *ShAn* 12, 1995). Previous editors, beginning
with Pascual de Gayangos in 1853, had thought it the work of an
anonymous Mudejar. M. T. Narváez, 'El Mancebo de Arévalo, lector
morisco de *La Celestina*', *BHS(L)*, 72, 1995:255–72, makes a surprising
discovery: the prologue of the *Celestina* was quoted in Arabic
characters in one of the most famous Aljamiado MSS, the *Tafsira* of
the Mancebo de Arévalo. N. also reflects on why the Mancebo quoted
a text that presents a chaotic view of the world: his historical context
forced him into constant struggle with a society that drove him and
his co-religionists into conversion. Hence the inclusion of the
Celestina's prologue, which points at a pessimistic view of the world.
A. Vespertino Rodríguez, *'La literatura aljamiado-morisca: últimos
estudios y estado de la cuestión', *REEI*, 27, 1995:181–93. L. F.
Bernabé Pons, *'Zur Wahrheit und Echtheit des Barnabasevangeli-
ums', pp. 133–88 of *Wertewandel und religiöse umnbrüche*, ed. R. Kirske,
U. Tworushka, and P. Schwarzenan, Balve, Zimmermann, 1996,
671 pp. Z. D. Zuwiyya, 'Royal fame and royal honor in the
Rrekontamiento del rrey Alisandre', *La corónica*, 25.1, 1996:128–45, traces
the evolution of the concept of 'fama' associated with Alexander the
Great from the pagan *Pseudo-Callisthenes*, through the Christianized
versions and finally the Muslim renditions, in order to assess the
originality of the Aljamiado version. A. García Pedraza, *'La vida

religiosa de los moriscos en el pensamiento historiográfico', *RHMag*, 87–88:315–70.

For the reader of Arabic the following articles from Binebine, *Manuscrit arabe*, will be of interest: H. Buzineb, 'Li-mādha kutibat ʿammiyat al-muriskiyyūn bi-ḥurūf ʿarabiyah' [Why was the Romance of the Moriscos written with Arabic characters?] (99–112), and M. J. Viguera, 'Baʿḍu al-mulahiẓāt ʿan al-makhṭuṭāt al-ʿarabiyah al-maktūbah bi-l-ʿajamiyah li-l-muslimīn fī Qastālah wa Araghūn' [Some observations on the Arabic manuscripts written in Aljamiado by the Muslims in Castile and Aragon] (113–29).

Studies of language continue to be of value for students of Aljamiado literature. A. Galmés de Fuentes, 'La literatura aljamiada nos revela el secreto: ant. esp. *consograr* "emparentar por afinidad o por razón de matrimonio" ', *BRAE*, 74, 1994:7–11, corrects the definition of the term in question in the Academy dictionary: a calque on Arabic, it denotes, ultimately, 'to establish alliance with a tribe'. Id., 'La lengua de los moriscos', Alvar, *Manual*, 111–18, provides the kind of introductory survey that befits a general volume. A better introduction, more informative on sociolinguistic and semantic aspects, is O. Hegyi, 'Die Sprache der Aljamiado-literatur und der Moriscos', Holtus, *Lexikon*, II/2, 736–53; in Spanish, despite the German title. Two pieces of the same year and almost identical title take different approaches: C. López-Morillas, 'Language and identity in late Spanish Islam', *HR*, 63, 1995:193–210, praises the Moriscos' affirmation of group solidarity through linguistic creativity; G. Wiegers, 'Language and identity: Muslim use of non-Arabic languages in the Muslim west', pp. 303–26 of *Pluralism and Identity in Ritual Behaviour*, ed. J. Platvoet and K. van der Toorn, Leiden, Brill, 1995, 376 pp., discusses the history, especially in Spain, of the translation of Islamic religious texts, concluding that it was tolerated from the 12th c. onward. T. Raczek, 'Editionstypen bei Aljamiadotexten', Glessgen, *Philologie*, 347–57, provides a basic introduction to the different editorial criteria employed by editors of Aljamiado manuscripts.

LITERATURE, 1490–1700
(PROSE AND POETRY)

By J. A. JONES, *Senior Lecturer in Hispanic Studies in the University of Hull*

1. GENERAL

B. W. Ife,'The literary impact of the New World: Columbus to Carrizales', *JIRS*, 3, 1994–95:65–85, fruitfully reflects on the birth of America and the novel. Golden Age connections with the New World are also highlighted in A. Martinengo, '"Indias de allá" e "Indias de acá": estrategias demoníacas asechando a la ciudadela de la Ortodoxia', *Actas* (AISO 1993), I, 115–32; L. Schrader, 'La invención de una ciencia de las religiones: Las Casas y el universo "no canónico" de los dioses paganos', *ib.*, 133–47; R. Gardes de Fernández, 'Metáforas contextuales en la literatura hispano-americana', *ib.*, 175–82; D. de Armas Wilson, '"The territory of these women": Amazon sightings from India to Las Indias', *Herrero Vol.*, 211–61; B. Mujica, 'Jorge Luis Borges and the Spanish Golden Age', *ib.*, 194–210. V. Infantes, 'Tipologías de la enunciación literaria en la prosa aúrea. Seis títulos (y algunos más) en busca de un género: obra, libro, tratado, crónica, historia, cuento, etc. (I)', *Actas* (AISO 1993), III, 265–72, usefully defines and categorizes. C. Strosetzki, 'Historia e historias en torno a la poética de la historiografía en el Renacimiento español', *ib.*, 513–19, relates history and fiction. V. Pineda, '"Dum viguit eloquentia, viguit pictura" (De literatura artística y arte literario, con ejemplos del libro segundo de Pacheco)', *ib.*, I, 191–98, analyses rhetorical techniques in Pacheco's *Arte de Pintura*. French connections are pursued in M. A. Etayo-Piñol, 'Impacto del Siglo de Oro español en Francia a través de la edición lyonesa', *ib.*, 169–74; S. Collet Sedola, 'Gramáticos y gramáticas: España en Francia (1600–1650)', *ib.*, 161–68. *BH*, 97, 1995, is devoted to 'La culture des élites espagnoles a l'époque moderne', and contains 12 studies of interest. Lesser known aspects of Golden Age writing are studied in: A. Egido, 'Linajes de burlas en el Siglo de Oro', *Actas* (AISO 1993), I, 19–50; H. Ettinghausen, 'Hacia una tipología de la prensa española del siglo XVII: de "hard news" a "soft porn"', *ib.*, 51–66; M. Joly, 'Dignificación y desprecio en la recuperación de lo marginado', *ib.*, 67–77; R. L. Kagan, 'La corografía en la Castilla moderna: género, historia, nación', *ib.*, 79–91; C. Lisón Tolosana, 'Retablo de máscaras gitanescas', *ib.*, 93–114; P. Vega Rodríguez, 'Resonancias erasmianas en los refraneros de paremiología aúrea', *ib.*, 207–14; M. García-Bermejo, 'La parodia en la génesis de los "gallos" universitarios', *ib.*,

III, 203–11; L. Rodríguez Cacho, 'Los epitafios curiosos en las misceláneas', *ib.*, 435–46. M. A. Martínez San Juan, 'Revisión del concepto "lo horaciano" en las epístolas morales del Siglo de Oro español', *BH*, 98, 1996:291–303, attempts to establish the meaning of this concept.

2. THOUGHT

Pierre Civil, *Image et dévotion dans l'Espagne du XVIe siècle: Le traité 'Norte de Ydiotas' de Francisco de Monzón (1563)*, Paris, Presses de la Sorbonne Nouvelle, 1995, 197 pp., and Id., 'Imagen y devoción: el *Norte de Ydiotas de Francisco de Monzón (1563)*', *Actas* (AISO 1993), III, 109–19, highlight the role of images in 16th-c. spirituality. C. Bouzy, 'Dios como arquetipo actancial en los *Emblemas Morales* de Juan de Horozco (Segovia, 1589): retórica y resorte dramatúrgico del emblema-predicación', *ib.*, I, 151–60, looks at emblematic representations of God. N. Fernández Marcos et al., *Cipriano de la Huerga. Obras completas. Volumen* IX. Estudio monográfico colectivo, León U.P., 1996, 427 pp., and *Pedro de Valencia. Obras completas* VII. Discurso acerca de las brujas, ed. M. A. Marcos Casquero and H. Riesco Alvarez, León U.P., 320 pp., continue the excellent León series. Aspects of humanism are illustrated in J. F. Alcina, 'Dos notas sobre Benito Arias Montano (1527–1598)', *Salinas*, 9, 1995:37–44; A. Sanz Cabrerizo, 'Lecturas y reescrituras de Padre Mariana en la Francia del siglo XVII', *Actas* (AISO 1993), III, 501–11; J. A. Jones, '"Con la pluma en la mano": the bond of words between Benito Arias Montano and Pedro de Valencia', *Cueto Vol.*, 33–53. *Faith and Fanaticism: Religious Fervour in Early Modern Spain*, ed. Lesley Twomey, Aldershot–Brookfield U.S.A.–Singapore–Sydney, Ashgate, viii + 181 pp., contains: R. Cueto, '*Fervor/Fanatismo* or *Entorno/Enfoque*: the problem of the female visionary in the Catholic Monarchy' (7–21); L. Twomey, '"Cechs són aquells que tenen lo contrari": fanatical condemnation of opponents of the Immaculate Conception in fifteenth-century Valencia' (23–35); T. O'Reilly, 'Meditation and contemplation: monastic spirituality in early sixteenth-century Spain' (37–57); A. Gordon Kinder, 'Spain's little-known "noble army of martyrs"' (61–83); M. Alpert, 'Did Spanish crypto-Jews desecrate Christian sacred images and why? The case of the *Cristo de la Paciencia* (1629–32), the *Romance* of 1717 and the events of November 1714 in the *Calle del lobo*' (85–94); N. Griffiths, 'Popular religious scepticism and idiosyncracy in post-Tridentine Cuenca' (95–126); H. Pomeroy, 'The religious background of the Sephardic ballad' (129–39); E. Sánchez García, 'A comparison of the devotional systems of the *Viaje de Turquía*' (141–57); J. A. Jones, '*Fervor sin fanatismo*: Pedro de Valencia's treatise on the *moriscos*' (159–74). E. Rummel, 'Marino Sículo: a protagonist of humanism in Spain', *RQ*, 50:701–22, studies writings of this royal historian. A. Moreno Mengíbar and J. Martos Fernández, 'Mesianismo y Nuevo Mundo en fray Luis de León: *In Abdiam Prophetam Expositio*', *BH*, 98, 1996:261–89, links Old Testament prophecy to events in the New World. Aspects of heterodoxy are examined in L. A. Homza, 'Erasmus as hero or heretic? Spanish humanism and the Valladolid assembly of 1527', *RQ*, 50:78–118; M. Firpo, 'The Italian Reformation and Juan de Valdés', *SCJ*, 27, 1996:353–64; J. San José Lera, 'Límites ideológicos de la exégesis romance. Al hilo de Juan de Valdés, Fray Luis de León y Francisco de Quevedo', *Actas* (AISO 1993), III, 471–84. M. J. Mancho Duque, 'Neologismos cultos en los *Ejercicios* de Ignacio de Loyola', *ib.*, 307–22, analyses the linguistic resources of St. Ignatius's work. A. Morel d'Arleux, 'Régimen de sanidad y arte de bien vivir', *ib.*, 335–46, offers advice on life as preparation for death. O. Perotti, '*San Nicolás el Magno* . . . de Ceferino Clavero de Falces', *ib.*, 399–407, illuminates 17th-c. hagiography. M. I. Toro Pascua, 'Literatura popular religiosa en el siglo XVI: los sermones impresos de San Vicente Ferrer', *ib.*, 521–29, usefully fills in aspects of religious background. M. A. Rees, 'The gaze of God. Doña Luisa de Carvajal y Mendoza and the English mission', *Cueto Vol.*, 92–114, depicts Anglo-Spanish religious experience and writing.

3. Lyrical and Narrative Poetry

GENERAL. D. G. Walters, 'Petrarquismo y pornografía: el *Jardín de Venus*', *Actas* (AISO 1993), I, 543–50, traces the narrow dividing line between these two elements. H. Janner, 'Friedrich Christian Rassman y la lírica del Siglo de Oro', *ib.*, 373–76, looks at Golden Age influence on this poet. E. Dudley, 'The lady is out of this world: erotic conceits and carnal displacements in three protocols of desire', *Herrero Vol.*, 176–93, considers the treatment of love. A. Rossich, 'Formas del plurilingüismo literario: textos de doble y triple lectura', *Actas* (AISO 1993), I, 501–12, illustrates textual tensions. J. M. Pedrosa, 'Rey Fernando, Rey Don Sancho, Pero Pando, Padre Pando, Pero Palo, Fray Príapo, Fray Pedro: metamorfosis de un canto de disparates (siglos XIV–XX)', *BH*, 98, 1996:5–27, traces the development of a poetic formula. O. Gorse, '*La cueva de Meliso*: el poder demoníaco en un ciclo satírico antiolivarista', *Actas* (AISO 1993), I, 359–66, portrays political satire and its effects. J. Toledano Molina, 'Una academia gaditana en honor de la reina Mariana de Austria Walters', *ib.*, 535–41, further illustrates the role of poetic academies. M. R. Couture, '*El agua más recordada*: Golden Age poetry in Lezama's "Ah, que tu escapes"', *His(US)*, 80:21–30, shows influence of baroque poetry on José Lezama Lima.

GARCILASO. Aspects of the sonnets are considered in A. Azaustre Galiana, '*Compositio*, puntuación y lectura del soneto 1 de Garcilaso', *BH*, 98, 1996:29–35; G. W. Dubois, 'Tradition, technique, and personal involvement in Garcilaso's Sonnet xvi', *HR*, 65:47–59; B. L. Creel, 'Canción 1 y Soneto 11 de Garcilaso y el problema del masoquismo en la lírica amatoria renacentista', *Actas* (AISO 1993), 1, 299–307; A. Gargano, 'Garcilaso y la *aegritudo canina*: el soneto *A la entrada de un valle, en un desierto*', *ib.*, 339–49; N. Ly, 'El trabajo de la reina en los sonetos de Garcilaso de la Vega', *ib.*, 387–93. E. L. Rivers, 'Garcilaso leído por Lapesa', *ib.*, 467–73, is an appraisal of a distinguished *garcilasista* by another. A. Roig, 'Correlaciones entre Sá de Miranda y Garcilaso de la Vega', *ib.*, 475–86, provides a useful comparison. M. C. Sigler, 'Apuntes para un estudio de la *interrogatio* en Garcilaso y Quevedo', *Salinas*, 10, 1996:44–50, illustrates the use of Classical rhetorical techniques.

LOPE DE VEGA. *Edad de Oro*, 14, M, Universidad Autónoma, 1995, 328 pp., contains 14 articles on Lope and includes F. J. Díez de Revenga, A. Egido, C. Guillén, B. López Bueno, and J. Moll. M. L. García Rodrigo, 'Algunas notas sobre la piratería en *La Dragontea* de Lope de Vega', *Actas* (AISO 1993), 1, 329–37, brings out the links between fiction and history. A. Ramajo Caño, 'Las huellas clásicas en un poema de Lope de Vega ("En la muerte de Baltasar Elisio de Medinilla")', *ib.*, 449–56, highlights Lope's use of Classical sources in treating the subject of death.

QUEVEDO. M. A. Candelas Colodrón, 'La Silva "El pincel" de Quevedo: la teoría pictórica y la alabanza de pintores al servicio del dogma contrarreformista', *BH*, 98, 1996:85–95, discusses Q.'s defence of art in transmitting dogma. Id., 'Algunos aspectos de la *dispositio* en la poesía de Quevedo', *BHS(G)*, 74:353–70, illustrates Q.'s refashioning of Classical models. S. Dale, 'La filosofía amorosa de Fedro y Ersímaco en el "Himno a las estrellas" de Quevedo', *Hispanófila*, 120:29–40, studies Q.'s use of Platonic concepts. F. J. Martin, 'Más allá del soneto amoroso: Quevedo y la preocupación metafísica', *RoN*, 38:25–35, establishes metaphysical links. M. Roig Miranda, '¿Existe el presente en los sonetos metafísicos de Quevedo?', *Actas* (AISO 1993), 1, 487–94, searches for the elusive present. A. Azaustre Galiana, 'El destinatario en los sonetos morales de Quevedo', *ib.*, 237–46, addresses the use of the Classical technique of apostrophe. M. A. Candelas Colodrón, '"¡Qué de robos han visto del invierno!": ¿una égloga de Quevedo?', *ib.*, 267–74, considers Q.'s treatment of pastoral. E. L. Rivers, 'Quevedo against "culteranismo": a note on politics and morality', *MLN*, 112:269–74, discusses Q.'s concern with moral truth. R. Morales Raya, 'Un dato para la revisión cronológica del romancero de Quevedo', *Actas* (AISO 1993), I, 405–13, brings out Q.'s interest in *romances*. C. Orobitg, '*Exclusus amator*: en torno a un poema de Quevedo ("A la puerta de Aminta")', *ib.*, 415–24, analyses Petrarchan themes. M. C. Sigler, 'La transmisión de los textos poéticos de Quevedo y la evidencia de la silva Farmaceutria', *Salinas*, 9, 1995:45–50, provides documentary material.

GÓNGORA. E. L. Rivers, '*Soledad* de Góngora y *Sueño* de Sor Juana', *ib.*, 10, 1996:69–76, reflects on G.'s influence on Sor Juana. Aspects of *Soledades* are highlighted in F. Carrasco, 'Transformaciones de un modelo textual: el *Beatus ille* en las *Soledades* de Góngora', *Actas* (AISO 1993), I, 287–98; J. Roses, 'Hibridaciones dramático-poéticas: égloga y disfraz en las *Soledades*', *ib.*, 495–500; E. Cancelliere, 'La realidad virtual en las *Soledades* de Góngora', *ib.*, 257–66. A. Cardona, 'Comentario a dos estrofas del *Polifemo* ("La fugitiva ninfa en tanto, donde" y "Salamandria es del Sol, vestido estrellas")', *ib.*, 275–85, provides further analysis. L. Terracini, 'Camas de batallas gongorinas', *ib.*, 525–33, searches under the beds. A. C. López Viñuela, 'Quevedo y "el pobre Lope de Vega" en un soneto gongorino', *ib.*, 377–85, deals with literary polemics.

OTHERS. *Ínsula*, 610, celebrates the fourth centenary of Herrera's death and contains ten articles of interest. L. Rabin, 'Speaking to silent ladies: images of beauty and politics in poetic portraits of women from Petrarch to Sor Juana Inés de la Cruz', *MLN*, 112:147–65, looks at the tension between external and internal images of the beloved. M. L. García Macho, 'Algunas notas sobre los sustantivos en -*dad* y -*ura* en San Juan de la Cruz', *Actas* (AISO 1993), I, 319–28, displays San Juan's command of language. D. M. Murphy, '"Oda a Francisco Salinas", Fray Luis de León's celestial air', *BHS(L)*, 74:159–78, looks at generic influences. I. Pepe Sarno, 'El *Ejemplar poético* de Juan de la Cueva entre intertextualidad e interdiscursividad', *Actas* (AISO 1993), I, 425–33, considers poetic academies in Seville. L. Gutiérrez Arranz, 'La poesía de tema mitológico de Villamediana', *ib.*, 367–72, examines Villamediana's use of Classical material. C. Clavería, '"Placet vinum." Ahora sobre "la silva" de Pérez de Moya', *HR*, 65:307–16, considers the sources of a little known poem. J. Acebrón Ruiz, 'El Orco: monstruo, ciego, enamorado. Anotaciones al canto III de *Las lágrimas de Angélica*', *Actas* (AISO 1993), I, 225–36, studies an unlikely love in Luis Barahona de Soto's poem. C. Vaíllo, 'Las teorías poéticas de Antonio López de Vega', *ib.*, 199–206, continues the rediscovery of this writer. T. O'Reilly, 'Jorge de Montemayor and the poetry of the Psalms', *Cueto Vol.*, 1–18, highlights Montemayor's poetic skills and familiarity with the Psalter.

Relatively unknown poets are brought to our attention in J. Sanz Hermida, 'Ensoñación y transformismo: la parodia erótica en *El sueño de la viuda* de Fray Melchor de la Serna', *Actas* (AISO 1993), I, 513–23; A. Madroñal Durán, 'Don Luis de Vargas Manrique (1566–1591?) y su círculo de amigos en torno al romancero nuevo', *ib.*, 395–404; V. Campo, 'De lectores y lecturas: la *Respuesta* de Fr. Tomás Quixada en *El peregrino curioso* de Bartolomé de Villalba', *ib.*, 247–55; S. Pérez-Abadín Barro, 'Las canciones de Francisco de la Torre', *ib.*, 435–48; R. González Cañal, '*La Fábula de Vulcano y Minerva* del Conde de Rebolledo', *ib.*, 351–58; I. Ravasini, 'John Owen y Francisco de la Torre y Sevil: de la traducción a la imitación', *ib.*, 457–65.

4.   PROSE AND THE NOVEL

GENERAL.   *Ínsula*, 584–85, 1995, is dedicated to 'La caballería antigua para el mundo moderno' and contains ten articles of interest. A. Bognolo, 'La desmitificación del espacio en el *Amadís de Gaula*: los "castillos de la mala costumbre"', *Actas* (AISO 1993), III, 67–72, relates the decline of Arthurian adventures to imperial expansion. J. Durán Barceló, 'La teoría historiográfica de Bartolomé de las Casas', *ib.*, 161–68, illustrates influence of Greek historiography on Golden Age writing. S. M. Carrizo Rueda, 'Los libros de viajes medievales y su influencia en la narrativa aúrea', *ib.*, 81–87, follows the reception and influence of medieval works in Golden Age Spain. F. Copello, 'Las *Aplicaciones* de Diego Rosel y Fuenllana: una reflexión sobre la geografía del relato en la España del siglo XVII', *ib.*, 129–38, debates views concerning geographical locations in short stories. L. González Martínez, 'Título y onomástica en la novela corta y en el drama del Seiscientos', *ib.*, 183–90, compares Lope's *La prudente venganza* and *El castigo sin venganza*. D. E. Sieber, 'The frontier ballad and Spanish Golden Age historiography: recontextualizing the "Guerras civiles de Granada"', *HR*, 65:291–306, relates literature, history and modern readings of older texts. J. A. Aldaz, 'Predicación divina, palabra y tópica ejemplar en los siglos de oro: *magis movent exempla quam verba*', *Salinas*, 10, 1996:55–68, raises questions of moral, didactic intentions.

PICARESQUE.   Studies on *Lazarillo* continue with: C. E. Armijo, '*Lazarillo de Tormes* y la crítica a la utopía imperial', *Actas* (AISO 1993), III, 29–38; M. Ferrer Chivite, 'El escudero del *Lazarillo*, cristiano nuevo', *ib.*, 177–84; A. Sánchez Romeralo, 'El triunfo de Lázaro (la estrategia del texto)', *ib.*, 485–92; R. Sánchez Sarmiento, 'Algunos cabos sueltos en una traducción italiana del *Lazarillo de Tormes*', *ib.*, 493–99. F. J. Sánchez, 'Subjetividad literario-política y riqueza en *Guzmán de Alfarache* y en Gracián', *BHS(L)*, 74:299–306, makes a useful contribution concerning the representation of the concept of wealth. M. Cavillac, 'Política y poética en el *Guzmán de Alfarache*', *Actas* (AISO 1993), III, 89–95, considers aspects of the conversion. H. Guerreiro, 'Tradición y modernidad en la obra de Mateo Alemán', *ib.*, 247–58, brings out another duality. S. López Poza, 'Imágenes emblemáticas en el *Guzmán de Alfarache*', *ib.*, 297–305, provides a contextual background which influenced Alemán. N. von Prellwitz, 'Presencias luciferinas en el *Guzmán de Alfarache*', *ib.*, 419–24, ventures into dark, Satanic recesses. M. Rubio Arquez, 'Situación actual de los estudios sobre el *Guzmán* apócrifo', *ib.*, 463–70, takes stock of the state of scholarship. M. Dimitrova, 'Aspectos espacio-temporales en la configuración del personaje picaresco femenino', *ib.*, 147–54, examines space and time. V. Roncero López, 'La novela bufonesca: *La pícara Justina* y el *Estebanillo González*', *ib.*, 455–61, considers the picaresque as vehicle for the *bufón*. L. P. Aguirre de Cárcer Casarrubios, 'El elemento árabe en *Marcos de Obregón*', *BH*, 98, 1996: 397–418, brings out ambiguity from a *morisco* perspective.

OTHERS. T. Hart, '*Retraer munchas cosas retrayendo una*: Delicado's art of representation', *BHS(G)*, 74: 145–53, raises questions of genre, readers and texts. J. Joset, 'De los nombres de Rampín (II)', *Actas* (AISO 1993), III, 273–78, pursues associations and meanings of this name. S. G. Artal, 'Nuevas notas acerca de la deshumanización del cuerpo humano en la prosa satírica de Quevedo', *ib.*, 39–44, proposes a classification. F. Cerdan, 'Quevedo predicador: la *Homilía de la Santísima Trinidad*', *ib.*, 97–108, highlights Quevedo's sacred eloquence. S. Fernández Mosquera, 'Situación y contexto de la *Execración contra los judíos* de Quevedo', *ib.*, 169–75, points to the targets of Quevedo's attack. V. Nider, 'Algo más sobre el problema textual de las *Migajas* de Quevedo', *ib.*, 369–76, picks up crumbs left by previous critics. C. Peraita, 'En torno a la circunstancia histórica de la *Política de Dios i* de Quevedo: " . . . aviendo de tener lado"', *ib.*, 389–98, looks at the political context. Useful contributions on Gracián are: M. Borrego Pérez, 'Algunas notas sobre las "cortes" en *El Criticón*', *Actas* (AISO 1993), III, 73–80; E. I. Deffis de Calvo, 'El discurso narrativo y el cronotopo en *El Criticón* de Baltasar Gracián', *ib.*, 139–46; F. Gil Encabo, '"injurias a tu mayor amigo . . . ": Gracián y Lastanosa entre *El Criticón* y la *Crítica de Reflección*', *ib.*, 221–27; F. Gambin, 'Anotaciones sobre las traducciones al italiano de *El Comulgatorio* de Gracián', *ib.*, 195–202; G. C. Marras, '*Elocuencia española en arte* de Jiménez Patón y *Agudeza y arte de ingenio* de Baltasar Gracián', *ib.*, 323–26; S. Neumeister, 'Visualización verbal en *El discreto* de Gracián', *ib.*, 355–67. A. del Río Noguera, 'Lastanosa y la celebración del nacimiento de Felipe Próspero en la Huesca de 1658', *ib.*, 425–34, finds some Gongoresque elements. J. González Rovira,

'Mecanismos de recepción en *El peregrino en su patria* de Lope de Vega', *ib.*, 239–46, analyses didactic techniques. M. Morrás, 'Una versión catalana desconocida de las *Epístolas familiares* de Antonio de Guevara', *ib.*, 347–54, considers the reception of this work. S. Hutchinson, 'Genealogy of Guevara's barbarian: an invented "Other"', *BHS(L)*, 74 : 7–18, explores idealization of non-existent others. J. Drinkwater, 'María de Zayas: la mujer emparedada y los *Desengaños amorosos*', *Actas* (AISO 1993), III, 155–59, extends implications of the treatment of woman. S. Hutchinson, 'Economía ética en las novelas de María de Zayas', *ib.*, 259–63, focuses on economic terminology. M. Aldoma García, 'Los *Hecatommithi* de Giraldi Cinzio en España', *ib.*, 15–21, studies a Spanish translation of 1590. J. Romera Castillo, 'Otro asalto a *El Patrañuelo*: la patraña octava', *ib.*, 447–53, confirms Timoneda's borrowings. E. Suárez-Galbán Guerra, 'Sobre un supuesto cambio en la estructura de la *Vida* de Torres Villarroel', *BH*, 98, 1996 : 419–27, rejects the view of a hybrid novel. A. Gallego Barnes, 'Otro enigma en torno a Julián Iñiguez de Medrano: las dos Orcavellas', *Actas* (AISO 1993), III, 185–93, provides biographical/bibliographical material. J. E. Laplana Gil, 'Historiografía local y literatura. El caso de Ambrosio Bondía', *ib.*, 279–88, ponders the relationship between history and literature. Relatively little-known writings are highlighted in E. Juárez, 'Alonso de Contreras: política del vestido y construcción del sujeto autobiográfico en el Barroco', *BHS(L)*, 74 : 179–95; A. Madroñal Durán, '*Los Comentarios de erudición* del Maestro Jiménez Patón, unas obras supuestamente perdidas', *BH*, 98, 1996 : 385–95.

CERVANTES

GENERAL. E. C. Riley, 'Tradición e innovación en la novelística cervantina', *Cervantes*, 17.1 : 46–61, looks at the influence of antecedents. J. M. Martín Morán, 'Cervantes: el juglar zurdo de la era de Gutenberg', *ib.*, 122–44, sees tension between oral and written culture. A. Estévez Molinero, 'La poética picaresca, Cervantes y "un postre agridulce como granada"', *BH*, 98, 1996 : 305–26, makes picaresque comparisons. T. L. Darby, 'Cervantes in England: the influence of Golden Age prose fiction on Jacobean drama, c.1615–1625', *BHS(L)*, 74 : 425–41, provides valuable evidence particularly concerning Cervantes. *Atti delle Giornate Cervantine, Venezia, 7 maggio 1991 (II Giornata), Padova, 4 maggio 1992 (III Giornata), Venezia, 23 aprile 1993 (IV Giornata)*, ed. C. Romero Muñoz, D. Pini Moro, and A. Cancellier, Padua, Unipress, 1995, 135 pp., contains ten articles of interest, including E. C. Riley, Aurora Egido and other well known *cervantistas*. A. Sánchez, 'Revisión del cautiverio cervantino en Argel', *Cervantes*, 17.1 : 7–24, attempts answers to controversial questions. J. Canavaggio, 'Aproximaciones al proceso Ezpeleta', *ib.*, 25–45, contextualizes this case. K. Sliwa, 'Perspectivas en los documentos cervantinos', *ib.*, 174–79, considers further documentary material. M. C. García de Enterría, 'Marginalia cervantina', *Actas* (AISO 1993), III, 213–20, looks at various writings about Cervantes. J. Montero Reguera, 'Miguel de Cervantes: el Ovidio español', *ib.*, 327–34, illuminates aspects of C.'s reading and learning. K. Sliwa and D. Eisenberg, 'El licenciado Juan de Cervantes, abuelo de Miguel de Cervantes Saavedra', *Cervantes*, 17.2:106–14, provides details of family background.

DON QUIXOTE. M. Joly, *Etudes sur 'Don Quichotte'*, Paris, Publications de la Sorbonne, 1996, 366 pp., brings together previously published articles. A. Rodríguez, *La conversación en el 'Quijote': subdiálogo, memoria y asimetría*, South Carolina, Spanish Literature Publications Company, 1995, 141 pp., studies the interaction of speakers and listeners. Interpretations of *DQ* are discussed in S. P. Cravens, 'Manuel Gutiérrez Nájera, Benigno Pallol and the former's review of the latter's esoteric "Interpretación del Quijote"', *Hispanófila*, 119:23–29. E. H. Friedman, 'The fortunes of chivalry: Antonio José da Silva's *Vida do Grande D. Quixote de la Mancha e do Gordo Sancho Panza*', *Cervantes*, 17.2:80–93, looks at a dramatic adaptation. L. Garrett, 'The Jewish *Don Quixote*', *ib.*, 94–105, tells us about a 19th-c. version. R. M. Flores, '*Don Quijote de la Mancha*: perspectivismo narrativo y perspectivismo crítico', *RCEH*, 21:273–93, concentrates on the narrative mode. S. A. López Navía, 'Algunas consideraciones acerca del tratamiento de la pseudohistoricidad en el *Quijote* apócrifo', *Actas* (AISO 1993), III, 289–95, brings out Avellaneda's looser handling of fact and fiction in comparison with Cervantes. R. L. Hathaway, '"A quien se humilla ... " ¿la homilía del *Quijote*?', *Cervantes*, 17.2:59–79, helpfully analyses the theme of humility and religiosity. The feminine in *DQ* is studied in L. López Grigera, 'Las causas de las acciones en el *Quijote*: acciones femeninas', *Salinas*, 10, 1996:83–87; C. A. Nadeau, 'Recovering the Hetaire: prostitution in *Don Quijote I*', *Cervantes*, 17.2:4–24. P. Campana, '"Et per tal variar natura è bella": apuntes sobre la *variatio* en el *Quijote*', *ib.*, 17.1:109–21, details C.'s variations. J. D. Vila, '"Lo que no dijo el desterrado a Ponto". Texto y contextos de las referencias a Ovidio en el *Quijote*', *Actas* (AISO 1993), III, 531–41, adds to our knowledge of C.'s debts to Ovid. A. Rodríguez and J. F. Dykstra, 'Cervantes's parodic rendering of a traditional *topos*: *locus amoenus*', *Cervantes*, 17.2:115–21, gives reasons for C.'s treatment of a passage in Pt.I, Ch.15. F. M. Pagan, 'Geografía, ansiedad e "imitatio" en la penitencia de la Sierra Morena', *Neophilologus*, 81:551–62, discusses different perspectives. M. Alcalá Galán, 'Algunos aspectos intertextuales en *El Curioso Impertinente*',

Actas (AISO 1993), III, 9–14, identifies connections with Ariosto and Tansillo. P. J. Pardo García, '*Don Quijote, Tirant el Blanco* y la parodia realista. De nuevo sobre "el pasaje más obscuro del Quijote"', *ib.*, 377–87, provides support for the curate's comments. *Edad de Oro*, 15, M, Universidad Autónoma, 1996, 216 pp., is devoted to *DQ* and contains 11 articles of interest.

OTHER WORKS. Joseph V. Ricapito, *Cervantes's Novelas ejemplares: Between History and Creativity*, West Lafayette, Indiana, Purdue U.P., 1996, ix + 164 pp., is a stimulating exploration of the influence of C.'s life on his creative process. F. Luttikhuizen, '¿Fueron censuradas las *Novelas ejemplares*?', *Cervantes*, 17.1:165–73, looks at types of extra-official censorship. M. Aranda, '*La Ilustre Fregona*, novela de aguadores', *Actas* (AISO 1993), III, 23–27, looks at the role of the water-carriers. M. A. Bel Bravo, 'El mundo social de *Rinconete y Cortadillo*', *ib.*, 45–54, compares social and documentary aspects. B. P. E. Bentley, 'El narrador de *Rinconete y Cortadillo* y su perspectiva movediza', *ib.*, 55–65, perceptively examines narrative levels. W. H. Clamurro, 'Redención e identidad en *La fuerza de la sangre* de Cervantes', *ib.*, 121–27, raises questions of identity. E. C. Riley, 'The antecedents of the *Coloquio de los perros*', *Herrero Vol.*, 161–75, continues tracing influences. J. Rodríguez Luis, 'Autorrepresentación en Cervantes y el sentido del *Coloquio de los perros*', *Cervantes*, 17.2:25–58, looks at the narrative mode in *Coloquio*, and three aspects of *El casamiento engañoso*. P. Alcalde, 'El poder de la palabra y el dinero en *La gitanilla*', *ib.*, 122–32, emphasizes aspects which counterbalance idealistic elements. M. T. González de Garay Fernández, 'Una profecía de Cervantes en *El Persiles*', *Actas* (AISO 1993), III, 229–37, studies references to Francisco López de Zárate and Torquato Tasso. C. Brito Díaz, '"Porque lo pide así la pintura": la escritura peregrina en el lienzo del *Persiles*', *Cervantes*, 17.1:145–64, highlights the relationship of novel-writing with history and painting. G. Serés, 'La ira justa y el templado amor, fundamentos de la *virtus* en *La Galatea*', *BH*, 98, 1996:37–54, depicts C.'s humanizing treatment of pastoral. P. Ruiz Pérez, 'Contexto crítico de la poesía cervantina', *Cervantes*, 17.1:62–86, reassesses critical and interpretative perspectives. J. Ignacio Díez Fernández, 'El soneto del rufián "arrepentido" (en dos series)', *ib.*, 87–108, puts in doubt C.'s authorship of this sonnet.

LITERATURE, 1490–1700 (DRAMA)

POSTPONED

LITERATURE, 1700–1823

By Gabriel Sánchez Espinosa, *Lecturer in Hispanic Studies,
The Queen's University of Belfast*

1. Bibliography and Printing

bibliography

*Eighteenth-Century Spanish Chapbooks in The British Library. A Descriptive
Catalogue*, ed. H. G. Whitehead, London, British Library, 145 pp.,
identifies and catalogues all the 18th-c. items — some 345 in total —
that were listed in the 1994 *Short-Title Catalogue* (*YWMLS*, 58:312)
under the composite headings 'Spanish Chapbooks', 'Catalan Chapbooks' and 'Villancicos'. The cataloguing of the graphic element of
the *pliegos de cordel* is particularly useful. F. Durán López, *Catálogo
comentado de la autobiografía española (siglos XVIII y XIX)*, M, Ollero &
Ramos, 403 pp., brings together the work of 479 authors born
between 1694 and 1875. Each reference is accompanied by a critical
bibliography.

books and printing

F. Lopez, 'Libros y papeles', *BH*, 99:293–307, reflects on 'libros' and
'papeles' in the book world of 18th-c. Spain, and distinguishes them
by the presence of a binding, albeit a modest one, in the case of the
'libros'. As is well known, a large section of 18th-c. printing, the
'papeles', has escaped detailed inventory. G. Sánchez Espinosa, *La
biblioteca de José Nicolás de Azara*, M, Calcografía Nacional, 294 pp., is
a study of the library of this *ilustrado*, who was Spanish Ambassador to
Rome, based on the sale catalogue of 1806. Azara was an important
bibliophile, owning some 80 incunabula, and was the principal
sponsor of Giambattista Bodoni, the neoclassical printer and typo-
grapher. The main body of the book is taken up with the reconstruction of his library, in which 3,106 works are recorded, a collection
that allows us to evaluate more precisely the presence of books of the
European Enlightenment among the Spanish enlightened minority.

2. Thought and the Enlightenment

H. C. Jacobs, *Schönheit und Geschmack. Die Theorie der Künste in der
spanischen Literatur des 18. Jahrhunderts*, Frankfurt, Vervuert, 1996,
418 pp., chronicles the problematic relationship between Art and
Science, the intense theoretical debate around the concept of beauty,
the success of the *no sé qué* as an aesthetic concept and the evolution of

the concept of *buen gusto* throughout the 18th c. in Spain. Id., *Organisation und Institutionalisierung der Künste und Wissenschaften. Die Akademiegründungen der Spanischen Aufklärung in der Tradition der europäischen Akademiebewegung*, Frankfurt, Vervuert, 1996, 115 pp., provides an outline of the ideological and institutional principles that brought about the creation and development of the different Royal Academies of arts and sciences in 18th-c. Spain, and a synopsis of their history during the Enlightenment period, without neglecting to include the projects of I. Luzán and T. Iriarte. The Spanish situation is continually set against the context of the European academic movement during the 17th and 18th centuries. His comprehensive bibliography will be extremely useful. Sally-Ann Kitts, *The Debate on the Nature, Role and Influence of Women in Eighteenth-century Spain*, Lewiston–Queenston–Lampeter, Mellen, 1995, 319 pp., rigorously reconstructs the stages and episodes of this ideological and social debate from its literary manifestations, beginning with B.-J. Feijoo's 'Defensa de las mujeres' in 1726, which opened the positive reevaluation of the nature and social role of the women, and concluding with an examination of the return to traditional misogynism as a reaction to the French Revolution in the years leading up to the *Guerra de la Independencia*. The pages dedicated to the contradictory development of the debate in the press in the 1770s and 1780s, in the most traditional as well as in the openly pro-enlightenment press, are particularly complete and will undoubtedly stimulate debate. W. Krauss, *Aufklärung iii. Deutschland und Spanien*, Berlin, de Gruyter, 1996, 810 pp., contains chapters i-iv, of Krauss's 1973 book *Die Aufklärung in Spanien, Portugal und Lateinamerika* (313–528). *Del Barroco a la Ilustración. Actas del simposio celebrado en McGill University, Montreal, 2 y 3 de octubre de 1996*, ed. J. Pérez Magallón (Anejos de *Dieciocho*, 1), 172 pp., focuses its attention on this period of transition. The following contributions stand out: P. Álvarez de Miranda, 'Las controversias sobre los cometas de 1680 y 1682 en España' (21–52), is a study of the series of publications dealing with the subjects of astronomy and astrology which appeared in Spain at that time. Although none of these works are comparable to C. de Sigüenza y Góngora's *Libra astronómica y filósofica*, this controversy highlights another facet of *novator* thought. J. Pérez Magallón, 'El hacerse un teatro nuevo entre los siglos xvii y xviii' (131–54), examines three aspects of theatre in the transition between the 17th and 18th cs: popular taste, the dramatic theory of Bances Candamo, and the development of the *comedia de figurón*. R. P. Sebold, ' "Mena y Garcilaso, nuestros amos": Solís y Candamo, líricos neoclásicos' (154–71), examines Antonio de Solís and Francisco Antonio de Bances Candamo as neoclassical poets. He situates them in the literary context prior to Gregoria Francisca de Santa Teresa, fray Juan Interián de Ayala, Gabriel Álvarez de Toledo, and Eugenio Gerardo Lobo. Solís y Bances Candamo were published posthumously in 1692 and 1720, respectively. M. Marti, 'Emblèmes et devises des sociétés économiques d'amis du pays: analyse d'un discours d'intention', *BH*, 98:97–120, analyses the emblems and mottos of these Societies in reference to the cultural, economic and social context of the time.

3. LITERARY HISTORY

GENERAL. R.-M. Aradra, *De la retórica a la teoría de la literatura (siglos XVIII y XIX)*, Murcia U.P., 359 pp., includes a useful review of 18th-c. Spanish rhetorical works. J. Cebrián, *Nicolás Antonio y la Ilustración Española*, Kassel, Reichenberger, 268 pp., is dedicated to the study of the different literary ventures carried out in the 18th c. in Spain following the example of the Sevillan bibliographer. The first part of the book is taken up with the unfinished *Historia literaria de España* (1766–91) by the franciscans Pedro and Rafael Rodríguez Mohedano, and with the controversy that the academician Ignacio López de Ayala mantained with them. Chapter v deals with the problems surrounding the *Biblioteca Española* (1781–86) of the hebraist José Rodríguez de Castro, victim of the editorial projects of Juan de Santander, the Royal Librarian; Chapter vi examines the *Ensayo de una Biblioteca Española* by J. Sempere y Guarinos (1785–89), as a contemporary literary history. The second part of the book focuses on the *Bibliotheca de traductores* (1778) of Juan Antonio Pellicer, the editing of medieval Spanish poetry by Tomás Antonio Sánchez, and the success of the Spanish version of *Dell'origine* by the exiled Jesuit Juan Andrés, printed by A. Sancha between 1784 and 1806, and adopted for the teaching of literary history in the *Reales Estudios de San Isidro*. *Españoles en Italia e italianos en España. IV encuentro de investigadores de las universidades de Alicante y Macerata (mayo, 1995)*, ed. E. Giménez, M.-A. Lozano, and J.-A. Ríos, Alicante U.P., 1996, 179 pp., contains various articles on exiled Spanish Jesuits in Italy, most notably E. Giménez López y M. Martínez Gomis' 'El padre Isla en Italia' (13–25), which examines the exiled F. de Isla's activity as a polemicist in Italy on behalf of the expelled *Compañía de Jesús*, and contains interesting notes on the insecurity of the Spanish reformers when faced with the possibility of becoming the target of his terrifying satirical skill.

DRAMA. Carnero, *Teatro*, gathers and occasionally expands articles published during the past few years in journals and conference proceedings; particular attention is given to the change in Calderón's reception in Spain between the end of the 17th c. and the second decade of the 19th c. (highlighting especially the controversy between Juan Nicolás Bohl, on the one hand, and José Joaquín de Mora and Antonio Alcalá Galiano on the other), and the hybrid genre of the *comedia sentimental-tragedia burguesa* in relation to the dramatic productions of Zavala y Zamora. *El teatro español del siglo XVIII*, ed. J.-M. Sala Valldaura, 2 vols, Lleida U.P., 828 pp., is the proceedings of the conference held in Lérida in October 1994. The following contributions stand out: P. Deacon, 'La ironía en *El sí de las niñas*' (289–307), centres on this characteristic feature of L. Moratín's drama, with which the playwright forges a relationship between the message and the structure of the play; J. Dowling, 'Ramón de la Cruz en el teatro lírico del XVIII: el poema y la música' (309–27), examines the relationship between literary and musical elements in the theatre of R. de la Cruz, beginning with the 'drama armónico' *Quien complace a la deidad, acierta a sacrificar*, first performed in 1757 with music by Manuel Pla; R. Froldi, 'La tragedia *Polixena*, de José Marchena' (397–415), for whom the play, printed in Madrid in May 1808, appears to have been written before Marchena left for France in the spring of 1792, and is, therefore, contemporaneous with the ideas expressed by P. Estala in his *Discurso sobre la tragedia*; F. Lopez, 'La comedia suelta y compañía, "mercadería vendible" y teatro para leer' (589–604), deals with the way in which the *comedia suelta*, belonging to the varied family of the *pliegos sueltos*, is of greater economic benefit to publishers than the *partes* or collections of plays.

PERIODICAL LITERATURE. E. Larriba and G. Dufour, *El Seminario de Agricultura y Artes dirigido a los Párrocos (1797–1808)*, Valladolid, Ámbito, 291 pp., is an anthology of more than 30 articles which appeared in this periodical promoted by M. Godoy with the aim of developing Spanish agriculture, taking advantage of the mediation of the rural clergy before the farmers. Juan Antonio Melón was the principal editor of this semi-official publication until January 1806. The introduction analyses the factors that prevented this publication being widely read, when it came up against the indifference of the majority of the rural clergy.

VERSE. J. Cebrián, 'Poesía didáctica y ciencia experimental en la Ilustración española', *BH*, 98:121–35, studies the poetry written during the *Ilustración* which glorified the sciences, new discoveries and improvements; special attention is given to I. López de Ayala's poem *Termas de Archena* (1777) on the foundations and benefits of termal waters and to J. Viera y Clavijo's *Los aires fijos* (1780) on Joseph Priestley's discoveries regarding carbon dioxide, nitrogen dioxide and oxygen, and Cavendish's method of obtaining hydrogen.

J. Pérez Magallón, 'Lo actual en lo intemporal de la bucólica: Forner e Iriarte ante las églogas de 1780', *Dieciocho*, 20:7–24, studies the differing aesthetic positions in the wake of the controversy following the *Academia de la Lengua*'s decision to award its prize to J. Meléndez's eclogue 'Batilo'. Contrasting with the arcadian view of Nature in Meléndez, T. Iriarte advocated a more contemporary concept of the countryside which was closer to the ideas of the Enlightenment.

4. INDIVIDUAL AUTHORS

ANDRÉS. M. Garrido Palazón, *Historia literaria, enciclopedia y ciencia en el literato jesuita Juan Andrés*, Alicante, Instituto de Cultura Juan Gil-Albert, 384 pp.

GONZÁLEZ DEL CASTILLO. J.-M. Sala Valldaura, *Los sainetes de González del Castillo en el Cádiz de finales del siglo XVIII*, Cadiz, Fundación Municipal de Cultura, 1996, 281 pp., deems J.-I. González del Castillo's ideology to be less conservative than that of R. de la Cruz. The detailed typology of the characters, related to their models in cosmopolitan Cadiz at the end of the century, and always contrasted to those of Cruz, is particularly notable.

LOBO. J.-M. Escribano Escribano, *Biografía y obra de Eugenio Gerardo Lobo*, Toledo, Instituto Provincial de Investigaciones y Estudios Toledanos, 1996, 172 pp., offers little more than documentary evidence.

LUZAN. I. de Luzán, *La virtud coronada*, ed. M.-A. Figueras Martí, Zaragoza, Institución Fernando el Católico, 1995, 275 pp., a 1742 play (Persian in theme, influenced by Metastasio) is classified by the editor as a tragedy. The protagonist is presented to us as an exemplary prince in accordance with the ideology and policies of Enlightened Absolutism. G. Carnero, 'Las *Memorias literarias de París* y la supuesta modernidad de Ignacio de Luzán ante la ciencia y la literatura de su tiempo', Carnero, *Teatro*, 44–65, presents L. as a cultural bureaucrat who was unable to capture what was most modern in mid-18th-c. Paris, unable to conceive of any culture other than that which passed through bureaucratic channels. This bureaucratic and institutional bias is particularly evident in his complete omission of the contemporary novel.

JOVELLANOS. G.-M. de Jovellanos, *Espectáculos y diversiones públicas. Informe sobre la Ley Agraria*, ed. G. Carnero, M, Cátedra, 437 pp., is preceded by an extensive and rigorous introduction to the bibliography and work of the *ilustrado*, which as well as combining his very varied literary facets allows us to appreciate the political, ideological and literary significance of these two fundamental works of the Spanish Enlightenment.

SAMANIEGO. F.-M. Samaniego, *Fábulas*, ed. A.-I. Sotelo, M, Cátedra, 523 pp., has an introduction highlighting the historical development of the genre and the relationship between Samaniego and his models La Fontaine, Phaedrus and Gay. Unfortunately the rest of Samaniego's poetic work is not included in this edition with the *Fábulas*, and this gives the impression that his work consists of very separate unrelated units, each the product of a different poet.

VIERA Y CLAVIJO. J. de Viera y Clavijo, *Los aires fijos*, ed. J. Cebrián, Frankfurt, Lang, 235 pp., is an exemplary edition of this long didactic poem (six *cantos*), with a physico-chemical theme, composed by one of those magnificent minor figures of the Spanish Enlightenment. The poem is preceded by a scholarly and very accesible introduction which centres on Viera's European experiences (his journeys through France, Italy, and Austria between 1777 and 1781); his contact with the scientists Sigaud de Lafond and Ingenhousz) and the relationship between Science and Poetry in the context of the European and Spanish Enlightenment. Viera's poem and biography afford us an excellent opportunity of approaching Spain's contradictory relationship with Europe during the period of the Enlightenment.

VILLANUEVA. J.-L. Villanueva, *Vida literaria de Joaquín Lorenzo Villanueva*, ed. G. Ramírez Aledón, Alicante, Instituto Juan Gil-Albert, 1996, 865 pp., is a re-edition of his memoirs based on the original 1825 London edition, published during his exile in England. A biographical introduction precedes the text.

ZAVALA Y ZAMORA. C. Carnero, 'Comedia seria/comedia sentimental/tragedia doméstica: una definición (a propósito de *Las víctimas del amor* de Gaspar Zavala y Zamora)', Carnero, *Teatro*, 91–134, relates this *comedia sentimental* by Zavala to its narrative source (*Anne Bell* by Baculard d'Arnaud) and the contemporary aesthetic controversy around the *tragedia burguesa*, and analyses the motives and characters of Zavala's *teatro sentimental*.

LITERATURE, 1823–1898

POSTPONED

LITERATURE, 1898–1936

By K. M. Sibbald, *McGill University*

1. General

BIBLIOGRAPHY. Useful summations covering 1994–96 can be found in the following: M. C. Simón Palmer, 'Información bibliográfica', *RLit*, 59:221–348, see particularly references to the 20th c. (310–44) for reviews from the general press about our period and items on Antonio Machado, Ramón Gómez de la Serna, Blasco Ibáñez, and Juan Ramón Jiménez; and 'Bibliografía', *NRFH*, 44, 1996:689–705, see section 'Siglo XX' (689–705) for specific criticism on Alejandro Casona, García Lorca, Gómez de la Serna, and Miguel Hernández, and *ib.*, 45:233–301 (particularly 287–301), for material from 1994–96 on Francisco Ayala, Azorín, Juan Larrea, and Valle-Inclán, not dealt with here. A more specialized compilation comes from Alberto Sánchez Álvarez-Insúa, *Bibliografía e historia de las colecciones literarias en España (1907–1957)*, M, Libris, 1996, 165 pp., in the form of a non-canonical bibliography of collections, designed to appeal to the general reading public, of histories, eroticism, general novels, film literature, political texts, and the odd volume of poetry, all clearly important for students of reception theory but only a first step in this enormous enterprise of cataloguing all levels of literary phenomena; the information given here is uneven in both length and quality.

LITERARY AND CULTURAL HISTORY. *La Torre* (3rd ser.), 1–2, 1996, begins a new series with a double number dedicated to 'El modernismo', weighted heavily towards José Martí, Manuel Gutiérrez Najera and Puerto Rico; it is of marginal interest here. Nearer home, L. F. Cifuentes, 'Apasionadas simetrías: sobre la identidad del 98', *ALEC*, 22:103–30, is an excellent refocusing on these authors to show how each rejected the vision of Paris as the metropolis of the modern world as mediated by the anecdotes, diaries, and chronicles of Americans in Paris like Darío, Gómez Carillo, Manuel Ugarte, and Amado Nervo, in order to concentrate on Spain. In revenge, J. Fornet, 'El síndrome del 98 en la literatura cubana', *CAm*, 205, 1996:117–27, concentrates on contact with the 'other' Generation of 1898 composed of Regino Boti, José Manuel Poveda, and Agustín Acosta. Ciriaco Morón Arroyo, *El 'alma de España': Cien años de inseguridad*, Oviedo, Ediciones Nobel, 1996, 308 pp., revisits the nationalism debate as seen by Unamuno, Julián Marías, Joaquín Costa, Ortega y Gasset, and Laín Entralgo. D. Romero López, 'Fortuna de Francis Jammes en España (1899–1907). Afinidad entre el jammismo y el krausismo como sistemas afiliados', *Neophilologus*,

81:381–401, uses a critical mix of Dinoiyz Durisin's typologies, I. Even-Zohar's polysystems and Edward Said's affiliated systems to adduce parallels between Krausism's anti-hegemonic discourse, that proposed an alliance between religion and science, a return to Nature and the search for Spanish *intrahistoria* in the pursuit of moral values through aesthetic criticism, and the Protestant ethic, cult of Nature and determinism found in Jammes's poetry, and suggests this influenced Juan Ramón, Unamuno and Pérez de Ayala. Quoting from the confidential reports filed in the archives of the Ministerio del Estado, D. de Lario, 'Ambassador at large: Rafael Altamira's mission to Spanish America 1909–1910', *BHS(G)*, 74:389–408, pays timely homage to the 'pacifista humano' whose tour of Cuba, Colombia, Mexico, Peru, Argentina, and Uruguay was designed to foment 'el americanismo español' and realign cultural ties after 1898. With more on the personalities than their writings: J. G. Cobo Bonda, 'Las dos orillas de la poesía hispánica', *Thesaurus*, 47, 1992:643–52, proposes the unusual triangle of Neruda, Herrera y Reissig, and Gómez de la Serna, and wanders back and forth between continents on Alberti in the Pampas and Juan Ramón under the Caribbean sun; whilst M. A. Zapata, 'Siluetas literarias de Arturo Torres-Ríoseco', *ALEC*, 22:299–326, digs up some unedited 'instantáneas' of such figures as Xavier Villaurrutia, Anderson Imbert, Reyes, Arciniegas and Ricardo Palma, and, of interest here, quotes malicious asides about Juan Ramón, the 'hombrecito neurasténico de lengua viperina', Jorge Guillén as 'un gallito picando granos de maíz', Pedro Salinas's poem 'Far West', and José Montesinos as 'un matador intelectual, Sánchez Mejías, aún vivo'. Rafael Lapesa, **De Berceo a Jorge Guillén. Estudios literarios*, M, Gredos, 288 pp., reprints some interesting work. José Manuel Losada-Goya, Kurt Reichenberger, and Alfredo Rodríguez López-Váquez edit a mammoth reference work with full critical apparatus, *De Baudelaire a Lorca. Acercamiento a la modernidad literaria*, 3 vols, Kassel, Reichenberger, 1996, 322, 313, 314 pp. Emilio Barón Palma, *T. S. Eliot en España*, Almería U.P., 1996, 138 pp., is a short but ambitious study of translators, intertextualities, and echoes in the writings of García Lorca, Salinas, Jiménez and Dámaso Alonso, Fernando Ortiz and Jon Juaristi and the Barcelona School (following an earlier collection on *T.S. Eliot and Hispanic Modernity*, *YWMLS*, 56:382, 393). Sounding off, C. C. Soufas, Jr., 'The "Generation of 1927" and the question of modernity', *ALEC*, 22:283–97, rightly rejects Dámaso Alonso's parameters and intellectual premises of 1948 to define this group's existence, but somewhat unfairly uses Andrew Debicki (*YWMLS*, 56:385–86) as the whipping-boy to denounce narrow, insular criticism in order to demand a global approach using universal rather than elitist,

332 *Spanish Studies*

ultranationalistic models of literary history to incorporate the Spanish writers into European modernism. S. Fortuño Llorens, 'La poesía de la otra generación del 27 (Edgar Neville, Jardiel Poncela y López Rubio)', *CH*, 18, 1996:281–97, merely reprints comments on the poetry of these dramatists and the influence of Gómez de la Serna (see *YWMLS*, 57:359). Francisco Javier Díez de Revenga, *Páginas de literatura murciana contemporánea*, Murcia, Real Academia Alfonso X el Sabio, 330 pp., collects in a handy volume earlier articles around a regional theme: of interest here and not reviewed previously, 'Juan Guerrero Ruiz, *Verso y Prosa* y un texto olvidado de Dámaso Alonso' (127–34), unearths Dámaso's exaltation of the Mount of Venus published in 1927 as 'Acuario en virgo', that was prudently or prudishly not collected in the *obras* of the illustrious philologist; 'Gerardo Diego: poemas con Murcia al fondo' (141–46), gives the text of Diego's 1926 radio broadcast on the Easter processions; 'Raimundo de los Reyes y la generación del 27' (147–55), explores the relationship between the co-directors of *Página Literaria de La Verdad*, the *Supplemento Literario de La Verdad* (1923–26), and *Sudeste* (1930–31); 'Valbuena Prat y los poetas del 27 (1930)' (157–66), remarks on *La poesía contemporánea* (1930) as the work of a sympathetic contemporary; 'Dos cartas de Jardiel Poncela' (173–75), reproduces two letters dated 12 May and 15 July 1948, respectively, on the possible staging by the amateur group directed by Felipe Palacios in Murcia of *El sexo débil ha hecho gimnasia*; 'Glosando la juventud de Carmen Conde' (179–87), deals with the poet's earliest publications in *El Liberal* and *Verso y Prosa* (Murcia), *El Porvenir* (Cartagena) and *La Tarde* (Lorca) in the period 1923–29, while 'Carmen Conde y el mar' (189–97), comments on some of *Los poemas de Mar Menor* (1962); and 'Análisis de una fidelidad: Julián Andújar—Miguel Hernández' (199–206), traces the master-disciple relationship. *Spanish Studies: An Introduction*, ed. Helen Graham and Jo Labanyi, OUP, 1995, 455 pp., provides a 'new' manual for the current interest in cultural studies; relevant here are Parts I and II, 'Elites in crisis 1898–1931' (21–94) and 'The failure of democratic modernization 1931–1939' (95–166), with short essays on the themes of national identities, ideological tensions, *modernismo* and *modernisme*, the avant-garde and popular culture, and sexual politics, intellectuals and power, the political debates on monolithism versus pluralism, and the cultural politics of the Civil War, respectively. On related art forms: C. A. Hess, 'Juan Manuel Bonet and Jorge de Persia's *Manuel de Falla y Manuel Ángeles Ortiz: "El retablo de Maese Pedro", bocetas y figurines'*, *ALEC*, 22:611–18, reviews the catalogue that accompanied the 1996 exhibition in the *Residencia de Estudiantes* in Madrid and points out how, in his first

neoclassical composition, Falla found his true voice and, by eliminating overt *andalucismos* and combining music and literature from the
Golden Age with modern harmony and the popular environment of
puppet theatre, the maestro won himself the admiration of musical
Europe and his own place in the Spanish vanguard; whilst, taking
care of the seventh art form, L. S. Maier, 'First take: origins and
images in two versions of Buñuel's *Un perro andaluz*', *HisJ*, 17,
1996:385–95, recounts the 'vampiración' of Buñuel's literary work
for the film and notes parallels with mentor Gómez de la Serna and
admiration for Lautréamont and Max Ernst, and J. Jones, 'Fatal
attraction: Buñuel's romance with *Wuthering Heights*', *ALEC*,
22:149–63, comments upon the deeply flawed film of 1954, saddled
with an impossible cast and the histrionics popular at the time, but
finds surrealistic undertones and Freudian implications not in the
book. Celebrating the first centenary of the cinema in Spain, José
Antonio Pérez Bowie, **Materiales para un sueño. (En torno a la recepción
del cine en España, 1896–1936)*, Salamanca, Librería Cervantes, 1996,
covers the first appearance of the cinema as such in Madrid on
15 May 1896, the 'consagración' of the art form about 1911–13 in
the special reviews of the day, and the cinema's triumphant entry into
literature in authors like Ramón Gómez de la Serna, Luis Carranque
de Ríos, Pedro Salinas, Vicente Aleixandre, Benjamín Jarnés, and
Azorín.

2. POETRY

GENERAL

Wilcox, *Women Poets*, questions traditional androcentric reading
habits and demonstrates what gynopoetic strategies might uncover in
order to make a substantial contribution to the *corpus* of a female
literary tradition running from the middle of the 19th until the late
20th c. (from Rosalía de Castro until Amparo Amorós, Ana Rossetti,
and Blanca Andréu); thus, of interest here is Chapter 2 (87–133),
building on earlier work (*YWMLS*, 57:340), which focuses on
Ernestina Champourcín and Concha Méndez, two marginalized
women of the male-dominated Generation of 1927, and comments
on a role model particularly in the Francoist years, Carmen Conde
(137–71). M. Lentzen, 'Lyrische Kleinformen Zum Haiku und
Haiku-ähnlichen Texten in der modernen Spanischen Dichtung',
Iberoromania, 45:67–80, finds Japanese influence in the forms used in
French, English and Spanish end-of-the-century poetry, and takes a
hard look at the occidental content in an oriental mode as practised
by Antonio Machado, Juan Ramón Jiménez, Luis Cernuda and,
particularly, Jorge Guillén and Juan José Domenchina. *Calas*

(Málaga), 2, ends the anniversary year with a general *homenaje* offered
to the Generation of 1927 which runs from poetic and artistic tributes
to serious criticism and contains: G. Torres Nebrera, 'Un tríptico
teatral albertiano: Aitana, Altea y Gallarda' (112–27), dealing with
El trébol florido (1940), *El adefesio* (1944) and *La gallarda* (1944–45);
A. Marchant, 'Vicent Aleixandre. ¿Poeta surrealista?' (90–99), looks
at the received wisdom and concludes, with Dámaso Alonso, that
more important is the 'sentido poético' of Aleixandre's special brand
of surrealism in *Espadas como labios, La destrucción o el amor* and *Pasión de
la tierra*, while F. J. Diez de Revenga, 'Un poema de Vicente
Aleixandre: "La primavera y el mar"' (158–67), is a close reading of
the poem from *Sombra del paraíso*, and P. J. de la Peña, 'Una
correspondencia con Vicente Aleixandre' (183–88), comments on
letters from the period 1970–73; N. Dennis, 'José Bergamín. Primer
historiador del 27' (38–49), explicates the work of those called by
Diego 'gusanos de luz', Bergamín and José María de Cossío, the real
promoters of the writers of their generation; E. Barón, 'Reverdy en
Cernuda' (56–73), combs through the poetry and criticism to find
more connections with Baudelaire, Mallarmé, Rimbaud and Reverdy
connections (see *YWMLS*, 57:342); A. Romero Márquez, 'Cernuda:
un destino' (189–95), explores the impossibility of gybing between
realidad and *deseo* in Cernuda's work; M. D. Molina, 'El jardín
provinciano de García Lorca' (179–82), surveys all manner of literary
landscapes; K. M. Sibbald, 'Estrategias "transgresoras" o aquel
múltiple *alter ego* generacional' (50–55), takes a brief look at generational pseudonyms in general and those of Jorge Guillén *alias* Félix de
la Barca and Pedro Villa, and García Lorca as don Isidoro Capdepón
Fernández, in particular; A. M. Couland-Maganuco, 'El amor en *Aire
nuestro V: Final* de Jorge Guillén' (100–10), exalts the poetic representation of the 'amor-plenitud' relationship with Irene, while C. Meneses,
'Dos tardes con Jorge Guillén' (175–78), tells of Guillén's honeymoon
in Mallorca with Germaine; J. C. Zerón Huguet, 'Walt Whitman y
Miguel Hernández' (169–74), finds affinities between two apparently
very different poets; J. M. Díez de Guereñu, 'Larrea: oficio de
insensateces' (26–37), investigates Larrea's dedication to his *métier*;
F. Chica, 'Norma y espíritu de la poesía. Emilio Prados y Gerardo
Diego a la luz de su correspondencia' (4–25), transcribes seven of
Diego's letters (to be read together with Id., 'Cartas de Emilio Prados
a Gerardo Diego', *RO*, 187, 1996:114–40), which describe Diego's
plans to visit Mexico, comments by Carlos Blanco Aguinaga on
Prados's later poetry and Diego's own enthusiasm. Y. Pascual Solé,
'Estética impresionista en *A la pintura* de Rafael Alberti', *BHS(L)*,
74:197–214, hails the poet as knowledgeable art critic and historian
who translates into words the works of the great masters from

classicism to impressionism. J. Malpartida, 'Dossier Vicente Aleixandre. Cartas inéditas a Emilio Nivero Díaz', *CHA*, 559:7–28, reproduces letters from the 1939–60 period with news of the illness that made of his 'cuerpo-cárcel' the 'mezquina prisión' of so much of his life, interesting comments on the genesis of *Sombra de paraíso* and *Corcel*, gossip about Vicente Gaos's impecunity, the Adonais Prize and public taste in the 1950s. J. Valender, 'Dos libros de Manuel Altolaguirre: nuevos poemas de *Las islas invitadas* y *Fin de un amor*', *BHS(L)*, 74:59–72, outlines how the love theme predominates in a complex world vision arrived at after a loss of faith, the stormy relationship with his Cuban lover, María Luisa Gómez Mena, following separation from his wife, Concha Méndez, and the final realization of the definitive nature of exile. R. Alvarado Ballester, 'Carmen Conde Abellán (1907–1996)', *BRAE*, 76, 1996:21–34, remembers a woman poet of the 1927 Generation who became 'Florentina del Mar' and, later, the first woman to enter the Spanish Royal Academy in 1979. Emilio Miró introduces and Amelia de Paz edits with full critical apparatus Juan José Domenchina, *Obra poética*, 2 vols, M, Castalia-Comunidad de Madrid, 1995, 385, 452 pp., documenting in her 'Introducción' (I, 15–55) parallels with Darío, Guillén and Quevedo, an alignment with Moreno Villa, Bacarisse, Espina, León Felipe, Basterra and Villalón, the singular technique and personal style of *Margen* (1933), and the importance of the dark poetry of exile in the difficult and troubling collection *El extrañado* (1958). F. J. Díez de Revenga, 'La guerra civil y el teatro de Miguel Hernández', *BFFGL*, 19–20, 1996:215–29, explicates context and contents of the wartime *teatro breve* known as *La cola*, *El hombrecito*, *El refugiado*, *Los sentados* and *Pastor de la muerte*. H. Huergo, 'Lo sublime y la vanguardia. Forma y finalidad en *Jacinto la pelirroja*', *NRFH*, 44, 1996:489–540, usefully characterizes the modernity of José Moreno Villa's poetics. In a limited edition, A. Carreira, 'Presentación de un epistolario de amistad. Cartas entre Emilio Prados y Camilo José Cela', *Iria Flavia* (Corunna), 5, 1996:11–166, contains some 33 letters from Prados full of doubts about his self-worth and work, and 23 replies from Cela showing comfort and understanding, in a collection full of perspicacious comments on Spanish literature of the 1950s and 1960s.

INDIVIDUAL POETS

BERGAMÍN. *Anthropos*, 172, dedicates a special number to uncritical homage that includes: G. Penalva Candela, 'Autopercepción intelectual de un proceso histórico. Instantáneas del recuerdo' (6–23), a bio-bibliographical record intended to bring into the limelight a poet rarely appreciated by either the general or a specialized public; J. Esteban, 'Bergamín de viva voz' (24–27), picks through conversations held in 1981 to come up with B.'s opinions on Claudel, Max Jacob and Cervantes, the aphorism as literary form and B.'s favourites of all time, Darío, Valle-Inclán, Unamuno, and Azorín; G. Torrente Ballester (28) pinpoints B. as the prose-writer of his generation; A. Sastre, 'Un episodio en la vida de José Bergamín' (29–30), is personal testimony about the events that led to B.'s second exile in Uruguay after he signed the petition against the torture of Asturian miners in 1963; G. Penalva Candela (31–34) offers a chronology of B.'s life and work, and Id. (34–39) comes up with a bibliography of both work by and about B.; Y. Rovillère (40–42) discerns the 'música callada' in B.'s poetry; N. Dennis, 'Tiempo y muerte en la poesía de José Bergamín' (42–49), elucidates B.'s so-called *barroquisimo* in a close reading of *La claridad desierta* (1973); C. Gurméndez, 'El pensamiento cristiano de José Bergamín' (49–55), identifies B. as a true metaphysical poet and revolutionary Christian; J. Monleón, 'Bergamín: el Madrid del 37 en dos obras del exilio' (56–67), reconsiders *La hija de Dios* and *La niña guerillera*, both staged and published in exile, in the light of B.'s presidency of the *Alianza de Intelectuales Antifascistas* in 1936; J. M. Mendibourne (68–70) wanders inconclusively from the aphorism to the essay; M. Aznar Soler, 'Discurso de José Bergamín en el X Congreso Internacional de Teatro (París, junio de 1937)' (71–73), reprints the text and documents the context; J. M. Amado (73–74) extols B. as perhaps the leading literary figure of the day and prime mover in the coming together of the generation of poets who emerged in *Litoral* and reached plenitude in *Cruz y Raya*; M. Suárez, 'Morirse de veras' (74–77), quotes B. on theatre and language, Unamuno, and B.'s considered opinion of André Malraux, from a letter dated 2 December 1957; G. Heras, 'Divagaciones sobre el primer teatro de José Bergamín' (77–80), muses about what B. himself called his 'teatro para leer, teatro para la butaca de casa'; J. Sanz Barrajas, 'El gran miedo del mundo, o la cornucopia' (81–84), makes quite a tour of the ring to explain B.'s aesthetic of the *toreo*; R. M. Grillo, 'De unas cartas senequistas (1939–1949)' (84–90), documents 26 letters sent by B. to Pedro Salinas containing news of the Editorial Séneca and the review *España peregrina* (1940), comments on his eurocentrism that made difficult integration in the countries of his exile, and his loneliness after the death of his wife, Rosario, as well as details about the polemic surrounding *Laurel*, and the project with Salinas as director for a 'Diccionario general de literatura' that never reached fruition; all brought to a close by M. Arroyo-Stephen, 'Región luciente' (90–92), some personal reminiscing about B.'s love of books

and paradoxical habit of leaving behind his libraries. (See also
POETRY: GENERAL.)

CERNUDA. María Cristina C. Mabrey, *La obra poética de Luis
Cernuda: entre mito y deseo*, M, Pliegos, 1996, 190 pp., offers a non-
traditional reading of C.'s work but rather heavy-handedly examines
the process whereby C. mythologizes his poetic language to express
simultaneously the axes of *realidad* and *deseo* in his poetry. E. Barón,
'Baudelaire en Cernuda', *RLit*, 49:67–87, adduces some interesting
information about French influence in C.'s criticism and creative
work (see also *YWMLS*, 57:342). Ranging over the possibilities of
comparative criticism: S. J. Fajardo, 'Ekphrasis and ideology in
Cernuda's *Ninfa y pastor por Ticiano*', *ALEC*, 22:29–51, outlines how
C. dissents from (visual) canonical values with respect to the viewing
subject, and, by producing a deviation of readerly desire, critiques
traditional codes of control and power relationships in a close reading
from *Desolación de la quimera* (1956–62), which transforms Titian's
painting into an erotic generator of creativity; while M. F. Varela,
' "El deseo es una pregunta cuya respuesta no existe": la poesía de
Cernuda a la luz de la filosofía de Schopenhauer', *CA*, 61:33–57,
investigates the effect of C.'s readings of Nietzsche, Schopenhauer
and the pre-Socratic philosophers, particularly Heraclitus. (See also
POETRY: GENERAL.)

DIEGO. The complete works come out in timely fashion: Francisco
Javier Díez de Revenga edits with an introduction, chronology and
bibliography, the edition prepared by D. himself, *Obras completas.
Poesía*, 3 vols, M, Alfaguara, 1996, followed up nicely by his edition of
Obras completas. Prosa. Memoria de un poeta, 2 vols, M, Alfaguara, 816,
802 pp., complete with exhaustive preliminary study (1, 23–108). The
centenary celebrations get into print with the mammoth *homenaje* that
derives from the congress held in Murcia in 1996, *En círculos de lumbre.
Estudios sobre Gerardo Diego*, ed. Francisco Javier Díez de Revenga and
Mariano de Paco, Murcia, CajaMurcia, 509 pp., which contains:
J. Siles, 'Gerardo Diego, crítico literario' (13–48); J. L. Bernal,
'Gerardo Diego: aproximaciones a su teoría poética y visión del
mundo' (49–64); J. M. Díaz de Guereñu, 'Diego: una poética
necesaria' (65–83); J. M. Pozuelo, 'Las poéticas de la *Antología* de
Gerardo Diego' (85–102); G. Morelli, 'Nuevos datos y documentos
en torno a la *Antología* de Gerardo Diego' (103–19); J. Pérez Bazo,
'Tres poemas franceses de Gerardo Diego y el problema de la
traducibilidad del texto creacionista' (121–52); J. Cano Ballesta,
'Pasión y "línea pura": Gerardo Diego y el cubismo' (153–72); M. C.
Ruta, 'Las caricias de las campanas: las tentaciones musicales de
Gerardo Diego' (173–87); F. Florit Durán, 'El mester filológico de
Gerardo Diego' (189–204); F. J. Díaz de Castro, 'Las *Odas morales*

de Gerardo Diego' (205–30); D. Chicharro, 'San Juan de la Cruz en la sensibilidad de Gerardo Diego: su perspectiva crítica' (231–74); F. J. Díez de Revenga, 'Gerardo Diego y varias estrofas de Lope' (275–94); M. J. Ramos Ortega, 'Gerardo Diego y Andalucía' (295–305); G. Torres Nebrera, 'La poesía taurina de Gerardo Diego (primera aproximación)' (307–33); J. Issorel, '*La suerte o la muerte*: belleza y ambigüedad' (335–55); V. Serrano and M. de Paco, 'Gerardo Diego y el teatro' (357–82); J. M. Balcells, 'Gerardo Diego y los poetas del cincuenta' (383–98); some personal testimony from daughter Elena Diego about D.'s various homes (401–05) and the brothers Sandalio and Gerardo (405–15), Pureza Canelo and her own poetry (417–29), Jaime Campmany (431–32) on the *jinojepa*, and some shared reminiscing from Salvador Jiménez (433–37), Antonio Martínez Cerezo (439–51) and Manuel Muñoz Cortés (453–60); all rounded off by a very useful compilation by F. J. Díez de Revenga, 'Bibliografía del centenario de Gerardo Diego' (479–506), which amasses a wealth of material covering works by and about the author, as well as anthologies, *homenajes*, conferences and compact disks, that complements coverage here of 1996–97. (See also POETRY: GENERAL.)

GARCÍA LORCA. C. Brian Morris, *Son of Andalusia. The Lyrical Landscapes of Federico García Lorca*, Liverpool U.P., xiv + 480 pp., explores in great depth the fundamental influence of G.L.'s Andalusian heritage, quoting sources in folk culture, popular verse, plant lore and traditional song to reveal how G.L. transformed and/or concealed the identity of real people and real places in the major works of his poetry and drama. A. A. Anderson, 'Bibliografía lorquiano reciente', *BFFGL*, 19–20, 1996:393–403, adds an update for 1995–96 of doctoral theses, reviews and audiovisual material not usually recorded here. John London edits and introduces *The Unknown Federico García Lorca: Dialogues, Dramatic Projects, Unfinished Plays and a Filmscript*, London, Atlas Press, 1996, 128 pp., and provides a useful translation for those unable to read the originals in the *obra completa* or *teatro inconcluso* collections. B. Urrea, 'Silencio, amor y muerte: el homosexual y la mujer en la obra de García Lorca', *BHS(L)*, 74:37–58, traces the triangle through G.L.'s earliest poetry to his last theatre plays to illustrate the images of homosexuality, but in fact adds little to the ground already covered by Paul Binding or Ángel Sahuquillo (*YWMLS*, 48:387). Going off in opposite directions: S. Handley, 'García Lorca: poet of the *inmensa minoría*? or voice of the Andalusian *pueblo*?', *CH*, 18:298–312, examines how G.L. turned to traditional Andalusian sources for inspiration and finds that his apparently abstruse images are often adaptations of colloquial Andalusian speech or popular beliefs; whilst R. Salvat i Ferrer, 'Federico García Lorca y las vanguardias', *BFFGL*, 19–20,

1996:175–86, explores the ups and downs of G.L.'s friendship with Dalí but defends only Dalí's view of modernity. Now that the dust has settled after the critical flurry occasioned by the unauthorized edition of 1983, A. A. Anderson, 'New light on the textual history of García Lorca's *Sonetos del amor oscuro*', *Herrero Vol.*, 109–26, establishes a stemma to summarize the composition and publication history of the collection; whilst Id., '*Et in Arcadia ego*: thematic divergence and convergence in Lorca's "Poema del lago Edén"', *BHS(G)*, 74:409–29, reads closely to analyse the metapoem that is all about writing poetry. To be read together: M. Ucelay, 'El teatro juvenil de Federico García Lorca', *BFFGL*, 19–20, 1996:157–73, takes a hard look at the relative literary value of G.L.'s early drama and finds *Jehová*, *Sombras* and *Elenita* the pick of what are for the most part unfinished pieces of the workshop variety; whilst evincing G.L.'s interest in subversive innovation, A. M. Gómez Torres, 'Un teatro desde los márgenes: Federico García Lorca y los dramaturgos renovadores de los años 20', *Primer Acto*, 271:9–19, documents G.L.'s escape from the bourgeois straitjacket tied tight by Benavente, the Quinteros and Marquina, to the experimental revisionism that would either kill or cure the Spanish theatre of its malaise. Interest centres on the first play of the rural trilogy: Brendan Kennelly, *Blood Wedding: A New Version*, Glasgow, Bloodaxe, 1996, 80 pp.; F. Smith-Kleiner, 'The cultural process of adaptation: *Bodas de sangre*', *HisJ*, 17, 1996:285–306, presses Seymour Chatman into service to explain how Andalusian song as the carrier of *duende* functions in the process variously illustrated in drama, Gades's choreography and Saura's film; while G. Edwards, '*Bodas de sangre* in performance', *ALEC*, 22:469–91, makes good use of contemporary interviews and reviews of productions by Josefina Díaz de Artigas and Manuel Collado (1933), Lola Membrives (1933), Margarita Xirgu (1935), the first production in English staged off-Broadway in New York (1935), and, more recently, by José Luis Gómez at the Edinburgh Festival (1986), all to underscore G.L.'s ideas on set design, speech rhythm, movement on stage, lighting and musical effects. N. R. Orringer, 'Lorca's *Así que pasen cinco años*: a symbolist vision of crisis', *Bleznick Vol.*, 101–15, insists that a symbolist interpretation *via* Mallarmé clarifies G.L.'s difficult, abstract dramas. A. M. Gómez Torres, 'Historia de una recepción teatral: los estrenos de *El público* de Federico García Lorca', *RLit*, 49:505–19, merely enumerates first-night performances in London (1972), Austin, Texas (1973), Murcia (1977), Puerto Rico (1978), Lodz, Poland (1984), Geneva and Milan (1986) and, finally, Madrid (1987), with details of later versions put on in London, Paris and Lisbon (see also *YWMLS*, 52:367); but A. A. Anderson, '"Una desorientación absoluta": Juliet and the shifting sand of García

Lorca's *El público'*, *RHM*, 50:67–85, is an excellent close reading of this 'adventurous, daring, exploratory, disconcerting, edgy and forward-looking play'. P. Menarini, 'Federico García Lorca y el teatro de su época. En torno a *El sueño de la vida'*, *BFFGL*, 19–20, 1996:145–55, analyses in some detail the *Comedia sin título* (1935) as 'una tragedia política' that was, in part, G.L.'s revenge on the public that had catcalled his *El maleficio de la mariposa* some 15 years before. T. Huerta, 'Tiempo de inciativa en la *Fuenteovejuna* de García Lorca', *HisC*, 80:480–87, departs from Paul Ricoeur's premise of the passage from history past, 'suspended and interrupted', and history yet to be made or 'transposed into a responsible decision', in order to justify G.L.'s resolution to cut by about a third his acting version of Lope's play for *La Barraca* so that his audience might appreciate and share a Brechtian 'learning play' that would enhance the collective understanding of their social environment and how to change it. (See also POETRY: GENERAL.)

JIMÉNEZ. Carmen Alfonso Segura edits with critical apparatus, **De poética en verso*, Seville U.P., 1996, 147 pp.; and Christopher Maurer edits with an impeccable translation, *The Complete Perfectionist. A Poetics of Work*, NY, Doubleday, 194 pp., taken mainly from the aphorisms of *Ideolojía* (1990). In one of the examples of the intertextual games played by those whose work forms part of the already impressive *corpus* of apocryphal writing in Spanish, L. Romero Tobar, 'La superchería literaria: esquema para un tipo de literatura mimética en español', Mildonian, *Parodia*, 205–18, plays detective to suggest that José García Nieto used the pseudonym of Juana García Noreña to win the Adonais Prize of 1950 for *Dama de soledad*; the clue is J., whose 'Eco de la dama de soledad' is the intertext here in much the same manner that the 'Carta a Georgina Hübner' in *Laberinto* (1913) derived from the fun and games at J.'s expense perpetrated by José Gálvez and Carlos Rodríguez Hübner in the apocryphal correspondence written under Georgina's hand to a young and amorous Juan Ramón.

MACHADO, A. L. Caparrós Esperante, ' "Hoy es siempre todavía": la plasticidad del ayer en los pensamientos de Antonio Machado', *Peers Vol.*, 317–45, follows up images of the struggle with time through the crystallization of personal symbols to express concurrence in the poem of different moments, and quotes examples from *Campos de Castilla*, a poem dated 4 April 1913, *Nuevas canciones (1917–30)*, and the last known poem written on a stub of paper found in A.M.'s overcoat on his death. G. Ribbans, 'Machado's "Ciclo de Leonor"', *Herrero Vol.*, 76–91, looks at some 14 poems written between the autumn of 1912 and the middle of 1913, and notes how the special calibre of poetic fervour disappears as A.M. turns, with varying success, to social critique, the writing of aphorisms and proverbial poetry, metaphysical reflection and a renewed classicism. A. Herrero, 'La "sibilación escrita": anagramatismo en la poesía de A. Machado', *BH*, 98, 1996:203–19, uses Saussure on the anagrammatical poetics of antiquity to decipher the proper names inside A.M.'s verse. A. Rodríguez and J. P. Ledoux, 'La presencia ornotológica en *Campos de Castilla*', *Hispanófila*, 120:41–45, note 42 bird names, but concentrate on *águilas*, *buitres*, *cigüeñas*, and *ruiseñores*, arguing that their presence accentuates certain poetic attitudes so that pride and cruelty are softened by pacific conviviality and the poetic tradition. (See also THEATRE.)

SALINAS. J. Serrano Alonso, 'Pedro Salinas y el modernismo: dos textos críticos recuperados (1914)', *ECon*, 10:75–80, reprints two brief reviews from the *Revista de Libros. Boletín mensual de bibliografía española e hispanoamericana*, of February-March 1914, on work by Amado Nervo and E. Gómez Carillo, which show S.'s early interest in *modernismo*, a term used 'a veces como pelota de entretenimiento, a ratos como jabalina de combate' and always unsatisfactorily. In comparative vein: Carmen Pérez Romero, **Ética y estética en las obras dramáticas de Pedro Salinas y T. S. Eliot* (*AEF*, Anejos, 17), Cáceres, Universidad de Extremadura, 1995 (see also *YWMLS*, 56:395–96); and J. W. Robb, 'Amistades literarias: Alfonso Reyes y Pedro Salinas (un americano en España / un español en América)', *Bleznick Vol.*, 159–69, documents once again a literary correspondence spanning the period 1916–42 (see *YWMLS*, 55:414).

3. PROSE

José Manuel del Pino, *Montajes y fragmentos: una aproximación a la narrativa española de vanguardia*, Amsterdam-Atlanta, Rodopi, 1995, 201 pp., sets up a theoretical framework in which to study the 'novela decadente' or 'novela deshumanizada' as the 'proyecto renovador de la novela' taken on by authors like Salinas, Espina and Ayala within the cultural orbit of the *Revista de Occidente*, which is then done in detailed individual analyses of *Víspera del gozo* (1926), *Pájaro pinto* (1927) and *Cazador en el alba* (1930). Rafael Cansinos-Asséns, **El divino fracaso*, ed. Juan Manuel de Prada, M, Autores Españoles, 1996, 219 pp., dissects the problems of art and creativity in prose 'sembrada de duras piedras, en que se hiera la planta de los visitantes'. M. P. Rodríguez, 'Desviación y perversión en *El veneno del arte* de Carmen de Burgos', *Symposium*, 51:172–85, points to an unusually sharp critique of rigid social mores in the figure of Luis de Lara, the quintessential dandy and homosexual eccentric; while M. S. Fernández Utrera, *RCEH*, 21:501–21, explicates the construct of the 'new woman' in the discourse of the Spanish vanguard as exemplified in *Estación. Ida y vuelta* by Rosa Chacel. A. Llorente Hernández, 'El crítico de arte Eugenio d'Ors', *CHA*, 561:37–39, explains how d'Ors's esthetics marked both Catalan *noucentisme* and the Madrid-based Francoist *españolismo*, but concludes sadly that his only true legacy to the art world is the style of his writing. B. J. Dendle, 'Solar imagery in three novels of Concha Espina', *ALEC*, 22:199–209, neatly documents a sacred realism running through *La esfinge margata, El cáliz rojo* and *Altar mayor*. In time for the various centenary celebrations, Antonio Gallego Morell, *Sobre Ganivet, Granada U.P., 220 pp., is a collection of 22 articles on the familiar, albeit important, themes of the early biographical criticism of this precursor of the Generation of 1898. Amelina Correa Ramón, *Isaac Muñoz (1881–1925). Recuperación de un escritor finisecular*, Granada U.P., 1996, 538 pp., disentangles truth and fiction in a bio-bibliographic study of an author who modelled much of his lifestyle on Baroja's novels, a fascination for Morocco, and a penchant for decandentism, all in a lifespan stretching from 3 June 1881 to 7 March 1925, not 1885–1924 as usually reported; while the same author edits a companion volume **La serpiente de Egipto*, M-Granada, CSIC-Diputación de Granada, a MS unpublished at Muñoz's death. María Alejandra Zanette, *La pintura y la prosa de Santiago Ruisiñol: un estudio comparativo* (*Siglo diecinueve*, Anejos, 2), Valladolid, Universitas Castellae, 114 pp., analyses in some detail signs common to both media to elucidate a negative realism concentrated on decadence, solitude, marginalization, sickness, and death that after 1905 is redeemed by the cult of beauty.

INDIVIDUAL WRITERS

BAROJA. J. Ruedas de la Serna, 'Vida y verdad en *Camino de perfección* de Pío Baroja', *La Torre* (3rd ser.), 3:87–99, uses Unamuno to explicate deftly this example of the 'novela excursionista' or 'alpinismo' along the *via crucis* or *via sacra* of life; while, on quite a different tack, W. O. Deaver, Jr., 'Una deconstrucción feminista de *Camino de perfección*', *CH*, 18:267–80, uses Annette Kolodny, Elaine Showalter and Lacanian theory to good effect. (See also POETRY: GENERAL.)

ORTEGA. M. López de la Vieja, *Política y sociedad en José Ortega y Gasset. En torno a 'Vieja y nueva política'*, B, Anthropos, 222 pp., is standard fare; while more worthy of critical attention is John T. Graham, *Theory of History in Ortega y Gasset: The Dawn of Historical Reason*, Columbia, Univ. of Missouri, xiv + 384 pp.

PLA. *CHA*, 567, organizes a *homenaje* in which A. Caballé, 'I aixi estem' (7–15), highlights P.'s importance as a writer in both Catalan and Castilian; A. Espada, 'El triunfo del periodismo' (17–20), compares P.'s periodical output with that of Azorín, Wenceslao Fernández Flórez or Julio Camba; X. Pla Barbero, 'Josep Pla: biografía, autobiografía, autoficción' (21–29), makes extravagant claims of equality with Víctor Català, Joaquim Ruyra and Mercè Rodoreda in prose, and Carles Riba, Salvador Espriu, Josep Carner, and J. V. Foix in poetry; citing his productive scepticism, B. Matamoro (31–39), characterizes P. as 'Montaigne in the Ampurdán'; A. Sotelo Vázquez, 'Josep Pla y los escritores del 98' (41–51), documents P.'s personal dealings with and critical opinions of this 'naturalist' group of intellectuals, and describes how P. inherited their feel for Spain and a particular sympathy for Baroja; E. Bou, 'Pla(nes) de viaje: de la URSS a los USA' (53–60), compares visits to Russia in the 1920s and to America in 1954; while L. Busquets (61–69), reviews P.'s 1953 book of poetry *Les hores*.

SENDER. M. J. Schneider, 'Thematic representation and "skiascopic" vision in Ramón J. Sender's *El rey y la reina*', *MLN*, 112 : 166–81, reads the novel as a cautionary tale about reception and perception, a true allegory of thematic representation, and countermanding Eugenio de Nora's oft repeated early critical assessment, uses Dolezel's 'structural thematics' to good effect in order to declare *the* theme to be the conjunction of history and individual fate. Ara Torralba, Juan Carlos, and Fermín Gil Encado duly edit the proceedings from the Huesca conference of 1995 as **El lugar de Sender. Actas del I congreso sobre Ramón J. Sender*, Huesca, Institución de Estudios Altoaragoneses, 760 pp., a mammoth volume of uneven worth.

UNAMUNO. †Victor Ouimette edits a pristine volume with useful notes to the 55 articles from the many published in Buenos Aires as *De patriotismo espiritual. Artículos en 'La Nación' de Buenos Aires 1901–1914*, Salamanca U.P., 352 pp., whose range is astonishing, from Kipling and the French, to alcoholism in Bolivia, *via* Vico, Pérez de Ayala, Edison and, best of all, Jane Austen. A. Villar Ezcurra, 'Aproximación al pensamiento de Unamuno', *RyF*, 1187–88 : 227–37, says little new. D. J. Pratt, 'Las analogías interartísticas y *El Cristo de Velázquez*', *ALEC*, 22 : 15–27, presses Hans-Gorg Gadamer, Wendy Steiner and Paul Ricoeur into service to explain how analogies between poetry and painting take on the same form as U.'s *búsqueda vital* for God. N. R. Orringer, 'Philosophy and tragedy in two newly discovered *Fedras* by Unamuno', *ib.*, 549–64, digs into the archives of the *Casa-Museo* to trace the process whereby U. starts off with Euripides and slowly approaches Seneca and Racine, making a noteworthy attempt to 'Christianize' his classical intertexts by endowing his three main characters with a 'tragic sense of life' and thus subverting the classical plot. All in a distinctly comparatist vein: E. I. Fox, 'Unamuno, Ganivet y la identidad nacional', *Herrero Vol.*, 54–75, uses Benedict

Anderson and Ernest Gellner to explicate similarities between Ganivet's 'constitución ideal' and U.'s 'intrahistoria'; T. R. Franz, 'Unamuno and the Poe-Valéry legacy', *RHM*, 50:48–56, explores some interesting affinities between Auguste Dupin, M. Teste and *Cómo se hace una novela* (1925), and 'Le Cimetière marin' and *La novela de Don Sandalio, jugador de ajedrez* (1930); D. Johnston, 'Buero Vallejo y Unamuno: la maldición de Caín', pp. 85–110 of *El teatro de Buero Vallejo: homenaje del hispanismo británico e irlandés*, ed. Victor Dixon and David Johnston, Liverpool U.P., 1996, 200 pp., compares uses of the myth as a dialectical metaphor for human relationships of fraternity and rivalry in, particularly, *Abel Sánchez* and *El otro* and *El tragaluz* and *Casi un cuento de hadas*; N. Palenzuela, 'Unamuno y Borges: disfraces del tiempo', *CHA*, 565–66:79–89, builds on such shaky ground that Shakespeare seems to be the only point in common; while M. J. Valdés, 'Life as a parody of writing: Unamuno's *Amor y pedagogía* (1902) and Updike's *S.* (1988)', Mildonian, *Parodia*, 353–61, takes in both the satire of Comte's scientific sociology and Spencer's social Darwinism and the post-modern continuation in Updike's parodic use of the ancient Indian Tantric cult of ecstasy as the promise of self-knowledge through sex in the Arizona desert. *'En torno al casticismo' de Unamuno y la literatura en 1895*, ed. Ricardo de la Fuente and Serge Salaün (*Siglo diecinueve*, Anejos, 1), Valladolid, Universitas Castellae, 215 pp., contains 15 essays of which the following are relevant here: J. Amezúa Amezúa, 'En torno al casticismo de Manuel Díaz Rodríguez' (7–19), uses U.'s definition of 'casticismo' to elucidate the concept of 'alma nacional' set out in *Ídolos rotos* (1901) and *Sangre patricia* (1902); J.-F. Botrel, 'En torno al lector del primer Unamuno' (21–33), explicates how U. learnt both to movilize and to co-opt the reader; R. de la Fuente Ballesteros, *'En torno al casticismo* y el *Quijote*: un apunte' (35–45), reads Schopenhauer to understand both U. and Cervantes; G. Gullón, 'La discursividad en la obra de Unamuno' (71–78), looks at U.'s method of argumentation and establishes the Larra-Unamuno-Ortega line of Spanish progressive thought; J. M. Lasagabaster, 'El otro clasicismo de *Paz en la guerra* a *Guerra en la paz*' (79–88), makes a comparison with Arturo Campión, founder of the Asociación Euskara de Nabarra; M. A. Lozano Marco, 'La otra intrahistoria' (89–95), comments upon *España negra*, the result of the journey made in 1888 by poet Émile Verhaeren and painter Darío de Regoyos; B. Magnien, 'Unamuno y la ciudad moderna' (97–107), briefly compares differences in attitude of Baroja, Ganivet and U. towards urban modernization; L. Robles, 'Unamuno, escritos y lecturas de 1895' (117–49), catalogues periodical literature, translations and readings for the year; to be read together, A. Romero Ferrer, 'Historia y casticismo en el teatro español hacia 1895'

(151–72) and S. Salaün, 'En torno al casticismo ... escénico' (173–86), both look at the serious theatre and, in lighter vein, the *zarzuelas*, *género chico* and *juguetes cómicos* of the period; C. Serrano (187–97) finds U. 'entre Herder y Rousseau'; whilst A. Sotelo Vázquez (199–212) considers the reception of *En torno al casticismo* in Spain from the turn of the century until the First World War.

VALLE-INCLÁN. By rifling through the then contemporary press, M. d'Ors, 'Dos estancias de Valle-Inclán en Granada, y una de Antonio Machado, con noticias de dos adaptaciones perdidas ("Andrés Sarto" y "Musette")', *RHM*, 50:205–13, tracks down details of V.-I.'s adaptations of Alfred de Musset's *André del Sarto* (1831) and Guy de Maupassant's *Musette* and the *estrenos* in March 1903 and October 1906, respectively, with useful quotations from the Granadine newspapers. J. Serrano Alonso, '*La corte isabelina* (1926), primera edición de *La corte de los milagros* de Ramón del Valle-Inclán', *BH*, 98, 1996:161–73, documents the work's genesis in *La Nación* (1926) and adds some useful diagrams to date the various versions and fragments (166–73). E. Drumm, 'Valle-Inclán's *acotador*: bridging the gap between the moment of creation and the moment of production', *ALEC*, 22:449–67, argues for a connection in the *acotaciones* between the text as text to be read and the text as a theatrical representation in the *Comedias bárbaras*. D. Dougherty, 'Poética y práctica de la farsa: *La Marquesa Rosalinda*, de Valle-Inclán', *BFFGL*, 19–20, 1996:125–44, gives a succinct history of farce (125–32) and a close reading of V.-I.'s 'farsa sentimental y grotesca' of 1912 as a true dislocation of the genre; while Id., 'La ciudad moderna y los esperpentos de Valle-Inclán', *ALEC*, 22:131–47, is an excellent study of Madrid as the modern metropolis and essential *locus* of V.-I.'s avant-garde theatre. W. de Ràfols, 'Nonworded words and unmentionable *pharmaka* in O'Neill and Valle-Inclán', *CDr*, 31:193–212, discovers with panache in (Derrida's) 'Plato's pharmacy' the panacea for the irony and ambiguity that make for suspense and suspension of disclosure.

ZAMBRANO. R. Johnson, 'María Zambrano as Antigone's sister: towards an ethical aesthetics of possibility', *ALEC*, 22:181–94, focuses on Z. as Ismene in order to elucidate the power of literature as an ethical force. F. La Rubia-Prado, *HR*, 65:199–216, zeroes in on Z.'s 'retórica de la reconciliación'. At the two ends of the scale, J. I. Equizabal, 'Filosofía y carnaval: el pensamiento político de María Zambrano', *Claves de Razón Práctica* (Madrid), 69:63–68, finds in Z.'s first book, *Nuevo liberalismo* (1930), the beginnings of her tutelage and interdependence with regard to father Blas Zambrano, mentor Ortega y Gasset, and beloved poet Antonio Machado; while S. J. Summerhill, 'Toward the postmodern sublime: the late essays of

María Zambrano', *Bleznick Vol.*, 185–202, uses Lyotard to explain Z.'s singular metaphorical arabesques in *Claros del bosque* (1977) and *De la aurora* (1986).

4. THEATRE

Critical work on the drama of the period is also noted above under GARCÍA LORCA, SALINAS, UNAMUNO, and VALLE-INCLÁN. Items not recorded here on Alberti, Carlos Arniches, Casona, García Lorca, and Valle-Inclán may be found in L.M. Pottie, 'Modern drama studies: an annual bibliography', *MoD*, 40: 183–278, see particularly section E: Hispanic (226–38). Manuel Gómez García, *El teatro de autor en España (1901–2000)*, M, Asociación de Autores de Teatro, 1996, 260 pp., is a summary history and a useful compendium of socio-political and bio-bibliographic details about 20th-c. authors of the Spanish stage. María Francisca Vilches de Frutos and Dru Dougherty guest edit *Teatro, sociedad y política en la España del siglo XX* (*BFFGL*, 19–20, 1996), 251 pp., which starts with Galdós and covers the rest of the century. José Antonio Pérez Bowie, **La novela teatral*, M, CSIC, 1996, amasses a wealth of general information about such economical collections as *El teatro moderno*, *La farsa* and others of that ilk, and documents the nine years and 450 titles of *La novela teatral*, which published Galdós and Arniches together with examples of a more ephemeral repertory of *quisicosas*, *pasillos veraniegos*, *operetas bíblicas* and *juguetes cómicos tetralingües*. P. Beltrán Núñez, 'Las parodias del género chico. *La golfemia*', *ALEC*, 22: 379–404, uses Salvador María Granés's 1900 parody of Puccini's *La Bohème* (1897) as the paradigm for a theory of parody in the *género chico* taking in such authors as Enrique López Marín, Gabriel Merino, Celso Rubio, Enrique García Álvarez, and Antonio Paso, while exemplifying the theatrical transformation of the romantic myth of bohemian Paris into an ironical vision of a seamy Madrid that foreshadows Valle-Inclán's *Luces de Bohemia*. S. Salaün, 'Política y moral en el teatro comercial a principios del siglo XX', *BFFGL*, 19–20, 1996: 27–47, examines with great lucidity and in depth the double standard regulating (sex) entertainment for the enjoyment of the bourgeoisie and the control, both of appetite and political power, of the lower classes, so maintaining class hegemony until the advent of the Franco regime. J. P. Ayuso, 'El teatro de la subjetividad y la influencia del psicoanálisis freudiano', *ib.*, 69–85, outlines two basic divisions between, first, the pyschological intrigue with manifestations of a certain pathological behaviour as found in Unamuno from *La esfinge* to *El otro*, *Las adelfas* by the Machado brothers, Ignacio Sánchez Mejías's *Sinrazón* and Valentín Andrés Álvarez's *Tararí*, and, secondly, the fantasy works which explore the pysche in an oneiric construction outside the parameters of time and space found in Claudio de la Torre's *Tic-tac*, Azorín's one act plays and García Lorca's *teatro imposible*. P. Nieva de la Paz, 'Mujer, sociedad y política en el teatro de las escritoras españolas del primer tercio de siglo (1900–1936)', *ib.*, 87–105, takes on 'the woman question' to explore the debate centring on the issues of marriage and maternity, sexual freedom and divorce as summed up in the 'Angel of the Hearth' versus the 'New Woman' dichotomy illustrated in the work of a whole slew of little known women dramatists (see also *YWMLS*, 55:422); while in 'El teatro de María Teresa Borragán: una contribución al feminismo reformista de preguerra', *Estreno*, 23.2:27–29, 41, the same author zeroes in on a particular example of partisan politics, showing how the Benavente-like models *Ilusión* (1917) and *A la luz de la luna* (1918) in support of education, equal rights and economic independence for women led to the thesis play *La voz de las sombras* (1924), inspired in Ibsen's *Ghosts*, and hailed as 'sanamente doctrinal' by Manuel Machado. In two articles 'Dos estéticas en contacto: lo cinético y lo dramático', *RLit*, 59:465–81, and 'Cine y teatro: dependencias y autonomías en un debate periodístico (1925–1930)', *ALEC*, 22:493–509, T. García-Abad elucidates relations between the muse Talia and the seventh art form in excellent use of the periodical literature, first enunciating the debate between the arch-*cinematofobo*, Antonio Machado, and the devoted *cinematofilos* Manuel Machado, García Lorca, Francisco Ayala, Antonio Espina, Azorín, and Antonio Hoyos y Vinent, in order, secondly, to focus on less well-known, albeit key, players such as Alberto Insúa, *Andrenio*, Juan del Brezo, Luis Araquistáin, Melchor Fernández Almagro, José Luis Mayoral, and Emilio Carrere; while C. B. Morris, 'La ciudad babilónica en el cine y el teatro', *BFFGL*, 19–20, 1996:49–67, traces the trajectory of the urban vision from Baudelaire and Dickens through Fritz Lang (*Metropolis* [1927]) and D. W. Griffth (*Intolerance* [1915]), the silent comics Buster Keaton, Laurel and Hardy, Chaplin, and Harold Lloyd, via G. W. Pabst and Karl Grüne to *La hija del capitán* and *El hombre deshabitado*. C. García Antón, 'Max Aub. *San Juan*: génesis y sentido de un teatro épico', *RLit*, 59:521–32, analyses the play as a reworking of the historical incident of the sinking of the *Saint Louis* in 1939 and, written as Aub was transferred from one concentration camp at Vernete to another at Djelfa in Algeria, as a vivid depiction of the plight of the Jews in Nazi Europe and part of his 'crítica y denuncio' vision of art. L. T. González-del-Valle, 'Ideología política en varias obras de Jacinto Benavente', *BFFGL*, 19–20, 1996:187–212, rescues the Nobel Prize winner from the usual chilly critical reception, offering instead the image of a playwright 'relativista, quizá posmoderno' of less defined political stripe. M. T. García-Abad García, 'Crítica, teatro y sociedad: Melchor Fernández Almagro en *La Voz* (1927–1933)', *ib.*, 107–22, looks at theatre reviews written for the Madrid newspaper that voice the need for social and aesthetic responsibility in revamping the art form by working towards a National Theatre. Carmen Herrero Vecino, *La utopía y el teatro: la obra dramática de Ramón Gómez de la Serna*, SSSAS, 1995, 279 pp., includes brief semiotic analyses of 20 of G. de la S.'s 24 plays but concentrates on *La utopía* for the full treatment, all complemented by an excellent bibliography. J. A. Ríos Carratalà, *A la sombra de Lorca y Buñuel: Eduardo Ugarte*, Alicante U.P., 1995, 190 pp., highlights a career in theatre and film in collaboration with García Lorca and *La Barraca*, Luis Buñuel, and José López Rubio as co-author of the prize-winning play *De la noche a la mañana* (1928), but concludes that, working with Ricardo María Urgoiti and Buñuel at the Filmófono Studios and, later, in exile during Mexico's cinemato-graphic Golden Age, Ugarte was definitely overshadowed by the major players. A. Gómez Yebra, 'El teatro de humor como escape social: el exilio de Jardiel Poncela', *BFFGL*, 19–20, 1996:285–98, finds humour that lasts and outlasts the political prejudices of many critics in a revindication of this dramatist's subliminal vision of post-war Spain. A. Romero Ferrer, *Los hermanos Machado y el teatro (1926–1932)*, Seville, Diputación de Sevilla, 1996, 318 pp., publishes part of his doctoral thesis as a hard new look at the historico-aesthetic context of the brothers' theatrical activity; while Id., 'Los apócrifos en el teatro de Manuel y Antonio Machado', *RLit*, 59:483–504, demystifies the ideologically based silence about Antonio's authorship during the Franco years, to find that both brothers actively particip-ated in the writing of their plays that were put on by the best actors and companies of the period, well received by the most serious critics, and later were published in the leading theatre reviews. (See also VALLE-INCLÁN.)

LITERATURE, 1936 TO THE PRESENT DAY

By OMAR A. GARCÍA, *Queen Mary and Westfield College, University of London*

1. GENERAL

C. E. Nimmo, 'The poet and the thinker: María Zambrano and feminist criticism', *MLR*, 92:893–902, establishes a parallel between Z. and Hélène Cixous, with particular emphasis on Z.'s concept of *razón poética*. R. Johnson, 'María Zambrano as Antigone's sister: towards an ethical aesthetics of possibility', *ALEC*, 22:181–94, highlights Z.'s attention to ethics in her philosophical discourse as approached from a literary stance, and the relation of her essays to her views on poetry and politics; particular attention is given to *Delirio y deseo*, Z.'s novelized autobiography where she places herself in Ismene's position as spectator, revealing Z.'s social concerns where Antigone 'embodies Z.'s notion of possibility'. F. LaRubia-Prado, 'Filosofía y poesía: María Zambrano y la retórica de la reconciliación', *HR*, 65:199–216, explores the dialectical marriage of writing and thought in Z.'s synthesis of poetry and philosophy, contradicting the traditional postulates that see philosophy's view of language simply as a necessary evil.

2. POETRY

GENERAL

Some welcome attention has been given this year to experimental poetry in *Ínsula*, but to a large extent critics' attention continues to centre on *poesía de la experiencia*, and to follow the norm established by publishing houses; the *novísimos* is the other group that has deserved some attention as it relates to those groups that follow them in time. Insertion into groups and tendencies or overt rejection of them continues to dominate the poetic trends towards the end of the millennium in what Luis García Montero, 'Nueva poesía joven', *El País* (Babelia), 26 July, p. 14, points out as the need to 'buscarse un antólogo, dos o tres rasgos generacionales ... maestros a los que respetar y gente pasada de moda a la que embestir ... El poeta solitario bordea el abismo del olvido'.

Antología de la poesía española (1975–1995), ed. José Enrique Martínez, M, Castalia, 260 pp., provides yet another anthology for this period, but despite some editorial infelicities and what at times may be perceived as an odd criterion for classification (e.g. year of birth regardless of year of publication) its strength lies in including and giving much needed attention to names often left out because they do not follow the main trends (8–43); M. includes 34 poets, broadly classified as mimetic (if they follow the *poesía de la experiencia*, which continues as the main trend) or experimental. Among those listed, we find: Luis Alberto de Cuenca, Ana Rossetti, Olvido García Valdés, Jon Juaristi, Andrés Sánchez Robayna, Margarita Merino, Concha García, and others; M. includes a section on 'Documentos y juicios críticos' (209–33), and a general orientation section which covers themes, structures, and styles (235–55). Peter E. Browne, *El amor por lo (par)odiado: la poesía de Gloria Fuertes y Ángel González*, M, Pliegos, 174 pp., uses a semiotic and structuralist approach to evaluate writing as process, and establishes the aesthetic similarities between F. and G., claiming that they both use the same creative principles with reference to their use of ludic, ironic, social, and self-referential elements; he pays particular attention to semantics, polyglossia, and hypertextuality, focusing on F.'s *Obras incompletas* and G.'s *Poemas*. Andrew P. Debicki, *Historia de la poesía española del siglo XX: desde la modernidad hasta el presente*, M, Gredos, 342 pp., is the Spanish version of the well-respected 1994 *Spanish Poetry of the Twentieth Century: Modernity and Beyond* (*YWMLS*, 56:408), covering the period from 1915 to 1990; unfortunately, no credit is given to the translator. Luis Antonio de Villena, *10 menos 30: la ruptura interior en la 'poesía de la experiencia'*, V, Pre-Textos, 265 pp., has an important introduction (9–42) that examines the characteristics of Spanish poetry of the last decade. He selects for the anthology section ten poets that are meant to be younger than 30 years old; unfortunately, by the year this book appeared 60 per cent would fall out of that range. Included are: Álvaro García, Ángel Paniagua, Lorenzo Plana, Luis Muñoz, Juan Bonilla, José Luis Piquero, Alberto Tesán, José Luis Rendueles, Juan Carlos Abril, and Carlos Pardo, listed in chronological order from eldest to youngest. Each collection of poems is preceded by the poet's answer to a series of questions: '1. ¿Cómo definirías el proyecto de tu poesía ahora mismo?, 2. ¿Podrías trazar — brevemente — un esquema de la actual poesía española en castellano?, 3. ¿Crees que el poema evoluciona? ¿Que en cualquier poesía hay que ir más lejos? ¿O el poema está ya y es un logro histórico?, 4. ¿Qué poetas prefieres — íntimamente — en este momento? No importa que sean o no españoles'; V. claims that these poets are all trying to reach a deeper, more radical stance within the *poesía de la experiencia*. *Poesía y cine*, ed. Carmen Peña Ardid, coord. María Ángeles Naval (*Poesía en el Campus*, 36), Zaragoza U.P., 1996, 36 pp., records opinions on the relationship between literature and film in a century marked by its emphasis on the image. Janet Pérez, *Modern and Contemporary Spanish Women Poets* (TWAS, 858), 1996, xxxii + 198 pp., includes: ch. 6, 'Major postwar poets' (89–114), which covers the work of Concha

Zardoya, Ángela Figuera Aymerich, and Gloria Fuertes; ch. 7, 'Postwar poets in Castilian' (115–41), with the inclusion of minor poets and their bio-bibliographical details; and ch. 8, 'Postwar poets in Galician and Catalan' (142–56). Overall, and according to the usual style of the series, P. offers an introduction to the life and work of the authors selected, surveying the poetry of Spanish women from the modern period to the death of Franco, trying to offset the 'perpetuating patriarchally inscribed boundaries of generational canons, androcentric focus and the consequent silencing of women's voices'; it is a rescue effort and as such comes across in more than one chapter as a collection of names, with over 25 poets included in some 40 pages for chs 7 and 8. J. Páez Martín, 'Poesía: de la posguerra a los setenta', *Quimera*, 153–54:119–23, offers a panoramic view of poetic language in the Canary Islands, pinpointing differences between Tenerife and Grand Canary. M. Persin, 'Reading Goya's gaze with Concha Zardoya and María Victoria Atencia', *ALEC*, 22:75–90, mainly taking as its theoretical starting point Robert Scholes's *Protocols of Reading*, sets out to examine the role of the reader of Z.'s and A.'s ekphrastic poems, with particular attention to issues of referentiality and artistic gaze, focusing on Z.'s sonnets 'Doble muerte', and 'Desastres, disparates' from *Corral de vivos y muertos*, and on A.'s 'Condesa de Chinchón' and 'Duquesa de Alba' from *Compás binario*, indicating that Z. and A. 'read and write the traditionally silenced woman's voice back into dialogue with the patriarchy, as metamorphosed into Goya's art'. A. Gracia, 'Una revisión de los "novísimos"', *Ínsula*, 607:16–18, stresses Castellet's myopia when he generalized the *novísimos*, an element already pointed out by Ángel Luis Prieto de Paula in 1996. G. goes on to make brief mention of the origins, culturalist aesthetics, and decline of the movement, and of what remains of it. J. A. Sarmiento, 'Comen besugos mientras interpretan (es un decir...) 1962–1972', *ib.*, 603–04:38–40, emphasizes the importance of the Argentinian writer Julio Campal in Spanish experimental poetry of the 1960s in all its forms (concrete, visual, semiotic, spatial, and others) together with Ángel Crespo's efforts as the first to vindicate the avant-garde in Spain. S. covers the group Zag including poets such as Juan Hidalgo and José Luis Castillejo, N.O. which started in 1968 with Fernando Millán as the leading figure, and the independent group exemplified by Felipe Boso's poetics which makes an ironic use of the vows of the Opus Dei applying them to experimental poetry; he also includes a list of others who tried a new form of writing, among them the best known are perhaps Celaya and Labordeta. F. Muriel, 'La escritura poética vanguardista de los setenta', *ib.*, 40–42, examines the dissemination of experimental poetry after it reached its highest period (1967–72), indicating that while Madrid seemed to reach the end of visual poetry, experimentation spread to other parts of the country, to Palma, Valencia, Barcelona, and Santander, among others; M. pays attention to two of the main currents: poetry of action which rejected the status quo, and visual poetry which concentrated on the materiality of the signifier. G. Vega and J. M. Calleja, 'La creación visual en España. Los últimos veinticinco años', *ib.*, 42–44, deal with visual poetry and its role in a search for alternatives to the official culture. They highlight the marginality to which experimental poetry has been set: the 70s saw a decrease in the generational groupings which had characterized the experimental poets of the 1960s; the 1980s saw visual poetry flourish, and the term continued into the 1990s together with the new term of 'polipoesía', the latter with the advantage of the internet; they also document events taking place in the 1990s which are a sign that visual poetry is finding a medium for expression. J. M. Parreño, 'La poesía visual en el territorio de las artes plásticas', *ib.*, 44–46, is an excellent article that examines the possibility of seeing visual poetry as a painted poem or written art, expressing the usual error of placing such a poem within the realm of the literary, forgetting the world of art to which it also belongs; it centres the argument on painters who use the verbal element as the key to their art, among them Rogelio López Cuenca, the Sociedad de Trabajo no Alienado, Ramón Bilbao, and Elena del Rivero, and stresses the erosion of genre divisions which make it hard, if not impossible, to classify the works as art or poetry alone. F. J. Díaz de Castro, 'La poesía de los ochenta y Manuel Machado', *ib.*, 608–09:47–49, establishes similarities between M.'s break with the aesthetics of the modernists, and the *poetas de los ochenta*'s break with that of the *novísimos*; D. also highlights the paradox of having some *novísimos* playing a role in recuperating M., and the importance of Gil de Biedma as bridge between the Machado brothers and the poets of the 1980s, especially Javier Salvago.

INDIVIDUAL AUTHORS

ARZE. J. Kortazar, 'La poesía visual de Joxe Anton Arze', *Ínsula*, 603–04:46–48, explores the use of collage in A.'s 1969 revolutionary book *Isturitzetik Tolosan barru* (*Desde Isturitz dentro de Tolosa*); it underlines the element of freedom in his work, and the active role of the reader when examining the phonic and visual aspects of A.'s poetry.

ATENCIA. I. J. López, '*Marta & María* de María Victoria Atencia', *ALEC*, 22:235–51, is on A.'s 1976 collection which is portrayed as a *ménage à trois* of three tendencies: her production of the 1950s and 1960s, akin with *poesía de la experiencia*, the culturalism of the *novísimos*, and the influence of the *Cántico* group. The weakness lies in the author's attempt to make A. stand out from her contemporaries yet without delving into a serious comparative approach or pinpointing referential documentation in endnotes to support her uniqueness; it crudely groups all other poets of the 1950s and the *novísimos*.

BENEYTO. D. R. Fisher, 'Negotiated subjects: multiplicity, singularity, and identity in the poetry of María Beneyto', *Symposium*, 51 : 95–109, indicates that B.'s is a poetic voice continually negotiating between self-representation and heterogeneity where the self occupies various subject-positions; F. reanalyses the work of this Valencian poet beyond the usual classification accorded to her of 'social poet', and concentrates on issues of subjectivity and identity of the poetic voice in the collections *Eva en el tiempo* (1952) and *Criatura múltiple* (1954).

BRINES. A. López Castro, 'La escritura en tensión de Francisco Brines', *Alaluz*, 29.1 : 13–40, concentrates on analysing six poems covering B.'s production from *Las brasas* (1960) until now, indicating that his craft is one of tension kept by an equilibrium between opposite poles integrated from the particular to the universal, towards a synthesis in totalized harmony, highlighting the fusion between past and present through the memory of the poetic subject, a poetry seen as 'juego o pasión del lenguaje y del conocimiento'.

CANELO. C. Newton, 'Intertextualidad, escritura femenina y postmodernidad en la poética de Pureza Canelo', *HisJ*, 17, 1996 : 169–82, situates the theoretical discourse with reference to the topics in the title, and sets out to insert within it C.'s poetics, as presented in *Habitable* and *Tendido verso*.

CASADO. A. Méndez Rubio, 'Escritura de la materia y material de la escritura en Miguel Casado', *HisJ*, 17, 1996:211–20, is a theoretical approach to C.'s poetry, analysing praxis and poiesis, and presenting his work as abandoning all teleological predispositions.

COLINAS. J. L. Puerto, 'Hacia otra luz', *Ínsula*, 607 : 22–23, is on C.'s *Libro de la mansedumbre* which shows its debt to meditative language, especially that of Miguel de Molinos.

CUENCA. J. M. Barrajón, 'La poesía de Luis Alberto de Cuenca, diversa y semejante', *RLit*, 59 : 113–25, pays particular attention to C.'s anthology *Poesía 1970–1989*, mentioning those poems from his previous collections which do not appear here, and indicating that C.'s production in the 1970s is similar to that of the *novísimos* in terms of culturalism, but identifies *La caja de plata* (1984) as the turning point to join the dominant aesthetics of the 1980s: 'la centrada en la reelaboración de la tradición clásica'. T. J. Dadson, 'Art and the distancing of grief: Luis Alberto de Cuenca's *La caja de plata* and its

Golden-Age antecedents', *RHM*, 50:363–81, sees this collection as a unit that has its origins in Garcilaso's First and Third Eclogues.

FERNÁNDEZ. J. L. Fernández de la Torre, 'Miguel Fernández: la retórica del yo y del silencio. A propósito de *Solitudine*', *RLit*, 59:89–111, labels F. with what he calls 'poesía de pensamiento' and concentrates on poetic subjectivity and the use of language.

GIL DE BIEDMA. J. O. Jiménez, 'Borrar, borrarse: la escritura poética de Jaime Gil de Biedma', *RHM*, 49:341–50, presents the poem as synthesis of dialectical conditions between writing and erasure, concentrating on his first collection *Compañeros de viaje* (1959), indicating that it is not nothingness that concerns the poet but his awareness of time unfolding towards the end of existence, and the end of true life with the end of youth.

HIDALGO. F. Ruiz Soriano, 'No perdonar a Dios', *Quimera*, 155:24–28, pays homage 50 years after H.'s death, in a brief thematic encounter with his poetry through *Raíz*, *Los animales*, and *Los muertos*.

IGLESIAS. M. Casado, 'Nudo. Espejo', *Ínsula*, 607:23–24, is on Amalia Iglesias's *Dados y dudas*, indicating the dynamics of a collection constituted on the sway 'según una lógica de *fusión* y según una lógica de *separación* y desdoblamiento'.

JIMÉNEZ. J. J. Lanz, 'La palabra en el tiempo de Diego Jesús Jiménez', *Ínsula*, 607:12–16, sets in context the poetry of the 1960s and pays particular attention to J., winner of the Premio Nacional in 1968, yet with the triumph of the *novísimos* he experiences a long silence until his next collection in 1976, and then again until 1990; it emphasizes the role of the oneiric, magic, memory, and time in his poetry, stressing that 'la función de la poesía no es conocer la realidad, sino habitar su misterio soñándola'.

MALPARTIDA. J. Doce, 'El canto redondo de Juan Malpartida', *Ínsula*, 605:19–21, is a brief approach to *Canto rodado*, presented as the highest point in a spiral that has taken M. through Octavio Paz, and claims that 'sus poemas más afortunados son pura *jouissance*'.

MASOLIVER RÓDENAS. A. Sánchez Robayna, 'Juan Antonio Masoliver Ródenas y *En el bosque de Celia*', *Ínsula*, 606:23–24, claims that M.R.'s poetry stands against tendencies and generations, indicating that the collection mentioned in the title reads like one long poem, where Eros and time dominate the discourse.

NÚÑEZ. F. R. de la Flor, 'Aníbal Núñez: el desmontaje impío de la ficción poética', *Ínsula*, 606:7–9, claims N.'s work deconstructs all absolutes of an idealist teleology to establish itself on capturing the instant and the ephemeral. C. Nicolás, 'Poesía y recepción. El caso de Aníbal Núñez', *ib.*, 9–12, highlights the work of a poet neglected in life yet notorious after his death, blaming the manipulation of the poetry market for its 'intereses creados'; he examines the period of the *novísimos* onwards to insert the poet within the literary tradition of this period, and emphasizes N.'s readjustments throughout his poetic evolution in an effort to please the dominant aesthetics ruling literary prizes. J. F. Ruiz Casanova, 'Sintaxis tridimensional', *ib.*, 13–14, is critical of the cultural aesthetics of the *novísimos*, and exalts the figure of N., underlining the three-dimensional aspect occupied by time, place, and word in his attention to the process of writing. M. Casado, 'Sea el agua quien lo diga: (una lectura de *Alzado de la ruina*)', *ib.*, 15–18, considers the process between language and reality in Wittgenstein style, and the themes present in N.'s work.

OTERO. J. J. Lanz, 'Poesía y metapoesía en la trilogía social de Blas de Otero. Sobre la función del lenguaje en el compromiso poético', *BHS(L)*, 74:443–72, places a Derridean emphasis on writing and gives attention to the element of reception, falling into a hermeneutic circle; the author examines O.'s defiance of power and censorship through his use of language. L. M. Alonso Gutiérrez, 'La poesía de Blas de Otero: *Ancia*, poemario de la angustia', *RLit*, 59:533–76, is a detailed study of O.'s anthology of 1958. A.G. observes that the tone holds together the poems of this collection; he analyses the anguish expressed before death, the role of God, and the philosophical implications present in the book; and he devotes space to metrics, figures of speech and language in general, claiming that the variety of structures show a synthesis of the avant-garde and tradition.

PERUCHO. *Juan Perucho*, ed. José-Carlos Mainer (*Poesía en el Campus*, 38), Zaragoza U.P., 44 pp., claims that due to the poet's bilingualism (Catalan-Spanish) his poetry must be examined as original text in both languages. The critical section (5–26) includes writings that range from the eulogistic and anecdotal to those that concentrate on his poetry (12–23); one should keep in mind that the purpose of the series is to honour the writer.

RIDRUEJO. J. V. Saval, 'Espiritualidad y proyecto fascista en los "Sonetos al Escorial" de Dionisio Ridruejo', *Hispanófila*, 121:1–10, analyses the portrayal of the *Monasterio de San Lorenzo de El Escorial* as the main imperial sign of the country, which R. uses to write from a nationalist perspective in his collection *Sonetos a la piedra*, and his later shift in 'Montserrat, 1946' from *Cuaderno catalán* (1965) rejecting his previous pro-fascist claims. S. observes that while the political symbols disappear in R.'s poetic evolution, the spiritual ones remain.

RODRÍGUEZ. P. W. Silver, 'Claudio Rodríguez, poeta "muy siglo xx": Nueva lectura de sus poéticas', *RHM*, 49:446–52, offers a brief look at the relationship between experience and poetic creation, and the Heideggerian sense of 'being in the world'.

ROSSETTI. J. Kruger-Robbins, 'Poetry and film in postmodern Spain: the case of Pedro Almodóvar and Ana Rossetti', *ALEC*, 22:165–79, claims that starting with the *novísimos* there is increased affinity between film and poetry, and posits an interesting new reading of R. and A. as 'presenting the eroticized body as a coded construction of ambiguous gender' in order to 'heighten our awareness of the artificiality of the gendered and heterosexual erotic stimulus without substituting for it a new model of eroticism'; the infelicitous element is that some issues of sexuality seem based on personal assumptions rather than on existing sociological research on sexuality. R.'s *Los devaneos de Erato* and A.'s *La ley del deseo* are both presented as creators of simulations through shared erotic codes that lure readers/spectators into what they dismantle through ambiguities and 'perversions' when analysed based on displaced 'social norms'. J. Nantell, 'Writing her self: Ana Rossetti's "Anatomía del beso"', *ALEC*, 22:253–63, is on the poem from R.'s first poetry collection, and highlights acts of discovery that link R.'s poetry to that of the so-called second postwar generation; N. examines R.'s polysemy that reveals a discourse of female desire rich in gendered images and R.'s usual subversion of established symbolism, and pinpoints the essence of the female self in R.'s work and that of other contemporary women writers.

SAHAGÚN. M. D. García Selma, 'La poesía de Carlos Sahagún', *Alaluz*, 28.1–2:26–39, is a thematic study of S.'s poetry and his insertion in the so-called second postwar generation. It is divided into five parts: the first gives background information, while the others concentrate each on a poetry collection starting with his second one *Profecías del agua*.

SALAS. J. L. Rozas, '*La sed*, de Ada Salas: "Hablar como la luz"', *Ínsula*, 607:25–26, is on S.'s third collection, and its place within her creative output up to the present, indicating the continuity it offers, with echoes of the mystics and the role of the 'voz secreta'.

SIMÓN. R. M. Belda Molina, 'La poesía de César Simón: *Extravío* (1991), el poeta en su "cumbre"', *RLit*, 59:607–16, examines the meditative aspect that S.'s poetry shares with that of other poets of his generation, that of the 1950s (though his first collection is written from 1965–69 and was published at the beginning of the next decade); B.M. stresses the constant ontological preoccupation which characterizes S.'s entire production.

TRAPIELLO. *Andrés Trapiello*, ed. María-Ángeles Naval (*Poesía en el Campus*, 37), Zaragoza U.P., 48 pp., as typical of this series, includes bio-bibliographical details accompanied by an anthology, and some studies which range from the personal and anecdotal to more insightful ones. D. Romero López, 'El conflicto entre el texto y el intertexto en la poesía de Andrés Trapiello', *ALEC*, 22:265–81, analyses the echoes of European symbolism in T., following T. S. Eliot's claim that every author is to be valued in light of a literary tradition. The first part is in line with post-structuralist postulates of intertextuality, the second is mainly based on Bloom's *The Anxiety of Influence* and historical discourse as related to textual production, drawing to some extent from studies by Richard Cardwell on the political ideology of Republicanism in Spain; the third and last part is perhaps the weakest due to its generalizations and briefness for such a broad topic, where no room is left to examine in detail T.'s work in light of the arguments raised.

VALENTE. J. Mayhew, 'Valente/Tàpies: the poetics of materiality', *ALEC*, 22:91–102, presents V. working towards the materiality of art and T. towards a poetic discourse, concentrating on 'El signo' from *La memoria y los signos*, 'Albada' from *Mandorla*, 'Cuerpo volcado' from *Al dios del lugar*, and the 'Cinco fragmentos para Antoni Tàpies' from *Material memoria*; M. identifies V.'s favouring of metonymy in his craft, where the index is presented as analogous to synecdoche with alliteration as the materiality of the poem, connecting with T.'s art.

3. PROSE

POSTPONED

4. DRAMA

GENERAL

The debate this year seems to focus attention on the usual debate between the health of theatre today, and its reception. John London, *Reception and Renewal in Modern Spanish Theatre: 1939–1963* (MHRA Texts and Dissertations, 45), xiv + 273 pp, is a serious, well-researched study of the reception of foreign theatre under Franco's censorship laws, and sets the period in context, aware of the eulogistic attention received by some authors. Ch. 6 concentrates on Buero Vallejo's *Historia de una escalera*, Sastre's *Escuadra hacia la muerte*, and the theatre of the absurd; ch. 7 covers Arrabal, highlighted in the introduction as 'the only post-Civil War Spanish dramatist to have made any impact on the international scene'; the first four chapters examine four genres: escapist theatre, religious and didactic theatre, serious North-American drama, and Parisian avant-garde, in that order, mentioning Spanish equivalents where relevant. L. draws on reception theory but without unquestionably subscribing to any one methodology; the book offers an important contribution to the field. O. Cornago Bernal, 'Historia del teatro en España: la escena madrileña 1969–70', *ALEC*, 22:405–48, contributes to the important research project based at the CSIC on documentation on the history of theatre this century; C.B. concentrates on the 148 plays staged in Madrid in 1969–70, both foreign and national. V. García Ruiz, '"La guerra ha terminado", empieza el teatro. Notas sobre el teatro madrileño y su contexto en la inmediata posguerra (1.IV–31.XII.1939)', *ib.*, 511–33, concentrates on plays staged in the immediate postwar period, based on information collected from the *ABC* of 1939, overall defining it as low quality theatre; the author opts for discarding the first six months covered as transitional, and presents the autumn of 1939 as a period of stabilization for postwar theatre. M. F. Vilches de Frutos, 'La temporada teatral española 1994–1995', *ib.*, 565–609, is part of her important ongoing research on theatre documentation: of particular relevance are sections on contemporary texts staged (570–74), on alternative theatre (581–83), and on staging in the different Autonomous Communities (597–603). G. Torres-Nebrera, 'La sociedad española en los dramaturgos de la promoción realista (1949–1965)', *BFFGL*, 19–20:231–51, offers a brief coverage of several authors from Buero Vallejo's 1949 *Historia de una escalera* to 1965 works by Agustín Gómez Arcos, José Martín Recuerda, Carlos Muñiz, Lauro Olmo, Alfonso Paso, Adolfo Prego, and José María Rodríguez Méndez; the title takes into account the dates of writing the plays and not that of staging them. L. Iglesias Feijoo, 'La polémica del posibilismo teatral: supuestos y pre-supuestos', *ib.*, 255–69, acknowledges its intention of expanding on the well-known article on *posibilismo* and *imposibilismo* by Kessel Schwartz, addressing the issues surrounding the Buero-Sastre polemic; the article does not pick up momentum until the third page. P. Zatlin, 'Atacando al patriarcado: los ejemplos de Gala y Nieva', *ib.*, 301–16, claims that despite G. and N.'s obvious differences, their point of similarity rests on their attack on patriarchal society which places them alongside feminist writers; particular attention is given to N.'s *Coronada y el toro*. K. Pörtl, 'Teatro universitario de Murcia: *El Fernando*, crítica del absolutismo como mensaje para la sociedad en la dictadura de Franco (1972)', *ib.*, 317–26, is on this play of collective authorship (José Arias Velasco, Ángel García Pintado, Jerónimo López Mozo, Manuel Martínez Mediero, Luis Matilla, Manuel Pérez Casaux, Luis Riaza, and Germán Ubillos) which uses the figure of Ferdinand VII to reflect on Spain under Franco; it is a thematic approach that examines the relationship of the play with the Civil War and its importance today. A. Peláez Martín, 'Fondos documentales para el teatro de posguerra en España', *ib.*, 335–47, is a personal approach to his relation with the *Centro de Documentación Teatral*; the most important part is the information it offers on the archival material available (340–45). M. T. Halsey, 'Teatro histórico y visión dialéctica: algunas obras dramáticas en la posguerra española', *ib.*, 351–67, selects seven works by four authors: *Las meninas* and *La detonación* by Buero Vallejo; *Las arrecogías del Beaterio de Santa María Egipciaca* and *El engañao* by Martín Recuerda; *Bodas que fueron famosas del Pingajo y la Fandanga* and *Historia de unos cuantos* by Rodríguez Méndez; and *Pablo Iglesias* by Olmo; H. claims that these authors look into the past not to re-create history but to address the present and look towards the future, seeing theatre as taking part in the transformation of society, establishing a dialectic between historical past and staging present in a Hegelian/Marxist continuity from past to present where hope lies in the reception of the work, and shows that the seven plays studied follow the way opened by Buero Vallejo's *Un soñador para un pueblo* (1958). M. F. Vilches de Frutos, 'Teatro público/teatro privado: un debate abierto en el teatro español contemporáneo', *ib.*, 369–87, underlines the hegemony of state-supported theatres over private ones during the period of 1983–93, stressing 1993 as the year marking the beginning of the most important debate between public and private after the public financing model starts to change. V. points out that the problems raised now were also present in the 1920s and 30s, as documented in the local press; analyses the pros and cons as well as the middle ground of the debate with reference to state supported theatres; and ends with an optimistic call for adaptability that could turn theatre into a 'género mayoritario'. R. Mahieu, 'El teatro español: estado de la cuestión', *CH*, 559:101–05, is a commentary on the present situation faced by theatres in Spain, constantly under threat yet alive. P. L. Podol, 'The father-daughter relationship in recent Spanish plays: a manifestation of feminism', *HisJ*, 17, 1996:7–15, deals with Buero Vallejo's *Diálogo secreto* and *Música cercana*, María Manuela Reina's *La cinta dorada*, and Paloma Pedrero's *Una estrella*; P. pinpoints that B.V. presents generational changes more than gender problems, while R. presents feminist issues unlike in her other plays (as already indicated by Patricia O'Connor), and Pedrero is the one who has a clear feminist agenda. I. Amestoy Egiguren, 'La literatura dramática española en la encrucijada de la posmodernidad', *Ínsula*, 601–02:3–5, in yet another obsessive generation attempt, lists 24 writers (including himself) as belonging to the generation of 1982 (authors born in the 1940s); in general terms he highlights how theatre is perceived by that generation, using Alfonso and Fernando de Toro's views on postmodern theatre. E. Centeno, 'Una historia del teatro representado', *ib.*, 5–6, has as its *raison d'être* his recent book *La escena española actual. Crónica de una década: 1984–1994*, concentrating on what has been stated in that decade by new as well as veteran playwrights. J. F. Cimarro, 'Nuevas empresas de teatro privado en la España actual', *ib.*, 7–10, posits the need for theatre legislation that takes into account the difference of the theatre business with reference to the rest of the enterprise world, and pinpoints the work of two private companies created in the late 80s: *Focus, S.A.* in Barcelona, and *Pentación Espectáculos, S.L.* in Madrid which he manages. W. Floeck, 'Escritura dramática y posmodernidad. El teatro actual, entre neorrealismo y vanguardia', *ib.*, 12–14, makes problematic Alfonso de Toro's model of postmodernist theatre, by adjusting it to the Spanish case in the last two decades, accentuating the importance of textual theatre today, and the coexistence as well as integration of heterogeneous elements in today's theatre. 'Encuesta al mundo del teatro', *ib.*, 17–18, 23–24, asks four questions: '1. ¿Cuáles son, a su juicio, las líneas predominantes en el teatro actual?, 2. ¿Cuáles sus valores y limitaciones?, 3. ¿Quiénes sus representantes más significativos?, 4. ¿Hacia dónde va el teatro?'. Those invited to answer are: Andrés Amorós, Eugenio Arocena, Vicente Ayala, Antonio Buero Vallejo, Jordi Coca, Comediants, Josep Maria Flotats, Antonio Gala, Manuel Lourenzo, Xavier Mendiguren, José Monleón, Francisco Nieva, and Alfonso Sastre; answers range from the specific (Amorós, Monleón) to the more diplomatic ones (Buero Vallejo) to those that avoid the subject by invalidating the questions (Sastre). R. Torres, 'Encuentro con el mundo del teatro: resistencia y pasión', *ib.*, 19–22, opens a debate with the participation of actors, directors, writers, and theatre people in general, addressing the problems faced today by the dramatic arts. M. Halsey, 'Vigencia y universalidad de Antonio Buero Vallejo y su generación', *ib.*, 26–28, claims that it is their interest in the particular, framed in time and space, which makes the realist generation (with Buero Vallejo and Sastre in the lead) have a universal appeal; special attention is given to B.V.'s *La fundación*, Olmo's *La camisa*, Martín Recuerda's *Las arrecogías del Beaterio de Santa María Egipciaca*, and Rodríguez Méndez's *Bodas que fueron famosas del Pingajo y la Fandanga*. G. Heras, 'La muestra de teatro español de autores contemporáneos de Alicante: el pulso firme de nuestra dramaturgia', *ib.*, 29–30, points out that now that four generations of playwrights coexist in Spain, it is important to create a receptive medium for innovation, which he sees in the creation four years ago of the *Muestra de Alicante*, which now has 83 stagings to its credit under his direction; he reiterates what by now is a familiar topic: the existence of playwrights, but the lack of support. I. Pascual, 'Teatro alternativo: un intento de panorámica', *ib.*, 32–33, posits that the conditions under which alternative theatre has developed has shaped the plays themselves, making them more intimate, in a desire for direct communication; one of the problems accentuated is what the author calls 'the Peter Pan syndrome' of a group always expecting to reach full maturity. E. Pérez-Rasilla, 'La escritura teatral, hoy', *ib.*, 33–36, registers that the dramatic text is now back after a period that gave emphasis to collective works and to the role of the director; P.-R. portrays contemporary writing in an equilibrium between tradition and innovation, citing Barcelona as a case apart, and pays particular attention to the independent groups, first concentrating on those born in the 1940s such as José Sanchis Sinisterra, José Luis Alonso de Santos, Ignacio Amestoy, Fermín Cabal, and Rodolf Sirera, among others; he highlights the generational disenchantment, and their emphasis on revitalizing old structures, their use of metatheatre and intertextuality, and their compromise with contemporary society. P.-R. also covers Madrid's 'segunda promoción' which includes Ernesto Caballero, Ignacio Moral and Paloma Pedrero, claiming they follow Alonso de Santos and Cabal; he moves on to the counterpart second group in Barcelona which follows Sanchis Sinisterra, and which includes Joan Casas, Josep Pere Peyró, Lluisa Cunillé, and Sergi Belbel; and he finally moves on to cover younger writers and the most recent tendencies, as well as including a list of established novelists who have made incursions into the theatre. P. Zatlin, 'El teatro español contemporáneo en los escenarios norteamericanos', *ib.*, 39–40, informs us of the lack of success of the Spanish plays in Broadway for this second half of the century, but pinpoints the efforts that have been successful and the present state of affairs; Z. also alludes to a somewhat misleading interview with Tessa Schneideman, the director who staged Buero Vallejo's *The Sleep of Reason* in London at the Battersea Arts Centre in 1991, who made the impressionistic affirmation that the spectators (*por lo general*) knew nothing of Goya, leading Z. to draw the conclusion that being able to do something similar in the United States would be virtually impossible.

INDIVIDUAL AUTHORS

ARRABAL. A. Berenguer, 'Arrabal en el teatro occidental', *BFFGL*, 19–20:327–34, is historical in approach, placing the author within the wider context of the avant-garde movement and its repercussions on later theatre.

AUB. C. García Antón, 'Max Aub. *San Juan*: Génesis y sentido de un teatro épico', *RLit*, 59:521–32, frames this play within the scope of testimonial theatre dated in time and space, and observes a parallel with some characteristics of Brecht's epic theatre; the article mainly centres on the plot of *San Juan* (1942).

BUERO VALLEJO.   M. Halsey, 'Music as sign and symbol: Buero's *Lázaro en el laberinto* and *Música cercana*', *Hispanófila*, 120:47–55, concentrates on the relevance of music to the plot of these two relatively recent plays of the late 80s, where music is seen as a sign of salvation and hope, and a spatial connector of the inner self, indicating that when the protagonists of the respective plays fail to hear the melody, freedom and happiness are threatened. S. Sanz Villanueva, 'En el 80 aniversario de Buero Vallejo: la soledad del corredor de fondo', *Ínsula*, 605:8, presents the author as an 'incomprendido hoy en día'; it is really a brief impressionistic eulogy commenting on how B.V. transcends the present day.

FALCÓN.   J. P. Gabriele, 'Toward a radical feminist stage rhetoric in the short plays of Lidia Falcón', *Symposium*, 51:3–19, is on F.'s feminist commitment that 'views dramatic art as a communicative process that carries both a personal and a political message'; G. focuses on *¡No moleste, calle y pague, Señora!*, *Tu único amor*, and *¡Parid, parid, malditas!*.

JARDIEL PONCELA.   A. Gómez Yebra, 'El teatro de humor como escape social: el éxito de Jardiel Poncela', *BFFGL*, 19–20:285–98, is in defence of J.P.'s role during the postwar years, offering a vindication and a new reading other than the one given at face value to his postwar production; it focuses on *Eloísa está debajo de un almendro*.

RUIBAL.   J. Hoeg, 'El nuevo teatro español a través de *Los ojos* de José Ruibal', *ALEC*, 22:535–47, examines the manipulation of language as one of many theatrical elements, and the issue of totality in this play as a recontextualization that combines all possible systems of communication; H. offers an analysis of *Los ojos* in the light of R.'s own theories on theatre and the development towards irrationality that characterized the *Nuevo Teatro* vs the *realistas*.

SASTRE.   *Alfonso Sastre o la ilusión trágica*, ed. Eva Forest, Hondarribia, Argitalatxe HIRU, 207 pp., is a homage volume edited by his wife, containing an autobiographical section covering his life and works (17–52); a collection of personal photographs (54–118); Mariano de Paso's 'El teatro de Alfonso Sastre' which first appeared in 1995 (119–38); interviews with S. (139–70); César de Vicente Hernando's 'Las otras escrituras de Alfonso Sastre (Un enfoque histórico)' (171–88); and a selected bibliography (191–207). Overall it is revealing with reference to S.'s opinions on his theatre and on contemporary theatre in general. M. de Paco, 'El teatro de Alfonso Sastre en la sociedad española', *BFFGL*, 19–20:271–83, is on S.'s intention to transform society through theatre from his creation of *Arte Nuevo* in 1945 to his work in the 90s after his unkept promise not to write another play after *¿Dónde estás, Ulalume, dónde estás?* (1990).

V. CATALAN STUDIES

LANGUAGE

By PEP SERRA, *Universitat de Girona*, SÍLVIA LLACH, *Universitat de Girona*, and BERNAT JOAN I MARÍ, *Universitat de les Illes Balears*

1. PHONETICS AND PHONOLOGY

D. Recasens, M. D. Pallarès, and J. Fontdevila, 'A model of lingual coarticulation based on articulatory constraints', *JASA*, 102:544–61, analyse the magnitude and temporal extent of consonantal and vocalic coarticulation in VCV sequences in Catalan. Different degrees of articulatory constraint (based on articulatory knowledge) are assigned to consonants and vowels; the vowel-dependent anticipation of tongue body is linked to the mechanico-inertial constraints associated with the tongue during the production of consonants. D. Recasens and J. Romero, 'An EMMA study of segmental complexity in alveolopalatal and palatalized alveolars', *Phonetica*, 54:43–58, report on an electromagnetic midsagittal articulometry study of the palatal nasal stop [ɲ]. Catalan and Russian data are studied and compared, showing that this phoneme can be considered as a single segment. P. Harrison, 'The relative complexity of Catalan vowels and their perceptual correlates', *Working Papers in Linguistics*, Department of Phonetics and Linguistics, University College London, 9:385–402, analyses the Catalan mid front vowels, as well as the procedures that identify the formant values for these vowels in vocalic space, to test claims made by perceptual studies and studies of acquisition about the greater complexity of [e] relative to [ɛ]. E. Bonet and J. Mascaró, 'On the representation of contrasting rhotics', Martínez-Gil, *Issues*, 103–26, approach the problems posed by rhotics at a descriptive level; their proposal makes extensive use of syllabic information by assigning the flap and the trill to different points in the sonority scale and by claiming that in all cases but one the feature that distinguishes flaps and trills receives one value or the other depending on which one satisfies best the principle of the 'Sonority Cycle'. M. R. Lloret, 'Consonant dissimilation in the Iberian Languages', *ib.*, 127–50, shows that sonorant dissimilation is not as marginal as it may appear since it is frequently found in the history of the Iberian languages, among others, and still synchronically occurs in many substandard (colloquial and dialectal) forms. Lloret argues that sonorant dissimilation shows enough subregularity to be taken into account if we are to capture the inherent similarities of sounds. B. Palmada, 'Continuant spreading and feature organization', *ib.*,

151–72, presents a detailed study on spirantization processes and concludes that the existence of well-attested phonological processes applied after spirantization leads us to the conclusion that spirantization itself has to be described as a phonological operation. T. Cabré Monné, 'Sobre processos fonològics i normes gràfiques: a propòsit de l'epèntesi vocàlica en català', *RCat*, 115:11–34, describes Catalan vocalic epenthesis and the justification of different normative regulations that maintain these vowels in word composition strategies.

P. Prieto, 'Prosodic manifestation of syntactic structure in Catalan', Martínez-Gil, *Issues*, 173–94, investigates how Catalan speakers disambiguate structurally ambiguous sentences and whether listeners are able to recognize their corresponding meaning; she also explores Bonet's hypothesis about the relationship between F_0 scaling and constituent boundaries in Catalan, and, more generally, the influence of syntactic/prosodic structure on pitch downtrend patterns. P. Serra, 'Prosodic structure and stress in Catalan', *ib.*,195–231, presents a system of word-stress assignment in Catalan. The incorporation of the basic elements of the 'Simplified Bracket Grids' theory and 'Optimality Theory' allows a homogeneous formulation of unmarked characteristics and special lexical cases.

2. LEXIS AND MORPHOLOGY

I. Creus, 'Aspectes metodològics del treball empíric en morfologia verbal', *Sintagma*, Universitat de Lleida, 9:75–89, aims to clarify the concept of verb as a research topic, demonstrates the advantages and disadvantages of some techniques used in studies of verb morphology, and suggests strategies for a pragmatic approach to the verbal component. G. Vázquez, 'El clític *es* i la construcció anticausativa', *ib.*, 61–73, defends the responsibility of the lexical component for the presence (or absence) of the pronoun in anticausative constructions, showing that syntax, morphology and semantics (event structure) are unable to explain the behaviour of all verbs concerning this structure. R. Saurí, *Tractament lexicogràfic dels adjectius: aspectes a considerar* (Papers de l'IULA, Sèrie Monografies, 2), B, IULA, analyses the information that normally appears in dictionary entries, and presents a proposal to describe the real uses of adjectives in dictionaries, focusing on syntax and semantics. T. Badia and C. Colominas, *The Predicate-Argument Structure* (Papers de l'IULA, Sèrie Monografies, 4), B, IULA, present a proposal for the representation of the Predicate-Argument Structure in typed feature-structure formalisms, giving a thorough exemplification of these structures for all major categories and of some modification relations. *Documents normatius 1962–1996: amb les novetats del diccionari*, ed. J. Rafel (Biblioteca Filològica, 32), B, IEC, contains the normative papers of this institution from the period in question, and introduces new criteria for the current normative dictionary of Catalan. M. T. Cabré et al., *Cicle de conferències 95–96: lèxic, corpus i diccionaris*, B, IULA, contains a selection of papers giving different perspectives on lexical entries and the elaboration of extensive corpora. C. Bach et al., *El corpus de l'Iula: descripció* (Papers de l'IULA, Sèrie Informes, 17), B, IULA, explain the criteria used in the construction of the plurilingual Iula corpus, its evolution, and the different thematic areas involved. J. Morel et al., *El corpus de l'Iula: etiquetaris* (Papers de l'IULA, Sèrie Informes, 18), B, IULA, explain the criteria used in the construction of the mark-up of the IULA corpus, and describes proposals for Catalan and Spanish. *Neologismes documentals a la premsa en català* (Observatori de Neologia, Papers de l'IULA, Sèrie Informes), B, IULA, includes the neologisms which appeared in the media during the period 1989–95, focusing on their use.

3. Syntax, Semantics, and Pragmatics

O. Bladas, 'Expressions lexicalitzades: anàlisi i comparació', *EMarg*, 59:23–44, compares two types of lexicalized sentences in Catalan. Dictionaries present these two types under the same format, but there are many obvious differences, one of which is the flexive verbal marks concerning one of the types. A. Arnal, 'Sobre el significat d'algunes construccions amb *hi* locatiu duplicat', *ib.*, 58:108–16, focuses on the determinate syntactic uses of the pronoun *hi*, which sometimes appears reduplicated in the sentence. A. shows that there are syntactic requirements at the levels of verb structure and discourse; in both cases, the pronoun must reduplicate because it has became an obligatory argument, not only a complement. A. Bel, 'Variació paramètrica i adquisició del català', *LlLi*, 8:249–68, uses an extensive corpus of data to demonstrate a new model of parameter setting, arguing that parameters do not follow the Instantaneous Acquisition model, but that acquisition is gradual and conditioned by parameters previously acquired. M. Capdevila and M. Llinàs, 'La pobresa gramatical del primer estadi de l'adquisició lingüística: raons i evidència', *ib.*, 269–87, support the Maturation Hypothesis of language acquisition, describing the first manifestations of speech in the Catalan child, where they detect the absence of functional categories. Following Rizzi's Continuist Hypothesis of language acquisition, A. Gavarró, 'La truncació de les categories funcionals en l'adquisició del català', *ib.*, 289–308, adduces bilingual data to demonstrate Truncation Theory, and J. Rosselló, 'Arguments nuls i perifèria de la frase a les gramàtiques infantils i adultes', *ib.*, 309-41, cites examples of Majorcan grammar.

4. SOCIOLINGUISTICS

SOCIOLINGUISTIC HISTORY. Pere Anguera, *El català al segle XIX. De la llengua del poble a llengua nacional*, B, Empúries, 296 pp., studies the transition from the subordinate and minority status of Catalan to its conception (and revindication) as the national language of Catalonia, and gives a fine picture of the Catalonian Renaissance. Miquel Almirall, *Milà i Fontanals*, B, La Busca, 77 pp., the first in a new collection on sociolinguistics, uses extracts from the works of M.F. to show changing views on the status of Catalan.

SLANG. Joan Pujolar, *De què vas, tio?*, B, Empúries, 320 pp., on youth slang, analyses the ideas about language use of young people in Barcelona, and their awareness of language use.

SOCIOLINGUISTICS AND EDUCATION. *Immersió lingüística, rendiment acadèmic i classe social*, comp. Josep Maria Serra, B, 156 pp., has several articles proving the relation between social class and academic progress in the context of the use of Catalan in education in towns where most of the population is Spanish-speaking. The experience of language immersion in Catalonia follows the example of Quebec, where the use of French is usual for English-speaking students; there is a close relation between Catalan and Quebequois Education departments in order to improve Catalan and French language in their respective areas.

LANGUAGE PLANNING. Bernat Joan, *Balears, Zona d'Urgent Intervenció Lingüística*, Eivissa, Res Publica, 97 pp., shows the precarious state of the use of Catalan in different areas in the Balearic Islands. In spite of the fact that there is a Language Normalization Law to regulate the official status of Catalan and Spanish within the Balearics, Catalan is placed in a subordinate position. In some areas, like law, the security forces or business, Catalan is relegated in the face of Spanish dominance. In education, the position of Catalan language is somewhat better; this is also true for local media, but not for Spanish media. *Política i planificació lingüístiques*, ed. Toni Mollà, Alzira, Bromera, 257 pp., brings together papers giving a broad view of politics and language planning in the Catalan regions: Toni Mollà on politics and language planning; Josep Lacreu on standard Catalan and its problems and perspectives; Rafael L. Ninyoles on the future of language use; Maria Pilar Garcia on the concepts of monolingualism and plurilingualism in Spain; Josep M. Puig on the official status of Catalan and Spanish as a legal issue; Emili Boix on language ideology in young generations; and Rafael Xambot on ideologies in the mass media in Valencia.

LANGUAGE USE. Joan Melià, *La llengua dels joves*, Palma, Majorca, Balearic Islands U.P., 248 pp., is the result of Melià's investigations of upon language knowledge and language use within young people in Majorca. M. analyses language uses, ideas about language, and positions in relation with language conflict in this population group. Antoni Babia, *La franja de la Franja*, B, Empúries, 387 pp, analyses the language uses and language characteristics of the Benasc Valley, in *La Franja* (a fringe of Catalan-speaking territory in the autonomous region of Aragon). Benasques (the dialect spoken in Benasc Valley) is a variety transitional between Catalan and Aragonese. The second part of the book offers us a description of Benasques. J. Solé i Camardons and J. M. Romaní, 'Els usos lingüístics en l'activitat comercial', *Llengua i ús:*58–61, conclude that most of the population (84.8%) think that the seller has to use the language of the buyer (Catalan or Spanish) and, therefore has to know these two official languages. Most of the population can read a commercial letter written in Catalan (74%) and half of the population (50.6%) have the opinion that products, medicines etc., have to show their instructions and trademarks in Catalan.

Noves SL publishes a special tenth anniversary issue, with a summary of all its papers and book reviews.

STANDARDIZATION. Gabriel Bibiloni, *Llengua estàndard i variació lingüística*, V, Tres i Quatre, 149 pp., analyses the functions of a standard language (understood as the means of intercommunication within a community, i.e. a national language), the processes of standardization (in general) and the nature of language variation (geographical, social, and stylistic). B. comments on the process of standardization of Catalan (from Pompeu Fabra's codification to the present), in terms of intralinguistic matters — standard pronunciation, verbal morphology, or interference — and social problems like functional ones or language secession in some parts of the Catalan area.

MEDIEVAL LITERATURE

By LOLA BADIA, *Professor of Catalan Literature at the Universitat de Girona*

1. GENERAL

BIBLIOGRAPHY AND COMPUTERIZED MATERIALS. *BAHLM*, 10:1–53, includes information on Catalan for the year 1996. *Qüern. Repertori bibliogràfic biennal de la literatura i llengua catalanes de l'Edat Mitjana i de l'Edat Moderna*, vol. 2, Girona U.P., 150 pp. R. Beltran and J. Izquierdo, compile a *Butlletí 'Tirant'*, for *LEMIR* (also published electronically, http://www.uv.es/lemir/). (See also AUSIÀS MARCH and VICENT FERRER AND OTHER RELIGIOUS WRITERS.) *Els cançoners catalans. Concordances*, B, UAB Seminari de Filologia i Informàtica, inaugurates the *Arxiu informatitzat de textos catalans antics*, with four of the ten scheduled volumes: *Cançoner L (B, Biblioteca de Catalunya, ms. 9)* ed. J. Torruella (AITCA, 3); *Espill de Jaume Roig. Vatican City, Bibliotheca Apostolica, ms. lat. 4806*, ed. A. Carré (AITCA, 5); *Cançoner del Marquès de Barberà (Montserrat, Biblioteca del Monestir, ms. 992)*, ed. S. Martí (AITCA, 9); *Cançoneret de Ripoll (B, Arxiu de la Corona d'Aragó, ms. Ripoll 129)*, ed. L. Badia (AITCA, 10).

COLLECTED ESSAYS OF A SINGLE AUTHOR. E. Colomer compiles all his writings on Catalan medieval thought, *El pensament als països catalans durant l'Edat Mitjana i el Renaixement*, Barcelona, PAM–IEC, 288 pp. S. Galmés, *Lul·lisme*, B, PAM, 244 pp., is exclusively on Llull. Two linguists gather their articles, some with medieval concern: G. Colón, *Estudis de filologia catalana i romànica*, V, IIFV—B, PAM, 508 pp., and J. Veny, *Onomàstica i dialectologia*, B, PAM, 1996, 232 pp.

2. LYRIC AND NARRATIVE VERSE

AUSIÀS MARCH

The sixth centenary of March's birth (1397) has produced a large amount of printed matter. First of all, a comprehensive edition by R. Archer, *Obra completa*, 2 vols., B, Barcanova, 715, 630 pp., with a full commentary of the poems and a new critical apparatus. X. Dilla publishes a didactic tool: *Guia de lectura d'Ausiàs March*, B, Empúries, 216 pp., and J. L. Martos, an approach from literary criticism: *Cant, queixa i patiment. Estudi macroestructural de 55 poemes d'Ausiàs March*, Alicante U.P., 182 pp. J. Chiner Gimeno, *Ausiàs March i la València del segle XV (1400–1459)*, V, Generalitat Valenciana, 607 pp., is a rich collection of documents on the March family and on the biography of the poet. C. proposes a new date of birth (1400) and gives fresh information about M.'s public and private life. *Afers*, 26, gathers some contributions to the March colloquium, held at the Universitat of Girona in July 1996: R. Archer, 'Ausiàs March i la invenció' (69–86); X. Dilla, 'Temporalitat i formes cançoneresques en la poesia d'Ausiàs March' (47–67); A. Terry, 'Introspecció i imaginació dins l'obra d'Ausiàs March' (87–102), and M.-C. Zimmermann, 'Ausiàs March. Construcció de la veu poemàtica i recerca de sentit' (33–46); there is also a bibliographical contribution, 'La recepció d'Ausiàs Marc. Assaig d'actualització bibliogràfica d'ençà de 1985' (117–43). Most of the papers from the March symposion in Valencia (October 1996) can be found in *Ausiàs March: Textos i Contextos*, ed. R. Alemany, Alicante U.P. — B, PAM, 407 pp., including: R. Archer, 'Ausiàs March i les dones' (13–30); L. Badia, 'Ausiàs March i l'enciclopèdia natural: dades científiques per a un discurs moral' (31–58); L. Cabré, 'Dos lectors antics del mestre Ausiàs i un context' (59–73); G. Colón, 'Ausiàs March interpretat al segle XVI per Juan de Resa i Jorge de Montemayor' (89–116); A. Hauf, 'L'apocalipsi marquià. Ausiàs March, místic i profeta de l'amor humà' (191–220); C. Miralles, 'Sobre les comparacions marines en la poesia d'Ausiàs March' (281–96); J. Pujol, 'Amor i desmemòria. Notes per a la interpretació del poema X d'Ausiàs March' (297–320); P. Ramírez, 'Ausiàs March: el saber del sentiment' (321–42); A. Terry, 'Ausiàs March i la imaginació medieval' (343–54); M. C. Zimmermann, 'El poema LXXXI d'Ausiàs March: d'un tòpic revisitat a un metallenguatge' (355–64), and R. Alemany and V. Martines, 'Bibliografia d'Ausiàs March' (365–408). *Deyermond Vol.* contains: L. Cabré, 'From Ausiàs March to Petrarch: Torroella, Urrea, and other *Ausiasmarchides*' (57–74), and A. Terry, '*Per la mort és uberta carrera*: a reading of Ausiàs March, poem 92' (469–80). See also C. Clausell, '*Donchs, mal deçà e dellà mal sens terme*: petjades anselmianes en el *Cant espiritual*, d'Ausiàs March', *ELLC*, 34:47–50; C. Di Girolamo, 'Medievalisme i modernitat d'Ausiàs Marc', *EMarg*, 57, 1996[1997]:5–13, and, by the same author, 'Tradurre Ausiàs Marc', *LlLi*, 8:369–400; V. Fàbrega Escatllar, '*Oh tu, mal fat!* (110,9). La problemàtica del fat en la poesia d'Ausiàs March', *RevAl*, 7, 1996:251–67, and R. Pinto, 'Fuentes médicas de Ausiàs March: una imagen de licantropia', Fragonard, *Transfert*, 87–94.

OTHER POETS

M. de Riquer, *Antologia de poetes catalans. Un milleni de literatura. I. Època medieval*, B, Cercle de Lectors, 484 pp., is a selection of the best poems of all the writers producing poetry in Catalonia during the Middle Ages (in Latin, Hebrew, Occitan, Catalan, Castilian or Italian). Two primary contributions on a secondary genre are R. Archer, 'Tres *maldits* inéditos contra hombres', *RFR*, 13, 1996:107–22, and I. de Riquer, '*Lo canviador* de Jordi de Sant Jordi: maldit', *BRABLB*, 45, 1995–96[1997]:239–58, who also studies the Catalan troubadour tradition in 'Presencia trovadoresca en la Corona de Aragón', *AEM*, 26, 1996:933–66, and edits new materials in *Poemes catalans sobre la caiguda de Constantinoble*, Vic, Eumo — B, Barcelona U.P., 86 pp.

NARRATIVE VERSE

Francesc de la Via, *Obres*, ed. A. Pacheco, B, Quaderns Crema, 415 pp., is a new edition of all the narrative verse of the 15th-c. author from Girona. *Blandín de Cornualla*, ed. M. Guisado and S. Cingolani, B, La Magrana, 217 pp., is a popular edition. On Jaume Roig, X. Vellón Lahoz, 'Literatura misògina i moral burgesa: la corporalitat com a espai de la sàtira a l'*Espill*', *ZK*, 9, 1996:20–32, and Michael Solomon, *The Literature of Misogyny in Medieval Spain: the Arcipreste de Talavera and the Spill*, NY–Cambridge, CUP, vii + 221 pp., the last from a medical point of view.

3.   DOCTRINAL AND RELIGIOUS PROSE

RAMON LLULL AND LULLISM

La versione occitanica della 'Doctrina pueril' di Ramon Llull, ed. M. C. Marinoni, Milan, Edizioni Universitarie di Lettere, Economia e Diritto, 329 pp., is a critical edition. J. E. Rubio *Les bases del pensament de Ramon Llull*, V–B, IIFV–PAM, 221 pp. is a study on the *Llibre de contemplació*. *SLu*, 35, 1995[1997], contains: A. Bonner, 'Correccions i problemes cronològics' (85–95), and F. Domínguez Reboiras, 'Geometría, filosofía, teología y Arte' (3–29). *Actes del Simposi Internacional de Filosofia de l'Edat Mitjana (1993)*, ed. P. Llorente, A. Boadas, F. J. Fortuny, A. Grau, and I. Roviró, Vic, Patronat d'Estudis Ausonencs, 1996, 678 pp, contains: E. Colomer, 'El problema de la relació fe-raó en Ramon Llull: proposta de solució' (11–20); A. Maduell, 'Assaig de síntesi de metafísica lul·liana' (312–18); I. Roviró Alemany, 'De la bellesa sensible a la font de la bellesa: la bellesa en Ramon Llull' (389–95); S. Trias Mercant, 'La relación natural-artificial en el *Libre de Home* de Ramon Llull' (450–56), and A. Vega, 'Cuerpo espiritual y espíritu corporal en Ramon Llull' (470–84). J. Perarnau Espelt, *De Ramon Llull a Nicolau Eimeric*, B, Facultat de Teologia de Catalunya, 129 pp., analyses the antilullism of N. Eimeric, as does J. de Puig Oliver, 'La *Incantatio studii Ilerdensis* de Nicolau Eimerich. O.P. Edició i estudi', *ATCA*, 15, 1996:7–108.

VICENT FERRER AND OTHER RELIGIOUS WRITERS

J. Perarnau Espelt, 'Els quatre sermons catalans de sant Vicent Ferrer en el manuscrit 476 de la Biblioteca de Catalunya', *ATCA*, 15, 1996:109–340, edits and studies some of Ferrer's texts. Other materials on the saint from a colloquium held at Valencia in May 1996, are found in *Paradigmes de la història, 1*, V, Saó, 213 pp.: A. Ferrando Francès, 'Vicent Ferrer (1350–1419), predicador políglota de l'Europa Occidental' (71–95); T. Martínez, 'Alguns aspectes de l'estructura del sermó vicentí' (109–34); A. Robles, 'Sant Vicent Ferrer en el context de diàleg. Les Minories religioses' (15–46), and M. Bas Carbonell, 'Bibliografia sobre sant Vicent Ferrer' (197–208). L. Cabré and X. Renedo, '*Et postea applicetur thema*: Format in the Preaching of St. Vincent Ferrer, OP', *Archivum Fratrum Praedicatorum*, 66, 1996:245–56, clarify Ferrer's popularising rhethorical devices. J. M. Perujo Melgar, 'Vers una classificació de les semblances de sant Vicent Ferrer', *Actas* (AHLM 6), 1179–1205, is a contribution on *exempla*. A. Hauf, 'La *Scala de contemplació*, de fra Antoni Canals, i el *De XV gradibus contemplationis* o *Viridiarium Ecclesiae*', *AABC*, 8:97–120, finds new sources for A. Canals. *Concordança de la 'Vita Christi' de sor Isabel de Villena*, ed. R. Alemany Ferrer, Alicante U.P., CD-ROM, contains the full text following R. Miquel's 1913 edition.

4. HISTORICAL AND ARTISTIC PROSE, NOVEL

HISTORIOGRAPHY

Pere Miquel Carbonell, *Cròniques d'Espanya*, ed. A. Alcoberro, 2 vols., B, Barcino, 278, 308 pp., is the critical edition of the history of the Crown of Aragon by the royal archivist Carbonell (1434–1517). On the *Cronica de Jaume I*, G. Colón, 'La *torra que és forcada* a la *Crònica* de Jaume I', *AABC*, 8:87–96, and J. Bruguera, 'La Crònica de Jaume I: projecció filològica i lingüística', *ELLC*, 33:5–16. A. Olivar, 'Sobre el manuscrit Q de la Crònica de Desclot', *BRABLB*, 45, 1995–96[1997]:223–29 deals with a Montserrat MS of Desclot. L. Badia, 'Dos creaciones retóricas olvidadas en el epítome catalán de la *Historia gothica*', *Actas* (AHLM 6), 233–42, studies the Catalan reception of Giménez de Rada.

TIRANT LO BLANC

Two contributions to the reception of *T*: V. Martines, *El Tirant políglota. Estudi sobre el «Tirant lo Blanch» a partir de les seues traduccions espanyola, italiana i francesa dels segles XVI–XVIII*, B, PAM–Curial, 206 pp., and *Partinoples. Précis sur la romance catalane. Histoire du vaillant chevalier Tirant le Blanc*, ed. P. Vila, Girona, Diputació, 130 pp. J. Chiner Gimeno, 'El *consell* d'Abdal·là Salomó al *Tirant lo Blanch* (cap. 143) i la *Lletra de reials costums*', *AABC*, 8: 47–66; J. Pujol, 'De Guido delle Colonne a l'Ovidi epistolar: sobre el rendiment narratiu i retòric d'unes fonts del *Tirant lo Blanch*', *ib.*, 133–74. This last is to be related to the same author's 'El desenllaç tràgic del *Tirant lo Blanc*, *Les Troianes* de Sèneca i les idees de tragèdia al segle xv', *BRABLB*, 45, 1995–96[1997]: 29–66, which establishes a turning point in the study of *Tirant* sources. Two other excellent articles are: X. Renedo, 'Raó i intuïció en Plaerdemavida', *ib.*, 317–60, and S. Cingolani, 'Clàssics i pseudo-clàssics al *Tirant lo Blanc*. Reflexions a partir d'unes fonts de Joanot Martorell', *ib.*, 361–88; see also G. Grilli, 'Viatges a Orient: la descoberta del cos adolescent', *ib.*, 273–93. Not all the contributions of the *Tirant* colloquium (Aix-en-Provence, 1994), in *Estudis crítics sobre 'Tirant lo Blanc' i el seu context*, ed. J. M. Barberà, B–V, Centre Aixois de Recherches Hispaniques — IIFV–PAM, 487 pp., deserve the same attention. Some remarkable ones are: R. Beltran, 'La muerte de Tirant: elementos para una autopsia' (75–93); J. Chiner Gimeno, 'A l'entorn d'un full manuscrit del *Tirant lo Blanc*' (43–59); A. Hauf, '*Manus habent*: entorn als eufemismes amorosos de tipus militar en el *Tirant lo Blanc*' (145–85); T. Martínez, 'De la comtessa de Varoic a la princesa Carmesina: per la presència de Sèneca al *Tirant lo Blanc*' (285–305); also worthy of attention are D. Siviero, 'Il modello della narrativa cortese e della precettistica cavalleresca nel *Tirant lo Blanc*', *ZK*, 9, 1996: 33–71; T. D. Stegmann, 'Aspectes del *realisme tècnic* i del *no-detallisme* al *Tirant lo Blanc*', *ib.*, 10: 7–38, and R. Beltran, 'Urganda, Morgana y Sibila: el espectáculo de la nave profética en la literatura caballeresca', *Deyermond Vol.*, 21–48.

JOAN ROÍS DE CORELLA

R. Cantavella, 'Dames a l'aigua: el tema del debat entre el Príncep de Viana i Joan Roís de Corella', *AABC*, 8: 37–46; S. Cingolani, 'D'Aquilles a Jesús. Reflexions sobre la cronologia de les obres de Joan Roís de Corella', *ib.*, 67–86, and C. Wittlin, 'La *Biblis*, *Mirra* i *Santa Anna* de Joan Roís de Corella: traduccions modulades, amplificades i adaptades', *ib.*, 175–89. R. Cantavella, 'On the Sources of the Plot of Corella's *Tragèdia de Caldesa*', *Deyermond Vol.*, 75–90. J. Turró, 'El mite de Caldesa: Corella al *Jardinet d'orats*', *Atalaya*, 7, 1996: 103–16, relates the creation of Caldesa, the 'fallen' Corella's beloved, to his immediate reception; S. Cingolani, 'Joan Roís de Corella o la interioritat de la moral', *RCat*, 120: 83–98, focuses the moral background of C.'s literary models, and T. Martínez, 'Per a una interpretació del *Triümfo de les dones*, de Roís de Corella: claus ecdòtiques', *ELLC*, 33, 1996:37–70, studies the text, and the theological context of C.'s *Triümfo*.

OTHER NARRATIVE TEXTS

Llibre de tres, ed. M. de Riquer, B, Quaderns Crema, 74 pp., is a critical edition. J. J. Morales Gómez, 'Un fragmento de narrativa catalana bajomedieval en el Archivo Histórico de Protocolos de Zaragoza', *BRABLB*, 45, 1995–96[1997]:231–38, presents a fragment of an unknown Catalan text. J. Ainaud, 'Un traductor al Purgatori: a propòsit del *Viatge al Purgatori de sant Patrici*, de Ramon de Perellós', pp. 133–41 of *Traducció i Literatura. Homenatge a Angel Crespo*, ed. S. González and F. Lafarga, Vic, Eumo — B, Universitat Pompeu Fabra, clarifies ecdotic problems. Three contributions on Turmeda: R. Beier, *Anselm Turmeda. Eine Studie zur interkulturellen Literatur*, Bonn, Romanistischer Vlg, 1996, 197 pp.; M. Garcia Sampere, Marinela and L. Martín, 'Algunes fonts occidentals de l'obra d'Anselm Turmeda, *Disputa de l'ase*', *RFR*, 13, 1996:181–214, and A. Espadaler, 'L'ombra amb vida d'Anselm Turmeda', Fragonard, *Transfert*, 95–103.

5. TRANSLATIONS AND OTHER GENRES AND TEXTS

J. Izquierdo offers two items on biblical translations: *La Bíblia en valencià. De la lecció de la sagrada escriptura en llengua vulgar*, V, Saó, 157 pp., and 'Sobre l'edició de les traduccions bíbliques catalanes medievals: el cas de la Bíblia valenciana', *AABC*, 8:121–32. William of Conches, *Dragmaticon philosophiae; Summa de philosophia in vvlgari*, ed. I. Ronca, L. Badia, and J. Pujol (CCCM, 152), Turnhout, Brepols, contains a study and critical edition by B. and P. (275–497) of the 14th-c. Catalan version of this 12th-c. Chartrian encyclopedia. L. Cifuentes, '*Translatar sciència en romans catalanesch*. La difusió de la medicina en català a la baixa Edat Mitjana i el Renaixement', *LlLi*, 8:7–42, explores the Catalan scientific materials of the 14th and 15th c.; on the same field, G. Avenoza, 'Els "Graus de les medicines" de l'*Inventari o col·lectari di cirurgia* de Guy de Chauliac', *ELLC*, 33, 1996:17–36, and I. de Riquer, 'Un roi catalan à la recherche d'une licorne', *RLaR*, 102, 1996:141–61. On other subjects: L. Badia, '*Fa che tu scrive*: variaciones profanas sobre un tema sagrado, de Ramon Llull a Bernat Metge', *Deyermond Vol.*, 3–20; L. Martín Pascual, *La tradició animalística en la literatura catalana medieval*, Alicante U.P., 304 pp.; B. Schlieben-Lange, 'Die *Torsimany* und die scholastische Grammatik', *ZK*, 9, 1996:7–19; B. Taylor, 'Un texto breve catalán sobre cortesía: texto y edición', *Actas* (AHLM 6), 1491–99; I. de

Riquer, 'La réception du Graal en Catalogne au Moyen Age', Fragonard, *Transfert*, 49–60, and T. M. Vinyoles Vidal, 'L'amor i la mort al segle xv: cartes de dones', pp. 111–98 of *Miscel·lània de Textos Medievals*, 8, B, CSIC, 1996.

6. DRAMA

A. J. Soberanas Lleó, 'El fragment passionístic de Vallclara del segle xv', *ELLC*, 33, 1996: 71–88. *La Festa d'Elx*, 49, Elx, Ajuntament, 224 pp, contains: J. Castaño Garcia, 'La Festa d'Elx i els seus intèrprets' (103–11); F. Massip and L. Kovács, 'Fent camí amb la Mare de Déu: el seguici marià a la Festa d'Elx' (115–17); R. Miró Baldrich, 'L'Assumpció a Tàrrega, primera part: nostra Senyora d'agost, festa major (segles xv–mitjan xvii)' (121–37), and P. Vila, 'El culte assumpcionista i el llit de la Mare de Déu de Vic' (173–83).

LITERATURE (NINETEENTH AND TWENTIETH CENTURIES)

By MARGARIDA CASACUBERTA, *Lecturer in Catalan Literature at the Universitat de Girona,*
and MARINA GUSTÀ, *Lecturer in Catalan Literature at the Universitat de Barcelona*

1. GENERAL

J. Castellanos, *Literatura, vides, ciutats*, B, Edicions 62, 193 pp., is a partial collection of the author's scholarly contributions on two writers, Verdaguer and Víctor Català, and on two cities, Girona and Barcelona, with regard to literary myths. Other contributions are collected in: L. Meseguer, *Literatura oberta*, PAM, 266 pp., with a preface by J. Molas. From the point of view of the history of translation, R. Pinyol i Torrents, 'Les traduccions de literatura russa a Catalunya fins a la guerra civil. Esbós d'una bibliografia', pp. 245–64 of *Traducció i literatura. Homenatge a Àngel Crespo*, Vic, Eumo, 272 pp. Finally, the appearance of *Homenatge a Arthur Terry*, ed. Joan Veny (ELLC, 35), 2 vols, Montserrat, Abadia-AILLC, 303, 276 pp., must be noted.

2. RENAIXENÇA

Two years after the commemoration of the 'Segle Romàntic', papers from one of the symposia held in 1995 and 1996 are finally available through *El Segle Romàntic. Actes del Col·loqui sobre el Romanticisme*, Vilanova i la Geltrú, Biblioteca Museu V. Balaguer, 551 pp., with papers by R. Torrents, A. Terry, E. Barjau, M. González, A. Marí, J. Massot, V. Salvador, M. Jorba, J. Mas i Vives, A. Tayadella, E. Miralles, M. Cuccu, J. M. Fradera, J. Fontana, and others. The figure of the woman in art and literature is studied in: *La dona i el Romanticisme. Quaderns del Museu Frederic Marès. Estudis*, 1, 1996, with contributions by M. Jorba, F. Fontbona, and P. Vélez. P. Anguera, *El català al segle XIX. De llengua del poble a llengua nacional*, B, Empúries, 298 pp., studies linguistic, social and cultural behaviour. One more volume of J. Verdaguer's complete works has appeared: *Montserrat. II. Llegenda de Montserrat*, ed. Maur M. Boix, Vic, Eumo–Societat Verdaguer, 245 pp. On the novel, there is E. Cassany, 'Narcís Oller i l'art de la novel·la', *EMarg*, 58:5–19; *Zola y España. Actas del Coloquio Internacional Lyon, set. 1996*, ed. S. Seillard and A. Sotelo Vázquez, Univ. de Barcelona, contains: R. Pla i Arxé, 'El naturalisme a *L'Avenç*' (1–12); R. Cabré, 'La preceptiva de Zola i la seva recepció en la crítica positivista' (13–28); M. Pons, 'Zola i la premsa catalana en llengua catalana' (29–33); J. Castellanos, 'Carles Bosch de la Trinxeria, un escriptor a recordar', *RCat*, 124:130–39. Three authors are studied from different perspectives: J. Requesens i Piqué, 'L'epistolari de Jaume Collell a A. M. Alcover', pp. 165–87 of *Estudis de llengua i literatura en honor de Joan Veny*, vol. I, ed. J. Massot, B, Abadia de Montserrat, 457 pp. J. Mas i Vives, 'Actualitat de Josep M. Quadrado', *SdO*:274–75; *Escalante i el teatre del segle XIX (Precedents i pervivència)*, ed. F. Carbó, R. X. Rosselló, and J. L. Sirera, B, IIFV-PAM, 398 pp.

3. MODERNISME

The figure and work of Santiago Rusiñol has been the object of several contributions: M. Casacuberta, *Santiago Rusiñol: vida, literatura i mite*, PAM, 616 pp., highlights the relationship between art and literature; *Santiago Rusiñol (1861–1931)*, B, Museu Nacional d'Art de Catalunya — M, Fundación Cultural Mapfre Vida, 317 pp., includes, among others: M. Casacuberta, 'Santiago Rusiñol i la novel·la de l'artista' (35–43); V. Panyella, 'El pati blau, un capítol de la biografia artística de Santiago Rusiñol (1891–1903)' (93–108). On Rusiñol as a dramatic author two works have appeared: F. J. Corbella, 'Santiago Rusiñol (1861–1931). Un dramaturg vuitcentista en els inicis de la modernitat', *RCat*, 123:21–53; M. Casacuberta, 'Les auques del senyor Esteve', pp. 29–52 of S. Rusiñol, *L'auca del senyor Esteve*, B, Edicions del Teatre Nacional, 113 pp. Scenic life in Modernisme is also the subject of another contribution: M. Cerdà i Surroca, '*La fada* (1897). Compendi de l'imaginari modernista a Catalunya', *SdO*:958–61. Two poetic works are studied in: M. Corretger, 'L'obra poètica d'Alfons Maseras', *LlLi*, 8:149–69; A. Camps, 'L'obra poètica de D'Annunzio en català: la raó d'una tria', *ib.*, 119–48. Also of interest is: M. A. Bosch, *Pous i Pagès. Vida i obra*, Figueres, Institut d'Estudis Empordanesos, 354 pp. In spite of its title, V. Martínez-Gil, *El naixement de l'iberisme catalanista*, B, Curial, 299 pp., contains several chapters on literary topics.

4. NOUCENTISME

J. Murgades, 'Usos del Noucentisme', *EMarg*, 58:73–92, outlines the latest historical and critical trends with regard to this movement. J. Aulet, *Antologia de la poesia noucentista*, B, Edicions 62, 200 pp., is a high point in the studies on poetry of Noucentisme. A new contribution to the study of Eugeni d'Ors is: V. Cacho Viu, *Revisión de Eugenio d'Ors (1902–1930). Seguida de un epistolario inédito*, B, Quaderns Crema — Publicaciones de la Residencia de Estudiantes, 382 pp.

Josep Carner is the author who has attracted the most attention: *Epistolari de Josep Carner*, vol. III, ed. A. Manent and J. Medina, B, Curial, 517 pp.; A. Camps, 'Josep Carner, traductor de Dante', *RCat*, 117:87–102; M. Ortín, 'Josep Carner davant el micròfon', *SdO*: 318–21. Finally, A. Manent, *Del Noucentisme a l'exili*, B, PAM, 258 pp., is a collection of several of M.'s papers on the role of the intellectual in this period.

5. PRE-WAR AND POST-WAR LITERATURE

J. M. Llompart, *Els nostres escriptors*, Palma de Mallorca, Moll, 1996, 254 pp., is a partial collection of the author's critical papers on 20th-c. writers, as well as J. Romeu, *D'assaig i crítica*, B, Columna-Faig, 244 pp., specially devoted to poets: Salvat-Papasseit, Foix, Garcés, Torres, and Vinyoli. Romeu is also studied by M. Enrich, *Josep Romeu i Figueras, l'intel·lectual i el poeta*, B, PAM, 176 pp. Poetry reading is the goal of J. Navarro Santaeulàlia, *Fusions. Comentaris de poesia catalana del segle* XX, B, La Magrana, 144 pp. J. Aulet, 'Uns quants epistolaris publicats recentment: comentari i reflexió', *EMarg*, 57:83–95, is a review of several collections of letters, with special regard to editorial problems.

Les literatures catalana i francesa al llarg del segle XX. *I Congrés Internacional de Literatura Comparada*, ed. C. Benoit, F. Carbó, D. Jiménez, and V. Simbor, B, PAM, 440 pp., contains contributions by V. Alonso, E. Balaguer, V. Simbor, J. Massot, C. Gregori, P. Rosselló Bover, and X. Vall, concerning, among other subjects, the avant-garde, existentialism, and Catholic trends. *Els anys vint en els Països Catalans (Noucentisme/Avantguarda)*, B, PAM, 247 pp. includes works by J. Murgades, J. Aulet, M. Roser i Puig, and M. Prudon. Two contributions on Carles Riba should be mentioned: X. Farré Vidal, 'Bibliografia ribiana recent', *LlLi*, 8:502–15; and J. Malé, 'Un editor d'Ausiàs March poc conegut: Carles Riba', *RCat*, 123:92–103. We must also point out: M. Subiràs i Pugibet, 'Les *Vint cançons*, de Tomàs Garcés, i el neopopularisme. Entre els *Boscos de la retòrica* i els *Camps oberts de l'emoció*', *LlLi*, 8:171–88, and J. Castells-Cambray, 'Salvador Dalí: obra de joventut', *ib.*, 499–502. The novel of the thirties is studied by J. M. Balaguer, 'La creació del Club dels Novel·listes i els fils de la història', *EMarg*, 57:15–35.

Some works focus on discussions of the duties of the intellectual after *Noucentisme*: R. Torné Teixidó, 'Carles Riba, sobre la didàctica del grec. (Dues cartes a Francesc Cambó sobre les activitats docents a la Fundació Bernat Metge)', *EMarg*, 57:53–69; M. A. Bosch, 'L'inèdit *Per Catalunya (1936–1939)*, de Josep Pous i Pagès', *SdO*: 395–97; J. Massot i Muntaner, 'La trajectòria vital de Miquel Batllori', *ib.*,

660–62; M. Ferrà, *Cartes a Joan Pons i Marquès (1915–1947)*, ed. Isabel Gràcia i Zapata, B, Curial-PAM, 171 pp.; P. Gómez i Casademont, '*Hores angleses*, de Ferran Soldevila', *SdO*: 743–45; J. Vilà i Folch, 'Un badoc incorregible. Sebastià Gasch (1897–1980)', *ib.*, 766–67; M. Vilà and J. Molar, 'El fons Lluís Nicolau d'Olwer de l'arxiu de l'Abadia de Montserrat', *LlLi*, 8:437–71; *Miscel·lània Joan Estelrich*, Palma, El Tall, 271 pp., contains papers by I. Graña, J. Massot, A. Manent, A. Manresa, J. Melià, G. Coll i Mesquida, M. Batllori, J. Medina, M. Corretger, and B. Peñarrúbia. A. Manent, 'Santiago Albertí, el dinamisme cultural en solitari', *RCat*, 122:103–11, Id., *Sobre Jordi Sarsanedas*, B, PAM, 220 pp., and T. Férriz Roure, 'Bartomeu Costa Amic, un editor català a Mèxic', *RCat*, 122:113–37, deal with the same subject under post-war circumstances. One more contribution to the understanding of writers in exile is M. C. Gibert, 'Visió global del teatre en català a l'exili. Buenos Aires: 1939–1975', *RCat*, 118:43–50. Also on theatre: F. Carbó and S. Cortés, *El teatre en la postguerra valenciana (1939–1962)*, B, Tres i Quatre, 264 pp. On the social role of literature, G. Casals 'La cultura a Barcelona. 1939–1975', pp. 341–372 of *Història de Barcelona*, vol. VII, B, Ajuntament de Barcelona – Enciclopèdia Catalana, 438 pp., and M. Gustà, 'La cultura a Barcelona. 1975–1997', *ib.*, 373–401. On postwar novelists: *Pere Calders o la passió de contar*, ed. R. Cabré, Vic, Eumo — Univ. de Barcelona, 108 pp., which includes papers by J. Melcion, J. Aulet, G. Tavani, and J. Triadú; P. Joan i Tous, 'Schreiben in schwierigen Zeiten. Poetik, Wahrheit, und List in Víctor Moras Roman *Els plàtans de Barcelona*', *ZK*, 10:90–108; L. van der Hout, 'Sobre la censura: L'obra de Manuel de Pedrolo. El cas d'*Acte de violència*', *RCat*, 124:113–29, and I. Cònsul, 'El territori narratiu de Vicenç Villatoro', *SdO*:113–16. Finally, the appearance of a critical edition of M. Rodoreda, *La mort i la primavera*, ed. C. Arnau, B, Fundació Mercè Rodoreda – IEC, 452 pp., must be noted. On poetry, one more volume of the critical edition of Espriu's complete works must be mentioned: *Miratge a Citerea. Letícia. Petites proses blanques. La pluja*, ed. M. Edo i Julià, B, Edicions 62, 368 pp. Also on this writer: M. Gómez, 'Cartes de Salvador Espriu a Aurora Bertrana', *EMarg*, 58:53–72. Two works are devoted to Brossa's poetry: G. Bordons, '50 anys de publicacions de Joan Brossa. Bibliografia 1948–1997', *ZK*, 10:120–26, and T. D. Stegmann, 'Kreativität in Joan Brossas Gedichten', *ib.*, 9:72–102. The sixties are focused, with regard to poetry, in J. Arévalo, 'La revista *Nous Horitzons* i la poesia catalana dels anys seixanta', *EMarg*, 57:96–104.

Several aspects of the relationship between literature and readers are studied in: J. Molas, *Fragments de memòria*, Lleida, Pagès, 188 pp., Id., 'La literatura: ahir, avui, demà?', *SdO*:583–84; V. Martínez-Gil,

'Correctors i escriptors en la literatura catalana: el concepte de coautoria lingüística', *LlLi*, 8 : 189–218, and J. Murgades, 'Cara i creu de l'aniversarisme a la literatura catalana', *RCat*, 124 : 7–15. We owe a lot of works of interest to a number of anniversaries. N. Perpinyà, *Gabriel Ferrater: recepció i contradicció*, B, Empúries, 96 pp., deals with Gabriel Ferrater's personality and work, as does M. Pessarrodona, 'Gabriel Ferrater de prop', *SdO* : 374–75. Unpublished Fuster is available in: J. Fuster, *Correspondència*, ed. F. Pérez Moragon, V, Tres i Quatre, 336 pp., with letters from J. Carner, M. Manent, C. Riba, J. Pla, S. Espriu, and L. Villalonga. Also, V. Pitarch, 'Repensar Fuster. Renegar-lo', *SdO* : 468–69. Relating to Llorenç Villalonga's life and works: D. Ferrà-Ponç, *Estudis sobre Llorenç Villalonga*, B, PAM, 280 pp.; *Llorenç Villalonga*, ed. A. Santa, Lleida U.P.- Pagès, 187 pp., which contains articles by J. Pomar, J. Murgades, J. Oleza, B. Porcel, P. Rosselló Bover, R. Mataix, E. Bou and M. C. Bosch; P. Rosselló Bover, 'En la cruïlla del centenari. Els estudis sobre Llorenç Villalonga i la seva obra', *SdO* : 674–76; L. Johnson, 'Villalonga i els seus lectors', *ib.*, 941–43; J. Pomar, 'Dos articles inèdits de Villalonga del temps de guerra', *RCat*, 123 : 77–91, and X. Duran, 'La idea de progrés en Pla i Villalonga', *SdO* : 212–13.

1997 was the commemorative year of Josep Pla's centenary. Among the great amount of works, some must be noted: X. Pla, *Josep Pla. Ficció autobiogràfica i veritat literària*, B, Quaderns Crema, 527 pp.; M. Gustà, '"Relacions", de Josep Pla: preludi i fuga', pp. 9–73 (introd.) of J. Pla, *El primer pròleg de 'Relacions'*, B, Biblioteca de Catalunya; J. Pla, *La diabòlica mania d'escriure*, ed. X. Pla, B, Fundació Josep Pla – Destino, 215 pp., with contributions by M. Gustà, N. Garolera, J. Vallcorba, V. Panyella, A. Marí, X. Pla, J. M. Castellet, J. F. Mira, and A. Puigverd, among others. Also of interest are: X. Pla, 'El realisme sintètic de Josep Pla', *SdO* : 44–46; M. J. Gallofré i Virgili, 'El retorn de Josep Pla', *ib.*, 124–26; P. Ballart, 'Josep Pla i la poesia: una passió culpable', *ib.*, 208–09; N. Comadira, 'La cuina segons Josep Pla', *ib.*, 210–11; J. Castellanos, 'Pla, un novel·lista contra la sintaxi', *ib.*, 309–11; M. Prats, 'La literatura i el futur de la llengua', *ib.*, 393–94; G. Casals, 'Per què no dir-ne intertextualitat? A propòsit de la biografia de Maragall', *ib.*, 483–84; M. Casacuberta, 'Josep Pla i el senyor Esteve', *ib.*, 587–89; A. Camps, 'Josep Pla i el poeta dels *Canti*', *ib.*, 665–67; C. Badosa, 'Josep Pla i el liberalisme com a mètode', *ib.*, 741–42; M. Gustà, 'Eternitat amb subtítols', *ib.*, 829–30; V. Martínez-Gil, 'Sobre l'edició crítica de l'obra planiana', *ib.*, 939–40; M. Casacuberta, 'Bibliografia planiana recent', *LlLi*, 8 : 491–98, and 'Josep Pla, biògraf de Rusiñol', *RevG*, 180 : 81–84; 'Josep Pla, la història i els historiadors', *L'Avenç*, 219 : 27–49, with articles by J. Canal, M. J. Gallofré, M. Gustà, and F. Vilanova; J. Triadú, 'Sobre Josep Pla i els exiliats', *RCat*, 123:92–103, and M. Llanas, '12 cartes de Josep Pla a l'Editorial Selecta', *ib.*, 118:99–116.

VI. PORTUGUESE STUDIES

LANGUAGE

By STEPHEN PARKINSON, *Lecturer in Portuguese Language and Linguistics, University of Oxford*

1. GENERAL

GENERAL. *Língua e Cidadania*, ed. E. Guimarães and E. P. Orlandi, Campinas, Pontes, 1996, 163 pp., collects readings designed to highlight the lack of recognition of Brazilian distinctiveness at the level of language planning and standardization; new material includes E. Guimarães, 'Sinopse dos estudos do Português no Brasil: a gramatização brasileira' (127–38); J. H. Nunes, 'A Gramática de Anchieta e as partes do discurso' (139–50), on the 16th-c. grammar of Tupi. *Die romanischen Sprachen im Vergleich*, ed. C. Schmitt and W. Schweickard, Bonn, Romanistischen Verlag, 1995, ii + 466 pp., has comparative articles by A. Denschlag on newspaper interviews (Ptg./It.), A. Monjour on word-formation (Ptg./Span.), and J. L. A. do Campo and J. Schmidt-Radefeld on compound nouns (Ptg./Ger.).

EARLY GRAMMARIANS. M. A. Kossárik, 'A doutrina linguística de Amaro de Roboredo', *Actas* (APL 1996), ii, 429–43, demands greater recognition of the place of this 17th-c. grammarian in the development of linguistic and pedagogical ideas. M. C. Rosa, 'Línguas *bárbaras e peregrinas* do Novo Mundo segundo as gramáticas jesuitas', *RevEL*, 6:97–149, traces early intimations of universality in 17th-c. Jesuit grammars of indigenous languages. L. L. Fávero, *As concepções lingüísticas no século XVIII*, Campinas, UNICAMP, 1996, 306 pp., is a compendium of quotations on and from 18th-c. grammarians, with an appendix of decrees regulating the teaching of grammar. J. Teixeira, '"Sons, signaes, ou accenos". A comunicação na *Gramática Filosófica* de Melo Bacelar', *Actas* (APL 1996), ii, 581–86, finds some modern ideas in M.B., as does A. Torres, 'Bernardo de Lima e Melo Bacelar e a sua Grammatica Philosophica no contexto cultural setecentista', *AAPH*, 35, 1995:367–80, who emphasizes the novelty of a grammar based on syntax rather than morphology. C. C. Assunção, 'Uma leitura da Introdução da *Arte da Grammatica da Lingua Portugueza* de Reis Lobato (1770)', *RFLUP*, 14:165–81, sees R.L.'s emphasis on the understanding of the mother tongue as a crucial factor in forming the great writers of the late 18th century. M. G. Funk, 'A questão da ordem das palavras na Gramática Portuguesa tradicional', *Actas* (APL 1996), ii, 419–27, traces the fading of the distinction between grammar and rhetoric. I. Castro, 'Os ossos de Camões', *ib.*, 403–09, reveals the detective work behind the identification of José Tavares de Macedo, as an object lesson in philological practice; A. L. Barros, 'António das Neves Pereira, fonte de Tavares de Macedo', *ib.*, 393–402, and F. M. Menéndez, 'Para uma abordagem do conceito de Língua em António das Neves Pereira', *ib.*, 483–93, give appreciations of his precursor and inspiration. In the same volume, more recent linguists are commemorated by A. C. Silva on Adolfo Coelho as linguist (549–58); E. d'Andrade and A. Kihm on C.'s foreshadowing of the bioprogram hypothesis (385–92); D. Kremer on Piel and Meier (445–55); R. Veloso on Rodrigues Lapa (587–604); C. Albino and L. Prista on the relations between philologists of the last 100 years (359–76), as remembered in Id., *Filólogos Portugueses entre 1868 e 1943*, L, APL-Colibri, 1996.

I.T. AND CORPORA. M. H. Mateus and A. H. Branco, *Engenharia da Linguagem*, L, Colibri, 1995, 150 pp., has overviews of IT applications to Portuguese: particularly useful are M. Correia and P. Guerreiro (43–69) on lexical databases, and C. Hagège and I. Duarte (71–93) on formal grammars. On child language, A. M. M. Guimarães and R. R. Lamprecht, 'The use of CHILDES database for Brazilian Portuguese', Faria, *Portuguese*, 207–14. L. F. Duarte, 'Para uma edição interactiva de textos antigos', *Actas* (APL 1996), II, 411–17, outlines a system of interconvertible editions of medieval documents.

2. HISTORICAL

GENERAL. J. Mattoso, 'Perguntas dos Historiadores aos Linguistas', *Actas* (APL 1996), II, 607–19, highlights among many elements the importance of critical editing and dating of documents for historical research. R. V. M. Silva, 'Desenvolvimentos recentes no Brasil dos estudos histórico-diacrónicos sobre o Português', *ib.*, 567–79, celebrates a revival. A. H. A. Emiliano, 'A língua notarial latino-bracarense e a reforma gregoriana', *ib.*, 91–109, argues that notarial *latim bárbaro* was not just tolerated but taught as a standard. C. A. Maia, 'A abordagem dos textos medievais. (Reflexões sobre alguns fragmentos das *Partidas* de Afonso X)', *ib.*, 157–69, emphasizes the need for chronological studies, and extracts relevant data from newly discovered Ptg. translations of the Alfonsine *Partidas*. A. Cortijo Ocaño, 'O Livro do Amante: the lost Portuguese translation of John Gower's Confessio Amantis (Madrid: Biblioteca de Palacio MS II-3088)', *PortSt*, 13 : 1–6, reconstructs the chronology of the transmission of the newly rediscovered MS, which he describes in 'La traducción portuguesa de la Confessio Amantis de John Gower', *Euphrosyne*, 23,

1995:457–66. R. Lorenzo, 'Documentos portugueses de Monte-derramo', *Actas* (APL 1996), II, 135–56, compares 14th-c. Ptg. and Galician documents from a monastic archive. C. Noia Campos, 'O galego escrito no Portugal do século XV', *Vázquez Vol.*, 69–76, compares parallel Ptg. and Galician versions of a 1486 synodal document from Viana do Castelo. On the 17th c., E. P. S. Verdelho, 'Sobre a língua portuguesa do séc. XVII. Estudos realizados e trabalhos em curso', *Actas* (APL 1996), II, 325–39.

ORTHOGRAPHY. M. H. Paiva, 'Variação e evolução da palavra gráfica: o testemunho dos textos metalinguísticos portugueses do século XVI', *Actas* (APL 1996), II, 233–52, gives a detailed account of graphemics and word separation in early grammarians. R. Mar-quilhas, 'Níveis de alfabetização no Portugal de Seiscentos', *ib.*, 171–78, discusses what can be deduced from signatures on Inquisition documents.

PHONOLOGY. R. M. Silva, *O português arcaico. Fonologia*, SP, Con-texto, 1995, 97 pp., is a valuable summary. E. Cardeira and M. A. Fernandes, 'Aspectos do português algarvio na transição do séc. XIV para o XV', *Actas* (APL 1996), II, 55–68, extract useful data on vocalic hiatus, falling diphthongs, and possessives, from the *Vereações de Loulé*. K. J. Wireback, 'On the palatalisation of /kt/, /ks/, /k'l/, /g'l/, and /gn/ in Western Romance', *RPh*, 50:276–94, argues that only /kt/ and /ks/ involve syllable-final velars becoming yod, and that the other palatalizations involve other (assimilatory) processes; the failure of previous accounts to explain the preservation of falling diphthongs in the relevant Ptg. forms is crucial. Id., **The Role of Phonological Structure in Sound Change from Latin to Spanish and Portuguese*, Frankfurt, Lang, 152 pp. Hajek, *Nasalization*, refers widely to Portug-uese to establish cross-linguistic nasalization parameters, though his model for the emergence of distinctive nasality owes more to Italian. M. A. Oliveira, 'Reanalisando o processo de cancelamento do (r) em final de sílaba', *RevEL*, 6:31–58, argues for lexical diffusion of BPtg. *r*-effacement.

MORPHOLOGY AND SYNTAX. G. Salvi, 'L'ordine delle parole nella frase subordinata in galego-portoghese antico', *Vázquez Vol.*, 317–33, assembles data on adverbs and clitic position. M. L. Crispim, 'Artigos definidos e demonstrativos num corpus do sec. XIII', *Actas* (APL 1996), II, 79–90, compares 13th-c. notarial texts and a 15th-c. literary text. A. P. Banza and H. Garvão, 'As formas verbais em documentos notariais do século XIII. Alguns aspectos', *ib.*, 31–38, give statistics of occurrence of Tense/Mood forms, confirming some early sightings of ã < õ. A. Torres, 'Na pista do Prof. Azevedo Ferreira: os verbos *ter* e *haver* em dois cartulários nortenhos', *ib.*, 303–13, studies *tenere* and *habere* in Latin documents from Braga. M. F. Xavier, 'Léxico em diacronia. Dados da história do Português e do Inglês', *ib.*, 347–56, compares evolutions in verbal syntax. L. Chacoto, 'Predicados nominais com *fazer*, no português medieval', *ib.*, 69–77, has obvious cases of support verb constructions. M. C. V. da Silva, 'As construções causativas em textos notariais dos séculos XIII e XIV', *ib.*, 289–95, collects data on *mandar*, *fazer*, and *deixar*. C. Barros, '*Porque* e *ca*: aspectos do discurso justificativo no texto do *Foro Real*', *RFLUP*, 12, 1995 : 149–57, distinguishes *porque* as a rationale for legislation and *ca* as a reason for individual decisions. M. M. Matos and S. A. Muidine, '*Acó* e *aló*', *Actas* (APL 1996), II, 211–17, find a simpler than expected O Ptg. adverb system.

LEXICON. A. G. Cunha, 'O lat. *dulcis* e seus derivados no vocabulário do português medieval', *Diacritica*, 11, 1996[1997]: 93–112, documents *doce* and its related forms.

3. PHONETICS AND PHONOLOGY

GENERAL. *Introdução a estudos de fonologia do Português brasileiro*, ed. L. Bisol, Porto Alegre, EDIPUCRS, 1996, 261, pp., has useful summaries of work on the vowel system (162–204), the consonant system (205–46) and phrasal phonology (247–59). Luiz Carlos Cagliari, *Fonologia do Português. Análise pela geometria de traços*, Campinas, p.p., 151 pp., is a concentrated account of BPtg. phonology, adding some original elements to Clements's feature geometry and Wetzels's analysis of vowel processes; see also his *Análise fonológica*, Campinas, p.p., 119 pp., for more elementary phonemics. S. Parkinson, 'Aspectos teóricos da história das vogais nasais portuguesas', *Actas* (APL 1996), II, 253–72, demonstrates the importance of phonological perspect-ives: distinguishing allophonic variations and phonological change clarifies issues of historical ordering of processes; the diphthongal status of nasal vowels is crucial to the understanding of nasalization and nasal diphthongization. Faria, *Portuguese*, contains: R. R. Lam-precht, 'A non-linear representation of some aspects of normal and deviant phonological acquisition' (35–42); C. L. M. Hernandorena, 'Palatal consonants in the acquisition of Brazilian Portuguese: representation in modern phonology' (43–53); M. J. Freitas, 'Alveolar trill(ions of problems): evidence from children acquiring European Portuguese syllables' (55–69), S. Frota and M. Vigário, 'The intona-tion of one European Portuguese infant: a first approach' (17–34). M. H. M. Mateus, 'Redundâncias lexicais e subespecificação: o sistema do português', *Actas* (APL 1996), I, 203–13, applies Radical Underspecification to Portuguese, with less than convincing results. H. Barroso, 'Os sistemas fonemático e grafemático do português actual ou das relações fone-fonema-grafema-letra', *Diacritica*, 11, 1996[1997]:265–93.

CONSONANTS. S. Mendonça, 'Oclusivas orais em discurso espontâneo: variação intra- ou interpessoal', *Actas* (APL 1996), 1, 215–25, has duration data for plosives in a range of styles. J. Veloso, 'Vozeamento, duração e tensão nas oposições de sonoridade das oclusivas orais do português', *RFLUP*, 14:59–80, uses perception tests to show duration to be a key cue to voicing contrasts.

VOWELS. V. Delplancq and B. Harmegnies, 'Les phonétiques et les phonologies du vocalisme portugais', *RevP*, 1:41–58, review issues in vowel phonology, with no new insights. F. Leite, 'Vogais silenciosas?', *Actas* (APL 1996), 1, 157–63, reports a flawed perception experiment on effaced [ə]. V. Delplancq and B. Harmegnies, 'Étude phonétique du système vocalique do portugais de Viseu', *ib.*, 125–37, give formant data.

SUPRASEGMENTALS. E. d'Andrade, 'Some remarks about stress in Portuguese', Martínez-Gil, *Issues*, 343–58, reviews previous analyses. E. d'Andrade and B. Laks, 'Stress and constituency: the case of Portuguese', pp. 15–42 of *Current Trends in Phonology: Models and methods*, ed. J. Durand and B. Laks, 2 vols, Salford, European Studies Research Institute, 1996, 1–395, 395–788 pp., distinguish verbs and nouns in a wave analysis of stress; quantity is irrelevant and extrametricality is avoided. On similar lines, S.-H. Lee, 'O acento primário do português do Brasil', *RevEL*, 6:5–30, gives an account of word stress in terms of prosodic constituency, and I. Pereira, 'O acento latino e o acento em português: do troqueu moraico ao troqueu silábico', *Actas* (APL 1996), 1, 269–75, gives a parametric account of regular and irregular nouns. S. Frota, 'On the prosody and intonation of Focus in European Portuguese', Martínez-Gil, *Issues*, 359–92, gives an intonational phonology account of declarative intonation and Focus; in a similar vein, M. C. Vigário, 'Marcação prosódica em frases negativas no Português europeu', *Actas* (APL 1996), 1, 329–49. M. H. M. Mateus, 'A prosódia nas gramáticas portuguesas', *Diacritica*, 11, 1996[1997]:619–38.

MORPHOPHONEMICS. W. J. Redenbarger, 'Apocope and lenition in Portuguese', Martínez-Gil, *Issues*, 439–65, argues that apocope has survived synchronically only in a subset of verbs. A. Morales-Front and E. Holt, 'The interplay of morphology, prosody and faithfulness in Portuguese pluralization', *ib.*, 393–437, give an unconvincing Optimality Theory account.

4. SYNTAX AND MORPHOLOGY

GENERAL. João Andrade Peres and Telmo Móia, *Áreas críticas da língua portuguesa*, L, Caminho, 1995, 538 pp., use a corpus of journalistic texts from the period 1986–94 to identify six areas in which grammatical norms are under strain: there are extended treatments of verbal syntax (valency and *regência*), relativization, coordination, and agreement, and lighter sections on passivization (mainly on passives formed from prepositional objects) and raising constructions. The absence of criteria for acceptability make the dividing line between descriptive and normative grammar difficult to define. Mário A. Perini, *Gramática descritiva do português*, SP, Ática, 1996, 380 pp., is an exemplary linguistic grammar of BPtg. firmly rooted in syntax and construction-types rather than morphology and word-classification. The variety described is the *padrão* of journalism and technical writing (seen as non-regional and less variable than literary language). Solange de Azambuja Lira, *The Subject in Brazilian Portuguese*, New York, Lang, 1996, 101 pp., a revised 1982 thesis, looks for functional factors in a variationist study of pronoun selection, subject position and null subjects. *Gramaticalização no Português do Brasil. Uma abordagem funcional*, ed. M. E. Martelotto, S. J. Votre, and M. M. Cezário, RJ, UFRJ-Tempo Brasileiro, 1996, 316 pp. Castilho, *Português falado*, IV, contains a series of articles on the marking (*preenchimento*) of syntactic boundaries: D. M. Callou et al. (169–92) on subordinate clauses; G. M. Silva, F. Tarallo, and M. L. Braga (193–217) on discourse markers; R. E. L. Moinho, 'Preenchimento de fronteiras V...V' (219–44); M. Kato and M. Nascimento (245) on adverb position as boundary marking, and M. A. F. Rocha (341–77) on headless adjuncts (PrepP and NP). Faria, *Portuguese*, contains: I. Leiria and A. Q. Mendes, 'Acquisition of tense and aspect in European Portuguese' (97–113); M. Vasconcelos, 'Relative clauses acquisition and experimental research: a study with Portuguese children' (115–28), H. J. Batoréo, 'Spatial expression in children's narratives: a study in European Portuguese' (191–206); L. Scliar-Cabral and G. Seco, 'Evidence for bound morphemes in a Brazilian child's corpus, MLU 1.45' (87–96). M. Sedano, 'Estructura y forma de las hendidas en cinco lenguas románicas: tensión entre economía y claridad', *HisL*, 8 : 123–53, surveys clefting.

GB SYNTAX. A. Gonçalves et al., *Quatro estudos em Sintaxe do Português. Uma abordagem segunda a teoria dos princípios e parâmetros*, L, Colibri, 1996, 188 pp., contains: A. Gonçalves, 'Aspectos da sintaxe dos verbos auxiliares do Português europeu' (7–50), proposing new criteria for identifying auxiliaries in Ptg., and distinguishing true auxiliaries from those satisfying only some criteria; M. Colaço, 'O princípio "Across-the Board" e o movimento sintáctico em estruturas de coordenação' (51–99); M. Miguel, 'A preposição *a* e os comple-mentos genitivos' (101–47); T. Móia, 'A sintaxe das orações relativas sem antecendente expresso do Português' (149–88), identifying the antecedent of free relatives as *pro*, and proposing distinct structures for infinitive relatives with and without antecendents. M. A. Kato and E. Raposo, 'European and Brazilian Portuguese word order: questions, focus and topic constructions', *Papers* (LSRL 24), 267–77, draw together some hitherto unconnected BPtg.-EPtg. differences (familiar data on clitic placement combined with V-S inversion in questions, topic, and focus constructions), all of which can be explained by postulating a FocusP constituent with different properties in the two varieties. A. M. B. Brito, 'Sobre algumas construções pseudo-relativas em português', *RFLUP*, 12, 1995:25–54, detaches non-relative *que*-constructions such as *E eu que ...*, *eis X que...* from true relatives. J. Costa, 'Word order and constraints interaction', *SemL*, 1:65–102, gives an Optimality Theory account of discourse conditions on word order.

TENSE AND ASPECT. O. G. Campos, A. C. S. Rodrigues, and P. T. Galembeck, 'A flexão modo-temporal no portugués culto do Brasil', Castilho, *Português falado*, IV, 35–78, focus on the values of past tenses. S. Matos, 'Aspectos da semântica e pragmática do imperfeito do indicativo', *RFLUP*, 13, 1996:435–73, attempts to relate modal and pragmatic values to the imperfectivity of the imperfect. M. D. Savić, 'Un probléme du portugais, envisagé dans le cadre des langues romanes et européennes (application du passé simple et du passé composé)', *Vázquez Vol.*, 265–75, notes the very low frequency of the Ptg. perfect tense. L. C. Travaglia, 'O uso do futuro do pretérito no português falado', *LetL*, 12.2, 1996:89–112, uses the concept of posteriority to reunite temporal and modal values of the conditional. F. Oliveira, 'Aspecto, referência nominal e papéis temáticos', *RFLUP*, 12, 1995:55–73, spells out the relationships between individualization and argument structure. D. Santos, 'Uma classificação aspectual portuguesa do português', *Actas* (APL 1996), I, 299–315, elaborates a language-specific classification of situation types, with *propriedades*, *estados*, and *acontecimentos* as major types.

MOOD AND MODALITY. R. Marques, 'Sobre a selecção de modo em orações completivas', *Actas* (APL 1996), I, 191–202, defends a modal interpretation of the subjunctive, which represents [-verídico] and/or [-epistémico]. B. Moreira, 'Para a caracterização de alguns marcadores enunciativos de intermodalidade', *ib.*, 241–51, describes the expression of near misses (*pouco, por pouco, quase*).

VERBS. M. E. Macedo, 'Os verbos *ensinar*, *deixar*, *fazer* e *mandar*: nova proposta de análise de algumas das suas construções', *Vázquez Vol.*, 303–07, proposes analysing *fazer/mandar/deixar* as operators, so that considerations of argument structure apply to the complex predicates they form. J. Baptista, 'Conversão, nomes parte-do-corpo

e restruturação dativa', *Actas* (APL 1996), I, 51–59, analyses constructions such as *dar/levar uma facada na barriga* in all their variant forms;
Id., '*Sermão, tarefa e facada*. Uma classificação das construções
conversas *dar - levar*', *SemL*, 1 : 5–37.

PRONOUNS.   E. V. Negrão and A. L. Muller, 'As mudanças no
sistema pronominal do Português brasileiro: substituição ou espe-
cialização de formas?', *DELTA*, 12, 1996: 125–52, see null subjects
and possessive *seu* surviving in specialized functions. R. Ilari, C. Franchi, and M. H. M. Neves, 'Os pronomes pessoais do português falado:
roteiro para a análise', Castilho, *Português falado*, IV, 79–166, is a
detailed study of BPtg. pronouns in their deictic, textual, anaphoric,
and thematic functions. M. Maia, 'The comprehension of object
anaphora in Brazilian Portuguese', *Papers* (LSRL 24), 293–311,
reports on perception experiments distinguishing topic-bound and
subject-bound gaps, and 'strict' and 'sloppy' interpretations of
pronouns. S. M. L. Cyrino, 'O objeto nulo do Português brasileiro',
DELTA, 12, 1996: 221–38, postulates a combination of ellipsis and
reconstruction. C. Novaes, 'Representação mental do sujeito nulo no
português do Brasil', *RevEL*, 6: 59–80, proposes that 1st person null
subjects are pronouns, and other null subjects are variables. E. Mou-
rão, 'Restrições à ocorrência da CV e do pronome lexical sujeitos no
português', *ib.*, 189–212, looks for restrictions on pro-drop in BPtg.
coordinate and complement structures.

CLITICS.   I. Duarte, G. Matos, and I. Faria, 'Specificity of
European Portuguese clitics in Romance', Faria, *Portuguese*, 129–54,
argue that EPtg. clitics are heads hosted in verbs, and that enclisis is
the unmarked pattern. C. Galves, 'Clitic placement and parametric
changes in Portuguese', *Papers* (LSRL 24), 227–39, explains the
emergence of enclisis in 19th-c. EPtg. as a change in the Agr-feature
of Comp from weak to strong, as part of a move away from Verb-
second structures. C. Galves and M. B. M. Abaurre, 'Os clíticos no
português brasileiro: elementos para uma abordagem sintáctico
fonológica', Castilho, *Português falado*, IV, 273–319.

ADVERBS.   T. Móia, 'Sintagmas com *Durante* e *Em* como expressões
de localização temporal ou de duração', *Actas* (APL 1996), I, 227–40,
argues that such time expressions are primarily of temporal location,
durational values being contextually determined. On *então*, A. C. M.
Lopes, '*Então*: elementos para uma análise semântica e pragmática',
ib., 177–90, distinguishes temporal and discourse values; M. M.
Risso, 'O articulador discursivo "então"', Castilho, *Português falado*,
IV, 423–51, details discourse uses; A. B. Afonso, 'Da especifidade de
alguns enunciados interrogativos (valores particulares com a ocorrência de *então*)', *Actas* (APL 1996), I, 25–37, highlights the interrogative
use of *então* to correct or contradict.

NEGATION. A. M. Martins, 'Aspectos da negação na história das línguas românicas. (Da natureza da palavras como *nenhum, nada, ninguém*)', *Actas* (APL 1996), II, 179–210, finds an evolution of polarity values.

DISCOURSE. Castilho, *Português falado*, IV, contains L.C. Travaglia, 'Tipologia textual e coesão/coerência no texto oral: transições tipológicas' (453–71); L. L. Fávero et al., 'Perguntas e respostas como mecanismos de coesão e coerência no texto falado' (473–508). J. Fonseca, 'O funcionamento discursivo de "se não A, pelo menos B"', *Diacritica*, 11, 1996[1997]:309–47. A. T. Alves, 'Acerca da selecção temporal no discurso', *Actas* (APL 1996), I, 39–46, has a simplistic view of sequence of tenses. H. J. Batoréo, 'Factores linguísticos, cognitivos e culturais na definição do modelo espácio-temporal do texto', *ib.*, 61–71, highlights the Ptg. dynamic conception of textual progression typified by the use of *recuar/avançar* for orientation in texts. D. P. Oliveira, 'O tópico em língua escrita', *LetL*, 12.2, 1996:149–61, argues that Ptg. is 'uma língua que tem tópico, e não uma língua de tópico'.

5. SEMANTICS AND LEXICON

SEMANTICS. A. S. Silva, 'A mudança semântica como reorganização de protótipos. O verbo *deixar*', *Actas* (APL 1996), I, 317–27, applies prototype theory to the evolution of *leixar/deixar*: there are always two protypes, but passive values come to the fore. M. Vilela, 'Do campo lexical à explicação cognitiva: *risco* e *perigo*', *Diacritica*, 11, 1996[1997]:639–65. G. Funk, 'O provérbio entre a oralidade e a escrita', *RevL*, 15, 1996:29–38. *Theoretical Issues and Practical Cases in Portuguese-English Translations*, ed. Malcolm Coulthard and Pat Odber de Baubeta, NY-Lampeter, Mellen, 1996, 144 pp.

LEXICOLOGY AND LEXICOGRAPHY. P. E. L. Mendes, 'O dicionário inédito de José Leite de Vasconcellos, *Folhas para um Dicionário da Língua Portuguesa*', *Actas* (APL 1996), II, 475–82, gives samples. J. A. Sábio and C. Jiménez, 'O *Dicionário Castelhano y Português* de Rafael Bluteau: um dicionário moderno?', *ib.*, 537–47. M. H. S. Sereno, 'Entre gostar e amar: análise sintáctico-semântica e textual', *RFLUP*, 14:141–63, finds case frames and syntax the major differenciating factors. A. Iriarte Sanromán, 'Co-ocorrência léxica no dicionário de Espanhol-Português', *Actas* (APL 1996), I, 149–56, emphasizes the need to recognize collocations. M. A. Marques, 'Siglas: um caso marginal de renovação lexical', *Diacritica*, 11, 1996[1997]:603–18. I. A. S. Stamato, 'Estudo dos nomes abstratos de acordo com a gramática de valência', *LetL*, 12.1, 1996:97–115, explores valency in different types of abstract nouns, with predictable results.

DERIVATION. C. A. V. Gonçalves and R. G. R. Costa, 'Um caso de distribuição complementar no léxico: os sufixos agentivos denominais', *LetL*, 13.1:25–35, finds a prestige hierarchy linking -*o*, -*ista*, -*ário*, and -*eiro*. M. Basilio, 'Formação e uso da nominalização deverbal sufixal no português falado', Castilho, *Português falado*, IV, 23–33, correlates register and functions of nominalizations.

ONOMASTICS. N. Nunes lists and studies 'Os prenomes de escravos na antroponímia primitiva da Madeira', *Actas* (APL 1996), II, 219–31.

6. SOCIOLINGUISTICS AND DIALECTOLOGY

SOCIOLINGUISTICS

GENERAL. M. Cook, 'Uma teoria de interpretação das formas de tratamento na língua portuguesa', *His(US)*, 80:451–64, adds a neutral term (the subjectless 3rd person verb forms) to the familiar V-T scheme; see by the same author 'On the Portuguese forms of address: from *vossa mercê* to *você*', *PSR*, 3.2, 1995:78–89, and 'Formas de tratamento do português actual: uma perspectiva sociolinguística', *JACIS*, 7.2, 1994:47–52.

BRAZIL. A. N. Isquerdo, 'Aspectos lexicais do português de fronteira', *Actas* (APL 1996), I, 125–34, looks at interactions in the vocabulary of foodstuffs on the Brazil-Paraguay frontier.

PORTUGAL. M. F. R. F. Matias, *Aspectos de estrutura sociolinguística da cidade de Aveiro*, Aveiro, Câmara Municipal, 1995, 259 pp., is a flawed study of urban sociolinguistics, showing maintenance of predictable regional features (*v/b* neutralization; lack of *e*-centralization; hiatus breaking in *a(j)agua*). F. Dantas-Ferreira, 'De "Por Senhor, que ainda há respeito" a "Por Tu, como havia de ser?": um estudo de variação em tempo aparente', *Actas* (APL 1996), I, 117–23, plots the advance of symmetrical *tu* usage in Northern Portugal.

DIALECTOLOGY

Eduardo Brazão Gonçalves, *Dicionário do falar algarvio*, 2nd edn, Faro, Algarve em Foco, 1996, 200 pp. B. F. Head returns to 'A "troca do V pelo B": uma alternância do norte de Portugal também encontrada no português popular do Brasil?', *Diacritica*, 11, 1996[1997]:767–81. I. A. Santos, 'Fenómenos de palatalização vocálica na România: valor dialectal em território português (continental)', *Actas* (APL 1996), II, 273–87, discusses French origins for dialectal /y/ (=/ü/).

7. PORTUGUESE OVERSEAS

W. Bal, 'Miettes de lexicologie afro-romane', *Vázquez Vol.*, 393–400, lists borrowings between Ptg. and African languages. J. S. Terra, 'A datação do primeiro texto em "língua de preto" na literatura portuguesa', *Diacritica*, 11, 1996[1997]:513–28. G. N. Batalha, 'O português falado e escrito pelos chineses de Macau', *Vázquez Vol.*, 203–12, has brief notes on the early use of Macau creole by the Chinese population, and on typical modern speech errors.

MEDIEVAL LITERATURE*

By STEPHEN PARKINSON, *Lecturer in Portuguese Language and Linguistics,
University of Oxford*, and KIRSTIN KENNEDY, *The Queen's College, Oxford*

(This survey covers the period 1989–97)

1. GENERAL

Dicionário da literatura medieval galega e portuguesa, ed. Giulia Lanciani
and Guiseppe Tavani, L, Caminho, 1993, 698 pp., is a rich and
authoritative reference work, with extensive sections on texts, terminology, authors and genres. Hugo Kunoff, *Portuguese Literature from
its Origins to 1990: A Bibliography Based on the Collections of Indiana
University*, Metuchen, NJ, Scarecrow Press, 1994, ix + 497 pp. A.
Deyermond, 'The lost literature of medieval Portugal: further
observations', *Willis Vol.*, 39–49, extends his earlier catalogue
(*YWMLS*, 49:401), including mention of some recent recoveries.
Ribeiro, *Género*, contains T. Amado, 'Os géneros e o trabalho textual'
(9–28); A. A. Nascimento, 'Traduzir, verbo de fronteira nos contornos
da Idade Média' (113–38); A. P. Morais, 'Alguns aspectos da retórica
do exemplo: lógica do modelo e hipóteses da ficção do *exemplum*
medieval' (227–37). Nuno Júdice, *O espaço do conto no texto medieval*, L,
Vega, 1991, 270 pp., from the perspective of critical theory, attempts
to differentiate between oral and written modes of *contar*, referring to
a wide range of short narratives. Godinho, *Imagem*, overwhelmingly
general in content, contains several items of Portuguese interest:
A. Rocha, 'O mar na literatura portuguesa antes dos descobrimentos'
(253–59), collecting a range of references, from the 'barcas novas' of
the *cantigas de amigo* to D. Duarte's allegory of 'Da barca sã e rota';
M. F. Pimentel Fontes, 'A lenda do rei Rodrigo: o herói e a decifração
do mundo' (155–60); J. V. Pina Martins, 'Entre a Idade Média e a
modernidade. Imagem de uma igreja decadente no "Tratado de
Confissom"' (267–80).

On texts and translations, Isabel Cepeda, *Bibliografia da prosa
medieval em língua portuguesa*, L, IBNL, 1995, 265 pp., is a much needed
updating of Cintra's 1960 bibliography. A. A. Gonçalves Rodrigues,
A tradução em Portugal, 1: 1495–1834, L, INCM, 1992, 428 pp., lists five
works up to 1500. A. L. F. Askins transcribes, '"Os Doze Manda-
mentos": an early Portuguese translation of the *Doctrina mandatorum*

* This article was compiled with the assistance of Dr Lisa Barber (University of
Oxford) and Maria Manuela Carvalho (University of Birmingham). The authors
gratefully acknowledge financial support from the Faculty of Medieval and Modern
Languages, University of Oxford.

duodecim Athanasii', *RFLUL*, 13–14, 1990:67–75. J. de Azevedo Ferreira, 'Traduction et paraphrase dans les premiers textes juridiques portugais', *CLHM*, 14–15, 1989–90:63–77. A. M. Espírito Santo, 'Problemas de imitação e tradução literária no Noroeste peninsular: para uma reinterpretação da figura de Martinho de Braga', *Actas* (Granada), II, 219–27, is concerned with Greek and Latin texts. C. B. Faulhaber, 'Sobre la cultura ibérica medieval: las lenguas vernáculas y la traducción', *Actas* (AHLM 6), I, 587–97, is a general survey of the number of translations made from Latin and other languages, into Span., Cat. and Ptg. M. G. Simões, *'D. Duarte e a teoria da tradução em Portugal no sec. XV'*, *Del Tradurre*, 2, 1995:19–27. J. M. Fradejas Rueda, '¿Una versión catalana del *Livro de Falcoaria* de Pero Menino?', *Actas* (Lisbon), III, 187–90, argues that the Catalan text is derived from the Ptg. work by Pero Menino, rather than López de Ayala's later treatise. T. García-Sabell Tormo, 'Sobre a traducción de textos literarios franceses na edade media: o capítulo 6 de *Erec*', *ib.*, IV, 315–24, concludes that the Gal.-Ptg. version is not a faithful rendition of the French text. A. Cortijo Ocaño, 'O Livro do Amante: the lost Portuguese translation of John Gower's Confessio Amantis (Madrid: Biblioteca de Palacio MS II-3088)', *PortSt*, 13:1–6, reconstructs the chronology of the transmission of the newly rediscovered MS, which he describes in 'La traducción portuguesa de la Confessio Amantis de John Gower', *Euphrosyne*, 23, 1995:457–66; see also B. Santano Moreno, 'The fifteenth-century Portuguese and Castilian translations of John Gower, *Confessio amantis*', *Manuscripta*, 35, 1991:23–34. R. B. Bernard, 'The intellectual circle of Isabel of Portugal, duchess of Burgundy, and the Portuguese translation of *Le Livre des Trois Vertus* (*O Livro dos Tres Virtudes*)', pp. 43–58 of *Reception of Christine de Pisan from the Fifteenth through the Nineteenth Centuries: Visitors to the City*, ed. Glenda K. McLeod, NY, Mellen, 1991. J. L. Freire, 'Los códices gallegos basados en el Roman de Troie y sus ediciones: Bibliografia sumaria', *RevR*, 24, 1989:116–25. J. Mattoso, 'O imaginário do Alem-Túmulo nos *exempla* peninsulares da Idade Media', *Actas* (Granada), I, 131–46, discussing *Orto do Esposo*, *Libro de los exemplos por ABC*, *Espéculo de los Legos*, with passing references to the *CSM*, aims to show that although these works slavishly imitate the structure of French and English collections of *exempla*, the examples used are grounded firmly in Iberian traditions of wisdom literature. J. A. Sabio Pinilla, 'Aspectos medievales de *Os Lusíadas*', *ib.*, 253–59, claims that 'La Edad Media portuguesa fue una preparación para su Renacimiento', the mediæval aspects of *Os Lusíadas* being Camões's encyclopaedic view of national history, and the themes and ideas which spring from this. Sheila R. Ackerlind, *King Dinis of Portugal and the Alfonsine Heritage* (AUS, ser. 9, History, 69), NY, Lang, 1990,

220 pp., is an uncritical collection of commonplaces, doing justice to neither monarch. P. A. Odber de Baubeta, 'Confession and penitence in Medieval Portuguese literature', *Willis Vol.*, 69–83, finds resonances in a wide range of texts and genres.

2. THE GALICIAN-PORTUGUESE LYRIC

GENERAL

COLLECTIONS. *O Cantar dos Trobadores*, the most important meeting of scholars of the last few years, contains the following general articles: A. Roncaglia, 'Ecci venuto Guido 'n Compostello?' (Cavalcanti e la Galizia)' (11–29); X. Filgueira Valverde, 'Compostela e os trobadores' (99–106); C. Alvar, 'Poesía gallego-portuguesa y Materia de Bretaña: algunas hipótesis' (31–51); A. Resende de Oliveira, 'A caminho de Galiza. Sobre as primeiras composições em galego-português' (249–61); I. de Riquer, 'Poemas catalanes con citas de trovadores provenzales y de poetas de otras lenguas' (289–314); C. Segre, 'Gl'inserti popolareschi nella lirica e nel romanzo (sec. XIII) e la preistoria delle *cantigas d'amigo*' (315–28). *Colectanea de estudios filológicos (lingüística, léxico, lírica y retórica) de la Profesor Aurora Juárez Blanquer (in memoriam)*, ed. Antonio R. Rubio Flores, Granada U.P., 1994, 323 pp., reprints key articles on the medieval lyric, including introductory sections to the new edition of Pero da Ponte left unfinished at J.B.'s untimely death.

EDITIONS. *Lírica profana galego-portuguesa. Corpus completo das cantigas medievais, con estudio biográfico, análise retórica e bibliografía específica*, coord. Mercedes Brea, 2 vols, Santiago de Compostela, Xunta da Galicia — Centro de Investigacións Lingüísticas e Literarias Ramon Piñeiro, 1996, 1–560, 561–1071 pp., is the first publication of the *Arquivo Galicia Medieval* project. The whole secular corpus, computerized in an SGML-based text database, is republished in conventional format with supporting material, ordered by author and incipit following Tavani's *Repertorio metrico* (rather than the order of the MSS, with implications for the study of sequences), and following established 'safe' editions. The true value of the project will be realised when the searchable text database comes online (http://www.cirp.es/meddb). Richard Zenith, *113 Galician-Portuguese Troubadour Poems*, Manchester, Carcanet, 1995, xlii + 280 pp., bravely translates an anthology with all genres well represented, and expresses his angst at the difficulty of the task in 'A tradução das cantigas medievais, ou a arte de saber perder', *CoL*, 132–33, 1994:5–20. *Medieval Galician-Portuguese Poetry. An Anthology*, ed. and trans. F. Jensen, NY, Garland, 1992, cxxxviii + 624 pp., has a conservative selection, with staid translations, and a lengthy but unoriginal introduction. G. E. Sansone,

Diorama Lusitano: Poesie d'amore e di scherno dei trovatori galego-portoghesi, Milan, BUR, 1990, 346 pp., is a parallel text Italian-Ptg. edition with a substantial introduction and bibliography.

MANUSCRIPTS. The discovery of the *Pergaminho Sharrer* is documented in H. L. Sharrer, 'The discovery of seven cantigas d'amor by Dom Dinis with musical notation', *His(US)*, 74, 1991:459–61, and 'Fragmentos de sete cantigas d'amor de D.Dinis, musicadas: uma descoberta', *Actas* (Lisbon), I, 13–30, with paleographical and musical descriptions by A. J. R. Guerra (31–34) and M. P. Ferreira (35–42). *Fragmento do Nobiliario do Conde Dom Pedro. Cancioneiro da Ajuda. Edição facsimilada do códice existente na Biblioteca da Ajuda*, 2 vols, L, Távola Redonda — Instituto Português do Patrimonio Arquitectónico e Arqueológico — Biblioteca da Ajuda, 1994, unpaged + 70 pp., is a limited edition facsimile with useful accompanying material, especially M. A. Ramos (27–47). A. Askins, 'The Cancioneiro da Bancroft Library (previously the Cancioneiro de um Grande d'Hespanha). A copy c.1600 of the Cancioneiro da Vaticana', *Actas* (Lisbon) I, 43–47, reports on an interesting but less momentous MS. Antonio Resende de Oliveira, *Depois do espectáculo trovadoresco. A estrutura dos cancioneiros peninsulares e as recolhas dos sec. XIII e XIV*, L, Colibri, 467 pp., finally achieves a synthesis of the structure and compilation of the *cancioneiros* that allows conclusions about dating, origins, authorship, and genre to be drawn, and gives updated biographies of many trovadores (repeated in *Trobadores e xograres: contexto histórico*, Vigo, Xerais, 1995, 200 pp.). Earlier works in this direction by the same author include: 'Do *Cancioneiro da Ajuda* ao *Livro das cantigas* do conde D.Pedro. Analise do acrescento à secção das cantigas de amigo Ω', *RHI*, 10, 1988:691–751; 'Investigação histórica e compilações trovadorescas', *Actas* (Lisbon), II, 169–73, identifying Stevam Travanca as author of the unattributed A185. Works superseded by it include H. Livermore, 'The formation of the cancioneiros', *ArCCP*, 25, 1988:107–47. E. Gonçalves, 'O sistema das rubricas atributivas e explicativas nos cancioneiros trovadorescos galego-portugueses', *Actas* (Santiago de Compostela), VII, 979–90, interprets the indications of internal structure of the original *cancioneiro*. On *marginalia*, *Actes* (Zurich), V, contains M. Brea and F. F. Campo, 'Notas linguisticas de A. Colocci no cancioneiro galego-portugues B' (39–56), and M. A. Ramos, 'L'importance des corrections marginales dans le Chansonnier d'Ajuda' (141–52). M. A. Ramos, 'Tradições gráficas nos manuscritos da lírica galego-portuguesa', *Actes* (Trier), VI, 37–48, has important observations on orthography, abbreviations, and truncation of refrains. M. Ciceri, 'Burle spagnole per calze portoghesi', *Bellini Vol.*, I, 245–55, discusses and edits some 20 stanzas of a 16th-c. copy of a *cantiga* in Chantilly MS.

TROVADORES AND *JOGRAIS*.   G. Tavani, 'I giullari e i canzoneri', *Bellini Vol.*, ii, 999–1013, discusses the evidence for *joglar* activity and presents his case for their compositions to have been deliberately excluded from the later compilations; similar ideas are presented in Id.,'Os jograis galegos e portugueses: considerações sobre a censura', Rossi, *Jongleurs*, 175–89, focusing on the derogatory tone of what little material there is, and the impenetrably cryptic references found in the poetry. G. Vallín, 'Trovador versus juglar: conclusiones de la crítica y documentos', *Actas* (Salamanca), 1115–20, argues persuasively that the divisions between the supposed 'trovador' and 'juglar' class are too rigid. F. Jensen, 'Sobre la herencia de los trovadores en la lírica galaico-portuguesa', *ib.*, 485–92, takes a more conventional line in arguing that, unlike in France, the jogral was the lowest of the low while the troubador was a talented composer. Similarly, P. Lorenzo Gradín, '"Mester con pecado": la juglaría en la Península Ibérica', Rossi, *Jongleurs*, 99–129. On broader historical background, A. Resende de Oliveira, 'Trovadores portugueses na corte de Afonso X', pp. 3–16 of vol. ii of *Actas das ii Jornadas Luso-espanholas de Historia Medieval*, Porto, INIC, 1987; Id., 'A cultura trovadoresca no ocidente peninsular: trovadores e jograis galegos', *Biblos*, 43, 1987:1–22; Id., 'A Galiza e a cultura trovadoresca peninsular', *RHI*, 11, 1989:7–36. A. Víñez, 'Documentación de trovadores', *Actas* (Alcalá), 531–42, searches official documents, finding references to Afonso Lópes de Bayão, Airas Pérez Vuitoron, Johan López de Ulloa, Pero Amigo, Mem Rodrigues Tenoiro, Estevam Perez Froyan, Gonçalo Eanes do Vinhal, and others. J. A. Osório, 'Trovador e poeta do sec. xiii ao sec xv', *RFLUP*, 10, 1993:93–108, links the appearance of *poeta* in the 15th c. with the decay of the view of *trovar* as an aristocratic preserve.

THEMES AND INFLUENCES.   G. Tavani, 'As artes poéticas hispânicas do século xiii e do início do xiv, na perspectiva das teorizações provençais', *Actas* (Lisbon), ii, 25–34, concludes that the *Arte de trovar* is a retrospective guide to 'um património literário já não actual', possibly by one of the compilers of the original *cancioneiro*. Arabic influence is asserted in R. Boase, 'Arab Influences on European Love-Poetry', pp. 457–82 of *The Legacy of Muslim Spain*, ed. Salma Khadra Jayyusi, Leiden, Brill, 1992, ix + 1098 pp., and D. Wulstan, 'Boys, women and drunkards: Hispano-mauresque influences on European song', pp. 136–67 of *The Arab Influence in Medieval Europe: Folia Scholastica Mediterranea*, ed. Dionisius A. Agius and Richard Hitchcock (Middle East Culture Series, 18), Reading, Ithaca, 1994, xi + 181 pp., who argues that Arabic-Berber influence on Romance poetry occurred through the genre of the *zajal* rather than that of *muwashshah*. Conversely, M. J. Rubiera Mata, 'Jarchas de posible origen galaico-portugués', *Actas* (Lisbon), iv, 79–81, uses Arab accounts of music, and a comparison between themes of *kharjas* and themes of Galician-Portuguese cantigas to argue that the *kharjas* represent proto-romance Occitan lyric in Galician-Portuguese. M. Brea, 'La *fin'amor* et les troubadours galiciens-portugais', *RLaR*, 100, 1996:81–107, concludes that there was a great deal of overlap between Provençal and Iberian poetry. Similarly, E. Fidalgo Francisco and J. A. Souto Cabo, 'El amor de oídas desde la lírica gallego-portuguesa', *Actas* (Granada), II, 313–28, catalogue examples of the topos of 'amor de lonh' and the re-working of these ideas in *cantigas de escarnho* to claim that the Gal.-Ptg. lyrics were totally in keeping with European traditions. I. González, 'El apóstrofe en Guido Guinizzelli. Semejanzas y diferencias con la lírica gallego-portuguesa', *Actas* (Salamanca), 429–36, lists features in the Italian poet's œuvre which are then compared with Gal.-Ptg. poems, concluding that the apostrophe is placed in a greater variety of places in the Italian poems. V. Beltrán, 'Tipos y temas trovadorescas. Leonoreta / Fin Roseta, la corte poética de Alfonso XI y el origen del Amadís', pp. 111–25 of vol I of *Actas del X Congreso da la Asociación Internacional de Hispanistas, Barcelona, 21–26 de agosto de 1989*, ed. Antonio Vilanova, Barcelona, PPU, 1992, P. Picoito, 'Espaço e poder na épica medieval portuguesa', *CoL*, 142, 1996:65–81, is interesting on geographical aspects; see also S. Reckert, 'Espacio, tiempo y memoria en la lírica galaico-portuguesa', *Actas* (AHLM 6), I, 57–70.

T. R. Hart, 'New perspectives on the medieval Portuguese lyric', *Homenagem Stegagno Picchio*, 69–78, searching for meaningful micro-contexts, sees the study of interrelationships between poets and genres as a key feature. *Actas* (Alcalá), includes: C. Alvar, 'Épica y lírica románicas en el último quartel del siglo XIII' (13–24); V. Bertolucci Pizzorusso, 'La lirica galego-portogheses all'epoca di Sancho IV di Castiglia' (25–34); V. Beltrán, 'Tipos y temas trovadorescos XI. La corte poética de Sancho IV' (121–40); M. L. A. Juárez Blanquer, 'Afinidad entre la lírica de Afonso X y Pero da Ponte', *BCSM*, 2, 1988–89:3–11, is predictable. H. Livermore, 'Santillana and the Galaico-Portuguese poets', *Iberoromania*, 31, 1990:53–64, traces the influence of the poetry, with many historical facts thrown in. A. W. Hamos, 'Popular elements in late troubadour poetry: the Galician-Portuguese influence', *Tenso*, 7, 1991:12–22. S. Fortuño Llorens, 'La modernidad literaria de la lírica galaico-portuguesa', *Actas* (AHLM 6), I, 617–27, studies modern poets' use of old genres, revealing the 'perenne potencial expresivo' of Gal.-Ptg. poetry. T. López, 'Leituras poéticas dos Cancioneiros', *Actas* (Lisbon) I, 325–30, discusses Cunqueiro's re-working of mediæval Gal.-Ptg. poetic forms. J. S. Miletich, 'Early medieval Iberian lyric and archaic Croatian folk song', *La corónica*, 19, 1990:83–95, argues that the relationship between the Croatian folk and literary traditions offers an approach for the comparative study of the *cantigas de amigo* and *kharjas*.

LANGUAGE AND STYLE. T. García-Sabell Tormo, *Léxico Francés nos Cancioneiros Galego-Portugueses: Revisión Crítica*, Vigo, Galaxia, 1990, 371 pp., lists borrowings with commentary on occurrence, etymology, and appearance in early prose; see also her 'Puntualizacions á influencia da escola trobadoresca no léxico da lírica galego-portuguesa', *Homenaxe García*, I, 171–78, pointing out the importance of borrowings for rhyme. M. A. Ramos, 'Um provençalismo no Cancioneiro da Ajuda: senner', *Piel Vol.*, 621–37, finds it used mainly in satirical poetry. A. M. Mussons (Freixas), 'Los trovadores y el juego del lenguaje', *O Cantar dos Trobadores*, 221–33, looks at the use of *trobar* and *cantar*, which serve to distinguish the activity of the *trobador* (*trobar*, *fazer cantar*) and the jogral (*cantar*, *dizer cantar*). A. Juárez Blanquer, 'Datos de retórica literaria emanados de la poesía de los cancioneros', *Actas* (Lisbon), II, 193–201, trawls through the *cancioneiros* for words such as *cantiga* and *cantar*, as evidence on how the poets themselves defined these words. On labels for verse forms, X. Filgueira Valverde, 'Sobre a nomenclatura da cantiga galego-portuguesa medieval: leixapren, refran, cossaute', *Piel Vol.*, 547–67. E. Corral Díaz, 'A *donzela* na lírica profana galego-portuguesa', *ib.*, 349–56, concentrates on secular lyrics, noting that the word *donzela* rarely appears except in *cantigas de escarnho*, but fails to draw any overall conclusion. Id., 'A denominacion *donas* nas cantigas de amigo', *Homenaxe García*, II, 275–83, following M. Brea, '"Dona" e "Senhor" nas cantigas de amor', *Homenaje Rubio García*, I, 149–70. F. Magán Abelleira, 'Sobre algunos rasgos epigramáticos en textos monoestróficos gallego-portugueses', *Actas* (AHLM 6), II, 957–65, is a lively article which focuses on the epigrammatic qualities of nine *cantigas*. J. Sáez Durán and A. Víñez Sánchez, 'Expresiones fijas en las cantigas gallego-portuguesas', *Actas* (Granada), IV, 261–71, are at pains to distinguish between 'formulas' and 'expresiones fijas', which are used for reasons of metrics. J. Dionísio, 'Condições de produção da cantiga: os pagamentos com panos', *Actas* (Santiago de Compostela), VII, 683–95, collects examples of verse rewarded by gifts of clothes, noting their concentration in the middle of the 13th century. M. Manero Sorolla, 'La imagen del ave fénix en la poesía de cancionero: notas para un estudio', *AEM*, 21, 1991 : 291–305. J. M. Díaz de Bustamente, 'Sobre la tradición elocutiva en las cantigas con textos latinos de los cancioneiros gallego-portugueses', *Homenaxe García*, II, 293–307, looks at the variety of reasons for the incorporation of snippets of liturgical Latin in the secular and religious lyric.

METRICS AND MUSIC. E. Gonçalves, 'Atehudas ata a fiinda', *O Cantar dos Trobadores*, 167–86, definitively resolves problems of terminology, distinguishing the *cantiga atehuda* (of which she identifies 43) from its more complex variant the *cantiga atehuda ataa a fiinda*. A. Ferrari, 'Parola-rima', *ib.*, 121–36, compares the rigidity of the Gal.-Ptg. *dobre* and *mordobre* with Provençal devices. M. L. Meneghetti, 'Les refrains romains: une question d'ensemble', *Actas* (Santiago de Compostela), VII, 331–38, notes the complementary preferences for *formes fixes* in Fr. lyric and paralellism in Gal.-Ptg. M. Tyssens, 'Cantigas d'amigo et chansons de femmme', *ib.*, 329–47, suggests that *leixa-pren* was a device borrowed from Fr. *chansons à danser* as part of the enrichment of traditional parallelistic forms. Â. Correia, 'O sistema das coblas doblas na lírica galego-portuguesa', *Actas* (Granada), II, 75–90, gives tabular information on rhyme schemes. A. Ripoll, '"Levantou-s'a velida ... Levou-s' a velida": unha análise de métrica rítmica na lírica medieval galego-portuguesa', *BGL*, 14, 1995:47–70, gives a weighty analysis of rhythm, with diagrams. Id., 'Jarcha, cantiga de amigo e a orixe da seguidilla na mélica tradicional peninsular. Unha análise comparativa de métrica acentual', *O Cantar dos Trobadores*, 461–73. D. Prieto Alonso, 'A métrica acentual na cantiga de amigo', *Homenagem Stegagno Picchio*, 111–42, gives a generative account of accentual structures, thus explaining irregular syllable counts. A. Víñez and J. Sáez, 'Un rimario de las cantigas de amigo', *Actas* (AHLM 6), II, 1589–98, summarize previous work and their own work in progress. On contrafactions, P. Canettieri and C. Pulsoni, 'Contrafacta galego-portoghesi', *Actas* (Granada), I, 479–97, P. Canettieri, 'Il *contrafactum* galego-portoghese di un *descort* occitanico', *Actas* (Salamanca), 209–17; P. Lorenzo Gradin, '*Acessus ad tropatores*. Contribución al estudio de los "contrafacta" en la lírica gallego-portuguesa', *Actes* (Zurich), V, 99–112.

GENRES

GENERAL. E. Gonçalves, 'Sur la lyrique galego-portuguaise. Phénoménologie de la constitution des chansonniers par genres', pp. 447–68 of *La tradition des chansonniers. Actes du colloque de Liège 1989*, ed. M. Tyssens, Liège, Bibl. de la Faculté de Philosophie et Lettres, 1991, 516 pp. A. A. L. Diogo, 'Lírica galego-portuguesa. Genologia e generalização', Ribeiro, *Género*, 29–42, approaches the interlinking of genres and social conventions from the point of view of prototype theory. M. R. Ferreira, '*Nomina sunt res*? Do poder reificador das designações genéricas no corpus da lírica galego-portuguesa', *ib.*, 43–54, rejects *alba* and *cantiga de romaria* as separate genres.

CANTIGA DE AMIGO. General works on the genre include: P. Lorenzo Gradín, *La canción de mujer en la lírica medieval*, Santiago de Compostela U.P., 1990, 282 pp; U. Mölk, *Die fruhen romanischen

Frauenlieder: Uberlegungen und Anregungen', pp. 63–88 of *Idee, Gestalt, Geschichte: Festschrift Klaus von See. Studien zur europaischen Kulturtradition*, ed. G. W. Weber, Odense U.P. 1988. On sexuality, M. de Antunes-Rambaud, 'Mère et fille dans les chansons d'ami galiciennes-portuguaises', pp. 131–39 of *Les relations de parenté dans le monde médiéval: XIVe colloque du Centre Universitaire d'Études et de Recherches Médiévales d'Aix (Senefiance, 26)*, Aix-en-Provence, Univ. de Provence — CUER MA, 1989, 604 pp.; A. D. Deyermond, 'Sexual initiation in the woman's-voice court lyric', *Papers* (ICLS 5), 125–58; A. P. Ferreira, 'Telling woman what she wants: the cantigas d'amigo as strategies of containment', *PortSt*, 9, 1993:23–38, is a feminist reading. On relations with other lyric corpora, A. Juárez Blanquer, 'Cantiga de amigo y poesía popular', pp. 153–67 of vol II of *Homenaje al prof. Antonio Gallego Morell*, ed. C. Argente del Castillo et al, 3 vols, Granada, 1989; B. Spaggiari, 'Frammenti di Cantiga de amigo in testi oitanici del'ultimo '200', *MedRom*, 17, 1992:183–95. R. Cossío Vélez, 'Hacia un repertorio temático de la cantiga de amigo', *Actas* (Granada), II, 91–95, describes problems and methods of work in progress.

    CANTIGA DE AMOR.   Vicente Beltrán, *A *Cantiga de Amor*, Vigo, Xerais, 264 pp. Id. (as Vicenç Beltran), 'A estructura conceptual de la cantiga de amor', *O Cantar dos Trobadores*, 53–75, makes illuminating comparisons with 17th-c. *conceptista* poetry, showing that the medieval poets' cultivation of a cryptic and oblique mode of expression stems not from a desire to surprise but from 'la obsesión por la unidad del poema'. J. Weiss, 'On the conventionality of the *Cantigas d'amor*', *La Corónica*, 26.1:225–45, shows how scholars have ignored the possibilities of these poems, classifying them as monotonous and conventional; from comparisons with the *cantiga de amigo*, observations on the way men represent themselves in the *cantiga de amor*, and the identification of distinctive uses of syntax as motifs particular to individual poets, W. argues persuasively that 'we should in fact regard their conventionality as a very creative practice'. X. Ron Fernández, 'Os trobadores no tempo da frol', *O Cantar dos Trobadores*, 475–92, identifies the claims to sincerity of *vozes discordantes* such as Dinis as a rhetorical device to individualize *coita de amor*, and not a statement of poetics. J. Casas Rigall, 'Desdoblamiento del yo lírico y silepsis en la cantiga de amor gallego-portuguesa y el cancionero amatorio castellano', *ib.*, 387–402, looks at synonyms of the poetic 'I'. A. Correia finds 31 cases of 'A jura como prova na cantiga de amor galego-portuguesa', Ribeiro, *Género*, 55–69. J. A. Frazão, 'A razão e o afecto na lírica de amor galego-portuguesa', *Actas* (Lisbon), III, 125–28. M. E. G. de Vasconcellos, 'As cantigas de amor: um serviço de alta tensão erótica', *CLus*, 9, 1992:78–93, gets more and more excited as she moves from 'silêncio feminino' to suggestions of 'paixão transgressora'. M. Brea, 'El *escondit* como variante de las cantigas de amor y de amigo', *Actas* (Lisbon), IV, 175–87, identifies a class of poems in which poets rebut accusations by *miscradores*, showing it to be a borrowing from the *escondit;* see also her 'Anotaciones sobre la función de los *miscradores* en las cantigas de amor gallego-portuguesas', *CN*, 52, 1992:167–80. V. Bertolucci Pizzorusso, 'Motivi e registri minoritari nell lirica d'amore galego portoghese: la *cantiga "de change"'*, *O Cantar dos Trobadores*, 109–20, focuses on poems declaring a new love. X. Filgueira Valverde, 'A servidume de amor e a expresión feudal nos Cancioneros', *Homenagem Stegagno Picchio*, 185–207, illustrates the whole glossary of *serviço de amor*. M. C. Vilhena, 'A amada das cantigas de amor: casada ou solteira?', *ib.*, 209–21, argues that the purity of feelings involved in the *cantiga de amor* made the *senhor*'s marital status irrelevant. Word studies include E. Corral Díaz, 'O vocabulario bélico na cantiga de amor', *Actas* (AHLM 6), I, 533–42; L. Curado Neves, 'O campo semântico da partida na cantiga d'amor galego-portuguesa', *Actas* (Lisbon), III, 259–65. On word-play, E. Fidalgo, 'En torno al *mot-equivoc* en la cantiga de amor gallego-portuguesa', *Actas* (AHLM 6), I, 611–16, is a routine survey, mainly on *senhor*.

ESCARNHO E MAL DIZER. Graça Videira Lopes, *A sátira nos cancioneiros medievais galego-portugueses*, L, Estampa, 1994, 385 pp., is a major advance in the study of the genre, clearly identifying the different modes of satirical writing, and showing the extent of a little appreciated genre, the *maldizer aposto* in which the apparent narrator is in fact the butt of the satire. Giulia Lanciani and Giuseppe Tavani, *As cantigas de escarnio*, trans. Silvia Gaspar, Vigo, Xerais, 1995, 212 pp., is a useful introduction incorporating some previous work. Manuel Rodrigues Lapa, *Cantigas d'escarnho e de mal dizer dos cancioneiros medievais galego-portugueses*, Vigo, Ir Indo — Lisbon, João Sá da Costa, 3rd edn, 1995, 395 pp., is a glossily illustrated re-edition, not really for scholarly use. M. A. Ramos, 'La satire dans les *cantigas d'escarnho e de mal dizer*. Les péchés de la langue', *Atalaya*, 5, 1994:67–84, notes the inadequacy of the *Arte de trovar* definition of these poems, and observes that they are often not satirical in sense that they often do not criticize anyone or anything in particular; instead they subvert and extend the language of courtly love by focusing on the real, material aspects of this abstract concept. G. Vallín, 'Escarnho d'amor', *MedRom*, 21:132–46, suggests that some *escarnhos* are better classified as love poetry. A. A. L. Diogo, 'Escarnh' e mal dizer em contexto', *Diacritica*, 10, 1995:401–60, tries to reconstruct the social context and functions of the explosion of satirical poetry in the second generation of *trobadores*. Id., 'Algumas considerações sobre o escarnh' e mal dizer',

Actas (Santiago de Compostela), VII, 697–06, shows the difficulties in attempts to distinguish *escarnho* and *maldizer* on thematic or stylistic grounds. J. Ventura, 'Sátira e aldrabaxe entre trobadores e xograis', *O Cantar dos Trobadores*, 533–50, argues for a subclassification of the genre, and studies a subgroup of *cantigas de escarnho* in comparison with Provençal counterparts. X. X. Ron Fernández, '*Porque no mundo mengou a verdade*. As cantigas morais na lírica galego-portuguesa', *Actas* (AHLM 6), II, 1347–66, rejects the Fr. term 'sirventés' and considers only 18 cantigas to be 'morais', insisting rather obviously that such poems should not be lumped in with the more popular *escarnho e mal dizer* which superseded them. G. Gouiran, '*Os meum replebo increpationibus*. Comment parler à Dieu sans prier, ou la contestation contre Dieu dans les lyriques occitane et galaico-portugais', *O Cantar dos Trobadores*, 77–98, includes a small number of *cantigas de escarnho*. J. Dagenais, 'Cantigas de escarnho and serranillas: the allegories of careless love', *BHS*, 68, 1991:247–63. Several studies focus on the objects of satire. Patricia Anne Odber de Baubeta, *Anticlerical Satire in Medieval Portuguese Literature,* Lewiston–Queenston–Lampeter, Mellen, 1992, 346 pp., has rich materials on the state of medieval clergy; see also her 'Disciplina eclesiástica e sátira anticlerical na literatura galaico-portuguesa medieval', *BGL*, 6, 1991:39–50, on the figure of the priest. L. Jefferson, 'Use of canon law, abuse of canon lawyers in two cantigas concerning the deposition of D.Sancho II of Portugal', *PortSt*, 9, 1993:1–22, ably explains the many specific references to canon law in two much-cited *cantigas*. E. Corral Díaz, 'A figura da *velha* nos cancioneiros profanos galego-portugueses', *O Cantar dos Trobadores*, 403–14, finds *vella* used as a term of abuse, often applied to courtesans, as an inversion of the conventions of the *cantiga de amor*. A. Rey Somoza, 'Estamentos no cristianos en las cantigas satíricas gallego-portuguesas', *Actas* (AHLM 6), II, 1249–59, observes that Jews and Muslims are rarely targets of satirical attack, and gives a brief analysis of instances when they are, with passing references to the *CSM*. O. Mussi da Silva, 'O tipo judeu nas cantigas cortesas trovadas em Leão e Castela na época de Afonso o Sabio', *Historia* (São Paulo) 8, 1989:67–80, and 'A mulher nas cantigas satíricas trovadas em Leão e Castela na época de Afonso o Sabio', *ib.*, 9, 1990:137–56. On more clearly identified targets, J. Ventura, 'Toponimia nas cantigas de sátira obscena do cancioneiro medieval galego-portugués', *Actas* (Granada), IV, 475–89, lists references to places. M. C. Tato García, 'Las cantigas de ultramar gallego-portuguesas', *Actes* (Trier), VI, 190–201, relabels them as 'sátiras de cruzadas e peregrinacións'. On linguistic features, F. Nodar Manso, 'El uso literario de la estructura del signo genital: onomastica y alegoría genitales en las cantigas de escarnio', *Verba*, 16, 1989:451–57;

A. Juárez Blanquer, 'Estuj, maeta, cofre: su alusividad en las literaturas románicas', *Homenaje Rubio García*, I, 665–75, puts Maria Balteira's *maeta* in a wider perspective. G. Vallín, 'Las cantigas del "Sisón"', *Actas* (Alcalá), 521–30, brilliantly interprets the satirical references to a bird of evil odour.

PASTORELA. P. Lorenzo Gradín, 'A pastorela peninsular: cronoloxia e tradicion manuscrita', *Homenaxe García*, II, 351–59, shows the genre to be another late-13th-c. development, perhaps led by Johan d'Avoim. S. Gaspar, 'La pastorela gallego-portuguesa. Apuntes para el estudio de una estética propia', *Actas* (AHLM 6), I, 691–700, argues they are different from French and Provençal *pastourelles*, but are worthy to be considered as more than just a minor genre. C. A. Ribeiro, 'O lirismo e a emergência de subjectividade (a propósito da pastorela de Joan Arias de Santiago)', *Actas* (Salamanca), 79–83, arguing with the majority that the pastorela should be considered a separate genre and not a subset of the *cantiga de amigo*, claims that the poem in question is 'lírico' because it is subjective and the subjectivity is played out before us.

TENÇÃO. G. Lanciani, 'Per una tipologia della tenzone galegoportoghese', *Actas* (Granada) I, 117–30, notes the many different forms of exchanges between poets, and the need for critical approaches to recognize 'national' differences in the selection and definition of forms from this range. A. Vilariño, 'Concepto del "Amor Cortés" en el joc partit', *O Cantar dos Trobadores*, 551–67, compares two debates on love with the better characterized Provençal genre.

INDIVIDUAL POETS

AFONS'EANES DO COTON. Sílvia Gaspar, *Libro dos cantares de Afonso Eanes do Coton*, Negreira, Concello, 1995, xiii + 119 pp., gives Galician translations.

AFONSO LÓPEZ DE BAIÃO. P. Lorenzo Gradín, 'Don Afonso López de Bayão y la épica francesa', *Actas* (Santiago de Compostela), VII, 707–16, dates the parody around 1252, and sees imitations of the *Chanson de Roland*.

AIRAS NUNES. Á. M. Mussons, 'Los trovadores en los últimos años del siglo XIII. Ayras Nunez y la romería de Sancho IV', *Actas* (Alcalá), 227–33, links 'A Santiago en romaria ven' to Sancho's pilgrimage of 1284, and builds a picture of N. around it. X. Ron Fernández, 'Citar es crear. El arte de la cita en Airas Nunez', *ib.*, 487–500, links the different types of textual re-creation in N., with reference to the *cantiga de seguir*.

ALFONSO X. *Alfonso X el Sabio: Cantigas Profanas*, ed. and introd. J. Paredes Núñez, Granada, 1988, 82 pp. C. Alvar, 'O *genete* alfonsí

(18, 28). Consideraciones métricas', *Actas* (Lisbon), II, 203–08, argues that the structure of the poem has its ultimate origins in mediæval Latin forms, and is an adapted *lais*. J. T. Snow, 'The satirical poetry of Alfonso X: a look at its relationship to the *Cantigas de Santa Maria*', Márquez-Villanueva, *Alfonso X*, 110–31, stresses the common themes. A. Branco, 'A mulher e o homem na poesia obscena de D. Afonso X', *Actas* (Lisbon), II, 151–54, concludes that Alfonso has three visions of woman into which male desire is sublimated. C. Flores Varela, 'Malheurs royaux et bonheur bourgeois. A propos d'une chanson de Alphonse X le Sage', *Verba*, 15, 1988:351–59, is on 'Non me posso pagar tanto', as is M. L. Meneghetti, '*Non me posso pagar tanto* d'Alphonse le Savant et la transformation des modèles littéraires', *Actes* (Trier), VI, 279–88, presenting it as 'un conte moral énoncé en forme d'*enueg-plazer*'. C. Pulsoni, 'In margine ad un *partimen* giocoso di Alfonso X', *Actas* (Salamanca), 813–19, on a *tenção*.

BONIFACIO CALVO. M. Piccat, 'Le "cantigas de amor" di Bonifacio Calvo', *ZRP*, 105, 1989:161–77.

DINIS. E. Gonçalves, *Poesia de Rei: três notas dionisinas*, L, Cosmos, 1991, 79 pp., has three substantial articles: a plea for non-interventionist editing and acceptance of metrical irregularity; a reinterpretation of the *escarnhos* on Joan Bolo, as thinly veiled accusations of pederasty; and re-reading of 'Disse m'oj' un cavaleiro' which finally make sense of 'praga por praga', as a complex wordplay. her 'D. Denis: um poeta rei e um rei poeta', *Actas* (Lisbon) II, 13–23, aptly characterizes D. as a prince among poets and a poet conscious of his royal status. J. L. Rodríguez, 'O eco de Dom Denis na literatura posterior', *Actas* (Granada), IV, 179–201, compares accounts of D. by his contemporaries and later poets with 14th- and 15th-c. chronicle accounts of Alfonso X, noting that his poetry is not mentioned. R. Cohen, 'A renúncia nas cantigas de D. Dinis', *CoL*, 134, 1994:138–44, returns to the theme of his 1987 book (*YWMLS*, 49:403). T. R. Hart, 'The cantigas de amor of King Dinis: em maneira de Proençal?', *BHS(L)*, 71, 1994:29–38, discusses differences between the Ptg. *cantigas* and their Provençal models. X. L. Couceiro, 'Notas a unha cantiga dionisiaca', *Homenaxe Garcia*, II, 285–92, reflects on the difficulty of classifying the *pastorela* 'Vi oj' eu cantar d'amor', where an abrupt declaration of love results in 'o verdadeiro reverso da cantiga de amor'.

DIOGO GONÇALVEZ DE MONTEMOR-O-NOVO. I. Rodiño Caramés, 'Diogo Gonçalvez de Montemor-o-Novo: un exemplo de acrecentamento postrobadoresco nos cancioneiros galego-portugueses', *Actas* (AHLM 6), II, 1297–1314, argues that this is a 16th-c. poem inserted when the *cancioneiros* were copied.

ESTEVAM COELHO. A. Ripoll Anta, 'As cantigas de Estevam Coelho. Dúas composicións de ritmo periódico', *Actas* (AHLM 6), II, 1269–81, is a generative analysis of the rhythm of two poems.

FERNAN SOAREZ DE QUINHONES. J. Dionísio, '*Ai, amor, amore de Pero Cantone*, de Fernan Soarez de Quinhones', *Actas* (Granada), II, 173–80, notes the unusual metrical features of the poem, and argues for a more specific interpretation of it as 'sobre o vinho como amor'. C. Alvar, 'Apuntes para una edición de las poesías de Fernan Soárez de Quinhones', *Homenagem Stegagno Picchio*, 3–14, identifies him as a Leonese noble of the later 13th c., and draws attention to his distinctive use of the *zéjel* form.

GIL PEREZ CONDE. C. P. Martínez Pereiro, 'Nova proposta textual da cantiga B 1528 de Gil Perez Conde. Frustração amorosa e blasfémia', *Actas* (Lisbon), II, 215–20, proposes a new reading, which he places within the context of poet's other work, to conclude that P.C.'s poetry flies in the face of convention.

GOMEZ GARCIA. P. Lorenzo Gradín, 'Gomez Garcia, Abade de Valadolide', *Actas* (Alcalá), 213–26, discusses the life of this late 13th-c. *trovador*, and the position of his two *cantigas* in the MS tradition.

GONÇAL' EANES DO VINHAL. A. Víñez Sánchez, 'Reconstrucción histórico-biográfica del trovador Gonzalo Ibáñez de Aguilar', *Actas* (Santiago de Compostela), VII, 717–29, traces his biography and explains his multiple names; 'Súplica y réplica: el infante don Enrique en la lírica gallego-portuguesa', *Actas* (Salamanca), 1161–70, argues that two poems refer to an aspect of Alfonso X's troubled relationship with his brother; the poems are neither *cantigas de amigo* nor *cantigas de escarnho*, but were intended by the poet to make a political point — asking Alfonso to be clement with his brother.

JOAN AIRAS DE SANTIAGO. J. M. Pedrosa, 'Poesía trovadoresca de inspiración popular en el siglo XIII: Joan Arias de Santiago, Cielo d'Alcamo y el tópico folclórico románico de *El viajero enamorado*', *Actas* (Granada), IV, 17–27, shows the idea of the itinerant troubador to be a *topos*, concluding that *cantigas de amor* as well as *cantigas de amigo* make use of the 'tradición popular'.

JOHAN FERNANDEZ D'ARDELEYRO. M. del C. Rodríguez Castaño, 'Una cantiga de amor de Johan Fernandez d'Ardeleyro', *Actas* (AHLM 6), II, 1315–34, a critical edition of his sole surviving poem.

JOÃO GARCIA DE GUILHADE. R. Cohen, 'Dança jurídica: I. A poética da Sanhuda nas cantigas d'amigo; II. 22 cantigas d'amigo de Johan Garcia de Guilhade: vingança de uma Sanhuda virtuosa', *CoL*, 142, 1996:5–50, presents Guilhade's cantigas as a highly structured cycle, with a coded subtext of return to his true (Jewish) faith: an interpretation which is bound to enrage the establishment, but which links many otherwise obscure passages. As an offprint of the same issue, C. edits a new critical edition of the poems. A. Domingues, *Cantigas de João Garcia Guilhade: Subsídios para o seu estudo linguístico e literário*, Barcelos, Câmara Municipal, 1992, vii + 103 pp., is left trailing in his wake.

JOAN MENDEZ DE BRITEIROS.   C. Alvares, 'Le rêve d'amour dans deux cantigas de amigo de Joan Mendez de Briteiros', *Taira*, 3, 1991:11–19.

JOAM SOARES COELHO.   Â. Correia, 'O outro nome da ama. Uma polémica suscitada pelo trovador Joam Soares Coelho', *CoL*, 142, 1996:51–64, takes a new look at the 'polémica das amas'. Y. Frateschi Vieira, 'Joam Soarez Coelho e a moda popularizante nas cantigas de amigo', *Actas* (AHLM 6), I, 629–38, gives a brief biography of C., and argues that his desire for political and social advancement led him to exploit general tendencies towards the popular in poetry; he deliberately eschewed images and techniques from aristocratic poets, using instead 'popular' elements (taken from lowly *jograis*) for his *cantigas de amigo*, to start a whole new fashion.

MARTIM CODAX.   P. Meneses, *'Poetic worlds: Martin Codax', *Style*, 25, 1991:291–309.

MARTIN MOYA.   M. M. Fernández Vuelta, 'El "Mundo al revés" en Martín Moya y Peire Cardenal', *O Cantar dos Trobadores*, 415–24.

MEENDINHO.   R. Raña, '"Illa de illas", (A Cantiga de Meendinho e a n° 86 das *Cantigas de Santa María*)', *BGL*, 15–16, 1996:145–52, finds the thematic similarity between these two poems 'asombrosa' (both involve a woman about to drown in an 'ermida'). X. A. Montero, 'Fortuna literária de Meendiño', *Homenagem Stegagno Picchio*, 85–109, collects editions, commentaries and later appropriations. (See also GALICIAN STUDIES: MEDIEVAL LITERATURE).

NUNO RODRIGUES DE CANDAREY.   M. Russo, '*En gran coita vivo sennor* (A68, B[181bis]; B1451, V1061): un caso nella lirica galego-portoghese di doppia tradizione e dubbia attribuzione?', *Actas* (Lisbon), IV, 139–45, bases an attribution on an acute analysis of codicology, layout, and text.

PAY GOMES CHARINHO.   M. Brea, 'Pai Gómez Charinho y el mar', *Actas* (Alcalá), 141–52, relates the poems to historical background.

PAY SOAREZ DE TAVEIRÓS.   G. Vallín, 'Pai Soarez de Taveirós: datos para su identificación', *Actas* (Lisbon), III, 39–42, identifies him as a member of a minor noble Galician family, continuing in 'Pay Soarez de Taveirós y la corte del Conde de Traba', *O Cantar dos Trobadores*, 521–31, to associate him with the Trastámara household; applying this data to the continuing reinterpretation of the *cantiga da guarvaya*, in '*Filla de don Paay Moniz* ¿De Rodeiro?', *Actas* (Granada), IV, 431–37, V. identifies 'Paay Moniz' as a local Galician landowner called 'Pelagio Muniz de Rodeyro', with a daughter who, coincidentally, had the same name as the Portuguese princess; the poem is a literary exercise in 'naming and shaming', exposing woman's perfidious nature. This is more convincing than M. do R. Ferreira, 'A cantiga da *guarvaya*: uma nova proposta de interpretação', *Actas* (Lisbon), IV, 129–37, who interprets 'en saya' not as meaning 'half-dressed' but as referring to the dress of people of lower social class, and concluding somewhat speculatively that the poet was commissioned to write a song by Sancho's lover who had aspirations above her station, and, having been scorned by her, took his revenge by exposing her pretensions to move into another social class.

PEDRO, CONDE DE BARCELOS. M. Simões, *Il canzoniere di D.Pedro, Conde di Barcelos*, Rome, Japadre, 1991, 131 pp., is an edition with full critical apparatus, commentaries and glossary.

PERO GONÇALVEZ DE PORTOCARREIRO. M. Calderón Calderón, 'Las cantigas de amigo de Pero Gonçalvez de Portocarreiro', *Actas* (Alcalá), 232–42, gives a biography and an edition.

PERO GOTERRES. V. Beltrán, 'Pero Goterres y la retórica de la impiedad: Alfonso X, Pero García Burgales, Gil Pérez Conde y Vasco Gil', *Actas* (AHLM 6), I, 279–95.

PERO MAFALDO. V. Beltrán Pepió, 'Tipos y temas trovadorescos. VIII. Datos para la biografía de Pero Mafaldo', *Actas* (Lisbon), IV, 345–52, gives a new slant to old information, and detects Provençal influence in M.'s works. Id., 'L'infant Pere, Cerverí de Girona i Pero Mafaldo', *SMV*, 39, 1993:9–31, is more on on Cerverí than on Mafaldo.

PERO DA PONTE. A. J. Brea Hernández, '"Se eu podesse desamar", de Pero da Ponte: um exemplo da "mala cansó" na lírica galego-portuguesa', *O Cantar dos Trobadores*, 351–72, explores routes by which this form of poetry against the lady could have been borrowed from Provençal models. V. Beltrán continues his 'Tipos e temas trovadorescos' series of articles on P.'s poems on border skirmishes (*YWMLS*, 50:411): 'II, Pero da Ponte y la rebelión de Don Lope Díaz de Haro', *Homenagem Stegagno Picchio*, 15–35, reveals a political subtext to a poem about a *soldadeira*, which he dates to 1255; 'VI. García López de Alfaro y el ciclo de las hostilidades del norte', *Homenaje Rubio García*, 143–48.

REYMON GONÇALVES. R. Cohen, 'Reymon Gonçalves: taking him back', *Homenagem Stegagno Picchio*, edits G.'s single poem, and subjects it to a close reading to show it to be a rare example of a 'request for reconciliation'.

RODRIGU'EANES D'ALVARES. M. Ferreiro, 'A cantiga de Rodrigu'Eanes d'Alvares. Edição crítica', *Actas* (Lisbon), III, 319–23.

ROY FERNANDEZ. X. B. Arias Freixedo, 'Aspectos particulares na lectura e interpretación do cancioneiro de Roy Fernandiz', *Actas* (Santiago de Compostela), VII, 177–86, has editorial suggestions. G. Tavani, **'Per il testo della cantiga di Roy Fernandez: "Quand'eu vejo las ondas"'*, pp. 97–100 of *Estudos Universitários de Lingüística, Filologia e Literatura. Homenagem ao prof. Dr. Silvio Elia*, RJ, 1990.

ROY QUEIMADO. C. Pérez Varela, 'Ironía fronte a sentimentalismo nas cantigas de amor de Roí Queimado', *O Cantar dos Trobadores*, 439–48, integrates R.Q.'s *ciclo da morte do amor* into the mainstream: inside this *escola topificada*, it focuses on death from sentimental and ironic viewpoints.

3. CANTIGAS DE SANTA MARIA

GENERAL. Jesús Montoya Martínez, *O cancioneiro marial de Alfonso X o sabio* (Biblioteca de Divulgación, Serie Galicia, 6), Santiago de Compostela U.P., 1991, 118 pp., is an admirable concise introduction; see also Id., '*O Cancioneiro Marial* de Alfonso X. El primer cancionero cortesano español', *O Cantar dos Trobadores*, 199–219. J. Grüber, 'Porque trobar é cousa en que jaz entendimento. Zur Bedeutung von *trobar natural* bei Marcabru und Alfons dem Weisen', *Piel Vol.*, 569–79. J. W. Marchand, 'Singers of the Virgin in 13th c. Spain', *BHS(L)*, 71, 1994:169–84, is very general on Berceo and the *CSM*. M. E. Schaffer, 'Questions of authorship: the *Cantigas de Santa Maria*', *Papers* (MHRS 8), 17–30, clarifies many of the issues behind authorship debates, casts serious doubt on the presence of Airas Nunes in the MSS, and makes clear why conclusive textual or linguistic data will be very hard to find.

METRICS AND LANGUAGE. Maria Pia Betti, *Rimario e Lessico in Rima delle Cantigas de Santa Maria di Alfonso X di Castiglia*, Pisa, Pacini, 1996, x + 419 pp., is an invaluable compendium of information on rhyme. M. J. Duffell, 'Alfonso's cantigas and the origins of the *Arte mayor*', *JHR*, 2, 1994:183–204, gives greater weight to the independence of half-lines in metres normally considered long lines with caesura. D. Wulstan, 'Pero cantigas ...', *BCSM*, 6, 1994:12–29, identifies a number of cases of apparent metrical irregularity, some suggesting a general use of paragogy, others revealed by the music to be deliberate. (See *ib.*, 7, 1995:91, for a corrected print of p. 22 of this article.) S. Parkinson, 'Final nasals in the Galician-Portuguese cancioneiros', pp. 51–62 of *Hispanic Linguistic Studies in Honour of F.W. Hodcroft*, ed. D. Mackenzie and I. Michael, Llangrannog, Dolphin, 1993, xvi + 224 pp., shows the search for extended rhymes to underlie the surprisingly evolved forms *cão* and *aldrabão*. C. A. Vega, 'The refram in the Cantigas de Santa Maria', Márquez-Villanueva, *Alfonso X*,

132–58, highlights the thematic and structural importance of the *CSM* refrain.

MSS AND TEXTS. Amparo García Cuadrado, *Las Cantigas: El códice de Florencia*, Murcia U.P., digests the visual content of the Florence MS, with little literary insight. K. Kulp-Hill translates 'The captions to the miniatures of the códice rico of the CSM', *BCSM*, 7, 1995:3–64. General works on the MSS and iconography include G. D. Greenia, 'The court of Alfonso X in words and pictures: the cantigas', *Papers* (ICLS 5), 227–37, and 'The politics of piety: manuscript illumination and narration in the CSM', *HR*, 61, 1993:325–44; E. Kosmer and J. F. Powers, 'Manuscript illustration: the *Cantigas* in contemporary art context', Burns, *Emperor of Culture*, 46–58, Jacques Le Goff, *'Le Roi, la vierge et les images: le manuscrit des cantigas de Santa Maria d'Alphonse X de Castille', pp. 385–92 of *Rituels: Mélanges offerts à Pierre-Marie Gy, OP*, ed. Paul de Clerck and Eric Palazzo, Paris, Editions du Cerf, 1990. G. D. Greenia, 'A new manuscript illuminated in the Alphonsine Scriptorium', *BCSM*, 2, 1989:31–42, points out resemblances between the *códices ricos* and Toledo, Biblioteca del Cabildo, MS 47–15. M. E. Schaffer, 'Epigraphs as a clue to the conceptualization and organisation of the CSM', *La Corónica*, 19, 1991:57–88, is a very important study, showing that the rubrics or epigraphs to the CSM reveal the different orientation of the stages in the collections. Her 'Marginal notes in the Toledo Manuscript of Alfonso El Sabio's CSM: observations on composition, correction, compilation and performance', *BCSM*, 7, 1995:65–84, has many perceptive comments on the MSS, while drawing tentative conclusions on the organization and performance of the festal *cantigas*. M. P. Ferreira, 'The stemma of the Marian cantigas: philological and musical evidence', *BCSM*, 6, 1994:58–98 (replacing a defective version in *ib.*, 5, 1993:49–84), shows the way in close study of the MSS, giving a detailed account of palaeographical and musical features of the Toledo MS and proposing a new and more detailed stemma in which it is an expanded early copy of the first collection of *CSM*. We need much more work of this kind. A. J. Cárdenas, '"De una maravilla que acaeció": miracles in the prose and poetry of Alfonso X's royal scriptorium', *ib.*, 2, 1988–89:13–30, pursues his explorations of chancery involvement in the *CSM*. On the Castilian prosifications, R. Ayerbe-Chaux, 'Las prosificaciones castellanas de las CSM: ¿una obra perdida de don Juan Manuel?', *ib.*, 3, 1990:39–52, makes an intriguing attribution; D. M. Rodgers, 'Cantigas de Santa Maria 2–25 and their Castilian prose versions', Toscano, *Estudios alfonsinos*, 196–204, notes discrepancies between prose and verse versions, and suggests that some of the prose miracles may be independent miracle stories appended to the MS. S. Kirby,

'Cómo se comentaba una obra artística en el siglo XIV: las prosificaciones de las CSM', pp. 25–31 of *Studia Hispanica Medievalia* II, ed.
R. E. Penna and M. A. Rosarossa, Buenos Aires, Univ. Católica
Argentina, 1990, 156 pp., is closer to the mark in seeing them as
14th-c. descriptions of the miniatures. C. Benito-Vessels, 'Palabra
frente a palabra: notas para un estudio de la enunciación en la prosa
marginal de las *CSM* del ms. de El Escorial T.I.1', *Vázquez Vol.*,
309–16, sees no change in views of language between the poetic texts
and the prosifications. Her 'The San Ildefonso miracle in the margins
of the *CSM* and in the Estoria de España', *BCSM*, 3, 1990: 17–30,
sees the prosifications as *rejuvenatio*. D. Wulstan, 'Decadal songs in the
CSM', *ib.*, 8, 1996: 35–58, identifies the *loores* and *festas* as a 'collection
within a collection', on metrical and musical grounds. S. Parkinson,
'Miragres de maldizer?: dysphemism in the *CSM*', *ib.*, 4, 1992: 44–57,
reveals many affinities of content and style between the *CSM* and
cantigas de maldizer.

THEMES AND SOURCES. On the role of Alfonso himself, J. T.
Snow, '"Macar poucos cantares acabei e con son": La firma de
Alfonso X a sus *Cantigas de Santa Maria*', *Actas* (Salamanca), 1021–30,
conjectures that Alfonso personally wrote about 40 poems himself,
mostly *loores*, but including the opening and closing poems. The
closing three poems re-state themes already set out in prologue
poems; the fact that the collection closes with three poems (not one)
shows the tension (explored in poems) between finishing a collection
which recognising that it cannot be finished. See also his 'Alfonso as
troubador: the fact and the fiction', Burns, *Emperor of Culture*, 124–140,
247–48. J. García-Varela, 'La función ejemplar de Alfonso X en las
cantigas personales', *BCSM*, 4, 1992: 3–16, portrays Alfonso as an
exemplary 'mensajero de la gracia marial' in relation to his subjects
and family. W. Mettmann, 'Os *Miracles* de Gautier de Coinci como
fonte das *Cantigas de Santa Maria*', *Homenagem Stegagno Picchio*, 79–84,
discusses 22 less clear cases. C. P. Jayne, 'The Virgin's cures for lust',
Toscano, *Estudios alfonsinos*, 118–24, discusses cantigas 16, 125, 132,
137, 151, 152. M. Brea, 'Milagros prodigiosos y hechos maravillosos
en las *CSM*', *RLMe*, 5, 1993: 47–61; M. I. Pérez de Tudela Velasco,
'La imagen de la Virgen Maria en las cantigas de Alfonso X', *En la
España medieval* 15, 1992: 297–320. On pilgrim songs, Ewa Korput,
*'Piesni pielgrzymow w repertuarze cantigas de Santa Maria krola
Alfonsa X el Sabio (XIII w)', pp. 25–31 of *Pielgrzymki w kulturze
sredniowiecznej Europy*, ed. Jacek Wiesiolowki, Poznan, 1993. C.
Scarborough, 'Las *Cantigas de Santa María* como texto penitencial',
Actas (Salamanca), 941–46, argues that the themes of repentance and
the psychological state of sinners in the *CSM* link the collection to
penitential handbooks of the period. J. D. Pinto-Correia, 'Narrativa

e castigo nas Cantigas de Santa María de Afonso X — aspectos dos milagres de "sanção negativa"', *Actas* (Lisbon), III, 129–40, notes the common elements and the small number of miracles of correction. On the Devil, M. del M. Gutiérrez Martínez, 'Espacios y momentos peligrosos para el hombre medieval (Aparición del Maligno en algunos textos del XIII al XV)', *Actas* (AHLM 6), I, 757–68, catalogues places and moments with diabolical associations. J. Ventura, 'Tradición satánica e pacto co demo: o miragre de Teófilo nas *Cantigas de Santa Maria* de Afonso o Sabio e nos *Milagros de Nuestra Señora* de Gonzalo de Berceo', *Actas* (AHLM 6), II, 1573–80, attempts to set the Theophilus story in historical context. J. Escobar, 'The practice of necromancy as depicted in CSM 125', *BCSM*, 4, 1992:33–43, finds poetic descriptions of the summoning of devils consistent with contemporary accounts.

Many studies tap the texts and miniatures of the *CSM* for views of daily life in the Middle Ages. Prominent among these is Connie L. Scarborough, *Women in Thirteenth-century Spain as Portrayed in Alfonso X's Cantigas de Santa Maria*, Lewiston, Mellen, 1993, viii + 184 pp. M. L. Trivison, 'Monastic living and monastic dying in the CSM', *BCSM*, 6, 1994:1–11, shows Alfonso's religious as simple people. K. Kulp-Hill, *ib.*, 42–52, collects references to games, and M. I. Montoya Ramírez, *ib.*, 5, 1993:35–47, to hunting. S. Moreta Velayos, **La sociedad imaginada de las Cantigas', *Studia historica. Historia Medieval* (Salamanca), 8, 1990:117–38. T. L. Kassier, 'Widows in the CSM', *BCSM*, 2, 1989:43–53, and R. Zaid, 'Some adverse criticism of women in the CSM', *ib.*, 79–88, explore female stereotypes. R. Ocasio, 'Ethnic underclass representation in the Cantigas: the black moro as a hated character', Toscano, *Estudios alfonsinos*, 183–88, argues that blackness stands out as a literary device consistently used to symbolise evil. O. W. Santiago, 'Alfonso el Sabio's attitude towards Moors and Jews as revealed in two of his works', *BCSM*, 6, 1994:30–41, compares the tolerance of the *Partidas* towards non-Christians with their selective demonization in the *CSM*. See also R. Daid, 'The muslim / mudejar in the Cantigas of Alfonso X el Sabio', *ShAn*, 4,1987:145–52; J. Montoya Martínez, 'La presencia de lo africano en las Cantigas de Santa Maria', pp. 9–15 of vol. II of *España y el Norte de Africa: Bases historicas de una relación fundamental — aportaciones sobre Melilla. Actas del primer congreso hispano-africano de las culturas mediterráneas "Fernando de los Ríos Urruti", 11–16 junio de 1984*, 2 vols, ed. Manuel Olmedo Jiménez, Granada U.P., 1987. Critical theory has made few inroads into *CSM* studies. R. J. González-Casanovas, 'Marian devotion as gendered discourse in Berceo and the CSM: popular reception of the *Milagros* and *Cantigas*', *BCSM*, 4, 1992:17–31, substitutes theory for theology. *Ib.*, 8, 1996, has articles on 'intended

audiences' by A. G. Cash (3–13) and D. A. Flory (15–29) which
deliver little more than narrative.

NARRATIVE STRUCTURES.   In a series of related articles, E. Fidalgo
Francisco, 'Esquemas narrativos en las *Cantigas de Santa Maria* (1)',
SMV, 38, 1992:31–100; '"La abadesa preñada" (Berceo, 21). Seis
versiones románicas y tres en latín', *Actas* (Granada), ii, 329–44; 'De
los modos de narrar: Miracle ii, 18, Cantiga 25, Milagro 23', *Actes*
(Zurich), V, 265–76, identifies narrative structures imposed on
miracle stories by the *CSM*, in comparison with the different stylistic
techniques used by Gautier de Coinci and Gonzalo de Berceo; her
'La estructura narrativa de las cantigas marianas de Alfonso X:
aproximación a distintos tipos de análisis', *BCSM*, 3, 1990:5–15,
compares structural, rhetorical, and formalist approaches; 'El exordio
en las *CSM*', *ib.*, 5, 1993:25–34, focuses on introductory formulae.
J. E. Keller, 'Drama, ritual and incipient opera in Alfonso's Cantigas',
Burns, *Emperor of Culture*, 72–89.

PARTICULAR CANTIGAS.   M. A. Diz, 'Berceo y Alfonso: la historia
de la abadesa encinta', *BCSM*, 5, 1993:85–96, compares the rhyme-
driven humour of *CSM* 7 with the discourse of maternity in Berceo.
R. T. Mount, 'The treatment of the miracle of the devout thief in
Berceo and Alfonso el Sabio', Toscano, *Estudios alfonsinos*, 165–71,
compares *CSM* 13 with Berceo. J. E. Keller, 'The living corpse:
miracle 67 of the *CSM* of Alfonso X', *BCSM*, 2, 1989:55–67, narrates
the story and the miniatures. D. Devoto, 'El tiempo en las Cantigas',
Márquez-Villanueva, *Alfonso X*, 1–16, returns to *CSM* 103, with a
wide range of comparative references. R. D. Tinnell, 'Marisaltos and
the Salt de la Bella Donna', *BCSM*, 2, 1989:69–77, links *CSM* 107 to
a Mallorcan folktale. D. E. Carpenter, 'A sorcerer defends the Virgin:
Merlin in the *CSM*', *ib.*, 5, 1993:5–24, compares *CSM* 108 with the
Prophecies de Merlin. On the Salas cycle, A. Ubieto Arteta, 'Las
Cantigas de Alfonso X el Sabio relativas a Santa Maria de Salas
(Huesca)', *Mayurqa*, 22, 1989:615–22, P. Aguado Bleye, *Santa Maria
de Salas en el siglo XIII: Estudio sobre las cantigas de Alfonso X el sabio,* 1989,
is the republication of an influential 1916 thesis; T. L. Kassier, 'The
Salas miracles of the *CSM*: folklore and social reality', *BCSM*, 3,
1990:31–38. On French miracles, W. Mettmann, 'Die Soissons-
Wunder in den *CSM*', *Piel Vol.*, 615–20. On Granada, J. Paredes
Núñez, *La guerra de Granada en las cantigas de Alfonso X el sabio*, Granada
U.P., 1991, and 'Las cantigas de Alfonso X como fuentes historicas:
La guerra de Granada', *CEMed*, 14–15, 1987, 241–52. On the
lengthy *CSM* 235, R. P. Kinkade, 'Alfonso X, Cantiga 235, and the
events of 1269–1278', *Speculum*, 67, 1992:284–323, gives extensive
explanations of the historical events which match references in the
poem, accepting the traditional belief that the poem is a lament on

Alfonso's misfortune; a view which is insightfully countered by K. Kennedy, 'In sickness and in health: Alfonso X of Castile and the Virgin Mary in *Cantiga* 235', *GalR*, 1:27–42, who argues that the poem is a glorification of his kingship. J. Montoya Martínez, 'La "gran vingança" de Dios y de Alfonso X', *BCSM*, 3, 1990: interprets an obscure passage in this poem as referring to the execution of Simón de los Cameros and the Infante D. Fadrique as heretics. A. F. Bolanos, 'Cantiga 308 de Alfonso X: el romance más antiguo de España?', *Hispanófila*, 95, 1989:1–11. R. P. Kinkade, 'Don Juan Manuel's father, Infante Manuel, in the *CSM*', *BSCM*, 8, 1996:59–75, expands on the historical content of *CSM* 366, 376, and 382. J. Montoya Martínez, 'La "carta fundacional" del Puerto de Santa María y las *CSM*', *ib.*, 6, 1994:99–115, shows close textual links between the Puerto de Santa Maria *cantigas* and the document establishing the town.

MUSIC. I. J. Katz, 'Higinio Anglés and the melodic origins of the Cantigas de Santa Maria', Márquez-Villanueva, *Alfonso X*, 46–75. F. Nodar Manso, '*Cantigas de Santa María* y sistema musical grecolatino', *Actas* (AHLM 6), II, 1105–12. J. R. Cohen, 'A reluctant woman pilgrim and a green bird: a possible cantiga melody survival in a Sephardic ballad', *BCSM*, 7, 1995:85–89, finds resonances of *CSM* 153 in *El paxaro verde*. I. J. Katz, 'Melodic survivals? Kurt Schindler and the tune of Alfonso's Cantiga "Rosa das rosas" in oral tradition', Burns, *Emperor of Culture*, 159–81, 251–57, returns to the later manifestations of the melody of *CSM* 10. E. Madriguera, 'Guitarras moriscas and latinas in the *CSM*', Toscano, *Estudios alfonsinos*, 129–39, draws conclusions from iconography.

FIFTEENTH-CENTURY POETRY

Cancioneiro Geral de Garcia de Resende, ed. Aida Fernanda Dias, 4 vols, L, 1993, is a major re-edition; on a smaller scale, *O Cuidar e Sospirar [1483]*, ed. Margarida Vieira Mendes, L, CNCDP, 190 pp. S. Reckert, 'Facing both ways: some poems from the *Cancioneiro Geral*', *PortSt*, 9, 1993:39–52, shows that the contents and imagery of this poetry look back to 13th- and 14th-c. Gal.-Ptg. poetry and forward to 16th- and 17th-c. Spain. J. A. Frazão, 'Imagens do mundo e do amor no *Cancioneiro Geral*', Godinho, *Imagem*, 281–86, discusses a range of 'espaços do amor'. A. Simões, '*Perdi o sen e a razon* — fortuna do tópico da *loucura amorosa* no *Cancioneiro Geral* de Garcia de Resende', *Actas* (Lisbon), II, 187–92, shows how passion leads to the fragmentation of the poetic 'I'. V. Tocco, 'La elegia funebre portoghese: Diogo Brandão piange la morte di D. João II', *Actas* (Salamanca), 1049–74, edits and comments on the *pranto*, noting that the Portuguese did not follow Castilian fashions in the genre (Italianate style, varied forms). G. Pérez Barcala, 'La poesía trovadoresca y las manifestaciones del amor en Duarte de Brito', *Actas* (AHLM 6), II, 1159–68, is on his continuing use of 'la tradición trovadoresca de los siglos anteriores' in the midst of humanist tendencies; by extension, *Cancioneiro Geral* poets still make use of medieval traditions. H. Macedo, 'A *Cantiga de amigo* by Bernardim Ribeiro', *Deyermond Vol.*, 253–58, attributes a poem from the *Cancioneiro Geral* to R., noting formal links between the *cantiga de amigo* genre and *Menina e Moça*. M. Calderón Calderón, 'Las *Cantigas Espirituais* de André Dias y la herencia trovadoresca', *O Cantar dos Trobadores*, 373–85.

4. PROSE

GENERAL

On relations between different chronicles, S. Luongo, '"El que vengó a su padre et a sus hermanos": Mudarra nella Primera Crónica General e nella Crónica de 1344', *MedRom*, 19, 1994:301–23. J. Mattoso, *'Sur les sources du Comte de Barcelos', pp. 111–16 of *L'Historiographie médiévale en Europe: Actes du colloque organisé par la fondation européene de la science au Centre de Recherches Historiques et Juridiques de l'Université de Paris I, du 29 mars au 1 avril 1989*, ed. Jean-Philippe Genet, Paris, CNRS, 1991. J. I. Pérez Pascual, 'Relaciones entre la *Crónica de 1344* y la *Crónica de 1404*', *Actas* (Lisbon), III, 163–66, concludes that the relationship between the chronicles confirms Cintra and Catalán's theory that a great many historiographical (and other) compilations made on the orders of the Conde de Barcelos were used by later writers. P. E. Russell, 'Archivists as historians: the case of the fifteenth-century Portuguese royal chroniclers', pp. 67–83 of *Historical Literature in Medieval Iberia*, ed. Alan Deyermond (PMHRS, 2), 1996, 132 pp., focuses on the use of documents in Fernão Lopes and Zurara. What makes L. distinctive is the extent of his use of documentary evidence, rather than the fact of his using it; both L. and Zurara must be suspected of eliminating source material which conflicted or competed with their own accounts. T. Balse, 'Don Pedro Ier de Portugal et Ines de Castro: des sources historiques et littéraires portugaises à "La Reine Morte"', *ArCCP*, 32, 1993:389–416, refers to prose sources (Fernão Lopes, Ruy de Pina, Cristóvão Acenheiro) and poetry sources (Garcia de Resende, Anrique da Mota, Camões) to show that Portuguese writers were the first to turn the murder of Inês de Castro into a legend. E. Nunes Esteves, 'Relações entre as lendas de Fernão Gonçalves e Afonso Henriques', *Actas* (Granada), II, 229–35, is an object lesson on the dangers of tracing neat lines of influence between texts; E. questions Cintra's 1957 analysis of the

Crónica de 1419 and the Fernão Gonçalves legend as told in the *Cronica Geral de 1344*, and notes that while the two accounts are very different, both authors draw on the same medieval *topoi* to achieve similar aims such as that of presenting characters as receiving divine help. C. Sousa Pereira, 'Rei Lear: percurso de uma lenda', *Actas* (Lisbon), II, 289–93, argues for a continuity between oral and written versions because both have as their message the importance of service and vassalage; different images are used depending on whether the message is being delivered to nobles or to people.

CRÓNICA DE 1344

F. Figueiredo, 'O maravilhoso na Crónica Geral de Espanha de 1344', Ribeiro, *Género*, 97–104, shows the presence of the supernatural to be both a narrative device and a reflection of popular belief. E. Nunes Esteves, 'O motivo da tenda real na *Crónica Geral de Espanha de 1344*', *Actas* (Lisbon), II, 321–24, concludes simplistically that there is no difference between the image of the tent in literary or historiographical texts, its function being to increase the image of royal majesty. See also his 'A influência da retórica na historiografia portuguesa do séc. XIV. A *Crónica Geral de Espanha de 1344*', *Actas* (AHLM 6), I, 581–86, and 'A dimensão retórica na "Crónica Geral de Espanha de 1344"', *CoL*, 142, 1996:103–09.

FERNÃO LOPES

Teresa Amado, *Fernão Lopes, contador de história*, L, Estampa, 1991, 242 pp., is a detailed study of L.'s incorporation of material from the *Crónica do Condestabre* and the chronicles of López de Ayala into the *Crónica de D. João I*. See also her *Bibliografia Fernão Lopes*, L, Estampa, 1991, 42 pp. João Gouveia Monteiro, *Fernão Lopes, Texto e Contexto*, Coimbra, Minerva, 1988, 161 pp., sees L. as seeking to legitimize the events of 1383–85, echoed by L. de Sousa Rebelo, 'Millénarisme et historiographie dans les chroniques de Fernão Lopes', *ArCCP*, 26, 1989:97–120, and Margarida Garcez Ventura, **O Messias de Lisboa. Um estudo de mitologia política*, L, Cosmos, 1992. J. Dionísio, 'A leitura como diálogo. I. *Crónica de D. Fernando*', *Actas* (Lisbon), III, 141–45, a thought-provoking study, moves from a gloomy exposition of the difficulty of studying reader-reception of L.'s chronicles, to focus on his way of addressing his readers, and concludes that his text is designed to address either lone, silent, readers or a listening public. D. shows that silent reading had not completely taken over from reading aloud in the 16th c., and produces documentary testimony that L.'s job included reading aloud to D. Duarte. M. J. Almeida,

'Crónica de cidade. Particularidades de género no texto de Fernão Lopes', Ribeiro, *Género*, 205–15, analyses the contamination of the royal chronicle genre by the subjective foregrounding of Lisbon. A. A. Lindeza Diogo, 'Texto e metatexto historiográfico em Fernão Lopes', *Actas* (Lisbon), II, 95–99, is on how L. characterizes his discourse as true narrative. L. de Sousa Rebelo, 'The topos of procreation in a passage of Fernão Lopes', *Willis Vol.*, 51–54, finds parallels for a tale of a father refusing to barter the lives of his sons. A. Hutchinson, 'Nun'Álvares Pereira: a Portuguese hero in the Arthurian mould', *ib.*, 55–68, develops parallels between the *Condesta-bre* and Galahad.

ZURARA

Crónica de D. Pedro de Meneses, ed. Maria Teresa Brocardo, L, FCG-JNICT, 742 pp., is the first serious modern edition of this chronicle, with detailed descriptions of the MSS. See also her 'Os manuscritos da Cronica do Conde D. Pedro de Meneses de Gomes Eanes de Zurara', *Actes* (Zurich), V, 197–210, and 'Editar uma crónica de Zurara', *CLHM*, 20, 1995:257–67, which observes the flaws of previous editions in no uncertain terms. A. Figueiredo, 'A ideia da historiografia e sua materialização em Gomes Eanes de Zurara', Ribeiro, *Género*, 217–25, emphasizes the centrality of the *ideal de cavalaria*. J. M. de Almeida Araújo, 'A terra e as gentes africanas nas crónicas de Zurara', *Actas* (Lisbon), III, 245–51, traces changes in depiction of the Arabs between Z.'s *Crónica do Conde D. Pedro* (positive) and his *Crónica do Conde D. Duarte de Meneses* (negative); concludes vaguely that Z.'s chronicles reflect the spirit of his age.

OTHER HISTORICAL TEXTS

Ribeiro, *Género*, includes: I. Dias, 'De como o Mosteiro de S.Vicente foi refundado' (139–44), showing how Afonso Henriques gains prominence in the Portuguese rewriting; M. F. Ramos, 'A memória *In Sancta et admirabili Victoria Christianorum* como fonte da Chronica del Rei Affonso IV' (157–71); A. Fournier, 'A crónica da fundação do Mosteiro de S. Vicente: memória e ideologia' (173–88), accentuating its hybrid nature. On reconquest chronicles, A. Branco, 'Verdade factual e verdade simbólica na "Crónica da Conquista do Algarve", *CoL*, 142, 1996:111–19, and 'O lugar do mestre Paio Correia na história-1. A *Crónica de 1419* e a *Crónica da conquista do Algarve*', *Actas* (AHLM 6), I, 357–64. H. Livermore, 'The conquest of Lisbon and its author', *PortSt*, 6, 1990, 1–16, describes the 12th-c. MS (Cambridge: Parker Library, CCC) which is the best contemporary source for the events of 1147. T. Amado, 'A cada um a sua batalha de Tarifa', *Actas* (Lisbon), IV, 303–07, compares Arabic, Spanish and Portuguese narratives, observing that all are basically similar apart from the *Livro de Linhagens*, which may have taken an Arab eye-witness account from a Christian familiar with Moors. T. Amado, 'Investigação das origens: o reinado de D. Afonso Henriques', *Actas* (AHLM 6), I, 143–49. *Estoria de Dom Nuno Alvarez Pereyra*, ed. Adelino de Almeida Calado, Coimbra U.P., 1991, cxcv + 256 pp., edits the *Cronica do Condestabre* with a lengthy introduction. A. Branco, 'A representação das mulheres na *Coronica do Condestabre*', *Actas* (Granada), I, 401–13, observes that women are only ever referred to briefly and in relation to men, concluding that for the chronicler, good women are those who do nothing or who follow orders, whereas good men are men of action; where events show that women have done something on their own initiative, the chronicler records their actions with veiled criticism. On crusades and the reconquest, X. I. Pérez Pascual, 'A narración das cruzadas na Crónica xeral de 1404', *Homenaxe Garcia*, II, 387–92, and B. Vasconcelos e Sousa, 'A imagem do mouro nos *Anais* de D. Afonso Henriques', Godinho, *Imagem*, 147–54.

HAGIOGRAPHY

Ribeiro, *Género*, contains: M. Madureira, 'Género e significação segundo o *Orto do Esposo*' (249–55); A. M. Machado, 'A leitura hagiográfica no *Orto do Esposo* e e hermenêutica implícita na *Legenda aurea*' (257–69); C. Sobral, 'Um autor ignorado e a recepção da hagiografia no século XV' (271–81), on Paulo de Portalegre, author of a lost Ptg. *Flos Sanctorum* of 1484. M. C. de Almeida Lucas, 'O poder temporal na hagiografia de quinhentos', *Actas* (Lisbon), IV, 45–50, is on the deeper meaning of hagiographical collections: conflict between celestial kings and earthly kings (who always lose) and the importance of knowledge; L. observes that the saint is never personally involved in acting out how he 'wins' this battle with earthly powers. Á. Correia, 'Sobre a funcionalidade da narrativa hagiográfica', *Actas* (Lisbon), II, 121–24, takes hagiographical narratives as a case of medieval reworking of texts, and decides unsurprisingly that elements are changed in what are basically similar accounts in order to tailor them to the customs of a particular religious community, or for the purposes of religious instruction. C. Sobral, 'A imagem da sabedoria na lenda de Maria Egipcíaca', *RFLUL*, 15, 1993 : 133–42. C. Sousa Pereira, '*Conto do Amaro*: Intervenções da divindade feminina', *Actas* (Granada), IV, 29–33, is a lightweight study of the Virgin Mary in the context of female figures of other (pagan) religions. A. M. Díaz Ferrero, 'Algunas consideraciones en torno a la mujer en el *Orto do Esposo*', *Actas*

(Granada), II, 151–58, reaches the conclusion that, Saints aside, the treatment of women in *OE* is generally 'misógino'. Similarly, A. M. S. Machado, 'A mulher e a representação do mal na hagiografia medieval portuguesa: alguns aspectos', *Actas* (Lisbon), II, 111–15, notes that women's accounts of female saints do not differ from those written by men, and catalogues the ways in which women are represented and linked to evil. The same author focuses on the *Orto do Esposo* in 'A "Legenda Aurea" nos "exempla" hagiográficos do "Orto do Esposo"', *CoL*, 142, 1996: 121–36; 'O Orto do Esposo e as teorias interpretativas medievais', *Actas* (AHLM 6), II, 925–35. I. M. D. Braga, 'Milagres de Nossa Senhora de Montserrat num códice da Biblioteca Nacional de Lisboa', *ArCCP*, 33, 1994: 663–721, gives a general introduction to the importance of Montserrat in Marian devotion, and transcribes the Montserrat Marian miracles found on fols 27–99 of Lisbon: BN, MS. 77. The miracles it contains date from 'época medieval' to the early decades of the 16th c.; the text seems to have been translated into Portuguese from a Castilian or Catalan version. A. A. Nascimento, 'O pacto com o demónio em fontes medievais portuguesas: Teófilo e Fr. Gil de Santarém', *Actas* (Salamanca), 737–45, notes that the bits added to the legend of Gil de Santarém are not inspired by reality; then proceeds to a literary analysis and compares the treatment of the figures of Theophilus and Santarém. Id., 'Diálogo e impersonificação: modos de construção e intencionalidade no *Horologium fidei* de André do Prado em favor do Infante D.Henrique', *Actas* (AHLM 6), II, 1095–1104, suggests the work was destined to show the Pope that Henry was interested in theology. A. M. e Silva Machado, 'O testemunho dos prologos na prosa didáctica moral e religiosa', *Actas* (Granada), III, 131–46, is on topoi and themes in prologues to 15th-c. Ptg. works, showing the way in which authors classified their works.

ARTHURIAN

J. Paredes Núñez, 'La materia de Bretaña en la literatura Peninsular (la literatura genealógica)', *Actas* (Lisbon), III, 233–37, is an overview. Irene Freire Nunes, **A Demanda do Santo Graal*, L, INCM, 1995, is a new edition. H. Megale, 'Le texte portugais de la *Demanda do santo graal*: les éditions de 1944 et de 1955–70', pp. 436–61 of *Arturus Rex. Volumen II: Acta conventus Lovaniensis 1987*, ed. W.Van Hoecke, G.Tournoy, and W. Verbeke, Louvain, 1991. J. C. Miranda, **A Demanda do Santo Graal e o Ciclo Arturiano da Vulgata*, O, 1993. M. G. Carvalhão Buescu, 'O interdito e a ocultação: dois *topoi* na *Demanda do Santo Graal*', *Actas* (Lisbon), IV, 57–64, is on the Christian significance of the image of the Grail and Sir Galahad in the context of the story. A. S.

Laranjinha, 'Um microcosmo textual? O episódio de Pentecostes do Graal na Demanda portuguesa', Ribeiro, *Género*, 85–96, explores the centrality of this early episode. P. Gracia, 'Variaciones sobre un tema mítico: Edipo en la Demanda do Santo Graal', *CN*, 53, 1993:194–214. P. Michon, 'Marc de Cornouailles au royame de Logres dans les romans arthuriens de la péninsule ibérique', *LR*, 48, 1994:163–73, refers to the *Demanda*. P. Michon, 'Le Tristan en prose galaico-portuguaise', *Romania*, 112, 1991:259–68, describes a 14th-c. fragment discovered in 1928 but mistakenly identified as from the Lancelot romance, before being correctly identified in 1962. S. de Almeida Toledo Neto, 'Liuro de Josep ab Aramatia and the works of Robert de Boron', *Quondam et Futurus*. 3.3, 1993:36–45. J. C. Miranda, 'Realeza e cavalaria no *Livro de José de Arimateia*, versão portuguesa da *Estoire del Saint Graal*', *Actas* (Lisbon), III, 157–61, discusses how the *Estoire* and its Ptg. version expand on their sources, with a shift in ideas by which divine favour is bestowed particularly on knights; M. argues that these two accounts provide the basic themes for the later Arthurian cycles. On onomastic echoes, H. L. Sharrer, 'Briolanja as a name in early fifteenth-century Portugal: echo of a re-worked Portuguese Amadis de Gaula?', *La corónica*, 19, 1990:112–18.

DIDACTIC TEXTS

M. M. Gomes, 'O Livro da Montaria de D. João I de Portugal no contexto dos tratados medievais de caça', Ribeiro, *Género*, 189–204, looks for sources and influences. On memory in D. Duarte, J. Dionísio, 'Lembranças rebeldes, combates mnésicos e remédios vinícolas: sobre a arte do esquecimento no "Leal Conselheiro", de D. Duarte', *CoL*, 142, 1996:147–58. L. Prista, 'Apostila a uma genealogia proposta por Leite de Vasconcelos, a propósito de certas características sintácticas de *O Livro de Esopo*', *Actas* (Lisbon), III, 293–98, alters Leite de Vasconcelos' conclusion about the type of sources of the *Livro de Esopo*. M. da Costa Fontes, 'Fernando de Rojas, Cervantes and two Portuguese folk-tales', pp. 85–96 of *Hispanic Medieval Studies in honour of Samuel G. Armistead*, ed. E. M. Gerli and H. L. Sharrer, Madison, HSMS, 1992, shows how the medieval antecedents of a folk jest, a conundrum and an etiological joke inspired aspects of the language of *La Celestina*. Similarly, C. Flores, 'Sobre unha adivina galega e as suas relacions cum fabliau do seculo XIII', *Homenaxe Garcia*, II, 315–18; J. M. Fradejas Lebrero, 'Motivos medievales en los *Contos Tradicionais do Algarve*', *Actas* (Lisbon), III, 163–66, is just a short list of motifs.

5. THEATRE

Guillermo Serés, 'Ficción sentimental y humanismo: La Sátira de Don Pedro de Portugal', *BH*, 93, 1991: 31–60, is on the relationship between the work and its sources. J. P. da Cruz, 'Auto dos Pastorinhos: teatro de tradição oral na aldeia do Lamegal, concelho de Pinhel, na Beira Alta', *His(US)*, 77, 1994: 1–10, describes a popular survival. R. Faingold, 'Judíos y conversos en el teatro portugues pre-vicentino', *Sefarad*, 51, 1991: 23–50.

6. BALLADS AND TRADITIONAL POETRY

M. Aliete Galhoz, 'Cantigas paralelísticas de tradição oral de Trás-os-Montes e do Algarve', *Actas* (Lisbon), IV, 11–17, concludes that Trás-os-Montes and Algarve poems are similar to mediæval ones and should not be forgotten. M. da Costa Fontes, 'El romancero trasmontano: nueva recolección', Catalán, *Balada y Lírica*, II, 109–24; A. M. Martins, 'A edição de romances e o problema da pontuação', *ib.*, I, 359–73. S. G. Armistead and M. da Costa Fontes transcribe 'Three Azorean ballads from the MSS of Joanne B. Purcell', *La corónica*, 22, 1994: 52–60.

LITERATURE, 1500 TO THE PRESENT

POSTPONED

VII. GALICIAN STUDIES

LANGUAGE

POSTPONED

LITERATURE

By DOLORES VILAVEDRA, *Department of Galician Philology, Universidade de Santiago de Compostela,* and DEREK FLITTER, *Senior Lecturer in Modern Spanish Language and Literature, University of Birmingham*

1. GENERAL

Historia da literatura galega. II, Vigo, ASPG-A Nosa Terra, comprises pp. 324–640 of a literary history appearing in weekly instalments since 1996. This second volume embraces the period from Rosalía de Castro to the theatre of the *Irmandades da Fala*; like its predecessor it is of uneven quality and depth of analysis, with many chapters written by non-specialists chosen more for their ostensible links with the overall project than for their academic expertise. *Diccionario da literatura galega. II. Publicacións periódicas*, ed. Dolores Vilavedra et al, Vigo, Galaxia, 596 pp., marks the latest stage in a collective work dedicated to cataloguing and commenting on the presence of works of Galician literature in a medium that was often, for socio-economic or political reasons, the principal vehicle for its wider diffusion. A. Figueroa and X. González-Millán, *Communication littéraire et culture en Galice*, Paris-Montreal, L'Harmattan, 188 pp., sees the co-authors revisit several of their own earlier pieces in a rigorous analysis of those conditioning factors, deriving from sociolinguistics, affecting literary production and its function as collective cultural product. X. V. Freire Lestón, *A prensa de mulleres en Galicia (1841–1994)*, Lisbon, Edições Universitárias Lusófonas, 177 pp., provides a documentary and broad critical survey of the entire period. X. L. Axeitos, 'O celtismo, utopía trascendente na literatura galega', *Unión Libre*, 2:79–86, is an historically-based assessment of the presence of this pervasive myth, from its re-invention in the hands of *Rexurdimento* historians to the present day. The same author's 'A recepción das vangardas en Galicia', *BGL*, 17:7–55, offers some fresh material and a revisionary approach to the impact of the avant-garde on Galician culture. A. Pociña, 'A cultura latina nos autores e autoras galegos', *AELG*, 1996:77–102, takes a rather cursory look at Classical elements of the works of writers like Pintos, Leiras, Noriega, Crecente Vega,

Iglesia Alvariño and Díaz Castro. B. Fernández, 'Fadas e bruxas como arquetipos morais femininos nos contos', pp. 215–49, of *Corpo de muller*, ed. M. X. Agra, Santiago, Laiovento, 249 pp., appraises the role of women in fairy tales and other short fantasy fiction. F. Fernández Rei, 'O folclore musical galego do final do milenio: o *Cancioneiro* de Schubarth e Santamarina', *ATO*, 31:87–97, reviews the *magnum opus* of the article's title, with shrewd contextualization and detailed descriptive commentary.

2. NARRATIVE

D. Vilavedra, 'Narrativa do 96: unha colleita plural', *AELG*, 1996:187–92, is a panoramic survey of the year's novelistic production, while S. Gaspar, 'Paseo positivista e fugaz pola literatura fantástica galega', *Grial*, 135:311–22, provides a similar overview of fantasy fiction.

3. POETRY

T. López, *O neotrobadorismo*, Vigo, A Nosa Terra, 220 pp., studies this movement as an extension of the interest aroused by the medieval *cancioneiros* since their rediscovery in the 19th century. H. Golubeva and H. Zernova, 'Poesía galega en traducións rusas', *BGL*, 18:103–09, is a typological survey of the appearance of these translations that considers also their cultural reception. H. González, 'Da poesía no ano da morte de Lois Pereiro', *AELG*, 1996:193–200, is an assessment of the year's published poetry. M. X. Nogueira, 'Poesía galega dos 80', *BGL*, 18:57–84, offers a detailed and rigorous analysis of the poetry of that decade. F. Villares, 'A escola poética do Seminario de Mondoñedo', pp. 19–32 of *Os poetas do Seminario de Mondoñedo*, Lugo, Deputación, 335 pp., introduces an anthology, selected by V., of poems by this group, one of the most prolific in the history of Galician literature. J. Ventura, 'La religiosidad popular en la poesía gallega contemporánea (del Rexurdimento a las vanguardias)', pp. 1037–60 of *Actas del Simposium 'Religiosidad Popular en España, II'*, San Lorenzo del Escorial, RCU Escorial-Ma. Cristina, makes a thematically based survey of the period from Rosalía de Castro to the avant-garde.

4. THEATRE

L. Tato Fontaíña, *Teatro galego, 1915–1931*, Santiago, Laiovento, 291 pp., is a broad-based history that introduces new factual information and unpublished documentary evidence in chronicling one of the most fertile periods in Galician theatre. M. F. Vieites et al, *Teoría e técnica teatral*, Santiago, Laiovento, 379 pp., despite the overly ambitious title, furnishes a cluster of texts that serve as a point of departure for a considered discussion of and reflection upon dramatic theory and practice from a contemporary Galician perspective. M. F. Vieites, 'Sesenta anos despois: memoria (dramática) incompleta do 36', *RGT*, 14:58–64, appraises the processes of construction of a Galician national theatre embarked upon by the *Irmandades da Fala* but subsequently curtailed by the outbreak of the Spanish Civil War, while the same author's 'Texto dramático, texto espectacular e texto teatral', *AELG*, 1996: 103–25, makes a stimulating attempt at classifying the various levels of enunciation present in the dramatic text, furnishing many examples taken from Galician literature.

5. MEDIEVAL LITERATURE

Santiago Gutiérrez, *Merlín e a súa historia*, Vigo, Xerais, 321 pp., analyses the historical emergence and development of the literary character, drawing on a range of sources from early Celtic legends to the Castilian and Galician-Portuguese successors of the mediæval French romances. Clodio González Pérez, *Meendiño, Martín Codax, Xoán de Cangas*, Noia, Toxosoutos, 98 pp., makes a schematic introduction to the extant work of the three troubadours (all of which is reproduced here), briefly locating them within the context of the medieval lyric. R. Polín, 'O arcediago de Toro: señas galegas e trobas pioneiras', *ATO*, 30:63–70, adduces some new biographical information and evaluates his subject's literary innovations. A. Rossell, 'A música da lírica galego-portuguesa medieval: un labor de reconstrucción arqueolóxica e intertextual a partir das relacións entre o texto e a música', *AELG*, 1996:41–76, embraces the principal themes and motifs of medieval musical accompaniments to Galician-Portuguese texts, including a detailed musicological analysis of specific examples from the *cantigas*. X. Bieito Arias, 'Eu at'end'o meu amig(u), e un á. ¿É posible unha nova lectura da cantiga de Meendinho?', *BGL*, 18:119–23, volunteers a new reading of the famous refrain from the troubadour's single extant poem.

6. CIVIL WAR LITERATURE AND LITERATURE OF EXILE

Xesús Alonso Montero, *Os poetas galegos e Franco*, Madrid, Akal, 222 pp., provides an expert examination of pro- and anti-Franco verse written in Galicia. C. Rodríguez Fer, 'Emigración, exilio y guerra civil (1936–9)', Portela, *Jornadas*, 63–78, assesses the salient dates, authors and events of a Galician tradition displaced by the

Civil War, the continuity of which was ensured by literary production outside Galicia.

7. INDIVIDUAL AUTHORS

BLANCO AMOR. C. Laíño, *E. Blanco Amor. 'Morte do mi padre'. Bases para o estudio e recuperación dun manuscrito inédito*, Corunna, Espiral Maior, 87 pp., transcribes and assesses a previously unpublished piece of narrative. S. Mayo, 'Personaxes femininos na narrativa de Blanco Amor', *ATO*, 30:91–98, considers B.A.'s literary treatment of women and its implications. R. Nicolás, 'A poesía de Blanco Amor ante a crítica do seu tempo', *BGL*, 18:19–56, surveys critical responses to B.A.'s poetry during his lifetime. V. Álvarez, *Unha lectura de 'A esmorga'*, Vigo, Xerais, 50 pp., contextualizes the novel within Galician literature of exile and furnishes a rigorous fresh analysis of the text. P. Rus, *Imaxe do mundo en E. Blanco Amor: a muller, o conflicto social e os marxinados*, Vigo, A Nosa Terra, 339 pp., is a polemical and ideologically partial reading of B.A.'s work. Within the published proceedings of the *Xornadas Eduardo Blanco Amor*, Santiago, Xunta de Galicia, 210 pp., the following contributions are particularly noteworthy: A. Carreño, 'Antropoloxía dun espacio cultural: *A esmorga* de E. Blanco Amor' (11–26), a confusing title that disguises a mainstream analysis of the novel's fundamental components; X. Alonso, 'Blanco-Amor e García Lorca' (27–40) adduces some new information, shedding further light on a topic far from exhausted by existing criticism; A. Pociña, 'Para un achegamento á poesía galega de Blanco Amor' (59–84), initiates a fresh perspective on some of B.A.'s lesser-known material; M. Forcadela, 'Unha visión psicoanalítica de *A esmorga*' (95–118), makes a Freudian interpretation of the novel's characters and their relationship to the authorial psyche. In the same volume are published the deliberations of the round-table discussions: 'Falando de Blanco Amor' (133–62), 'O teatro de Blanco Amor' (163–86), and 'Blanco Amor xornalista' (187–201).

CABANILLAS. X. M. Fernández Castro, 'Cuestións teóricas e históricas en *O Mariscal* de R. Cabanillas e A. Villar Ponte', *AELG*, 1996:11–40, uncovers textual and contextual strategies underlying the much-celebrated mythification of the Mariscal.

CARBALLO CALERO. C. Blanco, **O trevo das catro follas*: un poemario popular inédito de Ricardo Carballo Calero', *Moenia*, 2:123–44.

CASARES. Silvia Gaspar, *Unha lectura de 'Ilustrísima'*, Vigo, Xerais, 45 pp., shrewdly outlines an interpretation of the novel within the context of contemporary European narrative.

CASTELAO. Manuel Rosales, *A narrativa de Castelao. Xénese e desenvolvemento*, Santiago, Sotelo, 274 pp., appraises C.'s fiction both as a product of its age and within its own artistic terms. I. Gómez, *'Castelao, ministro do Goberno Giral: o galeguismo situado nunha "simblica Fisterra"', *Moenia*, 2:21–34. H. Monteagudo, 'Estudio introductorio', pp. 1–99 of *De viva voz*, Santiago, Fundación Castelao, 300 pp., is a thoroughgoing study that, by way of prefacing this collection of speeches and lectures (the most complete to date), contextualizes C.'s political activity within his rather elusive personal history as well as within the broader cultural picture. E. R. Ruibal, 'A tradición popular en *Os vellos no deben de namorarse*', *Grial*, 132:453–72, assesses the many and diverse elements of this theatrical tradition present in C.'s play.

CASTRO. V. Álvarez, 'Un importante documento para a biografía de Rosalía de Castro', *Grial*, 136:479–501, is an enormously important source of fresh evidence concerning Rosalía's life, and a piece that necessarily prompts some rethinking and reframing both of her relationship with her mother and of her poetic output in general. C. Davies, 'O retorno á nai catedral, unha estranxeira en terra de ninguén. Rosalía de Castro a través de Julia Kristeva', *ib.*, 503–25, appraises three poems that focus on those 'sacred places' identified by Kristeva's brand of psychoanalysis. M. Figueroa, 'La realidad socio-económica de la Galicia decimonónica y tres poemas de Rosalía de Castro', Portela, *Jornadas*, 139–48, examines three Rosalía poems as putative social documents. A. López and A. Pociña, 'Rosalía de Castro en la obra de Camilo José Cela', *Extramundi. Los papeles de Iria Flavia*, 10:9–25, survey the various appearances of the figure of Rosalía within Cela's work, reproducing the earliest example. C. Moreiras, 'Lingua común e identidade nacional en Rosalía de Castro', *ATO*, 31:99–116, looks at the possible motives underlying Rosalía's abandoning Galician as a literary language. A. Sixto, 'Los médicos en la vida y en la obra de Rosalía de Castro', Portela, *Jornadas*, 101–13, reports on the various doctors who treated or subsequently studied Rosalía from a psychological and neurological, as well as physiological, perspective. E. Wimmer, 'Dolor y esperanza', *ib.*, 149–60, undertakes a typical journey through Rosalía's life in search of interpretative pointers to her work.

CRECENTE. Luz María Durán and Ricardo Polín, *José Crecente Vega. A poesía de 'Codeseira'*, Lugo, Fundación Caixa Galicia, 238 pp., provide a new edition of this collection with a broad and thoroughgoing critical apparatus and two introductory chapters covering the biographical and wider cultural context.

CUNQUEIRO. Rexina Rodríguez Vega, *Álvaro Cunqueiro: unha poética da recreación*, Santiago, Laiovento, 103 pp., makes a stimulating analysis of C.'s incorporation of a range of literary discourses into the texture of his fiction. M. X. Nogueira, 'Habitantes da Fisterra. A presencia do celtismo na obra de Cunqueiro', *Unión Libre*, 2:123–36, is a rather broad-brush survey of Celtic elements in C.'s work, with a strictly literary rather than ideological emphasis. Xesús Rábade, *Unha lectura de 'Os outros feirantes'*, Vigo, Xerais, 43 pp., champions C.'s use of a specific genre.

FERREIRO. M. Villar, 'Literatura galega na década da posguerra (1939–49). *Rogo a Yavé*, un poema en galego non recompilado de Celso Emilio Ferreiro', *BGL*, 17:131–35, analyses the text with a view to locating it within F.'s postwar production and within the contemporary Galician context.

FOLE. The dedication to F. of the *Día das Letras Galegas* for 1996 produced the now familiar avalanche of publications of uneven quality and interest. Perhaps the best of these is *Ánxel Fole. Aproximación temática á súa obra narrativa en galego*, Vigo, Cumio, 140 pp., an up-to-date theme-based analysis of F.'s work. The same author's 'A compoñente relixiosa na vida e na obra de A. Fole', *Encrucillada*, 102:6–15, and 'Ánxel Fole e o relato fantástico', *Grial*, 134:253–62, look respectively at F.'s religiosity and at his short fantasy fiction, the latter placed within a broader Galician context. *Ánxel Fole. Día das Letras Galegas 1997*, ed. X. Alonso Montero, Santiago U.P., 118 pp., contains the editor's 'Prólogo á edición facsímile do número 6 de *Yunque*' as an appendix. A.M. also contributes 'Ánxel Fole, García Lorca e os *Seis poemas galegos* (con tres apéndices)' (38–80), an evaluation of F.'s role in Lorca's decision to cultivate Galician as a literary language. The volume additionally includes: X. Gregorio Ferreiro's 'Ánxel Fole e Lorenzo Varela: lembranzas dun tempo de ilusión' (81–88), a biographical study, and A. Palacio's similarly informative 'Ánxel Fole, traductor' (89–103). *Ánxel Fole. A luz da fala*, ed. C. Sánchez (A Nosa Cultura, 17), Vigo, A Nosa Terra, 72 pp., contains L. Alonso, 'Na dramaturxia: achegamento a *Pauto do demo*' (28–31), an assessment of what is often considered a minor work; C. Blanco, 'Mulleres e feminismo nos artigos de Fole' (46–52), a detailed examination of F.'s literary treatment of women; I. Gómez, 'Os primeiros escritos periodísticos' (9–12), a largely descriptive account of these; M. Lopo, 'Testemuña do celtismo' (41–45), which examines those articles with a Celtic component; M. X. Nogueira, 'O didactismo na obra de Fole' (32–37), highlighting F.'s strategies aimed at engaging the non-academic reader; O. Novo, 'Os mundos outros á luz do candil' (23–27), considers the presence of the supernatural in F.'s short fiction; A. Requeixo, 'Xornalista en *El pueblo gallego*' (13–16), appraises F.'s writing for one of Galicia's most eminent prewar journals; C. Rodríguez, 'O itinerario cronolóxico de

Ánxel Fole' (66–72), is a synthesis of biographical and bibliographical information provided by the leading authority on F.'s life and work; M. Veiga, 'Unha vida truncada polo franquismo' (4–8), looks at the experience of the Franco régime as a determining factor in F.'s life. The published proceedings of the *Congreso Ánxel Fole*, Santiago, Xunta de Galicia, 265 pp., include: C. Blanco, 'Contemplando a paisaxe e testemuñando a historia: a muller nos artigos de Fole' (89–117), highlighting the presence of women in F.'s journalistic production as indicative of his progressive humanism, pro-feminist ideological stance and committed *galeguismo*; M. Lopo, 'Fole e o celtismo' (119–33), stressing F.'s use of Celtic elements not just as sources for cultural allusion but as a means of communicating a popular 'Atlantic' tradition; A. Risco, 'Ánxel Fole e a literatura fantástica' (151–63), describing the different modes of the fantastic employed by F. in four tales; 'Os relatos pacegos de Ánxel Fole' (165–82), evaluating F.'s contribution to a distinctive literary setting that has, in Galicia at least, become a sub-genre in its own right; X. Alonso, 'O primeiro Fole: poesía e ideoloxía' (195–203), identifying elements of Marxist ideology in F.'s pre-war poetry; A. Basanta, '*Á lus do candil*: tradición e modernidade' (211–20), examining the work as belonging to an enduring tradition, one of structured collections of tales subscribing to an identifiable overall frame.

LAMA. M. Quintáns, 'O camiño de Xavier Lama no teatro galego actual', pp. 59–127 of *O peregrino errante que cansou ó demo*, Santiago, IGAEM, 261 pp., rigorously locates L.'s drama within a contemporary Galician context.

MANUEL ANTONIO. *'Vangarda e ¡Máis alá!', Serta*, 2 : 177–92.

MARTÍNEZ RISCO. Xosé R. Freixeiro, *Sebastián Martínez Risco, ensaísta e poeta*, Sada, Castro, 258 pp., is a welcome study of the multifaceted writer who was one of the leading Galician intellectuals of the post-Civil War period.

MÉNDEZ FERRÍN. Iris Cochón, *Unha lectura de 'Con pólvora e magnolias'*, Vigo, Xerais, 68 pp., significantly enhances our understanding of the intricate network of intertextual references that underlies M.F.'s collection.

OTERO PEDRAYO. C. Millán-Varela, 'Nationalism vs. universalism in the 1926 Galician fragments of *Ulysses*', *GalR*, 1 : 73–82, from the perspective of translation studies, examines O.P.'s texts as symbolically representing Galician cultural identity.

PATO. A. Casas, 'De impurezas, epitafios, balbordos. Lectura non só sistémica de *Fascinio* de Chus Pato nas coordenadas líricas dos 90', *AELG*, 1996 : 129–48, locates the collection within the context of the most recent Galician lyric.

PEREIRO. T. Seara, 'O executor en "stand by": premonición da morte nos poemas de Lois Pereiro', *Dorna*, 23:121–26, points to the pervasive presence of the theme of death in P.'s verse.

PONDAL. Manuel Ferreiro, *De Breogán aos pinos*, Santiago, Laiovento, 50 pp., examines the genesis and history of the poem and recovers the original text by reproducing the autograph in facsimile form. C. Blanco, 'Mulleres na utopía celta de Pondal', *Unión Libre*, 2:101–18, analyses the role of women in P.'s male-centred mythical constructions, underlining the cosmic associations of woman within the Celtic collective imagination. T. López, '¿Nas orixes do neotrobadorismo? Notas sobre o "Canto do vigía" de E. Pondal', *Grial*, 132:491–502, provides a commentary on a text traditionally felt to be a forerunner of *neotrobadorismo*.

POZO. Helena González, *Unha lectura de 'Códice calixtino'*, Vigo, Xerais, 36 pp., is a rigorous exegesis of the collection.

QUINTANILLA. *Donosiña*, ed. L. Tato, Corunna, Biblioteca-Arquivo teatral Francisco Pillado, has an enormously informative introduction to this previously unpublished play, its author and its period, and constitutes a splendid opening volume of a welcome new collection.

RISCO, VICENTE. D. Villalaín, 'Vicente Risco e o teatro do seu tempo', pp. 59–85 of *O Bufón de El Rei*, Santiago, IGAEM, 181 pp. O. Rodríguez, 'Os camiños narrativos de V. Risco', *AELG*, 1996:149–61, attempts to systematize R.'s literary production according to theme. M. J. Lorenzo Modia, 'Stephen Dedalus into Spanish and back into English: genesis of the translations', *GalR*, 1:52–61, makes a thought-provoking examination of 'Dedalus en Compostela'.

RISCO, ANTÓN. A. López, 'Antón Risco: pantasma, excéptico, subversivo, teórico e mestureiro', *Grial*, 135:409–17, seeks a critical synthesis of R.'s life and work using *Viaxes á América Latina á procura da literatura fantástica* as its starting point.

VALCÁRCEL, XULIO. Marina Vázquez, *A tépeda luz dos días. Aproximación á obra poética de Xulio L. Valcárcel*, Ferrol, Sociedade Cultural Valle-Inclán, 147 pp., is a primarily theme-based analysis of the various collections of poetry published by V. to date, with a broad introduction locating his work within the period after 1950.

VALENTE. M. Lopo, *José A. Valente: *Cantigas de alén*', *Serta*, 2:193–203.

VALLE-INCLÁN. *Valle-Inclán y el fin de siglo. Congreso Internacional*, ed. L. Iglesias et al, Santiago, Universidade-Consorcio, 517 pp., contains X. Alonso Montero, 'Dúas presencias galegas no primeiro Valle-Inclán: o Banquete de Conxo e Manuel Murguía' (487–505), which reproduces an unpublished letter on the subject from 1888, and A. Risco, 'A procura da Idade de Ouro (Galicia na obra de Valle-Inclán)' (507–17), a personal reflection on the aesthetic factors that, for R., ultimately conditioned V.-I.'s ethical position.

VÁZQUEZ. T. Monteagudo, 'Noticias acerca de Manuel Lois Vázquez', *BGL*, 17:99–107, and 'M. Lois Vázquez e os seus pseudónimos', *ib.*, 18:131–38, provide valuable biographical information on a little-known author.

VERGARA. *Guieiros*, 4, is a monographic issue dedicated to the Lugo poet as a posthumous tribute, in which a series of brief articles chart diverse aspects of the writer's life and work.

VICETTO. J. Renales, 'B. Vicetto e a construcción dunha literatura galega', *Unión Libre*, 2:87–99, investigates V.'s projected construction of a Galician literary model in the Castilian language based upon the imaginative concept of the larger 'septentrión' and thus akin to V.'s own Scottish-inspired *celtismo*.

VIII.   LATIN AMERICAN STUDIES

SPANISH AMERICAN LITERATURE
THE COLONIAL PERIOD
POSTPONED

THE NINETEENTH CENTURY

By ANNELLA MCDERMOTT, *Department of Hispanic, Portuguese, and Latin American Studies, University of Bristol*

1.   GENERAL

CHA, 560, has a dossier on *modernismo:* B. Matamoro, 'El viejo modernismo' (45–47), is a short introductory article; A. G. Morales, 'El "frontispicio" de *Los raros*' (49–62), proposes that this text describes a little-known engraving, *Pan Mountain* by the English artist Sturge Moore, and that this fact has implications for the meaning of the text; J. Franze, 'Lugones, 1897: socialismo y modernismo' (63–78), stresses the point that *modernismo* arose from the artist's questioning of his role in a capitalist society in which art is a commodity; R. Oviedo Pérez de Tudela, 'Una paradoja en la corte europea: José Fernández' (79–88), examines Silva's *De sobremesa*. F. Denegri, 'Desde la ventana: women "pilgrims" in 19th-c. Latin American travel literature', *MLR*, 92 : 348–62, looks at Flora Tristan's *Mémoires et pérégrinations d'une paria* and Juana Manuela Gorriti's *Peregrinaciones de un alma triste*, noting that both women's journeys were, in one sense, a failure, yet both discovered from them a sense of mission. M. Grunfeld, 'De viaje con los modernistas', *RevIb*, 62, 1996 : 351–66, links travel to a desire for identification with the prestigious centres of culture, but notes that for many *modernistas* the journey was imaginary rather than real. J. I. Gutiérrez, 'Crítica y modernidad en las revistas literarias: la *Revista de América* de Rubén Darío and Ricardo Jaimes Freyre o el eclecticismo modernista en la publicaciones literarias latinomericanas de fin de siglo', *ib.*, 367–83, sees the magazine as the voice of a Latin American intelligentsia undergoing the process of modernization. Luis A. Jiménez, **El arte autobiográfico en Cuba en el siglo* XIX, New Brunswick, NJ, Ometeca Institute, 1995. N. Jitrik, 'La estética del romanticismo', *Hispamérica*, 76–77 : 35–48, while concerning itself with Romanticism in general, discusses some particular Latin American manifestations. *La Torre*, 1.1–2, 1996, is a special issue on *modernismo* and includes: A. Acereda,

'Versolibrismo martiano y modernista: la libertad poética de José Martí' (5–18), which examines the concept of free verse and proposes M. as the initiator of this form in Hispanic poetry; B. A. Heller, 'Suturando espacios: comunidad, sexualidad y pedagogía en José Martí' (33–54), explores the sexual implications of certain mythical allusions in *Nuestra América* and the vision of woman revealed in M.'s last letters to Carmen Miyares de Mantilla and her daughters; C. L. Jrade, 'Poesía y compromiso político: Martí ante la modernidad' (55–69), argues that it is easier to see M. as a *modernista* writer if we conceive of that movement as a modernizing project, rather than a purely aesthetic one; C. Suárez León, 'José Martí y Víctor Hugo por una modernidad ética y poética' (71–77), looks at the influence of the French writer on M.; P. P. Rodríguez López, 'Nueva York en Caracas. Las crónicas norteamericanas de José Martí para *La Opinión Nacional*' (79–99), suggests that these early texts already demonstrate the stylistic characteristics of M.'s mature writing; F. Burgos, 'Actuación, fantasía y poética en los cuentos de *Azul*' (101–11), stresses the innovatory nature of Darío's prose; B. Clark de Lara, '*Por donde se sube al cielo* de Manuel Gutiérrez Nájera. Primera novela modernista' (113–29), is a reworking of the author's introduction to the 1995 edition of this text, which she had recently unearthed; R. Colón Olivieri, 'Contenido y expresión en *La Venus del patio* de Manuel Martínez Dávila, novela modernista puertorriqueña' (131–49), argues that the novel demonstrates the fact that in Puerto Rico *modernismo* retained its vigour into the 1930s; A. E. Díaz Alejo, 'La narrativa najeriana y el positivismo mexicano' (151–65), draws attention to three themes in Gutiérrez Nájera's writing drawn from the positivist tradition, these being education, relations between the rich and the poor, and the attitude of society and the state towards their weakest members; E. Martínez Masdeu, 'La poesía modernista en Puerto Rico: sinopsis descriptivo' (167–89), concentrates on the period of genesis of *modernismo* on the island; I. A. Schulman, 'Una voz moderna: la poesía de Juana Borrero' (191–203), stresses the importance of the poetry, as opposed to the biography. F. J. López Alonso, 'Pero esto no es más que el principio. De Fernández de Lizardi a Machado de Assís', *CHA*, 570:45–58, sees both writers as expressing a typically modern moral uncertainty, particularly in the former's *Don Catrín de la Fachenda* and the latter's *O alienista*. *RevIb*, 178–79, 'Siglo XIX: fundación y fronteras de la ciudadanía', includes: H. Achugar, 'Parnasos fundacionales: letra, nación y estado en el siglo XIX' (13–32), an examination of the first anthologies of poetry published after Independence in several countries of Latin America; B. González, 'Fundar el estado/narrar la nación. (*Venezuela heroica* de

Eduardo Blanco)' (33–46); N. Shumway, 'La nación hispanoamericana como proyecto racional y nostalgia mitológica: algunos ejemplos de la poesía' (61–70), shows that poets rejected the notion that a Latin American identity had to be formed from zero, appealing instead to a myth of origin that denied their newness; E. von der Walde Uribe, 'Limpia, fija y da esplendor: el letrado y la letra en Colombia a fines del siglo XIX', (71–86), points to connections between philology and political ideology; M. Glantz, '*Astucia* de Luis G. Inclán, ¿novela nacional mexicana?' (87–98), draws attention to the differences between this writer — popular, marginalized — and the writers more commonly held to be representative of 19th-c. Mexico; E. Garrels, 'Sobre indios, afroamericanos y los racismos de Sarmiento' (99–114); S. Rotker, 'Lucía Miranda: negación y violencia del origen' (115–28), examines the reappearance in several authors after Independence of this legendary figure, a white woman taken captive by Indians; N. Gerassi-Navarro, 'La mujer como ciudadana: desafíos de una coqueta en el siglo XIX' (129–40), is concerned with the Colombian writer Soledad Acosta de Samper; A. Fernández Bravo, 'La frontera portátil: Nación y temporalidad en Lastarria y Sarmiento' (141–48); L. Area, 'El *Album de Señoritas* de Juana Manso (1854): una voz doméstica en la fundación de una nación' (149–74); J. Lasarte, 'Ciudadanías del costumbriso en Venezuela' (175–84), establishes a connection between literary *costumbrismo* and the modernizing project; C. Iglesia, 'Mejor se duerme en la pampa. Deseo y naturaleza en *Una excursión a los indios ranqueles* de Lucio V. Mansilla' (185–92); R. Rosa, 'Hostos en el mercado: raza y nación en *Mi viaje el sur*' (193–208); R. Ianes, 'La esfericidad del papel: Gertrudis Gómez de Avellaneda, la condesa de Merlín, y la literatura de viajes' (209–18); F. Unzueta, 'Género y sujetos nacionales: en torno a las novelas históricas de Lindaura Anzoátegui' (219–32); A. González, '"Estómago y cerebro": *De sobremesa*, el *Simposio* de Platón y la indigestión cultural' (233–48), is mainly concerned with Silva's use of irony in his novel; O. Montero, 'Escritura y perversión en *De sobremesa*' (249–62); G. Mora, 'Modernismo decadentista: *Confidencias de psiquis* de Manuel Díaz Rodríguez' (263–76). F. Opere, 'Cautivos de los indios, cautivos de la literatura', *Hispamérica*, 76–77 : 49–76, traces the evolution of this theme in Argentinian literature, and examines its ideological function. I. A. D. Stewart, 'Textual representations of religion in Rosas' Argentina', *BHS(L)*, 74 : 483–500, looks at Echeverría's *El matadero*, Mármol's *Amalia*, and Sarmiento's *Facundo*, focusing on their denunciation of what they saw as Rosas's manipulation of religion. Examination of a sermon by a contemporary Scottish minister demonstrates that there was concern also among non-Catholic settlers in Argentina.

2. INDIVIDUAL AUTHORS

CASAL, JULIÁN DEL. J. Fombona, 'Julián del Casal: el mal viaje a París o el gozo de su "mal de siglo"', *RevIb* 62, 1996:385–91, concentrates on *La última ilusión* proposing that it can be read as offering a counterview to the prevailing francophilia. O. Montero, 'La periferia del deseo: Julián del Casal y el pederasta urbano', pp. 99–111 of *Carnal Knowledge: Essays on the Flesh, Sex and Sexuality in Hispanic Letters and Film*, ed. Pamela Bacarisse (Supplement to *RevIb*, 61), Pittsburgh, Ediciones Tres Ríos, 1995, 223 pp., ties the poet, perhaps somewhat tenuously, to the gay scene in Havana in the late 1890s and to certain pseudo-scientific writings of the period on the subject of prostitution.

DARÍO, RUBÉN. Jacques Issorel, **El cisne y la paloma. Once estudios sobre Rubén Darío*, Perpignan U.P., 1995, 219 + 9 pp. F. Solares Larrave, 'Las *Palabras liminares* de Darío: una declaración de identidad cultural', *REH*, 31:302–20, sees in this text a response from the margins to the centre and a declaration of self-determination in the form of parody and carnivalisation.

GÓMEZ DE AVELLANEDA, GERTRUDIS. B. Pastor, 'Symbiosis between slavery and feminism in Gertrudis Gómez de Avellaneda's *Sab*?', *BLAR*, 16:187–96, sees the novel as establishing a parallel between slavery and the treatment of women in the Cuba of her time, slavery functioning essentially as a metaphor in the novel.

HEREDIA, JOSÉ MARÍA. A. M. Beaupied, 'Lo bello y lo sublime en dos poemas de José María Heredia', *REH*, 31:3–23, contrasts the notion of 'lo bello' in *En el teocalli de Cholula* with that of 'lo sublime' in *Niágara*, suggesting that the former work fluctuates between Neoclassicism and Romanticism, whereas the latter is more clearly Romantic.

ISAACS, JORGE. R. Borello, 'Sociedad y paternalismo en *María*', *CHA*, 562:67–79 questions the view usually taken by critics that the female protagonist of I.'s novel is passive, innocent and angelic.

RODÓ, JOSÉ ENRIQUE. O. Montero, 'Hellenism and homophobia in José Enrique Rodó', *REH*, 31:25–39, examines how and why R. excluded the homosexual element in his use of the story of Hylas and Heracles in his *Motivos de Proteo*.

THE TWENTIETH CENTURY

By D. L. Shaw, *Brown-Forman Professor of Spanish American Literature in the University of Virginia*

1. General

GENERAL WORKS include M. E. de Valdés et al., *Latin America in its Literature*, Whitestone, Council on National Literatures, 1995, 219 pp., on identity; L. Shirley, *Latin American Writers, NY, Facts on File, 144 pp. R. González Echevarría, 'Latin America and Comparative Literatures, *Procs* (Brasília), 1017–29, defends a westernizing approach. A Fass Emery, *The Anthropological Imagination in Latin American Literature*, Columbia, Missouri U.P. 1996, 156 pp. R. Fernández Retamar, *Para una teoría de la literatura latinoamericana*, Bogotá, Caro y Cuervo, 1995, 389 pp. F. García Sánchez, *Estudios sobre la intertextualidad*, Ottowa, Dovehouse, 1996, 182 pp. A. J. Pérez, *Modernismo, vanguardismo, posmodernidad. Ensayos de literatura hispanoamericana*. BA, Corregidor, 1995, 318 pp. *Postmodernidad y Postcolonialismo*, ed. A. de Toro, Frankfurt, Vervuert. Id. 'Postcolonialidad y postmodernidad', *Iberoromania*, 44, 1996:64–98, is densely argued using Borges as the main example. *The Postmodern in Latin and Latino American Cultural Narratives*, ed. C. Ferman, NY, Garland, 1996, 243 pp. E. Spielmann, 'Third World literature', *Procs* (Brasília), 982–86, a critique of recent postcolonial theory. R. de la Campa, 'Latinoamérica y sus nuevos cartógrafos: discurso poscolonial, diásporas intelectuales y enunciación fronteriza', *RevIb*, 176–77, 1996:697–717, discusses critical options. J. Zevallos-Aguilar, 'Teoría poscolonial y literatura latinoamericana. Entrevista con Sara Castro Klarén', *ib.*, 963–71, has much on postcolonialism, little on Spanish American literature. W. D. Mignolo, 'Posoccidentalismo: las epistemologías fronterizas y el dilema de los estudios (latinoamericanos) de area', *ib.*, 679–86, is too abstract. B. McGuirk, *Latin American Literature: Symptoms, Rules and Strategies of Poststructuralist Criticism*, London, Routledge, 1996, 312 pp. V. Cervera Salinas, *La palabra en el espejo*, Murcia U.P., 1996, 218 pp. O. R. López Castaño, *La crítica latinoamericana*, Medellín, Vieco, 1996, 153 pp. E. Spielmann, 'El descentramiento de lo posmoderno', *RevIb*, 176–77, 1996:941–52, thought-provoking on the alleged shift in criticism in the 80s and 90s. A. Vidal, 'Los derechos humanos, hermenéutica para la crítica literaria', *ib.*, 719–29, calls for a more sociological, 'cultural' approach to criticism. L. Santos, 'O *kitsch* na transição do moderno ao pós-moderno', *Procs* (Brasília), 1357–62, really discusses recent critical stances. *Papeles de Montevideo*, 1, has ten essays on aspects of 'La crítica

literaria como problema'. *NTC*, 19–20, has a dozen articles on Latin
American cinema and literature. M. Cipollini, 'Cinema e letteratura
in America Latina', *StLI*, 27, 1996:59–99, is chiefly on the history
and problems of Latin American cinema. J. Cruz, 'Discurso de la
modernidad en las culturas pereféricas: la vanguardia latinoamericana', *Hispamérica*, 76–77:19–34, a dubious interpretation of *van-
guardismo*. *The Faulkner Journal*, 11.1–2, 1995–96, is devoted to
Faulkner's influence on Latin American fiction, with interviews with
Piglia and Saer and a dozen articles. D. Cohn, '"He was one of us":
the reception of Faulkner and the United States South by Latin
American authors', *CLS*, 34:149–69, is a well-documented survey.
D. B. Lockhart, *Jewish Writers of Latin America: a Dictionary*, NY,
Garland, 618 pp. J. G. Cobo Borda, **De Sarmiento a Borges*, Bogotá,
Caro y Cuervo, 1995. J. Franco, **Marcar diferencias, cruzar fronteras*,
Santiago de Chile, Cuarto Propio, 1996, 134 pp., her most recent
essays. *Narrativa y poesía hispanoamericana (1964–1994)*, ed. P. Tovar,
Lérida U.P. 1996, 494 pp., has 49 items mostly of indifferent quality.
G. M. Aguilar, *Crítica de la ruptura en la literatura latinoamericana*, Buenos
Aires U.P., 1996, 187 pp., has essays on Lezama Lima, Palés Matos,
P. de Rokha, Vallejo, and Felisberto Hernández. *Monographic Review*,
11, 1995, is on Hispanic prison literature.

GENDERED WRITING. L. Trevisan, **Política y sexualidad. Nudo en la
escritura de mujeres latinoamericanas*, Lanham, U.P. of America. F. Masi-
ello, 'Tráfico de identidades: mujeres, cultura y política de representación en la era neoliberal', *RevIb*, 176–77, 1996:745–66, is on feminine
resistance to neoliberal culture. **Revista Iztapalapa*, Mexico D.F.,
Univ. Autónoma, 37, 1995, is dedicated to Latin American women
writers. **Contesting the Power of Latin American Gender Imagery*, ed.
M. Melhuus and K. A. Stolen, London, Routledge,1996, 224 pp.
L. Fox, *Mujeres: Escritura y subversión*, East Lansing, Nueva Crónica,
1995, 227 pp., has 21 essays on prose and poetry. L. Guerra, *La mujer
fragmentada: Historias de un signo*, Santiago de Chile, Cuarto Propio,
1995, 217 pp., has sections on Mistral, Castellanos, and V. Ocampo,
and comments by Eltit and others. M. I. Lagos, *En tono mayor: Relatos
de formación de protagonista femenina en Hispanoamérica*, Santiago de Chile,
Cuarto Propio, 1996, 170 pp., is on women's biographical narratives
1924–85. S. Reisz, **Voces sexuadas: Género y poesía en hispanoamerica*,
Lérida U.P., 1996, 217 pp. N. Novaes Coelho, 'A poesia feminina na
America Latina', *Procs* (Brasília), 1215–21, is on C. Meireles, Mistral,
and Ibarbouru. C. J. Craft, 'Latin American popular culture and
women's narrative', *IJHL*, 8, 1996:197–210, is on Allende's *De amor
y de sombra* and G. Belli's *La mujer habitada* as soap operas. R. Cornejo-
Parriego, 'Racialización colonial y diferencia femenina en "Love
Story" de Poniatowska y "Cuando las mujeres quieren a los hombres"

de Ferré', *AfHR*, 16.2:10–18, is on feminist criticism and race. Robinson, *Women*, includes entries on many women writers including, besides expected authors, lesser figures such as Mirta Aguirre, Sara de Etcheverts, and Carmen Naranjo, along with many others. A. Witte, *Politics and Feminism in the Works of Women Playwrights from Spain and Argentina*, NY, Lang, 1996, 167 pp.

POETRY. S. Millares, 'El viaje imaginario en la vanguardia poética latinoamericana', *StLI*, 27, 1996:31–38, a quick survey. T. Kamenzain, *La edad de la poesía*, Rosario, Viterbo, 1996, 111 pp., has essays on Vallejo, Pizarnik, Lezama Lima, and others. G. Maturo, *La mirada del poeta*, BA, Corregidor, 1996, 158 pp., has essays on Huidobro and Lezama Lima. J. E. Albada-Jelgersma, 'Las tecnologías políticas del ser en los sujetos poéticos de Nancy Morejón y Gioconda Belli', *RCEH*, 21:441–55, is on their ideology. C. Bollentini, 'Il tema del paese natale in Luis Palés Matos e L. A. Arango', *StLI*, 28–29, 1996:117–27, is on their yearning for authenticity. G. Puleo, 'Los dos abuelos: Nicolás Guillén y Luis Palés Matos', *RHM*, 50:86–98, is superficial. N. Binns, 'Herencias anti-poéticas: Vicente Huidobro y Nicanor Parra', *NTC*, 18, 1996:139–52, is on the former as precursor of anti-poetry.

FICTION. E. Becerra, *Pensar el lenguaje: escribir la escritura. Experiencias de la narrativa hispanamericana contemporánea*, M, Univ. Autónoma, 1996. W. H. Corral, 'Nuevos raros y la historia literaria del canon de la forma novelística', *RHM*, 49, 1996:267–84, criticizes canon-formation and suggests other names to include. M. Bustos Fernández, *Vanguardia y renovación en la narrativa hispanoamericana*, M, Pliegos, 1996, 153 pp., discusses Macedonio Fernández, Torres Bodet, and others. M. D'Alessandro Bello, *La novela urbana en Latinoamérica durante los años 1945 a 1959*, Canarias, Fundación CELARG, 1995. M. Kunz, *El final de la novela*, M, Gredos, 430 pp., examines the endings of novels from Spain and Spanish America. M. Giardinelli, 'Reflections on Latin American Narrative of the Post-Boom', *Review*, 52, 1996:83–87, an important statement by this major author. E. F. Coutinho, 'Post-modernism and contemporary Latin American fiction', *Procs* (Brasília), 163–68, correctly argues that political agendas have to be recognized. M. Domínguez, *Historia, ficción y metaficción en la novela latinoamericana*, BA, Corregidor, 205 pp., has essays on Allende, Arenas, Carpentier, Vargas Llosa, Fuentes, and others. E. Dehennin, *Del realismo español al fantástico hispanoamericano*, Geneva, Droz, 222 pp., has much discussion of Borges, Cortázar, and García Márquez. *The Real Thing. Testimonial Discourse and Latin America*, ed. G. M. Gugelberger, Durham, Duke U.P., 328 pp., with essays full of interest on this important topic. L. J. Craft, *Novels of Testimony and Resistance from Central America*, Gainesville, Florida U.P., 237 pp., has meaty chapters on C. Alegría, M. Argueta, A. Arias and G. Belli. P. Elmore, *La fábrica de la memoria*, Lima, FCE, 233 pp., analyses historical novels by Carpentier, Roa Bastos, Vargas Llosa, Del Paso, and García Márquez and their reflection of modern problems. M. C. Pons, *La novela histórica de fines del siglo* xx, Mexico D.F., Siglo XXI, 1996, 285 pp., examines novels by Saer, Del Paso, and others. *Asesinos de papel*, ed. J. Lafforgue and J. B. Rivera, BA, Colihue, 1996, 302 pp., has interviews on detective fiction in the River Plate area with Borges, Cortázar, Denevi, Giardinelli, Martínez Estrada, Roa Bastos, and others. G. Mina, **Un continente desaparecido*, Mexico D.F., Diana, 1996, has interviews with García Márquez, Galeano, Menchú, and others. F. Garramuño, 'Genealogía y rescritura: novelas rioplatenses de fin de siglo', *Hispamérica*, 76–77:77–87, considers novels by C. Aira, Saer, E. Belgrano Rawson, T. de Mattos, and N. Ponce de León; another version in *RPl*, 17–18:597–87.

MORE THAN ONE AUTHOR. J. G. Cobo Borda, **Silva, Arciniegas, Mutis y García Márquez*, Bogotá, Imprenta Nacional. H. Méndez, 'Simón Bolívar y la imaginación literaria americana: García Márquez, Borges y Neruda', *BHS(G)*, 74:197–212, is excellent on the evolution of his literary image. S. Schlickers, **Verfilmtes Erzählen*, Frankfurt, Vervuert, is on the film versions of Puig's *El beso de la mujer araña* and García Márquez's *Crónica de una muerte anunciada*. J. Hoeg, 'The social imaginary/symbolic: technology and Latin American literature', *Mosaic*, 30.4:95–108, examines responses by García Márquez and Allende. S. Yurkievich, *La movediza modernidad*, M, Taurus, 1996, 339 pp., is on Borges, Girri, Paz, and others. L. Gregorich, *Escritores del futuro: Notas sobre literatura y teatro*, BA, Latinoamericano, 1995, 143 pp., has essays on Borges and Cortázar among others. M. E. Gilio, *Entrelíneas*, Montevideo, Brecha, 1996, 140 pp., has interviews with Benedetti, Roa Bastos, Borges, García Márquez, Puig, Onetti, Bioy Casares, and others. *Confesiones de escritores. Escritores latinoamericanos. Los reportajes de The Paris Review*, BA, El Ateneo, 1996, 249 pp., reprints interviews with Borges, Bioy Casares, Cabrera Infante, Cortázar, Fuentes, García Márquez, and others. G. Nudelstejer, *Las voces perdurables*, Mexico D.F., UNAM, 1996, 305 pp., has essays on Borges, García Márquez, Sábato, Carpentier, and others. Wing, *Belief*, includes conference papers on Yáñez, Fuentes, and E. A. Westphalen. N. Jitrik, *Atípicos en la literatura latinoamericana*, Buenos Aires U.P., 431 pp., has essays on A. Somers, A. Cancela, F. Hernández, D. Eltit, A. Porchia, G. Zani, and others. W. Rowe, *Hacia una poética radical: Ensayos de hermenéutica cultural*, Rosario, Viterbo, 1996, 253 pp., has essays on Donoso, Parra, Roa Bastos, Vallejo, Vargas Llosa, and others. A. M. Hernández de López, *Narrativa hispanoamericana contemporánea. Entre la vanguardia y el posboom*. M. Pliegos, 1996, 321 pp., has essays on Allende, García Márquez, Fuentes, Puig, Giardinelli, and others. S. Lipp, _Crucible of Ideas_, NY, Lang, 1996, 310 pp., has chapters on F. Romero, Sábato, Mariátegui, and other thinkers. M. Solotorevsky, 'Estética de la totalidad y estética de la fragmentación', _Hispamérica_, 75, 1996:17–35, is on Borges's 'La escritura del Dios', Sarduy's _Cobra_ and García Márquez's _Crónica de una muerte anunciada_. S. Magnarelli, 'Images of exile/exile(d) images: Valenzuela and Donoso', _REH_, 31:61–75, is on _El jardín de la lado_ and _Novela negra con argentinos_. R. M. Galindo, 'Feminismo y política en _Despierta, mi bien, despierta_ de Claribel Alegría y _La mujer habitada_ de Gioconda Belli', _Hispanófila_, 119:73–80, criticises apolitical feminism. D. K. Danow, _Magical Realism and the Grotesque_, Lexington, Kentucky U.P., 153 pp., uses Bakhtin on Rulfo's _Pedro Páramo_ and García Márquez's _El otoño del patriarca_. N. Jitrik, _Suspender toda certeza_, BA, Biblio, 220 pp., includes essays on García Márquez and Donoso. M. Martínez-Richter, _La caja de la escritura_, Frankfurt, Vervuert, 137 pp., has interviews with Saer, Roffé, Eloy Martínez, and others.

THEATRE. E. Neglia and F. Smieja, *_Medio siglo de teatro latinoamericano: una bibliografía_, Mississanga, Canada, 139 pp. *_Estudios sobre el teatro iberoamericano y argentino_, ed. O. Pellettieri, BA, Galerna, 409 pp. *_Del escenario a la mesa de la crítica_, ed. J. Villegas, Irvine, Gestos, 194 pp., has 14 essays. _Perspectives on Contemporary Spanish American Theatre_, ed. F. Dauster, Lewisburg, Bucknell U.P., 1996, 160 pp., has items on Triana, Arlt, Villaurrutia, Cossa, Gambaro, and others. B. H. Reynolds, 'Voz y memoria en el teatro hispanoamericano reciente', _LATR_, 30.2:31–43, discusses plays by A. Dorfman, R. Ramos-Perea, C. J. Reyes, and G. Schmidhuber. E. Neglia, 'Commedia dell'Arte en el teatro hispanoamericano', _StLI_, 27, 1996:101–11, documents its influence up to the 60s. E. Thomas, 'Metáforas de la identidad en el teatro hispanoamericano contemporáneo', _RCL_, 50:39–50, examines Usigli's _Corona de sombra_, Fuentes's _Todos los gatos son pardos_ and I. Aguirre's _Lautaro_. D. Zalacaín, 'La criollización de las heroínas griegas en el teatro caribeño', _SELA_, 40.3–4:24–28, is on V. Piñera's _Electra Garrigó_, L. R. Sánchez's _La pasión según Antígona Pérez_, and Franklin Domínguez's _Lisistrata odia la política_.

OTHER GENRES. C. de Mora, *_El cuento hispanoamericano contemporáneo_, Seville U.P., 1995, 204 pp., and W. Matzat, *_Lateinamericanische Identitätsentwürfe: Essayistische Reflexion und narrative Inszenierung_, Tubingen, Narr, 1996, 204 pp.

2. INDIVIDUAL COUNTRIES

ARGENTINA

Libros argentinos IBSN, 1982–97, BA, Cámara Argentina del Libro, is a CDRom covering more than 90,000 items. J. Amícola, 'La literatura argentina desde 1980', *RevIb*, 175, 1996:427–38, is on crucial dates and the arrival of women writers. N. M. Flawia de Martínez, *Ensayos de literatura argentina*, BA, Corregidor, 1996, 143 pp., has essays on Giardinelli, H. Tizón, T. Eloy Martínez, and others. R. P. Herrera, *Ensayos sobre poesía*, BA, Nuevo Hacer, 1996, 190 pp., has essays on Borges, Lugones, C. Mastronardi, R. Molinari, and others. J. Fondebrider, *Conversaciones con la poesía argentina*, BA, Tierra Firme, 1995. V. Kamer, 'Ironía y lenguaje en *Lunario sentimental* de Leopoldo Lugones', *LNL*, 300:57–66, is on irony and 'sociolects'. G. Marini, 'Origen y continuidad del expresionismo: *Lunario sentimental* (1909) de Leopoldo Lugones', *RPl*, 17–18:95–109, defines the term and its application. M. Soriano, '*Las fuerzas extrañas*. Positivisme et fantastique en Argentine', *Imprévue*, no. 1–2:177–221, is on Lugones's rejection of positivism. R. Antelo, 'Expedición a Quilmes', *RPl*, 17–18:251–66, is on *Versos al campo* by O. Girondo. L. García Moreno, 'A. Pizarnik: the poet as hostage', *LALR*, 48:67–93, is on her 'décriture'. S. Gregory, 'A. Pizarnik's *La condesa sangrienta*', *BHS(G)*, 74:293–309, overpraises Pizarnik's courageous insight. E. M. Martínez, 'Mercedes Roffé: poeta en Nueva York', *Chasqui*, 25.1, 1996:96–102, is an interview on her work.

FICTION. M. I. Lichtblau, *Annotated Bibliography of the Argentine Novel*, Metuchen, Scarecrow, 1136 pp. G. Speranza, *Conversaciones con quince narradores argentinos*, Bogotá, Norma, 1995. *Narrativa argentina*, BA, Fundación Noble, 302 pp., contains papers on 'La historia en la literatura'. M. Bermúdez Martínez, 'Ficción y verdad en la literatura argentina', *RPl*, 17–18:111–21, is too brief on Macedonio Fernández, R. Walsh, Saer, and Piglia. N. Ulla, *La insurrección literaria*, BA, Torres Agüero, 252 pp., is on colloquiality in Puig, Cortázar, Bioy Casares, and others. *La historia y la política en la ficción argentina*, Santa Fe, Univ. del Litoral, 1995. M. J. Punte, 'Una mujer en busca de autor. La figura de Eva Perón en dos narradores argentinos', *Iberoromania*, 46:101–27, discusses T. Eloy Martínez's *Santa Evita* and Abel Posse's *La pasión según Evita*. N. Girona, *La novela argentina de los años 80*, Valencia U.P. 1996. J. Ludmer, 'Mujeres que matan', *RevIb*, 176–77, 1996:781–97, finds examples in Arlt, Borges, Puig, and others. F. Aínsa, 'Del coraje de los guapos al país del miedo', *RPl*, 17–18:359–69, rather superficial. C. Correas, *Arlt literato*, BA, Atuel, 1995, 346 pp. O. Borre, *Arlt y la crítica, 1926–1990*, BA, Suarez-América Libre, 1996, 382 pp. V. Martínez, *The Semiotics of a Bourgeois. An Analysis of the Aguafuertes porteñas by Roberto Arlt*. Potomac, Scripta Humanistica, 210 pp. R. Gnutzman, 'Bibliografía de y sobre Roberto Arlt', *Chasqui*, 25.2, 1996:44–62, is very full and useful. H. González, *El filósofo cesante. Gracia y desdicha en Macedonio Fernández*, BA, Atuel, 1995, 223 pp. *Hablan de Macedonio Fernández*, ed.

G. L. García, 2nd edn augmented, BA, Atuel, 1996, 159 pp., has numerous interviews, with Borges and others. U. Kröptl, 'Der Nachlaβ Leopoldo Marechal's', *CHLR*, 21:393–415, is on *Megafón*. J. de Navascués, 'El viaje y la teatralidad en *Adán Buenosaires*', *RCEH*, 21:353–71, is on the novel as a penitential exercise. *Actas del Segundo Congreso Internacional sobre Martínez Estrada*, Bahía Blanca, Fundación Martínez Estrada, 1996, 232 pp., contains seven articles and 23 papers; henceforth indispensible. D. Civitanovi, **De Berceo a Borges*, BA, García Cambeiro, 1995, has essays on Mallea and Borges.

BORGES. V. Teitelboim, *Los dos Borges, Mexico D.F., Hermes, 1996, 341 pp., apparently a biography. A. Vaccaro, *Georgie 1899–1930*, BA, Proa-Alberto Casares, 1996, 447 pp., the first part of a superbly detailed biography. B. Josef, *Borges, Rio de Janeiro, Alves, 1996. C. Meneses, *Borges en Mallorca*, Alicante, Altea, 1996, 117 pp., very important on his early years as a writer. F. Mateo, *El otro Borges: Entrevistas 1960–1986*, BA, Equis, 203 pp., offers 16 interviews. A. Balderston, **Referencialidad y expresión de la realidad en Borges*, Rosario, Viterbo, 1996. R. Alifano, *El humor de Borges*, BA, Urraca, 1996, 133 pp., is non-literary gossip and odd fragments by his secretary. J. Woscoboinik, **Indagación psicoanalítica de la obra de Borges*, BA, Latinoamericano, 1996, 139 pp. E. Volker-Schmahl, 'Borges en el contexto del modernismo europeo', *Iberoromania*, 44, 1996:52–63, is chiefly on his philosophical irony. *Variaciones Borges*, 4, has an article by Eco and some fine bibliography, not all copied here. A. Sierra, *El mundo como voluntad y representación: Borges and Schopenhauer*, Potomac, Scripta Humanistica, 156 pp., a badly needed first book-length approach to this vital topic. S. Cueto and E. Giordano, **Borges: Ocho ensayos*, BA, Viterbo, 1995, 128 pp. **Borges, Calvino y la literatura 1*, Poitiers U.P., 1996, 2 vols. B. Mujica, 'Jorge Luis Borges and the Spanish Golden Age', *Herrero Vol.*, 194–210, compares Golden Age scepticism with his. J. Rigoli, 'Borges au jardin des espèces', *Compar(a)ison*, 1, 1996:133–83, is well researched on animal imagery in his work. M. Garate, 'Los textos del joven Borges', *Procs* (Brasília), 1232–37, is on his *poesía arrabalera*. M. Garate, 'La poética borgeana de la década del veinte', *RPl*, 17–18:297–306, is rather vague, on *Fervor*. R. Sanger, 'Words, action and anecdote in Borges's poetry', *BHS(L)*, 74:73–93, is on the contrast between writing and action. G. Ricci, 'Borges y la pérdida como recuperación del centro', *RPl*, 17–18:319–31, is on losing and finding identity in sundry poems. M. Fuentes, 'El narrador narrado (en torno al poema "Góngora" de Jorge Luis Borges)', *Salinas*, 11:135–37, is unsystematic. I. T. Agheana, 'The meaning of abstraction in the prose of Borges', *IJHL*, 8, 1996:127–44, is on man's need to structure space. B. Bosteels, 'Borges, hacia una lectura espacial', *La Chispa '95*, 49–58, is chiefly on 'La penúltima versión de la realidad'. M. E. Schwartz, 'Tradition and treason: sacred translation in two stories by Borges and Chekhov', *CRCL*, 23, 1996:1085–95, includes 'The Gospel according to Mark'. C. Bulacio de Medici, 'Ficciones e ironías', *RPl*, 17–18:283–95, is on Borges, Rorty and language. A. Louis, 'Las tensiones del presente. El guapo en Borges', *ib.*, 307–17, is on the evolution of the *guapo* theme. E. Amman, 'Time and creation in "Herbert Quain"', *IJHL*, 8, 1996:145–58, the only really convincing account of the tale. S. Juan-Navarro, 'La alquimia del verbo: "Tlön, Uqbar, Orbis Tertius" de Jorge Luis Borges y la sociedad de la Rosa-Cruz', *Hispanófila*, 120:67–80, sees the story of the *Rosa Cruz* as the model for the tale. F. Martínez-Bonatti, 'Ambigua parabola', *RHM*, 49, 1996:351–56, seems poorly researched on 'Pierre Menard'. A. N. Fragola, 'Postmodern time in "Theme of the Traitor and the Hero" and A. Robbe-Grillet's *The Man who Lies*', *NNR*, 4.2:49–65, emphasizes Borges's influence on the latter. H. Núñez-Faraco, 'In search of the Aleph: memory, truth and falsehood in Borges's poetics', *MLR*, 92:613–29, is chiefly on Daneri. T. Franco Carvalhal, 'Le "manuscrit trouvé" chez Borges et Piglia', *Procs* (Brasília), 271–76 is on 'Pierre Menard' and *Respiración artificial*. A. Mansbach, '"El inmortal" de Borges a través de la concepción heideggeriana de la muerte y la individualidad', *RHM*, 50:110–15, makes obvious points. N. de Marval-McNair, 'Borges's "Guayaquil" or the romance of the withheld', *ib.*, 49, 1996:368–94, is a dubious interpretation. A. Moreiras, 'Elementos de articulación teórica. Para el subalternismo latinoamericano. Cándido y Borges', *RevIb*, 176–77, 1996:875–91, offers an odd interpretation of 'La lotería en Babilonia'. C. X. Ardavín, 'Hacia una definición borgeana de la literatura: Dante y la Divina Comedia', *Chasqui*, 25.2, 1996:81–87, is on *Nueve ensayos dantescos*. S. J. Levine, 'Notes to Borges's notes on Joyce: infinite affinities', *CL*, 49:344–59, is on the connections between the two writers. M. Servodidio, 'Surfing the internet with Borges and Carme Riera', *RHM*, 49:434–45, is an eccentric comparison of the two writers. P. Spinato, 'I misteri di Borges', *StLI*, 27. 1996:115–27, is on comic-strip Borges in Italy. O. Peyrou, 'M. Peyrou, el hermano secreto de Borges', *CHA*, 562:81–86, is on their friendship. N. Fürstenberger, 'Emprunts mythologiques et modernité du roman argentin', *RPl*, 17–18:349–57, is on the minotaur in Borges and Cortázar. R. Bonceli, *Borges-Bioy*, BA, Sudamericana, 252 pp., contains interviews and commentary. J. Hernández Martín, 'Honorio Bustos Domenq's *Seis problemas para don Isidro Parodi*', *RCEH*, 21:295–311, is on its parodic language.

OTHER FICTION WRITERS. *QIA* is a special issue on Bioy Casares with nine articles and an unpublished story. N. Díaz, 'Itinerario de

Bioy Casares', *RPl*, 17–18:267–78, is on his earliest work. S. Sosnowski, 'Entrevista: Bioy Casares', *Hispamérica*, 75, 1996:49–59, a handful of memories. M. Lebron, 'The *compadrito* figure in Latin American fiction: a sociocritical approach', *Procs* (Brasília), 1197–1201, is on Bioy Casares's 'El sueño de los héroes'. H. Cavallari, 'La tramoya de la escritura en *La invención de Morel*', *BHS(L)*, 74:95–104, is wordy on the novel's strategies. J. Constenia, **Sábato el hombre. Una biografía*, BA, Espasa Calpe, 267 pp. M. R. Lojo, **Sábato, en busca del original perdido*, BA, Corregidor, 335 pp. K. Kohut, 'Buenos Aires en la obra de Ernesto Sábato', *Salinas*, 9, 1995:83–90, sees it as an existential metaphor. S. M. Frame, 'Vanishing point: the world view of Juan Pablo Castel in *El túnel*', *Hispanófila*, 121:1–10, is on his visual interpretation of reality. C. Serafín, '*Sobre héroes y tumbas*', *StLI*, 27, 1996:39–57, is on Sábato and the absolute. A. Mangin, **Temps et écriture dans Silvina Ocampo*, Toulouse-le-Mirail U.P., 1996. A. Ostrov, 'Vestidura/ escritura/ sepultura en Silvina Ocampo', *Hispamérica*, 74, 1996:21–28, is on dress and identity in some of her stories. R. Silva Cáceres, **Etude des motifs fantastiques dans l'oeuvre de Julio Cortázar*, Paris, L'Harmattan, 1996. Id., **El árbol de las figuras*, Santiago de Chile, LOM, 243 pp. **Visiones cortazarianas*, ed. R. Padilla López, Mexico D.F., Aguilar, 1996. M. D. Blanco Amejo, **La novela lúdica experimental en Cortázar*, M, Pliegos, 1996, 224 pp. L. H. Kahn, **Los paisajes en la obra de Cortázar*, NY, Lang, 1996, 218 pp. J. P. Shafer, **Los puentes de Cortázar*, BA, Latinoamericana, 1996, 227 pp., is apparently on the bridge metaphor in his work. P. Frölicher, **La mirada recíproca. Estudio sobre los últimos cuentos de Julio Cortázar*, Bern, Lang, 1996. T. J. Peavler, 'Something old, something new? Cortázar's final fictions', *La Chispa '95*, 291–300, is on his late socio-political themes. A. M. Rodríguez, 'La cultura francesa como componente de la especificidad de Buenos Aires', *RPl*, 17–18:511–18, is on French influence, especially on Cortázar. P. Standish, 'Los compromisos de Cortázar', *His(US)*, 80:465–71, is on his literary/ political stance. J. Boisen, 'Strange loops chez Julio Cortázar. Étude sur la recursivité', *OL*, 52:410–40, applies the ideas of D. Hofstadter to four stories. F. Zangrilli, **'Pirandello e Cortázar', *ItQ*, 33, 1996:15–29. M. Alcalá Galán, '"Todos los fuegos el fuego": reescritura fantástica de la tesis del eterno retorno', *BHS(L)*, 74:215–21, is on Cortázar's most Borgesian story. C. Henderson, '"Usted se tendió a su lado". Que ninguna gramática pondría en claro', *LNL*, 300:95–101, is on the end of the story as its beginning. C. S. Schmidt-Cruz, 'Desiring the maternal body in "Deshoras" and "Historias que me cuento" by Julio Cortázar', *LALR*, 49:7–21, is on incest fantasy. See also her 'Reclaiming the female consciousness in Cortázar's "Cambio de luces"', *HR*, 65:415–30, proposing a new feminist reading strategy.

J. Amícola, '"La noche boca arriba" como encrucijada literaria', *RevIb*, 180:459–64, contrasts it with Borges's 'El Sur'. J. F. Capello, 'Cortázar and Schrödinger's cat', *REH*, 31:41–60, is (again) on 'La isla a mediodía' and its paradoxical view of reality. P. Domínguez, 'Manuscritos inéditos de Julio Cortázar', *Procs* (Brasília), 1272–78, chiefly on miscellaneous poetry. J. I. Badenes, '*El laberinto* de Manuel Mujica Láinez', *His(US)*, 80:775–84, is on this 1972 novel as a parody of Larreta. M. J. Barra, 'Mestizos en Buenos Aires', *RPl*,17–18:499–510, is on Jewishness in the work of Mario Szichman. K. E. Hall, 'Visual media in the work of Mario Szichman', *Hispanófila*, 121:53–59, is chiefly on the cinematographic in his writings. D. Lagmanovich, 'Marco Denevi y sus *Falsificaciones*', *RCL*, 50:65–71, is on the fragmentation technique of this (1996) collection of microstories. M. A. Minelli, *Manuel Puig*, BA, Florida Blanca, 1995. G. Martí-Peña, **Manuel Puig ante la crítica. Bibliografía anotada y comentada (1968–96)*, Frankfurt, Vervuert. J. Amícola, 'Manuel Puig, el contra-canon borgeano', *RPl*, 17–18:373–83, is on Puig's work as a new beginning. A. Giordano, 'Manuel Puig: Discontinuidad y devenir en los comienzos de una literatura menor', *LNL*, 300:73–86,is on his earliest work. I. Logie, ***'Manuel Puig y el cine', *FoH*, 10, 1996. J. Amícola, *Materiales iniciales para La traición de Rita Hayworth*, La Plata, Revista Orbis Tertius, 1996, 504 pp., gathers up all the preparatory work. B. Schulz Cruz, 'Alimentando sueños en *El beso de la mujer araña*', *LNL*, 300:87–93, is on references to food. G. Martí, 'La magia de contar: estrategias narrativas de supervivencia en *Cae la noche tropical* de Manuel Puig', *Chasqui*, 25.1, 1996:12–24, is on the undermining of truth-telling. N. Bratosevich, **Ricardo Piglia y la influencia de la contravención*, BA, Atuel, 333 pp. B. Levinson, 'Trans(re)-lacions: dictatorship, disaster and the "literary politics" of Piglia's *Respiración artificial*', *LALR*, 49:97–120, is on Piglia's interpretation of Argentine history. T. Orecchia Havas, 'La literatura como infinita memoria. Sobre *La ciudad ausente*. Ricardo Piglia y Macedonio Fernández', *RPl*, 17–18:665–77, is on the shift in Piglia's work. E. H. Berg, 'Sobre *La ciudad ausente* de Ricardo Piglia', *Hispamérica*, 75, 1996:37–47, is too descriptive. J. Corbatta, 'Ricardo Piglia o la pasión de una idea', *NTC*, 18, 1996:153–73, is a useful interview. O. Steinberg, 'Novela histórica tradicional y nuevas maneras de novelar la historia', *RPl*, 17–18:611–23, is mainly on Eloy Martínez's *Santa Evita* (1995). F. Goldberg, '*La pesquisa* de J. J. Saer. Alambradas de la ficción', *Hispamérica*, 76–77:89–100, is on this socio-political detective novel. J. Premat, 'La novela policial según J. J. Saer', *LALR*, 48:19–38, similarly. S. Larrañaga, '*La pesquisa*', *RPl*, 17–18:601–10, is on Saer's renovation of detective fiction. J. Premat, 'El cataclismo de los orígenes: la pampa histórica de J. J. Saer', *ib.*, 689–700, is on the *pampa* in his *La ocasión*. C. Vásquez, 'Identidad y escritura, permanencia y cambio en la narrativa de Héctor Bianciotti', *ib.*, 641–51, surveys his use of the theme of exile. A. Llarena, '*A sus plantas rendido un león*', *ib.*, 471–82, is on O. Soriano's 1987 political novel. D. Palaversich, 'Postmodernismo, postcolonialismo y la recuperación de la historia subalterna', *Chasqui*, 24.1, 1995:3–15, is on Soriano's *Memoria del fuego* (1982–86) as postcolonial. Y. Germain, '*Una sombra ya pronto serás*', *RPl*, 17–18:701–10, is in French on Soriano and Arlt. H. Chaparro Valderrama, 'Osvaldo Soriano', *Quimera*, 157:24–28, is rather necrological. G. García-Corrales, '*Santo oficio de la memoria*: la memoria y la historia oficial: una lectura bajtiniana', *Chasqui* 24.1, 1995:53–59, discusses four textual strategies in Giardinelli's novel. O. Basabe, 'Autoritarismo y sátira en *El viento se la llevó* and *De pies y manos* de Roberto Cossa', *BHS(L)*, 74:223–34, contrasts their techniques. D. Boit, 'Abel Posse', *Secolas*, 28:134–42, discusses his historical novels. D. H. Bost, 'Reassessing the past: Abel Posse and the new historical novel', *La Chispa '95*, 39–47, is on the analysis of power in *El largo atardecer del caminante*. S. Menton, 'La *Historia verdadera* de A. Núñez Cabeza de Vaca en la última novela de Abel Posse, *El largo atardecer del caminante* (1992)', *RevIb*, 175, 1996:421–26, is on the novel's treatment of history. E. A. Cordeiro, **Haroldo Conti*, Córdoba, Narvaja, 1996, 105 pp. C. de Vallejo, 'Aspectos de la dialéctica especularia en *Una luz muy lejana* (1966) de Daniel Moyano', *RevIb*, 175, 1996:447–59, interprets the central figure, Ismael. R. de Grandis, 'Crítica a la razón histórica: *La astucia de la razón* de José Pablo Feinmann en la Argentina contemporánea', *ib.*, 180:449–58, is on its picture of the intelligentsia. E. Fisbach, '*El curandero del mal oscuro* de Gabriel Báñez', *RPl*, 17–18:653–63, is on its use of recent history. S. Contreras, '*La piel de caballo* de Ricardo Zelarayán', *ib.*, 203–15, is on style in this 1986 populist novel. N. Ponce. 'Un justiciero en busca de piedad', *ib.*, 567–77, is on Argentine detective fiction. M. L. de Arriba, 'El género negro en Argentina', *ib.*, 589–99, is on (kind of) detective novels by Juan Sasturain and Martín Caparrós. M. Crivelli, 'El género autobiográfico en Argentina', *ib.*, 679–88, is on Norah Lange. **Narrativa de Luisa Valenzuela*, ed. G. Díaz and M. I. Lagos, Santiago de Chile, Cuarto Propio, 1996, 264 pp. A. Parada, 'Metamorfosis del deseo femenino en "Ceremonias de rechazo" de Luisa Valenzuela', *La Chispa '95*, 281–90, is on the ceremonies' success. D. Niebylski, '"Ceremonias de rechazo": la parodia humorística como terapía reconstructiva', *LF*, 33:59–69, is on its (alleged) humour. A. Cook, '*Novela negra con argentinos* and the move towards reconciliation', *La Chispa '97*, 113–21, is illuminating on Valenzuela's new approach to repressive systems. V. Cox, 'Political and social alienation in Luisa Valenzuela's *Novela negra*', *LF*,

33:71–77, is too short, on Palant and writing. W. Caldwell, 'El laberinto del discurso', *RevIb*, 175, 1996:439–46, is on fear and exile mentality in *Novela negra*. E. Campello, 'Romanceando a arte de narrar o feminino', *La Chispa '95*, 59–70, is on *Novela negra* as a *Künstlerroman*. J. Logan, 'Valenzuela's *Simetrías*', *LALR*, 48:5–18, is on postmodernism vis-à-vis feminism. M. López Cabrales interviews Alina Diaconú in *RevIb*, 175, 1996:585–97, rather too biographical. M. C. Vargas, *Los cuentos de Liliana Heker*, NY, Lang, 1996, 154 pp., examines the work of this outspoken writer, and her polemic with Cortázar. R. Dahl Buchanan, 'Eros and writing in Tununa Mercado's *Canon de alcoba*', *Chasqui*, 25.1, 1996:52–61, is on the joys of sex. A. B. Dellepiane, 'El revés de la trama', *RPl*, 17–18:625–37, usefully surveys recent women writers.

THEATRE. O. Pelletieri, **Teatro argentino moderno, 1949–76*, BA, Galerna, 285 pp. See too his *Pirandello y el teatro argentino (1920–1990)*, BA, Galerna, 156 pp., and his *De Esquilo a Gambaro*, BA, Galerna, 126 pp., on classical influences on Argentine Theatre. A. Witte, *Guiding the Plot. Politics and Feminism in the Work of Women Playwrights from Spain and Argentina*, NY, Lang, 1996, xii + 163 pp., includes Gambaro and Aida Bortnik. E. Golluscio, 'La palabra en contraste', *RPl*, 17–18:419–31, is on *cocoliche* and standard Spanish in plays by Carlos Pacheco, A. Discépolo, and R. Arlt. S. Bonnardel, '*Un guapo del 900*', *ib.*, 335–47, ignores existing criticism. A. de Toro, *'Das postmoderne Theater von Eduardo Pavlovsky', *MK*, 38, 1996:69–94. I. del R. Moreno, 'Antígona en el teatro argentino y brasileño a partir de 1968', *LATR*, 30.2:115–29, is partly on Gambaro's *Antígona furiosa*. H. R. Morell, '*Penas sin importancia* y *Tío Vania*', *ib.*, 31.1:5–14, is on Gambaro's use of Chekhov in her 1991 play. L. Seda, '*. . . y a otra cosa, mariposa* de Susana Torres Molina', *ib.*, 30.2:103–14, is on her exploration of taboo themes. G. Tambascio, 'El teatro de Copi', *CHA*, 563:107–12, is a brief overview. D. S. Castro, 'The Argentine revista and the Uriburu Revolution', *LATR*, 31.1:43–58, is on popular theatre and politics in 1931. S. Pellarolo, 'Un precursor: Nemesio Trejo', *ib.*, 59–69, is on his organizational work, not his theatre.

REVIEWS. N. Salvador et al., *Revistas literarias argentinas, 1960–1990*, BA, Inca Seguros, 306 pp., a useful index. N. Salvador and E. Ardizzone, **Indice de Letras de Buenos Aires (1980–1995)*, BA, Sociedad de Estudios Bibliográficos, 1996, 110 pp. J. L. Trenti Rocamora, **Indice general y estudios de la revista Martín Fierro*, *ib.*, 1996 252 pp., and see O. Gallone's comments in 'Revista Martín Fierro', *Hispamérica*, 74, 1996:121–26.

BOLIVIA

J. C. Orihuela, 'Una aproximación a la narrativa boliviana de los últimos quince años', *RCL*, 49, 1996:95–101, very informative. M. Aronua, 'The vice of simulation in Alcides Arguedas's *Pueblo enfermo*', *Imprévue* no. 1–2:223–39, is on his pessimistic positivism. K. S. Leonard, 'Entrevista: Gaby Vallejo', *Hispamérica*, 75, 1996:61–74, is on her novels and plans.

CHILE

V. Teitelboim, **Gabriela Mistral. Pública y secreta*, Mexico D.F., Hermes, 1996, apparently biographical. S. Falabella, '"Desierto": territorio, desplazamiento y nostalgia en *Poema de Chile* de Gabriela Mistral', *RCL*, 50:79–96, is on her search for roots. E. R. Horan, 'Sor Juana and Gabriela Mistral: locations and locutions of the saintly woman', *Chasqui*, 25.2, 1996:89–103, is on their respective constructions of a 'public figure'. K. Hopfe, **Vicente Huidobro, der creacionismo und das Problem der Mimesis*, Tübingen, Narr, 1996. V. Teitelboim, **Huidobro, La marcha infinita*, Mexico D.F., Hermes, 1996, apparently biographical. M. Brescia, 'El creacionismo de Vicente Huidobro', *Procs* (Brasília), 1317–25, nothing new. A. Risco, '*Tour Eiffel* de Vicente Huidobro', *Salina*, 9, 1995:78–82, is on its verbal presentation. A. Pérez López, 'Castillos de palabras construídos sobre el aire', *RCL*, 50:141–46, is on literary relations between Huidobro and Unamuno. V. Teitelboim, *Neruda, Mexico D.F. 1996, apparently biographical. M. Urruria, **Mi vida junto a Pablo Neruda*, Barcelona, Seix Barral, 288 pp. L. Sainz de Medrano, **Neruda: cinco ensayos*, Rome, Bulzoni, 1996, 131 pp. H. Loyola, 'El uso del eneasílabo en Neruda', *RCL*, 49, 96:103–12, is a survey. O. Rodríguez, **La poesía póstuma de Neruda*, Gaitherburg, Hispamérica, 1995, 139 pp. M. Umeda, 'Del aislamiento hermético a la búsqueda del vínculo en *Residencia en la tierra*', *Atenea*, 475:11–29, is on Neruda's search for the 'other'. E. Parilla, **Humorismo y sátira en la poesía de Parra*, M, Pliegos, 209 pp. O. Sarmiento, 'Otro ejercicio de extrañamiento de Enrique Lihn', *RevIb*, 175, 1996:495–505, is on his *Pena de extrañamiento*. L. Correa-Díaz, **Lengua muerta: Enrique Lihn*, Cranston R. I., Inti, 1996. N. Nómez, 'Marginalidad y fragmentación en la poesía de los 60', *Atenea*, 474, 1996:105–26, very good on Post-Parra. R. Olea, 'La mujer ha salido al escenario. Poesía chilena de los ochenta', *Hispamérica*, 76–77:101–12, is on S. Fariña, E. Brito and C. Berenguer. O. Sarmiento, 'Teillier y Lara', *Atenea*, 474, 1996, 93–104, analyses 'La portadora' by Teillier and 'El lenguaje más querido' by Lara. A. C. Flores, **"Sujeto a la poesía. Conversaciones con Jorge Torres Ulloa, un poeta del sur de Chile', *Confluencia*, 12.1, 1996:210–18. J. Campos, 'Poesía y ecología', *RCL*, 50:111–17, examines two collections of poems by Carlos A. Trujillo. A. Villanueva-Collado, 'El puer virginal y el doble: configuraciones arquetípicas en *La pasión y muerte del cura Deusto* por Augusto D'Halmar', *Chasqui*, 25.1, 1996:3–11, is on this early gay novel. M. G. Berg, 'Marta Brunet's *La mampara*', *La Chispa '97*, 39–48, on the meaning of the image of the *mampara*. G. García-Corrales, *Relaciones de poder y carnavalización en la novela chilena contemporánea*, Santiago de Chile, Asterión, 1995, 120 pp., is on Donoso's *El jardín de al lado*, Skármeta's *Ardiente paciencia* and Eltit's *El cuarto mundo*. D. Oelker, 'La vanidad en L. Orrego Luco', *Atenea*, 474, 1996:67–79, is on his critique of the upper class. F. Schopf, 'La escritura de José Donoso', *ib.*, 127–38, interesting but too personal. J. Pérez, 'Masks, gender expectations . . . in the fiction of José Donoso', *Hispanófila*, 119:47–58, is on his subversion of *machismo*. C. Gaspar, 'Metaficción y productividad en José Donoso', *RevIb*, 180:419–35, discusses *El obsceno pájaro* and *Casa de Campo*. B. Schultz-Cruz, 'Bibliografía sobre Jorge Edwards', *Chasqui*, 24.1, 1995:60–75, goes up to December 1992. D.Flores, '"Nupcias", sentido y forma en su contexto literario', *RCL*, 50:5–19, superbly argued on this Skármeta short story. G. Yovanovich, 'The rebirth of the *pícara* and Skármeta's *Match Ball*', *Procs* (Brasília), 1207–14, is superficial on Sophie. C. Heymann, 'Les chemins de la lecture dans *Un viejo que leía novelas de amor*', *LNL*, 300:141–62, is descriptive on reading in this novel of L. Sepúlveda. R. Neustadt, 'Alejandro Jodorowsky: reiterating chaos, rattling the cage of representation', *Chasqui*, 26.1:56–74, is rather general on chaos in his work. M. I. Lagos, 'Cuerpo y subjetividad en narraciones de A. Maturana, A. M. del Río y D. Eltit', *RCL*, 50:97–109, is on the theme of illness in female characters. L. A. Martínez, 'La dimensión espacial en *Vaca sagrada* de Diamela Eltit', *ib.*, 49, 1996:65–82, is on the city and the individual. D. Eltit, 'Cuerpos nómadas', *Hispamérica*, 75, 1996:3–16 (formerly in English in *Review*) is on Luz Arce's *El infierno* (1993) and M.A. Merino's *Mi verdad* (1993). F. Moreno Turner, '*Hijo de mí* o la recuperación poética de la historia', *RCL*, 50:119–32, examines historical vision in this 1992 novel by Antonio Gil. R. Martínez, '*Ay Mamá Inés* de Jorge Guzmán: Entre la crónica y el testimonio', *ib.*, 21–37, studies this prize-winning 1993 novel. O. López Cotin, '*El tono menor del deseo* de Pía Barros', *La Chispa '95*, 209–20, is on feminine sexuality and the dictatorship. C. Morel Montes, **Identidad femenina en el teatro chileno*. Santiago de Chile, Univ. Pontificia, 1996, 238 pp. C. Loisel, 'El teatro del absurdo: a propósito de *El cepillo de dientes*', *La Chispa '97*, 255–64, is on social pressures in the play by Jorge Díaz. S. Gregory, **Ariel Dorfman and Harold Pinter*', *CDr*, 30, 1996:325–45. E. M. Gilmore,

'Gardel, tango y cultura popular en *Matatangos* de M. A. de la Parra', *His(US)*, 80:472–79, is on its debunking of Carlos Gardel.

COLOMBIA

Apuntes sobre literatura colombiana, ed. K. Kline, Bogotá, Ceiba, 143 pp., is useful especially on García Márquez. M. Jaramillo, B. Osorio, and A. Robledo, *Literatura y diferencia: escritoras colombianas del siglo xx*, 2 vols, Bogotá-Medellín, Uniandes-Antioquia U.P., 1995, 451, 405 pp., collect essays on both prose and poetry. C. Hernández de Mendoza, *La *poesía de Gerardo Valencia*, Bogotá, Caro y Cuervo, 1996. I. A. Quintana, 'La escritura de los cuerpos en *La vorágine*', *RevIb*, 175, 1996:393–403, is rather odd, on suffering.

GARCÍA MÁRQUEZ.   F. Moretti, *Modern Epic from Goethe to García *Márquez*, London, Verso, 1996, 272 pp. J. L. Cebrián, *Retrato de Gabriel García Márquez*, BA, Galaxia, 104 pp., a too brief biography. D. Saldívar, *García Márquez: El viaje a la semilla. La biografía*, Mexico D.F., Alfaguara, 612 pp., the best biography so far. J. G. Cobo Borda, *Para *llegar a García Márquez*, Bogotá, Temas, 256 pp. L. Walford, 'Violence in three early novels of Gabriel García Márquez', *Hispanófila*, 119:31–45, is on his dismantling of myths. F. Perus, 'Historiography and regionalism in Latin American narrative', *JLACS*, 6:173–81, is really on *Leaf Storm*. A. Herrmann, *Intertextualität und Textsemiotik in *Cándida Eréndira*, Hamburg, Kovac, 1995. J. C. Pettey, 'Nietzsche's *Birth of Tragedy* and Euripides's *Bacchae* as sources for aspects of *Chronicle of a Death Foretold*', *Hispanófila*, 121:21–34, is too speculative. G. D. Carillo, 'La dialéctica de la historia: Colón, Bolívar y Santander en la obra de G.M.', *RevIb*, 175, 1996:477–83, is on G.M.'s angry vision of history. K. Mose. '*El amor en los tiempos del cólera*', *Procs* (Brasília), 1186–91, is on its universal themes. A. M. Penuel, 'Symbolism and the clash of cultural traditions in G.M.'s *Del amor y otros demonios*', *His(US)*, 80:38–48, is on transcending orthodoxy. J. Cussen, 'G.M.'s *Of Love and Other Demons*', *The Explicator*, 55.1:53–4, is on the allusion behind the name Cayetano.

OTHER WRITERS.   J. Zambrano, *La violencia en Colombia: La ficción *de Alvarez Gardeazábal y el discurso histórico*, NY, Lang, 168 pp. Z. also interviews Alvarez Gardeazábal in *Hispamérica*, 76–77:113–24, with quotable remarks. E. Montes Garcés, *El cuestionamiento de los *mecanismos de representación en la novelística de Fanny Buitrago*, NY, Lang, 208 pp. A. Escobar Mesa, 'El goce del verbo: la narrativa de Armando Romero', *RevIb*, 175, 1996:485–94, is on its 'heterología'. G. Alzate, '¡*Que viva la música*! de A. Caicedo', *LALR*, 48:39–55, is on its counter-cultural theme. M. Malin, 'Andres Caicedo's ¡*Que viva la música*!: an implicit dialogue with the modern and postmodern',

Chasqui, 24.2, 1995:103–11, is on its reflection of Colombia's 'bourgeois modern project'. L. Garavito, '*Golpe de muerte* y *El paso de la candelaria*', *LALR*, 30.2:73–88, is on these two collectively-authored plays of protest.

COSTA RICA

M. Rojas and F. Ovares, *Cien años de literatura costarricense, San José, Farben, 1995. C. Kargleder, 'J. León Sánchez and *La isla de los hombres solos*', *Secolas*, 26, 1995:20–25, describes this 1963 novel of protest. C. Helmut, 'Entrevista: Carmen Naranjo', *Hispamérica*, 74, 1996:47–56, is on her feminism.

CUBA

M. R. Couture, 'El agua más recordada: Golden Age poetry in Lezama Lima's "Ah, que tu escapas"', *His(US)*, 80:21–30, is on his re-use of classic Spanish techniques. E. J. Mullen, 'Nicolás Guillén and the Notion of Race in Latin American Literature', *REH*, 31:533–50, discusses criticism of Guillén's work. A. G. Dahl, 'Resolving the question of identity: Nicolás Guillén's "La balada de los dos abuelos"', *AfHR*, 14.1, 1995:10–17, is on bringing together ethnic legacies. S. Bella, 'Ecriture et image dans *Muestrario del mundo* d'Eliseo Diego', *LNL*, 301:97–116, is on this 1988 collection. *AfHR*, 15.1, 1996, has eight articles on Nancy Morejón and an interview. G. Puleo, 'A Pan-africanist politics of the imagination: Nancy Morejón's "Mujer negra"', *RHM*, 49, 1996:419–29, is on this poem as a metaphorical statement. L. D. Bertot, *The Literary Imagination of the Mariel Generation*, Miami, Endowment for Cuban American Studies, 1995, 105 pp., studies the generation to which Arenas belonged. C. Davies, *A Place in the Sun? Women Writers in Twentieth Century Cuba*, London, Zed, 256 pp., superbly informative and critical. E. Matibag, *Afro-Cuban Religious Experience: Cultural Reflections in Narrative*, Gainesville, Florida U.P., 1996, 300 pp., examines the impact on Carpentier and others. M. R. Capeles, *El cuento fantástico en Puerto Rico y Cuba*, Kassel, Reichenberger, 1995, 138 pp., includes criticism of R. Ferré, Gustavo Agrait, J. Martínez Tolentino, L. Acosta, R. Arenas and R. González. J. B. Alvarez, 'La generación literaria sin trauma: una mirada socio-histórica a los novísimos narradores cubanos', *La Chispa '97*, 17–27, is on writers born between 1959 and 1972. F. López Sacha, 'Current tendencies in the Cuban short story', *SAQ*, 96.1:181–97, is informative. A. Nuño, 'Visto desde Cuba: entrevista con Cintio Vitier y Fina García Marruz', *Quimera*, 163:8–19, with interesting reminiscences of Lezama Lima. J. J.

Barquet, 'Epica, negrismo y actualidad cubana: *En el vientre del trópico de Alina Galliano*', *La Chispa '97*, 29–38, is on the enrichment of the *poesía negra* tradition by this 1994 collection. D. Cvitanovic, **Alejo Carpentier*, BA, García Cambeiro, 222 pp. B. Levinson, 'The death of the critique of eurocentrism', *REH*, 31:169–201, uses Carpentier. J. Ordiz, 'La aventura del héroe en *Los pasos perdidos*', *StLI*, 28–9, 1996:145–57, is too obvious. M. A. Cuevas, 'Estética y parodia: El capítulo sexto de *Concierto Barroco*', *Iberoromania*, 45:81–88, analyses the discussion therein. K. Stolley, 'Death by attrition: the confessions of Christopher Columbus in Carpentier's *El arpa y la sombra*', *REH*, 31:505–31, is on his two irreconcilable discourses. J. C. Hewitt, 'In(ter)vención y (sub)versión en *Tres tristes tigres*', *La Chispa '95*, 117–32, is on two modes of reading the novel. E. Perassi, 'Frammenti di un discorso mimetico: da *Tres tristes tigres* di Guillermo Cabrera Infante', Mildonian, *Parodia*, 303–15, is on his rebellion against older Cuban writers. D. T. Frost, 'Parallel worlds, convergent aesthetics: Cabrera Infante's *Tres tristes tigres* and Fellini's *La dolce vita*', *RoN*, 38:3–13, is on their similarities. *CHA*, 563:7–67, has a 'Dossier Sarduy' with five articles and an unpublished essay. I. Chiampi, 'La literatura neobarroca ante la postmodernidad', *Procs* (Brasília), 1030–41, is on Sarduy's ideas. A. Vorderi, **Severo Sarduy and Pedro Almodovar*, M, Pliegos, 239 pp. A. Kanzepolsky, 'Virgilio Piñera, la generosa provocación', *Hispamérica*, 75, 1996:137–49, contains fragmentary notes. **Matías Montes Huidobro*, ed. J. Febles and A. González-Pérez, Lewiston, Mellen, 258 pp. *El arte narrativo de Hilda Perera*, ed. L. A. Jiménez and E. Lismore, Miami, Universal, 1996, 180 pp., contains critical essays on both content and formal aspects of her work. **Reinaldo Arenas*, ed. O. Ette, M, Iberoamericana, 1995. B. Epps, 'Estado de deseo: homosexualidad y nacionalidad (Juan Goytisolo y Reinaldo Arenas a vuelapluma)', *RevIb*, 176–77, 1996:799–820, includes commentary on *Arturo, la estrella más brillante*. M. G. Paulson, 'Los exilios de Reinaldo Arenas en *Viaje a la Habana*', *La Chispa '97*, 343–53, is on exile and the biblical sub-text. D. Vilaseca, 'On the constitution and uses of homosexuality in Reinaldo Arenas's *Antes que anochezca*', *BHS(L)*, 74:351–71, is poorly laid out. S. Kaebnick, 'The *Loca* freedom fighter in *Antes que anochezca* and *El color del verano*', *Chasqui*, 26.1:102–14, is on uncovering the sexual/national self. M. G. Paulson, 'Antecedentes mitológicos de *Otra vez el mar* de Reinaldo Arenas', *Secolas*, 28:50–58. E. Bejel, '*Antes que anochezca*', *Hispamérica*, 74, 1996:29–45, comments on Arenas's autobiography. J. C. Hewitt, 'Crónica de un deseo: *El mar de las lentejas* de Antonio Benítez Rojo', *RevIb*, 175, 1996:461–76, is on its ambiguous treatment of history. A. Azougarh, **Miguel Barnet*, Geneva, Slatkine, 1996. M.A. Gutiérrez, **Lydia Cabrera*, M, Verbum, 1996. E.

González, *'Reflexiones sobre "Fresa y chocolate"', *FoH*, 10, 1996. E. Bejel, 'Strawberry and Chocolate', *SAQ*, 96.1:65–82, is on the film version. M. Resik, 'An interview with Senel Paz', *ib.*, 83–93, contains the usual prudent statements. P. Rosensveig, 'La complicidad del lenguaje en *La nada cotidiana*', *RHM*, 49, 1996:430–33, is on rebellion in Zoe Valdés's 1959 novel. R. I. Boudet, 'Current Cuban theatre', *SAQ*, 96.1:31–51, mentions some new playwrights. V. Martínez Tabares, 'Interview with Alberto Pedro', *ib.*, 53–63, introduces this new dramatist. T. L. Palls, 'Los Testigos de Jehová y el Teatro Escombray', *LATR*, 30.2:17–30, documents the latter's critique through theatre. N. Lie, *La revista cubana Casa de la Américas*, Gaithersburg, Hispamérica, 1996, 310 pp.

DOMINICAN REPUBLIC

W. García, '*Antígona-Humor* de Franklin Domínguez', *LATR*, 31.1:15–29, is on his re-writing of the myth. R. V. Williams, 'The inscription of sexual identity in Aída Cartagena's *Escalera para Electra*', *MLN*, 112:219–31, is on her recasting of the Electra story in committed terms. I. Z. Brown, 'Modernidad y nacionalismo en *Sólo cenizas hallarás (bolero)*', *SELA*, 40.3–4:13–73, is on this 1980 social novel by Pedro Vergés.

ECUADOR

'Jorge Carrera Andrade y la cultura japonesa', *StLI*, 28–29, 1996:107–16, is chiefly on his interest in the *haiku*. A. Ortiz interviews the Afro-ecuadorian poet Adalberto Ruiz in *RevIb*, 175, 1996:599–612, on *poesía negra* and on his fiction. O. Arbeláez, 'Cinco facetas del resentimiento nietzscheano en *Juyungo* [1942] de Adalberto Ortiz', *AfHR*, 14.2, 1995:3–9, examines five characters. M. Handelsman, 'Una doble y única lectura de "Una doble y única mujer" de Pablo Palacio', *Chasqui*, 24.2, 1995:3–23, is on its use of 'border identities'; see too his 'Mujeres del Ecuador dentro y fuera del burdel', *LF*, 33:79–107, on E. Viteri's 1984 novel *Las alcobas negras* and A. Yáñez Cossío's *La Casa del Sano Placer* (1989). A. Gladhart, 'Padding the virgin's belly', *BHS(L)*, 74:235–44, is on Yáñez Cossío's hilarious novel *La cofradía del anillo del vestido de la Virgen Pipona* (1985).

EL SALVADOR

E. Waters Hood interviews Roberto Castillo in *Hispamérica*, 76–77:125–31, on his life and fiction.

GUATEMALA

J. Berry-Bravo, *Romelia Alarcón Folgar: Palabra y poesía de Guatemala*, Guatemala City, Serviprensa, 1996, 437 pp., anthologizes and comments on this little-known poet. J. C. Galeano, 'Ana María Rodas: poesía erótica y la izquierda de las patriarcas', *LF*, 33 : 171–81, is on her rebellious feminism. M. R. Morales, 'Aldea oral/ ciudad letrada: el caso de Miguel Angel Asturias y las *Leyendas de Guatemala*', *RevIb*, 175, 1966:405–20, defends Asturias against Beverley. A. Rotti, 'Il circo de Miguel Angel Asturias', *StLI*, 28–29, 1996:129–43, is on humour in *El ahijado*. S. Henigan, 'Lands of Corn', *RoS*, 29:85–96, is on Asturias's interest in Romania. J. A. Serna, 'La mujer en *Solima* de Miguel Angel Asturias', *LATR*, 31.1:71–78, is on patriarchalism in this 1955 play. L. A. Jiménez, 'Autobiography as History', *SELA*, 40.3–4:29–36, is rather obvious on *I, Rigoberta Menchú*. G. Brotherston, 'Regarding the evidence in *Me llamo Rigoberta Menchú*', *JLACS*, 6:93–103, criticizes Levinson's approach. See the A. Moreiras's reply, *ib.*, 6:227–32. R. K. Sitler, 'Gaspar Pedro González: the first Mayan novelist', *Secolas*, 28:67–72, is on his *La otra cara* (1972).

HAITI

M. Chaney, **Framing Silence. Revolutionary Novels by Haitian Women*, N. Brunswick, Rutgers U.P., 224 pp.

MEXICO

J. L. Martínez, **Problemas literarios*, Mexico D.F., CNCA, seems to contain essays on 20th-c. Mexican Literature. C. Domínguez, *Tiros en el concierto literario mexicano del siglo v*, Mexico D.F., Era, 570 pp., contains essays on 20th-c. Mexican writers including Revueltas, Reyes, Vasconcelos, and Jorge Cuesta. J. Agustín, **La contracultura en México*, Mexico D.F., Grijalbo, 1996, 168 pp. A. V. Vento, **La generación Hijo pródigo*, Lanham, U.P. of America, 1996, 306 pp. C. Schaefer, *Danger Zones: Homosexuality, National Identity and Mexican Culture*, Tucson, Arizona U.P., 1996, 159 pp., is on M. Barbachano Ponce, Luis Zapata, J. R. Calva, S. Levi Calderón, and J. J. Blanco. A Trejo Villafuerte, *La esponja en la lanza*, Mexico D.F., Conacultura, 1996, 162 pp., has essays on Reyes, Paz, and other contemporary writers and themes. J. J. Villareal, *Los fantasmas de la pasión*, Mexico D.F., Aldus, 237 pp., has essays on López Velarde, Novo, Julio Torri, Chumacero, and Pacheco. G. Zaid, *Tres poetas católicos*, Mexico D.F., Océano, 352 pp., is on López Velarde, Pellicer and Ponce. R. Lozano Herrera, **Las veras y las burlas de J. J. Tablada*, Mexico D.F., Univ.

Iberoamericana, 1995, 319 pp. R. Hernández Rodríguez. 'El poeta
en la quinta avenida: modernidad o el tropiezo con el cuerpo
femenino', *LALR*, 49:43–61, is on Tablada's vision of woman.
G. Ramos et al., *Ensayos sobre la obra de Carlos Pellicer*, Mexico D.F.
Conacultura, 141 pp. S. Oropesa, 'La representación del yo y del tu
en la poesía satírica de Salvador Novo', *Chasqui*, 24.1, 1995:38–52, is
on Novo as a gay writer. M. Pinho, *Volver a ser: Un acercamiento a la
poética de Octavio Paz*, NY, Lang, 133 pp. B. Peralta, *El poeta en su tierra:
Diálogos con Octavio Paz*, Mexico D.F., Grijalbo, 1996, 178 pp., contains
sundry interviews. E. M. Santí, *El acto de las palabras*, Mexico D.F.,
FCE, 406 pp., is an intellectual biography of Paz with interviews.
X. Rodríguez Ledesma, *El pensamiento político de Octavio Paz*, Mexico
D.F., UNAM, 1996, 557 pp. M. C. Mabrey, 'Paz y Cernuda', *Secolas*,
27, 1996:97–106, compares *El laberinto de la soledad* and *Variaciones
sobre tema mexicano*. R. Mata Sandoval, '*Trasblanco*: una apropiación
creativa de Octavio Paz por Haroldo de Campos' *Procs* (Brasília),
1380–85, is on the introduction of Paz's poetry to Brazil. M. Jong,
'Un poème de Octavio Paz', *ib.*, 1279–84, is on 'Concorde' from
Ladera este. M. J. Bas Albertos, *La poesía cívica de J. García Terres*,
Alicante, Alicante U.P. 1996. A. Millán Chivite, *El costumbrismo
mexicano en las novelas de la revolución*, Seville U.P., 1996, 382 pp.
E. Montes de Oca Navas, *Protagonistas de las novelas de la revolución
mexicana*, Mexico D.F., Instituto Mexiquense de Cultura, 1996,
210 pp., is on character presentation. J. P. Duffey, 'Documentaries of
the Mexican Revolution: the influence of film on Martín Luis
Guzmán's *El águila y la serpiente*', *La Chispa '95*, 143–52, gives instances.
C. Clark D'Lugo, *The Fragmented Novel in Mexico. The Politics of Form*,
Austin, Texas U.P., 296 pp. P. Earle, 'Underdogs and top dogs in the
Mexican novel', *RHM*, 49, 1996:299–307, is rather slight on *Pito
Pérez*, *Artemio Cruz*, and *Noticias del Imperio*. *Escribir la infancia: Narradoras
mexicanas contemporáneas*, ed. A. M. Domenella, Mexico D.F., Colegio
de Mexico, 1996, 374 pp. *Insula*, 611, contains 11 chatty articles on
modern Mexican prose, including Alicia Llarena's very helpful
'Piedra de toque' (28–30) on contemporary women novelists. D. J.
Anderson, 'Difficult relations, compromising positions. telling
involvement in recent Mexican Narrative', *Chasqui*, 24.1,
1995:16–29, considers novels by M. L. Puga, S. Molina, F. Prieto,
F. Patán, and Carlos Fuentes. M. R. González, *Imagen de la prostituta
en la novela mexicana contemporánea*, M, Pliegos, 1996, 160 pp. L. M.
Scheider, *La novela mexicana entre el petróleo, la homosexualidad y la política*,
Mexico D.F., Nueva Imagen, 134 pp., is on fiction since the 80s.
S. Poot Herrera, *El cuento mexicano*, Mexico D.F., UNAM, 1996,
647 pp. K. Ibsen, *The Other Mirror: Women's Narrative in Mexico
1980–95*, Westport, Greenwood, 204 pp. M. I. Lagos, '*Balún-Canán*,

una novela de formación de protagonista femenina', *RHM*, 50:59–79, is on Castellanos's heroine's problematic identity. F. Leinen, 'Freunde im eigessen Land', *Iberoromania*, 44, 1996:109–32, is on ethnic relations in her *Cuidad Real*. R. K. Sitler, 'Rosario Castellanos's *Oficio de tinieblas*: the Maya otherworld through Ladina eyes', *La Chispa '95*, 437–56, is on her opaque vision of the Mayan world. K. S. López, 'Discourse and "desire to be other" in José Rubén Romero's *La vida inútil de Pito Pérez*', *Chasqui*, 26.1:75–92, is on the novel's ideological ambiguity. D. Cohn, 'A wrinkle in time: time as structure and meaning in *Pedro Páramo*', *RHM*, 49, 1996:256–66, is cogent but narrow in focus. L. A. Figuroa, 'Rulfo: el llano y los cielos', *NNR*, 4.2:68–85, is on his photography. *Antípodas*, 8–9, has seven essays on Fuentes. J. A. Rivas, 'Tres lecturas de una novela de Carlos Fuentes', *Salinas*, 10, 1996:190–94, analyses *La campaña* (1990). G. J. Pérez, 'La configuración de elementos góticos en "Constancia", *Aura* y "Tlactocatzine, del jardín de Flandes" de Carlos Fuentes', *His(US)*, 80:9–20, is on irony and ambiguity. M. Hardin, 'The language of the fathers: the conquering and colonizing tongue of *Cristóbal Nonato*', *Chasqui*, 25.2, 1996:30–43, is on Fuentes's unwitting acceptance of the 'colonizing male tongue'. P. Jay, 'Translation, invention, resistance: rewriting the conquest in Carlos Fuentes's "The two shores"', *MFS*, 43:405–31, is on the novella's modern relevance. **Ibarguengoitía a contrareloj*, ed. A. R. Domenella, Guanajuato, Ediciones de la 56a Legislatura, 1996, 153 pp. **Fernando del Paso ante la crítica*, ed. A. Toleda, Mexico D.F., UNAM, 315 pp. (essays). T. Granados Salinas, 'Al mal del paso, darle prisa', *Quimera*, 155:67–69, introduces Del Paso's new novel *Linda 67*. **Juan García Ponce ante la crítica*, ed. A. Pereira, Mexico D.F., UNAM, 274 pp. (essays, some by fellow writers). *Miradas a la obra de Sergio Galindo*, ed. J. L. Martínez Morales, Mexico D.F., Univ. Veracruzana, 1996, 257 pp. (essays). R. Prado Oropeza, **La narrativa de Sergio Pitol*, Mexico D.F., Univ. Veracruzana, 1996, 104 pp. E. Slater Gould, 'Construction of the Self in Gustavo Sainz's *Gazapo*', *Hispanófila*, 119:59–72, is Bahktinian on carnivalesque devices. S. Lemus, 'El más allá de la escritura', *Nexos* (Mexico), 238:65–69, is a useful interview with Salvador Elizondo. M. F. Medina, 'Interpretando el archivo: las estrategias de la novela detectivesca en *Morir en el golfo*', *Chasqui*, 24.2, 1995:24–31, discusses this (1985) novel by H. Aguilar Carmín. A. R. Reckley Vallejos, 'Expiating the scapegoat in Mexican fiction: [G.] Laveaga's contemporary transformation of Christ', *ib.*, 25.2, 1996:63–70, is on the Christ figure in his 1987 novel *Valeria*. C. Perilli, 'La increíble y triste historia de Angelina Beloff y de su amante desalmado', *RCL*, 50:133–39, is under-researched on Poniatowska's *Querido Diego*. I. M. López, '*Tinísima*: la (re)escritura de un mito', *LF*, 33:149–61, is on Poniatowska's personal vision of history in this biography of Modotti. I. Mathews, **Nellie Campobello*, Mexico D.F., Cal y Arena. I. M. López, **La novelística de M. L. Puga*, NY, Lang, 1996, 140 pp. M. A. Umanzor, **La visión de la mujer en Elena Garro*, Miami, Universal, 1996, 158 pp. R. Torniño, **Tiempo, destino y opresión en Elena Garro*, Lewiston, Mellen, 228 pp. J. A. Winkler, 'Marginality in *Los recuerdos del porvenir*', *IJHL*, 8, 1996:177–95, is on Garro's view of the destruction of the (social) centre. C. Schaeffer Rodríguez, '*Puerto libre* de Angeles Mastretta', *RCEH*, 21:373–84, is on its vision of a changing Mexico. G. de Beer, 'Historia, escritura y autobiografía en los juegos narrativos de Silvia Molina', *RHM*, 49, 1996:243–48, is on her novels and history. J. Payne, 'The novels of Angela Muñoz-Huberman', *BHS(G)*, 74:431–59, is on her themes of exile. S. Lucas Dobrian, 'Romancing the cook', *LALR*, 48:56–66, is (again) on parody in Esquivel's *Como agua para chocolate*. C. Ramón-Odio, 'Clarividentes, curanderas ...', *Secolas*, 27, 1996:41–48, is on the supernatural in that novel. E. Bejel, '*Como agua para chocolate* o las estrategias ideológicas del arte culinario', *NTC*, 19–20:177–94, is on its questioning of myth. J. Saltz, 'Laura Esquivel's *Como agua para chocolate*. the questioning of literary and social limits', *Chasqui*, 24.1, 1995:30–37, is on its parodic and transgressive elements. E. Frauman-Smith, 'Women and the problem of damnation in the short fiction of Inés Arredondo', *LF*, 33:163–70, is on gender relations in three stories. K. Ibsen, 'Entrevistas: Bárbara Jacobs/Carmen Boullosa', *Chasqui*, 24.2, 1995:46–63, is useful on these two new women writers. V. Leñero and V. H. Rascón Banda, **La moderna dramaturgía mexicana*, Mexico D.F., Consejo Nacional, 1996. L. M. Schneider, *Fragua y gesta del teatro experimental en Mexico*, Mexico D.F., UNAM, 1995, 372 pp., is on the *Ulises, Escolares del Teatro*, and *Orientación* groups. O. Harmony, *Ires y venires del teatro en Mexico*, Mexico D.F., Conaculta, 1996, 383 pp., is on modern dramatists and directors, including Magaña, Ibargüengoitía, Carballido, and Leñero. *LATR*, 31.1, contains several short papers on Mexican theatre given at the 1997 Kansas Conference. **El teatro de género chico en la revolución mexicana*, ed. A. de María y Campos, Mexico D.F., CNCA, 1996. F. W. Burgess, 'Five summers of Mexican theatre', *LATR*, 30.2:61–72, covers 1992–96. D. Meyran, **Tres ensayos sobre teatro mexicano*, Rome, Bulzoni, 1996, 141 pp., two appear to be on Usigli. R. Layera, **Usigli en el teatro: testimonios*, Mexico D.F., UNAM, 1996, 282 pp. *Lecturas desde afuera*, ed. K. F. Nigro, Mexico D.F., UNAM, 286 pp., has nine essays on Leñero. D. Cohen, 'Defining and defying woman in four plays by Luisa J. Hernández', *LATR*, 30.2:89–102, is on her refusal to stereotype. J. Hoeg, 'Retórica y negación freudiana en *Esta noche juntos* de Maruxa Vilalta', *ib.*, 31.1:31–41. J. E. Bixler,

'The postmodernization of history in the theatre of Sabina Berman', *ib.*, 30.2:45–60, is on her undermining of historical truth. B. M. García Monsiváis, **El ensayo mexicano en el siglo xx, Reyes, Novo, Paz*, Mexico D.F., UNAM, 1995.

J. Chen Sham, 'La oración del creyente', *LetD*, 76:225–34, is dull on Cardenal's 'Salmo 2'. J. Yviricu, 'El arte pop en la poesía de Ernesto Cardenal', *Chasqui*, 24.2, 1995:93–102, is on his mixed views on it. C. Giudicelli, 'Gioconda Belli et le détour par le mythe', *LNL*, 302:5–22, is on her 1996 novel *Waslala*.

B. J. Carbajal, **Paraguay en la obra de Augusto Roa Bastos*, M. Pliegos, 1996, 152 pp. B. Partyka, 'Conceptual imagery and the Ayvú Rapytá in Roa Bastos', *RHM*, 50:116–31, is on the linguistic influence of Guaraní. See too her 'Traditional oral narrative techniques in the fiction of Augusto Roa Bastos (1953–74)', *Chasqui*, 26.1:93–101, on certain modes of storytelling up to *Yo el Supremo*. A. Albónico, 'Roa Bastos y el "Napoleón del Plata"', *RevIb*, 180:467–84, is on his interest in F. Solana López.

A. Escobar, *Patio de letras*, Lima, Luis Alfredo, 1995, has essays on Vallejo, Arguedas and Ribeyro. D. Sobrevilla, **Introducción bibliográfica a César Vallejo*, Lima, Amaru, 1996. H. Machín, 'El individualismo colectivo en César Vallejo', *RevIb*, 175, 1996:507–21, is too general. H. Costa, 'A questão do registro literário em *Poemas humanos*', *Procs* (Brasília), 1067–76, attacks current criticism. C. Saylor-Javaherian, 'Tragic irony in *Poemas humanos*', *Secolas*, 26, 1995:90–97, analyses 'Fue domingo en las claras orejas. . .'; see too his 'Vallejo's "Marcha nupcial"', *CH*, 18, 1996:350–60, which sees it as a prelude to the last poems. O. Espejo, 'Un poeta peruano contemporáneo. [Carlos J.] Belli: Ensayo bibliográfico 1958–95', *RevIb*, 175, 1996:545–75, very painstaking. See too his handy 'Contribución a la bibliografía de Javier Heraud', *ib.*, 180:509–23. J. E. Albada-Jelgersma, 'Blanca Varela's *Casa de cuervos*', *BHS(L)*, 74:105–15, analyses the mother-son relationship in the poem. The same critic's 'Antonio Cisneros and Bram Stoker: continuities and discontinuities', *Chasqui*, 25.2, 1996:19–29, is on the poet's refiguring of the discourse of psychoanalysis. A. Cornejo Polar, 'Una heterogeneidad no dialéctica', *RevIb*,

176–77, 1996:837–44, is slight on migrants mostly in modern Peruvian fiction. W. Rowe, *Ensayos arguedianos*, Lima, SUR, 1996, 149 pp. H. Favre, 'J. M. Arguedas y yo', *CAm*, 56, 1996:23–31, rather biographical. *J. M. Arguedas, Reconsiderations for Latin American Studies*, ed. C. A. Sandoval and S. M. Boschetto-Sandoval, Athens, Ohio U.P., 220 pp. *Las cartas de Arguedas*, ed. J. V. Murra and M. López-Baralt, Lima, Univ. Católica, 1996, 364 pp. M. Schwartz, 'La política transnacional de la cultura en *La danza inmóvil* de Manuel Scorza', *RevIb*, 180:437–48, is on his ridicule of obsession with Paris. S. M. Nagy, '*Los ilegítimos* de [H.] Pérez Huarancca y la legitimidad del neo-indigenismo', *Chasqui*, 24.2, 1995:32–45, is on its socio-economic, not racial, approach. *Asedios a Julio Ramón Ribeyro*, ed. J. P. Márquez and C. Ferreira, Lima, Univ. Pontificia, 1996, 321 pp., has essays by Vargas Llosa, Bryce, J. M. Oviedo, and many others. S. Köllmann, *Literatur und Politik: Mario Vargas Llosa*, Bern, Lang, 1996, 408 pp. N. Lentzen, *Literatur und Gesellschaft-Mario Vargas Llosa*, Bonn, Romanistischer Vlg, 1996, 206 pp. M. A. Rodríguez Rea, *Tras las huellas de un crítico: Mario Vargas Llosa*, Lima, Univ. Pontificia, 1996. *Antípodas*, 8–9, has eight essays on Vargas Llosa including one by Vargas Llosa and one by Juan Goytisolo. M. G. Berg, 'Narrative multiplicity in Vargas Llosa's *Lituma en los Andes*', *La Chispa '95*, 25–38, is on simultaneity in the novel's technique. H. Habra, 'Revelación anamórfica en *Elogio de la madrastra*', *La Chispa '97*, 175–85, is on the novel's visual elements. J. Krapp, 'Figural castration in Vargas Llosa's *In Praise of the Stepmother*', *Hispanófila*, 121:35–43, is on the disempowerment of Rigoberto. H. Habra, 'Reminiscencias órficas en *¿Quién mató a Palomino Molero?*', *REH*, 31:77–91, is on the novel's complexity of meaning. M. E. Davies, 'Memory and Vargas Llosa', *ib.*, 221–33, is chiefly on *El pez en el agua*; so too is L. Rebaza-Soraluz's 'Out of failure comes success', *RCL*, 17.1:70–75 (see too his 'Demons and lies: motivation and form in Mario Vargas Llosa', *ib.*, 15–24, an important interview). E. Dipple, 'Outside, looking in: Aunt Julia and Vargas Llosa', *ib.*, 58–68, is on the 'deep problematic' in Vargas Llosa's fiction. E. Kristal, '*Captain Pantoja and the Special Service*: a transitional novel', *ib.*, 52–57, sees it as marking a turning point in Vargas Llosa's political outlook. C. Ferreira, 'Viaje al fondo del espacio de *Un mundo para Julius*', *RHM*, 50:144–57, is on Bryce's use of symbolic space. M. R. Corticelli, '*La vida exagerada de Martín Romaña*: towards cultural syncretism', *Iberoromania*, 44, 1996:99–108, is on contact with Europe. See too his '*La última mudanza de Felipe Carrillo*: novel set to the bolero rhythm', *ib.*, 45:89–98, is on Bryce's use of pop music. C. Arroyo Reyes, 'El incaísmo modernista de Augusto Aguirre Morales', *CA*, 69:186–96, discusses his novel *El Pueblo del Sol* (1924–27). A. Ferrari, 'La crítica literaria en la obra de J. C.

Mariátegui', *Hispamérica*, 76–77:5–17, a superficial survey.
N. Larsen, 'Indigenismo o lo "postcolonial"': Mariátegui frente a la
actual coyuntura teórica', *RevIb*, 176–77, 1996:863–73, discusses
him as possibly postcolonial.

PUERTO RICO

M. López-Baralt, *La poesía de L. Palés Matos*, San Juan, Puerto Rico
U.P., 1995, 764 pp. M. A. Gutiérrez, 'La victoria del discurso
semiótico kristevano en "Nicharrirí" de Lydia Cabrera', *LF*,
33:109–27, is on the story's language. R. González Orozco, *La
historia puertorriqueña de E. Rodríguez Juliá*, San Juan, Puerto Rico U.P.,
122 pp. A. Puleo, 'Ana Lydia Vega and the caribbean storyteller',
AfHR, 15.2, 1996:21–25, is on her story 'Otra maldad de Pateco'.
M. Murphy, 'Rosario Ferré en el espejo', *HR*, 65:145–57, is vague
on her vision of women. I. Balseiro, 'Through the looking glass
darkly: Rosario Ferré's "Cuando las mujeres quieren a los hombres"',
AfHR, 16.2:3–9, is on reflections of class and race. M. I. González,
'El efecto liberador de la oposición oralidad/escritura en *Maldito amor*
de Rosario Ferré', *LF*, 33:129–37, is on the deconstruction of
Hermenegildo's narrative. Y. Montalvo Aponte, 'La música en
Maldito amor', *RICP*, 100, 1996:49–56, is on musical references as
commentary. M. E. Filer, 'Polifonía y contrapunto: la crónica
histórica en *Maldito amor* and *The House on the Lagoon*', *RHM*, 49,
1996:318–28, is on Ferré's double vision of Puerto Rican history.
N. Gray Diaz, 'Performing *soledad*, the demythification of identity in
Giannina Braschi's *El imperio de los sueños*', *RoN*, 37:331–38, is on her
original view of identity and solitude. L. Rojas-Trempe, 'Lectura
bajtiana (sic) de *Este ojo que me mira* de Lorena Santos Silva'. *LF*,
33:139–48, is on its autobiographical stance. F. Kolma Agyor,
'Racial prejudice, racial shame: reading F. Arriví's *Máscara puertorriqueña*', *BHS(L)*, 74:501–12, criticizes the author's racial stance.
(See also CUBA.)

URUGUAY

Historia de la literatura uruguaya contemporánea 1, ed. H. Raviolo and
P. Rocca, Montevideo, Banda Oriental, 1996, 286 pp., is on modern
fiction. M. Trambaioli, 'La estatua y el ensueño: dos claves para la
poesía de Delmira Agustini', *RHM*, 50:57–66, is too general on her
'dionysian' poetry. L. V. Williams, 'Difference and identity in the
poetry of Cristina Rodríguez Cabral', *AfHR*, 14.2, 1995:27–34, is on
her voicing of the Afro-Uruguayan identity. See too her interview on
similar themes, *ib.*, 57–63. H. Verani, *De la vanguardia a la posmodernidad: narrativa uruguaya 1920–1995*, Montevideo, Linardi and Risso,

1996. E. L. Pasteknic, **El mito en la obra de Horacio Quiroga*, BA, Plus Ultra, 311 pp., a prize-winning work. H. Xaubet, *Autobiografía y metaficción en tres relatos de Felisberto Hernández*, Montevideo, Linardi and Risso, 1995, deals with 'Por los tiempos . . .', 'El caballo perdido', and 'Tierras de la memoria'. F. de Cesare, 'Le vite possibili di Onetti', *StLI*, 28–29, 1996:159–67, is rather introductory on *La vida breve*. O. Prego, 'Onetti y Faulkner: dos novelistas de la fatalidad', *CMar*, 129:56–60, is on Faulkner's influence on Onetti. M. Paoletti, *Benedetti, M. Alfaguara, 1996, 267 pp. H. Geldrich-Leffman, 'Body and voice: the dialogue of marriage in the short stories of Mario Benedetti', *Chasqui* 25.1, 1996:39–51, is on conjugal communication. C. Tisnado, 'Mario Benedetti's "Corazonada": silence that reverses power', *Hispanófila*, 121:45–52, is on silence, communication and oppression. T. M. Mackey, 'Reverse Stockholm syndrome in *Pedro y el capitán*', *LitP*, 43.4:1–15, is on implicit contradiction in Benedetti's 1986 play. V. Kaner, 'La anécdota vivida y la escritura del fragmento en F. Aínsa', *RPl*, 17–18:529–38, is on the theme of exile in *De aquí y de allá* (1991). T. Frugoni, 'El relato gótico: el modelo y sus reformulaciones en la literatura del Río de la Plata'. *ib.*, 555–65, is chiefly on Abelardo Castillo. L. Bravo, 'Armonía Somers: tríptico de la rama dorada', *CMar*, 130:61–67, is on her *El hacedor de girasoles* (1994). C. B. Moore, 'El papel del lector activo en "La inmigrante" de Armonía Somers', *Chasqui*, 26.1:45–55, is on this tale's difficult technique. M. Rowinski, **Las imágenes en la obra de Cristina Peri Rossi*, Montevideo, Trilce, 224 pp. H. A. Cochrane, 'Androgynous voices in the novels of Cristina Peri Rossi', *Mosaic*, 30.3:97–114, is on her undermining of gender assumptions. M. D. Blanco Arnejo, 'Metamorfosis e identidad en *La nave de los locos* de Cristina Peri Rossi', *His(US)*, 80:441–50, is on its challenge to the reader. R. Gnutzmann, 'Civilización y barbarie en *¡Bernabé! ¡Bernabé!* de Tomás de Mattos', *RPl*, 17–18:191–202, is on the theme of this 1988 historical novel. R. Pessoa, 'Entrevista a Tomás de Mattos', *CMar*, 123:56–61, 124:56–62, has useful declarations by the author of the best-seller *La fragata de las máscaras*. L. Bravo, 'Entrevista a Carlos María Domínguez', *ib.*, 134:71–75, with interesting remarks by the author of *La mujer hablada* (1995) etc. C. Vich, 'El diálogo intertextual en *Maluco*', *RevIb*, 180:405–18, is on the sources of this 1989 novel by Napoleón Baccino. F. Noguerol, 'La literatura asqueante rioplatense: el caso de Julio Ricci', *RPl*, 17–18:435–47, is on repulsive themes in *Los perseverantes* (1993). Y. Perron, 'Mario Levrero: la escritura fuera de los casillos', *ib.*, 461–69, introduces this author. M. Renard, 'Avatares de lo fantástico: el caso Mario Levrero', *ib.*, 449–59, is on strangeness in his *Desplazamientos* (1987). B. Castro Morales, 'Picaresca posmoderna', *ib.*, 519–28, is on Carlos Liscano's *El camino de Itaca* (1994).

R. Mirza, *Situación del teatro uruguayo contemporáneo*, Montevideo, Banda Oriental, 1996, 120 pp. J. Pignataro Calero, *La aventura del teatro independiente uruguayo*, Montevideo, Cal y Canto, 180 pp. J. Cordones-Cook, *El teatro afro-uruguayo de Andrés Castillo*, Montevideo, Graffiti, 1996, 167 pp. C. Gilman, 'Política y crítica literaria. El semanario *Marcha*', *RPl*, 17–18:217–27, examines its development 1939–74.

VENEZUELA

M. L. Canfield, 'Las estructuras poéticas de J. A. Ramos Sucre', *StLI*, 27, 1996:17–29, is basically thematic. J. Lisarte Valcarcel, **Juego y nación: Posmodernismo y vanguardia en Venezuela*, Caracas, Fundarte, 1995. E. Pandis Pavlakis, 'Aproximación a *La rosa cuántica* de Luala Velásquez', *CAm*, 60, 1996:217–24, discusses this 1992 collection. E. Duno and A. Hidalgo, *Narradoras venezolanas del siglo xx*, Caracas, Monte Avila, 1996, 247 pp., has essays on 12 authors and three interviews. J. Ortega, *El principio radical de lo nuevo*, Lima, FCE, 300 pp., is on postmodernity, especially in Venezuelan fiction. J. Castro-Urioste, 'Desde la escritura de Rómulo Gallegos a la búsqueda de la voz de otro', *La Chispa '95*, 81–89, is on the voicing of two cultures in *Doña Bárbara*. D. Miliani, 'Trilogía de artífices', *CAm*, 60, 1996:201–16, is on I. J. Pardo, A. Palacios, and A. Uslar Pietri. A. Isea, 'Regionalismo y estereotipos raciales en *Las lanzas coloradas*', *AfHR*, 16.1:25–31, is on the shortcomings of Uslar Pietri's picture of class and race. R. Esquenazi-Mayo, 'Arciniegas y Havel: dos generaciones, dos continentes, un pensamiento', *RHM*, 49, 1996:308–16, is on their attitudes to Europe. A. Martínez, 'La novela venezolana ante la crisis modernizante', *Procs* (Brasília), 1053–66, is on Luis Brito García's *Abrapalabra* (1980). C. Hernández, **Alvaro Mutis*, Caracas, Monte Avila, 1995. M. Gomes, **Poética del ensayo venezolano del siglo xx: la forma de lo diverso*, Providence R.I., INTI, 1996.

BRAZILIAN LITERATURE

By MARK DINNEEN, *Spanish, Portuguese, and Latin American Studies, University of Southampton*

1. GENERAL

B. McGuirk, *Latin American Literature: Symptoms, Risks and Strategies of Post-Structuralist Criticism*, London, Routledge, 265 pp., includes reference to Guimarães Rosa and Mário de Andrade, among other Brazilian writers, in a series of post-structuralist analyses of Latin American writing. S. H. S. Borelli, *Ação, suspense, emoção: literatura e cultura de massa no Brasil*, SPo, EDUC, 1996, 244 pp., offers an interesting discussion on relations between literature and the mass culture industry in Brazil, referring to such popular forms of fiction as the detective story, novels of adventure, and the *picaresque* tradition, and focusing particularly on the writing of Marcos Rey. L. H. Costigan, 'O diálogo Brasil/América hispânica: balanço/questões teóricas', *RCLL*, 45:13–26, examines attempts to integrate literary practice in Brazil and Spanish America and argues for the need for more comparative studies of the two bodies of literature. I. L. C. Walty, 'Cópia ou ruptura: um movimento pendular', *ib.*, 131–39, refers to a range of Brazilian critics in a discussion of their different responses to the question of the autonomy of Brazilian literature, and of theories which propose a revision of Brazil's literary history. B. J. Chamberlain, 'Dependente porém (truncada e) múltipla: a literatura brasileira vista pela teoria literária na década de 80', *ib.*, 46:255–68, considers the ways in which Brazilian literary theorists have dealt with the issue of cultural dependency, and how that has affected understanding of the country's literary history. C. S. de Tejada, 'Raya e género en la narrativa afro-brasileña', *ib.*, 269–85, discusses novels by Maria Firmina dos Reis, Carolina Maria de Jesús, and Marilene Felinto, whose work is seen as representing three distinct phases of resistance against racial discrimination. *Gender, Ethnicity and Class in Modern Portuguese Speaking Culture*, ed. H. Owen, Lampeter, Mellen, 1996, 235 pp., contains articles on several 20th-c. Brazilian writers. Robinson, *Women*, gathers together extracts from critics on women writers and includes entries on Cecilia Meireles, Lygia Fagundes Telles, Nélida Piñon, Rachel de Queiroz, Zulmira Ribeiro Tavares, Clarice Lispector, and Lya Luft. *Encyclopedia of Latin American Literature*, ed. V. Smith, London, Fitzroy Dearborn, 926 pp., is a useful work of reference, with entries on over 30 Brazilian writers and brief essays on such topics as African-Brazilian literature, Modernism, regionalism, and Indianism.

2. COLONIAL

Flavio R. Kothe, *O cânone colonial,* Brasília U.P., 416 pp., is a valuable discussion of colonial literature, arguing that existing concepts employed by critics, like *brasilidade,* have limited understanding of the period. Through sections on Caminha, Botelho, Anchieta, Matos and the *Escola mineira,* a reassessment is attempted. L. M. Bernucci, 'Disfraces gongorinos en Manuel Botelho de Oliveira', *CHA,* 570:73–94, discusses the poet's work in the context of the Spanish baroque, arguing that, having been forthrightly dismissed as a servile imitation of Góngora by Romantic and positivist critics, its original qualities have not been fully appreciated. J. S. Dean, 'Politics and pulpit in John Donne and Antônio Vieira', *LBR,* 34.1:43–55, is a comparative study which seeks to establish common characteristics of style in the work of the two priests in order to explain their effectiveness as writers. R. Budasz, 'A presença do cancioneiro ibérico na lírica de José de Anchieta: um enfoque musicológico', *Latin American Music Review,* 17.1, 1996:42–77, examines the relationship between A.'s poetry and Spanish *romancero* tradition. L. M. Bernucci, 'No espírito da épica: formações e variações discursivas na América hispánica e portuguesa', *RCLL,* 45:168–75, compares Ercilla's *La Araucana* and *O Uraguai* by Basílio da Gama to examine the way the two writers rework the European epic. J. A. Hansen, 'Ut pictura poesis e verossimilhança na doutrina do *conceito* no século XVII colonial', *ib.,* 45:177–91, discusses the cultural and literary models that helped to shape the work of such writers as Gregório de Matos and António Vieira, who are studied alongside Spanish American counterparts.

3. THE NINETEENTH CENTURY

Maria M. Lisboa, *Machado de Assis and Feminism: Re-reading 'The Heart of the Companion',* Lampeter, Mellen, 1996, 284 pp., highlights M.'s originality as a writer and importance as a social critic. It explores the way the work challenges deeply-rooted attitudes in 19th-c. Brazilian society through his treatment of the role of, and relations between, the sexes. Aleilton Fonseca, *Enredo romantico, música ao fondo,* R, Sette letras, 1996, 171 pp., examines musical references in the work of Alencar, Joaquim Manuel de Macedo, and Manuel Antonio de Almeida in order to discuss what they reveal about the ideology of the romantic writer. E. Boaventura, **Estudos sobre Castro Alves,* Salvador, Univ. Federal de Bahia, 1996, 192 pp. Maria M. Lisboa, 'A mother's boy's best friend: birth and kingslaying in the Brazilian foundation novel', *PortSt,* 13:95–107, is a perceptive study of Alencar's *Iracema* and Bernardo Guimarães's *A escrava Isaura*. It seeks to demonstrate how the two novels embody the contradictions that emerged in 19th-c. Brazil between the search for national identity on one hand, and the importation of European schemes of thought on the other. F. J. López Alfonso, 'Pero esto no es más que el principio: de Fernández de Lizardi a Machado de Assis', *CHA*, 570:45–57, shows how in his short story, *O alienista*, M. challenges and satirizes the unquestioning faith in science and reason of the modernizing elite in Brazil at the end of the 19th century. M. A. da Costa Vieira, 'Las relaciones de poder entre narrador y lector: Cervantes, Almeida Garret y Machado de Assis', *ib.*, 59–71, refers to M.'s *Memórias póstumas de Brás Cubas* to show how M., like the other two writers, plays on the diverging interests of narrator and reader in order to reflect upon the nature of fiction. M. C. Pinero Valverde, 'Don Juan Valera y el indianismo romántico brasileño', *ib.*, 107–23, highlights the importance of Valera's mid-19th-c. study of Brazilian literature as one of the first texts to investigate the distinctive features of Brazilian writing, and, anticipating the arguments of romantic writers, to identify indianism as a vital force for national expression. E. Botelho Junqueira, 'O bacharel de direito no século XIX: herói ou anti-herói?', *LBR*, 34.1:77–93, looks at the way lawyers and the application of the law are represented in Brazilian fiction, particularly in the work of Machado de Assis, A. de Azevedo, and R. Pompéia, and considers what that indicates about the writers' search for national identity. G. Pinheiro Passos, **A poética do legado: Presença francesa em Memórias póstumas de Brás Cubas*, SPo, Annablume, 1996, 158 pp. Helder Macedo, 'Garrett, Machado de Assis, and the impossible option', *Willis Vol.*, 199–204, is a comparative study of M.'s *Esaú and Jacó* and G.'s *Viagens na minha terra* identified as the two texts which show the different visions of the two writers most closely converging. J. Gledson, 'A history lesson: Machado de Assis's *Conto de escola*', *ib.*, 217–26, argues that the story, most frequently read as a simple narrative on a child's initiation into the adult world, also makes significant observations on political developments in 19th-c. Brazil. S. A. Peixoto, 'Gonçalves Dias: a consciência das ilusões perdidas?', *Caravelle*, 68:101–08, refers particularly to the prologue of D.'s *Primeiros cantos*, to discuss his approach to poetry, especially his attitude towards classical literary tradition. R. Antelo, '*Per Speculum in Aenigmate*: construção de identidades culturais nas ficções de inter-pretação nacional', *RCLL*, 45:155–66, looks at journalistic articles by Euclydes da Cunha and D. Sarmiento to analyse their interpreta-tions of late 19th-c. Latin American society. E. E. Fitz, 'Metafiction in Latin American narrative: the case for Brazil or if Brás Cubas were here today what would he say about Spanish American fiction?',

Mester, 26:43–69, looks at Machado's *Memórias póstumas de Brás Cubas* as the starting point of a tradition of self-conscious narrative, which, it is argued, is more pronounced in Brazil than in Spanish America.

4. The Twentieth Century

POETRY

Charles Perrone, *Seven Faces: Brazilian Poetry Since Modernism*, Durham, Duke U.P., 1996, 234 pp., the most important study published in English to date on Brazilian poetry of the last 50 years, highlights, above all, its diversity. Beginning with the legacy of Modernism, it traces the major phases and tendencies that have emerged, with sections on concrete poetry, political verse, and youth poetry, and a particularly interesting discussion on the relationship between poetry and popular song. Highly informative, the work also engages in lively debate, most notably in the final chapter, when different critical responses to postmodernism are considered. J. Castello, *João Cabral de Melo Neto: o homem sem alma*, R, Rocco, 1996, 184 pp., takes a biographical approach to look at M.N.'s poetry. Based on interviews with the poet, it seeks to understand the development of his work through the friendships, travels, and experiences of different periods of his life. L. M. Bernucci, 'That gentle epic: writing and elegy in the heroic poetry of Cecília Meireles', *MLN*, 112:201–18, highlights the technical achievements of M., who, the article argues, has been unjustly regarded by many critics as a poet of secondary importance in comparison with others of the modernist legacy. B. J. Vinkler, 'The anthropophagic mother/other: appropriated identities in Oswald de Andrade's *Manifesto Antropófago*', *LBR*, 34.1:105–11, examines how A. condemns patriarchy in his manifesto and constructs an oppositional utopian matriarchy, the limitations and contradictions of which are then discussed. T. F. Carvalhal, 'La tradition de la parodie et la parodie de la tradition dans les litteratures Latino-Américaines', Mildonian, *Parodia*, 297–302, briefly considers the role of parody in Oswald de Andrade's *Manifesto Antropófago*. Sara Castro Klarén, 'Corporización Tupi: Léry y el Manifesto Antropófago', *RCLL*, 45:193–210, examines the different ways in which the cannibal myth has been developed by writers, with particular reference to Mário de Andrade and Oswald de Andrade. R. Araújo, 'La nueva poesía visual brasilena', *CHA*, 559:39–43, is a brief account of recent experiments, involving Augusto and Haroldo de Campos among others, to produce poetry with the assistance of computer graphics. 'Folha de São Paulo, "la certeza de la influencia"', *ib.*, 568:73–84, marks the 40th anniversary of the Concrete Poetry movement in Brazil by reproducing an interview with Décio Pignatari, Augusto de Campos, and

Haroldo de Campos, in which they talk of the contribution made by the movement and its significance today. L. Villares, 'Ana Cristina Cesar and Adélia Prado; two women poets of 1970s Brazil', *PortSt*, 13:108–23, is a comparative study of the two poets, showing how their work embodies opposing responses to the oppressive social, cultural and political conditions imposed by authoritarian government in the early 1970s. *Fronteiras do literário: literatura oral e popular, Brasil/França*, ed. Z. Bernd and J. Migozzi, Porto Alegre, UFRGS, 1995, 143 pp., contains a series of studies of *literatura de cordel* by well-known scholars in the field, with emphasis on theoretical problems and the relationship between written popular poetry and oral popular tradition. M. Curran, 'Brazil's *literatura de cordel* ("String literature"): poetic chronicle and popular history', *SLtcPC*, 1996, 15:175–88, looks at the treatment of historical topics in popular verse.

DRAMA

Catarina Sant'Anna, *Metalinguagem e teatro: a obra de Jorge Andrade*, Cuiba, EduFMT, 370 pp., offers in-depth analysis of A.'s plays and extensive information on his career. It particularly examines how the plays explore the nature of theatre itself. I. R. Moreno, 'La recontextualización de Antígona en el teatro argentino y brasileño a partir de 1968', *LATR*, 30.2:115–29, refers to Jorge Andrade's plays of the 1970s, highlighting how he makes use of the myth of Antigone to create a theatre of social criticism. Iná Camargo Costa, *A hora do teatro épico no Brasil*, R, Paz e Terra, 1996, 233 pp., is a detailed and well-researched study, tracing the development of radical, anti-bourgeois theatre in Brazil in the 1960s, and the difficulties it faced after the 1964 coup. Particular reference is made to the work of Boal, Guarnieri, and Vianna Filho. S. J. Albuquerque, 'Luis Alberto de Abreu's *O Livro de Jó* and the representation of AIDS in Brazil', *RoS*, 29:65–73, studies how A. adapts the Book of Job for his play, which uses allegory to challenge deeply rooted perceptions and prejudices in Brazilian society about AIDS. E. E. Fitz, '*A pecadora queimada e os anjos harmoniosos*: Clarice Lispector as dramatist', *LBR*, 34.2:25–39, is a study of L.'s only published play, demonstrating how it reveals her growing political awareness, and how, in theme and style, it relates to her better-known prose works. D. W Foster, 'Lenguaje y espacio escénico: el italiano en dos textos teatrales', *RCLL*, 45:55–65, compares Juca de Oliveira's 1989 play *Meno male!* with *Babilonia*, by the Argentine Armando Discepolo, two works which focus on Italian immigrants in Latin America, to examine how the problems of the integration of the immigrant into mainstream society are presented. R. Roux, '*Vestido de noiva* de Nelson Rodrigues, un voyage au centre de l'Homme', *Caravelle*, 68:43–69, is a detailed analysis of R.'s play, emphasizing the psychological insight it gives into the Rio bourgeoisie.

Anna M. H. Baptista, *Tempo-memória no romance*, SPo, Catalise, 127 pp., is a study of the work of Graciliano Ramos, with particular reference to *Memórias do cárcere*, focusing on his treatment of memory and time. A. Quintella et al., *Cadernos de literatura brasileira, 4: Rachel de Queiroz*, SPo, Instituto Moreira Salles, 127 pp., collects together brief essays which give considerable information on Q.'s life and work, but no critical analysis. Tania Pellegrini, *Gavetas vazias: ficção e política nos anos 70*, SPo, Univ. Federal de São Carlos, 1966, 192 pp., is a very informative study of the relationship between fiction and politics in the era of military dictatorship. It focuses on work written in the 1970s by Veríssimo, Ignácio de Loyola Brandão, and Fernando Gabeira, showing how each employs different aesthetic forms to express resistance to the repression and censorship of the period. R. Dalcastagne, **O espaço da dor: o regime de 64 no romance brasileiro*, Brasília U.P., 1996, 155 pp. T. Marshall, 'Marxist feminism in Brazil', *RoN*, 1996, 36.3:283–92, is a sociological study of the writing of Patricia Galvão, in particular her novel *Parque industrial*. O. Messer Levin, **As figurações do Dândi: um estudo sobre a obra de João do Rio*, Campinas, Unicamp, 1996, 240 pp. Vilma Areas, 'A idéia e a forma: a ficção de Modesto Carone', *NovE*, 49:119–39, traces the development of C.'s work from the late 1970s, characterizing it in terms of thematic content and technique, and attempting to assess the place of the author within the Brazilian literary tradition. C. Ferreira-Pinto, 'Escrita, auto-representacão e realidade social no romance feminino latino-americano', *RCLL*, 45:81–95, makes reference to Helena Parente Cunha's *Mulher no espelho* in a discussion of how such writers attempt to unite social commitment with concern for the female subject. A. L. Andrade, 'A linguagem territorial e o intertexto cultural utópico latino-americano: Graciliano Ramos e Juan Rulfo', *ib.*, 97–106, compares the language employed by the two writers to highlight the role language plays in the writers' search for Latin American identity. R. M. Wasserman, '*O tempo e o vento* de Erico Veríssimo e as complicações do conceito de identidade nacional', *ib.*, 107–18, explores how V. seeks to define Brazilian national identity in his trilogy. M. N. S. Fonseca, 'Traços para a construção de imagens', *ib.*, 119–30, studies Ubaldo Ribeiro's *Viva o povo brasileiro* alongside novels by Carpentier and Vargas Llosa to compare how the writers confront the contradictions of Latin American culture. H. Vilhena de

Araújo, *O roteiro de Deus: dois estudos sobre Guimarães Rosa*, SPo, Mandarim, 1996, 556 pp., consists of in-depth studies of R.'s *Grande sertão: veredas* and *Corpo de baile*, which seek to identify the philosophical influences within those works. Emphasis is placed on the role played by various forms of Christian mysticism. F. Granato, *Nas trilhas do Rosa*, SPo, 1996, Scritta, 107 pp., is a brief but interesting work which uses R.'s notes to retrace the journey the novelist made through the interior of Minas Gerais in 1952, in order to identify places and people that provided inspiration for *Grande sertão: veredas*. L. Lobo, 'Sonia Coutinho revisits the city', pp. 162–78 of *Latin American Women's Writing*, ed. A. Brooksbank Jones and C. Davies, Oxford, Clarendon Press, 1996, 250 pp., examines how C.'s female characters escape the constraints of their traditional domestic space and emerge into the streets of the city, which become the site where a new independence can be found. Alaor Barbosa, *O ficcionista Monteiro Lobato*, Brasiliense, SPo, 1996, 113 pp., traces the development of technique and style in L.'s prose work, emphasizing his experiments with language, and attempts to assess the author's contribution to Brazilian literature. T. P. Waldemer, 'Revenge of the cannibal: surrender and resistance in Antônio Callado's nativist novels', *LBR*, 34.1:113–23, argues that C. fuses the cannibal metaphors of Montaigne and Brazilian modernism in his novels, to present an indigenous culture that both assimilates and resists Western culture. T. Hendrick, 'Mother, blessed be you among cockroaches: essentialism, fecundity and death in Clarice Lispector', *ib.*, 34.2:41–57, argues that L.'s novels are essentialist, privileging the reproductive capacity of women as the essence of what it means to be female. N. H. Vieira, 'Bruxaria (witchcraft) and espiritismo (Spiritism): popular culture and popular religion in contemporary Brazilian fiction', *SLAPC*, 15, 1996:175–88, deals with the assimilation of popular culture in the work of Roberto Drummond, Lispector, and Trevisan. R. Oakley, 'Lima Barreto's Menippean satire *Numa e a ninfa* in its historical context', *Willis Vol.*, 265–84, challenges the many critics who have regarded the novel as considerably inferior to B.'s better known works, arguing that they have failed to appreciate the true significance of the formal differences found in *Numa*. C. Pazos Alonso, 'Exploring women's destinies: *As três Marias* by Rachel de Queiroz', *ib.*, 285–95, re-examines the role of the three protagonists of the novel in order to highlight the originality of Q.'s treatment of the constraints imposed on women in patriarchal society. C. Kelley, 'Some observations on narrative processes in Guimarães Rosa's *Grande sertão: veredas*', focuses on R.'s narrative technique and the ways in which the novel deliberately refers to the processes of narrative creation. R. M. Levine and J. C. Sebe Bom Meihy, *The Life and Death of Carolina Maria de Jesús*,

Albuquerque, New Mexico U.P., 1995, 162 pp., assess the life and legacy of the *favelada* whose diary became a bestseller in Brazil and abroad. On the same subject, E. R. P. Vieira, 'Can another subaltern speak/write?', *ReMS*, 38, 1995:96–125, uses the theories of Spivak as a starting point for an analysis of the diary. **Women, Literature and Culture in the Portuguese Speaking World*, ed. C. Pazos Alonso and G. Fernandes, Lewiston, Mellen, 1996, 202 pp.

IX. ITALIAN STUDIES

LANGUAGE

By MAIR PARRY, *Senior Lecturer in Italian, University of Bristol,*
and RODNEY SAMPSON, *Senior Lecturer in French, University of Bristol*

1. GENERAL

The continuing increase in publications relating to the Italian dialects reflects an awareness of their importance for every branch of Italian linguistics, the profusion of dialectal variation offered within such a limited geographical area providing an ideal fount of data for testing linguistic and sociolinguistic theory. This emerges clearly from several Festchriften such as *Cortelazzo Vol.*, *Studi Giacomelli*, and *Fest. Pfister*, as well as from two very different volumes that provide up-to-date introductory overviews. Maiden, *Dialects*, a multi-authored English-language publication, draws on the expertise of an international range of specialists including many Italians, with the first main section dedicated to a cross-dialectal comparative perspective of structural features (phonological, morphological, syntactic, and lexical), followed by individual chapters on the various regions and a final section devoted to modern sociolinguistic issues, particularly the interaction between the dialects and the standard language. Just as Italian dialectology has been rejuvenated by modern theoretically oriented grammatical studies, as emerges in many of the contributions to this work, so the relevance of recent developments in sociolinguistic and pragmatic theory is stressed in Corrado Grassi, Alberto A. Sobrero, and Tullio Telmon, *Fondamenti di dialettologia italiana*, Bari, Laterza, xv + 424 pp. This is a comprehensive manual, richly illustrated and with clear language and lay-out, divided into five main sections: 'Dialettologia generale e dialettologia italiana', 'Cenni di storia della dialettologia italiana', 'I dialetti in Italia', 'L'uso del dialetto in Italia: aspetti sociali e pragmatici', 'Strumenti e metodi', which will provide excellent guidance for university students. Practical assistance relating to the interpretation of linguistic atlases, different phonetic transcription systems, and the compilation of questionnaires is especially useful. The theoretical relevance of a particularly topical aspect of dialect study to the burgeoning sphere of contact linguistics is cogently argued for in G. Berruto, 'Linguistica del contatto e aspetti dell'italianizzazione dei dialetti', *Fest. Pfister*, III, 13–29, which perceptively reviews the appropriateness for the Italian situation of the theoretical models available. A. L. Lepschy, G. Lepschy, and M. Voghera, 'Linguistic variety in Italy', Levy, *Italian*

Regionalism, 69–80, provides a lucid summary of three key aspects of the kaleidoscopic situation: its historical roots, its modern socio-linguistic characteristics, and language policy and linguistic legislation.

2. HISTORY OF THE LANGUAGE, EARLY TEXTS, AND DIACHRONIC STUDIES

R. Sornicola, 'L'oggetto preposizionale in siciliano antico e in napole-tano antico. Considerazioni su un problema di tipologia diacronica', *ItStudien,* 18:66–80, presents persuasive textual evidence in favour of a multiple origin for the prepositional accusative (some complements are to be interpreted as datives or locatives) and, in highlighting the crucial role of tonic personal pronouns, confirms earlier findings by Ibero-Romance scholars. Massimo Palermo, *L'espressione del pronome personale soggetto nella storia dell'italiano,* Ro, Bulzoni, 374 pp., is a rigorous quantitative and qualitative examination of a vast number of texts from two periods (up to Bembo; up to Manzoni), that reveals the crucial, normative, role effected by B. in halting the steady develop-ment towards the compulsory use of subject pronouns in Tuscan. In B.'s usage the author identifies a new stylistic criterion that gradually replaced the old syntactic one that had determined the use of subject pronouns, and it was eventually against the preciosity of this literary style that Manzoni was to act, drastically reducing the number of subject pronouns used and laying the foundations of the present discourse/pragmatically governed usage. L. Vanelli, 'Perché "lui" vince su "egli"', *IO,* 12:70–78, identifies as crucial the interaction of syntactic constraints (on "egli") and the relaxing of the conservative and normative rejection of non-standard variants. Francesco Sabatini, **Italia linguistica delle origini. Saggi editi dal 1956 al 1996,* ed. Vittorio Coletti et al., 2 vols, Lecce, Argo, 1996, xv + 660 pp., brings together important articles relating to two main themes: the relationship between vulgar Latin and Romance and the linguistic history of southern Italy. Ignazio Baldelli, **Dante e la lingua italiana,* F, Accademia della Crusca, 31 pp. M. Piccone, 'The formation of literary Italian. Aspects of poetic tradition and translation in the thirteenth century', *The Italianist,* 16:5–19. F. Sberlati, 'Sulla dittologia aggettivale nel *Canzoniere.* Per una storia dell'aggettivazione lirica', *StIt,* 12, 1994:5–69. L. Banfi, 'La redazione in versi della leggenda di Santa Margherita di Antiochia secondo un manoscritto quattrocentesco bergamasco', *QFLR,* 12:5–39. A prose version appears in R. Mona-celli Tommasi, 'Leggenda di Santa Margherita di Antiochia', *ib.,* 41–57. C. Curina, 'I capitoli dei gabellieri dal Libro VIII degli Statuti di Osimo del 1371 (ms. inedito)', *ib.,* 59–87. Aldo Rossi, *Cinquanta lezioni di filologia italiana,* Ro, Bulzoni, 245 pp. Marine terminology in some early texts is studied in G. B. Mancarella, 'Alcuni termini del mare nel codice pugliese', *Cortelazzo Vol.*, 199–208; G. B. Bronzini, 'Da Durazzo a Molfetta con un carico di legname: 5 luglio 1269', *ib.*, 209–18; C. Milani, 'I dialetti e il mare in un testo del 1434', *ib.*, 231–43. B. Richardson, 'Fulvio Pellegrino Morato and Fortunio's *Regole grammaticali della volgar lingua*', *Villari Vol.*, 43–54, documents an ambitious, eventually abandoned, attempt at a revised edition of Fortunio's *Regole*. E. Mattesini, 'L. Pacioli e l'uso del volgare', *SLI*, 22, 1996:145–80, is a fascinating account of the linguistic choices of an able mathematician at a momentous period of regeneration for both the vernacular and mathematics. In his contribution to *Laurea honoris causa a Carlo Dionisotti*, Soveria Mannelli, Rubbettino, 1996, 58 pp., J. Trumper pays tribute to a distinguished career that furthered in particular our understanding of the complexities of the Italian *Questione della Lingua*. The address (23–46), comprising two sections entitled, 'Riflessioni comparative sulla Questione della Lingua' and 'L'umanesimo e il concetto di dialetto: storia di un'idea', compares the process of linguistic standardization in England and France with that of Italy, noting the debt of the former countries to Italian discussions despite the very different outcomes. Another illuminating comparison is made in E. Banfi, 'The Language Question in Italy and Greece: a comparative approach', *Fest. Pfister*, III, 3–12, while the apparently puzzling vitality of dialect literature in 17th-c. Naples is given a sociolinguistic explanation in E. Radtke, 'La questione della lingua e la letteratura dialettale a Napoli nel Seicento', *ib.*, 73–85. J. de Bruijn-van der Helm and Tatiana Bruni, 'Aspetti linguistici di un libro di dialoghi italiano-neerlandese per mercanti', *RLFRU*, 16:1–16, discuss the earliest bilingual Italian-Dutch text (early 16th c.), probably compiled by a Flemish merchant while learning the trade in Venice. Anna Siekiera, **Giorgio Bartoli: lettere a Lorenzo Giacomini*, F, Accademia della Crusca, 375 pp. S. Bozzola, 'Glossario frugoniano', *SLeI*, 14:153–282, relates to Francesco Fulvio Frugoni's writings on style and rhetoric. I. Della Corte, 'Gli aggettivi composti nel Cesarotti traduttore di *Ossian*', *ib.*, 283–346. P. Manni, 'Il *Novo dizionàrio universale della lingua italiana* di Policarpo Petrocchi', *SLI*, 22, 1996:181–223, continues previous contributions. G. Fiorentino, 'Considerazioni sull'uso delle clausole relative e delle relative "deboli" ne *I promessi sposi*', *AGI*, 82:59–81, pays special attention to relative clauses introduced by the complementizer *che*.

3. HISTORY OF LINGUISTIC THEORY

L. Renzi, 'Come gli umanisti non scoprirono le leggi fonetiche', *Hommage Brunet*, 571–84, pursues a fascinating inquiry into the puzzle of why perceptive Italian humanists, especially Castelvetro and Varchi, failed to make the breakthrough achieved in the 19th century. D. Droixhe, '"Es bildet keine Philologen" — Christophe Cellarius et sa *Dissertation sur l'origine de la langue italienne* (1694)', *Baum Vol.*, 81–91, assesses the ideas of the German scholar in the intellectual context of his time. M. Lieber and C. Weyers, 'Giovan Giorgio Trissino: i Manoscritti Castiglioni 8/1, 8/2 e 8/3 della Biblioteca Braidense di Milano', *ib.*, 221–54, report a number of original and 18th-century copies of texts by T. of philological interest. Linguistic aspects in Vico's writings figure in F. Botturi, *Tempo, linguaggio e azione: le strutture vichiane della storia ideale eterna*, Na, Guida, 1996, 194 pp. S. C. Sgroi, 'Terminologia saussuriana. Retrodatazioni italiane di termini del *Cours de linguistique générale*', *CFS*, 49, 1995–96 [1997], 197–212. M. L. Porzio Gernia, 'Lo storicismo linguistico di Benvenuto Terracini', *ASGM*, 35–36, 1996:7–18.

4. Phonology

On pedagogical approaches to Italian pronunciation there is G. Curro, 'Five manuals of Italian pronunciation: Castiglione (1957), Agard and Di Pietro (1965), Chapallaz (1979), Noble (1986) and Canepari (1992)', appearing in a new Belgian journal *RevP*, 1:17–39, which offers a useful comparative presentation. Various contributions in Maiden, *Dialects*, address phonological topics: M. Maiden, 'Vowel systems' (7–14), provides a useful sketch of the varying patterns of vowel evolution found across Italo-Romance. Neat outlines of the broad characteristics of major developments of a segmental nature are found in L. Savoia and M. Maiden, 'Metaphony' (15–25), E. Tuttle, 'Palatalization' (26–31), L. Giannelli and T. D. Cravens, 'Consonantal weakening' (32–40), M. Loporcaro, 'Lengthening and *raddoppiamento fonosintattico*' (41–51), while higher level phonological units are considered by L. Repetti, 'The syllable' (52–57), and I. Vogel, 'Prosodic phonology' (58–67), in the latter of which an exclusively synchronic approach is adopted. M. Maiden, 'La dissimilation à la lumière des pronomes clitiques en roman', *ZRP*, 113:531–62, examines the widespread dissimilation of /l/ in sequences of 3rd person direct and indirect object clitics in Romance, including much Italian material, and argues that dissimilation is not just a phonetic process but may also involve morphological or lexical conditioning. L. Bafile, 'La spirantizzazione toscana nell'ambito della teoria degli elementi', *Studi Giacomelli*, 27–38, advances an interpretation of the *gorgia toscana* in terms of particle phonology. By the same author, 'Parole grammaticali e struttura prosodica: dati dell'italiano e del napoletano', *LS*, 32:433–69, deals with the phonological reduction of functional elements, and 'Sulla rappresentazione delle strutture metriche ternarie', *QDLF*, 7 : 1996 : 45–67, discusses antepenultimate stress, ever a controversial issue, in Italian and related dialects, in particular regarding loan words and the pronounciation of foreign words.

In addition to the outline by Loporcaro mentioned above, there are other significant contributions to the long-running debate on *raddoppiamento fonosintattico*, most notably the monograph of the same author, *L'origine del raddoppiamento fonosintattico: saggi di fonologia diacronica romanza*, Basel, Francke, xii + 181 pp. Following a judicious review of the incidence of *raddoppiamento* in the modern norm variety and recent phonological interpretations advanced for its description, the author impressively uses a rich array of comparative data from Romance and philological materials to chart the likely diachronic development of the phenomenon. His proposal is that it operated in two stages: the first came about with the assimilation of word-final consonants (DAT PANE(M) > *da* [pp]*ane*) already in Imperial times, the second involved a later abductive development in medieval times whereby speakers, especially in central Italian dialects, re-analysed the existing pattern so that *raddoppiamento* came to operate after all words ending in a stressed vowel. Some independent support for the early chronology proposed for the first stage is offered by F. Fanciullo, 'Anticipazioni romanze nel latino pompeiano', *AGI*, 82 : 186–98, who claims that Pompeiian inscriptions already indicate the presence of *raddoppiamento fonosintattico*, although the evidence adduced is far from overwhelming. By the same author there is also **Raddoppiamento sintattico e ricostruzione linguistica nel sud italiano*, Pisa, ETS, 65 pp.

Nasal vowels receive attention in a work of major importance, Hajek, *Nasalization*, in which northern Italian dialects, and especially those of Romagna, are taken as a test-case for a detailed investigation of the implementation of vowel nasalization in language. Impressively exploiting findings from experimental phonetics and theoretical phonology as well as drawing on a wide range of other primary language data from outside Italy, the author identifies and explores various parameters along which nasalization appears to operate. Three cognitive studies on aspects of phonology using Italian data appear in *Linguaggio e cognizione. Atti del XXVIII Congresso della Società di Linguistica Italiana*, ed. M. Carapezza et al., Ro, Bulzoni, 507 pp.: F. Albano Leone et al., 'Percezione, categorizzazione, riconoscimento di vocali italiane naturali e sintetiche' (315–28); E. Magno Caldognetto, L. Tonelli, and M. Panzeri, 'Evidenze dai *lapsus* per modelli di produzione del parlato' (329–56); M. Vayra, 'Regole formali vs. regolarità fonetiche: un caso di *accorciamento compensativo* in italiano' (357–82). M. Frascarelli, 'The phonology of Focus and Topic in

Italian', *LRev*, 14:221–48, presents evidence of the influence of focusing and topicalizing constructions on the application of phonological rules in Italian. A. G. Boano, 'Analisi contrastiva delle varietà regionali di italiano parlate a Genova e alla Spezia: vocalismo', *ASGM*, 35–36, 1996:160–76. A. Romano, 'Accent et intonation des parlers du Salento: une approche théorique et instrumentale', *Géolinguistique*, 7:93–132, examines prosodic structures in the regional Italian and dialects of the area.

5. MORPHOLOGY

Concise outlines of a wide range of individual topics appear in Maiden, *Dialects:* M. Maiden, 'Inflectional morphology of the noun and adjective' (68–74); L. Savoia, 'Inflectional morphology of the verb' (75–86); P. Cordin, 'Tense, mood and aspect in the verb' (87–98); N. Vincent, 'Synthetic and analytic structures' (99–105); L. Vanelli (with L. Renzi), 'Personal pronouns and demonstratives' (106–15); T. Telmon and M. Maiden, 'Word structure and word formation' (116–22). G. Crocco Galéas, **Metafora morfologica: saggio di morfologia naturale*, Padua, Unipress, viii + 97 pp. Pluralization of nominals is treated in M. R. Manzini, 'Alcuni casi di distribuzione del plurale nei sintagmi nominali', *Studi Giacomelli*, 227–39, which investigates theoretical aspects raised by data drawn from the dialects of Lunigiana and Val Bregaglia, and in J. Herman, 'À propos du débat sur le pluriel des noms italiens (et roumains): à la recherche d'une conclusion', *Fest. Pfister*, II, 19–30, where cogent arguments are advanced for not tracing modern plural nominal forms back directly to either the Latin nominative or accusative; instead it is proposed that in Late Latin there arose growing syncretism between the two case-forms leading to near-free variation which was only later resolved with regional differences in favour of one or other original form. F. Fanciullo, 'In italiano, *bontà* e *gioventù:* vicende di uno "stampo"', *ib.*, II, 71–80, claims that these truncated noun forms arose through influence from northern Italian dialects and Gallo-Romance. C. Agostinelli, 'Sull'origine degli infiniti sincopati "corre", "scerre", "sciorre", "sverre", "torre"', *SLI*, 22, 1996:65–73. G. Ineichen, 'Zur Übereinstimmung des Perfektpartizips mit HABERE', *ib.*, 3–5, briefly compares patterns of (non-) agreement in Italian, French, and Spanish. In a richly documented cross-dialectal study, E. F. Tuttle, 'Minor patterns and peripheral analogies in language change: à propos of past participles in *-esto* and the cryptotype *cerco* "searched", *tocco* "touched"', *AGI*, 82:34–58, identifies two conflicting tendencies in past participle formation, one towards hypercharacterization through the use of the additional suffixal -*esto* (widely found in Veneto dialects), the other towards hypocharacterization by deleting the original marker, this being most commonly encountered in Tuscan dialects.

G. Ernst, 'Die Nachfolger von lat. EX- im LEI', *Fest. Pfister*, II, 45–70, considers the fortunes of prefixal EX- for word formation. L. Serianni, '"O no"/ "O non"/ "O meno"', *ib.*, 81–85, reviews the incidence and earlier attestations of these coordinated sentence-final phrases. P. Ramat, 'Why *veruno* means "nobody"', *RPh*, 51 : 1–14, traces the shift in meaning from positive 'someone, any' (< VERE UNUM 'truly one') to negative 'nobody, no'. Already in 14th-c. Italian, the word figured in predominantly negative contexts, and R. claims that the key stage in negativization came with the use of the word in comparative constructions such as *maggiore che veruno coltello* where the implied non-existence of the *coltello* conveys negativity. I. Burr, 'Morphosemantische Veränderungstendenzen bei Nomina agentis in kontrastiver Sicht', *Baum Vol.*, 51–70, examines the vexed question of finding acceptable lexical forms to designate female professionals in Italian and other Romance languages. H. Baayen, C. Burani, and R. Schreuder, 'Effects of semantic markedness in the processing of regular nominal singulars and plurals in Italian', *YM*, 1996 : 13–33. M. Orsolini and W. Marslen-Wilson, 'Universals in morphological representation: evidence from Italian', *LCP*, 12 : 1–47.

6. SYNTAX AND SEMANTICS

G. Cinque, 'L'italiano', *Actas* (Santiago de Compostela), I, 1107–13, contributes a brief, lucid exposition in generative terms to the round table discussion on Romance word order, showing how the apparently 'free' ordering of the basic constituents (Subject, Verb, Object) is strictly controlled by syntactic, pragmatic, and prosodic factors. The order of sentential constituents also serves as the yardstick for G. Salvi, 'La posizione tipologica dell'italiano fra le lingue romanze', *ItStudien*, 18 : 25–38, which confirms L. Renzi's (1976) view that Italian is an 'average' Romance language, neither excessively innovative nor conservative. Concise comparative overviews of particular syntactic structures appear in Maiden, *Dialects:* P. Beninçà, 'Sentence word order' (123–30) and 'Conjunctions' (131–36); C. Poletto, 'Pronominal syntax' (137–44); M. Cennamo, 'Passive and impersonal constructions' (145–61); L. Renzi, 'The structure of the noun phrase' (162–70); N. Vincent, 'Complementation' (171–78); M. Parry, 'Negation' (179–85); G. Cinque, 'Quantifiers' (186–89); M. Cennamo, 'Relative clauses' (190–201); M. Mazzoleni, 'The syntax of conditional sentences' (202–07); N. Vincent, 'Prepositions' (208–13). In L. Giannelli, 'La risalita del possessore: restrizioni dell'italiano alla luce di raffronti interlinguistici', *Studi Giacomelli*, 153–65, a careful analysis of the contexts that allow the expression of the possessor as a clitic pronoun (e.g. *ti vedo le carte*) reveals the importance of the semantic feature relating to the possessor's control over the possessed object. I. Roberts, 'Restructuring, Head Movement and Locality', *LI*, 28:423–60, draws on Italian examples to argue for a new analysis of restructuring and clitic climbing in terms of the incorporation of the infinitive with the restructuring verb (the resulting complex verb cannot, however, be spelled out as such, owing to constraints that prevent more than one morphological word being realized under a single head position). Research inspired by Chomsky's Minimalist Program also makes frequent use of Italian examples: C. Donati and A. Tomaselli, 'La sintassi del soggetto nel quadro minimalista. Riflessioni su EPP e *pro-drop*', *LS*, 32:223–45, considers the impact of the Program on two central aspects of subject syntax: the Extended Projection Principle and the Null Subject Parameter, while M. Frascarelli, 'Focus and feature-checking: un'ipotesi minimalista', *ib.*, 247–72, argues for a syntactic analysis of Focus within a feature-checking framework, paying particular attention to the postverbal position of subjects in Italian. A. Moro, 'Dynamic antisymmetry: movement as a symmetry-breaking phenomenon', *SL*, 51:50–76, uses mainly Italian and English sentences (e.g. 'small clauses' and interrogatives) to argue for a weaker version of Kayne's 1994 theory of the antisymmetry of syntax, whereby syntactic movement is not triggered by morphological requirements as upheld in Chomsky's Minimalist Program, but by purely geometrical ones. G. Graffi, 'Frasi "complete" e frasi "ridotte". Recenti proposte di analisi', *LS*, 32:273–91, reviews recent theories using examples from Italian. Verner Egerland, *The Syntax of Past Participles. A Generative study of Nonfinite Constructions in Ancient and Modern Italian*, Lund U.P., 1996, 350 pp., presents an exhaustive generative analysis under three main headings: '*Avere* + Past Participle', 'The Absolute Past Participle', and 'Null Pronouns and notes on the syntax of adjectives'. C. Donati, 'Comparative clauses as free relatives: a raising analysis', *Probus*, 9:145–66, draws on mainly French and Italian data to argue that, while displaying all the properties associated with wh-movement, comparative clauses exhibit a number of unusual features that distinguish them clearly from other movement constructions. G. Fiorentino, 'Le clausole relative "deboli" in italiano', *LS*, 32:53–76, analyses clauses corresponding to Italian prepositional relatives but introduced by *che* in *italiano popolare*. A. Bonomi, 'Aspect, quantification and when-clauses in Italian', *LPh*, 20:469–514. G. Cocchi, 'A note on impersonal *si*', compares reflexive and impersonal *si* structures, focusing on auxiliary selection and past participial agreement; the difference between the two types of constructions deriving from the different nature of the element binding the anaphoric clitic *si*. B. Wehr, 'A proposito di una nuova categoria grammaticale: diatesi con SE in italiano', *Actas* (Santiago de Compostela), 1 791–97, seeks to resolve the long-standing debate about the status of constructions deriving from the Latin reflexive, traditionally known as *si passivante* and *si impersonale*, by postulating on the basis of morphological and functional distinctiveness a separate voice ('diathesis'), distinct from both active and passive constructions.

P. Benincà and C. Poletto, 'The diachronic development of a modal verb of necessity', Kemenade, *Parameters*, 94–118, offer a diachronic study of the grammaticalization of *bisogna* to illustrate their theory that verb syntax and morphology are determined in some of their aspects by the presence of a thematic grid; comparisons are drawn with *andare* + past participle, dialectal *volere* + past participle and Venetan *toca*. M. Bertuccelli Papi, 'Italian -*to* participle clauses as (quasi-) converbal constructions', *FLin*, 31 : 1–23, argues that clauses such as *Arrivato Gianni, (la festa si animò)*, and *Criticato da tutti, (Gianni fu costretto a dimettersi)* can be interpreted as being syntactically dependent on the matrix verb, as gerunds are. M. A. Cortelazzo, 'Perfetto semplice e perfetto composto in italiano', Taylor Torsello, *Grammatica*, 199–208, is a useful, clear review of differences in use between the two tenses: despite the steady extension of the latter at the expense of the former, the rapid demise of the simple past is considered unlikely, thanks to its persistence in narrative texts and the unsuitability of the compound tense in a number of other contexts. New light is thrown on Sicilian regional usage in G. Alfonzetti, '"Ora la luna si nascose, ma prima era bellissima". Passato prossimo e passato remoto nell'italiano di Sicilia', D'Agostino, *Aspetti*, 11–48. A. Giorgi, 'Nel mondo dei sogni *ovvero* Sulle dipendenze temporali create dai predicati di immaginazione', *LFB*, 5 : 125–46. M. Berretta, 'Sul futuro concessivo: riflessioni su un caso (dubbio) di de/grammaticalizza-zione', *ib.*, 7–40, discusses the development of the Italian usage illustrated by *'Sarò piemontese, ma mica scema!'*, raising probing questions about the exact nature of such linguistic change. A. Monjour, 'Verkürzte Partizipien im Italienischen, Spanischen und Portugiesischen: Funktionale Beschreibung und historische Interpretation', *RomGG*, 3 : 151–81. D. Calleri, *'L'acquisizione della frase infinitiva in italiano L1', *LFB*, 5 : 41–58. A. Valentini, *'Frasi relative in italiano L2', *ib.*, 195–221. A currently buoyant area of research involves constructions with a postverbal (quasi-) subject, existentials, and the role of *ci* in such structures, with Italian or the dialects often the language of exemplification, for instance A. Cardinaletti, 'Agreement and control in expletive constructions', *LI*, 28: 521–33, which relates non-agreement of the verb to the nominative case marking of the expletive in subject position; N. La Fauci and M. Lopocaro, 'Outline of a theory of existentials on evidence from Romance', *SILTA*, 26:5–55. C. Tortora, 'Two types of unaccusatives: evidence from a northern Italian dialect', *Papers* (LSRL 25), 251–62, argues on the basis of syntactic evidence from Borgomanerese (north-eastern Piedmont) for two classes of unaccusative verbs, one of them possessing two internal arguments, so that in addition to the object which becomes the surface 'subject' there is also a locative argument.

G. Brugger and M. D'Angelo, 'Movement at LF triggered by mood and tense', *FLin*, 29:195–221, includes in the analysis based on Italian examples a discussion of the semantic position of sentential negation. H. Glinz, 'Aspetti semantici nella sintassi', in *Baum Vol.*, 139–51. Iørn Korzen, **L'articolo italiano fra concetto ed entità. Uno studio semantico-sintattico sugli articoli e sui sintagmi nominali italiani con e senza determinante — con un'indagine particolare sulla distribuzione del cosiddetto 'articolo partitivo'* (Études Romanes 36), 2 vols, Copenhagen, Museum Tusculanum Press, 1996, 743 pp. J. Visconti, '"Deverbal" conditional connectives in English and Italian', *The Italianist*, 305–25, is an interesting comparative analysis of neglected elements such as *ammesso che, dato che*. Federica Casadei, **Metafore e espressioni idiomatiche. Uno studio semantico dell'italiano*, Ro, Bulzoni, 496 pp. T. Chardantseva, 'Semantica e grammatica dei modi di dire in italiano', *SLeI*, 14:347–411. P. Blumenthal and G. Rovere, 'Valenza, polisemia e traduzione', Renzi, *Linguistica*, 53–80, explores the inter-relationship between syntax and semantics, valency, and meaning, through a detailed analysis of one lexical family *(interesse)* and its possible German equivalents. T. Krefeld, '"Wahrnehmung" auf Italienisch. Zur verbalen Kategorisierung der Perzeption im Italienischen', *ItStudien*, 18:5–24. Italian is the language of exemplification in G. Chierchia, 'Considerazioni informali sui rapporti fra sintassi e semantica formali', *Della Casa Vol.*, 663–93; in C. Bazzanella and R. Damiano, 'Il fraintendimento linguistico nelle interazioni quotidiane: proposta di classificazione', *LS*, 32:369–95; and in M. Moneglia, 'Prototypical vs. non-prototypical predicates: ways of understanding and the semantic partition of lexical meaning', *QDLF*, 7:163–81. Id., 'Lungo, largo, alto, grande e grosso: teoria empirica del senso e sistema delle misure dimensionali in italiano', *Studi Giacomelli*, 257–77.

7. PRAGMATICS AND DISCOURSE

A. L. Lepschy, G. Lepschy, and M. Voghera, 'Intonazione del parlato e del recitato', *The Italianist*, 16, 1996:220–33, presents objectively measured differences between the two types of text and between Italian and English, in particular the speed of delivery. M. R. Caputo,

'Vocativi eloquenti', *IO*, 12 : 19–26, shows an interesting correlation between the melodic structure of the vocative and the sentence type that follows. M. Pettorino, 'Pause politiche', *ib.*, 12–18, offers a detailed analysis of the distribution and role of pauses in the speeches of Italian politicians. S. Schneider, 'Osservazioni sul verbo fattivo cognitivo *sapere*', *ItStudien*, 18 : 39–46, examines the modality of the complement clauses introduced by *che*. M. Frescura, 'Strategie di rifiuto in italiano: uno studio etnografico', *Italica*, 74 : 542–59. Dario Paccino, **Manuale di autodifesa linguistica*, Varese, Artigere, 1996, 104 pp., lists words used to conceal unjustified violence in capitalism.

8. LEXIS

A major new dictionary of Italian has appeared, F. Sabatini and V. Coletti, *DISC : Dizionario italiano Sabatini Coletti*, F, Giunti, xv + 3037 pp., while there are updated versions of *Lo Zingarelli in CD-ROM*, ed. M. Dogliotti and L. Rosiello, Bo, Zanichelli, which is based on the 12th printed edition, and the bilingual CD-ROM *Dizionario Garzanti: inglese-italiano, italiano-inglese*, Mi, Garzanti. E. Savino, *Guida ai sinonimi delle parole di base e a più alta frequenza: etimologie, significati primari, esempi fraseologici*, Mi, Mursia, 1996, v + 253 pp., presents a compact treatment of some 4,000 lexical items. Michele A. Cortelazzo, *Annali del Lessico Contemporaneo Italiano. Neologismi 1996*, Padua, Esedra. *Archivio di parole. Quaderno primo*, ed. Michele A. Cortelazzo and Claudio Vela, Lucca, Una Cosa Rara. C. Marello, **Le parole dell'italiano: lessico e dizionari*, Bo, Zanichelli, 1996, xii + 259 pp. T. Franceschi, 'In margine alle ricerche dell'Atlante Paremiologico Italiano', *Studi Giacomelli*, 129–45, notes fascinating grammatical and lexical features of Italian proverbs.

The third and final volume of a major project on legal language (vol. 1 in 1993) has appeared: *Indice della lingua legislativa italiana: inventario lessicale dei cento migliori testi di legge tra il 1723 e il 1973*, ed. P. M. Biagini, F, Giuntina, xv + 993 pp., which is complemented by S. Novelli and G. Urbani, **Dizionario della seconda Repubblica: le parole nuove della politica*, Ro, Editori Riuniti, xiii + 170 pp. M. Lanzarone, 'Note sulla terminologia informatica', *SLeI*, 14 : 427–507. Addressing rather a different lexical stratum is V. Boggione and G. Casalegno, *Dizionario storico del lessico erotico italiano*, Mi, Longanesi, 1996, lii + 684 pp., which offers an admirable historical panorama of this neglected area; following a solid introductory review of the varying fortunes of euphemism and eroticism in literature, there is a wide-ranging, thematically arranged coverage of the data completed by detailed indices. On a related theme is W. Schweickard, 'Tabu und Euphemismus in der italienischen Lexikographie', *Baum Vol.*, 303–10, which charts the increasing receptivity to sexually taboo words over the history of Italian lexicography. In E. Borello, 'Comunicazioni di massa e gergo', *Studi Giacomelli*, 65–78, the characteristics of *gergo* are examined using examples from northern Italy. R. Librandi, 'Sul lessico dell'economia negli scritti di Antonio Genovesi e Ferdinando Galiani', *Atti* (AISLLI 15), I, 239–52. G. L. Beccaria, 'L'automobile, un'officina di parole', *ib.*, II, 1147–87, is a fascinating account of loan words and neologisms and the cross-fertilization of technical jargon and everyday language. G. Lepschy, 'La lingua dell'industria', *ib.*, II, 1189–96, considers the lexical consequences of industrialization taking as examples *industria* and *chiave*. *Lessico e grammatica*, ed. T. De Mauro and V. Lo Cascio, Ro, Bulzoni, 462 pp., contains a number of interesting articles on the themes lexicon and language learning, collocations, lexicography, semantics and the lexicon, semantic and syntactic theory, and computational lexicography: P. P. Izquierdo, 'L'informazione sintagmatica in un vocabolario pedagogico monobilingue spagnolo-italiano italiano-spagnolo' (9–15); M. Boni, 'Le parole di "alta disponibilità" nell'italiano lingua straniera' (17–24); P. Guil, 'Gli aggettivi relativi e le liste di frequenza' (25–29); M. del Pilar Rodríguez Reina, 'Terminologia specializzata nei dizionari bilingui: il caso del lessico nautico' (31–44); U. Heid, 'Proposte per la costruzione semi-automatica di un dizionario elettronico delle collocazioni' (47–62); V. Lo Cascio, 'Semantica lessicale e i criteri di collocazione nei dizionari bilingui a stampa ed elettronici' (63–88); A. Puglielli, 'Quale e quanta grammatica in un dizionario?' (91–111); L. Renzi and A. Elia, 'Per un vocabolario delle reggenze' (113–29); C. Marello, 'Il dizionario come informatore del linguista: il caso dell'ellissi' (131–53); R. Simone, 'Esistono verbi sintagmatici in italiano?' (155–70); S. Scalise, 'Rappresentazione degli affissi' (171–91); L. Mereu, 'Sulla morfologia flessiva: tra lessico e sintassi' (193–215); A. Bisetto, 'Morfologia lessicale e lessicografia: alcuni punti di interazione' (217–27); G. Chierchia, 'Sulla distinzione fra Nomi Numerabili e Nomi Massa' (231–58); M. Moneglia, 'Teoria empirica del senso e proprietà idiosincratiche del lessico: note sulla selezione' (259–91); D. Marconi, 'La competenza referenziale in un dizionario tradizionale' (293–308); C. Schwarze, 'Strutture semantiche e concettuali nella formazione delle parole' (311–29); L. Dini, 'Problemi sintattici e soluzioni lessicali: il caso delle participiali assolute' (331–60); M. Leonetti, 'La struttura argomentale e le frasi completive nei sintagmi nominali' (361–73); D. Russo, 'Semantica dei termini e comprensibilità delle operazioni di formalizzazione e informalizzazione del significato' (375–94); M. de Palo, 'Il Vocabolario di base a confronto con il Lessico italiano del parlato'

(395–411); A. Elia, 'Standards informatici per la lessicografia computazionale' (415–30); R. Delmont, 'Rappresentazioni lessicali e linguistica computazionale' (431–62).

Vol. 16 of the *Glossario degli antichi volgari italiani*, ed. Giorgio Colussi, covers *stabbio — stragreve*, while *Fest. Pfister*, I, contains a number of contributions on diachronic aspects of the Italian lexicon: M. Cortelazzo, 'Il prestito come recupero lessicale' (47–52); P. Caratù, 'Garganico *fracchia* "torcione, falò". Proposta di etimologia' (115–24), argues for *FLACCULA < FACULA as the etymon; O. Lurati, 'Problemi di metodo, di approccio semantico e di datazioni: una nuova proposta su *mafia*' (137–49), notes 16th-c. attestations in mainland Italy but none in Sicily until 1865 and proposes a base etymon *maff-/baff-* 'puffed up, worthless'; A. Varvaro, 'Per la storia del lessico dell'Italia meridionale: Aversa normanna' (151–63), explores medieval documents from Aversa (prov. Caserta) for gallicisms; A. Zamboni, 'It. *stallìa*' (165–70), proposes STATIVA as etymon; A. Calabrò and F. Fazio, 'Descrizione del codice palermitano del *Thesaurus pauperum*: preliminari per una ricerca delle sue fonti' (203–18); A. Castellani, 'Un inventario quattrocentesco in fiorentino periferico' (219–40), reproduces a text which may come from Prato or Vinci; R. Coluccia and M. Aprile, 'Lessico quotidiano e cultura materiale in inventari pugliesi del secondo Quattrocento' (241–63); A. Cornagliotti, 'Il volgarizzamento della Bibbia di Ghinazzone da Siena: una fonte lessicale da acquisire' (265–81); G. Gasca Queirazza, 'Sotto il velo del latino: lessico volgare in un documento torinese del secolo XIV' (291–305); T. Hohnerlein-Buchinger, 'Giuseppe Acerbis *Classificazione geoponica delle viti*. Über die Bedeutung einer Ampelographie für die etymologische Bestimmung von Trauben- und Rebenbezeichnungen' (307–28); S. Lubello, 'Per una filologia delle fonti antiche: i libri di cucina antico-italiani nel *LEI*' (329–39); F. Sboarina, 'La vita acquatica in Mattioli: attestazioni ragionate' (355–69), presents selected items from M.'s 16th-c. compendium; A. Stussi, 'Versi in Archivio' (371–82), presents a 14th-c. Tuscan-Venetan sonnet; C. Vela, 'Materiali per la datazione di termini musicali (1491–1508)' (383–90); M. A. Cortelazzo, 'La seconda edizione del *Vocabolario della Crusca* (1623)' (393–402), notes significant advances from the first edition of 1612; W. Schweickard, 'Neue Medien und historische Lexikographie: die *Letteratura Italiana Zanichelli (LIZ)* auf CD-ROM' (441–49); F. Spiess, 'Grossräumige und kleinräumige etymologische Wörterbücher' (451–55); G. Tancke, 'Note per un *Avviamento al Lessico Etimologico Italiano (LEI)*' (457–87). In *Fest. Pfister*, II, there are also G. Colón, 'El adjetivo *tonto* entre Italia y España' (233–44), where this item is interpreted as a hispanism in Italian, ultimately of phonosymbolic origin, and F. Marri, 'Parole nuove tra Germania e Italia'

(245–64), in which recent Italian loans from German are reviewed. M. Pfister, 'Les éléments français dans le *LEI*, it. *ARCHIBUGIO*', *Martin Vol.*, 303–10, uses the item *archibugio* 'arquebus', a germanicism which entered Italian via French, to demonstrate the principle adopted for the *LEI* of treating such items, which were introduced into Italo-Romance via an intermediary, in special fascicles separate from the main text containing Latin and Germanic items which entered the lexicon of Italo-Romance through direct transmission. C. Schwarze, 'Struktur und Variation im Lexikon', *ItStudien*, 18:47–65, uses Italian data to explore how the lexicon can express new values, attributing major importance to polysemy. A. Varvaro, 'Lexical and semantic variation', Maiden, *Dialects*, 214–21, is a succinct though comprehensive overview of Italo-Romance variation.

Despite the title, E. Marques Ranchhod and M. De Gioia, 'Comparative romance [sic] syntax. Frozen adverbs in Italian and Portuguese', *LInv*, 20, 1996:33–85, is arguably more lexical than syntactic in coverage, exploring idioms functioning as adverbs, such as *(fuma) come una ciminiera*. L. Bertolini, 'Servi albertiani', *SLI*, 22, 1996:223–30, argues that Alberti uses 'servo' with the value 'slave'. G. Alvino, 'Onomaturgia darrighiana', *ib.*, 74–88, 235–69, M. Arcangeli, '"Clono", "clonazione" e dintorni', *ib.*, 89–100. C. A. Mastrelli, 'Per l'etimologia di *solluc(c)herare/ solluc(c)hero*', *Studi Giacomelli*, 247–55, proposes as the base etymon for this colloquial lexical family meaning '(to go into) ecstasy' a form *solleticherare 'to excite', and A. Nesi, '*Vócero*, italiano?', *ib.*, 301–11, sees this word as a loan from Corsican. The etymology of names for medicinal plants is the subject of G. A. Sirianni, 'L'erba di Artemide', *ib.*, 377–92. F. Möhren, 'Lexicographie critique: l'étymologie de fr. gris, it. grigio', *TLP*, 35–36: 299–316. A number of works examine loan words into Italian: N. Onorati, *Checkpoint: 5.500 vocaboli inglesi immigrati nella lingua italiana*, Ro, Star, 1996, 208 pp.; R. Tesi, *Aristotele in italiano: i grecismi nelle traduzioni rinascimentali della Poetica*, F, Accademia della Crusca, 204 pp.; M. R. Ansalone, **I francesismi in italiano: repertori lessicografici e ricerche sul campo*, Na, Liguori, x + 364 pp. M. Pfister, 'It. *arazzo*, un prestito francese in italiano', *TLP*, 35–36: 337–44. H. Thomassen, 'Les emprunts à l'allemand ("tedeschismi") dans quelques dictionnaires italiens de mots étrangers', *ib.*, 427–39. K. Jorgaqui, 'Contributo allo studio dei prestiti lessicali italiani nell'albanese', *SLeI*, 14:413–25.

Marking the centenary of the birth of Bruno Migliorini, a number of fascicles of *LN* are dedicated to this scholar. Two articles directly relate to his work: M. Fanfani, 'La terminologia linguistica di Bruno Migliorini', *LN*, 57, 1996:117–23, and Id., 'Onomaturgia migliori-niana', *ib.*, 58:12–29. Other articles are A. Dardi, 'Note su "spirito filosofico" e linguaggio scientifico nel settecento', *ib.*, 57, 1996:99–116; C. Cordié, 'Letteratura industriale e alimentare', *ib.*, 116, which looks at the history of these collocations, and also Id., 'Iperuomo', *ib.*, 123–24, where the fate of this unsuccessful rival to 'superuomo' is traced. P. Cherchi, 'San Bindo', *ib.*, 58:29, discusses the origin of this 16th-c. allusion. F. Marri, 'Parole non più nuove (I)', *ib.*, 45–56, presents early attestations for various Italian neologisms, and M. Fanfani, 'Linguista, purista e linguaiolo', *ib.*, 56–58, explores the uses of these terms over the past two centuries. E. Schafroth, '*Zapping* im Italienischen. Eine korpusgestützte Wortgeschichte', *RomGG*, 3:183–201.

G. Mastrelli Anzilotti, 'Denominazioni di masi e cognomi tedeschi nel Trentino', *AAA*, 90:43–53. D. Soranzo, 'I corsi d'acqua chiamati Seriola e Candelora', *ib.*, 125–37. Id., 'Le radici germaniche dell'onomastica Scaligera', *ib.*, 140–46. C. Weyers, 'Italienische Familiennamen in Málaga', *RomGG*, 3:63–81. R. Bracchi, 'Frammenti etimologici bormini', *ib.*, 147–74. M. G. Arcamone, '"Ad brettescham Scherancii (?) duo": c'era forse uno Scheraggio anche a Pistoia?', *Studi Giacomelli*, 19–25. F. Granucci, 'Appunti di idronomia toscana', *ib.*, 167–73, identifies river names of Etruscan origin.

9. SOCIOLINGUISTICS

The current sociolinguistic situation of the dialects is neatly summarized in three contributions to Maiden, *Dialects:* Ž. Muljačić, 'The relationship between the dialects and the standard language' (387–93); G. Berruto, 'Code-switching and code-mixing' (394–400); A. Sobrero, 'Italianization of the dialects' (412–18). Id., 'Italianization and variations in repertoire: the Koinai', *Sociolinguistica*, 10, 1996:105–11, stresses the need for research into the phenomenon of dialect koinization (especially sub-regional) in modern Italy. The complex interaction between Italian and the dialects in the various parts of Italy provides the theme of several studies, for example A. Miglietta, 'Il "code-switching" nella zona 167 di Lecce', *RID*, 20:89–121, is a detailed account of field work that reveals the lack of any functional diversification in the use of the two codes and the inadequacy in this transitional part of Lecce of the traditional distinction between rural and urban areas. A point of theoretical import is the apparent irrelevance of certain constraints that have been proposed regarding switching between different codes. Research linked to the *ALS (Atlante linguistico della Sicilia)* is also stimulating much theoretical discussion, for instance M. D'Agostino, 'Spazio, città, lingue. Ragionando su Palermo', *RID*, 20, 1996:35–87, investigates linguistic attitudes in Palermo as to the appropriateness of

standard Italian and the local dialect in specific situations, within a
thought-provoking re-evaluation of the notion of space for a convincing (sociolinguistic) analysis of linguistic behaviour. The contribution
of linguistic attitudes and speakers' sense of identity to linguistic
change also emerges clearly in D'Agostino's article, 'Un programme
sociolinguistique de l'espace: l'*Atlante linguistico della Sicilia (ALS)*',
Géolinguistique, 7 : 159–79, based on the analysis of phonetic variation
in the regional Italian and dialect of different age groups; the
important methodological issue of the balance between quantitative
and qualitative approaches is also introduced. D'Agostino, *Aspetti*,
includes by the editor, 'L'oggi e i diversi frammenti del passato: note
sulla lenizione delle occlusive sorde in Sicilia' (97–114), as well as
M. Criminisi, 'Variabilità linguistica e conservazione dialettale a
Grotte, un paese dell'Agrigento' (115–28); A. Colonna Romano and
G. Mammana, 'Italiano regionale di Sicilia in prospettiva diatopica'
(129–38); G. Mammana, 'Fra "italiano regionale" e "italiano parlato.
Appendice a una ricerca' (139–54); C. Battaglia, 'I giovani siciliani
"abbordano" ma spesso si "scantano". Una indagine sulle varietà
giovanili nell'area di Palermo' (155–73). I. Tempesta, 'Evoluzione
linguistica e mutamento sociale: una comunità di emigrati rientrati
in Sila', *BALI*, 3, 20: 115–36.

REGIONAL VARIETIES OF ITALIAN.   T. Poggi Salani, 'L'italiani di
Toscana', *IO*, 12:226–32, and N. Binazzi, 'Italiano di Toscana. Dove
si parla, dove se ne parla', *ib.*, 233–36. T. Telmon, 'La lingua di Tino
Faussone', *ib.*, 89–95, takes his cue from the protagonist of Primo
Levi's *Chiave a stella* to describe Piedmontese Italian. C. Schirru,
'Ulteriori considerazioni prosodiche sul vocalismo italiano del Pie-
monte', *BALI*, 3, 20:79–100. *Forme e percorsi dell'italiano nel Trentino-
Alto Adige,* ed. Vittorio Coletti, Patrizia Cordin, and Alberto Zamboni,
F, Istituto di Studi per l'Alto Adige, 1995, iv + 315 pp.

ADOLESCENT VARIETIES.   Neri Binazzi, *Le parole dei giovani fiorentini:
variazione linguistica e variazione sociale,* Ro, Bulzoni, 411 pp., raises
important methodological issues relating to the study of regional
Italian. Although responses to the written questionnaire presented to
a random sample of 790 young Florentines cannot be considered as
providing an objective description of actual usage, the detailed
analysis yields valuable evidence about the sociolinguistic connotations of lexical items in the region that appears least disposed to
conform to lexical standardization. Id., 'Dimensioni della dialettalità
a Firenze: spunti in margine a tre indagini lessicali', *Studi Giacomelli*,
55–64, raises related methodological issues. M. Danesi, 'Investigating
Italian adolescent talk: are there any implications for the teaching of
Italian as a second language?', *Italica*, 74: 455–65. C. Marcato, '*In
para totale . . . una cosa da panico:* sulla lingua dei giovani in Italia', *ib.*,

560–75. A. Nascimbeni, 'Indagine sul lessico dei ragazzi di Bussolengo (VR)', *ASGM*, 1996, 35–36:181–93.

SECTIONAL VARIETIES Francesca Sboarina, *La lingua di due quotidiani veronesi del secondo Ottocento (ZRP*, Beiheft 266), Tübingen, Niemeyer, 1996. Valentina Ruffin and Patrizia D'Agostino, *Dialoghi di regime: la lingua del cinema degli anni trenta*, Ro, Bulzoni, 209 pp., contains four fascinating chapters that document: 1. 'L'autarchia linguistica' (with a section on the use of *Lei* and *Voi*); 2. 'La dialettofobia' (with section on regional Italian); 3. 'Le lingue straniere'; 4. 'L'italiano'. M. A. Cortelazzo, 'Lingua e diritto in Italia. Il punto di vista dei linguisti', Schena, *Lingua del diritto*, 35–50, takes a comprehensive look at the many possible approaches to studying a special language that has been sadly neglected by linguists. P. Bellucci, 'La lingua "in divisa". I verbali nella pratica giudiziaria', *Studi Giacomelli*, 39–54, raises some disturbing questions about the language of written statements. Alfredo Fioritto, *Manuale di stile. Strumenti per semplificare il linguaggio delle amministrazioni pubbliche*, Bo, Il Mulino, 169 pp., which has the immediate practical aim of improving communication with the public, also offers interesting examples of the language of bureaucracy. Alberto Sensini, **Caro Silvio, caro Massimo: la neolingua della politica*, Ro, RTM, 111 pp., analyses the language used by the leaders of Forza Italia and the PDS. Lorella Cedroni, **Il lessico della rappresentanza politica*, Soveria Mannelli, Rubbettino, 1996, 217 pp. **Gli italiani trasmessi: la radio. Incontri del Centro di studi di grammatica italiana, Firenze, Villa Medicea di Castello, 13–14 maggio 1994*, F, Accademia della Crusca, 837 pp.

MINORITY LANGUAGES. Gabriele Birken-Silverman, *Sprachkontakt Italienisch–Albanisch in Kalabrien*, 3 vols, Frankfurt, Lang, xxx + 765, viii + 97, xii + 263 pp., is an in-depth sociolinguistic analysis of language contact in the Albanian linguistic enclaves that provides valuable information on the use of the two codes in the various domains and the transfer and integration of loan forms into Arberesche. Further studies of minority languages include T. Telmon, 'Aspetti sociolinguistici e culturali delle minoranze linguistiche in Piemonte e Valle d'Aosta', *Quaderni della Regione Piemonte, Montagna*, 1:9–13, and G. M. Scalia, 'Minoranze linguistiche ed ambiente: la diversità culturale come risorsa', *AAA*, 90:5–36, providing an interesting update on the fate of a bill relating to minority languages approved by the Italian Chamber of Deputies in 1991 but then shelved at the dissolution of Parliament (an amended text, strongly supported by the author, is appended). Pier Francesco Bellinello, **Minoranze etniche e linguistiche nel Nord Italia*, Cosenza, Editoriale Bios, 1996, 114 pp. A. Petralli, **Lingue sciolte. Dalle minoranze linguistiche loxAli* [sic] *alle nuove tecnologie internazionali*, Bo, CLUEB, 186 pp.

10. DIALECTOLOGY

L. Savoia, 'The geographical distribution of the dialects', Maiden, *Dialects*, 225–34, examines several crucial isoglosses from a perspective that also takes into account the relationship between the Italo-Romance linguistic continuum and varieties traditionally excluded. M. T. Romanello, 'Sulla rappresentazione dei confini linguistici', *RID*, 20, 1996: 7–33, uses data from the Salento peninsula to highlight the problems and sometimes the artificiality of using isoglosses as criteria for establishing dialect boundaries, whilst S. Canobbio, 'Un etnotesto e alcune proposte per la sua lettura; il *radon* dei laghi di Avigliana', *StP*, 26: 401–24, underlines the value of this sort of text (recorded for the *Atlante Linguistico dei Laghi Italiani*) not only for dialectology but also for sociolinguistic and pragmalinguistic study. The unpublished U. Pellis, *Il Questionario dell'Atlante Linguistico Italiano*, II, *L'allevamento e i suoi prodotti*, appears in *BALI*, 3, 20: 169–86. **Il lago...uno spazio domestico. Studi in memoria di Alessandro Alimenti*, ed. G. Moretti et al., S. Feliciano di Magione (PG), Museo del Pesce, 511 pp. *Cortelazzo Vol.* is a fitting tribute to a scholar whose outstanding contribution to Italian dialectology and lexicology, especially in relation to seafaring, thanks to his lifelong association with the *Atlante linguistico mediterraneo*, is honoured and reflected in a wide range of studies. The analysis of lexical variation is informed by sociolinguistic, cultural, and methodological discussion, for example, A. Nesi, 'I dialetti e il mare: area alto tirrenica' (33–48); F. Fanciullo, 'I dialetti e il mare: il caso del sud-tirreno' (49–64); V. Valente, 'Migrazioni lessicali dal mare di Venezia ai lidi di Puglia' (65–76); A. G. Mocciaro, 'Gli atlanti linguistici e le inchieste marinare e pescherecce: dall'ALM all'ALS' (101–20). M. Cortelazzo, F. Ursini and P. G. Tiozzo, 'Supplemento al *Saggio di bibliografia italiana*, Chioggia 1996', closes the volume (479–82).

NORTHERN DIALECTS. Concise overviews appear in Maiden, *Dialects:* M. Parry, 'Piedmont' (237–44); W. Forner, 'Liguria' (245–52); G. Sanga, 'Lombardy' (253–59); P. Cordin, 'Trentino' (260–62); E. Tuttle, 'The Veneto' (263–70); J. Hajek, 'Emilia-Romagna' (271–78); L. Vanelli, 'Friuli' (279–85); G. Salvi, 'Ladin' (286–94). The first volume of *QASIS* is dedicated to *Strutture interrogative dell'Italia settentrionale*, with contributions by P. Benincà, 'Gli elementi interrogativi nel dialetto di Monno', revealing in the Monno dialect a surprising interrogative use of a support verb corresponding to Italian *fare* with full verbs (cf. English 'do' support), e.g. *fe-t comprà-la?* 'do-you buy it?' (13–29); M. Cuneo, 'Il pronome interrogativo *koelu ke* nel dialetto di Cicagna' (31–61) deals with an interesting Ligurian phenomenon, also found in some Piedmontese varieties; N. Munaro,

'Proprietà distribuzionali dei sintagmi interrogativi in alcuni dialetti veneti settentrionali' (63–74); C. Poletto, 'Tipi di pronomi interrogativi in friulano occidentale' (75–81); C. Tortora, 'I pronomi interrogativi in Borgomanerese' (83–88); M. Parry, 'Variazione sintattica nelle strutture interrogative piemontesi' (91–103); C. Poletto and L. Vanelli, 'Gli introduttori delle frasi interrogative nei dialetti settentrionali' (105–18). S. Canobbio, 'Spunti di semiolessicologia diatopica: ancora a proposito del tipo *baciás*', *QS*, 18:65–93, explores the range of meanings associated mainly in north-west Italy with this reflex of Late Latin **bacca* 'container for water' (possibly of Celtic origin). L. Zörner, 'Der Adhortativ in den oberitalienischen Dialekten', *Mondo Ladino*, 21:321–31.

PIEDMONT. M. Loporcaro, 'L'importanza del piemontese per gli studi di tipologia linguistica', pp. 11–29 of *Convegno Piemonte: Mille anni di lingua, di teatro e di poesia, Vercelli, 11–12 ottobre 1997*, ed. Sergio Gilardino and Bruno Villata, Vercelli, Gallo, 214 pp., concentrates on vowel harmony and past participle agreement. B. Villata, 'Lessico e strutture grammaticali dei *Sermoni Subalpini* ancora usati nel piemontese di oggi', *ib.*, 31–65. M. Parry, 'Preverbal negation and clitic ordering, with particular reference to a group of north-west Italian dialects', *ZRP*, 113:243–70, discusses a sequence (almost unique in Romance) whereby the preverbal negative *follows* complement clitics (first and second persons and third reflexive). T. Telmon, 'Il patois delle Valli di Lanzo: una rassegna', pp. 63–74 of *Miscellanea di studi storici sulle Valli di Lanzo in memoria di Giovanni Donna d'Oldenico*, ed. B. Guglielmotto Ravet, Lanzo Torinese, Società Storica delle Valli di Lanzo, 1996, is a useful sociolinguistic and bibliographical overview of an alpine valley where Piedmontese and Italian have gradually encroached on the indigenous Franco-Provençal. Id., 'I nomi dell'aratro in Piemonte e Valle d'Aosta', pp. 283–95 of *Il seme l'aratro la messe. Le coltivazioni frumentarie in Piemonte dalla preistoria alla mecanizzazione agricola*, ed. R. Comba and F. Panero, Cuneo, Rocca de' Baldi, 1996. Michelangelo Bruno, *Alpi sud-occidentali tra Piemonte e Provenza: i nomi di luogo, etimologia e storia: dizionario toponomastico*, Cuneo, L'Arciere, 1996, 190 pp.

LIGURIA. *Bibliografia dialettale ligure. Aggiornamento 1979–1993*, ed. Fiorenzo Toso and William Piastra, Genoa, A Compagna, 1994, xxii + 345 pp., is an important sequel to the 1980 publication and contains F. Toso, 'Per una storia dell'identità linguistica ligure in età moderna' (5–43). Id., *Grammatica del genovese, varietà urbana e di koinè*, Genoa, Le Mani, x + 295 pp., deserves to succeed in its declared dual aim of promoting use and knowledge of the dialect among the general public and providing a reliable source of data for linguists (hence the use throughout of both a traditional orthography and phonetic transcription). Generous exemplification based on modern everyday usage supports a clear traditional description of phonology, morphology, syntax and word formation, making this an excellent reference grammar. Id., 'Un capitolo in volgare dello Statuto di Apricale (1474). Appunti per una storia linguistica della liguria occidentale in età tardo-medievale', *Intemelion*, 2, 1996:5–18. F. Toso is currently the driving force behind a spate of dialect publications (linguistic and literary), editing for example the following texts: *Trionfo dro pòpolo zeneise*, Genoa, A Compagna, 96 pp., and, published by Le Mani: Gaetano Gallino, *Caenna zeneise (Catena genovese e poesie anonime sulla guerra del 1746–1747)*, 62 pp.; Gian Giacomo Cavalli, *In servixo dra patria e dra coronna (Encomi dogali, canzone per la guerra del 1625)*, 70 pp.; *L'angonìa dra prepotença (Poesie, canzoni e libelli della rivoluzione del 1797)*, 64 pp.; *Ne scrìvan d'Arensen (Ci scrivono da Arenzano. Un paese di riviera attraverso le corrispondenze di 'O Balilla' e 'O Stafì' (1872–1904)*, 62 pp., and with others: Pier Giovanni Capriata, *Ra finta caritè (Intermezzo burlesco)*, 1996, 63 pp.; *La raxone de la Pasca*, 63 pp., the first printed Genoese text (1474) and probably the first calendar printed in Italy. *Et io ge onsi le juncture. Un manoscritto genovese fra Quattro e Cinquecento: medicina, tecnica, alchimia e quotidianità*, ed. Giuseppe Palmero, Genoa, Le Mani, 63 pp. Id. 'Il lessico del manoscritto inedito genovese "Medicinalia quam plurima". Alcuni esempi', *SLeI*, 14:123–51. L. Còveri, '"Traducte sunt suprascripte littere ex lingua gallica in Italam nostram': un testo cancelleresco genovese del 1499', *Croce Vol.*, 65–72, offers a valuable insight into the sociolinguistic complexities of the age, 'sembra farsi strada, all'alba del nuovo secolo, non solo una più netta coscienza degli ambiti d'uso di volgare locale, latino, *scripta* sovradialettale tendenzialmente toscana, ma anche una sorta di "preitalianità" linguistica'. Werner Forner highlights interesting conservative features of an 18th-c. text composed in an alpine Ligurian dialect (e.g. preservation of -*s* through -*i* epenthesis in 2sg. verb forms and acc. – dat. ordering for complement clitics) in the introduction to Luca Maria Capponi, *A canzun de Franzé u peguror*, ed. Sandro Oddo and Werner Forner, Triora, Pro Triora Editore, 188 pp. Marco Cuneo and Giulia Petracco Sicardi, *Vocabolario delle parlate liguri. Lessici speciali*, 2, II: *Mare, pesca e marineria*, Genoa, Consulta ligure, xxxii + 271 pp., completes the description of this particular semantic field. M. Cuneo, 'Tassonomia popolare dei pesci e tassonomia scientifica nei dialetti liguri', *Cortelazzo Vol.*, 303–18; P. Landini, 'Varietà sociolinguistiche nel lessico marinaresco di Camogli (GE)', *ib.*, 319–28.

EMILIA-ROMAGNA. Fabio Foresti, *Bibliografia dialettale dell'Emilia-Romagna e della Repubblica di San Marino (BDER)*, Bo, Compositori, xi + 198 pp., is another significant bibliographical compilation, in which a primary geographical classification (panregional, main towns and provinces) is in each case submitted to sub-division according to theme, a brief description or comment normally accompanying each entry.

LOMBARDY. P. Benincà, 'Note di dialettologia lombarda', *Della Casa Vol.*, 531–41, demonstrates eloquently the value of Italian dialect data for checking linguistic theories and indicating new avenues of research. G. Bonfadini, 'Le opposizioni vocaliche di durata nel dialetto di Novate Mezzola (So)', *ib.*, 583–604, is a descriptive and typological analysis of phonological oppositions of vocalic length in a rural West-Lombard variety. R. Broggini, 'Sul dialetto di Lodrino e della Riviera', *ASGM*, 1996, 35–36: 155–60. J. Kramer, 'Zur Bedeutung von alt lombardisch *lain* < LATĪNUS', *RomGG*, 3: 109–18.

TRENTINO ALTO ADIGE. G. Mastrelli Anzilotti, 'I dialetti dell'altipiano della Predaia', *AAA*, 90: 37–42, is a brief typological description.

VENETO. E. Tuttle, 'Profilo linguistico del veneto', in Renzi, *Linguistica*, 125–59, gives a rich and fascinating diachronic insight into the dialectal complexities of the area. C. Marcato, 'Per la storia del veneto lagunar orientale. A proposito della varietà di Caorle (dai rilievi di Ugo Pellis per l'ALI del 1926 e 1932), *Fest. Pfister*, III, 53–57. Lotte Zörner, *Il Pagotto, dialetto dell'Alpago: descrizione fonologica, storico-fonetica e morfologica*, Padua, Unipress, vi + 179 pp., offers a clear, detailed analysis, within a broadly structural and distributional framework, of a group of northern Veneto dialects belonging to the Belluno-Feltre-Treviso group; a useful syntactic commentary on a selection of oral texts is included. *I lavori dei contadini*, ed. Giovan Battista Pellegrini, Vicenza, Neri Pozza, 603 pp., is a beautifully produced and richly illustrated volume, documenting traditional agricultural and rural activities in the province of Vicenza and the associated dialect terminology, for which ample etymological and comparative details are furnished, for example C. Marcato, 'La fienagione' (319–32); P. Rizzolatti, 'La stalla e il governo degli animali' (333–84), and 'La lavorazione del latte e del malga' (385–447) and M. T. Vigolo, 'La pastorizia' (449–84). G. Marcato and A. A. Abdallah, 'A proposito di *madresia* - una presenza lessicale originale nel litorale veneziano', *Cortelazzo Vol.*, 357–67. P. G. Tiozzo, 'Dialetto e folklore a Chioggia', *ib.*, 451–61; G. Boscolo, 'Gli strumenti della pesca', *ib.*, 463–70; A. Padoan, 'Un monumento del dialetto chioggiotto "É descorso del pescaóre ciozoto"', *ib.*, 471–77, rescues from oblivion a 200-year-old text rich in lexical and grammatical as well as cultural detail. *Quaderno di bordo di Giovanni Manzini prete notaio e cancelliere (1471 -1484)*, ed. Lucia Greco, Venice, Comitato per la Pubblicazione delle Fonti relative alla Storia di Venezia, viii + 153 pp. D. Beria, 'Caratteri della lingua cancelleresca

e della cultura umanistica nella *Cronaca Veneziana* di Raffaino Care-
sini', *BALI*, 20: 101–14, analyses a late 14th-c. vernacular text.

CENTRAL DIALECTS. Concise overviews appear in Maiden, *Dialects:* L. Giannelli, 'Tuscany' (297–302); M.-J. Dalbera Stefanaggi,
'Corsica' (303–10). U. Vignuzzi, 'Lazio, Umbria and the Marche'
(311–20); R. Hastings, 'Abruzzo and Molise' (321–29). M. Loporcaro,
'L'esito dei nessi -GR-, -GN-: un mutamento di struttura sillabica nei
dialetti italiani centro-meridionali', *Atti* (Perugia), 337–74.

TUSCANY. A. Cresti, 'La risalita dei pronomi clitici con l'infinito',
QDLF, 7: 123–36, analyses clitic climbing constructions in San
Gimignano. Lexical topics are considered in E. Carpitelli, 'Continu-
atori di GLAREA in Lunigiana', *Studi Giacomelli*, 91–102, and
A. Nocentini, 'Tre zoonimi casentinesi', *ib.*, 313–22, which investi-
gates the origin of *ciúcola* 'lizard', *cuccusillo* 'type of coleoptera', *sbórro*
'wren' in the isolated northern Tuscan dialect zone of Casentino.
S. Montemagni and M. Paoli, 'Esplorazioni nel mondo dell'*ALT:*
itinerari alternativi', *ib.*, 280–300, highlight the rich pickings to be
gained from judicious consultations of the Atlante Lessicale Toscano.
G. Giacomelli, '"Riccio", "Cardo", "Peglia" nell'Atlante Lessicale
Toscano', pp. 601–09 of *Le vie della ricerca. Studi in onore di Francesco
Adorno*, ed. M. Serena Funghi, F, Olschki, 1996. E. Vassalle,
**Vocabolario del vernacolo viareggino: con accenni sulla pronuncia e scrittura
vernacole, appunti grammaticali e sintattici e costrutti particolari*, Viareggio,
Pezzini, 1996, 681 pp., and *Dizionario dei vocaboli di lingua corrente in
vernacolo viareggino: con accenni sulla pronuncia e scrittura vernacole, appunti
grammaticali e sintattici e costrutti particolari*, Viareggio, Pezzini, 1996,
240 pp. G. Malagoli, *Vocabolario pisano*, Sala Bolognese, Forni,
xix + 475 pp., elegantly reproduces the original edition of 1939.

UMBRIA AND LAZIO. A. Ciurnelli Fioroni, *Scritti linguistici: San
Martino in Campo nell'area urbana di Perugia*, Ellera Umbra, Era Nuova,
207 pp. F. Pompeo, 'Spazi vissuti: territorio e identità in una
comunità montana dell'Apennino laziale', *BALI*, 3, 20: 137–48.

SOUTHERN DIALECTS. An historical overview of southern dialects
appears in F. Fanciullo, *Fra oriente e occidente. Per una storia linguistica
dell'Italia meridionale*, Pisa, ETS, 1996, 171 pp. M. C. Strumbo, 'I
costrutti della frase dipendente in alcuni dialetti meridionali', *QDLF*,
7: 137–55, analyses sentential complementation in Salento, southern
Calabria, and north-eastern Sicily, dialects lacking infinitival clauses.

CAMPANIA. R. Sornicola, 'Campania', Maiden, *Dialects*, 330–37,
offers a useful conspectus. E. Radtke, 'Tortorella — eine
bislang unbekannte galloitalienische Sprachkolonie in Cilento', *ZRP*,
113: 82–108, shows that Tortorella (prov. Salerno) forms part of the
Gallo-Italian dialect zone of Policastro, offering substantial primary
data and critical evaluation of the present state and future prospects

of the dialect. Id., *I dialetti di Campania*, Ro, Il Calamo, 179 pp., helpfully brings together articles originally written in German by this distinguished scholar, the work being completed by a substantial bibliography and indices. A practical pocket dictionary of Neapolitan is provided by B. Amato and A. Pardo, *Dizionario napoletano: italiano-napoletano, napoletano-italiano*, Mi, Vallardi, vi + 262 pp. Neapolitan cant usage is studied by M. T. Greco, *I vagabondi, il gergo, i posteggiatori: dizionario napoletano della parlèsia*, Na, ESI, 162 pp. M. Guarino Amato and A. Nesi, 'La pesca alle costardelle a Forio d'Ischia', *Cortelazzo Vol.*, 121–30, presents the practice and lexicon of saury pike fishing.

BASILICATA AND CALABRIA. Two contributions to Maiden, *Dialects* provide introductory surveys, F. Fanciullo, 'Basilicata' (349–54), and J. Trumper, 'Calabria and southern Basilicata' (355–64). P. Soria-nello, 'Indici fonetici delle occlusive sorde nel cosentino', *RID*, 20, 1996: 123–59, uses instrumental data to demonstrate the presence of aspiration in onset voiceless plosives of the Cosenza dialect when they appear postconsonantally. The characteristics and historical background of the vocalism found in the border zone between Basilicata and Calabria are analysed by L. M. Savoia, 'Il vocalismo a tre gradi dell'area calabro-lucana', *Studi Giacomelli*, 363–70. P. A. Carè, 'La pesca del pesce spada e del tonno in Calabria', *Cortelazzo Vol.*, 157–72, explores the lexicon associated with local fishing practices. M. Lopor-caro et al., 'Micro- e macrofenomeni di centralizzazione vocalica nella variazione diafasica: rilevanza dei dati acustici per il quadro dialettologico del calabrese', pp. 157–75 of *Fonetica e fonologia degli stili dell'italiano parlato. Atti delle sette giornate di studio del Gruppo di Fonetica Sperimentale (A.I.A.)*, ed. F. Cutugno, Na, Collana Atti A.I.A., 1966.

PUGLIA AND SALENTO. M. Loporcaro, 'Puglia and Salento', Maiden, *Dialects*, 338–48, presents a helpful outline of dialectal patterns. The second volume of P. Ricciardelli, **La parlata di Torremaggiore*, Foggia, Leone, 1995, 277 pp., contains proverbs. M. Grimaldi, 'Salento meridionale e metafonia: una questione da riaprire', *QDLF*, 7:69–108, finds evidence in this archaic, conservat-ive area of widespread metaphony of Ĕ and Ŏ, similar to Sardinian. R. Coluccia and M. Aprile, 'Lessico quotidiano e cultura materiale in inventari pugliesi del secondo Quattrocento', *Fest. Pfister*, I, 241–63.

SICILY. A clear introductory overview appears in G. Ruffino, 'Sicily', Maiden, *Dialects*, 365–75. D'Agostino, *Aspetti*, includes D. Bentley, 'Modalità e futuro nel siciliano antico e moderno' (49–66), which gives the lie to traditional views about the expression of the future in Sicilian; R. Sornicola, 'Tra tipologia e storia: i pronomi soggetto e le colonie gallo-italiche' (67–84); M. Mazzoleni, 'Inversioni morfosintattiche nei costrutti condizionali lombardo-siculi' (85–96). V. Mortillaro, *Nuovo dizionario siciliano-italiano*, Sala

Bolognese, Forni, 1220 pp., is a handsome facsimile version of the massively detailed edition of 1876–81. The fourth volume has appeared of the extensive *Vocabolario siciliano*, ed. G. Tropea, Catania, CSFLS, xxx + 886 pp. Of more modest proportions is the anonymous *Vocabolario siciliano-italiano*, n. pl., Martin, 1996, 184 pp. Rosario Zappalà, *L'io visto dagli altri: i soprannomi in un paese dell'Etna*, Soveria Mannelli, Rubbettino, 182 pp., investigates the origins and meanings of nicknames used in Sant'Alfio near Catania. A. Michel, *Vocabolario critico degli ispanismi siciliani*, Palermo, CSFLS, 1996, 542 pp. G. Petrolini, 'Ittionomi siciliani nei *Banchetti* (1684) di Carlo Nascia', *Cortelazzo Vol.*, 173–81, presents a substantial repertoire of dialectal marine lexicon from Palermo assembled by N., who was a cook.

11. ITALIAN ABROAD

A lucid outline of the fortunes of Italian dialects carried outside Italy through emigration is found in H. W. Haller, 'The dialects abroad', Maiden, *Dialects*, 401–11. Rich in materials on the cultural diffusion and influence of Italian in Europe is the volume dedicated to the memory of Gianfranco Folena, *Italiano: lingua di cultura europea*, ed. H. Stammerjohann, Tübingen, Narr, 395 pp., which contains D. Goldin Folena, 'Seguendo Da Ponte: l'italiano lingua dei teatri musicali europei' (19–36); R. Simon, 'Geopolitica delle lingue tra Cesarotti e Leopardi' (37–48); S. Schwarze, 'Die italienische Sprache als Mitglied einer *gran famiglia europea*' (49–89); R. Bernecker, 'Italienisch in Paris: Giosafate Biagiolis *Grammaire italienne élémentaire et raisonnée* (1805)' (91–106); M. Lieber, 'L'italiano alla corte di Augusto il Forte' (107–31); F. Marri, 'Un caso di italiano nel Settecento e i suoi riflessi sulla cultura europea: la lingua del *Cristianesimo* di L. A. Muratori dall'originale alla traduzione tedesca' (133–84), which complements Id.,'Un po' di Germania nell'Italia del Settecento', *Baum Vol.*, 255–67, where lexical novelties in the correspondence of Gherardi with Muratori on Germanic topics are examined; M. Stegu, 'Italianismen und Pseudoitalianismen im Deutschen (unter besonderer Berücksichtigung des österreichischen Sprachgebrauchs' (185–203); J. Albrecht, 'Italienische Grammatikographie im Deutschland des 18. und in der ersten Hälfte des 19. Jahrhunderts' (205–21); K. Bergdolt, 'Deutsch-italienische Wissenschaftsbeziehungen und das Sprachenproblem im 19. Jahrhundert' (223–36); J. Lindon, 'L'italiano in Albione: la dimensione universitaria 1724–1903' (237–46); V. Lo Cascio, 'L'italiano nel secolo d'oro olandese' (247–81); A. Sanesi, 'Tracce nostrane in Bellman, poeta svedese settecentesco' (283–98); G. Skytte, 'L'immagine dell'italiano attraverso gli esempi della grammaticografia danese' (299–305); S. Stati,

'Gli italianismi nella lingua romena' (307–11); F. Brugnolo, '"Questa è lingua di cui si vanta Amore'. Per una storia degli usi letterari eteroglotti dell'italiano' (313–36); M. Carrera Díaz, 'Le ragioni della lingua: le prime grammatiche italiani per ispanofoni' (337–45); P. Silvestri, 'L'*Arte muy curiosa por la cual se enseña muy de rayz el entender, y hablar de la Lengua Italiana* di Francisco Trenado de Ayllón (1569)' (347–61); T. Giermak-Zielinsza, 'Les mots d'origine italienne en polonais contemporain' (363–73); Z. Fábián, 'La cultura italiana e l'insegnamento dell'italiano in Ungheria' (375–95). L. Bray, 'Lexicographie et néologie au XVIIe siècle. Le cas des italianismes néologiques dans la première édition du dictionnaire de l'Académie française', *TLP*, 35–36:149–64. A. L. Lepschy and G. Lepschy, 'From *antipasto* to *zabaglione*: italianisms in the *Concise Oxford Dictionary*', *Villari Vol.*, 242–59, discusses the nature of the italianisms listed in the *COD* (1995 edn), classifying them according to date of borrowing and semantic area. U. Gorini, *Storia dei manuali per l'apprendimento dell'italiano in Germania (1500–1950)*, Frankfurt, Lang, viii + 431 pp., reviews over 300 works published in Germany, analysing in detail the content and approach of 21 of these. D. Gheno, 'Influsso dialettale italiano in ungherese', *Studi Giacomelli*, 148–52. A. M. Raffo, 'Gli italianismi delle *bugarstice*', *ib.*, 355–62. **Scuola, lingua e cultura nell'emigrazione italiana all'estero: bibliografia generale 1970–95*, ed. G. Tassello and M. Vedovelli, Ro, Centro Studi Emigrazione, 127 pp. H. Stammerjohann, 'L'immagine della lingua italiana in Europa', Renzi, *Linguistica*, 27–51, reviews varying perceptions of the Italian language from the 16th c. onward. M. Mormile and R. Matteucci, *Le grammatiche italiane in Gran Bretagna: profilo storico, secoli XVI, XVII, XVIII*, Lecce, Argo, 218 pp. C. Bettoni and A. Rubino, **Emigrazione e comportamento linguistico. Un'indagine sul trilinguismo dei siciliani e dei veneti in Australia*, Galatina, Congedo, 1996, 226 pp.

12. SARDINIAN

M. A. Jones, 'Sardinia', Maiden, *Dialects,* 376–84, offers a clear outline of the phonology, morphology, and syntax of indigenous Sardinian varieties. L. Molinu, 'L'alternance /k/ — [?] dans les parlers de la "Barbagia d'Ollolai", une approche géophonologique non-linéaire', *Géolinguistique*, 7:133–57. **Il Condaghe di San Pietro di Silki, testo logudorese inedito dei secoli 11–13*, ed. Ignazio Delogu, Sassari, Dessì, 311 pp. *Leggende e tradizioni di Sardegna*, ed. Gino Bottiglioni, Ro, Meltemi, iv + 159 pp., appears as a facsimile reprint. A. Dettori, 'Pesce e mercati del pesce nella documentazione sarda medioevale', *Cortelazzo Vol.*, 219–30. G. Mondardini, 'Nomi, luoghi del mare e mutamento fra i pescatori del nord Sardegna', *ib.*, 291–301. M. Lörin-czi, 'Falsi, flauti, fiabe e fenicotteri, aerofoni e volatili venuti dal mare nella tradizione di Sardegna', *ib.*, 437–47. E. Blasco Ferrer, 'Contri-buti alla conoscenza dell'italianizzazione in Sardegna nel tardo Settecento e nell'Ottocento', *Fest. Pfister*, III, 31–52.

DUECENTO AND TRECENTO 1
DANTE
POSTPONED

DUECENTO AND TRECENTO II
(EXCLUDING DANTE)

By JOAN HALL, *Cambridge*

1. GENERAL

Some useful background studies this year have focused on language and education. R. Coluccia, 'La situazione linguistica dell'Italia meridionale al tempo di Federico II', *MedRom*, 20, 1996:378–411, surveys the southern dialects and the various influences affecting them — a field hitherto little studied. R. Black, 'The vernacular and the teaching of Latin in thirteenth and fourteenth-century Italy', *SM*, 37:703–51, is a historical-linguistic study covering organization and pedagogical methods, authors, and texts studied, and the use of the vernacular in teaching. *Studio e scuola in Arezzo durante il Medioevo e il Rinascimento. I documenti d'archivio fino al 1530*, ed. R. Black, Arezzo, Accademia Petrarca di Lettere Arti e Scienze, 1996, 874 pp., provides a rich fund of documents a few of which go back to the 14th c., together with a 78-page introduction on the history of educational institutions in Arezzo (mostly post 1384).

J. Lacroix, 'Essai d'interprétation de l'archétype hiérosolymitain dans la pensée médiévale italienne (XIIᵉ–XIVᵉ siècles)', Berriot-Salvadore, *Jerusalem*, 153–79, argues that in medieval Italian literature the concept of Jerusalem evolved into a myth whereby, for lay and religious poets and prose writers, it represented the 'pendant' of Rome as the holy city. P. Evangelisti, 'Per uno studio della testualità politica francescana tra XIII e XV secolo. Autori e tipologia delle fonti', *SM*, 37:541–623, points out that Franciscan texts contributed much to the development of Italian political language (which should not be seen as independent of religious discourse). A survey of the historiography and range of this material, with a long section on Sicilian Franciscanism, is followed by an examination of the lexis and the ethical-political models in these texts.

F. Suitner, 'Alle origini della lauda', *GSLI*, 193, 1996:321–47, surveys the varieties of religious poetry (sung, chanted, or recited) from the early 13th century. The author traces the development of the form, motifs, and language of the *lauda* and shows the close metrical relationship between it and the *ballata*, and the links between prayer, flagellation, and dance. Elena Landoni, *La grammatica come storia della poesia. Un nuovo disegno storiografico per la letteratura italiana dalle origini attaverso grammatica, retorica e semantica*, Ro, Bulzoni, 370 pp., discusses conceptions of poetic language, syntax as rhetorical strategy, the evolution of lyric vocabulary, and rhetoric as organization of meaning — all with reference to the Sicilians, Iacopone, Guittone d'Arezzo, Dante, and Cecco Angiolieri. Stefano Carrai, *La lirica toscana del Duecento. Cortesi, guittoniani, stilnovisti*, Bari, Laterza, 632 pp.; E. Sanguineti, *'Elementi poetici della scuola siciliana', *Omaggio Federico II*, 83–97; I. Li Vigni, *'Il cavaliere di carta: la figura del cavaliere e l'ideologia cavalleresca in letteratura', *ib.*, 98–111; Corinna Desole, *Repertorio ragionato dei personaggi citati nei principali cantari cavallereschi italiani*, Alessandria, Orso, 1995. G. Allaire, 'The use of owners' jingles in Italian vernacular manuscripts', *Viator*, 27, 1996:171–87, presents colophons written in vernacular MSS dating from the late 13th c., often rhymed, many with admonitions to return borrowed books promptly and to keep them away from lamps and children.

2. BOCCACCIO

R. Hollander, *Boccaccio's Dante and the Shaping Force of Satire*, Ann Arbor, Michigan U.P., 226 pp., contains six essays from the past 15 years, dealing with B.'s Dantean borrowings and his desire to shape his work as satire (prominently indebted to Ovid's early amatory works). The appendix, previously unpublished, is a *hapax legomenon* comparing the *Decameron* with Dante's *Commedia*. V. Kapp, *'Exempelerzählung und Amstandslehre bei Guazzo: zur Bedeutung der Exempla nach Boccaccio', Engler, *Exempla*, 97–114. Douglas Biow, *Mirabile dictu: Representations of the Marvelous in Medieval and Renaissance Epic*, Ann Arbor, Michigan U.P., 1995, 220 pp., argues in ch. 3, 'The value of marvels', that unlike Dante, B. 'does not aim to shape or understand the universe through the use of marvels. His distinctive aim is to investigate the social value of marvels in a world where processes of exchange (both linguistic and financial) are constantly taking place'. The discussion centres mainly on the *Decameron*, but also deals with the *Filocolo*.

T. Pisanti, 'Boccaccio in Inghilterra tra Medioevo e Rinascimento', Pisanti, *L'un lito e l'altro*, 171–82, begins with the question of how much Chaucer knew of B.'s works, examining several hypotheses: that B. was well known but considered too popular to mention; that Chaucer knew the works but not the author's name (as works were often circulated anonymously); that Chaucer thought B.'s works were written by 'maister Petrak'. Later sections deal with John Lydgate (who translated the French translation of *De casibus)*, and several 16th-c. writers. N. S. Thompson, *Chaucer, Boccaccio, and the Debate of Love. A comparative study of 'The Decameron' and 'The Canterbury Tales'*, Oxford, Clarendon, 1996, 354 pp., offers a thoughtful and broadly based examination of the two narrative collections (each taken as a whole), comparing their moral and literary preoccupations and internal dynamics. The author wisely sidesteps the vexed question of whether Chaucer knew the *Decameron*, though the affirmative view is strongly supported. The book is remarkable for its comprehensive mastery of both works and for the felicity of its presentation. G. Mazzacurati, *All'ombra di Dioneo. Tipologie e percorsi della novella da Boccaccio a Bandello*, F, La Nuova Italia, 1996, xviii + 218 pp., includes six previously published essays, three on B. (characterization, structure, the *novella* of Alatiel), and three on the later development of the *novella*.

K. L. Selig, 'Boccaccio's *Decameron* and "natural history" and compendia: some observations', *Leube Vol.*, 409–16, considers the 'encyclopedic' aspect of the *Decameron:* the vast range of experience, history, folklore, magic, and herbalism, and the contemporary knowledge expounded in popular 'compendia' such as Pliny's *Natural History*. Jill M. Ricketts, *Visualizing Boccaccio. Studies on Illustrations of 'The Decameron' from Giotto to Pasolini*, CUP, x + 214 pp., is an ambitious, perhaps rather forced, attempt to combine art-historical and literary criticism in a feminist study of the *Decameron*, with particular reference to the *novelle* of Griselda, Tancredi, and Nastagio, and two chapters on Pasolini's film of the *Decameron*. J. Levenstein, 'Out of bounds: passion and the plague in Boccaccio's *Decameron*', *Italica*, 73, 1996:313–35, develops an interesting analogy between the plague described in the Introduction and the sexual passion of love in Day 4 — the latter counteracted (successfully) by the *onestà* of the *brigata*. E. Urgnani, 'Censura e tolleranza religiosa nel *Decameron* da una prospettiva bachtiniana', *ItQ*, 33:5–16, argues that the comic perspective provides a secular ideological basis for the work, detached from dogmatic ecclesiastical schemes. In the discussion, focused on Days 1, 2, and 3 and the introduction to Day 4, the author maintains that for B., as for Bakhtin, the body represents the 'low' but fundamental material world; the nearness of death induces a critical freedom and reassessment of dogmas.

For M. Picone, 'Les avatars du récit-cadre du *Décaméron*', *REI*, 42, 1996:163–72, the frame-tale has less to do with the ten *giovani* than with the development of narrative in that historical moment, setting the *novella* against the *exemplum* or *fabliau:* B.'s aim was less to reconstruct the moral and social norms destroyed by the plague than to reconstruct the literary and artistic order destroyed by the *fabulatores*, whom he considered usurpers of *l'arte della parola*. This article studies the ways in which B.'s immediate followers responded to the *Decameron*, which they already took as a model of a 'book' as distinct from a mere collection of *novelle*. The discussion covers the

frame-tales of Ser Giovanni's *Pecorone,* Sercambi's *Novelle,* and Sacchetti's *Trecentonovelle.* V. Branca, 'Tenerezza affettiva e ironia ana-
grammatica nell'onomastica del *Decameron.* Conversazione per lettera
con Antonio', *D'Andrea Vol.,* 163–70, is an informal note on possible
interpretations of B.'s choice of names in the *Decameron,* in particular
Brunetta (VI, 4), Alatiel (II, 7) and Torello (X, 9) — some of them
based on anagrams. W. Krömer, *'L'eco del sistema di avantesti e
retrotesti del *Decameron* nelle raccolte di novelle del Cinquecento',
Peron, *Strategie,* 183–91.

Della Terza, *Strutture poetiche,* includes two 'Letture del *Decameron'.*
The first, '"Navis Fragium": la catastrofe come prolessi o conclusione
epifanica dell'evento narrato. Il naufragio da Properzio a Boccaccio'
(113–34), begins with a general discussion of the narrative uses of the
shipwreck theme, then (121–34) concentrates on its functions in the
novelle of Landolfo Rufolo (II, 7), Alatiel (II, 7), Gostanza (V, 2),
Gerbino (IV, 4), and Torello (X, 9); the second, 'Il *Decameron* e la
favola comica di Calandrino' (135–50), discusses the four *novelle* in
which Calandrino appears, in terms of his character and that of his
Florentine cronies, and the nature of the *beffa.*

E. Peters, 'Henry II of Cyprus, "Rex Inutilis" — Boccaccio and
the history of narrative art in thirteenth-century vernacular prose: a
footnote to *Decameron* I, 9', *Speculum,* 72:763–75, examines the story
of the 'gentil donna di Guascogna' in relation to its sources and
analogues and to B.'s political connections and interests. L. Rossi, 'I
tre "gravi accidenti" della *novella* di Andreuccio da Perugia (*Dec.* V, 2
[sic])', *StCrit,* 11:385–400, links the novella with the *fabliau* 'Boivin de
Provins' and (especially) with Apuleius (*Golden Ass* II, 2). M. Bendinelli
Predelli, 'Lettura in filigrana della novella di Zinevra (*Decameron* II,
9)', *D'Andrea Vol.,* 171–88, concerns the *novella*'s relationship with
possible oral and written sources, illustrating B.'s capacity to transform old material and give it new life. P. M. Forni, 'Boccaccio tra
Dante e Cino', *QI,* 16, 1995:179–95, identifies several sources for the
novella of Zima (III, 5), including Andreas Capellanus and Dante,
but most prominently Cino da Pistoia's sonnet 'Ora che rise lo spirito
mio' which B. had parodied earlier in the *Filostrato.* The critic
comments on the complex nature of B.'s parody and his relationship
with other authors. A. M. Babbi, 'L'"industria" femminile: dalla figlia
del visir alla contessa d'Artois', *Atti* (Naples), places the *novella* of
Giletta di Narbona (*Dec.* III, 9) midway in a narrative tradition
leading from an oral Tatar source to the 15th-c. *Roman du Comte
d'Artois.* C. März, *'Die Destille des Hans Sachs. Boccaccios Falkenno-
velle im Meisterlied', *Poetica,* 27:254–72; A. Bisanti, *'Una probabile
fonte della novella di Chichibio', *EL,* 22.2:47–58.

Studi sul Boccaccio, 24, includes: V. Branca and V. Zaccaria, 'Un altro codice del *De mulieribus claris* del Boccaccio' (3–6); D. Drusi, 'La *Lettera intorno a' manoscritti antichi* di Vincenzo Borghini e un suo nuovo reperto testuale in un codicetto per la rassettatura del *Decameron* del 1573' (7–58); P. Rafti, '"Lumina dictionum". Interpunzione e prosa in Giovanni Boccaccio' (59–122); G. D'Agostino, 'Le ballate del *Decameron:* note integrative di analisi metrica e stilistica' (123–80); B. Porcelli, 'Nomi in coppia nel *Decameron'* (181–92); V. Branca, 'L'Atteone del Boccaccio fra allegoria cristiana, evemerismo trasfigurante, narrativa esemplare, visualizzazione rinascimentale' (193–208); S. Contarini, 'La voce di Guido Cavalcanti: Jolles interprete di *Decameron* VI, 9' (209–17); A. Jolles, 'La facezia di Guido Cavalcanti' (218–30); R. Ferreri, 'Ciacco, Biondello e Martellino' (231–50); G. Padoan, 'Filologia e filologismo. A proposito dell'edizione del *Corbaccio'* (251–60); and A. Andreoli, 'Boccaccio fra le carte di un apprendista filologo: D'Annunzio e il "falso antico"' (261–82).

M. Sannelli, 'Fenomenologia di amore e stile lirico nella *Teseida',* *MedRom,* 20, 1996:437–45, finds the most decisive structural characteristic of the work in 'la contaminazione della sostanza epica con l'io e con l'eros'. W. C. Maisch, 'Boccaccio's *Teseida.* The breakdown of difference and ritual sacrifice', *AnI,* 15:85–98, defines the *Teseida* as Teseo's struggle to preserve the coherence of society against forces of 'nondifferentiation', or 'confusion of identity'; his weapons — reason, logic, language, and law — are finally ineffective without the 'ultimate referentiality' of Christianity. C. Carpinato, **Altre osservazioni sulla tradizione greca della *Teseida',* *Atti* (Naples), 173–89.

V. Baldassari, '"Adfluit incautis insidiosus amor": la precettistica ovidiana nel *Filostrato* di Boccaccio', *ib.,* 20–24, aims to bring out the importance of Ovid for the *Filostrato,* especially B.'s use of the *Heroides* as a model for some parts of the work. M. A. Calabrese, 'Feminism and the packaging of Boccaccio's *Fiammetta',* *Italica,* 74:20–42, contests the view of M. Causa-Steindler, who, in her commentary on a new translation, defines Fiammetta as a 'proto-feminist' and sees the book as a 'milestone in feminist literature'. Calabrese argues that in fact the 'myth of female falsehood makes it, rather, antifeminist'. With a vigorously contemporary approach, the writer rejects the 'literary matrix', explores the Ovidian context, and suggests 'ways of responding to the sexual poetics of the *Fiammetta* that respect both medieval literary history and contemporary critical imperatives'. M. Veglia, 'Ultimo viene il corvo: appunti sul *Corbaccio',* *Italianistica,* 25, 1996:265–80, argues that the title holds the key to the theme of the book, and its significance must have been clear to contemporaries. Boccaccio, the protagonist of the *Corbaccio* (the name rhymes and is almost an anagram), repents and repudiates carnal love, which was traditionally represented by bird images. P. Budra, '"Exemplify my frailty": representing English women in De Casibus tragedy', *PQ,* 74:359–72, defining 'De Casibus tragedy' as 'non-dramatic tales of the falls of great men and women written in imitation of B's *De casibus virorum illustrium,* studies its attitudes to English women.

F. S. Stych, *Boccaccio in English: A Bibliography of Editions, Adaptations and Criticism,* Westport CT, Greenwood, 1995, xix + 254 pp., is extensive and fully annotated, covering printed works from the 16th c. to the early 1990s, and listing reviews of the works cited.

3. PETRARCH

Petrarca e la cultura europea, ed. Luisa Rotondi Secchi Tarugi, Mi, Nuovi Orizzonti, 374 pp., includes: P. O. Kristeller, 'Il Petrarca nella storia degli studi' (7–30), dealing with P.'s treatment, in various works, of each of the five *Studia Humanitatis;* H. D. Jocelyn, 'Petrarch and classical drama' (31–54); U. Rombach, 'Francesco Petrarca ed Ercole al bivio' (55–70), arguing that Hercules' choice stands for P.'s moral choice of the contemplative over the active life; I. Rowland, 'Il Petrarca lettore di Vitruvio' (71–82); B. Lavillatte, 'Petrarca fra il nulla e l'essere' (83–94); J. L. Charlet, 'La beauté sublimée en lumière: le coup de foudre (Petrarque, *Africa* 5, 1–76)' (95–110); J. Petrie, 'Anniversario e memoria nei *Rerum vulgarium fragmenta*' (111–20); G. Ponte, 'I consigli politici del Petrarca a Francesco da Carrara (*Sen.* XIV, 1) (121–28); A. Ughetto, 'Le paysage dans les *Rime* de Petrarque entre convention et réalité' (129–38); E. Haywood, '"Inter urinas liber factus est". Il commento dell'Ilicino ai *Trionfi* del Petrarca' (139–60); L. Patetta, 'Petrarca e l'architettura delle città italiane' (161–80); S. Benassi, 'La vertigine del sublime: moralità della poesia e razionalità della morale in Petrarca' (181–202); G. Dell'Anna, 'Il Petrarca e la medicina' (203–22); L. Sozzi, 'Presenza del Petrarca nella letteratura francese' (243–62); J.-C. Margolin, 'De la *Vita solitaria* de Pétrarque à l'*Epistola de vita solitaria* de Bovelles: fonds communs de la rhétorique chrétienne' (263–90); H. Heintze, '*As Petrarchicus Tristium* das is ein Dutzend trawriger Lieder, cioè una dozzina di canti tristi' (291–98); E. Bigi, 'Una stroncatura preromantica del Petrarca' (299–310); G. Borri, 'Petrarca e Ungaretti' (311–26); M. Rivella, 'Il motivo dell'usingolo nei sonetti X e CCXI dei *Rerum vulgarum fragmenta* di Petrarca. Alcune riflessioni attinenti alla relazione triangolare fra la poesia classica, la poesia occitanica e la poesia italiana del Trecento' (327–40); L. Secchi Tarugi, 'Petrarca e l'umanesimo' (341–50). Giuseppe Billanovich, *Petrarca e il primo umanesimo,* Padua, Antenore, 1996, 632 pp., assembles 25 of the author's published essays on the poet.

B. D. Schildgen, 'Petrarch: a restless humanist's dialogue with Christian antiquity', *RStI*, 14.2, 1996: 1–19, defines P. as a continuer of the model of life expounded by the Latin Fathers, though he did not fully adopt that model. A. Bolland, 'Art and humanism in early Renaissance Padua: Cennini, Vergerio and Petrarch on imitation', *RQ*, 49:469–85, contains a brief discussion on P's theories of imitation and his assimilation of the arts of poetry and painting.

Maurizio Vitale, *La lingua del Canzoniere ('Rerum Vulgarium Fragmenta') di Francesco Petrarca*, Padua, Antenore, 1996, lv + 567 pp., presents an exhaustive linguistic analysis of the *Canzoniere*, covering phonetic elements, morphology, syntax, and lexis. Part III, 'La *actio* poetica', discusses P.'s linguistic education, his ideas about poetic language, and the origins and derivations of his linguistic forms. F. Brunori, 'Il mito ovidiano di Orfeo ed Euridice nel *Canzoniere* di Petrarca', *RoQ*, 44:245–54, argues that P.'s memory of the Orpheus myth in Books 10 and 11 of the *Metamorphoses* influenced his diction in the first part of the so-called 'rime in morte'. R. Caputo, 'Versi di Silio e rime di Petrarca (contributo all'ipotesi di un "confronto impossibile")', *D'Andrea Vol.*, 141–61, examines P.'s undeclared and ambiguous interaction with the *Punica* of Silius Italicus. C. F. Blanco-Valdés, *'Significado y función de la "fiera" en *Il Canzoniere* de Francisco Petrarca', *Actas* (Granada) 1, 333–46.

E. Fenzi, 'Note petrarchesche: *RVF* XXVI, "Movesi il vecchierel"', *Italianistica*, 25, 1996:43–62, explores the significance of the basic simile and the relationship between Laura and the "donna" whose "forma vera" the poet seeks. The article includes a critical survey of earlier commentators on the subject, especially De Sanctis, and explores the implications of the motif in the *Dolce Stil Novo*, in Dante and in other poems of the *RVF*. N. Tonelli, 'Noterella sulla pastoralità di Petrarca: Giraut de Bornelh in *RVF* CCXLV, 2', *ib.*, 1996:261–64, links P.'s poem with the *pastourelle* tradition; the sequence of conventional phases in the approach to the lady is derailed by Laura who gestures towards the future. B. D. Schildgen, *'Overcoming Augustinian dichotomies in defence of the laurel in canzoni 359 and 360 of the *Rime sparse*', *MLN*, 111, 1996:149–63; K. Stierle, *'Francesco Petrarca, Rime 312', *Italienisch*, 33, 1995:74.

D. Goldin Folena, '*Frons salutationis epistolaris:* Abelardo, Eloisa, Petrarca e la polimorfia del *Titulus*', *D'Andrea Vol.*, 41–60, speaks of P.'s epistles in relation to the letters of Abelard and Héloïse, and of the handling and significance of the introductory *salutatio* also in the *Canzoniere*. J. Pfeiffer, *'Petrarca und der Mont Ventoux (zu *Familiares IV, I*)', *GRM*, 47:1–24, places P. in the tradition of Augustinian theology, finding the interest of the epistle more in its literary aspect than in the content. On the same letter, J. Theisen, *'Sebastien Brant,

Dr. Griff und Petrarch auf dem Mont Ventoux. Das Titelblatt als Verstandnisvorgabe des *Narrenschiffs'*, *Euphorion*, 90, 1996:62–75. U. Kuhne, 'Brieftheoretisches in mittelalterlichen Briefen', *RF*, 109:1–23, devotes a few pages to Petrarch's *Epistolae familiares*. C. Pulsoni, 'Per la descrizione d'una postilla petrarchesca', *Anticomoderno*, 1995:175–78, argues that a note evidently written by P. in the margin of the copy of the *Commedia* given him by Boccaccio (MS Vaticano Latino 3199) has to do with the corruption of the church as discussed by Dante elsewhere in the work. **'Le varie fila'. Studi di letteratura italiana in onore di Emilio Bigi*, ed. F. Danelon, H. Grosset, and C. Zampese, Mi, Principato, 352 pp., includes: M. Santagata, 'Pellegrine, forosette e pastorelle: per un madrigale di Petrarca *(RVF* 54)'; G. Crevatin, 'In margine a Petrarca, *Triumphus Fame* Ia 30: il "mal vedere" di Pompeo'. L. C. Rossi, 'Presenze di Petrarca in commenti danteschi fra tre e quattrocento', *Aevum*, 70, 1996:441–76, surveys and quotes P.'s comments on Dante from various 14th- and 15th-c. sources.

4. Other Authors

Maria Pia Alberzoni et al., *Francesco d'Assisi ed il primo secolo di storia francescana*, T, Einaudi, xvi + 456 pp., covers various aspects of Franciscan history; of particular interest in the context of modern language studies are G. Miccioli, 'Gli scritti di Francesco' (35–70), E. Princivalli, 'Un santo da leggere: Francesco d'Assisi nel percorso delle fonti agiografiche' (71–116), E. Menestò, 'La "questione francescana" come problema filologica' (117–44), and A. Bartoli Langeli, 'I libri dei frati. La cultura scritta dell'Ordine dei Minori' (283–306). Cristiana Garzena, *Terra fidelis manet: humilitas e servitium nel 'Cantico di Frate Sole'*, F, Olschki, 178 pp., after a survey of criticism on the *cantico*, focuses on the ninth *versetto* which speaks of 'nostre matre Terra, la quale ne sostenta e governa . . .', exploring the history of the concept and role of 'mother earth' in pagan and Christian texts. Franco Mancini, *Il tempo della gioia. Un'interpretazione del 'Laudario di Cortona' con appendice e note esigetiche*, Ro, Izzi, 1996, 181 pp., studies the 'laudario cortese' in relation to the secular literature of the period; the aim is to place the *Laudario* within the Franciscan spiritual movement. P. Lachance, '"Celle qui ment" (The one who lies): Angela of Foligno', *SM*, 36, 1995:945–55, deals with Angela's *Libro* and a play written about her by Bérangère Bonvoisin and Philippe Clévenot (1984).

C. Delcorno, 'Censimento dei manoscritti delle *Vite dei Santi Padri* di Domenico Cavalca. Le biblioteche straniere', *LettI*, 49:93–112 and 427–70, covers France and Germany in Part I and Britain, Spain, the U.S.A., and Hungary in Part II. C. Beretta, 'Il *De ortu et tempore "Antichristi"* di Adso di Montier-en-Der e l'"istoria dello pseudo-Uguccione"', *MedRom*, 20:170–97, deals with 13th-c. MSS based on Adso's 10th-c. Latin treatise on the Antichrist, in particular the so-called *storia* attributed by Ezio Levi to Uguccione da Lodi. The author criticizes Levi's analysis and shows how the Latin text was used by the vernacular poet as a sermon to scare people away from sin. Enzo Colonna, *Le poesie di Liutprando di Cremona. Commento tra testo e contesto*, Bari, Edipuglia, 1996, 264 pp., concerns verse passages inserted in the medieval Latin historical writings of the 10th-c. bishop and diplomat Liutprando.

K. Brownlee, 'The practice of cultural authority: Italian responses to the French cultural dominance in *Il Tesoretto, Il Fiore*, and the *Commedia*', *FMLS*, 33:258–69, studies the status accorded to the French language in these three works, considering the function of the *Roman de la Rose* as a model, especially the *locus amoenus* as a setting and the God of Love as an authority figure. S. Carrai, 'Sulla prima traduzione metrica dal francese', *RLettI*, 13:9–23, looks at an anonymous 13th-c. rhymed sermon, explaining the background of its Tuscan translation. F. Bruni, 'Tra francese e fiorentino nella Sicilia del Trecento: postilla al *Libru di li vitii et di li virtuti*', *MedRom*, 20:204–08, sketches the relationship between the *Libru* (composed 1360–70 in the Benedictine monastery of San Martino delle Scale) and Zucchero Bencivenni's Florentine version of *Somme le Roi*. Bencivenni also produced a Florentine version of the *Libru*, which in various ways influenced the history of translations, *volgarizzamenti*, etc. F. Minetti, 'Autore o protagonista il Sordello non d'Oc d'una "nouvelle acquisition" cremonese?', *MedRom*, 20:56–74, examines eight poems edited by G. Dotti and attributed to Sordello. The critic suggests a different order from that of Dotti, and argues they are not by but about Sordello.

Simonetta Bianchini, *Cielo d'Alcamo e il suo contrasto. Intertestualità romanze nella scuola poetica siciliana*, Soveria Mannelli, Rubbettino, 1996, 222 pp., contains a substantial introduction on Old French literature and the Sicilian School, then essays on Cielo d'Alcamo in relation to Provençal literature (finding the origin of the sonnet not in the *canzone* but in the *tenzone)*, to Giacomo da Lentini and the Sicilian School (with a note on Dante's negative view of Cielo), and to the anonymous misogynistic 13th-c. *Proverbia quae dicuntur super natura foeminarum*. Cielo, like the *anonimo*, is seen as basically a moralist and severe social critic; his *contrasto* in that light becomes 'un'amara polemica' directed against the Sicilian courtly poets. A. Valori, 'La spera del canto: la soggettività letteraria nella scuola poetica siciliana', *CLett*, 25:3–29, notes that moments of subjectivity and originality are rare in the uniform corpus of the Sicilian School. While this poetry is often dismissed as lacking originality, the author argues that its originality lies precisely in its abstract and rarefied quality, breaking all links with real life. It represents the effort of one social group to separate poetic diction, by successive exclusions, from the language of everyday life: to declare the autonomy, nobility, and self-sufficiency of poetry. R. Schrott, *'Giacomo da Lentino, oder Von der Erfindung des Sonnetts und seiner Logik', *Akzente*, 6, 1996:528–61.

M. L. Ardizzone, 'Guido Guinizelli's "Al cor gentil": a notary in search of written laws', *MP*, 94:455–74, argues that it is 'Guinizelli's cosmological process in its guise of a physical process of love, together with the notion of intelligences as movers moved by God as light, that gives a new role to poetry'. J. Bartuschat, 'Visage et fonctions de la Philosophie dans l'allégorie de Bono Giamboni', *REI*, 43:5–26, considers the central role of the figure of Philosophy in the *Libro de' vizî e delle virtudi*. S. U. Baldassari, 'Alcuni appunti su Giotto e la poesia', *LItal*, 49:373–91, concerns a *canzone* attributed to Giotto, which appears in two MSS. The article supports the attribution and discusses the biographical, religious, and political context of the poem. G. Tanturli, *'La tenzone del Cavalcanti, XLV, con Giovenale, III', *Antonini Vol.*, 33–40. R. Bettarini, *'Croci e delizie', *ib.*, 25–32, deals with *interventi di restauro* on the text of the canzone *O cari frati miei* by Guittone d'Arezzo. S. Chessa, *'Forme da ritrovare: i due discordi di Bonagiunta da Lucca', *SFI*, 53, 1995:5–21.

C. Segre, 'È possibile un'edizione critica del *Novellino?*', *D'Andrea Vol.*, 61–68, answers in the affirmative; indeed Prof. Segre is working on just such an edition. In view of certain difficulties and complications he proposes an ingenious presentation of the material. He comes down firmly in favour of the *stemma* of Aruch and Monteverdi rather than that of Favati. The new edition will undoubtedly supersede all previous attempts and will provide a definitive text for the future. A. Conte, 'Ur-*Novellino* e *Novellino:* ipotesi di lavoro', *MedRom*, 20:75–115, returns to the question of the *stemma* of *Novellino* (like Segre he accepts that of Aruch and Monteverdi) and the order of the *novelle*. C. Animosi, 'Un caso curioso nella tradizione del *Novellino*', *ib.*, 198–208, argues that a post-*Decameron* copyist of the *Novellino* was influenced by Boccaccio's treatment of the *novella* of the *re di Cipri*, which Boccaccio knew from an earlier copy of the *Novellino:* 'In altre parole, il rapporto non è unidirezionale'. O. Rampin, 'Rassegna sacchettiana (1954–95)', *LettI*, 49:112–58, in an ample footnote summarizes the earlier history of Sacchetti criticism; then, beginning with a thoughtful discussion of the contributions of Franca Ageno, the survey is brought up to date. The aim is to 'fornire una valutazione critica dei singoli contributi, un resoconto, oggettiva senz'essere indifferente, dei risultati raggiunti dalla ricerca'. D. Pirovano, *Modi narrativi e stile del 'Novellino' di Masuccio Salernitano*, F, La Nuova Italia, 1996, 281 pp., is a technically oriented study of narrative mechanisms, rhetorical figures, lexis, and syntax, concluding with a few pages of general commentary on the special features of this little-studied work. G. Frosini, 'Il principe e l'eremita. Sulla tradizione dei testi italiani della storia di "Barlaam e Iosafas"', *SM*, 37, 1996:1–63, aims to bring order into the confusing mass of early literary, dramatic, sung, and anthologized versions of the legend, including *volgarizzamenti* from French, Provençal, and Latin. An appendix surveys manuscript and printed versions, mostly in Italian libraries, a few in France and Britain. L. Bartolucci, 'Il doppio nei *Reali di Francia:* Berta e Falisetta', Piva, *L'ombra*, 23–30, explores the story of how Bertha, the mother of Charlemagne, was replaced on her wedding day by her companion Falisetta, identical but for Bertha's 'gran pié'. The legend, derived from earlier sources, is given narrative consistency and functionality by Andrea da Barberino in the *Reali di Francia*. L. Bartolucci, *'L'Oriente nelle versioni italiane della *Lettera del Prete Gianni*. I rifacimenti', *Atti* (Naples), 221–34. A. Di Benedetto Zimbone, *'Dal *Cantare di Fiorio e Biancifiore* al *Florio e Platziaflore*', *ib.*, 191–202.

G. Billanovich, 'Come nacque un capolavoro: la "cronica" non più anonimo romano. Il vescovo Ildebrando Conti, Francesco Petrarca e Bartolomeo di Iacovo da Valmontone', *RANL*, 6, 1995:195–211, identifies Bartolomeo as the author of the *cronica*. M. Berisso, 'Preliminari per una lettura narrativa e tematica della *Cronica* di Dino Compagni, *Italianistica*, 25, 1996:9–42, maintains that the study of Compagni's book has always been conditioned by extra-textual factors such as the search for documentation of historical facts or its relationship with Dante and other literature. Here the author seeks to bring out the narrative organization of Compagni's historical discourse and the ideological-thematic poles around which it revolves, reading the *Cronica* as 'autobiografia militante' — within the genre of historiography, but eccentric. Frances Wood, *Did Marco Polo go to China?*, Secker & Warburg, London 1995, 182 pp., is a scholarly but informally written survey of the arguments, concluding that, although Marco Polo's Chinese travelogue was evidently based on contemporary written sources and family legends rather than personal experience, it provides much valuable information.

L. Pagnotta, 'Sulle tracce di un libro d'autore. Il manoscritto marciano', It. IX 175 e la tradizione delle opere di Tommaso di Giunta', *SM*, 36, 1995:169–97, through analysis of the MS of Tommaso's *Conciliato d'Amore*, concludes that its diverse elements represent a projected *libro* designed to represent Tommaso and preserve his life's work for the future, rather than a mere juxtaposition of texts. S. Pittaluga, *'L'abito buono di Riccardo da Venosa', *Omaggio Federico II*, 70–82, studies Riccardo's comedy *De Paulino et Polli*, especially with respect to forms of dress.

HUMANISM AND THE RENAISSANCE

By PAOLO L. ROSSI, *Senior Lecturer in Italian Studies, Lancaster University* and
GERALDINE MUIRHEAD, *Lecturer in Italian, Manchester Metropolitan University*

1. GENERAL

Alberto Asor Rosa, *Genus italicum: saggi sulla identità letteraria italiana nel corso del tempo*, T, Einaudi, xxix + 810 pp., looks at *italianità* and how 'insieme con il tema delle origini e della genesi [...] ricorre continuamente il tema del rapporto tra il "génie" e la lingua'. An essay on Guicciardini's *Ricordi* examines the implications inherent in its production for private as opposed to public consumption, while a study of Sarpi's *Istoria del Concilio di Trento* points to the echoes of Guicciardini's *Storia d'Italia* and shows that Sarpi's analysis, which has a secular rather than a religious thrust, was aimed at revealing the politics and ambitions that lay behind the deliberations. *Stefano Guazzo a Casale tra Cinque e Seicento*, ed. Daniela Ferrari, Ro, Bulzoni, 450 pp., is the collected conference proceedings for the 400th anniversary of his death with 15 essays that explore social, political, religious, and cultural life at Monferrato and the movement of noble families between there and Mantua, all within the context of Guazzo's activities at Court. There are studies of the *Civil conversazione, Lettere volgari, Dialoghi piacevoli* and the texts of 23 unpublished *lettere diplomatiche*. C. Nissen, 'Apostolo Zeno's phantom author: the strange case of Gentile Sermini da Siena', *Italica*, 74:151–63, re-evaluates the evidence for the existence of, and works attributed to, this figure. *Besomi Vol.* has a section of nine essays on the 15th and 16th cs including: history and antiquarian studies in Flavio Biondo; early editions of Da Porto's *Giulietta e Romeo;* morality and tragedy in Bandello's *novella Il signor Didaco Centiglia;* rewriting in the 1560 Milanese edition of the first three parts of Bandello's *novelle* edited by Ascanio Centorio; Chirico Strozzi and a missing passage from the ninth book of Aristotle's *Metaphysics*. Raffaele Ajello, *Una società anomala. Il programma e la sconfitta della nobiltà napoletana in due memoriali cinquecenteschi*, Na, ESI, 1996, 462 pp., examines the attempts by the Neapolitan nobility to assert its independence and cope with foreign domination by abandoning old-fashioned attitudes and adopting new strategies. It gives a critical edition of Caracciolo's *Discorso sopra il regno di Napoli*, correcting the Volpicella edition of 1880, and the text of F. Carafa's *Memorie*. Richard Cooper, *Litterae in Tempore Belli*, Geneva, Droz, xx + 414 pp., has updated versions of 17 previously published articles which look at the connections and relationships between France and Italy during the wars of Italy. Of particular interest to Italian scholars are: Marguerite de Navarre's interest in Italian literature, especially the works of Alamanni, Paradiso, Fregoso, Bandello, and Scaliger; Du Bellay and Rabelais, and the intellectual milieu in Rome, which looks at the make-up and activities of the academies. The complex background to the Angevin claims to the South, which legitimized the French invasions, is the subject of David Abulafia, *The Western Mediterranean Kingdoms 1200–1500. The Struggle for Dominion*, London, Longman, xix + 300 pp., which examines the turbulent economic and political activities in Sicily and Southern Italy in the 13th c. and the factors that drew the dynasties of Anjou and Aragon to seek dominion over this area.

Martin L. McLaughlin, *Literary Imitation in the Italian Renaissance*, Oxford, Clarendon, 1995, 314 pp., is an excellent scholarly study, which tackles a complex problem that preoccupied the major writers from Petrarch to Bembo. It concludes that theoretical positions were varied, precise, and sophisticated; that practice outstripped theory; and that there were close parallels in the textual strategies for writing in Latin and in the vernacular. Marco Lorandi, *Il mito di Ulisse*, Mi, Jaca Book, 1996, 635 pp., examines the myths surrounding the figure of Ulysses and the different levels of meaning relating to power, control, the struggle of vice and virtue, and the aspirations of those who made use of this imagery. *Vocabulary of Teaching and Research between Middle Ages and Renaissance*, ed. Olga Weijers, Turnhout, Brepols, 1995, 254 pp., has 14 essays which set out to 'define the development of concepts and realities by concentrating on the vocabulary used to express them'. The analysis of grammar, definitions, changes in terminology, commentaries, and the concepts of teaching and research will undoubtedly inspire further studies seeking to describe the past in its own terms instead of ours. Mia Lecomte, *Animali parlanti*, F, Atheneum, 1995, 125 pp., traces the genre of talking animals from antiquity and analyses the use made of them in the Renaissance. Antonio Stäuble and Walter Lenschen, *Traduire les classiques italiens*, vol. 2, Lausanne, Centre de Traduction Littéraire, 1995, 79 pp., has a chapter on the difficulty of translating particular terms in Alberti. Lucia Nadin, *Carte da gioco e letteratura fra Quattrocento e Ottocento*, Lucca, Pacini Fazzi, 278 pp., traces how playing cards developed from their use as a simple mnemonic device in the mid 15th c. to become part of the more complex and philosophical art of memory. It investigates the use of *tarocchi*, explores narrative techniques in recipes, books of secrets, and manuals for games, and gives a real insight into the social and intellectual world of the users and readers. This is a perceptive study that sheds new light on the works of Ragone, L. da Pirano, L. Giustinian, Marcolini, Conte, Pomeran, Boiardo, and Barbo.

Angelo Romano, *L'officina degli irregolari*, Viterbo, Sette Città, 237 pp., contains six already published studies and the following new essays on Aretino and his circle: 'Appunti su personaggi della "Cortigiana" dell'Aretino'; 'Biografia e bibliografia di Giovanni Giustiniani da Candia'; '"Dalla casuppola del Biondo", sei sonetti inediti di Michelangelo Biondo'. *Rewriting the Self: Histories from the Renaissance to the Present*, ed. Roy Porter, London, Routledge, xii + 283 pp., contains an essay by Peter Burke that raises questions about the nature of individual identity and its relationship to the cultural movement we call the Renaissance. It explores the language used to describe the self and offers possible reasons for the development of the autobiography (ego document) and the nature of biography. It points to contradictions in the way that portraits were executed, raises questions about the varieties of conceptions of the self, sees the response to ancient models as a reason for the rise in autobiographies and explores the relationship between the sense of self and Western individualism.

A number of studies trace the close relationship between literature and art. Jill M. Ricketts, *Visualizing Boccaccio. Studies on Illustrations of the Decameron from Giotto to Pasolini*, CUP, x + 214 pp., presents a feminist critique of Boccaccio, including a chapter which considers Botticelli's depiction on a *spalliera* of the story of Nastagio. The differences in the two narratives are noted and used to give 'a subversive reading' of the story's overtly didactic content. *The Eye of the Poet. Studies in the Reciprocity of the Visual Arts and Literary Arts from the Renaissance to the Present*, ed. Amy Golahany, Lewisburg, Bucknell U.P., 1996, 254 pp., has 11 essays on the theme of ekphrasis as a means of interpretation, with studies by: R. Smith on the topos of the living stone, which looks at Varchi's assessment of Michelangelo's *Pietà* and explores later adaptations of this theme in G. B. Strozzi il Vecchio, Bocchi, Lomazzo and Marino; G. Maiorino on the Renaissance Pastoral in Titian and Sannazaro; L. Freedman on Titian's portraits in the letters and sonnets of Aretino. Jaynie Anderson, *Giorgione: the Painter of Poetic Brevity*, Paris, Flammarion, 391 pp., examines a quality in his work that was first noted by P. Pino in 1548. This is an excellent well-researched study which explores the sensitivity in depicting humanist themes and subject matter that made Giorgione's works greatly sought after during his lifetime. It assesses his biographers and connoisseurs and gives a full *catalogue raisonné*. *Tasso, Tiziano e i pittori del parlar disgiunto*, ed. Andrea Emiliani and Gianni Venturi, Venice, Marsilio, 127 pp., has two essays: A. Emiliani, 'Parlar disgiunto e forma aperta in alcuni grandi artisti del Cinquecento Italiano', and C. Molinari, 'Torquato Tasso e il parlar disgiunto', which take as their points of departure the letter of

Scipione Gonzaga on 'parlar disgiunto' and investigate how this literary device was adapted by artists. Collaboration can also be traced in Riccardo Naldi, *Girolamo Santacroce*, Mi, Electa, 216 pp., where the links to Sannazaro and to members of the Accademia Pontaniana led to an acquaintance with the humanists' interests in classical texts and the study of antiquity.

Vitruvius, *De architectura*, ed. Pierre Gros, trans. Antonio Corso and Elisa Romano, 2 vols, T, Einaudi, xcv + 795, x + 796–1563 pp., gives the Latin text and facing translation with excellent critical apparatus and notes. There are essays by M. Losito, 'L'analemma vitruviano e il IX libro del *De architectura* di Daniele Barbaro (1556–67)'; 'La ricostruzione della voluta del capitello ionico vitruviano nel Rinascimento italiano (1450–1570)'. Marco Spesso, *Enea Silvio Piccolomini: scritti di architettura*, T, Testo e Immagine, 93 pp., gives extracts, mainly from the *Commentarii*, which, imbued with the spirit of Lucretian pessimism, reveal a sophisticated appreciation of town-planning and different architectural styles, an interest in archaeology, and an anxiety about the spoliation of antique remains. Vaughan Hart and Peter Hicks, *Sebastiano Serlio, On Architecture*, New Haven, Yale U.P., 1996, xxxv + 484 pp., is the first accurate translation of the most influential and innovative architectural treatise of the 16th c. with an excellent introduction, notes, and appendices containing the Venetian copyrights and the prefatory letter. Andrea Palladio, *The Four Books on Architecture*, trans. Robert Tavernor and Richard Schofield, London, MIT, xxv + 436 pp., has a good introduction which reviews the influence of Vitruvius, Serlio, and the cultural circle of Trissino, and the reception of the text. There are excellent notes and glossary.

Jerzy Miziolek, *Soggetti classici sui cassoni fiorentini alla vigilia del Rinascimento*, Warsaw, Polish Academy of Sciences, 1996, 158 pp. + 60 pls, is a detailed scholarly study which presents painted panels, literature, and archive documentation as evidence for a taste for antiquity in the late 14th c. Stories were based on mythological tales and ancient history, revealing a taste in Florence for the antique much earlier than previously accepted. Classical tales, seen as having religious significance, were fused with biblical works, and the humanists, particularly the circle around Salutati, were responsible for the stories depicted on the *cassoni*. G. Clarke, 'Ambrogio Traversari: artistic adviser in early 15th-c. Florence?', *RenS*, 11 : 161–78. Cecilia De Carli, *I deschi da parto e la pittura del primo Rinascimento toscano*, T, Allemandi, 254 pp., investigates the social background to the patronage behind these relatively expensive objects. It points to a 'romantic' strain in early 15th-c. humanism, as opposed to the later more moralistic tone, by examining the importance of children, the festivities surrounding birth, literary influences, and medieval versions of classical tales and histories. The study traces the creation of a new iconography which departs from the original texts, and its importance for assessing the metamorphosis of literary genres and themes as they were re-invented and adapted to new circumstances and uses. *Pietro da Cortona e il disegno,* ed. Simonetta Prosperi Valenti Rodinò, Mi, Electa, 283 pp., has a chapter by G. Fusconi on 'Cortona e l'antico' which traces the links with the Museo Cartaceo of Cassiano del Pozzo and his interpretation of classical themes.

The Oxford Illustrated History of Italy, ed. George Holmes, OUP, xiv + 386 pp., has 12 well-illustrated essays including: M. Mallett, 'Politics and Society 1250–1600', which treats political autonomy, the courts, and the power of the church; G. Holmes, 'Renaissance Culture', which looks at the influence of the church and humanism on culture, the Florence of Lorenzo de' Medici, and Venice and the High Renaissance. Mary Hollingsworth, *Patronage in Sixteenth Century Italy,* London, John Murray, 1996, 452 pp., is a well-documented study that takes into account the culture of humanism, but is careful to qualify the appeal to classical antiquity by different patrons and states, and examines in detail the complex relationship between patron, design, and execution.

FEMINISM AND WOMEN'S STUDIES. Henricus Cornelius Agrippa, *Declamation on the Nobility and Preeminence of the Female Sex,* ed. and trans. Albert Rabil Jr, Chicago U.P, 1996, xxxii + 109 pp., is the first volume in the series *The Other Voice in Early Modern Europe,* ed. Margaret L. King and Albert Rabil Jr. Each volume includes the series editors' introduction and an essay exploring the cultural and historical context, as well as an analysis of the text. This particular text had a great influence, after its publication in 1529, with translations into Italian, French, English, and German. Laura Cereta, *Collected Letters of a Renaissance Feminist,* ed. and trans. Diana Robin, Chicago U.P., xxv + 216 pp., divides the corpus of letters, written at the end of the 15th c., under specific headings and presents the texts which 'mingling themes anticipating modern feminism makes her work as different from that of any writer of her time'. The text of her only dialogue *On the Death of an Ass* is given at the end and the introduction examines humanist and anti-humanist themes. Cecilia Ferrazzi, *Autobiography of an Aspiring Saint,* ed. and trans. Anne Jacobson Schutte, Chicago U.P., 1996, xxix + 101 pp., gives an extract from the record of the trial before the Venetian Holy Office when she was charged with the 'pretence of sanctity' and where she tells her own story without inquisitorial prompting. The debate on human love was regarded as the province of males, and Tullia d'Aragona, *Dialogue on the Infinity of Love,* ed. and trans. Rinaldina Russell and Bruce Merry, Chicago

U.P., 114 pp., represents the first dialogue by a woman on this theme, voicing forthright views on sexuality and morality. Antonia Pulci, *Florentine Drama for Convent and Festival. Seven Sacred Plays*, ed. and trans. James Wyatt Cook and Barbara Collier Cook, Chicago U.P., xxx + 281 pp., is the first ever collection of Pulci's plays where 'female saints and [...] secular women are typically more intelligent, more rational, more constant in their purposes, more compassionate, and more emotionally stable than their male conterparts'. Moderata Fonte (Modesta Pozzo), *The Worth of Women. Wherein is Clearly Revealed their Nobility and their Superiority to Men*, ed. and trans. Virginia Cox, Chicago U.P., xxvii + 290 pp., is an excellent presentation of a text that revitalized the debate about the worth of women when it was in danger of degenerating into a sterile academic exercise. The volume also contains an extract from the *Floridoro* on the theme of women's equality. *Women and Art in Early Modern Europe. Patrons, Collectors and Connoisseurs*, ed. Cynthia Lawrence, University Park, Pennsylvania State U.P., viii + 263 pp., has 13 essays which include: Isabella d'Este's unquenchable thirst for collecting and antiquities; the impact of Eleonora of Toledo on court life and how her tastes, religious beliefs and piety contrasted to the dynastic and political propaganda of Cosimo I. The essays raise important questions about patronage and influence at court. Fredrika H. Jacobs, *Defining the Renaissance Virtuosa: Women Artists and the Language of Art History and Criticism*, CUP, xii + 229 pp., is a stimulating study concerned with the terms used to 'differentiate the artistic productions of women from those of men [...], and the organizational principles used to delineate a history of art monopolized by *pittori* and *cultori* and visited only marginally by *pittrici* and *scultrici*'. It covers writings by Vasari and Lomazzo, investigates conventional topoi, analyses the contextual meanings of aesthetic terms like *ritrarre, imitare, invenzione, fantasia*, and *grazia*, and sheds new light on classical and contemporary writings. Paola Tinagli, *Women in Italian Renaissance Art: Gender, Representation, Identity*, MUP, xii + 206 pp., draws on images and writings by Alberti, Aretino, F. Barbaro, Bembo, Dolce, Palmieri, and Savonarola to investigate women as 'embodiments of a set of ideals and values, both aesthetic and social shared by the artists and the patrons', and reveals the specific conventions appropriate to women and the creation of new genres. Samuel K. Cohn Jr, *Women in the Streets. Essays on Sex and Power in Renaissance Italy*, Baltimore, Johns Hopkins U.P., 1996, xi + 250 pp., traces the decline in women's status from the late 14th c. to the period of the Counter-Reformation when constraints were eased and women were to the forefront of new forms of spirituality. These seven studies take issue with previous interpretations and do much to clarify the changing role and status of women in Renaissance society. Francesco Saverio Toppi, *Maria Lorenza Longo. Donna della Napoli del '500*, Pompeii, Pontificio Santuario di Pompei, 270 pp., gives an insight into social interventions in the religious world of the Catholic reform movement by examining one of the major figures of the Oratory of Divine Love. Christa Grossinger, *Picturing Women in Late Medieval and Renaissance Art*, MUP, xiii + 173 pp., though concerned with Northern Europe, where the effects of the Reformation had an important impact, the conclusions of this study could be applied with profit to Italy and to literature as well as art.

TRAVEL. Paolo Emilio Taviani, *Cristoforo Colombo*, 3 vols, Ro, Società Geografica Italiana, 1996, 391, 376, 559 pp., contains a feast of well-documented scholarly studies on: history and biography; Colombus's correspondence with P. Toscanelli; his use of medieval and classical sources; his annotations; the *Giornale di Bordo;* the possible influences of the *Milione.* Robert C. Melzi, *Bartolomeo Fontana: itinerari (MS ital. 226, Univ. of Pennsylvania). Due viaggiatori veneziani attraverso l'Europa del Cinquecento*, Geneva, Slatkine, 1995, xciv + 94 pp., is an edition with an insightful study that looks at, and resolves, the texual problems raised by the description of five voyages, in five different literary styles, aimed at five different audiences. *Quaderno di bordo di Giovanni Manzini. Prete-notaio e cancelliere (1471–1484)*, ed. Lucia Greco, Venice, Comitato, viii + 153 pp., is an edition of a MS in the Archivio di Stato, Venice, containing notarial documents and a *libro di spese* which gives a fascinating glimpse into life on board ship. *The Book of Privileges Issued to Christopher Columbus by King Fernando and Queen Isabel 1492–1502*, ed. and trans. Helen Nader and Luciano Formisano, Berkeley, California U.P., xxix + 441 pp., presents for the first time all the documents both in chronological order and as a critical edition with translations. The way they are ordered in the MS both raises and answers many questions about the historical events and motives. This collection is essential for understanding the evolution of the political stance taken towards the New World and towards Columbus. *The Book of Prophecies Edited by Christopher Columbus*, ed. and trans. Roberto Rusconi and Blair Sullivan, Berkeley, California U.P., xiv + 419 pp., was to be presented to Isabella and Ferdinand and is a collection of biblical texts and *auctoritates* drawn from the Fathers of the Church, medieval theologians, and canonists. Its purpose was to locate the discovery of the Indies within the historical schema of the salvation of the human race as a final step towards the liberation of Jerusalem and the Holy Land from Muslim domination, and to assign a prominent role in these events to himself. Maria Giulia Barberini and Idalberto Fei, *Relazioni di Moscovia scritta da Raffaello Barberini*, Palermo, Sellerio, 1996, 110 pp., is a long account of a journey to

Russia in 1565 written, after Barberini's return, at the instigation of Count Leonardo Nagarola who had himself been to Russia. Giovanni Bockenheym, *La Cucina di Papa Martino V*, ed. Giovanna Bonardi, Mi, A. Mondadori, 1995, xxix + 81 pp., was written by a German cleric and cook at the court of Martin V. The introduction explores the curious style of the 75 Latin recipes which are set out as appropriate to specific social classes or races.

BIBLIOGRAPHY, PRINTING AND PUBLISHING. *Biblioteca Trivulziana, Milano*, ed. Angela Dillon Bussi and Giovanni M. Piazza, Fiesole, Nardini, 1995, 256 pp., is a study of late 15th-c. MSS of classical texts, humanist treatises, and works by Dante and Petrarch. Each entry is accompanied by excellent illustrations. L. Parri, 'Un Esopo fiorentino del XV secolo', *ASI*, 155:399–415, discusses the dating, attribution, and patron of the illuminated 'Spencer MS 50' in the print room of the New York public library. *Libri a corte. Testi e immagini nella Napoli aragonese*, ed. Emilia Ambra et al., Na, Paparo, 155 pp., is a beautifully produced volume that looks at the works created for the court and examines the plan and reason for the great collection of illuminated MSS produced for Alfonso and Ferrante. It includes studies of the epithets in the dedications and the bookbinding. Gianpaolo Garavaglia, *Gli incunaboli di Varallo Sesia*, T, Regione Piemonte, 1995, 231 pp., lists, with full critical apparatus, 53 incunables in the Biblioteca Civica Farinone Centa and the Società d'Incoraggiamento allo Studio del Disegno. There is also an essay on the problems of cataloguing early texts, while the introduction discusses the formation of the collections. R. Castellano, 'Due incunaboli di Antonio da Bitonto: un'analisi bibliologica', *Studi Bitonti*, 63:71–8, examines the *Expositiones evangeliorum dominicalium* (1496) and the *Sermones in epistolas dominicales et quadragesimales* (1496). *Le cinquecentine della Biblioteca Panizzi*, Reggio Emilia, Biblioteca Panizzi, ed. Eletta Zanzanelli and Valter Pratissoli, 1995, xxviii + 465 pp., gives short catalogue entries for 6,353 items with introductory essays by L. Balsamo and N. Harris discussing the collection. *Le edizioni italiane del XVI secolo. Censimento nazionale*, IV: C. *Chiesa di S. Barbara — Czernius*, Ro, Istituto Centrale per il Catalogo Unico, 1996, xxiii + 327 pp., continues an excellent project with full critical apparatus and excellent indexes. **Dizionario dei tipografi e degli editori italiani. Il Cinquecento, A-F*, ed. Marco Menato, Ennio Sandal, and Giuseppina Zappella, Mi, Bibliografica, 400 pp. *L'attività editoriale di Gershom Soncino 1502–1527*, ed. Giuliano Tamani, Edizioni del Soncino, 157 pp., has nine essays which reveal the complexity and vicissitudes of Soncino's career and examine prefaces, colophons, vernacular works, Latin alphabets, the 1503 edition of Petrarch, and the statutes of Fano (1508) and Jesi (1516). An appendix contains a chronological index of the Latin and vernacular editions. K. M. Stevens, 'Liturgical publishing in mid-16th-c. Milan: the contracts for the *Breviarium Humiliatorum* (1548) and the *Breviarium Ambrosianum* (1557)', *La Bibliofilia*, 99: 111–34, examines the interaction between the considerations of profit, editorial policy and publishing schedules. J. M. de Bujanda, *Index des livres interdits*, IV: *Index de l'Inquisition Portugaise 1547, 1551, 1561, 1564, 1581*, Quebec, Sherbrooke U.P. — Geneva, Droz, 1995, 875 pp., comprises a facsimile of each Index as well as a complete transcription accompanied by full critical apparatus for each work listed. There are also excellent indices and tables. Id., *Thesaurus de la littérature interdite au XVIe siècle. Auteurs, ouvrages, éditions avec addenda et corrigenda*, vol. 10, Quebec, Sherbrooke U.P. — Geneva, Droz, 839 pp., apart from the excellent critical apparatus contains new documents relating to the Florentine Index of 1553–54, and MS indexes (1576) by Giovanni di Dio Fiorentino and the Master of the Sacred Palace. These volumes complete the project which gives a detailed analysis of all the Indexes issued in the 16th c. One cannot overemphasize the great contribution which this meticulously planned and executed project has made to scholarship in opening up a corpus of hitherto inaccessible data. The most significant contribution this year to our understanding of the world of books is however *La censura libraria nell'Europa del secolo XVI*, ed. Ugo Rozzo, Udine, Forum, viii + 336 pp., which contains 13 essays that owe a great debt to the Sherbrooke project. The studies assess the importance of the Indexes as research tools for investigating cultural and social values, and the history of *mentalités*, the control of Jewish publishing, censorship as a stimulus to reading, strategies of prohibition and how works aimed at different social classes were affected, administrative procedures involved in book control, the effect of censorship on printers and the stategies used to evade it. An excellent essay by U. Rozzo on the expurgation of texts reveals 'un grandioso progetto di rilettura e riscrittura per ragioni dottrinali ed ideologiche, di tutta la nostra letteratura'. Gigliola Fragnito, *La Bibbia al rogo: la censura ecclesiastica e i volgarizzamenti della Scrittura (1471–1605)*, Bo, Il Mulino, 345 pp., also makes good use of the Sherbrooke project and shows how the authorities viewed the Bible as a dangerous work. This well-researched study looks at: the attempts to restrict the *volgarizzamenti* through the many indexes and decrees issued from 1559 to 1596; the history of the Bible in Europe after the Clementine Index and the implementation of the Index itself, with the sequestration and destruction of texts. The vernacular text was eradicated, leaving the Latin text inaccessible to the majority of the population. The importance of the Bible in popular and élite culture, which eventually led to its censorship, is attested to in *La Bibbia nel Medio Evo*, ed.

Giuseppe Cremascoli and Claudio Leonardi, Bo, Ediz. Dehoniane, 485 pp., which contains 24 essays including studies of political thought, hagiography, literature, prophecy, and parody. F. Sberlati, 'La pia ecdotica. L'edizione censurata degli *Inferni* di Anton Francesco Doni', *LItal*, 49 : 3–39. *La città e la parola scritta*, ed. Giovanni Pugliese Carratelli, Mi, Scheiwiller, xiv + 473 pp., traces the relationship between society and documentation. There are studies of printing investigating every aspect from finance to font; of the libraries of humanists and princes, and the development of the library as a public utility; and of the church and censorship. Every aspect is accompanied by excellent, carefully chosen illustrations. David Woodward, *Maps as Prints in the Italian Renaissance. Makers, Distributors and Consumers*, London, British Library, 1996, viii + 127 pp., contains the texts of the 1995 Panizzi lectures which examine the 'roles of authors and engravers, printers and distributors and patrons and consumers in the map trade that began in Florence in the late 15th c., but later developed in Rome and Venice'. Sissi Aslan, *L'Italia delle stampe*, Ro, Rendina, 237 pp., looks at the impact of prints as a means of promoting cultural trends. *Immagini di Roma. Libri e incisioni della Collezione Kissner*, ed. Emilia Lamaro, Ro, Biblioteca della Camera dei Deputati, 1996, xii + 146 pp., will be a useful resource for early descriptions and images of the city. It lists 169 items with numerous illustrations divided into three sections: 'Guide di Roma'; 'Itinerario romano'; 'Viaggi e paesaggi'. Each section is accompanied by a short essay outlining the methodology and features of the individual genres. *Guida inventario dell' Archivio della Curia vescovile di Rovigo*, ed. Francesca Bianchini and Giacomo Prandini, Rovigo, Minelliana, 1995, liv + 421 pp.

2. HUMANISM.

Paul Oskar Kristeller, *Studies in Renaissance Thought and Letters*, IV, Ro, Storia e Letteratura, 1996, xvii + 631 pp., is a rich feast of scholarship with 31 studies followed by tributes, obituaries, an essay, and an appendix with seven unpublished humanist letters. The first section deals with humanism, Italian universities, neoplatonism and philosophy, Latin and the vernacular, and the Jewish contribution to the Renaissance. The section 'The search for mannerism' includes an important study on the editing of 15th-c. texts. James Hankins, *Repertorium Brunianum: A Critical Guide to the Writings of Leonardo Bruni*, I: *Handlist of Manuscripts*, Ro, Istituto Storico Italiano per il Medio Evo, lxxv + 265 pp., is an invaluable bibliographical research tool which, as well as the handlist, provides multiple indexes — of scribes, annotators, illuminators, owners, etc. Two further volumes are planned giving a catalogue of genuine works, pseudobruniana, and Renaissance translations of his writings. Bartolomeo Scala, *Humanistic and Political Writings*, ed. Alison Brown, MRTS, xxxvi + 572 pp., gives the original texts with a critical apparatus and excellent notes. This selection reveals the variety of Scala's interests and his contacts with other humanists such as Filelfo, Marullo, and Platina. The excitement generated by ancient philosophical and literary texts, and the effect they had on his own compositions, are evident, and the letters reveal his stoic, ironic, and unconventional nature. Antonietta Iacono, *La 'Guerra d'Ischia' nel 'De Bello Neapolitano' di G. Pontano*, Na, Accademia Pontaniana, 1996, 90 pp., has a well-researched introduction that reveals Pontano's work as an important historical document as well as examining his methodology in writing history. There follows an anthology of relevant extracts from the autograph manuscript. Liane Lefaivre, *Leon Battista Alberti's Hypnerotomachia Poliphili. Re-Cognizing the Architectural Body in the Early Italian Renaissance*, London, MIT, 297 pp., is a stimulating study which makes use of poems, biographies, songs, novels, travel journals, memoirs, letters, diaries, and plaques on walls to examine the 'gradual eroticization of the body and its role in the aestheticisation of architectural thinking'. It charts the transformation of the body from the source of all evil to its acceptance as the highest good. Roswitha Stewering, *Architektur und Natur in der 'Hypnerotomachia Poliphili' (Manutius 1499) und die Zuschreibung des Werkes an Niccolò Lelio Cosmico*, Hamburg, Lit, 1996, vi + 596 pp. + 54 pls, is in two parts. The first gives an analysis of the first book in terms of the microcosm-macrocosm analogy, where the relationship between virtue, beauty, and ornament in L. B. Alberti and the concept of *natura artificiosa* is used to explore links with Vitruvius and Albertus Magnus. The second part examines the question of authorship and looks at humanist circles in Rome, the study of antiquity in Venice, and literary culture. One of the aims of Wolfgang Jung, *Über szenographisches Entwerfen Raffael und die Villa Madama*, Wiesbaden, Vieweg, viii + 320 pp., is to clarify the Renaissance's, and Alberti's, concept of beauty. It also investigates perspectival construction and takes issue with Wittkower's *Architectural Principles in the Age of Humanism*.

Rinascimento, 36, 1996, includes: G. Tanturli, 'Sulla data e genesi della *Vita civilis* di Matteo Palmieri' (3–48), and A. M. Adorisio, 'Nota dei codici appartenenti a Francesco e Stefano Guarnieri di Osimo' (195–205). A. Maggi, *'Della magia d'amore* di Guido Casoni: un compendio della trattatistica rinascimentale sull'amore', *REI*, 43:67–77. P. Murgatroyd, 'Landino, *Xandra* 2.20: a Renaissance paraclausithron', *BHR*, 59:105–09, shows how variations were introduced into a collection of elegies based on the classical locked-out lover's serenade. Id., 'Landino's *Xandra* 3.3 and its Latin models', *RenS*, 11:57–60. *RQ,* 50, includes: K. Gouwens, 'Discourses of vulnerability: Pietro Alcionio's orations on the Sack of Rome' (38–77), and E. O'Connor, 'Panormita's reply to his critics: the *Hermaphroditus* and the literary defense' (985–1010). *ASI*, 155, includes: P. Viti, 'Storia e storiografia in Leonardo Bruni' (49–98); G. M. Cao, 'Tra politica fiorentina e filosofia ellenistica: il dibattito sulla ricchezza nelle *Commentationes* di Francesco Filelfo' (99–126); and L. Santoro, 'Una biografia sconosciuta di Leon Battista Alberti' (143–52). T. Gargano, 'Sopravvivenza di un mito umanistico nel *Lorenzo* di Giordano de' Bianchi Dottula', *Studi Bitonti*, 63:79–90. N. Zorzi, 'A proposito di una lettera greca del Traversari', *LItal*, 49:624–36. R. M. Comanducci, 'Politica e storiografia nella visione di un oligarca', *AIISS*, 13, 1995–96:361–400, examines Bernardo di Giovanni Rucellai's *De Bello Italico*. Frank Fehrenbach, *Licht und Wasser. Zur Dynamik Naturphilosophischer Leitbilder im Werk Leonardo Da Vincis*, Tübingen, Wasmuth, 379 pp. + 105 pls, looks at the problems inherent in making connections between Leonardo's disparate areas of activity. It is particularly concerned with the aesthetics of 'effect', whose roots are traced back to classical rhetoric, and stresses how a methodology based on rhetoric fused science and art.

INDIVIDUAL CENTRES. Charles M. Rosenberg, *The Este Monuments and Urban Development in Renaissance Ferrara*, CUP, xvi + 329 pp., on the rise of Ferrara, inter alia examines the contribution of humanists and their treatises. Michele Savonarola, *Del felice progresso di Borso d'Este*, ed. Maria Aurelia Mastronardi, Bari, Palomar, 1996, 290 pp., written between 1454 and 1461 as a panegyric, has an introduction discussing the context of the textual strategies involved, the reasons for writing the text in terms of Ferrarese court politics, and the humanist influences on the structure and themes. *Torquato Tasso e l'Università*, ed. Walter Moretti and Luigi Pepe, F, Olschki, xvi + 536 pp., focuses on Ferrarese learning in relation to the poet in 30 essays falling into five sections that include: 'T., le scienze matematiche e l'università', 'T. e il sapere universitario', and 'Miti e ossessioni del T. e della cultura del suo tempo'. The individual essays give insights into (among other things) classical scholarship and the particular nature of Ferrarese mathematical studies. *La corte di Mantua nell'età di Andrea Mantegna 1450–1550*, ed. Cesare Mozzarelli, Robert Oresko, and Leandro Ventura, Ro, Bulzoni, 429 pp., the proceedings of the conferences held in London and Mantua in 1992, dealing with literature and humanism, with studies on the literary sources of Mantegna's *Triumphs*, identity in L. B. Alberti, the study of antiquity, and the theme of *renovatio urbis*. Michela Marangoni and Manlio

Pastore Stocchi, *Una famiglia veneziana nella storia: I Barbaro*, Venice, IV, 1996, 543 pp., contains excellent and wide-ranging essays covering the humanist interests of Ermolao and Francesco Barbaro, the voyage of Giosafat Barbaro to Persia, the Barbaro book collection, Daniele Barbaro and garden design, the political activities of F. Barbaro, the *epistolario* of F. Barbaro, F. Barbaro and Alberti, Poliziano, E. Barbaro and Pliny, Pico Della Mirandola and E. Barbaro, and E. Barbaro on worldly honour. Although the central focus is the Barbaro family the volume gives an insight into Venetian culture and its literary world. Gaetano Cozzi, *Ambiente veneziano, ambiente veneto. Saggi su politica, società cultura nella repubblica di Venezia in età moderna*, Venice, Marsilio, xii + 364 pp., has 10 essays, including a penetrating study of *pubblica storiografia* in 16th-c. Venice which examines the appointments and careers of Sabellico, Sanuto, Navagero, Bembo, D. Barbaro, Valier, Paruta, A. Morosini, and N. Contarini in the context of the ever-changing parameters for the writing of Venetian history. Other essays deal with: 'Marin Sanudo il giovane dalla cronaca alla storia'; 'Domenico Morosini, Niccolò Machiavelli e la società veneziana'; Paolo Paruta's *Della perfettione della vita politica*. All the essays display the same high level of erudition and clarity. *Perugia nel Rinascimento: una cultura oltre i confini. Il secolo di Benedetto Bonfigli attraverso i documenti della Biblioteca Augusta*, ed. Maria Pecugi Fop, Perugia, Comune di Perugia, 119 pp. + 8 pls, an exhibition catalogue, comprises eight sections of primary sources — MSS, incunables, and later printed works — which help to trace developments in publishing, printing, the university, writing, religion, science, town planning, economic and social life. *Storia di Torino*, i: *Dalla preistoria al comune medievale*, ed. Giuseppe Sergi; ii: *Il Basso medioevo e la prima età moderna (1280–1536)*, ed. Rinaldo Combra, T, Einaudi, xxvi + 923 + 35 pls, xxv + 850 pp., are the first two volumes of a planned nine-volume project, and the high standard of scholarship we have come to expect from Einaudi is maintained. There are excellent essays on orthography, language, literary production; the organization of learning; schools and the university; the development of a local artistic style; the advent of printing; the court of Amedeo III; letterati and cultural models. As with the volumes on the other cities these will become points of reference for future studies.

PHILOSOPHY AND HISTORY OF IDEAS. *Cambridge Translations of Renaissance Philosophical Texts*, i: *Moral Philosophy;* ii: *Political Philosophy*, ed. Jill Kraye, CUP, xiv + 281, xii + 315 pp., is an anthology with 40 new translations of important works not available in English and intended to be used in conjunction with the *Cambridge History of Renaissance Philosophy* (1988), in which all the texts are discussed. Of particular interest are extracts from Ficino, Bracciolini, Acciaiuoli,

F. de' Vieri, Salutati, Poliziano, Filelfo, Raimondi, Campanella, Pontano, B. Sacchi, Vergerio, Palmieri, Scala, F. Guicciardini, Vettori, and F. Piccolomini. The passages are divided into categories, give a real insight into Renaissance proccupations, and will be welcomed by both teachers and scholars. Maurizio Merlo, *Vinculum concordiae: il problema della rappresentanza nel pensiero di Nicolò Cusano*, Mi, Angeli, 302 pp., is a scholarly investigation of the theme of *repraesentatio* against the background of the intense philosophical theorizing about spiritual and secular power generated by the crisis in the Church at the time of the Council of Basle. Michela Marangoni, *L'armonia del sapere: i 'Lectionum antiquarum libri' di Celio Rodigino*, Venice, IV, 212 pp., examines a work written in 1516 by Ludovico Maria Ricchieri, divided into 16 books and presenting a vast panoply of quotations from antiquity and the Middle Ages. This incisive study reveals a man of scholarly enterprise who hoped to produce a synthesis of human knowledge in the manner of an encyclopaedia. *L'etica del Rinascimento tra Platone e Aristotele*, ed. Antonino Poppi, Na, Città del Sole, 303 pp., contains studies on the nature of philosophy and ethics, the supremacy of the *vita activa* in Speroni, A. and F. Piccolomini, free will in a letter of G. Contarini to V. Colonna, the structure of moral discourse in Zabarella, and Patrizi and Zabarella on philosophical methodology. D. A. Lines, 'The importance of being good. Moral philosophy in the Italian universities 1300–1600', *Rinascimento*, 36, 1996:139–93. *Repubblica e virtù. Pensiero politico e Monarchia Cattolica fra XVI e XVII secolo*, ed. Chiara Continiso and Cesare Mozzarelli, Ro, Bulzoni, 1995, 611 pp., has 26 essays which ask new questions about: the relationship between politics, justice, and prudence; the nature of republican and monarchical government; how the Ciceronian-Stoic model coped with post-Tridentine preoccupations; and the dynamism of political and social renewal. Of particular Italian interest are the essays on: E. Tesauro's *Filosofia morale;* the nature of politics in Campanella; G. Bragaccia's *L'ambasciatore;* Castiglione, B. Gracian, and the language of the court; kingship in Tasso's *Dialoghi*.

The relationship between collecting, the study of the natural world, and philosophy is finally receiving investigation. *L'erbario dipinto di Ulisse Aldrovandi*, ed. Antonella Maiorino et al., F, Ace International, 368 pp., contains five essays dealing with the methodology in the study of natural history within the context of 16th-c. philosophical currents, Aldrovandi as an investigator of natural history, the founding of the *orto botanico* in Bologna, the importance of the *erbario* for scientific classification, and its importance for philosophers, writers, and artists. Mina Gregori et al., *Magnificenza alla corte dei Medici*, Mi, Electa, 471 pp., the memorably illustrated catalogue of an exhibition held in the Pitti Palace, comprises upwards of a score of essays investigating Buontalenti's *Intermedi*, the scientific interests of the ruling élite, its passion for collecting which led to the manufacture of glass, rock crystal, porcelain, *pietre dure*, and tapestries. The figure of Giorgio Vasari il Giovane as one such collector is highlighted in his *Raccolto fatto dal Cavaliere Giorgio Vasari di varii instrumenti per misurare con la vista*, ed. Filippo Camerota, F, Giunti, 1996, 423 pp., edited from MS Ricc. 2138, Florence, with essays pointing to the current vogue for collecting at the Medici court and to the types of measuring device then available, followed by a catalogue of the instruments mentioned in the text, with explanations of their use. The Renaissance fascination with the natural world and the cultural activities linked to it can also be seen in *Rudolf II and Prague. The Court and the City*, ed. Eliska Fucikova et al., London, Thames & Hudson, ix + 792 pp. This massive catalogue of the Prague exhibitions, in its very unwieldiness, reflects the mania for collecting and the bountiful patronage of Italians at the Imperial court, which was tolerant of people of all races and faiths. Important for cultural historians is Rudolf's fascination with wonders, mysticism, philosophy, alchemy, and cosmological speculation which attracted scholars from every corner of Europe. Vincenzo Gheroldi, *Ricette e ricettari. Tre fonti per la storia delle tecniche delle arti alla Biblioteca Queriniana di Brescia (secoli XVI-XVII)*, Brescia, Comune di Brescia, 1995, 206 pp., is a scholarly study with a wealth of archive material that adds much to our understanding the nature of the books of secrets tradition. It first examines the principles and methodology employed by the compilers, and this is followed by three essays, including 'Le fonti di un ricettario della metà del Cinquecento'. Alfred W. Crosby, *The Measure of Reality. Quantification and Western Society 1250–1600*, CUP, xii + 245 pp., traces the changes in perception of reality in terms of visualiziation and quantification aided by the invention of printing. It examines the contribution made to art (perspective), exploration (cartography), and cosmology, and sees the West's advantage over other cultures not in science and technology but in the *mentalité* which allowed the displacement of the old qualitative model by a quantative model. J. V. Field, *The Invention of Infinity. Mathematics and Art in the Renaissance*, OUP, xii + 250 pp., examines the period 1300–1650 and traces a slow evolution as mathematics became increasingly important to craftsmen, tradesmen, and intellectuals. It reveals how the mathematics taught in 'abacus schools' differed from that taught at the universities and how the two traditions eventually came together. It covers the activities of Piero della Francesca, Tartaglia, D. Barbaro, E. Danti, Commandino, Benedetti, and del Monte. Though there is much technical detail, this is a clear, lively study which reveals how science and art were once inseparable. Miguel A. Granada, *El debate cosmologico en 1588: Bruno, Brahe, Rothmann, Ursus, Roslin*, Na, Bibliopolis, 1996, 165 pp., examines the *Camoeracensis Acrotismus* (1588) and assesses its place in Bruno's cosmology and the debate about the anticipated end of the world. *La diffusione del Copernicanesimo in Italia 1543–1610*, ed. Massimo Bucciantini and Maurizio Torrini, F, Olschki, vii + 272 pp., contains a dozen essays examining the reaction to Copernicus by both institutions and individuals. It covers the first Roman reaction to the *De revolutionibus*, the use of Copernican illustrations, the treatment of Copernicus in Italian centres of learning, and Copernicus in the writings of G. A. Magini, Della Porta, Cardano, Bruno, and Galileo. Rivka Feldhay, *Galileo and the Church: Political Inquisition or Critical Dialogue?*, CUP, 1995, viii + 303 pp., proposes that 'the different interpretations of the theologians' ban on Copernicus and of the possible limits of Galileo's campaign expressed two cultural orientations of two rival intellectual élites within the church, the Dominicans and the Jesuits, who attempted to implement the decrees of the Council of Trent and were engaged in a struggle over cultural hegemony', and how the Jesuits ultimately withdrew their support for Galileo and cooperated in his condemnation. Michele Cioni, *I documenti galileiani del S. Uffizio di Firenze*, F, Giampiero Pagnini, 1996, xxxvii + 76 pp., is a reprint of the 1908 edition together with the review by Antonio Favaro which pointed out the many errors. L. Valcke, 'Jean Pic de la Mirandole et Johannes Kepler', *Rinascimento*, 36, 1996:275–97.

The cross-fertilization between art and science is explored in Eileen Reeves, *Painting the Heavens. Art and Science in the Age of Galileo*, Princeton U.P., x + 310 pp. + 8 pls, which focuses on Galileo's theories concerning the new star of 1604 and his writings on the nature and substance of the moon. This influenced artists who painted a corruptible lunar surface, leading to a change in religious iconography, while Galileo himself used the term 'secondary light' in his polemical writings, a term widely used by artists and found in treatises on optics. The neoplatonic-hermetic side of religious symbolism is examined in Mauro Zanchi, *Lorenzo Lotto e l'immaginario alchemico*, Bergamo, Ferrari, xviii + 213 pp., which investigates the *imprese* on the intarsia panels of the choir in the Basilica of Santa Maria Maggiore, Bergamo, and places the images within the context of Medieval and Renaissance hermeticism. Lotto's contacts with philosophers and alchemists are examined together with the meaning of the word *impresa* and the alchemical message of the project is revealed. Giovanni Pico Della Mirandola, *Heptaplus: la settemplice interpretazione dei sei giorni della genesi*, trans. Eugenio Garin, Carmagnola, Arktos, 1996, 143 pp., has a succint introduction by A. C. Ambesi followed by a text without any notes or critical apparatus. Pietro Pomponazzi,

Gli incantesimi, ed. Cristiana Innocenti, F, La Nuova Italia, xli + 211 pp., has an introduction assessing the Renaissance debate on magic. The complex lines of transmission for magical and hermetic texts are studied in Charles Burnett, *Magic and Divination in the Middle Ages. Texts and Techniques in the Islamic and Christian Worlds*, Aldershot, Variorum, 1996, xii + 370 pp., which includes meticulously researched studies on necromancy among the Seven Liberal Arts; Arabic, Greek, and Latin works on astrological magic; Arab culture and the transmission of hermetic magic; chiromancy; onomancy; scapulimancy; astrology. The textual traditions which these studies map out add much to our understanding of what the Renaissance inherited. A. M. Piemontese, 'Il corano latino di Ficino e i corani arabi di Pico e Monchates', *Rinascimento*, 36, 1996: 227–73.

A number of studies focus on the nature of medical practice. Winifred Schleiner, *Medical Ethics in the Renaissance*, Washington, Georgetown U.P., 1995, xiv + 230 pp., examines books on the duties and procedures of physicians, and questions accepted interpretations of writing on the body and gender, giving new readings of well-known texts. *Umanesimo e medicina: il problema dell'individuale*, ed. Roberto Cardini and Mariangela Regoliosi, Ro, Bulzoni, 1996, viii + 99 pp., opens up new avenues of research into the nature of Early Modern medical practice with C. Crisciani on the link between the *consilia* of early Renaissance doctors and the methodology of the humanist historians; N. G. Siraisi on works by Benivieni and Cardano, who gave great attention to collecting instances of *mirabilia*, and the relationship beween this, the practice of medicine, and the notes on real cases; G. Federici Vescovoni on the psychological, astrological, and humanist elements of M. Savonarola's *Speculum physiognomiae*. Andrew Cunningham, *The Anatomical Renaissance*, Aldershot, Scolar, xiv + 283 pp., is an important study that questions the accepted notion that modern 'scientific' anatomy started with Vesalius. It proposes a more complex evolution whereby different Renaissance anatomists, mainly working in Italy, carried on different dialogues with the past, and argues that there were many anatomical projects and many different concepts of what constituted the body. It rejects the notion of any 'Renaissance' causality for these different anatomistic agendas and looks to the world of religion for answers to this difficult question. Piero Camporesi, *Il sugo della vita: simbolismo e magia del sangue*, Mi, Garzanti, 121 pp., uses a wide range of sources from medical treatments, anatomical experiments, and descriptions of torture to the writings of Ficino, Campanella, Della Porta, and the visions of Christian mystics. The study explores the religious, medical, cosmological, and superstitious connotations of this essential bodily fluid. Id., *Camminare il mondo. Vita e avventure di Leonardo Fioravanti medico del Cinquecento*, Mi, Garzanti, 309 pp., is a most enjoyable study that charts the extraordinary career of one who was doctor, alchemist, herbalist, and engineer, from his beginnings in Bologna to his voyages with the Imperial fleet and his activities at the courts of Rome and Florence. He was an intimate of Cosimo I de' Medici and Alfonso d'Este, a writer of treatises and books of secrets, an observer of contemporary events, and a protagonist in that feverish, futile attempt to master nature and harness power. Maria Rosa Davi, *Bernardino Tomitano, filosofo, medico e letterato (1517–1576): profilo biografico e critico*, Trieste, Lint, 1995, viii + 187 pp., concentrates on T.'s career as a doctor and philosopher and gives a bio-bibliographical profile based on archive sources. This will help to give a balanced picture of Tomitano who is perhaps better known as a writer on rhetoric and an experimenter with new literary forms. V. Nutton, 'The rise of medical humanism: Ferrara 1464–1555', *RenS*, 11 : 2–19. Ivana Ait, *Tra scienza e mercato. Gli speziali a Roma nel tardo medioevo*, Ro, Istituto Nazionale di Studi Romani, 1996, 317 pp., examines apothecaries as an active economic force and how they interracted with the social, cultural, political, and religious world of Renaissance Rome.

RELIGIOUS THOUGHT AND THE CHURCH. Gary Remer, *Humanism and the Rhetoric of Toleration*, University Park, Pennsylvania State U.P., 1996, x + 318 pp., is a thorough study that emphasizes the fact that humanists did not place the right of conscience at the centre of the Renaissance defence of religious toleration. Toleration stemmed from the study of classical rhetoric in a preference for persuasion over force, for scepticism and toleration in non-essentials and an emphasis on ethical living over dogma. *Archivio Italiano per la storia della Pietà*, 10, includes E.-M. Jung-Inglessis, 'Il pianto della Marchesa di Pescara sopra la passione di Christo' (115–204), on the publishing history, with text, of a work by V. Colonna, together with the *Sermone* of Varchi; and G. Mongini, '"Nel cor ch'è pur di Cristo il tempio". La *Vita del serafico e glorioso S. Francesco* di Lucrezia Marinelli tra influssi ignaziani, spiritualismo e *prisca theologia*' (359–453). Post-Tridentine efforts to re-invigorate and reorganize the church are examined in Giovanni Pinto, *Il governo episcopale di Antonio Puteo nella chiesa di Bari (1562–1592)*, Bari, Cacucci, 1995, 151 pp. Bard Thompson, *Humanists and Reformers. A History of the Renaissance and Reformation*, Michigan, Eerdmans, 1996, x + 742 pp., gives a good general survey clearly setting out of the nature of humanism and the religious issues. It explores the preoccupations and enthusiasms that linked Italy to the Northern Europe. Aldo Landi, *Concilio e papato nel Rinascimento (1449–1516) un problema irrisolto*, T, Claudiana, 472 pp., looks at the tensions between conciliarists and Papacy concerning ultimate authority. This is a scholarly well-documented study that clarifies the

wider political context particularly the power of the French and
Imperial factions.

Girolamo Savonarola, *La semplicità della vita cristiana*, ed. and trans.
Tito S. Centi, Mi, Ares, 1996, 170 pp., presents the text with few
notes of one of Savonarola's major works, first published in Latin
(1496), then translated by Benivieni. It is based primarily on Aquinas
and promotes a reformation of man rather than of the church. *Studi
Savonaroliani: verso il V centenario*, ed. Gian Carlo Garfagnini, F, Sismel,
1996, xviii + 344 pp. + 9 pls, a rich collection, contains 30 essays
divided into three sections ('Savonarola a Firenze', 'La cultura al
tempo di Savonarola', and 'Il movimento Savonaroliano') with an
initial historiographical survey (D. Weinstein) and a concluding
review of the issues raised during the conference (C. Leonardi). G. C.
Garfagnini, 'La *Vita savonarolae* di Gianfrancesco Pico', *Rinascimento*,
36, 1996: 49–72, looks particularly at the historical stance taken with
regard to prophecy and politics. Marcello Vannucci, *Girolamo Savonarola frate e capopopolo: dall'amore per Laudomia al rogo nella piazza della
Signoria*, Ro, Newton Compton, 191 pp., is a good general biography.

Stregoneria e streghe nell'Europa moderna, ed. Giovanna Bosco and
Patrizia Castelli, Pisa, Pacini, 1996, 583 pp., is a weighty collection
investigating methodology, historiography, and case histories. There
are good essays on witch-hunting (W. Stephens), demonology
(C. Balducci), and law (P. Peruzzi, M. Milani, P. Portone). Francesco
Renda, *L'inquisizione in Sicilia*, Palermo, Sellerio, 474 pp., is in two
parts. The first investigates the inquisition between 1487 and 1782,
and looks at the tension and jurisdictional conflicts between the
Spanish and the local population with regard to the imposition of a
Spanish inquisition. The second part considers the activity of the
inquisition, its effect on Jews and Muslims, the Holy Office and
abuses in the church, and the reaction against witchcraft and magic.
Aldo Migliorini, *Tortura, inquisizione, pena di morte*, Poggibonsi, Lalli,
157 pp., is a rather macabre volume that gives a facsimile of the *Sacro
arsenale ovver pratica dell'uffizio della santa inquisizione*, followed by
illustrations of instruments of torture. Domenico del Rio, *I Gesuiti e
l'Italia*, Mi, Corbaccio, 1996, 522 pp., gives a good account of the
Order's early organization and activities, though it lacks any critical
apparatus. Alete dal Canto, *Aonio Paleario*, Foggia, Bastogi, 1995,
127 pp., traces the activities which led to his execution for heresy.
D. S. Chambers, *Renaissance Cardinals and their Wordly Problems*,
Aldershot, Variorum, xii + 360 pp., has 11 essays, the majority
relating to Cardinal Francesco Gonzaga and his entourage, that
revolve around what was expected of a prince of the church in terms
of magnificence and the problems of finance. The volume also traces

the tensions set up when family obligations conflicted with duty to the church.

On the links between religion and art: Eugenio Marino, *Estetica, fede e critica d'arte. L'arte poetica di Savonarola, l'estetica di Ficino e la Primavera di Botticelli*, Pistoia, Provincia Romana di Frati Predicatori, 279 pp., examines the relationship between faith, theology, intuition, and poetic and visual images. It includes a consideration of the allegorical interpretation of pagan myths, theology as poetry and poetry as theology. This is a well-documented, scholarly study that examines the writings of Alberti, E. Barbaro, F. Guicciardini, Leonardo, G. Pico Della Mirandola, Poliziano and Pulci. Leo Steinberg, *The Sexuality of Christ in Renaissance Art and in Modern Oblivion*, Chicago U.P., 1996, viii + 417 pp., adds to the original study (1983) a substantial chapter incorporating new evidence and answering criticisms to the original thesis. It will no doubt give rise to more lively debate. Paolo Berdini, *The Religious Art of Jacopo Bassano. Painting as Visual Exegesis*, CUP, xiv + 208 pp., emphasizes the importance of the act of reading over the text and claims that 'what the painting visualises is not the narration of the text but its expanded reading as it emerges from the painter's reading'. There is a good discussion of the literary genres promoted, and the positions taken, after Trent and how these might have been read. Unfortunately, at times the argument is buried in jargon. Massimo Firpo, *Gli affreschi di Pontormo a San Lorenzo. Eresia, politica e cultura nella Firenze di Cosimo I*, T, Einaudi, xxiv + 446 pp. + 62 pls, reconstructs the lost frescoes of the choir in terms of their political and religious significance. This is an extremely well researched and methodologically resourceful study, documenting the circulation of Juan de Valdés's and other reformers' writings on the eve of the Council of Trent and Cosimo's struggle to consolidate his independence while maintaining his reputation as a true son of the church. The use of the theoretical pronouncements of the Counter-Reformation for analyses of cultural production is criticized in Pietro Amato, *Simone De Magistris: picturam et sculturam faciebat*, Macerata, Cassa di Risparmio, 1996, 362 pp., which emphasizes the need to study individual projects in terms of specific influences and circumstances.

Richard C. Trexler, *The Journey of the Magi. Meanings in History of a Christian Story*, Princeton U.P., xii + 277 pp., establishes the Magi as a high social and political icon and looks at the evolution of the image and its meaning. The chapter 'The pageant of the two kings' examines outdoor magi spectacles, popular in Florence in the latter part of the 15th c., which were controlled by the Medici and seen as a legitimizing icon for the government or for an individual family.

3. POETRY

AnI, 12, 1994, overlooked at the time, contains 13 high-quality essays discussing the Italian epic, all noted below under individual authors with the exception of: J. Vitullo, 'Contained conflict: wild men and warrior women in the early Italian epic' (39–59), analyses the absorption of marginal figures such as the noble savage into the early Italian epic and how the treatment of these problematic figures often indicated a 'democratization' of the chivalric mythology of the Carolingian cycle; this rapprochement between 'feudal' and 'bourgeois chivalric epics' led to a more confident portrayal of the female warrior by women writers of succeeding generations; D. Anderson, 'The Italian background to Chaucer's epic similes' (15–38). *Gli amici amanti coppie eroiche e storie notturne nell'epica italiana*, ed. M. C. Cabani, Na, Liguori, 1995, 141 pp., takes the model of the night excursion by a pair of friends/warriors in the Italian epic and compares it with its classical sources. Using Ariosto as the starting point — indeed that section is the most satisfying — the model is traced through Tasso down to the 17th c., to include the works of Francesco Bracciolini and Nicola Villani. D. Quint, 'Narrative interlace and narrative genres in *Don Quijote* and the *Orlando Furioso*', *MLQ*, 58:241–68, argues that Cervantes' indebtedness to Ariosto is clear (in *Don Quijote*) in the technique of multiple story-telling and contrapuntal narrative genres, and that both works by exemplifying these strategies demonstrate how 'narrative interlace becomes a formal technique of novelization'. A. Maggi, 'L'identità come impresa in *Rime degli Accademici Occulti*', *EL*, 22.1:43–61, explores the common late-16th-c. fashion for academies to publish volumes of *imprese* and verse relating to their members. Although each of the 14 chapters has a classic tripartite emblem structure (*impresa* to represent identity of *accademico*, commentary 3–10 pages and a series of lyric verses), M. declares them to be *imprese* purely on the grounds of 'il loro carattere essenzialmente privato'. In a further emblematic twist, the 'secretario' of the Academy becomes the 'auctoritas' of the personal symbol as he inserts a comment on the *impresa* itself, thus controlling the interpretation of the *accademico*'s public image. L. C. Rossi, 'Presenze di Petrarca in commenti danteschi fra Tre e Quattrocento', *Aevum*, 70, 1996:441–76, gives a systematic list of commentaries on Dante from 1360 to 1478. All of these texts use Petrarch and his works as a critical yardstick by which to judge Dante, but Rossi shows how the change in reference from Petrarch's Latin works to Petrarch the *volgare* poet marks the change in cultural climate between late Middle Ages and Renaissance. A. Fongaro 'Quatre remarques à propos d'Apollinaire et de l'Aretin', *REI*, 41, 1995:89–97, exposes a mistranslation of a comment Aretino made about Dante (from *L'Oeuvre du Divin Aretin* published in 1909 in the collection *Maîtres de l'Amour*, ed. Briffaut) — 'Più non val Dante o il terso Serafino' (Dante ne vaut pas plus que le limpide Acquilano) — which caused Apollinaire unjustly in turn to criticize the Italian poet for his lack of literary judgement.

ARIOSTO. R. J. Rodini, 'Selected bibliography of Ariosto criticism', *AnI*, 12, 1994:299–317, synthesizes the principal topics of interest to critics: allegory and intertextuality in A., the continuing study of the *Furioso*'s protagonists and its socio-historical background. E. J. Bellamy, 'Alcina's revenge: reassessing irony and allegory in the *Orlando Furioso*', *ib.*, 62–85, aims to prove that the 16th-c. insistence upon allegorizing A.'s poem was an attempt to confer, indeed impose, great (Virgilian) prestige upon the work, but that this simultaneously suppressed the essence of the text, the author's *ingegno* and irony. F. Masciandoro, 'Ariosto and the myth of Narcissus: notes on Orlando's folly', *Studi Aguzzi*, 22:147-68, discusses the link between the Greek myth and Ariosto's central episode of Orlando's madness, noting the scant attention it has received from critics. P. J. Cook, 'The epic chronotope from Ariosto to Spenser', *ib.*, 115–42; L. F. Rhu, 'Ariosto moralisé: political decorum in Spenser's imitations of *Orlando Furioso*', *ib.*, 143–58.

BERNI. M. Montanile, 'Le Chiome anti-petrarchiste di Berni', *EL*, 21.2, 1996:59–67, focuses upon the well-known sonnet XXIII, 'Chiome d'argento fino irte e attorte', to depict Berni's distrust of 'la poesia alta' and his defence of his identity as 'poeta comico'. B. overturns the traditional Petrarchan topos of the *chioma* (standardized in 16th-c. treatises on poetry and aesthetics) by celebrating female ugliness in an ironically high style so that this sonnet becomes a 'vituperatio contro l'uso umanistico dell'encomio'.

BOIARDO. Matteo Maria Boiardo, **Orlando Innamorato*, ed. Riccardo Bruscagli, 2 vols, T, Einaudi, 1995, lxvi + 523–1266 pp., in its systematic analysis of each canto with narrative summary and index of names, is a useful work for students although it does not relate Boiardo's work to the tradition of *letteratura cavalleresca*. M. Bregoli-Russo, 'Rassegna della critica boiardesca: 1983–1994', *AnI*, 12, 1994:267–97, looks at 132 studies dealing with such issues as intratextuality and intertextuality in B., and philological and stylistic approaches to him, while with an eye to the future of B. studies, she criticizes the lack of comprehensive analyses of B. works which would otherwise indicate the future evolution of B. criticism.

CATTANEO. **La poesia scolpita. Danese Cattaneo nella Venezia del Cinquecento*, ed. M. Rossi, Lucca, Pacini Fazzi, 268 pp., attempts to restore the reputation of the neglected 16th-c. sculptor/artist. By focusing on his poetry, the 13 canti of *L'amor di Marfisa* (1562), they put Cattaneo in the literary context of his times.

ERASMO DI VALVASONE. Erasmo di Valvasone, *Le Rime*, ed. Giorgio Cerboni Baiardi, Valvasone, Circolo Culturale Erasmo di Valvason, 1993 xix + 389 pp., is a handsome volume published in commemoration of the quatercentenary of the death of the neglected Friulan poet. His entire collection of vernacular lyric poetry is brought together for the first time in one volume along with a valuable bibliography of his known works.

FALAMONICA. G. Ponte, 'Sulla datazione del poema di Bartolo-meo Falamonica', *EL*, 22.3:5–14, reassesses the shadowy figure of a Genoese poet of some note from the end of the 15th c. By dating his didactic-religious poem *La Scoperta* to 1500–03, P. shows how F.'s work was steeped in the concerns of his time: condemnation of corrupt clergy, fear of Turkish expansion, and war between Christian princes. So his poem can be said to belong to the 'letteratura escatologica del tempo'.

FOLENGO. A. P. Russell, 'Epic agon and the strategy of reform in Folengo and Rabelais', *CLS*, 34:119–48, uncovers the unusual accolade accorded an Italian humanist in influencing Rabelais's work. The mock-epic *Baldus*, by Teofilo Folengo, was acknowledged soon after Rabelais's death as a model for the Pantagrueline stories.

LORENZO DE' MEDICI. Lorenzo de' Medici, *Poesie*, ed. Ilvano Caliaro, Mi, Garzanti, li + 301 pp., is a most readable student's guide to *Il Magnifico* and his poetry. Caliaro's introduction juxtaposes the two sides of *Il Magnifico*, prince/man of politics and man of letters, while the detailed notes illuminate the poetry and place it in the literary context of the time.

MANNARINO. The 16th-c. Apulian scholar Cataldo Antonio Mannarino's first published work (1596), the heroic poem *Glorie di guerrieri e d'amanti*, ed. Grazia Distaso, Fasano, Schena, 263 pp., while clearly showing its indebtedness to Tasso nevertheless puts its own individual stamp on epic poetry. Mannarino's eye-witness testimony of the siege of Taranto by the Turks in 1594, which is the specific subject of the poem, is striking for the richness of its regional focus and the recent nature of the events.

MICHELANGELO. T. E. Mussio, 'The Augustinian conflict in the lyrics of Michelangelo: Michelangelo reading Petrarch', *Italica*, 74:339–59, maintains that, although there is no concrete evidence suggesting a direct line of influence between St Augustine's *Confessions* and M.'s *Rime*, the link can be perceived through M.'s concerns in his verse regarding spiritual insecurity and the question of the soul and its salvation. For Mussio, Petrarch was the mediator between M. and St Augustine, and to illustrate this point he shows how M. manipulates

Petrarchan conceits and images in his *Rime*. George Bull, *Michelangelo: A Biography*, London, Viking, 1995, 504 pp., a well-documented study, takes account of the literary dimension, including M.'s encounters with Vasari, Varchi, and Beccadelli.

MOLZA. What is perhaps Molza's best-known work is studied by A. Bisanti, 'La *Ninfa Tiberina* di Francesco Maria Molza', *CLett*, 95:225–31. Considered of an equal stature with the mythological-bucolic poetry of Poliziano and Lorenzo, the poem in 81 *ottave* was composed in 1537 in honour of Faustina Mancini.

PULCI. E. Lebano, 'Un decennio di studi pulciani: 1984–1994', *AnI*, 12, 1994:233–65, presents a comprehensive bibliographical overview of the many studies on Pulci from 1984 (41 in total). His often in-depth critical analysis of these texts documents the clear trends in Pulci studies from 1984 while underlining the major critical currents of 1994, which include gender and hermeneutics.

TASSO. G. Da Pozzo, 'Last assaults and delayed victory in Tasso's *Liberata*', *Italica*, 74:319–38, rejects the term Mannerism in reference to Tasso. Focusing upon the description of the final attack upon Jerusalem which preludes the ultimate victory of the Christian armies, he explores the characteristics of Tasso's narrative style in comparison with other works like the *Aminta*. He attempts to resolve the unsatisfactory nature of the term Mannerism in reference to literary works of the late 16th c. In its stead, he suggests syncretism. Torquato Tasso, **Lettere poetiche*, ed. C. Molinari, Parma, Guanda (Fondazione Pietro Bembo), 141 pp., discusses the letters written by Tasso reflecting on his own poetry during the period of the Roman revision of the *Liberata* from February 1575 to the summer of 1576. The dense commentary can at times complicate reading of these lesser-known letters which have suffered from a poor publishing history in our century. P. Luparia, '"Trinitas Creatrix". Appunti sulla teologia platonica del Tasso nel *Mondo Creato*', *REI*, 42, 1996:85–116, explores the nature of Tasso's concept of God and the Trinity to unlock a new reading of the poet's last work, the *Mondo Creato*. A. Ghessi, 'Gli Elegiaci latini nella *Gerusalemme Liberata*', *Italianistica*, 26:61–73, examines the problematic influence of Latin elegy on 16th-c. poetry. She focuses upon the specific case of Tasso drawing the link between Catullus *Carmina LXIV* and the figure of the abandoned lover Armida (who recalls C.'s Ariadne) and showing how 16th-c. authors had to filter the erotic images of Catullus and Propertius through Christian morality. C. Bandera, 'Tasso and the epic: a Girardian reading', *AnI*, 15:101–24, explores the ironic juxtaposition of the zenith and decline of the epic. In Christian Europe it achieved its greatest prestige at the very moment when it was becoming unviable and historically irrelevant. C. Scarpati, **Tasso, i classici e i moderni*, Padua, Antenore,

1995, 182 pp., divides his book into three sections respectively dealing with the stylistic influence of Petrarch in the *Gerusalemme Liberata*, the fundamental influence of Ovid in the *Aminta*, and the fusion of classical and contemporary influences in *Torrismondo*. S. seeks to show how the three genres (epic, tragedy, and the pastoral) combine to form Tasso the poet. F. Betti, 'Woman-made-angel and otherwise in Italian poetry of the Middle Ages and Renaissance', *Studi Aguzzi*, 22:173–92, focuses on love poems to women from 1190, but gives particular emphasis to Tasso, Ariosto, and their works: the *Liberata*, *Aminta*, and *Furioso*. These texts reveal an uncertain, problematic attitude towards love, and with Tasso specifically the object of real love is shown to be unattainable. A. Ascoli, 'In liberating the tomb: difference and death in *Gerusalemme liberata*', *AnI*, 12, 1994:159–80, focuses upon the last two lines of the poem to explore the narrative axis of the text, the quest for the Holy Sepulchre, and the central themes of death, vow, and tomb which it exemplifies. W. Stephens, 'Tasso and the witches', *ib.*, 181–202. E. Salvaneschi, *Gerusalemme liberata: utopia per un regista*, Pisa, ETS, 121 pp., systematically analyses the principal characters, themes, and images with a view to their visual presentation on screen.

Torquato Tasso e l'università, noted above under INDIVIDUAL CENTRES, has sections on T.'s poetry and its reception, as well as papers on his links with Ferrara and the multifarious cultural context, from mathematics to the Counter-Reformation.

4. THEATRE

Luigi Alamanni, *Tragedia di Antigone*, ed. F. Spera, T, RES, 121 pp., has an introduction which identifies A.'s refined Petrarchan style and explores the tragic themes in his translation of Sophocles' play, a work which is seen as a bridge between the previous tradition (Trissino, Rucellai) and its continuation in the 1540s with Giraldi, Speroni, and Aretino. F. Doglio, *Il Teatro in Italia*, 1: *Medio Evo e Umanesimo*, Ro, Studium, 259 pp., presents an ambitious account of the origins and evolution of poetic drama in the Italian language. He charts the influence of classical culture through the Latin Middle Ages and quotes from little-known texts from the High Middle Ages down to the 15th c., illustrating as he does so the direct influence between epic/courtly poetry and Italian theatre. Following an interdisciplinary approach, Günsberg, *Gender*, applies a feminist reading to dramatic representations of women in plays from the Renaissance to Goldoni, D'Annunzio, Pirandello, and through to the contemporary works of playwright-actress Franca Rame. Politics and the political function of drama concern M. J. Flaumenhaft, in *Civic*

Spectacle, Essays on Drama and Continuity, Lanham, MD, Rowman and Littlefield, 1994, x + 168 pp. Dedicating a chapter each to the major plays of Aeschylus, Euripides, Machiavelli, and Shakespeare, she explores the purpose of the play-performance, the society it reflects, and ultimately its political impact upon the spectator. *Origini della commedia improvvisa o dell'arte. Atti del XIX Convegno, Centro Studi sul Teatro Medioevale e Rinascimentale (Roma, 12–14 ottobre 1995, Anagni, 15 ottobre 1995)*, ed. M. Chiabò and F. Doglio, Ro, Torre d'Orfeo, 541 pp., includes *inter alia*: N. Borsellino, 'Fra testo e gesto. Drammaturgie di transizione nel Cinquecento' (13–22); I. Innamorati, 'Il ri-uso della parola: a proposito della parentela fra generici e centoni' (163–85); S. Maraucci, 'Un suggello alla Commedia dell'Arte in area meridionale: lo Zibaldone di Placido Adriani' (247–71); M. Rousse, 'Comédiens français et comédiens italiens' (303–27). It also includes a very extensive *bibliografia ragionata internazionale* divided into four sections, the first being an exhaustive and selective bibliography of the genre up to 1988 (437–38), the second listing the major modern critical editions authored mainly by the comic actors themselves (439–51), the third covering general studies on the *commedia dell'arte* from its 16th-c. beginnings through to its influence upon 19th-c. theatre (451–58), and the fourth including the largest and most eclectic range of texts, which cover for example the interaction between music and comedy, and the biographies of some of *commedia*'s major protagonists (458–541). Giorgio Padoan **L'avventura della commedia rinascimentale*, Padua, Piccin, 1996, 230 pp., synthesizes P.'s writings on Renaissance comedy into one large compendium which is useful not simply for individual authors but as a general history of the genre. The vast range of works considered allows scope for analysis of other theatrical genres such as allegorical spectacles, masks, and *commedie alla burlesca*. P.'s insightful critical focus goes beyond the individual texts to analyse the impact of other factors such as techniques of acting, scenography, location of performance (court or academy), editorial history, and the success of the work in Italy and beyond. The book concludes with the *commedia dell'arte* and the reforms instituted by Goldoni.

ARIOSTO. Lodovico Ariosto, *Commedie*, I: *La Cassaria, I Suppositi*, ed. Luigina Stefani, Mi, Mursia, 223 pp., includes a lengthy introduction rehabilitating two of Ariosto's comedies which until now have been dismissed by critics as marginal to his development as a poet. In her extremely detailed analysis of the plays, Stefani reveals how they represent an important moment in the refinement of Ariosto, poet of the *Furioso*. M. Scalabrini, 'La schiatta di Mastro Iachelino. Una proposta per il Negromante', *LS*, 31, 1996:161–75, shows through an analysis of the character of Mastro Iachelino (particularly in comparison with Pulci's Margutte in the *Morgante)* how Ariosto's theatre illustrates his concept of social ethics whereby, within human relationships constructed upon power, truth is impossible.

MACHIAVELLI. Niccolò Machiavelli, *Mandragola*, ed. T. Piras, Mi, Garzanti, xlv + 83 pp., benefits greatly not only from the editor's illuminating and detailed linguistic commentary, but particularly from P. Gibellini's preface, which provides a most readable account of Machiavelli's life and of the play's characters and plot, as well as an accessible critical overview of Renaissance dramatic convention. Niccolò Machiavelli, *Mandragola*, ed. G. Inglese, Bo, Il Mulino, 126 pp., is a more erudite edition which takes as its base text the only manuscript version of the play (1519), preserved at the Laurentian Library in Florence. While providing a scholarly account of the publishing fortunes of the play and standardizing certain of its linguistic features, this edition is notable for including the texts of the songs written by Machiavelli for the 1526 performance of the play at Faenza. P. Baldan, 'La musica della (e nella) Mandragola di Machiavelli', *Italianistica*, 25, 1996:53–59, examines the relationship between literature and music in Machiavelli's play: the music which was present in the most sumptuous productions is presented as an essential accompaniment, woven into the action of the play. The Florence of Cosimo de' Medici and the Accademia is illustrated in Niccolò Machiavelli, *Tizia*, ed. Paolo Caserta, Ro, Bulzoni, 198 pp. The informative notes and introduction to this lesser-known play are complemented by an illuminating biography of the author himself.

NICCOLÒ DA CORREGGIO. R. L. Martinez, 'De-Cephalizing Rinaldo: the money of tyranny in Niccolò da Correggio's *Fabula de Cefalo* and *Orlando Furioso*, 42–43', *AnI*, 12, 1994:87–114.

TASSO. Torquato Tasso, *King Torrismondo*, ed. M. Pastore Passaro, NY, Fordham U.P., viii + 332 pp., is an elegant translation which ably fulfils the stated intention of bringing this neglected work to 'those students who do not command the language of the original text'. A. Oldcorn's general introduction to Tasso's life and Passaro's shorter informative essays on his *oeuvre* combine to put Tasso and this text in the context of their times.

5. PROSE

Giancarlo Mazzacurati, *All'ombra di Dioneo: tipologie e percorsi della novella da Boccaccio a Bandello*, F, La Nuova Italia, 1996, xviii + 218 pp., comprises six essays, which include: 'Dopo Boccaccio: percorsi del genere novella dal Sacchetti al Bandello'; 'La narrativa di Giovan Francesco Straparola e l'ideologia del fiabesco'; 'La narrazione policentrica di Matteo Bandello'. These essays explore narrative structure and strategies mixing echoes of the past with innovations.

ARETINO.   Pietro Aretino, *Lettere,* vol. 1, pt. 1, ed. Paolo Procaccioli, Ro, Salerno, 705 pp., the first volume of an Edizione Nazionale of the correspondence, is based on the second Marcolini edition of 1542, but the variants of the two 1538 Marcolini editions are duly registered. The thorough introduction explores A.'s strategies and criteria in selecting and ordering his letters for publication. There is a full critical apparatus including notes that give detailed descriptions of the early editions with all the variants. Pietro Aretino, *Dialoghi,* 1, *Ragionamenti della Nanna e della Antonia,* ed. Guido Davico Bonino, Mi, ES, 217 pp., has excellent notes and a scholarly introduction, and is based on the text of the 1975 Einaudi edition of the *Sei giornate.*

BRUNO.   J. R. Poulin, 'Giordano Bruno, une éthique e l'infini', *BHR,* 59:305–20. *Bruniana & Campanelliana,* 2, 1996 [1997], contains: D. von Wille, 'Bruno, Campanella e l'ateismo del Rinascimento nell'*Apologia* di Johann Jakob Zimmerman' (247–71); G. Aquilecchia, 'Paralipomeno nella documentazione di Bruno in Inghilterra' (359–60); and T. Provvidera, 'On the printer of Giordano Bruno's London works' (361–67). F. Tomizza, 'Quattro varianti significative nel dialogo 7 della *Cena de le ceneri* di Giordano Bruno', *Rinascimento,* 36:431–56.

CAMPANELLA.   John M. Headley, *Tommaso Campanella and the Transformation of the World,* Princeton U.P., xxv + 399 pp., is a meticulous piece of scholarship that sheds much light on a complex corpus of philosophical, political, and social writings. It looks at his works within their specific genre traditions but also goes beyond this to examine his correspondence, treatises, occasional writings, and statements, as he reacted to events and sought to impose some order upon the chaos of his age.

CARTARI.   Vincenzo Cartari, *Le immagini de i Dei de gli antichi,* ed. Ginetta Auzzas et al., Vicenza, Neri Pozza, 1996, lxxxviii + 618 pp., investigates the textual tradition listing the variants, discusses the publishing history of C.'s works and looks at the originality of this compilation. What emerges is a systematically organized source of information on mythology where the images are verbal rather than figurative.

CASTIGLIONE   S. Kolsky, 'Making and breaking the rules: Castiglione's *Cortegiano*', *RenS,* 11:358–80.

CELLINI.   M. Orsino, 'Il fuoco nella *Vita* di Benvenuto Cellini: aspetti di un mito dell'artista-fabbro', *ISt,* 52:94–110, examines the symbolism of fire but applies too many criteria derived from general theories, and shows no real understanding of Renaissance astrology. V. C. Gardner, '*Homines non nascuntur, sed figuntur:* Benvenuto Cellini's *Vita* and self-presentation of the Renaissance artist', *SCJ,* 28:447–65, looks at strategies aimed at personal advancement and immortality.

DE' ROSSI. Giovangirolamo De' Rossi, *Vita di Giovanni de' Medici detto delle Bande Nere,* ed. Vanni Bramante, Ro, Salerno, 133 pp., presents without critical apparatus the text of a composition which closely follows the established biographical tradition of Giovanni's life.

DOLCE. Ronnie H. Terpening, *Lodovico Dolce: Renaissance Man of Letters,* Toronto U.P., vi + 310 pp., is a call for a re-evaluation of D.'s repututation as a scholar, critic, and writer. Given the unwieldy variety of D.'s writings this study does not attempt a comprehensive literary biography. It points to areas for further study and concentrates on charting his changing interests from Ariosto and the chivalric romances, to the theatre and activity as critic and editor, and finally to his 'pre-encyclopedism'.

GARZONI. Tomaso Garzoni, *La piazza universale di tutte le professioni del mondo,* ed. Giovanni Battista Bronzini, 2 vols, F, Olschki, 1996, xlviii + 706, 707–1424 pp., is based on the 1589 editon, emended in the light of other editions. The variants are duly registered in an appendix. P. Cerchi, 'Onomastica e critica testuale nella *Piazza universale* di T. Garzoni', *Besomi Vol.,* 258–71, is a most enjoyable study which identifies the origin of misnomers and the reasons behind the invention of names.

GIOVIO. T. C. Price Zimmermann, *Paolo Giovio: The Historian and the Crisis of Sixteenth-Century Italy,* Princeton U.P., 1995, xii + 391 pp., is a well-documented biography which lays bare the faults and strengths of G.'s character, points up the perceptive nature of his writings, and at the same time presents the characters, events, and places that formed the setting for G.'s life's journey.

LEONARDO. Leonardo da Vinci, *Scritti scelti,* ed. Anna Maria Brisio, T, UTET, 1996, 702 pp., is a reprint with an up-dated, but disappointing, bibliography.

MACHIAVELLI. Alfredo Oriani, *Nicolò Machiavelli,* ed. Gennaro Maria Barbuto, Na, Guida, 153 pp., was first published in 1889 and seen as an attack on the lionization of M. by De Sanctis. Oriani, who had inherited the Risorgimento's antipathy for the Renaissance, sees M. as a great prose-writer rather than as a true political theorist. The introduction sets out the positions taken by De Sanctis, Villari, and Oriani within the context of 19th-c. historical and intellectual currents. G. Inglese, 'Postille machiavelliane. Codici del *De principatibus:* il MS Par.It.709', *AIISS,* 13, 1995–96:471–75, examines the MS written by B. Buonaccorsi between 1515–26 now in the Bibliothèque Nationale. Vickie B. Sullivan, *Machiavelli's Three Romes: Religion, Human Liberty and Politics Reformed,* De Kalb, Northern Illinois U.P., 1996, 235 pp., identifies three different concepts: the republican Rome of antiquity with its pursuit of glory; Christian Rome; the Rome of M.'s imagination, which would allow human liberty to flourish. The study postulates that M. wanted humanity to extricate itself from the grip of the Christian god, and that for him Christianity alone had made the practice of true political life impossible. For M. a compromise solution which avoids the pitfalls and brings together the strengths of both the Christian and Pagan Romes would provide a better alternative. Georges Faraklas, *Machiavel: le pouvoir du prince*, Paris, PUF, 127 pp., attempts to reconstruct M.'s theory of political power. It points out his desire for social justice and how, for him, power was to be defined not according to who wielded it but how, and to what ends, it was deployed. Niccolò Machiavelli, *Breviario*, ed. Gabriella Brusa Zappellini, Mi, Rusconi, 1996, 285 pp., is a collection of extracts from M.'s works organized under 14 headings. V. Cox, 'Machiavelli and the *Rhetorica ad Herennium:* deliberative rhetoric in *The Prince*', *SCJ*, 28:1109–41. J. D'Amico, 'Machiavelli and ambition', *ItQ*, 34:5–16, examines the connotations, mostly negative, of ambition and its relationship to *virtù*.

PEROTTI. Martine Furno, *Le cornu copiae de Niccolò Perotti*, Geneva, Droz, 1995, 251 pp., reconstructs P.'s methodology and acquaintance with classical and medieval texts, and examines the purpose of the work as an attempt to distil the essentials of knowledge.

SABADINO DEGLI ARIENTI. Carolyn James, *Giovanni Sabadino degli Arienti: A Literary Career*, F, Olschki, 1996, 160 pp., is a biography of the humanist known as the Bolognese Boccaccio. It traces the effects of patronage on his literary output and shows how other aspects of his expertise were valued more than his skill as a professional writer.

TASSO. S. Bozzola, '"Questa quasi arringo del ragionare": la tecnica dei *Dialoghi* tassiano', *Italianistica*, 26:253–74, presents a very detailed analysis to prove that the dialogue, as found in T., is not a true *disputatio*, but monological. His exploration of the dynamics and locutory roles of the dialogues themselves, and then, more broadly, of their relation to the dialogue tradition of the 16th c., leads him to conclude: 'se insomma Tasso distingue metodologicamente il dialogo dal testo filosofico, inversamente cerca nel dialogo la sobrietà e l'asciuttezza stilistica del filosofo'. Torquato Tasso, *Discorso della virtù feminile e donnesca*, ed. Maria Luisa Doglio, Palermo, Sellerio, 80 pp., has a perceptive introduction which places the work in the context of court culture and discusses the classical and philosophical influences and the textual tradition.

VASARI. K. A. McIver, 'Maniera, music and Vasari', *SCJ*, 28:45–55, examines the function of music to elevate, distract, and edify, and shows how V. used the language of music in discussing painting. Giorgio Vasari, *Le tecniche artistiche. Introduzione e commento di G. Baldwin Brown*, trans. Francesca Diano, Vicenza, Neri Pozza, 1996, xxxviii + 313 pp., gives the text of the commentary, which examines the first part of V.'s *Vite* and explains the terminology and technical details.

SEICENTO

By MAURICE SLAWINSKI, *Lecturer in Italian Studies, University of Lancaster*

I. GENERAL

LITERARY HISTORY, POETICS, GENERAL CRITICISM.   Matteo Peregrini, *Delle acutezze,* ed. Erminia Ardissino, T, RES, 176 pp., is the first complete modern edition of this earliest and most ambivalent of treatises on the rhetorical conceit: Peregrini begins by declaring that his concern is to correct its indiscriminate use, which has contaminated 'la facondia prosaica' (the greater part of his examples are drawn from Latin prose writers), but ends by focusing on vernacular verse; he dismisses 'acutezze e loro studio' as an amusement for 'ingegni leggieri', yet devotes considerable effort to explaining how to produce them; he condemns their indiscriminate and over-mechanical application, yet carefully sets down rules by which they may be 'assembled' to order. The text is clearly and scrupulously presented, with a minimum of explanatory notes, on the basis of a collation of the two known editions: in keeping with the publisher's aim of providing the major poetic and theoretical works of the Early Modern period in editions uncluttered by intrusive critical commentary, there is no introduction — only the most concise (but thorough) bio/bibliographical appendix; Pellegrino's quotations have been carefully yet unfussily identified; orthography and punctuation subjected to the right amount of 'conservative' modernization to make the text as accessible as possible without falsification. Having been well served by editor and publisher, one can only hope that Pellegrino's text will cease to be what it has been since Croce's 'rediscovery', arbitrary 'evidence' for this or that view of the *Seicento,* and begin to be read in terms of its own reasons and contradictions.

The Cambridge History of Italian Literature, ed. Peter Brand and Lino Pertile, CUP, 1996, xxxiv + 702 pp., devotes just 40 pages to the *Seicento* (the *Settecento* gets 20 more) containing irritating errors of fact (the Dukes of Savoy become kings 150 years early): the sections on lyric poetry, mock-epic and satire, and treatises, by Paolo Cherchi, are hurried and unenlightening, with half a page on *concettismo,* and not even a mention of, among others, Rinaldi or Casoni; half a page on the New Science; two short paragraphs that amount to no more than lists for Campanella; disproportionately more space for Marino, but marked by dubious assertions (are the *Epitalami* really 'more original' than the 1602 *Rime?*); Albert N. Mancini's contributions on narrative prose and theatre are equally brief, but a good deal more thoughtful and balanced, giving good sketches of the varieties of the *romanzo*, for instance, and the transformations which the classical dramatic genres undergo during the period. Even more constrained by space are David Kimbell's five pages on opera, whose literary (never mind musical) importance deserved better — which leaves the impression that the root of the problem is the editors' disregard for the *Seicento*, and conversely the 300-odd pages given over, I suspect for commercial reasons, to the 19th and 20th centuries. (This is despite the fact that documentation in English was already abundant for this period, while its international significance is modest.)

Storia della Letteratura Italiana, ed. Enrico Malato, v: *La fine del Cinquecento e il Seicento*, Ro, Salerno, 1207 pp., is an altogether weightier and more balanced summary of the current 'state of the art', with substantial contributions by some of the leading specialists in their fields (for example, Giuseppe Galasso on Spanish hegemony; Andrea Battistini on Baroque culture and society; Giorgio Fulco on Marino; Lina Bolzoni on Campanella) accompanied by up-to-date, intelligently selected bibliographies. Yet coming as it does in a long series of 'new' literary histories (from the Laterza history-anthology of the early 1970s, through the vast and still growing Einaudi *Letteratura italiana*, to the UTET *Storia della cultura letteraria italiana* earlier this decade), each of which in turn has devoted considerable space to re-interpreting the *Seicento*, one wonders whether a more daring editorial brief might not have been opportune, giving the distinguished contributors a greater chance to offer their own insights; as it stands the purpose and potential market for this enterprise escape me.

THEMES AND TOPICS. *Le parole e le ore. Gli orologi barocchi: antologia poetica del Seicento*, ed. Vitaniello Bonito, Palermo, Sellerio, 1996, 130 pp., is a by-product of the editor's long-term research on the theme, which has now reached fruition in Id., *L'occhio del tempo. L'orologio barocco fra scienza, letteratura ed emblematica*, Bo, CLUEB, 1996, 284 pp., a study which, after an interesting historical-theoretical introduction (albeit more at ease with generic, metaphysical statements about time than the precise historical reasons why, in the 17th c. it came to be configured and experienced in new ways) drifts off into rather unstructured exemplifications of the *topos*, uncritically placing side by side texts which share little else stylistically, historically, or in terms of the meaning attributed to time's passing. Gino Rizzo, *Filologia e critica tra Sei e Ottocento*, Galatina, Congedo, 1996, 180 pp., contains several useful new contributions concerning the literary culture of southern Italy: 'M. Rigillo, il Seicento e tre "Oziosi" (G. B. Basile, G. Battista e G. P. D'Alessandro' (7–15); 'Una serata tra gli "Umoristi" con Pietro Della Valle: le "tre nuove maniere di verso sdrucciolo"' (17–29); 'Con Poliziano, Marino e i marinisti tra api ingegnose e miele barocco' (57–70), plus one previously published (cf. *YWMLS*, 56:522) and another which now appears in a fuller form in *StSec* (see below). M. Lollini, 'Vico, Salvator Rosa e le maschere del Barocco', *FoI*, 29, 1995:245–65, argues that Rosa's painting *La menzogna* (1649), like Vico's later observations on the subject, moves beyond the Baroque preoccupation with appearance and self-representation and towards a 'poesia moderna in grado di esprimere parole di verità riguardo alla condizione umana' (an Enlightenment project which may reasonably apply to Vico, but seems to me rather problematic in connection with Rosa). R. Colapietra, 'L'Ercole glorioso: realtà socio-ambientale e costruzione letteraria nel grande banditismo abruzzese del secondo Seicento', *Bullettino della deputazione abruzzese di storia patria*, 85, 1995[1996]:235–79, compares documentary evidence with literary representation (though far from exhausting the latter, given the way banditry became a staple of prose and verse narratives). Similarly, M. R. Tamblé, 'Santi patroni e mutamenti sociali a Lecce nella svolta di metà Seicento', *Itinerari di ricerca storica*, 9, 1995:55–107, in addition to being of particular interest for the Salento, an area of some literary importance in the later *Seicento*, may be of general significance in relation to the minor but very popular sub-genre of hagiographies of local saints, suggesting that more was at stake than heavenly protection: conflicts between different sectors of the nobility; city oligarchs and the Viceroy in Naples; Jesuits and Theatines, all intent on monopolizing piety.

BIBLIOGRAPHY, PRINTING AND PUBLISHING. Roberto L. Bruni and D. Wyn Evans, *Italian 17th-Century Books in Cambridge Libraries*, F, Olschki, 590 pp., is a major contribution to our still very imperfect knowledge of 17th-c. publishing. Almost 6,000 editions are listed, in a total (allowing for duplicates) of 8,288 volumes, almost half of them in college and departmental libraries: a relatively modest collection compared to the holdings of the British Library, but very significant nevertheless when one considers that they include a substantial number not listed in other modern catalogues (of the 381 editions listed under the letter A, for example, 50 were previously unrecorded). Of greatest interest from the point of view of Anglo-Italian intellectual connections (apart from the well-documented Acton and Bute libraries, acquired in 1902 and 1949 respectively) are the Grills and Henry Newton bequests at Trinity, and that of the master of Emmanuel and Archbishop of Canterbury William Sancroft to his college, including 388 Italian editions, and one of the most comprehensive collections of Marino's works put together by a 17th-c. Englishman, dating from his youthful travels (surprisingly though, the Pepys Library at Magdalene holds only a modest number of *secentine*, just over one hundred, which may suggest that interest in what was, after all, the contemporary culture of the day, had waned by the end of the century, only to revive again as antiquarianism in the second half of the next). The catalogue is extensively indexed (by title, publishers, places of publication, editors, commentators) though not by individual library, which might have been useful, as would have slightly longer title entries, which for reasons of space no doubt are kept to the minimum. These, and the decision to reproduce to the exact orthography of the title-page, combined with a machine-generated alphabetical order which does not exclude articles, prepositions, etc., are the only quibbles concerning an otherwise immaculately thorough work of scholarship, and one can only hope that the holdings of Oxford college libraries, and the Taylorian, will one day soon be subjected to a similar comprehensive census.

On a smaller scale, the *Catalogo del fondo antico della biblioteca del Collegio Ghislieri di Pavia. Edizioni del XVII secolo*, ed. Annamaria Mauro, Pavia, Collegio Ghislieri, 148 pp. + 19 pls, lists 623 editions (plus 40 incunabula and *cinquecentine* omitted from the 1983 catalogue of pre-1600 imprints): a small and surprisingly heterogeneous collection with a strong medical-scientific component, in addition to the more predictable law-books, and including a significant number of books from Protestant northern Europe.

I also note Marie-France Viallon, **Catalogue du Fonds Italien du XVIIe siècle Auguste Boullier de la Bibliothèque municipale de Roanne*, Saint-Étienne U.P., 1995, 287 pp.; M. Capucci, 'L'onomastico inquinato', *StSec*, 38: 3–9, which traces some examples of biographical misinformation in the writings of the early 18th-c. literary 'journalist' Giovan Pellegrino Dandi, which found their way into the works of more distinguished annalists: a warning to present researchers to beware of their sources, and a revealing glimpse into the 'workshop' of a provincial *letterato* at the turn of the century; F. Tomasi, '"La malagevolezza delle stampe". Per una storia dell'edizione Discepolo del *Mondo creato*', *StT*, 42, 1994[1995]: 43–78, which is of *Seicento* interest for what it tells us of the activities of Discepolo, and another major Venetian printer of the early *Seicento*, G. B. Ciotti; P. F. Gehl, 'The 1615 statutes of the Sienese Guild of Stationers and Booksellers. Provincial publishing in Early Modern Tuscany', *I Tatti Studies*, 6, 1995[1996]: 215–53.

CHURCH HISTORY, RELIGIOUS ORDERS. W. V. Hudon, 'Religion and society in Early Modern Italy — old questions, new insights', *AHR*, 101, 1996: 783–804, is an excellent survey of the studies of the last 20 years, the various conceptual debates (Counter Reformation vs Catholic Reform; the usefulness of categories like *spirituali* and *intransigenti)*, and particularly the 'rise' and subsequent critique of the Foucault-inspired 'social control' interpretation of Tridentine reforms. But perhaps of most value to literary scholars will be the extensive notes, which cite all the major studies of the last two decades, many of them omitted from *YWMLS* for reasons of space.

M.-L. Rodén, 'Cardinal Decio Azzolino and the problem of papal nepotism', *AHP*, 34, 1996:127–57, discusses Azzolino's part in the long and tortuous debate leading to the banning of nepotism, drawing on his brief manuscript treatise on the subject.

Giovanni Baffetti, *Retorica e scienza. Cultura gesuitica e seicento italiano*, Bo, CLUEB, 312 pp., is particularly useful for its account of the Order's cultural and educational policies, with the debates surrounding them; the material concerning the work of Jesuit scientists is more derivative, and tends to suggest a less complicated and contradictory relationship between their work and the hierarchy's directives than was the case even for the kind of Roman establishment figures (Bartoli, Clavius, Pallavicino, Possevino) on which it concentrates. The theoretical first chapter, based largely on the now classic history and sociology of science of the 1970s, is the least original and satisfactory, leading I think to an overestimation of Jesuit science, which produced valuable data, but was ultimately forced into an epistemological cul-de-sac. The tensions and limitations of Jesuit culture are better brought out in Denise Aricò, *Scienza, teatro e spiritualità barocca. Il gesuita Mario Bettini*, Bo, CLUEB, 1996, 416 pp.: the six essays which make up the bulk of the volume, exploring Bettini's production as a (Latin and vernacular) poet and scientist, are expanded and corrected versions of articles already in print, prefaced by a long and detailed reconstruction of his career, and followed by appendices which include the text of his *Rubeno. Ilarotragedia satiro-pastorale* (in a manuscript version differing from the published version of 1614), and unpublished Latin verse.

Craig A. Monson, *Disembodied Voices: Music and Culture in an Early Modern Italian Convent*, Berkeley–Los Angeles, California U.P., 1995, xxiv + 354 pp., deals with Santa Cristina della Fondazza in Bologna, home to a large number of noblewomen of the city.

COURT SOCIETY. M. L. Doglio, 'Charles-Emmanuel Ier de Savoie, Honoré Laugier de Porchères et Isabella Andreini entre poèmes d'amour, devises et "théâtre" encomiastique (avec un sonnet inédit de Charles-Emmanuel Ier)', *DSS*, 49:647–57, illuminates the courtly role of post-Petrarchan poetic exchange in a Baroque court, where the poet-prince's own efforts, with their emphasis on morality and *regole di governo*, are the continuation-confirmation of the praise heaped on the absolute ruler by his writer-servants.

EPISTOLARY RELATIONS. G. Rizzo, 'Lettere di Giuseppe Battista al Padre Angelico Aprosio', *StSec*, 38:267–318, publishes 51 extant letters now in Genoa University Library, packed with information concerning the literary events of the day, as well as the biographies of the two, who corresponded for 30 years, but never met. G. Fulco, 'Marino, "Flavio" e il Parnaso barocco nella corrispondenza del "Rugginoso"', *Besomi Vol.*, 297–331, reproduces letters to Ridolfo Campeggi from Marino (four of them already published, for which see *YWMLS* 58:559), Maiolino Bisaccioni, Lodovico Tesauro (of considerable interest in relation to the 1614 *querelle* between Marino and Ferrante Carli), Flaminio Scala, and one from Campeggi himself to his cousin Lorenzo; but the article is perhaps most useful for a brief description of some hundred further letters to Campeggi by other notable *letterati* (virtually everyone who is anyone in the years 1600–24), and a chronology of this important gentleman-amateur's life and writings.

I also note G. L. Betti, *'Lettere di argomento scientifico conservate nell'archivio della famiglia Manzini presso l'Archivio di Stato di Bologna', *Nuncius*, 10, 1995:691–714; E. Trotta, 'Il carteggio tra Cassiano dal Pozzo e Fabio Chigi', *NRLett*, 1995, no. 2:87–110.

GENDER. Andrea Genuzio, *Satira ed antisatira*, ed. Girolamo de Miranda, Ro, Salerno, 130 pp., consists of two invectives 'contra gli abbigliamenti degli uomini e delle donne', first published by this 'cavalliero napoletano' under the pseudonym Ernando Tivega in 1640, notable for their lively style as well as the even-handedness of their rebukes, and referred to in the controversies between Aprosio and Tarabotta.

Donna, disciplina, creanza cristiana dal XV al XVII secolo. Studi e testi a stampa, ed. Gabriella Zarri, Ro, Storia e Letteratura, 1996, 804 pp., incorporates an extensive bibliography of 2627 Early Modern texts, as well as a collection of some 20 essays including T. Plebani, 'Nascita e caratteristiche del pubblico di lettrici tra medioevo e prima età moderna' (23–44); P. Gehel, 'Libri per donne. Le monache clienti del libraio fiorentino Piero Morosi (1588–1607)' (67–84); A. Scattigno, 'Maria Maddalena de' Pazzi. Tra esperienza e modello' (85–102); B. Majorana, 'Finzioni, imitazioni, azioni: donne e teatro' (121–40); G. Palumbo, 'Dalla disciplina al disciplinamento. Il corpo, l'anima, il libro nelle storie di monache e recluse' (141–64); E. Graziosi, 'Scrivere in convento: devozione, encomio, persuasione nelle rime delle monache fra Cinque e Seicento' (303–32); S. Urbini, 'Sul ruolo della donna "incisore" nella storia del libro illustrato' (367–91).

S. Datta, 'La presenza di una coscienza femminista nella Venezia dei primi secoli dell'età moderna', *SV*, 32, 1996:105–35, is too methodologically and critically naive to make any significant contribution to the subject: terms like 'feminism' and 'social reform' are used without ever pausing to ask what they might mean in an Early Modern context. A. Chiantera, 'Le donne e il "governo della lingua" nei trattati di comportamento cinque-seicenteschi', pp. 329–39 of

Donna e linguaggio. Convegno internazionale di studi: Sappada/Plodn (Belluno) 1995, ed. G. Marcato, Padua, CLUEP, 1995, 632 pp., discusses, among others, V. Nolfi's *Ginipedia overo avvertimenti civili per la donna nobile* (1631). S. Evangelisti, 'Moral virtues and personal goods: the double representation of female monastic identity', pp. 27–54 of *Women in the Religious Life*, ed. O. Hufton, F, European University Institute, 1996, 159 pp., contains some information on the personal book collections of nuns, as well as their private lives in the cloister. A. Malena, 'Il processo inquisitoriale contro Francesca Fabbroni (1619–1681)', *RSLR*, 32, 1996:349–89, reconstructs the trial and posthumous condemnation (complete with the burning of her remains in 1689) of this Pisan abbess, whose claims to sanctity were resented by her sisters and ultimately rejected by the Florentine inquisitor (a sorry tale of conventual rivalry, compounded by dogged self-assertion and lack of theological sophistication on the part of the victim). E. Weaver, 'Un falso editoriale: la *princeps* (1644) dell'*Antisatira* di Arcangela Tarabotti', *Besomi Vol.*, 393–404, points out that this edition is in fact two wholly different imprints, with identical frontispieces, with the second a not entirely satisfactory correction (almost certainly demanded and supervised by the author) of the error-riddled first imprint.

LANGUAGE. I note: G. Gandellini, 'Il Vocabolario della Crusca e la tradizione manoscritta dell'"Epitoma rei Militaris" di Vegezio nel volgarizzamento di Bono Giamboni', *SLeI*, 13, 1996:43–121; F. Rossi, 'La musica nella Crusca. Leopoldo de' Medici, Giovan Battista Doni e un glossario manoscritto di termini musicali del XVII secolo', *ib.*, 123–83; E. Durante and A. Martellotti, 'Il lessico musicale del tardo rinascimento e del barocco. Alcune puntualizzazioni', *NRMI*, 30, 1996:7–29.

PATRONAGE, ACADEMIES, ORGANIZATION OF CULTURE. Barbara Agosti, *Collezionismo e archeologia cristiana nel Seicento. Federico Borromeo e il Medioevo artistico tra Roma e Milano*, Mi, Jaca Book, 1996, 214 pp., is a source of valuable information concerning the development of antiquarian culture as well as the Counter-Reformation study of church history and Borromeo's intellectual biography. C. Bevilacqua, 'L'Accademia degli Innominati: un'istituzione culturale alla corte farnesiana di Parma', *AP*, 81:3–32, brings together the little that is known of this academy, founded in 1574, including details of its few extant publications and a (partial) list of its membership. I also note A. Morelli, 'Mecenatismo musicale nella Roma barocca: il caso di Cristina di Svezia', *QSt*, 95:387–408; T. Montanari, 'Il cardinale Decio Azzolino e le collezioni d'arte di Cristina di Svezia', *StSec*, 38:187–264.

TRANSLATION, TRANSMISSION, INFLUENCE. M. Saccenti, 'La "gran machina del mondo" e la congiuntura Tasso-Marchetti', *Italianistica*, 24, 1995:615–32, discusses the influence of the *Mondo creato* on Alessandro Marchetti's late-*Seicento* translation of *De rerum natura*.

MISCELLANEOUS CONTRIBUTIONS. Of some documentary evidence in relation to literary studies may be G. Cozzi, *Giustizia 'contaminata'. Vicende giudiziarie di nobili ed ebrei nella Venezia del Seicento*, Venice, Marsilio, 1996, 132 pp.; E. Grendi, *I Balbi. Una famiglia genovese fra Spagna e Impero*, T, Einaudi, xxv + 345 pp.; F. Fineschi, 'Insults of the living and fear of the dead: defaming the dead in Early Modern Italy', *IHC*, 3:35–65.

2. POETRY

G. M. Rinaldi, 'Il repertorio delle *canzuni* siciliane dei secoli XVI–XVII', *BCSS*, 18, 1995:41–108, gives an overview (mainly linguistic) of the material to be found, and provides a description of the printed and manuscript sources up to 18th c. (presentation of work in progress). G. Pedroietta, 'Un esempio di umiltà: una versione popolare, in ottava rima, di un capitolo del *Prato fiorito*', *Besomi Vol.*, 405–18, publishes an anonymous verse paraphrase dating from the second quarter of the century of Valerio da Venezia's 1605 compendium of morally edifying exempla, *Il prato fiorito*.

C. Sensi, 'La poésie lyrique: état des lieux, II: Constellations', *DSS*, 49:727–52, surveys the studies, and above all the critical editions of the last 30 years, though his comments are more general and less incisive than those of D. Chiodo (see *YWMLS*, 57:527), who now gives us 'Variazioni della bucolica: l'idillio barocco', pp. 29–39 of *Pastorale italiana. Pastorale francese*, ed. D. Dalla Valle, Alessandria, Orso, 184 pp., establishing some parameters for the study of this short-lived but not unimportant new genre (a phenomenon essentially of the first quarter of the century), and identifying its specificity in the combination of musicality, pathos, and the representation of a 'natura animata'.

BASILE. *Il Basile spirituale. Il Pianto della Vergine, Sacri Sospiri e altre rime*, ed. S. Ussia, Vercelli, Mercurio, 1996, 190 pp., brings together B.'s religious verse (the *Pianto* of 1608, the *Sospiri*, a cycle of 100 sonnets published in 1630, and compositions culled from other collections), prefaced by a long, largely descriptive introduction.

DOTTI. *Odi e altre rime inedite*, ed. Valter Boggione, Brescia, Biblioteca Queriniana, 272 pp., is chiefly notable, alas, for its combination of insensitivity to the finer points of orthography and punctuation and of numerous howlers in the notes ('l'Ercole gallo', the standard epithet for Henri IV throughout the *Seicento*, is absurdly glossed as G. B. Marino, on the strength of his stay in France). Not much more can be said of Id., *'Poi che tutto corre al nulla': le rime di Bartolomeo Dotti*, T, Università degli Studi, 320 pp., which manages to be at one and the same time sententious and prosaic, to talk airily about complex issues of literary-rhetorical codification and take everything terribly literally and autobiographically.

LUBRANO. M. Guglielminetti, 'Giacomo Lubrano, poète baroque', *DSS*, 49:715–25, takes a traditional, topic-based approach to a poet whose extreme, hallucinatory qualities have been better summarized by Marzio Pieri in the introduction to his 1982 edition of the *Scintille poetiche*.

MARINO. *Il Barocco: Marino e la poesia del Seicento*, ed. Marzio Pieri, Ro, IPS, xxvi + 1066 pp., is essentially a briefly annotated edition of *L'Adone*, followed by a small anthology of other verse (mainly lyrics): a new edition rather than simply a revision of Pieri's 1975–77 edition, since he has gone back to the two authorized imprints of 1623, giving us a text significantly closer to the orthography and punctuation of the original. It should be the standard *Adone* for many years to come, but Pieri's cares are vitiated by poor correction from proofs (including a series of computer induced transpositions) as well as an absurd editorial policy (it is part of a 100-volume luxury edition of classics which may only be bought *en bloc)* and one can only hope that a cheaper, better corrected reprint will soon be produced.

F. Giambonini, 'Bibliografia delle opere a stampa di G. B. Marino: 1700–1940 (III: Raccolte di opere singole di vari autori tra cui Marino)', *StSec*, 38:357–94, is the penultimate instalment of this valuable contribution to the history of the reception and circulation of M.'s works.

G. Bárberi Squarotti, 'Le silence de la tragédie: *Adone*, V', *DSS*, 49:659–76, makes some interesting observations concerning the representation of the 'tragedy of Acteon' and its place in M.'s 'epic of peace', though occasionally off target because of the absence of detailed comparison to the actual practices of *Seicento* court theatre, whose critique seems to me an essential part of his discourse. P. Palma, 'Sleep as a Baroque metaphor in Marino's *Adone'*, *RStI*, 14.2, 1996:43–51, argues that the various instances in which Adone falls asleep should be read as representing on the one hand abandonment to the senses and, on the other, the entry to the 'realm of the fantastic, which leads ultimately to a way of knowledge shaped by the imagination': a rather solemn reading which scarcely seems to do justice to the multiple ironies of the text. A. Casadei, 'Il telescopio, "ammirabile stromento": variazioni su *Adone*, X.39–47', pp. 75–83 of Id., *La fine degli incanti. Vicende del poema epico-cavalleresco nel Rinascimento*, Mi, Angeli, 190 pp., suggests that M.'s appropriation of the new science is more aesthetic than methodological, a view from which I beg to differ. E. Fumagalli, 'Marino, Lucano e la scuola umanistica', *Besomi Vol.*, 332–47, provides convincing evidence for M.'s indebtedness not only to Lucan's *Pharsalia*, but to its Renaissance commentators for the necromancy episode of *Adone* XIII: further evidence, if any were needed, of his 'composizioni ad intarsio'.

C. Sensi, 'La poésie lyrique: état des lieux, 1: Marino le prince astucieux', *DSS*, 49: 677–713, surveys the studies of the last 30 years, a useful, though sometimes rather uncritical, reminder of what has been done and what remains uncharted. F. Guardiani, 'Dieci pezzi sacri per un'edizione della *Lira II*', *Besomi Vol.*, 348–70, gives a foretaste of his and A. Martini's forthcoming edition of the *Madrigali e canzoni:* commentaries on ten madrigals on the birth, life, and sacrifice of Christ, stressing, rightly I am sure, that whatever his attitude to the religion of his day (Guardiani shows among other things how M. effectively rewrites more conventional texts by Angelo Grillo and the much less well-known Giuseppe Policreti) his efforts in this sphere are motivated by more 'spiritual' impulses than simply the perceived need to make show of orthodox devotion. A further sample of this work is Id., 'Oscula mariniana', *QI*, 16, 1995: 197–243, dealing with the much better known cycle of *Rime II* poems dedicated to kisses (and even orgasm and impotence) notable for Guardiani's emphasis on the complex architecture of the sequence.

M. Slawinski, 'Intorno a tre lettere "inglesi" di Giovan Battista Marino', *RLI*, 101.2–3:39–57, explores the significance for M.'s literary biography of two hitherto overlooked letters documenting his links with English court circles. L. Pedroia, 'Un'ignoto corrispondente del Marino: Annibale Mancini, "pittore d'istorie"', *Besomi Vol.*, 371–80, reconstructs, on the basis of a newly discovered letter from Mancini to M., the poet's relations with this minor painter.

NOMI. *Santuario — Poesie sacre. Un calendario liturgico in versi di fine '600*, ed. Giovanni Bianchini, Ro, Bulzoni, 1996, 340 pp., is the first edition of a collection of 331 poems (mostly sonnets) about, and following the order of, the liturgical calendar: a work of erudition as well as piety and literature, since N. draws on the latest hagiographic sources (the dedication is to the Bollandist Daniel Papeborch). As the editor's introduction admits, this *Santuario* may not be notable as a literary achievement, but 'può forse interessare [...] più altri versanti, da quello storico-antropologico a quello più propriamente religioso-agiografico-devozionale'.

TASSONI. Giovanni Bruno, 'Un glorioso antenato del conte di Culagna', *Besomi Vol.*, 381–92, argues that the principal source for the *Secchia*'s conte di Culagna is to be found in the Astolfo of Pietro Aretino's *Orlandino*, rather than the oft-cited Don Quixote.

TORCIGLIANI. Michelangelo Torcigliani, *Anacreonte e altre versioni poetiche,* ed. E. Taddeo and F. Ciccolella, Bo, Commissione Testi di Lingua, 1996, cxxvii + 253 pp.

3. DRAMA

DRAMATIC TEXTS. *Meraviglie e orrori dell'aldilà. Intrecci mitologici e favole cristiane nel teatro barocco,* ed. Silvia Carandini, Ro, Bulzoni, 1995, 202 pp., includes F. Taviani, 'Christus Iudex: tragoedia P. Stephani Tuccii saepius habita' (25–52), concerning one of the earliest Jesuit dramas, first performed in 1569, edited and published in 1673, then translated and adapted into Italian in 1698; P. Petronelli, 'Orfeo all'Inferno: Monteverdi e Dante' (97–109), on Dantesque echoes and borrowings in Monteverdi's opera; S. Carandini, 'La rivolta di demoni e titani. Prospettive cosmologiche nel teatro barocco' (135–55), exemplifying the role of cosmological themes in the 'production' of Christian *meraviglia* in *L'Adamo* (1613) and *Il convitato di pietra* (1651) of Giovan Battista Andreini.

R. Puggioni, 'Generi retorici e strutture drammatiche della pastorale barocca', *Pastorale italiana. Pastorale francese,* cit., 53–88, considers the presence of the rhetorical modes (forensic, deliberative, and epideictic) in Italian and French pastoral, and its role in determining dramatic form. Most of the essay is descriptive rather than analytical, identifying the (clearly quite conscious) deployment of formal oratory without really touching on its function. One interesting observation concerning the centrality, from *Il pastor fido* onwards, of marriage, family, and inheritance laws in the genre raises the interesting question (not taken up in the essay) of whether its baroque 'explosion' might not be related to this (perhaps involving an attempt to present them as 'natural' by placing them in an ahistoric fiction).

A. Sana, 'Eliodoro nel Seicento italiano, II: La *Carichia* di Ettore Pignatelli', *StSec,* 38:107–83, examines in great detail a tragedy (published in 1628, but probably written some 15 years earlier) drawn from the Greek novel. Sana suggests that the fact that Heliodorus was imitated most closely in Naples, by members of the Accademia degli Oziosi, is due to the influence of Spain, and of Cervantes in particular.

D. Isella, '"L'è pur la mala cossa ess servitoru". Un prologo milanese del Seicento', *Besomi Vol.,* 419–28, consists of the annotated (dialect) text of the prologue to a *Farsa musicale* of 1664, which Isella asserts (without adducing any evidence) 'metrica, lingua e immaginario poetico' ascribe to Carlo Maria Maggi. Its chief interest would be that it was written some 30 years before the bulk of Maggi's dialect verse. D. Zardin, 'Carlo Maria Maggi e la tradizione culturale milanese tra sei e settecento', *ASMC*, 3, 1997:9–50, argues, to my mind convincingly, that the attempt to see Maggi as a proto-Enlightenment figure, a precursor of Goldoni in the reform of the theatre, and of Parini in poetry, has been significantly overstated: more than a starting point of the Milanese enlightenment, Maggi is to be seen as a spokesman for the moderate paternalistic conservatism of the pro-Spanish patriciate of the mid *Seicento*.

DRAMATIC THEORY. R. di Ceglie, 'Il *Dialogo sopra la poesia dramatica* di Ottaviano Castelli', *StSec*, 38:319–55, reproduces the text (originally published in 1638, though curiously di Ceglie gives no bibliographical details) of this brief treatise by a Roman physician otherwise known for his opera libretti and an anti-Spanish satirical play.

COMMEDIA DELL'ARTE. Robert Henke, 'The Italian mountebank and the *Commedia dell'Arte*', *Theatre Survey*, 38.2:1–29, considers street entertainers, and their conflict with *Commedia* actors, who saw them as an obstacle in their effort to gain higher status and serious recognition for their art.

THEATRES. S. Monaldini, 'Teatri a Ravenna tra XVI e XVIII secolo', *Studi Romagnoli*, 44, 1993[1997]:327–58, includes an appendix of mainly 17th-c. documents.

OPERA AND ORATORIO. M. Emanuele, 'Arione e il melodramma alla corte dei Savoia', *StMus*, 26:313–29, documents music theatre at the court of Charles Emmanuel I, in the first three decades of the *Seicento*. A. N. Mancini, 'Retorica e spettacolo del potere in alcuni libretti d'opera del medio Seicento veneziano', *RStI*, 15.2:93–121, discusses Busenello's *Poppea* and Cicognini's *Orontea*. A. F. Ivaldi, 'Dialetto genovese e dramma per musica nel 1655', *NRMI*, 29,1995:607–28, considers a curious hybrid: a libretto written partly in dialect for a *melodramma (L'Ariodante)* combining Ariosto's story with low-life comic scenes derived from Anton Giulio Brignole Sale's *I due anelli simili* (1637). P. Maione, 'Giulia de Caro "seu ciulla" da commediante a cantarina', *RIM*, 32:61–80, reconstructs the remarkable mid-Seicento career of this Neapolitan prostitute, comic actress, and singer-turned-*impresario*. A. Morelli, 'La circolazione dell'oratorio italiano nel seicento', *StMus*, 26:105–86, documents the 'exportation' of some 700 oratorios from their original place of composition or performance to other Italian (and European) cities, based on extant MS copies in libraries and archives.

4. PROSE

BIOGRAPHY, AUTOBIOGRAPHY. Luigi Ferdinando Marsili, *Il ragguaglio della schiavitù*, ed. Bruno Basile, Ro, Salerno, 1996, 80 pp. + 16 pls, is the Bolognese nobleman's account of his capture at the siege of

Vienna and subsequent enslavement (1683–84), together with later political commentaries and a *Memoriale* to the future Emperor Joseph I concerning his role in the defence of Vienna. The introduction covers aspects of Marsili's style, highlighting its 'rationalism', and places the *Ragguaglio* in the context of related works of the period. Also by Basile, 'La più antica biografia del Tasso', *Italianistica*, 24, 1995:525–39, being the manuscript *Compendio* compiled in 1619 by G. B. Manso's lawyer, Francesco De Pietri, from the latter's *Vita di Torquato Tasso*, but why this 'esatta sintesi' needed to be published, especially now that Basile has given us an edition of the original (see *YWMLS*, 58:548) escapes me.

HISTORY AND HISTORIOGRAPHY. Silvia Bulletta, *Virgilio Malvezzi e la storiografia classica*, Mi, IPL, 1995, 276 pp., focuses on Malvezzi's political thought (particularly the *Discorsi sopra Cornelio Tacito* and the moralized biographies derived from Tacitus) and is prefaced by the most extensive reconstruction of his career to date. An appendix gives the text of the hitherto unpublished *Vita di Numa Pompilio*. Denise Aricò, 'Martiri e storiografia in lettere inedite di Daniello Bartoli', *StSec*, 38, 1997:57–105, discusses Bartoli's attempt to reconcile the religious and literary demands of hagiography with the demands of historicity in the light of observations in two letters to fellow Jesuits. A. Piscitello, 'La peste del 1630 a Clusone narrata da Bernardino Baldi', *ASB*, 3, 1995:62–81, transcribes the manuscript in the Biblioteca Angelo Mai.

NARRATIVE. Maria Di Giovanna, *La trilogia mondana di Girolamo Brusoni*, Palermo, Palumbo, 1996, 202 pp., is an important milestone in the study of this most original *Seicento* contribution to the genre and to its decline (which the unfolding of the trilogy itself, as Di Giovanna describes it, could be said to prefigure). Like many studies of the last few years, however, it could well do with exchanging traditional commonplaces concerning the link between literature and society, based on second-hand, and generally out-of-date, historiography, with a (moderate) dose of new-historicism. A. Morini, 'Giovan Francesco Loredano: sémiologie d'une crise', *REI*, 43:23–50, raises some interesting questions concerning an author whose (mild) youthful heterodoxy has perhaps encouraged critical over-estimations (was his Accademia degli Incogniti really that significant, or was it not rather a sort of 'vanity press', the self-publicizing whim of a rich amateur?), but the attempt to find the signs of his narcissistic failure (and that of Venice and his whole class) in a series of rhetorical habits (from his *romanzi* and *novelle*) common to most writers of the period is rather superficial. Denise Aricò, 'Prudenza e privanza nel *Davide perseguitato* di Virgilio Malvezzi', *FC*, 21, 1996:321–69, examines this text of 1634 (one of many hybrids retelling biblical history with an eye both to religious instruction and political comment) in the light of contemporary debates on the court. I also note A. Coppola, **L'Albergo di Maiolino Bisaccioni'*, *NLe*, 4–6, 1996: 147–54.

SACRED ORATORY. E. Ardissino, 'Rassegna di studi sulla predicazione post-tridentina e barocca' (1980–1996)', *LItal*, 49: 481–517, does not attempt anything more ambitious than a summary of recent studies (including a number overlooked in earlier volumes of *YWMLS*), but is no less useful for that, and for pointing up some of the major gaps in our knowledge. Frederick J. McGuinness, *Right Thinking and Sacred Oratory in Counter-Reformation Rome*, Princeton U.P., 1995, xii + 337 pp., studies the homilies delivered before the Pope from the Council of Trent to mid 17th c., discussing first the development of Cicero's and Quintilian's ideal *bene dicere* (moral as well as elegant oratory) into a theory of Christian oratory, then the practice and content of the homilies, ceremonially delivered to project the desired image of the centre of Catholicism and offer models *urbi et orbi*, with 16th-c. sermons full of the rhetoric of battle while those of the *Seicento* strive to project an image of triumphant order and peace under a revitalized Papacy. P. Zito, 'Francesco Marchese nemico della quiete', *EL*, 21.4, 1996: 73–93, surveys the career and religious writings of an interesting member of the Roman Oratory (1623–97) and is followed by the text of his pithy refutation of Quietism.

SATIRE. Lucia Rodler, *Una fabbrica barocca. Il 'Cane di Diogene' di Francesco Fulvio Frugoni*, Bo, Il Mulino, 1996, 221 pp., is an unusually readable doctoral dissertation, as well as (to my knowledge) the first modern monograph on a work whose interest and importance are often talked up, but which few (I am no exception) have read. It remains to be seen whether the careful architecture identified by Rodler really is the correlative of serious moral concern rather than misanthropic moralizing, and for that nothing short of a modern edition of this vast text may be necessary.

5. THOUGHT

ARISTOTELIANISM. *Heinrich C. Kuhn, *Venetischer Aristotelismus im Ende der aristotelichen Welt: Aspekte der Welt und des Denkens des Cesare Cremonini (1550–1631)*, Frankfurt, Lang, 1996, 864 pp.; G. Belgioioso, 'Philosophie aristotélicienne et mécanisme cartésien à Naples à la fin du XVIIᵉ siècle', *NRLett*, 1995, no. 1: 19–47.

ETHICS AND POLITICS. E. Mazzocchi, 'La riflessione secentesca su retorica e morale', *StSec*, 38: 11–56, examines the work of Matteo Pellegrino, Sforza Pallavicino, and Emanuele Tesauro, concluding that the 'proverbializzazione' of ethics has its correlative in the formalization of rhetorical *ingegno*, and both are fundamentally conservative devices, a view which is doubtless correct but which may not go to the roots of the phenomenon. The formalization of rhetoric involves a reversal of its Aristotelian foundations: where Aristotle had seen *doxa*, the accepted views of the *polis*, as the cornerstone of persuasion, the *Seicento* attributes that role to figures and tropes, while moral commonplaces become raw material to be 'dressed up' precisely in order to make it persuasive, an exercise which vainly strives to conceal the disintegration of that view of the human subject which the commonplaces were supposed to enshrine. D. Taranto, 'Sull'antimachiavellismo italiano della seconda metà del Seicento', *PenP*, 29, 1996: 374–401, consists of a rather piecemeal series of notes on the writings of Giambattista Mucci (*La sicurtà del trono*, 1679; *Il soldato*, 1691), and Carlo Maria Carafa (*Scrutinio politico*, 1692).

ACCETTO. Torquato Accetto, *Della dissimulazione onesta*, ed. Salvatore S. Nigro, T, Einaudi, xl + 75 pp., is prefaced by an introduction detailing the treatise's context (post-Reformation Nicodemianism, the decline of *cortegianeria* into servility; the professional code of the *secretario)* and providing a comprehensive bibliography of A. studies.

CAMPANELLA. New editions of C.'s works (some well known, others not at all) continue to appear. They include: **Apologia per Galileo*, ed. P. Ponzio, Mi, Rusconi, 262 pp., which makes available a text long out of print, together with Paolo Antonio Foscarini's *Lettera* arguing the compatibility of heliocentrism with Scripture, and an up-to-date bibliography; *La Città del Sole e Questione quarta sull'ottima repubblica*, ed. G. Ernst, Mi, Rizzoli, 176 pp., with a lucid introduction detailing the circumstances of the *Città*'s writing, and its place in C.'s thought, and with a new Italian translation alongside the Latin text of the thematically related *Quaestio;* **De libris propriis et recta ratione. Studendi syntagma*, ed. A. Brissoni, Soveria Mannelli, Rubbettino, 1996, 102 pp.

Angelamaria Isoldi Jacobelli, **Tommaso Campanella. 'Il diverso filosofar mio'*, introd. E. Garin, Ro–Bari, Laterza, 1995, xii + 215 pp., is principally concerned with interpreting and evaluating the gnoseological foundations of C.'s philosophy. Michel-Pierre Lerner, *Tommaso Campanella en France au XVIIᵉ siècle*, Na, Bibliopolis, 1995, 164 pp., discusses C.'s French reputation prior to his 1634 flight to Paris, and chronicles his residence there and the subsequent reception of his thought in 17th-c. France.

BrC, 2, 1996 [1997], is chiefly dedicated to C.: G. Ernst, '"Oscurato è il secolo". Il proemio allo Schoppe del ritrovato *Ateismo trionfato* italiano', *ib.*, 11–32, announces the finding of the autograph manuscript of the Italian version of the *Atheismus* (for further details of which we must await a future publication) and publishes its introductory epistle to Caspar Schoppe (withdrawn from the Latin version after Schoppe revealed himself a less than trustworthy custodian of C.'s scholarly confidences) accompanied by a commentary on the circumstances of their friendship and falling out. A further new discovery by Ernst is published in full in 'L'opacità del male e il disincanto del profeta. Profezia, ragion di stato e provvidenza divina in un testo inedito di Campanella', *ib.*, 89–155, a text dating from 1627, and the final stages of his imprisonment, in which C. attempts to demonstrate (largely, it would seem, for his own benefit) the futility of princes' persecution of philosophers, since even the most callous and immoral application of *ragion di stato* has its unwitting part in the fulfilment of a grander divine plan; G. Fulco, 'Il fascino del recluso e la sirena carceraria: Campanella, Ottavio Sammarco e Napoli in una scheggia inedita di carteggio (dic. 1614)', *ib.*, 33–56, is the account of another Neapolitan friendship, and another falling-out, this time with a young lawyer (later known for an original political treatise, the 1629 *Mutatione de' Regni*) who attempted to pass off C.'s *Aforismi politici* as his own: what stands out here in the Dominican's rebuke is the mixture of hurt pride at this misappropriation and unwillingness to forsake the link with the outside world that the relationship brings; G. Ernst and L. Salvetti Firpo, 'Tommaso Campanella e la cometa del 1618. Due lettere e un opuscolo epistolare inediti', *ib.*, 56–88, reproduce texts relating to C.'s attempt to turn the comet to his advantage by addressing an epistolary essay on the subject to Paul V which is notable for its attempt to combine up-to-date scientific discussion, traditional astrology, and grander claims as to the prophetic significance of such phenomena. Also on C.'s attempt to explain comets, P. Ponzio, 'La disputa sulle comete nelle *Quaestiones physiologicae* di Tommaso Campanella', *ib.*, 195–213; J. M. Headley, 'Campanella on freedom of thought: the case of the cropped pericope', *ib.*, 165–77, discusses an example of C.'s (mis)use of his sources, or rather, his (largely unconscious) tendency to draw on his formidable memory selectively to seek biblical and philosophical authority for his own views. The volume also contains shorter contributions by M.-P. Lerner, 'Un portrait suédois de Campanella', *ib.*, 157–61, and Id., '"Campanellae Deliramenta in Tartarum Releganda": une condemnation méconnue du *Sensu rerum et magia* en 1629', *ib.*, 215–36, a doctoral thesis defended at Fribourg; M. Fintoni, 'Impostura e profezia nelle poesie filosofiche di Tommaso Campanella', *ib.*, 179–93; G. Landolfi Petrone, 'Gli scritti su Campanella di Bertrando Spaventa (Torino, 1854–1855)', *ib.*, 273–93; D. Giovannozzi, '"Libero, ma cattolico pensatore". Tommaso Campanella nei manuali italiani di storia della filosofia del XIX secolo', *ib.*, 295–305;

M. L. Bianchi, 'La filosofia di Tommaso Campanella in *Das Erkenntnisproblem in der Philosophie und Wissenschaft der neuren Zeit*', *ib.*, 307–23; E. Baldini, 'Luigi Firpo e Campanella: cinquant'anni di ricerche e di pubblicazioni', *ib.*, 325–58, which rapidly surveys Firpo's production and provides a complete bibliography).

MARSILI. *I filosofi e le chiocciole. Operette di Anton Felice Marsili (1649–1710)*, ed. Gregorio Pala, Assisi, Porziuncola, 1996, 152 pp., consists of two essays, *Delle sette de' filosofi e del genio di filosofare* (1671), and the *Relazione del ritrovamento dell'uova di chiocciole* (1683) prefaced by an account of M.'s career.

GALILEO AND THE NEW SCIENCE. F. Motta, 'Due copie della lettera di Galileo a Cristina di Lorena tra Sei e Settecento', *ASE*, 12, 1995:129–43, takes the study of the two manuscript copies of the *Lettera* in Bologna University Library as the starting point for an interesting wide-ranging discussion of the work's significance and fortunes. Pietro Redondi, 'I fondamenti metafisici della fisica di Galileo', *Nuncius*, 11, 1996:267–89, is an elegant exposition of the presuppositions and implications of Galileo's physics, stressing his debt to classical and Christian metaphysics, while avoiding the temptation to fit him into too narrow a Platonist pigeon-hole. Massimo Bucciantini, 'Una difficile eredità: Galileo e le raccolte galileiane tra mito e storia', *ib.*, 311–28, discusses the continuing significance of the collections still being expanded by Florence's Museo di Storia della Scienza. I also note Egidio Festa, **L'erreur de Galilée*, Paris, Austral, 1995, 431 pp.

On Galileo's sources we have G. Aquilecchia, 'Possible Brunian echoes in Galileo', *NRLett*, 1995, no. 1:11–18, and Id., 'I *Massimi sistemi* di Galileo e la *Cena* di Bruno (per una comparazione tematico-strutturale)', *Nuncius*, 10, 1995:485–96; G. Nonnoi, 'Galileo e Pascal. Idee ed esperienze', pp. 152–65 of *Filosofia, scienza, storia: Studi in onore di Alberto Pala*, ed. Francesco Cadeddu, Mi, Angeli, 1995, x + 320 pp.

Aspects of Galileo's research are covered by R. Feldhay, 'Producing sunspots on an iron pan: Galileo's scientific discourse', pp. 119–43 of *Science, reason and rhetoric*, ed. H. Krips et al., Pittsburgh U.P., 1995, xii + 322 pp., and R. Gigli, 'L'"errore fruttuoso". L'argomento galileiano delle maree nella critica recente', *RSF*, 51, 1996:641–58, alternatives to which are the subject of F. Bonelli and L. Russo, 'The origin of modern astronomical theories of tides: Chrisogono, de Dominis and their sources', *BJHS*, 29, 1996:385–401.

The Medici court's continued commitment to Galileo is documented in T. Frangenberg, 'A private homage to Galileo. Anton Domenico Gabbiani's frescoes in the Pitti Palace', *JWCI*, 59, 1996:245–73, concerning 'heliocentric' frescoes painted in 1696 in the private apartments of hereditary prince Ferdinand, while

D. Topper and C. Gillis, 'Trajectories of blood: Artemisia Gentileschi and Galileo's parabolic path', *Woman's Art Journal*, 17.1, 1996: 10–13, suggest the influence of Galileo's parabolic law of projection behind her 'Judith beheading Holofernes'.

M. Biagioli, 'Etiquette, interdependence and sociability in 17th-century science', *CI*, 22, 1996: 193–238, has already been published in French (see *YWMLS*, 58: 571), and Id., 'La scienza e la corte. Alcune riflessioni sul "patronage" in Italia', *GCFI*, 74, 1995: 287–308, deals with related themes. Biagioli's 'social anthropology of science is discussed in M. H. Shank, 'How shall we practice history? The case of Mario Biagioli's *Galileo courtier*', *Early Science and Medicine*, 1, 1996: 106–50.

D. Aricò, '"Onestissime liti". Dispute scientifiche a Bologna tra Cinque e Seicento', *Intersezioni*, 17: 19–43, documents vigorous debates in and around the *Studio* concerning a whole range of topics from atomism, through Copernicanism and comets, to the accuracy of old and new methods of astronomical observation. Scientific debate is also the subject of A. Romano, 'I problemi scientifici nel *Giornale de' Letterati*' (1668–1681)', *Dimensioni e problemi della ricerca storica*, 1: 17–37, though here the emphasis is more on the Roman constraints on discussion, leading to a split betwen the co-founders of the *Giornale*, and the appearence of two rival publications of the same title. A more private mode of scientific exchange is documented by O. Trabucco, 'Scienza e comunicazione epistolare: il carteggio epistolare fra Marco Aurelio Severino e Cassiano Dal Pozzo', *GCFI*, 76: 204–45, on the extensive correspondence between the Neapolitan physician and medical theorist and the better-known Roman *virtuoso*, collector and *linceo*.

Giovan Battista Hodierna, *Scritti di ottica. Inediti e rari*, ed. Corrado Dollo, Mi, Angeli, 1996, 480 pp., brings together the works of a Sicilian 'neoteric' (as Dollo qualifies him in the extensive and wide-ranging introduction). Y. Conray, 'L'organizzazione dello spazio dei viventi nell'opera di Federico Cesi, fondatore dell'Accademia dei Lincei', *Nuncius*, 11, 1996: 185–203, discusses Cesi's attempt to classify the fauna and flora of the new world, as described in Francisco Hernandez's *Rerum medicarum Novae Hispaniae Thesaurus* (1628), arguing that it represents one of the first modern systems of scientific taxonomy (though oddly Conray does not make the obvious and possibly more pertinent link to the logical tables of Ramus).

SETTECENTO

By G. W. SLOWEY, *Lecturer in Italian, University of Birmingham*

1. GENERAL

LIBRARIES, PUBLISHING.　M. Callegari, 'I libri di un pubblico perito della città di Padova: la biblioteca di Giovanni Andrea Pasini', *AVen*, 149:87–110, drawing on an analysis of his library, shows how P., a surveyor, had cultural interests outside his work, in that nearly half the books in his library were on the humanities. M. R. Rescigno, 'Ascesa sociale e identità culturale di un avvocato di provincia: la biblioteca Ravizza di Chieti (1785)', *Fabbrica del libro*, 3.1:8–12, illustrates the wide-ranging coverage of this library, which, alongside the expected law books, contained editions of the classics and Italian authors from Dante to Metastasio, together with a number of historical items, including Pietro Giannone's *Storia del Regno di Napoli*. Elena Bonatti, **Vincentius Bellini rector Cassanae sibi et civibus: la biblioteca del Museo di Ferrara nel Settecento ed il suo catalogo*, Ferrara, Deputazione Provinciale Ferrarese di Storia Patria, 1996, 240 pp. Renato Pasta, **Editoria e cultura nel Settecento*, F, Olschki, xiii + 296 pp. F. Cancedda, **'Un tipografo romano del primo settecento: Francesco Gonzaga', Il Bibliotecario*, n.s., 1:133–55.

LITERARY HISTORY AND BACKGROUND.　As a follow-up to their previous work on the Seicento, Horizons Unlimited have issued *Encyclomedia: il Settecento*, Mi, Opera Multimedia, a CD-ROM which covers the European 18th c., with many sections on Italy. *L'Italia del secondo Settecento*, ed. Gigliola Pagano De Divitiis and Vincenzo Giura, Na, ESI, 1996, 606 pp., casts an interesting light on non-Italian views of the period through the eyes of British diplomatic representatives. **Scienza e donne nel Settecento: gli scritti di tre intellettuali dell'epoca: Olivi, Compagnoni, Algarotti*, ed. Cizio Gibin, Conselve, T & G Edizioni, 1996, 115 pp. Giulio Bollati, **Da Verri a Cattaneo: la prosa morale e civile in Italia tra Settecento e Ottocento*, T, Bollati Boringhieri, 119 pp. A. Borrelli, **'Scienza e accademie negli stati italiani del Settecento', StS*, 38:572–77. A. Dardi, 'Note su "spirito filosofico" e linguaggio scientifico nel Settecento', *LN*, 57:99–116, traces the origin of the term 'spirito filosofico' to France and examines references to it in such writers as Bettinelli and Parini. The article also deals with the way in which some thinkers of the period saw a contrast between 'spirito filosofico' and poetry, drawing at length on Clemente Sibiliato's *Sopra lo spirito filosofico nelle belle lettere* of 1779. R. Bufalini, 'Saverio Scrofani's *Viaggio in Grecia* and late eighteenth-century travel writing', *Italica*, 74:43–51, describes the fashionable literary themes on which

Scrofani drew while claiming not to be writing a typical travel book. The article also touches upon Scrofani's *Relazione sullo stato attuale dell'agricoltura e del commercio della Morea* and claims that it shows the way in which such imaginative travel writing was often dressed in a scientific garb. Paola Di Pietro Lombardi, *Girolamo Tiraboschi*, Rimini, Luisè, 1996, 183 pp., is a biography containing, in an appendix, a useful list of all Tiraboschi's correspondents. Giorgio Simoncini, *La città nell'età dell'illuminismo: le capitali italiane*, 2 vols, F, Olschki, 256 + 109 pp. R. Abbruggiati, 'Avec ou sans guillemets? Le rapport narration/dialogue dans *Il Caffè*', *REI*, 42, 1996:203–17, discusses the editorial choices to be made in indicating dialogue as opposed to narration in two modern editions of the periodical, that of Sergio Romagnoli for Feltrinelli (1960) and Gianni Francioni's for Bollati Boringhieri (1993). M. Ambrogi Mann, 'Twentieth-century thoughts on feminism and rights in eighteenth-century Milan: a view from *Il Caffè*', *RStI*, 15:196–202, reviews Pietro Verri's ideas on education and upbringing and Sebastiano Franci's essay 'Difesa delle donne'. G. Addeo, '*Il Corriere di Napoli e di Sicilia*', *ASPN*, 113, 1995[1996]: 381–408, examines another periodical, a bilingual French-Italian publication, financed by the government for 20 issues between February and April 1799. Addeo demonstrates that it attempted to reconcile the political authorities in Naples and the South with military and religious powers. G. Scherillo, 'Galvani-Volta. Scienza, politica, conformismo', *AAPN*, 45, 1996[1997]:159–68, addressing the celebrated controversy between the two eminent scientists about nerve and muscle structures which led directly to Volta's invention of the battery, sees the confrontation as representing the old world versus the new Enlightenment. B. Capaci, 'Il tavolino della dama. Lettere e letture di Caterina Dolfin-Tron', *SV*, 31, 1996[1997]: 191–228, investigates the library of this leading light of Venetian society to demonstrate not only her level of culture, but also her interest in the political world of her husband; the article also draws on her letters, which illustrate her influence and the range of her correspondents. L. Perini, 'L'epistolario di Elena Soranzo Mocenigo (1776–1781)', *AVen*, 149:41–70, analyses the correspondence between Elena and Francesco Pesaro, Venice's ambassador to Spain, which documents many aspects of the society of the period. Giulio Monteleone, *Padova tra Rivoluzione e Restaurazione, 1789–1815*, Padua, Programma, 200 pp., gathers together a number of the author's previously published essays. B. Stevanin, 'La società padovana di fine Settecento in un manoscritto inedito di Girolamo Polcastro', *SV*, 31, 1996[1997]:229–47, considers the contribution of Padua to Enlightenment thought in the period immediately preceding the arrival of Napoleon, basing itself on P.'s account of the period

1787–94 in *Compendio istorico degli avvenimenti accaduti alla città di Padova*.
Polcastro emphasizes the importance of philosophy in the development of the new ideas, and gives much information on the theatrical
and literary life of the city, as well as analysing the economic situation.
G. Zalin, 'Contatti epistolari tra Giovanni Arduino e Girolamo
Silvestri', *AVen*, 148:149–66, deals with A.'s literary-scientific correspondence with various secretaries of Rovigo's Accademia dei Con-
cordi. The importance of the universities in the continuing intellectual
debate is demonstrated by D. Tongiorgi, 'Angelo Teodoro Villa e gli
insegnamenti letterari nell'Università pavese riformata', *BSPSP*, 48,
1996:21–34, which analyses V.'s almost single-handed efforts to
maintain the teaching of *belle lettere* over several decades and his
opposition, rooted in an 'aspirazione enciclopedica', to increasing
specialization. See also M. Aglietti, 'L'Università di Pisa in età
leopoldina. La riforma degli esami di laurea 11 dicembre 1786', *BSP*,
65, 1996:115–62, a detailed discussion of Peter Leopold's plan to rid
the university of excessive bureaucracy and other abuses of the degree
system by instituting a commission, whose reforms continued until
the turn of the century. Donatella Balani, *Toghe di stato. La facoltà
giuridica dell'Università di Torino e le professioni nel Piemonte del Settecento*, T,
Centro Studi per la Storia dell'Università, 1996, xii + 334 pp., also
deals with the involvement of universities in public life, tracing the
activities and influence of the university in 18th-c. Turin with
particular reference to the educational reforms proposed by the pre-
revolutionary regime and the problems they gave rise to. Another
article on the House of Savoy is T. Ricardi Di Netro, 'Carlo
Emanuele Cavalleri di Groscavallo. Ascesa sociale e committenze
artistiche alla corte sabauda tra Sei e Settecento', *StP*, 26:47–60,
recording the artistic and literary activities of this governor of the
royal palaces. L. Guerci, 'Incredulità e rigenerazione nella Lombar-
dia del Triennio Repubblicano', *RSI*, 109:49–120, discusses the
Italian translation of the atheistic *Traité des trois imposteurs* and
Voltaire's *Histoire de l'établissement du christianisme*, and particularly the
part they played in the political and religious debates in Lombardy
and Milan in the late 18th c. **Politica, vita religiosa, carità: Milano nel
primo Settecento*, ed. Marco Bona Castellotti, Edoardo Bressan, and
Paola Vismara, Mi, Jaca Book, 294 pp. A. Borelli, 'Dall'innesto del
vaiolo alla vaccinazione jenneriana: il dibattito scientifico napoletano', *Nuncius*, 12:67–85, illustrates the contribution to the scientific
side of the Enlightenment debate of writers such as Galiani, Genovesi,
and Angelo Gatti. G. Bentivegna, 'Filosofia e politica nella tradizione
nella Sicilia del primo Settecento', *ASSO*, 91, 1995 [1997]:35–141, is
a substantial contribution to our understanding of the reception of
Enlightenment ideas in the South, which examines works such as

Giambattista Caruso's *Sogno accademico* (1723) and *Memorie istoriche* (1716). According to the author, these show a positive approach to tradition, which was opposed by the Jesuit Domenico Bandini and the apologist for the nobility, Pietro Vitale. The article notes the activities of the Inquisition, the impact of Muratori's work, and the importance of Agostino Pantò and Francesco Emanuele Cangiamila in the founding of the Accademia del Buon Gusto (1718), and examines the impact of writers such as Tommaso Natale, Vincenzo Gaglio, and Carlo Santacolomba, who were also linked to the influential masonic movement. Norbert Jonard, **L'Italie des Lumières. Histoire, société et culture du XVIIIe siècle italien*, Paris, Champion — F, Cadmo, 1996, 295 pp.

2. PROSE, POETRY, DRAMA

Ettore Bonora, *Dall'Arcadia al Leopardi. Studi di letteratura italiana*, Modena, Mucchi, 282 pp., gathers together seven previously published articles, including pieces on Arcadia and Europe, Parini and Baretti. *AARA*, 246, 1996 [1997], is devoted to the proceedings of a conference on Girolamo Tartarotti, held at Rovereto in October 1995 at Rovereto, and contains: C. Mozzarelli, 'Dal cosmo dell'Antico Regime all'illuminismo' (11–15); S. Vareschi, 'Le rivisitazioni storico-agiografiche di Girolamo Tartarotti: progetti, temi, metodo' (17–43); R. Filosi, 'Credere e sapere negli scritti di Girolamo Tartarotti sull'arte critica' (45–66); M. Allegri, 'Tra Vienna e Venezia: la formazione di una società colta nella Rovereto di primo Settecento' (67–89); G. P. Marchi, 'Storia di un'amicizia rifiutata: Scipione Maffei e Girolamo Tartarotti tra "scientifica cognizione" e "compassionevoli debolezze"' (91–115); E. Garms-Cornides, 'I rapporti tra Girolamo Tartarotti e gli eruditi ultramontani' (117–36); A. Trampus, '"Dottrina magica" e "scienza cabalistica" nei rapporti fra Tartarotti, Gianrinaldo Carli e Scipione Maffei' (137–51); G. P. Romagnoni, 'Girolamo Tartarotti, Lodovico Antonio Muratori e il "Tiranno delle lettere"' (153–86); E. Ferraglio, 'I rapporti tra Girolamo Tartarotti ed il cardinale Angelo Maria Querini nella corrispondenza privata degli anni 1741–1755' (187–205); A. Valle, 'Girolamo Tartarotti e la famiglia Rosmini' (207–20); P. Cordin, 'Girolamo Tartarotti e la nostra propria lingua volgare' (221–34); M. R. Di Simone, 'La stregoneria nella cultura giuridica del Settecento italiano' (235–53); S. Ferrari, 'Sulle tracce di Girolamo Tartarotti fra Vienna, Rovereto e Venezia' (255–88); G. Dall'Olio, 'L'immagine dell'Inquisizione romana nel *Congresso notturno delle Lammie*' (289–317); M. Nequirito, 'L'assetto istituzionale roveretano nel Settecento' (319–46); M. Farina, 'La chiesa tridentina nel travaglio tra vecchio e nuovo alla metà del Settecento' (347–69); S. Benvenuti, 'Il busto di Girolamo Tartarotti e l'interdetto alla chiesa di San Marco in Rovereto' (371–88); W. Neuhauser, 'Organisation der Bibliotheken in Tirol in der Mitte des 18. Jahrhunderts' (389–410); E. Sfredda, 'I luoghi dell'aggregazione sociale' (411–32); E. Schweizer, 'Girolamo Tartarotti poeta' (433–58); L. Frascio, 'Girolamo Tartarotti e i letterati bresciani' (459–515); S. Gagliardi, 'La biblioteca di Girolamo Tartarotti' (518–34); A. Spada, 'Gli accademici "taxiani" di Innsbruck e il loro contributo alla cultura roveretana' (535–55). E. Guagnini, *'Di alcuni viaggi immaginari del Settecento italiano: romanzo e dintorni', *Studi di teoria e storia letteraria*, 1996: 165–75. Giovanna Finocchiaro Chimirri, *Nel Parnaso siciliano del Settecento*, Catania, CUECM, 1996, 148 pp. G. Carnazzi, 'Berneschi e satirici nella Milano del Parini: tra lingua tosca e "cruschell de Beltramm"', *Acme*, 50.1: 127–46, discusses Domenico Balestrieri's *Lagrime in morte di un gatto* (1741), Vittore Vettori's *Della gelosia* from his 1744 *Rime piacevoli*, and the Accademia dei Trasformati, which Parini joined in 1753, with its opposition to the rigid Tuscanism of Bembo. The transition 'da un'ispirazione giocosa e piacevole a una satira di tono più alto' is traced through the poetry of Parini, and his use of the *capitolo* as an instrument of satire is set against the work of the two major dialect poets of this period, Carl'Antonio Tanzi and Balestrieri himself. A. Battistini, 'Miti di rigenerazione al tempo della Rivoluzione francese', *LItal*, 49: 572–99, touches on the impact of Foscolo's *Ultime lettere di Jacopo Ortis*. E. Gennaro, 'Il mito tassiano nel Settecento, I: il dibattito critico', *Bergomum*, 91.4, 1996 [1997]: 213–29, examines the contribution to the critical debate of the *Raccolta di opuscoli scientifici e filologici* of Angelo Calogerà, and specifically his work in the years 1730–39. The article continues with further assessment of the reception of Tasso by writers such as Goldoni, Monti, Zanotti, Bettinelli, and Baretti, whose reaction the author describes as 'una specie di riverente antipatia'. B. Brumana, 'Il cantante Giacinto Fontana detto Farfallino e la sua carriera nei teatri di Roma', *Roma moderna e contemporanea*, 4, 1996: 75–112, details the career of this most famous of *castrati*, who was closely linked to all the main theatres of Rome in the early part of the century. On a similar topic is B. M. Antolini and T. M. Gialdroni, 'L'opera nei teatri pubblici a Roma nella prima metà del Settecento', *ib.*, 113–42, which examines various sources of research material in this period. Still on Rome is a new edition of Saverio Franchi, *Drammaturgia romana*, II: *1701–1750: Annali dei testi drammatici e libretti per musica pubblicati a Roma e nel Lazio dal 1701 al 1750*, Ro, Storia e Letteratura, cxxvi + 410 pp. Francesco Cotticelli and Paologiovanni Maione, *Onesto divertimento, ed allegria de' popoli: materiali per una storia dello* *spettacolo a Napoli nel primo Settecento*, Mi, Ricordi, 1996, 437 pp. **Libretti d'opera italiana dal Seicento al Novecento*, ed. Giovanna Gronda and Paolo Fabbri, Mi, Mondadori, lxxxv + 1886 pp. S. Calabrese, **'Funzioni del romanzo italiano del Settecento'*, pp. 47–107 of Stefano Calabrese, *Intrecci italiani. Una teoria e una storia del romanzo (1750–1900)*, Bo, Il Mulino, 1995, 251 pp. **Tra commediografi e letterati: Rinascimento e Settecento. Studi per Giorgio Padoan*, ed. Tiziana Agostini and Emilio Lippi, Ravenna, Longo, x + 274 pp.

3. INDIVIDUAL AUTHORS

ALFIERI.   Pier Carlo Masini, **Alfieri*, Pisa, BFS, 95 pp. E. Del Cerro, *Vittorio Alfieri e la contessa d'Albany*, preface Pier Massimo Prosio, T, Druetto, 318 pp., is a republication of the 1905 work.

BARETTI.   Bartolo Anglani, **Il mestiere della metafora. Giuseppe Baretti intellettuale e scrittore*, Modena, Mucchi, 1997, 381 pp.

BARUFFALDI.   Maria Angela Novelli, **Storia delle 'Vite de' pittori e scultori ferraresi' di Girolamo Baruffaldi: una vicenda editoriale e culturale del Settecento*, San Giovanni in Persiceto, Aspasia, 159 pp.

BECCARIA.   Vol. 5 of the Edizione Nazionale of B.'s works is Cesare Beccaria, *Carteggio*, II: *1769–1794*, ed. Carlo Capra, Renato Pasta, and Francesco Pino Pongolini, Mi, Mediobanca, 1996, 814 pp., which also contains an appendix with a list of letters which have been lost.

BIANCHI.   A. Montanari, 'Modelli letterari dell'autobiografia latina di Giovanni Bianchi (Iano Planco, 1693–1775)', *Studi Romagnoli*, 45, 1994[1997]:277–99, discusses B.'s autobiography which appeared in the first volume of Giovanni Lami's *Memorabilia* and which followed a common 18-c. pattern of an account of a youthful experience (again not uncommonly, as in this case, untrue) and a later brilliant scientific career. The work had aroused criticism because of its excessive self-praise, but it is clear that B. is not concerned to write a historical document, but to offer a literary work in which due importance is given to narration and background.

CAPECI.   M. Di Martino, 'Oblio e recupero di un librettista settecentesco: Carlo Sigismondo Capeci (1652–1728) e il melodramma arcadico', *NRMI*, 30, 1996 [1997]:31–55, analyses the career of a Roman who worked at the court of Maria Casimir, Queen of Poland, producing melodramas which were set to music by the great composers of the day, such as Alessandro and Domenico Scarlatti and Handel. He also wrote comedies, and his work was praised by Quadrio and Martelli, and seen as being on a level with his contemporaries Zeno and Metastasio.

CESAROTTI. S. B. Chandler, 'La versione del Cesarotti del *Cartone di Ossian*', *EL*, 22.2:3–15, assesses the difficulties faced by C. in working on Ossian's *Carthon*, showing how sometimes C. alters the original and frequently embellishes it. C. O'Brien, *'From Fionn MacCumhaill to Melchiorre Cesarotti', pp. 15–24 of *Cross-currents in European Literature*, ed. Stephen F. Boyd et al., Dublin, UCD Department of Italian, 1996, 125 pp.

CHIARI. Luca Clerici, *Il romanzo italiano del Settecento: il caso Chiari*, Venice, Marsilio, 231 pp.

FEDERICI. G. Piaia, 'Un singolare antidoto poetico ai "Paradossi" pedagogico-religiosi di Rousseau', *AtV*, 34, 1996[1997]:145–58, deals with Domenico Maria Federici's *Emilio religioso*, which attempted, on the occasion of a noble wedding, to present an anti-Rousseau programme of family upbringing.

FILANGIERI. I. Sisto, 'La scienza dello stato nel pensiero di Gaetano Filangieri', *ArSP*, 49, 1996:153–61, examines F.'s *Scienza della legislazione*, assessing its position in the reform movement in Naples, with its emphasis both on the legislative programme as the most suitable means of producing an adequate public administration and on the liberation of the individual.

GOLDONI. There are new titles in the Marsilio edition of Goldoni's works: Carlo Goldoni, *Il giocatore*, ed. Alessandro Zaniol, Venice, Marsilio, 246 pp.; Id., *Sior Todero brontolon*, ed. Giorgio Padoan, Venice, Marsilio, 278 pp. Id., *La famiglia dell'antiquario*, electronic edition on CD-ROM, ed. Luigi Toschi, Venice, Marsilio, 1996, 182 pp. Id., *La serva amorosa*, introd. Luigi Lunari, ann. Carlo Arrigo Pedretti, Mi, Rizzoli, 167 pp. Id., *Il servitore di due padroni*, adapted by Talia Ottoboni and Alessandra Pistolese, Ro, Alta Marea, 1996, 125 pp., is aimed at younger readers. Carlo Goldoni, *La locandiera*, ed. Deirdre O'Grady, Dublin, UCD, 174 pp., is a very useful addition to the Belfield Italian Library series, with notes and introduction in English and Italian-English vocabulary. *Carlo Goldoni alla luce della ragione, all'ombra della passione*, ed. Paola Trivero, T, Tirrenia, 1996, 132 pp. M. Günsberg, 'Artful women: morality and materialism in Goldoni', Günsberg, *Gender*, 88–120, addresses G.'s moralizing and its influence on the portrayal of female characters. The chapter is divided into two sections, 'Angel in the house', which looks in detail at the characters of Bettina and Pamela, and 'Artful women', which examines, amongst other characters, Rosaura of *La donna di garbo* and Mirandolina, explaining how the different types produce different forms of theatricality and pointing out how, in both cases, the 'moral/patriarchal order is finally restored'. Jackson I. Cope, *Secret Sharers in Italian Comedy*, Durham NC, Duke U.P., 1996, x + 221 pp., has a chapter on Goldoni (139–84), where there is a description of *La bottega del caffè* as one of a number of 'exquisite cynical vignettes' and which deals at length with unfulfilled desire in the *Villeggiatura* trilogy, ending with an examination of *Una delle ultime sere di carnovale*. *Problemi di critica goldoniana*, ed. Giorgio Padoan, Ravenna, Longo, 1996, 284 pp., contains: G. Padoan, 'Correzioni d'autore al *Sior Todero brontolon*' (9–37), scrutinizing the Pasquali and Savioli editions; F. Fido, 'Un sonetto di Goldoni perduto e ritrovato' (35–37), examining a sonnet addressed to Pietro Correr; Id., 'Ancora sulla *Bottega del caffè*' (169–78), looking at the background of the coffee-shop culture; A. Scannapieco, 'Lo statuto filologico dell'opera goldoniana nella singolare prospettiva del *Padre di famiglia*' (39–157), which discusses in detail the linguistic challenges of the play as addressed by the author in her Marsilio edition; I. Crotti, 'Gli spazi della parola nei primi intermezzi goldoniani (1730–1736)' (159–67), which refers to the *intermezzi* as a 'ricerca sperimentale' by a playwright serving his apprenticeship; N. Jonard, 'L'image de la femme dans les comédies de Goldoni' (179–98), which claims that with the two images of the siren and the good wife, G. never makes woman the equal of man; M. Bordin, '"Figurare nel mondo". La trilogia della *Villeggiatura* o la commedia del desiderio' (199–281), which discusses the generational, moral, and ideological dimensions of the trilogy and G.'s growing unease with the 'veterocapitalismo mercantile', though the author identifies a certain ambiguity in G.'s response. Bartolo Anglani, *Le passioni allo specchio. Autobiografie goldoniane*, Ro, Kepos, 1996, 316 pp., while basing himself primarily on the *Mémoires*, also draws on material from the prefaces of the Bettinelli edition after 1750, in a collection of articles emphasizing the tension between G.'s desire for reform and theatre practice. R. Turchi, 'Laboratorio goldoniano. Rassegna di studi', *GSLI*, 174: 261–86, is an extremely useful survey, emphasizing recent discussion of the texts themselves, G.'s relationship with his publishers, and the various editions. Elisabetta De Troja, **Goldoni, la scrittura, le forme*, Ro, Bulzoni, 175 pp.

GOZZI. C. Perrone, 'Il "meraviglioso" in una fiaba senza magie: la *Turandot* di Carlo Gozzi', *FC*, 21, 1996:370–90, discusses G.'s sources for the play and their modification. The language of the characters, also touched upon, is said to show 'la corrispondenza fra varietà linguistica e stratificazione sociale dei personaggi'. N. Mangini, 'Le *Memorie inutili* di Carlo Gozzi: il problema della cronologia', *AtV*, 34, 1996 [1997]:131–44, points out the absence of a critical edition of the *Memorie*, and draws on printed and manuscript sources to demonstrate the misleading nature of much of what G. writes, particularly about his relations with Teodora Ricci and Pier Antonio Gratarol.

METASTASIO. *Studies in Music*, 16, is devoted to Metastasio, following a symposium at the University of Western Ontario in 1996, and includes: K. Markstrom, 'Metastasio's delay in reaching Vienna' (1–25), examining M.'s libretti for performances in Rome in the period 1728–30, before his departure for Vienna; F. A. J. Szabo, 'The cultural transformation of the Habsburg monarchy in the age of Metastasio, 1730–1780' (27–50); A. Sommer-Mathis, '*Il lamento di Metastasio*: Metastasio and the Viennese theatre in a changing society' (51–85), drawing extensively on M.'s correspondence; D. Neviele, 'Metastasio: beyond the stage in Vienna' (87–109), based on the diaries of Count Karl Zinzendorf; M. Burden, 'Metastasio on the London stage: adaptations and permutations' (111–34); A. Stonehouse, '*Demofoonte* and democracy, or the taming of a French tyrant' (135–53), discussing the reception of M. in France and the limited performance of his works; V. Meredith, 'The Old World in the New: Metastasio's verse and diversity in North America' (155–71). L. Tufano, 'Per l'epistolario di Pietro Metastasio', *FC*, 21, 1996:242–54, investigates various holdings of M.'s letters in Italian libraries in order to suggest changes to Bruno Brunelli's edition (Mi, Mondadori, 1943–54). R. Candiani, 'Il mestiere di "poeta del teatro": la produzione di Pietro Metastasio durante il soggiorno a Roma', *Roma moderna e contemporanea*, 4, 1996:143–65, discusses the importance of M.'s Roman period in forming his own model for theatrical production, examining *Didone abbandonata*, *Semiramide*, *Siface*, and *Siroe* in particular.

MONTI. G. Pegoraro, 'Fuochi e stelle. Un passo dell'*Iliade* montiana', *FC*, 21, 1996:458–81, looks at M.'s approach to a text he could not read since he knew no Greek. It examines his use of Samuel Clarke's Latin version and Cesarotti's Italian version to explain how M., drawing also on Virgil, was able to produce something 'musicalmente aggraziata e sottile'. On the same subject, F. Gavazzeni, 'Monti tra imitazione e tradizione', *BSPSP*, 48, 1996:11–20, considers M.'s approach to the *Iliad* and the *Odyssey* in the context of Cesarotti's work on them and discusses his desire to produce a modern translation while depending on the translations of others. A. Colombo, 'Vincenzo Monti fra metafisica e poesia. Intorno a due autografi ritrovati', *CLett*, 93, 1996:39–52, gives the text of two letters (1779–80) illustrating M.'s interest in restoring the dignity of the literary arts, and in the pedagogic function of literature, tragedy, and philosophy. P. Palmieri, 'Il cuore di Monti. In margine ad una recente antologia dall'*Epistolario*', *Studi Romagnoli*, 45, 1994[1997]:337–48, discusses Alfonso Bertoldi's Florence edition (1928–31) of M.'s letters and the more recent (1993) anthology, *Lettere d'affetti e di poesia*, edited by Angelo Colombo, which consists of 154 letters dealing with the development of M.'s poetry and aspects of his family life.

MURATORI. Lodovico Antonio Muratori, *Della pubblica felicità oggetto de' buoni prìncipi*, ed. Cesare Mozzarelli, Ro, Donzelli, 1996, xxxix + 276 pp., has an introduction outlining the critical debate on the work and dealing with the different stages of its composition.

NANI. S. Stoppato, 'I *Discorsi sul governo della Repubblica di Venezia* (1782–1784). L'approdo del percorso politico di Giacomo Nani', *SV*, 32, 1996 [1997]: 211–22, underlines N.'s awareness of the absence of political vision among his fellow patricians and his effective resignation to the collapse of the system.

PANSUTI. B. Alfonsetti, 'Trionfo dell'eroismo tragico: gli applausi all'*Orazia* di Saverio Pansuti nella Napoli asburgica di primo Settecento', *RLI*, 101.1 : 64–88, on the creation of a Habsburg myth in the early years of the century, refers to paintings by such as Francesco Paresi before turning to discuss P.'s *Orazia* (1719), a drama praising rulers such as Charles VI but destined to be forgotten with the passing of Naples to the Bourbons in 1734.

PARINI. Giuseppe Parini, *Il giorno*, vol. 1, ed. Dante Isella, vol. 2, comm. Marco Tizi, Parma, Guanda, 1996, cxxv + 276 pp., clxiii + 499 pp., is an updated version, with a new commentary, of the 1970 edition. G. Benvenuti, 'I rapporti del Cardinale Durini con Giuseppe Parini e l'ode *La gratitudine*', *Acme*, 49.3, 1996: 205–22, explores the links between these two temperamentally very different people, examining Durini's patronage of letters and his support of P., and including in an appendix various of Durini's Latin poetic compositions in praise of Parini. Marco Tizi, *La lingua del 'Giorno' e altri studi*, Lucca, Pacini Fazzi, 154 pp.

PIAZZA. A. Fabiano, 'Prolégomènes à l'étude du roman italien au XVIIIᵉ siècle: *La virtuosa ovvero la cantatrice fiamminga*, roman à sujet théâtral d'Antonio Piazza', *ChrI*, 50–51 : 99–126, describes the Italian 18th-c. novel as an 'objet mystérieux', but points out how the novel in general was characterized by a high degree of experimentation in order to produce a new kind of literature. Piazza wrote a number of novels with theatrical subjects, of which this (1770) was his first.

VERRI. Pietro Verri, *Meditazioni sulla felicità*, ed. Gianni Francioni, Como-Pavia, Ibis, 1996, 80 pp., is a welcome edition of a work important for an understanding V.'s intellectual development. G. Santato, 'L'Europa di Pietro Verri', *GSLI*, 174: 161–205, draws widely on the material in *Il Caffè*, showing how it fits into the cosmopolitan view of the Enlightenment in Europe and demonstrating how the *Caffè* group set out to awaken Italian society by addressing themselves particularly to the young through discussions on literature, politics, economics, and medicine. The article also examines V.'s collaboration in the *Estratto della Letteratura Europea*, describing V. as 'l'intellettuale più autenticamente europeo del secondo Settecento italiano'. C. Capra, 'Una lettera inedita di Pietro Verri sulla *Storia di Milano*', *Acme*, 50.1:117–26, gives the text of a letter to Joseph Sperges of 1779 in which V. discusses his plans for the history of Milan.

VICO. M. Martirano, 'Giuseppe Ferrari editore ed interprete di Giambattista Vico: una linea di ricerca', *AASN*, 107, 1996 [1997]:5–34, appraises Ferrari's attempts in the early 19th-c. to produce an edition of V.'s works and his disputes with another aspiring editor, Francesco Predari. M. Cassa, 'Vico, Goethe e il meccanismo', *QLL*, 21, 1996:57–67, looks at the 1995 Italian translation of Ernst Cassirer's *Goethe und die geschichtliche Welt*, examining anti-Enlightenment aspects of Goethe's work, comparing his anti-mechanistic approach with the work of V., interpreting the work of the latter as continuing, and ending, the 'tradizione tardo-rinascimentale'. G. Costa, 'Malebranche e Vico', *NRLett*, no. 2:31–47, appraises in particular the influence on V. of *La Recherche de la verité*. Id., **Vico e l'Europa, contro la 'boria delle nazioni*', Mi, Guerini, 1996, 183 pp. Andrea Battistini, **La sapienza retorica di Giambattista Vico*, Mi, Guerini, 1995, 138 pp.

OTTOCENTO

By JOHN M. A. LINDON, *Professor of Italian Studies, University College London*

(This survey covers the years 1996 and 1997)

1. GENERAL

Norbert Jonard, *Le Romantisme italien,* Paris, PUF, 1996, 127 pp., an incisive introduction, moves from romantic propaganda, romantic drama, and the historical novel to 'Leopardi et la poésie romantique', seeking to demonstrate the diversity of Italian romanticism via the contrasting figures of Manzoni and Leopardi. F. Betti, 'Key aspects of romantic poetics in Italian literature', *Italica,* 74:185–200, covers in some detail Berchet's *Lettera semiseria* and Visconti's *Idee elementari* before turning to writings by Foscolo, Leopardi, and Manzoni. Giovanni Battista Bronzini, *La letteratura popolare italiana dell'Otto-Novecento. Profilo storico-geografico,* [Novara,] Istituto Geografico De Agostini—[F,] Le Monnier, 1994, 263 pp., covers the Ottocento from Romanticism to Verga in three clear and concise chapters: 'La rivincita del popolare' (33–57); 'Prima e dopo l'unità: letterature regionali e cultura nazionale' (58–83); 'Comparativismo, verismo e critica storica' (84–108). *Atti* (AISLLI 15), the papers of the 1994 Turin conference on *Letteratura e industria,* overwhelmingly 'modern' (Ottocento/Novecento) in scope, afford a rich mine of information, ideas, and proposals for future research. On popular literature at the end of the century, they include A. Chemello, 'La filosofia del "buon operaio" nei primi "romanzi industriali" della letteratura popolare tardo-ottocentesca', *ib.,* 363–97; and P. Getrevi, 'L'alfabeto corporativo: da Cantù a Cena', *ib.,* 399–414. Many other individual items are separately noted below.

Once again there is a substantial body of writing on Ottocento narrative in particular. Stefano Calabrese, *Intrecci italiani. Una teoria e una storia del romanzo (1750–1900),* Bo, Il Mulino, 1995, 251 pp., largely consists of a historical core contained in three chapters which constitute a stimulating overview: 'Funzioni del romanzo italiano del Settecento' (47–107); 'Trame romantiche' (109–49); and 'Intrecci e finzioni di eventi nel romanzo post-romantico' (151–93). Its analysis of the evolution of plot is based on the work presented in Id., *Cento romanzi dell'Ottocento. Repertorio romanzesco dell'Ottocento italiano,* Modena, Mucchi, 1996, 410 pp., which assembles 100 résumés from Compagnoni's *Veglie di Torquato Tasso* (1803) to Graf's *Il riscatto* (1900), together with a general introduction and a brief bio/bibliographical note on each author. On the historical novel: K. Ley, 'Anmerkungen zum historischen Roman in Italien als Problem der Literaturgeschichte (mit einem bibliografischen Anhang', *ASNS*, 148:286–94. Franca Ruggieri et al., *Romanzo storico e romanticismo. Intermittenze del modello scottiano*, Pisa, ETS—Geneva, Slatkine, 1996, 152 pp., the proceedings of a 1994 colloquium organized by the Seminario di Filologia francese at the Fondazione Primoli in Rome, include: C. Leri, 'Manzoni e Scott. Folle in rivolta' (101–22); and G. Bardazzi, 'Tommazo Grossi. Tra storiografia e modelli scottiani' (123–44). M. Ganeri, *'Vicende ottocentesche del romanzo storico', *Filologia antica e moderna*, 10, 1996:59–81. Arnaldo Di Benedetto, *Ippolito Nievo e altro Ottocento*, Na, Liguori, vi + 289 pp., sandwiches the main Nievo section (for which see NIEVO, below) between essays largely devoted to narrative forms, from 'I racconti storici di Niccolò Tommaseo' (3–16), 'Il carattere della narrativa campagnola italiana' (53–67), and 'Per un profilo della narrativa campagnola' (69–94), to work on *scapigliatura* and 'Il romanzo antimilitarista di I. U. Tarchetti' (241–47). Giovanna Rosa, *La narrativa degli scapigliati*, Ro–Bari, Laterza, 187 pp., presents a clear, comprehensive, and well-structured account which will be of value to specialists as well as students. Oliva, *L'operosa stagione*, gathers essays mostly concerned with *verista* narrative (as well as Verga, for whom see below, Ciampoli, on whom see also Id., 'Lingua, dialetto e stile nel Ciampoli novelliere', *EL*, 22.2:47–58), but some of them dealing with D'Annunzio and *scapigliatura*. Also on the *scapigliatura* in general, I note David Del Principe, **Rebellion, Death and Aesthetics in Italy: The Demons of Scapigliatura*, Madison NJ, Fairleigh Dickinson U.P.—London, Associated University Presses, 1996, 179 pp.

Miscellaneous topics, themes, and figures are addressed in G. Bárberi Squarotti, 'Il mito di Omero', *REI*, 41, 1955:9–22, containing much on Vico, Foscolo, Leopardi, and Pascoli; Angelo Fabrizi, *Destino dell'antico da Dante a Saba*, Cassino, Lamberti, 252 pp., the fruit of wide reading and versatile intellect, gathering in revised form essays which converge on the *Nachleben* of the classics in the writings of Dante, Scamozzi, C. Gozzi, Alfieri, Foscolo, Manzoni, Saba, and A. La Penna; William Spaggiari, **La favolosa età dei patriarchi. Percorsi di classicismo da Metastasio a Carducci*, Ro, Izzi, 224 pp.; A. Colombo, 'Commentare Dante e Petrarca fra Sette e Ottocento. Scheda per una recente indagine attorno alle *sposizioni* da Muratori a Carducci (e oltre)', *ON*, 19.3–4, 1995:129–38, stressing the importance of Monti, Cesari, Carrer, Tommaseo, Leopardi, and Carducci; S. Timpanaro, 'Ancora sul padre Cesari: per un giudizio equilibrato', pp. 1–29 of Id., *Nuovi studi*, a revised and expanded version of the author's entry on C. in the *Dizionario biografico degli Italiani;* Gino Tellini, **L'arte della prosa. Alfieri, Leopardi, Tommaseo e altri*, F, La Nuova

Italia, 1995, 366 pp.; A. Di Benedetto, '"La sua vita stessa è una poesia": sul mito romantico di Torquato Tasso', *EL*, 22.4:17–34, focusing on the romantic myth with particular attention to Italy, but within a European frame of reference; Carmine Chiodo, *Ottocento minore. Pananti–Borsini–Fusinato–Baravalle*, Ro, Bulzoni, 1995, 331 pp., juxtaposing with frequent quotation four satirists who, to a degree, converge in their themes and values; C. Chellino, **Am Ufer der Fremde: Literatur und Arbeitsemigration (1870–1991)*, Stuttgart–Weimar, Metzlar, 1995, 502 pp., opening with a section documenting the late-Ottocento literary response to mass emigration; P. Rossi, 'Il mito della macchina nella letteratura positivista e futurista', *Atti* (AISLLI 15), 481–90; L. Pavan, '"Visioni urbane" nella letteratura e nell'iconografia di Scapigliati e Futuristi', *ib.*, 491–508; A. Martini, 'Pianoforti in poesia: da Verlaine a Montale', *Besomi Vol.*, 679–715, building on Pistone's *Le piano dans la littérature française* (1975) in a systematic investigation into the topos of the piano-plus-pianist (usually female) in poetry (French as well as Italian) before Montale's 'Tentava la vostra mano la tastiera'; Robinson, *Women*, introducing English readers to such late-Ottocento figures as Neera and Serao; Flavia Bacchetti, *I bambini e la famiglia nell'Ottocento. Realtà e mito attraverso la letteratura per l'infanzia*, F, Le Lettere, 155 pp., from a specialist in history of education and children's literature, passing from the rise of the bourgeois family, England, and Charles Dickens to the Tuscany of Pietro Thouar, Caterina Franceschi Ferrucci, Ida Baccini, and Hector Malot, with good analysis and an appendix of extracts.

A number of other items focus on particular regional phenomena or figures. For our period, in *Atti* (AISLLI 15) the northern industrial base inevitably looms largest: for the sociology of literature in an age of industrialization, D. Forgacs, 'Produzione di testi e pratiche di lettura nell'Italia protoindustriale', *ib.*, 141–62, recommends applying to Italy models such as those offered by Pierre Bourdieu and Raymond Williams. Milan in particular, which led the way in applying the new technology and produced the earliest illustrated novels to come out *a puntate* (including the definitive edition of *I promessi sposi*), is investigated in R. Tacchinardi, 'Per una storia del mercato editoriale milanese preunitario', *StIt*, 16, 1996[1997]: 17–41. For the period after unification, and in particular for what the 1881 Exhibition meant for the nascent *industria culturale:* D. Valencia Mirón and V. Peña Sánchez, '*Milano 1881:* vita letteraria e città industriale', *Atti* (AISLLI 15), 447–58. E. Bottasso, 'Le radici dell'industria editoriale in Piemonte', *StP*, 25, 1996:295–308, traces the causes of Piedmont's relative backwardness and the history of attempts in the 1830s and 40s (modelled on those of Milan and aided by the steam press) to reach a popular readership (the 'borghesia media e minuta'). Giuseppe Zaccaria, *Ottocento letterario in Piemonte*, Lecce, Milella, 324 pp. A. Di Benedetto, 'La scapigliatura piemontese secondo Gianfranco Contini', *CLett*, 24, 1996:305–09, also in Id., *Ippolito Nievo e altro Ottocento* (see above), 249–55. J. Graciliano González-Miguel, 'Il ruolo di don Bosco nello sviluppo della stampa popolare e per la gioventù', *Atti* (AISLLI 15), 283–335. Fr Callisto Caldelari, with Beatrice Lampietti, *Bibliografia ticinese dell'Ottocento*, 2 vols, Bellinzona, Casagrande, 1995. Angelo Nessi, *Scrittori ticinesi*, ed. Renato Martinoni and Clara Caversasio Tanzi, Locarno, Dadò, 303 pp. A. Brambilla, 'Una difficile identità: appunti bibliografici sulla cultura giuliana tra Otto e Novecento', *Versants*, 31:65–76, develops considerations prompted by *Poesia piranese dell'Ottocento*, ed. Paolo Blasi, Trieste, Ediz. Italo Svevo, 1995, 82 pp., and Elvio Guagnini, *'La cultura. Una fisionomia difficile'*, in *Trieste*, ed. E. Apih, Bari, Laterza, 1988, 280 pp. Umberto Pagani, *Olindo Guerrini uomo e poeta. Originalità e debiti*, pref. Gennaro Barbarisi, Ravenna, Girasole, 1996, 248 pp., is the first documented monograph to be devoted to the Romagnol socialist writer (1845–1916, pseud. Lorenzo Stecchetti), comprising chapters on his life, ideology, poetics, and sources, and his verse in dialect and in Italian, followed by a series of appendixes of illuminating documents. N. Costa-Zalessow, 'Teresa Carniani Malvezzi's correspondence with Giovanni Fabbroni: a testimony of early nineteenth-century Florentine and Bolognese cultural milieu', *RStI*, 15.2:121–60, illustrates, mainly through her correspondence with her scientific uncle, Fabbroni, Carniani's life to 1822 and her multiple relations with academics and intellectuals. S. Romagnoli, 'Considerazioni in margine ai *Toscani dell'Ottocento*', *RLI*, 99.3, 1995[1996]:92–101. C. Chiodo, 'Un poeta romantico calabrese: Filippo Greco', *CLett*, 25:349–94. Antonio Palermo, *Il vero, il reale e l'ideale. Indagini napoletane tra Otto e Novecento*, Na, Liguori, 1995, x + 174 pp.

There are also a few interesting items with a comparative or otherwise international dimension. L. Bottoni, 'La scena di Caino e le sue metamorfosi: da Alfieri a Benigni', *RLMC*, 50:21–41, concerns Byron and his 19th-c. Italian *fortuna*. G. G. Amoretti, 'Una poetessa romantica tra Francia e Italia: Agathe Sophie Sassernò', *Versants*, 31:45–64, illustrates the life and poetry of a native of Nice, 'poetessa francese per lingua e cultura letteraria, italiana per sentimenti e appassionata adesione al progetto risorgimentale', and well known in Piedmontese society. P. Pellini, *'La casa del sonno* di Bertolazzi e il "teatro finanziario" fra Otto e Novecento', *Italianistica*, 25, 1996 [1997]:329–55, explores the French-inspired theatre of financial speculation, noting a characteristic petty-bourgeois rigorism in Milanese plays like Bertolazzi's (1902), in contrast to the more restrained Tuscan moralism of Cesare Calvi in *I falliti* (1867) and the anti-capitalist protest of Cletto Arrighi's novel *La scapigliatura e il 6 febbraio* (1861). C. Giunta, 'Contatti letterari tra Italia e Germania nel secondo Ottocento: la rivista *Auf der Höhe*', *RLettI*, 13, 1995[1997]:245–82. For Italy's most noted 19th-c. *comparatista*, I note the welcome reprint: Bonaventura Zumbini, **Studi di critica e letteratura comparata*, ed. Epifanio Ajello, Ro, Izzi, 1996, 156 pp. Antonella Salomoni, *Il pensiero religioso e politico di Tolstoj in Italia (1886–1910)*, F, Olschki, 1996, 269 pp., is a major contribution on the circulation of T.'s ideas among groups interested in the relation between religion and politics. An impressive body of reactions to the challenge of his message is lucidly organized in chapters on 'Guerra, esercito e patria' (49–99), 'Un cristianesimo senza chiese' (101–74), 'Anarchismo e antimilitarismo' (175–23), and 'Socialismo e morale' (225–60).

2. INDIVIDUAL AUTHORS

ANGELI. R. Silvestri, 'Cultura e mondanità nella Roma umbertina: Diego Angeli', *CLett*, 24, 1996:213–39.

BELLI. The 'theatricality' of B.'s representation of Rome in his sonnets is discussed by L. De Nardis, 'Belli e il teatro', *StRo*, 44, 1996:364–66, an article prompted by Franco Onorato, **A teatro col Belli: il sublime ridicolo del melodramma nei sonetti romaneschi*, Ro, Palombi, 1996, 127 pp. Id., 'Spunti belliani in alcune lettere di Zenaide Wolkonskaia', *StRo*, 44, 1996:308–16. C. Ceresa, **I Borboni di Napoli nei sonetti romaneschi del Belli*', pp. 107–17 of *Strenna dei Romanisti*, 56, 1995.

BERCHET. I. Bertelli, 'Impeto politico e intensità poetica nelle *Romanze* del Berchet. *I profughi di Parga*', *CLett*, 25:449–63.

BINI. B.'s passionately dissident *Manoscritto di un prigioniero* (1833), antithetical to Pellico's *Le mie prigioni*, is the subject of B. S. Anglani, 'Sul *Manoscritto* di Carlo Bini', *StIt*, 15, 1996:19–33, also discussed by G. Tellini in *L'arte della prosa* (see GENERAL, above). The nature of Bini's political involvement is clarified in 'Due cospiratori che negarono di aver cospirato (forse Giordani, certamente Bini)', Timpanaro, *Nuovi studi*, 103–25, one of the wholly new essays of the collection.

BOITO, A. P. Paolini, 'Sull'elaborazione del *Mefistofele* di Arrigo Boito', *Italianistica*, 26:111–22. B.'s 'polyphonic' and colloquial *Falstaff*, highly original in relation to the comic opera tradition, deservedly figures with introduction, notes, and bibliography (text at pp. 1487–569) in the excellent anthology *Libretti d'opera italiani*, ed. Giovanna Gronda and Paolo Fabbri, Mi, Mondadori, lxxxv

+ 1880 pp. Di Benedetto, *Ippolito Nievo* (see GENERAL, above), analyses one of B.'s more memorable poems in '*Case nuove* di Arrigo Boito o le rovine di Milano' (217–39), and finds antecedents in Tarchetti, Fontana, Bouilhet, and Baudelaire. *Arrigo Boito, ed. Giovanni Morelli, F, Olschki, 1994.

BOITO, C. R. Rampini, 'Il contributo di L. Sterne alla genesi di un viaggiatore "vano"', *Italianistica*, 25, 1996[1997]:285–99, and C. Mazzoni, 'Gazing at the veil, unveiling the fetish: the case of Camillo Boito's short stories', *ItQ*, 129–30, 1996:29–43, explore B.'s *Storielle vane* from disparate points of view.

BORSIERI See GIORDANI, below.

CAMERANA. P. M. Prosio, 'Percorso figurativo di un poeta: Camerana e i suoi rapporti con la pittura di Fontanesi', *StP*, 26:257–75, shows how Camerana's poetry was variously linked with the work of the Reggian painter.

CANALE. Michele Giuseppe Canale, **Il viaggio da Genova all'isola di Corsica di un proscritto politico nel giugno 1833*, ed. Matilde Dillon Wanke, Modena, Mucchi, 1996, liii + 97 pp., presents C.'s fictionalized memoirs as an experiment aimed at replacing the dominant Manzonian model with a more popular form of historical novel based on the contemporary struggle and closer to Foscolo's *Ortis*.

CANTONI. The only previously unpublished item in Roberto Salsano, *Novellistica in nuce. Abbozzi, esempi, schizzi, 'smorfie' fra Ottocento e Novecento*, Na, Liguori, 1996, 73 pp., was also published as Id., 'Novellistica critica nel secondo Ottocento: *Il demonio dello stile* di Alberto Cantoni', *CLett*, 24, 1996:151–65. The Liguori volume also includes earlier work on Cantoni (cf. *YWMLS*, 55:600).

CAPUANA. M. Gadebusch Bondio, 'La vita oltre la morte: spiritismo, ipnotismo ed esperienze metapsichiche nei romanzi e nelle novelle di Capuana', *Italienisch*, 38:38–50, seeks to demonstrate that C.'s interest in death and spiritualism was not at odds with his *verismo*. V. Pappalardo, 'Dalle "eroine" di Capuana alle "isteriche" di Sigmund Freud', *CLett*, 25:253–69. F. Manai, 'Fenomenologia delle corna in Capuana e Pirandello', *Italianistica*, 25, 1996[1997]:357–66. A. Pagliaro, '*Il Marchese di Roccaverdina* di Luigi Capuana: crisi etica o analisi positivistica', *ItS*, 52:111–30. R. Fedi, 'Capuana favolista (con appendice)', *CLett.*, 25:493–512. C. Musumarra, 'Capuana e la critica testuale', *ib.*, 25:45–58. Oliva, *L'operosa stagione*, includes '*Il piccolo archivio:* un esperimento per il teatro verista' (85–92).

CARDUCCI. M. Martelli, *'Carducciana minima adnotanda', pp. 649–60 of ΟΔΟΙ ΔΙΖΗΣΙΟΣ. *Le vie della ricerca. Studi in onore di Francesco Adorno*, ed. M. Serena Funghi, F, Olschki, 1996, elucidates borrowings from Poliziano and F. Cassoli, and the intricate history of the hoopoe in Italian poetry from Parini and Foscolo to Carducci and beyond. A. V. Nazzaro, 'Note intertestuali su *A una bottiglia di Valtellina* del 1848 del Carducci', *CLett*, 24, 1996:113–27. L. Orsenigo, 'Rilevazioni carducciane', *ib.*, 25:31–44. B. Londero, 'Carducci tra streghe e fate della Carnia', *ItStudien*, 17, 1996:57–67. M. Pazzaglia, 'Carducci fra Panzini e Serra', *ib.*, 24, 1996:129–49.

COMPAGNONI.   Giuseppe Compagnoni, **Cinquantotto lettere e una supplica*, introd. and ann. Marcello Savini, Ravenna, Longo, 1996, 146 pp., brings to light material (1780–1833) from the Fondo Piancastelli at Forlì.

D'ANNUNZIO.   Pietro Gibellini, **D'Annunzio dal gesto al testo*, Mi, Mursia, 1995, 224 pp. Guido Baldi, **L'inetto e il superuomo. D'Annunzio tra 'decadenza' e vita ascendente*, T, Scriptorium, 322 pp. Oliva, *L'operosa stagione*, has a section of miscellaneous essays devoted to D'Annunzio. D. Fedele, 'I nuovi commenti dell'opera dannunziana', *CLett*, 25:169–88, surveys the commentaries published in recent collections of D'A.'s works. Carlo Santoli, *Gabriele D'Annunzio. La musica e i musicisti*, Ro, Bulzoni, 645 pp., systematically researches the import-ant and multifarious links with music and musicians under four heads: poetry and music (with particular reference to Malipiero, Pizzetti, Respighi, and Tosti, and their settings); the theatre (operatic settings, ballet music, incidental music for them and their cinematic versions; the collaboration with Debussy); references to music in his prose writings; miscellaneous writings, including D'A.'s musical journalism. This impressive compilation promises to be an extremely useful work of reference.

For the early verse we now have **Concordanza del 'Canto novo' di Gabriele D'Annunzio*, comp. Giuseppe Savoca and Alida D'Aquino, F, Olschki, 1995, xl + 252 pp. Later poetry is represented by Oreste Macrì, *Simbolo e ritmo nel 'Poema Paradisiaco' di Gabriele D'Annunzio*, Ro, Bulzoni, 202 pp., originally published in instalments in *L'Albero*, but without para. 29, 'Anatolia nelle *Vergini delle rocce* o della pietà familiare' (160–67), which develops the link (already noted by others) between that novel and the *Poema*. The study sets out to offer a selection, from the *Poema*, of the 'elementi vitali e poetici autentici e interiormente coerenti della linea romantico-simbolista nell'opera dannunziana', a line continued not only in *Maia* and *Alcyone*, but in the work of the epigones who emerged in the decade 1910–20: Ungaretti, Rebora, Saba, Campana. D. Rieger, '"O Giovinezza! . . ." — Ästhetizismus und Brüderlichkeit', *Italienisch*, 37:72–74, offers both a commentary on, and a German translation of, the D'Annunzio sonnet, the earliest composition in *Poema Paradisiaco*. A. Camps, '"Urbs inferna": dalla "Città infetta" alla "Città terribile" in *Maia*, primo libro delle *Laudi*', *Atti* (AISLLI 15), 535–45.

Marinella Cantelmo, *Il 'Piacere' dei leggitori. D'Annunzio e la comunicazione letteraria*, Ravenna, Longo, 1996, 276 pp., valuably brings together and integrates work on D'A.'s novels partly published in article form (cf. *YWMLS*, 57:563): leading themes are the aesthetics of *riscrittura* and the *funzione autore*, explored mainly with reference to *Il piacere*. The same author also focuses on *Il piacere* in her discussion of D'A.'s unfailing exploitation of the 'circuito comunicativo' with the public: 'Il futuro abortito: D'Annunzio e l'industria culturale', *Atti* (AISLLI 15), 509–34. On the basis of the novels, but in psychoanalytical terms, Lisetta Renzi, 'Come in uno specchio. Il "feminile" in d'Annunzio', *Intersezioni*, 16, 1996:327–55, concludes that 'nell'incontro con la propria dimensione femminile rimossa, come davanti ad uno specchio, si scopre un volto sconosciuto al quale non si tollera di riconoscersi simile'. What the hero sees is 'il volto dell'eterno feminino, la Medusa pietrificante che si nasconde nelle profondità del proprio essere'. On the same ground, D. Duncan, 'Choice objects: the bodies of Gabriele D'Annunzio', *ItS*, 52:131–50, argues that 'it is D'Annunzio's concern for the male gender which underpins his rhetoric of gender': what his novels reveal is 'the ceaseless, self-concealing effort to attain the masculine position'. C. Mazzoni, 'Rappresentazione della violenza, violenza della rappresentazione: *La Leda senza cigno* e *La Violante dalla bella voce* di G. D'Annunzio', *FoI*, 29, 1995:266–85.

Luisetta Elia Chomel, *D'Annunzio. Un teatro al femminile*, Ravenna, Longo, 247 pp., re-examines one by one the whole corpus of D'A.'s plays, to overturn the critical commonplace of his superman preoccupation, arguing that in his reaction against bourgeois drama he also transcends male prejudice, restores woman's subjective autonomy, and projects heroines superior to their male antagonists. A. Netti, 'Il teatro di Gabriele D'Annunzio nella Vienna di fine secolo', *ItStudien*, 17, 1996:91–105, explores D'A.'s changing fortunes on the Viennese stage in relation to figures such as Duse and Hofmannsthal, and also his growing anti-Habsburg reputation. N. Lorenzini, 'Il mito della parola. Riflessioni in margine alla *Figlia di Iorio*', *LS*, 32:505–17, explores the significance of myth in the drama by the aesthete for whom 'il verbo è tutto'. A. Bentoglio, 'Interpretazioni registiche della *Figlio di Iorio* sulle scene italiane del Novecento', *Ariel*, 12:51–57, discusses individual productions, noting contrasting tendencies: to create a hyper-real Abruzzo or an imagined archaic world at several removes from reality.

Annamaria Andreoli, *D'Annunzio archivista. Le filologie di uno scrittore*, F, Olschki, 1996, 339 pp., traces a series of engrossing excursions into the vast and still imperfectly catalogued collection of papers preserved at the Vittoriale. She suggests that D'A., having given them to the

Italian people, during his last years at Gardone may have intentionally set future scholars abstruse puzzles by planting references and allusions. Among new documents she brings to light is the autograph of the pasquinade on Hitler. Research both at the Vittoriale and in Paris brings much data to light on D'A.'s friendship with Romain Rolland and various Umbrian intellectuals, notably Romeo Gallenga Stuart, in Maurizio Pistelli, *Il 'divino testimonio'. D'Annunzio e il mito dell'eroica Rinascenza,* Modena, Mucchi, 1995, 284 pp., which concerns D'A.'s projected homage to Raphael and Perugia, the tragedy *Atalanta Baglioni,* which then gave way to the eight sonnets to Perugia (1902) included in *Città del silenzio.* Pistelli gives a critical edition of the sonnets and a historical commentary on them.

D'Annunzio himself remains a constant object of interest and has attracted numerous partial contributions: Francesco Giardinazzo, **D'Annunzio 1895: un viaggio in Grecia,* F, Aletheia, 189 pp.; Beningno Palmerio, **Con D'Annunzio alla Capponcina,* introd. Marco Marchi, F, Vallecchi, 1995, 240 pp.; S. Bartolini, 'Da Firenze a Fiume. Storia di un'amicizia fra giornali e "giornalini". Il carteggio d'Annunzio-Vamba (1900–1919)', *Luti Vol.,* 139–59; Alfredo Bonadeo, **D'Annunzio and the Great War,* Cranbury, NJ, Associated University Presses, 1995, 176 pp., perpetuating D'A.'s legend of himself, for which see the review article: J. R. Woodhouse, 'Caveat lector: D'Annunzio's autobiographical prestidigitation', *MLR,* 91, 1996:610–18, based on his long-awaited biography; C. Picariello, 'Il patto marino di Gabriele D'Annunzio', *RLI,* 101.1:156–76, which re-edits the *Pactum sine nomine* after an account of D'A.'s involvement in the FILM affair and an investigation into the history and sources of the text; Gabriele D'Annunzio, **Siamo spiriti azzurri e stelle. Diario inedito (17–27 agosto 1922),* ed. Pietro Gibellini, F, Giusti, 1995, 212 pp.

DE AMICIS. A. Brambilla, 'Edmondo De Amicis', *StP,* 25, 1996:357–76, a valuable review article noting renewed interest and recent research, which has led to De A.'s being seen in a fresh light, subjects to critical scrutiny the edition Edmondo De Amicis, **Opere scelte,* ed. Folco Portinari and Giusi Baldissone, Mi, Mondadori, 1996. Timpanaro, *Nuovi studi,* includes, on the *Idioma gentile,* 'De Amicis di fronte a Manzoni e Leopardi' (199–234), highlighting the limits of his *manzonismo* and his admiration for Leopardi as a stylist. B. Basile, 'De Amicis nei *Pirati della Malesia*', *FC,* 21, 1996 [1997]:482–86. Anita Gramigna, *'Il romanzo di un maestro' di Edmondo De Amicis,* F, La Nuova Italia, 283 pp., illuminatingly contextualizes (G. is a historian of education) and analyses the ideological programme of nation-building through education inherent in the 1890 companion-piece to *Cuore,* which was aimed, however, at the rural primary-school teacher, not (as was *Cuore*) at the urban elementary-school pupil. She includes a generous selection of extracts from the work.

DE ROBERTO. Annamaria Cavalli Pasini, *De Roberto*, Palermo, Palumbo, 1996, 286 pp., will be very useful both as an introduction and as a work of reference, comprising summary accounts of De R.'s career (11–95) and critical reception (99–206), followed by biographical (209–14) and bibliographical (215–38) notes, which latter, particularly full and valuable, make the concluding anthology of criticism (241–76) seem 'thin' and somewhat superfluous. M. Cantelmo, 'Silenzio d'autore: mito e modi dell'impersonalità narrativa nei *Viceré* di Federico De Roberto', *StCrit,*, 11, 1996:449–77. M. Chu, 'Federico De Roberto e le ragioni del potere', *MLN,* 111, 1996:74–88. G. Lopez, 'Federico De Roberto e Sabatino Lopez cent'anni fa', *Belfagor,* 52:332–40, also features Verga at a time when he was absorbed in his passion for photography.

DI BREME. G. Bolognesi, 'Byron e l'armeno', *Aevum,* 71:755–68, relates Byron's Venetian interest in Armenian and the Venetian monastery of San Lazzaro with his earlier association with Di B. in Milan. S. Gentili, '"Demostene" e il "sofista pericoloso" (Foscolo in di Breme)', *StIt,* 14, 1995 [1996], 123–34, sketches the new type of intellectual that emerges from Di Breme's letters in contrast to the heroic model of *letterato-tribuno* represented by Foscolo.

DI GIACOMO. A. Benevento, 'Il punto su Salvatore Di Giacomo (1984–1996)', *EL,* 22.2:83–102.

DOSSI. C. Gigante, 'Marziale in Dossi: un episodio della *Desinenza in a*', *EL,* 20.4, 1995:53–59, illustrates D.'s interest in Martial, identifying a second Latin literary reminiscence (to add to *Pervigilium Veneris,* noted by D. Isella) in the *Incendio di legna vecchia:* epigram 37 of the fifth book of Martial. P. Montefoschi, 'Carlo Dossi: dalla diligenza alla locomotiva', *Atti* (AISLLI 15), 471–80, traces D.'s hostility to the world of machines. Antonio Saccone, **Carlo Dossi. La scrittura del margine,* Na, Liguori, 1995, 154 pp.

FOGAZZARO. M. Colin, 'Un roman engagé d'Antonio Fogazzaro: *Daniele Cortis*', *REI,* 42, 1996:237–51. E. Travi, 'Valori attuali di *Piccolo mondo antico*', *Cenobio,* 45, 1996:149–51. Id., 'Antonio Fogazzaro scrive a Paolo Arcari', *ib.,* 152–56.

FOSCOLO. Useful recent re-editions are: Lanfranco Caretti, *Foscolo: persuasione e retorica,* Pisa, Nistri-Lischi, 1996, 154 pp., which reproduces in handier form the author's 1969 essay for the Garzanti *Storia della letteratura italiana;* and Mario Scotti, *Foscoliana,* Modena, Mucchi, 368 pp., which gathers 15 miscellaneous essays by Italy's foremost *foscolista.* Luigi Carrer, **Vita di Ugo Foscolo,* ed. Carlo Mariani, Bergamo, Moretti & Vitale, 1995, 440 pp., reproduces the best of the early biographies with an introduction and an appendix of other

19th-c. biographical documents. Vol. 1 of the new Einaudi-Gallimard edition of F.'s works is scrutinized in V. Di Benedetto, 'A proposito di un'edizione foscoliana', *GSLI*, 173:1996:267–80; and N. Trotta, 'Foscolo e i suoi contemporanei: la raccolta Acchiappati', *Autografo*, 31, 1995:143–50, surveys the part of the collection consisting of MSS, which has been donated to Pavia University: 53 letters (1800–27) by F. and many others to or about him. M. Paoli, **Lo specchio del poeta: contributo all'iconografia di Ugo Focolo', *Rara volumina*, 1995:39–76. B. Danna, 'Rassegna foscoliana (1980–1995)', *LItal*, 48, 1996:451–92, though not exhaustive, is nonetheless a comprehensive and competent survey, which will be an invaluable source of bibliographical and critical orientation.

E. Neppi, 'Foscolo e la crisi della cosmo-teologia', *Intersezioni*, 16, 1996:467–91, traces F.'s intellectual development from the theocentrism of the early poetry (1795–97) to the world-view of *Le Grazie* ('il corso del suo pensiero è attraversato [...] da una frattura epistemologica di dimensioni europee, che capovolge il suo modo di vedere le cose'); yet in suppressing the Judaeo-Christian God he replaces Him with 'meccanismi diversi' that have the same function. Id., 'Foscolo e i dilemmi della rappresentazione di sé', *RLMC*, 1995 [1996]:357–78. S. P. Sondrup, 'Werther, Jacopo, and the narrative constitution of the self', Mildonian, *Parodia*, 131–41, sees *Ortis* as not only 'a subtly crafted and ingeniously parodistic subversion of *Werther*, but also a subversion of itself as narrative and the process of narration': Jacopo turns out to be an unreliable narrator and becomes 'progressively less focused and articulate'. His use of words from Alfieri's tragedies, however, is astonishingly interpreted as a gesture of resignation: Alfieri is said to represent the values against which Jacopo's revolutionary fervour had been directed. G. Fogli, 'La "canzoncina di Saffo" e il tramonto della luna nelle *Ultime lettere di Jacopo Ortis*', *StCrit*, 11, 1996:431–48. M. Palumbo, *'Ultime lettere di Jacopo Ortis:* strategie di commento', *EL*, 22.3:15–18. Id., **Saggi sulla prosa di Ugo Foscolo*, Na, Liguori, 1994, 177 pp.

On the short poems: Pierantonio Frare, **L'ordine e il verso. La forma canzoniere e l'istituzione metrica nei sonetti del Foscolo*, Na, ESI, 1995, 226 pp.; M. Brose, 'Back to the body of the mother: Foscolo's *A Zacinto*', *Italica*, 74:164–84, psychoanalytical and verging on the *extravaganza;* and V. Vianello, 'Il "liber" di Foscolo: l'edizione pisana delle poesie', *QVen*, 21, 1995, 99–134. Research (cf. *YWMLS*, 57, 1995:566) into the relationship between the 1803 *Poesie* and F.'s study of Lucretius and Catullus-Callimachus is continued by G. Melli Fioravanti, 'Mito e poesia negli scritti foscoliani del 1802–1803', *Studi Blasucci*, 389–404, also in **Humanitas*, 48.4 1996, an issue (ed. P. Gibellini) devoted to *Il mito nella letteratura italiana moderna.*

F. Longoni, 'Foscolo e Virgilio. A proposito di due edizioni virgiliane appartenute a Ugo Foscolo, con postille inedite', *SFI*, 55:141–71, relates to F.'s copies of editions of Heyne's and Masvicius's Virgil: L. points to the interest of the *postille,* which show, for example, that F. planned at one point to demonstrate the Lucretian ascendency of Virgil. M. Salvini, 'La riflessione foscoliana sul mito', *ON*, 19.6, 1995:31–51, and 'Il mito nell'opera del Foscolo', *CLett*, 25:465–92. Carla Doni, *Il mito greco nelle tragedie di Ugo Foscolo (Tieste- Aiace),* Ro, Bulzoni, 119 pp., already published at least in part (but this is not acknowledged), pays particular attention to Greek, French, and (for *Ajace)* Foscolian precedents.

M. M. Lombardi, 'Sull'attribuzione al Foscolo dell'*Edippo,* tragedia di Wigberto Rivalta', *SFI*, 54, 1996:291–309, raises doubts over the tragedy's attribution to Foscolo, showing by linguistic analysis, in the process, that it is modelled on Bentivoglio's translation of Statius's *Thebaid* and on Alfieri's *Polinice* and *Antigone.* S. Carrai, 'Foscolo milanese tra Manzoni e Pellico', *GSLI*, 174:321–48. E. Bellini, 'Pellico, Foscolo e la "donna gentile"', *Aevum*, 71:769–99. R. Turchi, 'L'orazione inaugurale di Ugo Foscolo', *RLI*, 100.2–3, 1996 [1997]:26–73, lacks a clearly defined argument, but proposes some interesting derivations, notably from Mario Pagano's *Saggi politici.* C. Del Vento, 'Foscolo e Marc-Antoine Jullien: note in margine ai *Discorsi su Lucrezio*', *LItal*, 49:392–426. Id., 'Foscolo e "gli antichi amici dell'indipendenza"', *RLettI*, 13, 1995[1997]:79–136, draws on documents in the Milan state archives to shed new light on F.'s clandestine political involvement between 1813 and 1815. Carlo Torchio, *Fra romanticismo e decadenza. Studi sulla letteratura e sulla lingua letteraria,* T, Tirrenia, 1995, 250 pp., opens with 'La polemica "milanese" del Foscolo (Foscolo tra romanticismo e decadenza?)' (11–33), hitherto unpublished, which interprets F.'s romantic discontent and incompatibility with Milan in terms of decadentism.

S. Gentili, 'Autoritratto e apologia in Foscolo: la *Notizia bibliografica* e il terzo *Ortis*', *Luti Vol.*, 87–113. E. Lombardi, 'Per l'edizione critica delle *Lettere scritte dall'Inghilterra*', *SFI*, 53, 1995:249–344, points out the shortcomings of Fubini's edition (incompleteness, conflated *montage* of material from discrete phases of composition in order to achieve a unified text, and failure to apply rigorous philological criteria in the apparatus) before reconstructing the process of composition from all available sources and in relation to the Livorno MSS Foscoliani XV–XVI. J. Lindon, 'Foscolo e Łabenski. In occasione del ritrovamento di lettere foscoliane inedite', *StIt*, 17:83–93, draws attention to letters (1824, recently sold at Sotheby's) to a little-known correspondent, a Polish count in Russian diplomatic service, who went on to make his mark in France with poetry

modelled on Lamartine's and (as Lindon shows) also influenced by
Foscolo's. K. Ley, '"sii grand'uomo e sii infelice". Zur Umwertung
des Tasso-Bildes am Beginn des Ottocento: Vorraussetzungen und
Hintergründe im europäischen Rahmen (La Harpe/Gilbert–
Goethe–Foscolo)', *GRM*, 46, 1996:131–73.

GARIBALDI. M. Martinengo, *'Garibaldi narratore. Vicende edito-
riali e stato attuale dei manoscritti', *Il Risorgimento*, 48, 1996:89–112.

GIORDANI. *Carteggio Giordani–Vieusseux 1825–1847*, ed. Laura
Melosi, F, Olschki, 273 pp., presents 138 letters (almost entirely
written after G.'s residence in Florence, from 1824 to 1830; Vieusseux's are published for the first time) in an exemplary annotated
edition, with a particularly well-judged and illuminating introduction.
This is a very substantial documentary contribution, of relevance to
a multiplicity of subjects, from the Vieusseux circle, the *Antologia* and
its contributors, Grand-Ducal reform, Capponi and Niccolini, to
Leopardi, Manzoni, and Tommaseo. Timpanaro, *Nuovi studi*, includes
essays on or concerning G.: 'Un'operetta di Pietro Borsieri ed una di
Pietro Giordani' (310–54), where G.'s *operetta* is *Il peccato impossibile;*
'Le lettere di Pietro Giordani ad Antonio Papadopoli' (55–67); 'Pietro
Gioia, Pietro Giordani e i tumulti piacentini del 1846' (69–101); and
a fourth item noted under BINI, above. See also LEOPARDI, below.

GIUSTI. E. Ghidetti, 'Preliminari all'epistolario del Giusti', *RLI*,
99.3, 1995[1996]:16–33. L. Trenti, *'"Un'ombra di quel brio".
Giusti ed Orazio', pp. 79–87 of *Convergenze testuali*, Ro, Bagatto, 1995,
stresses the contradiction between G.'s strictures on Horace as a
'court' poet, based on an Alfierian literary ideology, and his ongoing
indebtedness to Horace's verse in his own.

GRAF. C. Allasia, '"Uomo instancabile, ringraziamenti e congra-
tulazioni": lettere inedite di Arturo Graf ad Angelo Solerti', *Italianistica*, 25, 1996 [1997]:301–27, introduces and transcribes 56 missives
(1886–1905), many of the earlier ones referring to Solerti's *Vita di
Torquato Tasso*.

GROSSI. P. Paradisi, 'Considerazioni fonomorfologiche sul *Marco
Visconti* di Tommaso Grossi', *ASNP*, 24, 1994[1995]:743–818. A. Sar-
genti, 'Notizie dal carteggio di Tommaso Grossi', *Cenobio*, 45,
1996:135–48.

LEOPARDI. To judge from the sheer quantity of books and articles
published, attention has been increasingly concentrated on L. in the
run-up to the 1998 bicentenary. In the sequel to *Il nulla e la poesia. Alla
fine della tecnica: Leopardi* (1990), not noted in *YWMLS* at the time,
Emanuele Severino, *Cosa arcana e stupenda. L'Occidente e Leopardi*, Mi,
Rizzoli, 527 pp., the theoretical philosopher continues to champion
the 'unità rigorosa e potente, la continuità profonda' of L.'s thought
and to view it as crucial for the present and future of the age of

technology. Mario Rigoni, *Il pensiero di Leopardi*, Mi, Bompiani, 243 pp. Elio Gioanola, *Leopardi, la malinconia*, Mi, Jaca Book, 1995, 505 pp., a substantial new intellectual biography, stresses the conditioning received from Monaldo and 'what L. made of what was made of him'. Poetry and philosophy are viewed as two ways of expressing the same existential intuition. Prompted by G.'s work is E. Fenzi, *'Leopardi, oltre la malinconia', *NC*, 43, 1996:83–117. Adriano Mariani, *Leopardi. Nichilismo e cristianesimo*, Ro, Studium, 170 pp., a challenging critique of L.'s thought, stresses his 'Platonic' (and in a fundamental respect un-Christian) conception of the Christianity he rejected, his arguments on God as infinite possibility (1820–21), the inherent contradictoriness of L.'s nihilism and of his 'heroic protest' in *La Ginestra*, and the untenability of a world-view in which evil is ontological: in this last connection M. conducts a searching critique of Luporini, Prete, Negri, Severino, Rigoni, and others. The conclusion reverses S. Timpanaro's views by asserting that L.'s thought, 'essendo essenzialmente incentrato sul tema dell'infinito, ha un preciso limite proprio in quanto nega, alla fine, la speranza religiosa'. E. Landoni, 'Giacomo Leopardi: la poesia come nostalgia del sacro', *Testo*, 33:13–35, seeks to substantiate a distinction between L.'s stance as unbeliever in his ratiocinatory prose (the *Zibaldone*) and religious impulses expressed in his poetry, which can thus be seen as a sort of religious quest. G. Barthouil, 'Leopardi et la Bible', *RLC*, 70, 1996:163–93, traces a three-phase evolution in L.'s views on religion and scripture through a detailed catalogue of *loci* in his writings. Giorgio Ficara, *Il punto di vista della natura*, Genoa, Il Melangolo, 1996, 140 pp., expands the author's introductions to his Mondadori edition of the *Canti, Operette morali e Lettere* and stresses the mythical character of L.'s Nature. On similar lines, Alberto Folin, *Pensare per affetti. Leopardi, la natura, l'immagine*, Venice, Marsilio, 1996, 173 pp., continuing work noted in *YWMLS*, 55:607–08, in the first part of the volume again stresses the essentially evocative, non-discursive nature of poetic language.

For the *Zibaldone* we have the edition Giacomo Leopardi, *Lo Zibaldone*, ed. R. Damiani, 3 vols, Mi, Mondadori, 4615 pp., and various textual studies: M. Dondero, 'Filologia leopardiana. Sul decimo volume dell'edizione fotografica dello *Zibaldone*', *RLI*, 101.1:89–98, commenting on the results emerging from the work of the Neapolitan team cataloguing L.'s MSS and responsible for the photographic edition of the *Zibaldone:* this latter is seen as complementary to Pacella's critical edition, while neither can completely exclude the need for direct examination of the autograph — with regard to which, new evidence confirms Panizza's hypothesis that it is not a first draft but the result of careful preparatory work;

F. Gavazzeni, *'Come copiava e correggeva il Leopardi' and G. Panizza, *'Un problema di ecdotica: la distinzione dei pensieri nello *Zibaldone* di Leopardi', pp. 281–92 and 293–305 of *'Operosa parva' per Gianni Antonini. Studi raccolti da Domenico De Robertis e Franco Gavazzeni*, Verona, Valdonega, 1996; and Id., *'Un indice dello *Zibaldone* e la storia delle *Operette morali'*, pp. 599–614 of *Per Cesare Bozzetti. Studi di filologia e letteratura italiana*, ed. Simon Albonico et al., Mi, Fond. Mondadori, 1996. After 42 years the classic study on L.'s own philology has reached a third edition complete with the author's addenda (219–43): Sebastiano Timpanaro, *La filologia di Giacomo Leopardi*, Ro–Bari, Laterza, 263 pp.

Miscellaneous aspects of L.'s thought and work are addressed in Id., 'Epicuro, Lucrezio e Leopardi', Timpanaro, *Nuovi Studi*, 143–97, which contains numerous additions and revisions; G. Barthouil, 'Guerra e pace nell'opera di Giacomo Leopardi', *Italianistica*, 25, 1996:91–109; N. Jonard, 'Leopardi e la politica', *ib.*, 26:237–49; Id., 'Leopardi: Romanticisme et révolution', *REI*, 42, 1996:173–87; K. Stierle, 'Poesia, industria e modernità. La polemica di Leopardi contro Lodovico di Breme', *Atti* (AISLLI 15), 163–75; G. Conversi, 'Leopardi e il romanzo di Maria Antonietta', *Intersezioni*, 16, 1996:309–26, exploring themes and imagery prompted by L.'s early reading of J.-J. Régnault-Warin's *Le Cimetière de la Madeleine* (1800–01) in the 1812 Italian translation; P. Possiedi, 'Favole antiche e favole moderne nella poesia e nel pensiero di Leopardi', *Italica*, 73, 1996:24–43; Id., 'La "mutazione totale" in Leopardi nel 1819: soggettività, maschere e scrittura', *FoI*, 30, 1996:24–54, reconstructing L.'s development through the 1819 crisis in terms of his confronting the problematic essence of writing and his recourse to the *personaggio-maschera* of Tristan; C. Torchio, 'Quale Leopardi? (Leopardi e il "sentimento della decadenza")', Id., *Fra romanticismo* (see FOSCOLO, above), 41–56; D. Bini, 'Giacomo Leopardi's *Ultrafilosofia'*, *Italica*, 74:52–66, taking its cue from L.'s own expression in the *Zibaldone*, but applying it to the conception of man as creator of his own meaning ... the poet-philosopher, author of his own reality', and concentrating on the *Operette* in particular; M. A. Bazzocchi, *'La potenza del riso. Lettura delle *Operette morali'*, pp. 45–67 of *L'immaginazione mitologica. Leopardi e Calvino, Pascoli e Pasolini*, Bo, Pendragon, 1996. A. Prete, ' "Scir detarnegòl bara letzafra". Sulla biblioteca fantastica di Leopardi', Mildonian, *Parodia*, 143–50, briefly looks at L.'s taste for philological mystification ('la traduzione da testi inesistenti, la costruzione dell'apocrifo e dell'anonimo, il gioco artificiale delle varianti e delle attribuzioni, l'esercizio di una filologia surreale e metafisica ...'), taking as starting point the *Cantico del gallo silvestre*, inspired by the entry *tarnegòl bar* in Buxtorf's *Lexicon Chaldaicum*

Talmudicum et Rabbinicum, and presented as a translation whose original title is not (as usually supposed) mere pastiche, but an adaptation of the Aramaic of the *Lexicon* entry. Also discussed are other *Operette,* and the bogus 'translations from the Greek', *Inno a Nettuno* and *Odae Adespotae,* which antedate the *Canti.* On the reception of the *Operette:* L. Melosi, 'Giordani, Leopardi, *l'Antologia* (con una redazione inedita del discorso sulle *Operette morali*)', *Luti Vol.,* 115–37.

For the *Canti* as a whole: Luigi Blasucci, *Il tempi dei 'Canti'. Nuovi studi leopardiani,* T, Einaudi, 1996, x + 262 pp., the third collection of Leopardi essays from B.'s pen, with its textual emphasis and unusual clarity of exposition makes a refreshing change from the current preoccupation with L.'s 'philosophy' and with 'speculative' interpretation of the poetry. B. aims at an 'articulated and differentiated' view of L.'s poetic output which does justice to its variety of style and quality while recognizing its characteristic 'carica conoscitiva'. Of 13 pieces only three have not already appeared in print (but the rest, all 1991–95, tend to be hidden away in *atti* or *Festchriften*): 'I tre momenti della *Quiete*' (123–40), 'Schede su *Amore e morte*' (141–61), and 'Quattro modi di approccio allo *Zibaldone*' (229–42). The volume takes its title from ch. 10, written for *Manuale di letteratura italiana,* ed. F. Brioschi and C. Di Girolamo, III, T, Bollati Boringhieri, 1995, 331–62, which is probably the best short account of the *Canti* now to hand. F. Gavazzeni, 'L'unità dei *Canti:* varianti e strutture', *Besomi Vol.,* 447–75, is a substantial contribution on the linguistic revision and evolving unity of the collection through the various editions; particular attention is paid to the *idilli* and the late insertion of *Il passero solitario,* seen as intended to effect the transition from the *canzoni* to the *idilli* and to have dictated the addition of lines 13–14 of *Alla luna.* Pietro Pelosi, **I fiumi del tempo, i luoghi dell'anima. Tempo e spazio nei 'Canti' leopardiani,* Na, Federico & Ardia, 1996, 119 pp. F. Pierangeli, '"Cara beltà", "cara speranza": un "logoro" denotativo per l'inno tra Leopardi e Pavese', *Italianistica,* 25, 1996 [1997]: 367–74, studies the function of the epithet 'caro' and of female beauty in the *Canti* and in this respect identifies a Leopardian dimension in Pavese. J. Alcorn, 'Giacomo Leopardi's art and science of emotion in memory and anticipation', *MLN,* 111, 1996:89–122, analyses the emotions aroused in L. by memory and anticipation: a first section elaborates a detailed classification; the second applies it to *Le Ricordanze,* which is considered to be its completest expression. Giacomo Leopardi, *Canti,* introd. Franco Fortini, trans. Paul Lawton, Dublin, UCD Centre for Italian Studies, 173 pp., is a welcome addition to the literature of and on L. in English: Fortini's selection and presentation of 24 of the *Canti* in a skilful and sensitive translation. F. stresses 'the intensely vivifying character of L.'s poetry, in seeming contradiction with his pessimistic and even desperate statements . . .'.

On individual *canti:* G. Orelli, 'Per leggere *L'Infinito* di Leopardi', *Besomi Vol.*, 476–86, offers a reading that stresses structural assonance but also makes copious reference to antecedents in sonnets by Tasso, Alfieri, Foscolo, and especially Petrarch. G. Savoca, *'Per una semantica dell'*Infinito*' , pp. 242–51, of *Simbolo, metafora e senso nella cultura contemporanea. Atti del Convegno internazionale (Lecce 27–29 ottobre 1994)*, ed. Carlo A. Augieri, Lecce, Milella, 1996. S. Sconocchia, *'Il mito in Leopardi', *Humanitas*, 48, 1996:611–29, sees L. as being in a constantly evolving relationship with myth, but concentrates more especially on the *canzoni*. T. Piras, *'Spunti mitologici ed echi virgiliani nelle prime canzoni di Leopardi', *ib.*, 630–43. G. Rando, 'Contraddizioni leopardiane: la canzone "censurata" del 1819', *EL*, 21.4, 1996:3–14. M. N. Muñiz, 'Lettura interlineare dell'epistola *A Carlo Pepoli*', *Belfagor*, 51, 1996:517–36, confirms the centrality of the epistle 'quale nodo strategico' with an analysis of a composition-process largely consisting of 'dialogic' manipulation of Horatian and Virgilian subtexts. S. Giovannuzzi, 'Per *A Silvia* di Leopardi', *StIt*, 14, 1995[1996]: 135–49, seeks to demonstrate that the main subtext of *A Silvia* is Tasso's sonnet 'Sposa regal', which L. had recently selected for the *Crestomazia italiana de' poeti*. A. Girardi, '*Il sabato* e la prosa dei *Canti*', *LN*, 56, 1995:116–22, extends a linguistic analysis from the 1829 lyric to the *Canti* as a whole, arguing that the presence of 'prosaic' diction is paralleled at the level of syntax by 'un periodare argomentativo' and that both are dictated by the thought component inseparable from L.'s poetry. A. Sole, 'I due pastori di Leopardi (lettura del *Canto notturno*)', *GSLI*, 174: 349–83. G. Savoca, 'Dall'auto-grafo (e dal Meyendorff) al finale del *Canto notturno*', *CLett*, 93, 1996:53–83. C. La Porta, 'Confronting the artifact: interrogative ekphrasis in Keats and Leopardi', *RStI*, 14.1, 1996:36–47, contrasts *Sopra un bassorilievo antico sepolcrale* with Keats's *Ode on a Grecian Urn*. C. Torchio, 'Appunti per un commento dell'inno leopardiano *Ad Arimane*', Id., *Fra romanticismo* (see FOSCOLO, above), 57–75. Vittorio Panicara, *La nuova poesia di Giacomo Leopardi. Una lettura critica della Ginestra*, F, Olschki, 156 pp., a notable contribution, clearly organized and methodical as befits a doctoral thesis, defines and explores three relationships — between heroic 'solidarism' and pessimism/nihilism, reason and nature, philosophy and poetry. The third is seen as *the* crucial question, and L.'s new poetic, his 'rifondazione della liricità', strenuously affirmed. M. de las N. Muñiz Muñiz, 'Le tracce dell'antico nella *Ginestra*', *Besomi Vol.*, 487–504, presents the poem as 'una summa di motivi catastrofici e rovinistici' drawn from a vast tradition going back to Lucretius and Virgil: the image of the broom itself ('traduzione in negativo del circuito che Foscolo stabilisce nei *Sepolcri* tra la natura e le tombe consolate dall'"arbore amica"') is not the antithesis of the sepulchral but actually incorporates it, 'diventando una sorta di tomba vivente'. A. Pappalardo, *'L'epigrafe della Ginestra* leopardiana', *Riscontri*, 17, 1995:105–09.

On other moments or aspects of L.'s later years: *Lettre inédite de Giacomo Leopardi à Charlotte Bonaparte retrouvée à Paris en 1993*, ed. Giorgio Panizza, Paris, Allia, 1993, brings to light a letter of March 1833 documenting L.'s friendship with Charlotte, based on shared disaffection towards the liberalism of the Tuscan *milieu*, and declaring: 'Vous savez que l'état progressif de la société ne me regarde pas du tout'. E. Benucci, 'Per un profilo di Aspasia. Dal carteggio Fanny Targioni Tozzetti — Antonio Ranieri', *RLI*, 99.3, 1995[1996]: 136–62. Liana Cellerino, *'L'io del topo. Pensieri e letture dell'ultimo Leopardi*, F, La Nuova Italia, 176 pp. F. Fedi, in '"In nome del nostro Giacomo". Saggio di edizione del carteggio Ranieri–Melchiorri', *Besomi Vol.*, 506–28, anticipates a projected edition of the extant letters of the *carteggio* (1833–54) with a sample dating from the early years, when the presence of L., the two correspondents' common friend, was strong. The sample shows the letters' potential relevance to L.'s biography, with a request for permission to read prohibited books, references to students of antiquities and the fine arts, some of whom are called friends of Giacomo, and L.'s possible involvement in such interests, which were shared by Ranieri and Melchiorri.

For L.'s recent fortunes in France and Germany, N. Bellucci, 'Della *Lettre inédite de Giacomo Leopardi à Charlotte Bonaparte retrouvée à Paris en 1993* e di alcune iniziative leopardiane in Europa: le edizioni Allia e la "Deutsche Leopardi Gesellschaft"', *RLI*, 101.1:99–102, gives particular weight to the 11 volumes published by Allia since 1992, which include a new edition (1994) of Sainte-Beuve's historic *Portrait de Leopardi*. This has also reappeared recently in Italy, in Novella Bellucci, **Giacomo Leopardi e i contemporanei. Testimonianze dall'Italia e dall'Europa in vita e in morte del poeta*, F, Ponte alle Grazie, 1996, 541 pp., and in C. A. Sainte-Beuve, **Ritratto di Leopardi*, ed. Carlo Carlino, Ro, Donzelli, 1996, xxix + 65 pp. G. Dignös, 'Leopardi', *Italienisch*, 37:56–71, inter alia rehearses the well-known topic Leopardi–De Sanctis–Schopenhauer. On Nietzsche's relationship to L.: A. Del Gatto, 'Leopardi e Nietzsche. Pensiero poetante e pensiero danzante', *Cenobio*, 46:221–47, and the second part of Folin, *Pensare per affetti*, where 'Intorno al rapporto Leopardi–Nietzsche' (131–54) is coupled with 'Il silenzio del nulla e la speranza del pensiero: Leopardi e Jabès' (155–69). O. Di Fidio, 'La fortuna di Leopardi in area anglosassone', *Testo*, 29–30, 1995:119–38, and 34:57–67, finds (in the second instalment) 'risonanze leopardiane' in poems by Matthew Arnold, James Thomson, and Thomas Hardy.

A few other items have not been seen: Giuseppe Antonio Camerino, *Le forme del diletto. Aspetti e fenomeni naturali nella percezione di Leopardi*, Lecce, Milella; Arturo Mazzarella, *I dolci inganni. Leopardi, gli errori e le illusioni*, Na, Liguori, 1996, 128 pp.; Vincenzo Guarracino, *Guida alla lettura di Leopardi*, Mi, Mondadori, 146 pp., while Carmelo Musumarra, *Le gemme perdute della poesia e altri saggi leopardiani*, Fasano, Schena, 1996, 112 pp., consists wholly of published essays, as apparently do Michele Dell'Aquila, *Leopardi. I viaggi, la luna*, Fasano, Schena, 1996, 96 pp.; and Id., *La linea d'ombra. Note sulla elegia di Leopardi*, Fasano, Schena, 1994, 241 pp. In contrast, Paolo Rota, *Lune leopardiane. Quattro letture testuali*, Bo, CLUEB, 133 pp., adds 'Epifanie di luna' (23–38) and 'Leopardi e il *Newtonianismo per le dame* di Francesco Algarotti' (79–91) to work already noted in *YWMLS*, 55: 569 and 571. Renato Minore, *Leopardi. L'infanzia, le città, gli amori*, Mi, Bompiani, 299 pp., is the second edition, with additions, of a readable, but light-weight and rather *romancée*, biography.

Lingua e stile di Giacomo Leopardi. Atti dell'VIII Convegno internazionale di studi leopardiani (Recanati 30 settembre–5 ottobre 1991), F, Olschki, 1994, xv + 593 pp., and *Leopardi in seiner Zeit. Leopardi nel suo tempo: Akten des 2. internationalen Kongresses der Deutschen Leopardi-Gesellschaft, Berlin, 17. bis 20. September 1992*, Tübingen, Stauffenburg, 1995, 341 pp., were not noted at the time.

LUZZATTO. G. Tamani, 'Ironia, parodia e satira nelle poesie di Samuel David Luzzatto', Mildonian, *Parodia*, 163–77, highlights (without pointing to Leopardi's *Palinodia*) L.'s ironic exaltation of 19th-c. 'progress' in *Derek ere.s o Atticismus*, published in Hebrew at Frankfurt in 1840 and in Esdra Pontremoli's Italian translation *(Il falso progresso)* at Padua in 1879.

MAMIANI. A. Nacinovich, 'Gli *Inni Sacri* di Terenzio Mamiani', *RLettI*, 13, 1995 [1997]: 413–49, analyses M.'s poetic debut, published in Paris in 1832, in terms of its important ideological position, prompted by the search for a new model of national literature in direct polemic with Manzoni and Leopardi.

MANZONI, A. Andrea Ciccarelli, *Manzoni: la coscienza della letteratura*, Ro, Bulzoni, 1996, 201 pp., constructs an introductory monograph about the ethical imperative governing M.'s writing, with chapters on his poetics, on the *Inni sacri*, on the novel and its 'polyphonic realism', and on M.'s Risorgimento commitment and the ethics of the 'just war'. Vincenzo Paladino, *Manzoniana e altri saggi tra Otto e Novecento*, Mi, IPL, 1996, 230 pp. Pier Carlo Masini, *Manzoni*, Pisa, F Edizioni, 1996, 81 pp.

For M.'s pre-conversion period: E. Farina, 'Il *Trionfo della libertà*. Classicismo e giacobinismo in uno scritto del giovane Manzoni', *Italianistica*, 26:425–40; and I. Botta, 'Giudizî di Manzoni sulla *Vita di Alfieri*', *Besomi Vol.*, 558–73, usefully fixing limits *post* and *ante quem* for the distribution of Alfieri's *Vita* (March and October 1808) and giving a careful transcription of M.'s letter to Fauriel (6 December 1808) expressing his immediate reaction to the work: she rightly underlines how M. characteristically 'homes in' on A.'s (unheroic) self-contradictions, but she regrettably indulges in biased moralizing herself with regard to Alfieri's tendentious account of his dealings with Ginguené over his books and MSS, sequestered in Paris during the Terror.

For the *Inni sacri* and tragedies there have been notable editions: Alessandro Manzoni, *Inni sacri, ed. Franco Gavazzeni, Parma, Guanda, 349 pp., and Alessandro Manzoni, *Le Tragedie, ed. Gino Tellini, Ro, Salerno, lxxiv + 1054 pp. F. Mattesini, 'Sull'innografia religiosa', *Testo*, 33:3–12, dwells more on Rebora, in contrast to M., than on M. himself. M. Sansone, 'Le *Réflexions* di Claude Fauriel, la poesia idilliaca, Manzoni e i primordi del romanticismo italiano (con un "Ricordo di Mario Sansone" di Michele Dell'Aquila)', *Italianistica*, 25, 1996[1997]:217–25. Id., 'Manzoni, Fauriel e la *Lettre* à Chauvet', *ON*, 19.6, 1995:5–29. Carlo Annoni, *Lo spettacolo dell'uomo interiore. Teoria e poesia del teatro manzoniano*, Mi, Vita e Pensiero, 298 pp., gives prominence to the analogies between M.'s dramatic theory and Lessing's *Drammaturgie*, and to the recently published first draft of the *Lettre à M. Chauvet* (cf. *YWMLS*, 52:497) containing interesting passages not included in the original edition. A. Bruni, 'Postilla al "coro" del *Carmagnola*', *Versants*, 29, 1996:105–17, among other things traces the *incipit* 'S'ode a destra uno squillo di tromba...' back to *Iliad* XVIII, 292–93, in Monti's translation: 'Come sonoro / D'una tuba talor s'ode lo squillo ...'. M. C. Albonico, 'Paternità conflittuali in Sofocle, Virgilio, Manzoni', *Testo*, 34:68–79, highlights M.'s predilection for Sophocles and Virgil in relation to the Desiderio–Adelchi relationship. Torchio, *Fra romanticismo*, noted under FO-SCOLO, gathers five essays on the language of *Adelchi*, one of them, 'Manzoni, Virgilio e la lingua dell'*Adelchi*' (137–51), hitherto unpublished. I. Becherucci, 'Sulla "crisi" dell'*Adelchi*', *RLettI*, 12, 1994[1996]:383–400, and 'La traduzione francese delle tragedie manzoniane', *SFI*, 54, 1996:311–27. The latter documents the history of the translation from M.'s *Epistolario* and in relation to M.'s changing relationship with Fauriel. G. Pedrojetta, 'Una lettera inedita di Alessandro Manzoni', *StCrit*, 12:215–19, edits the complete text, from the Neuchâtel MS, of M.'s letter to Alessandro Torri of

November 1826 refusing to co-operate in the Pisan reprint (Capurro, 1826) of his tragedies.

I promessi sposi is addressed as a whole from a variety of perspectives. Salvatore Nigro, **La tabacchiera di don Lisandro. Saggio sui 'Promessi Sposi'*, T, Einaudi, 1996, 206 pp., corresponds, with additions, to the author's engaging contribution on M. in *Letteratura italiana: Le Opere*, III, T, Einaudi, 1995, pp. 429–89; and Ezio Raimondi, *La dissimulazione romanzesca. Antropologia manzoniana*, Bo, Il Mulino, 195 pp., is an expanded edition of the 1990 volume (cf. *TWMLS*, 52:498) discussing convergent aspects of *I promessi sposi* within an unusually broad frame of reference. P. Frare, 'Una struttura in movimento: sulla forma artistica dei *Promessi sposi*', *The Italianist*, 16, 1996[1997]:62–75, presents an illuminating analysis of the dynamic nature of the often admired, but only apparently symmetrical, binary 'sistema dei personaggi'. Elena Parrini, *La narrazione della storia nei 'Promessi sposi'*, F, Le Lettere, 1996, 256 pp., considers M.'s developing strategy as historical novelist with regard to the combination of history and fiction, showing how the original dichotomy between the two in *Fermo e Lucia* gives way to the subordination of history to fiction in *I promessi sposi*. R. Scrivano, '*I promessi sposi:* il vero della storia e la finzione della favola', *EL*, 22.2:17–26. Riccardo Verzini, *Il paragone delle parole. La voce dei personaggi nei 'Promessi Sposi'*, T, Tirrenia, 1995, 116 pp., is a clear and useful *mise au point* on M.'s use of dialogue and inner monologue, and (in the final chapter) of his characteristic combination of the two. Sergio Calzone, *La giovine del miracolo. I 'Promessi sposi' e la cultura di ispirazione religiosa*, T, Tirrenia, 162 pp., maintaining that the importance of religious culture for Italian literature is not sufficiently recognized, brings a fresh approach to bear by exploring a series of elements present, or considered so, in the novel, such as the Marian tradition (Lucia), popular religiosity (Agnes), the religious art of the mountain chapels, the attributes of the saints and Manzoni's 'onomastics', etc. Some of the paths of enquiry pursued seem distinctly unfamilar, for example, Manzoni's metaphorical bestiary, or the treatment of architecture, i.e. buildings of all kinds, in the novel. N. Casella, 'Lucia tra Fermo e Renzo', *Besomi Vol.*, 538–57, usefully tabulates alongside each other narrative summaries of *Fermo e Lucia* and *I promessi sposi* with the latter redistributed in parallel to the former and with the appropriate indication for each narrative segment: 'identical', 'variant', 'omitted', or 'added'.

On individual episodes: M. Dillon Wanke, 'La commedia di un capitolo *(Promessi sposi*, VIII)', *Croce Vol.*, 391–411, follows Raimondi/Bottoni and other recent commentators in her theatrical (and Shakespearian) reading of the chapter, dubbed a comedy of errors without the happy ending, but stresses its function as subservient to moral comment on intrigue and 'furberie': M. draws on 'le strutture artificiose del comico' only in order to 'dimostrare le ragioni di Lucia'; C. Weiand, 'Manzoni und die Novelle', *ASNS*, 149:66–77, seeks to demonstrate from the process of revision of the Gertrude episode how M. uses the 'advantages' of the *novella* form 'als Reflexionshintergrund bei den Überarbeitungen seines Romans'; A. Chiari, 'La notte di Lucia', *CLett*, 24, 1996:85–96; Gian Carlo M. Rivolta, **Il collega Don Ferrante*, Carnago, SugarCo, 1995, 156 pp. P. A. Perotti, 'Spunti autobiografici nei *Promessi sposi*', *CLett*, 25:233–52. H. Meter, 'Die *Promessi sposi* und ihre Illustrationen. Francesco Gonins Zeichnungen für die Edition Guglielmini-Redaelli', *ItStudien*, 18, 1997:165–87. J. Goudet, '"Manzoni rivisitato"? L'*Anticritica* manzonienne d'Aldo Spranzi', *REI*, 42, 1996:219–35, responds at length to the arguments of Spranzi's *Anticritica dei 'Promessi Sposi'. L'efficienza dell'industria culturale: il caso de 'I Promessi Sposi'*, Mi, Giuffrè, 1995, 1210 pp., a work rejecting the whole critical tradition in favour of an antireligious interpretation of the novel. Ezio Raimondi, 'La storia e l'olocausto', *Besomi Vol.*, 529–38, gives a brief but incisive analysis of M.'s moral stance in *Storia della colonna infame*.

The bicentenary of the birth of Antonio Rosmini in 1797 has been marked by the 'reprint' (sponsored by the Centro Internazionale di Studi Rosminiani at Stresa and a local bank): *Carteggio fra Alessandro Manzoni e Antonio Rosmini, raccolto e annotato da Giulio Bonola*, Stresa, Ediz. Rosminiane Sodalitas, 1996, xv + 599 pp. (original edition, Milan 1901). I also note: E. Travi, 'Curiosità manzoniane', *Aevum*, 71:861–63; L. Parisi, 'Borgese e Manzoni', *MLN*, 112:38–56; and Hugo Blank, **Manzonis Napoleon-Ode in deutschen Übersetzungen, mit einem Beitrag von Vito R. Giustiniani*, Bonn, Romanischer Verlag, 1995, 312 pp.

MANZONI, M.   P. Spedicato, 'Una presenza bianca. Il *Journal* di Matilde Manzoni, figlia di Alessandro, lettrice di Leopardi', *EL*, 21.4, 1996:95–107, of the journal first published in 1992 comments: 'si tratta di una lettura sorprendente e per il suo valore intrinseco di piccola gemma psicologica e di gusto, e perché obbliga a ripensare le forme dell'autocoscienza moderna in Italia tra Sette e Ottocento'.

MARCHESA COLOMBI.   E. Pierobon, 'Maternità e conflittualità in alcune opere della marchesa Colombi', *Italica*, 74:201–16, focuses on the mother–daughter relationship in three short stories (1878–1900) and *Troppo tardi* (1880); and, by the same scholar, 'L'"enormità" del reale: una lettura di *Un matrimonio in Provincia* della Marchesa Colombi', *FoI*, 30, 1996:291–310, discusses the text (1885) said to be the most complete expression of her poetic.

MAZZINI.   P. M. Sipala, 'Il punto su Mazzini: dall'autobiografia alle biografie', *CLett*, 24, 1996:97–111.

MONTI.   A. Bruni, '"Apografi, non deteriores?" Ancora per il testo della *Pulcella d'Orléans* del Monti', *SFI*, 54, 1996:261–89, takes issue with G. Barbarisi and M. Mari over their continued attachment to the unreliable Andrea Maffei's copy of the translation, even after the rediscovery of the autograph in 1984. G. Pegoraro, 'Un passo dell'*Iliade* montiano', *FC*, 21, 1996 [1997]:458–81.

NIEVO.   The main section of Di Benedetto, *Ippolito Nievo e altro Ottocento* (see GENERAL, above), assembles: 'Ippolito Nievo: le *Confessioni d'un Italiano* e altro' (97–147); 'Il padre Pendola e l'"ingenuo" Carlino: un'astuzia della Provvidenza' (149–60); 'Caratteristiche formali del Nievo nelle *Confessioni d'un Italiano*' (161–79); 'Da Manzoni a Nievo' (181–92); and 'Ippolito Nievo nelle lettere' (193–214). Taken together, these probably represent the most substantial contribution on N. to have appeared for a number of years. Ippolito Nievo, *I giorni sommersi*, ed. Fausta Samaritani, Ro, Fond. Ippolito Nievo — Venice, Marsilio, 1996, 104 pp., gathers, from archives and libraries in several Italian cities, papers and other documents relating to Nievo and his disappearance in the shipwreck of the vessel *Ercole*.

PASCOLI.   M. Marcolini, 'La rivoluzione consapevole. Rassegna di studi pascoliani (1980–1995)', *LItal*, 48, 1996:101–48. Giovanni Pascoli, **Myricae*, ed. Giampaolo Borghello, Bo, Zanichelli, 1996, 438 pp. G. Bárberi Squarotti, 'Pascoli: Orfeo e l'eden', *RStI*, 15.2:161–75, analyses the poems of *Il ritorno a San Mauro* in terms of a return to Eden and the 'orphic' myth of poetry as that which alone can compensate and resuscitate the dead. P. Pepe, 'Giovanni Pascoli e la visione dell'"autre": i piani della prevedibilità', *CLett*, 25:59–68. L. Pitino, 'Pascoli tra critica e poetica', *ib.*, 159–63. P. L. Cerisola, 'Espressionismo pascoliano', *Testo*, 29–30, 1995:139–71. E. Elli, 'Pascoli e l'antico: i *Poemi conviviali*', *Aevum*, 70, 1996:721–40. F. Audisio, 'Pascoli: metrica "neoclassica" e metrica italiana', *RLI*, 99.3, 1995[1996]:34–91. M. Gragnolati, 'Giovanni Pascoli. Varianti "conviviali" 1895–1905', *REI*, 41, 1995:133–56. A. Zollino, 'Tasso e D'Annunzio nella "siepe" di Pascoli', *LItal*, 48, 1996:95–100. M. Ciccuto, 'Pascoli in filigrana. Tre saluti inediti a Ugo Brilli', *CLett*, 24:205–11. G. Capecchi, 'La commedia del fanciullino. Le lezioni inedite di Pascoli alla Scuola pedagogica di Bologna', *RLI*, 100.1, 1996:125–58.

PORTA.   Claudio Beretta, *Carlo Porta. Fonti letterari milanesi, italiane, europee*, Bellinzona, Ist. Editoriale Ticinese, 1994, 284 pp., overlooked in *YWMLS*, 57, continues in greater depth a *chasse aux sources* begun by the author for his 1988 Bompiani anthology of P.'s letters and verse. A historical and methodological introduction is followed by investigations into a lengthy series of individual poems. The recognition of English sources (notably Swift, Pope, and Sterne) would appear to constitute the particular originality of what is in any case a major contribution to P. studies.

PRATESI. T. Fiorino, 'Rileggendo Mario Pratesi', *CLett*, 24, 1996:167–203.

ROMANI. S. Verdino, 'I "bellissimi versi" di Felice Romani', *Croce Vol.*, 413–26, pinpoints the exceptional qualities of Romani's verse with examples from the masterpieces of Donizetti and Bellini: *Anna Bolena, La sonnambula, Norma, L'elisir d'amore, Beatrice di Tenda, Lucrezia Borgia*. The first and third can now be read with notes and bibliography in the anthology *Libretti d'opera italiani dal Seicento al Novecento* (see BOITO, A., above).

ROSMINI. Crillo Bergamaschi, **Bibliografia rosminiana*, vol. 8, Stresa, Ediz. Rosminiane Sodalitas, 1996. See also MANZONI, A., above.

ROSSETTI. Gabriele Rossetti, *Carteggi*, IV:*1837–1840*, ed. Alfonso Caprio, P. R. Horne, and J. R. Woodhouse, Na, Loffredo, 1995, 548 pp., the penultimate volume of the important Anglo-Neapolitan edition of R.'s correspondence, like previous ones is largely devoted to his intense exchange with his Scots patron, Charles Lyell; it assembles for the first time all extant letters relating to the completion and suppression of *Il mistero dell'amor platonico* after it had become clear that its historical-religious theses (particularly, organized religion as a sham) made it unpublishable in Victorian England.

ROVANI. Silvana Tamiozzo Goldmann, *Lo scapigliato in archivio: sulla narrativa di Giuseppe Rovani*, Mi, Angeli, 1994, 175 pp., primarily an analysis of *Cent'anni*, looks for what is uniquely new in R.'s writing, in contrast to the traditional biographical preoccupation with the Bohemian writer himself.

SALGARI. Silvino Gonzato, *Emilio Salgari. Demoni, amori e tragedie di un 'capitano' che navigò solo con la fantasia*, Vicenza, Neri Pozza, 1995, 207 pp., a biography bringing new documents to light, also includes a summary bibliography of S.'s writings by Vittorio Sarti, author of *Nuova bibliografia salgariana*, T, Pignatone, 1994. C. Gallo, 'Ritrovamenti e curiosità sui romanzi d'appendice di Emilio Salgari', *StP*, 26, 1996:101–10, sheds light on the editorial history of *La tigre della Malesia* and *La favorita del Mahdi*.

SERAO. Tommaso Scappatici, *Introduzione a Serao*, Ro–Bari, Laterza, 1995, 187 pp., following the established format of the Laterza series 'Gli scrittori', privilege S.'s development as a writer, while interweaving it with an account of her exceptional career in journalism. This relationship is reversed, by one who is himself a journalist, in Antonio Ghirelli, *Donna Matilde. Una biografia*, introd. Miriam Mafai, Venice, Marsilio, 1995, 231 pp., which sets out to tell 'la storia di una donna straordinaria' and does so with gusto.

SOLERTI.   See GRAF, above.

TARCHETTI.   D. Del Principe, 'Misbegotten, unbegotten, forgotten: vampires and monsters in the works of Ugo Tarchetti, Mary Shelley, Bram Stoker and the gothic tradition', *FoI*, 29, 1995:3–25.

TOMMASEO.   Niccolò Tommaseo, **Fede e bellezza*, ed. Donatella Martinelli, Parma, Guanda, cv + 382 pp. Niccolò Tommaseo, **Fede e bellezza*, ed. Fabio Danelon, Alessandria, Orso, 1996, 255 pp., purports to be a critical edition. F. Danelon, 'Un racconto antiromantico. Lettura di *Due baci* di Niccolò Tommaseo', *Italianistica*, 26:23–40, sets T.'s demystification of romantic love in the broader European context of its time. D. Martinelli, 'La formazione del Tommaseo lessicografo', *SFI*, 55:173–340. Flavia Bacchetti, *Niccolò Tommaseo e il 'Giornale della Caterina'. Un'immagine d'infanzia nell'Ottocento italiano*, F, Le Lettere, 195 pp., analyses T.'s diary (1852–60) of his daughter's early development, showing it to be his verification of educational theory he had formulated in the 1830s.

VALERA.   P. M. Sipala, '*La folla* di Paolo Valera: zolismo e populismo agli esordi dell'industrializzazione milanese', *Atti* (AISLLI 15), 459–69.

VERDI.   F. De Rosa, 'Letteratura e opera italiana in una recente monografia su Verdi (con una postilla sull'*Ernani*)', *Italianistica*, 25, 1996[1997]:385–408, is prompted by G. De Van, *Verdi, un teatro in musica*, F, La Nuova Italia, 1994.

VERGA.   C. Musumarra, 'Verga, le banche e le imprese industriali', *Atti* (AISLLI 15), 415–45, sketches stimulating reflections on V.'s work as hinging about a Catania–Milan axis and as his response to capitalist 'progress'. Oliva, *L'operosa stagione*, assembles substantial sections of material on Verga: 'Itinerario del Verga novelliere' (13–38); 'Esercizi di anatomia per il Verga milanese' (39–66); and 'Preliminari al *Mastro-don Gesualdo*' (67–84). N. Cacciaglia, '*Eros*, personaggi diabolici e immagini macabre nella narrativa verghiana', *FoI*, 31:15–30, traces the continuity of the theme of *eros* and its destructive power throughout V.'s narrative output. G. P. Biasin, **Lo zoo di Verga', pp. 17–28 of *Le periferie della letteratura. Da Verga a Tabucchi*, Ravenna, Longo. Lina Jannuzzi, *Sul primo Verga*, Na, Loffredo, 1995, 136 pp., revises and expands her 1988 contribution on V.'s early historical and patriotic novels, adding, as a final chapter, 'La doppia ottica verghiana nel romanzo *Sulle lagune*' (111–22), which finds Greek and Gothic (-novel) antecedents in V.'s third narrative. R. Luperini, 'L'Eva verghiana', *Belfagor*, 51, 1996:293–302. G. Rando, **L'abbozzo di *Fantasticheria* e la trama di *Padron 'Ntoni*', *NAFMUM*, 12–14, 1995–96:561–77, advances the hypothesis that the *novella* was conceived from the outset as an anticipation of the main text. Giovanni Verga, **I Malavoglia. Testo critico*, ed. F. Cecco, T,

Einaudi, 400 pp. P. Zambon, 'La città industriale nelle novelle di Giovanni Verga: lettura di *Per le vie* e altri testi', *Atti* (AISLLI 15), 415–31. Salvatore Rossi, *La nausea nel cuore e altri saggi vergiani*, Palermo, Palumbo, 92 pp., assembles scattered V. essays from volumes of *atti*, or lesser-known periodicals, and adds 'La nausea nel cuore' (69–75), on the pessimism of *Mastro-don Gesualdo*, and 'Un maestro degli studi verghiani' (83–85) on Carlo Musumarra's interpretation of Verga. M. Durante, **Dagli scarti del *Mastro-don Gesualdo:* la storia di *Mondo Piccino*', *Annali della Fondazione Verga*, 8, 1991[1995], studies the *novella* published in French in 1884, one of three derived from discarded parts of the the first draft of the novel. Lia Fava Guzzetti, *Verga fra Manzoni e Flaubert*, Ro, Studium, 278 pp. R. Melis, 'Verga, Selvatico e il teatro italiano negli anni di *Cavalleria rusticana*', *GSLI*, 174:211–42. S. B. Chandler, 'Verga's view of the theatre', *RStI*, 14.2, 1996[1997]:193–97. See also DE ROBERTO, above.

VISCONTI. S. Stroppa, '"La marque suprême de l'exil". Ermes Visconti e la pratica mistica delle aspirazioni', *LItal*, 49:40–65.

ZANELLA. J.-J. Marchand, 'L'elaborazione della poesia di Giacomo Zanella (da manoscritti inediti con postille di Fogazzaro)', *FC*, 21, 1996[1997]:412–57.

NOVECENTO

POSTPONED

X. ROMANIAN STUDIES*

LANGUAGE

By MARTIN MAIDEN, *Professor of the Romance Languages, University of Oxford*

GENERAL. Victor Iancu, **Limbă şi rostire românească, ieri şi azi*, Cluj-Napoca, Dacia, 1996, 165 pp. P. Ţugui, 'Cîteva precizări privind editarea lucrării lui Sextil Puşcariu "Limba română", vol. II. "Rostirea"', *LiL*, 41.2, 1996:91–100, offers an insight into the potential sensitivity in 1959 of publishing a volume with maps showing the 1939 Romanian frontiers, including Bessarabia and Bucovina, which led to distribution of the first edition of Puşcariu's directly to libraries and institutes, rather than to bookshops. Ţ. is also critical of the historical accuracy of some of M. Vulpe's comments in her introduction to the 1994 edition of the volume, but V. responds in 'Precizări la precizări ... (în legătură cu editarea lucrării *Limba Română*, II, *Rostirea* de Sextil Puşcariu)', *LiL*, 42.1:49–51. Another major figure of Romanian linguistics is the object of E. Coşeriu, 'Alexandru Rosetti, "un ascet al ştiinţei"', *FD*, 15, 1996:5–10, N. Saramandu, 'Alexandru Rosetti şi institutul de Fonetică şi Dialectologie', *ib.*, 11–13, and G. Brâncuş, 'Unitatea limbii în concepţia lui Al. Rosetti', *ib.*, 15–18.

Attention is drawn to a possibly useful research tool in M. Onofraş, 'Sistematizarea şi utilizarea eficientă a fişierului limbii române de la institutul de lingvistică al A[cademiei] Ş[tiinţe] M[oldova]', *RLSL*, no.5:64–69.†

HISTORY OF THE LANGUAGE. Grigore Brâncuş, *Cercetări asupra fondului traco-dac al limbii române*, Institutul Român de Tracologie, 1995, 118 pp., contains nine studies (seven of them published previously) covering aspects of substrate influences on vocabulary, phonology, morphology, and syntax, and stressing particularly the evidence of a common substratal inheritance in Romanian and Albanian. The two previously unpublished studies deal respectively with the transfer of onomastic terms from the substrate and with the postposition of the article, the latter purportedly reflecting the characteristic word order of the indigenous substrate. A. Avram, 'Despre originea vocalei [î] în limba română', *FD*, 15, 1996:19–26, develops Rosetti's view that [î] results from indigenous closure of [ă]. M. Maiden, 'A propos d'un changement analogique remarquable en

---

* The place of publication of books is Bucharest unless otherwise stated.

† It has not been possible to consult numbers 1 and 2 of *RLSL* for this survey.

roumain: le type *carte – cărţi*', *VR*, 56:24–57, is a detailed historical and comparative examination of the emergence of the stressed *a – ă* alternation in feminine nouns, and of the problems it presents for iconicity-based theories of morphological 'naturalness'. M. Manoliu Manea, '*A* atributiv în româna veche', *RLSL*, no.3:96–101.

L. Lindgren, 'Mărturii despre limba română ale cărtularului suedez Georg Stiernhelm (1598–1672)', *ib.*, 1996:85–90. F. Zgraon, 'Scrieri populare într-un colligatum budapestean', *ib.*, 91–99, deals with material dating from the period 1797–1821. R. Windisch, '"Emanciparea" limbii naţionale şi conştiinţa identităţii naţionale la români', *FD*, 15, 39–42, emphasizes the importance of Romanians' beginning to make use of the language in private correspondence. R. Piotrowski, 'Sinergetica şi ocrotirea limbii române în Republica Moldova', *RLSL*, no.3:88–95.

O. Sitaru, 'Influenţe latino-romanice în texte româneşti traduse in secolul al XVIII-lea', *LiR*, 45, 1996:77–84, deals with Latin and Romance influence at all levels of linguistic structure. Mihai Mitu, *Cercetări lingvistice şi literare româno-slave*, Editura Universităţii, 1996, 310 pp., contains a number of discussions of the history of Slavisms in Romanian: 'Conceptul de "împrumuturi în serie" (cu referire la polonismele limbii române)' (18–27), examines lexical borrowings as groups of terms entering the language within a brief chronological period, and suggests that recognition of such 'loan series' may help in identifying the source of loans of unknown origin; Slav loans are also the subject of 'Slavonisme şi polonisme la Dosoftei' (28–37) and 'O pagină necunoscută din istoria slavisticii româneşti: cercetările de etimologie slavo-română ale lui Iosif Naniescu' (78–92); the essay 'Între bibliologie şi lingvistică (însemnările pe cărţi vechi româneşti – izvor pentru cercetarea lexicologică' (93–110), underscores, with appropriate lexical examples, the value of early books as sources for lexicological investigation.

TEXTS. F. Dimitrescu, 'Texte româneşti vechi în haină latină (pe marginea unei antologii italiene)', *FD*, 15, 1996:103–09, discusses Piccillo's 1991 anthology of texts. J. Kramer, 'Asupra principiilor de editare a textelor vechi româneşti', *LiR*, 44, 1995:200–03, addresses the vexed question of the appropriateness of producing editions of early texts transliterated into the Roman alphabet. C. Moroianu, 'O versiune semirotacizantă a *Legendei Duminicii* din a doua jumătate a secolului XVII-lea', *ib.*, 48–58, offers a linguistic analysis of the text, and suggests that rhotacism was still at work in the late 17th c. in the Bihor dialect. M. Stanciu, 'Un *strastnic* românesc de la începutul secolului al XVIII-lea', *ib.*, 189–200, concludes, after a linguistic analysis, that the texts included in the manuscript were probably copied in Hunedoara by the hand of deacon Pătru of Băcăinţi.

F. Zgraon, 'Două tipărituri romînești vechi la "Orszagós Széchényi Könyvtar"', *ib.*, 139–45, draws attention to two 18th-c. texts, and publishes extracts from them. G. Piccillo, 'În legătură cu glosarul trilingv greco-aromâno-albanez de la muntele Athos: copie sau original?', *FD*, 15, 1996:87–93, concludes that the glossary is original. A study of the variant orthographical representations of /f/ in old Romanian texts is A. Mureș, 'O particularitate grafică rar întâlnită in scrierea românească veche [...]', *LiR*, 45, 1996:173–78. E. Pavel, 'Mihai Iștvanovici și normele limbii române literare (II, III)', *LiR*, 44, 1995:107–23; 205–19, compares innovations in the lexicon of Iștvanovici's Belgrade *Chiriacodromion* with that of Varlaam's *Cazanie*.

ORTHOGRAPHY AND PHONOLOGY. Ioan Teodor Stan, *Studii de fonetică și dialectologie*, Cluj, Presa Universitară Clujeană, 1996, 216 pp. M. Oprescu, 'Amendamente la normele utilizării punctelor de suspensie', *LiR*, 44, 1995:25–27. I. Chițoran, 'Prominence vs. rhythm: the predictability of stress in Romanian', *Papers* (LSRL 25), 47–58, deals both with primary and secondary stress patterns, revealing two different lexical primary stress patterns, one for nouns and adjectives, based on foot structure, and one for verbs based on word layer prominence. M. Mărdărescu-Teodorescu, 'Frecvența tipurilor de structuri silabice în limba română', *FD*, 15, 1996:71–86, finds, hardly surprisingly, a preference for CV structures.

MORPHOLOGY AND SYNTAX. A discussion of the implications for native linguistic awareness of Romanian grammatical terminology as reflected in didactic grammars from the 18th c., is M. Metzeltin and P. Lindenbauer, 'Terminologie und allgemeiner Wortschatz im Spiegel didaktischer Grammatiken. Ein rumänisches Beispiel', *Fest. Pfister*, I, 172–81. M. Gabinschi, 'Este oare româna o limbă de același tip analitic ca și limbile romanice apusene?', *RLSL*, no.5:46–54. Dan Barbu, *Structura logică a morfosintaxei limbii române*, Scripta, 1995, 198 pp. C. Moroianu, 'Observații asupra radicalului verbelor onomatopeice', *LiR*, 44, 1995:92–98, examines the way in which onomatopeic verbs, such as *a fleșcăi* or *a croncăni* preserve their onomatopoeic quality by failing to undergo otherwise normal inflectional modifications (interestingly, similar phenomena are observable for some Italian onomatopoeic verbs). D. Crașoveanu, 'Observații privind infinitivul prezent al unor verbe din conjugarea a II-a', *LiR*, 45, 1996:22–27, deals with conjugation-shifts of the type *a părea* > *a pare* in colloquial usage. V. Zagaevschi, 'Un sincretism analogic dialectal la unele forme ale verbelor de conj. a III-a și a II-a', *RLSL*, no.3:167–76. P. Zugun, 'Morfeme ale categoriei determinării', *LiR*, 44, 1995:167–72, is concerned particularly with the treatment of word-final vowels in the environment of suffixed articles. Id., 'Condițiile de existență a derivării și derivatelor', *RLSL*, no.4:50–53.

T. Capotă, 'Sistemul comparaţiei în limba română', *LiL*, 41.2, 1996:11–22, is a critical analysis of the types of comparative structures available in Romanian. Also Ş. Găitănaru, 'Sistemul comparaţiei în româna contemporană', *LiR*, 45, 1996:19–22. T. Cotelnic, 'Adjective incompatibile cu gradele de comparaţie', *RLSL*, no.3:128–32. A.-I. Rădulescu, 'Analyse contrastive des formes *être prép X* en français et en roumain', *LInv*, 19, 1995:289–324, applies to Romanian Gross's analysis of such constructions in French, examining differences between the two languages and some techniques for expressing the equivalents of French prepositional constructions in Romanian. Some light is thrown on the diachronic evolution of Romanian prepositions by Ş. Găitănaru, 'Descrierea locuţiunilor prepoziţionale cu genitivul', *LiR*, 44, 1995:87–92, who uses lexical and semantic criteria to establish whether prepositional phrases such as 'în baza', 'la nivelul', 'în preajma', 'în pofida' + genitive are analysable as lexicalized prepositions or as preposition + noun. F. Vicario, 'Sul tipo *a da afară, a veni înapoi*: verbi con avverbio in rumeno', *RRL*, 40, 1995:149–64, draws attention to the existence of such phenomena in Romanian as well as in other Romance varieties such as Italian, and suggests that they represent a purely 'internal' Romance development, rather than being due to the influence of non-Romance languages. I. Bărbuţă and E. Constantinovici, 'Structura actanţială a verbului în limba română vorbită: modificarea şi actualizarea ei în enunţ', *RLSL*, no.4:40–49. A.-I. Rădulescu, 'Vision contrastive sur les prépositions et les locutions prépositionnelles prolatives — domaine français-roumain', *RRL*, 40, 1995:179–89. M. Oprescu, 'Articolul ca marcă a individualizării', *LiR*, 45, 1996:27–29, is a critical review of remarks on the function of the article in an earlier discussion by A. Vrăjitoru. M. Van Peteghem, '*Autre* et ses correspondants en roumain', *RevR*, 32:27–50, explores contrastively the role of definiteness and reference in *un alt(ul), celălalt* and its French counterparts. A. Vrăjitoru, 'Sensul fundamental al cazurilor şi relaţia actant – actat la substantivele din limba română', *LiR*, 45, 1996:5–19.

C. Dominte, 'Esquisse de caractérisation typologique de la négation roumaine', *BalS*, 36, 1995:5–10, is keen to discern characteristic 'Romanceness' in the Romanian negation system. But the safest conclusion one could draw from this study is that features of Romanian negation, such as the 'double' negative of the *nu văd nimic* type, might just as easily be of Romance as of non-Romance origin. A. Voineag-Merlan, 'Coordonarea "discontinuă" în româna vorbită populară', *LiL*, 41.2, 1996:5–10, deals with anacoluthic structures (common in speech in many — perhaps all — languages) where conjunctions link elements of different, non-matching, syntactic status. Id., 'Pragmatica şi sintaxa semantică a structurilor bumerang în româna vorbită', *RLSL*, no.5:70–81.

LEXICON AND ONOMASTICS. F. Vasilescu, *'Micul dicţionar academic* şi "Dicţionarul Tezaur al Limbii Române"', *LiR*, 45, 1996: 71–76, contains methodological reflections on proposals to include all the information from the DLR in a single volume. S. Munteanu, 'Sinonimia — o perspectivă funcţională', *LiL*, 41.3–4, 1996:8–16, looks critically at the criteria used for determining relations of synonymy. C. Moroianu, 'Dublete etimologice – sinonimie şi diacronie', *ib.*, 42.2:20–27. M. Avram, 'Despre sinonimele cu bază comună din limba română', *RLSL*, no.3:70–73. G. Chiperi, 'Diferenţieri semantice între cuvintele *apartenenţă* şi *posesiune* (pe baza definiţiilor lexicografice)', *RLSL*, no.5:115–16. Stelian Dumistrăcel, *Expresii româneşti*, Iaşi, Institutul European, 314 pp., is a detailed scholarly account of the origins and motivations of Romanian sayings and set expressions, presented by alphabetical order of their key words. F. L. Ionilă, 'Cîteva observaţii asupra unităţilor frazeologice din limbile romană şi polonă, referitoare la denumiri ale corpului omenesc', *SRoP*, 21, 1996:59–64, discusses idioms involving names for body parts in Romanian and Polish. Nicolae Felecan, *Dicţionar de paronime*, Vox, 1995, viii + 312 pp., lists words of different meaning but similar form which are potentially liable to be confused — although one may wonder how many of them are ever really confused.

An exciting new project is announced by M. Sala, 'Il dizionario etimologico della lingua rumena (DELR)', *Fest. Pfister*, 1, 434–40, which discusses plans for the production of the new Romanian etymological dictionary coordinated by S. (which will also involve the formation of an 'etymological data bank of the Romanian language' extracted from existing publications by a large number of Romanian scholars). A. Avram, 'Note etimologice', *LiR*, 44, 1995:11–15, 99–106, 173–79; *ib.*, 45, 1996:57–63, examines the etymology of entries *mandalău, mangal, mangălăi, manişcă, mastroacă, mazdroancă, mazdrop, măgulică, mândăi, mândău, mâscăi, micăcior, mimiligi, mirtăţi, mişcute, mondroi, mordie, moară, modolău, modoran, mangul, marbotin, măzălui, mârsolit, minciog, mosoli, stajnic, steji, stihui, stimosi, strântori, sturluiba, suflintătură, sulhar, sulhău, sulig, sulzui, supşig, surhan, suvăiţă* from volumes VI and X of *Dicţionarul limbii române* (DLR). Other etymologies from this dictionary (*clipcă, comornic, corăbioară, harapnic, horeţ, huludeţ, mazdrac, mocni, pavăză, păguri, păţoancă, petină, petiţă, plav, reşcă, zăngăni*) are discussed by E. Vrabie in *LiR*, 44, 1995:15–16, 180–82, and *ib.*, 45, 1996:163–69. V. also asks 'Este cuvântul *scorţişoară* o formaţie românească independentă?', *ib.*, 63–66, and modifies the DLR view to conclude that the word is from *scoarţă* + suffix *-işoară*, probably calqued on Slav *korica*. A. Mareş, 'Un slavonism de cancelărie: METE(A)H "amestec"', *LiR*, 44, 1995:179–80. N. Ursu, 'O atestare a lui *frământă* "fermentă"', *ib.*, 16–17, supports the claim that Latin FERMENTA is the origin of *frământă*, by citing examples from a late-18th-c. text in which the word clearly means 'yeast'. M. Negraru, investigates the etymology of *(a) adia*. V. Ţara, 'Neologisme "româno-romanice"', *RLSL*, no.3:153–57.

Romanian toponymy and onomastics are at present the object of intensive scholarly interest. A. Rezeanu and F. Modoran, 'Modele în toponimia urbană', *ib.*, 225–32, examines the processes of giving names to street, neighbourhoods, bridges, etc. From the same authors are 'Toponimia urbană dinamica numelor de străzi' and 'Termeni entopici în toponimia urbană', *ib.*, 45, 1996:115–22 and 179–86, focusing on Bucharest. V. Ţurlan, 'Note de toponimie gălăţeană', *LiR*, 44, 1995:65–71. M. Dobre, 'Elemente metaforice în terminologia geografică populară şi în toponimie', *ib.*, 59–65. H. Stamatin, 'Toponimul *horăiată*', *ib.*, 45, 1996:122–29. A. Surjicov, 'Abrevierea şi omonimia în limba română', *ib.*, 44, 1995:9–10, surveys the use of acronyms and abbreviations as homonyms of the names from which they are derived. V. Goicu, 'Nume de localităţi de origine neolatină în Transilvania şi Banat', *SCO*, 2, 1996:179–84. S. Goicu, 'Termeni creştini în toponimia din Transilvania', *ib.*, 185–200. E. Bureţea, 'Cu privire la unele nume de locuri româneşti de origine antroponimică', *ib.*, 229–33. A. Andrei-Franca, 'Din toponimia judeţului Ialomiţa. Nume de sate dispărute din bazinul Ialomiţei (II)', *ib.*, 235–52. V. Urucu, 'Câteva precizări privind denumirea satului Dioşti din Câmpia Romanaţilor', *ib.*, 253–61. D. Bugă and S. Dobre, 'Formarea reţelei de aşezări în Subcarpaţii Getici. Consideraţii istorice şi toponimice', *ib.*, 263–70. E. Şodolescu-Silvestru, 'Raportul dintre antroponime şi toponime sub aspect termenologic', *ib.*, 297–302.

Alexandru Pele, *Etnonimele românilor: valah – etimologie ancestrală şi areal istoric*, Oradea, Abaddaba, 1996, 198 pp. Victor Vascenco, *Studii de antroponimie*, Editura Academiei, 1995, 280 pp., deals with Romanian and Slav anthroponymy, and their mutual influences. Viorica Goicu, *Nume de persoane în Ţara Zarandului*, Timişoara, Amphora, 1996, 200 pp. G. Bolocan, 'Dicţionarul numelor de familie din România', *SCO*, 2, 1996:7–44. T. Oancă, 'Nume standard şi variante antroponimice. Probleme de terminologie' and '*Cioban, mocan, pastor* şi antroponimele corespunzătoare', *ib.*, 45–53 and 85–98. V. Nestorescu, 'Din antroponimia românilor timoceni din Bulgaria', *ib.*, 55–58. L. Lazia, 'Structuri antroponimice dobrogene (secolul XIX — început de secol XX)', *ib.*, 59–73. L. Ionescu, 'Câteva consideraţii asupra elementului de compunere *cara-* în antroponimele româneşti', *ib.*, 75–78. D. Dincă, 'Valori semantice ale numelui propriu de persoană articulat cu articol nehotărât în română şi franceză', *ib.*, 79–84. I. Burci, 'Rolul şi răspândirea sufixului *-ete* în antroponimie', *ib.*, 99–105. V. Urucu, 'Consideraţii privind area de răspândire şi înţelesul termenului *uruc*', *ib.*, 107–10. I. Roşianu, 'Câteva observaţii privind scrierea şi pronunţarea numelor proprii', *ib.*, 111–17. D. Nedelcuţ, 'Astronime ştiinţifice moştenite', *ib.*, 119–77. I. Toma, 'Onomastica românească: evoluţie, tendinţe, realizări', *ib.*, 201–27. E. Faiciuc, 'Materialul onomastic existent în arhiva "Sextil Puşcariu"', 271–96. A. Dîrul, 'Porecla din perspectiva semiologică', *RLSL*, no.3:118–23. I. Ionescu, *LiR*, 44, 1995:71–72, relates the name 'Năsturel' to the saint's name 'Nestor'. The word for 'Christmas', ever problematic in Romanian lexicology, is the object of S. Goicu and V. Goicu, '*Crăciun* în onomastica românească', *FD*, 15, 1996:27–37.

DIALECTOLOGY. A most useful and detailed historical survey of the methodology of classification of the dialects of Romania is V. Frăţilă, 'La struttura dialettale del dacoromeno. Excursus storico del problema, cause e antichità delle aree dialettali', *BALI*, 20, 1996:5–47. F. ultimately favours a quadripartite division for modern Daco-Romanian into 'Walachian', 'Moldavian', 'Banat', and 'Transylvanian' subdialects, the last further articulated into the varieties of Crişana, Maramureş, north-eastern Ardeal and southern and central Ardeal. But he stresses that the modern situation should not be projected into antiquity, and explores also earlier dialect configurations. He proceeds to examine the historical *raisons d'être* of the divisions he establishes, both in terms of the languages with which Romanian was in contact, and in terms of political and social developments. A welcome addition to the Romanian linguistic atlases is *Atlasul lingvistic român pe regiuni. Muntenia şi Dobrogea*, ed. Teofil Teaha, 2 vols, Editura Academiei, 1996, xviii + 301 pp., xiii + 372 pp., which has over 300 maps, with further maps illustrating the areas covered by each of the investigators (Teofil Teaha, Mihai Conţiu, Ion Ionică, Bogdan Marinescu, Valeriu Rusu, Nicolae Saramandu, Magdalena Vulpe), and the official and local names of the localities investigated. V. Pavel, 'Probleme ale elaborării Atlasului lingvistic român pe regiuni. *Basarabia, Nordul Bucovinei, Transnistria*, vol. I–II', *FD*, 15, 1996:111–16. A. Mareş, 'Trei note de dialectologie istorică (secolul al XVII-lea)', *LiR*, 44, 1995:183–89, deals with: 'Epenteza luĭ (*să aiiubu, să aiubă, Roiubul*) în documente scrise în Ţara românească', 'Atestări muntene ale termenilor *ciobotă* şi *ciobotar*', and 'Despre prezenţa termenului *socaci* în Lexiconul lui Mardarie'. T. Teaha, 'Rom. *ord* "urzesc" — Formă dialectală refăcută', *FD*, 15, 1996:121–27. I. Mărgărit, 'DR *broaştină*', *ib.*, 135–36. M. Marin and I. Mărgărit, 'Glosar dialectal Muntenia. Partea a III-a: M-P', *FD*, 15, 1996:137–246.

A. Ulivi, 'Observații asupra metatezei în dialectele românești sud-dunărene', *ib.*, 15, 1996:95–101. Radu Sp. Popescu and Todor Balkanski, **Aromânii din Rodopii și graiul lor*, Craiova, Universitatea din Craiova, 1995, 168 pp. + 2 maps. H. Campos, 'Full and reduced clitics in Megleno-Romance', *Probus*, 7, 1996:247–78, (a study which gratuitously asserts the contentious view that Megleno-Romanian constitutes a separate branch of Romance from Romanian) deals with the distribution of full clitic versus reduced clitic pronouns, such as *au* vs. *u* 'her', where 'a reduced clitic appears when the clitic can lean on a head whose maximal projection dominates the clitic, otherwise a full form is used'. Although the central theoretical point is well made (with interesting comparisons with Galician), the argumentation is in places none too sound: it is surely not true that 'reduced' forms of clitics are generally used in Romanian before verbs beginning with *a*-, and given that the reduced forms are used specifically after *nu* and with auxiliary *am* etc., the conclusion that the Romanian clitic is 'phonologically determined' seems overstated; nor is *a avea* the infinitive of the auxiliary. It is irritating that *Probus*, whose subject matter is after all Romance linguistics, should have permitted in this article repeated errors of Romanian orthography (e.g. *vâd* for *văd*).

W. Dahmen, 'Die Bedeutung Venedigs für die Balkanromania', *Fest. Pfister*, 1, 313–25, discusses, inter alia, the lexical influence of Venetian on Aromanian. N. Saramandu, 'O colecție inedită de narațiuni populare aromâne', *FD*, 15, 1996:117–19. T. Ferro, 'Etimoane atestate și etimoane postulate pentru lexicul de origine latină al aromânei. Observații pe marginea *Dicționarului dialectului aromân* al lui Tache Papahagi', *ib.*, 57–70. Some information on a much-neglected domain, the use of Vlach (Aromanian) by communities in Australia, America, Albania, and Romania, may be gleaned from T. J. Winnifrith, *Shattered Eagles — Balkan Fragments*, London, Duckworth, 1995, 171 pp., who includes some interesting critical observations, based particularly on the Vlach of Romania, bearing on Trudgill's ideas concerning the relation between related minority and majority languages.

PRAGMATICS AND STYLISTICS. I. Condrea, 'Televiziune și normele limbii române literare', *RLSL*, no.4:62–66. V. Guțu-Romalo, 'Stilul "relaxat" în uzul limbii române actuale', *ib.*, 20–24, examines the penetration of aspects of casual style into formal discourse. L. Groza, 'Despre jocurile de cuvinte în frazeologia limbii române', *ib.*, 32–36, contains interesting reflections on the productivity in modern Romanian of puns based on long-established fixed expressions. The second edition of *Dicționarul Explicativ al Limbii Române* is considered in

A. Bidu-Vrănceanu, 'Mărcile stilistice (diastratice) în DEX și importanța lor normativ-didactică', *LiL*, 42.1:27–36. M. Mihail Deleanu, 'Stilul religios al limbii române literare', *ib.*, 42.2:28–29. A. Stoichiţu Ichim, 'Strategii persuasive in discursul publicitar (I)', *ib.*, 51–56, and also 'Observaţii privind influenţa engleză în limbajul publicistic actual', *ib.*, 41.1, 1996:37–46; 41.2, 1996:25–34, which contains useful information on English borrowings not listed in dictionaries but current in journalistic usage. M. Ciolac, 'Despre sociolectul unor categorii de intelectuali: registrul formal oral şi varianta standard a limbii', *FD*, 15, 1996:43–55. H. Pârlog and S. Vultur, 'Conştiinţa metalingvistică şi niveluri de limbaj în povestirea orală', *LiR*, 44, 1995:83–86. I. Ştefan, 'Prefixele negative în *Craii de Curtea-Veche* şi funcţia lor stilistică', *ib.*, 123–28, is concerned with the stylistic use of an aspect of derivational morphology in M. I. Caragiale's novel.

LITERATURE

POSTPONED

XI. RHETO-ROMANCE STUDIES

By KENNETH H. ROGERS, *University of Rhode Island*

1. BIBLIOGRAPHICAL AND GENERAL

G. A. Plangg, '*Spiglia(ta)* und Verwandtes aus dem Rätoromanischen', *Fest. Pfister*, I, 173–83, deals with both meanings and origins of a number of grape-growing and associated terms in Swiss Romansh, with comparisons to Ladin varieties.

2. FRIULAN

GENERAL.   A. Cuna and F. Vicario, 'Altri testi e frammenti friulani dall'Archivio di Stato di Udine', *Ce fastu?*, 72, 1996: 7–39, continues earlier contributions on the 14th- and 15th-c. documents from the Cividale region; the authors note the Italianizing nature of the Friulan used. Sergio Zuccolo, *Da Celti a Friulani: una storia dell'Occidente*, Venice, Marsilio, 1996, v + 465 pp. Of the six chapters contained in this work, only the fourth, 'la lingua' (201–33), concerns us. Z. takes up, once again, and in a somewhat humorous manner, the question of whether Rheto-Romance is a separate branch of Romance or whether, as especially Battisti and Pellegrini maintain, 'le varietà ladine si riducono a semplici varianti degli adiacenti dialetti italiani' (202). Z.'s chapter also contains handy reference lists of comparative Friulan and Italian vocabulary, to demonstrate (1) the greater influence of Celtic upon Friulan (108), and (2) the comparative impact of Ostrogothic (210–11), of Langobardic (213–14), and of Frankish (215) upon Friulan and Italian.

PHONOLOGY.   F. Vicario, 'Una predica in friulano del 1840', *Sot la Nape*, 48, 1996: 65–76, contains the text of the sermon (66–72), along with comments concerning, among other features, the Italianized spellings and lexicon of the text.

MORPHOSYNTAX.   G. Faggin, 'I verbi "analitici" in friulano', *Ladinia*, 20, 1996: 175–81, is an excerpt from the author's **Grammatica friulana* (Udine, Campoformido, 1996). While Friulan is not as intensively characterized by an abundance of these verb + adverb combinations (e.g., *tirâ sû*, *clamâ sot*) as are Swiss Romansh and Dolomitic Ladin, F. asserts that these verbs are more frequent in Friulan than in Italian. L. Spinozzi Minai, 'Rilevanza e potenziale scientifico dei materiali inediti del *Glossario del diletto del Torre* di Jan Baudouin de Courtenay', *Ce fastu?*, 72, 1996: 203–22. Luigi Salvatore d'Asburgo Lorena, *Frasi d'affetto e vezzeggiativi in friulano / Zärtlichkei-tausdrücke und Koseworte in der friulanischen Sprache*, Udine, Gaspari, 1996, is a facsimile reprint of the 1915 edition. ONOMASTICS. E. Costantini and L. Zanier, 'Fra Pracuncét e Ceséps: notule sulla toponomastica di Luìncis', *Sot la Nape*, 48, 1996:57–64. This tiny part of the commune of Ovaro has only about a hundred people, down from 262 in 1898; the place-names, according to the authors, fit in perfectly with the Carnic Alps region, with such examples as Cjamplùnc and Pràdas; very good maps are included in the article. P. Rizzolatti, 'Fuochi di paglia: su *pignarûl* e le denominazioni friulane e venete del falò epifanico', *Ce fastu?*, 72, 1996:175–202, contains a list of the terms associated with the ritual fire at Epiphany, and a discussion of their geographical distribution. Cornelio Cesare Desinan, *Itinerari friulani: i nomi di luogo fra storia e leggenda*, Udine, Società Filologica Friulana, 1996, 215 pp. Also by Desinan, *'Osservazioni sulla toponomastica del Canale di Gorto', *Memorie Storiche Forogiuliesi*, 75, 1996:135–88.

SOCIOLINGUISTICS AND LANGUAGES IN CONTACT. G. Osualdini, 'I corsi pratici di lingua friulana', *Sot la Nape*, 48, 1996:113–14, summarizes ten years of these courses, now held in 19 communities, with a number of non-Friulan students attending as well.

3. LADIN

GENERAL. R. Bauer, H. Goebl, and E. Haimerl, 'Arbeitsbericht 10 zum *ALD-I*', *Ladinia*, 20, 1996:191–221. H. Berschin, 'Questione ladina, Grundrechnungsarten und Dialektometrie', *Ladinia*, 20, 1996:187–89. Walter Belardi, *Breve storia della lingua e letteratura ladina*, San Martin de Tor, Istitut Cultural Ladin 'Micurà de Rü', 1996. H. Böhmer, *'L'Atlas linguistique du ladin central et des dialectes limitrophes (première partie — ALD-I)', pp. 275–79 of *CILL*, 22.3–4 and 23.1–2, 1996–97. Also by Böhmer, *'L'informatisation de l'Atlas linguistique du ladin central: le point de vue du dialectologue', *Actes* (Corte), 213–20.

MORPHOSYNTAX. R. Bauer, 'Strumenti e metodi di rilevamento per la raccoltà dei dati di ALD I', pp. 445–53 of *Neue Wege der romanischen Geolinguistik: Akten des Symposiums zur empirischen Dialektologie*, ed. Edgar Radke and Harald Thun, Kiel, Westensee, 1996, is a detailed description of vol. 1, which deals with morphosyntax and 'elementary' phonology; the research, based on 806 questions prepared by Hans Goebl and Dieter Kattenbusch, was undertaken from 1985 to 1992 and was limited to 200 localities. Vol. 2 will deal with the lexicon and 'morfosintassi elaborata'.

SEMANTICS. W. Belardi, 'Casi di "mediatas" e di "contradditto-rietà" semantiche nella storia del lessico ladino sellano', *Fest. Pfister*, I, 53–61, deals with semantic evolution as an additional technique for validating etymologies, among others, affirming that Latin SUBCUTERE > Ladin *sochedì*.

SOCIOLINGUISTICS AND LANGUAGES IN CONTACT. R. Bauer, 'Die romanische Geolinguistik im Spannungsfeld von Wirtschaft und Wissenschaft: Kooperationsmodelle im Projekt ALD I (con un epilogo in italiano)', *Neue Wege der romanischen Geolinguistik*, 430–44, asserts that, if done properly, three types of contact possibilities will be exploited: between universities and institutes, between private and public endeavours, and between academe and industry. A transfer-able geolinguistic model will certainly be the result. Also by Bauer, *'Le système de base de données de l'Atlas linguistique du ladin central', *Actes* (Corte), 195–211. P. Videsott, 'Wortschatzerweiterung im Ladin Dolomitan', *Ladinia*, 20, 1996:163–73, does not believe that a uniform Ladin written language is absolutely necessary for Ladin lexical expansion; he demonstrates his point with such potentially productive suffixes as Italian *-aggio*, which can be rendered in Ladin as *-aje/ -ac/ -agio/ -aso*. V. goes so far as to assert that such uniformity of word formation can even facilitate the development of a single written standard (164). N. Chiocchetti, *'SPELL — Servisc de Planificazion y Elaborazion dl Lingaz Ladin', pp. 89–92 of *La Gestion du territoire linguistique*, ed. Jean Chiorboli, Corte, Université di Corse, 1996. Johannes Kramer et al., *Etymologisches Wörterbuch des Dolomitenladinischen (EWD)*, VII (T–Z), Hamburg, Buske, 1996, 413 pp. Manuela Zappe, *Das ethnische Zusammenleben in Südtirol. Sprachsoziologi-sche, sprachpolitische und soziokulturelle Einstellungen der deutschen, italien-ischen und ladinischen Sprachgruppe vor und nach den gegenwärtigen Umbrüchen in Europa* (E. H. Linguistik, 174), Frankfurt, Lang, 321 pp.

4. SWISS ROMANSH

GENERAL. Žarko Muljačić, 'Una menzione del romanzo grigione dell'847', *Ladinia*, 20, 1996:183–85, maintains that, in the AD 847 Council of Frankfurt, the Latin 'in rusticam Romanam linguam …' refers to Romansh. Arthur Baur, *Allegra genügt nicht! Rätoromanisch als Herausforderung für die Schweiz*, Chur, Bündner Monatsblatt, 179 pp. G. Gangale, *'Bericht über meine Sprachuntersuchungen im rätoro-manischen Gebiet', *ASR*, 109, 1996:27–48. I. Gartmann, *'Publicaz-iuns: Tscherna bibliografica', *ASR*, 109, 1996:245–49. *DRG*: *Dicziunari Rumantsch Grischun*, 125: *Interim–intoppar*; 126: *intoppar–ints-chess*; 127: *Intschess–investir*; 128: *Investir–involar*, ed. Felix Giger et al., Chur, Inst. dal Dicziunari Rumantsch Grischun, 1996. Daniela

Gloor et al., *Fünf Idiome – Eine Schriftsprache: Die Frage gemeinsam Schriftsprache im Urteil der romanischen Bevölkerung*, Chur, 1996. Manfred Gross et al., *Rätoromanisch: Facts and Figures*, Chur, Lia Rumantscha, 1996.

MORPHOSYNTAX. Th. Krefeld, 'Dame Phonétique, Dame Sémantique et les autres. Bemerkungen zur bündnerromanischen Negation', *Fest. Pfister*, 1, 23–29, deals with the three types of negation used in Swiss Romansh: *buca, betga, brischa*, and attempts to trace the relations among them; K. believes that the *buca* type is the earliest of the three.

SOCIOLINGUISTICS AND LANGUAGES IN CONTACT. W. Carigiet and R. Cathomas, 'Schola romontscha e bilinguitad', *ASR*, 109, 1996:9–26, is a study of the degree of motivation and linguistic competence in Romansh of 260 school children (elementary and secondary) in the Grisons. The results are encouraging for the future of the language: students' abilities in Romansh increase with schooling, the attitudes of most (70–90%) of the students favours continuing instruction in Romansh, and German-Romansh bilingualism turns out not to be a problem — nor is the Romansh students' progress in German impaired.

3

CELTIC LANGUAGES

I. WELSH STUDIES

LANGUAGE

By DAVID THORNE, *Reader in Welsh Language and Literature,*
University of Wales, Lampeter

1. GENERAL

D. E. Evans, 'Celticity, Celtic awareness and Celtic Studies', *ZCP*,
49–50:1–27, is a thorough discussion of varied approaches and
definitions of the term Celtic which focuses attention upon the
legitimate concerns of scholars in the field. W. P. Lehmann, *ib.*,
440–54, highlights some of the changes which occurred in Celtic
from the proto-language in the light of the analysis of the Celtiberian
inscriptions. B. F. Roberts, 'Translating Old Welsh; the first attempts',
ib., 770–77, traces Edward Lhuyd's careful attempts to translate and
interpret examples of OW texts in the 18th century.

2. GRAMMAR

David A. Thorne, *Taclo'r Treigladau*, Llandysul, Gomer, 131 pp., is a
dependable introduction to the consonantal and vowel mutations of
the contemporary language and includes a large number of useful
examples from a variety of sources and registers. P. Russell, '*Gur
Gwynn y lau*: figures of speech in *Gramadegau'r Penceirddiaid* and Latin
grammarians', *CMCS*, 32:95–104, proposes that the compiler of the
grammar was able to exploit a range of Latin source material, but
that the identification and justification of faults was his own and
probably did not derive from a Latin original. L. Bednarczuk, 'A
typological contribution to the disappearance of p in Common
Celtic', *ZCP*, 40–50:43–49, examines the extinction of PIE p in
Common Celtic. J. de Hoz, 'When did the Celts lose their verbal
-i?', *ib.*, 107–17, is a rather inconclusive discussion of the loss of *-i*
of the verbal primary endings in Celtic. J. F. Eska, 'Allophony,
Chamalières *eððic* and related matters,' *ib.*, 170–78, reviews earlier
discussions of *eððic* in the Chamalières inscription and proposes that
the form is a quasi-phonetic orthographic representation of /*eððic*/.
D. S. Evans, 'The comparative adjective in Middle Welsh', *ib.*,

179–97, presents a detailed classification of the form and use of the comparative adjective throughout the Middle Welsh period, concluding that it is possible to trace its change from a mainly predicative to attributive function. F. O. Lindemann, 'On some "laryngeal" reflexes in Celtic', *ib.*, 455–68, thoughtfully reviews earlier discussions on laryngeal reflexes in Celtic and presents a series of other possible explanations. P. Mac Cana, 'Ir. *ba marb*, W. *bu farw*', *ib.*, 469–81, has notes on the similarities between the Ir. and W. copula + *marb*, expressions; the similarities indicate that it was a shared feature of insular Celtic and although the idiom has survived in W. it has been long obsolete in Irish. F. Villar, 'The Celtiberian language', *ib.*, 898–949, visits certain areas of Celtiberian which demand reconsideration in the light of recent epigraphic discoveries.

3. ETYMOLOGY AND LEXICOGRAPHY

G. O. Pierce, T. Roberts, and H. W. Owen, *Ar Draws Gwlad: Ysgrifau ar Enwau Lleoedd*, Llanrwst, Carreg Gwalch, 118 pp., provides an enlightening commentary on a wide selection of place names from all over Wales. G. R. Jones, 'The *gwely* as a tenurial institution', *SC*, 30:167–88, discusses the evolution and development of the term *gwely* by evaluating instances of its usage on the ground. J. F. Eska and M. Weiss, 'Segmenting Gaul. *tomedeclaï*', *ib.*, 289–92, conclude that the text of the inscription of Voltino is to be edited *to = me = declaï*. E. P. Hamp, 'Voteporigis Protectoris' *ib.*, 293–94, has a note on the possible status of the gentleman commemorated on the Castelldwyran stone. N. Jacobs, *ib.*, 295–90, has a note on *tors*. Part 47 of *GPC* (ed. G. A. Bevan) covers PUREN – RHADUS. D. Parsons, 'British *Caraticos*, Old English *Cerdic*', *CMCS*, 32:95–104, discusses the British origin of the name of the West Saxon king Cerdic and suggests that the transmission of the form into English is not indicated solely by linguistic evidence. P. Anreiter, 'Gallisch *brigantes*', *ZCP*, 49–50:31–42, examines the Gaulish *brigantes*. A. Falileyev, 'Cambro-Slavica', *ib.*, 198–203, has notes on W. *gweryd*: Russ. *vereteya*, and W. *hyd(d)er*: Russ. *zdorovyi*. J. E. C. Williams, Welsh *iawn*, *ib.*, 1000–12, explores the etymology and semantics of *iawn*. A. Breeze, 'Does *scripulum* in the Book of Llandaf mean "piece of gold"?', *THSC*, 3:5–8, presents an argument for interpreting the form *scripulum* which occurs in an 8th-c. document in the 12th-c. Book of Llandaf as 'a certain weight of gold'.

4. SOCIOLINGUISTICS

D. G. Jones, *John Morris Jones a'r 'Cymro Dirodres'*, Llangefni, Undeb y Gymraeg, 22 pp., discusses the state of contemporary spoken and written Welsh and emphasizes the role of *papurau bro*, community newspapers in giving the language grammatical stability. Robert Owen Jones, *Hir Oes i'r Iaith: Agweddau ar Hanes y Gymraeg a'r Gymdeithas*, Llandysul, Gomer, 462 pp., examines the social history of the Welsh language up to the present day showing that the experience of other countries is invaluable in understanding the factors which cause erosion.

Y Gymraeg yn ei Disgleirdeb: Yr Iaith Gymraeg cyn y Chwyldro Diwydiannol, ed. G. H. Jenkins, Cardiff, Univ. of Wales Press, xiv + 450 pp., is the first of a series of studies exploring the social history of the Welsh language; it contains 12 chapters each of which makes a substantial contribution to a much neglected area of scholarship. Ll. B Smith, 'Yr iaith Gymraeg cyn 1536' (15–44), discusses the history of the Welsh language from the time of the Welsh memorandum inserted in the book of St Chad up to the language clause included in the 1536 Act of Union. G. H. Jenkins et al., 'Yr iaith Gymraeg yn y Gymru fodern gynnar' (45–119), plot the geographical distribution of Welsh speakers, the status of the language in the home and in the work place and oral usage as recorded in civil and ecclesiastical court records during the early modern period. P. R. Roberts, 'Deddfwriaeth y Tuduriaid a statws gwleidyddol "yr iaith Frytanaidd" ' (121–50), examines the social and political considerations which formed the political backdrop to the language clause in the 1536 Act of Union. R. Sugget, 'Yr iaith Gymraeg a Llys y Sesiwn Fawr' (151–79), shows how the Welsh language was used in the Court of Great Session between 1543 and 1830 although the language clause in the Act of Union had declared that English was to be the only language of that court. J. G. Jones, 'Yr iaith Gymraeg a llywodraeth leol: ustusiaid heddwch a'r llysoedd chwarter *c.* 1536–1800' (181–205), discusses the use of the Welsh language in the administration of justice in the Courts of Quarter Sessions and shows how those charged with translation of evidence from Welsh into English frequently faced problems in understanding the evidence being presented because of the colourful language of defendants and plaintiffs. G. Williams, 'Unoliaeth crefydd neu unoliaeth iaith? Protestaniaid a Phabyddion a'r iaith Gymraeg 1536–1660' (207–32), emphasizes the influence of the Welsh Bible and devotional works in safeguarding standard literary Welsh. E. M. White, 'Yr eglwys sefydledig, anghydffurfiaeth a'r iaith Gymraeg c. 1660–1811' (233–85), shows how the Welsh were irritated, annoyed, and angered by the practice of appointing non-Welsh speakers to well endowed livings in Wales where they proceeded to hold church services in English. W. P. Griffith, 'Dysg ddyneiddiol, addysg a'r iaith Gymraeg 1536–1660' (287–314), explores the influence of English education on Welsh scholarship during the Renaissance and Reformation period. E. M. White, 'Addysg boblogaidd a'r iaith Gymraeg 1650–1800' (315–38), writes of the efforts to teach the common people basic literacy and assesses the impact of the circulating schools and the Sunday schools movement on the prospects and status of Welsh. R. G. Gruffydd, 'Yr iaith Gymraeg mewn ysgolheictod a diwylliant 1536–1610' (339–64), assesses the condition of Welsh scholarship in the 16th c. and the cause and effect of the demise of the native bardic tradition. G. H. Jenkins, 'Adfywiad yr iaith a'r diwylliant Cymraeg 1660–1800' (365–400), discusses the revival of interest in Welsh language and letters during the period 1650–1800. B. F. Roberts, 'Ieithoedd Celtaidd Prydain' (401–36), analyses the external history of the other Celtic languages of Britain.

Kathryn Jones and Delyth Morris, *Gender a'r Iaith Gymraeg: Arolwg Ymchwil*, Caerdydd, Y Comisiwn Cyfle Cyfartal, xii + 89 pp., investigate to what extent the Welsh language has, and will, impact on the equality between men and women in Wales, Gwenllian Awbrey, *Y Gymraeg yn y Gweithle a'r Ddeddf Gwahaniaethu ar Sail Rhyw*, Caerdydd, Y Comisiwn Cyfle Cyfartal, iv + 30 pp., debates the use of Welsh in a non-gender-specific context.

EARLY AND MEDIEVAL LITERATURE

By NERYS ANN JONES, *Department of Celtic, University of Edinburgh*

Our understanding of the genesis and transmission of the earliest Welsh poetry is greatly enhanced by the publication of John T. Koch, *The Gododdin of Aneirin: Text and Context from Dark-Age North Britain*, Cardiff, Univ. of Wales Press, cxliv + 262 pp. Thanks to his reconstructed text soundly based on principles of textual criticism and historical linguistics, it is now possible to distinguish clearly between the 6th-c. stratum in the Book of Aneirin and later accretions and also to identify modifications to the older material. The reconstruction is based on a detailed theory of the text's history outlined in the introduction which will provide food for thought and discussion among *Hengerdd* scholars for many years to come. Other contributions to the study of the *Gododdin* include, P. R. Wilson et al., 'Early Anglian Catterick and Catraeth', *Medieval Archaeology*, 40:1–61, and C. Cessford, 'Northern England and the Gododdin Poem', *Northern History*, 33:218–22. R. G. Gruffydd continues his series of short studies on the additions to the *Gododdin* corpus with 'The Strathcarron interpolation (*Canu Aneirin*, lines 966–77)', *SGS*, 17:172–78, and 'The *Englynion* of *Llyfr Aneirin*', *O Hehir Vol.*, 32–39. A new interpretation of another interpolated text is provided in K. A. Klar and E. E. Sweetser, 'Reading the unreadable: "Gwarchan Maelderw" from *The Book of Aneirin*', *ib.*, 78–103. Metrical analysis of this most obscure composition reveals a four poem sequence understood by a later copyist as a single unit and attributed to Tailiesin. M. Haycock examines the meaning, nature, and possible sources of the questions posed by the Taliesin persona in 'Taliesin's questions', *CMCS*, 33:19–79, while S. L. Higley, 'The Spoils of Annwn: Taliesin and material poetry', *O Hehir Vol.*, 43–53, shows how coherence can be given to the disparate parts of *Preiddeu Annwn* by interpreting the raid upon the otherworld as a depiction of Taliesin's seizure of poetic knowledge.

New insights into two *Gogynfeirdd* poems are provided by M. P. Bryant-Quinn, ' "*Archaf weddi*": rhai sylwadau ar farwysgafn Meilyr Brydydd', *LlC*, 20:12–24, a reinvestigation of the themes of Meilyr's death bed poem in the light of what is known of the devotional and theological tradition of 12th-c. Wales, and C. McKenna, 'The hagiographic poetics of *Canu Cadfan*', *O Hehir Vol.*, 121–37, which focuses on the hagiographical dimension of a mid 12th-c. *awdl* to St Cadfan of Tywyn and speculates as to the relationship between the early *Gogynfeirdd*'s poems to saints and the prose *vita* which began to

be produced in Wales in the same period. J. E. C. Williams, 'Yr
Arglwydd Rhys ac Eisteddfod Aberteifi 1176: y cefndir diwylliannol',
YB, 22:80–142, is an updated, fuller version of an article on the
culture of the court of Rhys ap Gruffudd of Deheubarth which
appeared in *Yr Arglwydd Rhys*, ed. N. A. Jones and Huw Pryce (see
YWMLS, 58:639). R. M. Jones, 'Gogynghanedd y Gogynfeirdd', *YB*,
22:41–79, takes a fresh look at the development of proto- *cynghanedd*
in medieval Welsh court poetry by applying the distinction first noted
by Saussure between levels of *langue* and *discours* to analysis of the
ornament used by the Poets of the Princes. A most welcome index of
the personal and place names of the *Gogynfeirdd* corpus is provided in
A. Parry Owen, 'Mynegai i enwau priod ym marddoniaeth Beirdd y
Tywysogion', *LlC*, 20:25–45.

Three volumes have been published in the University of Wales
Centre for Advanced Studies in Welsh and Celtic series, *Cyfres Beirdd
yr Uchelwyr*, under the general editorship of Ann Parry Owen, *Gwaith
Goronw Gyriog, Iorwerth ab y Cyriog ac eraill*, ed. Rhiannon Ifans et al.,
Aberystwyth, UWCASWC, xvii + 166 pp. contains editions of the
work of five 14th-c. poets from north-west Wales, Goronw Gyriog,
his son Iorwerth ab y Cyriog, Mab Clochyddyn, Gruffudd ap Tudur
Goch and Ithel Ddu. *Gwaith Einion Offeiriad a Dafydd Ddu o Hiraddug*,
ed. R. Geraint Gruffydd and Rhiannon Ifans, Aberystwyth,
UWCASWC, xviii + 204 pp. is an edition of the poetry associated
with Einion Offeiriad, author of the first version of the bardic
grammars, 1320–25, and his contemporary Dafydd Ddu o Hiraddug
who was responsible for a later edition of the grammar. *Gwaith Dafydd
Gorlech*, ed. Erwain H. Rheinallt, Aberystwyth, UWCASWC,
xvi + 106 pp. brings to light the work of a learned vaticinatory poet
of the second half of the 15th century. Editions and discussions of
individual poems from the 14th and 15th cs include Rh. Ifans, 'Cerdd
Freuddwyd', *YB*, 22:143–60, on the earliest complete dream poem
in Welsh, the work of 14th-c. Gruffudd ap Tudur Goch; G. A.
Williams, 'Cywydd Gwilym ap Sefnyn i Afon Ogwen ac Afon Menai',
Dwned, 3:83–89, on a praise poem to Robin ap Gruffudd of
Cochiwllan, Arfon in which Gwilym ap Sefnyn describes the perilous
journey from Anglesey to his patron's home; R. I. Daniel, 'Cywydd
moliant a brud i Ddafydd Llwyd ap Dafydd ab Einion o'r Drenew-
ydd', *Dwned*, 3:53–61, on a poem of uncertain authorship containing
a combination of praise and prophecy addressed to a nobleman of
South Wales who was a supporter of the Yorkist cause. Finally,
D. Johnston, 'Gwenllïan ferch Rhirid Flaidd', *ib.*, 3:27–32, deals
with the debate poem which contains a stanza attributed to Gwenllian
daughter of Rhirid Flaidd, hitherto thought to be the first Welsh

woman poet whose work survives, but identified here as the daughter of 15th-c. poet Tudur Penllyn.

Among the crop of articles on Dafydd ap Gwilym are L. Jones, ' "Gwyn eu byd yr adar gwylltion": golwg ar gerddi Dafydd ap Gwilym', *Dwned*, 3:9–26, an examination of the poet's portrayal of birds, especially in those *cywyddau* where he converses with them, and G. Morgan, 'Helyntion Dafydd ap Gwilym', pp. 13–24 of Gerald Morgan, *Helyntion y Cardi, Ysgrifau ar Hanes Ceredigion*, Aberystwyth, Cymdeithas Lyfrau Ceredigion, x + 180 pp., a lively account of the documentary evidence for Dafydd, Morfydd and her husband, and a discussion on the nature and social context of his love poetry. P. K. Ford, 'Re-reading Dafydd ap Gwilym', *O Hehir Vol.*, 20–31, presents to English readers examples from Eurys Rowland's inspired study of *Cywydd i fis Mai* in *LlC* 5 which showed that deliberate ambiguity and play on words were an important part of Dafydd's artistry. Ford then goes on to demonstrate how Dafydd's choice of end-rhyme and *cynghanedd* also subtly enhances the meaning in many of his poems. R. Bromwich, 'Dafydd ap Gwilym: influences and analogues', *CMCS*, 33:81–92, warmly welcomes Huw M. Edwards, *Dafydd ap Gwilym. Infuences and Analogues* (1996), and outlines the influence on Dafydd's work of his local background, family, and personal contacts. R. G. Gruffydd, 'Love by toponymy: Dafydd ap Gwilym and place-names', *Nomina*, 191:29–42, is a detailed study of *Taith i Garu (GDG* 83) which contains 14 place names, most of which can be identified as places in the vicinity of the poet's birth-place in northern Ceredigion. Gruffydd also examines the authenticity of a short poem attributed to the poet in two late manuscripts in '*Englynion* to a mill attributed to Dafydd ap Gwilym', *ZCP*, 49–50:273–81, concluding that on lexical grounds it is more likely to belong to the 15th c. or 16th c. than to the 14th c. D. Huws, 'Apocryffa Dafydd ap Gwilym', *Y Traethodydd*, 152:200–04, gives a mixed welcome to Helen Fulton's *Selections from the Dafydd ap Gwilym Apocrypha* (1996), and reacts to some of the author's more provocative statements on questions of authorship, editorial techniques and on the development of *cynghanedd*. A. C. Lake, 'Awduraeth cerddi'r Oesoedd Canol: rhai sylwadau', *Dwned*, 3:63–67, refutes Fulton's claim that modern scholars overemphasize the question of authorship of medieval Welsh poems by listing examples of *cywyddwyr* poetry which show that the poets themselves were very aware of the identities of their predecessors and of their authorship of specific poems or types of verse.

D. Johnston, 'Lewys Glyn Cothi, clerwr Dyffryn Tywi', *THSC*, 3:9–20, and G. W. Owen, 'Lewys Glyn Cothi — bardd sagrafennaidd', *Dwned*, 3:73–81, both survey and evaluate the work of 15th-c. poet Lewys Glyn Cothi, drawing attention to his humane vision of life. B. O. Huws, 'Dyddiadau Ieuan Gethin', *LlC*, 20:46–55, reasses the dates of another 15th-c. poet, Ieuan Gethin, while A. Breeze, 'Ieuan ap Rhydderch and Welsh *rhagman* 'game of chance', *ZCP*, 48:29–33 sheds light on a boasting poem of the same period by means of allusions to *ragman* in English verse. D. J. Bowen, 'B'le bu'r ymryson rhwng Siôn Cent a Rhys Goch Eryri?', *YB*, 23:100–17, is a particularly illuminating article which places a famous literary debate of the 15th c. in its historical and social background. J. Hunter is also concerned with the social context of the bardic debates of the *cywyddwyr* in 'Cyd-destunoli ymrysonau'r cywyddwyr: cipolwg ar 'yr ysbaddiad barddol', *Dwned*, 3:33–52, where he demonstrates that there is a close realtionship between debate poems and *englynion testuniaw* which are associated with the tradition of *cyff clêr* where the *pencerdd* was made the butt of satirical poems by lower grades of poets. In 'A feast of words: conspicuous consumption and praise poetry in medieval Wales', *Procs* (Harvard), 14, 39–48, Hunter draws attention to the image of the feast in the Welsh bardic tradition and examines in detail a praise poem by Dafydd Nanmor to Rhys ap Maredudd of Tywyn where this traditional *topos* has been 'reworked into an unique piece of poetic artistry'. D. J. Bowen, 'Pynciau cynghanedd: odli *I*, *U* a *Y*', *LlC*, 20:138–43, scrutinizes some of the rhyming practices of the *cywydd* poets.

The poetry of the *cywyddwyr* is used as a source of evidence for religious activity in late medieval Wales in M. Gray, 'Penrhys: the archaeology of a pilgrimage', *Morgannwg*, 40:10–32, and in J. Cartwright, 'The desire to corrupt: convent and community in Medieval Wales', pp. 20–48 of *Medieval Women in their Communities*, ed. Diane Watt, Cardiff, Univ. of Wales Press, xii + 250 pp., which also discusses the poets' perception of the nun as a corruptible virgin. A. T. E. Mationis, 'Textual culture and its assimilation in fourteenth-century Wales', *ZCP*, 49–50:576–90, demonstrates how Latin and continental learning was appropriated by Dafydd ap Gwilym and his contemporaries by examining the vocabulary and imagery of their religious poetry. J. G. Griffiths, 'Tarddiad syniadol y *Dialogus Inter Corpus et Animam* a'r ffurfiau Cymraeg', *LlC*, 20:1–11, traces the origins of the 'Dialogue of the Soul and Body' which is found in prose, verse, and dramatic form in medieval Welsh. I. Mittendorf, 'The Middle Welsh Mary of Egypt and the Latin source of the *Miracles of the Virgin Mary*', pp. 205–36 of Poppe, *Mary of Egypt*, is a thorough study of pp. 205–36 of the Welsh version of the miracle of Mary of Egypt which includes an edition and English translation as well as a comparison of the Welsh text with a Latin version in Oxford, Balliol College 240 which is shown to be the source of *Gwyrthyeu e Wynvydedic Veir*. Further light is shed on the text and its transmission in J. Fife,

'The Syntax of the Middle Welsh *Mair o'r Aifft*', *ib.*, 237–54. The aim of R. Iestyn Daniel, *A Medieval Welsh Mystical Treatise*, Aberystwyth, Research Papers of UWCASWC, 40 pp., is to present to non-Welsh readers the 14th-c. prose treatise on mysticism, *Ymborth yr Enaid*. Daniel reaffirms his view that it is largely an original composition and argues that it shows close affinities with texts such as the bardic grammars and the verse translation of the *Officium Parvum* and that some passages share stylistic characteristics with the *Mabinogion*. He closes by calling for a reconsideration of the dating of these tales.

S. Davies, 'Cyfieithu's Mabiongion', *YB*, 23:16–30, is a thought-provoking discussion on the translation into English of the medieval native tales of Wales, drawing on the comments of past translators of these texts and on recent theories in the field of translation studies. M. P. Bryant-Quinn, 'Adeiledd dioddefaint: sylwadau ar rai themâu yn yr ail Gainc', *YB*, 23:31–43, suggests, on the basis of an enlightening study of the structure of PKM 2, that the author of the Four Branches was mainly concerned with the nature of human society and with the boundaries which man has to adhere to in order to survive. Two more studies of the structure of PKM are provided in S. Ito-Morino, 'The sense of ending in the *Four Branches of the Mabinogi*', *ZCP*, 49–50:341–48, a brief analysis of the idealogical framework of PKM in which particular attention is paid to the use of the feast as an 'ending mark' to episodes within the tales, and M. Goldwasser,' What drives the *Mabinogi*?', *Procs* (Harvard), 14:49–57, where the driving mechanism behind the creation of PKM is identified as 'the manifestation of uncontrolled excess, mediated through the act of disappearance'. F. Winward, 'Some aspects of the women in *The Four Branches*', *CMCS*, 34:77–106, explores the portrayal of the female characters in PKM concluding that it is their manipulation of social convention, together with a measure of authorial sympathy, that makes them so much more memorable than their male counterparts. D. H. Evans, 'Cyfeiriad at Chwedl Blodeuwedd', *LlC*, 20:144, contains an additional reference to an oral version of the tale of Blodeuwedd found in a poem by Lewys Menai. S. Zimmer, 'Sprachliche Archaismen in *Culhwch ac Olwen*', *ZCP*, 49–50:1033–53, discusses lexical, morphophonematic, syntactic, and stylistic characteristics of *Culhwchac Olwen* which seem to reflect usages of the poetic tradition or of earlier stages of the language.

In *The Horse in Celtic Culture: Medieval Welsh Perspectives*, ed. Sioned Davies and Nerys Ann Jones, Cardiff, Univ. of Wales Press, xvi + 190 pp., use is made of Welsh literary sources in the study of medieval horses and horsemanship. Its chapters include R. Bromwich, 'The triads of the horses' (102–20), S. Davies, 'Horses in the *Mabinogion*' (121–40), N. A. Jones, 'Horses in medieval Welsh court poetry' (82–101) and B. O. Huws, 'Praise lasts longer than a horse': poems of request and thanks for horses' (141–61). Light is shed on the figure of Rhiannon in PKM 1 and her relationship with Celtic goddess Epona in J. Wood, 'The horse in Welsh folklore: a boundary image in custom and narrative' (162–82).

D. Huws, 'Llyfrau Cymraeg yn yr Oesoedd Canol', *Cof Cenedl*, 12:1–32 is a masterly survey of medieval manuscripts containing Welsh material which looks especially at the identity and cultural background of the scribes and at the social context of the production of the manuscripts. C. James, 'Ysgrifydd anhysbys: proffil personol', *YB*, 23:44–72, demonstrates to what extent a medieval scribe can reveal himself through his work, by presenting a portrait of the anonymous copier of two mid 15th-c. lawbooks, BL Add 22,356, and NLW Llanstephan 116. One of the many approaches used by James is the study of dialect features found in the texts of the two manuscripts which place the scribe in the Teifi Valley. Analysis of dialect features is also employed in P. W. Thomas, 'Haenau *Breudwyt Maxen*: ymarferiad mewn archaeoleg destunol', *YB*, 23:73–99, in order to reconstruct as far as possible the textual history of *Breudwyt Maxen*. A. Breeze, 'A manuscript of Welsh poetry in Edward II's library', *NLWJ*, 30:129–31 examines the incipit of a lost Treasury manuscript deducing that it was an early 14th-c. copy of an anthology of religious and possibly secular verse by official court poets. G. Conway, 'Towards a cultural context for the eleventh-century Llanbadarn manuscripts', *Ceredigion*, 13:9–28, examines possible influences on the script and decoration of Ieuan ap Sulien's copy of Augustine's *De Trinitate* and Rhigyfarch's Psalter and Martyrology.

Carol Lloyd Wood, *An Overview of Welsh Poetry Before the Norman Conquest*, Lewiston-Queenston-Lampeter, The Edwin Mellen Press, iv + 118 pp., and Stephen S. Evans, *The Heroic Poetry of Dark-Age Britain*, Lanham–New York–London, University Press of America, 156 pp., both suffer because of their authors' obvious lack of first hand knowledge of early Welsh poetry. The former is derivative, twenty years out of date in its references and peppered with inaccuracies, the latter's claims are based on slender evidence and a rather literal and simplistic interpretation of *Cynfeirdd* poetry. Equally disappointing, but for different reasons, is Andrew Breeze, *Medieval Welsh Literature*, Dublin, Four Courts Press, 174 pp., an unbalanced and rather self-indulgent survey written for the general reader but containing many gaps in its discussion and bibliography. It is not likely that this volume will surplant the new edition of *A Guide to Welsh Literature 1282–c. 1550 Volume II*, ed. A. O. H. Jarman and Gwilym Rees Hughes, Cardiff, Univ. of Wales Press, 386 pp., revised by Dafydd Johnston with up-to-date bibliographies.

LITERATURE SINCE 1500

By KATHRYN JENKINS, *Lecturer in Welsh, University of Wales, Lampeter*

Glanmor Williams, *Wales and the Reformation*, Cardiff, Univ. of Wales Press, xii + 440 pp., is a detailed and wide-ranging historical study of the circumstances surrounding the Reformation in Wales and contains a chapter on the translation of the Welsh Bible that notes that the Act of 1563 was a turning point in the history of the Welsh language and its literature. I. R. Edgar, *Llysieulyfr Salesbury*, Cardiff, Univ. of Wales Press, xxxvii + 216 pp., edits National Library of Wales MS 4581, noting in his introduction the context that inspired Salesbury to undertake such a study. *A Guide to Welsh Literature 1530–1700*, ed. R. G. Gruffydd, Cardiff, Univ. of Wales Press, 293 pp., is an exceptionally useful and valuable study dealing with such issues as the decline in the bardic tradition, the significance for Welsh nationhood of Renaissance prose and linguistic activity, and presents cogent arguments for the vitality of indigenous culture at this time. J. G. Jones, *Beirdd yr Uchelwyr a'r Gymdeithas yng Nghymru c. 1536–1640*, Denbigh, Gee, xxii + 243 pp., discusses the gulf between patron and poet and analyses the poets' awareness of unification images in their work. Id., 'Robert Holland a *Basilikon Doron* y Brenin Iago', *YB*, 22:161–88, brings to our attention an almost forgotten translator belonging to the second generation of Renaissance humanists in Wales who made a significant contribution to the religious prose of the period. C. L. Morgan, 'Portread Elis Gruffydd o'r Brenin Arthur', *ib.*, 23:118–32, studies an incomparable Arthurian source of the 16th c. that enlightens the modern-day reader on that century's opinion of Arthur and the oral traditions surrounding him. N. Lloyd, 'Catecism y Ficer Rhys Prichard', *ib.*, 164–83, analyses the religious and educational context to a work that is traditionally attributed to Prichard. G. W. Owen, 'Eschatoleg Morgan Llwyd', *ib.*, 22:189–203, emphasizes that while Llwyd certainly concentrated on the inner life of the soul as the cornerstone of his spirituality, he also considered heaven and hell as external and eternal phenomena.

R. L. Brown, 'Spiritual nurseries: Griffith Jones and the circulating schools', *NLWJ*, 30:27–50, looks at the theological and historical context of Jones's activities and notes his cultural connections with the leaders of Welsh Methodism. D. L. Morgan, 'Pa weledigaeth sy'n *Y Drych*', *Y Traethodydd*, 152:163–69, considers the historiographical aspects of Theophilus Evans's *magnum opus*, comparing it with *Y Ffydd Ddi-ffuant* and concluding that it contains no prophetical elements.

M. Morgan, 'Ellis Wynne, Kafka, Borges', *LlC*, 20:56–61, concludes that Wynne's vision of life is truly hell-like and that the nightmarish aspects of his work bear comparison to modern prose writers, particularly Kafka. *A People's Poetry: Hen Benillion*, trans. G. Jones, Bridgend, Seren Books, 170 pp., pays worthy tribute to T. H. Parry-Williams's pioneering work in 1940 in editing for a 20th-c. reader 17th-c. oral verses, the first printed collection of which appeared in 1710. Jones praises these self-contained stanzas and places them in their performative context noting their social function. G. Morgan, 'Baledi Dyffryn Conwy', *Canu Gwerin*, 20:2–12, surveys that form of oral performative literature in the Llanrwst and Trefriw area looking at topics, collectors, and performers from mid 18th c. to mid 19th c. D. Jones, 'Baledwyr, telynorion, a beirdd gwerin Arfon', *ib.*, 13–25, is a similar survey. E. M. White, ' "Myrdd o wragedd": merched a'r Diwygiad Methodistaidd', *LlC*, 20:62–74, looks at the role of women in the Methodist Revival, noting the portrayal of their spirituality in the literature of the period but concentrating on the implications of the nature of Methodist meetings to women's development in society. Id., ' "The world, the flesh and the devil" and the early Methodist Societies of south west Wales', *THSC*, 3:45–61, analyses the organization, spirituality, and conduct of religious meetings, recording accounts of Methodist dealings with the Mob and quoting evidence from the work of William Williams, Pantycelyn. D. S. Evans, 'Y peraidd ganiedydd Morgan Rhys', *YB*, 22:227–49, offers an appreciation of the work of the hymnist and considers some of the significant events of his life, particularly his educational activities, before commenting on the quality of his hymns. R. Rhys, ' "Yn erbyn tylau'n tynnu": llên a llafar Morgan Rhys, Cil-y-Cwm a Llanfynydd', *YB*, 23:184–207, is a comprehensive treatment of the themes and theology in the literature of Morgan Rhys. G. P. Owen, *Atgofion John Evans Y Bala: Y Diwygiad Methodistaidd ym Meirionnydd a Môn*, Caernarfon, Pantycelyn, 158 pp., is an exceptionally detailed study of the Methodism of the town of Bala as observed by John Evans and includes the text of the discourse between Scrutator and Senex, which is Thomas Charles's record of his dealings with Evans, 1799–1813. A. C. Lake, 'Rhys Jones: y golygydd a'r bardd', *YB*, 22:204–26, notes the background to the publication in 1773 of *Gorchestion Beirdd Cymru*, but further discusses the poetry of the editor himself who was clearly steeped in the traditional art of *cywyddau*. A. Llwyd, *Goronwy Ddiafael, Goronwy Ddu: Cofiant Goronwy Owen 1723–1769*, Swansea, Barddas, 464 pp., is an impressive study of the life, the disproportionate influence of literary criticism, and the poetry of the leader of the neo-classical movement in Welsh poetry.

J. Aaron, ' "Anadnabyddus neu weddol-anadnabyddus": cyd-awduresau Ann Griffiths yn hanner cyntaf y bedwaredd ganrif ar bymtheg', pp. 103–35 of *Cof Cenedl*, 12, looks at devotional literature by women in the 19th c. and in particular the work of Jane Hughes, daughter of John Hughes, Pontrobert, who was Ann Griffiths's theological adviser. Jane Hughes, it appears, wrote a substantial body of work and is one of the few authors of her period to display the continuing influence of religious passion first observed in the mid 18th c. during the Methodist Revival. E. R. L. Jones, 'Wil Bryan a Twm Nansi', *Taliesin*, 98:72–86, considers the similar roles taken by two characters in different novels by Daniel Owen. D. B. Rees, 'Gwalchmai (1802–1897)', *Barddas*, 239:10–13, recounts the career of an almost forgotten poet who achieved considerable notoriety in his day and who was influenced by Caledfryn. M. Ellis, 'Cyfeillion awenyddgar', *Y Casglwr*, 59:11–13, deals with the literary activities of a learned group of parsons. D. L. Hughes, 'Caneuon y degwm', *ib.*, 60:16–17, looks at the protest songs at the time of the tithe campaigns. P. H. Jones, ' "We only publish what we think will pay for publishing": agweddau ar hanes Hughes a'i Fab, Wrecsam, 1820–1920', *THSC*, 3:118–35, discusses the output of an influential Welsh press with particular reference to literary and religious publications, noting their pioneering spirit in publishing the novels of Daniel Owen.

J. Hunter, 'Y nos, y niwl a'r ynysig: estheteg fodernaidd T. Gwynn Jones', *Taliesin*, 98:37–54, suggests that the poet's medieval predilections were not an escape from modern society. B. L. Jones and G. Thomas, *R. Williams Parry*, Cardiff, Univ. of Wales Press, x + 188 pp., present the first full biography of the poet whose work is considered to be the epitome of Romanticism in Welsh, based on his letters and articles in magazines. The volume also includes critical material on his work. T. E. Prichard, 'I'r addfwyn rhowch orweddfa', *Barddas*, 244:42–44, looks at the family history behind R. Williams Parry's memorial *englyn* to his aunt. E. W. James, ' "Osborne druan!"': gohebiaeth R. Williams Parry a Leila Megane', *Taliesin*, 99:32–52, is a comprehensive account of the circumstances surrounding the said correspondence. Id., ' "Digymar yw fy mro": R. Williams Parry a Gwynfor, "yr hen actor" ', *YB*, 23:208–40, discusses the friendship of the poet with a notable figure of the first half of this century, namely Thomas Owen Jones. R. G. Gruffydd, 'Saunders Lewis ar y ffordd i Emaus', *ib.*, 22:250–54, suggests that Emaus in the poem is a symbol of the gradual disappearance of Christian civilization in the West in the 20th c. B. Griffiths, '*The Eve of Saint John* and the significance of the stranger in the plays of Saunders Lewis', *Welsh Writing in English*, 3:63–77, considers Irish influence, particularly

Synge, in Lewis's use in his theatre of the character of the unusual outsider who challenges the hero or, more often, the heroine. G. Davies, 'Rhagfur a rhagfarn', *Taliesin*, 100:61–77, looks at the possibility of anti-Semitic attitudes in the work of Saunders Lewis, T. S. Eliot, and Simone Weil, concluding that Lewis's opinions were formed by attitudes toward Wales at this time. M. Morgan, 'Rhwystrau ym *Monica*', *YB*, 23:263–69, analyses the open door as a motif in Lewis's prose and suggests that he feared his own sexuality. B. O. Hughes, 'Cyfieithiad Thomas Parry o olygfa gyntaf y ddrama *Saint Joan* gan George Bernard Shaw', *NLWJ*, 30:107–25, is an appreciation of Parry's work as translator and notes his general interest in English drama. *Goreuon Storïau Kate Roberts*, ed. H. P. Jones, Denbigh, Gee, 189 pp., is a collection of 23 of Roberts's short stories. The Introduction compares her to Chekhov in her delineation of common humanity and also presents her as stoic in the face of tragedy. F. Rhydderch, 'Cyrff yn cyffwrdd: darlleniadau erotig o Kate Roberts', *Taliesin*, 99:86–97, uses Roland Barthes to study the portrayal of the mother's body and the role of women in Roberts's work. G. Miles, 'D. Tecwyn Lloyd a Gwenallt: beirniad blaenllaw a bardd yr adwaith', *Barn*, 414–15:74–77, pays tribute to the former and analyses the poetry of the latter. *D. Tecwyn Lloyd 1914–1992*, ed. E. Edwards, Swansea, Barddas, 76 pp., is a further volume in the *Bro a Bywyd* series. R. Chapman, *W. Ambrose Bebb*, Cardiff, Univ. of Wales Press, 207 pp., is a biography of one of Wales's most noted men of letters in the first half of this century. The variety of Bebb's literary activity is noted and the biography is based on the author's unrivalled access to his diaries. S. Richards, 'Waldo: rhai o'i eiriau mawr', *YB*, 23:241–62, looks at poetic diction and notes Waldo's predilection for abstract nouns. M. Strange, 'Gwilym R. Jones fel cystadleuydd eisteddfodol', *Barddas*, 242:25–31, concentrates on the poet's winning compositions at the National Eisteddfod. M. W. Thomas, 'Pennar Davies y llenor', *Y Traethodydd*, 152:83–88, notes the influence of confessional Nonconformity on Davies's extreme and exceptional literary imagination.

G. Williams, 'Hiroshima a'r holocaust: archwilio ymateb llenyddiaeth Gymraeg', *Taliesin*, 100:105–17, considers the political engagement of Welsh poets and surveys the literature produced during 1939–45. J. Schimanski, 'Hen wraig y Bala', *Barn*, 414–15:72–73, analyses the implications of Islwyn Ffowc Ellis's novel, *Wythnos yng Nghymru Fydd*. D. D. Morgan, 'Gweledigaeth gyfannol Bobi Jones: gwerthfawrogiad beirniadol', *LlC*, 20:120–37, is a theological study of Jones's Calvinism as displayed in his literary criticism. S. L. Jones, 'Ambell nofel wledig', *ib.*, 108–19, analyses Welsh writers' usages of landscape and considers the presentation of rural issues together with the tendency to eulogize pre-industrial Wales. C. M. Jones, 'Golwg ar y llafar a'r llenyddol', *TB*, 23:270–77, looks at the justification for writers' use of colloquial language and suggests that only a talented writer could today maintain the quality of his work and make realistic use of such language. D. Johnston, 'Making history in two languages: *Y Pla* and *Griffri*', *Welsh Writing in English*, 3:118–33, looks at the work of two post-modern novelists, W. O. Roberts and Christopher Meredith, both of whose second novels have medieval settings, and analyses their attitudes to tradition and society. Bobi Jones, 'Pa bryd y bu ôl-foderniaeth?', *Barddas*, 241:2–3, considers the intellectual challenges of post-modernism. E. Lewis, 'Y beirniad a llysoedd barn', *Barn*, 414–15:68–69, tries to establish the nature of literary criticism at work in the National Eisteddfod. Marion Eames, *A Private Language?: a Dip into Welsh Literature*, Llandysul, Gomer, 202 pp., is an outline survey in 19 chapters and describes highlights in Welsh literature for the newcomer to the tradition. *Y Patrwm Amryliw: Cyfrol 1*, ed. R. Rhys, Swansea, Barddas, 279 pp., contains 23 short portrayals of varying quality of a mixed collection of this century's poets. A. Llwyd, *Y Grefft o Greu*, Swansea, Barddas, 308 pp., is a worthwhile collection of critical essays on poetic art in general and individual poets and poems in particular; much emphasis is placed on textual analysis and reader response. *Y Bywgraffiadur Cymreig 1951–1970*, ed. Brynley F. Roberts, London, Honourable Society of Cymmrodorion, xvi + 304 pp., is an invaluable biographical index to eminent Welshmen and women during most of the third quarter of the century. *Cydymaith i Lenyddiaeth Cymru*, ed. Meic Stephens, Cardiff, Univ. of Wales Press, xiii + 831 pp., is a new edition of a reference work first published in 1986 and does much to compensate for the former's omissions, but still contains many unexpected bibliographical references and entries of uneven quality.

II. BRETON AND CORNISH STUDIES

By Humphrey Lloyd Humphreys, *School of Modern Languages,
University of Wales, Lampeter*

1. Breton

There are a number of works dealing with sociological aspects of
Breton. F. Broudic, *L'Interdiction du breton en 1902 — la IIIe République
contre les langues régionales*, Spézet, Coop Breizh, 183 pp., examines in
considerable detail the situation of the language and the attitudes of
the parties involved, on the basis of the only substantial and
reasonably systematic direct documentation to be had on the
linguistic situation — that generated by the conflict between Church
and State. *Le français, le breton, l'école — Actes du Colloque de Trégarvan
(1994)*, Trégarvan, Musée de l'école rurale en Bretagne, 168 pp., in
addition to some 20 pages of discussion contains the following five
articles: H. Cadiou, 'Présence de la langue bretonne dans l'enseignement' (15–24), F. Broudic, 'Breton et français au XIXe siècle: les
pratiques scolaires' (27–42), C. Brunel, 'Le comité de préservation
du breton — entre raison d'Etat et raison d'Eglise' (53–90), C. Le
Du, 'Les pratiques pédagogiques à l'égard du breton à l'école
publique et privée (1900–1950)' (93–115), R. Le Coadic, 'Paroles de
marins-pêcheurs, d'agriculteurs et de chefs d'entreprises à propos de
la langue bretonne' (119–49). A new periodical, *Cahiers de sociolinguistique*, comes from Rennes U.P., vol. 1, *Langues et parlers de l'Ouest*, is
mainly concerned with matters of Romance interest but also contains
J. Le Dû, 'La situation linguistique de la Basse-Bretagne' (129–43), in
which he returns to the question of *badumes*, standards, and the
problematical norm, and F. Favereau, 'Poullaouen revisité:
1984–1994. Impressions d'enquête de terrain sur la pratique du
breton dans le Poher' (145–58), examines changes largely through
the eyes of residents. J. Le Dû, 'Le Breton au XXe siècle: renaissance
ou création?', *ZCP*, 49–50:414–31, is wider in scope than the title
suggests, for it presents, concisely but with deep reflection, key factors
concerning the material sociocultural functions of Breton and
conflicting attitudes towards the language.

F. Favereau, *Grammaire du breton contemporain / Yezhadur ar brezhoneg a
vremañ*, Morlaix, Skol Vreizh, 478 pp., is a very substantial work
which presents in a critical perspective not only what is too often
simplistically labelled 'standard' morphology and syntax, but fairly
systematically identifies more localized usages or generalized usages
not considered respectable from a puristic standpoint. This means
that there is considerable graphic variation, arising partly from the

use of original spelling in quotations, partly from the fact that a number of dialectal variants are often given. The basic spelling used is the majority *peurunvan*, the apostrophes so numerous in the large number of variants that they could perhaps have been replaced by superscript versions of missing 'standard' letters. There is a high ratio of concrete examples to commentary, but a certain lack of clarity arising from the density of detailed information that could often have been compensated by much more use of careful tabulations and specific status labelling. A real weakness is the complete absence of any explicit phonological presentation and this probably accounts for the fact that the initial mutations are oddly housed in a corner of the section dealing with the noun phrase. Source references within the text are numerous but neglect certain important works; the bibliography is compendious though not without a few omissions. This is a work of major importance, attempting pretty successfully a polylectal presentation of Breton with its centre of gravity in the central diagonal rather than the extreme north-west. P. Le Besco, *Parlons breton — langue et culture*, Paris, L'Harmattan, 211 pp., is on a very much smaller scale, being a summary presentation of 'standard' Breton; although sometimes carelessly put together it has a number of positive features, such as an attempt to put Breton into its sociolinguistic context.

H. Pilch, 'Word formation in Welsh and Breton', *ZCP*, 48:29–88, contains a number of valid observations, though frequent approximations and inaccuracies in the basic data for both languages rather suggest the quack — particularly preposterous is the claim that the everyday word *kroazhent* 'crossroads', 'must have been loan-translated . . . from W[elsh] *croesffordd*'. R. Delaporte, 'An anvioù tud e-keñver ar yezhadur hag ar reizhskrivadur', *Hor Yezh*, 210:5–20, discusses grammatical aspects of surnames and provides a corpus of over 400 names for which feminine and plural forms are indicated.

P. Le Besco, 'Le breton de Belle-Ile-en-Mer, 2ᵉ partie', *ZCP*, 48:89–258 (see *YWMLS*, 54:594), concludes with a glossary of some 2,500 words, including paradigms and a number of place names, and a selection of texts. A. Heusaff, *Geriaoueg Sant-Ivi (Kernev-Izel)*, Lesneven, Hor Yezh, 1996, 333 pp., is a glossary of well over 2,000 words compiled largely during the author's prolonged absence from his native parish and representing the usage of the 30s. Glossing and definitions are quite variable in their precision and the approximately phonological transcription becomes morphophonological in some cases; however, this is a generally useful piece of work. G. Goyat, *Chañsoniou eur Vigouden — étude d'un répertoire*, Brest, Emgleo Breiz–Ar Skol Vrezoneg, 442 pp., gives phonemic transcriptions of 15 songs, identifying non-local forms and in particular the melody-induced distortions which distance the phonology of orally transmitted song from that of speech. Quite a long section demonstrates the phonological oppositions observed by this native speaker who is also a sound musicologist.

G. Le Menn has started the publication of an important body of pre-modern lexicographic material, reproducing the original texts and making the corpus more accessible by providing a full index working from modern spellings. Two of these are dictionaries: *Le Premier Dictionnaire vannetais (Pierre de Châlons, 1723)*, n.p. [Spézet], Skol, 1996, 511 pp., text (39–219), presentation (7–39) and index (221–510). *Les Dictionnaires français-breton et breton-français du R. P. Julien Maunoir (1659)*, 2 vols, 1–252, 253–706 pp., n.p. [Spézet], Skol. The third is a literary text '*Cantiquou spirituel' (1642) — premier recueil de cantiques bretons*, ed., transl. and annotated, n.p. [Spézet], Skol, 1997, 517 pp., including preface (7–33), general index (320–501) and music (503–15–I. His-Ravier).

There are a number of other items of lexicological interest, notably Klerg [M. Le Clerc], 'Notennoù Klerg da c'heriadur Vallée', *Hor Yezh*, 209:5–52, which amount to about a 1,000 items; some of them are neologisms, many have been noted from the speech of traditional speakers. 'Notennoù Yezh' in *Hor Yezh* present individual words or lexemes, generally with full historical documentation often including etymological discussion. G. ar Menn, *c'hoantiz*, 210:45–47, *demat, mekaat*, 211:47–57, *fes(aj)*; H. ar Bihan, *kornandon, pant(enn), tata, Ben-*, 210:47–52, *eien*, 211:72; A. Botrel, *demat*, 210:52–55; D. Kervella, *ifomiñ, Ben-*, 211:57–58; G. Pennaod, OBr. *hebe*, MBr. *hambrouc*. TermBret gives short normative lists of plant and fungus names, *Hor Yezh*, 210:27–31 and 211:13–16.

In the field of toponomy, P. Pondaven and M. Madeg, *Renabl anoiou lehiou arvor Goueled Leon. Gwitalmeze, Lambaol — etre an Aberig hag Aod Vraz Lambaol*, Brest, Emgleo Breiz/Ar Skol Vrezoneg, 1997, 210 pp., continues work on the important oral inventory of coastal features. Ar Greizenn-Enklask war an Anvioù-lec'h, 'Treuzskrivadur anvioù-lec'h Breizh', *Hor Yezh*, 210:21–26, makes proposals for standardizing the Breton spellings of place names.

'Scenn comiq detachet', *Hor Yezh*, 211:17–34, is a secular theatrical fragment, perhaps of the 1790s, summarily presented and annotated and accompanied by a *peurunvan* transcription. L. Dujardin and R. Hemon, 'Dornskrid Botmeur ha Gwerz Santez Eoded', *ib.*, 211:35–45, presents the MS and gives the text of the 63 stanza narrative *cantiq* of about 1700, with subheadings but no notes. H. ar Bihan, 'An Dialog etre Arzur roe d'an Bretounet ha Guinglaff', *ib.*, 212:31–70, gives Pelletier's text of this isolated 250-line Arthurian vaticinatory poem of *c.* 1450, followed by an editorially reconstituted original; it is a pity that the two are not on facing pages. The text is abundantly annotated and there follows a section giving much fuller notes on the proper names occurring in it. The 19th-c. texts of four related pieces of oral literature are given in appendices.

2. CORNISH

L. Toorians, 'French loan-words containing nasal vowels in Middle Cornish', pp. 327–32 of A. Lubotsky, ed., *Sound Law and Analogy*, Leiden U.P., suggests that the doubling of nasal consonants in Middle Cornish words of French origin may be an indication of direct borrowing. This generally happens with final or preconsonantal nasals and is assumed to indicate perception of strong, if only allophonic, nasalization in French. L. Olson, 'Tyranny in *Beunans Meriasek*', *Cornish Studies*, 5:52–59, draws attention to the topicality of the political allusions in this work belonging to the aftermath of the 1497 rebellion.

III. IRISH STUDIES

EARLY IRISH

POSTPONED

MODERN IRISH

POSTPONED

IV. SCOTTISH GAELIC STUDIES

By RICHARD A. V. COX, *Lecturer in Celtic, University of Aberdeen*

Survey of the Gaelic Dialects of Scotland: Questionnaire Materials Collected for the Linguistic Survey of Scotland, ed. Cathair Ó Dochartaigh, 5 vols, Dublin, Dublin Institute for Advanced Studies, I. 1997, II–V. 1994, xiv + 178, iv + 453, iv + 453, iv + 447, iv + 441 pp., is the long-awaited first fruit of the work of the Gaelic section of the Linguistic Survey of Scotland, with phonetic material published directly from the field records of seven researchers, working mostly between 1950–63 under the leadership of the late Professor Kenneth Jackson, covering 207 collection points. Although it was originally intended to publish only the interpreted material, access to the raw data has advantages, not least because indigenous Gaelic speakers have now disappeared over the greater part of the area of survey collection (e.g. Aberdeenshire, the Trossachs, and St Kilda). The first, introductory, volume reviews the background and history of the survey and provides detailed and necessary guidance on transcriptions. W. Gillies, 'Scottish Gaelic *leugh* "read" ', *ZCP*, 49–50:243–49, discusses possible derivations for the /L'e:v/ forms of this word, adding *léamh-* (future/secondary future stem of Early Gaelic *lamaid* 'dares') with the developed sense 'experience' to the list. A. Breeze, 'Etymological notes on *Kirkcaldy*, *jocteleg* "knife", *kiaugh* "trouble", *striffen* "membrane" and *cow* "hobgoblin" ', *Scottish Language*, 16:97–110, stirs debate on the place name with a derivation from *Caer Caled with a personal name as specific; but given only the dismissive treatment of the suffix (surviving as -<y>) this is unlikely to be the final word on the subject. More convincing derivations are given of Burns' *kiaugh* (cf. Scots *in a kaugh* 'in a flutter') through Gaelic from Irish *cíach* [cf. G. *ceathach*], and of Scots *striffen* from Gaelic *sreabhann* (though the development [f] < [v] needs clarification). H. D. MacLennan, 'Shinty: some fact and fiction in the nineteenth century', *TGSI*, 59:148–274, cites some Gaelic shinty terminology. *Index of Celtic Elements in Professor W. J. Watson's 'The History of the Celtic Place-Names of Scotland' (1926) together with an Index of Subjects*, compiled by Eric B. Basden, Edinburgh, School of Scottish Studies, vii + 81 pp., is a printed version of the scarce 1978 typescript. Mutated, oblique or variant forms of words are indexed separately and accents and length marks are absent, but the preface notes that a future edition will correct these (large) inconveniences; it will also excise non-place name related elements, though the presence of these adds to the index's usefulness as a research tool. The subject index is idiosyncratic, and obvious omissions include sections on phonology and morphology. George Broderick, *Placenames of the Isle of Man*, III. *Sheading of Ayre*, Tübingen, Niemeyer, xli + 513 pp., continues this important survey. A. Falileyev, 'Irish references in early Scottish Gaelic grammars: a typological parallel', *Scottish Language*, 16:74–81, discusses innovations in the Scottish Gaelic grammatical tradition chiefly as reflected in William Shaw, *An Analysis of the Galic Language*, 1778, and Alexander Stewart, *Elements of Gaelic Grammar*, 1812, and draws attention to parallel developments in the Russian tradition.

C. Ó Baoill, 'The Scots-Gaelic interface', pp. 551–68 of *The Edinburgh History of the Scots Language*, ed. Charles Jones, Edinburgh U.P., x + 690 pp., is a clear and detailed survey of a range of points of contact between Gaelic and Scots, with discussion of the effects of this both on the Gaelic language and on perceptions of the language. A detailed analysis of possible infuences of Scottish Gaelic on Scots is found in C. I. Macafee and C. Ó Baoill, 'Why Scots is not a Celtic English', Tristram, *Celtic Englishes*, 245–86. R. D. Clement, 'Highland English', *ib.*, 301–07, is a looser study noting that 'Highland English . . . partakes of some of the phonetic features of Gaelic'. B. Bird, 'Past and present studies of Hebridean English phonology', *ib.*, 287–300, summarizes the work of others, especially Cynthia Shuken, in this field, noting some proposed Gaelic influences including preaspiration (non-phonemic) in Barra English (noted as not noticed by Borgstrøm). In J. Shaw, 'Gaelic and Cape Breton English', *ib.*, 308–19, attention is also drawn to the feature of preaspiration in the English speech of Inverness County, which is among a list of Gaelic influences, some tentative, proposed for this little researched area. Also in the New World, G. Shorrocks, 'Celtic influences on the English of Newfoundland and Labrador', *ib.*, 320–61, has an interesting section reviewing the small extent of Scottish Gaelic settlement, dating back to the 1840s, mostly via Cape Breton, in the Codroy Valley of Newfoundland, noting scope for further research on Gaelic influence on English there. G. Broderick, 'Manx English: an overview', *ib.*, 123–34, gives a broad account of the phonology of Manx English but also lists lexical borrowings and syntactical influences from Manx Gaelic. Also in the area of language contact, B. Sandnes, 'The Bu of Orphir, Burn of Gueth — a Gaelic pattern in Orkney place-names?', *Northern Studies*, 32:125–28, looks at the origin of the syntax of names such as those of the title and, arguing against W. F. N. Nicolaisen's earlier thesis that they are the result of Gaelic influence, unconvincingly favours a French rather than a Norse provenance. G. MacAoidh, 'Luchd-imrich Gaidhealach agus buaidh nan Gaidheal ann an Innis Tile', *Gairm*, 178:137–44, gives a summary account of evidence for Gaelic influence in Iceland.

N. MacGregor, 'Gaelic in Strathspey', *TGSI*, 59:488–606, is a social history of the language and its decline in the district, but its description of the dialect is unscientific and idiosyncratic. M. Caimbeul, '"An t-eilean beag riabhach": "eilean suairce na Gàidhlig" ', *ib.*, 59:21–48, is a partly reminiscing social history of the Island of Scalpay, Harris, with an emphasis on sea-faring and fishing. S. Walker, 'Gàidhlig an Cinntìr', *Gairm*, 180:327–28, continues his trawl through place names of Kintyre for evidence of Gaelic. C. N. Parsons, 'Naidheachd na Gàidhlig bho Albainn Nuaidh', *ib.*, 179:269–80, offers a short history on the resurgence of interest in Gaelic in Nova Scotia, on efforts to maintain the language, and on its position there today. Also in Canada, D. Livingston-Lowe, 'Some Gaelic place names of Upper and Lower Canada', *Garm Lu*, 20:12–14, is a useful starting point for sources on the history of the Gael in the region through its place names, which include commemoratively reused names (*Tobermory*), independently created names (*Am Baile Ùr*), as well as forms inspired by folk etymologies (*An t-Àth a Tuath* ← *Ottawa*). Debora Livingston-Lowe, 'The Gaelic-speaking community of Glengarry County, Ontario: a survey of the literature', *ib.*, 20:68–83, is a lightweight consideration of the sources for the social history of its area, including stories and incidents, travellers' account, fiction, and three Gaelic poems written by emigrants to Glengarry — though the significance of some of the images set in the context of homeland/exile verse is overplayed.

J. MacInnes, 'Looking at legends of the supernatural', *TGSI*, 59:1–20, lays a framework for the study of the nature and origin of, in particular, the *sìthichean* 'fairies' and the *samhla* or *co-choisiche*, the 'co-walker' or other self. D. Thomson, 'Influences on medieval thinking in the Gaelic world in Scotland, in the sixteenth century and later', pp. 17–26 of *The Middle Ages after the Middle Ages*, ed. Marie-Françoise Alamichel and Derek Brewer, Cambridge, ix + 166 pp., is a detailed summary of a range of aspects (both literate and oral) of Gaelic society of medieval provenance. Michael Newton, *Gaelic in Scottish History and Culture*, Belfast, An Clochán, iii + 37 pp., is a generalized, extended essay on its subject with tendencies of the propagandist tract. Vincent MacKee, *Gaelic Nations: Politics of the Gaelic Language in Scotland and Northern Ireland in the 20ᵗʰ Century*, London, The Bluestack Press, ix + 127 pp., focuses on the historical and contemporary politics of the language in both countries; it is a broad-brush description, with some misprints and a few errors of fact, overstating some recent developments, but noting the generally apolitical aspect of pro-Gaelic campaigning in Scotland compared to that in Northern Ireland. J. Leerssen, 'Celticism', Brown, *Celticism*, 1–20 is a theoretical discussion on the nature of Celticism which is described as a multi-genre, multinational phenomenon. D. Meek, 'Modern Celtic Christianity', *ib.*, 143–57, points to the unsound interpretations of the Celtic Church and of early Celtic literature and art, including Pictish, made by present-day Celtic Christianity in an exposé of the claims for the origins of this fashionable movement. G. Watson, 'Celticism and the annulment of history', *ib.*, 207–20, looks at the contribution in literature to the denial of history that the primitivist nature of Celticism ensures, noting also Iain Crichton Smith's own remark on 'a conservative force which drives Gaelic writers towards writing on Gaelic subject matter'. L. Gibbons, 'This sympathetic bond: Ossian, Celticism and colonialism', *ib.*, 273–91, also underlines the negative effect of Celticism and notes the influence of MacPherson's Ossian upon it: 'Celticism may be said to have achieved for Gaelic culture what the clearances did for the Highlands'. F. Stafford, 'Primitivism and the "primitive" poet: a cultural context for MacPherson's Ossian', *ib.*, 79–96, describes the literary and political environments in which MacPherson's 'Fragments of Ancient Poetry' appeared in 1760, and works toward an understanding of his motivation in producing 'an art form dictated by a sophisticated, urban culture's view of an alternative society'. M. Mac Craith, 'The forging of Ossian', *ib.*, 125–41, is a closer study of the steps taken by MacPherson toward the production of his 'forged' translations and contains a critically annotated bibliography. P. Sims-Williams, 'The invention of Celtic nature poetry', *ib.*, 97–124, makes passing reference to the influence of MacPherson's translations on the earliest translations from Irish in the 1780s. D. Droixhe, 'Ossian, Hermann and the Jew's Harp: images of the Celtic languages from 1600 to 1800', *ib.*, 21–33, notes a role of MacPherson's Ossian in the development of ideas about language. Gaskill, 'Herder, Ossian and the Celtic', *ib.*, 257–71, is a reminder of the broad influence of Ossian in German literary history, and examines the discerning fascination which the poet Johann von Herder had for the translations, and the extent to which he was influenced by MacPherson's mentor, Hugh Blair.

J. Bannerman, 'The Scottish takeover of Pictland and the relics of Columba', *Innes Review*, 48:27–44, is a closely argued case against the traditionally accepted view of a union between Picts and Scots in 842/3, and for a later date of 849 for what was conceived of then as a permanent Scots takeover of Pictland; it was in this context that the relics of Columba were divided and sent from Iona to new administrative church centres in Kells, for Ireland, and Dunkeld, for Scotland. There is an apparent gap between this period and the point at which the term *rí Alban* is used in preference to *rex Pictorum* in the annals, by the end of the 9th c., the context for which is discussed in Dauvit Broun, 'Dunkeld and the origin of Scottish identity', *ib.*, 48:112–24; one which needs to be filled. S. Taylor's survey in 'Seven-century Iona abbots in Scottish place names', *ib.*, 48:45–72, considers an earlier period from the abbacy of Columba's successor, Báithéne (d. 600), to that of Adomnán (d. 704), as well as the significance of Iona activity in the Athol area of the time. Benjamin T. Hudson, *Prophecy of Berchán*, Westport, Connecticut, Greenwood Press, xiii + 273 pp., is a valuable, new and complete edition of this poem following the fortunes of Irish and Scottish kings from the mid 9th to the late 11th centuries. Discussion of the literary context and significance of the prophetic genre, and of the historical context and reliability of the contents of the poem, underlines the importance of the text as an early source of Scottish history. D. E. Meek, "Norsemen and noble stewards": the Macsween poem in the Book of the Dean of Lismore', *CMCS*, 34:1–49, provides a welcome re-edition of this early 14th-c. poem as well as an analysis of its historical context and its literary position, and has an important bearing on the question of Norse-Gaelic contact. T. O. Clancy, 'Columba, Adomnán and the cult of saints in Scotland', *Innes Review*, 48:1–26, touches upon links between aspects of Gaelic hagiographical tradition and praise poetry. *Duanaire Colach 1537–1757*, ed. Colm Ó Baoill, Aberdeen, An Clò Gaidhealach, lv + 119 pp., is a collection of 17 mostly praise poems drawn from MS sources and associated with the Island of Coll. This Gaelic edition provides an introduction to the genre as well as to the subjects of the poems, and there are notes to the texts including the metres (from syllabic-based *rannaigheacht* to strophic) and airs. *General Robertson's Gaelic Manuscript*, ed. Colm Ó Baoill and Donald MacAulay, Aberdeen University Department of Celtic, v + 49 pp., is a detailed description of the MS, datable to the early 19th c. and written mostly in the old Gaelic hand, which belonged to William Robertson of Lude, near Blair Atholl, containing two previously unpublished poems and three Ossianic ballads (including two previously unpublished texts). M. Ní Annracháin, 'Vision and quest in Somhairle MacGill-Eain's "an Cuilithionn" ', *Lines Review*, 141:5–11, extends to this long poem her thesis on the interplay of vision and quest in Maclean's poetry. R. Black, 'Mac Mhaighstir Alastair in Rannoch: a reconstruction', *TGSI*, 59:341–419, is a very detailed examination of events and circumstances in Rannoch and surrounding the life of Alasdair Mac Mhaighstir Alasdair, establishing the poet as author of a series of notes written in 1739 upon a 17th-c. MS.

4

GERMANIC LANGUAGES

I. GERMAN STUDIES

LANGUAGE

By Charles V. J. Russ, *Reader in the Department of Language and Linguistic Science, University of York*

1. General

SURVEYS, COLLECTIONS, BIBLIOGRAPHIES

P. Stevenson, *The German-Speaking World*, London, Routledge, xx + 254 pp., is a textbook for students with tasks for them to do. The work is in three parts, covering ideas about German, variation in German, and current issues. Most of the topics are what linguists would agree on. There is an index of technical terms, one or two oversimplified, but a useful aid. The student will need to know the IPA for some sections of the book. The text is broken up with illustrative quotations and tasks at three levels: a quick reaction, a practical activity, and a more extensive study. This pedagogic method makes the text frustrating to read. Also, the demands of even the most elementary tasks are such that a teacher would be essential. The content assumes a semester: not all universities have these! Only time and experience will tell how successful this will prove to be, but it should be given a good chance. F. Debus, *Kleinere Schriften*, ed. H.-D. Grohmann and J. Hartig, 2 vols, Hildesheim, Olms, viii + 885 pp., is the collected works of a distinguished German linguist. The status of German in different countries features in U. Ammon, *Nationale Varietäten des Deutschen* (Studienbibliographien Sprachwissenschaft, 19), Heidelberg, Groos, 55 pp.; Id., 'Schwierigkeiten bei der Verbreitung der deutschen Sprache heute. Mit einem Ausblick auf die zukünftige Stellung des Deutschen in Europa', *Muttersprache*, 107:17–34; Id., 'Language-spread policy', *Language Problems and Language Planning*, 21:51–57; Id., 'Vorüberlegungen zu einem Wörterbuch der nationalen Varianten der deutschen Sprache', *Neue Forschungsarbeiten zur Kontaktlinguistik*, ed. W. W. Moelleken and P. J. Weber, Bonn, Dümmler, 1–9; U. Ammon, 'Gibt es eine österreichische Sprache?', *Unterrichtspraxis*, 29, 1996:131–36. The linguistic characteristics of German feature in T. Roelcke, *Sprachtypologie des Deutschen. Historische, regionale und funktionale Variation*, Berlin, de

Gruyter, 248 pp. The development of German studies is treated in *Germanistik als Kulturwissenschaft. Hermann Paul, 150. Geburtstag und 100 Jahre Deutsches Wörterbuch*, ed. A. Burkhardt and H. Henne, Braunschweig, Ars & Scientia, 94 pp., and *Funktionale Sprachbeschreibung in der DDR zwischen 1960 und 1990: Beiträge zur Bilanz und Kritik in der 'Potsdamer Richtung'*, ed. K. H. Siehr et al. (SST, 21), Frankfurt, Lang, 402 pp. Also noted: D. E. Zimmer, *Deutsch und anders: die Sprache in Modernisierungsfieber*, Reinbek, Rowohlt, 382 pp. The language of post-unification continues to be treated: *Probleme der Sprache nach der Wende. Beiträge des Kolloquiums in Rostock am 16. November 1996*, ed. I. Rösler and K. E. Sommerfeldt (SST, 23), Frankfurt, Lang, 160 pp.; J. Schiewe, 'Sprachwitz — Sprachspiel — Sprachrealität. Über die Sprache im geteilten und vereinten Deutschland', *ZGL*, 25 : 129–46; *Allgemeinwortschatz der DDR-Bürger: nach Sachgruppen geordnet und linguistisch kommentiert*, ed. M. Schröder and U. Fix (Sprache, Literatur und Geschichte, 14), Heidelberg, Winter, 197 pp.; *Von 'Buschzulage' und 'Ossinachweis': Ost-West-Deutsch in der Diskussion*, ed. R. Reiher and R. Lenz, Berlin, Aufbau, 1996, 320 pp.; and D. Herberg et al., *Schlüsselwörter der Wendezeit: Wörter-Buch zum öffentlichen Sprachgebrauch 1989–90* (Schriften des Instituts für deutsche Sprache, 6), Berlin, de Gruyter, vii + 521 pp.

The status and history of German in other countries receives attention in *Beiträge zur Geschichte der deutschen Sprache im Baltikum*, ed. G. Brandt (SAG, 339), 254 pp.; *Verstehen und Verständigung in Europa: Konzepte von Sprachenpolitik und Sprachdidaktik unter besonderer Berücksichtigung des Deutschen als Fremdsprache*, ed. H. Funk and G. Neuner (Deutsch als Fremdsprache: Mehrsprachigkeit), Berlin, Cornelsen, 1996, 242 pp.; M. Waas, *Language Attrition Downunder. German Speakers in Australia* (Studien zur allgemeinen und romanischen Sprachwissenschaft, 3), Frankfurt, Lang, 1996, 212 pp.; M. Zappe, *Das ethnische Zusammenleben in Südtirol: sprachsoziologische, sprachpolitische und soziokulturelle Einstellungen* (EH, XXI, 174), 1996, 321 pp.; and I. M. Tornqvist, *'Das hon ich von meiner Mama' — zu Sprache und ethnischen Konzepten unter Deutschstämmigen in Rio Grande do Sul* (USH, 137), x + 210 pp.

Aspects of written and spoken German are treated in M. Becker-Mrotzek, *Schreibentwicklung und Textproduktion: der Erwerb der Schreibfertigkeit am Beispiel der Bedienungsanleitung*, Opladen, Westdeutscher Vlg, 372 pp.; *Mündlichkeit und Schriftlichkeit im Deutschen*, ed. B. U. Biere and R. Hoberg (Studien zur deutschen Sprache. Forschungen des Instituts für deutsche Sprache, 5), Tübingen, Narr, 1996, 206 pp.; and C. Osburg, *Gesprochene und geschriebene Sprache: Aussprachestörungen und Schriftspracherwerb*, Baltmannweise, Schneider, ix + 205 pp. Politics rubs shoulders with language in **Politische Leitvokabeln in der Adenauer-Ära*, ed. K. Böke et al. (Sprache, Politik, Öffentlichkeit, 8), Berlin, de Gruyter, 1996, vii + 496; **Politische Betrachtungen einer Welt von Gestern. Öffentliche Sprache in der Zwischenkriegszeit*, ed. H. Bartenstein et al. (SAG, 279), 1995, 508 pp.; R. Reiter, 'Der "heimtückische" Witz im Dritten Reich als politisches Gleichnis', *Muttersprache*, 107:226–32; and J. Kilian, **Demokratische Sprache zwischen Tradition und Neuanfang: am Anfang des Grundrechte-Diskurses* (RGL, 186), viii + 410 pp.

Advertising language is the subject of A. Greule and N. Janich, **Sprache in der Werbung* (Studienbibliographien Sprachwissenschaft, 21), Heidelberg, Gross, 53 pp.

German as a foreign language occurs in many items: U. Häussermann and H-E. Piepho, **Aufgaben-Handbuch: Deutsch als Fremdsprache: Abriß einer Aufgaben- und Übungstypologie*, Munich, Iudicium, 1996, 528 pp.; J. S. Hohmann, **Deutschunterricht in SBZ und DDR 1945–1962: zur Geschichte und Soziologie sozialistischer Erziehung* (Beiträge zur Geschichte des Deutschunterrichts, 29), Frankfurt, Lang, 617 pp.; H. Helmers, **Didaktik der deutschen Sprache: Einführung in die muttersprachliche und literarische Bildung*, ed. J. Eckhardt and J. Diekneite, WBG, xi + 319 pp.; W. Knapp, **Schriftliches Erzählen in der Zweitsprache* (RGL, 185), xii + 275 pp.; K. U. Kickler, **Wortschatzerwerb im bilingualen Unterricht: Pilotstudie zur Evaluierung der lexikalischen Fähigkeiten bilingual unterrichteter Schüler* (Arbeitsberichte und Materialien zu bilingualem Unterricht und Immersion, 5), Kiel, l & f Vlg, 1995, 211 pp.; R. Hessky, 'Feste Wendungen — ein heißes Eisen? Einige phraseodidaktische Überlegungen für den DaF-Unterricht', *DaF*, 34:139–43; **Facharbeiter und Fremdsprachen: Fremdsprachenbedarf und Fremdsprachbenutzung in technischen Arbeitsfeldern: eine qualitative Untersuchung*, ed. E. Ros et al., Bielefeld, Bertelsmann, 1996, 93 pp.; S. Mahlstedt, **Zweisprachigkeitserziehung in gemischtsprachigen Familien: eine Analyse der erfolgsbedingenden Merkmale*, Frankfurt, Lang, 1996, 240 pp.; A. Stenzel, **Die Entwicklung der syntaktischen Kategorien Normen und Verb bei ein- und zweisprachigen Kindern* (Language Development, 20), Tübingen, Narr, 280 pp.; S. Luchtenberg, 'Zwei- und Mehrsprachigkeit in Kinder- und Jugendliteratur', *Muttersprache*, 107:168–86; K. Schramm, **Alphabetisierung ausländischer Erwachsener in der Zweitsprache Deutsch*, Münster, Waxmann, 1996, 179 pp.; **Deutsch für Ausländer: eine Bibliographie berufsbezogener Lehrmaterialien mit Kommentierung*, ed. G. Kühn, Bielefeld, Bertelsmann, 1996, 194 pp.; R. Esser, **'Etwas ist mir geheim geblieben am deutschen Referat': kulturelle Geprägtheit wissenschaftlicher Textproduktion und ihre Konsequenzen für den universitären Unterricht von Deutsch als Fremdsprache*, Munich, Iudicium, 1996,

266 pp.; D. Hansen, *Spracherwerb und Dysgrammatismus: Grammatik, Diagnostik und Therapie* (Uni-Taschenbücher, 1949), Munich, Reinhardt, 1996, 249 pp.; *Multimedia — eine neue Herausforderung für den Fremdsprachenunterricht*, ed. M. Hahn et al. (Deutsch als Diskussion in der Diskussion, 3), Frankfurt, Lang, 1996, vii + 278 pp.; E. Kwakernaak, *Grammatik im Fremdsprachenunterricht: Geschichte und Innovationsmöglichkeiten: am Beispiel Deutsch als Fremdsprache in den Niederlanden* (Deutsch, 1), Amsterdam, Rodopi, 1996, 473 pp.; *Sprachenpolitik Deutsch als Fremdsprache: Länderberichte zur internationalen Diskussion* (Deutsch. Studien zum Sprachunterricht und zur interkulturellen Didaktik, 2), Amsterdam, Rodopi, 103 pp.; *Deutsch in Japan: Interkulturalität und Skepsis zwischen Vergangenheit und Zukunft: Dokumentation eines Seminars in Minakami, Japan*, ed. G. Gad, Bonn, Deutscher Akademischer Austauschdienst, 216 pp.; and R. Köppe, *Sprachtrennung im frühen bilingualen Erstspracherwerb Französisch/Deutsch* (TBL, Serie A. Language Development, 21), x + 309 pp.

Translation studies and metaphors feature in D. Pirazzini, *Cinque miti della metafora nella Überseztungswissenschaft: problemi di traduzione delle imagini figurate nella copia di lingue; tedesco (lingua di partenza) — italiano (lingua d'arrivo)* (EH, IX, 27), 1996, 242 pp.; I. Kurz, *Simultandolmetschen als Gegenstand der interdisziplinären Forschung*, Vienna, WUV, 1996, 201 pp.; C. Baldauf, *Metapher und Kognition: Grundlagen einer neuen Theorie der Alltagsmetapher* (Sprache in der Gesellschaft, 12), Frankfurt, Lang, 428 pp.; M. Ulrich, *Die Sprache als Sache: Primärsprache, Metasprache, Übersetzung: Untersuchungen zum Übersetzen und zur Übersetzbarkeit anhand von deutschen, englischen und vor allem romanischen Materialien* (Romanica Monacensia, 49), Tübingen, Narr, xxii + 434 pp.; and I. Stengel-Hauptvogel, *Juristisches Übersetzen Spanisch-Deutsch: Immobilienkaufverträge* (Forum für Fachsprachenforschung, 41), Tübingen, Narr, xii + 229 pp.

Psychological aspects of language surface in J. Grabowski, *Bedeutung — Konzept, Bedeutungskonzepte. Theorie und Anwendung in Linguistik und Psychologie* (Psycholinguistische Studien), Opladen, Westdeutscher Vlg, 1996, 309 pp.; *Kognitive Aspekte der Sprache: Akten des 30. Linguistischen Kolloquiums, Gdansk 1995*, ed. K.A. Sroka (LA, 360), 1996, xxi + 306 pp.; and F. Pulvermüller, *Neurobiologie der Sprache: gehirntheoretische Überlegungen und empirische Befunde zur Sprachverarbeitung* (Psychologia universalis, n.s., 2), Lengerich, Pabst, 1996, 132 pp.

GENERAL LINGUISTICS, PRAGMATICS, AND TEXTLINGUISTICS

Some general linguistic and sociolinguistic items are P. Bærentzen, 'Zur Handhabung des linguistischen Instrumentariums', *Fest. Bergmann*, 199–206; N. Dittmar, *Grundlagen der Soziolinguistik: ein*

Arbeitsbuch mit Aufgaben (Konzepte der Sprach- und Literaturwissenschaft, 57), Tübingen, Niemeyer, xiv + 359 pp.; H. J. Simon, 'Die Diachronie der deutschen Anredepronomina aus Sicht der Universalienforschung', *STUF*, 50:267–81; and F. Malliga, **Tendenzen in der geschlechtsabhängigen Sprachverwendung und Spracheinschätzung: am Beispiel der Stadt Villach in Kärnten* (Schriften zur deutschen Sprache in Österreich, 19), Frankfurt, Lang, 243 pp.

Dialogue studies include F. Hundsnurscher, 'Der definite positive Bescheid', *Fest. Werner*, 129–41, E. Weigand, 'Dialogic competence and consciousness', *ib.*, 287–93, and **Dialoganalyse V.: Referate der 5. Arbeitstagung, Paris 1994*, ed. E. Pietri (Beiträge zur Dialogforschung, 15), Tübingen, Niemeyer, ix + 536 pp. Conversational analysis encompasses W. Nothdurft, *Schlichtung. 2. Konfliktstoff. Gesprächanalyse der Konfliktbearbeitung in Schlichtungsgesprächen* (Schriften des Instituts für deutsche Sprache, v, 2) Berlin, de Gruyter, vi + 195 pp.; **Schlichtung. 3. Schlichtungsgespräche: ein Textband mit einer exemplarischen Analyse*, ed. P. Schröder (Schriften des Instituts für deutsche Sprache, v, 3), Berlin, de Gruyter, vi + 277 pp.; B. Schönherr, **Syntax — Prosodie — nonverbale Kommunikation: empirische Untersuchungen zur Interaktion sprachlicher und parasprachlicher Ausdrucksmittel im Gespräch* (RGL, 182), xii + 233 pp.; K. Bremer, **Verständigungsarbeit. Problembearbeitung und Gesprächsverlauf zwischen Sprechern verschiedener Muttersprachen* (TBL, 420), viii + 249 pp.; *'Jeder deutsch kann das verstehen': Probleme im interkulturellen Arbeitsgespräch*, ed. R. Kokemohr and H.-C. Koller (Interaktion und Lebenslauf, 11), Weinheim, Deutsch Studien Vlg, 1996, 467 pp.; **Sprechen — reden — mitteilen: Prozesse allgemeiner und spezifischer Sprechkultur*, ed. S. Thiel (Sprache und Sprechen, 32), Munich, Reinhardt, 1996, 339 pp.; K. Luttermann, **Gesprächsanalytisches Integrationsmodell am Beispiel der Strafgerichtsbarkeit* (Rechtslinguistik, 1), Münster, Lit, 1996, 480 pp.; **Gesprächsrhetorik: rhetorische Verfahren im Gesprächsprozeß* (Studien zur deutschen Sprache: Forschungen des Instituts für deutsche Sprache, 4), Tübingen, Narr, 1996, 421 pp.; A. P. Müller, **'Reden ist Chefsache.' Linguistische Studien zu sprachlichen Formen sozialer 'Kontrolle' in innerbetrieblichen Arbeitsbesprechungen* (Studien zur deutschen Sprache, 6), Tübingen, Narr, 371 pp.; K. Steyer, **Reformulierungen: sprachliche Relationen zwischen Äußerungen und Texten im öffentlichen Diskurs* (Studien zur deutschen Sprache, 7), Tübingen, Narr, 294 pp.; K. Bührig, **Reformulierende Handlungen: zur Analyse sprachlicher Adaptierungsprozesse in institutioneller Kommunikation* (Kommunikation und Institution: Untersuchungen, 23), Tübingen, Narr, 1996, xii + 325 pp.; A. Deppermann, **Glaubwürdigkeit in Konflikt: rhetorische Techniken in Streitgesprächen. Prozeßanalysen von Schlichtungsgesprächen* (EH, xxi, 184), 350 pp.; and I. Bose, **Zur temporalen Struktur frei gesprochener Texte* (Forum Phoneticum, 58), Frankfurt, Hector, 1994, 176 pp.

The linguistic study of a variety of texts can be seen from C. Diem et al., 'Usertalk — Beobachtungen und Überlegungen zu einer Sprache über den Computer', *Muttersprache*, 107 : 149–67; J. Bauer, **Der 'Leittext' als (fach-)textlinguistisches Phänomen: Analyse und Optimierungsmöglichkeiten einer betriebsinternen Textsorte* (Forum Linguisticum, 34), Frankfurt, Lang, 414 pp.; W. Franke, 'Ratgebende Aufklärungstexte. Überlegungen zur linguistischen Beschreibung ratgebender Beiträge der Massenmedien', *ZGL*, 24, 1996 : 249–72; *'*Kohle' für die Kohle! Textoptimierung mit Hilfe der Sprechaktsanalyse am Beispiel von Pressemitteilungen der Ruhrkohle AG*, ed. M. Hack (Kleine Schriften zur Betriebslinguistik, 3), Paderborn, IFB-Vlg, 1996, 57 pp.; R. Geier and J. Sternkopf, 'Ich schwöre . . . Linguistische Anmerkungen zur Textsorte Fahneneid', *Muttersprache*, 107 : 217–25; E. Ockel, 'Wie Sprach- und Sprech- und Literaturwissenschaft beim Textverstehen zusammenwirken', *ib.*, 243–56; **Texte im Text: Untersuchungen zur Intertextualität und ihren sprachlichen Formen*, ed. G. Hassler (Studium Sprachwissenschaftliche Beihefte, 29), Münster, Nodus, 263 pp.; **Dortmunder Korpus der spontanen Kindersprache*, ed. K. R. Wagner and S. Wiese, *Teilkorpus Nicole 1.8* (Kindersprache, 12), Essen, Die Blaue Eule, 1996, xiii + 185 pp.; and *Teilkorpus Andreas 2.1* (Kindersprache, 13), Essen, Die Blaue Eule, 1996, xiii + 270 pp.

2. HISTORY OF THE LANGUAGE

There is a new edition of W. Schmidt, *Geschichte der deutschen Sprache*, 7th edn, Stuttgart, Hirzel, 1996, 383 pp., which brings the bibliography up to date and keeps the tried and trusted structure. The buoyant state of the study of the history of German can be measured by *Sprachgeschichte des Neuhochdeutschen. Gegenstände, Methoden, Theorien*, ed. A. Gardt et al. (RGL, 156), 1995, x + 468 pp., which contains the following articles: K. J. Mattheier, 'Sprachgeschichte des Deutschen: Desiderate und Perspektiven' (1–18); U. Knoop, 'Ist der Sprachwandel ein historisches Phänomen? Überlegungen zu den Gegenständen der Sprachgeschichtsschreibung' (19–38); P. Von Polenz, 'Sprachsystemwandel und soziopragmatische Sprachgeschichte in der Sprachkultivierungsepoche' (39–67); F. Hermanns, 'Sprachgeschichte als Mentalitätsgeschichte. Überlegungen zu Sinn und Form historischer Semantik' (69–101); V. V. Pavlov, 'Die Form-Funktion-Beziehungen in der deutschen substantivischen Zusammensetzung als Gegenstand der systemorientierten Sprachgeschichtsforschung' (103–25); H. Schmidt, 'Wörter im Kontakt. Plädoyer für historische Kollokationsuntersuchungen' (127–43); A. Gardt, 'Das Konzept der *Eigentlichkeit* im Zentrum barocker Sprachtheorie' (145–67);

O. Reichmann, 'Die Konzepte von "Deutlichkeit" und "Eindeutigkeit" in der rationalistischen Sprachtheorie des 18. Jahrhunderts' (169–97); U. Hass-Zumkehr, 'Daniel Sanders und die Historiographie der Germanistik' (199–225); T. Roelecke, 'Lexikalische Bedeutungsrelationen und Sprachwandel' (227–48); U. Maas, 'Ländliche Schriftkultur in der Frühen Neuzeit' (249–77); J. Gessinger, 'Kommunikative Verdichtung und Schriftlichkeit: Lesen, Schreiben und gesellschaftliche Organisation im 18. Jahrhundert' (279–306); I. Reiffenstein, '"Oberdeutsch" und "Hochdeutsch" in Bayern im 18. Jahrhundert' (307–17); P. Wiesinger, 'Die sprachlichen Verhältnisse und der Weg zur allgemeinen deutschen Schriftsprache in Österreich im 18. und frühen 19. Jahrhundert' (319–67); A. Linke, 'Zur Rekonstruierbarkeit sprachlicher Vergangenheit: Auf der Suche nach der bürgerlichen Sprachkultur im 19. Jahrhundert' (369–97); H. H. Munske, 'Ist eine europäische Sprachgeschichtsschreibung möglich?' (399–411); C. Schmidt, 'Affinitäten und Konvergenzen in der Entwicklung westeuropäischer Sprachen. Für eine soziokulturell ausgerichtete Wortbildungslehre der romanischen Nationalsprachen und des Deutschen' (413–37); R. Willemyns, 'Sprachliche Variation und Sprachgeschichtsforschung: Überlegungen zur Historiographie des Niederländischen' (439–54); and finally a podium discussion 'Was soll Gegenstand der Sprachgeschichtsforschung sein?' (455–59). All the authors provide an informative and stimulating impulse to the subject.

Fest. Arndt contains the following general items on the history of German: R. Brandt, 'Die Eselsbrücken der Periodisierung oder das wahre Walten des Weltgeistes in der deutschen Sprachgeschichte — Anmerkungen zu einem sprachextern-sprachinternkriteriellen Korrelationsmodell sprachhistorischer Periodisierung' (49–60); M. Kotin, 'Das Verhältnis von "Verbalaspekt" und Genus verbi in der deutschen Sprachgeschichte — Zum Problem der Kategorisierung sprachlicher Inhalte' (103–16). Also noted: H. Glück, 'Altdeutsch als Fremdsprache', *Fest. Bergmann*, 251–69. An innovative slant on the history of German is shown by *Bausteine zu einer Geschichte des weiblichen Sprachgebrauchs. II. Forschungsberichte — Methodentreffen Internationale Fachtagung Lübbben/Spreewald 16.-19.07.1995*, ed. G. Brandt (SAG, 341), 1996, 254 pp., which contains the following: E. Berner, 'Dialekt, Umgangssprache und Standardsprache im Sprechurteil von Frauen und Männern — Zur Wahrnehmung des aktuellen Sprachgebrauchs im Land Brandenburg' (5–28), showing a wide range of usage, not strictly historical; I. Keiler, 'Täter und Opfer im Diskurs von Frauen — Ergebnisse einer Studie zum Sprachgebrauch von Gegnerinnen des Naziregimes' (29–48), a lexical study; M. Rössing-Harder, '*Verhoffen essey eynem yden verstendigen klag gnug an tag geben* — Verständlichkeit als erklärtes Ziel der reformatorischen Flugschrift Ursulas von Münsterberg' (49–70), an examination of the structure of a difficult text; C. Zeiher, 'Rhetorische Mittel in den Schriften Katharina Zells' (71–94), showing the use of rhetorical figures by a well-educated woman who published regularly; B. M. Schuster, '*Ja wend das blat vmb, szo findistu es.* Zum Gebrauch textstrukturierender und textkommentierender Äußerungen in frühneuhochdeutschen Flugschriften' (95–118), surveying similarities and differences in four texts; B. Franz, 'Zu Reflexionen von Sprech-sprachlichkeit in Argula von Grumbachs *Antwort in gedichtß weiß* (1524)' (119–38); G. Brandt, 'Ursula von Zschöpperitz-Weyda-Fehem. Individueller Sprachgebrauch und zeitgenössischer Usus' (135–56), an interesting contrastive study which hints at female usage of the adverbial suffix -*lich*; E. Skvairs, 'Frauenstimmen im russisch-hansischen Dialog (nach hansischen Quellen des 16. Und 17. Jh.)' (157–66); I. Rösler, '"... mit zauberej behafftete personhen." Zur Selbst- und Fremddarstellung der wegen Hexerei beschuldigten Personen' (167–90); K. Bercker, 'Variationstechnik in Sophie La Roches Roman "Geschichte des Fräuleins von Sternheim". Zum Verhältnis von poetologischer Reflexion und ihrer Anwendung' (191–210); S. Pavidis, 'Schwarz und Schulz oder: Schwarz gegen Schulz?' (211–26); and R. Hünecke, 'Die schreibende Frau in einer sächsischen Kleinstadt des 18. und beginnenden 19. Jahrhunderts. Eine Fallstudie' (227–54), referring mostly to women who are left on their own. The role of women in the history of German has been underinvestigated but it is not yet certain whether there is a clear difference between female and male usage.

Textarten im Sprachwandel — *nach Erfindung des Buchdrucks*, ed. R. Grosse and H. Wellmann (Sprache- Literatur und Geschichte, 13), Heidelberg, Winter, 1996, 325 pp., focuses on another important aspect in the history of German. The volume has contributions which deal with three areas. First, the general and societal influence of printing: H.-J. Künast, '*Auf gut verstendlich Augspurger Sprach* — Anmerkungen zur "Augsburger Druckersprache" aus der Sicht des Buchhistorikers' (9–15); H. Nickel, 'Deutsch im Leipziger Buchdruck während der Inkunabelzeit' (17–27); A. Šimečková, 'Zur Produktion der ältesten Druckerstädte in Böhmen: Sprachen, Themen, Adressaten' (29–39); M. Kopecký, 'Die tschechischen Wiegendrucke und die Literaturgeschichte' (41–51); J. Rusek, 'Krakau als Wiege des kyrillischen Buchdrucks und ihre Bedeutung für die orthodoxen Slawen' (53–61); V. Vašnoraš, 'Baltische Frühdrucke aus heimischen und fremden Offizinen' (63–68). Second, early printing and the history of German: G. Kettmann, 'Städtische Schreibzentren und früher Buchdruck (Beispiel Wittenberg): Medienwandel und Graphematik' (69–76); C. J. Wells, 'Uneingewandte Einwände. Unfertiges Referat zur vernachlässigten sprachgeschichtlichen Rolle Westmitteldeutschlands in der zweiten Hälfte des 16. Jahrhunderts' (77–99); R. Metzler. Gedruckte und ungedruckte ostmitteldeutsche Rechtstexte aus der ersten Hälfte des 16. Jahrhunderts — Kanzleisprachliches in den Zwickauer Druckereien' (101–18). Third, the development of the language of different text types: O. Reichmann, 'Autorenintention und Textsorte' (119–33); N. R. Wolf, 'Das Entstehen einer öffentlichen Streitkultur in deutscher Sprache' (135–46); R. Bentzinger, 'Textsortenspezifika in Erfurter Flugschriften der Reformationszeit — Heinz Mettke zum 70. Geburtstag' (147–60); H. Blosen, 'Von Flöhen und Bosselieren im "Ständebuch" des Hans Sachs' (161–69); V. Hertel, 'Orientierungshilfen im frühen deutschen Sachbuch — Sachsenspiegelausgaben des 15. und 16. Jahrhunderts' (171–204); G. Bellmann, 'Das bilinguale Sprachlehrbuch als Textsorte und als Zeugnis drucksprachlicher Entwicklungen in frühneuhochdeutscher Zeit' (205–23); E. Glaser, 'Die textuelle Struktur handschriftlicher und gedruckter Kochrezepte im Wandel. Zur Sprachgeschichte einer Textsorte' (225–45); I. Rösler, '*Navigare necesse est.* — Texte der späten Hansazeit: Navigation' (251–68); M. Walch, 'Zur Sprache von frühen deutschsprachigen Buchanzeigen und Rezensionen' (269–88); H. Wussing, 'Einige Bemerkungen zur Entwicklung der frühen deutschen mathematischen Fachsprache' (289–96); R. Kössling, 'Buchdruck und Humanistenbriefe' (297–304); H. Wellmann, 'Textarten- und Sprachwandel. Zur Vorgeschichte' (305–07); and finally a concluding podium discussion on the formation of standard NHG: J. Erben, 'Überblick über die Diskussion' (309–10); J. Schildt, '3 Thesen zur Herausbildung der neuhochdeutschen Schriftsprache — ihre Voraussetzungen, Bedingungen, regionalen Schwerpunkte und Erscheinungsformen' (311–14); P. Wiesinger, '5 Thesen zur Regionalität und Überregionalität in der schriftsprachlichen Entwicklung: Der bayerisch-österreichische Raum vom 16. bis 18. Jahrhundert' (315–18); W. Besch, '6 Thesen zur Sprengung der Raumfessel: Überregionalität in der Schriftlichkeit' (319–22); and R. Grosse, 'Schlußwort' (323–25). A stimulating, well produced volume. It is interesting to notice the shedding of ideological baggage in this discussion. The history of modal verbs features in *Untersuchungen zur semantischen Entwicklungsgeschichte der Modalverben im Deutschen*, ed. G. Fritz and T. Gloning (RGL, 187), ix + 455, which contains the following articles: G. Fritz, 'Historische Semantik der Modalverben. Problemskizze — Exemplarische Analysen — Forschungsüberblick' (1–157), a potted history of the modals with useful diagrams of their development; R. Lühr, 'Zur Semantik der althochdeutschen Modalverben' (159–75), seeing *sollen* as the main motor in the changes; Id., 'Modalverben als Substitutionsformen des Konjunktivs in früheren Sprachstufen des Deutschen? Die Verhältnisse in der Hypotaxe' (177–208); R. Peilicke, 'Zur Verwendung der Modalverben *können* und *mögen* im frühneuzeitlichen Deutsch (1500 bis 1730)' (209–47); G. Fritz, 'Deutsche Modalverben 1609. Nicht-epistemische Verwendungsweisen' (249–305), on newspaper usage; and T. Gloning, 'Modalisierte Sprechakte mit Modalverben. Semantische, pragmatische und sprachgeschichtliche Untersuchungen' (307–437), with some examples going back to the 11th c. The volume covers a full range of problems throughout the history of German. There is a useful index of authors and concepts.

Germanic is, as always, well represented: R. B. Howell and J. C. Salmons, 'Umlautless residues in Germanic', *AJGLL*, 9:83–111; R. D'Alquen, 'Non-reduplication in Northwest Germanic: the problem that will not go away', *NOWELE*, 31–32:69–91; F. van Coetsem, 'Reconditioning and umlaut in Germanic, and the question of $\bar{e}^{2*}$', *NOWELE*, 31–32:423–37; G. W. Davis and G. K. Iverson, 'The *Verschärfung* as feature spread', Lippi-Green, *Linguistics*, 103–20; M. Niepokuj, 'Germanic Class IV and V preterites', *ib.*, 121–35; E. C. Polomé, 'Germanic in early Roman times', *ib.*, 137–47. Old Saxon appears in C. Arnett, 'Perfect selection in the Old Saxon *Heliand*', *AJGLL*, 9:23–72. Old Frisian is represented by D. Boutkan, *A Concise Grammar of the Old Frisian Dialect of the First Riustring Manuscript* (*NOWELE*, supp., 16), Odense U. P., 1996, 203 pp., which provides a much-needed synchronic description of an Old Frisian text.

Gothic is represented by R. Sternemann, 'Gedanken zum "Artikel" im Gotischen', *Fest. Arndt*, 151–72. Articles on OHG include K. Donhauser, 'Gibt es einen Indefinitartikel Plural im Althochdeutschen?', *ib.*, 61–72; K. G. Goblirsch, 'Notker's Law and consonant strength', *NOWELE*, 31–32:135–43; E. Leiss, 'Genus im Althochdeutschen', *Fest. Bergmann*, 33–48; A. Masser, 'Wege zu gesprochenem Althochdeutsch', *ib.*, 49–70; I. Reiffenstein, '*theodiscus* in den althochdeutschen Glossen', *ib.*, 71–84; R. Schmidt-Wiegand, '*Quod theodisca lingua harisliz dicitur*. Das Zeugnis der Lorscher Annalen (788) im Kontext frühmittelalterlicher Rechtssprache', *ib.*, 85–91; F. Simmler, 'Interpungierungsmittel und ihre Funktionen in der Lorscher Beichte und im Weißenberger Katechismus des 9. Jahrhunderts', *ib.*, 93–114; H. Tiefenbach, 'Zur frühen Werdener Sprachgeschichte. Die Namengraphien der Vita Liudegeri', *ib.*, 169–83; C. Moulin-Fankhänel, 'Althochdeutsch in der älteren Grammatiktheorie des Deutschen', *ib.*, 301–27; J. Riecke, *Die schwachen Verben jan-Verben des Althochdeutschen: ein Gliederungsversuch* (SA, 32), 1996, 702 pp.; Id., 'Ahd.

dwesben, fehtan und die starken Verba der III. Ablautreihe', *Sprachwis-senschaft*, 27 : 207–19; and A. Vanó-Cerdá, 'Die Verbindung *ist* + Part. Prät. als Perfektum passivi im (Alt-)Hochdeutschen', *ib.*, 221–86.

O. W. Robinson, *Clause Subordination and Verb-Placement in the Old High German Isidor Translation* (Germanische Bibliothek. 3. Reihe, n. F., 26), Heidelberg, Winter, 157 pp., is an excellent example of the combination of linguistics and philology. R. assumes a basic know-ledge of concepts such as constituent and leads us step by step through his description. Despite the title the volume contains a whole chapter on the position of the verb in main clauses. Verb first position chiefly occurs in questions and imperatives, otherwise verb second order is to be found. Nonfinite complements, participles and infinitives usually appear at the end of the main clause. The position of the verb in subordinate clauses is treated under the heading of the conjunction, e.g. *dhazs*, or type of clause, e.g. relative, concessive, etc. Unsurpris-ingly verb last is the preferred position with a small number of predicted constituents occurring in some instances after it. The whole volume is clearly written and all the quotations, of which there are many, are glossed in English. This could serve as an excellent starting point for the history of word order in German. The interplay between syntax and semantics in Old High German is seen by the contribu-tions to *Semantik der syntaktischen Beziehungen. Akten des Pariser Kolloquiums zur Erforschung des Althochdeutschen 1994*, ed. Y. Desportes (Germanische Bibliothek, n. F. Untersuchungen, 27) Heidelberg, Winter, 253 pp., which contains: M. T. Z. Ruiz-Ayucar, 'Die Lexikalisierung non-verbaler Kommunikationskomponenten in althochdeutschen litera-rischen Quellen'; (9–22); H. Eilers, 'Parataxe und Hypotaxe in Notkers Psalmenübersetung' (23–45); J. Haudry, 'Die privaten Konstruktionen im Altgermanischen' (46–53); B. Meineke, 'Syntakti-sche und semantische Aspekte althochdeutscher Prudentiusglossen' (54–91); M. Krause, 'Zur Modalisierung bei Otfrid' (92–106); A. Greule, 'Probleme der Beschreibung des Althochdeutschen mit Tiefenkasus. Ein Erfahrungsbericht' (107–22); A. Masser, 'Syntax-probleme im althochdeutschen Tatian' (123–40); S. Sonderegger, 'Syntaktisch-semantische Beziehungen bei Notker dem Deutschen von St. Gallen: Das Problem der Markierung von Kommentarein-schüben' (141–60); Y. Desportes, 'Zur Semantik der akkusativischen Beziehung in Otfrids Evangelienbuch: syntaktisch-semantische Ana-lyse der Okkurenzen von "duan"' (161–85); P. Valentin, 'Der Modusgegensatz im Althochdeutschen' (186–99); R. Lühr, 'Althoch-deutsche Modalverben in ihrer semantischen Leistung' (200–22); E. Oubouzar, 'Syntax und Semantik des adnominalen Genitivs im Althochdeutschen' (223–44); and P. Marcq, 'Zur Determination des

Raumteils "vorne" in einigen Altsprachen' (245–52). The *Althochdeutsches Wörterbuch* has continued on its long way with vol. 4, fasc. 12, *heilîg — gihulfin,* cols 832–916, 1993; fasc. 13, *zuo-helfan — herling,* cols 917–996, 1994; and fasc. 14, *hermalta — himil,* cols 997–1076, 1995.

MHG is well represented by J. Tao, *Mittelhochdeutsche Funktionsverbgefüge. Materialsammlung, Abgrenzung und Darstellung ausgewählter Aspekte* (RGL, 183), vi + 206 pp., a corpus-based work, using both verse and prose texts. The examples from the corpus are given in an appendix. As in NHG functional verbs are difficult sometimes to delimit in MHG. Most verbs occur in a phrase with a simple noun, the formations with *-ung* are much less frequent. The most frequent verbs are *bringen* and *komen.* The whole construction shows only gradual changes between MHG and NHG. A well-presented account based on solid evidence. Also noted: G. Kramer, 'Was bewirkt die Mystik für die Erweiterung des deutschen Wortschatzes? — Zur sprachlichen Entwicklung im 14. Jahrhundert', *Fest. Arndt,* 117–24; S. Dentler, **Zur Perfekterneuerung im Mittelhochdeutschen: die Erweiterung des zeitreferentiellen Funktionsbereichs von Perfektfügungen* (GGF, 37), 197 pp.; and S. Habscheid, **Die Kölner Urkundensprache des 13. Jahrhunderts: flexionsmorphologische Untersuchungen zu den deutschen Urkunden Gottfried Hagens (1262–74)* (Rheinisches Archiv, 135), Cologne, Böhlau, xi + 280 pp. Middle Low German is represented by **Satz — Text — Sprachhandeln: syntaktische Normen der mittelniederdeutschen Sprache und ihre soziofunktionalen Determinanten,* ed. I. Rösler (Sprachgeschichte, 5), Heidelberg, Winter, xxv + 316 pp.; R. S. Nybøle, **Reynke de Vos. Ein Beitrag zur Grammatik der frühen Lübecker Druckersprache* (Forschungen zum Niederdeutschen, 1), Neumünster, Wachholtz, xvi + 295 pp.; and U. Björnheden, **Zum Vierkasussystem des Mittelniederdeutschen* (GGF, 38), 1996, 241 pp.

Word formation is the topic of B. Döring and B. Eichler, *Sprache und Begriffsbildung in Fachtexten des 16. Jahrhunderts* (WM, 24), 1996, ix + 342 pp., which takes a corpus of eight texts, covering theology, law, medicine and nature studies. After a theoretical section on word formation the examples of the corpus are studied, first, semasiologically, starting with the affix, and then onomasiologically, starting with their function. Copious tables show the results and compare them with NHG. Predictably, the diminutive *-lin* has vastly decreased, while *-heit* and *-er* have increased. This is another useful block in the coverage of the history of word formation in German. A general item on ENHG is W. Bonzio, 'Kontinuität und Diskontinuität in der Sprachentwicklung — Zur Verdrängung des Genitivus partitivus im Frühneuhochdeutschen', *Fest. Arndt* 13–28. Text types in the Reformation period are treated by J. Kampe, *Problem 'Reformationsdialog'. Untersuchungen zu einer Gattung im reformatorischen Medienwettstreit* (Beiträge zur Dialogforschung, 14), Tübingen, Niemeyer, vii + 359 pp. Included in dialogue are a variety of texts written between 1520 and 1525. K. comes to the conclusion that they are a mixture of genres. He wants to investigate what the authors intended to write and in chapter 5 he gives an analysis. Many linguists may find some of the Latinate literary terms he uses rather strange. He divides the dialogues into five blocks on the basis of the theological position of the writer; the text type; the figures portrayed in them; the structure and argumentation of the conversation; and formal structural features. The genre ceased to have much importance after 1525. This is not an easy work to tackle but covers a wide range of texts. Also noted: W. A. Benware, 'Processual change and phonetic analogy: ENHG <s> > <sch>', *AJGLL*, 8, 1996:265–87, and H. Puff, *'Von dem Schlüssel aller Künsten/nemblich der Grammatica': Deutsch im lateinischen Grammatikunterricht 148–1560* (BSDSL, 70), 1995, 424 pp. Items on Luther include B. Eichler, 'Animisierungen in Luthers Sprache — Eine ideolektale Erscheinung?', *Fest. Arndt*, 73–82; R. Peilicke, 'Modalverbgebrauch bei Luther — Zur Verwendung von /können/ und /mögen/', *ib.*, 125–36; A. Greule, 'Zur Diachronie der Textgrammatik am Beispiel von Bibelübersetzungen', *Fest. Bergmann*, 287–300; J. Erben, 'Einige Bemerkungen zu *Christ(en), christ(en)-lich* und *Christen-mensch* in der Luthersprache', *ib.*, 407–13.

M. Lefevre, *Die Sprache der Lieselotte von der Pfalz. Eine sprachliche Untersuchung der deutschen Briefe (1676–1714) der Herzogin von Orleans an ihre Tante, Kurfürstin Sophie von Hannover* (SAG, 231), 1996, 381 pp., is based on a new corpus of original letters. L. describes the sociopragmatic conditions of the letters, e.g. censorship. Lieselotte's rank determines her language which is of the highest standard befitting her rank. The French influence amounts to only 12 per cent of the vocabulary, but there are traces of a more subtle syntactic and stylistic influence. Regional influence is more difficult to determine, but consonant lenition is evident. Most of the traditional linguistic areas are covered but some paradigms would have made the presentation more accessible. Mostly the linguistic usage is described solely for the letters and what is lacking is a wider view of the usage within a regional framework. For instance, there is no hint that the separation of *da* from *mit* is chiefly North German. This volume is a very solid foundation for the study of Early NHG.

C. Moulin-Fankhänel, *Bibliographie der deutschen Grammatiken und Orthographielehren*. II. *Das 17. Jahrhundert* (Germanische Bibliothek, n. F., 6. Reihe, Bibliographien und Dokumentationen, 5), Heidelberg, Winter, 501 pp., contains descriptions of works by 51 grammarians. There are biographical information, bibliographical references, detailed accounts of the works themselves, including which libraries have them (many are in the British Library), and some facsimiles.

The 17th c. is characterized by a wide variety of grammatical (and lexical) works and there is a tendency for complete grammars of German to be undertaken. This an essential research tool for the history of German. Also noted: A. Abramowski, '"…. weil die Zeitungen darzu nicht in Gebrauch kommen/ daß man daraus die Wolredenheit erlerne" (Kaspar Stieler) — Untersuchungen zu strukturellen Varianten der Satzgefüge in den ersten Berliner Zeitungen', *Fest. Arndt*, 5–12; P. Ewald, 'Zur Ausprägung des morphemidentifizierenden Prinzips in frühneuhochdeutschen Drucken', *Fest. Bergmann*, 237–50; U. Götz, 'Die *Sprachkunst* des Johann Ludwig Prasch. Zur Hochsprache in einer Grammatik des 17. Jahrhunderts aus Regensburg', *ib.*, 271–86; and N. R. Wolf, 'Herzog August der Jüngere von Braunschweig und Lüneburg und das Ende des Frühneuhochdeutschen', *ib.*, 357–67.

Items on the 18th c. include R. Hünecke, 'Sprache in Institutionen — Zum Sprachgebrauch in der kursächsischen Bergverwaltung des 18. Jahrhunderts', *Fest. Arndt*, 93–102; P. Wiesinger, 'Die Anfänge der Sprachpflege und der deutschen Grammatik in Österreich im 18. Jahrhundert. Zu Johann Balthasar Antespergers "Kayserlicher deutscher Sprachtabelle" von 1734', *Fest. Bergmann*, 337–55; A. Fleming-Wieczorek, **Die Briefe an Friedrich Justin Bertuch: eine Studie zu kommunikativen, sprachlichen und sozialen Verhältnissen im klassischen Weimar*, Aachen, Shaker, 1996, 180 pp.; I. Reiffenstein, 'Anton Roschmann (1694–1760), katholische Aufklärung und die deutsche Sprache', Holzner, *Literatur*, 123–42; and K. Faninger, **Johann Siegmund Valentin Popowitsch: ein österreichischer Grammatiker des 18. Jahrhunderts* (Schriften zur deutschen Sprache in Österreich, 18), Frankfurt, Lang, 1996, 257 pp.

The 19th c. features in I. Schmidt-Regener, '"Es giebt … kein Richtig und Falsch einer Sprachform" — Das Verhältnis der etablierten Germanistik zur öffentlichen Sprachkritik im letzten Drittel des 19. Jahrhunderts', *Fest. Arndt*, 137–50, and M. Klenk, **Sprache im Kontext sozialer Lebenswelt: eine Untersuchung zur Arbeiterschriftsprache im 19. Jahrhundert* (RGL, 181), viii + 390 pp. An item on the 20th c.: N. G. Jacobs, 'On the investigation of the 1920s Jewish speech', *AJGLL*, 8, 1996:177–217.

3. ORTHOGRAPHY

A description of the new orthography is P. Gallmann and H. Sitta, *Duden. Die Neuregelung der deutschen Rechtschreibung: Regeln, Kommentare und Verzeichnis wichtiger Neuschreibungen* (Duden Taschenbuch, 26), Mannheim, Bibliographisches Institut, 1996, 316 pp. The new orthography is discussed and criticized in *Zur Neuregelung der deutschen*

Orthographie. Begründung und Kritik, ed. G. Augst et al. (RGL, 179), 495 pp., which contains the following contributions: H. Zabel, 'Die Geschichte der Reformbemühungen von 1970 bis 1995 in der BRD' (7–14); S. Hellinger and D. Nerius, 'Die Geschichte der Reformbemühungen von 1970 bis 1990 in der DDR' (15–24); K. Blüml, 'Die Geschichte der Reformbemühungen von 1960 bis 1995 in Österreich' (25–36); R. Looser and H. Sitta, 'Die Geschichte der Reformbemühungen von 1970 bis 1995 in der Schweiz' (37–48); H. Zabel, 'Der Internationale Arbeitskreis für Orthographie' (49–66); 'Abschlusserklärung der 3. Wiener Gespräche zur Neuregelung der deutschen Rechtschreibung vom 22. bis zum 24.11.1994' (67–68); 'Gemeinsame Absichtserklärung zur Neuregelung der deutschen Rechtschreibung vom 1.7.1996' (69–70); G. Augst and B. Schaeder, 'Die Architektur des amtlichen Regelwerks' (73–92); P. Gallmann and H. Sitta, 'Zum Begriff der orthographischen Regel' (93–109); G. Augst and E. Stock, 'Laut-Buchstaben-Zuordnung' (113–34); P. Gallmann, 'Warum die Schweizer weiterhin kein Eszett schreiben. Zugleich eine Anmerkung zu Eisenbergs Silbengelenk-Theorie' (135–40); H. Zabel, 'Fremdwortschreibung' (141–56); B. Schaeder, 'Getrennt- und Zusammenschreibung — zwischen Wortgruppe und Wort, Grammatik und Lexikon' (157–208); P. Gallmann, 'Konzepte der Nominalität' (209–41); R. Baudusch, 'Zur Reform der Zeichensetzung — Begründung und Kommentar' (243–58); G. Augst, 'Die Worttrennung' (259–68); K. Heller and J. Scharnhorst, 'Kommentar zum Wörterverzeichnis' (269–90); M. Kohrt, 'Orthographische Normen in der demokratischen Gesellschaft' (295–315); 'Der Alternativentwurf der Studiengruppe Geschriebene Sprache' (317–19); P. Eisenberg, 'Die besondere Kennzeichnung der kurzen Vokale — Vergleich und Bewertung der Neuregelung' (323–35); U. Maas, 'Orthographische Regularitäten, Regeln und ihre Deregulierung. Am Beispiel der Dehnungszeichen im Deutschen' (337–64); D. Herberg, 'Aussageabsicht als Schreibungskriterium — ein alternatives Reformkonzept für die Regelung der Getrennt- und Zusammenschreibung (GZS)' (365–78); G. Augst, 'Das Problem des Regelaufbaus und der Regeloperationalisierung am Beispiel der Großschreibung von Substantiven und Substantivierungen' (379–96); H. H. Munske, 'Über den Sinn der Großschreibung — ein Alternativvorschlag zur Neuregelung' (397–417); P. Ewald and D. Nerius, 'Die Alternative: gemäßigte Kleinschreibung' (419–34); P. Gallmann, 'Zum Komma bei Infinitivgruppen' (435–62); B. Primus, 'Satzbegriffe und Interpunktion' (463–88); and R. Baudusch, '"Die unproblematischten Vorschläge sind die zur Zeichensetzung"' (489–95). The volume covers theoretical as well as historical and practical ground. Also noted: W. Kürschner, '"Entspricht den neuen amtlichen

Regeln..." — Zur Umsetzung der Orthografiereform in den Rechtschreib-Wörterbüchern von Bertelsmann und Duden (1996)', *Fest. Werner*, 173–92; H.-W. Eroms, 'Die Gewichtung des "historischen Prinzips" in der deutschen Orthographie', *Fest. Bergmann*, 221–35; D. Nerius, 'Zur Groß- und Kleinschreibung fester nominaler Wortgruppen in der gegenwärtigen und künftigen deutschen Orthographie', *ib.*, 329–35; R. Hoberg, 'Orthographie, Rechtschreibreform und öffentliche Meinung', *Sprachdienst*, 41: 189–93; W. H. Veith, 'Die deutsche Orthographie im Brennpunkt', *Sprachwissenschaft*, 22 : 19–44; T. Ickler, 'Woran scheitert die Rechtschreibreform?', *ib.*, 45–100; N. Willenpart and H. Kircher, **Diskussion Rechtschreibreform: kommentierte Bibliographie zur Reformdebatte 1970–1992*, Vienna, Österreichischer Bundesverlag, 1994, 208 pp.; **Kleine Wüteriche am Werk: Berichte und Dokumente zur Neuregelung der deutschen Rechtschreibung*, ed. H. Zabel, Hagen, Padligur, 1996, 448 pp.; **Die Rechtschreibreform: Pro und Kontra*, ed. H. W. Eroms and H. H. Munske, Berlin, Schmidt, 264 pp.; J. M. Zemb, **Für eine sinnige Rechtschreibung: eine Aufforderung zur Besinnung ohne Gesichtsverslust*, Tübingen, Niemeyer, 154 pp.; Id., 'Sans souci? Zur Ambiguität des deutschen Kommas: Melodie oder Kalkül?', *Sprachwissenschaft*, 22 : 101–32; W. P. Klein and M. Grand, 'Die Geschichte der Auslassungspunkte. Zu Entstehung, Form und Funktion der deutschen Interpunktion', *ZGL*, 25 : 24–44; C. Lindqvist, 'Schriftinduzierter Lautwandel: Synchrone und diachrone Auswirkungen im Deutschen', *Fest. Werner*, 193–212.

4. PHONOLOGY

Tonaufnahmen des gesprochenen Deutsch: Dokumentation der Bestände von sprachwissenschaftlichen Forschungsprojekten und Archiven, ed. P. Wagener and K.-H. Bausch (Phonai, 40), Tübingen, Niemeyer, xvi + 252 pp., is an excellent research tool which gives the details of recordings of spoken German, ranging from standard to dialect, which have been used for research. Most importantly for researchers is the information whether or not copies can be made or access given to the recordings in question. For each project there is a uniform description giving details such as date, place, and type of German recorded. Also noted: A. Lutz, 'Lautwandel bei Wörtern mit imitatorischem oder lautsymbolischem Charakter in den germanischen Sprachen', *NOWELE*, 31–32 : 213–28; F. Van Coetsem, **Towards a Typology of Lexical Accent: 'Stress Accent' and 'Pitch Accent' in a Renewed Perspective* (Monographien zur Sprachwissenschaft, 18), Heidelberg, Winter, 1996, 141 pp.; D. L. Fertig, 'Phonology, orthography and the umlaut puzzle', Lippi-Green, *Linguistics*, 149–84; A. Szulc, 'Außersprachliche Determinanten im phonologischen System der deutschen Hochlautung', *Fest.*

Werner, 275–86; H. P. Kelz, *Deutsche Aussprache: praktisches Lehrbuch zur Ausspracheschulung für den Unterricht Deutsch als Fremdsprache* (Sprachen und Sprachenlernen, 122), Bonn, Dümmlers, 1995, 167 pp.; and U. Hirschfeld, *Untersuchungen zur phonetischen Verständlichkeit Deutschlernender* (Forum Phoneticum, 57), Frankfurt, Hector, 1994, xv + 219 pp.

5. MORPHOLOGY

A general item on morphology is T. Becker, 'Bildungsregeln, Wohlgeformtheitsbedingungen und Prototypen in der Morphologie', *Sprachwissenschaft*, 22 : 161–80. A detailed historical and comparative investigation is S. Howe, *The Personal Pronouns in the Germanic Languages: a Study of Personal Pronouns, Morphology and Change in the Germanic Languages from the First Records to the Present Day* (SLG, 43), 1996, xxii + 390 pp. Items on inflectional morphology include: W. U. Wurzel, 'Natürlicher grammatischer Wandel, "unsichtbare Hand" und Sprachökonomie — Wollen wir wirklich so Grundverschiedenes?', *Fest. Werner*, 295–308; A. Pounder, 'Inflection and the paradigm in German nouns', *AJGLL*, 8 : 219–63; M. Kefer, 'Superlativbildung auf *st* oder *est?*', *ZGL*, 24, 1996:287–98. Derivational morphology features in the following: H. Altmann, '*miß-* als Wortbildungsbestandteil', *Fest. Werner*, 29–48; E. Ronneberger-Sibold, 'Sprachökonomie und Wortschöpfung', *ib.*, 249–61; M. Bues, 'Das Halbsuffix "-trächtig". Neue Mitteilungen zu Vorkommen und Verwendung', *Muttersprache*, 107 : 120–32; E. Donalies, '*Da keuchgrinste sie süßsäuerlich.* Über kopulative Verb- und Adjektivkomposita', *ZGL*, 24, 1996:273–86; C. Féry, 'Uni und Studis: die besten Wörter des Deutschen', *LBer*, 171 : 461–89; K.-N. Kim, *Leserzuschrift als textlinguistisches Objekt: unter besonderer Berücksichtigung der Wortbildungskonstruktionen mit einem gleichem Stamm-Morphem zum Zwecke der Textkohärenz*, Münster, Waxmann, 1996, 248 pp.; B. Ruf, *Augmentativbildungen mit Lehnpräfixen: eine Untersuchung zur Wortbildung der deutschen Gegenwartssprache* (Germanische Bibliothek, n. F., 3. Reihe, 25), Heidelberg, Winter, 1996, 451 pp.; D. Stoeva-Holm, *Farbbezeichnungen in deutschen Modetexten: eine morphologisch-semantische Untersuchung* (SGU, 34), Uppsala U.P., 1996, 134 pp.; Franz Hundsnurscher, *Das System der Partikelverben mit aus in der Gegenwartssprache* (BGS, 11), xvii + 241 pp.

6. SYNTAX

A wide-ranging volume is *German: Syntactic Problems — Problematic Syntax*, ed. W. Abraham and E. van Gelderen (LA, 374), vi + 323 pp., which contains: W. Abraham, 'The base structure of the German clause under discourse functional weight: contentful functional categories vs. derivative ones' (11–42); H. Haider, 'Projective economy — on the minimal functional structure of the German clause' (83–103); J.-W. Zwart, 'Transitive expletive constructions and the evidence supporting the multiple specifier hypothesis' (105–34); A. Alexiadou and E. Anagnostopoulou, 'Towards a uniform account of scrambling and clitic doubling' (143–61); K. K. Grohmann, 'Pronouns of the left periphery of West Germanic embedded clauses' (163–89); E. Mallen, 'Agreement and case matching in noun phrases in German' (191–230); J. R. te Velde, 'Deriving conjoined XPs: a Minimal deletion approach' (231–59); C. Platzak, 'The Initial Hypothesis of Syntax: A Minimalist perspective on language acquisition and attrition' (269–306), and R. A. Sprouse, 'The acquisition of German and the "Initial Hypothesis of Syntax": A reply to Platzack' (307–17). This is a stimulating volume but requires rather a lot of good knowledge of modern syntactic theory. Another item on the typology of German is J. O. Askedal, 'Zur typologischen Charakterisierung des Deutschen', *DaF*, 34 : 204–10. A major work is *Grammatik der deutschen Sprache*, ed. G. Zifonun et al., 3 vols (Schriften des Instituts für deutsche Sprache, 7/1–3), xi, ix, ix + 2569 pp.

The latest theoretical position on syntax, Minimalism, is represented by C. M. Schmidt, *Satzstruktur und Verbbewegung. Eine minimalistische Analyse zur internen Syntax der IP (Inflection-Phrase) im Deutschen* (LA, 327), ix + 287 pp., which is rather hard going but essential for syntax specialists. A more traditional approach is adopted by O. Leirbukt, *Untersuchungen zum bekommen-Passiv im heutigen Deutsch* (RGL, 177), ix + 342 pp., who undertakes a corpus-based study finding that there is a range of *bekommen* constructions. The structure of sentences features in J. R. te Velde, 'Coordination and antisymmetry theory. Some evidence from Germanic', *AJGLL*, 8 : 135–75; G. Fenk-Oczlon, 'Die Länge einfacher deutscher Aussagesätze im typologischen Vergleich', *Fest. Werner*, 101–10; M. Diesing, 'Yiddish VP order and the typology of object movement in Germanic', *Natural Language and Linguistic Theory*, 15 : 369–427; B. Staudinger, *Sätzchen: Small Clauses im Deutschen* (LA, 363), x + 241 pp.; P.-A. Mumm, *Parameter des einfachen Satzes aus funktionaler Sicht: Abriß ihrer onomasiologischen Systematik. 1. Relationierung der lexeme in Prädikation: Valenz* (Edition Linguistik, 11), Munich, LINCOM Europa, 1996, 117 pp.; J. Sabel, *Restrukturierung und Lokalität: universelle Beschränkungen für Wortstellungsvarianten* (Studia Grammatica, 42), Weinheim, Akademie, vii + 342 pp.; S. Heydenreich, *Prinzipien der Wortstellungsvariation: eine vergleichende Analyse* (Werkstattreihe Deutsch als Fremdsprache, 57), Frankfurt, Lang, 320 pp.; O. Önnerfors, *Verb-erst-Deklarativesätze: Grammatik und Pragmatik* (LGF, 60), 269 pp.

Prepositions in the noun phrase are treated in: J. Wilmots and E. Moonen, 'Der Gebrauch von Akkusativ und Dativ nach Wechselpräpositionen', *DaF*, 34:144–49; O. Kokov, 'Ein Präpositionstrainer', *ib.*, 235–38. Items dealing with the syntax of the verb include: S. M. B. Fagan, 'The epistemic use of German and English modals', Lippi-Green, *Linguistics*, 15–34; J.R. te Velde, 'Arguments for two verb-second clause types in Germanic. A comparison of Yiddish and German', *ib.*, 35–64; W. Abraham, 'Kausativierung und Dekausativierung: Zu Fragen der verbparadigmatischen Markierung in der Germania', *Fest. Werner*, 13–28; D. Wunderlich, 'Cause and the structure of the verb. Lexical decomposition grammar', *LI*, 28:27–68; M.-C. Koo, *Kausativ und Passiv im Deutschen* (EH, I, 1624), 260 pp.; and J. O. Askedal, 'drohen und versprechen als sogenannte "Modalitätsverben" in der deutschen Gegenwartssprache', *DaF*, 34:12–19. The treatment of the category tense features in: B.-M. Ek, *Das deutsche Präsens: Tempus der Nichtvergangenheit* (LGF, 59), 1996, 154 pp.; M. Itayama, 'Fragen zum System und Modell der deutschen Verbtempora von Viktor Myrkin', *DaF*, 34:26; R. Kozmová, 'Die Perfektauxiliare im Deutschen', *ib.*, 162–66; M. Hennig, 'Die Darstellung des Tempusystems in deutschen Grammatiken', *ib.*, 220–27. The passive is the subject of A. Mihailova, '*Man wird hier gut bedient.* Zur Analyse eines *man*-Passiv-Satzes', *DaF*, 34:80–82, and G. Helbig, 'Man-Konstruktionen und/oder Passiv?', *ib.*, 82–85.

Historical studies include: R. L. Lanouette, 'The attributive genitive in the history of German', Lippi-Green, *Linguistics*, 85–102; B. Primus, 'Der Wortgruppenaufbau in der Geschichte des Deutschen. Zur Präzisierung von synthetisch vs. analytisch', *Sprachwissenschaft*, 22:133–59; and S. Nässl, *Die 'okkasionelle Ereignisverben' im Deutschen: synchrone und diachrone Studien zu unpersönlichen Konstruktionen* (RBDSL, 62), 1996, 320 pp. Items on pronouns include: W. Abraham, 'German standard pronouns and non-standard pronominal clitics. Typological corrollaries', Lippi-Green, Linguistics, 1–14; *Pro-Formen des Deutschen*, ed. M.-H. Perennec (Eurogermanistik, 10), Tübingen, Stauffenberg, 1996, vi + 222 pp.; C. H. Lambine, 'Das Korrelat *es* bei Objektsätzen im Lichte der modernen Forschung', *DaF*, 34:93–97; *Verblose Sätze im Deutschen: zur syntaktischen und semantischen Einbindung verbloser Konstruktionen in Texten*, ed. I. Behr and H. Quintin (Eurogermanistik, 4), Tübingen, Stauffenberg, 1996, xii + 264 pp.; M. Ide, *Lassen uns lazen: eine diachrone Typologie des kausativen Satzbaus* (WBDP, 17), 1996, 282 pp.

Contrastive studies include: X. Zhu, *Die Aktionalität des Deutschen im Vergleich zum chinesischen Aspektsystem* (EH, XXI, 170), 276 pp.; J. O. Askedal, 'Indirekte Objekte im Deutschen und im Norwegischen', *Fest. Werner*, 49–66; S. Rolffs, *Zum Vergleich syntaktischer Strukturen im*

Deutschen und im Türkischen mittels der Dependenz-Verb-Grammatik: eine Untersuchung der Nebensatzstrukturen in beiden Sprachen (EH, XXI, 177), 409 pp.; M. T. Bianco, **Valenzlexikon deutsch-italienisch*, 2 vols (Deutsch im Kontrast, 17/1,2), Heidelberg, Groos, 1996, 952 pp.; D. Liu, **Verbergänzungen und Satzbaupläne des Deutschen und des Chinesischen: eine kontrastive Untersuchung im Rahmen der Verbvalenzgrammatik*, Hamburg, Kovac, 1996, 270 pp.; M. Nekula, **System der Partikeln im Deutschen und Tschechischen: unter besonderer Berücksichtigung der Abtönungspartikeln* (LA, 355), 1996, xiii + 220 pp.; U. Wandruszka, **Syntax und Morphosyntax: eine kategorialgrammatische Darstellung anhand romanischer und deutscher Fakten* (TBL, 430), 230 pp.; A. Ogawa, 'Argumenterhöhung im Sprachvergleich. Dativ im Deutschen vs. Postposition *-ni*, Multiple-Subject und Adversativ-Passiv im Japanischen', *Sprachwissenschaft*, 22:181–206; F. Freund and B. Sundqvist, '*Leichten Herzens = med lätt hjärta*. Eine deutsche genitivische Konstruktion und ihre Entsprechung im Schwedischen', *DaF*, 34:21–19; and E. Baschewa, 'Zur Anwendung des Valenzmodells in kontrastiven Untersuchungen (am Beispiel des Präpositionalobjektsatzes)', *ib.*, 156–61.

Also noted: **Studies in Comparative Germanic Syntax II*, ed. H. Thráinsson et al. (Studies in Natural Language and Linguistic Theory, 38), Dordrecht, Kluwer, 1996, xxxix + 302 pp.; H. Sinn, **The Lemma Access to German Temporal Conjunctions: Situational Focusings in Speech Production* (Mentale Sprachverarbeitung: psycho- und neurolinguistische Studien, 2), Freiburg, Hochschulverlag, 1994, 354 pp.; J. Geilfuss-Wolfgang, **Über gewisse Fälle von Assoziation mit Fokus* (LA, 358), 1996, 125 pp.; L. H. Cornelis, **Passive and Perspective* (Utrecht Studies in Language and Communication, 10), Amsterdam, Rodopi, 295 pp.; J. Jacobs, 'I-Topikalisierung', *LBer*, 168:91–133; V. Molnár and I. Rosengren, 'Zu Jacobs' Explikation der 'I-Topikalisierung'', *ib.*, 169:211–47; B. Tischer, 'Selbstkorrekturen in Dialogen: Regeln zur automatischen Syntaxverarbeitung', *ib.*, 170:312–44; G. Helbig, 'Grammatik und Kommunikation', *ZDL*, 64:259–71; F. Klumpp, 'Zu den Ursachen der Ungrammatikalität von Präpositionsstranden im Deutschen', *NMi*, 98:147–59; A. Peyer, **Satzverknüpfung — syntaktische und textpragmatische Aspekte* (RGL, 178), ix + 315 pp.; and B. J. Cheon-Kostrzewa and F. Kostrzewa, 'Der Erwerb der deutschen Modalpartikeln. Ergebnisse aus einer Longitudinalstudie', *DaF*, 34:86–92, 150–55.

7. SEMANTICS

The development of vocabulary through various means features in: I. Barz and A. Neudeck, 'Die Neuaufnahmen im Rechtschreibduden als Dokumentation der Wortschatzentwicklung', *Muttersprache*,

107:105–19; P. Braun, Germanismen im heutigen Italienisch', *ib.*, 201–05; H. Fink, **Anglizismen in der Sprache der Neuen Bundesländer: eine Analyse zur Verwendung und Rezeption* (Freiberger Beiträge zum Einfluß der angloamerikanischen Sprache und Kultur auf Europa, 4), Frankfurt, Lang, xi + 211 pp.

General items on semantics include L. Lemnitzer, **Akquisition komplexer Lexeme aus Textkorpora* (RGL, 180), viii + 258 pp.; K. von Heusinger, *Salienz und Referenz: der Epsilon-Operator in der Semantik der Nominalphrase und anaphorischer Pronomen* (Studia Grammatica, 43), Berlin, Akademie, x + 226 pp.; P. R. Lutzeier, 'Gegensinn als besondere Form lexikalischer Ambiguität', *LBer*, 171:381–95; C. Maienborn, **Situation und Lokation: die Bedeutung lokaler Adjunkte von Verbalprojektionen* (SDG, 53), 1996, vii + 292 pp.; I. Rapp, 'Fakultativität von Verbargumenten als Reflex der semantischen Struktur, *LBer*, 172:490–520; H.-U. Schmidt, '*Die Universität XY ist bestrebt* ..... Die *Vorlesung führt ein* ....Überlegungen zu Metonymie und Subjektschub im Gegenwartsdeutschen', *Sprachwissenschaft*, 22:1–18; R. Schumacher, **'Metapher': Erfassen und Verstehen frischer Metaphern* (BSDSL, 75), 271 pp.

Lexicography is represented by H. E. Wiegand, **Wörterbuchforschung: Untersuchungen zur Wörterbuchbenutzung, zur Theorie, Geschichte, Kritik und Automatisierung der Lexikographie*, Berlin, de Gruyter, 1200 pp.; **Das Lernerwörterbuch Deutsch als Fremdsprache in der Diskussion*, ed. I. Barz and M. Schröder (Sprache, Literatur und Geschichte, 12), Heidelberg, Winter, 1996, viii + 266 pp.; **Lexikon und Text: wiederverwendbare Methoden und Ressourcen zur linguistischen Erschließung des Deutschen*, ed. H. Feldweg and E. W. Hinrichs (Lexicographica. Series Maior, 73), Tübingen, Niemeyer, 1996, xii + 266 pp.; and R. Geier and J. Sternkopf, '"Bildungssprachliche" Phraseologismen? Zur Markierung im Duden, Band 11', *DaF*, 34:98–105. A new edition of *Wahrig Deutsches Wörterbuch*, ed. R. Wahrig-Burfeind, 6th edn, Gütersloh, Bertelsmann, 1420 pp., has appeared. The historical aspects of lexicography feature in U. Hass-Zumkehr, '"alle welt erwartet hier eine erklärung von mir" — Jacob Grimms Vorrede zum Deutschen Wörterbuch zwischen Apologie und Programm', *ZGL*, 25:1–23; H. Henne et al., 'Das Wörterbuch im Visier — Hermann Pauls systematische Arbeit. 100 Jahre Deutsches Wörterbuch (1897–1997)', *ib.*, 167–99. The *Deutsches Wörterbuch*, Stuttgart, Hirzel, wends its way with two fascicles. Vol. 2, fasc. 8, *Ankunftsort — anschicken*, cols 1121–280, has a number of interesting entries: *Anlage* and its various meanings goes back to the 18th c., *ankurbeln*, 1920s, when applied to the economy, *anläßlich* is 19th c., *Anlaut* is a coinage by Jacob Grimm, *Ansagerin* goes back to 1940, more recent words include *Anmache* (since the 1970s), *Anrufbeantworter* (1965), *anno dazumal* (1966). Vol. 8, fasc. 5, *erlauben — Erregung*, cols 1921–2080, focuses on the productivity of the *er-* prefix.

Semantic fields feature in U. Louis-Nouvertne, **Satzsemantik in der Kollokationsanalyse: ein Beitrag zur Methodendiskussion am Beispiel des Wortfelds 'Weiblichkeit'*, Aachen, Mainz, 304 pp.; C. Schottmann, **Politische Schlagwörter in Deutschland zwischen 1929 und 1934* (SAG, 342), 604 pp.; K.-E. Sommerfeldt, **Gestern so und heute anders: sprachliche Felder und Textsorten in der Presse*, Munich, Iudicium, 171 pp.; S. Schimpf, **Wissens- und Wortschatzvariationen im Bereich der Sexualität anhand ausgewählter Zeitschriftentexte* (GASK, 33), 340 pp.; **Bausteine Fachdeutsch für Wissenschaftler. Geschichte*, ed. M. A. Rieger, Heidelberg, Groos, 1996, vi + 135 pp.; and M. Bujalková, 'Fachdeutsch Medizin: spezifische Probleme der Ausbildung zukünftiger Ärzte', *DaF*, 34:106–08. Individual words feature in E. Ormelius-Sandblom, **Die Modalpartikeln ja, doch und schon: zu ihrer Syntax, Semantik und Pragmatik* (LGF, 61), 151 pp.; P. Braun, **Personenbezeichnungen: der Mensch in der deutschen Sprache* (RGL, 189), viii + 157 pp.; Y. T. Radday, 'Mephisto .... hebräisch?', *Muttersprache*, 107:133–48; R. Bloomer, '"Dopen" im Deutschen. Zur Geschichte eines aktuellen Wortes', *ib.*, 206–16; J. Knobloch, 'Das "Wissen um Sumpfhühner" oder Wie ein Wort in Verruf geriet', *ib.*, 233–39; Id., 'Etymologische Betrachtungen zum deutschen Wortschatz. Teil 3', *ib.*, 240–42; W. König, 'Zur Etymologie des Monatsnamen *Hornung*', *Fest. Bergmann*, 429–43; M. Schlaefer, 'Zum Problem des Bezeichnungsmotivs: das Meerschweinchen', *ib.*, 463–77; G. Zifonun, 'Ungewöhnliche Verwendungen von *mit* (II)', *DaF*, 34:20–25; H. Blosen and H. Pors, 'Das Verb *beanspruchen* als Verb des Forderns', *Fest. Bergmann*, 207–20; J. M. Zemb, 'Gehört "Behaupten" wesentlich zum "Setzen"?', *ib.*, 369–75; I. Rauch et al., '*Babysitter/in, lernbehindert*, and other German PC terms', *NOWELE*, 31–32:337–43; and F. Hammar, 'Okkasionelle Abwandlungen von Phraseologismen (am Beispiel der Paarformeln)', *DaF*, 34:228–34.

Contrastive semantic studies include C. von Stutterheim, 'Zum Ausdruck von Zeit- und Raumkonzepten in deutschen und englischen Texten', *ZGL*, 25:147–66.

8. DIALECTS

General items include: **Varietäten des Deutschen. Regional- und Umgangssprache*, ed. G. Stickel (Institut für deutsche Sprache, Jahrbuch 1996), vi + 476 pp., which contains the papers from a conference in Mannheim; H. J. Dingeldein, 'Dialekt als "Stigma", Dialekt als "Waffe". Zu einigen gesellschaftlichen Aspekten und zur Zukunft des Dialektsprechens', *Hessische Blätter für Volks- und Kulturforschung, n. F.*,

32:63–70, and M. Schröder, 'Brauchen wir ein neues Wörterbuch-kartell? Zu den Perspektiven einer computerunterstützten Dialektlexikographie und eines Projekts "Deutsches Dialektwörter-buch"', *ZDL*, 64:57–66.

Phonetic and phonological issues are treated in W. J. Barry and M. Pützer, 'Zur phonetischen Basis der Fortis-Lenis-Opposition bei Plosiven im moselfränkischen und rheinfränkischen Dialekten sowie in Übergangsgebieten im germanophonen Lothringen (Frankreich)', *ZDL*, 64:155–78, and J. Venema, *Zum Stand der zweiten Lautverschie-bung im Rheinland. Diatopische, diachrone und diatstratische Untersuchungen am Beispiel der dentalen Tenuis (voralthochdeutsch /T/)* (Mainzer Studien zur Sprach- und Volksforschung, 22), Stuttgart, Steiner, viii + 552 pp.

The *Bayerischer Sprachatlas. Sprachatlas von Bayerisch-Schwaben*, Heidel-berg, Winter, continues with vol. 1, *Einführung*, ed. W. König, 238 pp., and vol. 3, *Lautgeographie*, 1, ed. W. König and M. Renn, xx + 261 pp. Vol. 1 contains very varied background maps dealing with historical, geographical, and linguistic questions. There are metalinguistic questions on whether speakers in the next village are more Bavarian or Swabian. The whole thrust of the maps is to show how the dialects are embedded in a wider linguistic culture. There are, of course, the bread-and-butter lists of informants, with sociolinguistic and personal details. Most were born between 1897 and 1927 and several were interviewed for each locality for each of which the dialect form was given. The questionnaire and the transcription system, similar to that for the *Sprachatlas der deutschen Schweiz*, are given. All this careful preparation sets the scene for the actual linguistic data. Vol. 3 treats the short vowels, comparing them with High German. Most examples are treated by *Kombinationskarten* containing the distribution of up to four words. A minority of individual special cases are represented in smaller *Kommentarkarten*. One particularly interesting case is that of short vowels before /t/ which shows lack of lengthening in the dialect as against High German. A very useful help is a bookmark with the transcription symbols. All in all an excellent atlas which will deepen our knowledge of the dialects in this transitional area. Also continuing is *Mittelrheinischer Sprachatlas*, ed. G. Bellmann et al., vol.3: *Vokalismus*, III, Tübingen, Niemeyer, vii + pp. 178–313 maps. This volume deals with short vowels, unstressed vowels, and epenthetic vowels, grouped according to their MHG counterparts. Among the phenomena mapped, derounding lowering, including the leap from $i > a$ show up well. Somewhat frustrating is the treatment of *nichts* where mapping of the full form would have been more useful. The vocalization of *-er* is quite advanced in this region. Suprasegmental features such as the Rhenish *Schärfung* are also mapped. This atlas continues to provide a sound basis for dialect study.

Low German features in: W. Lammers, **Die plattdeutsche Sprache: Ursprung, Entwicklung, Verwandte, Prognose*, Neumünster, Wachholtz, 1996, 106 pp.; E. I. Biehl, **Norderneyer Protokolle: Beobachtungen zu einer niederdeutschen Mundart im Rückgang* (SGF, 62), 1996, 407 pp.; F. Möller, **Der typisierte Plattsprecher: Modalwertanalyse zum Niederdeutschen in Schleswig-Holstein anhand der GETAS-Umfrage von 1984* (Schriften des Instituts für niederdeutsche Sprache. Reihe Dokumentation, 18), Leer, Schuster, 274 pp.; and R. K. Seymour, 'Linguistic change and an historical continuum in German dialect studies', *NOWELE*, 31–32 : 345–59. An historical study is H. Kröger, *Plattdüütsch in drei Jahrhunderten. 1. 1700 bis 1900*, Hanover, Lutherisches Verlagshaus, 386 pp. In this thoroughly researched work the 18th c. is characterized by individual contributions, despite the official frowning on the use of Low German. The Enlightenment also had a positive attitude to the dialect. The sources for the 19th c. are much more copious. There are programmatic statements, sermons, and, encouraged by the development of literature in LG, the demand for a LG Bible. The work is divided into chapters on personalities and topics, e.g. LG Bible, LG in school. A fascinating book whose continuation is eagerly awaited. The subject of MLG loan words in Latvian features in S. Jordan, *Niederdeutsches im Lettischen* (Westfälische Beiträge zur niederdeutschen Philologie, 4), Bielefeld, Vlg für Regionalgeschichte, 1995, 124 pp., which is primarily a dictionary of MLG loans collected from dictionaries. After a short historical introduction, the loans are examined as to their sound substitution, for example MLG *sch* is replaced by *sk*. J. says that the semantic side of the loans has already been covered but it might have been nice to show which areas of the vocabulary were affected.

A thoroughly researched and well written work is A. R. Rowley, *Morphologische Systeme der nordostbayerischen Mundarten in ihrer sprachgeographischen Verflechtung* (*ZDL*, Beihefte, 93), Stuttgart, Steiner, xx + 277 pp. R. majors on the inflectional system of the noun. He sets out his theoretical position, taking up a word-and-paradigm model (something British linguists will approve of) and gives a clear history of the development of morphological research. L. Najdič, *Deutsche Bauern bei St. Petersburg-Leningrad. Dialekte — Brauchtum — Folklore* (*ZDL*, Beihefte, 94), Stuttgart, Steiner, 241 pp., treats the customs and folklore as well as the dialect of these German dialect enclaves which existed until 1942. N. has tracked down a number of informants and sources which build up a convincing but limited reconstruction of the dialect of a group of villages. She also confirms V. Schirmunski's theory that the dialect agrees best with that of the

Palatinate. A bold and nostalgic picture of a past age. Among other items on speech islands noted: G. Brandt, 'Deutsche Sprachinseln in Baschkirien', *Fest. Arndt*, 29–48, and **Wolgadeutscher Sprachatlas, aufgrund der von Georg Dinges 1925–29 gesammelten Materialien*, ed. N. Berend, Tübingen, Francke, 320 pp.

Central German dialects feature in R. Harnisch. 'Ein mittel-deutsches Tempusparadigma in textökonomischer Sicht', *Fest. Werner*, 111–28. A wide range of papers on Alemannic are featured in *Syntax und Stilistik der Alltagssprache*, ed. A. Ruoff and P. Löffelad (Idiomatica, 18), Tübingen, Niemeyer, 296 pp. They include papers on individual topics: H. Bausinger, 'Dialekt und Erzählstil' (13–26); M. Gyger, 'Zielspracheschweizerdeutsch — Beobachtungen zur Syntax dialek-taler Lernvarietäten von fremdsprachigen Kindern und Jugendlichen in der deutschen Schweiz' (27–36); D. Huck and A. Bothorel-Witz, 'Zum morphologischen und morphsyntaktischen Dialektwandel im Elsaß. Einige empirische Beobachtungen' (37–48); M. Hundt, 'Zum Prestige gesprochener Alltagssprache: Sächsisch und Schwäbisch' (49–64); H. Klausmann, 'Der Ellwanger Sprachraum — ein ost-schwäbisches Randgebiet' (65–84); A. Lötscher, '"Guet, sind si doo." Verbstellungsprobleme bei Ergänzungssätzen im Schweizer-deutschen' (85–95); Y. Matras, 'Zur stilistischen Funktion der Sondersprache *Lekoudesch* in südwestdeutschen Erzählungen' (97–106); D. Nübling, 'Der alemannische Konjunktiv II zwischen Morphologie und Syntax. Zur Neuordnung des Konjunktivsystems nach dem Präteritumschwund' (107–21); B. Siebenhaar, 'Stilistische Varianz in der Sprache eines in der Deutschschweiz lebenden Romands' (123–34); M. Vulpe, 'Die Leistung der Satzkonjunktion in gesprochener Sprache: Rumänisch — Schwäbisch kontrastiv' (135–43); K. Wild, 'Zur Verbstellung in den schwäbischen Mund-arten Südungarns' (145–54); P. Zürrer, 'Systemveränderung in Südwalser Sprachinseldialekten' (155–69). Recent and ongoing research is reviewed and recounted in short contributions: U. Bärnert-Fürst and B. Henne-Memmesheimer, 'Arbeitsbericht des Teilprojekts B6 des SFB 245: Standard/Nonstandard als Faktor bei der Struktu-rierung kommunikativer Situationen' (173–74); G. W. Baur, 'Die Arbeit am Badischen Wörterbuch in den Jahren 1993 bis 1996' (175–76); W. Besch, 'Zur Ortssprachenforschung am Beispiel Erp. Kritische Bilanz nach (gut) 20 Jahren' (177–80); A. Bothorel-Witz and D. Huck, '"Sprachbewußtsein der Mundartsprecher im Elsaß." Bilanz und neue Forschungswege' (189–90); S. Dal Negro, 'Morphsyntaktischer Sprachverfall bei den Walsern in Pomatt (Dis-sertationsbericht)' (191–95); H. Hilbe, 'Liechtensteiner Namenbuch' (197–98); T. Jauch, 'Tübinger Aktion zur Sammlung und Deutung von Flurnamen in Baden-Württemberg' (199–203); H. Klausmann,

'Vorarlberger Sprachatlas mit Einschluß des Fürstentums Liechtenstein, Westtirols und des Allgäus (VALTS). (Arbeitsbericht 1993–1996)' (203–04); P. Leuenberger, 'Stadtsprache — Sprachen in der Stadt am Beispiel Basels' (205–10); R. J. Ramseyer, 'Berner Personennamen im 16. Jahrhundert. (Arbeitsbericht)' (211–14); L. Reichardt, 'Zur historischen Dialektologie des Schwäbischen. Die baden-württembergischen Ortsnamenbücher' (215–22); M. Renn, 'Der Sprachatlas von Bayerisch-Schwaben (SBS). (Arbeitsbericht 1993–1996)' (223–26); A. Ruoff, 'Tübinger Arbeitsstelle "Sprache in Südwestdeutschland". Arbeitsbericht 1994–1996' (227–29); G. Schiltz, 'Dialektrometrischer Atlas von Südwest-Baden (DASB)' (231–33); R. Schrambke, 'Südwestdeutscher Sprachatlas (SSA). (Arbeitsbericht 1994–1996)' (235–36); F. Stäheli, 'Inventarisierung bestehender Tonaufnahmen — Dokumentation schweizerdeutscher Soziolekte im Phonogrammarchiv der Universität Zürich' (237–38); R. Trüb, 'Sprachatlas der deutschen Schweiz (SDS)' (239–41); E. Waser, 'Luzerner Namenbuch Arbeitsbericht)' (243–44); V. Weibel, 'Das Projekt "Orts- und Flurnamenbuch des Kantons Nidwalden"' (245–47). Also in this volume are: G. W. Baur, 'Grüßliches' (251–52); E. Gabriel, 'Zur Gliederung des Alemannischen' (253–56); E. Glaser, 'Hoi!' (257–62); D. Herz, 'Das "I freilich!" der Gustel aus Blasewitz in *Wallensteins Lager*' (263–65); R. Hildebrandt, 'Alemannische Parallelen zum Wortschatz der Hildegard von Bingen' (167–68); R. Hinderling, 'Zur sprachgeographischen Lage der Stadt Basel' (269–70); H. Klausmann, 'Der spätrömische Limes als Grenze romanischer Reliktwörter' (271–76); U. Knoop, 'Die zweite Lautverschiebung (p, t, k) und die Drucklegung des "Sprachatlas des deutschen Reichs"' (277–79); H. Kuhn, 'Ist das Öffentlichkeitsschweizerdeutsche noch Mundart?' (281–82); and A. Ruoff, 'Die Geschichte der Tübinger Arbeitsstelle "Sprache in Südwestdeutschland" 1955–1995. Mit einer Bibliographie' (283–96). The range and high standard of scholarship is to be envied. Alemannic is one of the best researched German dialects. Alemannic items also include *Stadtsprache — Sprachen in der Stadt am Beispiel Basels*, ed. A. Häcki Buofer and H. Löffler (BSDSL, 72), xiii + 306 pp.; R. Schrambke, 'Sprachraumforschung im alemannischen Dreiländereck. Zur dialektalen Gliederung in der Nordwestschweiz, im Oberelsaß und in Südwestbaden', *ZDL*, 64 : 272–320.

Bavarian articles include: F. Patocka, *Satzgliedstellung in den bairischen Dialekten Österreichs* (Schriften zur deutschen Sprache in Österreich, 20), Frankfurt, Lang, 433 pp.; E. Kühebacher, 'Die Mundartlichen Bezeichnungen des Schmetterlings in Tirol', Holzner, *Literatur*, 69–79; and *Werdenfelser altes Bairisch: ein unterhaltsames Mundart-Lexikon, gesammelt von Franz von Paula Ludwig Hoheneicher in den*

Jahren 1812–17, ed. W. Keller (Bairische Kulturzeugen, 1), Windach, Viktoria Presse, 1996, 92 pp. A general dialect dictionary is *Wörterbuch deutscher Dialekte: eine Sammlung von Mundartwörtern aus zehn Dialektgebieten im Einzelvergleich, in Sprichwörtern und Redewendungen*, ed. U. Knoop and M. Mühlenhort, Gütersloh, Bertelsmann, 478 pp. Items on dialect dictionaries include S. Sienarth, 'Das Siebenbürgsächsische Wörterbuch im Spannungsfeld zwischen wissenschaftlicher Verpflichtung und ideologischer Vereinnahmung', *Fest. Schwob*, 433–46. The following dialect dictionaries continue on their way: *Hamburgisches Wörterbuch*, fasc. 14, *Hillichaven — Huusdör(en)slötel*, Neumünster, Wachholtz, cols 641–768; *Pfälzisches Wörterbuch*, vol. 6, fasc. 49 *wie so — zappelig*, Stuttgart, Steiner, cols 1345–1563; *Preußisches Wörterbuch*, vol. 3, fasc. 7, *spielen — Stichlingsklippe*, Neumünster, Wachholtz, 1996, cols 769–896. An item on Rotwelsch is K. Siewert, 'Das Pfedelbacher Jenisch. Mit einem Glossar aus den schriftlichen Quellen', *ZDL*, 64:37–56.

Items on Yiddish include N. G. Jacobs, 'Towards a phonological description of *l* palatalization in Central Yiddish', Lippi-Green, *Linguistics*, 149–68.

9. ONOMASTICS

A work on North Frisian burial mound names which deals with the inflexion of personal names is V. F. Faltings, *Nordfriesische Grabhügelnamen mit anthropnymem Erstglied. Zur Form und Funktion nordfriesischer Rufnamen* (*NOWELE*, supp., 14), Odense U. P., 1996, v + 186 pp. F. examines written sources from the past and his corpus is analysed according to the structure of word, e.g. linking morphemes, etc. Most of the names are Frisian/West Germanic but some are Nordic and a few biblical. Personal names also feature in: F. Debus, 'Eigennamen in der literarischen Übersetzung', *Fest. Bergmann*, 393–405; R. Lühr, 'Werturteile in germanischen Personennamen — Lexemersatz von Galizismen?', *ib.*, 445–62; T. Berg, 'Lexical stress differences in English and German. The special case of proper names', *LBer*, 167:3–22; *Nomen et gens: zur historischen Aussagekraft frühmittelalterlicher Personennamen*, ed. D. Geuenich et al. (Reallexikon der germanischen Altertumskunde, Ergänzungsbände, 16), Berlin, de Gruyter, x + 303 pp.; H. Wellmann, 'Notburga, Burg(e)l(e), Burgi, Burga. Über Namenvariation in Tirol', Holzner, *Literatur*, 21–30; and L. Ortner, 'Benennung und Charakterisierung von Personen in den Sagen aus Tirol (Ignaz, Vinzenz Zingerle)', *ib.*, 31–52. More numerous are studies of place names: P. Hessmann, 'Ein lexikographisches Relikt als Flurnamen element: mnd. HUK', *Fest. Bergmann*, 415–28; *Historisch-philologische Ortnamensbücher. Regensburger Symposion*,

4. und 5. Oktober 1994, ed. H. Tiefenbach (*BNF*, n. F., Beihefte, 46), Heidelberg, Winter, 1996, 314 pp.; M. Besse, **Namenpaare an der Sprachgrenze. Eine lautchronologische Untersuchung zu den zweisprachigen Ortsnamen im Norden und Süden der deutsch-französischen Sprachgrenze* (Beihefte zur *ZRP*, 267), Tübingen, Niemeyer, xiv + 878 pp.; **Wort und Name im deutsch-slavischen Sprachkontakt*, ed. K. Hengst et al. (Bausteine zur slavischen Philologie, n. F., 20), Cologne, Böhlau, 569 pp.; **Bayerisches Flurnamenbuch für das Haus der bayerischen Geschichte.* iv. *Gemeinde Tapfheim*, ed. M. Henker and A. Freiherr von Reitzenstein, Augsburg, Haus der bayerischen Geschichte, 1996, 589 pp.; D. Wenninger, **Flurnamen im Kaiserstuhl: eine namenkundliche und sprachgeschichtliche Untersuchung der Vogtsburger Ortsteile Achkarren, Bickensohl et al.* (EH, 1, 1607), 450 pp.; E. Schneider, 'Beunde/Bünt — Einfang — Bifang/Beifang — Bütze/Bitze. Sonderland und Sonderrecht in Hegauer Flurnamen', *Hegau. Zeitschrift für Geschichte, Volkskunde und Naturgeschichte des gebietes zwischen Rhein, Donau und Bodensee. Jahrbuch*, 53, 1996:149–64; and N. Wagner, '*Thulbach* und *Dimbach*', *BNF*, 31, 1996:247–50. In a bold interpretation, T. Vennemann, 'Der Kastalische Quell, die Gastein und das Rätische. Mit einem Anhang zu Kassandra und Kastianeira', *Fest. Bergmann*, 479–503, suggests that the oldest language spoken in Europe was allied to Basque.

Plant names are the subject of P. Seidensticker, **die seltzamen namen all. Studien zur Überlieferung der Pflanzennamen* (*ZDL*, Beiheft, n. F., 101), Stuttgart, Steiner, 136 pp.; Id., 'Der Pflanzenname in der abendländischen Überlieferung. Geschichte und Linguistik', *BNF*, 31, 1996:260–91.

Also noted: A. Bammesberger, 'Gotisch *ansis* und urgermanisch **ans(u)-*', *ib.*, 231–40; N. Wagner, '*Prod(o)* und *Prod(i)*', *ib.*, 241–46.

MEDIEVAL LITERATURE

By DAVID A. WELLS, *Professor of German at Birkbeck College, University of London*

I. GENERAL

Literaturwissenschaftliches Lexikon. Grundbegriffe der Germanistik, ed. Horst Brunner and Rainer Moritz, Berlin, Schmidt, 372 pp., addresses student need with 150 articles selected for the relevance to *Germanistik.* Even though there is some overlap with other works of reference, most items occupy 2–3 densely printed pages and the amount of basic information conveyed is accordingly considerable. Of particular medieval interest are *Althochdeutsche Literatur, Frühmittelhochdeutsche Literatur* and *Germanische Dichtung* (E. Hellgardt), *Bibel* and *Mystik* (F. Löser), *Epos* and *Klassik, Mittelhochdeutsche* (H.-J. Behr), *Fabel* (R. Zymner), *Geistliche Dichtung, Legende, Mündlichkeit / Schriftlichkeit* and *Volksbuch* (E. Feistner), *Geschichtsschreibung* and *Spätmittelalterliche Literatur* (D. Klein), *Heldendichtung, Höfischer Roman, Minnesang,* and *Tagelied* (E. Lienert), *Kreuzzugsdichtung* (J. Theisen), *Lehrliteratur* (R. K. Weigand), *Lied, Meistergesang,* and *Sangspruch / Reimspruch* (H. Brunner), *Politische Dichtung* (S. Kerth), *Schwank* (H.-J. Bachorski), *Spielmannsepik* (U. Meves), and *Tierdichtung* (K. Düwel). Henry and Mary Garland, *The Oxford Companion to German Literature,* 3rd edn by Mary Garland, OUP, xv + 951 pp., appears eleven years after the previous edition (see *YWMLS,* 48:666). The work has been reset in a smaller but scarcely less legible typeface. The 80 new entries necessarily shift the balance of the work further towards contemporary literature, but there has also been substantial revision of many existing sections and a general improvement in quality as a result of the increasing involvement of numerous specialist scholars, acknowledged in the prefaces. R. Schröder, Sørensen, *Geschichte,* I, 15–38, gives a brief survey of the major OHG works and their background, while B. Murdoch, Watanabe, *History,* 1–39, supplies relatively more detailed information about the basic conditions of literary production and works in the period 750–1100. Compared with Sørensen, *Geschichte,* I, in which R. Schröder provides chapters surveying in turn the classical courtly period (39–65) and the later Middle Ages (66–88), N. F. Palmer, Watanabe, *History,* 40–91, has a little more space for the period 1100–1450 and manages to convey the essential facts about the main genres and developments, well amplified with informative statements about individual authors and works. H. Watanabe-O'Kelly, *ib.,* 92–146, carries the narrative into the early modern period. *Literaturgeschichte Österreichs. Von den Anfängen im Mittelalter bis zur Gegenwart,* ed. Herbert Zeman and Werner M. Bauer,

ADEVA, 1996, 604 pp., includes chapters by A. Wolf on the high Middle Ages and F. P. Knapp on Latin literature and the late Middle Ages. Jürgen Schutte, *Einführung in die Literaturinterpretation* (SM, 217), 4th edn, vii + 231 pp., remains a useful guide for the interpretation of literature of all periods and is now updated. The focus falls on the 1970s and later and the dense literature is surveyed in four substantial chapters concentrating on communication, production, structural analysis, and reception.

Max Wehrli, *Geschichte der deutschen Literatur im Mittelalter. Von den Anfängen bis zum Ende des 16. Jahrhunderts*, 3rd rev. edn, Stuttgart, Reclam, 1284 pp., is, with a slightly revised title, a third edition of the work which first appeared in 1980 as the first volume of a literary history (see *YWMLS*, 42:690). The text follows the second edition but the useful bibliographical leads have been wholly revised by D. Klein. A. Classen, *FCS*, 22, 1996:119–40, surveys late-medieval research published 1985–94. A. Classen and P. Dinzelbacher, *Mediaevistik*, 8, 1995 [1996]:55–73, comment on recent work on secular literature by poetesses. M. Maher, *Fest. Schwob*, 271–76, reports on medieval German studies in Egypt. H. Birus, *Fest. Worstbrock*, 13–28, is not the first to ask fundamental questions about the possibility of comparative medieval studies, while F. P. Knapp, *JIG*, 29.1:31–37, argues for a comparative approach as a pedagogical discipline, and U. Müller, *Runa*, 25, 1996:101–08, notes the affinity between medieval studies and 'intercultural *Germanistik*'.

Walter Haug, *Vernacular Literary Theory in the Middle Ages. The German Tradition, 800–1300, in its European Context*, trans. Joanna M. Catling (Cambridge Studies in Medieval Literature, 29), CUP, xiv + 426 pp., is a major work on medieval literary theory (see *YWMLS*, 54:650) which now achieves the rare distinction of an English translation. That this has been a labour of love is apparent both from the acknowledged difficulty of translating abstract German critical and theoretical terminology into English with the consequent need for paraphrase and adaptation, and from the highly readable quality of the resulting text. There are full indexes and the bibliography of the primary works helpfully includes English translations of the German and French texts cited where they exist, a useful accompaniment to a book which makes claims for the status of vernacular literary production transcending the legacy of Curtius. U. Peters, *DVLG*, 71:363–96, reviews new theoretical approaches to medieval studies, notably 'new philology', 'new historicism', and feminism, and W. Röcke, *MJ*, 31.2, 1996:21–37, comments on the 'new historicism' approach. In *ZDP*, 116, *Sonderheft*, S. G. Nichols (10–30) continues the debate about a new textual philology, favouring on the basis of Old French examples a 'philological scepticism' which treats each individual manuscript as a self-contained cultural monument. In a highly theoretical contribution H. U. Gumbrecht (31–45) links different versions of the New Philology to the philosophy of Derrida, and I. Bennewitz (46–61) pleads for the retention of the benefits of traditional textual criticism whatever new tasks may be impending, while P. Strohschneider (62–86) places the concept of situation at the heart of a critique of the new approaches. Glessgen, *Philologie*, is dedicated to 'alte und neue Philologie', and takes issue with the substance and consequences of the 'new philology' on a broad and interdisciplinary basis. General issues and problems are outlined by M.-D. Glessgen (1–14), while there are further critiques partly, but by no means exclusively, concentrating on individual disciplines, by P. Ménard (French, 17–33), A. Varvaro (Italian, 35–42), and J. Kramer (Classical antiquity and Romania, 43–59). For medieval German, R. Schnell (61–95) in a pungent and wide-ranging analysis argues that, while the overall picture is complex, editorial practice is far less archaic than the proponents of the new school allege. D. Rieger (97–109) criticizes 'new philology' from a literary view-point, and W. Oesterreicher (111–26) and W. Raible (127–41) consider different aspects of textual philology and editorial practice. M. Selig (201–25) considers the role of 'orality' in the debate, and R. E. F. Straub (227–35) the place of electronic textual editions. K.-E. Geith, pp. 9–20 of *Zwiesprache. Beiträge zur Theorie und Geschichte des Übersetzens*, ed. Ulrich Stadler and John E. Jackson, Stuttgart, Metzler, 1996, xi + 418 pp., comments on problems of translation in the Middle Ages.

Kerstin Bartels, *Musik in deutschen Texten des Mittelalters* (EH, I, 1601), 518 pp., is a comprehensive classified survey, if thin on detail. *Das Mittelalter*, 1.1, 1996, inaugurates a new journal with a range of articles on often interdisciplinary aspects of providence, fate, and fortune; *ib.*, 2.1, is dedicated to approaches to foreign languages in the period, and includes a substantial bibliography on the subject (K. Bosselmann-Cyran, 3–14), besides work on the high medieval conception of *imitatio* (D. de Rentiis, 83–92), and on late-medieval Latin teaching (U. Bodemann, 29–46); *ib.*, 2.2, is dedicated to the proverb and medieval literature, with a select bibliography (B. Janz, 3–6). Susann El Kholi, *Lektüre in Frauenkonventen des ostfränkisch-deutschen Reiches vom 8. Jahrhundert bis zur Mitte des 13. Jahrhunderts* (Ep, 203), 480 pp., is a Bonn dissertation which identifies its sources as chiefly library catalogues, works known to originate in convents and hagiographic texts probably linked to them, and works cited by women writers or commissioned by women. The greater part of the study (pp. 11–300) is an alphabetically arranged list of authors and works accompanied by the documentary evidence of their presence.

There follow systematic lists of works by chronology and subject-matter from which inferences are drawn about the relative popularity of specific types of work in different periods. The strength of this careful analysis ultimately derives less from any particular view of women's education than from the fact that the female religious houses supply a manageable body of data for fruitful analysis. Nevertheless, the conclusions include the important observation that, in view of the relative overall paucity of vernacular works, the level of Latinity in female religious houses must have been very high. Ernst Ralf Hintz, *Learning and Persuasion in the German Middle Ages* (GRLH, 1958), xv + 206 pp., considers the theme of Christian education in selected vernacular works of the early Middle Ages as delineated above all in Augustine's *De doctrina christiana*, an analysis of which forms the substance of the opening chapter on concepts of learning and teaching, followed by glances at Gregory the Great and Hrabanus Maurus. Subsequent chapters then focus on the *Muspilli*, *Memento Mori*, Frau Ava, whose works are perceived as embodying a unified pattern of *ascensus*, and the *Linzer Antichrist*. The analyses are quite detailed and include English translations of the passages cited. The emphasis on the pedagogical function of the texts is a useful corrective to some recent approaches, but begs the question of whether authors such as Otfrid or indeed the bulk of the corpus of Early MHG religious texts had a primarily educational purpose.

Karl Stackmann, *Mittelalterliche Texte als Aufgabe. Kleine Schriften*, 1, ed. Jens Haustein, Göttingen, Vandenhoeck & Ruprecht, viii + 445 pp., reprints in handsome format 30 articles spanning the whole period from 1955 to 1990. The seminal 'Mittelalterliche Texte als Aufgabe' introduces the collection, the contents of which are grouped according to the central focuses of S.'s research, the 12th-c. pre-courtly epic and the lyric of Frauenlob and Heinrich von Mügeln, while there is also much of interest here on the earlier history of *Germanistik*. Fritz Peter Knapp, *Historie und Fiktion in der mittelalterlichen Gattungspoetik. Sieben Studien und ein Nachwort*, Heidelberg, Winter, 213 pp., consists of reprints of seven essays previously published between 11980 and 1996. Although not especially inaccessible, the reproduction of these items together in book format is justified by their unified concern with the problems of *historia*, fictionality, rhetoric, and literary theory, based on the fundamental insight that the theocentric understanding of all medieval literature supplies an objective yardstick for its analysis in the poetics of the period. K.'s work draws on a very wide range of examples of both theoretical and creative literature and the index of authors and works is accordingly welcome. Xenja von Ertzdorff, *Spiel der Interpretation. Gesammelte Aufsätze zur Literatur des Mittelalters und der frühen Neuzeit* (GAG, 597),

1996, 552 pp. A. Masser, Holzner, *Literatur*, 143–56, publishes correspondence of Joseph Seemüller.

A. Mentzel-Reuters, *DAEM*, 53:179–203, supplies a bibliography of MS catalogues. New MS catalogues with a vernacular content include E. Overgaauw, *Die mittelalterlichen Handschriften der Universitäts- und Landesbibliothek Münster*, Wiesbaden, Harrassowitz, 1996, 300 pp.; H. Hoffmann, *Bamberger Handschriften des 10. und des 11. Jahrhunderts* (MGH. Schriften, 39), Hanover, Hahn, 1995, xiv + 210 pp.; *Die Handschriften des 12. Jahrhunderts der Staatsbibliothek Bamberg*, ed. G. Suckale-Redlefsen (Katalog der illuminierten Handschriften der Staatsbibliothek Bamberg, 2), Wiesbaden, Harrassowitz, 1995, xlvi + 206 pp.; *Handbuch der historischen Buchbestände in Deutschland. I. Schleswig-Holstein, Hamburg, Bremen*, ed. P. Raabe, ed. A. Müller-Jerina, Hildesheim, Olms-Weidmann, 1996, 382 pp.; *Die gotischen Handschriften der Württembergischen Landesbibliothek Stuttgart. I. Vom späten 12. bis zum frühen 14. Jahrhundert*, ed. C. Sauer, Stuttgart, Hiersemann, 1996, vi + 478 pp.; *Handbuch der historischen Buchbestände in Österreich. III. Burgenland, Kärnten, Niederösterreich, Oberösterreich, Salzburg*, ed. W. Buchinger and K. Mittendorfer, Hildesheim, Olms-Weidmann, 1996, 33 pp.; K. Gugel, *Welche erhaltenen mittelalterlichen Handschriften dürfen der Bibliothek des Klosters Fulda zugerechnet werden? I. Die Handschriften. II. Die Fragmente aus Handschriften* (Fuldaer Hochschulschriften, 23), 2 vols, Frankfurt, Knecht, 1995, 1996, 88, 72 pp.; Elisabeth Klemm, *Die illuminierten Handschriften des 13. Jahrhunderts deutscher Herkunft in der Bayerischen Staatsbibliothek* (Katalog der illuminierten Handschriften der Bayerischen Staatsbibliothgek in München, 4), 2 vols, Wiesbaden, Reichert, 256, 224 pp.; A. Fingernagel and M. Roland, *Die illuminierten Handschriften und Inkunabeln der Österreichischen Nationalbibliothek. Mitteleuropäische Schulen*, I (Österr. Akad. der Wiss., phil.-hist. Kl., Denkschriften, 245), 2 vols, Vienna, Österr. Akad. der Wiss., xxxii + 362, 70 pp.; and Hugo Alker, *Universitätsbibliothek Wien. Katalog der Inkunabeln*, ed. Leopold Cornaro, 2nd rev. edn, Vienna, Universitätsbibliothek, 1996, xv + 279 + xlv pp. I. T. Piirainen, *GeW*, 119:29–38, documents neglected vernacular manuscripts in Silesian archives in Poland. W. Milde, *Scriptorium*, 50, 1996:269–78, supplies essential information on the organization of medieval book catalogues, and T. Brandis, *GJ*, 72:27–57, attempts a classification of manuscripts from the end of the period, while R. Cermann, *Scriptorium*, 51:30–50, includes vernacular documents in a survey of the library of Duke Eberhard im Bart of Württemberg, and U.-D. Oppitz, *ZDA*, 125, 1996:404–10, describes manuscripts formerly in the possession of Karl Anton Josef von Kesaer. H. Taubken, *Fest. Möhn*, 29–38, comments on Stockholm MS Cod. Holm Vu 73. J. P. Gumbert, *ABÄG*, 48:149–53, asks fundamental questions about the role of manuscript punctuation. Also noted: Jürgen Römer, *Geschichte der Kürzungen. Abbreviaturen in deutschsprachigen Texten des Mittelalters und der frühen Neuzeit* (GAG, 645), 237 pp., while P. Czerwinski, *IASL*, 57.2 : 1–33, introduces work on the significance of the initial capital.

OTHER WORKS

E. P. Bos, *ABÄG*, 48 : 71–86, contributes to knowledge of medieval semantics, and W. Neuhauser, Holzner, *Literatur*, 157–64, publishes a 13th-c. complaint about the detrimental effect of bad proof-readers, while R. Härtel, *Fest. Schwob*, 119–31, reviews the anthroponymy of different types of medieval text, and O. G. Oexle, *Fest. Worstbrock*, 241–62, considers approaches to cultural history.

Karl Langosch, *Mittellatein und Europa. Führung in die Hauptliteratur des Mittelalters*, 2nd edn, WBG, xiv + 305 pp., is an admirable concise survey of the period to the early 13th c. divided into three phases. Each is in turn subdivided into the major geographical regions, within each of which the Latin literary activity is surveyed followed by reference to the chief vernacular developments. The sections on Old and Middle High German are not insubstantial and the perspective is a helpful corrective to the many recent treatments of the vernacular divorced from its 'roots'. *The Poems of Alcimus Ecdicius Avitus*, trans. and introd. George W. Shea (MRTS, 172), ix + 154 pp., is a most welcome rendering in a readable English prose of the standard MGH edition of A.'s works, the five based on Genesis and Exodus and of seminal importance for the medieval tradition of the biblical epic, and *On Chastity*. The no less admirable introduction occupies almost half the book: S. gives a general review of the life and works, followed by quite detailed analyses of each poem in turn, though refraining from systematic documentation of biblical and theological parallels. One can only regret that the Latin text was not also included. Boethius, *Trost der Philosophie. Zweisprachige Ausgabe*, trans. Ernst Neitzke, introd. Ernst Ludwig Grasmück (IT, 1215), xxxiv + 344 pp., gives the standard Latin text accompanied by a clear German translation on facing pages. The introduction reviews the historical background to the work and its content and structure. There is a short section of notes. P. Godman, *Fest. Worstbrock*, 177–98, has a survey of medieval Latin historiography. Constant J. Mews, *Peter Abelard*. V. I. J. Flint, *Honorius Augustodunensis of Regensburg* (Authors of the Middle Ages. II, 5–6. Historical and Religious Writers of the Latin West), Aldershot, Variorum, 1995, vi + vii + 80, vi + 89 pp., is simultaneously announced as two separate paperback titles. Both studies are admirably informative introductions to their respective subjects. M. supplies the chief established facts about Abelard's life and works in 35 pages, followed by a richly documented classified bibliography of manuscript and printed sources in 44 pages following the organization of the introductory text, and bibliography. F. summarizes her authoritative research on the career, chronology, and works of Honorius in 63 pages, followed by a provisional handlist of surviving Latin manuscripts and bibliography.

Zeitkonzeptionen, Zeiterfahrung, Zeitmessung. Stationen ihres Wandels vom Mittelalter bis zur Moderne, ed. Trude Ehlert, Paderborn, Schöningh, xv + 337 pp., is an interdisciplinary collection with an introduction and 18 essays on subjects indicating either reflection on attitudes to time or their implicit manifestation. Of central interest to the period are essays by H.-W. Goetz (the conceptions of time in high medieval historiography, 12–32), H. Appel (the development of conceptions of time in the natural sciences, 49–68), U. Lindgren (Albertus Magnus and astronomical time, 69–79), B. Pabst (atomic vs. continuous time in a range of medieval authors, 80–102), W. Knoch (time and eternity in Nicholas of Cusa, 103–16), G. Keil (sickness and time, 117–38), U. R. Jeck (Augustine and the early medieval theory of time, 179–202), and T. Ehlert (temporal aspects of the OHG confessional formulae and later hagiographical works, 256–73). Contributions on works in other languages are also included. J. Knape, *LiLi*, 105:6–21, traces the place of *memoria* in Classical and later rhetoric. Lothar Pikulik, *Warten, Erwartung. Eine Lebensform in End- und Übergangszeiten. An Beispielen aus der Geistesgeschichte, Literatur und Kunst*, Göttingen, Vandenhoeck & Ruprecht, 195 pp., treats the theme of waiting, expectation, and *fin de siècle* in different periods against the background of the forthcoming millennium. The section on the medieval period, which could obviously have been amplified with specifically historical information, dwells on the relevance to the topic of *Heilsgeschichte*, the liturgical cycle, and the sacraments. Other chapters focus on the Enlightenment and Romantic expressions of the theme, developments at the turn of the 20th c. with special emphasis on the sickness motif as exemplified in Thomas Mann's *Der Zauberberg*, and more recent treatments in exile literature and elsewhere.

Arnold Angenendt, *Geschichte der Religiosität im Mittelalter*, Darmstadt, Primus, xiii + 986 pp., is a truly monumental study of medieval religious practice within the context of religious history. The work takes account of all major approaches to medieval theology in the past generation and the sheer density of the material is made manageable by careful organization. After a preliminary chapter on fundamentals and periodization A. deals in turn with God, Christ, and the supernatural powers; revelation and doctrine; time, space, family, society, and the organization of the Church in practice; the liturgy; human conduct, sin, penance, and atonement; death, judgement, and the after-life. This is a substantial work of reference rather than a study to read from cover to cover and the very full and careful documentation means it can be used as a guide through a massive array of literature when the precise detail sought is lacking. Henning Graf Reventlow, *Epochen der Bibelauslegung. III. Renaissance, Reformation, Humanismus*, Munich, Beck, 271 pp., continues this attractively readable history (see *YWMLS*, 53:618; 56:721, for earlier volumes). The chapter on the Renaissance focuses on exemplary figures involved in the return to the original languages, Platonic, Judaizing, more evangelistic approaches, and Erasmus. The substantial second chapter addresses the Reformation in detail and there is a brief concluding section on its legacy in Lutheran orthodoxy and Counter-Reformation. Arvid Göttlicher, *Die Schiffe im Alten Testament*, Berlin, Gebr. Mann, 250 pp. + 212 pls, is a useful and relatively comprehensive survey of the subject and a source of examples in both literature and iconography. While theological considerations dominate, G. aims also to exemplify aesthetic, decorative, historical, and philological aspects, besides practical and ecological features more common in modern interpretations. The study is, not surprisingly, dominated by Noah's ark, Moses and Jonah coming far behind. A substantial number of medieval literary texts are cited, too many for detailed analysis. On a similar topic is Günter Kettenbach, *Einführung in die Schiffahrtsmetaphorik der Bibel* (EH, XXIII, 512), 1994, 538 pp. A. M. Bass, Debatin, *Metaphor*, 203–13, studies the metaphor of the human body in John of Salisbury and elsewhere, astonishingly without reference to the work of D. Peil (see *YWMLS*, 46:661–62). Heinz Schreckenberg, *Die christlichen Adversus-Judaeos Texte (11.-13. Jh.). Mit einer Ikonographie des Judenthemas bis zum 4. Laterankonzil* (EH, XXIII, 335), 3rd rev. edn, 739 pp., is a welcome revision of this monumental review of the major texts of the period. The work extends the equally comprehensive treatment of the early Middle Ages (see *YWMLS*, 58:718) and in fact goes beyond anti-Jewish polemic in the narrow sense to document much of more general significance as Christian apologetic, often with the chief purpose of didactic instruction of the Christian faithful for whom the unbelieving antagonist may be little more than a fictional construct. This volume is notable for the inclusion of a significant range of mainly Early MHG texts and authors, notably *Mittelfränkische Reimbibel, Kaiserchronik*, Lamprecht's *Alexander, St. Trudperter Hohelied, Anegenge, Der Wilde Mann, Esau und Jakob, Morant und Galie*, and 'Das Jüdel', besides other vernacular instances of common European themes such as the legend of the destruction of Jerusalem. S.'s description and bibliographical documentation of the works is never less than adequate if not always wholly up to date, and their integration into a catalogue of mainly Latin theological works points to the role of vernacular literature in the development of attitudes to the Jews in the period. *Shylock? Zinsverbot und Geldverleih in jüdischer und christlicher Tradition*, ed. Johannes Heil and Bernd Wacker, Munich, Fink, 304 pp., includes considerable documentation on the background to the attitude to interest in the medieval period. K. Werner (11–20) explains the Old Testament background with its unclear distinction between legal and moral prohibition, and M. T. Kloft (21–34) traces the attitude of the Church from early times through to the Baroque period. J. Heil (35–58) amplifies the exegetical tradition and considers literary examples, in particular the treatment of the Golden Calf episode in the late-medieval drama. F. Burgard (59–80) makes a detailed comparison of money-lending by Christians and Jews in medieval Trier. The remaining contributions treat Venice, Frankfurt, and more modern dimensions of the topic. Luther Link, *Der Teufel. Eine Maske ohne Gesicht*, trans. Heinz Jatho, Munich, Fink, 247 pp., is a richly illustrated study which draws on a range of literary, artistic, and scholarly sources, though in a somewhat haphazard and arbitrarily organized fashion. With chapters on the name and appearance of the devil, heresies and the depiction of hell, the Last Judgement in art, and the devil as rebel angel, L. distinguishes different strands in the portrayal of the devil and asks rather than answers difficult questions about the development of doctrine in this area. Hans Körner, *Grabmonumente des Mittelalters*, Darmstadt, Primus, v + 202 pp. with 142 illus., is an informative complement to current interest in the memorial culture of the period. The approach is substantially art historical, with a section on the dominant role of the Church in funerary practice from the earliest Christian period followed by an account of the development of types of monumental tomb. Among subsequent chapters those on on the idealized portrayal of the dead, the role of masses for the dead, and the generic distinction between tomb and monument, are of particular relevance. *Pictura quasi fictura. Die Rolle des Bildes in der Erforschung von Alltag und Sachkultur des Mittelalters und der frühen Neuzeit. Internationales Round-Table-Gespräch Krems an der Donau 3. Oktober 1994*, [ed. Gerhard Jaritz] (Österr. Akad. der Wiss. Phil.-hist. Kl. Forschungen des Instituts für Realienkunde des Mittelalters und der frühen Neuzeit. Diskussionen und Materialien, 1), Vienna, Vlg der Österr. Akad. der Wiss., 1996, 208 pp., includes an introduction by G. Jaritz and eight further contributions of the role of illustration in conveying perceptions of late-medieval culture. Besides theoretical discussions of the 'reality' of pictorial representation there is work by K. Schreiner (87–127) on the imagery of the milk and breasts of the Virgin Mary, W. Schmid (129–74) on

Dürer, and N. Schnitzler (175–90) on the cult of images. H. Kugler, *Fest. Worstbrock*, 77–93, relates the tradition of the medieval *mappae mundi* to literary descriptive technique. Jurgis Baltrušaitis, *Das phantastische Mittelalter. Antike und exotische Elemente der Kunst der Gotik*, Berlin, Gebr. Mann, 415 pp. incl. 188 illus., reinterprets the Gothic style in terms of the fantastic and exotic, so that from the opening pages we are treated to a whole host of examples of fabulous and monstrous beings and their like. B. attributes many aspects of the art of the period to Classical, Islamic, and Oriental, even Chinese, influences; Buddhist features, for example, presumably known to Oriental travellers, influence both the forms (mandala) and the themes (dance of death) of late-medieval art. While the possibility of polygenesis can rarely be wholly excluded, there is much food for thought here.

Wolfgang L. Gombocz, *Die Philosophie der ausgehenden Antike und des frühen Mittelalters* (Geschichte der Philosophie, 4), Munich, Beck, 513 pp., is part of a planned 12-volume history of philosophy which began in 1978. In spite of the immense ground to be covered G. succeeds in conveying a balance between names and clear surveys of the essential ideas. The first two chapters address the Platonic thought of late antiquity. The third deals with the beginnings of Christian philosophy with sections on early apologetics, the Greek Fathers, St Augustine, and Dionysius the Areopagite, while the final chapter takes us by way of Boethius and John Eriugena and the Carolingians to Anselm of Canterbury and the beginnings of scholasticism. *Das Licht der Vernunft. Die Anfänge der Aufklärung im Mittelalter*, ed. Kurt Flasch and Udo Reinhold Jeck, Munich, Beck, 191 pp., is a collection of 14 essays with the aim, outlined by K. Flasch in his introduction, of demonstrating, against popular prejudice, that ideas of the Enlightenment and the supremacy of reason date back to the high Middle Ages. The concise and readable contributions include work by F. Niewöhner (Maimonides), C. E. Butterworth (Averroes), P. von Moos (Abelard), L. Sturlese (Albert the Great), G. Mensching (Aquinas), L. Bianchi (Étienne Tempier), A. de Libera (logic in rational thought), K. Flasch (Boccaccio), O. Pluta (materialist thought), U. R. Jeck (magic and alchemy), and A. Murray (the social consequences of rational thought in the period).

Jagd und höfische Kultur im Mittelalter, ed. Werner Rösener (Veröffentlichungen des Max-Planck-Instituts für Geschichte, 135), Göttingen, Vandenhoeck & Ruprecht, 590 pp., is a very detailed treatment of the topic, with introductory survey of research (11–28) and summarizing conclusion (573–90) by W. Rösener. Besides contributions of direct literary relevance cited below there is also work by L. Fenske (the conditions of hunting in the early Middle Ages and the hunter's spiritual affinity with nature, 29–93); T. Zotz (the role and organization of royal forests, 95–122); W. Rösener (the relationship between hunting, chivalry, and the royal court, 123–47); J. Fried (Frederick II and the *Ars venandi*, 149–66); T. Szabó (hunting in Classical literature and in medieval exegetical tradition, 167–229); K.-H. Spiess (the peasants in relation to hunting, 231–54); J. Morsel (the social significance of hunting in late-medieval Franconia, 255–87); W. Störmer (the courtly hunt in Bavaria, with a mention of *Ruodlieb*, 289–324); K. Militzer (the Teutonic Order, 325–63); and W. Meyer (the archaeological dimension of hunting and fishing, 465–91). U. Müller, Erfen, *Fremdheit*, 93–146, studies the exotic associations of the surviving figures used in the medieval games of chess and *hnefatafl*. Werner Faulstich, *Das Medium als Kult. Von den Anfängen bis zur Spätantike (8. Jahrhundert)* (Die Geschichte der Medien, 1), Göttingen, Vandenhoeck & Ruprecht, 327 pp., follows the recently published volume on the medieval media (see *YWMLS*, 58:710). The aim here is to illustrate the thesis from the dawn of humanity to the early Middle Ages; what emerges is a canter through the major ancient civilizations focusing on whatever features of their archaeology, inscriptions, and rituals can be interpreted as 'media'. While the earliest history of the book forms a natural bridge to medieval civilization, the culmination of this volume in the druids as 'letztes genuines Menschmedium der Geschichte' points to the limitations of the approach. Eileen Power, *Medieval Women*, ed. M. M. Postan, CUP, xxviii + 104 pp., reprints a series of vivid and concisely informative chapters on medieval attitudes to women, the lady, working women, education, and nunneries, a timely reminder that much of the recent wave of publication in this area is less innovative than its authors sometimes appear to claim. The introductory biography of the author (1889–1940) by M. Berg is a thoroughly fascinating document in its own right. H.-W. Goetz, *Das Mittelalter*, 1.2, 1996:89–111, makes a quantitative analysis of the sexually specific features of miracles in hagiographical sources.

Das Mittelalter. Ein Lesebuch zur deutschen Geschichte 800–1500, ed. Rainer Beck (BsR, 1235), 283 pp., is an imaginatively conceived anthology of 35 pieces covering all aspects of German social, political, and cultural history in the period and based mainly, though not exclusively, on works from the Beck publishing house. The glittering array of specialists compensates for the fact that most items are, inevitably, of only a few pages in length, but there could hardly be a better way of advertising the wealth of readable work on the historical background to the period produced in the past 25 years. Roland Pauler, *Die deutschen Könige und Italien im 14. Jahrhundert. Von Heinrich VII. bis Karl IV.*, WBG, viii + 336 pp. + map, writes lucidly on a neglected period of history, showing above all the survival of the

Hohenstaufen ideal into the following century. While only Henry VII, made famous by Dante and later writers, sought to uphold the old theocratic view of monarchy in a manner impossible in Germany, Ludwig IV's partisanship effectively restricted the monarchy to Germany, while Charles IV was more successful than either through diplomacy. The text is copiously documented from the contemporary chronicles and elsewhere. A time chart and brief biographies of the chief personalities are included. Jörg K. Hoensch, *Geschichte Böhmens. Von der slavischen Landnahme bis zur Gegenwart*, 3rd rev. edn, Munich, Beck, 588 pp., is sufficiently detailed and documented to achieve the remarkable status of a complete short history within the covers of a single volume. H. adopts a straightforward chronological approach. The chapters on all periods pay more than lip-service to cultural developments, and the interaction of Germanic and Slavonic is clearly conveyed. Gerd Althoff, *Spielregeln der Politik im Mittelalter. Kommunikation in Frieden und Fehde*, Darmstadt, Primus, ix + 360 pp., contains 11 essays, seven of which were previously published in the recent past, forming a very coherent study of the manner in which conflict was conducted in medieval society and on forms of communication. Particularly illuminating is the detailed evidence on the manner in which conflict could be mitigated or terminated, the role of the adviser and the forms of counsel, the expression of the emotions, and the formalized, ritualistic aspects of both conflict and communication. Norbert Ohler, *Krieg und Frieden im Mittelalter*, Munich, Beck, 366 pp., is a broad-brush but effective account of the subject, though more concerned with war than peace. After a review of the relevant vocabulary and the basic conditions of topography, travel, and climate in medieval Europe, O. addresses religious attitudes to warfare, the conduct of military campaigns, relationship between commanders and warriors, aims and motivation of wars and their types, the rituals attending the opening and closing of hostilities, and forces tending to restrain the use of military power. *Norm und Praxis im Alltag des Mittelalters und der frühen Neuzeit. Internationales Round-Table-Gespräch Krems an der Donau 7. Oktober 1996*, [ed. Gerhard Jaritz] (Österr. Akad. der Wiss. Phil.-hist. Kl. Forschungen des Instituts für Realienkunde des Mittelalters und der frühen Neuzeit. Diskussionen und Materialien, 2), Vienna, Vlg der Österr. Akad. der Wiss., 126 pp., includes reference to a wide range of textual sources in a series of studies anchored in a thoughtful consideration of the implication of 'norms' for the study of various aspects of the everyday life of the period. G. Jaritz (7–19) illustrates the theoretical problem with a number of examples; G. Kocher (21–26) considers the relationship between concrete objects and rights and duties; K. Simon-Muscheid (55–74) examines the position of servants in relation to those in authority over them; H. Bräuer (75–93) surveys the situation of beggars and the place of almsgiving; and B. P. McGuire (107–24) writes on forms of norm and practice among the early Cistercians.

2. GERMANIC AND OLD HIGH GERMAN

Wilhelm Grönbech, *Kultur und Religion der Germanen*, pref. Otto Höfler, 12th edn, 2 vols in 1, Darmstadt, Primus, 440, 428 pp., makes available in handy format a classic study of early Germanic thought and culture from the early years of the century. While the work suffers from some obvious defects of *Geistesgeschichte* and tends to extrapolate from a primary focus on the early Norse evidence to Germania as a whole, many of the chapters on aspects of Germanic values and attitudes can still be read as useful surveys of ideas reflected in literature. C. T. Petersen, *MedS*, 59:301–56, updates the bibliography of work on Gothic, and H. Sivan, *RB*, 105, 1995:280–92, writes on Ulfila's biography, while E. A. Ebbinghaus, *NOWELE*, 31–32:101–03, points to the uncertain origin of Gothic manuscripts. Ingemar König, *Aus der Zeit Theoderichs des Großen. Einleitung, Text, Übersetzung und Kommentar einer anonymen Quelle*, WBG, x + 270 pp., supplies a critical edition with translation on facing pages (pp. 69–95) of a brief but seminally important work on the historical Theodoric, here named *Theodericiana* and previously *Excerpta Valesiana* or *Anonymus Valesianus* after its 17th-c. editor. The accompanying studies deal in detail with the transmission and relationship to other early medieval historians, historical value, and dating. The commentary is substantial (pp. 97–209). There are appendices of texts with cognate sources and full indexes. L. Hermodsson, *Fest Härd*, 99–112, poses some fundamental questions about the tribes in the Age of Migrations, and D. Poli, *NOWELE*, 31–32:325–29, writes on early Germanic and Romance conceptions of peace and war. *La funzione dell'eroe germanico: storicità, metafora, paradigma. Atti del convegno internazionale di studio Roma, 6–8 maggio 1993*, ed. Teresa Pàroli, Rome, Il Calamo, 1995, xiii + 376 pp., includes work on the early Germanic period by C. A. Mastrelli (the linguistic background, 1–5), A. Liberman (the heroic world-view, 259–72), W. Goffart (the Franks, 41–56), M. L. Ruggerini (the hero and his monstrous opponents, 202–57), and T. Pàroli (the anti-hero, 273–321), besides applications to Norse and Old English topics. Giangabriella Buti, *Mantica e mito nell'antica poesia germanica* (Biblioteca del Dipartimento di Lingue e Letterature Straniere Moderne dell'Università degli Studi di Bologna, 10), Bologna, Patròn, 1993, 206 pp. Patrick J. Geary, *Die Merowinger. Europa vor Karl dem Großen*, trans. Ursula Scholz, Munich, Beck, 1996, 249 pp., is a

German-language edition of a work which brings immense clarity to a difficult period. Following chapters on the Roman and the Germanic background G. explains the fusion of the two legacies and provides the essential detail on political developments, while not neglecting the wider cultural significance of figures such as St Martin of Tours, the missions, and the historiographical understanding of the early Franks. R. Boyer, *EG*, 52:581–92, attacks far-fetched mythical and magical interpretations of the runes, and T. Pàroli, *NOWELE*, 31–32:277–304, contributes to knowledge of the history of the Franks Casket, while B. Mees, *ZDA*, 126:131–39, reinterprets the Meldorf fibula inscription, and K. Düwel, *NOWELE*, 31–32:93–99, condemns the Illertissen (Ashmolean Museum) runic ring as a forgery.

G. Köbler, *ZDA*, 126:247–78, surveys OHG dictionaries, and H. Endermann, *CGP*, 25:1–10, reviews the development of OHG as a medium of translation from Latin, while A. Masser, *Fest. Bergmann*, 49–70, illustrates the scribal evidence of spoken OHG, and C. Moulin-Fankhänel, *ib.*, 301–27, reviews the treatment of OHG by early modern grammarians. D. H. Green, *MLR*, 92:xxix–xxxviii, shows how fundamental linguistic evidence, exemplified by the words *rîchi*, *wîn*, and **kirika*, taken in conjunction with historical data, can illustrate how Germanic, Roman, and Christian factors combined in the early Middle Ages. R. Gusmani, *HSp*, 109, 1996:133–43, analyses the HG Sound Shift in the *Pariser Gespräche*, and M. Gebhardt, *AION(FG)*, 5.1–2, 1995:9–24, interprets *cotinc* from the *Abrogans* glossary, while in *Fest. Bergmann*, S. Stricker (139–57) studies the glosses to the grammar of Donatus, I. Reiffenstein (71–84) documents *theodiscus* in OHG glosses, E. Glaser (3–20) amplifies her work on the Echternach scratch glosses, L. Voetz (185–95) identifies an OHG version of John 19. 38 as a translation rather than a mere gloss, R. Schmidt-Wiegand (85–91) notes legal language in the *Lorscher Annalen*, and F. Simmler (93–114) analyses punctuation in the Lorsch confessional formula and the *Weissenburg Catechism*. *Die lateinisch-althochdeutsche Benediktinerregel Stiftsbibliothek St. Gallen Cod. 916*, ed. Achim Masser (SA, 33), 382 pp., is the sixth edition to date of this important but neglected monument. A. seeks to facilitate access with a text close to the manuscript without being a mere diplomatic transcript such as P. Piper's edition which failed to relate the OHG interlinear glosses adequately to the Latin base text. A. sees this as his substantial achievement. Using different typefaces as necessary, each right-hand page corresponds to one manuscript folio, the line-lengths and the positioning of Latin and German words corresponding exactly. To make this possible abbreviations are not written out. The apparatus on the left-hand pages includes, among much else, information on the numerous later corrections. A substantial introduction and bibliography complement a very practical working edition for most study purposes, conceived along lines which deserve to be imitated for other glossed texts. Orrin W. Robinson, *Clause Subordination and Verb Placement in the Old High German 'Isidor' Translation* (Germanische Bibliothek, 3rd ser., 26), Heidelberg, Winter, x + 157 pp., is a significant contribution to the problem of word-order in OHG, based on the insight that the *Isidor* is the best example of early prose of sufficient size to allow meaningful conclusions. R. writes with lucidity, dealing in turn with finite and complex verbs, other non-finite constructions, the conjunction *dhazs*, indirect questions, relative, causal, concessive, and conditional clauses, and clauses of time, place, and manner. The numerous examples, with the index of passages cited, make this a useful guide to understanding a difficult text. H.-W. Eroms, *ZDA*, 126: 1–31, analyses the temporal system of verbs in *Isidor*, and K. Gärtner and G. Holtus, pp. 97–127 of *Beiträge zum Sprachkontakt und zu den Urkundensprachen zwischen Maas und Rhein*, ed. Kurt Gärtner and Günter Holtus (Trierer historische Forschungen, 29), Trier, THF, 1995, 315 pp. + supp., study the transmission of the *Straßburger Eide*. N. Wagner, *Sprachwissenschaft*, 22: 309–27, interprets some details of the *Hildebrandslied*, and L. Papo, *Prospero*, 3, Trieste, 1996: 172–80, considers the sources of the *Muspilli*, while H.-D. Schlosser, *ZDA*, 125, 1996: 386–91, links lines in Otfrid's dedication to Ludwig the German with the Treaty of Meerssen and hence finds a new *terminus post quem* of 8 August 870.

D. Hofmann, *NdJb*, 117, 1994: 7–23, statistically assesses metrical and alliterative usage in the *Heliand*, while in *NdJb*, 115, 1992, R. Veenbaas (159–73), T. Klein (174–77), and T. Hofstra (177–82) cautiously discuss the evidence that it was composed by Bernlef. G. R. Murphy, *MDU*, 89: 5–17, studies the light imagery of the *Heliand*, arguing that it is developed independently of the traditional sources. There is a Spanish translation, *Heliand*, trans. Carlos Búa, Madrid, Pons, 1996, xix + 353 pp. S. B. Mintz, *Neophilologus*, 81: 609–23, takes a feminist view of the Eve of *Genesis B*. H. Tiefenbach, *Fest. Bergmann*, 169–83, shows the value for the history of Old Saxon of the graphemic forms in the *Vita Liudgeri*.

Heinrich Götz, *Deutsch und Latein bei Notker. Ergänzungen zum Notker-Glossar von E. H. Sehrt*, Tübingen, Niemeyer, ix + 120 pp., is organized as an alphabetical dictionary designed to accompany the use of Sehrt's still invaluable work of 1962. The material has accrued with the increasing realization in the course of lexicographical work that Sehrt's assertion that each of his OHG words is accompanied by the corresponding Latin term is of only limited validity. Following an introductory survey classifying the new information G. presents over

3,600 new entries, more than enough to justify publication in this form and essential for integration in any new edition of Sehrt's glossary. Notker Labeo, *De musica*, ed., trans., and comm. Martin van Schaik, Utrecht, 1995, xii + 83 pp. E. S. Firchow, *Fest. Schwob*, 99–108, prints and discusses a 17th-c. life of Notker, and S. Sonderegger, *Fest. Bergmann*, 115–38, studies Notker's treatment of the Orpheus and Eurydice episode in his Boethius translation, while P. W. Tax, *ib.*, 159–68, examines Notker's procedure in some of his recently edited minor texts. A. Zissos, *MJ*, 32.2:53–78, studies the marriages in *Ruodlieb*.

3. MIDDLE HIGH GERMAN

GENERAL

Eberhard Nellmann, *Quellenverzeichnis zu den mittelhochdeutschen Wörterbüchern. Ein kommentiertes Register zum 'Benecke/Müller/Zarncke' und zum 'Lexer'*, Stuttgart–Leipzig, Hirzel, 212 pp., is a handy aid to the practical use of what remain, used in conjunction, the two major MHG dictionaries. N. addresses the haphazard and arbitrary documentation of the sources in the different volumes with a fairly comprehensive index of the abbreviations added, and supplies titles and dates of works, later editions than those cited, and the standard modern editions. Most useful of all is the breakdown of the contents of the 19th-c. collective editions which greatly enhances the ease of identification. U. Schaefer, pp. 50–70 of *Mündlichkeit—Schriftlichkeit—Weltbildwandel. Literarische Kommunikation und Deutungsschemata von Wirklichkeit in der Literatur des Mittelalters und der frühen Neuzeit*, ed. Werner Röcke and Ursula Schaefer (ScriptOralia, 71), Tübingen, Narr, 1996, vi + 225 pp., favours a fundamental change in communicative media in the 12th century. C. S. Jaeger, Wenzel, *Gespräche*, 177–92, notes the presence of irony in the stylized rhetoric of friendship and love in Latin letters of the 11th and 12th cs, and M. Wis, *Ginkgobaum*, 13, 1995:194–201, comments on *mîn vrouwe* as a form of address, while I. Bennewitz, *Das Mittelalter*, 1.2, 1996:11–26, characterizes dialogues between women in a range of MHG texts, and N. R. Wolf, *Fest. Schwob*, 557–66, emphasizes the narrative significance of the use of *lop* as a term of approbation in classical courtly literature, and corresponding terms to denote criticism or blame. C. S. Jaeger, *Exemplaria*, 9:117–37, traces 12th-c. aesthetic changes in terms of the transformation of the charismatic body into text, and R. De Pol, *Chloe*, 26:423–44, characterizes physical beauty in MHG works, while T. Nolte, *Fest. Laufhütte*, 39–60, studies the theme of *wilde* and its attributes. Also noted: Alois Wolf, *Das Faszinosum der mittelalterlichen*

Minne (Wolfgang Stammler Gastprofessur für Germanische Philologie. Vorträge, 5), Fribourg U.P., 1996, 66 pp. M. J. Schubert, pp. 237–73 of *Parody. Dimensions and Perspectives*, ed. Beate Müller (Rodopi Perspectives on Modern Literature, 19), Amsterdam, Rodopi, 313 pp., records parody in 13th-c. poetry. In *JRG*, 7, 1996, D. Buschinger (11–22), W. Spiewok (155–68), and M. Vittor-Lesaffre (181–91) discuss literature of the Teutonic Order. E. Wenzel, *ZDP*, 116:417–26, reports newly-discovered wall paintings in Zurich from *c.* 1330. D. E. H. de Boer, *ABÄG*, 48:87–113, studies Bavarian–Dutch political and literary relations *c.* 1390.

In Wenzel, *Gespräche*, H. Wenzel (9–21) introduces an important collection of essays focusing on the implications of new technology and communications theory for medieval literature and the insight that it is based on a 'performance culture'. W. Haug (23–41) exemplifies the forms of communication in three great love stories with the themes of message (*König Rother*), confession (*Tristan*), and ecstatic deed transcending speech (*Prosa Lancelot*), and B. Siegert (45–62) considers approaches to communication in pre-modern Europe, while H. Wenzel (86–105) discusses types and functions of messenger and message in a range of MHG works, and H.-J. Bachorski (344–64) studies the communicative function of the lie, seeing its relative effect as closely related to the genres in which it is used. Klaus Hofbauer, *Gott und der Welt gefallen. Geschichte eines gnomischen Motivs im hohen Mittelalter* (EH, 1, 1630), 404 pp., in a work originally inspired by F. Ohly investigates the background to a theme perhaps most familiar from Gottfried's *Tristan*. Over half the work is taken up with a chronological survey of the exegetical background to the equation of God and the world, a task made difficult by the discrete nature of relevant biblical texts. Somewhat arbitrarily, H. selects two gnomic passages from Proverbs and two verses from Luke. The presentation of the exegetical tradition, which includes due attention to homiletic literature, is not facilitated by a diffuse discussion of a whole range of work on the cultural and theological background. Nevertheless, H. does succeed in identifying a line of tradition which in the second part of the work is traced to a range of authors, courtly as well as more explicitly didactic, from the period 1150–1230. U. Herzog, *Fest. Tarot*, 231–36, reviews references to *gotes hantgetât*. E. Papp, *NdJb*, 120:33–58, surveys the literary characterization of the Saxons. In Erfen, *Fremdheit*, a collection dedicated to journeys and the concept of the foreign, K.-H. Spiess (17–36) surveys European-wide evidence of bridal journeys to foreign parts among the nobility, and D. Ruhe (37–51) links literary bridal journeys to contemporary matrimonial law. R. Bräuer (53–63) categorizes the forms of travel which constitute the existence of medieval epic heroes, and D. Kattinger (93–117) studies the experiences of Albrecht of Mecklenburg as a foreign ruler in 14th-c. Sweden. H.-P. Schmiedebach and M. G. Bondio (217–34) consider attitudes to the foreign arising from the spread of the plague in the 14th c., and C. Friedrich (235–41) points to the role of the itinerant apothecary. J. C. Frakes, *NOWELE*, 31–32: 119–33, identifies types of 'metamorphosis' in the literary treatment of 'Muslims', while real Muslims feature in Kiril Petkov, *Infidels, Turks, and Women. The South Slavs in the German Mind, ca. 1400–1600*, Frankfurt, Lang, 335 pp. C. Brinker-von der Heyde, *BGDSL*, 119: 399–424, surveys Amazons in MHG literature.

Claudia Brinker-von der Heyde, *Geliebte Mütter—Mütterliche Geliebte. Rolleninszenierung in höfischen Romanen* (SGAK, 123), 1996, 403 pp., focuses on the mother figures and roles in Gottfried, Wolfram, Hartmann, Ulrich von Zatzikhoven's *Lanzelet*, and Wirnt von Grafenberg's *Wigalois*. The opening chapters on the concept of the mother and the views of the Church have a feminist slant, but the subsequent analyses lack the reductive implications of the approach and cover a wide range of topics: the various qualities necessary to be the mother of a hero, procreation and birth, maternal functions, the death of the mother, and the plurality of maternal roles. Above all the secular poets are seen to reflect the separation in clerical literature of biological and spiritual motherhood, resulting in a constant elevation of motherhood into an unrealistic ideal. Ann Marie Rasmussen, *Mothers and Daughters in Medieval German Literature*, Syracuse U.P., xvi + 253 pp., uses 'contemporary feminist theory to interpret the mother-daughter relationship in male-authored medieval German literature'. The conventional discussion by mothers and daughters about love figures in many but not all of the texts discussed: Brother Hermann's *Leben der Gräfin Iolande von Vianden* (whose relationship with her mother is also analysed in *Das Mittelalter*, 1.2, 1996: 27–37), Veldeke's *Eneas*, the *Nibelungenlied*, *Kudrun*, Gottfried's *Tristan*, *Die Winsbeckin*, Neidhart songs, and a fabliau-type *Minnerede*, *Stiefmutter und Tochter*. Underlying the study is the assumption that the social contexts 'place all women at a disadvantage'. The huge generic and thematic range of these works results in the subjection of the often relatively slight passages of text to an interpretative weight they can sometimes scarcely bear; fortunately, the conclusions emphasize the diversity of notions of femininity in a patriarchal social order. J. W. Thomas, *GN*, 28: 22–24, draws attention to the number of high medieval narratives which deal with domestic tragedy. Ekaterini Kepetzis, *Medea in der Bildenden Kunst vom Mittelalter zur Neuzeit. 'So im Herzen bedrängt erglühte verderbliche Liebe'* (EH, xxviii, 305), 280 pp., includes a catalogue of 106 examples which form the basis for the analysis, and 27 illustrations. The extreme ambivalence of a figure whose love for Jason could be accommodated to courtly sentiment but whose subsequent behaviour could only reduce her to a negative *exemplum* emerges clearly from this study, which lays the groundwork for a treatment of Medea in literature while treating the art-historical aspect comprehensively. K. first takes us through the Classical literary and artistic background. The following chapter, which exploits manuscript illustration, substantially confirms the suggestion of W. Schröder in the context of Konrad von Würzburg's *Trojanerkrieg* (see *YWMLS*, 55 : 723) that the high Middle Ages distanced itself from the tragic implications of the love of Jason and Medea, for the initial positive reception of Benoît's *Roman de Troie* is not maintained and the later medieval examples are strictly moralizing and didactic, a situation which must surely be the case in literature. About equal space again is devoted to the review of examples from the Renaissance to the late 19th c., and the book as a whole supplies a rich and well-documented source of the subject-matter. Antje Holzhauer, *Rache und Fehde in der mittelhochdeutschen Literatur des 12. und 13. Jahrhunderts* (GAG, 639), 361 pp. E. Feistner, *BGDSL*, 119 : 235–60, surveys cross-dressing disguise in various MHG sources. H. Eckhardt, *Neophilologus*, 81 : 105–15, surveys spiders from MHG literature on.

H. Fromm, *Ginkgobaum*, 13, 1995 : 181–93, considers the programme of St Gall Codex 857. Helmut de Boor, *Die deutsche Literatur im späten Mittelalter. 1. 1250–1350*, rev. and ed. Johannes Janota (Geschichte der deutschen Literatur von den Anfängen bis zur Gegenwart, III/ 1), 5th edn, Munich, Beck, xii + 568 pp., represents a total revision of this portion of the late-medieval section of the standard literary history, following the completion of the second volume (see *YWMLS*, 49 : 628). In the present instance the advantages of revision by a single hand are clear and the text, with the bibliography concentrated in a single final chapter, can be read with confidence as an account of the period which does justice to the huge developments in research of recent decades without adopting transient approaches of current fashion. J. explains his carefully considered policy of eliminating de Boor's thesis of *Zerfall*. *Wortindex zu hessisch-thüringischen Epen um 1200*, ed. Thomas Klein, Joachim Bumke, Barbara Kronsfoth, and Angela Mielke-Vandenhouten (IDL, 31), xix + 510 pp., is part of an ambitious project for computerized grammatically parsed indexes to the corpus of Central German works of the 12th and 13th cs. The approach is justified by the systematic care with which the project has been undertaken, and the result is a superbly informative reference work of manageable size covering nine verse epics from the period 1160–1220: Trier and Höxter *Aegidius*, Strassburg *Alexander*, *Athis und Prophilias*, Der Arme Hartmann's *Rede von dem heiligen gelouben*, Herbort von Fritzlar's *Liet von*

Troye, Heinrich's *Litanei, Pilatus, Graf Rudolf,* and the *Trierer Silvester.*
The layout with grammatical forms and references, and a reverse
index, achieves a high degree of clarity. D. Kelly, *SMC*, 38:47–58,
includes examples from Hartmann von Aue and Konrad von
Würzburg in a study of the *fidus interpres* theme which argues that
'infidelity to source' is the expected norm. Gert Kaiser, *Der Tod und die
schönen Frauen. Ein elementares Motiv der europäischen Kultur,* Frankfurt,
Campus, 1995, 192 pp., includes brief chapters on Hartmann's *Erec*
and on the dance of death. P. Wapnewski, *JDASD*:42–64, considers
problems facing the translator of the *Nibelungenlied* and *Parzival.* In
Jagd und höfische Kultur (see pp. 670–71 above), H. Brackert (365–406)
supplies a substantial study of the portrayal of the hunt in high
medieval epic literature, while S. Schwenk (407–64) includes
Gottfried's *Tristan* in an account of hunting manuals, and H. Wolter-
von dem Knesebeck (493–572, incl. 29 pls) studies attitudes to the
courtly pastime in pictorial sources, including the Manesse MS. *Die
Wolfenbütteler Sammlung (Cod. Guelf. 1203 Helmst.). Untersuchung und
Edition einer mittelniederdeutschen Sammelhandschrift,* ed. Volker Krobisch
(NdS, 42), 360 pp. + 4 pls, is a Münster dissertation which forms a
comprehensive codicological and literary treatment of a significant
Low German monument, besides an edition of the contents: *Zeno,
Kranichhals, Vruwen Loff, Vogelsprache, The Nine Worthies, Alexander,
Marina, Brandan, Flos und Blankeflos, Theophilus,* and a 'carmen latinum'.
Besides a codicological and linguistic analysis of the whole K. supplies
brief chapters on the subject-matter, structure, and transmission of
the individual items; if most can be related to wider traditions, there
are convincing arguments that the essentially heterogeneous material
does possess certain coherent features in style and transmission. The
near-diplomatic edition (pp. 165–342) is appropriate in the context
and clearly legible.

EARLY MIDDLE HIGH GERMAN

Barbara Gutfleisch-Ziche, *Volkssprachliches und bildliches Erzählen
biblischer Stoffe. Die illustrierten Handschriften der 'Altdeutschen Genesis' und
des 'Leben Jesu' der Frau Ava* (EH, 1, 1596), 338 pp. with 65 illus., is the
first attempt for some time to interpret the relationship between text
and illustration in Early MHG biblical epic. A review of recent
approaches to the literature leads to the hypothesis that the illustrations, known since the work of H. Voss (1962) to derive from their
own established traditions much older than the vernacular epic itself,
actually influence the adaptation of the biblical source. This plainly
has implications for questions of audience and reception. For the
Genesis a meticulous analysis of the structural divisions and rubrics of

the Vienna and Millstatt versions leads to the conclusion that that the cycle of illustrations presented the poet with a structured and manageable pattern for presenting his text, reflected in its narrative sections. The application of a similar approach to Ava's poem is less convincing to the extent that the cycle of illustrations in the Görlitz MS has to be reconstructed with a degree of speculation, and the conclusion conflicts with the equally plausible thesis of liturgical influence. Nevertheless the care with which the argument is conducted justifies the claim to have identified a new and potentially very fruitful approach to illustrated manuscripts. J. Jacobs, *ABÄG*, 48:3–18, studies the concept of *praesumptio* in a range of EMHG religious poetry, focusing in particular on the procrastination of the raven's voice. I. Erfen, Erfen, *Fremdheit*, 243–65, links the line 'sô wir daz die Crîchen hôrin redin' to the theme of spiritual pilgrimage in the *Annolied*.

U. Friedrich, Harms, *Wahrnehmen*, 119–36, considers the dichotomy of nature and culture in the *Strassburger Alexander*, and M. Chinca, Pratt, *Roland and Charlemagne*, 127–47, reviews the background to the *Rolandslied*, emphasizing that it is a 'symbiosis of lay and clerical interests'. J. Haustein, *ZDP*, 116, *Sonderheft*, 115–30, considers synchronic and diachronic approaches to the transmission of *Herzog Ernst*, emphasizing the need for a 'polyphonous' approach which takes account of the different versions, and A. Stein, Harms, *Wahrnehmen*, 21–48, interprets *Herzog Ernst B* with particular reference to the monstrous beings, while T. Gärtner, *ZDA*, 126:279–300, comments on the text of Odo of Magdeburg's *Ernestus*. H. Fromm, *BGDSL*, 119:214–34, reconsiders *Graf Rudolf* in its essentials, and W. Kofler, *ZDA*, 126:301–13, studies a rediscovered manuscript of *Salman und Morolf*. Hildegard von Bingen, *Wisse die Wege. Ratschläge fürs Leben*, ed. and trans. Johannes Bühler (IT, 2164), 312 pp., is a reissue of a substantial selection of H.'s works in translation which originally appeared in 1922. There is brief introductory material and notes and full documentation of the sources. W. Knoch, *Das Mittelalter*, 1.2, 1996:39–53, examines feminine values in Hildegard, and M. Schultheiss, *Meine in Gott geliebte* (see p. 701 below), pp. 78–87, 139–40, studies Hildegard's images of herself and others.

MIDDLE HIGH GERMAN HEROIC LITERATURE

Das Nibelungenlied. Mittelhochdeutsch / Neuhochdeutsch. Nach dem Text von Karl Bartsch und Helmut de Boor, trans. and comm. Siegfried Grosse (UB, 644), 1019 pp., for study purposes replaces the standard Brockhaus text of MS B, adding to the 21st edition an unpretentious prose translation on facing pages and a substantial commentary

(pp. 719–935) containing a wealth of literary and linguistic information and textual parallels based on about 320 items of critical
literature included in a admirable basic bibliography (pp. 938–63).
The introductory 'Nachwort' (pp. 965–1001) includes an account of
the problems of translation, consciously placing G.'s effort in the
context of a long history of *Nl.* reception. The index of proper names
and the map are improvements on those accompanying the
Brockhaus text. The new edition is accompanied by an excellent
interpretative introduction, Ursula Schulze, *Das Nibelungenlied* (UB,
17604), 336 pp., with chapters on literary and cultural background,
dating and transmission, genesis, form, structure, and genre, the
narrator, courtly innovation and the uncourtly narrative skeleton,
and the interpretation and reception of the work. The bibliography is
helpfully classified. Edward R. Haymes and Susann T. Samples,
Heroic Legends of the North. An Introduction to the Nibelung and Dietrich Cycles
(GRLH, 1403), 1996, xix + 170 pp., is aimed both at the 'general
reader' and the student who needs guidance through the morass of
critical literature. Chapters on the background in the first part deal
with the medieval literary versions of the legends, the heroic tradition
and its formation and transmission, and surveys of the historical
background and the medieval chronicle sources. A separate chapter
is devoted to the question of oral transmission, with a sensitively
nuanced account of the controversy surrounding the oral-formulaic
theory. The second part takes us through the evidence of all the
relevant works, with summaries of content and comment on the main
scholarly issues, from the sporadic traces in early texts by way of the
major works of the Dietrich and Nibelungen cycles to related legends.
There are excellent basic bibliographies at every stage. Marten
Brandt, *Gesellschaftsthematik und ihre Darstellung im Nibelungenlied und
seinen hochmittelalterlichen Adaptionen* (EH, 1, 1643), 310 pp., is a Cologne
dissertation which reflects all the positive qualities of the school from
which it emanates to the extent that the aspects of the presentation of
society and social concerns emerge directly and convincingly from
the text of the *Nl.* rather than being read into the text from any
preconceived sociological theory. Social themes turn out to be legion,
and span the gamut from the basic linguistic usage of pronouns (*ich,
wir, man*) by way of rhetorical devices (forms of address to the
audience, epic premonition), authorial intention, courtly values
(loyalty, friendship, representation of the ruler, his generosity,
reliance on advice, etc), to the fundamental social conflicts which
form the substance of the action. B. helpfully distinguishes the usage
of the B and C versions, reserving a final chapter for the *Klage*. If the
view that C and *Klage* add a moral dimension to the evaluation of
events is not wholly new, the detailed evidence here presented

certainly makes the conclusion all the more convincing. M. Jönsson, *Fest. Härd*, 133–44, comments on anticipation and back-reference in the *Nl.*, and W. Mieder, *ib.*, 165–77, documents its use of aphorisms and their relation to fate, while P. Strohschneider, *Fest. Worstbrock*, 43–75, considers the implications for the motivation and structure of events in the *Nl.* of what the narrator either does or does not tell us. U. Schulze, *ZDA*, 126:32–52, interprets Siegfried's deception about his subordinate relationship to Gunther against the background of the feudal terminology of the *Nl.*, and I. R. Campbell, *Neophilologus*, 81:563–76, finds plausible positive reasons for Siegfried's conduct. C. Lecouteux, *Euphorion*, 91:279–90, assesses the mythological background to the Burgundian royal family, and L. Thelen, *JEGP*, 96:385–402, examines Hagen's association with a shield motif on five occasions in the work, arguing that he is not rehabilitated in Part II but remains *untriuwe*, while A. V. Murray, *FMLS*, 33:142–55, enhances Rumolt's status to that of a prominent and serious adviser whose counsel reflects the contemporary conception of royal responsibility. K. Smits, Obermayer, *Österreich*, 1–24, comments on the place of journeys and encounters with the foreign in the *Nl.*, and K. H. Ihlenburg, Erfen, *Fremdheit*, 267–75, studies journeys and the exotic, while M. Springeth, *JOWG*, 9, 1996–97:425–40, examines the reception of the *Nl.* in the late Middle Ages, W. Kofler, *ib.*, 441–69, its recension in the prose *Heldenbuch*, and O. Ehrismann, *GeW*, 116, 1996:23–42, Goethe's view of the *Nl.* and other medieval themes. A. Poltermann, pp. 245–69 of *Literaturkanon—Medienereignis—kultureller Text. Formen interkultureller Kommunikation und Übersetzung*, ed. Andreas Poltermann (Göttinger Beiträge zur internationalen Übersetzungsforschung, 10), Berlin, Schmidt, 1995, viii + 292 pp., addresses the cultural and canonic implications of the *Nl.* in the light of F. H. von der Hagen's 1807 translation. *3. Pöchlarner Heldenliedgespräch. Die Rezeption des Nibelungenliedes*, ed. Klaus Zatloukal (Philologica Germanica, 16), Vienna, Fassbaender, 1995, 202 pp., includes, besides work focusing on the 19th-c. reception of the material, studies equally relevant for the *Nl.* and its medieval understanding, among them I. Bennewitz (33–52) on attitudes to Kriemhilt, P. Göhler (67–79) on the transmission, J. Heinzle (81–107) on shared views in the medieval and modern periods, F. P. Knapp (109–26) on the wedding-night episodes, U. Müller (147–55) on a Spanish parallel, H. Reichert (157–71) on the Nibelungen in Norway, M. Springeth (173–85) on the Vienna MS k, N. Voorwinden (1–15) on Rüedeger, and U. Wyss (187–202) on Rumolt.

Joachim Bumke, *Die vier Fassungen der 'Nibelungenklage'. Untersuchungen zur Überlieferungsgeschichte und Textkritik der höfischen Epik im 13. Jahrhundert* (QFLK, 8 (242)), 1996, xiv + 746 pp., is a monumental text-critical study culminating in an edition of the four versions. While Bumke focuses on textual issues, a handy complement to his work is *Diu Klage mittelhochdeutsch—neuhochdeutsch*, introd., trans., and comm. Albrecht Classen (GAG, 647), xlvi + 248 pp., which returns pragmatically to the edition of Karl Bartsch and includes a line-by-line translation on facing pages. Besides documenting the MS tradition the introduction and notes (pp. 205–29) review all the literary issues of substance relating to the text. C. indefatigably supplies a brief survey of research, accounts of the ethical dimension of the content, comparison with the *Nl.* and the reception of the longer work, the presentation of the major figures, the contextualization of the tragic ethos, dating, and authorship. L. Tomassini, *SM*, 37, 1996:203–54, studies the figure of Dietrich in *Diu Klage*, T. M. Andersson, *NOWELE*, 31–32:13–27, makes interesting comments on the possible political associations of the Dietrich epic, and H. Beck and S. Kramarz-Bein, pp. 72–87 of *Zeitgeschehen und seine Darstellung im Mittelalter. L'actualité et sa représentation au Moyen Âge*, ed. Christoph Cormeau (Studium Universale, 20), Bonn, Bouvier, 1995, 259 pp., comment on the Low German-Norse Dietrich epic, while V. Bok, *Fest. Schwob*, 26–35, documents the reception of the Dietrich legend in Bohemia in both German and Czech, and D. Hempen, *MDU*, 89:18–30, interprets the Wild Woman Else in *Wolfdietrich B*, seeing her as ultimately no threat to civilization. M. Pearson, Harms, *Wahrnehmen*, 153–65, studies different sex roles in the exotic environment of *Kudrun*, and C. Händl, *AION(FG)*, 4.1–2, 1994:97–124, studies the Ermanarich legend within heroic tradition.

THE COURTLY ROMANCE

Frank Rossnagel, *Die deutsche Artusepik im Wandel. Die Entwicklung von Hartmann von Aue bis zum Pleier* (HS, S 11), 1996, 253 pp. H. Wandhoff, *JIG*, 28.2, 1996:80–99, summarizes his view of the courtly epic from the viewpoint of media history (see *YWMLS*, 58:725), and T. Tomasek, *Fest. Worstbrock*, 221–39, surveys the influence of the romance of Apollonius of Tyre on vernacular narrative of the 12th and 13th cs, while A. Masser, *Fest. Schwob*, 277–90, comments on the relationship of the Runkelstein frescoes to the romance, and K. Ridder, *LiLi*, 105:62–85, analyses the memorial visualization of the absent lover in Gottfried's *Tristan*, Konrad Fleck's *Flore und Blanscheflur*, and the *Prosa-Lancelot*. S. Onderdelinden, *ABÄG*, 48:175–91, notes some recent examples of Arthurian reception in Germany.

H. Wuth, Wenzel, *Gespräche*, 63–76, considers forms of communication in Veldeke's *Eneas*, distinguishing the decline of orality (Dido and Carthage) from the written word (Lavinia and Rome), while

C. Wöhrle-Naser, *Holler Vol.*, 24–78, discusses the pathology of love in Veldeke, and U. Liebertz-Grün, Kornbichler, *Liebe*, 51–93, looks at sexual politics in the *Eneas* and the French source. E. Schmid, *Fest. Worstbrock*, 199–220, studies Herbort von Fritzlar's treatment of his source in the *Liet von Troie*. Also noted: Brigitte Rücker, *Die Bearbeitung von Ovids Metamorphosen durch Albrecht von Halberstadt und Jörg Wickram und ihre Kommentierung durch Gerhard Lorichius* (GAG, 641), 407 pp.

HARTMANN VON AUE

Will Hasty, *Adventures in Interpretation. The Works of Hartmann von Aue and their Critical Reception*, Columbia, SC, Camden House, 1996, xiii + 123 pp., seeks to survey the critical literature on H. and at the same time serve as a general English-language introduction. After preliminary chapters on the approaches of scholars in different periods and on H.'s life and the problems of chronology there are separate treatments of the *Klage* and the lyrics followed by each major narrative work. Some account is given of problems of source, text, and transmission, but the weight of the treatment falls on interpretation and provides a good guide through the flood of literature even though the chronologically arranged bibliography of works consulted is by no means complete. Mary Vandegrift Mills, *The Pilgrimage Motif in the Works of the Medieval German Author Hartmann von Aue* (Studies in Medieval Literature, 13), Lewiston–Queenston–Lampeter, Mellen, 1996, x + 104 pp., is a well-written study focusing by no means exclusively on *Gregorius, Der arme Heinrich*, and the crusading lyric and anchored in a far from exhaustive reading of the critical literature, while a range of other vernacular and theological texts are invoked as corroborative evidence. The strength of the work is that it can be recommended to students as a competent summary of many ideas fundamental to the period. The weakness of the thesis that each work represents the fusion of a spiritual and secular quest lies in its association with a structural pattern so reductively archetypal that any journey whatever, real or metaphorical, is a 'pilgrimage' of some kind. S. Kishitani, *Fest. Iwasaki*, 179–99, addresses details of H.'s narrative technique. H. Kischkel, *ZDP*, 116:94–100, doubts the authenticity of the final poem of Hartmann's *Klage*, and E. Willms, *OL*, 52:61–78, reinterprets Erec's reasons for the harsh treatment of his wife, while S. Bauer, *Poetica*, 29:75–93, relates the theme of *wân* to love and chivalry in *Erec*, and C. Wand-Wittkowski, *Fabula*, 38:1–13, studies Feimurgan as a sorceress. Also noted: Wolfgang Wetzlmair, *Zum Problem der Schuld im 'Erec' und im 'Gregorius' Hartmanns von Aue* (GAG, 643), 197 pp.

Jens-Peter Schröder, *Arnolds von Lübeck 'Gesta Gregorii Peccatoris'. Eine Interpretation, ausgehend von einem Vergleich mit Hartmanns von Aue 'Gregorius'* (HBG, 23), 261 pp., is a most welcome detailed study of the neglected Latin work of 1209–13 which clarifies many misconceptions and effectively rehabilitates it as an object of study in its own right. S. is concerned to show that A. adapts rather than translates Hartmann: although he follows the source in close outline, his work does not provide a key to his theological understanding of H.'s poem, but rather an independent conception of the history of Gregorius. A. makes clearer than H. features such as the element of *superbia* in the decision to leave the monastery, the conception of an accumulation of sins as inherent in human nature, the lack of distinction between intended and unintended sin, and the attainability of grace through total dedication to God. The closeness of the textual comparison and the clarity of argumentation make this a thoroughly convincing treatment. Werner Schröder, *'Der arme Heinrich' Hartmanns von Aue in der Hand von Mären-Schreibern* (Sitzungsberichte der Wiss. Gesellschaft an der Johann Wolfgang Goethe-Univ. Frankfurt am Main, 35, no. 1), Stuttgart, Steiner, 30 pp., is in the same vein as his recent polemics against the value of the newly-discovered fragments of *Erec* (see *YWMLS*, 58:732). Proceeding from the insight that all MSS of the shorter poem are late and derivative, and reflect their transmission in corpora of minor works and literature of the fabliau type, S. argues in detail that the 24 new lines from the recently discovered Benediktbeuern fragments (E) are spurious and have no business in Kurt Gärtner's new edition (see *YWMLS*, 58:733). Werner Schröder, *Laudines Kniefall und der Schluß von Hartmanns 'Iwein'* (Akad. der Wiss. und der Lit., Mainz. Abh. der geistes- und sozialwiss. Kl., Jg 1997, no. 2), Stuttgart, Steiner, 31 pp., takes issue with the fact that Laudine's appeal for Iwein's forgiveness, lines 8121–36, appear only in MS B of the older manuscripts, and their appropriateness has been questioned by a range of scholars. Examination of the additions and omissions of B as a whole leads S. to the conclusion that a redactor is at work, that two versions of *Iwein* were indeed in circulation in the 13th c., and that the offending lines should be removed from an edition of H.'s text.

WOLFRAM VON ESCHENBACH

Joachim Bumke, *Wolfram von Eschenbach* (SM, 36), 7th rev. edn, xii + 274 pp., has been wholly reorganized since the previous edition (*YWMLS*, 53:643) but, regrettably, the work has reached its physical limits, so that new text on interpretative problems in the epics and on the narrator in *Parzival* has resulted in a recasting of the bibliography.

This now focuses on work of the past ten years: B. justifiably refers the reader to earlier editions of this indispensable handbook, besides the bibliographies of *Wolfram-Studien*. Alfred Raucheisen, *Orient und Abendland. Ethisch-moralische Aspekte in Wolframs Epen 'Parzival' und 'Willehalm'* (BBLI, 17), 198 pp. E. Nellmann, *Poetica*, 28, 1996:327–44, argues from *Parzival* that W. knew the works of Chrétien and other earlier romances in some detail, and A. Classen, *SN*, 69:59–68, interprets *P.* in terms of J. Habermas's concept of a communicative community, while K. Bertau, *Prospero*, 3, Trieste, 1996:96–101, reconsiders the theme of questions in *P.*, and K. Nyholm, *Fest. Härd*, 223–37, discusses the implications of Cunneware's laughter (*P.* 151, 11–19). S. Gilmour, *Euphorion*, 91:311–41, interprets textual cruces in *P.* 173,3, and 652,10, and J. M. Clifton-Everest, *ZDP*, 116:321–51, explores the ironic naming of the heroine of Book VIII after Statius's Antigone, and in particular the frustration of her potential role in reconciling brother and lover, while B. D. Haage, *Holler Vol.*, 1–23, returns to Gawan's miraculous medical skills, and M. Dallapiazza, *Prospero*, 3, Trieste, 1996:85–95, looks at Plippalinot's daughter Bene. Friedrich de la Motte Fouqué, *Der Parcival. Erstdruck*, ed. Tilman Spreckelsen, Peter Henning Haischer, Frank Rainer Max, and Ursula Rautenberg, Hildesheim, Olms, 628 pp., is an important example of *P.* reception but entirely neglected hitherto, the 1832 work having existed only in manuscript. The text follows Wolfram with remarkable accuracy and a distinctive feature is the introduction of dramatic dialogues between the characters, among whom is Wolfram himself. S. Obermaier, *Euphorion*, 91:467–88, studies medieval reception in Adolf Muschg's Parzival novel, and C. Carnevale, *Fest. Schwob*, 61–72, considers the treatment of Trevrizent in the same work.

J. Janota, pp. 93–104 of *Große Werke der Literatur. IV. Eine Ringvorlesung an der Universität Augsburg 1994/1995*, ed. Hans Vilmar Geppert, Tübingen, Francke, 1995, 254 pp., surveys *Willehalm*, and C. Fasbender, *ZDP*, 116:16–31, criticizes the emphasis in J. Heinzle's *Whm* commentary on the critique of crusading ideology. Sylvia Stevens, *Family in Wolfram von Eschenbach's 'Willehalm': mîner mâge triwe ist mir wol kuont* (STML, 18), ix + 201 pp., is a well-written analysis all aspects of the very ramified nexus of familial relationships in *Whm*. With close textual reference at every point, S. deals in turn with the concept of kinship, including the terminology used; father-child relationships; parents and children; Rennewart; uncles, nephews, and nieces; and siblings. The chief lines of W.'s treatment which emerge are not wholly surprising: in comparison with his source W. shifts the emphasis from the uncle-nephew relationship to that of father and child, and the heathen are capable of family bonds comparable to those of the Christians. References to *Aliscans*, however, often beg the question of the source, and the concluding chapter draws no threads together but comments on the theme in the light of the unfinished state of the poem. In general, the study fails to come to grips with controversial issues: thus, in the discussion of the religious analogies to kinship, S. cites the view that both Christian and heathen are perceived as children as well as creatures of God, but makes no mention of the current debate on this problem; nor does J. Heinzle feature in the bibliography.

GOTTFRIED VON STRASSBURG

Mark Chinca, *Gottfried von Strassburg, Tristan*, CUP, vii + 119 pp., is an introduction which provides an excellent combination of factual data relating to Gottfried and his predecessors and successors and an original interpretative reading of his work. C. is innovative in the critical language he brings to bear on the work and is particularly illuminating in his discussions of the use of religious analogy, the lovers' independent interior state, the prologue, and the distinction between microstructure and macrostructure. U. Jantzen and N. Körner, *Euphorion*, 91:291–309, interpret the Carlisle Thomas fragment and its significance for Gottfried's *Tristan*, and M. Javor Briški, *ANeo*, 29, 1996:13–25, studies the epic and symbolic function of education in *Tristan*, while W. Mieder, *Das Mittelalter*, 2.2:7–20, focuses on the proverbial aspects of Gottfried's metaphorical usage, K. Kucaba, Harms, *Wahrnehmen*, 73–93, emphasizes the dimension of courtly manners in the treatment of Isolde's trial by ordeal, and W. Hutfilz, *ib.*, 95–117, relates the courtly frame of the work to the European bucolic tradition. H. Bayer, *MJ*, 31.2, 1996:39–80, links Gottfried (for B., Gunther von Pairis) with heretical elements in the *Carmina Burana*. W. Hoffmann, *Euphorion*, 91:431–65, surveys *Tristan* reception. Also noted: Dorothee Grill, *Tristan-Dramen des 19. Jahrhunderts* (GAG, 642), vi + 250 pp.

OTHER ROMANCES

Stephan Fuchs, *Hybride Helden: Gwigalois und Willehalm. Beiträge zum Heldenbild und zur Poetik des Romans im frühen 13. Jahrhundert* (FBG, 31), 425 pp., seeks a theoretical framework for understanding the known contradictions of 13th-c. narrative works in contrast to the earlier relatively unified model of romances derived from Chrétien. Rejecting the old idea of 'epigonality' as an unsatisfactory label for the later narrative, F. works through the salient characteristics of two ostensibly quite different texts, arguing that Wirnt von Grafenberg in

Wigalois and Wolfram von Eschenbach in *Willehalm* share in common, in the treatment of their heroes, the introduction of a polyvalence of responses to inherited models and a heterogeneity of narrative strategies so substantial as to constitute the positive hallmarks of the later epic. E. Lienert, *ASNS*, 234:263–75, studies the narrator in Wirnt von Grafenberg's *Wigalois*. Ulrike Zellmann, *Lanzelet. Der biographische Artusroman als Auslegungsschema dynastischer Wissensbildung* (Studia humaniora, 28), Düsseldorf, Droste, 1996, 310 pp., propounds the interesting thesis that Ulrich von Zatzikhoven's work, so far from being a merely trivializing treatment of its hero as comparison with the French models might suggest, adopts his biography as a means of transmitting to its noble audience practical secular knowledge relating to their domestic situation. Z. rejects the model of the 'mirror of princes' type of literature, seeing the hero's career as an exemplification of the conventional medieval view of the stages of life, and relating successive episodes to a programme of education appropriate to the child, adolescent, youth, and mature adult. Hartmut Bleumer, *Die 'Crône' Heinrichs von dem Türlin. Form-Erfahrung und Konzeption eines späten Artusromans* (MTU, 112), ix + 298 pp., is an interpretative study proceeding from the apparently conflicting insights that the work is on the one hand bound to earlier Arthurian tradition above all through the given figure of Gawein, but on the other hand exhibits ironic or parodistic features. The study of the major episodes of the first half of the work leads to an emphasis on its affinities with, but by no means rejection of, the *Lancelot* tradition. The second part of the romance is viewed as substantially more complex, its difficulties largely avoided by critical focus on either the wider structural pattern or individual motifs. B. interprets the work as a rejection of the tradition of stories about a hero, rendered pointless because of his idealized supremacy, in favour of a discourse with the reader which has the effect of transforming the established aesthetic of the classical romance. It remains to be seen whether the currently fashionable concept of 'dialogue', in this case between the reader and the formal structure of the work, will retain enough substance to survive as a satisfactory aesthetic criterion for explaining away the otherwise apparently irreconcilable discrepancies of complex medieval texts. C. Brinker-von der Heyde, *Runa*, 25, 1996:109–18, suggests that Frou Saelde's castle is the key to the interpretation of *Diu Crône*, on which we also note Johannes Keller, *'Diu Crône' Heinrichs von dem Türlin: Wunderketten, Gral und Tod* (DLA, 25), 465 pp. W. Röcke, *Mündlichkeit* (see p. 676 above), pp. 85–108, adopts a communicative approach to romances of Konrad Fleck and Johann von Würzburg.

Lancelot. Nach der Kölner Papierhandschrift W. f° 46* Blankenheim und der Heidelberger Pergamenthandschrift Pal. Germ. 147. IV. *Namen- und Figuren-register,* ed. Hans-Hugo Steinhoff and Klaudia Wegge (DTM, 80), xiv + 135 pp., goes some way to fulfilling Reinhold Kluge's desire for a dictionary to the *Prosa Lancelot,* the three volumes of which (1948–74) are, somewhat ironically, out of print. The study of the names, which here include appellatives in the widest sense, emerges as a highly ramified subject in which not only linguistic variation plays a part but also the practice of endowing one figure with more than one name, or changing the name of an established figure. The index is extremely easy to use: it includes all textual references and brings together all relevant information relating to an individual figure, such as chief and alternative names, relationships, appellatives, and the first references to figures whose first appearance lacks the name. B. Smelik, *Queeste,* 4 : 16–26, comments on uncourtly behaviour by minor knights in versions of the *Prosa Lancelot.* A. Deighton, *ZDA,* 126 : 140–65, reopens the question of the sources of the *Tristan* continuations of Ulrich von Türheim and Heinrich von Freiberg, arguing that they must have had access to versions other than Eilhart's. W. Hofmeister, *Fest. Schwob,* 159–75, edits *Edolanz* fragment A. *Der Ritter mit dem Bock. Konrads von Stoffeln 'Gauriel von Muntabel',* ed., introd., and comm. Wolfgang Achnitz (TTG, 46), viii + 664 pp., is a monumental treatment of probably the last Arthurian romance in verse, dated to *c.* 1280–1300. A detailed study of the documentary, genealogical, and heraldic evidence identifies the author as a member of the Swabian Stöffeln/Gönningen family. Besides a full account of the complicated codicology and textual transmission a chapter is devoted to the literary analysis and interpretation of the neglected work: in spite of the obvious affinities with the classical romance and Hartmann's *Iwein* in particular, A. refrains from the older judgement of 'epigonal-ity', finding some merit in the adaptation of traditional structures to the poet's contemporary social and political situation. In the face of two very divergent manuscripts and the poet's obvious intention to imitate classical MHG, A. supplies a parallel diplomatic print of the Karlsruhe and Innsbruck texts and makes the former the basis for a readable critical edition on the right-hand pages. B. Kellner, *Wenzel, Gespräche,* 154–73, distinguishes between spoken and written language on the one hand and non-verbal communication on the other in *Friedrich von Schwaben.* J. Bumke, *ZDP,* 116, *Sonderheft,* 87–114, places the *Rappoltsteiner Parzifal* at the centre of a demonstration of how little we in fact know about the circumstances of literary production and reception and how fluid the boundaries are between the conceptions of author, redactor, and transmission. In *ABÄG,* 47, H. van Dijk (39–48) compares Dutch and German treatments of the romance of

Ogier of Denmark; B. Duijvestijn (49–64) studies the German reception of *Reinolt van Montalban*; T. Klein (79–107) places Augustijn's *Herzog von Braunschweig* at the centre of an analysis of the different types of reception of Dutch works in German; and R. Schlusemann (175–96) writes on Johann von Soest's translation of *Die Kinder von Limburg*. U. von Bloh, Harms, *Wahrnehmen*, 221–38, characterizes amazement and the marvellous in *Herzog Herpin*, and C. Kleppel, *ib.*, 177–91, considers the implications of letter-writing in Johann Hartlieb's *Alexander*. Ulrich Füetrer, *Das Buch der Abenteuer. I. Die Geschichte der Ritterschaft und des Grals. Von den Templeysen. Vom Kampf um Troja. Von Mörlin. Von Gamoreth. Von Tschionachtolander. Von Parzival und Gaban. Von Lohargrim. II. Das annder púech. Von Wigoleis. Von Seyfrid. Von Melerans. Von Iban. Von Persibein. Von Poytislier. Von Flordimar. Nach der Handschrift A (Cgm. 1 der Bayerischen Staatsbibliothek)*, ed. Heinz Thoelen and Bernd Bastert (GAG, 638), 2 vols, 601, 539 pp., is an immensely welcome service to scholarship which makes all these important texts accessible and will certainly stimulate research. The semi-diplomatic text seeks to maintain a balance between legibility and preservation of the scribal peculiarities of MS A, which is essentially transcribed verbatim with abbreviations written out and capitals reserved for proper names and the opening letters of strophes and headings. The brief but informative appendix gives a basic account of the author, his patrons, and the structure of his monumental work, and helpfully lists the disparate and often inaccessible earlier editions of its individual parts. B. Bastert, *JOWG*, 9, 1996–97:471–88, examines the social and political attitudes reflected in Ulrich Füetrer's *Buch der Abenteuer*, and R. Hahn, *AKG*, 74, 1992:125–46, comments on Marquard von Stein's *Ritter vom Turn*.

LYRIC POETRY

Gert Hübner, *Frauenpreis. Studien zur Funktion der laudativen Rede in der mittelhochdeutschen Minnekanzone*, 2 vols (Saecula spiritalia, 34, 35), Baden-Baden, Koerner, 1996, 353, 354–570 pp., takes a theme as fundamental to the essence of the Minnesang as the praise of the lady and finds the situation more complicated than received judgements might suggest. An introductory chapter helpfully surveys the fundamental concepts, themes, and arguments of 'courtly love'. The real value of the study lies in the detailed analyses of the laudative elements in different poets: following a section on the early Minnesänger the most substantial treatment is reserved for Reinmar, Morungen, and Walther, while Ulrich von Lichtenstein is chosen to exemplify the postclassical development. The often detailed annotations are conveniently printed in a second volume, which includes a tabulated summary of Morungen's metaphorical usage. H. Brunner, *Fest. Schwob*, 47–59, studies the renunciation of the beloved in a wide range of lyric texts. Jens Köhler, *Der Wechsel. Textstruktur und Funktion einer mittelhochdeutschen Liedgattung*, Heidelberg, Winter, xvi + 335 pp., fills an important lacuna in research with a comprehensive treatment of what is rightly identified as an ambivalent cliché in histories of the German lyric. K. is fully aware of the problem posed by the fact that the very selection of the texts traditionally associated with the sub-genre presuppose its definition. The problem is successfully resolved by a careful review of the attitudes displayed in previous scholarship followed by a systematic analysis of the chief features associated with the *Wechsel*. K. then sets up his own definition, and identifies all the texts which either conform to it or are relevant to the discussion of the *Wechsel* as a whole. The greater part of the study is given over to careful detailed analyses of the texts which emphasize more than hitherto the significance of their roles and their performative function. T. Bein, Schwob, *Edition*, 21–35, takes examples from the lyric tradition to illustrate the theory and practice of 'open text', while M. Chinca, *Paragraph*, 18, 1995 : 112–32, attacks recent approaches to the alleged ritual function of the love-lyric, arguing that medievalists have neglected social anthropology; Id., *FMLS*, 33 : 204–16, interprets some early love-lyric in terms of the 'theory of practice' of P. Bourdieu. Bertrand Michael Buchmann, *Daz jemant singet oder sait… Das volkstümliche Lied als Quelle zur Mentalitätengeschichte des Mittelalters*, Frankfurt, Lang, 1995, 341 pp.

P. Göhler, Wenzel, *Gespräche*, 77–85, reviews the role of the messenger in *Minnesangs Frühling* and in Walther. Andreas Hensel, *Vom frühen Minnesang zur Lyrik der Hohen Minne. Studien zum Liebesbegriff und zur literarischen Konzeption der Autoren Kürenberger, Dietmar von Aist, Meinloh von Sevelingen, Burggraf von Rietenburg, Friedrich von Hausen und Rudolf von Fenis* (EH, 1, 1611), 404 pp., takes issue with what is seen as the oversimplified approach to the early lyric as a series of developmental phases of theme and form. H. attributes this situation to an excessive preoccupation with text-critical problems and with the origins of the MHG lyric, and his own work has something to say on both. Its substance consists of a treatment of each of the named poets in turn with textual analysis followed by interpretation. Although the relatively modest scope of their work is seen as a reason for their relegation behind Hausen, Reinmar, Morungen, and Walther, A. is obliged in many cases to be selective in his approach to the 'minor' poets, and his studies do not always convince the reader that they have been as neglected in previous critical discussion as he claims. Particularly welcome, however, is the full and detailed interpretation of Rudolf von Fenis, and in general H. does succeed in demonstrating the individuality and variety of the whole corpus. Axel Eisbrenner, *Minne, diu der werlde ir vröude mêret. Untersuchungen zum Handlungsaufbau und zur Rollengestaltung in ausgewählten Werbungsliedern aus 'Des Minnesangs Frühling'* (HS, S 10), 1995, 473 pp.

R. J. Davies, *JOWG*, 9, 1996–97 : 495–508, studies the musical and formal problems of the German reception of Conon de Béthune's 'Ahi Amors' by Friedrich von Hausen and Albrecht von Johansdorf, and A. Fuss, S. Kirst, and M. G. Scholz, *Euphorion*, 91 : 343–62, interpret Hausen's *Mîn herze und mîn lîp* as a disputation, while H. Tervooren, *Queeste*, 4 : 1–15, links Veldeke's lyric to the minor courts of the Maas-Rhine region. Also noted: Rudolf von Fenis, *Die Lieder: unter besonderer Berücksichtigung des romanischen Einflusses. Mit Übersetzung, Kommentar und Glossar*, ed. Olive Sayce (GAG, 633), 1996, x + 202 pp. Rodney W. Fisher, *The Minnesinger Heinrich von Morungen. An Introduction to his Songs*, San Francisco–London–Bethesda, International Scholars Publications, 1996, x + 321 pp., is a most useful volume combining original scholarship with a welcome aid for students and medievalists of other disciplines. An introduction focusing on the context, performance, visual sense, and imagery of M. is followed by reprints of the songs from H. Tervooren's edition with (surprisingly) English verse translations which generally succeed in maintaining accuracy while conveying the sense in a readable modern idiom. The analytic interpretations of each song are of substantial length, combining original insights with material assimilated from existing scholarship. Id., *GLL*, 50 : 267–82, finds in Morungen's songs abundant evidence of how they might have been performed, and K. Skow-Obenaus, *GN*, 28 : 121–27, considers attitudes to women in Morungen, while B. Kellner, *BGDSL*, 119 : 33–66, delineates the role of violence in Morungen's lyric, and T. Cramer, *ZDP*, 116, *Sonderheft*, 150–81, notes that, in the manuscript transmission of authors in *Minnesangs Frühling*, the strophes of Morungen and Reinmar are most subject to variations in order. C. considers the consequences of this phenomenon for a literary aesthetic that takes account of the possibility of such variation.

Walther von der Vogelweide, *Gedichte. 11. Auflage auf der Grundlage der Ausgabe von Hermann Paul*, ed. Silvia Ranawake and Horst Brunner. 1. *Der Spruchdichter* (ATB, 1), liii + 167 pp., is an exciting new edition which marks a decisive change in the history of this seminal text, the ramifications of which are traced by R. in her preface. In effect the work marks a return to Hermann Paul's fourth edition (1911), a moderate and balanced treatment regarded as a desideratum by Hugo Kuhn in the tenth edition (1965). There is a substantial and welcome introduction on the codicological and literary background, amplified by a substantial section of notes (pp. 85–151) including

Brunner's appendix with the melodies. Use is facilitated by concordances to the other major editions. Thomas Bein, *Walther von der
Vogelweide* (UB, 17601), 299 pp., is an admirably comprehensive short
introduction, dealing all too briefly with biographical issues; the
cultural background, types of lyric, and performance; edition and
transmission; a survey of the Minnesang and of the political and
didactic poetry; and reception. B. is thoroughly contemporary in his
approach as when, for example, the term 'Mädchenlieder' is explicitly
dispensed with after a brief explanation. This handy work testifies to
the increasing dominance by Reclam of the quality student market.
R. W. Fisher, Obermayer, *Österreich*, 25–43, points to the implications
for the performance of W.'s songs of forms of address and gesture in
the context of variation in strophic order, and A. Classen, *SM*, 37,
1996:671–702, interprets songs of W. in the light of modern
communication theory. D. McLintock, *Fest. Stillfried*, 279–89, analyses
'Vil wol gelobter got' (L. 26,3), and in *Zeitgeschehen und seine Darstellung*
(see p. 684 above), P. Konietzko (136–72) interprets L. 19,5, and
T. Bein (118–35) studies L. 105,13. Id., *ZDP*, 116, *Sonderheft*, 182–90,
uses two versions of L. 52,23 to illustrate the need for editors to take
complex manuscript transmission into account, while L. Schneider,
Euphorion, 91:363–75, interprets L. 73,23 *Die mir in dem winter*, and
R.-H. Steinmetz, *ZDP*, 116:352–69, supports the editorial separation
of L.117,29 and L.118,12, regarding the latter as spurious. F. P.
Knapp, *Fest. Laufhütte*, 61–74, links Der Wilde Alexander's
'Kindheitslied' to W.'s *Alterslyrik*, and J. Haustein, *Poetica*, 29:94–113,
considers poetological reflection in encomiastic lyric from W. on.
Also noted: Dietlinde Heckt-Albrecht, *Walther von der Vogelweide in
deutschen Lesebüchern. Ein Beitrag zur germanistischen und schulischen
Rezeptionsgeschichte Walthers von der Vogelweide* (GAG, 629), 287 pp.

H. Vögel, Harms, *Wahrnehmen*, 167–76, points to the courtly and
the peasant aspects of the performance of Neidhart, on whom we also
note Elizabeth I. Traverse, *Peasants, Seasons and werltsüeze: Cyclicity in
Neidhart's Songs Reexamined* (GAG, 637), xiii + 160 pp. F. V. Spechtler,
Editio, Beihefte, 7, 1995:3–9, notes the biographical evidence for
Ulrich von Liechtenstein, and U. Müller, Kornbichler, *Liebe*, 27–50,
notes the place of masculine fantasy in Ulrich. J. Haustein, *ZDA*,
126:193–99, comments on the transmission of Marner's Latin works,
and J. Klinger, Wenzel, *Gespräche*, 106–26, interprets Ulrich von
Liechtenstein's *Frauendienst* in terms of direct and indirect communication, while P. Strohschneider, *ib.*, 127–53, uses Konrad von Würzburg's *Schwanritter* to illustrate forms of literary communication.
O. Reichmann, pp. 204–38 of *Wörterbücher in der Diskussion II. Vorträge
aus dem Heidelberger Lexikographischen Kolloquium*, ed. Herbert Ernst
Wiegand (Lexicographica: Ser. maior, 70), Tübingen, Niemeyer,

1996, xv + 364 pp., continues the debate about the dictionary to the Göttingen Frauenlob edition.

A. Classen, *JVF*, 42 : 13–37, contrasts popular and 'high' culture in late-medieval song books, and H. Endermann, Holzner, *Literatur*, 165–73, identifies Tyrolean elements in the Jena Song MS, while H. Tervooren, *ZDP*, 116, *Sonderheft*, 191–207, views the Hague Song MS 128 E 2 as a coherent monument in its own right opening new perspectives on Dutch-German literary traditions. F. Willaert, *ABÄG*, 47 : 213–27, argues that the Middle Dutch love-lyric uses Romance forms with vocabulary indebted to the German Minnesang, and C. de Haan, *ib.*, 48 : 115–27, considers the implications of the German forms in the Gruuthuse lyric manuscript, on which we also note Brigitte Schludermann, *A Quantitative Analysis of German Dutch Language Mixture in the Berlin Songs mgf 922, the Gruuthuse-Songs, and The Hague MS 128 E 2* (GAG, 338), 3 vols, 1996, xxvi + 402, viii + 367, viii + 458 pp. M. Tischler and P. Tischler, *BGDSL*, 119 : 459–62, edit a 1439 love song from Bartfeld/Bardejov, and K. Scheel, *LB*, 85, 1996 : 303–46, studies the depiction of wars in the 15th-c. political lyric, with texts and commentary.

DIDACTIC, DEVOTIONAL, AND RELIGIOUS LITERATURE

N. Voorwinden, *Queeste*, 4 : 27–41, compares the treatment of the Holy Family in Konrad von Fussesbrunnen, Konrad von Heimesfurt, and the Dutch *Vanden levene ons heren*. S. Tuchel, *Reinardus*, 10 : 153–67, studies rape and castration in the beast epic, and C. Fasbender, *ASNS*, 234 : 78–89, questions the degree of anti-clerical satire habitually attributed to *Reinhart Fuchs*. H. Wenzel, *ZDP*, 116, *Sonderheft*, 224–52, studies the relationship of text and illustration in manuscripts of Thomasin von Zerclaere's *Der Welsche Gast*, arguing that the different emphases given to a text by variable placing of the illustrations in different manuscripts means that such variation necessitates a different evaluation from that appropriate to unillustrated manuscripts. W. F. Carroll, Harms, *Wahrnehmen*, 137–52, notes exotic elements in didactic literature of Thomasin von Zerclaere and Hugo von Trimberg. Der Stricker, *Verserzählungen. II. Mit einem Anhang: Der Weinschwelg*, ed. Hanns Fischer and Johannes Janota, 4th rev. edn (ATB, 68), xix + 58 pp., appears 13 years after the previous edition (see *YWMLS*, 46 : 685). The present editor can fairly claim that Fischer's editorial principles have been justified by time, and accordingly the changes are confined to an updating of the now quite substantial bibliography on S.'s contribution to the genre and the five eminently entertaining texts. *Lemmatisierter Index zu den Werken des Strickers*, ed. Siegfried Christoph (IDL, 30), xvii + 582 pp., is a handy word-index covering both the long and the over 170 short works, the sole exception being *Karl der Große* for which U. von der Burg's reference work (see *YWMLS*, 36:638) is a satisfactory complement to the present volume. The different editions followed are clearly set out and abbreviated. C. is of course aware that users of the work are likely to have specialized linguistic knowledge, whereas the multiplicity of approaches in the numerous editions incorporated would, without intervention, make for a thoroughly cumbersome and heterogeneous format. Accordingly, a limited degree of parsing is applied to produce 'normalized' lemmata. The compromise adopted results in a thoroughly practical and user-friendly work of reference. H. Wuth, *ZDP*, 116:101–07, compares the painter episode in Stricker's *Pfaffe Amis* with the equivalent narrative in *Eulenspiegel*, and C. Dietl, *NMi*, 98:1–13, traces Arthurian references in the *Minnereden*.

A. Vizkelety, *Fest. Schwob*, 513–21, edits recently discovered fragments of the *Leipziger Predigten* from Sopron, and R. Schnell, *MJ*, 32.2:93–108, considers the oral-written tension in Berthold von Regensburg's treatment of marriage in his sermons. F. Pensel, *Schwob, Edition*, 85–96, supplies prolegomena for an edition in DTM of the prose version of *Der guote Gêrhart*. H. Thomas, *DAEM*, 52:509–45, pursues the links between Konrad von Würzburg and the House of Habsburg, and W. Woesler, *Editio*, 11:50–61, considers a new edition of Konrad von Würzburg's *Silvester*, while A. B. Mulder-Bakker, *ABÄG*, 47:131–42, studies the *vita* of the Magdeburg hermit Kreupele Margriet and its Dutch and German translations. Christian Naser, *'Der geistliche Streit.' Synoptischer Abdruck der Fassungen A, C, B und D. Kommentar und Motivgeschichte* (Texte und Wissen, 2), Würzburg, Königshausen & Neumann, 1995, iv + 252 pp., revives interest in the neglected MHG psychomachia text. N. has discovered two further manuscripts to complement to previously edited, and in view of substantial divergences towards the end of the work provides in a clear layout a synoptic print in parallel columns. No less useful are the accompanying studies which take us through the tradition in Latin theological literature and place the work against this background and the evidence of other MHG examples.

Harald Tersch, *Unruhe im Weltbild. Darstellung und Deutung des zeitgenössischen Lebens in deutschsprachigen Weltchroniken des Mittelalters*, Vienna, Böhlau, 1996, 406 pp., applies to the chronicle literature a new approach which seeks to take into account both its intellectual and social content and also its didactic function in adapting a relatively rigid genre to the needs of new lay audiences. The ambitious range of sources, which are introduced in a preliminary chapter, include *Kaiserchronik*, *Sächsische Weltchronik*, Jans Enikel, Ottokar's *Reimchronik*, *Oberrheinische Chronik*, Friedrich Closener, *Konstanzer*

Weltchronik, Detmar von Lübeck, Jakob Twinger von Königshofen, Johannes Rothe, *Weihenstephaner Chronik*, Johann Statwech: their chronology alone points to a huge development in function and audience. Besides the general changes of perspective in the view of *Heilsgeschichte*, piety, forms of didacticism, and historical consciousness, T. deals in some detail with aspects of ecclesiastical history, prosopography, social groups, war, political identities at Imperial and regional level, culture, and nature. If the approach is necessarily selective and heavily dependent on the standard critical literature in the discussion of detailed topics, it does show how historiography can illuminate innumerable facets of medieval life. J. Wolf, *NdJb*, 118, 1995:7–26, publishes a fragment of the *Sächsische Weltchronik* from Riga, and M. Zips, *ib.*, 119, 1996:7–60; 120:7–32, supplies a substantial monograph on the same work, while H.-W. Goetz, *Das Mittelalter*, 1.1, 1996:75–89, characterizes the figure of Fortuna in high medieval historiography. Monika Schwabbauer, *Profangeschichte in der Heilsgeschichte. Quellenuntersuchungen zu den Incidentien der 'Christherre-Chronik'* (*VB*, 15–16), Berne, Lang, 1993–94 [1997], vi + 414 pp., is a very detailed study, by no means restricted to the non-biblical subject-matter, and with much of interest on the medieval historiographical background as a whole. S. introduces the neglected text with a review of what is known of its origin and a survey of the content and structure. The account of previous research is substantially concerned with the lack of a complete edition of the text and with scholarly literature chiefly concerned with other chronicles. The sources are then reviewed in detail, and a catalogue of the usage of the various MHG terms referring to them will be valuable for other treatments of historiographical works. An account of the adaptation by the educated author of his material for a lay audience and a study of his modification of the structural principles of Rudolf von Ems's *Weltchronik* are also an essential foundation for the detailed study of the 23 secular *incidentia* added to the biblical history, which relates them to their sources. A tabulated analysis of their treatment of proper names is another welcome feature in an immensely informative work which will serve as a model and stimulus for further research on the neglected vernacular world chronicles. G. Dunphy, *ZDA*, 125, 1996:411–18, publishes and discusses fragments of Jans Enikel's *Weltchronik* in Weimar, and A.-D. von den Brincken, *DAEM*, 50, 1994:611–13, supplements her work on Martin von Troppau's chronicle, while D. Welter, Schwob, *Edition*, 123–32, examines the background to Gottfried Hagen's *Reimchronik der Stadt Köln*, and K. J. Kuepper, *ZDP*, 116:370–87, sees oral tradition behind different narrations of the same event in late-medieval Cologne chronicles. A. Kraus, *ZBL*, 60:5–69, includes medieval chronicles in a study of the historiographical treatment of Ludwig the Bavarian, S. Weigelt, Schwob, *Edition*, 109–21, studies the sources of Johannes Rothe's *Thüringische Landeschronik* in relation to its editorial potential, and D. W. Poeck, *Das Mittelalter*, 2.2:81–92, notes the prominent use of proverbs in late-medieval civic chronicles, while J. Wenta, *JOWG*, 9, 1996–97:323–39, reviews the manuscript evidence of historiography in 15th-c. Prussia, and A. Hetzer, *NdJb*, 117, 1994:24–57, examines text coherence in MLG chronicles. K. Schnith, *ZBL*, 60:479–89, reviews research on late-medieval Augsburg chronicles, and V. Honemann, *DAEM*, 52:617–27, studies the late-15th-c. chronicler Peter Eschenloer of Breslau.

The Medieval 'Gospel of Nicodemus'. Texts, Intertexts, and Contexts in Western Europe, ed. Zbigniew Izydorczyk (MRTS, 158), Tempe, Arizona, Arizona State Univ., xv + 573 pp., is a major new survey of this seminal apocryphal text and related works, with an introduction by I., 12 further chapters on the various Western literary traditions, a bibliography of 968 numbered items, and full indexes of authors, manuscripts, names, subjects, and texts. I. also writes the fundamentally important contribution on the *Gospel of Nicodemus* in the Latin Middle Ages, and, with J.-D. Dubois, an account of the work 'before and beyond' the medieval West which effectively places it in the wider context that tended to dominate older scholarship. W. J. Hoffmann supplies separate chapters on the High German (287–336) and Dutch and Low German (337–60) literary traditions respectively. This is an immensely useful handbook which will be the first point of reference for years to come. T. R. Jackson, Debatin, *Metaphor*, 113–24, relates medieval religious poetry, especially with Mariological themes, to the theory of metaphor, and A. Berteloot, *ABÄG*, 47:9–38, studies the language of vernacular translations of the *Legenda Aurea* from the border regions of Dutch and German, while M. J. Schubert, *ZDP*, 116:32–45, edits and discusses variant versions of Der Steyrer's mnemonic *Cisiojanus*, and J. Goossens, *ABÄG*, 47:65–78, relates the rhyme forms of the MLG translations of the legend of the wood of the Cross to their Dutch source. W. J. Hoffmann, *NdJb*, 116, 1993:72–108, surveys the 15th-c. Ripuarian and LG transmission of the *Vitaspatrum*, and B. Spreitzer, *Fest. Schwob*, 477–87, reviews examples of female transvestites in hagiographical literature, while P. Strohschneider, *Scientia poetica*, 1:1–34, surveys the Brendan legend, the perception of the marvellous and miraculous in which is interpreted by S. Demmelhuber, Harms, *Wahrnehmen*, 49–71. K. E. Geith, *Fest. Schwob*, 109–18, documents a German translation of the *Vita Sancti Udalrici*. Reinhold Schneider, *Elisabeth von Thüringen*, introd. Bernhard Vogel, ed. Karl-Josef Kuschel, Walter Schmitz, and Carsten Peter Thiede (IT, 2118), 135 pp., reprints the biographical essay which first appeared in a collective work in 1956. The work is both readable and scholarly and the attractive format lends itself to the reproduction of Moritz von Schwind's illustrations and supplementary essays on these and on the reception of the Elisabeth legend from the Romantic period on. L. Jongen, *ABÄG*, 48:41–55, studies texts relating to the Dominican martyr St Peter of Verona.

Meister Eckhart and the Beguine Mystics. Hadewijch of Brabant, Mechthild of Magdeburg, and Marguerite Porete, ed. Bernard McGinn, NY, Continuum, x + 166 pp., contains seven essays on various aspects of the relationship between the female mystics and E., with an introduction by McGinn (1–14) who highlights 'vernacular theology' as a new departure from the monastic and scholastic traditions. The authors are S. Murk-Jansen (the affinities between E. and Hadewijch, 17–30); P. A. Dietrich (the wilderness theme in E. and Hadewijch II, 31–43); F. Tobin (E. and Mechthild, 44–61); M. Lichtmann (E. and the work of Marguerite Porete, 65–86); A. Hollywood (Marguerite, E., and female spirituality, 87–113); M. Sells (categories of being in Marguerite and E., 114–46). There is a summarizing conclusion by R. Woods (147–64). In *Das Mittelalter*, 1.2, 1996:73–88, H. Röckelein studies the beguine community in Hamburg. Michael Egerding, *Die Metaphorik der spätmittelalterlichen Mystik. I. Systematische Untersuchung. II. Bildspender—Bildempfänger—Kontexte. Dokumentation und Interpretation*, 2 vols, Paderborn, Schöningh, 248, 752 pp., is an impressively detailed study of metaphorical usage which in spite of some inevitable selectivity includes all seven major mystics of the period 1250–1370. The opening chapter deals concisely but constructively with the problems of the identification of metaphors and their relative degrees of creativity or conventionality, and the specific implications of their use in mystical contexts, without becoming excessively immersed in theoretical issues in general. The close and carefully written analyses of the first volume address each author under the headings of the transformation and the transposition of man effected by the mystical process, God's activity towards man, and the body of metaphor concerned with aspects of the dichotomy between unity and diversity. The monumental second volume justifies its claim to be a kind of dictionary of mystical language: for each author in turn there appears an alphabetical listing of relevant metaphors with full references and quite detailed interpretations. Besides its immediate value for the study of the mystics this is likely to be an important source for wider lexicographical compilations. Also noted: Katharina Bochsler, *'Ich han da inne ungehortú ding gesehen.' Die Jenseitsvisionen Mechthilds von Magdeburg in der Tradition der mittelalterlichen Visionsliteratur* (DLA, 23), ix + 192 pp., and Maren Ankermann, *Gertrud die Große von Helfta. Eine Studie zum Spannungsverhältnis von religiöser Erfahrung und literarischer*

Gestaltung in mystischen Werken (GAG, 640), 275 pp. M. Ankermann and A. Sroka, *JOWG*, 9, 1996–97:275–91, place Gertrud von Helfta's *Legatus divinae pietatis* at the centre of a study of problems of late-medieval authenticity. G. Steer, Buckl, *Krisenzeit*, 33–51, writes on Eckhart. *Meister Eckhart: Lebensstationen—Redesituationen*, ed. Klaus Jacobi (Quellen und Forschungen zur Geschichte des Domini-kanerordens, n. F., 7), Berlin, Akademie, 405 pp., addresses the question of communicative speech and related themes running through E.'s work on the basis of a series of essays on the different periods of his career. In a theoretical introduction R. Margreiter (15–42) relates mystical thought to a 'medial noetic'. E. in Erfurt is treated by W. Wackernagel (the *redemeister* in the *Rede der underscheidunge*, 45–68) and M. Enders (a broader analysis of the same work, 69–92). The theology of the Paris period is analysed by E.-H. Wéber (95–114), M. von Perger (115–48) focusing on the theme of *disputatio*. On Strasbourg, E. Hillenbrand (151–73) characterizes the friars' convent in E.'s time, O. Langer (175–92) studies E.'s relationship to his audience, and M.-A. Vannier (193–204) the parallels to the mystics of the Rhineland and Flanders. The Cologne period is reviewed by W. Senner (207–37), R. Schönberger (239–59) on E.'s understanding of the *grobe liute* who oppose him, J. Kreuzer (261–78) on E.'s view of time, eternity, and the Incarnation, R. Manstetten (279–301) on the sermon suspected of heresy, and N. Largier (303–32) on *figurata locutio*. On Avignon, W. Trusen (335–52) criticizes modern interpreta-tions of the trial, which J. Miethke (353–75) places in the context of other proceedings against Dominicans. Finally, W. Goris (379–91) writes on the *Opus tripartitum* and its audience. B. Mojsisch, *Das Licht der Vernunft* (see p. 670 above), pp. 100–09, explains Eckhart's concep-tion of the self, and G. Stachel, *ZDA*, 125, 1996:392–403, rejects the authenticity of Eckhart's sermon 86, while in *FZPT*, 44, U. Kern (297–316) studies Eckhart on time and eternity, M. A. Vannier (317–34) the concept of the noble man in his Strassburg works, and T. Yamazaki (335–54) his theological doctrine of analogy. Franz Josef Schweitzer, *Meister Eckhart und der Laie. Ein antihierarchischer Dialog des 14. Jahrhunderts aus den Niederlanden* (Quellen und Forschungen zur Geschichte des Dominikanerordens, n. F., 6), Berlin, Akademie, cxx + 263 pp., is a fine critical edition along traditional principles, based on the identification of one MS from a complex stemma as close to the author's original. Besides a survey of the codicological and textual background the introduction includes a comprehensive study of an important monument of E. reception. The vexed question of the chronology, related to obscure details within the text, is sensibly resolved with a cautious dating to *c.* 1340/41. S. avoids a controversial approach to a definition of the subject-matter as either philosophical or mystical, focusing rather on the different interpretations of its 'antihierarchical' quality, the form of lay piety it represents, and its relationship to the beguine movement and the monastic issues topical in E.'s time. Also noted: Theresia Heimerl, *Waz mac ich, ob ieman daz niht enverstât? Die Rolle der Volkssprache im Prozeß gegen Meister Eckhart* (GAG, 635), 1996, 160 pp. F. Löser, *BGDSL*, 119:425–58, points to the changes in Eckhart's doctrine in its reception by Marquard von Lindau. In *Meine in Gott geliebte Freundin. Freundschaftsdokumente aus klösterlichen und humanistischen Schreibstuben*, ed. Gabriela Signori (Religion in der Geschichte, 4), Bielefeld, Vlg für Regionalgeschichte, 1995, 151 pp., a collection mainly focused on Latin texts, A. Kuhn (98–106, 141) discusses Heinrich von Nördlingen and Margareta Ebner, while H. E. Keller, *JOWG*, 9, 1996–97:341–59, writes on secular and spiritual marriage in *Christus und die minnende Seele*, and W. Beutin, *ib.*, 361–72, notes secular and spiritual oppositions in late-medieval poetry and mystical texts. Ernst Haberkern, *Funken aus alter Glut. Johannes von Indersdorf, Von dreierlei Wesen der Menschen. Die theologischen, philosophischen und weltanschaulichen Grundlagen eines mystischen Traktats des 15. Jahrhunderts* (EH, I, 1615), 544 pp.

E. Meuthen, *Fest. Worstbrock*, 263–94, writes on the education of the clergy in the 14th–16th cs, and C. Naser, *Holler Vol.*, 248–321, studies Mainz MS I 51 as a compendium of reading for lay brothers. Prominent among work on the Dominicans is Walter Senner, *Johannes von Sterngassen OP und sein Sentenzenkommentar. I. Studie. II. Texte* (Quellen und Forschungen zur Geschichte des Dominikanerordens, n. F., 4, 5), 2 vols, Berlin, Akademie, 1995, 472, x + 411 pp. + microfiche, while K. Ruh, *ZDA*, 126:166–73, draws attention to the significance of nine 14th-c. Dutch sorority books. M. Hubrath, *LiLi*, 105:22–38, studies the monastic concept of *memoria* in the early-14th-c. South German Dominican nuns' lives, which are the subject of Gertrud Jaron Lewis, *By Women, for Women, about Women. The Sister-Books of Fourteenth-Century Germany* (Studies and Texts, 125), Toronto, Pontifical Institute of Medieval Studies, 1996, xiii + 329 pp., a comprehensive survey of the nine works, focusing on the mixture of genres, their content, theological concerns, and background, the whole with a strongly feminist undercurrent. F. van Oostrom, *ABÄG*, 48:31–39, draws attention to a reference to *Arbogasto* in Engelbert of Admont's *Speculum virtutum moralium* and considers its implications for the Charlemagne legend exemplified in *Karel ende Elegast*. P. Ochsenbein, *ZDA*, 126:53–63, publishes a 14th-c. translation of the Pseudo-Senecan *De remediis fortuitorum*. A. T. Wright, *Harms, Wahrnehmen*, 9–19, comments on the reception of the fables of Avianus, and M. Backes and J. Geiss, *ZDA*, 125, 1996:419–47, edit newly discovered fragments of Konrad von Ammenhausen's *Schachzabelbuch*, while M. Sherwood-Smith, *GLL*, 50 : 390–402, studies gynaecological matters and their sources in the Dutch *Historiebijbel van 1360*, and J. Fournier, Schwob, *Edition*, 37–49, characterizes the neglected 14th-c. *St. Pauler Evangelienreimwerk*. A. Mentzel-Reuters, *Daphnis*, 26 : 209–61, studies the Teutonic Order *Judith* and Heinrich von Hesler's *Apokalypse*, and F. Löser, *Chloe*, 25 : 637–68, places Georg Kreckwitz's Apocalypse commentary in the context of other vernacular treatments, while B. K. Vollmann, *Fest. Worstbrock*, 151–62, examines the relationship of German and Latin in Johann von Neumarkt, and T. Mertens, *ABÄG*, 47 : 109–30, elucidates the High German transmission of four works of Jan van Ruusbroec.

Annette Volfing, *Heinrich von Mügeln, 'Der meide kranz'. A Commentary* (MTU, 111), viii + 422 pp., is a well-written and well-proportioned study which both interprets the work and places it against its medieval intellectual background, so that, aided by the indexes of subjects and of biblical references, the reader is informed on a vast array of subjects. V. compensates for the relative inadequacy of W. Jahr's 1908 edition with amendments to the critical apparatus. The text is accompanied by an excellent translation which ought to make the work known to a wider audience of medievalists. The commentary sections use footnotes when required by the detail of the argument but prefer to focus on the text rather than overburden the reader with references to secondary literature. Michael Stolz, *'Tum'-Studien. Zur dichterischen Gestaltung im Marienpreis Heinrichs von Mügeln* (BG, 36), 1996, xi + 522 pp., is an exhaustively detailed study, while K. Stackmann, *ZDP*, 116, *Sonderheft*, 131–49, considers the textual position of the shorter works of Heinrich von Mügeln to exemplify the practical problems raised by the demands of the New Philology to do justice to variants in the transmission. Michaela Krieger, Gerhard Schmidt, Elfriede Gaál, and Katharina Hranitzky, *Die Wenzelsbibel. Vollständige Faksimile-Ausgabe der Codices Vindobonenses 2759–2764 der Österreichischen Nationalbibliothek Wien. Kommentarband. 1. Erläuterungen zu den illuminierten Seiten* (Codices Selecti, 70/1*), ADEVA, 1996, 230 pp., begins the commentary on the monumental facsimile edition. *Die Vokabulare von Fritsche Closener und Jakob Twinger von Königshofen. 1. Einleitung. Text A-Im. 11. Text In-Z. 111. Register*, ed. Klaus Kirchert and Dorothea Klein (TTG, 40–42), 3 vols, 1995, vii + 140 + 716, vii + 717–1603, vii + 452 pp., is a monumental contribution to early lexicography, and R. Damme, *NdJb*, 117, 1994 : 75–92, studies the glossary of Dietrich Engelhus, while G. von Olberg, *Das Mittelalter*, 2.2 : 69–80, examines the relationship of German and Latin in late-medieval proverbial usage. H. Blosen, *Fest. Schwob*, 17–26, traces the reception of Peter Suchenwirt's *Würfelspiel*, and M. J. Schubert, *ZDA*, 126 : 314–32, publishes a 15th-c. fragment of the German *Speculum* *humanae salvationis*, while P. Wiesinger, *Fest. Schwob*, 523–38, studies the epic narrative of Andreas Kurzmann's version of the latter, and M. Schumacher, *JOWG*, 9, 1996–97:309–22, investigates Heinrich Kaufringer's 'Von den sieben Todsünden und den sieben Gaben des Heiligen Geistes'. A. M. Rasmussen, Harms, *Wahrnehmen*, 193–204, looks at femininity in *Stiefmutter und Tochter*, and M. Siller, *Fest. Schwob*, 447–62, addresses the question of the nobility in Hans Vintler's *Blumen der Tugend*, the proverbs of which are the subject of E. De Felip-Jaud, Holzner, *Literatur*, 175–98. Diebold Lauber's 15th-c. prose version of Bruder Philipp's *Marienleben* is the subject of Andrea Rapp, *bücher gar húbsch gemolt. Studien zur Werkstatt Diebold Laubers am Beispiel der Prosabearbeitung von Bruder Philipps 'Marienleben' in den Historienbibeln IIa und Ib* (*VB*, 18), 1996 [1998], xi + 452 pp., also A. Rapp, Schwob, *Edition*, 97–108. In *Chloe*, 25, U. Möllmann (595–609) discusses the editing of late-medieval *Regula Benedicti* texts, and F. Simmler (851–934) uses them to exemplify fundamental problems facing the text editor, while A. Margani, *NdJb*, 116, 1993:28–71, edits a 15th-c. MLG version of the Song of Songs and its Latin source, and I. Schröder, *ib.*, 115, 1992:7–23, comments on a MLG Gospel translation of *c.* 1480. M. Bärmann, *Daphnis*, 26:179–85, finds new documentary evidence relating to Antonius von Pforr, the illustrations to whose *Buch der Beispiele der alten Weisen* are analysed in detail by U. Bodemann, *BGDSL*, 119:67–129 + 16 pls. H. Moser, Holzner, *Literatur*, 219–59, edits a late-15th-c. collection of miracles from Maria Waldrast, and G. Signori, *Das Mittelalter*, 1.2, 1996:113–34, surveys late-medieval accounts of miracles related to childbirth, while W. Röll, *Chloe*, 25:621–36, studies the problems of editing a 15th-c. Yiddish translation of Job.

DRAMA. E. E. DuBruck, *FCS*, 22, 1996:163–91; 23:236–57, reviews recent research on late-medieval drama; Id., *ib.*, 23:171–83, identifies the reasons for the creation of late-medieval 'salvation theatre', and R. Warning, *Fest. Worstbrock*, 29–41, looks at basic theoretical problems arising from the study of the religious drama. *Frankfurter Dirigierrolle. Frankfurter Passionsspiel. Mit den Paralleltexten der 'Frankfurter Dirigierrolle' des 'Alsfelder Passionsspiels' des 'Heidelberger Passionsspiels' des 'Frankfurter Osterspielfragments' und des 'Fritzlarer Passionsspielfragments'*, ed. Johannes Janota (Die Hessische Passionsspielgruppe: Edition in Paralleldruck, 1), Tübingen, Niemeyer, 1996 [1997], xiv + 430 pp., is the first of three monumental volumes intended to present this group of plays in a reliable modern edition which takes the relationships between the texts fully into account. The volume begins, appropriately, with a diplomatic print of the *Frankfurter Dirigierrolle* followed by a user-friendly edition. The parallel texts of the four plays are introduced by convenient summaries of the scenic content of each. The *Frankfurter Passionsspiel* of 1493 is treated as the leading text against which the parallels are easily read off. The edition is both conservative and readable, standard abbreviations in both German and Latin being written out. A double apparatus distinguishes modifications to the texts by later hands from scribal corrections and variants. This superbly produced work is an immense service to scholarship on the drama. Other new editions include *Die geistlichen Spiele des Sterzinger Spielarchivs*. III. *Rabers Passion (1514)—Fragment einer Passion—Gründonnerstagspiel—Ludus Pascalis (1520)—Planctus Beate Marie Virginis—Ludus de Nativitate Domini (1511)*, ed. Hans-Gert Roloff (MDL, 16), 1996, 445 pp., and *Die geistlichen Spiele des Sterzinger Spielarchivs*. VI, 2. *Kommentar zur Edition der Melodien*, ed. Andreas Traub and Sabina Prüser (MDL, 19, 2), 1996, 183 pp. *The Alsfeld Passion Play*, trans. and introd. Larry E. West (SGLL, 17), xxxvii + 648 pp., will certainly encourage interest in the drama on an interdisciplinary basis. The detailed introduction reviews the content of the play, its background and relationship to its analogues, literary and dramatic qualities, performance, anti-Semitism, and important earlier scholarship. R. Froning's 1893 edition is printed on left-hand pages. The facing translation is generally successful in its intention primarily to capture the essence and mood of the original and uses a fusion of modern idiom and more archaic biblical language to achieve this, with occasional rhymes. E. Vijfvinkel, *EG*, 52:293–301, compares the stage directions of the *Donaueschingen Passion Play* and *Lucerne Easter Play* against the biblical background, and A. Schnyder, *NdJb*, 118, 1995:27–55, analyses and interprets the *Redentin Easter Play*, while in *Shylock?* (see p. 669 above), J. Heil (35–58) refers to the dramatic treatment of the Golden Calf of Exodus. A. Classen, *Daphnis*, 25, 1996:627–44, studies the religious mentality of the *Chur Last Judgement Play*, and H. Linke, *BGDSL*, 119:268–75, questions the existence of a Lucerne Last Judgement play attributed in the literature to Jakob am Grund, while F. V. Spechtler, *Fest. Schwob*, 463–67, links the 17th-c. Salzburg Passion play *Vom Leiden und Sterben Jesu Christi* with the late-medieval dramatic tradition. E. Simon, *ZDP*, 116, *Sonderheft*, 208–23, considers the text of the Lübeck *Fastnachtspiele* of relative insignificance compared with the wealth of documentation which points to the richness of medieval performance, and B. Quast, Harms, *Wahrnehmen*, 205–19, comments on poetological aspects of the Nuremberg *Fastnachtspiele* in the light of M. M. Bakhtin's theories.

SCIENTIFIC AND SPECIALIZED LITERATURE

W. Buckl, Buckl, *Krisenzeit*, 109–32, writes on Konrad von Megenberg, and J. G. Mayer, *Holler Vol.*, 322–35, on Konrad and Paracelsus, while A. Deighton, *ZDA*, 126:200–12, edits a manuscript of the *Mainauer Naturlehre* in York. R. Schmidt-Wiegand, *NdJb*, 116, 1993:7–27, studies the filiation of illustrated *Sachsenspiegel* MSS, B. Hennig, *Fest. Möhn*, 11–28, notes the use of the *Sachsenspiegel* in MHG lexicography, and R. Pilkmann-Pohl, *NdW*, 37:55–64, includes a legal text of 1449 in documentation of the application of the *Sachsenspiegel* in Minden. T. Bohn and A. Rapp, *Beiträge zum Sprachkontakt* (see p. 675 above), pp. 215–83 + supp., update the *Corpus der altdeutschen Originalurkunden*, and K. Gärtner, Schwob, *Edition*, 51–61, considers problems in the transmission of legal documents of the 13th and 14th cs, while J. Regge, Erfen, *Fremdheit*, 289–98, reviews the legal treatment of those identified as strangers or foreigners, and in *Norm und Praxis* (see p. 672 above), different aspects of legal theory and practice are the subject of work by C. Gauvard (27–38) and M. Dinges (39–53). G. Cornelissen, *NdJb*, 117, 1994:58–74, investigates the language of 14th-c. MLG documents, and G. Wittek, *ib.*, 120:59–78, studies the use of *fride* and *pax* in late-medieval civic documents. K. Kranich-Hofbauer, *Fest. Schwob*, 257–70, edits Tyrolean historical documents from 1434, and M. Will, *NdJb*, 115, 1992:41–69, surveys MLG diaries and autobiographies, while B. Schnell, *Holler Vol.*, 118–33, studies Michael de Leone's *Iatromathematisches Hausbuch*, and T. Ehlert, *Fest. Schwob*, 73–85, considers the oral and written aspects of 15th-c. cookery books. H.-P. Hils, *Holler Vol.*, 201–19, considers the legal status of the professional swordsman. Manfred Zollinger, *Bibliographie der Spielbücher des 15. bis 18. Jahrhunderts*, I. *1473–1700*, Stuttgart, Hiersemann, 1996, lxxxiv + 272 pp., is a major catalogue of early works concerned with games and pastimes in the widest sense, including texts on magic, divination, medicine, etc. In *Chloe*, 25, there are comments on the problems attending the editing of vernacular scientific texts by J. Paulus (the alchemical *Donum Dei*, 795–803), K. Pfister (the astrological *Buch vom Firmament*, 805–09), and G. Brey (15th-c. mathematical texts). Also noted: Walter L. Wardale, *Der Hochdeutsche Bartholomäus. Kritisch-kommentierter Text eines mittelalterlichen Arzneibuches auf Grund der Londoner Handschriften Brit. Mus. Add. 16,892, Brit. Mus. Arundel 164, Brit. Mus. Add. 17,527, Brit. Mus. Add. 34,304*, Dundee, James Follan, 1993, xii + [62] + [338] + [102] pp., also in English as *The High German Bartholomaeus. Text, with Critical Commentary, of a Mediaeval Medical Book Based on the London Manuscripts Brit. Mus. Add. 16,892, Brit. Mus. Arundel 164, Brit. Mus. Add. 17,527, Brit. Mus. Add. 34,304*, Dundee, James Follan, 1993, with some variation in the pagination of the separate sections; Walter L. Wardale, *Der deutsche Macer-Text aus der Handschrift Brit. Mus. Add. 16,892*, Dundee, Follan, 1995, xviii + 86 pp.; Britta-Juliana Kruse, *Verborgene Heilkünste. Geschichte der*

Frauenmedizin im Spätmittelalter (QFLK, 5 (239)), 1996, xi + 498 pp., includes editions, facsimiles, and discussions of major texts. D. Jacquart, *Das Licht der Vernunft* (see p. 670 above), pp. 84–99, outlines the rational dimension of medieval medicine, while in *Holler Vol.*, R. Spranger (98–117) writes on the *Breslauer Arzneibuch*, C. Weisser (79–97) edits prognostic medical texts from Darmstadt, J. G. Mayer (156–77) records the first printed herbals, and G. Keil (178–200) addresses the Alemannic *Rosmarin-Traktat*. Id., *Das Mittelalter*, 2.1:101–09, examines the interaction of German and Latin in medical texts, while R. Jütte, *Norm und Praxis* (see p. 672 above), pp. 95–106, studies the implications for medical theory and practice of the many texts on bleeding, and A. Berndzen, *NdW*, 37:87–118, edits the Lübeck *Bock van der pestilencien* of 1484.

OTHER LATER MEDIEVAL LITERATURE

Work on the fabliau includes Joëlle Fuhrmann, *La représentation de la femme dans la 'nouvelle' allemande du moyen âge tardif. Description de quelques schémas normatifs de l'imaginaire masculin et patriarcal* (WAGAPH, 34), 2 vols, 1996, 321, 293 pp., while M. Chinca, pp. 187–210 of *Framing Medieval Bodies*, ed. Sarah Kay and Miri Rubin, Manchester U.P., 1994, vii + 287 pp., interprets a number of sexual *Mären* in terms of body and gesture, A. Schnyder, *Euphorion*, 91:397–412, analyses Heinrich Kaufringer's *Der zurückgegebene Minnelohn*, and B. Lundt, Kornbichler, *Liebe*, 149–72, points to the transition in idealized masculine figures in works such as *Von den sieben weisen Meistern*. G. Niggl, Buckl, *Krisenzeit*, 227–37, writes on the *Ackermann aus Böhmen*. U. Zitzlsperger, *GLL*, 50:403–16, studies the late-medieval fool from the viewpoint of his absence of feminine characteristics, M. and R. Bräuer, *Fest. Schwob*, 37–45, place Heinrich Wittenwiler at the centre of a study of the conception of adventure, and W. Röcke, *Neohelicon*, 23.2, 1996:145–66, includes the *Ring* in a study of functions of laughter in medieval literature, while T. Cramer, Wenzel, *Gespräche*, 212–25, interprets the love-letter in the *Ring* in terms of the tension between oral and written communication, and D. Roth, *Euphorion*, 91:377–96, studies a topos in Wittenwiler's marriage debate.

JOWG, 9, 1996–97, in commemoration of the 550th anniversary of Oswald von Wolkenstein's death, presents work by A. Schwob (progress with the edition of the documentation of O.'s life, 3–15); S. K. Németh (Hungary in O.'s time, 17–29); F. J. Schweitzer (the Hussite songs in the context of the Bohemian Reformation and Revolution, 31–43); R. Schmidt-Wiegand (Imperial law in O. and in Wittenwiler, 45–58); W. Hofmeister (O.'s use of proverbial utterance, 59–70); F. Daxecker (O.'s injured right eye, 71–79); U. M. Schwob (fear of sudden death in O.'s literature and life, 81–98); K. Helmkamp (the prison songs, 99–109); E. Lienert (childhood in O., 111–20); T. Nolte (O.'s images and projections of woman, 121–38); J. Spicker (the marriage songs, 139–56); C. Berger and T. Tomasek (Kl. 68 and the Margarethe songs, 157–77); M. Schiendorfer (secular and spiritual in Kl. 40, 179–96); F. Fürbeth (Kl. 18 and medieval doctrines of sin, 197–220); E. Loenertz (Kl. 16 and the relationship of music and text, 221–37); M. Schadendorf (text and melody in Kl. 33–36); H. Lengenfelder (the editing of illustrated manuscripts of O. and other 15th-c. authors, 259–74); H. Straub (the translations of 'Mundi renovatio' and 'Mittit ad virginem' by O. and by the Monk of Salzburg (509–22); and R. Strohm (O.'s reworking of a French model in Kl. 47 and the wide questions it raises, 523–50). A. K. Wimmer, *Fest. Schwob*, 539–45, identifies aspects of Oswald's work appropriate for enlarging students' medieval horizons, J. Spicker, *ZDA*, 126:174–92, considers the conception of authorship in Oswald von Wolkenstein and Hugo von Montfort, and M. Winkler, *Fest. Schwob*, 547–56, speculates on Oswald's links with Scandinavia, while S. Hartmann, *ib.*, 133–39, documents Oswald's role at Emperor Sigismund's ceremonial entry into Perpignan, E. Koller, *ib.*, 251–56, his presence at the Portuguese attack on Ceuta, and N. R. Wolf, Holzner, *Literatur*, 81–91, considers his use of diminutives. M. Siller, *ib.*, 93–122, includes Oswald in a study of *solch* and *welch*, and A. Robertshaw, *ib.*, 199–210, studies his word-play on personal names. Id., *Fest. Schwob*, 379–87, comments on his use of numbers. R. Schmidt-Wiegand, *ib.*, 401–05, notes legal references in Oswald, and J. Spicker, *ZDP*, 116:413–16, links Kl. 18, 44, and 104 to the tradition of the French *malmariée* song, while K. Bartsch, *Fest. Schwob*, 1–9, writes on the poetry of Paul Wiens, an instance of Oswald reception.

Barbara Christine Stocker, *Friedrich Colner: Schreiber und Übersetzer in St. Gallen 1430–1436* (GAG, 619), 1996, 350 pp. E. Koller, *Runa*, 26, 1996:477–88, prints and studies German-language correspondence of Empress Eleonore of Portugal. Paul Weinig, *Aeneam suscipite, pium recipite! Aeneas Silvius Piccolomini. Studien zur Rezeption eines humanistischen Schriftstellers im Deutschland des 15. Jahrhunderts* (Gratia. Bamberger Schriften zur Renaissanceforschung, 33), Wiesbaden, Harrassowitz, vi + 167 pp., documents some 700 manuscripts, and B. Wachinger, *Fest. Worstbrock*, 163–76, discusses the Classical models relating to women and love in Piccolomini's *Historia de duobus amantibus*, while R. Glendinning, *FCS*, 23:101–20, relates the themes of the *Historia de duobus amantibus* to Gottfried's *Tristan* among other models, and W. Röcke, Wenzel, *Gespräche*, 226–43, studies letters as the expression of a 'literary culture of the emotions' in Niklas von Wyle's translation of the *Historia de duobus amantibus* and in Franciscus Florus's *De amore Camilli et Emiliae Historia.* C. Kiening, *ib.*, 320–43, studies 15th-c. humanist consolatory dialogues. Eleonora von Österreich, *Pontus und Sidonia*, ed. Reinhard Hahn (TSM, 38), 168 pp., fills an important lacuna with a clearly legible edition, including the woodcuts, of the A version, that of Eleonore, of this important prose romance. The introductory matter places the edition in the context of the history of the subject-matter in general and the German transmission in particular, the contemporary B version having already been edited by Karin Schneider (TSM, 14) in 1961. After recapitulating details of the B version, H. provides full descriptions of the single MS G and the 24 printed editions, following the older studies of P. Wüst to identify the 1483 print of Johann Schönsperger of Augsburg as the best text. D. Mertens, *Fest. Worstbrock*, 295–314, highlights the cultural and artistic associations of the Imperial Diet at the end of the period, and A. M. Haas, *JOWG*, 9, 1996–97:293–308, studies the conception of the wall of paradise in Nicholas of Cusa, while M. Jonas, Holzner, *Literatur*, 211–17, publishes correspondence of the Abbess Verena von Stuben.

C. Nolte, Erfen, *Fremdheit*, 65–92, surveys the salient characteristics of journeys to Jerusalem by 15th-c. princes, and M. Müller (147–63) shows the importance of the Holy Land and other foreign destinations in the dissemination of architectural and building technology, while M. Löwener (165–76) uses the founding of the Teutonic Order to illustrate the significance of itineraries as a guide to historical chronology, and H. Wernicke (177–92) illustrates the experiences abroad of Hanseatic merchants, included in a specific study of England by N. Jörn (193–216). W. Carls, *Chloe*, 25:611–19, discusses the editing of Felix Fabri's *Sionpilgerin*, H. Kästner, Wenzel, *Gespräche*, 280–95, analyses the conversations between Christian travellers and Oriental heathen rulers in travel literature, and U. Ganz-Blättler, *Das Mittelalter*, 2.1:93–100, documents references to foreign languages and their speakers in pilgrimage narratives, while W. F. Reddig, *ib.*, 135–50, is concerned specifically with Turkish language and customs, and K. Cieslik, Erfen, *Fremdheit*, 277–88, reviews the experience of foreign parts as a major attribute of the heroes of late-medieval romances. Andres Betschart, *Zwischen zwei Welten. Illustrationen in Berichten westeuropäischer Jerusalemreisender des 15. und 16. Jahrhunderts* (WDBP, 15), 1996, vi + 379 pp. + map, starts from the insight that, notwithstanding the resurgence of interest in travel literature in the past two decades, the illustrations in the various works have been largely neglected. The analysis is based on a substantial catalogue (pp. 245–376) which aims to be a comprehensive listing of all 14th–16th-c. pilgrimage books including illustrations. This is a major achievement in its own right. Following the iconographical-iconological approach of E. Panofsky, B. reveals a varied pattern: while the topography of Jerusalem is a constant focus of interest, in other areas a 'medieval' concern with the marvels of nature gives way to a more realistic depiction of foreign peoples.

Hans-Jörg Künast, *'Getruckt zu Augspurg.' Buchdruck und Buchhandel in Augsburg zwischen 1468 und 1555* (Studia Augustana, 8), Tübingen, Niemeyer, ix + 373 pp. + map, is an ambitious monograph which adds significantly to factual knowledge of early book production in Augsburg but particularly succeeds in placing the whole subject in a much wider historical, social, and cultural context than hitherto. Besides the expected statistical data on the books produced and their authors and genres (much of tabulated in a substantial appendix of charts and graphics) there is a wealth of information here on the organization of the book trade, censorship, the education of printers and readership, socio-economic factors conditioning the market, the role of the Reformation, pamphlets, and the Jews. U. Neddermeyer, *Gazette du livre médiéval*, 28, 1996:23–32, considers the problems associated with quantifying late-medieval book production; Id., *ib.*, 31:1–8, surveys results from a quantitative survey. *Laienlektüre und Buchmarkt im späten Mittelalter*, ed. Thomas Kock and Rita Schlusemann (Gesellschaft, Kultur und Schrift. Mediävistische Beiträge, 5), Frankfurt, Lang, 305 pp., is a thoughtful collection of essays on early printing, book production, and readership. H. Pleij (13–32) with numerous examples addresses the question of lay literacy, emphasizing the essential fluidity of a situation in which market forces dominated. R. Schlusemann (33–59) studies the specific book market in Antwerp, with statistical and other data, and F. Eisermann (109–27) the impact of Wilhelm von Velde's *Kleines Empyreal*, seen to be directed to an identified public. B. Schnell (129–45) finds no satisfactory or simple answer to the question of for whom medical literature was written in the vernacular, and V. Honemann (147–60) surveys instances of lay literary patronage. J. M. M. Hermans (161–85) characterizes conditions in the northern Netherlands, and L. Wierda (187–97) book production in Zwolle, while T. Kock (199–220) traces the practice of reading and book production, with the impact of printing, among the adherents of the Devotio Moderna. N. Staubach (221–89) casts new light on the latter movement with a substantial monograph on Gerhard Zerbolt of Zutphen's *De libris teutonicalibus*. *BW*, 29, 1996, includes studies of the drastic reduction in book prices at the end of the 15th c. (L. Hoffmann, 5–23), the gatherings of early incunabula (M. Boghardt, 24–58), early Bohemian printing (J. Vrchotka, 70–77), the Magdeburg printer Simon Koch (N. Suckow, 87–94), and the Göttingen collection of incunabula

(H. Kind, 126–32), besides other studies of early printed books and bindings.

S. Edmunds, *BGDSL*, 119:261–67, identifies Jörg Roggenburg, the patron of Clara Hätzlerin, and M. Dallapiazza, *JOWG*, 9, 1996–97:373–83, points to models of love, marriage, and domesticity in late-15th-c. literature, while C. Baufeld, *Fest. Schwob*, 11–18, notes literature on the activities of beggars, tramps, and other ruffians from the end of the period. Frank Piontek, *Ein Fürst und sein Buch. Beiträge zur Interpretation des Buchs der Beispiele* (GAG, 631), 241 pp., concerns Antonius von Pforr's work, and C. Reske, *GJ*, 72:95–106, adds to knowledge of the printing of Schedel's world-chronicle. W. Frey, *IASL*, 57.1:155–76, reviews recent work on the Dance of Death, and V. Leppin, *AKG*, 77, 1995:323–43, reconsiders the problem of the origin of the Dance of Death in the light of recent research. *Der Todtentanz in der Marienkirche zu Lübeck. Nach einer Zeichnung von C. J. Milde, mit erläuterndem Text von Professor W. Mantels, Lübeck 1866, H. G. Rahtgens*, 3rd rev. edn with supp. by Hartmut Freytag, Lübeck, Vlg DrägerDruck, 14 pp. + 8 pls, iv + 18 pp., is a handsome reissue of this large-format volume (see *YWMLS*, 51:668–69). H. Freytag updates his essay on the Lübeck Dance of Death and the related Reval (Tallinn) fragments in the light of the substantial recent research on the subject. Texts and translations are included. A. Krüger, *NdJb*, 117, 1994:109–29, surveys the theological reference of the Lübeck Dance of Death and related works, and H. Freytag, *ZDP*, 116:90–93, notes the affinities of the newly-discovered Kleve Dance of Death fragments to the Lübeck and Reval monuments.

Populäre Literatur des Spätmittelalters. Inkunabeln aus Zweibrücken (Jörg Geßler). Faksimileausgabe. Ink E 4817 der Universitätsbibliothek Freiburg i. Br. Ink F 10 Nr. 10 der Historischen Bibliothek der Stadt Rastatt, ed. Ute Obhof and Johannes Schöndorf, comm. Ute Obhof, Wiesbaden, Reichert, 27 pp. + 59 pp., is a beautifully produced and extremely clear facsimile reproduction of *Arnolt Buschmanns Mirakel* (1492) and Hans Ortenstein's *Das Fräulein von Britannien*, probably of the same date. The introduction is concise but has full scholarly documentation and ranges widely over the authorship, subject-matter, genre, and influence of the two quite different works, besides the Zweibrücken printing-house and its historical background and significance. W. Röcke, pp. 124–34 of *'Nicht allein mit den Worten.' Festschrift für Joachim Dyck zum 60. Geburtstag*, ed. Thomas Müller, Stuttgart-Bad Cannstatt, Frommann-Holzboog, 1995, 228 pp., writes on the demonization of the Jews in late-medieval civic literature. *Sébastien Brant, son époque et 'La nef des fols'* = *Sebastian Brant, seine Zeit und das 'Narrenschiff'. Actes du colloque international Strasbourg 10–11 mars 1994*, ed. Gonthier-Louis Fink (Collection recherches germaniques, 5),

Strasbourg Univ., Institut d'Études Allemandes, 1995, 187 pp., includes a range of work on many aspects of Brant and his work and the *Narrenschiff* in particular. H. Vredeveld, *Daphnis*, 26:553–651, supplies detailed notes for a new commentary on the *Narrenschiff*, and D.-R. Moser, *LiB*, 50:2–8, emphasizes the Augustinian dimension of the work, while F. Voss, *NdJb*, 116, 1993:109–17, considers the MLG *Narrenschiff* in relation to its sources. Also on Brant we note Silke Umbach, *Sebastian Brants Tischzucht (Thesmophagia 1490). Edition und Wortindex* (Gratia, 27), Wiesbaden, Harrassowitz, 1995, 201 pp., while W. Ludwig, *Daphnis*, 26:263–99, studies a newly-discovered version of his *Varia Carmina*, and E. E. DuBruck, *FCS*, 22, 1996:85–95, comments on his attitude to education. From the end of the period, F. Pensel, *ZDA*, 126:64–85, publishes a German verse translation of Prudentius's *Tituli historiarum* dated 1497, and H. A. Arnold, *FCS*, 23:93–100, reviews the chief themes of the *Buch der Hundert Kapitel*, while H. Freytag, *Fest. Möhn*, 39–54, comments on the relationship of verse and prose in *Reynke de vos*, and J. Goossens, *ib.*, 55–62, on the speech of the female ape in *Reynke de vos* and *Reinaerts historie*. P. Wackers, *ABÄG*, 47:197–211, examines the structure of *Reynke de vos* and its glosses, and B. Janz, *Das Mittelalter*, 2.2:21–29, studies its legal proverbs.

THE SIXTEENTH CENTURY

By PETER MACARDLE, *University of Durham*

1. GENERAL

BIBLIOGRAPHY

Werner Fechter, *Deutsche Handschriften des 15. und 16. Jahrhunderts aus der Bibliothek des ehemaligen Augustiner-Chorfrauenklosters Inzigkofen*, Sigmaringen, Thorbecke, xxiii + 219 pp., is a splendid catalogue of the German MSS of this house of Augustinian canonesses (whose books, apart from liturgical works, were all in the vernacular). The core is a detailed description and inventory of the 60 MSS, now dispersed over 14 libraries in Germany and elsewhere, which can be identified as coming from Inzigkofen. But it is also a contribution to our understanding of late medieval and early modern *Bildungsgeschichte*. A history of the convent, detailed biographical notes on the nuns, and an account of the fate of their books are added. The evidence of the texts allows F. to identify writers of the MSS and trace the work of the nuns' chaplains in reviewing and correcting books. The heterogeneity of the collection is convincingly demonstrated; about the 'literary relations' of the convent, in the sense of the exchange of texts and the provenance of MSS copied at Inzigkofen, something can be said. This is a model for the exploration of the library remains of other monastic houses. *Deutsche illustrierte Flugblätter des 16. und 17. Jahrhunderts. Kommentierte Ausgabe.* VII. *Die Sammlung der Zentralbibliothek Zürich. 2. Die Wickiana, 2. Hälfte*, ed. Wolfgang Harms and Michael Schilling, Tübingen, Niemeyer, 400 pp., continues this important series. *Repertorium deutschsprachiger Ehelehren der Frühen Neuzeit*, ed. Erika Kartschoke, Berlin, Akademie, begins with I, 1. *Handschriften und Drucke der Staatsbibliothek zu Berlin/Preußischer Kulturbesitz (Haus 2)*, xxxii + 338 pp.; the two remaining volumes will catalogue the material in Wolfenbüttel and Munich. *Editionsdesiderate zur Frühen Neuzeit. Beiträge zur Tagung der Kommission für die Edition von Texten der Frühen Neuzeit*, ed. Hans-Gert Roloff and Renate Meinicke (*Chloe*, 24), 2 vols, xiv + 592, 593–1063 pp., contains contributions by H. Blume, on Bote (17–36); L. Lieb, on Waldis (37–50); H. Thomke, on Swiss drama (67–71); U. Gaebel, on dialogues and plays on marriage (73–90); G. Dörner, on Reuchlin's correspondence (121–39); A. Kühne, on the Munich Copernicus edition (141–55); J. Jungo, on J. K. Lorcher (167–70); W. Ludwig, on the correspondence of W. Reichart (171–77); D. Peil, on three pamphlets of 1589 (209–29); S. Kura, on Broelman's play *Laurentias* (283–89); S. Looss, on Karlstadt (553–65); W. Held, on Müntzer (567–75); U. Möllmann, on 15th-c. and 16th-c. Rules of St Benedict (595–609); E. Mayerova, on 15th-c. and 16th-c. wills from Pressburg (617–19); G. van Gemert, on works of S. Franck preserved only in Dutch (669–85); M. Schilling, on the *Fuggerzeitungen* (717–27); P. Dilg, on V. Cordus's botanical and pharmaceutical writings (975–82); H. Kästner, on M. Schedel's autobiography (995–1003); and K. Jaeger, on H. von Rüte's plays (1005–11). I. Bezzel, 'Petrus Littinus Buscius, Drucker in Köln von 1527 bis 1531', *Gutenberg-Jb.*, 72:114–20; F. Schanze, *ib.*, 111–14, redates a printing of the *Bauernpraktik* previously assumed to be of 1508.

2. HUMANISM AND THE REFORMATION

Bard Thompson, *Humanists and Reformers. A History of the Renaissance and Reformation*, Grand Rapids, MI–Cambridge, Eerdmans, 1996, x + 742 pp., is a compendious account of the main lines of the Italian Renaissance and the European Reformation; pp. 331–537 deal with the Northern Renaissance and the Reformation in Germany and in the contiguous countries. Inevitably, an attempt to cover such a sweep cannot break new ground; rather it presents a modern scholarly consensus, but does so for the most part very fairly indeed, though not without some minor errors. Peter Matheson, *The Rhetoric of the Reformation*, Edinburgh, Clark, 288 pp., approaches the Reformation as a paradigm shift in the European religious imagination, an essentially rhetorical phenomenon. The study is largely concerned with the Reformation pamphlet. One chapter explores the ways in which this genre created a 'public opinion' in the German-speaking countries; others examine the themes, techniques, language, and polemic of such writers as Luther, Karlstadt, Müntzer, and Argula von Grumbach. Repeatedly, M. argues that 'propaganda' may not be the most helpful term to apply to the pamphlets: heuristic and ludic qualities are also of prime importance. He concedes, however, that with time this liberating polemic, aimed at creating a community of discourse, did indeed turn into manipulative and entrenched propaganda. Susan Karant-Nunn, *The Reformation of Ritual. An Interpretation of Early Modern Germany*, London–NY, Routledge, ix + 282 pp., examines the cultural meaning of the changes made by the Reformers to the Catholic rites of engagement and marriage, baptism, the churching of women, confession and the Eucharist, and death and burial. The conclusion is that the Protestant churches, in ostensibly 'purifying' these rituals, were in most cases censoring or controlling those elements in them which before had effectively belonged to the people. The new rituals became a means of increasing the status of the clergy and of disciplining the populace; this was resisted by the laity, who often found ways of clinging to vestiges of earlier ritual. Reforming attempts to emphasize community in rituals were often thwarted by the loss of the flexibility which had characterized Catholic practice. The partly anthropological method, and several conclusions, will be familiar from recent work on the English Reformation. Kurt Stadtwald, *Roman Popes and German Patriots: Antipapalism in the Politics of the German Humanist Movement from Gregor Heimburg to Martin Luther* (THR, 299), 1996, 237 pp., is a compact attempt to vindicate the relevance and importance of the German humanists' political programme, rooted in patriotic opposition to papal pretensions. After locating the origins of this anti-Roman stance in Barbarossa's confrontation with the Papacy, conducted by G. Heimburg, S. considers the political engagement of Celtis and the Vienna Circle, Erasmus, Hutten, J. Ziegler, J. Aventin, Vadian, and Luther. Throughout, he contends that the humanists were neither as politically naïve, nor as much under the thumb of princes and patrons, nor as ineffectual in disseminating their opinions, as has often been assumed. He also argues that Luther's attitudes to Rome and the papacy were more decisively formed by the humanist tradition than much Reformation scholarship has conceded. *Convents Confront the Reformation: Catholic and Protestant Nuns in Germany*, ed. Merry Wiesner-Hanks, trans. Joan Skocir and Merry Wiesner-Hanks, Milwaukee, Marquette U.P., 110 pp., prints and translates four early modern texts written by nuns, or women who had recently left the religious life. The first two are from the 16th c.: Katherina Rem (Augsburg 1523) and Ursula von Münsterberg (Freiberg 1528). The texts are of considerable interest, since the question of how the Reformation coped with female religious has been largely neglected (as W.-H.'s informative introduction shows). The project of editing inaccessible early modern works is admirable; but both the transcription and editing of the German texts leave a good deal to be desired, while the English translation is uneven, and often seriously inaccurate. A. Buck, 'Zum Selbstverständnis der Renaissance', *WRM*, 21:49–57. K. Jensen, *Atti* (Ferrara), II, 23–41, discusses the impact of Italian humanist grammatical textbooks on their German counterparts.

Several brief studies focus on particular towns and regions. U. Wagner, 'De urbibus Germaniae humanitate distinctis', *Vox Latina*, 33:41–60, concentrates on Bamberg and Jena. R. Hinterndörfer, 'Dichter des Späthumanismus im Donauraum beiderseits der Enns', *Chloe*, 26:547–75, studies relevant life and works. Ekrem, *Reformation*, contains several studies on Rostock University. J. Krēsliņš (30–41) details the factors — confessional, pedagogical and social — that made Rostock University particularly attractive to Lutheran students from northern Europe, while A. Tering (56–70) analyses its appeal to students from the Baltic countries, and R. Sarasti-Wilenius (71–82) studies the presence of Finnish students there and at Wittenberg; all three emphasize the importance of the prestige of D. Chytraeus. S. Rhein (42–55) shows that the progress of Greek studies at Rostock in the 16th c. was more halting and uneven than is often recognized; H. bei der Wieden (123–37) examines scholarly awareness of Iceland at the University in the late 16th c. Telling differences between the pattern of Reformation in Rostock, Wismar, and Stralsund are examined by W. Trossbach, *AR*, 88:118–6. The importance of educational reforms at Wittenberg in the early period of the Reformation is discussed by M. Treu, Ekrem, *Reformation*, 19–29. P. T. Ferry, *SCJ*, 28:143–66, writes on popular preaching in Saxony. B. Nischan, *AR*, 88:199–216, examines confessionalization in Lutheran preaching on Maundy Thursday, the Ascension, and Corpus Christi during the late 16th and early 17th cs. I. Ekrem, Ekrem, *Reformation*, 207–25, surveys historical writing and history teaching, particularly in the tradition of Melanchthon and D. Chytraeus, in Germany and Scandinavia. A. Schmid, 'Die Anfänge der Bistumshistoriographie in den süddeutschen Diözesen im Zeitalter des Humanismus', *Römische Quartalschrift für christliche Altertumskunde und Kirchengeschichte*, 91, 1996:230–62.

3. GENRES

DRAMA AND DIALOGUE

Stephen L. Wailes, *The Rich Man and Lazarus on the Reformation Stage: A Contribution to the Social History of German Drama*, Selinsgrove, Susquehanna U. P., 359 pp., examines ten 16th-c. dramatizations of this parable: the anonymous play from the Sterzing *Spielarchiv*, the Zurich play of 1529, and those of Funckelin, Frey, Krüginger, Müntzer, Hoffmann, Rollenhagen, and Ayrer. W. argues that the plays deal with wealth and poverty, explosive social and political issues in the Reformation, and as such are part of the public discourse on these issues. He is most convincing on the earlier material, particularly on the Zurich play, which he relates in various ways to anti-Roman polemic. Of Funckelin's recasting (1551) of the Zurich play, he argues persuasively that some of the changes reflect the need for diplomacy in the delicate confessional situation of the Swiss Confederation at mid-century. But with some other plays (Krüginger, Müntzer, and Hoffmann) the social approach seems less fruitful, and these works are either treated somewhat perfunctorily, or else the focus shifts, to concentrate on other aspects of their composition and effect. E. Simon, pp. 208–23 of *Philologie als Textwissenschaft. Alte und neue Horizonte* (*ZDP*, 116, Sonderheft), reconstructs the dramatic activity

of the Lübeck *Fastnacht* from the recently discovered records of the
Greveradenkompanie, a merchant guild. P. F. Casey writes on 'Children
and images of childhood in German biblical drama of the sixteenth
century', pp. 1–14 of *Life's Golden Tree. Essays in German Literature from
the Renaissance to Rilke*, ed. Thomas Kerth and George C. Schoolfield
(SGLLC), 1996, xiv + 282 pp. F. Rädle, *Ijsewijn Vol.*, 309–23, examines satirical and verbal comedy in the Latin drama of the 16th and
17th cs, particularly in Naogeorg, Frischlin, and the Jesuit theatre.
A. Zorzin, 'Einige Beobachtungen zu den zwischen 1518 und 1526
im deutschen Sprachbereich veröffentlichten Dialogflugschriften',
AR, 88:77–117.

PROSE AND VERSE

E. Hein, 'Die lateinischen Gesprächsbüchlein der Humanisten —
Eine Anregung für den modernen Lateinunterricht', *Der altsprachliche
Unterricht*, 39, 1996:83–100. U. Zitzlsperger, *GLL*, 50:403–16,
explores the reasons why the figure of the Fool in the 15th and 16th cs
was never female. E.-B. Körber, 'Der soziale Ort des Briefs im 16.
Jahrhundert', Wenzel, *Gespräche*, 244–58. A. Classen, '"Ach Gott,
wem soll ichs klagen." Women's erotic poetry in sixteenth-century
German songbooks', *NMi*, 98:293–313.

4. OTHER WORK

E. Rabbie, 'Editing Neo-Latin texts', *Editio*, 10, 1996:25–48. Recent
volumes in the series *Die deutschen Inschriften*, Wiesbaden, Reichert,
are: 39. Luise and Klaus Hallof, *Die Inschriften des Landkreises Jena*,
1995, lv + 326 pp. + 138 illus.; 41. Horst Hülse, *Die Inschriften der
Stadt Einbeck*, 1996, xxvii + 134 pp. + 47 illus. F.-H. Hye, *Fest. Schwob*,
229–37, examines bilingual inscriptions on Tyrolean monuments.
K. Zach, 'Bild — Gegenbild — Spiegelbild. Ethnotypische Chiffren
aus einer Region multikultureller Übergänge am Beispiel Siebenbür-
gens', *ib.*, 567–88.
　　Michaela Triebs, *Die medizinische Fakultät der Universität Helmstedt
(1576–1810). Eine Studie zu ihrer Geschichte unter besonderer Berücksichtigung
der Promotions- und Übungsdisputationen* (Repertorium zur Erforschung
der Frühen Neuzeit, 14), Wiesbaden, Harrassowitz, 1995, 354 pp.
W. Ludwig, '*Galli.* Syphilis unter deutschen Studenten des 16.
Jahrhunderts', pp. 345–64 of *Satura Lanx. Festschrift für Werner A. Krenkel
zum 70. Geburtstag*, ed. Claudia Klodt, Hildesheim, Olms, 1996,
xiv + 414 pp. A. Künzelbach, '"Wahnsinnige Weyber betriegen den

unverstendigen Poeffel": Anerkennung und Diffamierung heilkundiger Frauen und Männer, 1450 bis 1700', *Medizinhistorisches Journal*, 32 : 29–56, is a study based largely on Augsburg sources.

N. Jopek, Currie, *Object*, 139–52, discusses the fate of the Fugger Chapel in Augsburg and Albrecht von Brandenburg's *Neues Stift* in Halle; A. Schmitt, *ib.*, 153–76, analyses the post-Reformation iconography of painting and sculpture in the decorative scheme of the Lüneburg Town Hall. D. Wuttke, pp. 75–91 of Dieter Wuttke, *Dazwischen. Kulturwissenschaft auf Warburgs Spuren* (Saecula Spiritalia, 29–30), 2 vols, Baden-Baden, Koerner, 1996, xxiv + 454, vi + 455–883 pp., investigates the iconography of the Vischer family grave in Nuremberg. D.-R. Moser, *Fest. Schwob*, 299–322, interprets H. Bosch's Madrid table-top as a completely orthodox theological depiction of the Seven Deadly Sins.

5. INDIVIDUAL AUTHORS AND TEXTS

ABEL, MICHAEL. F. Rädle, Ekrem, *Reformation*, 151–78, demonstrates that A.'s verse presents a meditative allegoresis of the phenomena of the world, reflecting traditional Christian exegetical and poetic practice.

AGRIPPA VON NETTESHEIM, HEINRICH CORNELIUS. Marc van der Poel, *Cornelius Agrippa, the Humanist Theologian and his Declamations* (BSIH, 77), xiv + 303 pp., combats the potent image of A. as a charlatan whose *declamationes* were wilfully paradoxical and confrontational rhetorical set pieces. It argues that the works were in fact serious attempts to convince the reader about controversial moral and theological issues. After an examination of A.'s reasons for rejecting scholastic theology, and proposing in its place a modified scholastic reasoning, there follow examinations of several of A.'s writings, including detailed analyses of the three declamations *De nobilitate ... foeminei sexus*, *De originali peccato*, and *De sacramento matrimonii*. Id., 'Agrippa de Nettesheim (Henri Corneille)', *Chomarat Vol.*, 25–29. B. Newman, pp. 224–43 of Barbara Newman, *From Virile Woman to WomanChrist. Studies in Medieval Religion and Literature*, Philadelphia, Univ. of Pennsylvania Press, 1995, vi + 355 pp., argues that A. uses *De nobilitate ...* to 'explore some novel implications of both esoteric and evangelical theology' (p. 242).

ALBERUS, ERASMUS. Erasmus Alberus, *Die Fabeln. Die erweiterte Ausgabe von 1550 mit Kommentar sowie die Erstfassung von 1534*, ed. Wolfgang Harms, Herfried Vögel, and Ludger Lieb (FN, 33), vi + 412 pp., is a fine edition both of A.'s large collection of 49 fables published in 1550, and of the much smaller one (containing only 17) of 1534, which was the first fable collection by a Lutheran author.

Particularly helpful is the apparatus and the very extensive commentary, offering details on A.'s sources, on the illustrations, and on
relevant secondary literature on individual fables, as well as a
Stellenkommentar. Both the commentary and the introduction clearly
bring out the degree of freedom which A. enjoyed *vis-à-vis* many
narrative and moral conventions of the fable in earlier collections.
The editors also draw attention to the numerous questions of
interpretation, such as appropriate modes of reading the collection,
which await investigation.

BEBEL, HEINRICH. Carl Joachim Classen, *Zu Heinrich Bebels Leben
und Schriften* (NAWG, no. 1), 86 pp., represents an extremely scholarly
attempt to establish a reliable biography of B., and to clarify some
problems of dating of his works. Its third and largest section lists B.'s
writings, characterizing the positions he adopts in them. They are
shown to give important insights into the methods of Latin teaching
in his time. C. relates several of them to B.'s work at Tübingen, where
he taught many distinguished students; from the authors and methods
which B. approves or condemns there emerges a clear image of the
gradual replacement of medieval language manuals by new material
from Italy. B. saw the teaching of correct Latinity as a task of national
importance, necessary to keep Germany in the forefront of learning.
C. concludes that B.'s pedagogical works were ultimately less
influential than the *Facetiae* and the historical writings; he sees B.'s
lasting significance in a concern for linguistic exactness and critical
thinking. Id., 'Bebel (Heinrich)', *Chomarat Vol.*, 91–96.

BOTE, HERMANN. U. Seelbach, *Eulenspiegel-Jb.*, 36, 1996:13–47,
suggests four main desiderata for future research on *Till Eulenspiegel*;
H. Kokott, *ib.*, 85–109, reads the ninth *historie* of *T. E.* as an initiation
of T. as a *Schalk*; P. Derks, *ib.*, 131–35, considers the etymology of B.'s
name. H. Wuth, 'Till, Niemand und der Hof: Zur paradoxen
Auflösung von Repräsentation in der frühen Neuzeit', *ZDP*,
116:101–07.

BRANT, SEBASTIAN. H. Vredeveld, *Daphnis*, 26:553–651, presents
a substantial supplement to Zarncke's commentary on the *Narrenschiff*.
L. Lieb, Harms, *Wahrnehmen*, 239–53, reads B.'s 'Additiones' to his
edition of Aesop as an initiation of the (humanist) reader into a
critical perception and assessment of the often confusing phenomena
of the world. H.-G. Roloff, *EG*, 52:277–91, characterizes B.'s play
Tugent Spyl as a subtle and ambitious piece of dramatized social
criticism. D. Wuttke, *Ijsewijn Vol.*, 131–37, considers B.'s interpretation, as a political augury, of the hoof of an aged deer caught in
Nördlingen. W. Ludwig, 'Matern Hatten, Adam Werner, Sebastian
Brant und das Problem der religiösen Toleranz', *Zeitschrift für die
Geschichte des Oberrheins*, 144, 1996:271–99; Id., 'Eine unbekannte

Variante der *Varia carmina* Sebastian Brants und die Prophezeiungen des Ps.-Methodius. Ein Beitrag zur Türkenkriegspropaganda um 1500', *Daphnis*, 26 : 263–99.

CASTELLIO, SEBASTIAN. Hans R. Guggisberg, *Sebastian Castellio 1515–1563. Humanist und Verteidiger der religiösen Toleranz im konfessionellen Zeitalter*, Göttingen, Vandenhoeck & Ruprecht, ix + 353 pp. The late G.'s life's work on C. has issued in this fine volume, which deals very fully with this still comparatively neglected figure. G. brings out well the interrelatedness of the main aspects of C.'s work: his consistent attempts to combine philological and religious teaching, as exemplified in the immensely popular *Dialogi sacri* and the Latin and French Bible translations; his early championing of religious tolerance, particularly towards 'heretics'; and his belief in the freedom of the will, which caused him to dissent from Calvin's predestinationism. On the latter two counts it becomes clear why C. was regarded as such an outsider, vilified by magisterial Protestants, unmolested only in the liberal ambience of Basel. The two concluding chapters sum up C.'s theological thought, and chronicle the subsequent influence of his work, from the 'C. Renaissance' of the early 17th c. through Enlightenment neglect to modern rediscovery. M. Bracali, 'Il filologo ispirato. Sebastiano Castellione e l'edizione dei *Sibyllina Oracula* (Basilea 1555)', *Rinascimento*, 36, 1996 : 319–49.

CELTIS, CONRAD. D. Wuttke, 'Celtis Protucius (Conradus)', *Chomarat Vol.*, 261–67.

CNAUSTINUS, HEINRICH. R. Johne, 'Die Dido-Gestalt von Vergil bis Cnaustinus', pp. 83–93 of *Vergil: Antike Weltliteratur in ihrer Entstehung und Nachwirkung*, ed. Johannes Irmscher, Amsterdam, Hakkert, 1995, 224 pp.

CONCATENATIUS, JACOBUS. B. R. Jenny, 'J. C., der Herausgeber des Basler Bartolus von 1562. Ein historischer Steckbrief', *Basler Zeitschrift für Geschichte und Altertumskunde*, 96, 1996 : 91–93.

COPERNICUS, NICOLAUS. M. P. Lerner, 'Copernic (Nicolas)', *Chomarat Vol.*, 285–93; H. Kettenberg, 'De *Commentariolus* van Copernicus. De herontdekking van een manuscript', *Spiegel Historiael*, 32 : 270–74. F. Krafft, *Sudhoffs Archiv*, 81 : 138–57, argues for an earlier dating of the *De revolutionibus* on the basis of several previously unremarked quotations from Horace.

CORDUS, EURICIUS. Armgard Müller, *Das 'Bucolicon' des Euricius Cordus und die Tradition der Gattung. Text, Übersetzung, Interpretationen* (Bochumer Altertumswissenschaftliches Colloquium, 27), Trier, WVT, 363 pp. After material on C.'s life and works, and on his place in the bucolic tradition, there follows the text of the *Bucolicon* with a facing German prose translation, and substantial interpretative commentaries, though only on the first three eclogues. These discuss the Classical parallels and examine the ways in which C. has allegorized persons and events of his own time. The work is very much that of a Classicist: accurate on the language of the *Bucolicon* and its relationship to the Classical tradition, but sometimes less nuanced about the Renaissance and Reformation background. The treatment of 'humanism'—as a unified phenomenon in clear contra-distinction to medieval and Reformation thought—seems to reflect older views less typical of recent Renaissance scholarship. The bibliography is light on recent literature on humanism and the German Renaissance. P. G. Schmidt, 'Cordus' Gedichte auf die Bettelmönche', pp. 427–35 of *Hundert Jahre Historische Kommission für Hessen 1897–1997. Festgabe*, ed. Walter Heinemeyer (Ver-öffentlichungen der Historischen Kommission für Hessen, 61), Marburg, Elwert, xxviii + 1290 pp.

DIOGENES. Niklaus Largier, *Diogenes der Kyniker. Exempel, Erzählung, Geschichte in Mittelalter und Früher Neuzeit* (FN, 36), xi + 423 pp. The bulk is taken up with a (sparely annotated) edition of the anonymous *History von aller Leer unnd Läben Diogenis* ... (Zurich, 1550), and with a selection of 74 texts documenting the medieval and early modern reception of D. In a substantial first section, L. traces the development of the image of D., from the predominantly hostile patristic view to the increasingly positive medieval and early modern evaluations. He considers the interplay of exemplary and allegorical treatments of the anecdotes of D.'s life with the ever more 'novellistic' approach found in late-medieval and Renaissance texts.

EPISTOLAE OBSCURORUM VIRORUM. K.-H. Gerschmann, 'Wenn Dunkelmänner Briefe schreiben ...', *Neophilologus*, 81 : 89–103.

FEICHTER, VEIT. A. Hofmeister, *Fest. Schwob*, 141–58, examines what can be learnt from MS corrections and revisions in F.'s *Dommesnerbuch*; in Schwob, *Edition*, 63–72, H. discusses F.'s use of sources in this text and in his *Dommesnerurbar*.

FISCHART, JOHANN. C. Hoffmann, 'Bücher und Autographen von Johann Fischart', *Daphnis*, 25, 1996 : 489–579.

FLACIUS ILLYRICUS, MATTHIAS. J. Knape, *Chloe*, 26 : 197–210, discusses F.'s reception of Petrarch.

FUCHS, LEONHART. S. Kusukawa, *JHI*, 58 : 403–27, argues that both text and illustrations of *De historia stirpium* (1542) are central to F.'s project of reviving Galenic medicine.

GEILER VON KAYSERSBERG, JOHANNES. Susanne Eisenmann, **Sed corde dicemus. Das volkstümliche Element in den deutschen Predigten des Geiler von Kaysersberg* (EH, I, 1565), 1996, 211 pp.

GESNER, CONRAD. C. M. Pyle, *Viator*, 27, 1996 : 265–321, exam-ines Teodoro Ghisi's 'critical illustration' (*c.* 1590) of a mid-15th-c. Vatican MS, copying images from G.'s *Historia animalium*.

M. Cochetti, 'Gesner (Conrad), *Chomarat Vol.*, 391–97. C. Fiacchi, 'Il *De dialectis* di Angelo Rocca e il *Mithridates* di C. G.', *Atti* (Ferrara), II, 333–41.

HAGER, GEORG. M. Kern, Schwob, *Edition*, 73–84, examines the relation of three of H.'s *Meisterlieder* to their Classical sources.

HEYDEN, SEBALD. Sebald Heyden, *Nomenclatura rerum domesticarum*, ed. Peter O. Müller and Gaston van der Elst, Hildesheim, Olms, xlviii + 144 pp., reprints the 1534 edition of this important educational text. G. A. R. De Smet, *Fest. Möhn*, 127–42, examines a 1540 Dutch edition of H.'s *Formulae Puerilium Colloquiorum*.

HUTTEN, ULRICH VON. Ulrich von Hutten, *Die Schule des Tyrannen. Lateinische Schriften*, ed., trans., and comm. Martin Treu, WBG, 1996, 368 pp., provides a fluent German rendering of those Latin prose writings of H. which he himself did not translate into German: the polemical dialogues *Phalarismus, Febris, Fortuna, Bulla, Monitor, Praedones*, and *Arminius*, as well as his (immensely popular) treatise on guaiac wood as a cure for syphilis (1519). The detailed notes are extremely helpful, as is T.'s judicious afterword on H.'s career and significance. Ulrich von Hutten, *Gespräch büchlin, Bialogard, Danowski, 182 pp., is a facsimile reprint of the edition of 1521.

KEPLER, JOHANNES. A. Segonds, 'Kepler (Iohannes)', *Chomarat Vol.*, 457–72. E. Knobloch, '"Die gesamte Philosophie ist eine Neuerung in alter Unkenntnis." Johannes Keplers Neuorientierung der Astronomie um 1600', *Berichte zur Wissenschaftsgeschichte*, 20:135–46. C. Methuen, *Isis*, 87, 1996:230–47, examines the Copernicanism of K.'s mentor, the Tübingen professor Michael Maestlin (1550–1631).

LALEBUCH. A. Bässler, 'Die Funktion des Rätsels im *Lalebuch* (1597)', *Daphnis*, 26:53–84.

LIPSIUS, JUSTUS. *Juste Lipse (1547–1606) en son temps. Actes du colloque de Strasbourg, 1994*, ed. Christian Mouchel, Paris, Champion, 1996, 542 pp., contains 23 contributions by various hands on five aspects of L.'s activity: philosophy, philology and rhetoric, art and archaeology, literary and intellectual relations, and politics. Of particular relevance to German studies are those of A. Michel, on the influence of Cicero (21–30); P. Maréchaux, on L.'s 'allegorical paganism' (71–89); P.-F. Moreau, on L. and Erasmus (91–100); D. Sacré, on L.'s research into the pronunciation of Latin (117–31); J. Papy, on L.'s verse, with textual and bibliographical appendixes (163–214); M. Morford, on L.'s influence on visual art (235–73); R. Hoven, on critical reactions to the *De constantia* (413–22); and A. Moss, on the relation of the *Politica* to the commonplace-book tradition (471–78). The volume as a whole succeeds well in its aim of conveying the resonance of L.'s thought and writing in a wide range of late-Renaissance intellectual activity. *Lipsius en Leuven*, ed. Gilbert Tournoy, Jan Papy, and Jeanine De Landtsheer (Supplementa Humanistica Lovaniensia, 13), Leuven U.P., xiv + 387 pp., the catalogue of an exhibition in Leuven, magnificently transcends its genre. It begins with a detailed chronology of L.'s life, and essays by J. Ijsewijn on L. as a scholar of predominantly philological interests, and J. Roegiers on the stages of his university career in Germany and the Netherlands. The comments on the 125 exhibits themselves are effectively detailed essays, by 18 expert authors, on L. as philologist, historian, educator, and philosopher, and on the tradition of visual depiction of L. With its many well-chosen illustrations this amounts to an immensely informative volume. Justus Lipsius, *Principles of Letter-Writing: A Bilingual Text of 'Justi Lipsii Epistolica Institutio'*, ed. and trans. R. V. Young and M. Thomas Hester, Carbondale, Southern Illinois U.P., lvii + 76 pp., is a useful edition, with an extensive introduction, a good commentary, and a facing English version. M. Magnien and C. Mouchel, 'Lipse (Juste)', *Chomarat Vol.*, 505–13. M. Oosterbosch and G. Tournoy, 'Two unknown autograph letters by J. L. (1547–1606)', *Lias*, 23, 1996:321–26. M. Vielberg, 'Folgenreiche Fehlrezeption. J. L. und die Anfänge des Tacitismus in Jena', *Gymnasium*, 104:55–72. J. Waszink, 'Instances of Classical citations in the *Politica* of J.L.: their use and purposes', *HL*, 46:240–57.

LUTHER, MARTIN. Susanne Dähn, *Rede als Text. Rhetorik und Stilistik in Luthers Sakramentssermonen von 1519* (BBLI, 18), Frankfurt, Lang, 155 pp., submits three of L.'s 'Sermone' to literary examination. After sketching the theological background, D. performs a generic, then a stylistic-rhetorical analysis of the texts. Many conclusions are a little pedestrian, but D. makes useful points on the genre of the 'Sermon' and its use by L., and suggests some fruitful lines of research. *Luther mit dem Schwan. Tod und Verklärung eines großen Mannes*, Berlin, Schelzky & Jeep, 1996, 180 pp., the catalogue of a Wittenberg exhibition on the visual image of the Reformer in the 17th and 18th cs, brilliantly demonstrates not only the vast extent of this material, but also the degree to which it is still unknown, unclassified, unstudied, kept as much of it is in churches and other locations outside the normal run of museums and galleries. A dozen extremely informative essays by various hands, including J. Strehle and V. Joestel, deal with the figure of the swan, which dominates the L. iconography of the period in question; many of the numerous illustrations, particularly those of early L. 'monuments', are of the greatest interest. A. Dörfler-Dierken, *Lutherjb.*, 64:19–46, argues that the vow to St Anne in 1505 may have been a piece of late autobiographical reconstruction on L.'s part. M. Lieber, *Atti* (Ferrara), II, 45–56, compares L.'s lexical experimentation with the techniques of G. Trissino; G. Hassler, *ib.*, II, 273–81, compares L.'s method of translation with the process which Italian humanists knew as *volgarizzamento*. D. Bielfeldt, *SCJ*, 28:401–20, offers a critique of recent attempts to see *theosis* as the core of L.'s theology. V. J. Camden, *RQ*, 50:819–49, examines Bunyan's reception of L.'s commentary on Galatians. J. A. Schroeder, 'The Rape of Dinah: Luther's Interpretation of a biblical narrative', *SCJ*, 28:775–91. H. Düfel, *Lutherjb.*, 64:47–86, chronicles the activity of the *Luther-Gesellschaft* between 1925 and 1935. W. Ribhegge, 'Löwen und Wittenberg. Erasmus von Rotterdam, Martin Luther und zwei Gedenkjahre', *Stimmen der Zeit*, 214, 1996:457–66.

MANUEL, HANS RUDOLF. B. Steinbauer, *Fest. Schwob*, 489–502, situates M.'s *Weinspiel* (1548) in the theatrical and political context of the Swiss Confederation.

MELANCHTHON, PHILIPP. Philipp Melanchthon, *Enarratio secundae tertiaeque partis Symboli Nicaeni (1550)*, ed. and comm. Hans-Peter Hasse (Quellen und Forschungen zur Reformationsgeschichte, 64), Gütersloh, Gütersloher Verlagshaus, 1996, 220 pp. Heinz Scheible, *Melanchthon. Eine Biographie*, Munich, Beck, 294 pp., is written in a most accessible style by the editor of the monumental *Melanchthons Briefwechsel* (Stuttgart, Frommann-Holzboog); everywhere it shows the intimate knowledge of M.'s career and concerns which his vast correspondence has revealed. As S. points out, access to this rich source-material puts us in a better position to understand the man than many of his own contemporaries enjoyed. Again and again S. brings out the fullness and subtlety of M.'s thought and corrects the one-sided views of him (for example as a simple compromiser) still all too frequently found in scholarly literature. The nature of M.'s complex and often fraught relationship with Luther is particularly well expounded. In general, the biography communicates a vivid sense of how delicate and thankless a task was the practical defence of the Lutheran Reformation in the highly unstable Germany of the first half of the 16th c. Id., *Melanchthon und die Reformation. Forschungsbeiträge*, ed. Gerhard May and Rolf Decot (Veröffentlichungen des Instituts für Europäische Geschichte Mainz, Abteilung abendländische Religionsgeschichte, Beiheft 41), Mainz, von Zabern, 1996, viii + 578 pp., reprints 24 substantial articles of S.'s from the last three decades. *Philipp Melanchthon und Leipzig*, ed. Günther Wartenberg, Christian Winter, and Rainer Behrends, Leipzig, Universität Leipzig, 179 pp., is the catalogue of a fine exhibition which seeks to draw attention to the importance of M.'s relations with Leipzig, notably with Mosellanus, J. Pfeffinger, Camerarius, and Caspar Borner. Twelve essays by various hands deal with the history of Leipzig, with M.'s intellectual contacts there, and with the depiction of M. in monuments, pictures, medals, and book-bindings. These sections on the visual arts are particularly interesting; many of the illustrations are refreshingly unfamiliar, being outside the canon of images which reflect the Wittenberg-centred view of the Reformation. Wilhelm Hammer, *Die Melanchthonforschung im Wandel der Jahrhunderte. Ein beschreibendes Verzeichnis.* IV. *Register*, ed. Manfred Blankenfeld and Michael Reichert (Quellen und Forschungen zur Reformationsgeschichte, 65), Gütersloh, Gütersloher Verlagshaus, 1996. Stefan Rhein, Wolf D. Müller-Jahnke, and Jürgen Blum, *Melanchthon auf Medaillen 1526–1997*, Ubstadt-Weiher, Vlg Regionalkultur, 200 pp. + 270 illus. K. Meerhoff, 'Melanchthon (Philippe)', *Chomarat Vol.*, 537–49. N. Thiel, 'De Philippo Melanchthone, praeceptore Germaniae, ante quingentos annos nato', *Vox Latina*, 33:201–07. M. Pade, Ekrem, *Reformation*, 193–206, investigates a Hamburg MS containing a commentary on Thucydides written either by M. or by V. Winsemius. T. J. Wengert, *AR*, 88:57–76, shows how the edition of M.'s works published by C. Peucer (Wittenberg, 1562–64) presented to posterity an image of M. as theologian, exegete and Church politician, entirely suppressing his literary and philosophical activity. S. Bräuer, *Lutherjb.*, 64:87–126, recounts the political machinations behind the Wittenberg M. jubilee in 1960. Also noted: **Melanchthon und das Lehrbuch des 16. Jahrhunderts. Begleitband zur Ausstellung im Kulturhistorischen Museum Rostock 25. April bis 13. Juli 1997*, ed. Jürgen Leonhardt (Rostocker Studien zur Kulturwissenschaft, 1), Rostock, Universität Rostock, Philosophische Fakultät, 127 pp.

MORGANT DER RIESE. H. Sievert, Wenzel, *Gespräche*, 261–79, demonstrates how dialogue effects, and motivates, radical changes of plot-direction in the story.

MÜNSTER, SEBASTIAN. Sebastian Münster, *Spiegel der wyßheit*, ed. Romy Günthart, 2 vols, Munich, Fink, 1996, 149, 177 pp., is a fine edition of M.'s important but now rather neglected translation of the *Speculum sapientiae*, a very widely read 14th-c. fable-collection structured on the scheme of the four cardinal virtues. The excellent commentary volume contains copious information on the biblical and Classical background of the *Speculum*, the philosophical and theological import of its fables, an Upper German glossary and an index of characters, names, and subjects. F. Lestringant, 'Münster (Sébastien)', *Chomarat Vol.*, 571–74.

MURNER, THOMAS. M. Samuel-Scheyder, *RG*, 26, 1996:137–51, examines M.'s attack on Wimpfeling's assertion, in his *Germania* (1501), of an exclusively Germanic Alsatian identity.

NIEGE, GEORG. *Leben im 16. Jahrhundert. Lebenslauf und Lieder des Hauptmanns Georg Niege*, ed. Brage bei der Wieden, Berlin, Akademie, 1996, 224 pp., is a very welcome publication on this interesting figure, who left university to become a mercenary, but ended his life as a city official and vernacular poet. The volume offers a commented edition both of N.'s verse autobiography and of a selection of his secular and religious poems. The editorial decision constantly to interrupt the text of N.'s autobiography to intersperse the (copious) commentary was ill-advised; the text is thereby split up into 39 small sections. But this is a minor flaw in a work which draws a barely-known literary figure of the later 16th c. to scholarly attention.

PARACELSUS. U. Benzenhofer and K. Finsterbusch, *Sudhoffs Archiv*, 81:129–38, argue that P.'s anti-Semitism was neither racially motivated nor extreme by the standards of his time.

PEUTINGER, CONRAD. G. Tournoy, 'Peutinger (Conrad)', *Chomarat Vol.*, 613–16.

PIRCKHEIMER, WILLIBALD. S. Gysens, *Augustiniana*, 46, 1996:311–38, compares P.'s Latin translation of St Maximus's *Liber asceticus* with those of other humanists.

PLATTER FAMILY. Emmanuel Le Roy Ladurie, *Le siècle des Platter 1499–1628*. 1. *Le mendiant et le professeur*, Paris, Fayard, 1996, 527 pp., uses the P. diaries and travel-journals, and copious archival material, to construct a rich narrative of the 16th c. as lived out by Thomas P. the Elder and his son Felix. Much of this first volume concerns F.'s childhood and earlier adulthood, including his medical training at Montpellier, his return journey to Basel in 1557, and the start of his career in the medical faculty there. The book is effectively a re-narration, accompanied by a magisterially amplifying authorial commentary, of the Ps' own writings.

RANTZAU, HEINRICH. P. Zeeberg, Ekrem, *Reformation*, 138–50, concludes that Danish humanists did not regard the Holsteiner R. as a particularly important link with their German colleagues; W. Ludwig, 'Théodore de Bèze und Heinrich Rantzau über ihre Bücherliebe', *Philologus*, 141:141–44.

REICHART, WOLFGANG. W. Ludwig, *Ijsewijn Vol.*, 193–214, prints and comments on an address delivered by R. in his M. A. examination at Tübingen in 1509; possibly a unique surviving example of the genre. Id., *Medizinhistorisches Journal*, 32:121–77, recounts R.'s disagreement with A. Blarer's diagnosis of a case of diabolical possession (1533); Id., *Daphnis*, 26:653–90, examines the cost of R.'s son's studies at several universities.

REUCHLIN, JOHANNES. Johannes Reuchlin, *L'arte cabbalistica (De arte cabalistica)*, trans. and ed. Giulio Busi and Saverio Campanini (Eurasiatica, 38), Florence, Opus Libri, 1995, lxx + 292 pp., prefaces an annotated Italian translation of this treatise with introductory matter on R.'s biography and works, and essays on the *De arte* and on R.'s cabbalistic library. A. Cizek, 'Reuchlin (Johannes)', *Chomarat*

Vol., 667–78; W. Ludwig, 'Nachlese zur Biographie und Genealogie von Johannes Reuchlin', *Südwestdeutsche Blätter für Familien- und Wappenkunde*, 21, 1996:437–60.

RHENANUS, BEATUS. J. Hirstein, 'Rhenanus (Beatus)', *Chomarat Vol.*, 679–85. H. Meyer, *Annuaire des amis de la Bibliothèque Humaniste de Sélestat*, 47:17–24, writes on R.'s death and his heirs; R. Walter, *ib.*, 25–30, examines the art of J. Sturm's biography of R.; Id., J. S. Hirstein and F. Schlienger, *ib.*, 31–43, edit several of R.'s unpublished letters.

RÜSSOW, BALTHASAR. Paul Johansen, *Balthasar Rüssow als Humanist und Geschichtsschreiber. Aus dem Nachlaß ergänzt und herausgegeben von Heinz von zur Mühlen*, Cologne, Böhlau, 1996, xii + 313 pp. This study of an almost forgotten Reval clergyman represents an important addition to our knowledge of the writers of the later 16th c. The first part examines R.'s main work, the *Chronica der Provintz Lyfflandt* (1578–84), concentrating largely on R.'s sources. The second reconstructs R.'s biography, clearing up much that was previously unresolved, and the third deals with the reception of R.'s work, with R.'s friends and literary contacts, and with questions of *Mentalitätsgeschichte*. There are excellent indexes, genealogical information, and facsimiles of title-pages.

SELNECKER, NIKOLAUS. H. J. De Vries, *Daphnis*, 26:33–51, points out facial similarities between S. and the pictures of David in several editions of S.'s commentary on the Psalter.

SINAPIUS, JOHANNES. John L. Flood and David J. Shaw, *Johannes Sinapius (1505–1560). Hellenist and Physician in Germany and Italy* (THR, 311), viii + 304 pp., is a splendidly comprehensive treatment of the life and works of S. (Johann Senff), a once well known and universally respected but now almost forgotten humanist. The study, a model of detail and clarity, traces S.'s career from studies in arts at various German universities via the medical faculties in Padua and Ferrara to posts as a physician in Limoges, Ferrara, and Würzburg. Treated in particular detail are S.'s subjection to the guaiac 'cure' for syphilis in 1527, and the ultimately unanswerable question of his religious sympathies (at various times he worked for, or had contact with, Catholics, Lutherans, and Calvinists). His extensive network of important humanist friends is very fully documented, and appendices print material relevant to S., notably the full texts of all 76 extant letters to, from, or about him, and two of his declamations on humanist studies.

SLEIDAN, JOHANN. Emil van der Vekene, *Johann Sleidan (Johann Philippson). Bibliographie seiner gedruckten Werke und der von ihm übersetzten Schriften von Philippe de Comines, Jean Froissart und Claude de Seyssel. Mit*

einem bibliographischen Anhang zur Sleidan-Forschung (Hiersemanns Biblio-
graphische Handbücher, 11), Stuttgart, Hiersemann, 1996,
xxx + 398 pp., records the nearly 350 editions, both Latin and
vernacular, of S.'s *Commentarii* and the *De quattuor summis imperiis*,
printed between the 16th and 18th cs, as well as his pamphlets and
Latin translations from earlier historians. There are numerous
illustrations of title-pages and the usual indexes. L. Druez, 'Etat
présent des études sleidaniennes', *BHR*, 58, 1996:685–700.

SPENGLER, LAZARUS. *Lazarus Spengler als Übersetzer. (Ps.-)Eusebius*
De morte Hieronymi *Nürnberg 1514*, ed. Erika Bauer (Germanische
Bibliothek, 3rd ser., 28), Heidelberg, Winter, 170 pp., edits S.'s
translation of this popular devotional work, produced in the early
13th c., probably in Carthusian circles. As well as S.'s translation,
with critical apparatus and identification of the many biblical
quotations (but no other notes or commentary), the edition contains
sections on S., on H. Ebner, to whom the translation is dedicated,
and H. Höltzel, its printer. A substantial treatment of S.'s approach
to translation analyses in particular his techniques of dealing with
biblical material, making comparisons with the translation by the
Carthusian Heinrich Haller (1464). The original printing of S.'s
translation (Nuremberg, 1514) is described and analysed in detail,
bibliographically and linguistically.

STURM, JOHANN. C. J. Classen, 'Die Bedeutung Ciceros für
Johannes Sturms pädagogische Theorie und Praxis', *Ciceroniana*, n. s.,
9, 1996:47–66.

WICKRAM, GEORG. O. Neudeck, Harms, *Wahrnehmen*, 255–75,
explores the motivation of the social ascent of Lewfried in *Der
Goldtfaden*, relating it to a narratorial stance which partly anticipates
that of the modern novel. I. von der Lühe, Haferland, *Erzählungen*,
411–23, examines the use of letters and *exempla* to communicate a
'personaler Innenraum' in *Von guten und bösen Nachbaurn*.

ZELL, KATHARINA. E. A. McKee, 'Katharina Schütz Zell: A
Protestant Reformer', pp. 73–90 of *Telling the Churches' Stories. Ecumen-
ical Perspectives on Writing Christian History*, ed. Timothy J. Wengert and
Charles W. Brockwell, Jr, Grand Rapids, MI–Cambridge, Eerdmans,
1995, 134 pp.

ZWINGLI, HULDRYCH. M. Peronnet, 'Zwingli (Uldrych)', *Chomarat
Vol.*, 811–15.

THE SEVENTEENTH CENTURY

By JILL BEPLER, *Herzog August Bibliothek, Wolfenbüttel*

1. GENERAL

Two survey volumes this year contain sections dealing with the 17th c., both providing very useful introductions. Watanabe, *History*, 92–146, encompasses the period between 1450 and 1720 as 'early modern' and looks at the three main genres of poetry, prose, and drama, sticking not just to the standard authors, and showing the close links between Latin and the vernacular throughout the period. W. examines the problems facing women who wrote in the period, but also highlights the niches available to them. In the section 'Das Barock' by S. Arndal, Sørensen, *Geschichte*, i, 114–52, the approach of the section is defined by that of the whole volume. A general survey of the most important social, political, and cultural categories of the period is followed by the three main genres and sketches of six authors. In contrast to Watanabe, *History*, not one single woman writer of the period merits even passing mention by A., let alone ranking as a main author. Adam, *Geselligkeit*, contains the proceedings of an interdisciplinary Wolfenbüttel Baroque conference dealing with society and sociability in the 17th c. and how 'Geselligkeit' was reflected in the fields of architecture, philosophy and ethics, music, law and politics, and theology and literatures. Individual contributions are noticed below. A. J. Harper, 'Urbs litteraria: on researching the literary life of the town in seventeenth-century Germany', pp. 101–14 of *Life's Golden Tree: Essays in German Literature from the Renaissance to Rilke*, ed. Thomas Kerth and George Schoolfield, xiv + 282 pp., gives a succinct account of the political and cultural forces which have shaped work on German town culture in the Baroque over the past 30 years, with the main impetus often coming from *Auslandsgermanisten. Die Fruchtbringende Gesellschaft unter Herzog August von Sachsen-Weißenfels. Die preußischen Mitglieder Martin Kempe (der Erkorne) und Gottfried Zamehl (der Ronde)*, ed. M. Bircher and A. Herz (Die Deutsche Akademie des 17. Jahrhunderts Fruchtbringende Gesellschaft, ser. II, C, 1), Tübingen, Niemeyer, 464 pp., includes biographical sketches and commentated bibliographies of works by Kempe and Zamehl as well as reprints of Kempe's *Neugrünender Palm-Zweig Der Teutschen Helden-Sprache und Poeterey* and his *Bedencken/ Uber die Schrifften derer bekantesten Poeten hochdeutscher Sprache*, both with exhaustive annotations. Zamehl was admired in his day as an author of *rondeau* poetry and probably admitted to the Fruchtbringende Gesellschaft on the basis of his work in that genre, two of which are reproduced in facsimile here. *Die Fruchtbringende Gesellschaft unter Herzog August von Sachsen-Weißenfels. Süddeutsche und österreichische Mitglieder,* ed. M. Bircher and A. Herz (Die Deutsche Akademie des 17. Jahrhunderts Fruchtbringende Gesellschaft, ser. II, C, 2), Tübingen, Niemeyer, 361 pp., deals with a total of five members of the from this final phase of the society's existence, none of whom are poets, showing the very eclectic nature of the membership of this later period which also spans the three main religious confessions. As authors these members wrote devotional, political, legal, historical, and eulogizing texts. The section dealing with the artist Joachim von Sandrart d. Ä. is followed by a reprint of Sigmund von Birken and Martin Limburger's *Ehren-Preiß Des Durchleuchtigst-Fruchtbringenden Teutschen Palmen-Hains* from Sandrart's *Iconologia Deorum.* Ralf Georg Bogner, *Die Bezähmung der Zunge. Literatur und Disziplinierung der Alltagskommunikation in der frühen Neuzeit* (FN, 31), 233 pp., begins by conducting an intertextual analysis of a chorus from Gryphius's *Leo Arminius.* In typical dialectical structure (*Satz, Gegensatz, Zusatz*) the chorus deals with different aspects of the tongue, as being essential to human expression, as life-threatening in its capacity for evil and finally as a positive force which must be subject to restraint. B. interprets this dramatic speech in terms of the vast, mostly forgotten, ethical literature from the early modern period in which the tongue is the central focus. In his next section B. looks at the role of *lingua* texts in the process of civilization, surveying ethical manuals of statecraft and prohibitions against blasphemy and perjury as they are imparted in legal ordinances and sermons. In the main section of book B. examines the literary strategies by which norms of speech (the tongue) are conveyed both explicitly and implicitly. One of the very positive aspects of B.'s study is that he bases his findings on an equal number of Catholic and Protestant sources, highlighting how accusations of sins of the tongue were used in confessional defamation.

2. POETRY

INDIVIDUAL AUTHORS

BALDE. K. Töchterle, 'Zur Hölle in Schwaz, gen Himmel in Hall: Jacob Balde und Tirol', Holzner, *Literatur,* 303–38, deals with two Latin odes by B., reproduced in the original and in translation at the end of the essay, both of which are poetical responses to and allegorizations of stations on a journey undertaken by B. to Tyrol in 1640, one being a visit to a mine and the other an imaginary flight up to the heavens from the very real landscape of the mountains of the region.

GRYPHIUS. J. A. Steiger, 'Die poetische Christologie des Andreas Gryphius als Zugang zur lutherisch-orthodoxen Theologie', *Daphnis*, 26:85–112, sees Lutheran Christology as a central focus of G.'s verse, stressing the poet's very close links with the theological works of Luther, Arndt, Moller, Herberger, and Gerhard, whose teachings G. expresses in a poetical language of prayer, transforming a *rhetorica sacra* into a *poetica sacra*.

GUARINONI. U. Maley, 'Hippolytus Guarinonius' "Venus Liedle"', Holzner, *Literatur*, 289–302, looks at the didactic intentions of one of the verses contained in H.'s *Die Grewel der Verwüstung menschlichen Geschlechts* and its connections with a song by Jacob Regnart (1576) employing similar themes and imagery.

HOFFMANNSWALDAU. T. Borgstedt, 'Naturrecht der Geselligkeit und protestantische Emanzipation der Ehe in Hoffmannswaldaus *Heldenbriefe*', Adam, *Geselligkeit*, 765–80, interprets H.'s *Heldenbriefe*, tales of marriage and bigamy whose moral stance has often been called into question, in the light of the Protestant secularization of the marriage sacrament. B. posits that H. advocates a progressive ideal of marriages of love rather that of convenience based on natural law. M.-T. Mourey, 'Der Briefwechsel des Dichters und Diplomaten Christian Hoffmann von Hoffmannswaldau', *Daphnis*, 26:113–47, gives a survey of H.'s scattered extant letters, with a short characterization of the correspondence and the partners involved.

SCHERFFER. *Wencel Scherffer von Scherffenstein Geist- und weltliche Gedichte. Erster Teil Brieg 1652*, ed. Ewa Pietrzak (Rara ex bibliothecis Silesiis, 6), Tübingen, Niemeyer, 48 + 766 + 14 + 118 pp., is a well-produced facsimile edition with an excellent afterword. The volume provides us with a collection of occasional poetry from the first half of Scherffer's career (1630–51), which includes sections from his German verse translation of Hermann Hugo's *Pia Desideria*, on the basis of which Harsdörffer recommended that Zesen admit the poet to the Deutschgesinnte Genossenschaft in 1644. The occasional poetry reflects both S.'s associations with the court in Brieg, as well as the network of his friends and patrons among the courtiers and the ruling élites of his local area. As an organist, S. numbered many musicians among his friends and the last of the 11 books into which the collection is divided is entitled 'Der Music Lob'.

SCHWARZ. D. Niefanger, '"Fretowischer Fröhligkeit"—Die *laus ruris*-Dichtung von Sibylle Schwarz', Adam, *Geselligkeit*, 411–25, shows that S. adapted her Classical models to her own specific geographical and biographical situation in Frätow, her father's country estate, where, given her youth and inexperience, her pastoral idyll is based on a cult of friendship rather than centering on themes of love.

SPEE. J. J. Berns, 'Ahà, ahà, ahà — Unsägliches und Unsagbares in einem Weihnachtsgedicht Friedrich Spees', *Fest. Tarot*, 73–90, gives a reading of S.'s Christmas poem in which the wind and the Holy Spirit merge with the breath of the animals to warm the Infant Jesus in the crib. B. reflects on the precarious theological stance behind this and demonstrates S.'s dependence on the text of the Pseudo-Matthew Gospel.

OTHER WORK

Kerstin Heldt, *Der vollkommene Regent: Studien zur panegyrischen Casuallyrik am Beispiel des Dresdner Hofes Augusts des Starken* (FN, 34), 434 pp., examines the function of occasional poetry in a political context by using the Dresden court at the end of the 17th c. as a case study. The sheer mass of such texts, especially in a court context, and their apparent lack of originality and poetic value, have meant that they have hitherto received only fleeting attention. H.'s study is carefully documented and has an excellent bibliography. It combines an investigation of the social history of the court and the role of panegyric literature with a book-historical approach to questions of production and distribution. The results are highly illuminating and show how the genre adapted to changing values and reflected the new patterns of virtue and morals associated with them. Miroslawa Czarnecka, *Die 'verse = schwangere' Elysie. Zum Anteil der Frauen an der literarischen Kultur Schlesiens im 17. Jahrhundert* (AUW, 1882), Wroclaw U.P., 210 pp., must be greeted as a first attempt to survey the cultural activities by women in Silesia in the 17th c. After a general introduction C. deals with devotional literature written by women, which she defines as prose, and rather surprisingly separates it from what in the next section she calls 'geistliche Dichtung'. This is followed by an analysis of 'profane Literatur' written by women, in which all other texts are dealt with. A brief passage on Silesian duchesses and their patronage of the arts concludes the volume, which is somewhat marred by glaringly incorrect bibliographical citation. *Dichtungen schlesischer Autorinnen des 17. Jahrhunderts. Eine Anthologie*, ed. M. Czarnecka (AUW, 1906), Wroclaw U.P., 192 pp., offers a welcome selection of poetry by five Silesian women authors mentioned in the previous study with short biographical studies of each.

H. Watanabe O'Kelly, '"Sei mir dreimal mehr mit Licht beklei-det." German poems by women to their mentors in the seventeenth century', *ColGer*, 28, 1995:255–64, examines poetry by women authors which underscores their indebtedness to the male teachers and patrons who promoted their literary skills and arranged for the publication or preservation of their works. M. Basler, 'Zur Sprache der Gewalt in der Lyrik des deutschen Barock', Meumann, *Angst*, 125–44, posits that the portrayal of violence in Baroque poetry is always restricted to the context of rhetorical argument and never a subject *per se*. G. Braungart, 'Ein Ferment der Geselligkeit: Zur Poetik des Apophthegmas', Adam, *Geselligkeit*, 463–72, examines the way in which the use of the apophthegm or maxim changes in the 17th c. For Harsdörffer in particular the apophthegm is not a text which is an end in itself as it had been understood in the Humanist tradition, but a text which generates further texts, a motor in a process of communication. M. Schilling, 'Gesellschaft und Geselligkeit im *Pegnesischen Schaefergedicht* und seiner *Fortsetzung*', *ib.*, 473–82, reflects on the sociable aspects of the collective authorship of the *Schaefergedicht*, seeing the text's main purpose as the demonstration of the integrating power of art, music, and literature, of the necessity of taming nature and bringing it into harmony with man, and of the preservation of both history and the present in memory. A. Harper, 'Gesellige Lieder, poetischer Status und Stereotypen im Barockzeitalter', *ib.*, 855–58, reminds us that the seemingly realistic elements of the popular *Lied* are just as stylized as elements of other genres. E. Mannack, 'Barock-Dichter in Danzig', *Fest. Tarot*, 291–305, points to the need for a reappraisal of German poetry in Danzig in the 17th c., especially in the light of the politically dubious selection contained in Kindermann's 1939 volume *Danziger Barockdichtung*. J. V. Curran, '"Ut pictura poesis" in pyramid poems', *Simpliciana*, 19:167–77, gives no justification for her selection of material and interprets two pyramid-shaped pattern poems by Johann Helwig and Johann Christoph Männling in the light of Walter Benjamin's definition of allegory.

3. PROSE

INDIVIDUAL AUTHORS

BEER. E. Peter, 'Verhaltensethik und Erzählgeselligkeit in Johann Beers *Teutschen Winter-Nächten*', Adam, *Geselligkeit*, 781–91, sees B.'s novels not as the emanations of a naive spontaneous author, but as highly artificial narrative constructions in which story-telling in a sociable context functions as a didactic means of practising the strategies by which consensus can be achieved in conversation on a series of social and philosophical questions.

FRANCISCI. R. Kramer, 'Gespräch und Spiel im *Lustgarten*. Literatur und Geselligkeit im Werk von Erasmus Francisci', Adam, *Geselligkeit*, 505–29, looks at the very specific way in which games and conversations structure F.'s compendium on the East and West India and China, showing how F. is indebted to Harsdörffer for his models, using his own vast work to instruct the reader on contemporary political, religious and aesthetic controversy.

GRIMMELSHAUSEN. A. Merzhäuser, 'Über die Schwelle geführt. Anmerkungen zur Gewaltdarstellung in Grimmelshausens *Simplicissimus*', Meumann, *Angst*, 65–82, interprets the opening scene of the novel and sees the innovative aspect of G.'s portrayal of the violence of war in his use of the incomplete perspective of the young *ignotus* Simplicius and his eyewitness account of atrocities he cannot interpret correctly. P. Michel and R. Zeller, '"... auß andern Büchern extrahirt." Grimmelshausens Schwankvorlagen im *Simplicissimus*', *Fest. Tarot*, 307–22, explores how G. uses *Schwank* episodes at key points in the novel and reverses their original content to denote moments of progress in the protagonist's psychological development and to evoke a sense of confusion on the part of the reader familiar with his sources. R. Wimmer, 'Der Lügner Simplicissimus. Anmerkungen zur Poetik Grimmelshausens', *Fest. Tarot*, 537–58, investigates the various aspects of 'untruth' in the novel, which is used both as a means of unmasking truth, of practising deceit, and of entertaining, and which in the play between truth and fiction also provides a comment on the highly artificial structure of the work. A. M. Cordie, 'Modi des Handelns und Erzählens in Grimmelshausens *Erstem Beernhäuter*', *Simpliciana*, 19:9–28, gives a close reading and examination of narrative structures of G.'s little-known short tale. D. Breuer, 'Grimmelshausens *Wunderliche Antiquitäten*. Zu seinen Argutienreihen von 1667', *ib.*, 40–53, examines the earliest known work by Grimmelshausen, his appendix to the German translation of Francis Godwin's *Man in the Moone* published in 1667, which consists of a comical listing of biblical and historical relics. B. places this in the tradition of *argutia*, seeing its closest model in the work of Fischart. I. M. Battafarano, 'Erzählte Dämonopathie in Grimmelshausens *Courasche*', *ib.*, 55–89, carefully inspects the way in which witchcraft is used as a theme in *Courasche*. In reviewing her life Courasche recalls how in her youth she had been in peril of acquiring knowledge which could have made her a witch, implying that this had never been the case. B. shows how the accusation of witchcraft levelled at the protagonist at several points in the novel is always unmasked as the tactic of a male aggressor directed at an innocent female party. He sees her autobiography not as the confession of a woman who has made a pact with the devil, but as a depiction of her morally questionable attempts to reconcile her own volition with adverse circumstance. T. Kemper, '"Lufftfahrt" und "Hexentantz" — Zauberei und Hexenprozeß in Grimmelshausens *Simplicissimus*', *ib.*, 107–23, calls for moderation in judging G.'s stance on witchcraft, seeing him neither as reactionary nor progressive, but as a normal representative of his time and class possessed of a deeply-rooted belief in the existence and power of witches, whose appearance in the narrative of his novel *Simplicissimus* is used to denote the moral abyss into which the hero is about to sink.

GRYPHIUS. N. Kaminski, '"Der Kirchhoff dein Parnaß" — Poetische Inszenierung des *Kirchhoffs* als Ort von Geselligkeit', *ib.*, 821–32, takes the metaphorical and the actual role of the graveyard in G.'s *Leichabdankungen* and examines how G. uses the metaphor to create a vision of transcendent sociability with the dead in the certainty of the resurrection by using the metaphors of the stage or a wedding.

HARSDOERFFER. B. Becker-Cantarino, 'Frauenzimmer Gesprächspiele. Geselligkeit, Frauen und Literatur im Barockzeitalter', Adam, *Geselligkeit*, 17–41, looks at the way in which, even in the seemingly egalitarian atmosphere of H.'s conversation games, women's roles are restricted by the models of virtue they are forced to embody. R. Zeller, 'Die Rolle der Frau im Gesprächspiel und in der Konversation', *ib.*, 531–41, examines the same texts, but investigates how H. uses the contributions of the women involved in the games to demarcate the line between scholarship and non-intellectual amusement, indicating the careful balance which characterized the light-hearted ideal of conversation propagated by the Italian authors of the Renaissance, who were H.'s models. J. J. Berns, 'Gedächtnislehre und Gedächtniskunst bei Georg Philipp Harsdörffer und Christian Knorr von Rosenroth', *Morgen-Glantz*, 7 : 203–39, looks at the influence of the vast *ars memorativa* literature of the early modern period on the thought of H. and Knorr, showing that K.'s elaborations on the subject are drawn mainly from a work by Lambert Schenckel. In contrast to H., Knorr was not an admirer of Raymund Lull, whose theories were central to H.'s work. B. identifies the art of memory as a key to understanding H.'s *œuvre* in all its genre and discipline-transcending manifestations.

LOHENSTEIN. Cornelia Plume, *Heroinen in der Geschlechterordnung. Weiblichkeitsprojektionen bei Daniel Casper von Lohenstein und die 'Querelle des Femmes'*, Stuttgart, Metzler, 1996, 339 pp., is a fascinating study of L.'s novels and tragedies and the author's dependence on Le Moyne's *Gallerie des femmes fortes* for the patterns of virtue projected in them. A useful appendix juxtaposes texts from the two authors to show this relationship. P. sees L.'s work as primarily addressed to women of the upper nobility, calling it a *Fürstinnenspiegel*. Her study gives an introduction to the debates of the *querelle* and a close reading of L.'s novel using two comparable novels of state by Buchholtz and Anton Ulrich to interpret the specific character of L.'s depiction of female figures. A brief comparison with L.'s tragedies, where P. sees not virtues projected but an array of potential responses to political practicalities enacted, shows that L. incorporates both the misogynist and the pro-female arguments of the *querelle* into his works, while his basic premise remains that both sexes command equal intellectual and ethical potential.

ZESEN. J. D. Krebs, 'Manieren und Liebe. Zur Dialektik von Affekt und Höflichkeit in Philipp von Zesens *Adriatische Rosemund*', Adam, *Geselligkeit*, 401–10, takes Z.'s bourgeois novel and shows how Hardörffer's *Gesprächspiele* provide the model for what K. terms 'Konversation als Ritual der maskierten Affektkommunikation', in which the actual conduct and the subject-matter of conversation and correspondence create a diffuse erotic mood. K. sees affect control in Z.'s bourgeios milieu not as sublimation but as emotional repression which leads to the deadly melancholy of the main protagonist. S. Krump, 'Von der heiligen Schönheit. Zesens *Assenat* und die Romandiskussion des 17. Jahrhunderts', *Daphnis*, 26:691–713, takes Z.'s characterization of his novel as 'heilig' in the preface seriously and investigates how the two concepts of 'wahr' and 'heilig' are paralleled and reflect Z.'s particular concept of the novel.

OTHER WORK

A. Martino, 'Die Rezeption des *Lazarillo des Tormes* im deutschen Sprachraum (1555/62–1750)', *Daphnis*, 26:301–99, gives a critical survey of the German and Latin translations of *Lazarillo*, ending with a short section on evidence of the actual readership of the novel during the period under discussion.

4. DRAMA

INDIVIDUAL AUTHORS

GRYPHIUS. A. Solbach, 'Politische Theologie und Rhetorik in Andreas Gryphius' Trauerspiel *Leo Arminius*', *Fest. Tarot*, 409–25, interprets G.'s drama, both in its action and in its imagery, as a political demonstration of the interdependence of law and gospel in the sense of Luther's theology of the cross. By contrast, G. Spellerberg, 'Narratio im Drama oder: Der politische Gehalt eines "Märtyrerstückes". Zur *Catharina von Georgien* des Andreas Gryphius', *ib.*, 437–61, stresses the interdependence of the political and religious content of G.'s tragedies, lamenting the tendency of critics to see G. and Lohenstein as polar opposites, the former being religiously motivated and the latter concerned only with the secular. S. advocates a reading of the martyr dramas as political drama in which the martyr's death is a symbol of the upholding of a higher political order and rejection of chaos and in which the tyrant is shown as subject to this transcendental order. In a detailed investigation of just one play, R. Tarot, 'Die Kunst des Alexandriners im barocken Trauerspiel Andreas Gryphius *Papinian*', *Simpliciana*, 19:125–54, looks at the many ways in which G. achieves variety while complying with the dictates of comprehensibility for the spoken alexandrine, employing among other stylistic devices verses in which the rhetorical accent overrides the sense accent ('gegenmetrische Rhythmusakzente').

SCHIRMER.   J. P. Aikin, 'The musical-dramatic works of David Schirmer', *Daphnis*, 26:401–35, adduces internal evidence for S.'s authorship of hitherto anonymous or, in her opinion, falsely attributed *Singspiele* performed in Halle in the 1660s and in Dresden in 1678.

OTHER WORK

A. Beise, 'Verbrecherische und heilige Gewalt im deutschsprachigen Trauerspiel des 17. Jahrhunderts', Meumann, *Angst*, 105–24, begins with an analysis of Heinrich Julius von Braunschweig-Lüneburg's bloodthirsty Nero drama *Von einem ungerathenen Sohn*, showing how drastic violence is used as a radical underscoring of the evil nature of the protagonist and is made fully acceptable to audiences by virtue of its very theatricality. The reception of neo-Stoic ideas meant that stage violence perpetrated against the virtuous innocent could become a focus of identification for the audience, a means of inculcating the precepts of constancy and virtue. This primarily Protestant view of violence passively suffered was expanded in the Jesuit theatre to encompass an active pursuit of martyrdom, the portrayal of acts of violence on the part of infidels in order to justify and glorify enforced conversion and re-Catholicization. B. sees the works of Lohenstein as a synthesis of these earlier models in which violence no longer represents the stability-threatening violation of a norm but has become the norm itself. M. Titzmann, '"Verstellung." Semiotische, anthropologische, ideologische Implikationen im Drama des deutschen Barock', Adam, *Geselligkeit*, 543–57, divides the Baroque era into two distinct eras characterized by differing evaluations of dissimulation. In the first it is an identifiable emanation and proof of evil, whereas in the second it is legitimized, making the sphere of politics, in which dissimulation is most often presented in drama, a moral exclave. C. Caemmerer, 'Original und Übersetzung vs. Quelle und Text. Zur Bedeutung der Quellen bei der Edition von Schäferspielen des 17. Jahrhunderts am Beispiel von Jan Harmens Kruls *Cloris en Philida* und Hermann-Heinrich Schers *Daphnis und Chrysilla*', Schwob, *Edition*, 149–67, presents an editorial project which by a close reading of the original Dutch play by a Catholic

semi-professional dramatist contextualizes the German version produced by the unknown Scher and brings to light both the particular
forces at work in the German adaptation and the varying concepts of
the function of bucolic literature it embodies. S. Colvin, 'A pattern
for social order: women, marriage and music in early German opera',
Adam, *Geselligkeit*, 679–94, equating the portrayal of male and female
attributes on the opera stage with the biological sexes, sees the *Singspiel*
as a reinforcement of patriarchal standards of virtuous womanly
behaviour, where the *femme forte* must remain the exception. M. Wade,
'Emblems and German Protestant court culture: Duchess Marie
Elisabeth's Ballet in Gottorf (1650)', *Emblematica* 9:45–109, starts by
examining two emblematic ballets performed at weddings in Holstein
in 1649 and 1650, both of which represent significant developments
in the German *Singspiel* and in applied emblematics. By placing these
texts and their illustrations in the context of Gottorf court culture
with its emphasis on economic and scientific innovation and on the
cultivation of a deeply orthodox Lutheran piety, W. convincingly
demonstrates the major role played by the Duchess Marie Elisabeth
in the planning and publication of these festivities assisted by the
court mathematician and travel-writer Adam Olearius. The study
gives an excellent insight into the cultural interaction pursuant to
dynastic marriages. E. Hastaba, 'Vom Lied zum Spiel. Das Anderl-
von Rinn-lied des Hippolyt Guarinoni als Vorlage für Anderl-von-
Rinn-Spiele', Holzner, *Literatur*, 273–87, traces the way in which the
presumed ritual murder and martyrdom of a child in Rinn in 1462
was put into song by G. in 1642 and performed by Jesuits all over
southern Germany. The story remained a subject of folk drama up to
1935.

THE CLASSICAL ERA

By JEFF MORRISON, *Lecturer in German, National University of Ireland, Maynooth*

I. GENERAL

GENERAL STUDIES AND ESSAY COLLECTIONS. *IASL*, *Sonderheft* 8, entitled *Literatur, Politik und soziale Prozesse*, contains three articles on the reading habits of the broader 18th-c. public which make interesting contributions to our understanding of 'Kulturvermittlung' and its social/political implications: W. Greiling, '"... dem gesellschaftlichen Leben der Menschen zur Aufnahme, Vortheil und Beförderung." "Intelligenzblätter" in Thüringen' (1–39); R. Siegert, 'Die Lesegewohnheiten des "gemeinen Mannes" um 1800 und die Anfänge von Volksbibliotheken' (40–61); U. Puschner, '"Mobil gemachte Feldbibliotheken." Deutsche Enzyklopädien und Konversationslexika im 18. und 19. Jahrhundert' (62–77). *Almanach- und Taschenbuchkultur des 18. und 19. Jahrhunderts*, ed. York-Gothart Mix (Wolfenbütteler Forschungen, 69), Wiesbaden, Harrassowitz, 1996, 210 pp., gathers together a number of contributions on these more marginal literary publications, locating them in terms of the history of ideas, political history or literary history. Among them are: Y.-G. Mix, 'Lektüre für Gebildete und Ungebildete. Einleitende Bemerkungen zu H. C. Boies *Musenalmanach*, J. P. Hebels *Rheinländischen Hausfreund* und anderen literarischen Begleitern durch das Jahr' (7–20); W. Haefs, 'Aufklärung und populäre Almanache in Oberdeutschland' (21–46); N. Oellers, 'Die Französische Revolution im Spiegel deutscher Musenalmanache' (47–62); W. Bunzel, 'Publizistische Poetik. Goethes Veröffentlichungen in Almanachen und Taschenbüchern' (63–76); Y.-G. Mix, 'Der Literaturfreund als Kalendarnarr. Die Almanachkultur und ihr Publikum' (77–88); M. Zenker, 'Deutschsprachige Almanache und Taschenbücher in der Schweiz des 18. und 19. Jahrhunderts' (113–42). *'Öffentlichkeit' im 18. Jahrhundert*, ed. Hans-Wolf Jäger, Göttingen, Wallstein, 360 pp., is largely the product of a 1992 conference on this theme. The contributions are concerned to define the notion of *Öffentlichkeit* and examine its significant 18th-c. manifestations. We see how it is shaped by, or shapes, politics, the academy, the press and, importantly, literature and the arts. A. Grieger, 'Kunst und Öffentlichkeit in der zweiten Hälfte de 18. Jahrhunderts' (117–35), provides a reminder that the aesthetic debates of the late 18th c. were not taking place in a vacuum. The text also includes: W. Albrecht, 'Literaturkritik und Öffentlichkeit im Kontext der Aufklärungsdebatte: Fünf Thesen' (277–94); E. Schön, 'Publikum und Roman im 18. Jahrhundert' (295–326);

Y.-G. Mix, 'Über die ästhetische Erziehung des Dilettanten: Die literarische Öffentlichkeit, die Klassizität der Poesie und das Schema über den Dilettantismus von Fr. Schiller, J. W. Goethe und L. H. Meyer' (327–43); K. Wölfel, 'Ist die Poesie eine öffentliche Angelegenheit? Sind öffentliche Angelegenheiten poetisch?' (345–60). Peter Philipp Riedl, *Öffentliche Rede in der Zeitenwende: Deutsche Literatur und Geschichte um 1800* (SDL, 142), 418 pp., deals with developments in the study of the subject 'Rhetoric'. It also discusses manifestations of the skill in contemporary politics, law, academia and the Church and changing definitions of and responses to its nature and function. Direct literary connections are made in a study of (legal) rhetoric in Wieland's *Geschichte der Abderiten* and Goethe's *Reineke Fuchs* (42–87). Academic rhetoric is examined in part on the basis of the Schiller/Fichte debate (241–294). *Norm und Transgression in deutscher Sprache und Literatur: Kolloquium in Santiago de Compostela, 4–7 Okt. 1995*, ed. Viktor Millet, Munich, Iudicium, 1996, xi + 266 pp., reports several notable transgressions from our period. H. Cortés, 'Wilhelm Heinse als Normverstoßer' (30–40), deals with the complex genesis of his thinking, which draws upon material from antiquity, the Renaissance, and various streams of contemporary thought to create an original mixture. The treatment of Dionysiac elements in H.'s work is perhaps the most powerful component of this inevitably short study. Also of relevance are: M. Pfeiffer, 'Der Mythos zwischen ästhetischer Idealisierung und historischer Realität: Zum Homerbild der deutschen Klassik' (41–55); L. Pikulik, 'Schiller und die Konvention' (56–74); U. Wergin, 'Vom Symbol zur Allegorie?: Der Weg von der Frühklassik zur Frühromantik, verfolgt im Ausgang von Goethes *Iphigenie* über *Das Märchen* bis hin zu Novalis' *Glauben und Liebe*' (75–125). *Deutsch-Russische Beziehungen im 18. Jahrhundert: Kultur, Wissenschaft und Diplomatie*, ed. Conrad Grau et al. (Wolfenbütteler Forschungen, 74), Wiesbaden, Harrassowitz, 412 pp., contains contributions from a 1993 conference. They are largely concerned with politics and diplomacy but some focus on the international transmission of Enlightenment ideas (pp. 189–286). Some few are directly concerned with literature of our period, including: G. Robel, 'German travel reports on Russia and their changing function in the eighteenth century' (267–89); S. Karp, 'Grimm à Pétersbourg' (291–303); I. N. Kouznetsow, 'Herder und Rußland. Zur Fragestellung' (323–28); A. Michailow, 'Nikolaij Michajlovic Karamsin und die deutschen Dichter der Aufklärungszeit oder: Karamsins sechs Nebensätze als eine sentimental-rhetorische Skizze zur Geschichte der deutschen Literatur des 18. Jahrhunderts' (329–49).

AUFKLÄRUNG.   S. Arndal, Sørensen, *Geschichte*, 1, 154–205, offers an introductory survey of the political, religious, philosophical and cultural determinants and parameters of this period, followed by brief characterizations of its literary products and treatments of some major literary figures. It constitutes a useful means of orientation within the period, allowing for declared limitations. A more interesting introduction to the same period is contained in R.-E. Boetscher Joeres, Watanabe, *History*, 147–201, which focuses upon questions of gender and class and their implications for an understanding of German Enlightenment; in attempting to do less it reveals more. Wolfgang Albrecht, *Das Angenehme und das Nützliche: Fallstudien zur literarischen Spätaufklärung in Deutschland* (WSA, 23), xii + 341 pp., is concerned to redress the balance in Enlightenment studies from the mid-18th c. towards the study of the period 1770–1820, a period which A. finds interesting because of its somewhat contradictory nature; it can reveal a greater diversity and refinement of thought and yet simultaneously there is a fading of Enlightenment principles. The collection is particularly strong in dealing with the new reforming, socially-critical impulse in literature and with the difficulties of literary periodization. The essays (some revised republications) focus upon individual authors after a thematic introduction: 'Die Literatur im Ensemble der deutschen Spätaufklärung. Eine einleitende Problemskizze' (1–28). Also included: 'Christoph Martin Wieland—Priester der Musen im Dienst milder Humanität und Aufklärung' (29–72); 'Gefühl, Einbildungskraft, Gemeinsinn. Aspekte weiblicher Literatur und Aufklärung aus der Sicht Sophie von La Roches' (73–111); 'Zwischen patriotischer Spätaufklärung und religiöser Gegenaufklärung. Lorenz Westenrieder, der "Praeceptor Bavariae"' (113–45); 'Gemeinsinnige streitbare Publizistik im Glauben an Wirkungmacht der "Publizität." Wilhelm Ludwig Wekhrlin' (147–84); 'Von reformerischen zum revolutionär-demokratischen und liberalen Aufklärertum. Entwicklungen politisierter literarischer Spätaufklärung am Beispiel Georg Friedrich Rebmanns' (185–232); 'Berliner Spätaufklärung offensiv. Friedrich Nicolais Kontroverse mit den Klassikern und Frühromantikern' (233–297); '"Zwischen gebildeten und ungebildeten Lesern keinen Unterschied erkennend." Johann Peter Hebel's literarische Volksaufklärung in Kontext seines beruflichen Wirkens' (299–336). *Um Menschenwohl und Staatsentwicklung. Textdokumentation zur deutschen Aufklärungsdebatte zwischen 1770 und 1850, mit drei zeitgenössischen Kupfern*, ed. Wolfgang Albrecht (SAG, 302), 522 pp., is concerned with broadly the same period. The assumption which informs the text is that the Enlightenment was after 1770, and so 100 years as a measurable movement, increasingly self-conscious, divided and subject to counter-currents. There was correspondingly a high level of debate about the surviving nature of Enlightenment. By 1850 the Enlightenment was beginning to be seen as an historical phenomenon. This collection of primary material drawn from a massive range of treatises and journals is an extremely useful resource. It enables the reader to examine individual statements and developments in the thinking of central Enlightenment figures and, perhaps more importantly, to trace more popular renditions of Enlightenment debates. The main thematic interests are broadly political (including sexual politics, education, religion) and not literary, but the documents nevertheless provide potentially important supporting evidence for cultural/literary studies. Wolfgang Promies, *Reisen in Zellen und durch den Kopf. Ansichten von der Aufklärung* (Promenade, 7), Tübingen, Klöpfer & Meyer, 261 pp., is a good read. It brings together previously published essays (some in fuller form) to offer an interesting perspective upon the Enlightenment. The individual essays can be idiosyncratic but they are fascinating and even amusing. They also subvert our expectations inasmuch as they lack any conventional academic apparatus. The essays each in very different ways (since they include such disparate matters as psychiatric illness, corset wearing, and the French Revolution) test the assumption that the Enlightenment was characterized by an aspiration to 'Ebenmaß' in art and life, and indeed they provide evidence that at points the opposite was true. The contents include: 'Das Verlangen nach dem Ebenmaß, in der Kunst wie im Leben. An Stelle eines Vorworts' (6–46); 'Christian Heinrich Spieß, oder: Wahnsinn in guter Gesellschaft' (47–83); 'Über Schnürbrüste, Forster und Lichtenberg. Ein Paradigma für Aufklärung' (84–111); 'Von dem Vermögen deutscher Schriftsteller, Unruhe zu stiften. Eine Bagatelle zur Französischen Revolution' (112–39); 'Weltbürger oder vaterlandsloser Geselle. Georg Forsters eingedenk' (140–57); 'Wo ist Anschel? Rekonstruktion eines jüdischen Lebenslaufes am Ende der Aufklärung' (158–88); 'Welsche Wollust und teutsche Tugend. Ein Unterhaltungsstoff für mehrere Jahrzehnte' (189–213); 'Reisen in Zellen und durch den Kopf. Auch ein Beitrag zur Aufklärung' (214–39); '"Dieses Monster ist auch ein Mensch." Jean Jacques unter den Deutschen' (240–54). This is an interestingly subversive collection of criticism which helps to undermine conventional notions of the Enlightenment. The darker side of Enlightenment is dealt with in a number of contributions, including: G. Sauder, '"Dunkle" Aufklärung', *Das achtzehnte Jahrhundert*, 21:61–68, which is concerned with 18th-c. aesthetics (Sulzer, Meier, Wolff, Herder) and matters such as sexuality, disease, death, and superstition. It is particularly interesting in its treatment of the core notion of 'Prägnanz'. R. Schlögl, 'Die Moderne auf der Nachtseite der Aufklärung: Zum Verhältnis von Freimaurerei und Naturphilosophie', *ib.*, 33–60; U. Wunderlich, '"Aber, ihr Herren, der Tod ist so aesthetisch doch nicht": Über literarische Totentänze der Aufklärung', *ib.*, 69–84, deals with representations of death in literary texts and illustrations. Other problematic issues are presented by: J. Graf, 'Judentaufen in der Literatur der Spätaufklärung', *IASL*, 22:19–42; M. Schumann, *'Arminius redivivus:* Zur literarischen Aneignung des Hermannstoffs im 18. Jahrhundert', *MDU*, 89:130–47, which is concerned with the problematic place of patriotism in Enlightenment literature and the development of a brand of enlightened patriotism. *Die Philosophie und die Belles-Lettres*, ed. Martin Fontius and Werner Schneiders (Aufklärung und Europa: Beiträge zum 18. Jahrhundert), Berlin, Akademie, 183 pp., contains a range of essays on French and German themes. Interesting from the German perspective are: M. Fontius, 'Ein begriffsgeschichtlicher Rückblick' (171–73); W. Schneiders, 'Ob Philosophie schöne Literatur sein kann' (175–77); W. Schneiders, 'Nicht plump, nicht säuisch, nicht sauertöpfisch. Zu Thomasius' Idee einer Philosophie für alle' (11–20); F. Grunert, 'Von polylogischer zu monologischer Aufklärung. Die Monatsgespräche von Christian Thomasius' (21–38); C. Buschmann, 'Methode und Darstellungsform bei Christian Wolff' (41–52); U. Goldenbaum, 'Mendelssohns philosophischer Einstieg in die schönen Wissenschaften. Zu einer ästhetischen Rezeption Spinozas' (53–79); M. Pott, 'Philosophischer Untergrund. Clandestine Traditionen radikaler Aufklärung in Deutschland' (151–68). *Schweizer im Berlin des 18. Jahrhunderts*, ed. Martin Fontius and Helmut Holzhey (Aufklärung und Europa: Beiträge zum 18. Jahrhundert), Berlin, Akademie, 1996, 401 pp., contains papers from a 1994 conference with a broad remit concerning with cultural/political links between the two countries. It is an important document for an understanding of *Kulturvermittlung* and includes: H. Holzhey, 'Die Berliner Popularphilosophie. Mendelssohn und Sulzer über die Unsterblichkeit der Seele' (201–16); H. E. Bödeker, 'Konzeption und Klassifikation der Wissenschaften bei Johann Georg Sulzer (1720–1779)' (325–40); A. Gerhard, '"Man hat noch kein System von der Theorie der Musik." Die Bedeutung von Johann Georg Sulzers *Allgemeiner Theorie der schönen Künste* für die Musikästhetik des ausgehenden 18. Jahrhunderts' (341–54). E. Weigl, 'Wien oder das letzte Fest der Aufklärung', Obermayer, *Österreich*, 44–65, is a brief survey of the cultural and political conditions which enabled a late flowering of the Enlightenment in Vienna. In a similar connection see W. Baum, 'Wien als Zufluchtsort der Aufklärung: Josef Schreyvogel — die Philosophie Kants als Hilfsmittel im Kampf gegen Schlegels neue Schule "der Wiener Romantik"', *JWGV*, 99, 1995:83–102. Another geographical centre is examined in G.-L. Fink, 'Straßburg im Schnittpunkt der deutschen und der französischen Aufklärung. Das soziale und kulturelle elsässische Mosaik zur

Zeit Schoepflins', *RG*, 26, 1996: 153–204. E. Kleinschmidt, '*Um*schreibungen — Um*schreibungen*. Sprachphilosophische Selbstreflexivität im 18. Jahrhundert', *DVLG*, 71:70–91, deals with the development of language as a vehicle for developing systems of thought from Herder to Kant.

EMPFINDSAMKEIT, STURM UND DRANG. Hans-Georg Kemper, *Deutsche Lyrik der frühen Neuzeit*. VI/1. *Empfindsamkeit*, Tübingen, Niemeyer, xiii + 568 pp., does much more than the title might suggest. It is reviewed in this section since it constitutes more than a study of poetry alone; it takes on the whole complex genesis of *Empfindsamkeit*, a term which seems clumsily global after a reading of this text. K. investigates the complex synchronic and diachronic relationships between Pietism, neology and *Empfindsamkeit*. This involves the analysis of a vast body of material covering, on an often international and interdisciplinary basis, biography, theology, philosophy, aesthetics, and literature and serving to illuminate the complex mechanisms of reception and creativity which underlie literary periodizations such as *Empfindsamkeit*. The material is organized into two sections dealing with 'Pietismus und Empfindsamkeit' (19–148), centrally concerned with Zinzendorf, Tersteegen, Pyra and Lange, and secondly with 'Neologie und Empfindsamkeit' (151–498), a section which embraces a vast range of material and culminates in highly illuminating studies of Gellert, Wieland, and Klopstock. This text constitutes a major contribution to scholarship and an extraordinary act of synthesis. A single reservation concerns the intrusive academic apparatus in the body of the text which can serve to obscure the line of argument. B. A. Sørensen, Sørensen, *Geschichte*, 1, 206–51, offers an introductory survey of the political, religious, philosophical, and cultural determinants and parameters of the *Sturm und Drang*, followed by brief characterizations of its literary products and treatments of some major literary figures, although in the case of this contribution to the volume the treatment of non-literary material is very brief. It constitutes a useful means of orientation within the period within declared limitations, although the selection as representative literary figures of G. A. Bürger, J. M. R. Lenz, the young Goethe and Schiller is perhaps not the most productive. R. Krebs, 'L'idée d'energie dans l'esthétique du Sturm und Drang', *RG*, 26, 1996: 3–18.

CLASSICISM. B. A. Sørensen, Sørensen, *Geschichte*, 1, 252–89, contributes a chapter on 'Weimarer Klassik und Goethes Spätwerk' which constitutes a useful treatment of the period, its historical background, aesthetic principles and literary products subject to severe constraints of space. K. L. Berghahn, 'Weimarer Klassik & Jenaer Romantik = Europäische Romantik?', *MDU*, 88,

1996:480–88, attempts to redefine conventionally separate movements and see them as effectively aspects of the same thing. Volker Riedel, *Literarische Antikerezeption: Aufsätze und Vorträge* (Jenaer Studien, 2), Jena, Bussert, 1996, 444 pp., brings together in a more accessible form a number of previously published essays and lectures on the reception of literary material from antiquity from the 17th to the 20th c. A substantial portion of the material deals with our period, particularly the work on Winckelmann, Lessing, and Goethe which forms the backbone of the first two sections (9–179). Taken together these contributions constitute an interesting treatment of the developing taste for the antique, as well as of the wilful use of antique raw materials.

GENRES. '*Geist=reicher' Gesang: Halle und das pietistische Lied*, ed. Gudrun Busch and Wolfgang Miersemann (Hallesche Forschungen, 3), Tübingen, Niemeyer, viii + 381 pp., brings together contributions from a 1994 conference. It is a very interesting collection for students of our period since the connection between Pietism and literature is a fundamental issue there. The study of Pietist hymns (and so their texts) is a valuable intermediate stage for this investigation since these songs, like contemporary and later poetry, also have both a theology and an aesthetic, with the relationship between the two clearly a central point. Whilst the collection ranges back into the 17th c. and also deals with music there is much of interest, including: S. Arndal, 'Inspiration und subjektive Erfahrung. Zum Begriff des "Geist=reichen" bei Johann Anastasius Freylinghausen und Christian Friedrich Richter' (157–70); S.-P. Koski, '"Und sungen das lied Mosis daß Knecht GOttes/ und das lied des Lamms — Apoc. XV:3." Zur Theologie des *Geist=reichen Gesang=Buches* (Halle 1704) von Johann Anastasius Freylinghausen' (171–96); D. M. McMullen, 'Melodien geistlicher Lieder und ihre kontroverse Diskussion zur Bach-Zeit: Pietistische kontra orthodox-lutherische Auffassungen im Umkreis des *Geist=reichen Gesang=Buches* (Halle 1704) von Johann Anastasius Freylinghausen' (197–210); C. Bunners, 'Lieder Paul Gerhardts im Freylinghausenschen Gesangbuch' (211–40); T. Althaus, 'Entstehen aus dem Widerspruch. Das pietistische Lied bei Gottfried Arnold, dem Grafen von Zinzendorf und Gerhard Tersteegen' (241–54); A. Lindner, 'Der Kampf um das reformatorische Liedgut in der ersten Hälfte des 18. Jahrhunderts: Johann Martin Schamelius und sein *Evangelischer Lieder=Kommentarius*' (255–68); H.-G. Kemper, 'Der Himmel auf Erden und seine poetische Heiligung. Säkulisierungstendenzen in den *Freundschaftlichen Liedern* von Immanuel Jakob Pyra und Samuel Gotthold Lange' (269–86); G. Busch, '*Melodien zu der Wernigerödischen Neuen Samlung geistlicher Lieder* (Halle 1767) — ein pietistischer Hof und sein

Choralbuch' (287–312). Another poetry with religious overtones is discussed in J. Stenzel, '"Venus/komm vnd frewe dich." Hochzeitsgedichte von Opitz, Klopstock und Goethe', *JFDH*, 1997: 1–27.

GENRES. *Die dramatische Konfiguration*, ed. Karl-Konrad Polheim (UTB, 1996), 377 pp., offers a simultaneously varied and focused collection of essays, some of the best of which centre on our period. P.'s introductory essay, 'Die dramatische Konfiguration (mit Goethes *Iphigenie* und Hofmannsthals *Rosenkavalier* als Beispielen)' (9–32), emphasizes the need for clear configuration of figures in drama, since 'Im Anfang ist die Figur' (10). They are the source of contact with the audience, of action and expression. And figures are grouped to significant effect. The fundamental ordering of these figures, their place in 'der letzten und höchsten Schicht des Kunstwerkes' (12) is what P. understands as the essential configuration of a play. In contrast, transcient variations upon the basic configuration are 'Gruppierungen' or 'Konstellationen'. This structural distinction is maintained throughout the volume and helps the contributors towards extremely productive analyses of individual texts. Four contributions (including P.'s introduction) deal directly with our period: S. Schröder, 'Tödliche Ratio — Zur Konfiguration in Lessings *Emilia Galotti*' (33–56), revises conventional analysis of the drama in terms of *bürgerliches Trauerspiel*, since the deep structure of the work points to interest in more fundamental conflict between reason and passion; G. Slotosch, 'Goethes *Götz von Berlichingen* — Konstellationen und Konfiguration' (57–90), takes on conventional criticism of the formlessness of the text and reveals ingenious compositional principles; B. Bittrich, 'Zur Konfiguration von Friedrich von Schillers Trauerspiel mit Chören *Die Braut von Messina oder die feindlichen Brüder*' (91–100), in contrast reveals the unexpected organizational principles of a text which is readily, but casually, accepted as structured. Ruth B. Emde, *Schauspielerinnen im Europa des 18. Jahrhunderts* (Internationale Forschungen zur allgemeinen und vergleichenden Literaturwissenschaft, 26), Amsterdam–Atlanta, Rodopi, xv + 368 pp., reveals the theatre as an interesting site for the study of womens' position in social history. It is interesting since the theatre was one of the few places where women could achieve a degree of equality in their working environment; but the status of actresses was not entirely unproblematic. As E. suggests, during the Enlightenment people did not necessarily act reasonably; during the *Empfindsamkeit* there was not necessarily great fellow-feeling for women. The fact that women were acting women emerges as an interesting issue. E. suggests that femininity is not a property which women have but a role which they play. Hence all women could be seen as actresses. 'Real' stage actresses have a still more complex status since they play these (role-playing) women. They then play women as they appear to be and yet — importantly — they also have the potential to show them as they are. And, of course, they must still act out their own lives. The text interweaves evidence of the various layers of role play demanded of actresses in reality and fiction and reveals disturbing testimony of the limitations imposed upon those roles, limitations which amount to a refusal of the right to self-determination. Whilst some of the actresses studied are shown to battle against any constraints the general picture is negative. The drama of their lives and aspirations is largely tragic. The text has a European rather than exclusively German focus but this is in line with the European appeal of contemporary theatre. In this connection: S. Kord, 'The curtain never rises: femininity and theater censorship in eighteenth- and nineteenth-century Germany', *GQ*, 70:358–375, provides an illuminating treatment of contemporary censors' concern with/about actresses and female theatre-goers and contrasts this with apparent institutional indifference to women authors. More generally see: J. Purver, '"Zufrieden mit stillerem Ruhme"? Reflections on the place of women writers in the literary spectrum of the late eighteenth and early nineteenth enturies', *PEGS(NS)*, 64–65, 1993–95 [1996]:72–93. Further discussions of the drama of the period include: A. Beise, 'Untragische Trauerspiele. Christian Weises und Johann Elias Schlegels Aufklärungsdrama als Gegenmodell zur Märtyrertragödie von Gryphius, Gottsched und Lessing', *WW*, 47:188–203; B. Müller-Kampel, 'Sittenrichter gegen Possenreißer. "Österreichische Lösungen" auf dem Theater der zweiten Hälfte des 18. Jahrhunderts', *LitL*, 1996:221–37.

The general treatments of prose fiction received for review were scarcely concerned at all with the central genres of *Novelle*, novel, or short story and even when they were the interest was for the most part in works from outside the established canon. *Offene Formen: Beiträge zur Literatur, Philosophie und Wissenschaft im 18. Jahrhundert*, ed. Bernd Bräutigam and Burghard Damerau (BBNDL, 22), 352 pp., is a collection of essays with two common strands: an interest in 18th-c. anthropological thinking, and an interest in genres not always seen as belonging to 'literature'. There is a happy coincidence of these interests in the travel-writing, diaries, autobiographies, aphorisms, essays, etc. examined here. These are further the 'offene Formen' of the title for which the editors make grand claims. In their view 'Die Aufklärung etabliert sich durch Systeme', but importantly 'sie realisiert sich schließlich durch offene Formen' (p. 8) towards the end of the 18th c. The work covers some Italian and Romantic material but largely analyses texts from our period. The contents include:

A. Behrmann, 'Anmerkungen zum Begriff der offenen Form' (11–23);
R.-R. Wuthenow, 'Die Posse der Freiheit, das Schauspiel der Welt.
Zu Wilhelm Heinses Tagebüchern' (24–43); K. Weissenberger, 'Das
produktionsästhetische Spektrum des literarischen Reiseberichts in
der zweiten Hälfte des 18. Jahrhunderts' (44–70); B. Bräutigam,
'Szientifische, populäre und ästhetische Diktion. Schillers Überle-
gungen zum Verhältnis von "Begriff" und "Bild" in theoretischer
Prosa' (92–117); B. Damerau, 'Zwischen Hirngespinst und Herzens-
angelegenheit. Wieland im Gespräch: *Euthanasia*' (118–39);
G. Cantarutti, 'Edita inedita eines Kenners des menschlichen
Herzens. Ein unerforschter Aspekt bei J. K. Lavater' (208–40);
G. Marahrens, 'Über aphoristische Metaphorik und metaphorische
Aphorismen in Goethes *Maximen und Reflexionen*' (241–66). Ulrich
Klein, *Die deutschsprachige Reisesatire des 18. Jahrhunderts* (*Euphorion*,
Beihefte, 29), Heidelberg, Winter, 280 pp., provides a refreshing
treatment of this generally less well-known body of literature. The
introduction contains something of a disclaimer; K. refuses to get
bogged down in theoretical treatment of either travel writing or
satire. He will simply take on board texts which aid our cultural-
historical understanding. This approach has both advantages and
disadvantages for his text. The lack of a theoretical framework means
that the focus of the text is sometimes unclear, but it also means that
K. has scope for dealing with a wide range of material. This is
productively united in a final section which points out structural and
historical/thematic developments in these satires and suggests an
increasing disillusionment with the whole notion of getting to know
oneself through experience of the other. Texts are gathered together
under section headings; these are followed by brief surveys of uniting
themes. The sections are: 'Die Reisesatire als Pasquill' (34–41);
'Übernahme französischer Rokoko-Vorbilder in die Reisesatire'
(42–52); 'Die Hofmeister-Reise: von der moralischen zur sozialkri-
tischen Satire' (53–56); 'Curieuse Luftschiffer-Konquistadoren und
Gulliver-Epigonen' (71–98); 'Imaginäre Reisen zu spezifischen
Länder-Charakteristika' (99–110); 'Picarische und Don Quijote-
Vorbilder für das Reisethema' (111–42); 'Deutschsprachige Yorick-
Nachahmer' (143–71); 'Reisesatiren gegen den Literaturbetrieb'
(172–93); 'Spätaufklärerische Reisesatire gegen den Geniekult'
(194–206); 'Antiklerikale und kosmopolitische Reisesatiren' (207–37);
'Kulturelle Themen-Vielfalt und Regionalisierung der Reisesatire'
(238–51). In connection with satire see also F. Palmeri, 'The
metamorphoses of satire in eighteenth-century narrative', *CL*, 48,
1996:237–64. E. J. Weintraut, '"Islands in an archipelago": The
German dramatized novel', *GQ*, 70:376–94, provides an interesting
genre study. The focus is upon the nature and function of dialogue

presentation in this form of novel, in particular upon its ability to generate immediacy. It also investigates the socio-cultural reasons for the emergence and short-lived popularity of the genre. Barbara Potthast, *Die verdrängte Krise: Studien zum 'inferioren' deutschen Roman zwischen 1750 und 1770* (Studien zum achtzehnten Jahrhundert, 21), Hamburg, Meiner, x + 227 pp., deals with the discrepancy between theory and practice in the Enlightenment. More precisely it examines central figures from less well-known novels in terms of their life experience and shows how their expectations, shaped by the rationalizing, ordering principles of the Enlightenment are often sadly at odds with their experiences. We are shown how the inner world of characters, as well as the external world, cannot be made to conform to laws or rules. Virtue and happiness, the assumed products of life in this ordered world, are then correspondingly elusive. The analysis of protagonists is most compelling and P. makes full use of the fact that characters from 'inferior' novels reveal themselves more readily. The concluding sections on *Agathon* and *Werther* show how these characters too are shaped by similar difficulties in coping with reality, although P. must admit that the presentation is more sophisticated, revealing the psychology of the characters subtly rather than displacing psychological trauma into crude action which is often the case in lesser novels. *Werther* is seen as the culmination of a process of revelation of the limitations of Enlightenment in the novel. Another neglected genre is discussed in B. Witte, 'Emblematische Bilder. Die deutschsprachige Fabel des achtzehnten Jahrhunderts zwischen Oralität und Literalität', *Daphnis*, 25, 1996:713–38.

THEMES. *Ästhetische und religiöse Erfahrungen der Jahrhundertwenden.* 1. *Um 1800*, ed. Wolfgang Braungart, Gotthard Fuchs, and Manfred Koch, Paderborn, Schöningh, 230 pp., contains a number of contributions on the interrelationship between the terminologies and theories of religion and aesthetics in the 18th c. W. Braungart, 'Die Geburt der modernen Ästhetik aus dem Geist der Theodizee' (17–34), elucidates the core issues in a powerful opening essay, including treatment of Lessing, Moritz, and Klopstock; L. van Laak, 'Das Bild-Macht des erhabenen Gefühls. Ästhetische Theorie und literarische Praxis des Erhabenen im 18. Jahrhundert' (61–81), deals with variations upon the idea of the sublime in Bodmer, Brockes, Pyra, Klopstock, and Kant, and suggests that post-Kantian understanding of the idea amounts to an inversion of earlier interpretations; G. Kurz, 'Athen und Jerusalem. Die Konkurrenz zweier Kulturmodelle im 18. Jahrhundert' (83–96), has Hegel as theoretical starting-point but deals substantially with Herder, Hamann and Klopstock. Also included: M. Koch, 'Der Sündenfall ins Schöne. Drei Deutungen der Paradiesgeschichte im 18. Jahrhundert (Kant, Herder, Goethe)'

(97–114); H. Timm, 'Was die Welt im Innersten zusammenhält. Die neuspinozistische Nuklearästhetik der Goethezeit' (115–25). *Johann Dominicus Fiorillo: Kunstgeschichte und die romantische Bewegung um 1800*, ed. Antje Middeldorf Kosegarten, Göttingen, Wallstein, 501 pp., brings together a large number of contributions from a 1994 colloquium. Its subtitle is somewhat misleading since, whilst it does look forward to the 19th c., it also contains essays on important aspects of the study of aesthetics in the 18th c. and on the early development of art history in Göttingen, including: B. Steindl, 'Zwischen Kennerschaft und Kunsthistoriographie. Zu den Werkbeschreibungen bei Winckelmann und Cicognara' (96–113); M. Menze, 'Das künstlerische Schaffen Johann Dominicus Fiorillos vor dem Hintergrund seiner Ausbildung zum Zeichner und Maler in Rom und Bologna' (114–44), reminds us of the influence of the Roman scene for German art/aesthetics; H. G. Döhl, 'Johann Dominicus Fiorillo und Christian Gottlob Heyne. Interdisziplinäre Zusammenarbeit im 18. Jahrhundert' (145–66); H. Dilly, 'Hat Fiorillo den Merkur gelesen? Kunstgeschichten des Jahres 1794' (167–79). *RGI*, 7, provides a collection of articles in the fashionable area of landscape studies, some theoretical, some comparative, some focused on individual authors. Of most relevance to our period are: É. Décultot and C. Helmreich, 'Présentation. Paysage et modernité' (5–16); G. Oesterle, 'Révolutions des jardins et culture du souvenir' (17–30); T. Grosser, 'La perception du paysage chez les voyaguers allemands en France' (31–46); J.-P. Barbe, 'La tension ville/campagne dans les voyages fictifs allemands à la fin du xviiie siècle' (59–70); W. Scharfe, 'Cartographie et représentation du paysage au xviiie et au xix siècle: géometrisation, inventerisation, codification' (71–92); P. Penisson, 'Herder et le paysage italien' (93–100); M.-C. Hoock-Demarle, 'Le paysage allemand revisité: lectures du paysage dans les *Ansichten vom Niederrhein* de Georg Forster (1791)' (101–12); A. Ruiz, 'Les paysages de la Riviera et du Pays niçois vus par Ernst Moritz Arndt en 1799' (113–26); J. Mondot, 'Paysages du moi, nature de la mélancolie chez Karl Philipp Moritz' (183–92). However, the volume gains from being read as a whole, particularly through the drawing-in of material from the visual arts and from the Romantic period not mentioned above. *Garten und Wildnis: Landschaft im 18. Jahrhundert*, ed. Hansjörg Küster und Ulf Küster, Munich, Beck, 366 pp., is an extremely useful resource. It contains (in part extracts from) primary texts from our period concerned with this theme, covering thoeretical treatises—aesthetic and agricultural—and responses to gardens, parks, the natural countryside, exotic and foreign landscapes, woodland. Another interesting contribution to our understanding of aesthetics is offered by C. Zelle, 'Maschinen-Metaphern in der Ästhetik des 18. Jahrhunderts', *ZGer*, 7 : 510–20.

Winfried Löschburg, *Und Goethe war nie in Griechenland: Kleine Kulturgeschichte des Reisens*, Leipzig, Kiepenheuer, 192 pp., just about lives up to its subtitle, but within its declared limitations it is a useful book and in the sections concerning our period (pp. 63–112) briefly covers most aspects of contemporary travel with an emphasis on practical difficulties, or amusing and dramatic events—precisely those matters overlooked by more earnest volumes and probably precisely those remembered by the average traveller. There are a large number of useful reproductions of contemporary images of travel. Christian von Zimmermann, *Reiseberichte und Romanzen: Kultur-geschichtliche Studien zur Perzeption Spaniens im deutschen Sprachraum des 18. Jahrhunderts* (FN, 38), x + 516 pp., is, by contrast, an extremely exhaustive study of the interaction of two cultures built upon solid theoretical foundations. We are given a treatment of the pitfalls and creative aspects of exposure to another culture through literature or travel and then examples of vital interaction in travelogues and German literature exploiting individual Spanish sources or character-istic Spanish genres. The individual sections on many minor and some few major (Wieland, Gleim, Herder) German writers are individually illuminating and the whole marks an interesting contri-bution to the debate on the experience of the 'other' in or through literature and on international intertextuality, whilst at the same time presenting material which might be less familiar than, for example, writing on or from Italy.

Ingrid Altenhöfer, *Die Sibylle als literarische Chiffre bei Johann Georg Hamann / Friedrich Schlegel / Johann Wolfgang Goethe* (EH, 1, 1646), 346 pp., is informed by a Derridean understanding of, on the one hand, the elusiveness of language and meaning and, on the other, of the importance of language as the means to process reality. The presence of Sibyls or Sibylline motifs in texts by each of the authors mentioned does not mean that we get the clear delivery of clear messages we might expect from spokeswomen for the gods. The 'simple' Sibyl of ancient mythology is adapted over time to religious and literary ends and so her function becomes ambiguous. She at once crystallizes issues, focuses them, and makes us aware of their complexity; on this basis she does not just become potentially of thematic interest but also opens up literary/structural possibilities and reminds us of the difficulties and possibilities of her medium, language. This text is interesting on a theoretical and also on a literary-historical level, particularly when we are reminded of the mysterious absence of Sibyl figures during the Enlightenment which required a less mysterious sense of the nature and function of language.

2. GOETHE

EDITIONS. Johann Wolfgang Goethe, *Die Leiden des jungen Werthers: Synoptischer Druck der beiden Fassungen 1774 und 1787*, ed. Annika Lorenz und Helmut Schmiedt, Paderborn, Igel, 211 pp., is a very useful tool. Without engaging in discussion of the genesis of the later edition, which might obscure matters slightly, this volume presents in parallel the two authorized editions of the text and allows insight into the attempts to balance presentation of the central characters in the later version. It does, however, seem strange that a text with such intentions lacks conventional critical apparatus, although this would be widely (if less conveniently) available elsewhere. A parallel text enterprise of a different nature is offered in the very useful version of Johann Wolfgang von Goethe, *Erotic Poems*, introd. Hans Rudolf Vaget, trans. and ed. David Luke (The World's Classics), OUP, lii + 143 pp., which is a revised republication (of a text originally published elsewhere) with the addition of a selection from the *Venetian Epigrams* added to the previously included *Roman Elegies* and *The Diary*. Johann Wolfgang Goethe, *Wilhelm Meisters Theatralische Sendung*, Berlin, Aufbau, 352 pp., contains no critical apparatus.

GENERAL STUDIES AND ESSAY COLLECTIONS. Karl Maurer, *Goethe und die romanische Welt: Studien zur Goethezeit und ihrer europäischen Vorgeschichte*, Paderborn, Schöningh, 360 pp., brings together a collection of essays produced over 35 years (for the most part unrevised even in bibliographical terms) and otherwise less accessible. The subtitle is perhaps more illuminating than the full title since the focus is not exclusively on G. One contribution, 'Fénelons vergebliche Kritik der französischen Klassik und die Emanzipation der deutschen Literatur von der klassizistischen Norm' (99–179), is published for the first time in its full form in German. Another, 'Die verkannte Tragödie: Die Wiedergeburt der Tragödie aus dem Geist der Pastorale' (181–342), is published here for the first time and offers a compelling treatment of German tragedy in its relationship to related French and Italian traditions, culminating in an understanding of *Tasso* as the ultimate product of 200 years of complex, international theatre history. Also included: 'Goethe und die romanische Welt' (11–52); 'Das Leben des Bienvenuto Cellini' (53–72); 'Die verschlei-erten Konfessionen: Zur Entstehungsgeschichte von Goethes *Werther* (*Dichtung und Wahrheit*, 12. und 13. Buch)' (73–84); 'Entstaltung: Ein beinahe untergangener Goethescher Begriff' (85–97). Other general studies include: A. Fineron, 'Goethe's response to Jacobi's *Von den göttlichen Dingen und ihrer Offenbarung* and the influence of Hamann', *GLL*, 50:283–306; H. Hamm, 'Goethe und die französische Zeit-schrift *Le Globe*. Eine Lektüre im Zeichen der *Weltliteratur*', *Euphorion*,

91:207–11; P. Höyng, '"Was seh ich? Welch ein himmlisch Bild zeigt sich in diesem Zauberspiegel!"': Neuere Literatur zu und über Goethe: Ein Kommentar', *ColGer*, 30:171–87; J. Pfeiffer, 'Von Prometheus zum Wandererbund. Das Verhältnis von Künstlertum, Kreativität und Masochismus bei Goethe', *ib.*, 30:121–29.

POETRY. W. Braungart, 'Das Ur-Ei. Einige mediengeschichtliche und literaturanthropologische Anmerkungen zu Goethes Balladenkonzeption', *LitL*:71–84; M. Daley, 'Playing charades with Goethe: The identity of the beloved in *Charade*', *Seminar*, 33:95–106; F. Dieckmann, 'Imperative des erfüllten Augenblicks — Über Goethes Gedicht *Vermächtnis*', *SuF*, 49:506–23.

DRAMA. S. E. Gustafson, '"Don't See, Don't Tell." Gender transgression and repetition compulsion in Goethe's *Die natürliche Tochter*', *MDU*, 89:148–67, sees Eugenie's death as an expunction of her 'masculinity' as 'emasculation' for the sake of conformity. E. Denton, 'Satyr at play: Goethe's *Satyros*', *ib.*, 88, 1996:434–461.

FAUST. *Europe*, 813–14, offers a collection of articles about Faust, many inspired by Goethe's *Faust* and concerning the structure and meaning of that play, the myth or historical personnage of Faust or other related treatments of Faust materials. Of most direct relevance are: A. Dabezies, 'Miroirs du mythe' (3–9); C. Magris, 'Les métamorphoses de Faust' (10–14); G. Mahal, 'Le personnage historique de Faust' (15–22); G. Thinès, 'La trahison du disciple' (22–26); H. Henning, 'Goethe et la tradition de Faust' (39–46); A. Dabezies, 'Les structures du drame de Goethe' (47–53); A. Dabezies, 'Interprétations du drame de Goethe au XIXe siècle' (53–58); H. de Campos, 'La "trans-création" du *Faust* de Goethe' (59–65); F. Flamant, 'Le *Faust* de Goethe et le romantisme russe' (78–91). C. H. Niekerle, 'Sexual imagery in Goethe's *Faust II*', *Seminar*, 33:1–21, provides an interesting development of most treatments of sex in *Faust*. He examines the complex interplay between notions of 'sex' based upon biological conceptions of the body and socially-constructed definitions of 'gender'. An interesting analysis of modern Faust reception in literature is to be found in P. P. Brady, 'The black cook as Mater Gloriosa: Grass's *Faust* parodies in *Die Blechtrommel*', *ColGer*, 29, 1996:235–47. In the matter of reception see also H. Rölleke, '"Frau Marthe!"—"Was soll's?" Der Name der Nachbarin in Goethes *Faust* und anderwärts', *JFDH*:64–68. Other studies include: E. Grebel, 'Faust beschaut die Zeichen. Anmerkungen zum 1. Teil der Tragödie', *WB*, 43:271–85; J. Schmidt, 'Faust als Melancholiker und Melancholie als strukturbildendes Element bis zum Teufelspakt', *JDSG*, 41:125–39.

NARRATIVE. G.'s prose fiction is currently drawing a vast amount of attention. Julie A. Reahard, '*Aus einem unbekannten Zentrum, zu einer nicht erkennbaren Grenze': Chaos Theory, Hermeneutics and Goethe's 'Die Wahlverwandtschaften'* (Internationale Forschungen zur allgemeinen und vergleichenden Literaturwissenschaft, 25), Amsterdam–Atlanta, Rodopi, 87 pp., is a short but very provocative work. It is perhaps more of an introduction to the elusiveness of the text than a textual study in the conventional sense. We are shown how most critical methods when applied to the text provide unsatisfactory results or a sense of frustration at its slipperiness. R. appears to argue that in some senses the slipperiness is the point of the text and something that we can come to terms with given the right critical assumptions. We are introduced to two main brands of thinking, alongside G.'s own, which might help us adjust to the text. Firstly, Chaos Theory: this is presented as a brand of non-linear dynamics which suggests that there may not be a direct route to a clear understanding of a given phenomenon. Secondly, Gadamer's hermeneutics: R. focuses upon Gadamer's sense that understanding is a dynamic process and that in attempting to understand we enter an hermeneutic circle and cannot — once more — take a direct line towards an unequivocal conclusion. Interesting parallels are drawn between these theories and G.'s understanding of the world on the basis that they each tend towards an holistic approach rather than conventional scientific thinking. Furthermore each is concerned to find the hidden order within apparently chaotic systems whilst not seeing chaos as being in constant opposition to order; indeed they see chaos as driving systems towards a higher order. We are invited to visualize the implications of these related bodies of theory; we see the famous spirals of Chaos Theory, picture Gadamer's circle and are shown a graphic representation of the structure of G.'s novel. From our perspective the latter is certainly compelling in its presentation of 'mirror scenes' and the (unresolved) tensions which they reveal. The final chapter deals interestingly — and in part on the basis of alchemical theory — with the difficulty of achieving 'closure' in any reading, something which according to R. the reader simultaneously desires and fears. The brevity of the text does not give the reader the sense that the analysis is exhaustive but that may well be precisely the point; R.'s text may in the final analysis act as provocation and warning. Gabrielle Bersier, *Goethes Rätselparodie der Romantik: Eine neue Lesart der 'Wahlverwandtschaften'* (UDL, 90), viii + 217 pp., provides another approach to the elusive nature of G.'s novel. Inspired by the new respectability of parody in modern literary theory as one of the key sites of intertextuality, Bersier offers a virtuoso treatment of what she sees as a virtuoso parody — one so good that it enters literary history as an original. She also explores at length Romantic theory of parody, particularly Schlegel, and its input into G.'s work. Parody can be used to attack the old, or to defend the old against the new and both possibilities are shown. Parody is furthermore shown as highly self-conscious or self-reflexive and so we are shown in minute detail G.'s use of contemporary literary and theoretical texts. Despite his early resistance to parody we see how it becomes an increasingly useful and productive tool and in this novel is, ironically, at the heart of his originality. The core of the work consists of treatment of the parodistic elements in the treatment of central characters and in the self-presentation of G. as theorist and practioner and is extremely illuminating. We are forewarned of the quality of the analysis by a brief but marvellous treatment, by way of introduction, of the reception of the scenes concerning Ottilie's death (pp. 45–55). Another highlight and example of productive and, in literary-historical terms, highly significant intertextual interplay is provided by the examination of Rousseau parody (pp. 191–202). The Schlegel relationship is further explored in J.-M. Valentin, 'Les *Affinités électives*: Goethe contra Schlegel?', *EG*, 52:665–72. P. McIsaac, 'Exhibiting Ottilie: Collecting as a disciplinary regime in Goethe's *Wahlverwandt-schaften*', *GQ*, 70:347–57, provides an interesting treatment of the death and posthumous exhibition of Ottilie in terms of the pastime of collecting and the history of museum collecting.

John Blair, *Tracing Subversive Currents in Goethe's 'Wilhelm Meister's Apprenticeship'* (SGLLC), x + 204 pp., marks an attempt to read the novel outside the context of the *Bildungroman*. Wilhelm's integration into society is certainly not seen here as a seamless one. According to B. such a view of the novel can only be achieved by suppression of detail, particularly of subversive and vital elements of the text. The analysis is built upon an understanding of coercive power structures in the Enlightenment as expressed in the novel. A dark side is revealed to ideas such as utility and rationality since central characters find themselves in conflict with them. A comparison of the *Theatralische Sendung* and the *Lehrjahre* is highly productive in this connection. Whilst dealing with broadly the same material they are separated in historical terms by the French Revolution and in biographical terms by the Italian journey which is understood as an escape for G. from years of bureaucratic service. The consequence of this gap is a more radical scepticism in the later text; there is greater pessimism and distrust of authority and a diminution of human agency. This is shown in analysis of comic personages and women who are mar-ginalized by prevailing power structures, in the behaviour of charac-ters with a more assured position in the hierarchy/patriarchy, and, of course, in the torn central character Wilhelm. Particularly interesting are the study of marginalized voices in the final chapter and the earlier examination of the cold voice of literary theory which cast an interesting light upon this highly self-conscious work of art. Claudia Schwamborn, *Individualität in Goethes 'Wanderjahren'*, Paderborn, Schöningh, 187 pp., offers an interesting perspective on the novel, and indeed upon the process of reading the novel. Readings have often focused upon the point of absorption of the individual into the community or nature; S. focuses upon the problematic nature of the individuality of the characters and therefore sees their assimiliation as less than conclusive or self-explanatory. We are shown a world in which a clear sense of self is not a given and so where the individual is forced to examine his own boundaries; individuality is not fixed but in flux, dynamic; the individual's perception of it changes also. And the reader's perception of the individuals in the text is also problematic. S. suggests that the structure of the text means that the reader has to work hard to assemble a coherent view of characters, or in the theoretical terms of the text, to fill 'Unbestimmtheitsstellen'. In rising to the challenge the reader is tacitly acknowledging the elusive nature of individuality; for the reader, as for the characters themselves, clarity of vision is difficult to achieve. Other treatments of the Wilhelm Meister novels include: H. Ammerlahn, 'Goethe's *Wilhelm Meisters Lehrjahre*: An apprenticeship toward the mastery of exactly what?', *ColGer*, 30:99–119; I. Egger, '"... eine Art von Experiment." Goethes Kritik szientifischer Methoden und die *Wilhelm Meister*-Romane', *JFDH*, 1997:69–92; M. Koch, 'Serlo, Aurelie, Orest und Cornelia. Zu den Namen in Goethes Roman *Wilhelm Meisters Lehrjahre*', *GRM*, 47:399–414; H. Merkl, 'Die Hülle des Gewünschten als Gegenstand der Wunscherfahrung. Die Kästchen-Episode in Goethes *Wanderjahren*', *GRM*, 47:65–75. W. Albrecht, 'Zeitgenössische Alpen- und Italienbeschreibungen in Goethes *Reise-Tagebuch 1786*: Probleme ihrer Berücksichtigung für die Textkonstitution und Kommentierung innerhalb einer neuen historisch-kritischen Ausgabe der Tagebücher Goethes', Schwob, *Edition*, 179–85, provides interesting discussion of the degree of analysis of G.'s literary sources appropriate in a critical edition of G.'s work. Discussion centres upon G.'s use of J. J. Volkmann's guidebook to Italy and upon whether the editor should do more than make us aware of that source. Other treatments of G.'s prose writing include: S. P. Sondrup, 'Werther Jacopo, and the narrative constitution of self', Mildonian, *Parodia*, 131–41, which presents U. Foscolo's *Ultime Lettere di Jacopo Ortis* as a clever parodistic subversion of *Werther* but also as a subversion of itself as narrative and of the process of narration generally; H. Merkl, 'Gratisvorstellung im Burghof. Zur Deutung von Goethes *Novelle*', *ZDP*, 116:209–23; H. J. Becker, 'Raumvorstellung und selektives Sehen in Goethes *Italienische Reise*', *JDSG*, 41:107–24; B. Knauer, 'Im Rahmen des Hauses. Poetologische Novellistik zwischen Revolution und Restauration (Goethe, Arnim, Tieck, E. T. A. Hoffmann, Stifter)', *ib.*, 140–69.

THEMES. Hans-Peter Schwander, *Alles um Liebe? Zur Position Goethes im modernen Liebesdiskurs* (Historische Diskursanalyse der Literatur), Opladen, Westdeutscher Vlg, 385 pp., is concerned with the nature of ('romantic') love in G. and its unsustainabilty in a social context. It is shown in conflict with, for example, the institution of marriage which is intended to preserve it. More importantly, however, love is undermined by the historically-conditioned individuals involved. S. summarizes: 'Goethe hat seinen Gefühlsdiskurs als Entfaltungsmöglichkeit des egoistischen Subjekts produziert', and so love develops 'unter den Bedingungen der leistungsorientierten, egoistischen Persönlichkeitsstruktur, wie sie der aufkommende Kapitalismus hervorbringt' (p. 377). I cite these passages to indicate that the conclusion of the text may be slightly at odds with the introduction to the text which distances itself from other work in the field designed to serve some theoretical/critical method. Whilst this text is indeed based for the most part on close reading, surely its whole structure is shaped by the conclusion? Which does not mean that the study is uninteresting, indeed it is compelling. S. divides the business of love in his study of *Werther* and *Wilhelm Meister* (he ranges more widely later) into four characteristic phases: meeting; transformation of loved-one into fantasy figure; attempt to come to terms with discrepancy between dream and reality; collapse of union, feeling fails. In this context S. is most interesting on the role of women and in his thesis that love is a fiction, not only within fiction. The parallels drawn between bourgeois definitions of capitalist success and romantic love are also important. In both cases if success is achieved — in achieving a happy union or economic contentment respectively — then in some sense the system collapses. Bruno Hillebrand, *'Der Augenblick ist Ewigkeit': Goethes wohltemperiertes Verhältnis zur Zeit* (Abhandlungen der Akad. der Wiss. und der Lit., Mainz. Kl. der Lit., 1997, no. 1), Stuttgart, Steiner, 26 pp., was first delivered as a lecture and retains that character in contrasting, e.g. *Sturm und Drang* desires to experience eternity in the conventional sense with G.'s mature sense that we might experience it in moments, not understood in the first instance temporally but as 'Verdichtung eines Erfahrungskosmos' (p. 17). Other treatments of individual themes include: H. J. Becker, 'Die naturwissenschaftliche Prosa des späten Goethe', *JWGV*, 99, 1995:7–17; M. Bell, 'Goethe's two types of Classicism', *PEGS(NS)*, 65, 1993–95 [1996]:98–115; A. Käuser, 'Goethes Redeweise über die Farbe', *ZGer*, 7:249–61; M. Riedel, 'Zwischen Dichtung und Philologie. Goethe und Friedrich August Wolf', *DVLG*, 71:92–109; R. H. Stephenson, 'Goethe's prose style: making sense of sense', *PEGS(NS)*, 66, 1995 [1996]:33–41;

M. Swales, '"Das Bild, O König, soll uns nicht entzweien"': Image and image making in Goethe', *ib.*, 42–45.

INFLUENCE. RECEPTION. Nicholas Vazsonyi, *Lukács reads Goethe: From Aestheticism to Stalinism* (SGLLC), viii + 158 pp., provides a fascinating treatment of one man's wilful G. reception. The starting point is the understanding that ethics and aesthetics are interdependent in L. This has major implications for his understanding(?) of G., particularly in material written during Stalin's reign. Writing on G. is a regular feature of L.'s work even it is not a big part of the total output nor an exclusive focus. This study centres on two collections of essays, *Goethe und seine Zeit* and *Faust-Studien*, published under Stalin. L.'s adaptation to Stalin's dubious politics and ethics is reflected in his writing on G. in whose texts he locates the potential for radical ethics also. V. rejects the idea that these readings may be a response to direct political pressure on the critic and suggests that political violence had already been thematized by him before. Interestingly, G. was always a shadowy presence even when L. was largely tied up in work on political theory; G. was a useful cultural icon who could be made a useful vehicle for (dubious) politics and ethics. The connections made between the French and Russian Revolutions, between Enlightenment and Marxism as intellectual movements, could probably only have been carried off by someone with L.'s extraordinary knowledge of European cultural history. V.'s analysis is consciously in the tradition of reception theory and so does not try to legitimize L.'s views or otherwise, although we can sometimes hear the critical voice in the descriptions of L.'s conscious politicization of G. Other treatments of G. reception include: S. de Angelis, 'Le implicazione estetiche del giudizio di Goethe su Manzoni: Uno studio comparatistico sul significato della teoria letteraria del romanticismo italiano per la riflessione estetica tedesca del primo Ottocento', *ColH*, 24, 1996:61–94; J. Endres, 'Unerreichbar nah. Zur Bedeutung der Goetheschen *Novelle* für Stifters Erzählkunst', *JDSG*, 41:256–94; W. Hahl, 'Mann und Frau gehn durch die Krebsbaracke von Gottfried Benn — eine Replik auf Goethes Elegie *Die Metamorphose der Pflanzen*?', *JWGV*, 99, 1995:18–36; M. Ives, 'Angelika Kaufmann: A woman painter in Goethe's Italy', *WWAG*, 8, 1996:46–56; E. T. Larkin, 'Christian August Vulpius' *Rinaldo Rinaldini*: Beyond trivial pursuit', *MDU*, 88, 1996:462–479; W. Maierhofer, 'Vetter Grüne. Goetherezeption in Julian Schüttings *Zuhörerbehelligungen* und *Leserbelästigungen*', *ZDP*, 116:603–20; E. S. Schaffer, 'George Eliot and Goethe: "Hearing the grass grow"', *PEGS(NS)*, 66, 1995 [1996]:3–22; C. Ujma, 'Auf Goethes und den eignen Spuren: Fanny Lewalds *Italienisches Bilderbuch*', *WWAG*, 8, 1996:57–95. An interesting modern example of the popular cult of G. is provided by *Berühmte*

Liebespaare von Johann Wolfgang Goethe und Christiane Vulpius bis Simone Signoret und Yves Montand, ed. Hans Hillmann, Frankfurt–Leipzig, Insel, 229 pp., whose chapter on Goethe (pp. 9–20) is included, well, because Goethe is famous. See also Eva Klingler, *Warte nur, balde ruhest du auch*, Berlin, Rütten & Loening, 236 pp.

BIOGRAPHY. *Goethes Leben von Tag zu Tag: Eine dokumentarische Chronik*. VIII, ed. Angelika Reimann, Zurich, Artemis, 1996, 619 pp., continues the fine work of the earlier volumes which provide a very useful entry point or checkpoint for G. scholarship. This volume offers a very valuable means of orientation within the last period of G.'s life and work from 1828 to 1832 and even though at 600 or more pages it is subject to limitations of space it can be relied upon to guide the reader towards appropriate biographical and bibliographical sources. Since this volume covers the deaths of Großherzog Karl August (1828) and Großherzogin Louise (1830) (as well as that of G. himself), the production of the *Ausgabe letzter Hand* of his works (1830) and the last phase of the Faust projects (1831) it is clearly an important one. The only reservation at this stage concerns the access route to the material which remains chronological but this situation will be remedied by the forthcoming publication in volume IX of the indexes. Jules Keller, *Aus dem Alltagsleben einer Frankfurter Goethe-Freundin: Unveröffentlichte Briefe der Anna Elisabeth Schönemann geborene d'Orville an ihre Tochter Lili in Straßburg (1778–1782)* (Contacts ser. 3, Études et documents, 40), Berne, Lang, xxi + 311 pp. + 11 pls, offers — over and above any intrinsic interest — a refreshing perspective upon the social and, to a lesser extent, intellectual atmosphere prevailing in Frankfurt am Main in the late 18th c., although it provides no startling revision of our view of G. Doris Maurer, *Charlotte von Stein: Eine Biographie*, Frankfurt–Leipzig, Insel, 303 pp., revises a 1985 edition of the biography and adds illustrations. It offers a useful access point to S. and her relationship with G. and also to the culture and politics of the Weimar court. Wilhart S. Schlegel, *Goethe und andere Schwule*, Frankfurt, R. G. Fischer, 104 pp., contains a short essay 'Die Bisexualität Goethes — ein Essay' (pp. 7–18) listing some evidence of G.'s sexuality (particularly his interest in male bodies as represented in art and his relationships with other men) but the cursory presentation of the material prevents it from acting as anything other than a provocation to search further. The essay is perhaps more interesting as an instance of G. reception in terms of (homo-)sexual politics.

3. SCHILLER

EDITIONS. *Was heißt und zu welchem Ende studiert man Universalgeschichte?*, ed. Volker Wahl, Jena, Bussert, 1996, 30 pp. + lxix, provides a reprint of the text from *Der Teutsche Merkur* (from late 1789) with compact critical essay and critical apparatus (chronology, bibliography, related documentation). The handy volume Friedrich Schiller, *Der Geisterseher. Erzählungen*, Berlin, Aufbau, 205 pp., also contains *Der Verbrecher aus verlorener Ehre* (133–59) and *Merkwürdiges Beispiel einer weiblichen Rache* (161–203) but lacks any critical apparatus.

LITERARY WORKS. R. Harrison, '"Wer die Wahl hat, hat die Qual": Philosophy and poetry in Schiller's *Wallenstein*', *PEGS(NS)*, 64–65, 1993–95 [1996]: 136–60; W. Wittkowski, 'Können Frauen regieren? Schillers *Maria Stuart*: Poesie, Geschichte und der Feminismus', *RG*, 52:387–409; W. Wittkowski, 'Verzeichnet, verfälscht, verweigert: Schillers *Kabale und Liebe*. Tendenzen der Forschung, alt und neu', *JWGV*, 99, 1995:37–68; G. Vonhoff, 'Integration als Funktion: Aspekte editionsphilologischer Arbeit mit Quellen und anderen Vorlagen, dargestellt an Schillers *Semele*', Schwob, *Edition*, 195–202.

INFLUENCE, RECEPTION. Eva Zimmermann, *Die Harmonie der Kräfte: Casimir Ulrich Boehlendorffs dramatische Dichtung*, Weimar, Böhlau, 230 pp., sets out to establish a fairer place for B. in literary history and to liberate him from charges of epigonality. He is to be removed in particular from the shadow of Schiller. Z. claims that his conscious use and adaptation of literary models adds up to more than epigonality although at times this case seems a little stretched because of the quality of work produced. The study does, however, provide an interesting biographical/literary study of an intense period of dramatic production and an interesting case of S. reception.

4. INDIVIDUAL AUTHORS
(EXCLUDING GOETHE AND SCHILLER)

BAUMBERG. M. Ives, 'In praise of marriage: reflections on a poem by Gabrielle Baumberg (1766–1839)', *WWAG*, 7, 1995:3–17.

BAUMGARTEN. H. Reiss, 'The rise of aesthetics: Baumgarten's radical innovation and Kant's response', *BJECS*, 20:53–61.

BROCKES. M. Wagner-Egelhaaf, 'Gott und die Welt im Perspektiv des Poeten. Zur Medialität der literarischen Wahrnehmung am Beispiel Barthold Hinrich Brockes', *DVLG*, 71:183–216.

BÜRGER. An interesting example of Bürger reception is to be found in the new illustrations (to the older text edition) of Gottfried August Bürger, *Wunderbare Reisen des Freiherrn von Münchhausen*, illus. Uta Bettzieche, Frankfurt–Leipzig, Insel, 133 pp.

CLAUDIUS *Matthias Claudius 1740–1815: Leben-Zeit-Werk*, ed. Jörg-Ulrich Fechner (WSA, 21), 1996, xxviii + 344 pp., brings together 16 papers presented at an international conference in October 1990.

The range of contributions is large and they are gathered under three headings: 'Claudius in seiner Zeit' (3–65), 'Claudius' Verhältnis zu Zeitgenossen' (69–178), 'Zu Claudius' Werk' (181–331). Individual contributions investigate C.'s relationship to significant contemporaries (Klopstock, Lessing, Herder, Jacobi, Lavater) and his production of hymns, satire, reviews, translations. Collectively the volume goes some way to satisfying the editor's wish that we should not be satisfied with the conventional, stereotyped image of Claudius. Herbert Rowland, *Matthias Claudius: Language as 'Infamous Funnel' and its Imperatives*, Cranberry, NJ, Fairleigh Dickinson U.P.–London, Associated U.P., 335 pp., has a similar revisionist aim. Far from being the naïve poet, C. is presented as a writer whose work reveals a profound scepticism and it is a scepticism which the theoretical assumptions of this study make appear very modern. The most compelling chapters concern his use of language. C. is shown to confront a vacuum of meaning and the limitations of his chosen medium, something which he tries to overcome through linguistic innovation and in his use of metaphor and illustrations. The later chapters (5–7) are concerned with political and religious issues and in these matters C. is placed — significantly — besides famous contemporaries Wieland and Kleist. A dark, pessimistic side is revealed, particularly to the older C., something which little C. reception might have led us to expect. A further interesting contribution to the problem of language in C. is made by S. Donovan, 'Metaphor as an instrument of religious discourse and critique of pure reason in the works of Matthias Claudius', Debatin, *Metaphor*, 215–27.

FORSTER. B. Leuschner, 'Georg Forsters *Ansichten vom Niederrhein*: Tagebuch, Briefe, Reisebeschreibung', Schwob, *Edition*, 187–93, examines the three different forms in which reports of this journey survive, only to conclude that distinctions between the reporting styles cannot be maintained since the letter may have diary character and vice versa. On this basis, L. argues each version of events should be represented in a definitive edition.

GOTTSCHED (JOHANN CHRISTOPH). Susanne Niefanger, *Schreibstrategien in Moralischen Wochenschriften: Formstilistische, pragmatische und rhetorische Untersuchungen am Beispiel von Gottscheds 'Vernünfftigen Tadlerinnen'* (Medien in Forschung und Unterricht, ser. A, 45), Tübingen, Niemeyer, vii + 337 pp., is essentially a work of linguistic scholarship but makes an important contribution to our understanding of these (sub-literary?) cultural documents. They are generally regarded, after/with Blackall, as having an important input into the development of the German literary language, but this text goes much further in explaining how. N. reveals the characteristic formal structures and the sources from which they derive and explains how this might be seen as clear and simple 'model' prose well attuned to G.'s moral and linguistic precepts.

GOTTSCHED (LUISE). K. R. Goodman, 'Klein Paris and women's writing: Luise Gottsched's unknown complaints', *Daphnis*, 25, 1996:695–711, ranges more widely than the title might suggest. G. investigates the treatment of learned women in the literary world as well as investigating their often negative and distorted perceptions of their selves.

HAMANN. Eric Achermann, *Worte und Werte: Geld und Sprache bei Gottfried Wilhelm Leibniz, Johann Georg Hamann und Adam Müller* (FN, 32), viii + 368 pp., contains a complex treatment of Hamann's *Vermischte Anmerkungen* (pp. 150–256) connecting in an intriguing manner his understanding of language and economics/finance as sign systems and the broader history of ideas. Other treatments of H. include: E. Büchsel, '"Weitgefächertes Interesse": Hamannliteratur 1986–1995', *DVLG*, 71:288–356; S.-A. Jørgensen and Joachim Ringleben, 'Der "Eckelname" des Narziß. Interpretation einer rätselhaften Stelle in Hamanns *Aesthetica in nuce*', *JFDH*:28–63.

HERDER. J. Schneider, 'Herder und der deutsche *Kriegsgesang*', *GRM*, 47:53–64, examines a brutal irony in the promotion of this poetic sub-genre; it can elevate and ennoble the reader but it depends upon the implied presence of death and destruction. S. also deals with the fate of the *Kriegsgesang* after Herder. N. Wegmann and M. Bickenbach, 'Herders *Reisejournal*: Ein Datenbankreport', *DVLG*, 71:397–420, provides an interesting study of linguistic, stylistic, and generic innovation in the text in question. J. Barkhoff, 'Metaphors of the environment and the environment of metaphor in Johann Gottfried Herder's *Ideen*', Debatin, *Metaphor*, 39–49, examines Herder's use of metaphors which emphasize proximity to nature and to fellow men and explores modern difficulties in responding to these and indeed to nature itself. See also: I. Gombocz, 'The reception of Herder in Central Europe: idealization and exaggeration', *Seminar*, 33:107–18.

HIPPEL. J. Kohnen, 'Zu einem unveröffentlichten Hippel-Brief', *RG*, 26, 1996:127–36, refers to a letter of 22 December 1768.

KLINGER. The second volume of Friedrich Maximilian Klinger, *Werke: Historisch-kritische Gesamtausgabe*, ed. Sander L. Gilman, Georg Bangen, and Ulrich Profitlich, has appeared in the form of *Die Zwillinge: Paralleldruck der Ausgaben von 1776 und 1794*, ed. Edward P. Harris, Ekhard Haack, and Karl-Heinz Hartmann (Neudrucke deutscher Literatur, n. F., 47) Tübingen, Niemeyer, xlvi + 261 pp., which is an outstanding piece of textual scholarship (not really concerned with matters of interpretation) also containing as an appendix Friedrich Ludwig Schröder's treatment of the text.

LA ROCHE. P. Micha, 'Deuil et commémoration dans l'œuvre de Sophie von la Roche', *EG*, 52:365–92; P. Niklas, 'Aporie und Apotheose der verfolgten Unschuld: Samuel Richardson und Sophie von La Roche', *ColH*, 24, 1996:29–60.

LAVATER. Johann Kaspar Lavater, *Reisetagebücher* (Texte zur Geschichte des Pietismus, VIII, 3), ed. Horst Weigelt, 2 vols, xi + 839, viii + 401 pp., marks a enormous contribution to scholarship and to posterity in recording texts whose manuscripts are partly unstable and/or illegible. The two volumes do not, as the title might suggest, reproduce all of the diaries but those which are most significance to an understanding of Lavater — or rather of the Swiss/German cultural scene in general, such is the range of theme, cultural reference and personal contact recorded. The important diary of the journey to Bad Ems (1774) where he had contact with Goethe is not reproduced here since substantial parts have been published in connection with G. scholarship. Volume 1 contains the 'Tagebuch von der Studien- und Bildungsreise nach Deutschland 1763 und 1764'. Vol. 2 includes: 'Reisetagebuch nach Süddeutschland 1778' (1–26); 'Reisetagebuch in der Westschweiz 1785' (29–105); 'Brieftagebuch von der Reise nach Kopenhagen 1793' (109–363). In each case there is extensive coverage of textual history, the itinerary of the journey, and its significance.

LENZ. *EG*, 52.1, is entirely dedicated to L. with contributions from: G. Schneilin, 'L'écriture grotesque dans le théâtre de Lenz' (5–14);J.-P. Soulé-Tholy, 'Le personnage dramatique dans le théâtre de Lenz' (15–36); J. Mondot, 'Lenz, adapteur de Plaute' (37–48); G. Sauder, 'Lenz' eigenwillige *Anmerkungen über das Theater*' (49–64); R. Krebs, 'Lenz, lecteur de Goethe: *Über Götz von Berlichingen*' (65–78); G. Sautermeister, '"Unser Begier wie eine elastische Feder beständig gespannt": Der "Geschlechtertrieb" in Lenzens Theorie, Lyrik und Dramatik' (79–98); G. Niggl, 'Neue Szenenkunst in Lenzens Komödie *Die Soldaten*' (99–112); I. Haag, 'Die Dramaturgie der Verschiebung' (113–30); C. Klein, '"Ich weiß nicht, soll das Satire sein, oder —." Intertextualité et indétermination dans *Le Précepteur* de Lenz' (131–42); F. Genton, 'Lenz et la "misère allemande"' (143–58). Other articles published seperately include: M. Maurach, 'Aufklärung im Gespräch. Eine interaktionsanalytische Untersuchung des Dramendialogs im Sturm und Drang am Beispiel von Jakob Michael Reinhold Lenz', *Das achtzehnte Jahrhundert*, 21:176–88; S. Pfäffle, 'Die subversive Kraft von Liebe und Sexualität — J. M. R. Lenz: Moraltheorie und literarisches Werk am Beispiel ausgewählter Texte', *TeK*, 20, 1996:109–30.

LESSING. *GRM*, 47.3, is entirely devoted to analyses of Lessing's Italian journey, including: L. Ritter-Santini, 'Ohne Rosenkranz in der Tasche' (203–09); W. Lepenies, 'Zurück zur Aufklärung. Einleitende Bemerkungen zur Eröffnung der Ausstellung *Eine Reise der Aufklärung. Lessing in Italien*' (209–14); C. Wiedemann, 'Italien ohne Mythos. Lessings Reise in die italienische Gelehrtenrepublik' (215–26); G. Mattenklott, 'Lessings Grenzen. Anmerkungen zum *Tagebuch der Italienischen Reise*' (227–36); L. Ritter-Santini, 'Tagebuch oder Briefe italienischen Inhalts' (237–46); G. P. Romagnani, 'Turin im Jahre 1775. Kulturräume und ihre Protagonisten' (247–64); L. L. Momigliano, 'Lessing in Turin und seine Begegnung mit Giuseppe Vernazza' (265–82); M. Cavazza, '*Philocentria* und Pietramala. Lessing zwischen wissenschaftlicher Neugier und bibliophiler Leidenschaft' (283–94); P. Chiarini, 'Scipione Maffeis *Merope* und die Widersprüche der *Hamburgischen Dramaturgie*' (295–308); S. Matuschek, 'Lessing und Vico. Zum sprachphilosophischen Ursprung der *Erziehung des Menschengeschlechts*' (309–16); L. Ritter-Santini, 'Die Erfahrung der Toleranz. Melchisedech in Livorno'(317–40). Arno Schilson, '... *auf meiner alten Kanzel, dem Theater': Über Religion und Theater bei Gotthold Ephraim Lessing* (Kleine Schriften zur Aufklärung, 9), Göttingen, Wallstein, 56 pp., deals with the complex relationships between religion and reason, the sermon and the theatre. It focuses on the theological debate with Goeze and the drama *Nathan der Weise*. Other treatments of L. include: I. Morris, 'The symbol of the rose: a baroque echo in *Emilia Galotti*', *PEGS(NS)*, 64–65, 1993–95 [1996]: 53–71. W. Woesler, 'Lessings *Emilia* und die Virginia-Legende bei Livius', *ZDP*, 116:161–71. L. reception is covered in: A. Lagny and D. Thouard, 'Schlegel, lecteur de Lessing: réflexions sur la construction d'un classique', *EG*, 52:609–28; D. Arendt, 'Heine über Lessing oder: "derjenige Schriftsteller, den ich am meisten liebe"', *WW*, 47:204–20.

LICHTENBERG. Georg Christoph Lichtenberg, *Observationes: Die lateinischen Schriften*, ed. Dag Nikolaus Hasse, Göttingen, Wallstein, 240 pp., contains four L. lectures written in Latin and translated here (with commentary) for the first time. They are scientific works on subjects such as astronomy and electricity and remind us that L. was known to contemporaries more as a scientist than as a literary figure and that the worlds of art and science were inextricably linked in the 18th c.

LOËN. Johann Michael von Loën, *The Honest Man at Court*, trans. John R. Russell, Columbia, Camden House, xiv + 214 pp. This translation of *Der redliche Mann am Hofe* brings back to our attention an author who is interesting because of his exposure to the Enlightenment and Pietism at Halle, his religious views, and his knowledge of the German courts and their political and legal operations. The translation is certainly very readable but appears without the benefit of any academic apparatus.

MENDELSSOHN. *Gesammelte Schriften, Jubiläumsausgabe*, continues with vol. 24, *Porträts und Bilddokumente*, ed. Gisbert Porstmann, Stuttgart-Bad Cannstatt, Frommann-Holzboog, 401 pp., which is a very impressive supplementary volume containing documentary material relevant to M. It contains a wealth of images of M. himself and of contemporaries (many previously unpublished), text frontispieces and other pertinent illustrations and reproductions of manuscripts and handwritten texts. It constitutes an excellent resource for the study of M.'s life and times and of his contemporary reception, illustrating the myriad of projects in which he was involved and their contexts (Jewish and/or gentile) and helping to explain his central position in those contexts.

MEREAU. A. Harper, 'The novels of Sophie Mereau (1770–1806)', *WWAG*, 7, 1995:32–56; S. Jones, 'Sophie Mereau and Gryphius: some reflections', *ib.*, 57–67.

MORITZ. Karl Philipp Moritz, *Anton Reiser: Ein psychologischer Roman. Mit den Titelkupfern der Erstausgabe* (Bibliothek des 18. Jahrhunderts), Munich, Beck, 349 pp., is a second, slightly revised edition with extensive notes and useful concluding essay (pp. 379–410). Other treatments include: R. Charlier, 'Der heilige Rettich. Die Versinnlichung des Pneumatischen im *Andreas Hartknopf* von Karl Phillip Moritz', *GRM*, 47:379–98; O. Gutjahr, 'Das verdrängte Weibliche in Karl Phillip Moritz' *Anton Reiser*', *RG*, 26, 1996:19–40.

PICHLER. M. Garrard, '"Der Herrscher geheiligtes Haus": Caroline Pichler and Austrian identity', *WWAG*, 8, 1996:3–25.

SCHUMMEL. A. Hölter, 'Johann Gottlieb Schummels Empfindsame Reise durch Deutschland. Ein scheiternder Dialog zwischen Autor und Leser in der deutschen Sterne-Rezeption', *Euphorion*, 91:23–63.

STOLBERG. Dirk Hempel, *Friedrich Leopold Graf zu Stolberg (1750–1819): Staatsmann und politischer Schriftsteller* (Kontext, 3), Weimar, Böhlau, x + 329 pp., is a biography which attempts to present a subtle picture of the man (and to a lesser extent) the work and which certainly covers more than the subtitle might suggest. H. attempts to combat assumed critical prejudices about S. based on his adopted Catholicism and religious views generally, his reactionary politics and his ambiguous aesthetics. H. does indeed achieve some clarity and from a literary-critical standpoint provides useful, concrete detail of the intellectual/literary circles to which S. was exposed.

WEZEL. Johann Karl Wezel, *Gesamtausgabe in acht Bänden*, ed. Klaus Manger, Heidelberg, Mattes (the Jenaer-Ausgabe), has begun to appear, appropriately with the third volume, and W.'s most famous

work, *Hermann und Dorothea*, ed. Bernd Auerochs, 920 pp. The
publication coincides with the author's 250th birthday and when
complete will bring together W.'s entire published work, correspondence, and other contemporary testimony of the author's life and
work. This volume contains the text of the first edition with only
minor and sensible emendations (see pp. 811–15), facsimiles of the
plates of the four original volumes, a critical essay covering genesis,
structure, content, and reception of the text, a commentary, and a
bibliography. *Warum Wezel? Zum 250. Geburtstag eines Aufklärers*, ed.
Irene Boose, Heidelberg, Mattes, 94 pp., is a short text with a mission
to reawaken interest in W. whose position in literary history is seen as
unjustifiably obscure. The mission, of course, happily corresponds
with the publisher's parallel publication of the complete works, but
this is not to devalue the short contributions in this volume, all of
which make a good case for W. and introduce us to some of the
editors of the works. The individual contributions are: J. Heinz,
'Warum Wezel?' (9–15); K. Manger, 'Johann Karl Wezel — biogra-
phisch: Dichter und Schriftsteller, Anthropozentriker und Aufklärer'
(17–23); W. Hörner, 'Die Mär vom wilden Schreckensmann: Arno
Schmidt und Johann Karl Wezel — ein folgenreiches Mißverständnis'
(25–41); T. Joerger, 'Deutsche Lustspiele?—Wezel lesen!' (43–51);
A. Kosenina, '"zwey Blätter ..., die den Deutschen Ehre machen":
Wezel an Daniel Chodowiecki, zwei Beispiele aus der Briefedition'
(53–62); I. Boose, 'Wezel Konstruktionen: Ein Nachleben in Son-
dershausen' (63–69); 'Mythos Johann Karl Wezel; Biographische
Quellen und Dokumente', ed. W. Hörner (71–88).

WIELAND. Christoph Martin Wieland, *Von der Freiheit der Literatur:
Ausgewählte Publizistik und kritische Schriften*, ed. Wolfgang Albrecht,
2 vols, Frankfurt–Leipzig, Insel, 1530 pp., brings together a vast
range of material which would be otherwise difficult to assemble. It
unites reviews, journal publications and other marginal publications
which have a bearing upon important themes for W.'s work or for the
Enlightenment. The work is divided into six sections: 'Antike und
westeuropäische Geschichte, Literatur, Kunst' (9–160); 'Deutsche
Literatur und Sprache' (161–340); 'Philosophie, Theologie, Ästhetik'
(341–541); 'Staat, Politik, Aufklärung, Kultur' (541–720); 'Zur
Französischen Revolution' (721–888); 'Vorreden und
Selbstäußerungen zu eigenen Werken und im *Teutschen Merkur*'
(889–942). This arrangement is supported by a vast commentary
which enables connections within and beyond the text to be made
with ease. These volumes constitute a major contribution to scholarship. See also: N. Graap, 'Peregrins Geschichte: Die antike Welt als
Rederaum in Wielands *Geheime Geschichte des Philosophen Peregrinus
Proteus*', *LJb*, 38:9–26.

WINCKELMANN. J. Morrison, 'Johann Joachim Winckelmann: The body in question', pp. 39–46 of *Text into Image: Image into Text. Proceedings of the Interdisciplinary Bicentenary Conference held at St. Patrick's College, Maynooth (the National University of Ireland) in September 1995*, ed. Jeff Morrison and Florian Krobb (Internationale Forschungen zur allgemeinen und vergleichenden Literaturwissenschaft, 20), Amsterdam–Atlanta, Rodopi, 353 pp.

THE ROMANTIC ERA

By SHEILA DICKSON, *Lecturer in German, University of Strathclyde*

1. GENERAL STUDIES

Gerhard Schulz, *Romantik. Geschichte und Begriff*, Munich, Beck, 1996, 144 pp., offers a basic introduction to the concept of Romanticism in a broad, European sense. It covers a wide spectrum in readable style without claiming to contribute substantially to the academic debate. N. Saul, 'Aesthetic Humanism (1790–1830)', Watanabe, *History*, 202–71, is an authoritative analysis of the emergence, development, and decline of Romanticism within the wider picture of the Enlightenment, Classicism, and the Restoration. It does justice to the many complexities, and manages, while covering such well-trodden ground as Romantic ideas, personalities, and literary achievements, to achieve originality of approach and to yield new insights. B. A. Sørensen, 'Deutsche Romantik', Sørensen, *Geschichte*, I, 290–342, covers the same area and is also useful as a point of general reference without the same depth of analysis. Erika and Ernst von Borries, **Romantik* (dtv, 3345), DTV, 447 pp. U. Stadler, 'Esoterisch und exoterisch. Popularisierungsversuche bei Jean Paul, Novalis und Heinrich Heine', Winkler, *Heine*, 57–71, takes a comparative look at these authors' strategies to bring Romantic thought to a wider audience.

THEMES. Containing the proceedings of a conference, *Salons der Romantik*, ed. Hartwig Schultz, Berlin, de Gruyter, viii + 378 pp., covers a range of Romantic personalities and their theories of sociability. H. Eichner (1–19) considers the perception of women in early Romanticism with reference to the relationship of Caroline and Dorothea in Jena and to Friedrich Schlegel's *Lucinde*, and rejects the former's aesthetic contributions as inferior. A much more differentiated analysis of *Lucinde* is given by B. Becker (21–44), who recognises that Schlegel's emancipatory drive was purely male and narcissistic. The salon of Dorothea and Friedrich Schlegel in Paris is contrasted with the German version by I. Hundt (84–133), who uses this research to suggest a new understanding of Schlegel's attitude towards France. The theory behind the sociability of the salon is investigated by A. Arndt (45–61) with reference to Schleiermacher's 'Versuch einer Theorie des geselligen Betragens', and the ideal of free communication is revealed as an illusion. Also on theory, H. Scholz (135–46) uses A. W. Schlegel's lecture series as background to contemporary women's attempts at emancipation, with particular reference to Rahel Varnhagen's reception of them. Three further contributions examine Rahel's salon, K. Feilchenfeldt (147–69) placing her between Varnhagen and Schleiermacher, U. Isselstein (171–212) and B. Hahn (213–34) examining her correspondence with Karl Gustav von Brinkmann. On the presentation of the salon in Romantic literature, K. Hasenpflug (63–82) provides historical and biographical information to place *Phantasus* in context, and there are contributions on Bettine von Arnim's works *Goethes Briefwechsel mit einem Kinde* by I. Leitner (235–50), her *Königsbuch* by H. Schultz (251–70), her *Armenbuch* by U. Landfester (271–96), and her *Dämonenbuch* by U. Püschel (297–316). Of these, Leitner and Schultz examine Bettine's work in its contemporary setting; Leitner identifies her as a public relations expert working in all media, and Schultz compares the salon conversation to Romantic pseudo-folk art and sees the originality of Bettine's contribution in her recording of a *Naturstimme* (Goethe's outspoken mother), with a woman's voice being for the first time in the centre and in control, and in her (albeit necessarily disguised) social criticism. Also on Bettine's works, L. M. Hock (317–41) compares the presentation of Jews in factual and fictional writings and establishes a development from negative to positive, which remains, however, within the narrow confines of the stereotype (317–41). On Bettine's musical work, R. Moering (343–66) writes on 'Bettines Melodien als Inspirationsquelle' (343–66).

One particular centre of Romanticism, Dresden, is the subject of Klaus Günzel, *Romantik in Dresden. Gestalten und Begegnungen*, Frankfurt–Leipzig, Insel, 237 pp. G. illustrates the importance of this city as a meeting place for a range of Romantic writers, painters, and musicians. Their life and works are interlinked with the history of Dresden. This work, in the style of his earlier monograph on the Brentano family (see *YWMLS*, 56:847), is a documentation of cultural history, well researched and beautifully illustrated, and aimed at a wide, general readership.

Aurora, 57, contains the proceedings of a conference on 'Kunst — Literatur — Religion zur Zeit der Romantik', and has contributions on visual art by A. Perrig (65–91) on 'Der Tetschener Altar und Caspar David Friedrichs "Deutung"', and H. Eilert (93–111) on the Nazarene painters and their influence in the 19th c. W. Keil (113–27) writes on church music, and N. Jückstock (175–94) on the *Zauberflöte*.

'Fessellos durch die Systeme.' Frühromantisches Naturdenken im Umfeld von Arnim, Ritter und Schelling, ed. Walther C. Zimmerli, Klaus Stein, and Michael Gerten (Natur und Philosophie, 12), Stuttgart-Bad Cannstatt, Frommann-Holzboog, 533 pp., has a general essay on 'Naturforschung im Zeitalter der Romantik' by D. von Engelhardt (19–48), and comparative studies on 'Philosophie der Chemie:

Arnim, Schelling, Ritter' by K. Stein (143–202), on 'Kants naturphilosophisches Erbe bei Schelling und von Arnim' by F. Moiso (202–74), and on 'Schellings, Arnims und Justus Graßmanns Konstruktion der Dimensionen im Hinblick auf Kant und die Möglichkeit einer mathematischen Naturwissenschaft' by M.-L. Heuser (275–316). K. Richter (317–29) and J. Teichmann (331–39) introduce Johann Wilhelm Ritter's work, M. Durner (341–68) and W. Neuser (369–89) write on Schelling, and, on Arnim, there are analyses by R. Burwick of '*Hollin's Liebeleben* als "Übergangsversuch" von der Wissenschaft zur Dichtung' (49–89), and by M. Gerten of Arnim's research and writing methods (91–141). Further material on Arnim's work is provided in an appendix of unpublished archive material by K. Stein and M. Gerten (459–528). The volume is an important one as it offers reliable documentation of scientific and philsophical perspectives unfamiliar to many Germanists but vital to our understanding of Romantic thought. The link between literature and science is made particularly clearly by R. Burwick, who demonstrates the fusion of the two in *Hollin's Liebeleben* and clarifies the role each has to play in Arnim's world view.

Jugend. Ein romantisches Konzept?, ed. Günter Oesterle, Würzburg, Königshausen & Neumann, 358 pp., has contributions on the concept of youth from the *Sturm und Drang* period to the end of the 19th c. G. Oesterle provides an introduction, in German (9–22) and English (31–43). Of direct relevance to our period are essays by H.-H. Ewers, who argues that the Romantics linked youth backwards to the child, rather than forwards, as the stage beyond childhood, because the Romantic youth wishes to remain a child (45–60). A. von Bormann examines Romantic youth as self-reflexive (61–80). G. Neumann writes on the question of identity and in particular the processes of female socialization, with reference to *Der blonde Eckbert, Undine* and *Der Magnetiseur* in his first essay in the volume (81–103) and *Nußknacker und Mausekönig* in his second (135–60). The latter text is discussed under the same aspect by G. Brandstetter (161–79). H. Brüggemann (105–28) compares Tieck's *Waldeinsamkeit* and *Der blonde Eckbert* to highlight the problematical nature of the symbiosis of poetry and life, as reflected in Tieck's irony. Examples of the Romantic motif of *Verjüngung* are given by H. Hudde (213–23), who emphasises their sources in previous literature, and J. Neubauer (333–48) questions the cliché of the youthful Romantic wanderer (333–48). Rahel Varnhagen's concept of youth in her correspondence with Pauline Wiesel and with Friedrich Gentz is contrasted by B. Hahn (193–209). A wider view is provided in an essay by D. Richter (181–92), who gives examples of returning to the place of one's childhood in writings from the 18th and early 19th cs, and by further essays on Goethe's

Lehrjahre, by R. Käser (225–52), on the drama of the *Sturm und Drang* by T. Clasen (277–92), and on children's literature (1750–1850) by R. Steinlein (297–332).

Peter Duesberg, *Idylle und Freiheit. Ein Entwicklungsmodell der frühromantischen Landschaft in der Wechselwirkung von äußerer und innerer Natur* (EH, 1, 1546), 1996, 447 pp., takes a look at the interaction of outer and inner nature, or *Landschaft* and *Seele,* and contrasts organic Romanticism with mechanistic Enlightenment, the former discovering the infinite in nature. The study begins with a chapter on Kant, Fichte, and Schelling, but then moves backwards in time, not only to the Enlightenment but to the period of Middle High German. There is too much extraneous material, in addition to two extended excursuses, and the study loses clarity of focus as a result. The individual texts, particularly those of Tieck, are described, not analysed, the descriptions are not free of clichés, and *Der blonde Eckbert* is downgraded to a forerunner of *Franz Sternbalds Wanderungen.*

There are three essays on women in the early 19th c. in *Fest. Steinsdorff,* by U. Püschel, '"... übrigens sollest du nicht lesen ..." Maximiliane Brentanos "Tagesordnung" für ihre Tochter Sophie' (37–49), J. Purver, 'Die Erzählungen Caroline Auguste Fischers im Kontext ihrer Zeit' (59–68), and U. Landfester, '"Heute soll hier die Revolution losgehen ..." Anna von Arnims Briefe aus Berlin an ihren Mann Freimund vom Sommer 1848' (257–88). J. Purver has also published an informative article on this topic, '"zufrieden mit stillerem Ruhme"? Reflections on the place of women writers in the literary spectrum of the late 18th and early 19th centuries', *PEGS,* 64–65, 1993–95 [1996]: 72–93. Xu Pei, **Frauenbilder der Romantik: Sophie Mereau-Brentano, Karoline von Günderode, Annette von Droste-Hülshoff, Clemens Brentano, Joseph von Eichendorff, Heinrich Heine,* Düsseldorf, Grupello, 180 pp.

GENRES. A. Alm-Lequeux, 'Karoline Pichlers *Denkwürdigkeiten*: Ein Selbstbekenntnis', Obermayer, *Österreich,* 66–86, is an interesting investigation of autobiograhical writing by a little known Viennese writer (1767–1843). Sven Gesse, **'Genera mixta': Studien zur Poetik der Gattungsmischung zwischen Aufklärung und Klassik-Romantik* (Ep, 220), 265 pp.

2. INDIVIDUAL AUTHORS

ARNIM, BETTINE VON. Dagmar von Gersdorff, *B. und Achim v. A. Eine fast romantische Ehe,* Berlin, Rowohlt, 207 pp., gives a lively presentation of the two protagonists and G. does well in her presentation and interpretation of their correspondence. It is not a strictly academic study and there are small factual errors, but it is of interest to

Germanists as well as to a more general public. I. Leitner, '"... vom tausendfarbigen Morgenlicht umwebt ..." Die Lichtdramaturgie in B. v. As *Goethes Briefwechsel mit einem Kinde*', *Fest. Steinsdorff*, 131–42, analyses B.'s use of light constellations as a reflection of her conception of utopia and detects the triumph of poetic spiritualism. M. Ferber, 'Ein "Hauptpfeiler Weiblicher ... Abnormalitäten"? August Nodnagels B.-Porträt in seinen *Poetischen Frauenbildern*', *ib.*, 205–21, describes a contemporary's reaction to B., H. Härtl, 'Publizistische Beiträge B. von As 1844–1848', *ib.*, 237–56 documents material not included in the recent DKV edition, and G. Lauer, 'Der "rothe Sattel der Armuth". Talmudische Gelehrsamkeit oder die Grenzen der poetischen Technik bei B. v. A.', *ib.*, 289–319, re-evaluates B.'s conception and presentation of Jewish life, arguing that it is more ambivalent than sometimes assumed and thus typical of the transition period from Romanticism to Biedermeier. Ursula Püschel, '... *wider die Philister und die bleierne Zeit.' Untersuchungen, Essays, Aufsätze über B. v. A.*, Berlin, Seifert, 1996, 329 pp., is a collection of individual essays on B.'s life and influence.

ARNIM, L. A. VON. R. Moering publishes three new Arnim texts, 'A. v. As Weimar-Stanzen. Mit einem Gedicht auf Christoph Martin Wieland', *Wieland-Studien*, 3, 1996:244–72; 'A. v. A. an Jacob Grimm. Ein unbekanntes Brieffragment zur Debatte um den "altdeutschen Meistergesang"', *Brüder Grimm Gedenken*, 12:160–63; and 'Arabeske von Einsiedler. Eine Mischhandschrift von Bettine Brentano und A. v. A.', *Fest. Steinsdorff*, 51–57. Holger Schwinn, *Kommunikationsmedium Freundschaft. Der Briefwechsel zwischen L. A. v. A. und Clemens Brentano in den Jahren 1801 bis 1816* (EH, 1, 1635), 221 pp., examines the Romantic concept of friendship in terms of various syntheses, many of them paradoxical. These friends' letter-writing is characterized as a organ of literary experimentation.

BRENTANO, CLEMENS. G. Och, 'Spuren jüdischer Mystik in Bs *Romanzen von Rosenkranz*', *Aurora*, 57:25–43, examines the source and meaning of Jewish mysticism, including the figure of the golem. K. Hasenpflug, 'Gedichte C. Bs an Luise Hensel', Schwob, *Edition*, 203–21, compares Hensel's known texts with B.'s versions and in doing so analyses their relationship, both personal and poetic.

EICHENDORFF, JOSEPH VON. *Aurora*, 57, which contains the proceedings of the 1996 E.-Gesellschaft conference with the theme 'Kunst — Literatur — Religion zur Zeit der Romantik', has a minimum of contributions on E. himself. There is a short piece by P. H. Neumann (1–6) on art and religion in *Ahnung und Gegenwart*, in which N. argues that E. is a self-reflective not a naive writer, and I. Holtmeier (203–08) continues her E. bibliography. Wolfgang

Nehring, *Spätromantiker. E. und E. T. A. Hoffmann*, Göttingen, Vandenhoeck & Ruprecht, 246 pp., is not a new study but a collection of
reworked older material. The first essay introduces both writers and
considers their similarities and differences, while subsequent essays
are on one author only. Franz Xaver Ries, *Zeitkritik bei J. v. E.* (SLit,
11), 302 pp., is a careful study of E.'s perception and conception of
contemporary structures and their changing status in the period to
1848. There is a considerable amount of material on political, social,
and cultural life. E. is shown to move away from his Christian to a
more distanced and sovereign standpoint. H. Hollmer and A. Meier,
'"So oft der Lenz erwacht." Zu einigen Motivzusammenhängen in J.
v. Es *Das Marmorbild*', *Fest. Steindorff*, 69–80, regards the Novelle as a
victory of Christianity over paganism, both as a parable and as a
poetic text. Christoph Meckel, **J. v. E. 'Das Marmorbild', der Adel und
die Revolution: Merkmalminiaturen*, Stuttgart, Mayer, 143 pp.

FICHTE. *J. G. F. — Gesamtausgabe der Bayerischen Akademie der
Wissenschaften*, ed. Reinhard Lauth and Hans Gliwitzky, Reihe I,
Werke, vol. 7, *Werke 1800–1801*, ed. Reinhard Lauth, Hans Giwitzky
et al., Stuttgart-Bad Cannstatt, Frommann-Holzboog, ix + 519 pp.,
is the latest volume in this standard critical edition. In keeping with
previous volumes, the standard of editing is very high, providing F.
scholars with invaluable and reliable material.

FOUQUÉ. J. A. Kruse, 'Heine und F. Romantischer Ausgangspunkt mit emanzipierten Folgen', Winkler, *Heine*, 15–39, provides
interesting new detail on F.'s influence on Heine, and their relationship, in the course of which Heine's enthusiasm turned to ambivalence and F.'s patronage to distance. A. Solbach, 'Immanente
Erzählpoetik in Fs *Undine*', *Euphorion*, 91:65–98, attempts to place
this work in the context of F.'s œuvre as a whole.

GÖRRES, JOSEPH. J. Osinski, 'J. G. als Zeitkritiker: Revolution —
Nation — Konfession', *Aurora*, 57:11–24, addresses the development
of his opinions in these areas.

GRIMM, JACOB AND WILHELM. A volume of essays, *Brüder Grimm
Gedenken*, 12, has contributions on biographical, bibliographical, and
editorial issues. W. Meves (1–15) addresses the problems of constructing the text of J.G.'s lectures on German literary history by
means of written notes by students. Details of the Gs' relationships
with other scholars are provided by G. Ziegengeist (78–117), who
reproduces correspondence and diary entries by Varnhagen von
Ense, V. von Hammerstein (118–36), who traces the young theology
student Carl Wetli's admiration of the Gs and reproduces his detailed
account of his eventual meeting with J.G. in 1860, H. Schmidt
(137–46), who illustrates the fruitful relationship between J.G. and
Hans Ferdinand Massmann, and the possible co-operation which

never came about, D. Wagner (147–59), who reproduces evidence of the correspondence between J.G. and the Classical scholar Julius Maximilian Schottky, E. Ebel (164–69), who writes on the brothers' correspondence with Danish scholars, and E. Hexelschneider (170–85), who investigates the link between the Gs and the publishing house F. A. Brockhaus, concluding that it was neither close nor extensive. Also in this volume, L. Denecke et al. (16–58) note additions and corrections to the bibliography of the Gs' library, and M. Sutton (59–77) takes a look at the English-language reception of the Gs' tales, showing how they were adapted to contemporary British taste and often radically watered down and altered. K.-H. Ryu (186–98) publishes a bibliography of Korean editions of Gs' *Märchen*, 1920–89. Lothar Bluhm and Heinz Rölleke, '*Redensarten des Volks, auf die ich immer horche' Märchen — Sprichwort — Redensart*, Stuttgart–Leipzig, Hirzel, 192 pp., is an updated documentation (the original study was published in 1988), with a preface which poses the question of source and editorial emendation and establishes, predictably, the impossiblity of definitive answers.

GÜNDERODE, KAROLINE VON. Lucia Maria Licher, *Mein Leben in einer bleibenden Form aussprechen. Umrisse einer Ästhetik im Werk K. v. Gs (1780–1806)* (BNL, 150), vi + 490 pp., provides a wealth of material on this author's ideas and their representation in her works. Two major strands of politics and philosophy are explored and the research has been carefully done to construct a picture of G.'s achievement within the limitations of her situation as a young woman of the Romantic age. H. Dormann, *Athenäum*, 6, 1996:227–48, has a *Forschungsbericht* on this author.

HAUFF, WILHELM. W. Schmitz, '"Mutabor." Alterität und Lebenswechsel in den Märchen von W. H.', *Fest. Steinsdorff*, 81–117, sees H. as representative of his period and compares him with E. T. A. Hoffmann and Hans Christian Andersen.

HOFFMANN, E. T. A. This year's *E. T. A. H.-Jahrbuch*, vol. 5 in the new series, has K. Kanzog (7–18) address the question 'Was ist "hoffmannesk"?', in the context of international H. reception. A. Hildebrandt (37–46) analyses the title figure of *Klein Zaches* without doing justice to H.'s comic talent. J. Imada (47–53) writes briefly on the theme of the family in *Ignaz Denner*. There is a more substantial essay by G. Jaiser (19–336), 'Konstruktion als Prozeß. Leserführung als Formprinzip in E. T. A. Hs *Fantasiestücken in Callot's Manier*', which perceives the cycle as a *Gesamtkunstwerk* and divides it into two kinds of narrative, namely preparatory texts which train the reader to respond correctly and adequately to the main texts (the latter being *Ritter Gluck, Don Juan, Der goldene Topf*). Also in this volume is the second part of a bibliography of secondary literature, covering the period 1988–93, by A. Olbrich (67–119). Stephan Reher, *Leuchtende Finsternis. Erzählen in Callots Manier* (KGS, 37), ix + 267 pp., is a published doctoral dissertation and looks at H. in conjunction with Aloysius Bertrand and Wolfgang Hildesheimer. The author examines the *Nachtstück* as an attempt to create the effect of a painting in words. The camera obscura and tableau are identified as relevant for H. and their role and their significance are indicated by means of useful historical background information. At the end of the short section on H., however, R. argues for the development in H.'s work from the attempt to reproduce the painter's art to the achievement of his own means of presentation. This argument is not convincing as the later works are paid relatively scant attention, and the idea of a chronological development is thus overstated. Stefan Ringel, *Realität und Einbildungskraft im Werk E. T. A. Hs*, Cologne–Weimar–Vienna, Böhlau, 336 pp., is also a doctoral dissertation and does not go far beyond a restatement of previous research on the relationship of inner and outer world and the role of the imagination in H.'s work. R. differentiates between *Dualismus* and *Duplizität*, the latter being the ideal to strive for that removes the distinction between reality and imagination and allows a true, symbolic (as opposed to allegorical), understanding of reality and the infinite. Aline le Berre, *Criminalité et justice dans les 'Contes nocturnes' d'E. T. A. H. Une image noire de l'homme* (EH, 1, 1547), 1996, x + 466 pp., presents H. as a knowledgeable, rigorous legal expert, who observes reality closely and is aware of the contemporary debate on mental illness and the criminal mind and who is very sensitive to these psychological factors in assessing human behaviour. There are chapters on H. as judge faced with the problem of guilt, personal responsibility and punishment, and analyses both of H.'s works and of real cases. B. has gathered a large amount of material and the volume is a useful source of information on this aspect of H.'s life. Wolfgang Nehring, *Spätromantiker. Eichendorff und E. T. A. H.*, Göttingen, Vandenhoeck & Ruprecht, 246 pp., has no substantial new material on H. Sandro M. Moraldo, *Wandlungen des Doppelgängers. Shakespeare — E. T. A. H. — Pirandello*, Frankfurt, Lang, 1996, 236 pp., has a chapter on H.'s *Prinzessin Brambilla*, and the contribution of this work to the development in the motif is seen to be the internalization of the situation within the main character; an endangering of the self which is overcome on a higher level. The analysis does not develop further the research already done on this text. Hartmut Steinecke, *E. T. A. H.* (Literaturstudium; UB, 17605), 259 pp., provides an overview of H.'s life, works, and their reception, by a Germanist who knows H. scholarship well. The chapters on H.'s legal and musical writings and on his visual art cover less well-known ground and overall it will be useful as orientation for undergraduates.

F. Loquai, 'Kampf gegen das Böse. Zur Bedeutung literarischer Exorzismen bei E. T. A. H.', *Aurora*, 57:45–64, compares H.'s *Elixiere* with M. Lewis's *The Monk* and demonstrates how H. places the question of differentiating possession and psychosis at the centre of his work. He concludes that H.'s text uses devil and exorcism symbolism to confirm man's inability to control his destiny. G. M. Newman, 'Narrating the asymbolic subject in E. T. A. H.'s *Der Sandmann*', *Seminar*, 33:119–33, surveys psychoanalytical theories of the emergence of language to argue for the text both as a description of Nathanael's psychosis and also as its 'therapy'.

HÖLDERLIN, F. H.   Helmut Hühn, *Mnemosyne. Zeit und Erinnerung in Hs Denken*, Stuttgart, Metzler, 306 pp., looks at the poet as philosopher, following the development of his thought in works from *Hyperion* to *Mnemosyne*. The analysis of the works is well-informed, and the work contributes significantly to the literary-theoretical debate on H. Sieglinde Grimm, *'Vollendung im Wechsel.' Hs 'Verfahrungsweise des poetischen Geistes' als poetologische Antwort auf Fichtes Subjektphilosophie*, Tübingen, Francke, 415 pp., approaches H.'s work from a similar kind of angle, linking poet and thinker. It demonstrates very clearly H.'s understanding of Fichte's modern subjectivism, in relation to his reception of the ancient ideal of beauty. As poet H. uses the former to legitimize the latter. Ulrich Port, *Die Schönheit der Natur erbeuten. Problemgeschichtliche Untersuchungen zum ästhetischen Modell von Hs 'Hyperion'* (Ep, 194), 1996, ix + 358 pp., is a valuable investigation with chapters on philosophy, teleology, philosophy of history, theory of art, and landscape art, each in the framework of the aesthetic of nature. The general material is informative and in each case there is detailed reference to the text. Jorn Erslev Andersen, *Poetik und Fragment. H.-Studien*, Würzburg, Königshausen & Neumann, 183 pp., is a translation of a Danish study published in 1993. It is a well-structured chronological study of H.'s aesthetic theory and practice, emphasizing his shifting and ambivalent understanding of the opposing poles of *Vollendung* and *Abgrund*. A. covers a range of works, from *Hyperion* and the *Stuttgarter Foliobuch*, to 'Wie wenn am Feiertage' and 'Hälfte des Lebens', and he includes an analysis of certain specific traits of language and metaphor. Eva Kocziszky, *Mythenfiguren in Hs Spätwerk*, Würzburg, Königshausen & Neumann, 161 pp., contains five individual detailed analyses of mythical figures in H.'s work. The aim is to create a more differentiated picture of this aspect of H.'s writing in specific texts, and the author places her interpretation in the line of Peter Szondi's literary hermeneutics. It is a well-researched study with useful detail. Katrin Theile, *Historizität und Utopie. Quellenkritische und konzeptionell-strukturelle Aspekte des Griechenbildes in Hs 'Hyperion'* (EH, 1, 1625), 157 pp., is a broad historical study with background information on contemporary views of Greece as the wider context to H.'s work. Martin Vöhler, '*Danken möcht' ich, aber wofür?' Zur Tradition und Komposition von Hs Hymnik*, Munich, Fink, 231 pp., looks at the influence of Klopstock and Schiller on H.'s *Tübinger Hymnen* and analyses them thematically and structurally. V. demonstrates the consistency of H.'s work, and also the continuous evolving of his thought. The set form of the hymn was used as protection for the development of new ideas. *Bordeaux au temps de H.*, ed. Gilbert Merlio and Nicole Pelletier (Contacts, 20), Berne, Lang, viii + 360 pp., focuses on the German community in Bordeaux, where H. stayed for a few months. There are general articles on the relationship between Bordeaux and Germany, and on other visitors, such as Sophie von la Roche and Johanna and Arthur Schopenhauer, and essays on H. in Bordeaux by G. Routet (229–64) and A. Bennholdt-Thomsen (265–86), both of whom consider the philosophy and poetics of 'Andenken', and by B. Böschenstein, 'Réminiscences françaises dans les fragments hymnique de H.' (287–307). G. Merlio (311–32) and F. Colomès (333–51) document the reception of H. in France. Elisabeth Weibler, '*O seelige Natur!' Bezüge zwischen Hs 'Hyperion' und dem idealistischen Denken aus religionsgeschichtlicher Sicht* (TSL, 28), 1996, 304 pp., examines the theological and philosophical debate on the relationship between nature and religion. The study covers a lot of ground and has a broader base than the title implies. Annekatrin Pusch, *F. H. als Übersetzer Lucans* (EH, 1, 1578), 1996, 229 pp., is a textual analysis of H.'s translation in comparison with the original. The former is placed in the context of H.'s creative work. More detailed textual analysis is contained in Josefine Müllers, *Die Ehre der Himmlischen. Hs 'Patmos'-Hymne und die Sprachwerdung des Göttlichen* (EH, 1, 1639), 150 pp., which interprets each stanza, including those of different versions, and establishes different levels of consciousness of the divine, in particular achieved through the creative word or metaphor. *H. Lesarten seines Lebens, Dichtens und Denkens*, ed. Uwe Beyer, Würzburg, Königshausen & Neumann, 266 pp., has essays by U. Brauer, 'F. H. und Isaac von Sinclair — Stationen einer Freundschaft' (19–48), K. Dahlke, 'Der "Tod des Einzelnen" im Zeichen der Zäsur. Zu Hs *Empedokles*' (51–76), A. Ross, 'Sinnlichkeit und Gefährdung. "Andenken" als tragischer Prozeß' (77–100), M. Nottscheid, 'Der Editor als Kunstrichter — Die Behandlung der "spätesten Gedichte" Hs durch die Editionsphilologie unter besonderer Berücksichtigung von Jochen Schmidts Klassiker-Edition (1992)' (101–22), A. Schmitz, 'Die "heilige Stunde" dichterischer Inspiration. Vergleich einer Meerfahrtszene aus dem *Hyperion* mit der (Boden-)Seeszene in "Heimkunft"' (123–42), A. Schulz, 'Die gebildete Natur. Skizze über Hs Beziehung zur natürlichen Mitwelt und zur Technik' (143–55), W. Wirth, Transzendentalorthodoxie? Ein Beitrag zum Verständnis von Hs Fichte-Rezeption und zur Kritik der Wissenschaftslehre des jungen Fichte anhand von Hs Brief an Hegel vom 26.1.1795' (159–233), U. Beyer, '"Sein und Zeit" bei H.' (235–63). Eberhard Baumann, *Das Geheimnis wird Licht. F. Hs Gedicht 'Andenken'*, Essen, Die Blaue Eule, 314 pp., explores the poem as a deliberate deception or puzzle. Michael Knaupp, *F. H. 'Hyperion'* (Erläuterungen und Dokumente; UB, 16008), 344 pp., has helpful and important documentation, with earlier versions and later fragments, followed by the history of the work's genesis and reception. Commentary is restricted to textual annotations. Stephan Wackwitz, *F. H.* (SM, 215), x + 203 pp., is a second edition, reworked by Lioba Waleczek. The main new material is bibliographical. Also noted: Y. A. Elsaghe, '"Süßer als Gebären": Matriarchale und patriarchale Metaphern in Hs Feiertagshymne', *GR*, 72:119–29.

KLEIST. *H. v. K. Sämtliche Werke und Briefe*, ed. Ilse-Marie Barth et al., vol. 4, *Briefe von und an H. v. K. 1793–1811*, ed. Klaus Müller-Salget and Stefan Ormanns, DKV, 1279 pp., has all known letters to and from K., with no editorial modernization, and with a detailed commentary. The editors claim not to have answered perennial questions surrounding K.'s biography, but to have raised new ones and thus to be opening the way for new research. In any event, the volume shows evidence of careful research and sensitive editing. *K.-Material. Katalog und Dokumentation des Georg Minde-Pouet Nachlasses in der Amerika-Gedenkbibliothek, Berlin*, ed. Wilhelm Amann and Tobias Wangermann, Frankfurt, Stroemfeld/Roter Stern, 669 pp. *KJb* contains the proceedings of the 1996 conference on 'Der junge K.' held in Würzburg in 1996 and several essays focus on K.'s journey to Würzburg, analysing and speculating on the reasons behind it and his experiences there. G. Hess (21–37) comments on the influence of the Enlightenment in K.'s description of the city, and cites K.'s letters to show how he moves from this position to a more personal one. D. Grathoff (38–56) presents the theory that on the journey to Würzburg K. and his companion Ludwig von Brockes were trying to collect information to disprove the theory of a link between German freemasons and the French revolution; a theory based on information concerning the people they are known to have met. Similar themes on a more general level are discussed by R. Mohr (72–96), who examines the influence of the Enlightenment on K.'s religious belief system. He finds this mixed with pietism and concludes that the two actually have much in common. G.-L. Fink (97–125) compares K.'s descriptions of different cities, on the basis of a comparison between France and Germany, and establishes K.'s personal and ideological prejudices. From this basis, F. explains K.'s view of the foreign in terms of a search for something better than that which he left at home. Another experience in K.'s young life was study at the University in Frankfurt/Oder, and this is described by D. Willoweit (57–71). The argument is that K. was by then too independent a thinker to fit in with the way of teaching at this institution. K.'s letters from his travels are examined by A. Tanzer (149–63), who compares them with Franz Alexander von Kleist's letters. K.'s letters at this time are shown to be an experiment, a means of self-testing for the young writer. H. Pfotenhauer (126–48) contributes an essay on the role of visual art in K.'s early works and letters as a reflection of a crisis of language. P. argues that K. uses pictures to express the inexpressible and thus outdo language in its own medium. *BKF* has two essays on *Penthesilea*, by R. M. Schell (44–59), who examines the contradictions inherent to the amazon state, and K. Köhler (60–74), who places the work in the contemporary redefinition of the role of the sexes. W. Jordan and S. Feuchert (16–43) look for indications of K.'s reception of contemporary philosophical discourse and conclude that what K. found could not help him in his search to overcome insecurity and find happiness. Documentation on K. is provided by R. Loch (75–116), who publish extracts from *Stammbücher* kept by K.'s mother's family to demonstrate the warmth and community spirit K. was exposed to as a child and sorely missed in later life. H. F. Weiss (128–42) emphasizes the importance of an awareness of the factual elements and the historical context in our interpretation of the anecdotes K. published, and C. Kaiser (147–62) brings K. into contact with Günter Kunert. Volker Nölle, *H. v. K. Niederstiegs- und Aufstiegsszenarien* (PSQ, 140), 320 pp., has identified an important group of themes in K.'s works and discusses it in detail across a full range of texts. The individual analyses are carefully thought out but N. does not go beyond this to draw conclusions for K.'s work as a whole. Il-Sang Jin, *Die gesellschaftlichen Formationen in H. v. Ks Erzählungen* (EH, 1, 1619), 191 pp., highlights the importance of contemporary structures (the state, the church, the family) in K.'s works. It is a competent descriptive study which does not, however, analyse the significance of the interrelationship between the historic and the poetic. There is a chapter on body and sexuality in *Die Verlobung* in Herbert Uerlings, *Poetiken der Interkulturalität* (UDL, 92), x + 363 pp. S. Allan, '"... Auf einen Lasterhaften war ich gefaßt, aber auf keinen --- Teufel": H. v. K.'s *Die Marquise von O ...*', *GLL*, 50: 307–22, challenges the Freudian-based interpretations of the Marquise's experience of the rape and reinterprets the import of the angel/devil dichotomy. Also noted: B. Greiner, '"Repräsentationen" novellistischen Erzählens. Cervantes, *La fuerza de la sangre* (*Die Macht des*

Blutes), Kleist, *Die Marquise von O . . .*', *GRM*, 47:25–40; U. Abraham, 'Gotikbegeisterung und neugotische Pläne. Zu H. v. Ks Cäcilien-Erzählung', *ib.*, 77–90; H. F. Weiss, 'Eine unbeachtete Rezension zum ersten Band der *Erzählungen* (1810) H. v. Ks', *Neophilologus*, 81:423–31.

MEREAU, SOPHIE. **Harmonie stiftete unsere Liebe, Phantasie erhob sie zur Begeisterung und Vernunft heiligte sie mit dem Siegel der Wahrheit: der Briefwechsel zwischen S. M. und Johann Heinrich Kipp*, ed. Anja Dechant (EH, I, 1585), 534 pp.

NACHTWACHEN VON BONAVENTURA. L. Katrizky, 'Ort und Zeit in den *Nachtwachen* von Bonaventura', *E. T. A. Hoffmann-Jahrbuch*, 5:54–66, concludes that both time and place are flexible in this work, which she interprets as a structural parable.

NOVALIS. *Novalis und die Wissenschaften*, ed. Herbert Uerlings, Tübingen, Niemeyer, xi + 295 pp., contains the proceedings of the first confernce held by the newly-formed N.-Gesellschaft in 1994. The theme of the sciences is interpreted very broadly and so the contributions are wide-ranging. H. Uerlings begins the volume with a review of work done in this area (1–22), and G. Rommel sketches out the history of editing N.'s writings in this area (23–47). N. is placed in his contemporary context by means of comparisons with other writers by J. Neubauer (49–63), who writes on N. and Goethe as scientists, D. Lancereau (169–91) writes on N. and Leibniz, F. Strack (193–211) on N. and Fichte. Wider comparisons are drawn in the areas of *Naturphilosophie* in a contribution by F. Henderson (121–42) on the concept of the experiment for N., Ritter, and Schelling, and in the theory of the state by K. Peter (239–67), comparing N., Fichte and Adam Müller. This latter essay emphasizes N.'s optimism, as does D. F. Mahoney (107–20), who compares N.'s theories with present-day theories of chaos and concludes that N.'s certainty of a future golden age has now been lost, so arguing against N. as precursor of the modern theory. D. von Engelhardt (67–85) sets out N.'s interest in and knowledge of contemporary medical developments and debates under different headings in a very clear exposé. U. Stadler (87–105), writing on N.'s anthropology, makes a strong case for N.'s development beyond the ideas of his teachers and his rejection of the naïve idea that the outer person can reveal the inner person. M. Engel (143–68) considers contemporary dream theory and relates N.'s ideas to his works, particularly *Heinrich von Ofterdingen*, to conclude that N.'s literary dreams are *Kunst-* and not *Naturträume*. I. Kasperowski (269–83) also focuses more on N.'s literary work by taking *Heinrich von Ofterdingen* as the base for an analysis of N.'s and contemporary views of the Middle Ages, and of how N. builds on the latter in his novel. G. Schulz (213–37), in his examination of the theme of eroticism, is able to link N.'s philosophical and literary work. *Athenäum*, 6, 1996, has two essays with relevance to N., by M. Frank, 'Friedrich Karl Forberg — Porträt eines vergessenen Kommilitonen des Novalis' (9–46), which contains information of importance to N., and S. Matuschek, 'Über N' *Monolog* und kritische Erbauung' (197–206), which places this text in the historical parameters of early Romanticism. Regula Fankhauser, *Des Dichters Sophia: Weiblichkeitsentwürfe im Werk von N.*, Weimar, Böhlau, 320 pp. Georg Wenzel, *N. in den Anschauungen von Ricarda Huch, Thomas Mann und Hermann Hesse* (Texte aus dem Novalis-Schloss 2), Halle/Saale, Janos Stekovics, 96 pp., has essays on these writers' links with N.'s life and thought.

RICHTER, JEAN PAUL. Caroline Pross, *Falschnamenmünzer. Zur Figuration von Autorschaft und Textualität im Bildfeld der Ökonomie bei J. P.* (MSLKD, 26), 133 pp., looks at the problem of authorship within the framework of contemporary categories of economic possession, and identifies a metaphorical system of trade, exchange, and value underlying the intertextuality of J.P.'s writings. The angle of interpretation is not new, a fact recognized by the author, but the analysis contains original and interesting detail. Regula Bühlmann, *Kosmologische Dichtung zwischen Naturwissenschaft und innerem Universum: Die Astronomie in J. Ps 'Hesperus'* (EH, I, 1561), 1996, 201 pp., chooses a very specific angle of interpretation, but it yields very general results regarding the discovery of the unconscious, inner world as a response to Kant's philosophy. J.P. is seen to take up a paradoxical position to the subject/object dilemma. M. Huber, 'Der Text als Bühne. Zu J. Ps *Leben des vergnügten Schulmeisterlein Maria Wutz*', Fest. Steinsdorff, 23–35, argues for the importance of this work in terms of narrative self-reflexivity. Götz Müller, *J. P. im Kontext. Gesammelte Aufsätze*, Würzburg, Königshausen & Neumann, 1996, 179 pp., is a collection of essays previously published in the period 1977–94.

SCHLEGEL, FRIEDRICH. There are five essays on S. in *EG*, 52, written in honour of Ernst Behler, by B. Binoche, 'Condorcet, F. S. et la perfectibilité indéfinie' (593–607); A. Lagny and D. Thouard, 'S., lecteur de Lessing. Réflexions sur la construction d'un classique' (609–27); E. Décultot, 'F. S. et "l'art divin de la peinture"' (629–48); A. Muzelle, 'F. S. et l'arabesque picturale. Le débat néoclassique sur les ornements' (649–63); and J.-M. Valentin, 'Les *Affinités électives*: Goethe contra S.?' (665–72). Also noted: G. Naschert, 'F. S. über Wechselerweis und Ironie (Teil 1)', *Athenäum*, 6, 1996:47–90. Tae Won Yoon, *Der Symbolcharacter der neuen Mythologie im Zusammenhang mit der kritischen Funktion der romantischen Ironie bei F. S.* (EH, 1, 1570), 208 pp.

SCHLEGEL-SCHELLING, CAROLINE. *C. S.-S. Die Kunst zu leben*, ed. Sigrid Damm (IT, 1921), 517 pp., is a selection of her letters, based on the critical edition by Erich Schmidt, and thus a reading not a scholarly edition. There is a substantial introductory essay by D., originally written for her 1984 Reclam edition and now revised.

TIECK, LUDWIG. *L. T. Literaturprogramm und Lebensinszenierung im Kontext seiner Zeit*, ed. Walter Schmitz, Tübingen, Niemeyer, xiii + 279 pp., is a collection of essays designed to reflect the most recent positions in T. research and to challenge old clichés concerning his work. Many of the essays tackle aspects of T.'s philosophy of language and art in general, such as E. Ribbat (1–16) on *Sprachverwirrung* and intercontextuality, A. Hölter (17–41) on T.'s adaptation of mythology, and A. Bosse (43–62) on orientalism in his work. Other essays establish links between T. and other Romantics, such as R. Kolk (63–85) on the early Romantic group, S. Vietta (87–99) on Wackenroder and T., E. Richter (169–91) on T. and Karl August Böttiger, and S. von Steinsdorff (217–33) on Bettine von Arnim and T. On individual works U. Landfester (101–33) places *Der gestiefelte Kater* in its theatrical tradition and shows how T. makes this tradition the subject of his wit, W. Bunzel (193–216) takes *Der Wassermensch* as illustration of T. as 'Aktualisator kulturellen Gedächtnisses', and M. Neumann (265–77) places T. between Jacob Böhme and Sherlock Holmes, with reference to *Aufruhr in den Cevennen*. Writing on T.'s other activities, H. Uerlings (135–59) assesses T.'s editing of Novalis's work and finds it one-sided, and K. Günzel (161–67) describes the reading evenings at T.'s home in the *Dresdener Altmarkt*. C. Strosetzki (235–52) writes on the interest in Spain shared by T. and his contemporaries, and R. Paulin (253–64) on T.'s interest in Shakespeare, also placed in the contemporary situation. Heather I. Sullivan, *The Intercontextuality of Self and Nature in L. T.'s Early Works* (SMGL, 83), ix + 207 pp., reassesses the variously interpreted individualistic, dualistic, and ambiguous nature of T.'s work to demonstrate instead a system of intercontextuality that combines constant change with often rigid constraints. It is the interrelations of self and other, self and world that generate meaning, but often prove dangerous and uncontrollable. This model works well for *Der blonde Eckbert* and *William Lovell*. With *Der Runenberg* and *Franz Sternbalds Wanderungen* the author takes it a stage further to the level of textual communication and the desire to understand *per se*. One feels that the basis of interpretation has shifted or become too narrow for the study as a whole, but the individual analyses are generally convincing.

WACKENRODER. *Athenäum*, 6, 1996, includes the proceedings of a conference on the *Herzensergießungen* in 1996. S. Vietta (91–107) considers the influence of Moritz on W., and W.'s originality,

R. Paulin (125–35) compares Stolberg, as a representative of the past generation, with W., who represents the new. R. Littlejohns (109–24) proves the *Herzensergießungen* to be a polemical text based on a sound knowledge of contemporary debate, and emphasizes that the religious element in the work preaches relativism and tolerance, not Catholicism. W. Keil (137–51) explores the importance of this work for the history and theory of music. Edwin Lüer, *Aurum und Aurora. L. Ts 'Runenberg' und Jakob Böhme* (BNL, 151), 262 pp., provides almost 80 pages of background information on Böhme and on the reception of *Der Runenberg* before examining symbols and structures in T.'s work. The approach throughout is descriptive rather than analytical. K. Peter, *Aurora*, 57 : 129–47, compares presentations of Nürnberg in the works of T., Wackenroder, and Richard Wagner.

LITERATURE, 1830–1880

By BOYD MULLAN, *Senior Lecturer in German in the University of St Andrews*

1. GENERAL

REFERENCE WORKS AND GENERAL STUDIES. The second, revised edition of the *Quellenlexikon zur deutschen Literaturgeschichte: Personal- und Einzelwerkbibliographien der internationalen Sekundärliteratur 1945–1990 zur deutschen Literatur von den Anfängen bis zur Gegenwart*, ed. Heiner Schmidt et al., Duisburg, Verlag für pädagogische Dokumentation, has reached the letter H with the appearance of vols 6–9, 1996, 512 pp. per volume, and vols 10–13, 512 pp. per volume. Together with vol. 1, 1994, these volumes provide comprehensive information about the secondary literature on German authors in no fewer than 28 languages. Two books that invite comparison are Watanabe, *History*, and Eda Sagarra and Peter Skrine, *A Companion to German Literature: From 1500 to the Present Day*, Oxford, Blackwell, xiv + 380 pp. Both are written explicitly for the general reader and for students, and both have a similar amount of space (about 400 pp.) to cover the last five centuries of German literature. They are both attractively produced and printed, similarly priced, and well indexed. There however the similarities end. The Cambridge volume is the work of nine different contributors, all of them respected experts in their fields. It is acknowledged in the preface that 'no overall editorial line was imposed' (p. xii) and it has to be said that this shows, for the chapters differ markedly in their approach and are of uneven quality. It is of course very difficult to do justice to the huge bulk of the material, especially in the modern period, but the outstanding contribution of Ritchie Robertson shows that it is still possible. The chapter dealing with our period is contributed by Gail Finney, 'Revolution, resignation, realism (1830–1890)' (pp. 272–326). This is helpfully divided into three sections, the first on *Junges Deutschland* and the *Vormärz*, followed by one on *Biedermeier* and one on Realism. The broad general issues are treated clearly and intelligently; there are, for example, good definitions of the four terms just mentioned and good analyses of the representative authors' aesthetic and political concerns. But the devil is in the detail. Finney follows enthusiastically what appears to be an editorial recommendation that prominence be given to women's writing (i), but in doing so she presses the case too far. Approximately one quarter of her chapter, and a fifth of her bibliography, is devoted to women's writing. There is of course a place for challenging the canon, but it is surely not in a book which is aimed at the general reader and the undergraduate and which is presumably intended to remain a standard reference work for a good many years. Louise Otto-Peters and Louise von François are not worth the page or more that they each get when Heyse merits only a passing reference, Mörike gets just over half a page and — most surprisingly of all — Raabe is never once mentioned. Even in the list of women writers there are puzzling omissions; Charlotte Birch-Pfeiffer and Eugenie Marlitt, both enormously successful in their day, are completely ignored. Sagarra and Skrine undoubtedly gain from the closeness of their collaboration. It is impossible to tell from whose pen any particular chapter comes, and the whole book is more thoughtfully planned and more disciplined in execution than the Cambridge volume. In contrast to their Cambridge rivals they eschew all bibliographical data — which would anyway quite rapidly date — and are thus able to find room for a 100-page 'biographical index' containing useful short profiles of many hundreds of writers, including many lesser-known ones. Most of the biographical material in the book is relegated to this index, which has the advantage of making more space available in the main body of the text for discussion of the major writers and the social, political, and cultural context in which they worked. There are six helpful literary maps of Germany ranging from the 16th c. to the post-1945 era, and four 'thematic surveys' which treat diachronically such large topics as German political verse or popular literature for adults and children. Due attention is paid to women's writing without distortion of historical reality. Within the period 1830–80 Sagarra and Skrine are however less strong than Finney on the definition of important terms like *Vormärz* or *Biedermeier*. There are also a few factual errors — for example, Heyse won the Nobel prize in 1910, not 1912 (p. 141), and Storm wrote a Novelle with the title *Ein Fest auf Haderslevhuus*, not *Ein Festtag auf Hadlershuis* (p. 346). Yet overall it is fair to say that Sagarra and Skrine win on points over the Cambridge team. Professional Germanists interested in the second half of the 19th c. will find a use for both these books, but will turn even more often to *Bürgerlicher Realismus und Gründerzeit 1848–1890*, ed. E. McInnes et al. (Hansers Sozialgeschichte der deutschen Literatur, 6), Munich, Hanser, 1996, 896 pp. This is without any doubt the finest and fullest available survey of the period in question and likely to remain the best for a long time to come. Each of the 14 chapters, all of them excellent, treats a particular theme or aspect of the subject. For this reviewer the most fascinating contributions are probably those of E. Becker, 'Literaturverbreitung' (108–43), who discusses the growth of the reading public, the development of lending libraries, the rise of popular magazines like the *Gartenlaube*, the place of the serialized novel and the economic status of authors, and R. Werner, 'Ästhetische Kunstauffassung am

Beispiel des *Münchner Dichterkreises'* (308–43), who has illuminating comment on the history, the political stance, and the aesthetic ideals of King Maximilian's famous 'Berufene'. P. Stemmler (84–107) deals with the definition of realism; K.-M. Bogdal (144–75) with 'Arbeiterliteratur'; R. Parr and W. Wülfing (176–210) with the role of schools and educational associations; W. Rohe (211–41) with the impact of new scientific discoveries; E. McInnes (343–93) with drama and the theatre; J. Föhrmann (394–461) with the lyric; W. Freund (462–528) with the Novelle; G. Plumpe (529–689) with the novel; H. Müller (690–707) with the historical novel; and A. Drews and U. Gerhard (708–28) with the use of symbolism in Realist writing. H. Nielsen contributes two chapters on the 19th c. to Sørensen, *Geschichte*, II, 'Die Restaurationszeit: Biedermeier und Vormärz' (13–61), and 'Der bürgerliche Realismus' (62–99). The chapters are not ambitious but they are clear and readable and provide a good and reliable introduction for students and the general reader. The layout of the material is in each case similar. First comes a brief general characterization of the period, with useful definitions of the main concepts (*Biedermeier, Junges Deutschland*); this is followed by two or three pages on each of the main genres (lyric, epic, dramatic); finally there comes a page or two on some of the major canonical authors. *Literaturwissenschaftliches Lexikon (LL): Grundbegriffe der Germanistik*, ed. H. Brunner et al., Berlin, Schmidt, 372 pp., is aimed primarily at students of *Germanistik* and has entries on some 150 of the most important periods, genres and theories. *Yale Companion to Jewish Writing and Thought in German Culture 1096–1996*, ed. Sander L. Gilman and Jack Zipes, Yale U. P., xxxiv + 864 pp., has useful entries on a wide range of writers, including in our period Börne, Heine, B. Auerbach, K. E. Franzos, and F. Lewald; the comprehensive index makes it easy to use.

THEMES. Andrew J. Webber, *The Doppelgänger: Double Visions in German Literature*, OUP, 1996, xxii + 379 pp. + 4 pls, traces the history of the *Doppelgänger* motif from its high point in the the work of Jean Paul and the Romantics through the period of Poetic Realism to the renewal of its popularity in the literature of the *fin de siècle*. This is a fascinating topic that was waiting to be treated, and Webber has done it exceedingly well. He uses the long and interesting introductory chapter to define the meaning of the term *Doppelgänger* and to explore the philosophical and psychological dimensions of the subject. There then follow five very good chapters on the use of the motif in Jean Paul (*Leben Fibels*), E. T. A. Hoffmann (principally *Der Sandmann*), Kleist (with the emphasis on *Der Findling*), the Novelle of Poetic Realism (Droste-Hülshoff, Keller, Storm), and writers of the 20th c. (among them Rilke, Kafka, Hofmannsthal). In the chapter on the

Poetic Realists there are excellent discussions of a wide range of texts including Droste's *Die Judenbuche,* Keller's *Der grüne Heinrich, Die Leute von Seldwyla* and *Sieben Legenden,* and Storm's *Ein Doppelgänger.* The book is in every way an outstanding achievement. Ronald Taylor, *Berlin and its Culture,* Yale U.P., xv + 416 pp., is a beautifully produced and illustrated book which contains a wealth of information on the literary, theatrical, and cultural life of the city. Chapter 7 on 'Realism and Revolution' (pp. 114–52) and Chapter 8 on 'The Self-Assurance of Empire' (pp. 153–209) cover the middle and later years of the 19th c. Authors treated include Alexis, Büchner, Fontane, Gutzkow, and Wagner. F. Krobb, 'Between exile and assimilation: Language and identity in German-Jewish texts around 1848', *Exiles and Migrants: Crossing Thresholds in European Culture and Society. Papers Presented at a Conference Held in Dublin City University, 1994,* ed. A. Coulson, Brighton, Sussex Academic Press, pp. 43–54. Christian Essellen, *Babylon,* ed. Cora L. Nollendorfs (GLC, 19), 1996, xxxvii + 184 pp., is a long-forgotten dramatic poem about the 1848 Revolution by one who lived through the period and then emigrated to America. *Fremde und Fremdes in der Literatur,* ed. J. Jablkowska et al. (GANDLL, 16), 1996, 283 pp., is concerned with the themes of migration and encounter with the foreign; Hebbel and Karl May are among the authors studied. *Life's Golden Tree: Studies in German Literature from the Reformation to Rilke. Festschrift for Robert Browning,* ed. T. Kerth et al., Columbia, SC, Camden House, 1996, x + 169 pp., has contributions on the 19th-c. lyric, including Heine, and on Nietzsche. Florian Krobb, '"und setzten einen Triumph darein, abtrünnig zu werden": Spiegelungen der Salonepoche in der deutschen Literatur des 19. Jahrhunderts', *Menora. Jahrbuch für deutsch-jüdische Geschichte,* 6, 1995: 113–35. D. Arendt, 'Seiltänzer in der Literatur oder "Ein Philister kann nie ein Seiltänzer zu werden wünschen"', *WW,* 46, 1996: 345–58, has brief comment not only on Nietzsche but also on a range of other writers including Immermann, Heine, Raabe, Spielhagen, and Fontane. *Ton — Sprache: Komponisten in der deutschen Literatur,* ed. G. Brandstetter (Facetten der Literatur, 5), Berne, Haupt, 1995, 227 pp., has two contributions falling into our period: E. Tunner, 'Mozart begegnet Casanova in Prag' (29–37), who considers Mörike's *Mozart auf der Reise nach Prag* and Louis Fürnberg's *Mozart-Novelle* of 1947; and M. Schneider 'Wagner bei Nietzsche und Proust' (143–69).

MOVEMENTS AND PERIODS. Martin Swales, *Epochenbuch Realismus: Romane und Erzählungen* (Grundlagen der Germanistik, 32), Berlin, Schmidt, 204 pp., acknowledges (189) that the book is to a considerable extent a reworking of his 1995 publication *Studies of German Prose Fiction in the Age of European Realism* (see *YWMLS,* 57:820), though expanded and modified for the benefit of German-speaking readers.

The first five chapters (pp. 11–53) deal fairly briefly with the theory and definition of realism and attempt to place the literature of German realism in a wider European context, contrasting it with the English and French realist movements. Swales makes a good case for his view that German realism begins around 1830 rather than 1848 and extends beyond the death of Fontane in 1898; he not unreasonably sees *Buddenbrooks* as the crowning achievement of the movement. Most of the book is taken up with interpretations of individual texts by major representative authors. The chapters on Keller, Raabe, Fontane, and Mann re-use with minimal alteration the corresponding chapters in the 1995 monograph, but there are new interpretations — though some are very short — of Gotthelf's *Anna Bäbi Jowäger*, Sealsfield's *Das Cajütenbuch*, Gutzkow's *Die Ritter vom Geiste*, Freytag's *Soll und Haben*, Spielhagen's *Sturmflut*, Storm's *Schimmelreiter*, and Ludwig's *Zwischen Himmel und Erde*. The book is intended as an introduction to realism for the German student and general reader (p. 8) and breaks no significant new ground. *Forum Vormärz Forschung*, 2, 1996, *Autorinnen des Vormärz*, is devoted to the subject of women's writing of the period. It includes: K. Tebben, 'Erfahrung und politische Intention: Zu Aspekten des jüdischen Selbstverständnisses in Fanny Lewalds Roman *Jenny* (1843)' (93–111); G. Schneider, 'Aus der Werkstatt einer Berufsschriftstellerin: Unbekannte Briefe Fanny Lewalds an den Verleger Wilhelm Hertz aus den Jahren 1876 und 1877' (113–30); C. Otto, 'Emanzipation der Frau als literarische Innovation: Weibliche Vorbildfiguren und emanzipatorische Protestkomplexe im frühen Romanwerk (1843–1852) von Louise Otto-Peters' (131–61); G. Frank, 'Die Rolle kultureller Dispositive für weibliche Biographie, Autorschaft und Literatur und ein komplexes Beispiel des Vormärz: *Memoiren* der Lola Montez (1851)' (163–210); M. Lauster, '*Vormärzliteratur in europäischer Perspektive*: Vorstellung eines interdisziplinären Projekts (1994–1996)' (213–18); B. Füllner, '"Voilà du courage! Voilà la vérité!": Georg Weerths Rede auf dem "Congrès des Économistes de tous les Pays" in Brüssel am 18. September 1847' (219–39); A. Ritter, 'Über den Stand der Sealsfield-Forschung und des Autors literarische Österreichkritik' (245–59). Peter Hasubek, *Vom Biedermeier zum Vormärz: Arbeiten zur deutschen Literatur zwischen 1820 und 1850*, Frankfurt, Lang, 1996, 304 pp., reprints 11 articles first published by the author between 1968 and 1990. There is however nothing random about the collection, for all the articles are concerned with aspects of the *Restaurationszeit* and there is a special emphasis on the *Zeitroman*, which Hasubek sees as the most innovative genre of the period, and the *Zeitgedicht*. The individual articles are: 'Der Roman des Jungen Deutschland' (11–41); 'Der Zeitroman: Ein Romantypus des 19. Jahrhunderts' (43–71); '"Ruhe" und "Bewegung": Versuch einer Stilanalyse von Georg Büchners *Lenz'* (73–102); 'Heinrich Heines Zeitgedichte' (103–26); '"Hofdichter der Nordsee": Heines Naturgestaltungen in seinen *Seebildern* der *Nordsee*-Zyklen' (127–50); 'Ausbürgerung — Einbürgerung? Heinrich Heine als Schullektüre: Ein Beitrag zur Rezeptionsgeschichte' (151–81); 'Grabbes "kritische" Liebe zu Shakespeare: Der Essay *Über die Shakespearo-Manie* als Antwort auf die Shakespeare-Rezeption in den ersten Jahrzehnten des 19. Jahrhunderts' (183–210); 'Odysseus im 19. Jahrhundert: Zukunftsweisende Experimente zur Erneuerung des Romans: Karl Immermann *Die Epigonen*' (211–47); 'Karl Gutzkow: Der Begründer einer neuen Literatur?' (249–70); 'Karl Gutzkow: *Die Ritter vom Geiste* (1850–51): Gesellschaftsdarstellung im deutschen Roman nach 1848' (271–87); 'Georg Herwegh: Gedichte und Prosa. Ein Essay' (289–301). The articles have held their value, and *Restaurationszeit* specialists will be glad to have them in this handy form. W. Bunzel, 'Tradition und Erneuerung: Tiecks Versuch einer literarischen Positionsbestimmung zwischen Weimarer Klassik und Jungem Deutschland am Beispiel seiner "Tendenznovelle" *Der Wassermensch*', *Ludwig Tieck: Literaturprogramm und Lebensinszenierung im Kontext seiner Zeit*, ed. W. Schmitz, Tübingen, Niemeyer, pp. 193–216, is marginally relevant to our period. E. Bahr, 'Die Widersacher des alten Goethe: Die Jungdeutschen, die Nationalen und die Orthodoxen', *GJb*, 112, 1995:227–41. **Philosophie, Literatur und Politik vor den Revolutionen von 1848: Zur Herausbildung der demokratischen Bewegungen in Europa*, ed. L. Lambrecht, Frankfurt, Lang, 1996, 567 pp., is an interdisciplinary volume with some discussion of little-known writers of the *Vormärz*.

REGIONAL LITERATURE. Johannes Scherr, *Rosi Zurflüh: Eine Geschichte aus den Alpen*, ed. H. Amstutz, Berne, Haupt, 1995, 234 pp. Although Scherr, who was born in Swabia in 1817 and died in Zurich in 1886, is now almost forgotten, he was in his day a well-known and widely read man of letters and a controversial cultural and literary historian. Along with his novel, *Michel: Geschichte eines Deutschen unserer Zeit* (1858), *Rosi Zurflüh* (1860), a story in the tradition of the *Dorfgeschichte*, is the work by which he is best remembered. Amstutz reproduces the text of the story, which has been long out of print, and adds a brief but informative account of Scherr's chequered career. *Westfälisches Autorenlexikon. III. 1851 bis 1900*, ed. W. Gödden et al., Paderborn, Schöningh, 955 pp., is the third of four projected volumes on Westphalian writers since since 1750 and contains some 400 entries, mostly on authors now forgotten. *Literarisches Schreiben aus regionaler Erfahrung: Rheinland — Westfalen — Oberschlesien und darüber hinaus*, ed. W. Gössmann et al., Paderborn, Schöningh, 1996, 492 pp.

  Der literarische Umgang der Österreicher mit Jahres- und Gedenktagen, ed. Wendelin Schmidt-Dengler, Vienna, ÖBV Pädagogischer Vlg, 1995,

128 pp. E. Neumayr, G. Mühlberger, and K. Habitzel, 'Tirol im historischen Roman: Eine kommentierte Bibliographie (1792–1945)', Holzner, *Literatur*, 339–58, list 128 novels by 29 authors, most of them now forgotten. The favourite theme of these novelists is the uprising led by the Tyrolean hero Andreas Hofer against the French in 1809. Among the authors listed are Louise Mühlbach (Clara Mundt) and H. E. R. Belani (Karl Ludwig Häberlin), who both used the story of Andreas Hofer, Felix Dahn (*Die Kreuzfahrer*), and Carl Spindler. J. Le Rider, 'Peut-on parler d'une littérature autrichienne?', *RGI*, 8:201–11. H. Blaukopf, 'Moritz Hartmann (1821–1872)', *LK*, no.3:99–106, gives a brief account of the life and works of this minor Jewish writer from Bohemia.

DRAMA. *Hanswurstiaden: Ein Jahrhundert Wiener Komödie*, ed. J. Sonnleitner, Salzburg–Vienna, Residenz, 1996, 392 pp., reproduces in this attractive volume the text of five exemplars of the Viennese popular comedy of the 18th and 19th cs which are now difficult to obtain: Stranitzky's *Der große Überwinder*, Kurz's *Die getreue Prinzeßin Pumphia*, Hafner's *Der geplagte Odoardo*, Perinet's *Kaspar, der Fagottist*, and Bäuerle's *Die Bürger in Wien*. Catherine Rigby, *Transgressions of the Feminine Tragedy: Enlightenment and the Figure of Woman in German Classic Drama* (RS, 130), 1996, xii + 270 pp., is a Melbourne Univ. dissertation of 1991 which has been (apparently considerably) revised for publication. It nevertheless still reveals its origins as a dissertation in a tendency to be diffuse, to indulge in name-dropping, and to go in for rather heavy footnoting. It falls into two main parts, the first of which is largely theoretical while the second is concerned with individual authors and texts ranging from the 17th c. (Racine's *Phèdre*) to the 19th. There is a chapter each on Grillparzer's *Das goldene Vlieβ* and Hebbel's *Gyges und sein Ring*. The work, which has a strong feminist slant, aims primarily to explore the place of women 'in the conjuncture of tragedy and enlightenment' (p. 5) in French and — especially — German Classical drama. German Classical tragedy (Goethe, Kleist, Grillparzer, Hebbel) is seen as the product of a transitional period between the traditional (tragic) age and the (at least in some sense more enlightened) modern age, and Rigby sets herself the task of examining the ambivalent, and still often repressed, role of women both in such tragedy and more broadly in bourgeois culture and society. There is no denying that she is highly knowledgeable about important aspects of the history and theory of European tragedy, but most readers are likely to become frankly wearied by the over-lengthy perambulation through the theoretical undergrowth and by the use of awkward vocabulary like 'dissynchronicities' (p. 74) and 'dichotomisation of the figure of woman' (p. 122). Volker Klotz, *Radikaldramatik. Szenische Vor-Avantgarde: Von Holberg zu Nestroy, von

Kleist zu Grabbe, Bielefeld, Aisthesis, 1996, 238 pp. S. Kord, 'The curtain never rises: Femininity and theater censorship in eighteenth- and nineteenth-century Germany', *GQ*, 70:358–75, investigates possible reasons why traditional histories of censorship have little to say about women writers and the censors. P. Branscombe, '"bin offen für das Kreative": Some observations on Hofmannsthal's relationship to the Viennese *Volkskomödie*', *Fest. Strelka*, 103–13.

NARRATIVE PROSE. Henry H. H. Remak, *Structural Elements of the Novella from Goethe to Thomas Mann* (NASNCGL, 14), 1996, xx + 322 pp., reprints in unaltered form nine articles previously published over the period 1958–88. The majority of them are concerned with canonical Novellen of the 19th. There is a heavy emphasis on questions of theory, form, and structure in the genre, as the title of the collection indicates. Remak writes well and clearly in what he himself acknowledges to be a now old-fashioned tradition — intrinsic, 'pragmatic, text-driven' (p. 3) — but it is one which in his introduction he combatively defends! There is an index of names and titles and, helpfully, of topics ('Begebenheit', 'Dingsymbol', 'Falke'). The essays are thoughtful and informative and will be useful for students. *Eight German Novellas*, trans. Michael Fleming, introd. and ann. Andrew J. Webber, OUP, xxiv + 320 pp., provides new English translations of eight canonical Novellen, nearly all of them drawn from the 19th c. The texts are: Tieck's *Der blonde Eckbert*, Kleist's *Die Marquise von O …*, Büchner's *Lenz*, Droste's *Judenbuche*, Stifter's *Turmalin*, Mörike's *Mozart auf der Reise nach Prag*, Keller's *Kleider machen Leute*, and Storm's *Schimmelreiter*. The task of literary translation is of course widely regarded as one only for fools or heroes. Nevertheless Fleming has done a good job, for all the translations read well and convincingly. He succeeds admirably in his aim of remaining faithful to idiosyncrasies of style in the originals; thus he reproduces Kleist's complex syntax and extensive use of indirect speech, and renders Storm's Low German into Yorkshire dialect. Webber's introduction gives a brief account of the nature and history of the Novelle genre and an introductory page or two on each of the authors. There are also five pages of useful explanatory notes at the end, and users of the book are likely to wish only that there had been room for more. The book will certainly be a welcome aid to less experienced undergradu- ates and will perform a valuable service in making these outstanding texts available to a wider readership. *An Anthology of German Novellas*, ed. S. Weing, Columbia, SC, Camden House, 1996, xxii + 277 pp.; includes the texts of Droste-Hülshoff's *Die Judenbuche*, Stifter's *Bergkri- stall*, Heyse's *L'Arrabbiata*, and Ebner-Eschenbach's *Krambambuli*, and an introduction by the editor to the theory and history of the Novelle genre.

2. INDIVIDUAL AUTHORS

BIRCH-PFEIFFER. Helga W. Kraft, *Ein Haus aus Sprache: Dramatike-rinnen und das andere Theater*, Stuttgart, Metzler, 1996, xiii + 233 pp., has a chapter on the life and work of B.-P.

BÜCHNER. *Büchner-Opern: Georg Büchner in der Musik des 20. Jahrhunderts*, ed. Peter Petersen et al. (Hamburger Jahrbuch für Musikwissenschaft, 14), Frankfurt, Lang, 272 pp., surveys 15 operas based on texts of B. and considers their status as 'Literaturopern'. There are detailed analyses of several works, including those of Berg, Peter Maxwell Davies, and Gottfried von Einem. D. Müller Niebala, 'Das Loch im Fürstenmantel: Überlegungen zu einer Rhetorik des Bildbruchs im *Hessischen Landboten*', *ColGer*, 27, 1994 [1995]:123–40. R. Taylor, 'Danton's ontology of suffering', *MGS*, 20, 1994 [1996]:1–17. F. Cercignani, 'G. B. e la ricerca dell'esperienza autentica', *Studia theodisca*, ed. F. Cercignani (Critica letteraria), vol. 3, Milan, Ed. Minute, 1996, pp. 77–90. G. Reuchlein, '"... als jage der Wahnsinn auf Rossen hinter ihm." Zur Geschichtlichkeit von G. Bs Modernität: Eine Archäologie der Darstellung seelischen Leidens im *Lenz*', *JIG*, 28.1, 1996 [1997]:59–111. B. Tilp, 'Schnitter Tod: Das Regensburger Volkslied "Es ist ein Schnitter, der heißt Tod" und seine Rezeption bei Clemens Brentano, Georg Büchner, Joseph von Eichendorff und Alfred Döblin', *LiB*, 49:12–29. T. Buck, 'Der "gefährliche Gemütsmensch": Zu Bs Simon-Figur in *Dantons Tod*', *Mélanges Iehl*, 53–63. J. Walker, '"Ach die Kunst! ... Ach, die erbärmliche Wirklichkeit!" Suffering, empathy, and the relevance of realism in Bs *Lenz*', *FMLS*, 33:156–70. L Martin, '"Schlechtes Mensch, gutes Opfer": The role of Marie in G. B.'s *Woyzeck*', *GLL*, 50:429–44. E. de Angelis, '*Woyzeck*: Bs erstes Drama', *GRM*, 47:91–100, argues that *Woyzeck* was B.'s first drama and not, as is usually believed, his last. J. K. Lyon, 'B.'s "crisis" of 1834: The material basis of his sudden emergence as a writer', *Fest. Strelka*, 47–58. H. Müller-Sievers, 'Büchner — Cult', *MLN*, 112:470–85, is a review essay which considers the development of B. scholarship over the past quarter-century with particular reference to J.-C. Hauschild's *Georg Büchner* (1993) and J. Reddick's *Georg Büchner: The Shattered Whole*.

BURCKHARDT. J. R. Hinde, 'J. B. and nineteenth-century realist art', *JES*, 27:433–55, is concerned with B.'s interest in the visual arts.

BUSCH. **Max und Moritz von A bis Z in deutschen Mundarten von Aachen bis zur Zips*, ed. M. Görlach, Heidelberg, Winter, 1995, 201 pp. *Max und Moritz in aller Munde: Wandlungen eines Kinderbuches. Eine Ausstellung in der Universitäts- und Stadtbibliothek Köln 27. Juni — 30. September 1997*

von Manfred Görlach (Kleine Schriften der Universtitäts- und Stadtbibliothek, 3), Cologne, Univ.- und Stadtbibliothek, 112 pp., gives a good
idea of the world-wide interest aroused by B.'s famous poem and lists
over 280 translations into various German dialects and a large
number of foreign languages. K. H. Spinner, '*Max und Moritz*', *Große
Werke der Literatur*, ed. H. V. Geppert. IV. *Eine Ringvorlesung an der
Universität Augsburg 1994–95*, Tübingen, Francke, 1995, pp. 159–73.
T. Kohut, 'W. B.: Die Erfindung eines literarischen Nationalhelden
1902–1980', *LiLi*, 27 : 157–67.

DROSTE-HÜLSHOFF. Although the year 1997 brings both the
bicentenary of D.-H.'s birth and the 150th anniversary of her death,
surprisingly little has been done to mark the facts. A. v. D.-H.,
Historisch-kritische Ausgabe. Werke, Briefwechsel, ed. Winfried Woesler,
has added vol. IX, 2: *Briefe 1839–1842. Kommentar*, ed. B. Plachta et
al., Tübingen, Niemeyer, xiv + 926 pp. *Ich, Feder, Tinte und Papier: Ein
Blick in die Schreibwerkstatt Annette von Droste-Hülshoffs (Katalog zur
Wanderausstellung des Landschaftsverbands Westfalen-Lippe)*, ed.
W. Gödden et al., Paderborn, Schöningh, 1996, 128 pp., is a lavishly
illustrated bibliophile publication brought out with an eye to the
commemorative year. It contains numerous facsimiles of D.-H.'s
manuscripts and, if nothing else, it inspires a new respect for the
editors who have laboured long and hard to produce the definitive
critical editions that are now coming out. Thomas F. Schneider,
*Annette von Droste-Hülshoff: Die Balladen. Text/Dokumentation, Osna-
brück, Rasch, 1995, viii + 438 pp. Herbert Kraft, **Annette von Droste-
Hülshoff: Ein Gesellschaftsbild*, Münster, Aschendorff, 1996, 191 pp.
Winfried Freund, **Annette von Droste-Hülshoff: Was bleibt*, Stuttgart,
Kohlhammer, 130 pp.

The editors of *Droste-Jb.*, 3, 1991–96, have clearly had their
problems in recent years but, with the help of a new publisher
(Schöningh), have produced a new volume for the commemorative
year. Most of the articles are concerned with aspects of D.-H.'s
writing, but there is an interesting biographical contribution by
F. Mende, 'Die D. und Weimar' (212–28) concerning her acquaintance with Johanna and Adele Schopenhauer. J. Linder, 'Strafe oder
Gnade? Zur *Judenbuche der D.*' (83–113), argues on theological grounds
that Mergel dies not by suicide but through fateful 'magische Kräfte'.
Other valuable contributions include: O. Niethammer, 'Die literarische Zusammenarbeit zwischen A. v. D.-H. und Levin Schücking:
Referenzen, Korrespondenzen und Widersprüche' (115–26); E. Bla-
kert, J. Grywatsch, and S. Thürmer, 'Aschendorff, Velhagen oder
Cotta? Von den ersten Überlegungen der D. zur Wahl eines
geeigneten Verlegers bis zum Erscheinen ihrer Gedichtausgabe von
1844' (135–54); R. Nutt-Kofoth, 'Frühe postume Drucke von A. v.

D.-Hs Jugendgedicht *Das befreyte Deutschland*: Ein Beispiel zur Problematik, verlorene Handschriften zu erschließen' (155–75).

A. Palinieri, 'Die Judenbuche — eine antisemitische Novelle?', *Gegenbilder und Vorurteile: Aspekte des Judentums im Werk deutschsprachiger Schriftstellerinnen*, ed. R. Heuer et al., Frankfurt, Campus, 1995, pp. 9–38. W. Woesler, '"Entzauberung": Mein Indien liegt nicht in Rüschhaus. Die Droste und Grillparzer', *Literatur in Westfalen: Beiträge zur Forschung*, 3, ed. W. Gödden, Paderborn, Schöningh, 1995, pp. 289–91. P. Labaye, '"Durchwachte Nacht": Une peinture de l'éphémère chez A. v. D.-H.', *Mélanges Iehl*, 227–48. G. Weydt, 'Macht und Machtlosigkeit des Worts: Zu den Levin-Gedichten der A. v. Droste', *Fest. Tarot*, 519–35. F. E. Lenckos, 'The sublime, irony and "das Wunderbare" in A. v. D.-H.'s poetry', *ColGer*, 29, 1996:303–21. J. S. Chase, 'Part of the story: The significance of the Jews in A. v. D.-H.'s *Die Judenbuche*', *DVLG*, 71:127–45. A. Lange-Kirchheim, 'Der Arzt und die Dichterin: Zu einer Verserzählung der Droste (mit einem Blick auf Kafka)', *JDSG*, 40, 1996:244–61. K. R. Sazaki, 'The crippled text/woman: A. v. D.-H.'s *Ledwina*', *MDU*, 89:168–81. V. D. Huszai, '"Denken Sie sich, der Mergel ist unschuldig an dem Morde": Zu D.-Hs Novelle *Die Judenbuche*' *ZDP*, 116:481–99. B. Plachta, 'Der Verlust des festen Bodens: Sozialgeschichtlicher und literarischer Kontext des Droste-Gedichts "Der Knabe im Moor"', *JFDH*:206–31. M. Peterfy, 'Von William Carlos Williams zu A. v. D.-H.: Die weibliche Stimme des Dichters in einem Fall von "gendered translation"', *CGP*, 25:23–37.

EBNER-ESCHENBACH. The last of six planned volumes of E.-E.'s diaries, this one covering the last decade of her life, has now appeared, *Tagebücher*. VI. *(1906–1916)*, ed. K. K. Polheim et al., Tübingen, Niemeyer, viii + 412 pp. One supplementary volume containing a commentary and index is still awaited. E.-E.'s story *Unsühnbar* (1889) has been translated under the title *Beyond Atonement*, trans. and introd. V. van Ornam (SGLLC), xiv + 130 pp. Ulrike Tanzer, **Frauenbilder im Werk Marie von Ebner-Eschenbachs* (SAG, 345), 280 pp. I. Surynt, 'Die Problematik weiblicher Arbeit in der Erzählprosa M. v. E.-Es', *Filologia Germanska*, 2, 1996:15–36. A. Zsigmond, 'Leben und Person der M. v. E.-E.' *Jb. der ungarischen Germanistik*, 1995 [1996]:221–38. R. C. Ockenden, 'Unconscious poesy? M. v. E.-E.'s *Die Poesie des Unbewußten*', *ASt*, 7, 1996:36–46. E. Toegel, '"Vergangene Freuden, überstandene Leiden": Reflections on M. v. E.-E.'s autobiographical writings', *MAL*, 30:35–47, is mainly concerned with E.-E.'s *Meine Kinderjahre* (1905). K. K. Polheim, 'M. v. E.-E. — neu zu entdecken: Am Beispiel ihrer Erzählung *Der Muff*', *JFDH*:232–65.

FOLLEN, AUGUST ADOLF LUDWIG. E. Spevack, 'August Adolf Ludwig Follen (1794–1855): Political radicalism and literary romanticism in Germany and Switzerland', *GR*, 71, 1996: 3–22.

FONTANE. Theodor Fontane, *Unechte Korrespondenzen: Ein Jahrzehnt Redakteur der Kreuzzeitung*, ed. Heide Streiter-Buscher (Schriften der Theodor Fontane Gesellschaft, 1), 2 vols, Berlin, de Gruyter, 1996, 1,277 pp., reproduces a lengthy selection of the political reports and commentaries — mostly about British affairs — for which F. had some sort of editorial responsibility during the years 1860–70 when he was on the staff of the *Kreuzzeitung*. Streiter-Buscher acknowledges that it is difficult to establish the exact extent of F.'s input into the reports, but she argues that they do cast new light on him and reveal him to have been politically much more conservative than has hitherto been believed. Christian Grawe, *Führer durch Fontanes Romane: Ein Lexikon der Personen, Schauplätze und Kunstwerke* (UB, 9439), 1996, 365 pp., is a second, revised edition of the invaluable book first brought out by Ullstein in 1980 and contains some 750 informative articles. Helen Chambers, *The Changing Image of Theodor Fontane* (Literary Criticism in Perspective), Columbia, SC, Camden House, xiv + 172 pp., provides the first detailed account in any language of the history of F. literature, though for reasons of space only the reception of F.'s narrative fiction is considered; his verse, travel literature, and autobiographical writing are all excluded. The book contains five main chapters, the first of which is concerned with contemporary reviews and early academic criticism. The most interesting point to emerge here is that although F. himself was often disappointed with them the contemporary reviews were from the outset generally positive. Chapter 2 traces the unhappy tale of the 1930s and 1940s when significant parts of the unpublished *Nachlaß* were either sold off or lost through war damage. It was not until the 1960s that F. scholarship really took off, aided by the appearance of large and reliable critical editions of his works. Chapters 3 and 4 survey the enormous and diverse growth of the critical literature over the last three decades, giving a clear picture of the impact of sociology, reception history, comparative studies, psychoanalysis, and feminism on the study of an author by now firmly fixed in the canon. In chapter 5 there is an illuminating discussion of the reasons why F. is still often regarded by non-Germanists as a marginal figure in the history of European realism. (The existence in Germany of a strong Idealist tradition with little respect for realist writing and the status of the *Bildungsroman* are among the causes suggested.) The book is well-planned and clearly written, though the first word in the title of Schopenhauer's *Parerga und Paralipomena* is twice misspelt *Paregra*. Monika Wengerzink, *Klatsch als Kommunikationsphänomen in Literatur und*

Presse: Ein Vergleich von Fontanes Gesellschaftsromanen und der deutschen Unterhaltungspresse, Frankfurt, Lang, 308 pp., approaches its topic from a sociological viewpoint and pays particular attention to the dialogue in *Frau Jenny Treibel* and *L'Adultera*. Manfred Rösel, '*Das ist ein weites Feld': Wahrheit und Weisheit einer Fontaneschen Sentenz*, Frankfurt, Lang, 152 pp., sees Effi Briest's father as the fictional *alter ego* of Fontane himself. Edda Ziegler and Gotthard Erler, **Theodor Fontane: Lebensraum und Phantasiewelt*, Berlin, Aufbau, 1996, 299 pp. Christine Kretschmer, **Der ästhetische Gegenstand und das ästhetische Urteil in den Romanen Theodor Fontanes* (EH, 1, 1637), 256 pp. Eue-Choon Park, **Fontanes Zeitromane: Zur Kritik der Gründerzeit* (EH, 1, 1641), 205 pp.

Fontane-Blätter, 63, has: M. Horlitz, '"Aber das Reizende ist leider immer das weniger Wichtige": Vier Briefe Fs an seine Frau aus Frankreich 1871 und einige Reisenotizen' (10–25); H. Fischer, '". . . so ziemlich meine schlechteste Lebenszeit": Unveröffentlichte Briefe von und an T. F. aus der Akademiezeit' (26–47); R. Loew, 'Die Verleger Friedrich Fontane (Berlin) und Adolph Marcks (St Petersburg) im Disput um Leo Tolstois Roman *Auferstehung*' (48–63); C. Grawe, '"Einen frischen Trunk Schiller zu tun": T. Fs Schillerkritiken 1870–1889. Teil 2' (66–90); H. Nürnberger, '"Du hast den Sänger Rizzio beglückt . . .": Mortimer und Maria Stuart, Robert von Gordon-Leslie und Cécile von St Arnaud' (91–101); M. Kikawa, 'Von *Küstrin* zur *Katte-Tragödie*: Ein Beitrag zur Auseinandersetzung Fs mit dem Preußentum in den *Wanderungen durch die Mark Brandenburg*' (102–20); R. Muhs, 'Fs "Englische Berichte" 1854–55' (121–23); E. Volkov, 'Zum Begriff des Raumes in Fs später Prosa' (144–51); F. Franke and P. Schaefer, 'Bibliographie: Neuerscheinungen und -erwerbungen des F.-Archivs bis März 1997' (171–86). *Fontane-Blätter*, 64, is devoted mainly to contributions on *Effi Briest* and has: G. Radecke, '". . . möge die Firma grünen und blühen": T. F. Briefe an den Sohn Friedrich' (10–63); H. Aust, 'Effi Briest oder: Suchbilder eines fremden Mädchens aus dem Garten' (66–88); R. C. Zimmermann, 'Was hat Fs *Effi Briest* noch mit dem Ardenne-Skandal zu tun? Zur Konkurrenz zweier Gestaltungsvorgaben bei Entstehung des Romans' (89–109); R. Köhne, '*Effi Briest* und die Duellfrage: Zu einem Brief Fs an Maximilian Harden' (110–15); H. Patsch, 'Aischa auf der Schaukel: Zu einer möglichen literarischen Anregung für Fs *Effi Briest*' (116–23); S. Neuhaus, 'Geheimrat Zwickers Affären: Zur Funktion einer Nebenfigur in Fs *Effi Briest*' (124–32); K. Weber, '"Au fond sind Bäume besser als Häuser": Über T. Fs Naturdarstellung' (134–57). There is also a review article by R. Muhs on H. Streiter-Buscher's recent edition of F.'s journalistic work, '*Unechte Korrespondenzen, aber alles echter F.?* Zur Edition von Heide Streiter-Buscher' (200–20), and a reply by Streiter-Buscher, 'Gebundener Journalismus

oder freies Dichterleben?' Erwiderung auf ein Mißverständnis?'
(221–44). The volume is rounded off with a select bibliography of
recent F. literature (246–58).

C. A. Bernd, 'Die Politik als tragendes Strukturelement in Fs *Effi
Briest*', *Fest. Tarot*, 61–71; H. Eilert, 'Fs *Irrungen, Wirrungen*: Zum
Verhältnis von Gespräch und Handlung am Beispiel einer Aphasie
scheiternden Liebe', *ib.*, 111–27. R. Boeschenstein, '"Und die Mutter
kam in Salz"': Muttergestalten in Fs *Vor dem Sturm* und *Effi Briest*',
*Mutter und Mütterlichkeit: Wandel und Wirksamkeit einer Phantasie in der
deutschen Literatur. Festschrift für Verena Ehrich-Haefeli*, ed. I. Roebling et
al., Würzburg, Königshausen & Neumann, 1996, pp. 247–69. B. A.
Jensen, 'Die Entfachung der kindlichen Vitalität in T. Fs *Grete Minde*',
GLL, 50:339–53. R. von Heydebrandt, 'Der literarische Kanon und
die Geschlechterdifferenz: Vorüberlegungen am Beispiel von Gabri-
ele Reuter und T. F.', *JFinL*, 29:86–99, is concerned with Reuter's
Aus guter Familie: Leidensgeschichte eines Mädchens (1895) and F.'s *Effi
Briest*. T. Martins de Oliveira, 'Dienstmädchengestalten in den
Romanen *O primo Bazílio* von Eça de Queirós und *Effi Briest* von
T. F.', *Runa*, 26, 1996:553–61. M. Mandelartz, '"Das erste Kapitel
ist immer die Hauptsache"': Paradies und Sündenfall der Effi Briest',
DB, 98:71–79 (in German). S. Thielking, '"Nur wer im Wohlstand
lebt, lebt angenehm!"': Rührpoesie und Renommage in T. Fs *Frau
Jenny Treibel*', *LitL*, 20, 133–42. Also noted: L. Berg-Ehlers, 'T. F. für
die Schule: Die europäische Dimension im Deutschunterricht', *DD*,
26, 1995:246–55; F. Wippich, 'Aspekte des Umgangs mit einem
Klassiker: F. auf der Sekundarstufe', *DD*, 26, 1995:296–300.

FRANZOS. F. Krobb, '"Auf Fluch und Lüge baut sich kein Glück
auf..."': Karl Emil Franzos' novel *Judith Trachtenberg* and the question
of Jewish assimilation', *ASt*, 5, 1994 [1995]:84–93.

FREYTAG. W. Kunicki, 'Zur Problematik der Polenwahrnehmung
bei G. F. und Gottfried Keller', *GeW*, 119:63–75, considers the
portrayal of Poles in F.'s *Soll und Haben* and Keller's *Kleider machen
Leute*.

GOTTHELF. The bicentenary of G.'s birth in 1997 has produced
virtually no response in the critical literature. P. Utz, 'Gezügeltes
Erzählen: Die beiden Fassungen von Gs *Der Mordiofuhrmann*. Ein
Kalenderblatt zu Gs zweihundertstem Geburtstag', *DVLG*,
71:589–606. W. B. Hess-Lüttich, 'Dialog und Didaxe in Gotthelf's
Uli-Romanen. Mit einem Nachwort zur Mediendebatte', *ABNG*,
40:53–72.

GRABBE. Carl Wiemer, *Der Paria als Unmensch: Grabbe — Genealoge
des Anti-Humanitarismus*, 166 pp., is a collection of five essays in which
the author presents G.'s pessimistic work as the radically modern
inspiration of Walter Benjamin's 'Theologie der Hölle'. *Grabbe-Jb.*,

15, 1996, includes: A. Schulze-Weslarn, 'G. bei Künstlern unserer Zeit' (10–30); F. U. Krause, 'Nachahmung schwarz/weiß: Bilder zu und von Gs *Gothland*' (48–64); F. Höfer, 'Die Rezeption C. D. Gs im Naturalismus 1880 bis 1900' (65–88); R. Müller, 'Gs Einfluß auf Friedrich Dürrenmatts *Es steht geschrieben*' (89–107); M. Morgenroth, 'Die Liebe als Spiel — die Geliebte als Ding: Anmerkungen zur Liebe in Büchners *Leonce und Lena* und Gs *Scherz, Satire, Ironie und tiefere Bedeutung*' (108–29); A. Tullius, 'Gs Auseinandersetzung mit Shakespeares *Hamlet*' (130–42); M. Mitsuaki, 'Die Deutschen und die Julirevolution — C. D. Gs Haltung zu ihrem Ausbruch' (143–50); A. Schulz-Weslarn, 'Die *Gothland*-Inszenierung in Detmold: Nachbemerkung mit Ulf Reiher' (152–56); I. Schleier, 'Theater ohne Gehäuse: Eine bühnenkundliche Assoziation zu Gs *Scherz, Satire, Ironie und tiefere Bedeutung*' (161–66); E. Neuss, 'Zum Familiennamen G.' (167–74); K. Nellner, "Grabbe-Bibliographie 1995 mit Nachträgen' (218–24); Id., 'Freiligrath-Bibliographie 1995 mit Nachträgen' (225–31); Id., 'Weerth-Bibliographie 1995 mit Nachträgen' (232–33).

GRILLPARZER.   Karin Hagl-Catling, *Für eine Imagologie der Geschlechter: Franz Grillparzers Frauenbild im Widerspruch. Entwicklung und Anwendung eines theoretischen Gesamtkonzepts zur Analyse von Frauenbildern unter Berücksichtigung von kulturhistorischen und biographischen Aspekten anhand ausgewählter Beispiele* (EH, 1, 1588), 1996, 312 pp., attempts to reconcile traditional with feminist literary theory in detailed analyses of the portrayal of G.'s heroines Sappho, Medea, Libussa, and Rahel. Sima Kappeler, *First Encounters in French and German Prose Fiction, 1830–1883* (STML, 19), 1996, ix + 228 pp., includes one chapter each on Grillparzer and Stifter: 'Exchange and dispossession: Grillparzer's *Der arme Spielmann*' (91–117), and 'Displacement and recognition: Stifter's *Brigitta*' (119–60). *Fest. Stillfried* includes John Warren, 'The London of Dickens and Grillparzer' (485–98), and W. E. Yates, 'Nestroy zitiert Grillparzer: Zu Nestroys Anspielungskunst' (539–50). O. W. Johnston, 'Erzählte Kriminalität in Gs *Ahnfrau*', *Ethik und Ästhetik: Werke und Werte in der Literatur vom 18. bis zum 20. Jahrhundert: Festschrift für Wolfgang Wittkowski zum 70. Geburtstag*, ed. Richard Fischer (FLK, 52), 1995, pp. 419–44. H. Cerny, '"Vom Silberband der Donau rings umwunden!": Zur Tradition des *Locus amoenus* in F. Gs Lobrede auf Österreich', *Fest. Laufhütte*, 275–82. U. Baur, 'Die Uraufführung von Gs Lustspiel *Weh dem, der lügt!* und die Zensur', Schmidt-Dengler, *Komik*, 126–34. J.-M. Valentin, '"Den vielverschlungenen Knoten der Verwirrung/Zu lösen eines Streichs": Gegenreformatorisches und Aufklärerisches in Gs *Bruderzwist in Habsburg*', *Mélanges Iehl*, 30–52. M. Weber, 'Die Bedeutung des Namens "Jakob" in Gs *Der arme Spielmann*', *Neophilologus*, 81:583–99.

M. Hornung and H. Möcker, 'Das *Goldene Vließ*: Ein altösterreichischer Ritterorden — F. Gs Trilogie: Eine Orthographieproblem', *ÖGL*, 41 : 20–28.

GROTH. The highlight of the *Jahresgabe der K.-G.-Gesellschaft*, 39, is the article by B. Reetz, '"... denn ich habe ihn herzlich lieb gewonnen": Briefe zur Entstehung der Groth-Porträts von Hans Olde' (29–56), which sheds light on the arrangements leading to the painting of the best-known portrait of G. in old age. Other contributions include: U. Bichel, 'K. G. in seiner und in unserer Zeit' (9–24); P. Wapnewski, 'Brunnen, Mond und Stille: Eine Interpretation von Gs "Min Jehann" aus der von Marcel Reich-Ranicki besorgten Reihe "Frankfurter Anthologie' der FAZ' (25–27); J. Hartig and I. Bichel. 'Vor hundert Jahren: K. G. in den Jahren 1896 und 1897' (57–86); F. Schüppen, 'Liebe und Ökonomie: Hauptthemen der Erzählungen von K. G. VI. Von *Witen Slachters* zu *Sandburs Dochder*: Formen des Endes als Deutungen des Anfangs' (87–118).

GRÜN. *Anastasius Grün und die politische Dichtung Österreichs in der Zeit des Vormärz: Internationales Symposion Laibach/Ljubljana 3.-6. November 1994*, ed. A. Janko et al. (Veröffentlichungen des Südostdt. Kulturwerks, Reihe B, Wissenschaftliche Arbeiten, 68), Munich, Vlg Südostdt. Kulturwerk, 1995, 231 pp., contains 14 articles, most of them on the topic of G.'s place in the literary and social context of his time. The two most interesting contributions are those of A. Mádl, 'A. G. und Nikolaus Lenau: Eine Dichterfreundschaft' (55–79), and Z. Szendi, 'Zur Funktion der narrativen Elemente in den "Ungarn-Gedichten" Lenaus' (169–77).

HEBBEL. *Hebbel: Mensch und Dichter im Werk. Jubiläumsband 1995 mit Symposionsreferaten*, ed. I. Koller-Andorf (F.-H.-Ges., Schriftenreihe, 5), Vienna, Eigenverlag der F.-H.-Ges., 1995, 366 pp., is an important publication which has: H.-G. Werner, 'Die ästhetische Rettung des Subjekts durch den Tragödiendichter F. H.' (33–46); M. Ritzer, 'Der funktionalisierte Moloch: Zu Hs Kulturbegriff am Beispiel eines Dramenprojekts' (47–66); P. Leisching, 'Der Gesetzesbegriff im Weltbild F. Hs' (67–78); G. Häntzschel, 'Integration und Verantwortung in F. Hs Tagebüchern aus der Wiener Zeit' (79–90); W. Häusler, '"Der einzige Mensch in Wien, mit dem ich umgehe": Sigmund Engländer — Weggefährte und Antipode F. Hs' (91–105); H. Blume, '"... ein schwer wiegendes Opfer von meiner Seite": Zu Hs Ausgabe *Sämmtlicher Werke* des Ernst Freiherrn von Feuchtersleben. Mit drei unveröffentlichten Briefen aus der Verlagskorrespondenz H. — Carl Gerold' (117–61); R. Andraschek, 'F. H. und Robert Hamerling: Elemente der Rezeption' (163–70); J. Hein, 'H., Nestroy und das Wiener Volkstheater' (171–96); H. Kaiser, 'Subjektivität bei H. und Grillparzer' (197–209); H. Grundmann, 'Zur Aktualität der Lyrik F.

Hs' (211–24); H. Fröschle, 'Hs Verhältnis zu Uhland: Zur Problematik der Wirkung in der Literatur' (243–58); T. Trummer, 'Hebbel im deutschen Roman' (259–67); A. Mantler, 'Kontraste und Parallelen zu Hs Klara in *Maria Magdalena* bei Schnitzler und Horváth' (269–80); G. Scheit, 'Bürgerliches Trauerspiel und patriarchale Staatsaktion: Dramaturgie der Geschlechter bei F. H.' (281–91); R. Fourie, 'Hs Frauengestalten im Prozeß zwischen den Geschlechtern: Eine feministische Perspektive' (293–310); I. Koller-Andorf, 'Hs Dramen auf der Bühne: Kritische Anmerkungen, Regiekonzepte und Auszüge aus Kritiken' (325–38). Andrea Stumpf, **Literarische Genealogien: Untersuchungen zum Werk Friedrich Hebbels* (Epistemata, 229), Würzburg, Königshausen & Neumann, 168 pp.

G. Häntzschel, 'Hs Erfahrung der Fremde', *Ethik und Ästhetik: Werke und Werte in der Literatur vom 18. bis zum 20. Jahrhundert: Festschrift für Wolfgang Wittkowski zum 70. Geburtstag*, ed. Richard Fischer (FLK, 52), 1995, pp. 457–69. H. Kreuzer, 'Die paradoxen Skizzen in den Tagebüchern F. Hs', *ib.*, pp. 471–84. O. Ehrismann, '"Man wird heiliger und reiner, wenn man dieß Gedicht liest." F. H.: Die neue Welt, das Epos', *Fest. Schwob*, 87–98, deals with H.'s epic poem *Mutter und Kind*. *H.-Jb.*, 52, has 10 interesting and substantial articles. Of special importance is that of A. Hummel, '"Mein Buch ist wie eine Feuerkohle in der Tasche." F. Hs Lektüre (I): Lesegewohnheiten' (27–50), who demonstrates just how much and how widely H. read once he had left Wesselburen and gained the necessary means and opportunities. The other contributions are: O. Ehrismann, 'Das Mittelalter und die Philosophie der Geschichte: Zur Funktion der Mediävalismen bei H.' (7–26); U. H. Gerlach, 'Berufung oder Beruf — Dichtung oder Schriftstellerei? Hs Selbstverständnis als Autor' (51–65); D. Dethlefsen, 'Versehrungen: Hs Weg zu sozialer Anerkennung' (67–83); E. Streitfeld, '"Der Umgang mit einem großen Mann ist wie das Wohnen in der Nähe eines feuerspeienden Berges": F. H. und Emil Kuh: Phasen ihrer Beziehung' (85–107); G. Eversberg. 'Storm liest H.: Spuren der H.-Lektüre in Theodor Storms Werk' (109–20); H. Thomé, 'Aporien der "modernen Tragödie": Zur H.-Rezeption der Neuklassik' (121–50); H.-J. Knobloch, 'Hebbel, Un-Hebbel oder Anti-Hebbel? Die H.-Bearbeitungen von Franz Xaver Kroetz' (151–68); S. Nieberle, '"Warum bringen sie denn nicht auch die Musik in Worte. Es wäre doch verständiger": Überlegungen zur Musikauffassung F. Hs' (169–94); R.-R. Wuthenow, 'F. H. als kritischer Leser' (195–208).

HEINE. The bicentenary of H.'s birth has predictably produced an enormous flood of new publications. The Düsseldorf edition of his works, ed. M. Windfuhr, has now been completed with the appearance of vol. 16, *Nachträge und Korrekturen. Register*, ed. M. Tilch et al.,

Hamburg, Hoffmann & Campe, 840 pp. A most welcome and affordable volume for both specialists and students is H. H., *Sämtliche Gedichte*, ed. B. Kortländer, Stuttgart, Reclam, 1117 pp., which contains the entire lyric *œuvre*, including the posthumously published poems, and an extensive commentary. Kortländer has also edited a *Heine-Brevier*, Stuttgart, Reclam, 332 pp. Another useful addition to the Reclam series is H.'s *Zur Geschichte der Religion und Philosophie in Deutschland*, ed. J. Ferner (UB, 2254), 250 pp., with comprehensive notes and a *Nachwort*. H. H., *Deutschland: A Winter's Tale*, trans. T. J. Reed, London, Angel, 185 pp., reprints the text of Reed's translation of 1986, but the original German text has now been added on facing pages. There are 11 pages of explanatory notes and a 15-page introduction. H. H., *Roter König, Grüne Sau: Frivole Gedichte*, ed. J.-C. Hauschild, Cologne, Kiepenheuer & Witsch, 164 pp., reprints 77 of H.'s most erotic and blasphemous poems, the majority of them so offensive to public taste that he did not include them in the collections of verse published during his lifetime — though in truth they seem tame enough now. The poems are followed by a few pages of notes and short essay by the editor.

Jan-Christoph Hauschild and Michael Werner, *'Der Zweck des Lebens ist das Leben selbst': Heinrich Heine. Eine Biographie*, Cologne, Kiepenheuer & Witsch, 697 pp., provide a highly readable and astonishingly detailed account of all aspects of H.'s life from the cradle to the grave. It is clear that the book is aimed at a wide readership as well as the specialist academic one, for there are no footnotes and no references to the secondary literature. The authors' technique is as far as possible to allow H. to speak for himself, hence they build into their text numerous and extensive quotations from H.'s own writings and letters. The effect is to keep the focus at all times firmly on H. himself and to create an exceptionally vivid picture of his life and personality. The emphasis is very much on the poet's biography, though the biographical narrative is interwoven with short, usually undemanding, accounts of his works and with explanations of the cultural and political context within which they were written (political climate of the *Restaurationszeit*, implications of his Jewishness, his love of relatively liberal France). The perennial question of the nature of H.'s final illness is discussed (syphilis is the preferred diagnosis this time) and the intriguing point is made that DNA testing of a lock of his hair may soon provide final proof. This is not a book for those interested in critical interpretations of H.'s writings, but it is a scholarly and readable biography and one of the major publications of the year.

'Ich, Narr des Glücks': Heinrich Heine 1797–1856. Bilder einer Ausstellung, ed. J. A. Kruse, Stuttgart, Metzler, xxiii + 584 pp. + 207 coloured

and 178 monochrome pls, is a companion volume to the H. exhibition which was mounted in Düsseldorf and Paris in May–December 1997 to celebrate the 200th anniversary of H.'s birth. Appropriately, the book is also published simultaneously in French by Éditions du Cerf, Paris. The organization of the exhibition was a huge enterprise, involving a very long list of collaborators and the participation of academic and cultural institutions from many countries. But if the quality of the catalogue is anything to go by, the effort was well rewarded. Metzler deserve warmest congratulations, for this must be one of the most generously illustrated and beautifully produced catalogues of its kind ever published. The format and layout of the book are most attractive, and the quality of the colour printing is of the highest standard. The work is divided into eight thematic sections, each of which combines text and illustrations. The texts, which are written by a wide range of contributors, are of mixed quality and in no case very demanding or ambitious, though this does not matter much since the main interest of the book lies in the illustrations. There are good contributions from leading H. scholars like Edda Ziegler (on H.'s attitude to women) and Markus Winkler (on the Loreley myth), but that of Alice Schwarzer is redundant. The eight sections of the book deal with H.'s biography, his experience of Germany (Düsseldorf, the situation of the Jews), France (the 1848 Revolution, his marriage to Mathilde), and Europe (his many journeys in Germany, France, Poland, England, Holland, and Italy); his view of Nature (the Harz, the North Sea); his religious questing and conversion; his attitude to women; and the history of the Lorelei theme with which his name is most famously associated. All in all, this is an exceptionally attractive book which any Germanist will be delighted to own.

Gerhard Höhn, *Heine-Handbuch: Zeit-Person-Werk*, 2nd rev. edn, Stuttgart, Metzler, xvi + 570 pp., was first published in 1987. J. A. Kruse, *Heine-Zeit*, Stuttgart–Weimar, Metzler, viii + 401 pp., contains 20 articles by this leading H. expert dealing with a wide range of aspects of the poet's life, work, and times. Most of them have been published before but have been revised for this commemorative edition. The four new ones are: 'Herr von Schnabelewopski in Hamburg: H. Hs hansestädtische Reisebilder' (151–61); 'H. und die Provence', dealing with H.'s journey there in 1836 (171–85); 'Poesie der Angst, des Mitleids und des Respekts: Hs Ratten und ihre literarischen Verwandten', concerned with the unpleasant associations and symbolism of these creatures in H.'s poems (288–312); 'Heine trifft Brecht', considering the experience of exile which the two men shared (381–95).

Winkler, *Heine,* has: J. L. Sammons, 'The elusive Romantic: *Die romantische Schule* as evasion and misdirection' (1–14); J. A. Kruse, 'H. und Fouqué: Romantischer Ausgangspunkt mit emanzipierten Folgen' (15–39); R. C. Holub, 'Personal roots and German traditions: The Jewish element in H.'s turn against Romanticism' (40–56); U. Stadler, 'Esoterisch und exoterisch: Popularisierungsversuche bei Jean Paul, Novalis und H. H.' (57–71); J. Brummack, 'Das Narrenmotiv im Werk H. Hs vor dem Hintergrund der deutschen Romantik' (72–85); D. I. Behler, 'H. and early German Romanticism' (86–103); K. Kloocke, 'Madame de Staël, *De l'Allemagne,* H. H., *Die romantische Schule*: Literatur — Poetik — Politik' (104–15); E. Behler, 'H. H. und Madame de Staël zum Thema *De l'Allemagne*' (116–28); A. Seyhan, '"Jede Zeit ist eine Sphynx, die sich in den Abgrund stürzt, sobald man ihr Räthsel gelöst hat": (Re)dressing the Romantic text' (129–43); S. B. Würffel, '"Pflanzt die schwarz-rot-goldne Fahne auf die Höhe des deutschen Gedankens [...]": H. H. und die deutsche Nationalsymbolik' (144–58); G. Hoffmeister, 'Granada und Jerusalem oder "Poesie-Orient" versus Real-Orient: Referenzbeziehungen zwischen H., Arnim und Byron' (159–72); M. Winkler, Weltschmerz europäisch: Zur Ästhetik der Zerrissenheit bei H. und Byron' (173–90); H.-J. Schrader, 'Schnabelewopskis und Wagners *Fliegender Holländer*' (191–224).

Fritz J. Raddatz, *Taubenherz und Geierschnabel: Heinrich Heine. Eine Biographie,* Weinheim–Berlin, Beltz Quadriga, 392 pp., is aimed at a general readership but is nevertheless academically well founded. Albrecht Betz, *Der Charme des Ruhestörers: Heine-Studien, Ästhetik und Politik,* II, Aachen, Rimbaud, 95 pp., is more journalistic than academic in style. M. Reich-Ranicki, *Der Fall Heine,* Stuttgart, Deutsche Verlags-Anstalt, 128 pp., brings together several previously published essays by this lively critic. J. Hermand, *Deutscher, Jude oder Franzose? Heine im internationalen Kontext* (Bibliotheksgesellschaft Oldenburg, 17), Oldenburg, BIS-Vlg, 1995, 31 pp. R. Kreis, *Kafkas 'Prozeß': Das große Gleichnis vom abendländisch 'Verurteilten' Juden. Heine — Nietzsche — Kafka* (Nietzsche in der Diskussion), Würzburg, Königshausen & Neumann, 1996, 95 pp.

H.-Jb., 35, 1996, has: K. H. Kiefer, 'Descamps' *Türkische Patrouille*: Hs Bild vom Orient' (1–22); B. Bauer, '"Nicht alle Hebräer sind dürr und freudlos": H. Hs Ideen zur Reform des Judentums in der Erzählung *Der Rabbi von Bacherach*' (23–54); E. Lutz, 'Der Held in mehrfacher Gestalt: "Der Rabbi von Bacherach" als Held des mythischen Zirkels' (55–65); A. Schirmeisen, 'Hs *Aus den Memoiren des Herren von Schnabelewopski*: Eine parodistische Negation des Bildungsromans?' (66–80); R. E. Cook, '"Citronia" — "Kennst du das Land...?": A riddle of sexuality and desire' (81–112); H. Ferstenberg,

'H. H. und George Canning' (113–27); U. Pongs, 'H. A. Korff und H.' (128–51); G. Weiss, 'Ein Schriftsteller von größtem Talente und ein Mann von ehrenvollem Charakter: Auguste Luchet (1809–1872)' (152–62); M. M. Dobrinac, 'H. H. im ehemaligen Jugoslawien 1945–1981' (163–68); H. T. Siepe, '"Vive la France! quand même …"': H. in Frankreich. Bemerkungen anläßlich eines Essays und einer Edition' (169–75); I. Hermstrüver et al., 'Neue H.-Briefe (Berichtszeitraum 1983–1996)' (176–223); F. Sengle, 'Trommler und Dichter: Zum 175. Geburtstag H. Hs 1972', ed. M. Windfuhr (224–35); T.-R. Feuerhake, 'H.-Literatur 1994–95 mit Nachträgen' (265–80). *H.-Jb.*, 36, has: P. Peters, 'Die Frau auf dem Felsen: Besuch bei Hs Loreley' (1–21); S. Neuhaus, 'Warum sollen keine Poeten nach London fahren? Zur Intention literarischer Reiseberichte am Beispiel von H. Hs *Englischen Fragmenten*' (22–39); D. Arendt, 'H. H.: Aus den Memoiren des Herren von Schnabelewopski oder Ein Pikaro am Jungfernstieg' (40–69); M. Bergengruen, 'Warum Herodias "so kokett zugleich und schmachtend" nickt: Die Ironie als korrektiv der Mimesis im *Atta Troll*' (70–92); H. Czirnich, 'Die "temporelle Bärenhaut": Überlegungen zu den Capita vii und ix aus H. Hs *Atta Troll. Ein Sommernachtstraum*' (93–110); A. Pistiak, '*Bimini*: Eine Lesart' (111–23); A. Del Caro, 'Sendung, Blendung, Nichtvollendung: Heine on Romantic historiography' (124–33); G. Höhn, '"Farceur" und "Fanatiker des Ausdrucks": Nietzsche, ein verkappter Heineaner' (134–52); C. Höpfner, '"Jener Lieder süße Worte": Friederike Kempners Heine-Gedichte' (153–67); H. D. Tschörtner, 'Gerhart Hauptmann und H. H. Mit einem unbekannten Brief' (168–74); H. Baumeister, '"Das Lied der Loreley, meint man, könne nicht mehr gehört werden …": Zu den "Gnaden des souveränen Gedankens" bei Gerhart Hauptmann' (173–76); A. Bauer, 'H. H. und sein Werk in Argentinien' (177–82); W. Zöller, 'H.-Gedenkmünze zum 200. Geburtstag' (183–86); P. Stein, 'Sengles Heine: Eine Entgegnung' (187–93); T. Spreckelsen, '"Denn er ist Romeo und ich bin sein Mercutio!"': Karl Immermanns Schwank *Die Entführung, oder Das Lustspiel ohne Dame*' (194–226); T.-F. Feuerhake, 'H.-Literatur 1995–96 mit Nachträgen' (274–97). *DUS*, 49, is devoted entirely to articles on H. and contains: K. Fingerhut, 'H. als Symptom: Auch eine Einführung in die Literaturdidaktik' (5–18); G. Beste, 'Hs Sicht auf Berlin, mit heutigen Augen gesehen: Unterrichtsvorhaben zu Hs Briefen aus Berlin in einem Profilkurs der 11. Klasse' (19–26); G. Höhn, '(Ver-)Bildungsreisen: Zu Hs Kritik am modernen Tourismus' (27–33); M. Ponsard et al., 'H. europäisch' (34–48); G. Schiavoni, 'H. und die "Blutschuld" der Juden: Über die Erzählung *Der Rabbi von Bacherach*' (49–55); K.-R. Roth, 'H. — Tucholsky: Überlegungen zu einem problemorientierten Brückenschlag' (58–62);

K. Fingerhut and J. Stückrath, '"Wie man H. fressen kann und verdauen": Wolf Biermann im Gespräch' (63–77). Another journal dedicated this year exclusively to work on H. is *RGI*, 9, 1998 [1997], which has: J. Revel, 'Retour sur une histoire: H. entre l'Allemagne et la France' (11–25); M. Espagne, 'H. historien de la culture' (27–45); M. Werner, 'Réflexion et révolution: Notes sur le travail de l'histoire dans l'œuvre de H.' (47–60); J.-C. Hauschild, '"Différentes manières de considérer l'histoire: A propos des réflexions de H. en matière de philosophie de l'histoire dans les années 1830' (61–72); G. Höhn, '"Les salons disent le faux, les tombeaux disent le vrai": H., penseur de l'histoire' (73–87); O. Lämke, 'H., *Lutèce* et le communisme: Une nouvelle conception de l'histoire après 1848?' (89–101); F. Barbier, 'Eugène Renduel, éditeur de H. H.' (103–14); C. Trautmann-Waller, 'Du *Rabbin de Bacherach* aux "Mélodies hébraïques" du *Romancero*: Le judaisme entre science et poésie' (115–28); I. Kalinowski, 'L'histoire, les fantômes et la poésie dans le *Romancero*' (129–42); J.-P. Lefebvre, 'L'assassinat de Wilhelm Wisetzki' (143–49); B. Kortländer, 'H. H. et Annette von Droste-Hülshoff: deux poètes d'Allemagne' (151–65); É. Décultot, 'La réception de H. en France entre 1860 et 1960: Contribution à une histoire croisée des disciplines littéraires' (167–90).

G. Hoffmeister, 'The poet on the margin and in the center: H. H. and the German condition', *MGS*, 20, 1994 [1996]: 18–32. Y. Zhang, 'H. H. und deutsche Professoren', *Im Dialog der Kulturen: Festschrift für Tschong-Dae Kim zu seinem 60. Geburtstag*, ed. Tschong-Young Kim et al., Seoul, Hankuk, 1995, pp. 347–68. Peter U. Hohendahl, 'H. H.: Macht und Ohnmacht des Intellektuellen', *Responsibility and Commitment: Ethische Postulate der Kulturvermittlung. Festschrift für Jost Hermand*, ed. K. L. Berghahn et al. (FLK, 54), 1996, pp. 91–107. C. Stöcker, 'Die Korrespondenz zwischen H. H. und Franz Liszt. Mit einem ungedruckten Brief', *Das Goethe- und Schiller-Archiv 1896–1996: Beiträge aus dem ältesten deutschen Literararchiv*, ed. J. Golz, Weimar, Böhlau, 1996, 337–46. M. Winkler, '". . . exilirt in eine fremde Sprache": Zu einigen Unterschieden zwischen den deutschen und den französischen Fassungen von Hs Schriften über Deutschland', *Zwiesprache: Beiträge zur Theorie und Geschichte des Übersetzens*, ed. U. Stadler et al., Stuttgart, Metzler, 1996, pp. 105–20. Z. Yushu, '*Atta Troll* und Hs Angst vor dem Kommunismus', *Sprache, Literatur und Kommunikation im kulturellen Wandel: Festschrift für Eijiro Iwasaki anläßlich seines 75. Geburtstags*, Tokyo, Dogakusha–Munich, Iudicium, pp. 463–82. S. Belluzzo, 'D'Atta Troll à l'*Invocation de la grande ourse* — remarques sur le symbole de l'ours et quelques-uns de ses avatars de Heine à Ingeborg Bachmann', *Mélanges Iehl*, 317–38. E. Richter, 'Historische und literarische Quellen von Hs Tragödie *Almansor*: Zu ihrer Darstellung in einer historisch-kritischen Edition (HSA)', Schwob, *Edition*, 243–53.

M. C. Foi, '*Die Harzreise*: H. und die Rechtskultur seiner Zeit', *JDSG*, 41:236–55. D. Arendt, 'H. über Lessing oder: "derjenige Schriftsteller, den ich am meisten liebe"', *WW*, 47:204–21. Id., 'Heinrich Heine "Denk ich an Deutschland in der Nacht" oder: Zwischen Patriotismus und Kosmopolitismus', *OL*, 52:301–28. J. Habermas, 'H. H. und die Rolle des Intellektuellen in Deutschland', *Merkur*, 50, 1996:122–37. R. Martin, 'Hs Hymne an die Nacht: Zur Novalis-Rezeption in *Die Stadt Lukka*', *Aurora*, 57:149–73. J. A. Kruse, 'Düsseldorf und H. H.: Skizze einer unendlichen Geschichte', *DUB*, 50:506–13; H. Kaufmann, 'H. H. und Karl Kraus', *ib.*, 514–24. J. Hessing, 'Totgeborene Zeit: Zum 200. Geburtstag H. Hs', *Jüdischer Almanach des Leo Baeck Instituts*, 6, 1998 [1997]:45–58. R. Newman, 'Heine's Aristophanes: Compromise formations and the ambivalence of Carnival', *CL*, 49:227–40, considers the reception of Aristophanes by H. in his correspondence and in *Deutschland. Ein Wintermärchen*. D.-R. Moser, 'H. H.: Ein deutscher Dichter — ein Europäer', *LiB*, 50:36–38. T. Kinkel, 'H. und Goethe', *LiB*, 50:39–46, assesses H.'s changing view of Goethe and his debt to Goethe, paying special attention to H.'s little-known ballet scenario *Der Doktor Faust* (1847). H. Holzbauer, 'H. H. und Bayern', *LiB*, 50:46–49. J. Hein, 'Editorische Überlegungen zu Nestroys Possen und ihre Quellen', Schwob, *Edition*, 223–34. E. Richter, 'Historische und literarische Quellen von Heines Tragödie *Almansor*: Zu ihrer Darstellung in einer historisch-kritischen Edition (HSA)', Schwob, *Edition*, 243–53.

HEYSE. The large Hildesheim reprint edition of P. H., *Gesammelte Werke (Gesamtausgabe)*, ed. M. Bernauer et al., has added *Reihe* 4, vols 1–6, ed. M. Bernauer et al., Hildesheim, Olms, 1995. Vols 1–5 of the new *Reihe* contain photographic reprints of all of H.'s published Novellen that were not included in *Reihen* 1–3 of Petzet's 1924 edition. Vol. 6 reprints the second part of the 1912 edition of H.'s autobiography, *Jugenderinnerungen und Bekenntnisse*, together with the most important passages from the considerably different first edition of 1900. It is planned to bring out two further *Reihen* containing photographic reprints of the remaining dramas and H.'s voluminous translations. When these two *Reihen* appear we shall have in one edition all the works printed in the three collected editions that were published during his lifetime. This will unfortunately still not be a complete edition of H.'s writings, for it will contain none of his letters and diaries and will omit the occasional poems that appeared in various journals but did find their way into any of the collected editions, and it will be in no sense a critical edition. Nevertheless it

will be the best edition that we are likely to have for the foreseeable
future and will provide a very useful basis for future research.
  Ein Gefühl der Verwandtschaft: Paul Heyses Briefwechsel mit Eduard Mörike,
ed. Rainer Hillenbrand, Frankfurt, Lang, 106 pp., publishes the 21
surviving letters, of which nine are from H.'s pen and 12 from
Mörike's. All the letters by H. and three by Mörike are here printed
for the first time. Despite its modest length this is an important
correspondence and it is surprising that it has had to wait so long to
receive the attention it deserves. Although the two men met only
occasionally, their admiration for each other's work and a genuine
personal affection are everywhere evident. Literature is the main
topic of the exchange and there are many references, especially on
H.'s side, to work in progress. It is a measure of Mörike's esteem for
H. that he uncharacteristically took the trouble to make detailed
written comments on the latter's early verse (though H. followed only
some of them). Hillenbrand provides an informative 15-page introduction and some 30 pages of illuminating notes. See p. 809 below
for the publication of the correspondence between Heyse and Holtei.
R. Hillenbrand, 'In die Poesie verbannt: Poetologisches in P. Hs
Novellen', *MGS*, 20, 1994 [1996]: 94–137.
  IMMERMANN.   Peter Hasubek, *Karl Leberecht Immermann: Ein Dichter
zwischen Romantik und Realismus*, Cologne, Böhlau, 1996, x + 289 pp.,
is a collection of essays by the author, most of which have been
printed before. There is however a new one on Immermann and
Tieck. M. Springer, 'Kein Blick ins Offene: Immermanns *Papierfenster
eines Eremiten* und die Restauration', *LiLi*, 27 : 137–47.
  KELLER.   Y.-Y. Zhang, *Verschwiegene und schweigende Individuen im
realistischen Roman: Eine Untersuchung zum 'Grünen Heinrich' und zur Effi
Briest*, Pfaffenweiler, Centaurus, 1996, 211 pp., is a 1995 Bonn
dissertation. G. Niggl, 'G. K.: Dichtung und Politik', *Ethik und Ästhetik:
Werke und Werte in der Literatur vom 18. bis zum 20. Jahrhundert: Festschrift
für Wolfgang Wittkowski zum 70. Geburtstag*, ed. Richard Fischer (FLK,
52), 1995, pp. 485–96. C. Begemann, 'Ein weiter Mantel, doktrinäre
Physiognomisten und eine grundlose Schönheit: Körpersemiotik und
Realismus bei G. K.', *Fest. Laufhütte*, 333–54. H. Thomke, 'Töne und
Mißtöne: Musikalische Motive in G. Ks *Martin Salamander*', *ib.*,
355–66. W. Weber, '". . . allein vor den Werken Gottes zu sitzen . . .":
Bemerkungen zu G. Ks Bericht *Ein bescheidenes Kunstreischen*', *Fest.
Strelka*, 59–64. H. Zeller, 'Ein neuer Weg zur Textkonstitution: Die
Textverwitterung in der historisch-kritischen Keller-Ausgabe', *Eupho-
rion*, 91 : 213–32. T. Plagwitz, 'Tellurische Mädchengestalten in
Gottfried Kellers Romanen: Vom "Meretlein" in *Grünen Heinrich* zum
Märchen im *Martin Salander*', *ABNG*, 40 : 73–91. U. Mahlendorff,
'The crime of punishment: the psychology of child abuse and the

Meretlein incident in G. K.'s *Der grüne Heinrich'*, *GQ,* 70:247–60.
M. Böhler, 'Die falsch besetzte zweite Herzkammer: Innere und
äußere Fremde in G. Ks *Pankraz der Schmoller'*, *Figuren des Fremden in der
Schweizer Literatur*, ed. C. Caduff, Zurich, Limmat, pp. 36–61.
R. Charbon, 'Zweieiige [*sic*] Zwillinge?: Schweizer Schriftsteller und
Deutsches Reich 1871–1914', *ib.*, 109–29, discusses the attitudes
taken to the new Empire by G. K., C. F. Meyer, and the patriotic
Swiss lyricist Ferdinand Schmid (1823–88) who wrote under the
pseudonym Dranmor and is best remembered for his poem 'Eine
Nachtwache'. W. Goetschel, 'Love, sex and other utilities: K.'s
unsettling account', *Narrative Ironies*, ed. A. Prier et al. (Studies in
Comparative Literature, 5), Amsterdam–Atlanta, Rodopi,
pp. 223–35, deals very superficially with *Die Leute von Seldwyla*.

KOMPERT, L. **Der Dorfgeher: Geschichten aus dem Ghetto*, ed. F. Krobb,
Göttingen, Wallstein, 261 pp.

KÜRNBERGER. R. Robertson, 'German idealists and American
rowdies: F. K.'s novel *Der Amerika-Müde'*, *ASt*, 7, 1996:17–35.

LEWALD. *Freundschaftsbriefe an einen Gefangenen: Unbekannte Briefe der
Schriftstellerin Fanny Lewald an den liberalen jüdischen Politiker Johann Jacoby
aus den Jahren 1865 und 1866*, ed. G. Schneider, Frankfurt, Lang, 1996,
x + 228 pp. + 9 pls, prints 30 letters written by L. between 30 August
1865 and 13 March 1866 to the Jewish doctor and politician J. Jacoby,
who had provoked Bismarck's anger by his uncompromising resistance to the latter's high-handed and unconstitutional Indemnity Bill
and been sentenced to six months' imprisonment for treason. Jacoby
was a long-standing personal friend of L.'s — they were both from
Jewish families in Königsberg and shared liberal opinions — and the
letters were intended mainly to keep up Jacoby's spirits during his
captivity. The three main themes of the letters are private affairs (L.
is frank about her marital difficulties), literature, and cultural life,
and — rather surprisingly in the circumstances — politics (after initial
hesitation L. expresses strong indignation at the policy of the Prussian
government). The letters make lively and interesting reading and
convey an impression of L.'s strong and engaging personality. They
were long believed to be missing but were rediscovered several years
ago in the Lewald *Nachlaß* in Berlin. They are here published in full
for the first time, with the editor's extensive and informative
explanatory footnotes and a useful index. The book represents a
valuable contribution to the recent renaissance of interest in this
remarkable woman. F. L., *A Year of Revolutions: Fanny Lewald's
Recollections of 1848*, trans. H. B. Lewis, Providence, RI–Oxford,
Berghahn, 164 pp., provides a translation of most of L.'s *Erinnerungen
aus dem Jahre 1848* (1850) with a 20-page introduction and extensive
explanatory footnotes.

MEYER. The HKA of C. F. M.'s *Sämtliche Werke*, ed. H. Zeller et al., has been completed with the publication of vol. 5, 1, *Gedichte. Apparat zu den Abteilungen VIII und IX*, and vol. 5, 2, *Gedichte. Nachträge. Verzeichnisse. Register zu den Bänden 1–7*, ed. H. Zeller, 1996, Berne, Benteli, 718 pp. H. Zeller, 'Die synoptisch-textgenetische Darstellung: Dafür und dawider', *Editio*, 10, 1996:597–625, draws upon texts by Meyer. P. Sprengel, 'Schlachtfeld Alpen, Schweizer Identität? Kulturkampf als Strukturmodell in C. F. Ms Berglyrik', *GRM*, 46, 1996:450–62. R. Simon, 'Dekonstruktiver Formalismus des Heiligen: Zu C. F. Ms Novellen *Der Heilige* und *Die Versuchung des Pescara*', *ZDP*, 116:224–53.

MÖRIKE. Achim Nuber, *Mehrstimmigkeit und Desintegration: Studien zu Narration und Geschichte in Mörikes 'Maler Nolten'* (EH, 1, 1628), 278 pp. S. Schwabach-Albrecht, 'Die Ehrengabe der Dresdener Schillerstiftung zu Ms 70. Geburtstag: Briefe von Johann Georg Fischer, Eduard Duboc und Eduard Mörike', *JDSG*, 41:21–30. H.-H. Krummacher, 'Der junge M. und die Tradition des Epicediums. Mit einem unbekannten Gedicht auf den Tod der württembergischen Königin Katharina', *Fest. Tarot*, 267–89.

NESTROY. The HKA of N.'s *Sämtliche Werke*, ed. Jürgen Hein et al., Vienna, Deuticke (formerly Jugend und Volk), has added *Stücke*, 18, 2, *Die Papiere des Teufels oder Der Zufall. Die Ereignisse im Gasthofe*, ed. J. Hein, 1996, xvi + 352 pp.; *Stücke* 23, 2, *Der Unbedeutende*, ed. J. Hein, 1995, xvi + 560 pp.; *Stücke*, 27, 1, *Der alte Mann mit der jungen Frau*, ed. U. Helmensdorfer, xx + 572 pp.; *Stücke* 27, 2, *Höllenangst*, ed. J. Hein, xvi + 352 pp.; *Stücke*, 28, 1, *Der holländische Bauer*, ed. W. Obermaier, xxi + 537 pp. Despite the change of publisher the books retain the same attractive format and distinctive blue cover, all are illustrated, and all are copiously and expertly annotated. Eva Reichmann, *Konservative Inhalte in den Theaterstücken Johann Nestroys* (Ep, 158), 1995, 233 pp., in a 1994 Bielefeld dissertation rejects the conventional view that N.'s plays are essentially light-hearted fun written with no ulterior political or social purpose or that, if he has a political point at all, he should be seen as 'progressiv-liberal' (p. 13), a left-wing sympathizer with the cause of social revolution. Although many of his plays and letters may seem to support such an interpretation, Reichmann argues that the general picture that emerges is of a man with conservative views. While he favoured some reforms such as the abolition of the censorship that gave him so much trouble, he basically believed in the 'natural' conservative social order of the *Restaurationszeit*. Thus the feudal aristocracy and their loyal servants are normally portrayed favourably while *parvenu* members of the *Bürger* class, who care only about money and personal advantage (p. 25), are presented in a bad light. Most of the thesis is then devoted in support of this argument to an examination of the master-servant relationship and the importance of money as a dramatic motive in N.'s plays. Although Reichmann analyses many texts to back up her case, she has a tendency to ignore awkward facts that do not suit her. If her argument is to prevail, it will require corroboration by other researchers. Volker Mergenthaler, *Medusa meets Holofernes: Poetologische, semiologische und intertextuelle Diskursivierung von Enthauptung*, Berne, Lang, 153 pp., contains a discussion of Nestroy's *Judith und Holofernes*. *Nestroyana*, 15.3–4, 1995, includes: G. Magenheim, 'N. und Bäuerle, oder: Die beinahe uneigennützige Dankbarkeit' (93–95); F. Walla, '"Curiose Speiserln" in der Wiener Stadt- und Landesbibliothek: Ein Originalbeitrag zu Ns *Dreyßig Jahre aus dem Leben eines Lumpen*' (96–101); Id., 'Zeitungslesen als Inspiration: Ein kleiner Beitrag zu Vorlagenforschung bei N.' (102–11); H. Aust, 'Der Zopf oder Ns Requisitenspiel mit Zeit und Geschichte' (112–21); E. Reichmann, 'Gebrauch und Funktion von Klischees im Wiener Volkstheater und bei N.' (122–30); H. J. Koning, 'N. in Holland: Zur Rezeption seiner Stücke auf den holländischen Bühnen des 20. Jahrhunderts' (131–37); K. Ilgenfritz, 'J. N. und Ludwig Ganghofer: Eine Betrachtung anläßlich des 75. Todestages von Ludwig Ganghofer. 24. Juli 1920–24. Juli 1995' (138–43). *Nestroyana*, 16, 1996, has: M. Draudt, 'Zum Lokalkolorit in den Shakespeare-Parodien von Perinet, Kringsteiner und Meisl' (5–23); J. Hein, '"... bin Dichter nur der Posse": Ein Albumblatt Ns aus dem Jahr 1846' (24–25); W. E. Yates, 'Paul de Kock und N.: Zu Ns Bearbeitung französischer Vorlagen' (26–39); J. Hein, '"Nestroy und Konsorten" (Friedrich Engels) — "Deathless Nestroy" (Thornton Wilder): Notizen zur N.-Rezeption II' (40–51); J. Benay, 'Volksästhetischer Humanismus in der Spätdramatik Friedrich Kaisers' (52–65); G. Magenheim, 'Kostverächter war er keiner! Adolf Bäuerle und die nicht immer holde Weiblichkeit' (83–88); H. J. Koning, 'Raimund in Holland: Zur Rezeption seiner Stücke auf den holländischen Bühnen' (89–96); R. Theobald, 'Versteckte N.-Briefe: Eine Anregung zur Nachlese' (97–99); K. Stierstorfer, 'Oxenfords *A Day Well Spent* als Quelle von Ns *"Jux"*: Eine Neubewertung' (100–11); W. Hettche, 'Karl von Holtei und Paul Heyse: Elf bisher unbekannte Briefe' (112–31). Ten of the letters are from Holtei to Heyse, one from Heyse to Holtei; all date from the period May–November 1871. *Nestroyana*, 17, has: R. Reutner, 'Comparatio delectat: Zur rhetorischen Figur des Vergleichs bei Kringsteiner und N.' (5–12); S. P. Schleichl, 'N. den Österreichern! Oder: Darf Jürgen Hein N. edieren?' (13–23); G. Waidelich, 'Dokumente zu Ns Amsterdamer Engagement in Korrespondenzberichten über das dortige deutsche Theater' (24–38); A. Gulielmetti, '*Häuptling Abendwind* und *Präsident Abendwind*: N. und Elfriede Jelinek'

(39–49); R. Theobald, 'Raimund, Nestroy und Carl in der Theatersammlung Rainer Theobald: Ein Bestandsverzeichnis' (50–65); J. Benay, 'Theater im *kupferne[n] Zeitalter. Eine Wohnung ist zu vermiethen ... Mehrere Wohnungen zu vermiethen!* (Roche/Duflot, Angely, Malß, Nestroy' (77–97); R. Reuter, 'Idiolektal bedingte Dialektwörter bei Friedrich Kaiser — eine literarisch-dialektologische Quisquilie' (134–40). There is also a facsimile of the original edition of Angely's play which is discussed by Benay, 'L. Angely, "Wohnungen zu vermiethen!"' (98–133).

Also noted: H.-P. Ecker, '"Hausherrn haben noch selten hoffnungslos geliebt": Werttheoretische Betrachtungen zur Konfliktgestaltung und Gerechtigkeitsauffassung in Komödien (nicht nur) von N.', *Fest. Laufhütte*, 319–32; W. E. Yates, 'Sex in the suburbs: N.'s comedy of forbidden fruit', *MLR*, 92:379–91; G. Stieg, 'Ns Wagner-Parodien', Schmidt-Dengler, *Komik*, 135–44; J. Hein, 'Editorische Überlegungen zu Ns Possen und ihren Quellen', Schwob, *Edition*, 223–34; E. Kawano, 'Satire und Geschichte: Über Karl Kraus' Essay *Nestroy und die Nachwelt*', *DB*, 98:65–73 (in German); F. Walla, '"O Häuser! Häuser! Eure Macht ist groß! — Hausherrn haben noch selten hoffnungslos geliebt." Wien in Literatur und Geschichte: Die Rolle des Hausherrn bei N.' *ÖGL*, 41:334–45.

NIETZSCHE. *The Cambridge Companion to Nietzsche*, ed. B. Magnus et al., CUP, 1996, x + 403 pp., contains much that will be of interest to Germanists. Paul Bishop, *The Dionysian Self: C. J. Jung's Reception of Friedrich Nietzsche* (Monographien und Texte zur Nietzsche-Forschung, 30), Berlin, de Gruyter, 1995, xvi + 411 pp., is a detailed and penetrating study of the impact of N.'s thought on Jung's psychology, but only marginally relevant to Germanists. Another good piece of work, but one which is again of only marginal relevance, is Douglas Smith, *Transvaluations: Nietzsche in France, 1872–1972*, OUP, 1996, xiv + 250 pp. Rudolf Kreis, **Nietzsche, Wagner und die Juden*, Würzburg, Königshausen & Neumann, 1995, 227, pp. Ernst Behler, *Ironie und literarische Moderne*, Paderborn, Schöningh, 336 pp., has a chapter on 'Nietzsche und das Spiel der Masken'. David F. Krell, *Infectious Nietzsche*, Bloomington, Indiana U. P., 1996, xviii + 281 pp., is a collection of essays on N. about half of which have been published before.

Nietzsche-Studien, 26, includes: G. Gritzmann, 'Ns Lyrik als Ausdruckskunst: Poetisch und stilistisch konstitutive Merkmale in Ns 6. "Dionysos-Dithyrambus" *Die Sonne sinkt*' (34–71); C. Niemeyer, 'Ns rhetorischer Antisemitismus' (139–64); J. Salaquarda, 'Die *Fröhliche Wissenschaft* zwischen Freigeisterei und neuer "Lehre"' (164–83); D. Collins, 'On the aesthetics of the deceiving self in N., Pindar and Theognis' (276–99); D. Fuchs, '*Der Wille zur Macht*: Die Geburt des

"Hauptwerks" aus dem Geiste des N.-Archivs' (384–404); A. Fambrini, 'Ola Hannson und Georg Brandes: Einige Bemerkungen über die erste Rezeption Ns' (421–40). Gérald Froidevaux, 'La réception de Nietzsche dans les revues romandes vers 1900', *ColH*, 24, 1996 [1997]: 95–107, traces the developing interest in N. in French-speaking Switzerland.

M.-L. Haase, 'Todesarten: "Wenn Götter sterben..."' Gottes Tod in Ns *Also sprach Zarathustra*', *Das Goethe- und Schiller-Archiv 1896–1996: Beiträge aus dem ältesten deutschen Literaturarchiv*, ed. J. Golz, Weimar, Böhlau, 1996, pp. 395–414. Anette Horn, 'Immoralität als Gedankenexperiment: Musils *Törleß* und Nietzsches Machtbegriff', *AGJSG*, 24, 1996 [1997]: 65–80. E. Schaffer, 'Philosophie und Philologie bei N.: Neuere Tendenzen der N.-Forschung', *DVLG*, 71: 635–46. M. Wischke, 'Der Kampf der Moral mit den Grundinstinkten des Lebens: Über eine Ambivalenz im Perspektivismus F. Ns', *WB*, 43: 394–403. K. Zittel, 'Von den Dichtern: Quellenforschung versus Intertextualitätskonzepte, dargestellt anhand eines Kapitels aus Friedrich Nietzsches *Also sprach Zarathustra*', Schwob, *Edition*, 315–31.

OTTO-PETERS, LOUISE.   G. K. Friesen, '"Zählen Sie immer auf mich, wenn es sich um Verstandenwerden handelt": Briefe von Louise Otto-Peters an Karl Gutzkow', *Jb. der Internationalen Bettina von Arnim Gesellschaft*, 6–7, 1994–95 [1996]: 80–106. *Louise Otto-Peters: Ihr literarisches und publizistisches Werk. Katalog zur Ausstellung*, ed. J. Ludwig et al. (Louiseum, 2), Leipzig U. P., 1995, 144 pp. H. G. Morris-Keitel, 'Not "until earth is paradise": Louise Otto's refracted feminine ideal', *WGY*, 12, 1996: 87–99.

RAABE.   Rosemarie Schillemeit, **Antikes im Werk Wilhelm Raabes und andere Beiträge zur Raabe-Philologie*, Göttingen, Vandenhoeck & Ruprecht, vii + 211 pp. Peter O. Arnds, *Wilhelm Raabe's 'Der Hungerpastor' and Charles Dickens's 'David Copperfield': Intertextuality of Two Bildungsromane* (NASNCGL, 20), xi + 191 pp., shows how Raabe borrowed much of his plot and characters from Dickens. H. V. Geppert, 'W. R.: *Stopfkuchen. Eine See- und Mordgeschichte*', *Große Werke der Literatur*, ed. H. V. Geppert, vol. 4, *Eine Ringvorlesung an der Universität Augsburg 1994–95*, Tübingen, Francke, 1995, pp. 175–87. K. Grätz, 'Erbe und Sammler in W. Rs *Wunnigel*: Der Zerfall einer literarhistorischen Allianz', *ZDP*, 116: 525–44. *R.-Jb.*, 38, has: G. Kaiser, 'Erlösung Tod: Eine Unterströmung des 19. Jahrhunderts in Rs *Unruhige Gäste* und Meyers *Die Versuchung des Pescara*' (1–17); M. Winkler, 'Die Ästhetik des Nützlichen in *Pfisters Mühle*: Problemgeschichtliche Überlegungen zu W. Rs Erzählung' (18–39); W. Hettche, 'Raabennest und Adlerhorst: Aus dem Briefwechsel zwischen W. R. und Max Adler' (40–71); J. Hessing, 'Verlustmeldungen: *Zum wilden Mann* — drei Interpretationen' (72–83); C. Liebrand, 'Wohltätige

Gewalttaten? Zu einem Paradigma in Rs *Stopfkuchen*' (84–102); R. Haas, 'Einige Überlegungen zur Intertextualität in Rs Spätwerk. Am Beispiel der Romane *Das Odfeld* und *Die Akten des Vogelsangs*' (103–22); R. Hohl Trillini, 'Stimmengewirr aus schwierigen Zeiten: Erzählen über schlimme Frauen bei R. und Grimmelshausen' (123–46); C. Laumont, 'Aspekte allegorischen Erzählens im späten Realismus: W. R. im Vergleich mit C. F. Meyer' (147–60); W. Dittrich, 'R.-Bibliographie 1997' (233–39).

RAIMUND. E. Schwarz, 'Raimunds *Der Diamant des Geisterkönigs* und Hofmannsthals *Phantasie über ein Raimundsches Thema*', pp. 56–67 of *Weltbürger — Textwelten: Helmut Kreutzer zum Dank*, ed. L. Bodi et al., Frankfurt, Lang, 1995, 414 pp.

RIEHL. C. Schwarz, 'Wilhelm Heinrich Riehls kulturgeschichtliche Novellen', *LiB*, 50:9–25, reassesses the reputation of R. on the centenary of his death.

RÜCKERT. *Gestörte Idylle: Vergleichende Interpretationen zur Lyrik Friedrich Rückerts*, ed. M.-R. Uhrig, Würzburg, Ergon, 1995, 207 pp., contains 12 contributions in which poems of R. are compared with poems of other lyricists — most of them his contemporaries or near-contemporaries — in an attempt to uncover the true nature of his verse and clear away some of the over-hasty assumptions that still commonly obscure the understanding of him. He is in the opinion of the editor most accurately seen as 'ein bisher zu Unrecht vernachlässigter Indikator des Umbruchs zwischen Biedermeier und Bourgeoisie' (p. 10). D. Wittmann-Klemm (13–18) compares Brentano's 'Hör', es klagt die Flöte wieder' with R.'s 'Wie ist die Welt von Blumen voll und Tönen'; H.-U. Wagner (19–39) considers poems by R. and Eichendorff on the subject of the death of children; A. Hummel (41–62) compares R.'s 'Beatus ille' with Platen's 'Amalfi'; C. Haas (63–73) examines R.'s 'Amara' sonnet and Heine's 'Mein Herz, mein Herz ist traurig'; R.-B. Essig (75–92) compares R.'s Um Mitternacht' with Droste-Hülshoff's 'Durchwachte Nacht'; G. Riedel (93–107) looks at R.'s 'Parabel' and Lenau's 'Drei Zigeuner'; R. Dove (109–23) considers two poems written by R. and Mörike in old age; D. Gelbrich (125–42) compares R.'s 'Von Büblein und Buben' with other poems for children; J. Dirksen (143–57) looks at the political implications of R.'s 'Um mich her in weitem Wogen' and Hebbel's 'Nachtlied'; M.-R. Uhrig (159–69) compares R.'s 'Abendlied eines Wanderers' with Storm's 'Meeresstrand'; J. Barth (171–84) examines the motif of the water nymph in R. and Gottfried Keller; and F. Almai (185–201) considers the treatment of autumn in R.'s 'Herbsthauch' and Franz Werfel's 'Lied'.

SAAR. The HKA of F. v. S., *Kritische Texte und Deutungen*, ed. K. K. Polheim et al., Tübingen, Niemeyer (formerly Bouvier, Bonn), has added vol. 8, *Hymen*, ed. N. Nowak, 261 pp. F. v. S., *Wiener Elegien*, ed. K. Wagner, Vienna, Deuticke, 79 pp. + 21 monochrome pls, is a bibliophile edition of S.'s best-known lyric work. It reproduces the 15 poems of the cycle together with six more that celebrate Viennese notables like Radetsky and Grillparzer. The photographs give an impression of the contrasting sides of life in contemporary Vienna, or provide facsimiles of some of the pages of S.'s manuscript. The editor adds a brief but scholarly *Nachwort*. Ernst Kobau, *'Rastlos zieht die Flucht der Jahre …': Josefine und Franziska von Wertheimstein — Ferdinand von Saar*, Vienna, Böhlau, 728 pp. + 17 pls. I. Foster, 'F. v. S.'s *Doktor Trojan*: Politics, medicine and myth', *ASt*, 7, 1996:47–60. H.-J. Gerigk, 'Wo beginnt der Kitsch? Turgenjews *Frühlingsfluten* und ihre Varianten *Eugene Pickering* (Henry James), *Ginevra* (F. v. S.) und *Luischen* (Thomas Mann)', *Fest. Strelka*, 511–17.

SACHER-MASOCH.   Holger Rudloff, *Gregor Samsa und seine Brüder: Kafka — Sacher-Masoch — Thomas Mann*, Würzburg, Königshausen und Neumann, 102 pp. M. Sauter, 'S.-Ms *Venus im Pelz*: Emanzipation oder Dämonisierung der Frau?', *MAL*, 30:39–47.

SCHLÖGL.   Jo Ann M. Fuess, *The Crisis of Lower Middle Class Vienna, 1848–92: A Study of the Works of Friedrich Schlögl* (Austrian Culture, 13), NY, Lang, 120 pp., gives a competent account of Viennese social and cultural life in the middle and later years of the 19th c. as it is reflected in the *Wiener Skizzen* of the minor civil servant and feuilletonist Friedrich Schlögl (1821–92). After outlining the nature and the unique importance of the feuilleton in Vienna she analyses S.'s views on the social life of the city (with special emphasis on its taverns and tobacco shops), family life and education, the role of an entrenched and over-influential Church, and the still lively but declining tradition of the *Volkstheater*. She is interested in S. primarily as a social and cultural commentator, as the title of her book indicates, and ignores the question of his language and style, stating rather too readily in her conclusion that 'S.'s main contribution lay not in stylistic invention, but in choice of topics and his social perspective' (p. 93). That the way in which he uses language is certainly worth studying will be evident to anyone who dips into F.S., *Wiener Blut und Wiener Luft: Skizzen aus dem alten Wien*, ed. K. Rossbacher et al., Salzburg–Vienna, Residenz, 255 pp. The book reproduces 24 of the sketches drawn from the collections *Wiener Blut* (1873), *Wiener Luft* (1875), and *Wienerisches* (1883). They give a good impression of the humour and satire that made S. popular with the middle-class public of his time. The editor appends a (very necessary!) glossary and a short *Nachwort*.

SEALSFIELD (KARL POSTL).   *Neue Sealsfield-Studien: Amerika und Europa in der Biedermeierzeit*, ed. F. Schüppen (Schriftenreihe der Charles-Sealsfield-Gesellschaft, 7), Stuttgart, M & P, 1995, 493 pp., publishes the proceedings of a conference held in Marbach in 1993 to mark the bicentenary of S.'s birth. An attempt is made to situate him in the intellectual, political, and literary context of the *Biedermeierzeit*. The 22 contributions, which are of mixed quality, cover a wide range of topics dealing with his biography, his religious and political views (attitude to slavery in America), his journalistic writing, his novels, his views of the British, the Germans, and the French, and his reception both by contemporaries in the 19th c. and by modern critics (notably F. Sengle). *Zwischen Louisiana und Solothurn: Zum Werk des Österreich-Amerikaners Charles Sealsfield*, ed. Joseph P. Strelka (New Yorker Beiträge zur Österreichischen Literaturgeschichte, 6), Berne, Lang, 228 pp., publishes the proceedings of a conference held in Albany, NY, in 1992. The six most valuable contributions are concerned with aspects of S.'s narrative fiction: K. Krolop, 'C. Ss Poetik des Romans' (73–92); W. Kriegsleder, 'Zwischen Goethe und Balzac: C. Ss *Morton oder die große Tour*' (101–18); G. Marahrens, 'Über C. Ss Roman *Neue Land- und Seebilder: Die deutsch amerikanischen Wahlverwandschaften*' (119–59); A. Ritter, 'Agrardemokratische Botschaft und die gemiedene Stadt: C. Ss erzählerische Konsequenzen in seinem Roman *Das Kajütenbuch*' (161–84); J. P. Strelka, 'Österreichische Perspektiven Amerikas: C. Ss *Prärie am Jacinto*' (185–207); K. Weissenberger, 'Handlung, Bildlichkeit und Sprachrhythmus in *Süden und Norden*: Ein Kaleidoskop des Magischen' (209–24). Other articles deal with aspects of S.'s biography and politics. J. L. Sammons, 'An Austrian Jacksonian: C. S.'s political evolution 1829–1833', *ASt*, 7, 1996:3–13. A. Reiter, 'Austrophobia as it is: C. S., Thomas Bernhard and the art of exaggeration', *ib.*, 166–77.

SPINDLER, CARL. *Der Jesuit: Charaktergemälde aus dem ersten Viertel des achtzehnten Jahrhunderts. Roman in drei Bänden*, ed. M. Schardt (Edition deutschsprachiger Texte des 18. und 19. Jahrhunderts, 1), Paderborn, Igel, 1996, 369 pp.

STIFTER. The HKA of S.'s *Werke und Briefe*, ed. A. Doppler et al., has added vol. 8.1, *Schriften zu Literatur und Theater*, ed. W. M. Bauer, Stuttgart, Kohlhammer, 361 pp. A. S., *Die Mappe meines Urgroßvaters: Letzte Fassung*, ed. Alexander Stillmark (Manesse Bibliothek der Weltliteratur), Zurich, Manesse, 431 pp., is a most handsomely produced little volume and a welcome addition to Manesse's attractive series. Stillmark's 15-page *Nachwort* neatly situates the story in the context of S.'s life and work and in the wider context of 19th-c. German literature.

Adalbert Stifter. Studien zu seiner Rezeption und Wirkung. 1. 1868–1930. Kolloquium, 1, ed. Johann Lachinger (Schriftenreihe des A.-S.-Instituts, 39), Linz, A.-S.-Institut des Landes Oberösterreich, 1995, 262 pp., publishes the proceedings of a 1986(!) Linz conference. It has 13 contributions, most of them by leading Stifter scholars. O. Gutjahr, 'Das "sanfte Gesetz" als psychohistorische Erzählstrategie in A. Ss *Brigitta*', *Psychoanalyse und die Geschichtlichkeit von Texten*, ed. J. Cremerius et al. (*FLG*, 14), 1995, pp. 285–305. W. Wittkowski, 'Heimat genügt nicht: Ss Nachsommerprinzip, besonders bei den Erzählungen *Zuversicht* und *Das alte Siegel*', *MAL*, 29, 1996:75–100. A. Stillmark, 'A. S.: *The Eclipse of the Sun*', *Fest. Strelka*, 3–10. E. Tunner, 'Der komische Kauz: Tiburius Kneigt in Ss *Waldsteig*: Eine andere Art, S. zu lesen', Schmidt-Dengler, *Komik*, 145–54. H. Ragg-Kirkby, '"Äußeres, Inneres, das ist alles eins": S.'s *Der Nachsommer* and the problem of perspectives', *GLL*, 50:323–38. M. Ansel, 'Die künstlerische Vollendung Ss: Die Historisierung literarischer Wertung in der junghegelianischen Publizistik', *ZDP*, 116:500–24. K. Grätz, 'Traditions-schwund und Rekonstruktion der Vergangenheit im Zeichen des Historismus: Zu A. Ss *Narrenburg*', *DVLG*, 71:606–34. B. Knauer, 'Im Rahmen des Hauses: Poetologische Novellistik zwischen Revolution und Restauration (Goethe, Arnim, Tieck, E. T. A. Hoffmann, Stifter)', *JDSG*, 41, 140–69. J. Endres, 'Unerreichbar nah: Zur Bedeutung der Goetheschen *Novelle* für Ss Erzählkunst', *JDSG*, 41:256–94.

STORM. Regina Fasold, *Theodor Storm* (SM, 304), viii + 222 pp., is a great improvement on the tendentious and unsatisfactory volume of H. Vinçon (1973) which it replaces. Fasold is certainly helped by the fact that she has nearly three times as much space at her disposal as Vinçon had, but she needs it all given the large amount of work that has been done on S. in the past quarter-century. The book is very clearly and economically laid out so that the reader is able to access quickly and easily the great wealth of information that it contains. It is divided into three main parts, with a well-judged amount of space devoted to each. The first part has 65 pages on S.'s biography, the second 100 pages on his lyric poetry and Novellen, and the third 10 pages on such matters as the manuscripts and correspondence. All the bibliographical information, which takes account primarily of work published in the last 25 years, is relegated to a concluding section nearly 40 pages long. What emerges clearly from the book is the extent to which critics have played ideological games with S. — Stuckert, Vinçon, and in recent years David Jackson have all had their hobby-horses to ride. (They get away with it only because S. was not in the academic sense a rigorous thinker or scholar and the roots of his *Weltbild*, apart from personal experience, are genuinely hard to identify.) In this reviewer's opinion Jackson's speculative and unnecessary argument that S. was deeply influenced by Feuerbach has been pushed much too hard and done significant damage to S. scholarship. Fasold too seems to be unconvinced by it, for she tell us 'Jackson nimmt mit Recht an, daß sich Storm mit Feuerbach bereits vor 1848 beschäftigte' (p. 107) and then immediately qualifies her statement in the very next sentence with her reference to 'einer möglichen Feuerbach-Rezeption'!

Schriften der T.-S.-Ges., 46, contains: K. E. Laage, '"Culpa patris"': Zur Frage nach der Schuld des Vaters in Ss Novelle *Carsten Curator*' (7–12); W. Hettche, 'Alexander Julius Schindler (Julius von der Traun): Briefe an T. S.' (13–69); P. Goldammer, 'T. S. und Elise Polko: Ein Nachtrag. Mit einem unbekannten Brief Storms an Hans von Schellendorf' (71–75); J. Pizer, 'Mit wem ging T. S. spazieren? G. E. Lessing, Erich Schmidt und *Auf der Universität*' (77–83); W. Hettche, 'Neues zur Beziehung zwischen Raabe und Storm' (85–87); H.-S. Hansen, '"Denn die Vernichtung ist auch was wert"': Einige Überlegungen zu einem rätselhaften Vers von T. S.' (89–94); W. Zimorski, 'Neuentdeckte Musikalien der Storm-Familie: Ein Forschungsbericht' (95–98); K. E. Laage, 'K. H. Keck, "Storm-Stiftung zum Wohle der Arbeiter aus Anlaß des *Doppelgängers*"' (99–104); R. Leroy and E. Pastor, 'Redliche versus unredliche Attacke: Eine Replik' (105–06); E. Jacobsen, 'S.-Bibliographie' (107–15).

A. Cozic, 'Histoires de fantômes contées au coin du feu: Fonctionnement et fonctions du fantastique chez T. S. A propos du recueil *Am Kamin*', *Mélanges Iehl*, 163–90. J.-J. Pollet, 'Maisons hantées: *Das öde Haus, Bulemanns Haus, Das unbewohnte Haus*', *ib.*, 146–62. P. Wapnewski, 'Diese grünen Träume oder: Der Schwärmer im Feldlager. Zu T. Ss Novelle *Ein grünes Blatt*', *Euphorion*, 91:183–205.

UHLAND. W. Scheffler, 'L. U. privat: Der wohl letzte Nachlaßbestand aus Familienbesitz. Mit vier erstveröffentlichten Briefen des Dichters', *JDSG*, 41:11–20.

WAGNER. Franz W. Beidler, *Cosima Wagner-Liszt: Der Weg zum Wagner-Mythos. Ausgewählte Schriften des ersten Wagner-Enkels und sein unveröffentlichter Briefwechsel mit Thomas Mann*, ed. D. Borchmeyer, Bielefeld, Pendragon, 428 pp., is one of the most fascinating publications of the year. Beidler, until now an almost forgotten figure, was W.'s first grandchild, the son of Cosima's daughter Isolde who was legally regarded as the daughter of Hans von Bülow but whose real father was in fact Wagner. Beidler devoted much of his life to the writing of an unfinished biography of his grandmother Cosima, the main aim of which was to undo what he regarded as her damaging falsification of W.'s image and the dangerous influence of the Bayreuth circle on W. reception, for he believed that these had contributed materially to the ideological force of National Socialism. Beidler's biography, here published for the first time, occupies just over half the book. To it Borchmeyer has added a selection of other, shorter writings by Beidler on Cosima and W. and Beidler's previously unpublished correspondence with Thomas Mann. A lengthy and informative *Nachwort* (over 60 pages) concludes the book. The scholarship here on offer is of the highest order, as one would expect from this leading W. expert, so that it seems almost churlish to complain about the lack of an index. Daniel Schneller, *Richard Wagners 'Parsifal' und die Erneuerung des Mysteriendramas in Bayreuth: Die Vision des Gesamtkunstwerks als Universalkultur der Zukunft*, Berne, Lang, 373 pp., discusses the religious and cultural aspects of the work and interprets it as a modern mystery play. Jans-Joachim Bauer, **Richard Wagner: Sein Leben und Wirken oder die Gefühlwerdung der Vernunft*, Berlin, Propyläen, 1995, 640 pp. *Richard Wagner, 'Der Ring des Nibelungen': Ansichten des Mythos*, ed. U. Bermbach et al. (Metzler Musik), Stuttgart, Metzler, 1995, xii + 195 pp., has 14 contributions on various aspects of the tetralogy. R. Meyer-Kalkus, 'R. Ws Theorie der Wort-Tonsprache in *Oper und Drama* und *Der Ring des Nibelungen*', *Athenäum*, 6, 1996: 153–95. A. Le Feuvre, 'Lé récitant et son double: Villiers de l'Isle-Adam et R. W.', *RLC*, 71: 293–306, discusses W.'s reception by the French writer. P. Levesque, 'The double-edged sword: Anti-Semitism and anti-Wagnerianism in Thomas Mann's *Wälsungenblut*,' *GSR*, 20: 9–21. P. Russell, 'Sexuality, self-division and guilt: W.'s *Tannhäuser* 150 years on', *AUMLA*, 87: 21–36. K. Peter, 'Nürnbergs krumme Gassen: Zum Deutschlandbild bei Wackenroder, Tieck und R. W.', *Aurora*, 57: 129–47. *NGC*, 69, is devoted entirely to W. and has: S. Zizek, '"There is no sexual relationship": W. as a Lacanian' (7–35); C. von Braun, 'R. W.: A poisonous drink' (37–51); M. A. Weiner, 'Reading the ideal' (53–83); S. Bernstein, 'In Formel: W. und Liszt' (85–97); J. Deathridge, 'Post-mortem on Isolde' (99–126); D. J. Levin, 'Reading Beckmesser reading: Antisemitism and aesthetic practice in *The Mastersingers of Nuremberg*' (127–46); E. Bronfen, 'Kundry's laughter' (147–61); M. P. Steinberg, 'Music drama and the end of history' (163–80); A. Huyssen, 'Monumental seduction' (181–200).

WEERTH. B. Plachta, 'Das Feuilleton als Verbrecher! Georg Ws Roman *Leben und Thaten des berühmten Ritters Schnapphahnski* zwischen Quellendokumentation und Quelleninterpretation', Schwob, *Edition*, 235–42.

LITERATURE, 1880–1945

By D. H. R. JONES, *Lecturer in German in the University of Keele*

(This survey covers the years 1996 and 1997)

I. GENERAL

LITERARY HISTORIES AND SURVEYS. Brenner, *Literaturgeschichte*, contains chapters on 'Moderne' (189–221), 'Weimarer Republik' (223–45), and '"Drittes Reich" und Exil' (247–68). Herbert Lehnert, *Geschichte der deutschen Literatur vom Jugendstil bis zum Expressionismus*, Stuttgart, Reclam, 1996, 1077 pp., is a reprint of the comprehensive survey of literature from 1890 to 1918 which was published in 1978. As L. states in the introduction these dates coincide with the reign of Friedrich Wilhelm II, but he regards as characteristic of the writers of the period a proclamation of individuality and artistic freedom fundamentally at odds with the materialism of the Second Empire. The usefulness of L.'s work as an introduction to the period is reflected not only in the chapters on individual authors (George, Hofmannsthal, the Mann brothers, Hauptmann, Rilke, and Kafka) but also in the meticulous treatment of themes and genres. The work is a rich source of information, both of a biographical and literary nature, on the hundreds of writers of this period of German literature which can be compared in its vitality and the establishment of new directions with Weimar Classicism and Romanticism. The lucid and illuminating text is complemented by a selection of reproductions of drawings, photographs, paintings and posters which help to bring the whole period to life. B. A. Sørensen, Sørenson, *Geschichte*, II, contributes chapters on Naturalism (100–15), on Fin de siècle (116–73), and on German Literature 1910–45 (174–265). An eminently readable and illuminating survey of the period is offered by R. Robinson in his chapter, 'From Naturalism to National Socialism (1890–1945)', in Watanabe, *History*, 327–92.

MOVEMENTS AND PERIODS. Katja Grote, *Der Tod in der Literatur der Jahrhundertwende*, Frankfurt, Lang, 1996, 202 pp., considers works by Schnitzler, T. Mann, and Rilke. Joachim Pfeiffer, *Tod und Erzählen. Wege der literarischen Moderne um 1900*, Tübingen, Niemeyer, 260 pp. Anja Elisabeth Schoene, *'Ach, wäre fern, was ich liebe!' Studien zur Inzestthematik in der Literatur der Jahrhundertwende*, Würzburg, Königshausen & Neumann, 265 pp. Uwe Spörl, *Gottlose Mystik in der deutschen Literatur um die Jahrhundertwende*, Paderborn, Schöningh, 418 pp. D. A. Shepherd, 'Nature as political metaphor: four examples of Utopian literature, 1914–1930', *ColGer*, 29, 1996:191–207, considers H. Mann's *Der Untertan*, Döblin's *Berge, Meere und Giganten*, Heinrich Ströbel's *Die erste Milliarde der zweiten Billion: Die Gesellschaft der Zukunft*, and Erich Mühsam's *Alle Wetter*. Thorsten Bartz, *'Allgegenwärtige Fronten' — Sozialistische und linke Kriegsromane in der Weimarer Republik 1918–1933* (EH, I, 1623), 315 pp. G. Streim, 'Deutscher Geist und europäische Kultur. Die "europäische Idee" in der Kriegspublizistik von Rudolf Borchardt, Hugo von Hofmannsthal und Rudolf Pannwitz', *GRM*, 46, 1996:174–97. Anthony Grenville, *Cockpit of Ideologies. The Literature and Political History of the Weimar Republic*, Frankfurt, Lang, 1995, 394 pp. David F. Kuhns, *German Expressionist Theatre. The Actor and the Stage*, CUP, 311 pp., focuses on production and performance in Expressionist theatre. Central to this stimulating work is the concern with those plays where there is evidence in the research sources — contemporary reviews, statements by actors and directors and their personal memoirs, and stage directions — of a commitment to specific modes of Expressionist performance. The work supplements existing research on themes and staging with a new emphasis on the production — and the actor's part in it — as the means of liberating 'expression'. Michael Hahn, *Scheinblüte, Krisenzeit, Nationalsozialismus* (EH, I, 1542), 1995, 424 pp., considers a range of novelists of the Weimar period in relation to the relative strength of their sympathy for the Republic. Thus Feuchtwanger and Heinrich Mann are placed in the category of republic-friendly authors, whereas Frank Thiess is regarded as hostile and Werfel and Döblin are among those considered non-committed. R. Nenzel, 'Nicht der Dadaismus ist absurd, sondern die Gesellschaft, die er kritisiert. Über Walter Petrys Streitschrift "Die dadaistische Korruption"', *ZDP*, 115, 1996:137–55. Dieter Lang, *Staat, Recht und Justiz im Kommmentar der Zeitschrift 'Die Weltbühne'*, Frankfurt, Lang, 1996, 265 pp. Elke Matijevich, *The Zeitroman of the Late Weimar Republic* (SMGL, 77), 1995, 198 pp. *Reisekultur in Deutschland: Von der Weimarer Republik zum 'Dritten Reich'*, ed. Peter J. Brenner, Tübingen, Niemeyer, 294 pp. C. Schönfeld, 'The urbanization of the body: prostitutes, dialectics and Utopia in German Expressionism', *GSR*, 20:49–62. Ernst Behler, *Ironie und literarische Moderne*, Paderborn, Schöningh, 336 pp. Hans-Peter Kunisch, *Gefährdete Spiegel. Körper in Texten der Frühen Moderne (1890–1930): Musil — Schnitzler — Kafka*, Frankfurt, Lang, 1996, 320 pp. K. Ambrosy, 'Mädchenerziehung in der Weimarer Republik und die literarische Verarbeitung dieser Thematik', *Runa*, 25, 1996:187–95, includes reference to works by Christa Winsloe and Irmgard Keun. Michaela Enderle-Ristori, *Markt und intellektuelles Kräftefeld. Literaturkritik im Feuilleton von 'Pariser Tageblatt' und 'Pariser Tageszeitung' (1933–1940)*, Tübinger, Niemeyer, 432 pp., is a mine of meticulously researched information about the literary and political concerns of exiled writers. The exhaustive investigation of themes, influences and programmatic positions is complemented by a superbly detailed and informative index of reviews in chronological order. Izabela Sellmer, '*Warum schreibe ich das alles?' Zur Rolle des Tagebuchs für deutschsprachige Exilschriftsteller 1933–1945* (EH, I, 1617), Frankfurt, Lang, 246 pp. Bernhard Spies, *Die Komödie in der deutschsprachigen Literatur des Exils: ein Beitrag zur Geschichte und Theorie des komischen Dramas im 20. Jahrhundert*, Würzburg, Königshausen & Neumann, 199 pp. *Exil*, 16.1, 1996, contains the following articles on the German-speaking theatre in exile: B. Drewniak, 'Deutschsprachiges Theater in Polen zwischen 1933 und 1939' (59–73); H. Schneider, 'Die Kleinen neben den Großen. Deutschsprachige Bühnen im Prag der dreißiger Jahre' (46–58); N. Suhl, 'Die "Komödie" — ein Exiltheaterensemble in Luxembourg' (74–80). Katrin Diehl, *Die jüdische Presse im Dritten Reich*, Tübingen, Niemeyer, 362 pp. J. S. Hohmann, '"Deutschkundlicher Unterricht" in Thüringen im Zeichen nationalsozialistischer Ideologie', *WW*, 46, 1996:275–301. R. Klausnitzer, 'Blaue Blume unterm Hakenkreuz. Zur literaturwissenschaftlichen Romantikrezeption im Dritten Reich', *ZGer*, 7:521–42. R. Geissler, 'Zusammenbruch und Neubeginn. Zu den Rundfunkkommentaren von Thomas Mann (1940–1945) und Alfred Döblin (1946–1952)', *LitL*, 1, 1996:1–16.

AUSTRIA, PRAGUE AND SWITZERLAND. *Von Franzos zu Canetti. Jüdische Autoren aus Österreich*, ed. Mark H. Gelber, Hans Otto Horch, and Sigurd Paul Scheichl, Tübingen, Niemeyer, 1996, 424 pp. J. Holzner, 'Schule des Schauens. Oscar Walter Ciseks Roman *Vor den Toren'*, Fest. *Schwob*, 177–81. C. J. Hutterer, 'Über einige Probleme der ungarndeutschen Literatur in der ersten Hälfte des 20. Jahrhunderts', *ib.*, 209–18. W. Methlagl, 'Zum kulturellen Leben in Tirol nach dem Ersten Weltkrieg', Holzner, *Literatur*, 419–52. V. Obad, 'Das triviale Leseglück im alten Essek', *ib.*, 337–50. C. Ruthner, 'Die andere Seite Kakaniens. Österreichische Phantastik nach 1900', Obermayer, *Österreich*, 87–103. P. Rychlo, 'Der "Mythos Wien" in der deutschsprachigen Literatur der Bukowina', *MAL*, 30:13–23, refers to Rose Ausländer, Paul Celan, Alfred Kittner, and the popularity of Karl Kraus in Czernowitz between the wars.

2. POETRY

Wilhelm Grosse, *Expressionistische Lyrik: Kommentare, Diskussionsaspekte und Anregungen für produktionsorientiertes Lesen*, Hollfeld, Beyer, 1996, 125 pp.

3. Prose

Neues zu Altem. Novellen der Vergangenheit und der Gegenwart, ed. Sabine Cramer (Houston German Studies, 10), Munich, Fink, 1996, ix + 281 pp., contains essays on lesser-known examples of the genre. H. F. Glass considers the orientalist 'Novellen' of Paul Scheerbart, R. F. Nicolai traces links between Kafka's *Eine kleine Frau* and some of his other works, V. Greenberg writes on Ilse Faber and Tolstoy, S. Cramer contributes an essay on Gertrud Le Fort's *Die Letzte am Schafott*, and E.-M. Schulz-Jander writes on Gertrud Kolmar's *Susanna*.

4. Individual Authors

ANDRES, STEFAN. M. Braun, '"Ein kläglicher Prophet in seinem Fisch." Stefan Andres und die Probleme der inneren Emigration', *ZDP*, 115, 1996:262–78.

BALL, HUGO. *Dionysius DADA Areopagita: Hugo Ball und die Kritik der Moderne*, ed. Bernd Wacker, Paderborn, Schöningh, 1996, 273 pp.

BARLACH, ERNST. *Ernst Barlach: Briefwechsel 1900–1938*, ed. Wolfgang Tarnowski, Munich, Piper, 775 pp.

BENJAMIN, WALTER. E. Geulen, 'Toward a genealogy of gender in Walter Benjamin's writing', *GQ*, 69, 1996:161–80. Marianne Muthesius, *Mythos Sprache Erinnerung. Untersuchungen zu Walter Benjamins 'Berliner Kindheit um neunzehnhundert'*, Basel, Stroemfeld, 1996, 276 pp. H. Müller, 'Walter Benjamin's critique of historicism: a re-reading', *GR*, 71, 1996:243–51. A. Rauch, 'Culture's hieroglyph in Benjamin and Novalis: a matter of feeling', *ib.*, 253–66. D. Schöttker, 'Fragment und Traktat. Walter Benjamin und die aphoristische Tradition', *WB*, 43:503–19. D. Schöttker, 'Edition und Werkkonstruktion. Zu den Ausgaben der Schriften Walter Benjamins', *ZDP*, 116:294–315. C. Schulte, 'Krieger! Denk mal! Walter Benjamin's erster Versuch über Karl Kraus', *GR*, 71, 1996:267–78. G. Wagner, 'Dialektische Kontraste. Walter Benjamin über die mimetische Konkurrenz von Schrift- und Bildkultur', *WB*, 43:485–502.

BORCHARDT, RUDOLF. *Rudolf Borchardt und seine Zeitgenossen*, ed. Ernst Osterkamp, Berlin, de Gruyter, 409 pp.

BRECHT, BERTOLT. *Das Brecht-Jahrbuch*, 21, contains the following: J. K. Lyon, 'Collective productivity — Brecht and his collaborators' (1–18); H. Fehervary, 'Brecht, Seghers, and *The Trial of Jeanne d'Arc* — with a previously unpublished letter of 1952 from Seghers to Brecht' (21–47); T. Kuhn, '"Ja, damals waren wir Dichter": Hanns Otto Münsterer, Bertolt Brecht and the dynamics of literary friendship' (49–66); S. Mews, 'Bertolt Brecht and Frieda Bloom: *Loving Brecht?*'

(69–83); A. Führich, '"Dieses Chicago, das haben Männer aufge-
baut"? Elisabeth Hauptmanns Kurzprosa der zwanziger Jahre'
(85–99); M. Voigts, 'Brecht and the Jews' (101–22); C. Weber, 'The
Prodigal Son and the family *In the Jungle*: notes on Brecht's early
Chicago play and its contemporary American staging' (125–39);
V. Stegmann, '*La nuova commedia dell'arte*: Ferruccio Busoni als
Vorläufer von Brecht und Weill' (141–57); J. G. Highkin, '"Words
make you think, music makes you feel. And songs make you feel
thoughts": The function of song and music in Brecht and Eisler's *The
Measures Taken*' (159–77); N. Rivera, 'Bringing the culinary principle
under discussion: John Cage, Bertolt Brecht, and the opera' (179–89);
J. Hermand, 'Das Gemeinsame im Trennenden: Brecht und Fels-
enstein' (191–202); H. Knust, 'Brechts Fischschule — mehr aus dem
Wasser geholt, als aus der Luft gegriffen?' (205–18); P. Thompson,
'From Shen Te to Shui Ta: gendered reading, Utopian Communism
and Stalinism?' (221–42). Margaret Eddershaw, *Performing Brecht.
Forty Years of British Performances*, London, Routledge, 1996, 188 pp.
Der junge Brecht: Aspekte seines Denkens und Schaffens, ed. Helmut Gier and
Jürgen Hillesheim, Würzburg, Königshausen & Neumann, 1996,
278 pp. Werner Hecht, *Brecht-Chronik: 1898–1956*, Frankfurt, Suhr-
kamp, 1315 pp. *Brecht und Stanislawski — und die Folgen*, ed. Ingrid
Hentschel, Berlin, Henschel, 271 pp. Hans-Christian von Herrmann,
Sang der Maschinen. Brechts Medienästhetik, Munich, Fink, 1996, 220 pp.
Horst Jesse, *Brecht in Berlin*, Munich, Das Freie Buch, 1996, 346 pp.
Sabine Kebir, *Ich fragte nicht nach meinem Anteil: Elisabeth Hauptmanns
Arbeit mit Bertolt Brecht*, Berlin, Aufbau, 292 pp. Albrecht Kloepfer,
*Poetik der Distanz. Ostasien und ostasiatischer Gestus im lyrischen Werk Bertolt
Brechts*, Munich, Iudicium, 248 pp. Jan Knopf, *Gelegentlich: Poesie. Ein
Essay über die Lyrik Bertolt Brechts*, Frankfurt, Suhrkamp, 1996, 294 pp.
Hans Mayer, *Erinnerung an Brecht*, Frankfurt, Suhrkamp, 1996, 121 pp.
A. Oesmann, 'The theatrical destruction of subjectivity and history:
Brecht's *Trommeln in der Nacht*', *GQ*, 70:136–50. Günther
Schwarzberg, *Sommertage bei Bertolt Brecht. Tagebuchskizzen under dem
dänischen Strohdach*, Hamburg, Rasch & Roehring, 227 pp. Marielle
Silhouette, *Le grotesque dans le théâtre de Bertolt Brecht (1913–1926)*
(Contacts, 18), Berne, Lang, 1996, 544 pp. R. Witzler, 'Der Vater des
Dichters: Zur Person Berthold Friedrich Brechts', *LiB*, 50:51–58.

BROCH, HERMANN. L. Bornscheuer, 'Die apokalyptische "End-
schaft der Kunstperiode" in Hermann Brochs *Der Tod des Vergil* und
Thomas Manns *Doktor Faustus*', *LitL*, 1996, no.1:17–31. Jürgen
Heizmann, *Antike und Moderne in Hermann Brochs 'Tod des Vergil'. Über
Dichtung und Wissenschaft, Utopie und Ideologie* (MBSL, 33), 207 pp. Otto
Tost, *Die Antike als Motiv und Thema in Hermann Brochs Roman 'Der Tod
des Vergil'* (IBKG, 53), 1996, 230 pp., examines B.'s debt to classical

philosophy, his portrayal of various aspects of Roman life, and his depiction of historical figures from the emperor Augustus to the physician Charondos. On some topics, for example slavery or Virgil's relationship to other writers of his time, there is much that is factually informative and of help to the uninitiated reader. On others, such as rural life, T. the classicist offers persuasive insights. Elsewhere — in passages on Plato's thought, for instance, or on the Orpheus myth — the information level is more that of a basic encyclopaedia than an academic thesis.

CANETTI, ELIAS. W. C. Donahue, '"Eigentlich bist du eine Frau. Du bestehst aus Sensationen." Misogyny as cultural critique in Elias Canetti's *Die Blendung*', *DVLG*, 71 : 668–700. Petra Kuhnau, *Masse und Macht in der Geschichte: zur Konzeption anthropologischer Konstante in Elias Canettis Werk Masse und Macht* (Ep, 195), 1996, 423 pp. E. Nährlich-Slaweta, 'Das Meer und seine Tropfen im Zeitalter der Vereinzelung. Das erste Buch: "Die Blendung"', *GRM*, 46, 1996:198–215. *'Ein Dichter braucht Ahnen.' Elias Canetti und die europäische Tradition*, ed. Gerald Stieg and Jean-Marie Valentin (*JIG*, A 44), Frankfurt, Lang, 315 pp.

CELAN, PAUL. Christine Ivanovic, *Das Gedicht im Geheimnis der Begegnung. Dichtung und Poetik Celans im Kontext seiner russischen Lektüren*, Tübingen, Niemeyer, 1996, 379 pp. *Kommentar zu Paul Celans 'Die Niemandsrose'*, ed. Jürgen Lehmann and Christine Ivanovic, Heidelberg, Winter, 430 pp. *Stationen. Kontinuität und Entwicklung in Paul Celans Übersetzungswerk*, ed. Jürgen Lehmann and Christine Ivanovic, Heidelberg, Winter, 203 pp. Bernhard Paha, *Die 'Spur' im Werk Paul Celans. Eine 'wiederholte' Lesung Jacques Derridas*, Giessen, Kletsmeier, 161 pp. Bianca Rosenthal, *Pathways to Paul Celan* (SMGL, 73), 1996, 256 pp. Uta Werner, *Textgräber. Paul Celans geologische Lyrik*, Munich, Fink, 288 pp.

DÖBLIN, ALFRED. Armin Arnold, *Alfred Döblin* (Köpfe des 20. Jahrhunderts, 129), Berlin, Morgenbuch, 1996, 94 pp. Birgit Hoock, *Modernität als Paradox. Der Begriff der 'Moderne' und seine Anwendung auf das Werk Alfred Döblins (bis 1933)*, Tübingen, Niemeyer, 335 pp. Annette Keck, *'Avantgarde der Lust.' Autorschaft und sexuelle Relation in Döblins früher Prosa*, Munich, Fink, 280 pp. Anne Kuhlmann, *Revolution als 'Geschichte': Alfred Döblins 'November 1918'*, Tübingen, Niemeyer, 1996, 230 pp. Ingrid Maass, *Regression und Individuation. Alfred Döblins Naturphilosophie und späte Romane vor dem Hintergrund einer Affinität zu Freuds Metapsychologie* (HBG, 24), 208 pp. Yoshihito Ogasawara, *'Literatur zeugt Literatur.' Intertextuelle, motiv- und kulturgeschichtliche Studien zu Alfred Döblins Poetik und dem Roman 'Berlin Alexanderplatz'* (EH, I, 1579), 1996, 177 pp.

DODERER, HEIMITO VON. Torsten Buchholz, *Musik im Werk Heimito von Doderers* (EH, 1, 1573), 1996, 258 pp.

EBNER-ESCHENBACH, MARIE VON. *Tagebücher.* V. *1898–1905*, ed. Karl Konrad Polheim and Norbert Gabriel, Tübingen, Niemeyer, 1996, 628 pp. *Tagebücher.* VI. *1906–1916*, ed. Polheim and Gabriel, 412 pp. E. Toegel, '"Vergangene Freuden, überstandene Leiden": Marie von Ebner-Eschenbach's autobiographical writings', *MAL*, 30:35–47.

EINSTEIN, CARL. *Carl-Einstein-Kolloqium 1994*, ed. Klaus H. Kiefer (BBL, 16), 223 pp.

FALLADA, HANS. *Hans Fallada: sein Leben in Bildern und Briefen*, ed. Gunnar Müller-Waldeck, Roland Ulrich, and Uli Ditzen, Berlin, Aufbau, 270 pp.

GEORGE, STEFAN. *George-Jahrbuch*, 1, 1996–97, ed. Wolfgang Braungart and Ute Oelmann, Tübingen, Niemeyer, 1996, 160 pp. Wolfgang Braungart, *Ästhetischer Katholizismus. Stefan Georges Rituale der Literatur*, Tübingen, Niemeyer, 400 pp.

GOERING, REINHARD. Frank U. Pommer, *Variationen über das Scheitern des Menschen. Reinhard Goerings Werk und Leben* (EH, 1, 1575), 1996, 289 pp.

HASENCLEVER,WALTER. Bernhard F. Reiter, *Walter Hasenclevers mystische Periode. Die Dramen der Jahre 1917–1925* (EH, 1, 1632), 305 pp.

HAUPTMANN, GERHART. F. Marx, '"Schiller ganz anders." Gerhart Hauptmanns Spiel mit der Weimarer Klassik in der Tragikomödie "Die Ratten"', *ZDP*, 115, 1996:122–36.

HESSE, HERMANN. Christoph Gellner, *Weisheit, Kunst und Lebenskunst. Fernöstliche Religion und Philosophie bei Hermann Hesse und Bertolt Brecht*, Mainz, Matthias-Grünewald-Vlg, 366 pp. David G. Richards, *Exploring the Divided Self. Hermann Hesse's 'Steppenwolf' and its Critics*, Columbia, SC, Camden House, 1996, 169 pp.

HOCHWÄLDER, FRITZ. A. Obermayer, 'Hochwälders *Donnerstag* oder: Was ein Roman aus dem Jahre 1933 und ein Theaterstück aus dem Jahre 1959 außer dem Titel gemeinsam haben', Obermayer, *Österreich*, 155–70.

HODDIS, JAKOB VAN. Bernd Läufer, *'Entdecke dir die Häßlichkeit der Welt.' Bedrohung, Deformation, Desillusionierung und Zerstörung bei Jakob van Hoddis* (LU, 28), 1996, 494 pp.

HOFMANNSTHAL, HUGO VON. W. Nehring, 'Wien versus Österreich oder Die Spannung zwischen Hofmannsthal und Schnitzler', Obermayer, *Österreich*, 135–54. A. Thomasberger, 'Edition als Grundlage intertextueller Aufmerksamkeit. Beispiele aus der Kritischen Hofmannsthal-Ausgabe', Schwob, *Edition*, 301–06. P. Sprengel, 'Selbstmord in Berlin. Zum Anlaß von Hofmannsthals Gedicht

"Der Schatten eines Todten fiel auf uns"', *JDFDH*, 266–73. P. Sprengel, 'Mit dem Schattenbande. Kryptische Mythologie in Hofmannsthals Gedichten *Wo ich nahe, wo ich lande* und *Ein Knabe'*, *LitL*, no. 1:1–10. Ulrike Stamm, *'Ein Kritiker aus dem Willen der Natur'*: Hugo *von Hofmannsthal und das Werk Walter Paters* (Ep, 213), 308 pp. Gregor Streim, *Das 'Leben' in der Kunst: Untersuchungen zur Ästhetik des frühen Hofmannsthals* (Ep, 171), 1996, 229 pp.

HORVÁTH, ÖDÖN VON. Peter Gros, *Plebejer, Sklaven und Caesaren. Die Antike im Werk Ödön von Horváths* (EH, 1, 1550), 1996, 168 pp. Ingrid Haag, *Ödön von Horváth. Fassaden-Dramaturgie* (LU, 26), 1995, 228 pp. A. Mathäs, 'History, ideology, and false consciousness in Ödön von Horváth's "Das Fräulein wird bekehrt"', *GSR*, 20:305–21.

HUCH, RICARDA. Cordula Koepcke, *Ricarda Huch — ihr Leben und ihr Werk*, Frankfurt, Insel, 1996, 321 pp., is a lucid and accessible biography in which references to H.'s private life, and in particular to her affair with, marriage to, and eventual divorce from her brother-in-law take precedence over a detailed discussion of her major works. Through the frequent verse quotations which punctuate the text the reader is reminded that, apart from her authoritative works on German Romanticism and German history, H. had considerable strengths as a lyric poet.

JAHNN, HANS HENNY. Marion Boennighausen, *Musik als Utopie: zum philosophisch-ästhetischen Kontext von Hans Henny Jahnns 'Die Niederschrift des Gustav Anias Horn' und Thomas Manns 'Doktor Faustus'*, Opladen, Westdeutscher Vlg, 280 pp. Armin Schäfer, *Biopolitik des Wissens: Hans Henny Jahnns literarisches Archiv des Menschen* (Ep, 167), 1996, 357 pp.

JÜNGER, ERNST. *Images d'Ernst Jünger*, ed. Danièle Beltran-Vidal, Frankfurt, Lang, 1996, 176 pp. H. Esselborn, 'Die Verwandlung von Politik in Naturgeschichte der Macht. Der Bürgerkrieg in Ernst Jüngers *Marmorklippen* und *Heliopolis'*, *WW*, 47:45–61. A. Pütz, 'Ernst Jünger und Maurice Barrès. Begegnungen im Raum der Fiktion', *WB*, 42, 1996:188–206.

KAFKA, FRANZ. G. Blamberger, 'Kafka's death images', Debatin, *Metaphor*, 239–50. Elizabeth Boa, *Kafka: Gender, Class, and Race in the Letters and Fictions*, Oxford, Clarendon, 1996, 304 pp. I. Bruce, 'Seductive myths and Midrashic games in Franz Kafka's *Parables and Paradoxes'*, *CGP*, 25:57–77. D. Cohn, 'Kafka and Hofmannsthal', *MAL*, 30:1–19. Christian Eschweiler, *Kafkas Wahrheit als Kunst: Lichtblicke im Dunkel*, Bonn, Bouvier, 1996, 240 pp. S. Feldmann, '"Verstand geht dem Blödesten auf." Medien und Kultur in Kafkas "Strafkolonie"', *WB*, 42, 1996:357–78. Dagmar Fischer, *Kafkas Proceß-Prosa. Eine textimmanente Interpretation*, Frankfurt, Lang, 1996, 580 pp. S. L. Gilman, 'Die Rolle von Zeugnis und Glauben im Prozeß bei Franz Kafka und Arnold Zweig', *ZDP*, 116:254–71.

R. Heinemann, 'Kafka's oath of service: "Der Bau" and the dialectic of bureaucratic mind', *PMLA*, 111, 1996:256–70. *Kafka and China*, ed. Adrian Hsia (Euro-Sinica, 7), Frankfurt, Lang, 1996, 212 pp. Doris Kolesch, *Aufbauende Zerstörung. Zur Paradoxie des Geschichts-Sinns bei Franz Kafka und Thomas Pynchon* (SDLNZ, 35), 1996, 161 pp. Karoline Krauss, *Kafka's K. versus the Castle. The Self and the Other* (Austrian Culture, 14), Frankfurt, Lang, 1996, 110 pp. Rudolf Kreis, *Kafkas 'Process': das große Gleichnis vom abendländisch 'verurteilten' Juden; Heine — Nietzsche — Kafka*, Würzburg, Königshausen & Neumann, 1996, 95 pp. Se-Hoon Kwon, *Die moderne Schreibweise in den Werken von Franz Kafka und Günter Kunert* (EH, 1, 1583), 1996, 197 pp. C. Liebrand, 'Die verschollene (Geschlechter-) Differenz. Zu Franz Kafkas Amerika-Roman', *LitL*, no. 3:143–57. V. Liska, 'Stellungen. Zu Franz Kafkas "Poseidon"', *ZDP*, 115, 1996:226–38. F. Möbus, 'Kein "Engel über dem Ehebett": Mystische Metaphorik in Briefen Franz Kafkas', *GLL*, 49, 1996:217–24. M. Owari, 'Konstruktion des Ich durch Sprache — Zu Kafkas Erzählfragment "Der Bau"', *DB*, 99:91–99. R. Robertson, 'Mothers and lovers in some novels by Kafka and Brod', *GLL*, 50:475–90. Holger Rudloff, *Gregor Samsa und seine Brüder: Kafka — Sacher-Masoch — Thomas Mann*, Würzburg, Königshausen & Neumann, 101 pp. M. Schmidt, 'Katz und Maus: Kafkas "Kleine Fabel" und die Resonanz der frühneuzeitlichen Konvertitenbiographik', *GLL*, 49, 1996:205–16. Georg Ernst Weidacher, *Elemente des Kafkaesken. Problematische Kommunikationsstrukturen als Ursache einer Leseirritation* (ES, 113), 119 pp., is a stimulating investigation of communication problems which are both presented and encountered by K.'s characters and which compound the reader's difficulties in establishing a secure interpretation. The study is characterized by a lucid and subtle commentary on K.'s language and style and by effective reference to critical theory. J. Wolfradt, 'Der Text als Botschaft des Textes: Zu Franz Kafkas Roman *Der Verschollene*', *GR*, 71, 1996:211–28. H. D. Zimmermann, 'Jüdisches, Unjüdisches: Zur Frage der Gesetze bei Franz Kafka', *GLL*, 49, 1996:225–35.

KEYSERLING, EDUARD VON. Antoine Alm-Lequeux, *Eduard von Keyserling. Sein Werk und der Krieg*, Paderborn, Igel, 1996, 162 pp. offers a re-adjustment to the general perception of K. as a writer concerned wih issues of love and adultery within a degenerate aristocracy. On the basis of a close analysis of the texts A.-L. convincingly shows how K. was an enthusiastic supporter of the German cause in the First World War. Although, unlike some of his literary contemporaries, K. did not indulge in ideological glorification nor resort to propaganda, he nevertheless believed that the war was necessary in order to preserve German cultural values and that it provided the unifying force which brought all social groups together. She suggests that this sense of belonging to a greater whole was particularly important to K. as an alternative to the individualism, often the sense of isolation, which is characteristic of his pre-war novels. The volume contains a selection of K.'s articles on the war, the short story *Verwundet*, which testifies to K.'s enduring concern with the fate of the individual — here the wounded soldier — and a most useful bibliography. In addition to its importance as a contribution to K. scholarship, the work is a reminder of the widespread support given by German intellectuals to their political leaders at the outbreak of the Great War. W. Nehring, 'Jagdlust und Erotik: Zur Metaphorik der Jagdszenen bei Eduard von Keyserling', *ZDP*, 115, 1996:560–75.

KRAUS, KARL. *Karl Kraus — Otto Stoessl: Briefwechsel 1902–1925*, ed. Gilbert J. Carr, Vienna, Deuticke, 1996, 288 pp., is a welcome edition to the relatively few collections of K.'s correspondence and one which provides fascinating insights into his work on 'Die Fackel' in particular and his linguistic and literary ideas in general. The letters, most of which were written before 1916, are fully annotated and the introduction provides an illuminating commentary on the material and the friendship and mutual respect which developed between the correspondents. S. P. Scheichl, 'Quellen von Satiren. Am Beispiel von Karl Kraus', Schwob, *Edition*, 277–89. B. Spinnen, 'Einen Roman für Karl Kraus', Ingold, *Autor*, 173–82. John Theobald, *The Paper Ghetto. Karl Kraus and Anti-Semitism*, Frankfurt, Lang, 1996, 218 pp.

LASKER-SCHÜLER, ELSE. A. Bodenheimer, "Die Traurigkeit überlassen Sie mir." Else Lasker-Schülers Briefe an Emil Raas', *ZDP*, 116:588–602. Stephanie Bettina Heck, *'Und weckte doch in deinem ewigen Hauche nicht den Tag.' Prophetie im Werk Else Lasker-Schülers* (EH, 1, 1576), 1996, 166 pp. Sissel Lægreid, *Nach dem Tode — oder vor dem Leben. Das poetische Projekt Else Lasker-Schülers*, Frankfurt, Lang, 262 pp. A. U. Rohde, 'Translating cultural hybridity: conceptualizations of cultural identity in translations of Else Lasker-Schüler', *CGP*, 25:38–56. K. J. Skrodzki, '"[...] die stärkste und unwegsamste lyrische Erscheinung des modernen Deutschland." Stationen der Lyrik Else Lasker-Schülers', *ZDP*, 115, 1996:156–68. R. Stamm, 'Else Lasker-Schüler und das Folkwang-Museum', *WW*, 46, 1996:379–92.

MANN, HEINRICH. Andrea Bartl, *Geistige Atemräume. Auswirkungen des Exils auf Heinrich Manns 'Empfang bei der Welt', Franz Werfels 'Stern der Ungeborenen' und Hermann Hesses 'Das Glasperlenspiel'*, Bonn, Bouvier, 1996, 370 pp. Ekkehard Blattmann, *Heinrich Mann — Die Bildvorlagen zum Henri Quatre-Roman*, Frankfurt, Lang, 450 pp. H. Delbrück, 'Zur Bedeutung von H. Manns *Untertan* und F. Saltens Lueger-Essay für

das Wechselverhältnis der deutschen und österreichischen Literatur',
Obermayer, *Österreich*, 104–34. J. Schneider, '"The pleasure of the
uniform": masculinity, transvestism, and militarism in Heinrich
Mann's *Der Untertan* and Magnus Hirschfeld's *Die Transvestiten*', *GR*,
72:183–200. Michael Wieler, *Dilettantismus — Wesen und Geschichte:
am Beispiel von Heinrich Mann und Thomas Mann* (Studien zur Literatur-
und Kulturgeschichte, 9), Würzburg, Königshausen & Neumann,
1996, 439 pp.

MANN, THOMAS.   *Thomas Mann Jb.*, 9, ed. Eckhard Heftrich and
Thomas Sprecher, Frankfurt, Klostermann, 1996, 366 pp., presents
the following papers from the 1995 Lübeck colloquium: E. Heftrich,
'Der Zauberberg — nach siebzig Jahren' (15–27); J. Radkau,
'Neugier der Nerven. Thomas Mann als Interpret des "nervösen
Zeitalters"' (29–53); H. Lehnert, 'Familienfeindlichkeit. Über ein
literarisches Motiv der Wende zum zwanzigsten Jahrhundert'
(55–72); A. Bruns, 'Jahrhundertwende im Weltwinkel' (73–89);
J. Stoupy, 'Thomas Mann und Paul Bourget' (91–106); H. R. Vaget,
'Thomas Mann und Bayreuth' (107–26); M. Dierks, 'Typologisches
Denken bei Thomas Mann — mit einem Blick auf C. G. Jung'
(127–53); H.-J. Gerigk, '"Herr und Hund" und Schopenhauer'
(155–72); M. Wieler, 'Der französische Einfluß. Zu den frühesten
Werken Thomas Manns am Beispiel des Dilettantismus' (173–87);
B. Dotzler, '"... diese ganze Geistertummelage." Thomas Mann,
der alte Fontane und die jungen Medien' (189–205); P. Pütz,
'Götzendämmerung und Morgenröte bei Nietzsche und Thomas
Mann' (207–21); I. Jens, 'Seelenjournal und politische Rechenschaft.
Thomas Manns Tagebücher. Ein Bericht aus der Werkstatt' (231–48).
The proceedings of the 1996 Lübeck colloquium are contained in
Thomas Mann Jb., 10, ed. Eckhard Heftrich and Thomas Sprecher,
Frankfurt, Klostermann, 360 pp., and include the following: A. von
Schirnding '"Abdankung" — Phantasie über ein Thema Thomas
Manns' (37–51); V. Hage, 'Mit "Don Quijote" nach Amerika. Über
Thomas Manns "Seitensprung" im Jahre 1934' (53–65); E. Heftrich,
'Joseph in der Fremde' (67–82); D. Borchmeyer, 'Politische Betrach-
tungen eines angeblich Unpolitischen. Thomas Mann, Edmund
Burke und die Tradition des Konservatismus' (83–104); P. Grossardt,
'Ein kretischer Seefahrer, Odysseus und Joseph. Zur Verankerung
des Hermes-Motivs im vierten Teil von Thomas Manns Roman
Joseph und seine Brüder' (105–11); F. Marx, '"Die Menschwerdung des
Göttlichen." Thomas Manns Goethe-Bild in *Lotte in Weimar*' (113–32);
M. Neumann, 'Ein Bildungsweg in der Retorte. Hans Castorp auf
dem Zauberberg' (133–48); J. Rieckmann, '"In deinem Atem bildet
sich mein Wort": Thomas Mann, Franz Westermeier und *Die
Bekenntnisse des Hochstaplers Felix Krull*' (149–65); H. Siefken, 'Thomas

Manns "Dienst an der Zeit" in den Jahren 1918–1933' (167–85);
R. Wimmer, '"... mit dem Herausgeber und Vollstrecker nach
Gutdünken umgehen mochten." Gedanken zu einer Edition des
Doktor Faustus' (187–202). This volume also contains two papers given
at the 1996 annual meeting of the Thomas Mann Gesellschaft in
Zurich: R. Görner, 'Zauber des Letzten. Thomas Mann im spätbür-
gerlichen Zeitalter' (11–25), and F. Mann, 'Das Verhältnis von
Thomas Mann und seiner Familie zu Deutschland' (27–35). Bernd
Hamacher, *Thomas Manns letzter Werkplan — 'Luthers Hochzeit'* (TMS,
15), 376 pp. *Auf dem Weg zum 'Zauberberg'*, ed. Thomas Sprecher
(TMS, 16), 361 pp., is likely to become an indispensable source of
information on some of the central issues and ideas of the novel. It
contains the following contributions by acknowledged Mann scholars
to the Davoser Literaturtage, 12–16 August 1996: M. Dierks,
'Krankheit und Tod im frühen Werk Thomas Manns' (11–32);
H. Schott, 'Krankheit und Magie. *Der Zauberberg* im medizinhisto-
rischen Kontext' (33–48); S. B. Würffel, 'Mitbewohner des *Zauberbergs*.
Davoser Sanatoriumsgeschichten vor 1924' (49–75); H. Kurzke, 'Auf
dem Weg zum *Zauberberg*. Timpe und Schrenk: zwei Studien' (77–94);
B. Rüttimann, 'Die Lungentuberkolose im *Zauberberg*' (95–109); H. R.
Vaget, '"Ein Traum von Liebe." Musik, Homosexualität und Wagner
in Thomas Manns *Der Zauberberg*' (111–41); H. Wisskirchen, 'Der
Einfluß Heinrich Manns auf den *Zauberberg*' (143–64); C. Virchow,
'Katia Mann und der *Zauberberg*' (165–85); T. Sprecher, 'Kur-,
Kultur- und Kapitalismuskritik im *Zauberberg*' (187–249); R. Wimmer,
'Zur Philosophie der Zeit im *Zauberberg*' (251–72); H. Koopmann,
'Der *Zauberberg* und die Kulturphilosophie der Zeit' (273–97); T. J.
Reed, 'Von Deutschland nach Europa. Der *Zauberberg* im euro-
päischen Kontext' (299–318); D. von Engelhardt, 'Tuberkulose und
Kultur um 1900. Arzt, Patient und Sanatorium in Thomas Manns
Zauberberg aus medizinhistorischer Sicht' (323–45). Klaus Makoschey,
Quellenkritische Untersuchungen zum Spätwerk Thomas Manns (TMS, 17),
220 pp., considers *Joseph, der Ernährer, Das Gesetz*, and *Der Erwählte*.

M. M. Anderson, 'Jewish mimesis? Imitation and assimilation in
Thomas Mann's *Wälsungenblut* and Ludwig Jacobowski's *Werther, der
Jude*', *GLL*, 49, 1996:193–204. P. Bishop, '*Jung-Joseph*: Thomas
Mann's reception of Jungian thought in the *Joseph* tetralogy', *MLR*,
91, 1996:138–58. L. Blum, '"ein geistiger Wegbereiter und eiskalter
Wollüstling der Barbarei." Thomas Mann über Ernst Jünger', *WW*,
46, 1996:424–45. Peter V. Brinkemper, *Spiegel & Echo. Intermedialität
und Musikphilosophie im 'Doktor Faustus'* (Ep, 227), 520 pp. T. Buck,
'Loyalty and licence: Thomas Mann's fiction in English translation',
MLR, 91, 1996:898–921. P. Eisenstein, 'Leverkühn as witness: the
Holocaust in Thomas Mann's *Doktor Faustus*', *GQ*, 70:325–46. Joseph

Erkme, *Nietzsche im 'Zauberberg'* (TMS, 14), 1996, 388 pp. Elisabeth Galvan, *Zur Bachofen-Rezeption in Thomas Manns 'Joseph'-Roman*, Frankfurt, Klostermann, 1996, 176 pp. Anthony Heilbut, *Thomas Mann: Eros and Literature*, NY, Knopf, 1996, 636 pp. Werner Hickel, *'Freund Hain', die erotische Süssigkeit und die Stille des Nirwanas. Thomas Manns Rezeption der Erlösungsthematik zwischen Schopenhauer, Nietzsche und Wagner*, Hamburg, Kovac, 309 pp. E. Joseph, 'Hans Castorps "biologische Phantasie in der Frostnacht". Zur epischen Integration naturwissenschaftlicher Texte im *Zauberberg* von Thomas Mann', *WW*, 46, 1996:393–411. J. S. King, '"Most dubious": myth, the occult, and politics in the *Zauberberg*', *MDU*, 88, 1996:217–35. Michael Köhler, *Götterspeise. Mahlzeitenmotivik in der Prosa Thomas Manns und Genealogie des alimentären Opfers*, Tübingen, Niemeyer, 1996, 179 pp. Dietmar Krug, *Eros im Dreigestirn. Zur Gestaltung des Erotischen im Frühwerk Thomas Manns* (LU, 29), 247 pp. A welcome reprint of Hermann Kurzke, *Mondwanderungen. Wegweiser durch Thomas Manns Joseph-Roman* (FT, 11806), 212 pp., offers a guide to the structure, themes, and characters of the tetralogy, as well as an assessment of its importance in the context of M.'s work as a whole, an overview of his sources, and a summary of its reception. P. Levesque, 'The double-edged sword: anti-Semitism and anti-Wagnerianism in Thomas Mann's *Wälsungenblut*', *GSR*, 20:9–21. E. B. Lucca, '"Diesmal wird mit dem Namen herausgeplatzt." Bemerkungen zum vollständigen Buchtitel von Thomas Manns *Doktor Faustus*', *ColGer*, 29, 1996:223–34. Sonja Matthes, *Friedrich Mann oder Christian Buddenbrook: eine Annäherung*, Würzburg, Königshausen & Neumann, 118 pp., is a discursive and detailed portrayal of M.'s family background and, in particular, of his uncle, Friedrich Wilhelm Lebrecht Mann, the inspiration for Christian Buddenbrook. Although making no claims to scholarly rigour, the work nevertheless is a fascinating commentary on the Mann family at the turn of the century and on the unfortunate figure of Friedrich (Friedel) whose psychological problems, foreshadowing those of later members of the family, were not taken seriously. B. Müller, '"... über den Sprachen ist die Sprache." Mythogene narrative Strukturen in Thomas Manns Roman *Der Erwählte*', *WB*, 42, 1996:207–30. N. P. Nenno, 'Projections on blank space: landscape, nationality and identity in Thomas Mann's *Der Zauberberg*, *GQ*, 69, 1996:305–21. In Charlotte Nolte, *Being and Meaning in Thomas Mann's Joseph Novels* (MHRA Texts & Dissertations, 44; BSD, 22), Leeds, Maney, 1996, 170 pp., the inherent dialectic of the novel is illustrated by means of a detailed discussion of central pairs of opposites, motifs, and metaphors, and the gradual awareness of identity. The development of ego-consciousness is not only discussed in philosophical and psychological terms but also skilfully related to the narrative character of the tetralogy. The work is a stimulating contribution to research on the novel and reflects a discriminating understanding of Mann's creative application of contemporary psychological theory. W. H. Rey, 'Zuflucht im Idyll? Die Liebe zum Kind als Komponente in Thomas Manns erotischer Konstitution', *ColGer*, 30:149–70. H. Rudloff, 'Hetaera esmeralda: Hure, Hexe, Helferin. Anklänge ans "Märchenhafte" und "Sagenmäßige" in Thomas Manns Roman *Doktor Faustus*', *WW*, 47:61–74. M. Rupprecht, 'Thomas Mann und Ernst Jünger', *ib.*, 46, 1996, 411–23. Liisa Saariluoma, *Nietzsche als Roman. Über die Sinnkonstituierung in Thomas Manns 'Doktor Faustus'*, Tübinger, Niemeyer, 1996, 227 pp. Paul L. Sauer, *Gottesvernunft. Mensch und Geschichte im Blick auf Thomas Manns 'Joseph und seine Brüder'*, Frankfurt, Lang, 1996, 707 pp. Angelika Schaller, *'Und seine Begierde ward sehend': Auge, Blick und visuelle Wahrnehmung in der Prosa Thomas Manns*, Würzburg, Ergon, 407 pp. K. Schettler, '"Wort für Wort der Welt leserlich gemacht ..." Stationen aus dem Leben Hilde Reachs, Sekretärin von Thomas Mann', *Exil*, 17.1:18–32. Christoph Schmidt, *"Ehrfurcht und Erbarmen." Thomas Manns Nietzsche-Rezeption 1914 bis 1947*, Trier, Wissenschaftlicher Vlg Trier, 324 pp. J.-T. Siehoff, '"Philine ist doch am Ende nur ein Hürchen..." *Doktor Faustus*: Ein Bildungsroman? Thomas Manns *Doktor Faustus* und die Spannung zwischen den Bildungsideen der deutschen Klassik und ihrer Rezeption durch das deutsche Bürgertum im 19. und frühen 20. Jahrhundert', *MDU*, 89:196–207. A. U. Sommer, 'Thomas Mann und Franz Overbeck', *WW*, 46, 1996:32–55. Thomas Sprecher, *Davos im 'Zauberberg'. Thomas Manns Roman und sein Schauplatz*, Munich, Fink, 1996, 349 pp. A. Stephan, 'Thomas Mann und das FBI', *Procs* (Brasília), 699–705. H. R. Vaget, 'Thomas Mann und der deutsche Widerstand. Zur Deutschland-Thematik im *Doktor Faustus*', *Exilforschung*, 15:88–101. *Thomas Mann. Ein Leben in Bildern*, ed. Hans Wysling and Yvonne Schmidlin, Frankfurt, Fischer, 504 pp., is a compilation, divided into 15 chronological chapters, of selections from the texts, letters, comments by contemporaries, drawings, photographs and copies of title pages which together comprise a fascinating illustration of the background to M.'s life and work. The judicious selection of material and the discernment of the introduction will guarantee the success of this illustrated biography which is a fitting testimony to one of the great Mann scholars. Sigrid Zöller, *Der Begriff der 'Haltung' als literarisches Gestaltungsprinzip bei Thomas Mann* (EH, 1, 1562), 1996, 191 pp.

MÜNCHHAUSEN, BÖRRIES VON. K. K. Polheim, '"zersungen und vertan." B. v. Münchhausens Ballade *Jenseits* und das Lied *Jenseits des Tales*', *Fest. Schwob*, 351–61.

MUSIL, ROBERT. A. Daigger, 'Mit Robert Musil in Kakanien. Österreichbilder im Roman *Der Mann ohne Eigenschaften*', *MAL*, 30:158–69. C. Groppe, '"Das Theorem der Gestaltlosigkeit." Die Auflösung des "anthropozentrischen Verhaltens" in Robert Musils Roman *Der Mann ohne Eigenschaften*', *GRM*, 46, 1996:71–89. Christoph Hoffmann, *'Der Dichter am Apparat.' Medientechnik, Experimentalpsychologie und Texte Robert Musils 1899–1942*, Munich, Fink, 272 pp. Sun-Ae Hwang, *Liebe als ästhetische Kategorie. Zu 'Drei Frauen' von Robert Musil* (EH, I, 1544), 1996, 199 pp. B. Neymeyr, 'Musils skeptischer Fortschrittsoptimismus. Zur Ambivalenz der Gesellschaftskritik in seinen Essays', *ZDP*, 115, 1996:576–607. C. Niekerk, 'Foucault, Freud, Musil: Macht und Masochismus in den *Verwirrungen des Zöglings Törleß*', *ib.*, 116:545–66. A. Russegger, 'Schichtungen und Schaltungen. Zu Nachlaß-Projekten des Robert Musil Instituts der Universität Klagenfurt', Schwob, *Edition*, 351–60. E. von Schneider-Handschin, 'Kakanien im Schweizerhaus? — Zu Robert Musils *Mann ohne Eigenschaften* und Meinrad Inglins *Schweitzerspiegel*', *MAL*, 30:144–57. E. Schütz, '"Du brauchst bloß in die Zeitung hineinzusehen." Der große Roman im "feuilletonistischen Zeitalter": Robert Musils *Mann ohne Eigenschaften* im Kontext', *ZGer*, 7:278–91. S. T. de Zepetnek, 'Female sexuality and eroticism in Musil's *Die Versuchung der stillen Veronika*', *ColGer*, 30:131–47.

NIETZSCHE, FRIEDRICH. C. Zittel, 'Von den Dichtern. Quellenforschung versus Intertextualitätskonzepte, dargestellt anhand eines Kapitels aus Friedrich Nietzsches *Also sprach Zarathustra*, Schwob, *Edition*, 315–31.

REMARQUE, ERICH MARIA. T. F. Schneider, 'Das Genre bestimmt die Quelle. Anmerkungen zum Einfluß der Publikation und Rezeption auf die Entstehung und Quellenlage von Erich Maria Remarques *Im Westen nichts Neues* (1928/29)', Schwob, *Edition*, 361–68.

RILKE, RAINER MARIA. E.-M. Clauss, 'Orpheus in Paris. Zur Poetik der Erinnerung im *Malte Laurids Brigge*', *WW*, 47:31–45. Annette Gerok-Reiter, *Wink und Wandlung. Komposition und Poetik in Rilkes 'Sonette an Orpheus'*, Tübingen, Niemeyer, 1996, 319 pp. Alfred Grimm, *Rilke und Ägypten*, Munich, Fink, 384 pp. H. Holzkamp, '"Der Tod Brigges." Untergang und Verklärung in Rilkes *Aufzeichnungen des Malte Laurids Brigge*', *EG*, 56, 1996:481–512. A. Schwarz, 'The colors of prose: Rilke's program of *Sachliches Sagen*', *GR*, 71, 1996:195–210. Uwe C. Steiner, *Die Zeit der Schrift. Die Krise der Schrift und die Vergänglichkeit der Gleichnisse bei Hofmannsthal und Rilke*, Munich, Fink, 1996, 445 pp. A. Unterkircher, '*Unbekannter* Brief Rilkes an Wallpach, *erste* Gedichtveröffentlichung Trakls im Nachlaß Arthur von Wallpachs', *MBA*, 15, 1996:130–42.

ROTH, JOSEPH.   R. Cohen, 'Männerwelt, Gewalt, Weimarer Republik. Rechtsextremisten im Frühwerk Joseph Roths und in Ernst Ottwalts *Ruhe und Ordnung*', *MAL*, 30:48–68.

SCHLAF, JOHANNES.   J. Stüben, 'Zur Edition der von Johannes Schlaf und Arno Holz gemeinsam verfaßten Werke und ihrer Vorlagen', Schwob, *Edition*, 291–300.

SCHNITZLER, ARTHUR.   C. Benthien, 'Masken der Verführung — Intimität und Anonymität in Schnitzlers *Reigen*', *GR*, 72:130–41. D. von Boetticher, '"schließlich ist es ja Ihr bestes Buch, Sie Schmutzfink." Spiegelungen der "Reinheit" im Werk A. Schnitzlers', *WW*, 47:14–31. B. Dieterle, '"Keineswegs kann ich weiterleben" — Figurationen des Schreibens bei Arthur Schnitzler', *MAL*, 30:20–38. L. Gerrekens, 'Demontage verlorener Hoffnungen: Arthur Schnitzlers *Die Frau des Richters* oder die literarische Verdrängung eines Scheiterns', *MDU*, 89:31–58. M. Landwehr, 'Dream as wish fulfillment: eros, thanatos, and self-discovery in Schnitzler's *Casanovas Heimfahrt*', *MAL*, 30:1–18. Wolfgang Lukas, *Das Selbst und das Fremde. Epochale Lebenskrisen und ihre Lösung im Werk Arthur Schnitzlers*, Munich, Fink, 1996, 309 pp. M. Ossar, 'Individual and type in Arthur Schnitzler's *Liebelei*', *MAL*, 30:19–34. P. Plener, '"... und bin beruhigt weil ichs notire." Arthur Schnitzlers Tagebücher am Fin de siecle', *GM*, 45–46:15–34. Andrew C. Wisely, *Arthur Schnitzler and the Discourse of Honor and Dueling*, Frankfurt, Lang, 1996, 278 pp.

SUDERMANN, HERMANN.   Karl Leydecker, *Marriage and Divorce in the Plays of Hermann Sudermann* (EH, I, 1559), 1996, 278 pp.

TOLLER, ERNST.   J. Jordan, 'One of our war poets is missing: the case of Ernst Toller', *OGS*, 25, 1996:24–45. E. Piper, '"Ich will es mit Liebe umpflügen" — Ernst Toller 1919 bis 1939', *Exil*, 16.2, 1996:13–24. E. Röttger, 'Schriftstellerisches und politisches Selbstverständnis in Ernst Tollers Exildramatik', *ZDP*, 115, 1996:239–61. C. Schapkow, 'Judentum als zentrales Deutungsmuster in Leben und Werk Ernst Tollers', *Exil*, 16.2, 1996:25–39. Birgit Schreiber, *Politische Retheologisierung: Ernst Tollers frühe Dramatik als Suche nach einer 'Politik der reinen Mittel'* (Ep, 186), 251 pp.

TRAKL, GEORG.   *Zyklische Kompositionsformen in Georg Trakls Dichtung*, ed. Károly Csúri, Tübingen, Niemeyer, 1996, 268 pp. A. Doppler, 'Gewalt und Klage. Bemerkungen zu einem zentralen Thema in der Lyrik Georg Trakls', Holzner, *Literatur*, 381–89. Matteo Neri, *Das abendländische Lied — Georg Trakl*, Würzburg, Königshausen & Neumann, 1996, 173 pp. E. Sauermann, 'Dokumentation und Interpretation. Neue Möglichkeiten durch die Innsbrucker Trakl-Ausgabe', *ZDP*, 116:567–87. E. Sauermann, 'Edition und Funktion von Trakls Quellen. Über die Dunkelheit der Gedichte *Helian* und *Kaspar Hauser Lied*', Schwob, *Edition*, 255–75. L. Scheidl, 'Georg Trakls *Grodek*:

Die Vollendung eines dichterischen (Leidens) Wegs', *Runa*, 25, 1996: 153–62.

TUCHOLSKY, KURT. D. Grathoff, 'Kurt Tucholskys "Rheinsberg": Die Inszenierung der Idylle im Rekurs auf Theodor Fontane und Heinrich Mann', *MDU*, 88, 1996: 197–216.

WALSER, ROBERT. Thomas Bürgi-Michaud, *Robert Walsers 'mühse- ligkeitenüberschüttetes Kunststück'. Eine Strukturanalyse des 'Räuber'-Romans*, Frankfurt, Lang, 1996, 273 pp. K. Garloff, '"schimmern, glitzern, blöden, träumen, eilen und stolpern": Robert Walser's theatrical cities', *GR*, 71, 1996: 35–49.

WASSERMANN, JAKOB. E. von Schneider-Handschin, '"Schöpfer" vs. "Macher" — zur Produtkionsästhetik und Romanpoetik Jakob Wassermanns und Hermann Brochs', *MAL*, 30:84–100.

WEDEKIND, FRANK. A. Best, 'Fool's gold and false talismans: Frank Wedekind's *Hidalla* and the alchemy of human relationships', *GLL*, 49, 1996:459–78. Ward B. Lewis, *The Ironic Dissident: Frank Wedekind in the View of his Critics*, Columbia, SC, Camden House, 173 pp. E. Waldmann, 'Probleme der Quellendokumentation bei Frank Wedekinds *Bismarck*', Schwob, *Edition*, 307–13.

ZUCKMAYER, CARL. *BCZG*, 17, 1996, includes: G. van Roon, 'Das Bild des deutschen Widerstandes in Zuckmayers *Des Teufels General*' (37–48). *BCZG*, 18, includes: S. Mews, '"Der Brecht zeugte den Zuckmayer" — Zum persönlichen und literarischen Verhältnis Brechts und Zuckmayers' (57–75); F. Schüppen, 'Der Blick vom anderen Ufer — Staatsbegräbnis und Staatsbegründung in Zuckmay- ers Tragödie *Des Teufels General*. Eine literatur-philosophische Deutung' (77–99); H. Wagener, 'Die Carl-Zuckmayer-Forschung — Zwischen Vergessen und Volkstümelei' (37–55). A. Grenville, 'Authoritarianism subverting democracy: the politics of Carl Zuck- mayer's *Der Hauptmann von Köpenick*', *MLR*, 91, 1996:635–46.

ZWEIG, ARNOLD. Ursula Schumacher, *Die Opferung Isaaks. Zur Manifestation des Jüdischen bei Arnold Zweig* (BBNDL, 20), 1996, 240 pp.

ZWEIG, STEFAN. J. Holzner, 'Traumbilder: Stefan Zweigs Bilder aus Brasilien und Österreich', *Procs* (Brasília), 706–12.

LITERATURE FROM 1945
TO THE PRESENT DAY

By OWEN EVANS, *Lecturer in German, University of Wales, Bangor*

1. GENERAL

*Schreiben im heutigen Deutschland. Die literarische Szene nach der Wende, ed. U. E. Beitter (Contemporary German Literature and Society, 1), NY, Lang, xxviii + 196 pp. *Beyond 1989. Re-Reading German Literature since 1945*, ed. Keith Bullivant (Modern German Studies, 3), Providence-Oxford, Berghahn, xiii + 177 pp., builds on B.'s earlier surveys of German-speaking literature, although the editor assumes a more background role this time, allowing other academics based in the USA to explore and comment on the shifting cultural currents evident in Germany today. J. Michaels compares and contrasts FRG and GDR approaches to the Nazi past; C. Costabile-Heming explores State interference in the GDR cultural scene of the 1970s; B. Kosta and H. Kraft provide an overview of developments in women's writing since 1945; and W. Pape offers a fresh approach to Erich Fried, which rests a little uneasily with the other contributions. The most engaging articles of the study, however, offer insight into the different arguments surrounding the future of literature in Germany. Several of the articles focus naturally enough on the *Literaturstreit*. S. Mews identifies three phases of the debate in his exploration of Frank Schirrmacher's attempt to set a new post-unification agenda. Mews acknowledges that Schirrmacher may have provided impetus for a new cultural direction in Germany, but sees no evidence yet of any radical break with pre-1990 literature. S. Brockmann argues that greater cultural unity existed between the FRG and the GDR than the political situation suggested and traces evidence of the convergence between the two cultural spheres. He concludes by suggesting that *Was bleibt* marked the end of any convergence and a return to specific 'GDR literature'. Any criticism of Wolf was 'logical', therefore, as she appeared entrenched in the GDR at a time when the two Germanies were on the brink of unification. J. Rosellini ponders the apparent revival in conservative literature, offering insight into articles written for *Der Spiegel* in 1993 by Walser, Strauss, and Enzensberger, and juxtaposing their views with those expressed in the volume of right-wing articles entitled *Die selbstbewußte Nation* (1994). Rosellini finds some of the nationalist sentiments expressed in this work disturbing, but concludes that, as literature plays merely a peripheral role in the contributions, the text is unlikely to inspire a new generation of conservative authors. Indeed, he comments on the

disappearance of a cultural élite in a modern society which is less centred on 'bookish culture' (p. 128). N. Alter picks up the themes of nationalism and racism in her study of the disturbing film *Herzsprung* (1992). In a stimulating article, the author not only throws light on the complexity of the German situation with regard to resurgent neo-Nazism, but also makes a strong defence of film as a medium worthy of academic study. The volume closes with F. Trommler's provocative overview of post-1945 literature, in which he wonders whether literature can survive the existing media onslaught. It is a sober note on which to end an engaging volume which reinforces the complexity and challenge facing those who observe German culture, while offering detailed insight into recent debates. *Zwei Wendezeiten. Blick auf die deutsche Literatur 1945 und 1989*, ed. Walter Erhart and Dirk Niefanger, Tübingen, Niemeyer, viii + 168 pp.

Karl G. Esselborn, *Gesellschaftskritische Literatur nach 1945. Politische Resignation und konservative Kulturkritik, besonders am Beispiel Hans Erich Nossacks* (Kritische Information, 56), Munich, Fink, 221 pp. *Wende-Literatur. Bibliographie und Materialien zur Literatur der Deutschen Einheit*, ed. Jörg Fröhling, Reinhild Meinel, and Karl Riha (Bibliographien zur Literatur- und Mediengeschichte, 6), Frankfurt, Lang, 255 pp., represents a fine reference source for anyone engaged in research into the literary treatment of the *Wende* and its aftermath. The bibliography is divided into two sections, the first covering the period 1989–94 and the second 1995–96. Within each section, a list of primary and secondary texts is followed by a collection of short reviews of selected works cited in the bibliography and finally a list of articles from *Der Spiegel*. In addition, the first section also includes a useful catalogue of television programmes, ranging from documentaries to drama. The various sections are well-ordered and the bibliography should prove to be a valuable reference work. C. Gansel, 'Zwischen Wirklichkeitserkundung und Stereotypenbildung. Vom Dilemma einer Jugendliteratur zur "Wende"', *DUS*, 48.4, 1996:32–43. *Deutsche Literatur zwischen 1945–1995. Eine Sozialgeschichte*, ed. Horst A. Glaser (UTB, 1981), ix + 786 pp. U. Greiner, 'Die Vorzüge des Elfenbeinturms. Über Literatur und Engagement heute', *Merkur*, 41:1093–104. H. J. Hahn, '"Es geht nicht um Literatur": some observations on the 1990 "Literaturstreit" and its recent anti-intellectual implications', *GLL*, 50:65–81. J. Hermand, 'Der Kalte Krieg in der Literatur. Über die Schwierigkeiten bei der Rückeingliederung deutscher Exilautoren und -autorinnen nach 1945', *Argonautenschiff*, 4, 1995:26–44. *Zeitgenossische Utopieentwurfe in Literatur und Gesellschaft. Zur Kontroverse seit den achtziger Jahren*, ed. Rolf Jucker, Amsterdam, Rodopi, 377 pp. *Deutschsprachige Gegenwartsliteratur*, ed. Hans J. Knobloch and Helmut Koopmann (Stauffenburg

Colloquium, 44), Tübingen, Stauffenburg, 224 pp. *Das Loch in der Mauer. Der innerdeutsche Literaturaustausch*, ed. Mark Lehmstedt and Siegfried Lokatis (Schriften und Zeugnisse zur Buchgeschichte, 10), Wiesbaden, Harrassowitz, 364 pp. A. Opitz, '"Die Reise nach Lissabon." Zur Dekonstruktion der Fremde in der deutschen Gegenwartsliteratur', *Runa*, 26, 1996:563–71. Robinson, *Women*, includes entries on many German-speaking women writers of the postwar period, with each contribution comprising a selection of portraits and critical observations collated from diverse literary sources. The following authors are included: I. Aichinger, R. Ausländer, I. Bachmann, C. Busta, H. Courths-Mahler, H. Domin, I. Drewitz, J. Ebner, E. Erb, M. Fleisser, B. Frischmuth, C. Goll, R. Huch, M. L. Kaschnitz, I. Keun, S. Kirsch, A. Kolb, H. Königsdorf, E. Langgässer, G. Leutenegger, E. Lasker-Schuler, C. Lavant, G. von Le Fort, F. Mayröcker, B. Morgenstern, I. Morgner, H. Nowak, E. Plessen, C. Reinig, L. Rinser, F. Roth, N. Sachs, A. Seghers, I. Seidel, K. Struck, G. Wohmann, and C. Wolf. R. Rosenberg, 'Wiedervereinigung der deutschen Literaturgeschichte?', *Schiller Jb.*, 40, 1996:470–74.

E. Sagarra and P. Skrine, 'Literature after 1945', pp. 215–55 of Eda Sagarra and Peter Skrine, *A Companion to German Literature*, Oxford, Blackwell, xiv + 380 pp., is the last of nine chapters in a work covering German literature from 1500. A detailed survey of the entire work falls outside the scope of this review, but it is worth noting that the authors select four central thematic concerns throughout their study, namely the Faust myth, the role of translation in moulding German literary tastes, political poetry, and popular literature for adults and children, with the result that a degree of overlap exists between the various periodic divisions. Thus the authors devote a section of their concluding chapter to an analysis of poetry after Auschwitz, with special reference to the work of Paul Celan, but simultaneously ensure that this postwar material is set in its broader German, and indeed European, context. S. and S. provide a neat summation of the literary developments and themes in the post-1945 period, touching on the key cultural co-ordinates such as *Heimkehrerliteratur*, the *Gruppe 47*, *Vergangenheitsbewältigung*, the return of the exiles and the literary representation of the *Wirtschaftswunder*, but are careful to stress that there is more to German literature than merely the output of the Federal Republic. The influence of Frisch and Dürrenmatt in the 1950s is emphasized, and space is given to detailed overviews of East German, Austrian, and Swiss literature, allowing the reader to compare and contrast the coverage of themes in the different countries. A notable feature is the integration of women writers into the study, which ensures that due recognition is paid to the role of authors such as Ingeborg Bachmann and Ilse Aichinger, for example, in contemporary literary history. If there is a weakness, it is in the lack of any comment on trends since 1990, which results in the volume coming to a rather unsatisfactory conclusion. Nevertheless, the book as a whole is a fine achievement and will doubtless prove a valuable reference work for student and general reader alike. The chapter in question offers an informative and readable account of the development of German-language literature between 1945 and 1990, and places this period in its broader cultural and historical context. The alphabetical index of German-language authors provided at the end of the volume is also of great value. R. Schweikart, 'Adoleszenz im Medienzeitalter. Jugend und Medien in aktuellen Jugendromanen', *DUS*, 48.4, 1996:44–55. H.-G. Soldat, 'Die Wende in Deutschland im Spiegel der zeitgenössischen deutschen Literatur', *GLL*, 50:133–54. H. Steinecke, 'Von zwei deutschen Literaturen zu einer Literatur? Bemerkungen zu einigen Entwicklungen vor und nach der Wende', *Jb. der ungarischen Germanistik*, 1995 [1996]:13–29. M. Swales, 'Wie oft soll gefragt werden, wieviele deutsche Literaturen es gibt?', *Schiller Jb.*, 40, 1996:482–84. *Postwar Women's Writing in German. Feminist Critical Approaches*, ed. Chris Weedon, Providence-Oxford, Berghahn, 360 pp., sets out to formulate a 'reply, necessarily partial and selective, to the exclusion and marginalisation of women's writing in the post-war period' (p. 96). The result is a detailed and informative survey which, as the title indicates, does not just concentrate on the Federal Republic. In the first of five discrete sections, C. Weedon provides an historical overview of gender relations and an outline of different theoretical approaches to the literature in question which have evolved since the early 1970s. The second, and most substantial, section deals with work produced in the Federal Republic and includes F. Meyer's detailed investigation of the postwar period up to the 1960s spread over three chapters, the first of which examines the relative lack of recognition accorded authors such as E. Langgasser, whose short stories are described as 'among the most penetrating texts of the immediate post-war years' (p. 35). Meyer's second chapter outlines the peripheral role women writers were forced to play in the *Gruppe 47*, whilst the third examines the early novels of R. Rehmann. C. Rapisarda then casts light on the evolution of explicitly feminist writing in the 1970s, whilst M. Littler looks at developments in the 1980s and 1990s. The West German segment concludes with J. Bossinade's survey of A. Duden and I. Neubert's overview of publications by Turkish women, especially E. S. Özdamar. The third section, focusing on the GDR, opens with E. Kaufmann's comprehensive coverage of developments over the period 1945–89, in which she stresses that few GDR authors 'were (or are) prepared to use the term "women's writing" to describe their work' (p. 169). She then investigates the post-*Wende* period and finds no greater interest in feminism; the concerns remain more existential in nature. Indeed, she uncovers relatively little in works that have appeared since 1989 to indicate a decisive break has been made with the past. C. Weedon argues convincingly, however, that of all GDR women authors, C. Wolf had developed a 'female' aesthetic, especially in *Kassandra*. A. Fiddler opens the fourth section with her introduction to the situation in Austria. She argues that feminist writing is less radical than in the Federal Republic, but those writers in her survey are perhaps more linked 'to a political critique of societal structures [. . .] which is not held to be a characteristic of mainstream writing by Austrian men' (p. 245). The Austrian section is completed by E. Boa's examination of I. Bachmann's posthumous adoption by feminists and Fiddler's article on E. Jelinek, whose writing is presented as a contribution to feminist literature, precisely because it conforms neither with 'notions of how women should write, nor indeed with how feminists should write' (p. 302). The final section comprises C. Flittner's introduction to Swiss-German writing, with special reference to E. Hasler and G. Leutenegger. Both writers, it is argued, fit in with developments elsewhere in the German-speaking world, since both, in their very different ways, search for 'evidence of female repression and the repressed' (p. 323). The volume is an invaluable and accessible survey of the similarities and differences in the four countries. It deserves to be viewed as a seminal study, which underlines the significant contribution women writers have made to postwar German-language literature. *Wendezeiten — Zeitenwende. Positionsbestimmungen zur deutschsprachigen Literatur 1945–1995*, ed. Robert Weninger and Brigitte Rossbacher (Studien zur deutschsprachigen Gegenwartsliteratur, 7), Tübingen, Stauffenburg, xvi + 260 pp. Bernd Wittek, *Der Literaturstreit im sich vereinigenden Deutschland. Eine Analyse des Streits um Christa Wolf und die deutsch-deutsche Gegenwartsliteratur in Zeitungen und Zeitschriften*, Marburg, Tectum, 162 pp.

WEST GERMANY, AUSTRIA, SWITZERLAND. Marc Aeschbacher, *Tendenzen der schweizerischen Gegenwartsliteratur (1964–1994). Exemplarische Untersuchung zur Frage nach dem Tode der Literatur* (EH, 1, 1604), 472 pp. F. Aspetsberger, 'Eine Einritzung auf der Pyramide des Mykerinos. Von der relativen (geschlechtlichen) Identität des Banalen und des Erhabenen', Obermayer, *Österreich*, 190–213. *Banal und Erhaben. Es ist (nicht) alles eins*, ed. F. Aspetsberger and Günther A. Höfler (Schriftenreihe Literatur des Instituts für Österreichkunde:

Nützliche Handreichungen zur österreichischen Gegenwartsliteratur, 1), Bozen, Studien, 192 pp. **Nicht (aus, in, über, von) Österreich. Zur österreichischen Literatur, zu Celan, Bachmann, Bernhard und anderen. Beiträge des Debrecener germanistischen Symposions zur österreichischen Literatur nach 1945 im Oktober 1993*, ed. Tamas Lichtmann (Debrecener Studien zur Literatur, 1), Frankfurt, Lang, 1995, 319 pp. M. McGowan, 'German writing in the West (1945–1990)', Watanabe, *History*, 440–506. H. Nielsen and A. B. Petersen, 'Die deutsche Literatur 1945–1995', Sørensen, *Geschichte*, II, 266–436. C. Ruthner, 'Der ganz gewöhnliche Schrecken. Parallelaktionen zur Phantastik 1945–95 (Artmann, Bernhard, Jelinek et al)', *GM*, 43–44, 1996:201–18. **Neue Perspektiven zur deutschsprachigen Literatur der Schweiz*, ed. Romey Sabalius, Amsterdam, Rodopi, 248 pp. W. Schmidt-Dengler, 'Das neue Land. Die Konzeption einer neuen österreichischen Identität in der Literatur 1945–55', *GM*, 43–44, 1996:27–49. K. Zeyringer, 'Bestände — Aufnahmen. Österreichische Literatur der achtziger und beginnenden neunziger Jahre im Überblick', *ib.*, 125–39.

GDR. Frank Bechert, **Keine Versöhnung mit dem Nichts. Zur Rezeption Samuel Beckett in der DDR* (EH, 1, 1629), 428 pp. Peter Becker and Alf Ludtke, **Akten. Eingaben. Schaufenster. Die DDR und ihre Texte. Erkundungen zu Herrschaft und Alltag*, Berlin, Akademie, 313 pp. M. Behn, 'Neuere Gesamtdarstellungen der Geschichte der DDR-Literatur', *DUS*, 48.5, 1996:88–91. Peter Bothig, **Grammatik einer Landschaft. Literatur aus der DDR in den 80er Jahren*, Berlin, Lukas, 298 pp. Birgit Dahlke, **Papierboot. Autorinnen aus der DDR — inoffiziel publiziert* (Ep, 198), 386 pp. H. Fehervary, 'The literature of the German Democratic Republic (1945–1990)', Watanabe, *History*, 393–439. A. Herhoffer, '"… und heimatlos sind wir doch alle": Sinnverlust und Sinnstiftung in älterer und neuerer ostdeutscher Literatur', *GLL*, 50:155–64. U. Heukenkamp, 'Zwischen Heimatsinn und kaltem Blick. Lyrik der DDR in den 60er Jahren', *DUS*, 48.5, 1996:5–17. *'The New Sufferings of Young W.' and Other Stories from the German Democratic Republic*, ed. Therese Hornigk and Alexander Stephan (The German Library, 87), NY, Continuum, xviii + 350 pp., is a collection of translations which aims to introduce an array of authors from the former GDR to an English-speaking audience. An informative introduction by A. Stephan outlines the cultural atmosphere that existed in the GDR and rightly condemns disparaging Western judgements of some of the more challenging, innovative work produced before 1989, in spite of pressures from the state to adhere to the tenets of Socialist Realism. The anthology's strength is in revealing to a new audience the wide variety of work that did exist despite the monolithic cultural structures, and it thereby performs a welcome service in defending the reputation of GDR literature. The key text is K. P. Wilcox's translation of Plenzdorf's provocative 1972 story, which doubtless occupies its prominent position in the volume by virtue of both its unconventional, nonconformist nature and the American influences which Edgar Wibeau cites throughout. The colloquial style of the original German is neatly rendered into English by Wilcox, although certain Americanisms may jar with the British reader. The rest of the anthology provides a good mix of authors, both young and old, with texts grouped together in four categories: everyday life under socialism, women in the GDR, coming to terms with the Nazi past, and the end of the GDR. The absence of key figures such as Volker Braun and Jurek Becker due to copyright problems is regrettable, but a notable absentee is Monika Maron. Although such an anthology is always likely to provoke argument, and it should be recorded that the editors do achieve a good cross-section of GDR literature with 36 authors in all, the omission of Maron is still a surprise. An extract from her novel *Flugasche* would have been a good reflection of the ecological problems which plagued the GDR. Nevertheless, the volume is a pleasing and stimulating addition to the German Library series, and it is to be hoped that the editors succeed in reaching the wide audience they envisage. J. Lehmann, 'Die Rolle und Funktion der literarischen Intelligenz in der DDR. Fünf Anmerkungen', *DUS*, 48.5, 1996:59–67. **Literatur in der Diktatur. Schreiben im Nationalsozialismus und DDR-Sozialismus*, ed. Günther Rüther, Paderborn, Schöningh, 508 pp. Wolfgang Schneiss, **Flucht, Vertreibung und verlorene Heimat im früheren Ostdeutschland. Beispiele literarischer Bearbeitung* (EH, I, 1552), 1996, 356 pp.

MINORITY LITERATURE.   **Interkulturelle Konfigurationen. Zur deutsch-sprachigen Prosaliteratur von Autoren nichtdeutscher Herkunft*, ed Mary Howard, Munich, Iudicium, 200 pp. S. Klettenhammer, '"Mit den Ohren schauen" — Hörspiele von Tiroler Autorinnen und Autoren in den neunziger Jahren', Holzner, *Literatur*, 521–62. Marilya Veteto-Conrad, **Finding a Voice. Identity and the Works of German-language Turkish Writers in the Federal Republic of Germany to 1990* (AUS, III, 48), 1996, 92 pp. W. Wiesmüller, 'Die christlich-katholische Tradition im Spiegel der Tiroler Literatur nach 1945 am Beispiel des Jahrbuchs *Wort im Gebirge*', Holzner, *Literatur*, 465–81.

2.   LYRIC POETRY

T. Bleicher, 'Keine Zeit für Liebe? Zur deutschsprachigen Liebeslyrik nach 1945', *Convivium*, 1996:133–56.

3. DRAMA

M. Bobinac, '1968 und das neue Volksstück', *Jb. der ungarischen Germanistik*, 1995 [1996]: 63–72.

4. PROSE

M. Kublitz-Kramer, 'Drinnen und Draußen. Zur Analyse erzählender Texte von Gegenwartsautorinnen', *DUS*, 48.1, 1996: 78–86. Hans-Martin Plesske, **Beruf und Arbeit in deutschsprachiger Prosa seit 1945. Ein bibliographisches Lexikon. Ergänzung und chronologische Fortführung des Werkes 'Beruf und Arbeit in deutscher Erzählung' von Franz Anselm Schmitt*, Stuttgart, Hiersemann, xvi + 436 pp. **Von Böll bis Buchheim. Deutsche Kriegsprosa nach 1945*, ed. Hans Wagener (ABNG, 42), 421 pp. Gretchen E. Wiesehan, **A Dubious Heritage. Questioning Identity in German Autobiographical Novels of the Postwar Generation* (STML, 26), 186 pp.

5. INDIVIDUAL AUTHORS

AICHINGER, ILSE. N. E. Rosenberger, 'Ungefügte Optik. Zur Rolle der Sinneswahrnehmung in I. As Roman *Die größere Hoffnung*', *SCRIPT*, 12: 23–28. B. Thums, 'Name, Mythos und Geschichte in I. As Erzählung "Ajax"', *ZGer*, 7: 292–302.

ANDERSCH, ALFRED. Maria Elisabeth Brunner, **Der Deserteur und Erzähler A. A. 'Daß nichts dunkel gesagt werden darf, was auch klar gesagt werden kann'*, Frankfurt, Lang, 491 pp.

AUSLÄNDER, ROSE. A. Kita, 'R. A.: Begegnung mit Paul Celan', *DB*, 97, 1996: 49–60. M. Klanska, 'Biblische Motive im Schaffen R. As: Versuch einer ersten Bestandsaufnahme', *Fest. Schwob*, 239–49. Harald Vogel and Michael Gans, **R. A. Lesen. Lesewege — Lesezeichen zum literarischen Werk* (Leseportraits, 2), Baltmannweiler, Schneider Hohengehren, 223 pp.

BACHMANN, INGEBORG. *Austriaca*, 21, 1996, a special issue on B., includes: K. Bartsch, '"Muß einer denken?" Zur Problematik der Geschlechterpolarisierung im Werk der I. B.' (27–36); S. Belluzzo, 'Via negativa — passion et compassion — I. B. lit Simone Weil' (63–83); L. Cassagnau, '"Am Horizont ... glanzvoll im Untergang": structure d'horizon et allégorie dans la poésie d'I. B.' (121–40); F. Collin, 'Cet arc de deuil' (17–25); M. Couffon, 'I. B. et la musique' (107–20); H. Dorowin, 'Die schwarzen Bilder der I. B. Interpretation zu *Die gestundene Zeit*' (153–66); J.-P. Faye, 'Perspectivisme de Nietzsche à I. B.' (57–61); M. Kappes, 'Le motif de l'autodestruction dans la prose narrative d'I. B.' (167–81); H. Mahrdt, 'Zu den "Sitten" der

Zeit in I. Bs später Erzählung *Drei Wege zum See* (37–56); A. Puff-Trojan, '"Das Mögliche ist unmöglich unsagbar."' La littérature et le pouvoir des philosophes' (85–96); F. Retif, 'Le retour des enfers. I. B. en quête d'une autre écriture' (141–52); and I. von Weidenbaum, 'Ich bin eine Slawin' (7–16). M. Albrecht, 'Eine Quelle zu der Erzählung *Gier* und ihre Dokumentation in der kritischen Edition von I. Bs Todesarten-Projekt', Schwob, *Edition*, 333–39. Bettina Bannasch, *Von vorlebten Dingen. Schreiben nach 'Malina': I. Bs 'Simultan'-Erzählungen* (Ep, 216), 267 pp. G. Brokoph-Mauch, 'Österreich als Fiktion und Geschichte in der Prosa I. Bs', *MAL*, 30.3–4:185–99. C. Decker, '"wenn je etwas gut und ganz werden soll": B.'s "Unter Mördern und Irren" and the political culture of the *Stammtisch*', *ib.*, 29.3–4, 1996:43–56. Christa Dericum, *Faszination des Feuers. Das Leben der I. B.*, Freiburg, Herder, 1996, 153 pp. D. Dollenmayer, 'Schoenberg's "Pierrot lunaire" in I. B.'s *Malina*', *MAL*, 30.2:101–16. R. Duffaut, 'I. B.'s alternative "states": rethinking nationhood in *Malina*', *ib.*, 29.3–4, 1996:30–42. I. Dusar, 'Wie die Literatur Geschichte schreibt. Weibliche Existenz im Kontext von I. Bs "Haus Österreich"', *GM*, 43–44, 1996:51–67. I. Egger, 'Mehrsprachigkeit. Zu einem Motiv der österreichischen Literatur am Beispiel von I. B.', *DVLG*, 70, 1996:692–706. Stefanie Golisch, *I. B. zur Einführung* (Zur Einführung, 141), Hamburg, Junius, 168 pp. D. Gottsche, 'Intertextualität, Leitmotivik und Textgenese in I. Bs Todesarten-Projekt und in dessen kritischer Edition', *Editio*, 10, 1996:116–23. A. F. Grant, '"Kränkung" and "Verdrängung": the metaphor of hysteria in Marlen Haushofer's *Die Mansarde* and I. B.'s *Der Fall Franza*', Obermayer, *Österreich*, 171–89. H. Mahrdt, '"Society is the biggest murder scene of all": on the private and public spheres in I. B.'s prose', *WGY*, 12, 1996:167–87. U. Marquardt and L. Bluhm, 'Das vergiftete Buch. Zu einem intertextuellen Spiel in I. Bs zweitem *Todesarten*-Roman', *WW*, 47:353–58. N. Šlibar, 'Von einem, der auszog, das Fürchten zu lernen. I. Bs Gedichtzyklus *Von einem Land, einem Fluß und den Seen*, *ŻGB*, 5, 1996:139–56. M. Tzaneva, 'Die Welt ist meine Welt: Österreich und das Bild der Himbeere in I. Bs *Malina*', *MAL*, 30.3–4:170–84.

BAYER, KONRAD. D. Bartens, 'Orgie und Exorzismus. Szenische Elemente in Prosatexten von K. B. und Oswald Wiener', *GM*, 43–44, 1996:81–95.

BECKER, JUREK. M. Dubrowska, 'J. B. und sein Judentum', *Convivium*, 1996:179–90. D. Rock, 'Christoph Hein und J. B.: Zwei kritische Autoren aus der DDR über die Wende und zum vereinten Deutschland', *GLL*, 50:182–200.

BERNHARD, THOMAS. Paola Bozzi, *Asthetik des Leidens. Zur Lyrik T. Bs* (BLL, 16), 243 pp. Josef Donnenberg, *T. B. (und Österreich). Studien zu Werk und Wirkung 1970–89* (SAG, 352), 148 pp. Karl Fitzthum, **Eine Geschichte, die allen gefällt. Die Grundlegung von T. Bs Poetik in der Erzählung 'Der Kulterer'* (ES, 109), 61 pp. **T. B.-Symposium*, ed. Karin Hempel-Soos, Bonn, Bouvier, 124 pp. Bernhard Judex, **'Wild wächst die Blume meines Zorns . . .' Die Vater-Sohn-Problematik bei T. B. Biographische und werkbezogene Aspekte* (EH, 1, 1600), 137 pp. E. Leonardy, 'Das Verhältnis der Erzählfiguren zu den Dingen im Werk T. Bs', *GM*, 43–44, 1996:97–114. C. Lepschy, 'B. reads Kleist — I: a marionette theatre as a writing machine', Debatin, *Metaphor*, 13–24. Id., 'B. reads Kleist — II: a text as murderer', *ib.*, 251–57. Regine Meyer-Arlt, **Nach dem Ende. Posthistorie und die Dramen T. Bs* (GTS, 56), viii + 218 pp. Eckhart Nickel, **Flaneur. Die Ermöglichung der Lebenskunst im Spätwerk T. Bs*, Heidelberg, Manutius, 180 pp. **T. B.: Beiträge zur Fiktion der Postmoderne. Londoner Symposion*, ed. Wendelin Schmidt-Dengler, Adrian Stevens, and Fred Wagner, Frankfurt, Lang, 220 pp. Laura Sormani, **Semiotik und Hermeneutik im interkulturellen Rahmen. Interpretationen zu Werken von Peter Weiss, R. W. Fassbinder, T. B. und Botho Strauß*, Frankfurt, Lang, ix + 345 pp.

BÖLL, HEINRICH. Bernd Balzer, **Das literarische Werk H. Bs*, DTV, 416 pp. Helmut Bernsmeier, **H. B.* (UB, 15211), 151 pp. Viktor Böll und Markus Schäfer, **Fortbeschreibung. Bibliographie zum Werk H. Bs*, Cologne, Kiepenheuer & Witsch, 250 pp. Ingo Lehnick, **Der Erzähler H. B.* (BNE, 15), 181 pp. G. Sander, '"Verantwortlich sein fur eine weitere deutsche Geschichte." H. Bs politisches Engagement der fünfziger und sechziger Jahre in chronologischer Darstellung', *WW*, 47:358–98. M. Serrer, '"Todesursache: Hakennase." H. Bs Erzählung über eine Massenexekution', *DUS*, 49.4:76–78.

BRAUN, VOLKER. Karin Bothe, **Die imaginierte Natur des Sozialismus. Eine Biographie des Schreibens und der Texte V. Bs (1959–1974)* (Ep, 189), 488 pp. M. Jäger, 'Vollendung im Fragment. V. B.', *SuF*, 49:607–16. C. Cosentino, 'Ostdeutsche Autoren Mitte der neunziger Jahre: V. B., Brigitte Burmeister und Reinhard Jirgl', *GR*, 71, 1996:177–94.

BRINKMANN, ROLF DIETER. **Bibliographie R. D. B.*, ed. Günter Geduldig and Claudia Wehebrink, Bielefeld, Aisthesis, 279 pp. Claudia Schwalfenberg, **Die andere Modernität. Strukturen des Ich-Sagens bei R. D. B.* (Agenda Resultate, 6), Münster, Agenda, 260 pp.

BROCH, HERMANN. R. Duhamel, 'Von Vergil bis Ovid. Kunst und Kunstler bei H. B. und Christoph Ransmayr', *GM*, 43–44, 1996:191–200. Jürgen Heizmann, **Antike und Moderne in H. Bs 'Tod des Vergil'. Über Dichtung und Wissenschaft, Utopie und Ideologie* (MBSL, 33), 207 pp. Glenn R. Sandberg, **The Genealogy of the 'Massenführer'. H. B.'s 'Die Verzauberung' as a Religious Novel* (BNL, 153), x + 167 pp.

E. V. Schneider-Handschin, '"Schöpfer" vs. "Macher". Zur Produktionsästhethik und Romanpoetik Jakob Wassermanns und H. Bs', *MAL*, 30.2:84–100.

DE BRUYN, GÜNTER. *Verleihung des Literaturpreises der Konrad-Adenauer-Stiftung e. V. an G. d. B., Weimar, 15. Mai 1996*, ed. Günther Rüther, Weseling, Konrad-Adenauer-Stiftung, 1996, 44 pp. D. Tate, 'G. d. B.: The "gesamtdeutsche Konsensfigur" of post-Unification literature?', *GLL*, 50:201–13.

BUCH, HANS CHRISTOPH. Herbert Uerlings, *Poetiken der Interkulturalität. Haiti bei Kleist, Seghers, Müller, B. und Fichte*, Tübingen, Niemeyer, 363 pp.

BURGER, HERMANN. Christian Schön, *H. B.: Schreiben als Therapie. Eine Studie zu Leben und Werk*, Stuttgart, Ibidem, 186 pp. Claudia Storz, *Bs Kindheiten. Eine Annäherung an H. B.*, Zurich, Nagel & Kimche, 1996, 383 pp.

BURMEISTER, BRIGITTE. B. Alldred, 'Two contrasting perspectives on German Unification: Helga Schubert and B. B.', *GLL*, 50:165–81. See also BRAUN, VOLKER.

CANETTI, ELIAS. Eric Leroy du Cardonnoy, *Les 'Réflexions' d'E. C. Une esthétique de la discontinuité* (Contacts, Serie III, Études et documents, 38), Berne, Lang, 338 pp. C. Magrio, 'E. C. y el imperio en el aire', *CHA*, 565–66:247–54. I. Ookawa, 'Grenzüberschreitender Geist oder E. Cs "Möglichkeitssinn"', *DB*, 97, 1996:61–71. *Autobiographie zwischen Fiktion und Wirklichkeit. Internationales Symposium Russe, Oktober 1992*, ed. Angelova Penka and Emilia Straitscheva (Schriftenreihe der E.-C.-Gesellschaft, 1), St. Ingbert, Röhrig, 314 pp.

CELAN, PAUL. John Felstiner, *P. C.: Eine Biographie*, Munich, Beck, 432 pp. Ute Henjes, *Engführung. Kommentar zu P. Cs Gedichtzyklus* (Edition Wissenschaft, 28), Marburg, Tectum, 265 pp. Y. Hirano, 'Flora von "Buchenland". Ein Versuch über C.', *DB*, 97, 1996:39–48. *Kommentar zu P. Cs 'Die Niemandsrose'*, ed. Jürgen Lehmann (BNL, 149), 430 pp. *Stationen. Kontinuität und Entwicklung in P. Cs Übersetzungswerk*, ed. J. Lehmann (BNL, 156), xiii + 195 pp. Cindy Mackey, *Dichter der Bezogenheit. A Study of P. Cs Poetry with Special Reference to 'Die Niemandsrose'* (SAG, 306), 472 pp. Bernhard Paha, *Die 'Spur' im Werk P. Cs: Eine 'wiederholte' Lesung Jacques Derridas* (Wissenschaftsskripten 1, 4), Giessen, Kletsmeier, 184 pp. See also AUSLÄNDER, ROSE.

CZECHOWSKI, HEINZ. W. Ertl, '*Sonnenhang und Nachtspur*: Reiner Kunzes und H. Cs poetische Positionen im Zeitgeschehen um die Wende', *GR*, 70, 1995:145–52. I. Hilton, 'H. C.: Die überstandene Wende?', *GLL*, 50:214–26.

DELIUS, FRIEDRICH CHRISTIAN. B. Rossbacher, 'Unity and imagined community: F. C. D.'s *Die Birnen von Ribbeck* and *Der Sonntag, an dem ich Weltmeister wurde*', *GQ*, 70:151–67.

DODERER, HEIMITO VON. W. Riemer, 'The imperative of technology: D.'s "Divertimento No. IV"', *MAL*, 30.1:88–101.

DRAWERT, KURT. M. Hipp, 'Über den Umgang mit Schuld in K. Ds deutschem Monolog *Spiegelland*', *BBGN*, 10, 1996:69–83.

DREWITZ, INGEBORG. M. Shafi, 'Gazing at India: representations of alterity in travelogues by I. D., Günter Grass and Hubert Fichte', *GQ*, 70:39–56.

DUDEN, ANNA. E. Kleinschmidt, '"Das Schreiben der Texte hingegen erinnert sich wörtlich." Zur Poetik A. Ds', *WB*, 43:538–53. B. Lersch-Schumacher, 'Melencolia, Mnemosyne, Medusa. Zur Mythopoetik des Blicks in A. Ds *Das Judasschaf*', *SCRIPT*, 12:36–43.

DÜRRENMATT, FRIEDRICH. H. Masumoto, 'Eine Analyse zum Problem des Grotesken in der Prosafassung der *Panne* F. Ds', *DB*, 97, 1996:102–12.

ENZENSBERGER, HANS MAGNUS. Martin Fritsche, **H. M. Es produktionsorientierte Moral. Konstanten in der Ästhetik eines Widersachers der Gleichheit* (EH, 1, 1631), 264 pp. J. Monroe, 'Between ideologies and a hard place: H. M. E.'s utopian pragmatist poetics', *STCL*, 21:41–77.

ERB, ELKE. B. Mabee, 'Footprints revisited or "Life in the changed space that I don't know": E. E.'s poetry since 1989', *STCL*, 21:161–85.

FICHTE, HUBERT. Peter Braun, **Die doppelte Dokumentation. Fotografie und Literatur im Werk von Leonore Mau und H. F.*, Stuttgart, Metzler, vi + 391 pp. See also BUCH, HANS CHRISTOPH; DREWITZ, INGEBORG.

FLEISSER, MARIELUISE. Silvia Henke, **Fehl am Platz. Studien zu einem kleinen Drama im Werk von Alfred Jarry, Else Lasker-Schüler, M. F. and Djuna Barnes* (Ep, 200), 199 pp.

FRISCH, MAX. Chieh Chien, **Das Frauenbild in den Romanen 'Stiller' und 'Homo faber' von M. F. im Lichte der analytischen Psychologie C. G. Jungs* (EH, 1, 1648), 263 pp. L. Lob, '"Insanity in the darkness": anti-semitic stereotypes and Jewish identity in M. F.'s *Andorra* and Arthur Miller's *Focus*', *MLR*, 92:545–58.

FÜHMANN, FRANZ. P. Beicken, 'Stürzender Engel, verlorene Heimat. Zum Österreichischen bei F. F., *Böhme und Vagant*', *MAL*, 30.3–4:239–52.

GERNHARDT, ROBERT. **R. G.*, ed. Heinz Ludwig Arnold (TK, 136), 121 pp. G. Seibt, 'Zweite Unschuld. Über den Lyriker R. G.', *SuF*, 49:708–19.

GOES, ALBRECHT. Helmut Hornbogen, **Erinnerung an Anfänge. Tübingen. Vom Gedenken. Gespräche mit A. G. und Hermann Lenz*, Tübingen, Narr, 1996, 89 pp.

GOETZ, RAINALD.   J. Bertschik, 'Theatralität und Irrsinn. Darstellungsformen "multipler" Persönlichkeitskonzepte in der Gegenwartsliteratur. Zu Texten von Heinar Kipphardt, Unica Zürn, R. G. und Thomas Hettche', *WW*, 47:398–423. Thomas Doktor and Carl Spies, **Gottfried Benn — R. G. Mediumliteratur zwischen Pathologie und Poetologie*, Wiesbaden, Westdeutscher Vlg, 277 pp.

GRASS, GÜNTER.   Mark Martin Gruettner, **Intertextualität und Zeitkritik in G. Gs 'Kopfgeburten' und 'Die Rättin'* (Studien zur deutschsprachigen Gegenwartsliteratur, 6), Tübingen, Stauffenburg, 152 pp. C. Mayer-Iswandy, '"Danach ging das Leben weiter." Zum Verhältnis von Macht und Gewalt im Geschlechterkampf. Systemtheoretische Überlegungen zu G. G. und Ulla Hahn', *ZGer*, 7:303–20. **Der Fall Fonty. Ein weites Feld von G. G. im Spiegel der Kritik*, ed. Oskar Negt, Göttingen, Steidl, 1996, 495 pp. J. Osinski, 'Aspekte der Fontane-Rezeption bei G. G.', *Fontane-Blätter*, 62, 1996:112–26. D. Stolz, 'Nomen est omen. *Ein weites Feld* von G. G.', *ib.*, 321–35. See also DREWITZ, INGEBORG.

HAHN, ULLA.   C. Melin, 'Improved versions: feminist poetics and recent work by U. H. and Ursula Krechel', *STCL*, 21:219–43. See also GRASS, GÜNTER.

HANDKE, PETER.   C. Becker, '"Lebenswelten" oder Handke liest Hofmannsthal', *SuF*, 49:867–77. Thomas Hennig, **Intertextualität als ethische Dimension. P. Hs Ästhetik 'nach Auschwitz'* (Ep, 180), 1996, 250 pp. T. Karino, 'Die Dynamik der Verwandlung. *Die Angst des Tormanns beim Elfmeter* von P. H.', *DB*, 97, 1996:113–21. H. Kiesel, '"Es lebe der König!" Eine Apologie von P. Hs "Königsdrama" *Zurüstungen für die Unsterblichkeit*', *SuF*, 49:442–48. F. Pilip, 'Österreichbilder in P. Hs Erzählung *Die Stunde der wahren Empfindung*', *MAL*, 30.3–4:213–21. Tilmann Siebert, **Langsame Heimkehr — Studien zur Kontinuität im Werk P. Hs*, Göttingen, Cuvillier, 221 pp. M. Tabah, 'Von der *Stunde der wahren Empfindung* (1975) zum *Jahr in der Niemandsbucht* (1994). P. Hs ästhetische Utopie', *GM*, 43–44, 1996:115–23. U. Wesche, 'Metaphorik bei P. H.', *MDU*, 99:59–67. **Die Angst des Dichters vor der Wirklichkeit. 16 Antworten auf P. Hs Winterreise nach Serbien*, ed. Tilman Zülch, Göttingen, Steidl, 1996, 139 pp.

HARIG, LUDWIG.   *L. H.*, ed. Heinz Ludwig Arnold (TK, 135), 91 pp., was published to coincide with H.'s 70th birthday and offers welcome insight into a writer so often overlooked in studies of contemporary authors. Opening with a commemorative poem by Dieter Wellershoff and an autobiographical text by H. himself, the volume concentrates on the most important aspects of H.'s career. M. Reich-Ranicki identifies H. as one of the best chroniclers of 20th-c. German life, basing his assessment on the author's three autobiographical novels: *Ordnung ist das ganze Leben* (1986), *Weh dem, der aus der Reihe tanzt* (1990), and *Wer mit den Wölfen heult, wird Wolf* (1996). The significance of these texts is reflected in two further articles. H. Lenz explores the second text in the trilogy, which recounts H.'s experiences at an élite Hitler Youth school, and finds him a 'schonungsloser Registrator, besonders, was ihn selbst betrifft' (p. 48). B. Rech runs the rule over H.'s 'autobiographisches Erzählen' in general, arguing that it is not to be viewed merely as documentary or historical writing since it is not based on cold facts, but on the author's memory of events: 'Also ist für ihn Wahrheit gebunden an das Wahrnehmen und das Empfinden' (p. 53). In its conflation of memory and invention, H.'s autobiographical writing has much in common with that of Günter de Bruyn. In subsequent articles, R. Köhnen explores the linguistic experimentation of H.'s poetry, J. Kamps looks at the work written for radio, J. Hieber explores H.'s work as an interpreter of poetry and recounts how his inability to teach P. Celan effectively led to his abandonment of teaching as a profession, and W. Jung underlines the important role football plays in H.'s work. M. Sitter closes the volume with a detailed select bibliography. The volume gives a full picture of the variety of H.'s work and does much to underline his importance, in particular, as an observer of the recent German past.

HERMLIN, STEPHAN. T. Hörnigk, 'Interview mit S. H. am 30. 9. 1995 über die Geschichte des PEN nach 1945', *ŽGer*, 7 : 140–54.

HEYM, STEFAN. P. Maas, 'Der handelnde Zeuge oder: weshalb der *Ahasver* von S. H. kein postmoderner Roman ist', *GerLux*, 10 : 71–88.

HILBIG, WOLFGANG. Gabriele Eckart, **Sprachtraumata in den Texten W. Hs* (DDR-Studien, 10), NY, Lang, 1996, viii + 206 pp. Bärbel Heising, *'*Briefe voller Žitate aus dem Vergessen.*' *Intertextualität im Werk W. Hs* (BSDL, 48), 1996, 237 pp.

HILSENRATH, EDGAR. N. O. Eke, 'Planziel Vernichtung. Zwei Versuche über das Unfaßbare des Völkermords: Franz Werfels *Die vierzig Tage des Mesa Dagh* (1933) und E. Hs *Das Märchen vom letzten Gedanken* (1989)', *DVLG*, 71 : 701–23.

HODJAK, FRANZ. S. P. Scheichl, '*die brunnen, die einst anders rauschten, sind ausgedorrt.* F. H. — Lyriker eines kulturellen Zusammenbruchs', *Fest. Schwob*, 389–400.

JAHNN, HANS HENNY. J. Bürger, 'Am Anfang steht die Lektüre. Intertextualität als Kommentierungsproblem. Das Beispiel H. H. J.', Schwob, *Edition*, 341–49.

JANDL, ERNST. M. Berghoff, 'Hypermedia als weitere Chance für den Deutschunterricht? Skizze eines interaktiven Assoziations- und Interpretationsraums im Internet zu E. Js "wien: heldenplatz"',

MDG, 44:78–94. M. Schmitz-Emans, 'Zwischen Sprachutopismus und Sprachrealismus: zur artikulatorischen Dichtung Hugo Balls und E. Js', *Hugo Ball Almanach*, 20, 1996:43–117.

JELINEK, ELFRIEDE. Maria E. Brunner, *Die Mythenzertrümmerung *der E. J.*, Neuried, ars una, 198 pp. G. Finney, 'Komödie und Obszönität: der sexuelle Witz bei J. und Freud', *GQ*, 70:27–38. Heike Fischer, *Materialistische Theoreme in ausgewählten Werken E. Js, Herzogenrath, Shaker, 290 pp. B. Haines, 'Beyond patriarchy: Marxism, feminism, and E. J.'s Die Liebhaberinnen', *MLR*, 92:643–55. M. S. Pflüger, *Vom Dialog zur Dialogizität. Die Theaterästhetik von E.J. (MFDT, 15), 1996, 326 pp.

JOHNSON, UWE. *Internationales Johnson-Forum*, 4, 1996, includes: K. Fickert, 'The attitude of narration in J.'s *Jonas zum Beispiel*' (169–79); S. Golisch, 'J. auszählen. Einige kritische Bemerkungen zum gegenwärtigen Stand der J.-Forschung' (191–95); A. Last, 'Von *Ingrid Babendererde* zu *Jahrestage*. Ein stilistischer Streifzug durch U. Js Romane' (13–67); W. Martynkewicz, 'Doppelt belichtet. Einige Bemerkungen zum Stellenwert von Photographie und Bildfiktion in den *Jahrestagen* von U. J.' (143–54); M. Radtke, 'Überlegungen zum Begriff Erinnerung in U. Js *Jahrestage*' (111–24); N. Riedel, 'Neuere Forschungsarbeiten zum Werk U. Js. Eine Auswahlbibliographie der Sekundärliteratur 1981–1994' (197–217); S. A. Vischer, 'Zwischen Ende und Anfang. Zur Funktion der fiktionalen Verträge in der Struktur von U. Js Roman *Jahrestage*' (69–110); and W. Wittkowski, 'Zeugnis geben: religiöses Helden- und Pseudo-Heldentum in U. Js *Jahrestagen* (Bd. 2)' (125–42). *Ib.*, 5, includes: T. Buck, 'U. Js Utopie gegen die deutsche(n) Wirklichkeit(en)' (23–38); A.-Y. Galliot, 'L'image diffractée de l'Allemagne ou la quête d'identité dans les *Jahrestage* de U.J.' (55–75); M. Haslé, 'La réalité appréhendée dans *Mutmaßungen über Jakob* de U. J.' (159–75); L. Helbig, 'Der deutsche Osten aus amerikanischer Sicht. U. Js Protagonistin Gesine Cresspahl in New York' (109–26); B. Neumann, 'Aspekte des deutsch-deutschen Romans. U. J. und Christa Wolf' (39–53); I. Rabenstein-Michel, 'U. Js Collage *Eine Reise nach Klagenfurt* — mehr als ein biographischer Prospekt' (91–107); N. Riedel, 'Bibliographie zur Edition und Rezeption U. Js im französischen Sprachraum. Werk und Wirkung in Frankreich, Belgien und der Schweiz' (199–216); B. Schulz, "Derelict", der 25. Februar, 1968. Eine Art, U.Js *Jahrestage* zu lesen' (77–90); Id., 'Ein französischer Blick auf die Prosa U. Js: Jean-Louis de Rambures im Gespräch am 2. November 1994 in Frankfurt am Main' (191–97); J. Tailleur, 'U. J. — deux ans après le prix Formentor. Aus dem Französischen übersetzt und mit Anmerkungen von Ralf Zschachlitz' (179–90); and P. Wellnitz, 'Traumebenen in U. Js Prosa. Eine Ansicht zu *Zwei Ansichten*' (127–38). *Johnson-Jb.*, 4, includes: G. Bond, '"Sie hätten eine verdammt gute Zeit miteinander haben können." Erste Eindrücke zu U. Js *Heute Neunzig Jahr*' (56–71); G. Butzer, '"Ja. Nein." Paradoxes Eingedenken in U. Js Roman *Jahrestage*' (130–57); I. Hoesterey, 'Modern/postmodern: eine Rezeption der *Jahrestage*, USA 1977' (48–55); H.-J. Klug, 'Aus den Schulakten. U. Js *Darstellung meiner Entwicklung*' (15–16); I. Müller, 'Der Tischler als Oberbürgermeister. Über eine Vorlage für Heinrich Cresspahls Amtszeit als Bürgermeister von Anfang 1945 bis zum 22. Oktober 1945' (158–76); U. Neumann, '"Andere über mich." Schriftsteller (und Politiker) über U. J., Teil 1: Von Leipzig nach Berlin' (177–96); R. Paasch-Beeck, 'Bißchen viel Kirche, Marie? Bibelrezeption in U. Js *Jahrestage*' (72–114); D. Searls, '"Funny how the past catches up with you." U. J. in Sheerness, 12 years later' (197–200); G. Stübe, 'J. in Güstrow. Berührungen' (39–47); and O. Vogel, '"Make room for the lady! Make room for the child!" Zum Ort des Erzählens in U. Js *Jahrestagen*' (115–29). M. Hofmann, 'Erinnerung und Gedächtnis, Korrespondenz und Allegorie. Walter Benjamins Poetik der Moderne und U. Js *Jahrestage*', *ZDP*, 116:272–93. M. Scheffel, 'Das geteilte Deutschland im Spiegel der zeitgenössischen Literatur. Ein Rückblick auf zwei Romane von Arno Schmidt und U. J.', *Runa*, 25, 1996:265–73.

JÜNGER, ERNST. R. Schieb, 'Die Rezeption E. Js nach 1945', *Schiller Jb.*, 40, 1996:348–61.

KANT, HERMANN. T. Hörnigk, 'Interview mit H. K. am 8. 10. 1995 über die Geschichte des PEN nach 1945', *ZGer*, 7:357–71. W. Schemme, 'H. K.: *Abspann* — Erinnerung an meine Gegenwart. Vom schwierigen Versuch, "sich zu erklaren"', *DUB*, 48, 1995:246–56.

KASER, NORBERT C. B. Rabelhofer, '*es bockt mein herz*. Zur Organsprache N. C. Ks', *Fest. Schwob*, 363–74.

KIPPHARDT, HEINAR. Sven Hanuschek, **H. Ks Bibliothek. Ein Verzeichnis*, Bielefeld, Aisthesis, 240 pp. See also GOETZ, RAINALD.

KIRSCH, SARAH C. Cosentino, '"An affair of uncertain ground": S. K.'s poetry volume *Erlking's Daughter* in the context of her prose after the *Wende*', *STCL*, 21:141–60. *S. K.*, ed. Mererid Hopwood and David Basker, Cardiff, Wales U.P., xi + 123 pp., is the next volume in the fine series arising from the visit of writers and academics to Swansea's Centre for Contemporary German Literature. This volume follows the pattern already established, opening with five previously unpublished poems by K. which were written during her stay on the Gower Peninsula. An outline biography leads into a tantalizingly brief interview with the author, but the disappointment is assuaged by the fine contributions which follow. A tribute by Günter Kunert sets the tone by outlining K.'s predilection for solitude, a theme revisited in the ensuing chapters: M. Kane charts K.'s early career in the GDR and the growing innovation in her work; A. Bushell opts to concentrate on poetic theme and structure rather than politics in the early collections, uncovering an 'undiminished sense of unrest' (p. 35) which is common to them all; M. Butler focuses on the extent to which the author has largely devoted herself to prose over the past decade, and finds transience to be the overriding feature, with earlier playfulness giving way to a more sombre tone in *Das simple Leben*; and R. W. Williams offers a detailed and compelling analysis of this latter text, defending its self-referentiality as an attempt to impose aesthetic order on a chaotic and disturbing world, while simultaneously underlining K.'s awareness of the futility of her enterprise. In the most engaging chapter, however, M. Hopwood explores the poetry K. has written in Wales and places it in the broader context of her work. On an earlier visit to Swansea in 1989, K. produced three poems which appeared in *Erlkönigs Tochter*, and H. sees the influence of Dylan Thomas at work in them. The lighter tone of these poems is then contrasted with the darker mood of the later poems which open this study. H. L. Arnold's reminiscence of K. is the final article and the volume concludes with a detailed bibliography. Each of the contributions touches on the challenge of reading K.'s work, yet emphasizes the pleasures therein, and in this way the study represents a stimulating new appraisal of K.'s creative imagination.

KISCH, EGON ERWIN. C. G. Ervedosa, 'Der "Kalte Krieg" in der Germanistik. Studien zur unterschiedlichen Rezeption E. E. Ks in der BRD und der ehemaligen DDR', *Runa*, 25, 1996:257–63. Marcus G. Patka, **E. E. K. Stationen im Leben eines streitbaren Autors* (LGGL, 41), 581 pp.

KIWUS, KARIN. J. Rolleston, 'Modernism and metamorphosis: K. K.'s *Das chinesische Examen*', *STCL*, 21:111–22.

KOEPPEN, WOLFGANG. D. Basker, 'The author as victim: W. K., *Jakob Littners Aufzeichnungen aus einem Erdloch*', *MLR*, 92:903–11. Gerhard Pinzhoffer, **W. Ks 'Tod in Rom'. Entwurf einer Theorie literarischer Bildlichkeit aus anthropologischer Sicht* (Ep, 174), 1996, 243 pp. K. Prümm, 'Notate eines Reisenden. Zum Tod von W. K.', *DUS*, 47.3, 1996:81–86. Josef Quack, **W. K. Erzähler der Zeit*, Würzburg, Königshausen & Neumann, 324 pp. G. Vilas-Boas, 'Unglückliche Lieben. Zu zwei Texten von Annemarie Schwarzenbach und W. K.', *Runa*, 25, 1996:239–45.

KROETZ, FRANZ XAVER. H.-J. Knobloch, 'Hebbel, Un-Hebbel oder Anti-Hebbel? Die Hebbel-Bearbeitungen von F. X. K.', *Hebbel Jb.*, 52:151–68.

KUNERT, GÜNTER. **K.-Werkstatt. Materialien und Studien zu G. Ks literarischem Werk*, ed. Manfred Durzak and Manfred Keune, Bielefeld, Aisthesis, 1995, 239 pp. R. Grimm, 'Intertextualität als Schranke: Übersetzungsprobleme bei Zitaten und dergleichen am Beispiel G. Ks', *MDU*, 89 : 208–20. D. Hinze, **G. K.: Sinnstiftung durch Literatur. Literaturtheorie und dichterische Praxis* (BNE, 13), 1996, 127 pp. L. Olschner, 'A poetics of place. G. K.'s poem sequence "Herbstanbruch in Arkadien" from his volume *Fremd daheim*', *STCL*, 21 : 123–36. Werner Trömer, **Polarität ohne Steigerung. Eine Struktur des Grotesken im Werk G. Ks (1950–1980)*, St. Ingbert, Röhrig, 514 pp.

LANGGÄSSER, ELISABETH. B. Adler, 'Herkunft Rheinhessen. Literatur zwischen Heimat und Welt bei Anna Seghers und E. L.', *Argonautenschiff*, 4, 1995 : 167–73. M. Bircken, 'Begegnungen. Anna Seghers und E. L.', *ib.*, 174–88.

LASKER-SCHÜLER, ELSE. Sissel Laegrid, **Nach dem Tode — oder vor dem Leben. Das poetische Projekt E. L.-Ss*, Frankfurt, Lang, 262 pp.

LAVANT, CHRISTINE. **Die Bilderschrift C. Ls. Studien zur Lyrik, Prosa, Rezeption und Übersetzung. 1. internationales C. L. Symposion Wolfsberg, 11.–13. Mai 1995*, ed. Arno Russegger and Johann Strutz, Salzburg, Müller, 1995, 237 pp.

LEBERT, HANS. E. Reichmann, '"Dampfende Dunghaufen hegend versinken die Dörfer im Schmutz." H. Ls Österreichbild — eine parteibraune Landschaft', *MAL*, 30.3–4 : 130–43.

LEHMANN, WILHELM. R. Kiefer, '"Unberühmter Ort" — Die Geschichte im absoluten Text', *Ernst Meister Jb.*, 1994–95 [1996] : 87–104.

LENZ, HERMANN. **Begegnung mit H. L. Kunzelsauer Symposion*, ed. Rainer Moritz (UDL, 83), vii + 156 pp., includes: M. Durzak, 'Magischer Realismus bei H. L.' (106–20); W. Everling, 'Der Clown und das Licht. Zur Lyrik von H. L.' (72–105); H.-M. Gauger, 'Zum Stil von H. L.' (121–40); P. Hamm, 'H., der Held. Lobrede auf H. L.' (19–35); H. Maier, 'Der Roman als Geschichtsquelle. Anmerkungen zu H. L.' (141–51); R. M., 'Über H. Ls literarhistorischen Ort' (1–18); H. Schuhmacher, 'Realitätsflucht und Bewußtseinskritik. Zum Frühwerk von H. L.' (36–62); and H. Wallmann, 'H. Ls Erzählung *Die Abenteuerin* (1952) als frühes Spätwerk. Prolegomena zu einer künftigen Lektüre' (63–71). See also GOES, ALBRECHT.

LENZ, SIEGFRIED. Claus H. R. Nordbruch, **Über die Pflicht. Eine Analyse des Werkes von S. L. Versuch über ein deutsches Phänomen* (GTS, 53), 1996, 249 pp. Id., '*Deutschstunde*, eine Pflichtlektion. Zur Interpretation der "Antipoden" Jepsen und Nansen', *Germanica*, 24, 1996 [1997] : 91–100. Id., 'S. L.: Ein Kriegsende. Ist Pflichterfüllung mit Menschlichkeit zu verbinden?', *LiLi*, 27 : 148–58.

MALKOWSKI, RAINER. Christof Kneer, *R. M.: *Neue Objektivität in der Lyrik. Monographie zu Leben und Werk R. Ms* (LU, 30), 184 pp.

MARON, MONIKA. U. Niebergall, 'Das Mißverständnis der Liebe. Gedanken zu den Werken von M. M.', *MS*, 90, 1996:168–78.

MITTERER, FELIX. K. Müller-Salget, 'Die Realität der Satire der Satire der Realität. Bemerkungen eines Zugereisten zu F. Ms "Piefke-Saga"', Holzner, *Literatur*, 511–20. G. U. Sandford, 'Zum Heimatbegriff in einigen Stücken F. Ms', *MAL*, 29.3–4, 1996:117–30.

MONÍKOVÁ, LIBUŠE. B. Haines, '"New places from which to write histories of peoples": power and the personal in the novels of L. M.', *GLL*, 49, 1996:501–12. K. H. Jankowsky, 'Remembering Eastern Europe: L. M.', *WGY*, 12, 1996:203–15.

MORGNER, IRMTRAUD. J. Kormann, 'I. M.: Hoffnung auf Alternativen — befreiender Humor', *DUS*, 48.3, 1996:62–66. G. Plow, 'What became of "Notturno": the development of an early theme in I. M.'s work', *GLL*, 50:241–53.

MÜLLER, HEINER. R. Clauss, '"Zerstoben ist die Macht an der mein Vers/Sich brach wie Brandung regenbogenfarb./Im Zaun der Zähne starb der letzte Schrei" — Rückblick auf Leben und Theaterwerk von H. M.', *Grabbe Jb.*, 15, 1996:176–207. L. Fritze, 'Das Elend des moralischen Rigorismus. Überlegungen zu H. Ms Stück *Der Auftrag*', *SuF*, 49:699–707. C. Guimarães, 'Panoptikum, oder von der Kunst, mit Geschichte(n) umzugehen. Zum neuesten Stück von (über) H. M.', *Runa*, 25, 1996:367–73. J. Hermand, 'Blick zurück auf H. M', *ZGer*, 7:559–71. R. Kamath, 'Die manichäsische Welt. H. M.: *Der Auftrag*', *Arcadia*, 31, 1996:223–30. W. Schemme, 'H. M.: Krieg ohne Schlacht. Theater als Angriff auf die Wirklichkeit', *DUB*, 48, 1995:202–211. M. Streisand, 'Erfahrungstransfer. H. Ms *Die Umsiedlerin oder das Leben auf dem Lande*', *DUS*, 48.5, 1996:18–28. T. Zenetti, '"Des deux côtés du front, entre les fronts, au-dessus." H. M. et la réunification allemande', *RevA*, 28, 1996:565–75. See also BUCH, HANS CHRISTOPH.

MÜLLER, HERTA. F. Apel, 'Turbatverse: Ästhetik, Mystik und Politik bei H. M.', *Akzente*, 44:113–25. G. Beste, 'Kommunikation und Identität in H. Ms Erzählung *Der Mensch ist ein großer Fasan auf der Welt*', *DUB*, 50:124–29. Herta Haupt-Cucuiu, **Eine Poesie der Sinne. H. Ms 'Diskurs des Alleinseins' und seine Wurzeln* (Literatur- und Medienwissenschaft, 49), Paderborn, Igel, 1996, 188 pp. *Der Druck der Erfahrung treibt die Sprache in die Dichtung: Bildlichkeit in Texten H. Ms*, ed. Ralph Köhnen, Frankfurt, Lang, 183 pp., is a collection of essays which represents the proceedings of a colloquium held in Bochum during M.'s guest professorship there in 1995/96. The volume explores the author's use of figurative language in each of her major publications from *Niederungen* (1982) to *In der Falle* (1996), stressing the extent to which her essayistic work displays many of the characteristics of her fiction, while the editor provides a general overview of the imagery of motion and perception across M.'s canon. The fascination and irritation of reading M.'s hermetic texts permeates each of the contributions, a number of which endeavour to unpick the locks by adopting a highly theoretical approach. T. Roberg's essay on *Der Mensch ist ein großer Fasan auf der Welt* (1986) is one such example. The most successful chapters eschew the theoretical and focus more on isolating the themes and motifs which underpin the texts. U. Growe's exploration of the complex *Der Wächter nimmt seinen Kamm* (1993), which comprises 94 cards of text, silhouette and collage, is the most effective reflection of the difficulties facing any reader of M.'s work. Growe accepts that it is virtually impossible to instruct the reader on how to tackle this particular text, noting that 'Die Kluft, die sich zwischen Blick, Bild und Beschreibung auftut, scheint unüberbrückbar' (p. 102), yet points to the cohesion to be found in M.'s linguistic style and recurrent motifs. Be they words, phrases or people, these features link not only certain cards within *Der Wächter*, but also this collection with the rest of M.'s work. The volume suggests most convincingly that the apparent impenetrability of M.'s writing can be attributed to the author seeking to articulate the problems of describing the experience of life under Ceauşescu's terrifying dictatorship, where the state intruded into all aspects of the private sphere, including language. M. Hoffmann and K. Schulz outline the way in which even nature in Romania is presented as a threat, rather than a haven, in *Der Fuchs war damals schon der Jäger* (1992). This volume signals that M. is indeed being embraced by a wider audience. The contributors readily admit that their respective interpretations can in be no way be viewed as definitive, and it is hoped that this study will thus stimulate further interest in a challenging, yet fascinating, author. E. Kroeger-Groth, '"Der Brunnen ist kein Fenster und kein Spiegel" oder: wie Wahrnehmung sich erfindet. Ein Gesprach mit H. M.', *DD*, 26, 1995: 223–30. G. Melzer, 'Verkrallt in Aussichtslosigkeit. Eine rumänische Kindheit. Zu H. M. und ihrem Roman *Herztier*', *Fest. Schwob*, 291–97. A. Steets, 'H. M.: Sprache und Identität. *Der Mensch ist ein großer Fasan auf der Welt*', *DUB*, 50: 130–38.

NADOLNY, STEN. *S. *N.*, ed. Wolfgang Bunzel (Porträt, 6), Eggingen, Isele, 1996, 274 pp. Ü. Gökberk, '"Culture studies" und die Türken: S. Ns *Selim oder die Gabe der Rede* im Lichte einer Methodendiskussion', *GQ*, 70: 97–122.

NEUTSCH, ERIK. Andreas Fritsche, **Zur polyphonen Struktur in E. Ns Romanwerk 'Der Friede im Osten'* (Edition Wissenschaft, 35), Marburg, Tectum, 132 pp.

NÖSTLINGER, CHRISTINE. I. Wild, 'Vater — Mutter — Kind. Zur Flexibilisierung von Familienstrukturen in Jugendromanen von C. N.', *DUS*, 48.4, 1996:56–67.

NOSSACK, HANS ERICH. Gabriele Söhling, *Das Schweigen zum Klingen bringen. Denkstruktur, Literaturbegriff und Schreibwesen bei H. E. N.* (MR, 81), 1995, 379 pp.

NOWAK, HELGA. M. S. de Lugnani, 'Das Sibirien H. Ns', *Prospero*, 3, 1996:62–69.

ÖZDAMAR, EMINE SEVGI. K. Jankowsky, '"German" literature contested: the 1991 Ingeborg-Bachmann-Prize debate, "cultural diversity", and E. S. O.', *GQ*, 70:261–76. A. Seyhan, 'Lost in translation: remembering the mother tongue in E. M. O.'s *Das Leben ist eine Karawanserei*', *ib.*, 69, 1996:414–26.

PAUSEWANG, GUDRUN. R. Steinlein, 'Holocaust-Literatur zwischen Pädagogik und Innovation. G. Ps Erzählung *Reise im August*', *DUB*, 49, 1996:295–304.

PLENZDORF, ULRICH. Armin-Thomas Bühler, *U. P.: Personalbibliographie 1970–1993*, Giessen, Kletsmeier, 1996, 79 pp. E. Schütz, 'Old Wibeau oder Werthers Himmelfahrt. Zur Aktualisierbarkeit eines gealterten Jugendkult-Textes', *DUS*, 48.5, 1996:48–58.

RANSMAYR, CHRISTOPH. L. Cook, 'Variations of the lost hero: blood on the ice in C. R.'s *Schrecken des Eises und der Finsternis*', Obermayer, *Österreich*, 214–33. F. Decreus, 'Vom Chaos zur Ordnung und von der Ordnung zum Chaos. Über das Erfinden und Verlieren der Wirklichkeit in C. Rs *Die letzte Welt* (1988)', *GM*, 43–44, 1996:175–90. See also BROCH, HERMANN.

REHMANN, RUTH. F. Eigler, '"Gesinnung" und "Ästhetik". R. Rs kulturhistorische und autobiographische Spurensuche in *Unterwegs in fremden Träumen. Begegnungen mit dem anderen Deutschland*', *WB*, 43:255–70.

REICHART, ELISABETH. K. Müller, 'Gespräch mit E. R.', *DeutB*, 27:83–98.

REIMANN, BRIGITTE. K. McPherson, '"Kann man sich denn auf irgendeinen Briefpartner verlassen?" B. R. — Christa Wolf', *ZGer*, 7:543–58.

RICHTER, HANS WERNER. Sabine Cofalla, *Der 'soziale Sinn' H. W. Rs. Zur Korrespondenz des Leiters der Gruppe 47*, Berlin, Weidler, 140 pp.

SACHS, NELLY. Dorothee Ostmeier, *Sprache des Dramas — Drama der Sprache. Zur Poetik N. Ss* (CJ, 16), vii + 156 pp.

SCHÄDLICH, HANS JOACHIM. W. Jung, '"Es ist alles ein großes Spiel." Gespräch mit H. J. S.', *DUS*, 48.5, 1996:91–96. H. Krauss, 'Franz Kafka und der real existierende Sozialismus oder kleines Kolleg über den Realismus — vom Polizeistandpunkt aus', *Runa*, 25, 1996:385–92.

SCHMIDT, ARNO.   U. Japp, 'Rekapitulation der Weltliteratur. A. Ss Totengespräche', *DVLG*, 71 : 164–77. S. Jurczyk, *Symbolwelten. Studien zu 'Caliban über Setebos' von A. S.* (Literatur- und Medienwissenschaft, 61), Paderborn, Igel, 263 pp. Carsten Scholz, **'Ich lese nichts Geschriebenes mehr.' Literarische Mündlichkeit in A. Ss 'Kaff auch mare Crisium'*, Bielefeld, Aisthesis, 112 pp. See also JOHNSON, UWE.

SCHNEIDER, PETER.   J. Gomsu, '"Nicht einmal die Generäle dürfen ausreden. Der Pferdekopf kann es" oder Literatur als Medienkritik', *Germanica*, 24, 1996 [1997]: 131–39.

SCHNEIDER, REINHOLD.   Hjou-Sun Choi, **Christentum und christlicher Widerstand im historischen Roman der 30er Jahre. Studien zu Las Casas vor Karl V. — Szenen aus der Konquistadorenzeit von R. S. und zum Land ohne Tod von Alfred Döblin* (Theorie und Forschung, 407), Regensburg, Roderer, 1996, 198 pp.

SCHNEIDER, ROBERT.   B. A. Kruse, 'Interview mit R. S.', *DUS*, 48.2, 1996:93–101.

SCHNURRE, WOLFDIETRICH.   Ian Roberts, *'Eine Rechnung, die nicht aufgeht': Identity and Ideology in the Fiction of Wolfdietrich Schnurre* (HKADL, 20), 258 pp., makes a strong case for reassessing a writer whose career spanned 50 years and seeks to overturn the perception of S. as merely a purveyor of short stories. The study devotes chapters to the various key phases of S.'s career in turn, but examines his military career and the early work in particular detail. R. underlines how the themes of guilt, a loss of innocence, and a search for identity underpin the texts of the immediate postwar period, yet the extent to which S. wrestled with these problematic issues for the remainder of his career emerges throughout the work. Indeed, in S.'s only true novel, *Ein Unglücksfall* (1981), it is argued that these themes were tackled effectively for the first time. S. appears restless in his early publications, experimenting with literary styles as diverse as the American realism of Hemingway and magic realism, yet never rests with one. It is the themes, rather than the style, which unite the two key collections of short stories, *Die Rohrdommel ruft jeden Tag* (1950) and *Eine Rechnung, die nicht aufgeht* (1958). What truly fascinates is the picture of S.'s life which emerges: from the analysis of his childhood, through his military career, which appears more illustrious than S.'s own account suggests, to his controversial and provocative public pronouncements in the 1960s and ensuing debilitating illness. R.'s thesis is that S.'s fiction became a means of trying to resolve the personal disorientation caused by the experiences of his formative years under National Socialism, an ideology the young man embraced wholeheartedly at first. In piecing together the biographical details, R. has uncovered correspondence between S. and the Nazi *Reichsschriftumskammer* and documentation relating to his receipt of the Iron Cross (second class) in 1943. Doubt is therefore cast over S.'s claims that he opposed the Nazis during the war and suffered as a result of his dissent. R. seeks neither to judge nor condemn; he merely emphasizes that S.'s constant focus on guilt and wartime experiences, and the fluid relationship between fiction and autobiographical fact in his writing, are surely not a coincidence. By the end of the 1950s S. had lost his way and was prominent primarily for dogmatic public outbursts, most notably in the wake of the erection of the Berlin Wall. After the long hiatus enforced by his life-threatening illness, S. emerged a more introverted person and wrote the autobiographical *Der Schattenfotograf* (1978) which allowed greater scope for self-examination. R. contends that the author became more at ease with himself thereafter, which directly contributed to the success of *Ein Unglücksfall*. Despite the latter's good reception, S. was to remain an outsider, so much so that his death in 1989 'left critics uncertain as to how to review a career which had effectively ended (as far as many were concerned) in the 1950s' (p. 183). R. concludes that it was precisely S.'s failure to resolve fully his problems with identity and ideology that make his work worthy of consideration alongside that of his more successful colleagues.

SCHÜTZ, STEFAN. **S. S.*, ed. Heinz Ludwig Arnold (TK, 134), 91 pp.

SCHUTTING, JULIAN. W. Maierhofer, 'Vetter Grüne. Goetherezeption in J. Ss "Zuhörerbehelligungen" und "Leserbelästigungen"', *ZDP*, 116:603–20. H. Murphy, 'Jutta/Julian S.'s transfiguration of childhood in *Am Morgen vor der Reise*', *MAL*, 30.2:130–43.

SEGHERS, ANNA. *Argonautenschiff*, 3, 1995, includes: J. B. Bilke, 'Zwiespaltiges Gedenken. Begegnungen mit der Mainzerin A. S.' (45–56); U. Brandes, 'Auf dem Weg zu A. S. Biographie als Annäherung' (267–71); E. Haas, '"Post ins gelobte Land" — ein Requiem' (139–50); E. Kaufmann, 'Schöne Räubergeschichte' (117–26); S. Rottig, 'Menschen auf der Flucht. Zu den beiden Flüchtlingsromanen *Das siebte Kreuz* und *Transit*' (205–12); C. Z. Romero, 'A. S.: Schwierigkeiten mit der Biographie' (263–66); H. Scheuer, 'Biographik und Literaturwissenschaft: Konstruktion und Dekonstruktion. A. S. und ihre Biographen' (245–62); K. Schubert, 'A. S.: — *Die drei Bäume*' (199–204); S. Spira-Ruschin, 'Begegnungen mit A. S.' (163–66); C. Spirek, 'Autor und Heimat — erarbeitet am Beispiel des Werks von A. S. als literarische Spurensuche mit einem Leistungskurs 13' (213–18); and S. Thielking, 'Warten — Erzählen — Überleben. Vom Exil aller Zeiten in A. Ss Roman *Transit*' (127–38). T. Mast, 'Representing the colonized/ understanding the other? A rereading of A. S.'s *Karibische Geschichten*', *ColGer*, 30:25–45. J. Vogt, 'Geschichten eines Adjektivs. Was man

mit einem kleinen Text von A. S. machen kann', *DUS*, 49.4 : 20–27.
See also BUCH, HANS CHRISTOPH; LANGGÄSSER, ELISABETH.

SPIEL, HILDE. Waltraud Strickhausen, **Die Erzählerin H. S. oder
'Der weite Wurf in die Finsternis'* (Exil-Studien, 3), NY, Lang, 1996,
486 pp.

STRAUSS, BOTHO. T. Anz, 'Sinn fur Verhängnis und Opfer? Zum
Tragödien-Verständnis in B. Ss *Anschwellender Bockgesang'*, *Schiller Jb.*,
40, 1996 : 379–87. I. Drennan, 'The lost generation in B. S.'s *Kalledey'*,
Germanica, 24, 1996 [1997] : 111–29. W. Erdbrugge, 'Symptomatische
Bemerkungen zur Postmoderne, B. S. und einem Drama in
Jahrgangsstufe 12', *DUS*, 47.6, 1995 : 31–39. B. Greiner, 'Wiederge-
burt des Tragischen aus der Aktivierung des Chors? B. Ss Experiment
Anschwellender Bockgesang', *Schiller Jb.*, 40, 1996 : 362–78. H. Kiesel,
'Wovon uns nur Götter erlösen könnten. Eine Reflexion auf die
Wiederkehr der Götter. Aus Anlaß von B. Ss *Ithaka'*, *SuF*, 49 : 149–55.
C. Parry, 'B. S. zwischen Kulturpolitik und Poetik. Zur Aktualität des
konservativen Diskurses', *JFinL*, 28, 1996 : 181–88. See also
BERNHARD, THOMAS.

SURMINKSI, ARNO. H. Beyersdorf, 'Gespräch mit A. S.' *DeutB*,
27 : 1–17.

SÜSKIND, PATRICK. W. Frizen, 'P. Ss "postmoderne" Didaktik',
DUS, 48.3, 1996 : 26–31. C. Liebrand, 'Frauenmord für die Kunst.
Eine feministische Lesart', *ib.*, 22–25. K. H. Spinner, 'Stil-Etuden zu
S.', *ib.*, 32–36.

THELEN, ALBERT VIGOLEIS. Klaus-Jürgen Hermanik, **Ein vigolo-
trischer Weltkucker. Die Prosa des A. V. T. im Zusammenhang mit dem
deutschsprachigen Pikaroroman* (EH, 1, 1556), 1996, 218 pp.

TIŠMA, ALEKSANDAR. F. Hutterer, 'A. T. und seine Welt. Topogra-
phie einer multiethnischen Stadt', *Fest. Schwob*, 219–28.

TORBERG, FRIEDRICH. W. G. Klein, 'Remembering F. T.
1943–1979. A personal recollection', *MAL*, 30 : 117–29.

TURRINI, PETER. M.-F. Reygnier, 'Von der Zweistimmigkeit zur
Siebenstimmigkeit. P. Ts dramatisches Werk 1971–1995', *GM*,
43–44, 1996 : 151–64. G. K. Schneider, '"Und dennoch sagt der viel,
der *Heimat* sagt": Ts Ansichten über Österreich und die österreichische Seele', *MAL*, 29.3–4, 1996 : 169–86.

WALSER, MARTIN. G. A. Fetz, **M. W.*, Stuttgart, Metzler, 221 pp.
*He, Patron! M. W. zum Siebzigsten, ed. Josef Hoben, Uhldingen-
Mühlhofen, de scriptum, 244 pp. S. Taberner, 'M. W.'s *Halbzeit*:
stylizing private history for public consumption', *MLR*, 92 : 912–23.
M. Tambarin, 'Les intellectuels face à l'unification allemande: les cas
M. W.', *RevA*, 28, 1996 : 539–49.

WEIDENHEIM, JOHANNES. P. Motzan, '*Maresi — mein kleines Welttheater*. Der donauschwäbische Erzähler J. W. wird wiederentdeckt', *Fest. Schwob*, 323–36.

WEIL, GRETE. Carmen Giese, **Das Ich im literarischen Werk von G. W. und Klaus Mann. Zwei autobiographische Gesamtkonzepte* (EH, 1, 1640), 233 pp. Uwe Meyer, **'Neinsagen, die einzige unzerstörbare Freiheit.' Das Werk der Schriftstellerin G. W.* (FLK, 56), 1996, 377 pp. Id., '"O Antigone ... stehe mir bei." Zur Antigone-Rezeption im Werk von G. W.', *LiLi*, 26, 1996:147–57.

WEISS, PETER. Henning Falkenstein, **P. W.* (Köpfe des 20. Jahrhunderts, 125), Berlin, Morgenbuch, 1996, 93 pp. K. Garloff, 'P. W.'s entry into the German public sphere: on diaspora, language, and the users of distance', *ColGer*, 30:47–70. Anton Philipp Knittel, **Erzählte Bilder der Gewalt. Die Stellung der 'Ästhetik des Widerstands' im Prosawerk von P. W.* (Konstanzer Schriften zur Sozialwissenschaft, 39), Konstanz, Hartung-Gorre, 1996, 118 pp. G. Pakendorf, '"I have arrived twenty years too late ..." The intertext of P. W.'s investigation into Auschwitz', *Germanica*, 23, 1995 [1996]:69–78. **P. W. Jb.*, 6, ed. Martin Rector and Jochen Vogt, Opladen-Wiesbaden, Westdeutscher Vlg, 176 pp. See also BERNHARD, THOMAS.

WELLERSHOFF, DIETER. W. Delabar, 'Warum ich und nicht du? Zum Brudermotiv in D. Ws *Blick auf einen fernen Berg*', *JIG*, 28, 1996 [1997]:10–21.

WILDENHAIN, MICHAEL. E. Buhr, '"Und wir werden dich nun killen, alte, fettgewordne Wachtel Westberlin." M. Ws *Die kalte Haut der Stadt*', *JIG*, 28, 1996 [1997]:22–39.

WOLF, CHRISTA. M. Jäger, 'Noch einmal: Nachdenken über C. Ws Prosa', *DUS*, 48.6, 1996:39–47. Halina Ludorowska, **C. W. Das Leben im Tagebuch*, Lublin U.P., 1996, 125 pp. G. Paul, 'Schwierigkeiten mit der Dialektik: zu C. Ws *Medea. Stimmen*', *GLL*, 50:227–40. J. Sallis, 'C. W. und die Medien: der Weg zur Enttabuisierung?', *Germanica*, 24, 1996 [1997]:101–09. R. West, 'C. W. reads Joseph Conrad: *Störfall* and *Heart of Darkness*', *GLL*, 50:254–65. See also JOHNSON, UWE; REIMANN, BRIGITTE.

ZODERER, JOSEPH. H. Ortner, 'Heruntergekommene Subjekte. Die "Sprachbehinderten" in der "Walschen" von J. Z.', Holzner, *Literatur*, 53–67.

II. DUTCH STUDIES

LANGUAGE

POSTPONED

LITERATURE

By WIM HÜSKEN, *Lecturer in Dutch, University of Auckland*

1. GENERAL

Bibliographies are indispensable for anyone interested in Dutch language and literature. In 1970 a project was started under the auspices of the Royal Dutch Academy of Science to bring out comprehensive lists of publications in the field of Dutch language and literature. The *Bibliografie van de Nederlandse taal- en literatuurwetenschap*, 2 vols, 's-Gravenhage, Stichting Bibliographia Neerlandica, 1996, 1703 pp., covering the years 1993 to 1995, is part 29 in the series. Still available are the volumes related to the years 1940–45 and 1960–92, published between 1974 and 1994. The *Bibliografie van de Nederlandse taal- en literatuurwetenschap* is also accessible through the Internet. (Further information may be obtained from the Bureau voor de Bibliografie van de Neerlandistiek, c/o Royal Library The Hague, Prins Willem Alexanderhof 5, 2595 BE 's-Gravenhage.)

Nico Laan, **Het belang van de smaak: Twee eeuwen academische literatuurgeschiedenis*, Amsterdam, Historisch Seminarium van de Universiteit van Amsterdam, 352 pp., reviews the professional discipline of literary studies in Dutch at universities in the Netherlands during the last two centuries. In 1797 the first Chair in Dutch was established at the University of Leiden, with Matthijs Siegenbeek becoming the father of Dutch literary studies. During the second half of this century, literary studies have been thoroughly influenced by the work of one man, G. P. M. Knuvelder. Between 1970 and 1976, he published, in four volumes, his fifth edition of the *Handboek tot de geschiedenis van de Nederlandse letterkunde*, a comprehensive history of Dutch literature before 1916. However, after almost a quarter of a century this work needs a thorough revision. Bringing it up to date does not suffice because over the last decades research in Dutch literary history has changed significantly. In 1996 a seminar was therefore held in The Hague at which some 125 specialists from Flanders and the Netherlands exchanged their thoughts about a new literary history of the Low Countries. *Veelstemmig akkoord: Naar een nieuwe literatuurgeschie-denis*, ed. H. Bekkering and A. J. Gelderblom (Voorzetten van de Nederlandse Taalunie, 52), Den Haag, SDU, 122 pp., contains the papers and summarizes the discussions of the day. Plans were made for its realization and it is to be expected that this new literary history will be available by the year 2003.

The relation between religion and literature is discussed in *De god van Nederland is de beste: Elf opstellen over religie in de moderne Nederlandse literatuur*, ed. Goffe Jensma and Yme Kuiper, Kampen, Kok Agora, 191 pp. The essays study works ranging from 19th-c. authors such as François Haverschmidt and Multatuli to modern writers like W. F. Hermans and Harry Mulisch. Hans Heesen, Harry Jansen, and Ed Schilders, *Waar ligt Poot? Over de dood en de laatste rustplaats van Nederlandse en Vlaamse schrijvers*, Baarn, De Prom, 331 pp., deals with a rather morbid topic, the details regarding the deaths and the places of burial of no less than 570 Dutch and Flemish authors.

Een kwestie van stijl: Opvattingen over stijl in kunst en literatuur, ed. Caroline van Eck, Marijke Spies, and Toos Streng (Historische Reeks, kleine serie, 34), Amsterdam, Historisch Seminarium van de Universiteit van Amsterdam, 196 pp., is one of the first books attempting to survey conceptions and definitions of style in art and literature over the centuries, varying from what is called good style to personal and historically restrained style. Seven of the twelve articles relate to Dutch literature. Jeroen Jansen discusses a remarkable statement on style by the early-17th-c. playwright Abraham de Koning in 'Een Neolatijnse encyclopedie en een voorrede in de moedertaal: Twee opvattingen over *perspicuitas* in 1616' (79–95). Imagery in tragedies written *c.* 1700 is dealt with by Jan Konst in '"Vlie 't geen bespotbaar is": denkbeelden over beeldspraak in de tragedie rond 1700' (97–108). Jacob Geel, one of the most famous literary critics of the mid-19th c., and his ideas on style are discussed in Willem van den Berg's essay 'Sollen met de stijl' (119–29). Another literary critic from the same era is studied by Gert-Jan Johannes in 'Ras verdwijnt die waan: Stijl als probleem bij Busken Huet' (131–45). Gerard Raat and Monique van Dam explore conceptions of style in the works of two of the most important post-war authors in 'Stijl, de verleider: Stijlopvattingen in het werk van Willem Frederik Hermans' (165–76), and 'Architectonische zelfbevrediging: De architectuurme-tafoor in het stijlbegrip van Gerrit Komrij' (177–86). *Mooi meegenomen? Over de genietbaarheid van oudere teksten uit de Nederlandse letterkunde*, ed. Herman Pleij and Willem van den Berg, Amsterdam U.P., 193 pp., is a collection of 37 short essays in honour of E. K. Grootes, Emeritus Professor of the University of Amsterdam. The central question answered in these essays is whether one can really enjoy reading historical literature or is it merely a convenient topic of research? Are there any texts which are still capable of moving researchers emotionally?

An anthology of literary texts, the first in its kind, written by women from the early modern era is *Met en zonder lauwerkrans: Schrijvende vrouwen uit de vroegmoderne tijd, 1550–1850, van Anna Bijns tot Elise van Calcar*, ed. Riet Schenkeveld-Van der Dussen et al., Amsterdam U.P., xxi + 970 pp. Intended to be comprehensive it pays attention to some 160 women authors, many of whom most modern readers will, rightly or wrongly, never have heard of.

2. THE MIDDLE AGES

The Southern Low Countries were very prolific in the dissemination of copies of the *Speculum humanae salvationis*. The production of the text in this area is the subject of Bert Cardon, **Manuscripts of the Speculum humanae salvationis in the Southern Netherlands (c. 1410-c. 1470): A Contribution to the Study of the 15th-Century Book Illumination and of the Function and Meaning of Historical Symbolism*, Leuven, Peeters, 1996, xlvi + 450 pp. Special attention is paid to miniatures. In an appendix a complete list is given of all known *Speculum* manuscripts from the Low Countries. Wybren Scheepsma, *Deemoed en devotie: De koorvrouwen van Windesheim en hun geschriften*, Amsterdam, Prometheus, 379 pp., concentrates on the texts written by nuns in the 13 convents in the Low Countries belonging to the Windesheim congregation. Many underwent the influence of Johannes Brinckerinck, a fervent follower of the founder of the Devotio Moderna, Geert Grote, who advised them to further their spirituality by writing religious texts.

By the end of the 14th c. many a ducal court was frequented by troubadours who recited short tales set to rhyme named *sproken*. Dini Hogenelst, **Sproken en sprekers: Inleiding op en repertorium van de Middelnederlandse sproke*, 2 vols, Amsterdam, Prometheus, 276, 303 pp., studies this genre, comparable to the French *lai*, and lists 358 of them. Frederik Joris Lodder, *Lachen om list en lust: Studies over de Middelnederlandse komische versvertellingen*, Ridderkerk, De Ridderhof, 243 pp., concentrates on yet another genre in Dutch literature not extensively researched so far, the *boerde*. Where a *sproke* may include some serious instruction, *boerden* seem to be there for the sole purpose of amusement. However, as a genre-denomination Lodder prefers the expression 'comic narrative in verse' rather than *boerde*. Further aspects of the genre discussed are the comic procedures, the function of the text, the intended audience, and moral issues.

Frits van Oostrom, *Maerlants wereld*, Amsterdam, Prometheus, 1996, 563 pp., goes back to one of the most important authors of the

Middle Ages in the Low Countries, Jacob van Maerlant. He reflects not only on the large amount of texts of this author preserved for posterity, a remarkable fact in itself, but also on the world in which Maerlant lived and worked. The miniatures in Van Maerlant's world history, *Spiegel Historiael*, one of the treasures of the Royal Library at The Hague, are presented in a beautifully edited book, Jozef Janssens and Martine Meuwese, *Jacob van Maerlant, Spiegel Historiael: De miniaturen uit het handschrift Den Haag, Koninklijke Bibliotheek, KA XX*, Leuven, Davidsfonds/Clauwaert, 197 pp.

Hadewijch, *Visoenen, ed. Frank Willaert and Imme Dros, Amsterdam, Prometheus–Bakker, 1996, 226 pp., presents a bilingual edition, offering the text in its original medieval version as well as in modern Dutch. Hadewijch is considered to be one of the most important mystic female authors of the Middle Ages, renowned not only for her visionary prose but also for her strophic poems and letters to her religious sisters. **De burggravin van Vergi: Een middeleeuwse novelle*, ed. Ria Jansen-Sieben and Willem Wilmink, introd. W. P. Gerritsen (Nederlandse klassieken, 11) Amsterdam, Prometheus–Amsterdam, Bakker, 94 pp., also contains a bilingual edition, medieval and modern, of a text dating back to 1315 written by an unknown poet from Brabant. The story is a free adaptation of the French *Châtelaine de Vergi* and it may be regarded as a warning to those involved in a secret love relationship to keep their love concealed to themselves. One of the richest manuscripts of Dutch medieval literature is kept in Stuttgart. An integral edition of this codex is given in **Het Comburgse handschrift: Hs. Stuttgart, Württembergische Landesbibliothek, Cod. poet. et phil 2° 22*, ed. Herman Brinkman and Janny Schenkel (Middeleeuwse verzamelhandschriften uit de Nederlanden, 4), Hilversum, Verloren, 2 vols, 1562 pp. The edition contains, among other things, versions of *De roman van de roos*, *Van den vos Reynaerde*, and *De reis van Sente Brandane*. Texts by Jacob van Maerlant and Jan van Boendale also appear in this extremely important medieval manuscript. *Netherlandic Secular Plays of the Middle Ages: The 'Abele Spelen' and Farces of the Hulthem Manuscript*, ed. Theresia de Vroom (Carleton Renaissance Plays in Translation, 29), Ottawa, Dovehouse Editions, 246 pp., is the first edition in English of the complete play collection in the Van Hulthem manuscript, comprising four serious secular plays and six farces. The *abele spelen* belong to the oldest secular plays in Western Europe.

3. THE RHETORICIANS' PERIOD

A. A. den Hollander, **De Nederlandse bijbelvertalingen 1522–1545* (Bibliotheca bibliographica Neerlandica, 33), Nieuwkoop, De Graaf, xiv + 565 pp., presents a comprehensive bibliographical survey of

Dutch Bible translations at a time in which the establishment of the most reliable Bible text was much more than just a matter of philological concern. An interdisciplinary approach of literary studies and the history of fine arts is the collections of papers on *Anglo-Dutch Relations in the Field of the Emblem*, ed. Bart Westerweel (Symbola et emblemata, 8), Leiden, Brill, xxv + 310 pp., containing contributions by Werner Waterschoot on Van der Noot's *Theatre*, Paul J. Smith on emblematic fables, Michael Douglas on the *Emblemata Horatiana*, and Judith Dundas on Henry Peacham.

B. A. M. Ramakers, *Spelen en figuren: Toneelkunst en processiecultuur in Oudenaarde tussen Middeleeuwen en Moderne Tijd*, Amsterdam U.P., 1996, vi + 507 pp., presents a very rich study of late medieval cultural life in the Flemish city of Oudenaarde. On the day of Corpus Christi processions would go around the town including scenes of both religious and secular origin. The author studies the development of this important aspect of late medieval culture in a city which proves to have had a special inkling for things theatrical. Herman Brinkman, *Dichten uit liefde: Literatuur in Leiden aan het einde van de Middeleeuwen*, Hilversum, Verloren, 415 pp., researches 15th-c. and 16th-c. literature in Leiden, a medium-sized town in the province of Holland. A central position in this book is taken by the detailed scrutiny of the first part of a manuscript now in the State Library of Berlin, the Handschrift-Jan Phillipsz. (Hs. germ. qu.557). The author also addresses questions such as the function of making poetry in a medieval city, the reciting, copying and printing of it as part of an urban culture, and the civic morale expressed in the texts collected in the manuscript. In two appendices Brinkman reviews the evidence in relation to the possession and production of books in Leiden before 1540.

Herman Pleij, *Dromen van Cocagne: Middeleeuwse fantasieën over het volmaakte leven*, Amsterdam, Prometheus, 544 pp., concentrates on the three extant Dutch versions of a very colourful depiction of a land of Cocagne. The author does not fail to depict the rich cultural background of this late-medieval idealistic view of life as it unfolded in a society which felt an ever-growing desire to mirror itself against a time in which life was still relatively uncomplicated. In 1514 a remarkable text was published by the Brussels printer Thomas van der Noot: *Den triumphe ende 't palleersel van den vrouwen*, the Dutch translation of Pierre Desrey's adaptation of Olivier de la Marche's *Le parement et triumphe des dames*. In 26 poems women's clothes and apparel were described, each item referring to a female moral quality. Saskia Raue, *Een nauwsluitend keurs: Aard en betekenis van Den triumphe ende 't palleersel van den vrouwen (1514)*, Amsterdam U.P., 455 pp., studies this text, returning among other things to biblical allegory in order to explain its salient imagery. The symbolism of colours and the role of bridal mysticism are, according to Raue, further sources for the text.

Mireille Vinck-Van Caekenberghe, *Een onderzoek naar het leven, het werk en de literaire opvattingen van Cornelis van Ghistele (1510/11–1573): Rederijker en humanist*, Ghent, KANTL, 1996, xxvii + 685 pp., presents a lengthy study of the life and the works of a man whose most creative years were situated around the middle of the 16th c. Vinck-Van Caekenberghe frowns on Van Ghistele as a Rhetorician, mainly in his plays, but praises him for his translations into Dutch of various Latin texts, thus displaying the first signs of a genuine Renaissance interest in Classical Antiquity. Rather then describing him as someone who, by borrowing from and being inspired by Roman authors, attempted to improve the quality of the literature of his own day, Vinck-Van Caekenberghe sees Van Ghistele as torn between two very different eras. Karel van Mander became famous as the author of *Het Schilder-boeck* (1603–04), in part a translation and adaptation of Vasari's encyclopedia of Italian art. His essays on Dutch and German artists, *Het leven der doorluchtighe Nederlandtsche en Hoogduytsche schilders*, are entirely his own. Between 1994 and 1996, the first three volumes of an English translation of these essays appeared in print. *The Lives of the Illustrious Netherlandish and German Painters, Preceded by the Lineage, Circumstances and Place of Birth, Life and Works of Karel van Mander, Painter and Poet and Likewise his Death and Burial*, ed. Hessel Miedema, Doornspijk, Davaco, xiv + 234 pp., is volume 4 in this edition of the first collection of biographies of Dutch and German medieval and Renaissance artists.

The Haarlem Chamber of Rhetoricians left behind a large collection of plays dating back to the 16th and early 17th cs, collected in 14 volumes, only three of which have not survived. In 1992, the first volume, *Boek A*, was published in a facsimile edition accompanied by modern transcriptions. Five years later the editors have reached as far as volume VII, *Trou Moet Blijcken: Bronnenuitgave van de boeken der Haarlemse rederijkerskamer 'de Pellicanisten', Boek G*, ed. W. N. M. Hüsken, B. A. M. Ramakers, and F. A. M. Schaars, Assen, Quarto, [582 pp.].

4. THE SEVENTEENTH CENTURY

Marijke Meijer Drees, **Andere landen, andere mensen: de beeldvorming van Holland versus Spanje en Engeland omstreeks 1650* (Nederlandse cultuur in Europese context, 6), Den Haag, SDU, ix + 173 pp., depicts the way the Dutch looked at themselves by the middle of the 17th c. as opposed to or compared to the way the Spanish and the English did. Literary authors whose works are used to determine the image the nation held up to itself include Jacob Cats, Johan van Beverwijck,

Lambert van den Bosch, G. A. Bredero, D. V. Coornhert, Jacob Duym, and Roemer Visscher.

The Dutch 17th c. was, according to Wim Klever, *Mannen rond Spinoza (1650–1700): Presentatie van een emanciperende generatie*, Hilversum, Verloren, 249 pp., a time of radical enlightenment, instead of a mere preparation for the 18th c., the age of philosophy *par excellence*. Benedictus de Spinoza occupied a central position in the philosophical discussions of his day but, except for the specialists, his works are almost impossible to understand. Klever attempts to approach Spinoza via the circle of intellectuals surrounding him. Among the men thus introduced is the relatively unknown merchant Pieter Balling who, as one of Spinoza's fellow-Collegiates, composed a number of treatises in which he defended the right of self-determination for members of the Anabaptist Church in matters of dispute. Two of the better known figures discussed in this book are Lodewijk Meyer, a man of theatre who was a co-founder of *Nil volentibus arduum*, and Adriaan Koerbagh, lawyer, medical doctor and author of *Een ligt schijnende in duystere plaatsen* (1668). For writing this pamphlet Koerbagh was accused of heresy and sentenced to ten years' imprisonment. Before the end of the year he died of exhaustion in the Rasphuis, the Amsterdam prison where the convicted had to rasp Brazilian wood for the production of red stain.

Kort tijt-verdrijf: Opstellen over Nederlands toneel (vanaf ca. 1550) aangeboden aan Mieke B. Smits-Veldt, ed. W. Abrahamse et al., Amsterdam, A D & L, 1996, 286 pp., contains 34 essays on Dutch drama and theatre between the early Renaissance and the 18th c. Apart from studies on plays by famous authors such as Bredero, Hooft, and Vondel, this collection also contains articles on less well-known texts and minor authors such as Jan Thönisz, Gijsbrecht van Hogendorp, and Jan van Arp. Els Stronks, *Stichten of schitteren: De poëzie van zeventiende-eeuwse gereformeerde predikanten*, Houten, Den Hertog, 1996, 347 pp., discusses in her dissertation the poetry and the poetic conceptions of a number of ministers in the Dutch Reformed Church. She describes two different categories of authors, those who merely composed poetry with the intention to uplift their flock, and those who wrote non-religious poetry as well. Special attention is paid to Laurens Bake's treatise on biblical poetry, *Verhandeling over de Heilige ofte Bybelpoezy* (1685).

E. K. Grootes, *Terug naar Bredero*, Amsterdam, A D & L, 23 pp., returns to the late 1960s when the monumental edition of Bredero's works was conceived. Published in 15 volumes between 1970 and 1986, it became one of the most remarkable accomplishments of scholarly editing of the second half of this century. Grootes reviews the developments in research of early Renaissance literature in the two decades during which Bredero's works were published and he admits that present day researchers have proved to be able to add quite a few new insights.

The title of *Omnibus Idem: Opstellen over P. C. Hooft ter gelegenheid van zijn driehonderdste sterfdag*, ed. Jeroen Jansen, Hilversum, Verloren, 198 pp., refers to the motto used by one of Holland's most famous men living in the first half of the 17th c., Pieter Corneliszoon Hooft. The nine essays collected in this book discuss Hooft's relationship with nine other important men. Some lived in his direct environment or belonged to his circle of close intimates, others influenced his life and works via different channels or were influenced by Hooft himself. E. K. Grootes, 'Hooft and Bredero' (19–29) investigates the imprint of Bredero's works on Hooft's. H. Duits, 'Hooft en Hendrik IV' (31–50) returns to *Hendrik de Grôte* (1626), Hooft's *laudatio* of the French king, Henry IV, written in gratitude for his important contributions to the Dutch revolt. Mieke B. Smits-Veldt, 'Hooft en De Groot' (51–68), discusses the difficult relationship between Hooft and the dissident poet, scholar, and statesman Hugo de Groot who, in 1618, was expelled for life to Loevestein castle after having been accused of subversive activities against Stadholder Maurice. Ad Leerintveld, 'Hooft en Huygens' (69–82), reviews the first years of intimate friendship between two of the most important poets of the first half of the century. Paula Koning, 'Hooft en Mostart' (83–100), draws one of Hooft's lesser known friends into the limelight, the Amsterdam town secretary Daniel Mostart who, in 1635, wrote a manual on the writing of official letters, *Nederduytse secretaris of zendbriefschryver*, a book initially meant to be dedicated to Hooft. Leopold Peeters, 'Hooft, Tacitus en de Medici' (101–05), discusses a passage in Hooft's history of the Florentine House of the Medici, written in 1635–36, a text clearly influenced by the Roman historian, Tacitus. Ton Harmsen, 'Hooft en Nil Volentibus Arduum' (107–20), elaborates on the degree in which the so-called French-Classicist authors, active after 1669, appreciated Hooft's poetry and drama. Jeroen Jansen, 'Hooft en Huydecoper' (121–48), answers the question who was responsible for the large collections of positive testimonies to justify the publication of Hooft's letters in 1738. Finally P. Tuynman, 'Hooft en de filosoof' (149–88), shows that Hooft's phrase 'Nu leeven wij hier op zijn Philosoophs' ('Now we live here as Philosophers'), suggesting that Hooft aimed at secluding himself from the outer world and that he had changed his attitude towards life, has so far been misinterpreted. A second collection of essays on Hooft is *Zeven maal Hooft: Lezingen gehouden ter gelegenheid van de 350ste sterfdag van P. C. Hooft*, ed. Jeroen Jansen, Amsterdam, A D & L, 138 pp. This book contains articles by Jan Konst, Piet Verkruijsse, Tineke

868 *Dutch Studies*

ter Meer, K. Porteman, B. Hartlieb, Henk Duits, and Marijke van der Wal.

In 1996, Constantijn Huygens's 400th birthday was commemorated as well. In Groningen a colloquium was held in the poet's honour: *Constantijn Huygens 1596–1996: Lezingen van het tweede Groningse Huygens-symposium*, ed. N. F. Streekstra, Groningen, Passage, 151 pp. This collection of essays contains seven articles. In 'De groote Webb' (9–31), a title referring to Huygens's poem, *Hofwijck* (1653), N. F. Streekstra presents a review of Huygens scholarship during the last 20 years. Ad Leerintveld retraces Huygens's diary and reports on this *trouvaille* in 'Enkele vondsten en bevindingen naar aanleiding van de historisch-kritische editie van Huygens' vroege Nederlandse gedichten' (33–49). In 'Huygens als dialectkenner' (51–70), H. M. Hermkens studies the author's knowledge of Antwerp and Holland dialects, notably in Huygens's *Trijntje Cornelis* (1653). The reception of this play during the 19th c. is discussed by A. Keersmaekers, 'De (her)waardering van Huygens' *Trijntje Cornelis* in de 19de eeuw' (71–94). Huygens is also renowned for his music. Rudolf Rasch, 'Waarom schreef Constantijn Huygens zijn *Pathodia sacra et profana?*' (95–124), asks the reason for the composition of a work of 1647. In Huygens's family, Jean-Louis Calandrini, an Italian merchant whose ancestors had fled from Italy for religious reasons, was a welcome guest. Tineke ter Meer, 'De vriendschap tussen Huygens en Jean-Louis Calandrini: een gedicht en een verhaal' (125–35), writes on the friendship between the two men. After his wife, Susanna van Baerle, died in 1637 Huygens wrote four poems on her death. One of them, *Epimikta in mortem Stellae uxoris dilectissimae*, is dealt with in the final essay of this collection by J. P. Guépin, 'Epimikta' (137–51). Two editions of Huygens's *Trijntje Cornelis* (1653) have appeared in print. The first was published on the occasion of a season of performances of the play, with introductory essays by Michaël Zeeman and Wim Hüsken, Amsterdam, Het Toneel Speelt, 123 pp. Constantijn Huygens, *Trijntje Cornelis: Een volkse komedie uit de Gouden Eeuw*, ed. H. M. Hermkens and Paul Verhuijck (Nederlandse klassieken, 10), Amsterdam, Prometheus–Bakker, 213 pp., is a bilingual edition, in both 17th-c. Dutch and a modern translation.

A number of minor poets were also considered. Wouter Abrahamse, *Het toneel van Theodore Rodenburgh (1574–1644)*, Amsterdam, A D & L, ix + 218 pp., studies the plays of one of the innovators of early 17th-c. Dutch drama, Theodore Rodenburgh. In 1617, he became the leader of one of the Amsterdam Chambers of Rhetoric, De Eglantier (The Eglantine), after G. A. Bredero, P. C. Hooft and S. Coster had left it to found their own school, De Nederduytsche Academie. Abrahamse discusses, among other things, Rodenburgh's poetic principles, his world view and his activities as a translator of Guarini and Lope de Vega. A short biography of the author is given in an appendix. E. M. Beekman, *The Crippled Heart: An Introduction to the Life, Times and Works of Willem Godschalck van Focquenbroch* (Padde-moesreeks, 2), Leiden, Astraea, 174 pp., presents a biography of a truly colourful author of Dutch Renaissance literature, Willem van Focquenbroch. Trained as a medical doctor, Van Focquenbroch sailed to the west coast of Africa in an administrative function, where the Dutch West Indies Company had a settlement in the city of Elmina. There he died of an unknown cause. Beekman allows his readers a first introduction into the life and the works of this author in English.

*Hollantsche Parnas: Nederlandse gedichten uit de zeventiende eeuw, ed. Ton van Strien (Alfa reeks), Amsterdam U.P., x + 163 pp., presents an anthology of 17th-c. Dutch poetry. The poems are arranged accord-ing to a number of themes, such as love, religion, political propa-ganda, and poethood. Dirck Buysero and Carel Hacquart, **De Triomfeerende Min: Vredespel, gemengt met zang- en snaarenspel, vliegwerken en baletten, 1680*, ed. P. Andriessen and T. Strengers (Monumenta Flandriae Musica, 1), Leuven/Peer, Alamire, 1996, liii + 79 pp., is an edition of a play set to music, written on the occasion of the Nijmegen Peace Treaty of 1678. It is regarded as the oldest Dutch opera.

5. The Eighteenth Century

Satire and social criticism were the two main motifs for the painter and writer Jacob Campo Weijerman. Only in the 1970s was he recognized as an important author. In 1738 Weijerman was arrested after having insulted the local authorities of his then place of residence, Vianen. The subsequent year saw his conviction for life deportation to a prison in The Hague. *Geconfineert voor altoos: Stukken behorend bij het proces Jacob Campo Weijerman (1739)*, ed. Karel Bostoen and André Hanou, Leiden, 225 pp., publishes all documents relevant to Weijerman's trial as well as an autobiographical sketch written after his imprisonment.

6. The Nineteenth Century

Bernt Luger, **Wie las wat in de negentiende eeuw?*, ed. Wim van den Berg, Marita Mathijsen, and C. J. Aarts, Utrecht, Matrijs, 272 pp., contains a number of essays on 19th-c. reading and readers. During the first years of the 19th c. the novel was a popular genre in the Netherlands. However, translations were available in much greater quantity than original Dutch texts. Joost Kloek, *Een begrensd vaderland: De roman rond 1800 tussen nationaal karakter en internationale markt*, Amsterdam, Koninklijke Nederlandse Akademie van Wetenschappen, 38 pp., tries to give an explanation for this remarkable fact. The deficiency may be related to the Biedermeier trend of preferring homely conditions to a more outgoing, enterprising spirit. Ellen Krol, *De smaak der natie: Opvattingen over huiselijkheid in de Noord-Nederlandse poëzie van 1800 tot 1840*, Hilversum, Verloren, 380 pp., studies homeliness as the leading criterion for poetic criticism during the first four decades of the 19th c. Limited as it is to criticism, the treatment of the subject would have benefited greatly had the author included a survey of homely poetry in Flanders and the Netherlands as well. The oldest still extant journal in the Netherlands, *De gids*, was founded in 1837. During its lifetime of more then a century and a half it remained loyal to its liberal views, both culturally and politically. Its 19th-c. history is studied in detail by Remieg Aerts, *De letterheren: Liberale cultuur in de negentiende eeuw: Het tijdschrift De Gids*, Amsterdam, Meulenhoff, 697 pp. Understandably, a great deal of attention is paid to three of its editors, E. J. Potgieter, R. C. Bakhuizen-Van den Brink, and Conrad Busken Huet, who added some vibrant colours to the palette of insignificant and uninspiring men in a tiresome society. Conrad Busken Huet, *Een vastgeraakte lokomotief: Een portret in brieven*, ed. Olf Praamstra, Amsterdam, Veen, 317 pp., also pays due respect to the last mentioned of the three men, the famous literary critic of the second half of the 19th c., in an edition of a number of his letters.

Verhalen voor Vlaanderen: Aspecten van het Vlaamse fictionele proza tot aan de Tweede Wereldoorlog, ed. Koen Wauters, Kapellen, Uitgeverij Pelckmans, 308 pp., is a collection of essays on aspects of Flemish prose written between 1800 and 1940. The book contains articles by Ludo Simons, Kris Humbeeck, Marc Somers, Paul Pelckmans, Ludo Steynen, Piet Couttenier, Karel Wauters, Joris Gerits, and Luk Adriaens. An de Vos, *Gezelles 'Gouden eeuw': de Zuidnederlandse zeventiende-eeuwse literatuur in het werk van Guido Gezelle* (Antwerpse studies over Nederlandse literatuurgeschiedenis, 1), Leuven, Peeters, 485 pp., studies the most important Flemish poet of the second half of the 19th c. and his interest in 17th-c. Flemish literature.

As a young person, Willem Bilderdijk proved to be nothing less than a genius. In 1795, after the Dutch Republic had been overrun by the French, he was forced to leave the country because he refused to sign a Declaration of Human Rights. In London he met Catharina Wilhelmina Schweickhardt, a girl half his age, and, though married, started a relationship with her. Though officially still married to his first wife, on 18 May 1797 Bilderdijk single-handedly accepted Catharina as his new spouse without asking for an official sanction of this relationship by Church or civic authorities. *Liefde en ballingschap: Brieven 1795–1797*, ed. Marita Mathijsen, Amsterdam, De Arbeiderspers, 254 pp., contains Bilderdijk's correspondence with his wife, with his new object of affection, and with a number of his acquaintances. The edition allows the reader to reconstruct the development of the love-affair. Isaäc da Costa, *Dwaasheid, ijdelheid, verdoemenis! Een keuze uit het werk*, ed. G. J. Johannes, Amsterdam U. P., 1996, vi + 146 pp., is a selection from the works including Da Costa's *Bezwaren tegen de geest der eeuw* (1823) in which he expresses his aversion to rationalism and enlightenment, favouring a Protestant *reveille* instead.

Jacob David Mees, *Dagboek 1872–1874*, ed. Thimo de Nijs (Egodocumenten, 14), Hilversum, Verloren, 110 pp., offers us a glimpse into the short life of a son of a Rotterdam banker who, as a student of law at the University of Leiden, kept a diary noting in it everything from the exuberant joys of student life to his much more serious introduction to literature and the unfavourable situation of the Jews in an otherwise wealthy Dutch town. Mees died of tuberculosis at the age of twenty-four.

7. 1880 TO 1945

Jan-Willem van der Weij, *Beweging en bewogenheid: Het prozagedicht in de Nederlandse literatuur aan het einde van de negentiende eeuw*, Amsterdam, Thesis, 500 pp., discusses the relatively unknown sub-genre of the 'prose poem', *prozagedicht*. The term tries to capture a tendency to introduce rhyme, rhythm, and other repetitive characteristics into prose. The inauguration of 'prose poems' in the Netherlands may have been effected by a possible influence of the French *poèmes en prose* on Dutch authors. Two of them are dealt with in particular, Frans Erens and Lodewijk van Deyssel. Harry G. M. Prick, *In de zekerheid van eigen heerlijkheid: Het leven van Lodewijk van Deyssel tot 1890*, Amsterdam, Athenaeum–Polak & Van Gennep, 1080 pp., offers a biographical sketch of the first 25 years in Van Deyssel's life. One of the leading authors of the 'Tachtiger' generation, a group who introduced new literary trends in Dutch literature varying from naturalism in prose to sensitivism and symbolism in poetry. Prick describes the author's family background (Lodewijk van Deyssel being the pseudonym of Karel J. L. Alberdingk Thijm, son of a famous art historian), his years in Limburg at a Roman Catholic boarding school, his return to Amsterdam at the age of fourteen, and his adolescent years. Van Deyssel contributed to *De nieuwe gids*, a periodical founded in 1885 as mouthpiece of the 'Tachtiger' generation.

In 1916, Louis Couperus visited Nijmegen where he delivered two speeches. M. Klein, *Couperus in Nijmegen* (De achterkant van de literatuur, 2), [Nijmegen], Vantilt, 40 pp., takes these lectures as his starting point for a discussion of Couperus's homo-eroticism, claiming that ideas regarding sexuality, such as the ones expressed in the novels *Extaze* (1892) and *De berg van licht* (1905–06), were rather inspired by philosophical conceptions about androgyny than by overt homosexuality. As an appendix, Klein edits Couperus's humorous story *Arnaldo en Candido*.

Siem Bakker and Emy Thorissen, *De dichter Theo van Doesburg / I. K. Bonset: 1883–1931*, Nijmegen, Instituut Nederlands KUN, 78 pp., contains a number of bio-bibliographical essays on one of the most versatile artists of the early 20th c. However, writing under the pseudonym of I. K. Bonset, Van Doesburg was never regarded as a great poet. His essays on art and literature, many of them published in the periodical *De stijl* (1917–31), were much more influential. In a final chapter Bakker and Thorissen pay due attention to his impact on the poetry of the 1950s and 1960s generations, Jan Hanlo in particular. One of the leading poets of the inter-war period in Dutch literature was Hendrik Marsman. He drowned at sea on 21 June 1940 when the ship on which he tried to escape to England was torpedoed by the Germans. *Paradise Regained*, ed. Jaap Goedegebuure (Alfa), Amsterdam U. P., vii + 94 pp., contains the texts of his first two collections of poems, *Verzen* (1923), and *Penthesileia* (1925). In 1927 they were joined together and underwent some extension in *Paradise Regained*. In his introduction, Goedegebuure pays special attention to Marsman's popularity with the young readers of the 1920s, positioning himself between traditionalism and modernism.

In 1916 Martinus Nijhoff married Netty Wind. Nijhoff is regarded as one of the most important renewers of Dutch poetry after the Great War, and Wind was well-known in the circle of *avant-garde* artists and writers of the inter-war period. Barely within a year the couple separated but they kept writing letters to each other. *Brieven aan mijn vrouw*, ed. Andreas Oosthoek, Amsterdam, Bakker, 1996, 261 + 16 pp., contains an edition of 80 letters out of a total of 100 in this correspondence. Another collection of letters is J. C. Bloem, *De brieven aan Albert Verwey*, ed. Bart Slijper, Maarssen, Umbra, 108 pp. Bloem made his debut in 1910 when he published his first poems in *De beweging*, a literary journal led by Verwey. Their friendship came to an end in 1918 after Bloem published a critical essay on Verwey's poetry. This edition comprises 71 letters written by the young poet Bloem.

Dirk de Geest, *Literatuur als systeem, literatuur als vertoog: Bouwstenen voor een functionalistische benadering van literaire verschijnselen*, Leuven,

Peeters, [1996], 231 pp., attempts to apply a functionalist approach to modern literature, and to literary criticism in Flanders during the Second World War in particular. By concentrating on functionalism he tries to establish a connection between the study of methodology and literary history in a way most modern literary historians would prefer to see applied to literature in general, an opinion repeatedly voiced in *Veelstemmig akkoord* (see pp. 860–61 above). *Soms tussen tulpen: Poëzie uit Vlaanderen en Nederland 1916–1945*, ed. Hubert van Herreweghen and Willy Spillebeen, Leuven, Davidsfonds–Clauwaert, 277 pp., is an anthology from Dutch and Flemish poetry written between 1916 and 1945.

8. 1945 TO THE PRESENT DAY

Lisa Kuitert, *Het uiterlijk behang: Reeksen in de Nederlandse literatuur, 1945–1996*, 5 vols, Amsterdam, De Bezige Bij, 386 pp., discusses the popularity of literary series in the post-war period. A true revolution seems to have taken place in the consumption of literature after the phenomenon of the pocket edition had been introduced. Jaap Goedegebuure, *De veelvervige rok* (De bijbel in de moderne literatuur, 2), Amsterdam U.P., 146 pp., studies the influence of the Bible on modern authors, including Brakman, Claus, Kellendonk, and Reve. Biblical characters such as Jacob, Joseph, Bathsheba, and Lazarus are given special attention. Goedegebuure shows that the Bible invariably remains an important source of inspiration for many authors and that the Christian heritage still plays a significant role in modern literature.

World War II is still one of the most important topics in modern Dutch literature. Works on this theme in which authors such as Harry Mulisch, Marga Minco, Jeroen Brouwers, and Rudy Kousbroek view the events through the eyes of children are discussed by Jolanda Vanderwal Taylor, *A Family Occupation: Children of the War and the Memory of World War II in Dutch Literature of the 1980s*, Amsterdam U.P., viii + 211 pp., who argues that between the 1960s and the 1980s a gradual shift from stories of resistance heroes and Holocaust victims to tales of ordinary citizens took place. The author is astonished at the fact that most writers talk about 'the War' instead of 'the German Occupation': in the Netherlands, the actual fighting lasted only four days, after which the Dutch suffered a five-year period of being occupied by the Germans.

The 1950s have become famous in Dutch literary history for a movement in poetry which could be labelled as experimental. In the early 1990s some of the authors looked back to these years in interviews conducted with them on VPRO radio. The producers of the series of the radio programmes present a selection of the material broadcasted in printed form and compact disc: H. J. A. Hofland and Tom Rooduijn, *Dwars door puinstof heen: Grondleggers van de naoorlogse literatuur*, Amsterdam, Bas Lubberhuizen, 174 pp. + 78 mins CD. *... Die zo rijk zijn aan zichzelf ...: Over Hans Faverey*, ed. Hans Groenewegen (Over ..., 5), [Groningen], Historische Uitgeverij, 285 pp., contains nine essays on one of the better known poets of the 1960s. Among the authors are Maria van Daalen, Wiel Kusters, Martin Reints, and C. O. Jellema. Frans van Campenhout, *Willem M. Roggeman: dichter van het exotisme: een monografie*, Antwerpen, Paradox Pers–Leiden, Dimensie, 1996, 138 + 4 pp., presents a biography of the poet Roggeman followed by a number of essays on other aspects of his work: poetry, activities in the field of theatre and drama, social and political points of view, and the placing of his works in modern Dutch literature. Van Campenhout also discusses the author's critical activities and his contributions to art and music.

Lutgarde Nachtergaele, *Apollo op vrijersvoeten: Een onderzoek naar de thematische coherentie in de Verzamelde verhalen van S. Vestdijk*, Louvain, Edition Peeters, 1996, 477 pp., studies thematic coherence in the collected stories. In them the author appears to display a split personality, not knowing whether to concentrate on his own individuality or to yield to life as a creative yet destructive force. Firmin Asma, *Pen of penis bij Marnix Gijsen*, Antwerp–Rotterdam, De Vries-Brouwer, 1996, 336 pp., presents a psychoanalytical approach of the works of the Flemish author. According to Asma, Gijsen was a confirmed supporter of the Flemish movement as well as a sexually clumsy man, as a result of which he became a cynical follower of agnosticism in his later years. Hubert Lampo is known to be a writer interested in various kinds of occult phenomena such as a fourth dimension, UFOs and utopia, magic realism, the Holy Grail, and the Jungian concept of the subconscious. Paul van Aken, *Hubert Lampo: de schrijver van het onzichtbare*, Amsterdam, Meulenhoff–Antwerp, Manteau, 1996, 336 pp., researches Lampo as the writer of the invisible by trying to reach the essence of his authorship. As a poet, Cees Nooteboom did not receive much attention until he published, in 1980, his novel *Rituelen*. This work was instantaneously regarded as his masterpiece. Hilde van Belle, *Zichzelf kan hij niet zien: een lectuur van de roman 'Rituelen' van Cees Nooteboom* (Symbolae, Series D. Litteraria, 10), Leuven U.P., 252 pp., adds another study to the already long list of interpretations of this novel. Regarded by some as a writer of popular fiction, by others as a literary author *pur sang*, Antoon Coolen is gradually receiving more attention as one of our most succesfull writers of regional novels, all of whom are set in his beloved province of Brabant. *Antoon Coolen 1897–1961: Lezingenbundel met teksten over Antoon

Coolen, ed. Gerard Jansink, Deurne, Heemkundekring, 71 pp., pays due respect to this aspect of his varied authorship. Bart Vervaeck, **Lijf en letter: Over 'Het godgeklaagde feest' van Willem Brakman* (Brakman cahier, 2), Kaatsheuvel, Stichting Willem Brakman Kring, 246 pp., studies the metaphorical interrelationship between body and literature in Brakman's works, notably in his novel *Het godgeklaagde feest* (1967). Aleid Truijens, **Hella S. Haasse: Draden trekken door het labyrint* (De school van de literatuur), Nijmegen, Sun–[Antwerp], Kritak, 85 pp., reviews the works of the prolific post-war author of psychological and historical novels.

Jos Muyres, **Spoken van de Kapellekensbaan: Register bij het tweeluik De Kapellekensbaan/Zomer te Ter-Muren van Louis Paul Boon*, Oude Tonge, Huis-Clos, 48 pp., offers an index as well as brief descriptions of the basic features of the characters acting in two of the most important novels by the Flemish author Louis Paul Boon. *Dromen en geruchten: Over Boon en Claus, aangeboden aan Bert Vanheste*, ed. Jos Joosten and Jos Muyres, Nijmegen, Vantilt, 192 pp., contains five essays on each of the two authors mentioned in the title. L. Missinne, 'Boon en Walschap' (21–32), considers Gerard Walschap's influence on Boon. Jos Muyres, 'De zee, de wouden en God . . . ?' (33–55), concentrates on his novel *Mijn kleine oorlog* (1946). Paul de Wispelaere, 'Notities bij "Boontje"' (57–69), reiterates the implications of Boon's use of a pseudonym, Boontje. His literary style is discussed by Annie van den Oever, 'De stijl van de "Vlaamse volksschrijver" Louis Paul Boon' (71–98). The reception of one of Boon's masterpieces, *Zomer te Ter-Muren*, is dealt with by Jan van Avezaath, 'Een meesterwerk voltooid' (99–110). Hugo Claus is doubtless the most versatile Flemish author of the post-war period. Georges Wildemeersch, 'Hugo Claus in poëzie en poëtica' (113–25), elaborates on his poetry and poetic principles. Truth is central to Jos Joosten, 'Heeft waarheid haar gezicht verbrand' (127–44). Hedwig Speliers, 'Landschap als autobiografie' (145–58), reflects on Claus's edition of his collected poems published between 1948 and 1993. One of his poems, 'De zanger', is analysed by Anja de Feijter, 'Toppen scherend als een baard' (159–65). G. H. F. Raat, 'Een veredelde kruiswoordpuzzel' (167–79), criticizes the lack of interest on the part of literary critics in one of the central issues in Claus's novel *De geruchten* (1996), namely the author's misgivings about a society which has become disconnected from its roots. Flemish prose of the 1990s is discussed by Jooris van Hulle, **Wilde inkt en ambrozijn: Vlaams proza in de jaren negentig*, Leuven, Davidsfonds–Clauwaert, 206 pp.

*Tijd bestaat niet: leven en werk van Jan Wolkers, ed. Murk Salverda et al. (Schrijversprentenboek, 38), Amsterdam, De Bezige Bij–Den Haag, Nederlands Letterkundig Museum en Documentatiecentrum,

1996, 159 pp., is a documentary on one of the earliest rebels in post-war Dutch literature. The book contains a large quantity of photographic material and facsimiles of personal documents related to the author. It was written on the occasion of a 1996 exhibition on his life and works in The Hague. *Cees Nooteboom: Ik had wel duizend levens en ik nam er maar één*, ed. Harry Bekkering et al. (Schrijversprentenboek, 40), Amsterdam, Atlas–Den Haag, Nederlands Letterkundig Museum en Documentatiecentrum, 176 pp., is the catalogue of another exhibition in the same museum of 1997–98. Cees Nooteboom is regarded as one of the most important Dutch authors who has been attracting large audiences within and outside his country.

To the wealth of correspondence between Gerard Reve and various other people two more volumes were added: Gerard Reve and Willem Nijholt, *Met niks begonnen: Correspondentie*, ed. Nop Maas, Amsterdam, Veen, 142 pp., and Gerard Reve, *Brieven aan Matroos Vosch 1975–1992*, ed. Nop Maas, Amsterdam, Veen, 366 pp.

III. DANISH STUDIES*

LANGUAGE

By Tom Lundskær-Nielsen, *Queen Alexandra Lecturer in Danish,
Department of Scandinavian Studies, University College London*

1. General

The texts of the Parliamentary Acts concerning (a) Danish orthography and (b) the official status and composition of Dansk
Sprognævn (the Danish National Language Council), as the authoritative body charged with moniting the development of the Danish
language, giving advice and taking decisions on language issues, are
reprinted in *Nyt fra Sprognævnet*, no.3 : 5–10. This issue also contains an
informative article on these matters by H. Galberg Jacobsen,
'Ordnede forhold. Om retskrivningsloven og sprognævnsloven', *ib.*,
1–5. The same author deals with more general problems of norms in
Danish in 'Aktuelle normproblemer i dansk sprog', *Proceedings of the
Eleventh Biennial Conference of the British Association of Scandinavian Studies*,
Univ. of Hull, pp. 27–34. *Fra Egtvedpigen til Folketinget. Et festskrift til
Hendes Majestæt Dronning Margrethe II ved regeringsjubilæet 1997*, ed. Poul
Lindegård Hjorth et al., Det Kongelige Danske Videnskabernes
Selskab, Munksgaard, 310 pp., includes among its articles P. L.
Hjorth, 'Ret og galt at stave, om det juridiske grundlag for den
kodificering af staveformer som finder sted i Retskrivningsordbogen
set i historisk perspektiv' (109–32), and J. Rischel, 'Det færøske sprogs
mærkelige overlevelse, om det færøske sprogs skæbne, om dets nedtur
i sidste halvdel af 1600-tallet, da det var reduceret til mundtligt
almuesprog, om skabelsen af et færøsk skriftsprog i romantikkens
tidsalder og diskussionen om færøsk status som selvstændigt sprog
eller dansk dialekt og det færøske sprogs konsolidering i løbet af de
sidste 100 år' (189–212). *Sounds, Structures and Senses. Essays Presented to
Niels Davidsen-Nielsen on the Occasion of his Sixtieth Birthday*, ed. Carl
Bache and Alex Klinge, Odense U.P., 286 pp., contains several
contributions on Danish: B. L. Jensen, 'On the use of mood and
modal verbs in Italian and Danish' (109–25); P. A. Jensen, 'On the
semantics of agentive *af* in Danish' (127–48); F. Larsen, 'The Danish
and English sound systems: complications of a contrastive analysis'
(189–204); and Carl and Sten Vikner, 'The aspectual complexity of
the simple past in English. A comparison with French and Danish'

* The place of publication of books is Copenhagen unless otherwise indicated.

(267–84). M. Bæhring, 'Den eneste trussel mod det danske sprog er danskerne selv', *Modersmål-Selskabets årbog*, pp. 27–33. F. Hauberg Mortensen, 'Internationalisering: et indlæg på debatdagen om danskfagets fremtid', *Synsvinkler*, 6.17:5–20. The contentious issue of political correctness in language is discussed in Pernille Frost, *En strid om ord. Det politisk korrekte sprog*, Fremad, 114 pp., and in the same author's 'Politisk korrekthed i sproget — en moderat nyhed', *Mål & Mæle*, 20.4:11–17. P. Jarvad, 'Language policy and attitudes in Denmark', *Language and Cultural Hegemony* (Language and Cultural Contact, 13), Aalborg U. P., pp. 95–109. D. Nikulitjeva, 'Sprogstruktur og sprogbeskrivelse', *Danske Studier 1997*, C. A. Reitzel, pp. 15–31, examines the status of grammatical and linguistic theories in Danish language research and argues that the structure of a language influences the choice of descriptive model for analysing it. *NyS*, 22, ed. Anne Holmen et al., has semiotics as its theme, and contains C. Grambye and H. Sonne, 'Kompas' (13–41); H. Jørgensen, 'Aktanterne, aktørerne, figurerne — og den konkrete tekst' (43–64); J. D. Johansen and S. E. Larsen, 'Semiotic og lingvistik' (65–95); and I. Ulbæk, 'Teorien om altings betydning (TAB)?' (97–129). *Hermes. Tidsskrift for Sprogforskning*, 14, 15, ed. Henning Bergenholtz et al., Det Erhvervssproglige Fakultet, Handelshøjskolen i Århus, 255, 303 pp. Per Anker Jensen and Carl Vikner, *Natursprogsbehandling og unifikationsgrammatik*, I–II (Computational Linguistics, 2), Handelshøjskolen, Munksgaard, 1996, 202, 317 pp. *Mål & Mæle*, 20.1–4, ed. Carsten Elbro, Erik Hansen, Ole Togeby, and Pernille Frost, 32, 32, 32, 32 pp. *Sprog og Samfund*, ed. Rasmus Bjørgmose (Nyt fra Modersmål-Selskabet, 15).

2. History of the Language, Phonology, Morphology, Lexis, Syntax, and Semantics

Ord, Sprog oc artige Dict. Et overblik og 28 indblik 1500–1700. Festskrift til Poul Lindegård Hjorth, ed. Flemming Lundgreen-Nielsen, Marita Akhøj Nielsen, and John Kousgård Sørensen, UJDS, C. A. Reitzel. P. Frost, 'Om sprogets ulidelige foranderlighed: sproggenerationer og generationssprog', *Mål & Mæle*, 19.4:20–25. F. Gregersen and I. L. Pedersen, 'Hovedsætningsordstilling i underordnede sætninger', *Danske Folkemål*, 39, C. A. Reitzel, pp. 55–112, discusses word order in subordinate clauses in a historical perspective. E. Fischer-Jørgensen, 'Tryk i dobbeltsammensætninger i dansk', *Rask. Internationalt tidsskrift for sprog og kommunikation*, 5–6:67–159. A. Karker, 'Det tar sin tid. Om kortformer af nogle danske verber', *Nyt fra Sprognævnet*, no.1:6–11. A few short articles on lexis have appeared in *Nyt fra Sprognævnet*: E. Hansen, 'Høj(t)taler', no.1:11–12; E. Bojsen,

'Dramatisk talt', no.3:2–4; and V. Sandersen, 'Paparazzo', no.4: 1–2. H. Korzen, 'Det er svært at undgå ikke at fortale sig', **Mål & Mæle*, 20.1 : 7–11. Jens Martin Eriksen and Bent Møller, **Svære ord — og lette*, Statens Information, 88 pp. Henrik Holmboe, *Udforskning af dansk ordforråd og grammatik*, Datalingvistik, Handelshøjskolen, Århus, 140 pp. John Kousgård Sørensen, *Patronymer i Danmark 2. Nyere tid og nutid*, Institut for Navneforskning, C. A. Reitzel, 139 pp., is the second and last volume on patronyms in Denmark (vol. 1 in 1984). *The Valency of Nouns*, ed. Karen Van Durme (Odense Working Papers in Language and Communication 15), Odense U.P., 170 pp., includes K. van den Eynde, 'From verbal to nominal valency'; M. Herslund, 'Typological remarks on complex noun phrases in Danish'; S. Kirchmeier-Andersen, 'Verbal and nominal valency'; F. Sørensen, 'The nightmare of the genitive'; H. Wegener, 'Nominalizations revisited'; and B. Ørsnes, 'Towards an HPSG-analysis of Danish synthetic compounding'. Lene Schøsler and Sabine Kirchmeier-Andersen, *Studies in Valency*. II. *The Pronominal Approach Applied to Danish* (RASK supplement, 5), Odense U.P. Helle Wegener, *Studies in Valency*. III. *En undersøgelse af danske verbalsubstantiver med henblik på automatisk natursprogsbehandling* (RASK supplement, 7), Odense U.P. L. Fogsgaard and S. Østergaard, 'Udsagnsord', *Den blå port*, 41:53–73. Erik Hansen, *Dæmonernes port*, 4th edn, Hans Reitzel, 155 pp. This useful book on Danish grammar has been revised and a new chapter on phonetics has been added. E. Hansen, 'Kriterier for inddeling af ledsætninger', *Ny forskning i grammatik* (Fællespublikation 5), Odense U.P. L. Brink, 'Den danske *der*-konstruktion', *Danske Studier 1997*, C. A. Reitzel, pp. 32–83. Jørn Lund, **Professor Higgins' sproglige diagnoser*, Danmarks Nationalleksikon, 93 pp., contains a selection of the author's newspaper columns on language from the past two years.

3. DIALECTOLOGY, CONTRASTIVE LINGUISTICS, AND BILINGUALISM

Danske Folkemål, 39, C. A. Reitzel, 112 pp., contains two dialect studies: T. Kristiansen, 'Sprogbrug og sprogholdninger. Kommentarer og sammenligninger i anledning af "Moderne sjællandsk"' (3–30), and I. Ejskjær, 'Nogle gamle enstavelsesformer med vestjysk stød og disse formers tilsvar i sønderjysk' (31–53). H. A. Kofoed, **Gøbbanissa — og andre sære bornholmske ord og stednavne*, Bornholms Tidende, 109 pp. Arne Espegaard, **Nogle nordjyske mål: sproghistorie og dialektgeografi*, I–II, Vendsyssel, 1996, 333, 210 pp. Johanna Barðdal, Nils Jörgensen, Gorm Larsen, and Bente Martinussen, **Nordiska. Våra språk förr och nu*, Studentlitteratur, Lund, 536 pp., compares the grammar and pronunciation of the Scandinavian languages in a historical perspective. N. K. Grøftehauge, 'Hovedpand(s)karl eller kop-og-kande: lidt om integrering af fremmedord', *Ord & Sag*, 17:5–11. M. Herslund and N. Davidsen-Nielsen, 'Engelsk indflydelse på dansk — er der brug for sprogrøgt?', *Sprint*, 2:1–4, Handelshøjskolen. A. Holmen, 'Dansk som andetsprog: positioner og antagelser i uddannelsesdebatten', *Sprog forum*, 3.9:22–26. H. Korzen, 'Ser man det... Noget om at *se* på dansk og fransk', *Sprint*, 2:17–35, Handelshøjskolen. K. Lomholt, 'Viltus draugi latviešu un dāņu valodā: semantiska draudzība, bet stilistisks viltus', *Sastatāmā un Lietišķā Valodniecība: Kontrastīvie pētījumi*, vi, Latvijas Universitātes Zinātniskie raksti (Acta Universitatis Latviensis), Riga, pp. 22–30.

4. LEXICOGRAPHY, GRAMMARS, AND RHETORIC

Henrik Galberg Jacobsen and Peter Stray Jørgensen, *Politikens Håndbog i Nudansk*, 3rd edn, Politiken, 539 pp., has been extensively revised to bring it in line with the latest edition of *Retskrivningsordbogen* (1996) and the new rules on punctuation. Bente and Henrik Holmberg, *Politikens Pocket Fremmedordbog*, Politiken, 350 pp. Karl Hårbøl, Jørgen Schack, and Henning Spang-Hanssen, *Fremmedordbog*, Munksgaard, 1,008 pp. S. Lervad has written the Danish terms of *Dictionnaire Multilingue de l'Aménagement du Territoire et du Développement Local, français, anglais, portugais, italien, espagnol, allemand, danois, néerlandais et grec*, ed. Armelle Lebars, Paris, Maison du Dictionnaire, 695 pp. Barbara Fischer-Hansen and Ann Kledal, *Basis grammatikken: basishåndbog i dansk grammatik for udlændinge*, Herning, Special-pædagogisk forlag, 104 pp. Inger Lytje and Claus Donner, *Gratex. Dynamisk grammatik til dansk sprog*, Aalborg Univ.–Orfeus, 1996, 84 pp. (with disk), is a Danish grammar to be used in conjunction with the Gratex programme. Lis Gabers and Sten Høgel, *Retorik: Levende tale eller tom snak?*, Nyt Nordisk, 1996, 220 pp. Klaus Kjøller, *Få din vilje! Tal og skriv effektivt*, Akademisk Forlag, 1996. *Metaforer i sprog og tænkning. Proceedings fra metafornetværkets seminar i Odense den 8.-10. februar 1996*, ed. Carsten Hansen, Copenhagen Univ., 189 pp. *Metaforer i kultur og samfund. Proceedings fra metafornetværkets seminar i København den 24.–26. oktober 1996*, ed. Carsten Hansen, Copenhagen Univ., 211 pp. Dorrit Faber et al., *Introduktion til dansk juridisk sprogbrug — metoder og analyser*, Handelshøjskolen, 106 pp. Kirsten Rask has produced two manuals on written communication for specific professional groups, *Når pædagoger skriver: en håndbog i skriftlig kommunikation*, Grafisk Litteratur, 1996, 101 pp., and *Skriv sikkert: en skrivehåndbog for forsikringsfolk*, Rungsted Kyst, Forsikringshøjskolen, 1996, 91 pp.

LITERATURE

POSTPONED

IV. NORWEGIAN STUDIES*

LANGUAGE

By Arne Kruse, *Lecturer in Norwegian at the Department of Scandinavian Studies, University of Edinburgh*

1. General

An interesting debate has arisen around the (American) English translation of the Norwegian international fictional best-seller *Sofies verden* by Jostein Gaarder. The translator has chosen drastically to change many references to Norwegian culture and history, e.g. the Norwegian Nobel laureate Knut Hamsun has become the American Nobel laureate John Steinbeck. This is one of many examples cited in a very critical article by Gülay Kutal, 'Hva er galt med *Sophie's World?*', *Samtiden*, no. 2–3:53–58. In no. 5–6:102–04, the translator, Paulette Møller, gives a short answer, and then the author himself, Jostein Gaarder, gives his comments. *Nordens språk*, ed. Allan Karker, Birgitta Lindgren, and Ståle Løland, Novus, 215 pp., is a completely new edition of a book that was first published in 1983 under the title *Språkene i Norden*. This is a survey of all the eight native languages in the Nordic countries with separate chapters dealing with the relationship between the languages and with Nordic co-operation on language questions. A new textbook for the introductory courses in linguistics for all university language students is Rolf Theil Endresen, Hanne Gram Simonsen, and Andreas Sveen, *Innføring i lingvistikk*, Scandinavian U.P., 1996, 350 pp. From a structuralistic perspective, Svein Pedersen, *Språk og språkutvikling hos barn*, Samlaget, 155 pp., focuses on the language system in his description of how children develop language. A separate chapter deals with children growing up in multilingual surroundings. A varied *Festschrift* with articles mostly from the Bergen linguistic milieu is *Språket er målet. Festskrift til Egil Pettersen på 75-årsdagen 4. mars 1997*, ed. J. Bondevik, G. Kristoffersen, O. Nes, and H. Sandøy, Bergen, Alma Mater, 219 pp. Among the contributions are the following. M. Christoffersen (44–52) discusses three hypotheses on the origin of the special placement of the negation in dependent clauses in Mainland Scandinavian; A. Grannes (53–61) points to problems with the names of the inhabitants of the new republics of the former Soviet Union; J. E. Hagen (62–71) tries to establish rules for the prepositions *på* and *i* used for locations; J. R.

---

* The place of publication of books is Oslo unless otherwise indicated.

Hagland (72–77) returns to Hans Jacob Wille who in the 1780s published works on the dialect of Seljord in Telemark; G. Kristoffersen (78–90) discusses the use of the pronoun *du* in the object position, an innovation that has spread rapidly on the south coast of Norway; E. Lundeby (91–102) promotes the benefits of a normalized speech form of Norwegian, still a very unfashionable idea in the linguistic climate of Norway; J. Myking (103–10) discusses aspects of the theory of terminology; G. Nedrelid (111–21) shows how the dialect of Jostedalen treats new words that are given a feminine gender; O. Nes (122–28) looks at the etymology of *fanden* and establishes a background in Old Norse *fjándinn* and similar words; H. Omdal (129–49) reflects upon some of the dilemmas the language consultant ought to consider, e.g. whether it is useful to insist on certain 'correct' forms in the written language when they are no longer upheld in the spoken language; M. Rindal (150–59) considers whether the language in four medieval documents from Jämtland and Härjedalen is Swedish or Norwegian; H. Sandøy (160–77) outlines how the gender of nouns ending in *-ning* are distributed in the dialects and how they have been treated in Nynorsk; K. F. Seim (178–87) shows that *sin* in a runic inscription from Bergen is not a very early form of the so-called *garpegenitiv* — as was earlier believed — but rather a word for penis; K. Venås (188–99) investigates the language of the author Olav Sletto; and L. S. Vikør (200–14) looks at the relationship between the principles for orthography and the normalized spelling of place-names ('rettskrivingsprinsipp og normalisering av stadnamn'). There is a *Festschrift* for Kjell Venås, *Målvitskap og målrøkt*, ed. Andreas Bjørkum, Botolv Helleland, Erik Papazian, and Lars S. Vikør, Novus, 505 pp., which contains previously published articles by V. on dialects, sociolinguistics, grammar, language history, and onomastics, besides literature. The compilation demonstrates clearly the range of interests of that scholar. Ottar Grepstad, *Det litterære skattkammer. Sakprosaens teori og retorikk*, Samlaget, 624 pp., is an ambitious attempt to analyse Norwegian non-fictional prose from a number of different angles, including that of rhetoric. As a textual analysis it is quite unique, e.g. in that it presents one book per year between 1737 and 1996. *Tekstens mellommenn*, ed. Egil Børre Johnsen (Norsk sakprosa, 3), Scandinavian U.P., is partly based on G.'s book, where he is praised for his empiricism and criticized for his theory. Egil Børre Johnsen, *Oppgavetekst og dannelse*, Scandinavian U.P., 562 pp., is a doctoral thesis on the titles given for the Norwegian essay for the Eksamen Artium (Upper Secondary School) in the period 1880–1991. Another doctoral thesis is Anne Hvenekilde, *'Hvad gjør vi saa med arven?'*,

Scandinavian U.P., 1996, pp. 454, a study of text-books for primary education in Norwegian in America.

PERIODICALS AND JOURNALS. In *Språk i Norden 1997*, ed. Ståle Løland et al., Nordic Language Board, Novus, 157 pp., there is an excellent survey article by H. Sandøy, 'Fornorsking og norvagisering. Norsk språkrøkt i 1996', where he sums up e.g. the discussion that followed the suggestion to write some English loan-words according to Norwegian spelling rules. In *Syn og Segn*, no.4: 20–28, B. Furre writes on the making of Nynorsk into a language standard that could be used within the Church of Norway. In *MM*, no.2, Ottar Grønvik, 'Nissen' (129–48), is mostly on the folklore aspects of this goblin-like farm spirit but G. argues for a new etymology — not from Nikolaus — but from Old Norse **niðsi* (m.), 'the dear/little relative'; Oddrun Grønvik (149–56) presents the sources for the term *nisse* in *Norsk Ordbok*; and J. O. Askedal (191–206) analyses the linguistic nature of numerals and then uses his results to explore why the 'old' numerals have survived since they were changed in 1951.

2. HISTORY OF THE LANGUAGE AND TEXTUAL STUDIES

A CD-ROM called *Ivar Aasen*, Samlaget, provides a popular presentation of the influential linguist. In addition to sound, illustrations, and animation, Aa.'s collected works are included, which makes the publication a very useful and handy source of reference. The Ivar Aasen Society has published text no. 5 in its A series (which is for unpublished manuscripts left by Aa.): *Målsamlingar frå Tronhjems og Troms' Stifter av Ivar Aasen*, ed. Jarle Bondevik, Oddvar Nes, and Terje Aarset, Bergen, Norsk Bokreidingslag. *Nordica Bergensia*, 15, is dedicated to the poet Olav Nygard. G. Akselberg (23–46) outlines how the writer developed his language in constant search for a personal form in the midst of rapid development of the Landsmaal norm at the beginning of this century. R. Slagstad, 'Arbeiderpartistaten — reguleringspolitikk, økonomi og språk', *Ordet*, no.2: 10–14, suggests that government language planning reflects the wish to plan and regulate the development of the economy and society in the highdays of the Norwegian Labour Party. Jan Ragnar Hagland and Jørn Sandnes have translated and supplied a commentary on the oldest city law of Norway, the medieval law of Trondheim, *Bjarkøyretten*, Samlaget, 141 pp. An introduction, pp. xi–xxx, gives the history of the law, the relationship to the other local law — the Frostating Law — and attempts to plot the relationship between the different manuscripts containing extracts of the law. Rune Røsstad, *Á tveim tungum: Om stil og stilvariasjon i norrønt lovmål* (KULTs skriftserie, 73), Norwegian Council for Research, deals with stylistics in Old Norse legal language. Also noted is Audun Dybdahl and Jørn Sandnes, *Nordiske middelalderlover. Tekst og kontekst. Rapport fra seminar ved Senter for middelalderstudier 29.-30. november 1996*, Trondheim, Tapir, 129 pp. *Nordica Bergensia*, 14, is devoted to Old Norse philology. The late B. Fidjestøl is represented with several articles, firstly on the cognomens of the three famous characters *þambaskelmir, hárfagri*, and *hornklofi* (6–14), then (15–19) with a controversy based on the poem *Nesjavísur*: did King Olav win the battle because he had more people or in spite of having fewer people? I. H. W. Ingebretsen (54–78) outlines the word order in Old Norse nominal phrases; A.-G. Borch (79–105) discusses mood and tense in Old Norse conditionals; E. Veland (149–88) comments and publishes a five-page fragment manuscript of *Heimskringla*, AM 325 VIII 14°; R. Kyrkjebø (189–200) discusses which text(s) Peder Claussøn might have used for his translations from the first part of *Heimskringla*; O. E. Haugen, 'I den stemmatiske hagen' (201–29), reflects on the importance of establishing the stemma of texts; and J. Louis-Jensen (230–43) investigates the possibility that *Kringla* could have been edited by Snorri Sturluson's nephew Ólafr Þórarson. A special issue of *Multilingua*, 16.4, ed. Laura Wright and Ernst Håkon Jahr, is entitled *Language Contact through Trade in the late Middle Ages: Middle Low German and other North European Languages*. E. H. Jahr also has an article in the journal where he indicates new perspectives on the language contact between Middle Low German and mainland Scandinavian in the late Middle Ages. In *NOWELE*, 31–32, F. Amory (1–11) approaches the difficult metonymic and metaphoric kennings in Old Norse poetry from a semantic-syntactic angle; M. P. Barnes (29–42) asks 'How "Common" was Common Scandinavian?', pointing to the fact that scholars have a tendency to repeat certain 'facts' about the language situation in Scandinavia 550–1050, many of them established from 12th–13th c. manuscripts whereas other isoglosses than those supporting the classic east-west division are generally ignored; B. warns about unsound speculations but points to the likelihood of widespread social and geographical variations of speech within the period; J. L. Byock and M. Krygier (47–55) suggest how to explain the Old Norse u-umlaut to linguistically unprepared students, insisting that understanding the mechanism of the change saves students memorizing huge numbers of paradigms; H. Fix, 'Text editing in Old Norse: a linguist's point of view' (105–17) criticizes the standard editions of Old Norse manuscripts as interpretations that one should look upon with suspicion: F. further calls for a resuscitation of the editing tradition of the last century and for new editions that allow readers to judge for themselves. *MM*, no.1, contains articles by K. Bakken

(1–36) who establishes the use of various palaeographic and ortho-graphic patterns in order to identify hands in medieval manuscripts; K. Wolf (37–54) investigates the use of *me* and *vi* in Old Icelandic and Old Norwegian and finds the difference to be less great than expected; and K. E. Kristoffersen (55–76) writes on Fredrik Wilhelm Lund, the first person to write a major work on Old Norse syntax (1862). Hermann Pálsson, *Úr landnorri. Samar og ytstu rætur íslenskrar menningar* (Studia Islandica, 54), Reykjavík, 199 pp., deals with the influence from Northern Norway on medieval Iceland. The author concen-trates on the influence from the Sami people and claims this to be of much higher importance than previously thought. *Bjarne Fidjestøl: Selected Papers*, ed. Odd Einar Haugen and Else Mundal, trans. Peter Foote (Viking Collection Series, 9), Odense U.P., is a compilation of articles by the late, highly respected scholar of Old Norse.

3. RUNOLOGY

The first systematic analysis of the runic material from Dublin is Michael P. Barnes, Jan Ragnar Hagland, and R. I. Page, *The Runic Inscriptions of Viking Age Dublin* (National Museum of Ireland, Medieval Dublin Excavations 1962–81, ser. B, 5), Dublin, Royal Irish Acad-emy, ix + 82 pp. F. X. Dillmann, 'Les runes dans la littérature norroise. À propos d'une découverte archéologique en Islande,' *Proxima Thule*, 2:51–89. R. Hagland and R. T. Lorentzen, pp. 43–78 of *Runor och ABC: Elva föreläsningar från ett symposium i Stockholm våren 1995*, ed. Staffan Nyström (Runica et Mediævalia, Opuscula, 4), Stockholm Medieval Museum, 192 pp., investigate what research on children's early writing can tell us about runic inscriptions. *Spor — fortidsnytt fra Midt-Norge*, 12.1, has two popularizing articles: A. Beverfjord, 'Skrifter i stein — runer i Nidarosdomen' (40–41), and J. R. Hagland, 'Skrift i Trondheim kring år 1000' (36–38). J. E. Knirk, 'Galteland-steinen rekonstruert', *Årbok for Universitetets Oldsak-samling*, Univ. of Oslo (121–37); Id., *Archiv und Geschichte im Ostseeraum: Festschrift für Sten Körner*, ed. Robert Bohn et al. (Studia Septentrionalia, 3), Frankfurt am Main, pp. 25–37, comments on the runic love-poems from Bryggen in Bergen. Id., pp. 86–96 of *Nytt lys på middelalderen*, ed. Jørgen Haavardsholm, Sypress, 255 pp., looks at how runic inscriptions may be used as sources for historical events in the medieval period. Id., *Middelalderens symboler*, ed. Ann Christensson et al., Univ. of Bergen Centre for European Cultural Studies, pp. 83–105, investigates the function of runes as signs and symbols. There is a *Festschrift* in the form of articles by Lucien Musset, *Nordica et Normannica* (Studia Nordica, 1), Paris, Societé des Études Nordiques, 495 + xix pp. The articles are first and foremost about Norman history but several deal with runes and runology. Also noted is the very useful *Nytt om runer* published by the Runic Archive, Univ. of Oslo.

4. DIALECTOLOGY

Martin Skjekkeland, *Dei norske dialektane*, Kristiansand, Høyskoleforlaget, 249 pp. + 27 illus., aims at explaining the relationship between the various dialects and the two written forms of Norwegian. A very systematic approach with emphasis on the historical development, there are separate chapters on the phonology and morphology as well as a chapter describing the individual dialects.

Jan K. Hognestad, *Tonemer i en høytonedialekt. En undersøkelse med utgangspunkt i Egersund bymål*, Samlaget, 208 pp., is an investigation into tonemes or musical accents in the dialect of Egersund, a town within the so-called high-tonal dialect area. The book gives a presentation of the research into tonemes, and then an analysis of the realization of tonemes in the particular dialect, based on instrumental phonetics. Tor Erik Jenstad and Arnold Dalen, *Trønderordboka*, Trondheim, Tapir, 287 pp., is the first larger regional dictionary in Norway, covering the dialects of Nordmøre and Trøndelag. The dictionary is the product of a project that was started in 1981 and the current publication is meant as an intermediate and popular edition of what in the future hopefully will be a scientific and much bigger dictionary. The book covers c. 4,000 entries indicating meaning, usage, and where the word is documented, and there is a most useful introduction to the dialects of the area (pp. 13–36). In *MM*, no.2, E. Papazian (161–90) sums up the results of an investigation into the dialect of Numedal, where young people clearly and rapidly are giving up distinct dialect features. *Nordica Bergensia*, 13, ed. G. Akselberg, is devoted to sociolinguistics and the linguistic interpretation of data, and includes the following. B. Mæhlum, 'En apologi for den metodologiske individualismen' (9–28), discusses if the object for research within the spoken language should be the individual or the collective; A. Torp, 'Fonologisk regionalisering' (29–50), looks at the spread of the uvular *r* from a *sprachbund* perspective; O. Monsson (51–68) outlines how the phonological realization in West Norwegian of syllables with length on both the vowel and the consonant can be described within a theory on morphological-phonological interaction; J. A. Nergaard (88–104) gives the results of an investigation of the loss of vocabulary from one generation to the next; G. Akselberg (105–23) attempts to view the Norwegian linguistic community from the theoretical perspective of the French cultural sociologist P. Bourdieu; H. Dyvik (124–41) reflects on what should come first in linguistic research projects — the theory or the data; G. Kristoffersen (142–57) outlines how acoustic data can be used in phonological analyses; and finally R. O. Andersen (188–208) analyses data from the Test in Norwegian for foreigners and shows, among other things, that if the candidates are in a situation where they can use their Norwegian actively, this will have a positive effect on their Test results. Ove Orvik, *Vesterålsk ordbok*, Sortland, Målmann, 62 pp., is a collection of vocabulary from Vesterålen in Northern Norway. The contents of a periodical from the Dialect Archive, University of Oslo, *Talatrosten*, ed. A. Bjørkum, include A. Bjørkum and J. Bondevik (4–12) on a list of vocabulary from Lærdal in 1811; G. Harildstad (13–15) writes on the words *kovern* and *kornoteleg*; J. A. Schulze (19–28) sums up very briefly research on the Norwegian language since 1957 and looks in some more detail at works by P. N. Grøtvedt and G. Indrebø; and J. Øverby (32–98) has a most thorough review of N. Kjenstad, *Snåsamålet* (1993).

5. ONOMASTICS

There is an important new edition of *Norsk stadnamnleksikon*, ed. Jørn Sandnes and Ola Stemshaug, Samlaget, 536 pp. This is the fourth edition since the first in 1973 of this very useful dictionary of place-names in Norway. Errors have been corrected and more names, new interpretations and, not least, many more Sami names have been included as well as an article by K. A. Helander (57–60) on Sami names and a glossary on Sami toponymic elements (61–64). A new introduction to toponymics is Peter Hallaråker, *Innføring i stadnamn. Innsamling og metode*, Scandinavian U.P., 280 pp. There are two main sections, first a practical approach to the subject with directions on how to collect place-names, then a theoretical section meant for students at university level. Ivar Aasen, *Norsk Navnebog*, ed. Kristoffer Kruken and Terje Aarset (Skrifter frå Ivar Aasen-instituttet), Volda Regional College, 170 pp., is a new edition of the first book (1878) on personal names in Norway, with a new introduction and index. The report of the 8th National Conference on name research, *Namngransking som studie- og undervisningsfag*, ed. Kristin Bakken, Section for Name Research, Univ. of Oslo, 169 pp., has an article by G. Akselberg and K. Bakken (11–40) where they outline the position of onomastics in Norway today. They find that the discipline is rather conservative and that there is a great potential in developing new methods and theories by co-operating with other disciplines within language, history, and archaeology. Å. K. Hansen, 'Forskningsfaget navne-gransking' (83–107), is a general presentation about which fields of research Nordic onomasticians have concentrated upon. L. S. Vikør

(109–19) reflects upon the relationship between the disciplines onomastics and *nordisk* (Scandinavian Language and Literature); H. Otnes (121–40) and H. Vintermyr (141–58) discuss problems and possibilities related to engaging pupils in secondary and upper secondary school in name research; and P. Hallaråker (159–66) underlines the duty onomasticians have to publish their findings in a format that will reach a greater public. In *Namn og Nemne*, 14, Å. K. Hansen (21–38) studies names with the element *-tuit* in Normandy; K. Bakken (43–58) discusses the term *nedervd uttale* ('inherited pronunciation') of place-names; B. Sandnes (59–68) outlines possibilities with field-names as an object of research; M. Hovdenak (81–90) discusses geological names; and K. Flokenes (91–106) indicates the loss of place-names. In **Ortnamn i språk och samhälle: Hyllningsskrift till Lars Hellberg*, ed. Svante Strandberg (Nomina Germanica: Arkiv för germansk namnforskning, 22; Acta Universitatis Upsaliensis), Uppsala U.P., 311 pp., there are articles by B. Helleland on Norwegian names with a social and sacred background, J. Sandnes on the element *tun* in Norwegian farm-names, and O. Stemshaug on place-names linked to travelling. Id., *MM*, no.1:75–90, argues against the theory that says the element *finn* in toponyms derives from the people *Finn* with the meaning 'Sami' or 'Lapp'. S. would rather see an appellative *finn* meaning 'sharp edge, top, summit'.

6. SYNTAX, MORPHOLOGY

Tor A. Åfarli, *Syntaks. Setningsbygning i norsk*, Samlaget, 190 pp., gives an introduction to Norwegian syntax, aimed at students at university level. The book includes exercises and a glossary of definitions. From his base within generative syntax, Å. discusses various theoretical approaches to syntax in three sections, focusing on function, phrase structure, and sentence member position. H.-O. Enger, *MM*, no.1:91–102, contributing to a discussion he initiated, finds the use of the morpheme irrelevant or unhelpful in relation to inflected languages like Old Norse.

7. LEXICOGRAPHY AND DICTIONARIES

Nordisk leksikografisk ordbok, Scandinavian U.P., 348 pp., is a dictionary of Scandinavian terms used within lexicography. Around 1,000 terms are explained and equivalents are given in Danish, Finnish, Icelandic, Swedish, Nynorsk, English, French, and German. Valerij Berkov, *Norsk ordlære*, Scandinavian U.P., 224 pp., is the Norwegian edition of the Russian original published in 1994. The book is more an introduction to lexicography than a discussion of Norwegian word formation and much of the terminology discussed is from rhetoric and stylistics. The six chapters deal with the word as a unit, vocabulary, phraseology, lexical processes, the making of new words and, finally, Norwegian lexicography. *Terminologi — system og kontekst*, ed. Johan Myking, Randi Sæbøe, and Bertha Toft, Norwegian Council for Research, 1996, 298 pp., is a report from a Nordic symposium with articles on the terminology of medical language, off-shore industry, and the theory of text linguistics. Aagot Landfald and Kjell M. Paulsen, *Norsk ordbok. Bokmål*, Cappelen, 1996, 656 pp., has more than 45,000 entries with definitions. There is a useful mini-grammar and information about declension is also given with compound words, e.g. *galge-n* and *galgenhumor-en*. Stress is indicated when it does not fall on the first syllable. There are many practical examples of the entries in use. Another useful feature for foreign users is the marking 'fam.' or 'dial.' for words with an oral or dialectal use. *Norsk Ordbok — nynorskens leksikografiske kanon?*, ed. Lars S. Vikør, Dept of Scandinavian and Literary Studies, Univ. of Oslo, is a report of a seminar where the topic was the role of the dictionary *Norsk Ordbok*. Nils Martin Hole, *Kva heiter det? Bokmål — nynorsk ordliste*, Fagbokforlaget, 190 pp., is meant for those who use Nynorsk in their work or studies and are uncertain in their choice of vocabulary, morphology, and phraseology. The first part of the book gives information about verbs, nouns, and adjectives as well as how to express the genitive form in Nynorsk. The second part is the dictionary, with entries in Bokmål and with the Nynorsk equivalents and examples of texts with the Nynorsk word in use. A CD-ROM called *Norsk språk*, Kunnskapsforlaget, includes the largest spell-checker for Norwegian and electronic versions of *Norsk ordbok*, *Tanums store rettskrivningsordbok*, *Bevingede ord*, and *Kunnskapsforlagets blå fremmedordbok*. Anne-Line Graedler, *Anglisismeord. Engelske lånord i norsk*, Scandinavian U.P., 466 pp., contains more than 4,000 entries of originally English words used in Norwegian. In addition to their spelling, pronunciation, usage, and declension in Norwegian, we are also informed of the history of each word and the possible different usage in English and in Norwegian. Ivar Tryti, *Språkets ville vekster*, Aschehoug, 216 pp., is a new and bigger edition of the book that was first published in 1985, presenting the historical background of idiomatic expressions and metaphors in the Norwegian language. Similar, but focused on the word-level, is Johan Hammond Rosbach, *Polydoras bok. Etymologi — Kunnskap og kuriositeter*, Pax, 134 pp. Norwegian is one of nine European languages represented in Lars Melin, *Norstedts förbjudna ordbok*, Norstedts, Sweden, 1996, 187 pp., where 'forbidden' words are listed and explained in alphabetical order. The first of its kind in Scandinavia is *Kinesisk-norsk ordbok*, Kunnskapsforlaget, 1300 pp.

Entries are alphabetical after the pronunciation of the Chinese signs and they are also written in Latin letters. Per Moen and Per-Bjørn Pedersen, *Engelsk-norsk, norsk-engelsk ordbok*, Samlaget, 958 pp., is the long-awaited two-way dictionary between English and Norwegian (Nynorsk). The dictionary is comprehensive, with 90,000 entries, there is a small grammar of the English language, and IPA-based advice on the pronunciation of Norwegian words. This is finally a dictionary that is not meant for Norwegians only but also for foreign learners or users of Norwegian!

LITERATURE SINCE THE REFORMATION
POSTPONED

V. SWEDISH STUDIES*

LANGUAGE

By KERSTIN PETERSSON, *Lecturer in Swedish, University of East Anglia*
(This survey covers the years 1995–97)

1. GENERAL

Språk i Norden, 1995, ed. Ståle Løland (Nordisk Språksekretariats Skrifter, 19), 154 pp., contains articles on lexicography and language cultivation, some with a Nordic perspective, notably in relation to the European Union. *Språk i Norden*, 1996, ed. Ståle Løland (Nordisk Språksekretariats Skrifter, 20), 240 pp., is devoted to literary language and its potential influence on the linguistic norm. *Språk i Norden*, 1997, ed. Ståle Løland (Nordisk Språksekretariats Skrifter, 21), 154 pp., contains articles on language planning. U. Teleman and Margareta Westman, 'Behöver Sverige en nationell språkpolitik?', *ib.*, 5–22, offer a Swedish perspective. Margareta Westman, *Språkets lustgård och djungel* (SSSN, 79), 1995, 236 pp., is a delightful and unusual book. One can assume that it is intended for the general readership who might be interested in language but has not ventured into detailed study before. The author opens windows into the realm of language study with a rare combination of linguistic professionalism and intuitive skills. She shows us that we all share in creative language ability, advocating an awareness of grammar and norms, but insisting that a sign of a living language is that it is impossible to know or master all its facets. *Svenskan i tusen år: glimtar ur svenska språkets utveckling*, ed. Lena Moberg and Margareta Westman (SSSN, 81), 1996, 194 pp., is a refreshing and informative introduction to the history of the Swedish language. The examples of texts from different periods provide valuable insights into the flexibility and variation contained in a language. Gertrud Pettersson, *Svenska språket under sjuhundra år. En historia om svenskan och dess utforskande*, Lund, Studentlitteratur, 1996, 251 pp., is a welcome handbook for university students with its clear and useful information on the history of Swedish and on central issues in historical linguistics. *Nordiska studier: femton uppsatser om ord, namn, dialekter, filologi, stilhistoria och syntax*, ed. Christer Platzack and Ulf Teleman (LSNS, ser. A, 48), 1996, 199 pp., is a *Festschrift* in honour of Gösta Holm on his 80th birthday. *Samspel och variation*, ed. Mats Thelander and Lennart Elmevik, Uppsala Universitet, Institutionen

* The place of publication of books is Stockholm unless otherwise indicated.

för nordiska språk, 1996, 521 pp., is a *Festschrift* in honour of Bengt Nordberg on his 60th birthday. *En bra svenska?: om språk, kultur och makt*, ed. Annick Sjögren, Ann Runfors, and Ingrid Ramberg, Tumba, Mångkulturellt Centrum, 1996, vii + 111 pp., is an anthology which forms part of the project 'Språk och Miljö'. Catharina Grünbaum, *Strövtåg i språket*, Bonniers, 1996, 191 pp., is a collection of articles written for *Dagens Nyheter* on topics concerning correct usage, language cultivation, and language planning. Mikael Reuter, *Reuters rutor*, Esbo, Schildt, 1996, 232 pp., is a volume of articles discussing questions concerning Swedish usage, with an emphasis on Finland-Swedish. *Målande uttryck: en liten bok med svenska idiom*, 1996, 156 pp., contains Swedish idiomatic expressions, compiled by Språkdata at the University of Gothenburg. *Läroboksspråk: om språk och layout i svenska läroböcker*, ed. Siv Strömquist (Ord och Stil, 26), 1996, 195 pp., with an English summary, examines the language and layout in a sample of Swedish textbooks for schools. Hans Nyman, *Medicinens språk*, Liber, 1996, 216 pp., is a book about medical language. *Svenskan i IT-samhället*, ed. Olle Josephson (Ord och Stil, 28), 205 pp., examines the position of Swedish in the world of Information Technology.

2. RUNOLOGY AND OLDER TEXTS

Jan Owe, *Svenskt runnamnsregister*, 2nd enlarged edn, Hässelby, Jan Owe, 1996, 138 pp., is an index of Swedish rune names. *Runor och ABC*, ed. Staffan Nyström (Runica et mediævalia. Opuscula, 4), 192 pp., is a collection of 11 papers from a symposium in Stockholm in the spring of 1995. Another collection of articles on various rune topics is *Blandade runstudier* (Runrön, 11), 199 pp. Marit Åhlén, *Runristaren Öpir: en monografi* (Runrön, 12), 249 pp., with an English summary, is a doctoral dissertation on the famous rune master Öpir. Stefan E. Hagenfeldt, *Sandstone Rune Stones* (Runica et mediævalia. Scripta maiora, 2), 1996, 123 pp., examines the use of sandstone for erected rune stones. Surveys of runic inscriptions from specific local areas are Maria Cinthio, *En vägledning till runorna i Lund*, Lund, Kulturen facta, Drottens arkeologiska museum, 1996, 24 pp.; Lars Rask, *Trosatraktens runstenar*, Västerljung, Axplock, 1995, 71 pp.; and Palle Budtz, *Vikingatidens runstenar i Sorunda socken*, Sorunda, Sorunda hembygdsförening, 1996, 27 pp. Frank Hübler, *Schwedische Runendichtung der Wikingzeit* (Runrön, 10), 1996, 190 pp., is a volume on Swedish runic poetry. Björn Andersson, *Runor, magi, ideologi* (USH, 136), 1996, 459 pp., with summaries in English and German, is a study of runes and rune magic in the context of the history of ideas. *Svenskt diplomatarium / Diplomatarium Suecarium.* VII, fasc. 2. *1360–1369,* Kungliga Vitterhets-, historie-, och antikvitetsakademien–Riksarkivet, 1995, pp. 421–633. Bertil Albrektson and Christer Åsberg, *Det nya Gamla Testamentet. Från forntida hebreiska till nutida svenska / The New Old Testament. From Ancient Hebrew to Modern Swedish,* Örebro, Libris, 1996, 107 pp., describes the scholarly co-operation between exegetes and linguists in the preparation of a new translation. The authors illustrate the principles and methods of their work with a wealth of illuminating examples. Bo-A. Wendt, *Landslagsspråk och stadslagsspråk* (LSNS, ser. A, 53), 263 pp., diss., with a German summary, examines the law of King Kristoffer (1418–48) from a historical stylistic perspective.

3. ORTHOGRAPHY, PHONETICS, ACCENT, AND METRICS

Alexander Zheltukhin, *Orthographic Codes and Codeswitching: a Study of 16th Century Swedish Orthography* (SSSP, n. s., 21), 270 pp., diss., with a German summary, is a study of spelling variation. The author's hypothesis is that such variation is less random than it may seem. Claes-Christian Elert, *Allmän och svensk fonetik,* Norstedt, 1995, 172 pp., has appeared in its 7th revised edition. Per Hedelin, *Norstedts svenska uttalslexikon,* Norstedt, 1369 pp., is a comprehensive pronunciation dictionary. It has a very useful introduction by Claes Christian Elert (pp. 10–44), offering an outline of phonetic signs, speech production, variants in Swedish pronunciation, including the distinctive features of the standard speech norm of the south contrasted with those of the central Swedish norm, and also Finland-Swedish. Gunilla Söderberg, *Taga, bagare, Bragby: om g för äldre k i svenskan / Taga, bagare, Bragby: a Study of g for Older k in Swedish* (SINSU, 47), 203 pp., diss., with an English summary. Duncan Markham, **Phonetic Imitation, Accent and the Learner* (TILL, 33), 269 pp. Kristian Wåhlin, *Allmän och svensk metrik,* Lund, Studentlitteratur, 176 pp., is an introduction to metrics. David Kornhall, *Vers och tonaccent: om den svenska tonala accenten som poetiskt verkningsmedel* (Skrifter utgivna av Centrum för metriska studier, 4), 1995, 102 pp., is a study of the use of the Swedish tonal accent for poetic effect. Collections of papers have been published from two Nordic metrics conferences: in Lund, 1993, with the title *Rytmen i fokus,* ed. Sven Bäckman, Eva Lilja, and Bengt Landberg (Skrifter utgivna av Centrum för metriska studier, 6), 203 pp., and in Oslo, 1995, with the title *Metriska fäder och förnyare / Metrical Fathers and Innovators,* ed. Ulla-Britt Frankby and Jörgen Larsson (Skrifter utgivna av Centrum för metriska studier), 184 pp. Both volumes include summaries in English.

4. MORPHOLOGY, SYNTAX, AND SEMANTICS

Magnus Olsson, *Swedish Numerals in an International Perspective* (LSNS, ser. A, 50), 207 pp., diss. Gunlög Josephson, *On the Principles of Word Formation in Swedish* (LSNS, A, 51), 182 pp., diss. Lisa Christensen, *Framtidsuttrycken i svenskans temporala system* (LSNS, ser. A, 52), 222 pp., is a survey and analysis of temporal expressions denoting the future. Beatrice Silén, *Agentadverbialet i modern svenska* (StNF, 76), 222 pp., diss., with an English summary, examines agent phrases in modern Swedish. Kerstin Norén, *Svenska partikelverbs semantik* (NG, 17), 262 pp., on the semantics of Swedish phrasal verbs and verbal particles, has appeared in a new edition. Ulf Ottosson, *Kausalitet och semantik: ett bidrag till belysningen av förhållandet mellan lingvistisk språkteori och hermeneutisk fenomenologi* (NG, 19), 1996, 526 pp., diss., with an English summary, examines the relation between linguistic theory and hermeneutical phenomenology. Lennart Hellspong and Per Ledin, *Vägar genom texten*, Lund, Studentlitteratur, 303 pp., is a handbook on the analysis of factual texts. Mall Mölder Stålhammar, *Metaforernas mönster i fackspråk och allmänspråk*, Carlsson, 216 pp., compares characteristic metaphorical patterns in specialist and standard prose language. Torbjörn Lager, *A Logical Approach to Computational Corpus Linguistics* (GML, 14), 1995, 332 pp., Börje Gambäck, *Processing Swedish Sentences: A Unification-Based Grammar and Some Applications*, Stockholms Universitet, Tekniska Högskolan (SICS Dissertation Series, 21), 247 pp., with a short summary in Swedish.

5. RHETORIC, DISCOURSE ANALYSIS, AND SOCIOLINGUISTICS

Peter Cassirer, *Huvudlinjer i retorikens historia*, Lund, Studentlitteratur, 117 pp., is an outline of the main developments in the history of rhetoric. *Retorik och samhälle*, ed. José Luis Ramirez (Rapport: Nordiska Institutet för samhällsplanering, 1995, no. 2), 136 pp., is a volume with reports from a Nordic symposium on the place of rhetoric in social planning and public life held in November 1991. *Retoriska frågor: texter om tal och talare från Quintilianus till Clinton*, ed. Christer Åberg, Norstedt, 1995, 306 pp., is a volume of articles offered as a *Festschrift* to Kurt Johannesson. *Agitatorerna*, ed. Kurt Johannesson, Carlsson, 1996, 383 pp., is a collection of texts on the political campaigners and speakers within the Swedish Labour Movement. It is part of a survey project called 'Arbetarrörelsen och språket'/'The Labour Movement and Language'. Another report from the same project is *Arbetarna tar ordet*, ed. Olle Josephson, Carlsson, 1996, 367 pp. This examines the way in which representatives of the working classes find their voice on the political arena and adjust their linguistic skills to fit their political purpose. Per Ledin, *Arbetarnas är denna tidning: textförändringar i den tidiga socialdemokratiska pressen*, diss., with an English summary (SSSP, n. s., 20), 1995, 213 pp., investigates textual change in the social democratic press in the period 1892–1912. The author shows how the social democratic press was influenced by the centralization and bureaucratization which is a characteristic of political public life, and how this brought about stylistic change in the form of a move away from the spoken word. Barbro Wallgren-Hemlin, *Att övertyga från prediksstolen*, Nora, Nya Doxa, 331 pp., a Gothenburg Univ. diss., with an English summary, is a study of the rhetoric in 45 sermons held on the 17th Sunday after Trinity in 1990. Christina Melin-Köpilä, *Om normer och normkonflikter i finlandssvenskan: språkliga studier med utgångspunkt i nutida elevtexter* (SINSU, 41), 234 pp., diss., with an English summary. The material used in this study is a corpus of schoolchildren's essays and its main aim is to determine whether Finland-Swedish should be defined as a language in its own right or regarded as one of a number of regional variants of standard Swedish. Eva Aniansson, *Språklig och social identifikation hos barn i grundskoleåldern* (SINSU, 40), 1996, 303 pp., examines the connection between linguistic and social identification in 85 schoolchildren below the age of 16, using sound recordings of their speech over a period of three years as research material. Mats Eriksson, *Ungdomars berättande: Struktur och interaktion* (SINSU, 43), 307 pp., diss., with an English summary, is an investigation of the structural and interactive aspects of storytelling among adolescents. Brittmarie Öberg, **Negotiation Processes as Talk and Interaction: Interaction Analysis of Informal Negotiations* (Linköping Studies in Arts and Science, 133), 1995, 168 pp., diss. Ulla Melander-Marttala, *Innehåll och perspektiv i samtal mellan läkare och patient: en språklig och samtalsanalytisk undersökning* (SINSU, 39), 1995, 255 pp., diss., examines the content and interactive perspective in conversations between doctor and patient. Kerstin Nordenstam, *Skvaller i Kvinnliga och manliga gruppsamtal* (Meddelanden från Institutionen för svenska språket vid Göteborgs universitet, 12), 1996, 140 pp., compares the characteristic features of male and female group conversations in the context of everyday gossip. Another study of argumentative discussion in male and female group conversations is Karolina Wirdenäs, *Diskussion och gräl i vardagssamtal* (Meddelanden från Institutionen för svenska språket vid Göteborgs universitet, 20), 60 pp. *Language and Gender* (Meddelanden från Institutionen för svenska språket vid Göteborgs universitet, 11), 1995, 122 pp., is a collection of papers emanating from a course on gender issues held in the autumn of 1994.

6. FIRST AND SECOND LANGUAGE ACQUISITION AND BILINGUALISM

Från joller till läsning och skrivning, ed. Boel de Geer and Ragnhild Söderbergh, Malmö, Gleerup, 305 pp., is an anthology of texts on a child's linguistic development from the earliest speech sounds to reading and writing. Nils Jörgensen, **Barnspråk och ungdomsspråk*, Lund, Studentlitteratur, 1995, 241 pp. Gunilla Ladberg, *Barn med flera språk: tvåspråkighet i familj, förskola och skola*, 2nd edn, Liber utbildning, 1996, 124 pp., examines children with two or more languages in the context of the family, nursery school, and school environment. *Mer än ett språk*, ed. Eva Westergren and Hans Åhl, Norstedt, 244 pp., is a collection of articles on bilingualism and trilingualism in the north of Sweden. In her doctoral dissertation *Klara verba: andraspråksinlärares verbanvändning* (NG, 18), 1996, 253 pp., Ingegerd Enström investigates the way in which second language learners get to grips with Swedish verbs. Ingrid Andersson, *Bilingual and Monolingual Children's Narration* (Linköping Studies in Arts and Science, 156), 255 pp., diss., is a contrastive study of discourse strategies and narrative style. Inger Lindberg, **Second Language Discourse in and out of Classrooms* (Centre for Research on Bilingualism), 1995, 23 pp., diss., plus four articles, is a range of studies of the second language learner's discourse patterns in educational contexts. Kristina Korkman, *Tvåspråkighet och skriftlig framställning* (SSLF, 593), 1995, 374 pp., diss., is a survey of written work by bilingual and monolingual pupils in Finland-Swedish schools, focusing on bilingual pupils whose dominant language is Finnish. The author has extended her study to differences in language use between older and younger children and differences between boys and girls. Lisa Washburn, *English Immersion in Sweden: a Case Study of Röllingby High School 1987–1989*, Stockholms univ., 369 pp., diss. Monica Reichenberg Carlström, *Att på svenskarnas språk förstå Sverige* (Meddelanden från Institutionen för svenska språket vid Göteborgs universitet, 10), 1995, 175 pp., is a very interesting and illuminating survey of the difficulties encountered by immigrant pupils when faced with school textbooks in history, social sciences, and religion. The author advocates increased resources for developing readability, without simplifying the content, and properly meeting the needs of the growing number of immigrant pupils. Lars-Johan Ekerot, *Ordföljd, tempus, bestämdhet*, Lund, Gleerup, 1995, 187 pp., is based on a series of lectures for teachers of Swedish as a second language, dealing with central areas of the grammar of Swedish in a SLA perspective, i.e. word order, tense, the use of the definite, and, in addition, the acquisition of vocabulary. The book offers invaluable insights for anybody interested in SLA and the detailed analyses of texts written by second language learners are an asset, consolidating the SLA perspective.

7. DIALECTOLOGY

Lars Levander and Stig Björklund, *Ordbok över folkmålen i övre Dalarna* (SDFU, ser. D, Dialektordböcker från Dalarna, Gotland och andra landskap, 1), has reached volume 4, fasc. 33, *Skämne-Slå*, 1995, pp. 2295–374, and fasc. 34, *Slå-Sno*, 1996, pp. 2375–454. *Mål i sikte*, ed. Maj Reinhammar (Skrifter utgivna av Språk- och folkminnesinstitutet, genom Dialektenheten i Uppsala, ser. A, 27), 347 pp., is a volume of papers from a Nordic dialectology conference held in Sigtuna in August 1994. The articles are published in Swedish/Danish/Norwegian, with short summaries in English. Åke Hansson has issued an atlas of the dialects of the far north of Sweden, *Nordnorrländsk dialektatlas* (SDOFU, ser. A, Dialekter, 11), 2 vols, text, 99 pp., maps, 140 pp. Also noted: Jonny Ambrius, *Skånsk ordbok*, 4th rev. edn, Vällingby, Strömberg, 1995, 112 pp.; Knut Warmlund, *Värmländsk ordbok*, Wahlström & Widstrand, 399 pp.; Gunnar Fältskytt, *Lövångersmålet: böjt och rimmat*, Skellefteå, Gunnar Fältskytt, 1995, 150 pp., plus supp., 1996, 18 pp., a survey of a regional dialect from Västerbotten in the north of Sweden; Lars Grimbeck and Stefan Gustafsson, *Halländska ord och uttryck*, 3rd rev. edn, Varberg, Utsikten, 173 pp.

8. ONOMASTICS

Behövs en ortnamnslag?, ed. Eva Brylla (SOU, ser. B, Meddelanden, 10), 1995, 48 pp., is a collection of papers from a symposium on the potential need for legislation on place names. *Ortnamn i språk och samhälle*, ed. Svante Strandberg (Nomina Germanica, 22), 311 pp., is a *Festschrift* in honour of Lars Hellberg and contains articles on place names, both in a linguistic and a social context. *Från götarna till Noreens kor*, ed. Eva Brylla, Svante Strandberg, and Mats Wahlberg (SOU, ser. B, Meddelanden, 11), 1996, 216 pp., is a *Festschrift* in honour of Lennart Elmevik on his 60th birthday. *Ägonamn — struktur och datering*, ed. Gunilla Harling-Kranck (NORNA-rapporter, 63), 167 pp., is a volume with reports from a symposium held in September 1995 on the structure and dating of ownership names. The following have appeared: Gösta Franzén and Svante Strandberg, *Memmings härad: bebyggelsenamn* (SOU, ser. A, Sveriges ortnamn; Ortnamnen i Östergötlands län, D 16), 1995, 73 pp.; Bertil Flemström, *Bräcke Kommun: bebyggelsenamn* (SOU, ser. A, Sveriges ortnamn; Ortnamnen i Jämtlands län, D 3), 1995, 102 pp.; Gunnar Pellijeff, *Övertorneå kommun: bebyggelsenamn* (SDOFU; Ortnamnen i Norrbottens län, D 154), 1996, 140 pp. In addition to the instalments in the ongoing major surveys of settlement names listed above, some individual publications have been issued in the field, including Staffan Nyström, *Ortnamnen i Ornö socken* (Bygdemuseet Ornö sockenstugas skriftserie, 6), 1996, 127 pp.; Åke Axell, *Skärgårdsnamn i sörmländska farleder och arkipelager*, Saltsjöbaden, Författares bokmagasin, 120 pp.; Lars Dufberg, *Förklaringar till vägnamnen inom Höllviken, Kämplinge och Ljunghusen*, Vellinge, Stadsbyggnadskontoret, 1996, 47 pp.; Jan Agertz, *Bebyggelsenamn: socknarna Reftele och Villstad*, Smålandsstenar, Västbo härads fornminnesförening, 96 pp.; and Gunnar Jonsson, *Dalslands ortregister*, Forshaga, Värmlands släktforskarförening, 1995, 35 pp. Jens Corneliusson, *Växternas namn: vetenskapliga växtnamns etymologi — språkligt ursprung och kulturell bakgrund*, Wahlström och Widstrand, 602 pp., concerns the etymology and cultural and scientific background of plant names.

Two instalments of the dictionary of medieval personal names have appeared: *Sveriges medeltida personnamn: ordbok: förnamn* (Arkivet för ordbok över Sveriges medeltida personnamn), vol. 3, fasc. 11, *Hans — Harald*, cols 1–160, and fasc. 12, *Harardus — Henrik*, cols 161–320, Almqvist & Wiksell International. Gudrun Utterström, *Dopnamn i Stockholm 1621–1810* (Nomina Germanica, 29), 155 pp., with summaries in English and German, is a survey of baptismal names. Olof Brattö, *Personnamn i Bohuslän*, Gothenburg, Olof Brattö, 1995, 132 pp., is the third in a series of volumes. This one is dedicated to family names. Inger Larsson, *Dåpp Inger, Tupp Lars och Jacobs Olof* (Nomina Germanica, 21), 1995, 82 pp., is a study of naming practices in the parish of Nås in the province of Dalarna. The author has investigated the system of name-giving based on the 'farm-related personal name' + forename + patronymic (e.g. Tupp Anders Mattsson). This is a regional characteristic and the author focuses on its use in the period 1680–1900. Her purpose is to shed light on the sources of the names, the extent to which they became hereditary, and the function they had in the community. Gunnar Bergh, *Kejsare, huliganer och pappenheimare: en utflykt bland ord och uttryck bildade på personnamn*, Carlsson, 1996, 331 pp., is a survey of the background of *c.* 250 eponyms, i.e. words based on personal names, notably *banta* — *to slim*, referring to a Dr Banting. Aino Naert, *Ortnamn i språkkontakt* (Nomina Germanica, 20), 1995, 238 pp., diss., with a German summary, is a methodological discussion concerning an analysis of the place names in a Swedish-Finnish contact area, i.e. the parish of Nagu in the south-western archipelago of Finland.

9. LEXICOGRAPHY

The Swedish Academy's *Ordbok över svenska språket*, Lund, Svenska Akademien, continues with fascs 334–38, cols 13769–4504, *Stå an — Sulkyplog.* *Stora Svenska ordboken*, Norstedt, 1996, 1513 pp., is a new edition of *Norstedts stora svenska ordbok*, compiled by Språkdata at the University of Gothenburg under the direction of Sture Allén and Åsa Abelin. It contains 100,000 words and phrases. Sten Malmström, *Bonniers svenska ordbok*, 6th rev. edn, Bonnier Alba, 1995, 682 pp., is a modern dictionary of standard Swedish, including new words, foreign words, technical terms, and phrases. *Norstedts plusordbok*, Norstedt, 1349 pp., is another dictionary compiled by Språkdata in Gothenburg, which also contains encyclopaedic articles by Per Axelsson and Håkan Josephson. Elias Wessén, *Våra ord: deras uttal och ursprung*, Norstedt, 530 pp., a short etymological dictionary which is now a classic, has been republished. Ingvar Stenström, *Interlingua — svensk ordbok*, Lund, Studentlitteratur, 1995, 279 pp., is a dictionary of 25,000 international words. *Teknisk ordbok*, 7th rev. edn, Liber, 590 pp., offers technical terms in Swedish, English, German, Finnish, and five other languages. *Strömbergs handelsordbok* (Swedish/English/German/Finnish), Strömberg, 633 pp., is a dictionary of commerce which is also available as an electronic publication. Nils-Fritiof Edström, *Svensk-engelsk ekonomiordbok*, Fritze, 1996, 171 pp., has appeared in its 6th revised and enlarged edition. Roger Gourdon, *Svensk-fransk EU-ordbok*, Lund, Studentlitteratur, 1995, 329 pp., contains terminology for the European Union. The following dictionaries have appeared in various specialist fields: Ola Feust, *Engelsk-svensk ordlista i marknadsföring*, Malmö, Liber-Hermod, 1995, 79 pp., is a dictionary of marketing; Carlos Alvear, *Plast- och gummilexikon* (Swedish/English/German), Gothenburg, consulting European Association (CEA), 1995, 307 pp., covers plastics and rubber terminology; Carlos Alvear, *Massa — papper — förpackning* (Swedish/English/German/French), Gothenburg, Consulting European Association (CEA), 470 pp., offers terminology connected with the paper and packaging industry; Folke Dubell, *Lantbrukslexikon* (Swedish/English/German/French), LT, 311 pp., is an agricultural dictionary; Lambert Scherp, *Engelsk-svensk ordbok för fordonstekniker*, Liber utbildning, 1995, 128 pp., is a dictionary for motor vehicle technicians. Tekniska Nomenklaturcentralen has published a word list on rehabilitation in the workplace, *Ordlista för arbetslivsinriktad rehabilitering* (TNC, 97), 1995, 29 pp. Several dictionaries of immigrant languages have been issued, notably Issa F. Michael, *Mikaels lexikon: svenskt-arabiskt*, 2nd edn, Författares bokmagasin, 1995, 246 pp.; Boris Havel, *Bosnisk-svensk, svensk-bosnisk ordbok*, Utbildningsradion, 1995, 280 pp.; Solveig

Elsberga, *Svensk-lettisk ordbok*, Norstedt, 1995, 383 pp.; Lars Dahlerus, *Litauisk-svensk ordlista, historisk version*, Lidingö, Instructor, 1995, 272 pp.; Id., *Litauisk-svensk ordlista, modern version*, Lidingö, Instructor, 1996, 234 pp.; Srebre Milenkovski and Stevce Acevski, *Svenskt-makedonskt lexikon*, Statens skolverk, Norstedt, 1995, 806 pp.; and Ahmed Yousseuf Elmi and Jama Mohamoud Omar, *Svenskt-somaliskt lexikon*, 2nd rev. edn, Statens skolverk, Norstedt (distr.), 1995, 301 pp.

10. BIBLIOGRAPHY

Språk i Norden, 1995, includes 'Ny språklitteratur' (106–41), and 'Nye ordbøker og ordlister' (142–52). *Språk i Norden*, 1996, has 'Ny språklitteratur' (188–225), and 'Nye ordbøker og ordlister' (226–38). *Språk i Norden*, 1997, includes 'Ny språklitteratur' (119–49), and 'Nye ordbøker og ordlister' (150–57). *Nordiska Studier* (see p. 891 above), includes 'Gösta Holms tryckta skrifter 1976–96' (183–96), a bibliography compiled by Lars Svensson. *Mål i sikte* (see p. 897 above), a *Festschrift* for Lennart Elmevik, includes 'Lennart Elmeviks tryckta skrifter 1962–95', a bibliography compiled by Jan Axelsson and Marit Åhlén.

LITERATURE

By BIRGITTA THOMPSON, *Lecturer in Swedish at University of Wales Lampeter*

1. GENERAL

Å. Bertenstam, 'Svensk litteraturhistorisk bibliografi 112–113 (1993–1994); med tillägg och rättelser för tidigare år', *Samlaren*, 117.2, 1996[1997]: 1–183. Eva Hættner Aurelius, *Inför lagen. Kvinnliga svenska självbiografier från Agneta Horn till Fredrika Bremer* (Litteratur Teater Film, Nya serien, 13), Lund U.P., 1996, 448 pp., is an impressive study of Swedish women's autobiographies from the period 1647–1856 and the Swedish history of the genre. The aim has been to portray women's views on themselves, their world, their writings, and the female writer, using some of the material in the 1991 bibliography that lists women's autobiographies and diaries in the years 1650–1989 (no. 6 of the same series). The main focus is on Agneta Horn, Queen Kristina, and Fredrika Bremer, and reference is made to international research into language and fiction, genre, text, and the self. Less space is devoted to female religious autobiographers; mention is made of Jesper Swedberg, Hedvig Charlotta Nordenflycht, P. D. A. Atterbom, and Malla Silfverstolpe. Christina Sjöblad, *Min vandring dag för dag. Kvinnliga dagböcker från 1700-talet* (Litteratur Teater Film, Nya serien, 16), Lund U.P.–Carlssons, 384 pp., is another study within the same project; here the focus is on the diaries, or journals, of a handful of Swedish 18th-c. women in a general European context; future plans include the diary genre in the 19th c. After introductory surveys of the European diary and early diary writing in Sweden, four representative female journals are explored against the ideological background of women's status at the time, namely those of Metta Lillie (1737–50), Christina Charlotta Hiärne (1744–1803), Queen Hedvig Elisabeth Charlotta (1775–1817), and 'Årstafrun', Märta Helena Reenstierna (1793–1839). Magnus Röhl, *Kalliope på svenska cirka 1720–1830. Ett bidrag till vår kännedom om detaljer och dominanter i det versepiska Sverige* (Acta Universitatis Stockholmiensis. Stockholm Studies in History of Literature, 35), Stockholm U.P.– Almqvist & Wiksell International, 652 pp., is a huge work which presents a survey of epic writing in Sweden, both as literature and literary theory; it is not, however, a history of Swedish epic writing, as the author is keen to point out. According to him, it should not be read from cover to cover but used as a reference work; this aim is greatly facilitated by a detailed index. The first part deals with works on theoretical aspects of the genre, native as well as translations, such as Erik Brander, *Försök om epopée, poëme epique eller hjälte-dikt*, 1768, 'a unique contribution to Swedish literary theory'. The second part is about 'the six great epic writers' in translation, from Homer and Virgil to Voltaire. Finally, part three concentrates on native Swedish epic writing, its themes and reception at the time, from Brander's *Gustaviade*, the only national epic in the Age of Liberty, to attempts by Per Henrik Ling and Esaias Tegnér. A concluding essay summarizes details, explores fundamental aspects of this vast amount of material, and considers the place of the epic in a literary and ideological setting. Summaries, conclusions, and a disarmingly irreverent quotation from David Lodge's *Small World* bring the work to a conclusion. Bengt Lewan, *Renässansbilder. Den italienska renässansen i svensk diktning*, Carlssons, 1995, 357 pp., looks at the Italian Renaissance in Swedish literature, and analyses works by King Gustav III, C. J. L. Almqvist, Verner von Heidenstam, August Strindberg, Hjalmar Bergman, and Pär Lagerkvist. *Fiktionens förvandlingar. En vänbok till Bo Bennich-Björkman den 6 oktober 1996*, ed. Dag Hedman and Johan Svedjedal (Avdelningen för litteratursociologi, 33), SLIUU, 1996, 263 pp., published in honour of Bennich-Björkman's 70th birthday, includes: L. Bennich-Björkman, on female reality in women's weeklies 1960–90 (9–30); M. Björkman, on translating novels into Swedish in the late 18th c. and the impact on national literature (31–71); U. Boëthius, on modern research into children's and young people's literature (72–88); R. E. Du Rietz, on publishing and variant editions (89–107); L. Furuland, on proletarian literature (108–23); S. Hansson, on the study of social conditions and their significance for orality and literacy, especially before Romanticism (142–50); D. Hedman, on Harry Martinson's *Aniara* and science fiction (151–81); L. Lönnroth, on Snorri Sturluson's concept of genre (182–93); M.-C. Skuncke, on late-18th-c. parodies (194–217); J. Svedjedal, a chapter from his current Birger Sjöberg biography (218–39, see p. 923 below); A. N. Uggla, on the reception of Polish literature (240–49); L. Wendelius, on the criticism of American exceptionalism from the mid-19th c. to the early 20th (250–63). Henrik Grönroos and Ann-Charlotte Nyman, *Boken i Finland. Bokbeståndet hos borgerskap, hantverkare och lägre sociala grupper i Finlands städer enligt städernas bouppteckningar 1656–1809* (SSLF, 596), Helsinki, 1996, 638 pp., is an important tool for anybody interested in the history of reading among the middle and lower classes in Finland until the end of the union with Sweden. The lists and indexes are based on about 4,000 estate inventories in 19, mainly coastal, cities and towns. *Svenska Akademiens Handlingar*, 23, 1996 [1997], Svenska Akademien–Norstedts, 64 + 222 pp., briefly refers to the series of classics, currently being published by the Swedish Academy, and to Esaias Tegnér; the main part is devoted to 'Henrik Schücks anteckningar till Svenska Akademiens historia 1883–1912.

IV. Invalen 1901–1908', ed. Bo Svensén, pp. 1–222, which concerns the furore surrounding Schück's own election to the Academy and his controversy with its Secretary, Carl David af Wirsén, until he finally became a member as late as 1913. Like Karin Johannisson's *Den mörka kontinenten* (Norstedts, 1994), Ulla Manns, *Den sanna frigörelsen. Fredrika-Bremer-förbundet 1884–1921*, Eslöv, Symposion, 320 pp., is an essential study of the role of women and female emancipation round the turn of the century, based on the history of ideas. It should help to modify the historical perspective of some current literary feminist trends. *Skånes litteraturhistoria.* I. *Fram till 1940-talet.* II. *1900-talets senare del*, ed. Louise Vinge, 2 vols, Malmö, Corona, 284, 303 pp., is a stimulating and learned work on the literary map of the region, which did not acquire a cultural tradition of its own until the 1870s. However, evidence of it goes even further back to the 18th c., to Linnaeus's travels and the later works of Esaias Tegnér. Even well-known writers from Skåne, such as Victoria Benedictsson, Vilhelm Ekelund, and Birgitta Trotzig, emerge in a different light when the focus is on their regional roots. Vinge's well-written preface stresses the close links between academic Lund and its rural hinterland, and the lively interest in various forms of folk-art in addition to the provincial writing one takes for granted. Especially in view of the fact that the other five contributors are all academics in the Department of Literature at the University of Lund, it is perhaps not surprising that the spirit of Lund is a predominant feature of the work. Together with the lavish illustrations, this is a refreshingly modern approach to regional literary history. Helena Forsås-Scott, *Swedish Women's Writing 1850–1995* (Women in Context Series: Women's Writing 1850–1990s, 4), London–Atlantic Highlands, NJ, Athlone Press, xiv + 333 pp., is the fourth volume in this country-by-country survey of women's writing from the beginnings of the struggle for emancipation until the present day. It will no doubt establish itself as a standard reference work with its clear emphasis on writing in the context of historical, social, political, and cultural developments, which are presented with special attention to the situation of women. It makes available important aspects of both Swedish history and literature to readers without a grasp of Swedish. Anna Williams, *Stjärnor utan stjärnbilder. Kvinnor och kanon i litteraturhistoriska översiktsverk under 1900-talet* (Avdelningen för litteratursociologi, 35, SLIUU), Hedemora, Gidlunds, 287 pp., explores how women writers of the 1880s, the 1930s, and the years 1965–85 have been treated in 20th-c. literary handbooks. The approach is both quantitative and qualitative, and illustrates the process of how a literary canon is formed. The study confirms the view that norms which marginalize women writers dominate throughout the century, even in the most recent literary histories. *Italienska förbindelser. En vänbok till Bengt Lewan*, ed. Birthe Sjöberg (Absalon, 11), SLIUU, 191 pp., is an anthology of essays dedicated to Lewan and his interest in Italy: not that of his speciality, the 19th c., but a more varied selection, including Queen Kristina, Birgitta Stenberg, and Viktor Rydberg. Johan Elmfeldt, *Läsningens röster. Om litteratur, genus och lärarskap*, Eslöv, Symposion, 348 pp., is a doctoral dissertation, based on empirical research into reader response in two sixth-form classes; the literary texts are mainly from the late 19th c., but also include Agnes von Krusenstjerna's novel *Den blå rullgardinen*. P. Rydén, 'En möjlig kanon — och en omöjlig. Staffan Björck och Harold Bloom om det litterära arvet', *Fest. Vinge*, 51–64, compares Björck's *Swenska språkets skönheter*, 1984, with Bloom's *The Western Canon*, 1994. Dag Hedman, *Prosaberättelser om brott på den svenska bokmarknaden 1885–1920: en bibliografi* (Avdelningen för litteratursociologi, 34, SLIUU), Hedemora, Gidlunds, 472 pp., deals with the formative years of the book market for crime fiction, mostly translations from English, French, and German. B. Agrell, 'Konsten som grepp — formalistiska strategier och emblematiska tankeformer', *TidLit*, 26.1:26–58. D. Hedman, 'Bibliografering av populärlitteratur', *ib.*, 26.2:75–79. M. Mazzarella, 'Vilken historia berättar Ruth Hedvall?', *HLS*, 72:175–83 (SSLF, 608), is a critical reappraisal of Hedvall's *Finlands svenska litteratur*, published in 1917. *TidLit*, 26.3–4, is a special issue on poetics. L. M. Potte, 'Modern drama studies: an annual bibliography', *ModD*, 40:183–278, includes the entry 'Scandinavian', pp. 263–64.

2.   THE MIDDLE AGES

BIRGITTA.   M. Malm, 'Uppenbarelse och poetik', *TidLit*, 26.3–4:61–80.

3.   FROM THE RENAISSANCE TO THE GUSTAVIAN AGE

Jakob Christensson, *Lyckoriket. Studier i svensk upplysning*, Atlantis, 1996, 470 pp., is a doctoral dissertation and a comprehensive cultural history of Swedish Enlightenment from the early years of the Age of Liberty to the first few decades of the 19th c. To a large extent it deals with the world of contemporary minor writers and is therefore relevant to the literary historian, not least because it shifts the focus of interest to a different perspective from the usual. The study shows that even after the French Revolution Enlightenment continued to function as an ideology for the élite of the country, and that it was mainly socially conservative in character and was supported by the clergy and therefore far from opposing the Lutheran Swedish church.

I. Oscarsson, 'Nyhetsförmedling och nyhetsberättande i svensk 1790-talspress', *Fest. Vinge*, 332–50.

BELLMAN, CARL MICHAEL. Gunnar Hillbom, *Källorna till Fredmans sånger och 'Den svenske Anacreon'* (Filologiskt arkiv, 38), Vitterhetsakademien–Almqvist & Wiksell International, 1996, 106 pp., is the first textual study of Fredman's songs and their historic origins, complementing Hillbom's work from 1991 on the epistles. Both the collections comprise a single corpus of text, based on a common body of manuscript material. The study confirms previous conclusions related exclusively to the epistles. Apart from examining the authenticity of the original edition, the work demonstrates the similarities and differences in the many variant sources; included are two disks in different formats with these variants. Gunnar Hillbom and Hans Nilsson, *Sångernas värld: om verket, visorna och Bellman i utlandet*, Proprius, 159 pp., published together with the complete version of the songs on CD, it illustrates international interest in B. and examines various aspects of the work. *Freia und Bacchus. Hommage an den schwedischen Dichter Carl Michael Bellman*, ed. Maria and Peter Ulrich Hein, Cologne, Seltmann & Hein, 1996, 139 pp., includes recent essays by a number of authors. Jens Kristian Andersen, *Bellman og de danske guldalderdigtere. En studie i litteraer reception* (Skrifter udgivet af Selskabet Bellman i Danmark, 1), Copenhagen, Danmarks universitetsforlag, 1996, 137 pp., is a reception study, mainly of Fredman's epistles and songs in the early 18th c. Bengt-Olov Linder, *Vår försummade Bellman. Närläsning av ett urval epistlar, sånger, dikter*, Carlssons, 1995, 282 pp., analyses a number of B.'s texts, familiar as well as unfamiliar. *Bellman var där: en vägvisare till Bellmansmiljöer i och kring Stockholm*, ed. Marie Louise Andersén et al., Bellmanssällskapet–Norstedts, 183 pp., examines about 50 places in Greater Stockholm used as settings in the songs of B. that have survived reasonably intact since his days. The double perspective is enhanced by parallel illustrations both from the 18th c. and today. G. Hillbom et al., 'Kommentar', pp. 1–161 of B., *Översättningar*, ed. Sigbrit Swahn, Sven Christer Swahn, Andreas Sanesi, Birgit Stolt, and Gunnar Hillbom (Carl Michael Bellmans Skrifter. Standardupplaga, 19), Bellmanssällskapet, 282 + 161 pp., discusses the justification for including translations by B. in the final volume of the B. Society standard edition of his works together with introductions to the individual texts and textual commentary. The publication is a comprehensive selection of early and late translations of both prose and poetry from French, German and Italian.

DALIN, OLOF VON. *Olof von Dalin. Samhällsdebattör, historiker, språkförnyare*, ed. Ingemar Carlsson et al., Olof von Dalinsällskapet–CAL-förlaget, 127 pp., is the first biography of D. for almost a century, and has been published by the D. Society which was founded in 1995. It seems strange that the pioneer of Enlightenment and one of the first journalists of modern times should have been so thorougly forgotten. This study is a welcome remedy for the current neglect, and gives a rounded picture of different aspects of D. in eight chapters, together with a commented bibliography, stressing the need for a text-critical edition of D.'s works, especially his poetry.

KELLGREN, JOHAN HENRIC.   Carina and Lars Burman, 'Kommentarer och ordförklaringar till volym I och II', pp. 271–372 of Johan Henric Kellgren, *Skrifter.* II. *Dramatik* (Svenska klassiker), Svenska Akademien–Atlantis, 1995, 376 pp.; this two-volume edition of K.'s writings (vol. I comprises poetry and prose) is the first in the Swedish Academy classics series, which so far includes eleven authors from the 18th to the 20th cs with introductions by Academy members, and text versions, comments, and word definitions by experts in the field. C. Burman, 'Dikt och sanning. Om författarskap och forskning', *TsSk*, 18:63–70.

LENNGREN, ANNA MARIA.   A. Swanson, 'Anna Maria Malmstedt and the Swedish musical theatre', *Scandinavica*, 36:139–67.

LEOPOLD, CARL GUSTAF AF.   I.-B. Täljedal, 'Leopolds sunda förnuft', *Fenix*, 13.2:111–43.

LINNÆUS, CARL.   Sven Snogerup and Matz Jörgensen, *I Linnés hjulspår runt Skåne*, Atlantis, 152 pp., follows nearly 250 years later in the track of L.'s journey to Skåne in 1749, trying to retrace what he described in *Skånska resan* (1751): plants and buildings, meadows and towns, forests and mansions. Inevitably, things have changed, often beyond recognition when it comes to waterways, groundwater level, and arable land. The main culprit is current attempts to abolish our history and in the process destroy the natural countryside, an operation which seems to have intensified recently. E. Zillén, 'Hummeln och den gröna strilkannan. Om *Trädgården* som figura', *Fest. Vinge*, 494–505, explores Magnus Florin, *Trädgården* (1995).

LUCIDOR, LARS JOHANSON.   S. Hansson, 'Inledning', pp. 7–33 of Lars Johanson (Lucidor), *Samlade dikter*, ed. Stina Hansson (Svenska författare. Ny serie), Svenska Vitterhetssamfundet, 530 pp., is the first text-critical edition for almost 70 years of the 17th-c. writer L.'s collected poetry, in SVS's new series of Swedish authors. Unlike the earlier edition by Sandwall, Hansson presents the poems in the same order as when they were first published in *Helicons blomster* (1689); the new edition with explanatory comments in footnotes throughout is a welcome revised and updated version of its predecessor. The introduction explores the relation of L.'s verse to 'the repertory and rhetoric of the tradition of vernacular renaissance in 17th-c. Europe' in the light of recent research.

NORDENFLYCHT, HEDVIG CHARLOTTA. Torkel Stålmarck, *Hedvig Charlotta Nordenflycht. Ett porträtt*, Norstedts, 223 pp., is a study of the interplay between the life and work of N., with an emphasis on life rather than on the literary texts, although there are numerous quotations from her writings. Stålmarck has also edited and annotated the recent volume of N.'s *Skrifter*, 1996, in the Swedish Academy current classics series, 1995–. N. is one of the very first Swedish writers who made poetry out of her life and emotions. The mystery is how a woman at that time, widowed at the age of 23, could achieve such a success: establishing contacts with leading European intellectuals and being the leading light behind the literary society Tankebyggarorden and the hostess of the foremost literary salon at the time. Stålmarck's highly readable study goes some considerable way towards explaining this early feminist phenomenon.

4. ROMANTICISM AND LIBERALISM

Leif Landen, *Jacob Adlerbeth* (Filologiskt arkiv, 39), Vitterhetsakademien–Almqvist & Wiksell International, 136 pp., examines the driving force behind Götiska Förbundet and its journal *Iduna*, and evaluates Adlerbeth's contribution to early 19th-c. cultural life. Ingmar Stenroth, *Järnåren i svensk litteratur*, Hovås, Pierre Racine AB, 1996, 97 pp., reassesses the negative aspect of the so-called iron age that followed the golden age of Gustav III's reign and ended with the overthrow of absolute monarchy. Romanticism has traditionally been considered as the dawn of a new cultural climate; instead Stenroth emphasizes that later technical and industrial developments and inventions are decisive and more important for literary trends of a more lasting nature, and that changes in the course of events around the year 1840 are more influential than those in 1810. What was actually achieved during the period 1798–1809, he claims, raises doubts about the accuracy of the term 'iron age' as a suitable label for its cultural life. Ingeborg Nordin Hennel, *Mod och försakelse. Livs- och yrkesbetingelser för Konglig Theaterns skådespelerskor 1813–1863*, Hedemora, Gidlunds, 488 pp., is a pioneering work investigating the lives and professional conditions of actresses at the Royal Theatre in Stockholm, focusing on three years, namely 1813–14, 1838–39, and 1862–63. The ethical-didactic literature of the same period provides the background to the current norms of femininity, and it is obvious that actresses were trapped within the same social hierarchical gender system as other women at the time. For actresses, this was made even more poignant in their performance of stereotype roles. J. Mickwitz, 'Konst som socialt och politiskt symbolgods. Bildkonst, teater, litteratur och musik i Norden under den "borgerliga revolutionens" tidevarv', *HLS*,

17–68 (SSLF, 608). M. Gram, 'Malla Silfverstolpe och hennes salong', *NT*, 73:31–39.

ALMQVIST, CARL JONAS LOVE. *Carl Jonas Love Almqvist: konstnären, journalisten, pedagogen*, ed. Roland Lysell and Britt Wilson Lohse (Almqviststudier, 1), Gidlunds, Hedemora, 1996, 173 pp., contains lectures and essays published by the A. Society at a Scandinavian symposium to commemorate the 200th anniversary of A.'s birth. Three main aspects are evident in this selection: A. as a pedagogue and the didactic intention of his work; the wide range of A.'s journalistic activity; and A. the artist and professional writer, where the focus is on reading his texts as an aesthetic programme, the influence of Swedenborg, his musical production, and his relevance for current gender studies. *Fest. Vinge* includes in its extensive coverage: B. Romberg, 'Eremiten i världsbullret. Love Almqvists självkarakteristiker' (65–80); L. Larsson, 'Feministernas Almqvist från kvinnoförrädare till frigörande dekonstruktör' (97–106); U.-B. Lagerroth, '"Konsten är det enda fullt uppriktiga." C. J. L. Almqvist mellan konstarter och mellan konst och liv' (109–25). B. T. Thomsen, 'Nation og roman. Om konstruktionen af rum i Andersens *O. T.* og Almqvists *Det går an*', *Procs* (BASS 10), 230–42, discusses two Scandinavian novels from the 1830s. J. Svedjedal, 'Almqvist på Internet. Om publicering av en textkritisk edition som digital hypertext', *TidLit*, 26.2:60–74. L. Gustafsson, 'Uppsalaromantisk genrepoetik. Samuel Grubbe, genrernas renhet och romanen', *ib.*, 26.3–4:104–20. J. Staberg, 'C. J. L. Almqvist och 1810-talets religiösa renässans', *ib.*, 121–39. J. Almer, 'En götisk poetik. C. J. L. Almqvist om Lings *Asarne* och skaldekonstens hemligheter', *ib.*, 140–56. L. H. Holm, 'Almqvist och alkemin', *Fenix*, 13.1:7–45.

ATTERBOM, PER DANIEL AMADEUS. R. Lysell, 'P. D. A. Atterboms poetik i *Grundbegreppen af Ästhetik och Vitterhet*', *TidLit*, 26.3–4:157–79.

BREMER, FREDRIKA. *Fredrika Bremer: Brev. Ny följd. Tidigare ej samlade och tryckta brev*. I. *1821–1852*. II. *1853–1865*, ed. Carina Burman, 2 vols, Hedemora, Gidlunds, 1996, xii + 545, 501 pp., is the result of a six-year-long research project, and signifies the complete publication of all known letters by B. in archives and private collections in various countries. Over 800 letters have been added to those published previously in four volumes in 1915–20 by Klara Johanson and Ellen Kleman. With its detailed comments, careful textual editing, and consecutive references to letters in the earlier work plus comprehensive indexes of addressees, names and works, Burman's work will be of invaluable use to future research, which should include a comprehensive biography, long overdue for over a hundred years. Carina Burman, *Mamsellen och förläggarna: Fredrika Bremers förlagskontakter 1828–1865* (Litteratur och samhälle, 30/1), MLIUU,

1995, 103 pp., examines B.'s contacts with publishers, both Swedish and international, and is based on largely unpublished material. L. A. Lofsvold, 'Trädgårdarna i den nya världen', *Fest. Vinge*, 474–85. S. Death, 'Afterword', pp. 231–40 of Fredrika Bremer, *The Colonel's Family*, ed. and trans. Sarah Death, Norwich, Norvik Press, 1995, 240 pp., introduces this classic in a new English translation, the first having been made in 1843.

GEIJER, ERIK GUSTAF. *OB*, no. 3–4, is devoted to G., and includes U. Knutsson, on G. and Malla Silfverstolpe (79–85); J. Svedjedal, on G. and C. J. L. Almqvist (86–95); E. Hættner Aurelius, on G. and Fredrika Bremer (96–101).

HEBBE, WENDELA. Brita Hebbe, *Wendela. En modern 1800-talskvinna*, Natur och Kultur, 342 pp., explores the life of one of the more remarkable literary women of her time, who in spite of her talent never became a serious rival to the leading female writers Fredrika Bremer, Emilie Flygare-Carlén, and Sophie von Knorring. Instead, she worked mainly as a journalist on *Aftonbladet*, and was involved in relations or on friendly terms with some of the leading literary names, such as Esaias Tegnér, Lars Johan Hierta, and C. J. L. Almqvist.

KNÖS, THEKLA. L. Elleström, 'Thekla Knös — en idealrealistisk ironiker?', *Fest. Vinge*, 143–53.

LIVIJN, CLAS. O. Fischer, 'Clas Livijn. Tecken och offentlighet', *TidLit*, 26.2 : 3–17.

RUNEBERG, JOHAN LUDVIG. M. Ekman, 'Den katastrofala kärleken — en läsning av *Kung Fjalar*', *HLS*, 72 : 69–86 (SSLF, 608).

TEGNÉR, ESAIAS. Kurt Johannesson, *Ögonblickets genius*, Lund, Tegnérsamfundet, 31 pp., investigates the very different assessments of T. through the ages, especially T. as the outstanding orator of his day. C. Svensson, 'Dikternas tillkomsthistoria' and 'Kommentar', pp. 338–441 of *Esaias Tegnérs Samlade dikter*. VII. *1840–1846*, ed. Christina Svensson, Lund, Tegnérsamfundet, 1996, 445 pp., is the final volume of T.'s poetry; published by the T. Society, it contains writings from his final years when T. suffered from mental illness. Even though considerable material from this period might have been lost, the volume still includes about one third of the total number of T.'s poems in their original MS form; many of them are published here for the first time. The editing has been executed with admirable scholarly precision. Id., 'Skattkammare eller avgrund? Några underjordsskildringar under romantiken', *Fest. Vinge*, 169–80, on T.'s *Gerda*.

TOPELIUS, ZACHARIAS. M. Lehtonen, 'Brasaftnar i vindskammaren. Fältskärns gestalt och ramberättelsen i *Fältskärns berättelser*', *HLS*, 72 : 87–114 (SSLF, 608).

5. THE LATER NINETEENTH CENTURY

A continuation of the three-volume work by Göte Klingberg and Ingar Bratt, *Barnböcker utgivna i Sverige 1840–89*, 1988, is Ingar Bratt, *Barnböcker utgivna i Sverige 1890–1899: en kommenterad bibliografi* (SSBI, 60), Lund U.P., 1996, 695 pp. The completion means that 19th-c. publications for children and young people (including the popular Christmas magazines typical of the decade) have been thorougly covered bibliographically, carefully commented and provided with additional references about illustrators, composers and suggestions for further reading. Together with the four indexes of publishers, series, titles and personal names it is an invaluable tool for any future research. *Fest. Vinge* includes: C. Fehrman, 'Georg Brandes och Lunds litteraturhistoriker' (21–39); C. Sjöblad, 'Blicken och rummet hos sekelslutets flanörer: Laura Marholm och Ola Hansson' (383–99); J. Westerström, 'Lundabohemer' (271–86), on Emil Kléen, Bengt Lidforss, and Axel Wallengren. Anna Williams, *Åttitalister och kvinnliga åttitalister. Genus och kanon i litteraturhistoriska översiktsverk* (Litteratur och Samhälle, 31/1), MLIUU, 1996, 94 pp., deals with literary history from the point of view of gender, and is part of the author's extended study published in 1997, *Stjärnor utan stjärnbilder* (see p. 903 above).

BENEDICTSSON, VICTORIA. E.-L. Hultén, 'Victoria Benedictsson och hennes dagbok', *Horisont*, 44.2 : 4–15.

FRÖDING, GUSTAF. *Jag! utropar Fröding. Femton författare, hundra år efteråt*, ed. Staffan Söderblom, Gustaf Fröding-sällskapet–Wahlström & Widstrand, 128 pp., brings together views on F. by 15 contemporary writers, who were asked to write anything they wanted about him and his work. The result is a stimulating and personal book that proves F. is still a living classic. It is a pity the volume is so slim, and somewhat longer essays would have been welcome.

GEIJERSTAM, GUSTAF AF. Carl-Henrik Ankarberg, *Nennies saga. En författarhustrus livsöde i slutet av 1800-talet*, Carlssons, 320 pp., is a biography of G.'s wife, and inevitably throws light not only on G.'s writings but also on other writers at the time, not least Strindberg.

KARLFELDT, ERIK AXEL. Jöran Mjöberg, *Många maskers man: vad dikterna berättar om Karlfeldt* (Karlfeldtsamfundets skriftserie, 29), Wahlström & Widstrand, 287 pp., presents an admirably varied picture of K. in his poems, and also stresses the presence of recurring confessional works from different periods in his life. True to an old 19th-c. tradition, each of K.'s collections of poetry is introduced by a poem with a 'policy statement' for that particular work, and concluded by one that summarizes its literary intentions. Ingegärd Fries, *Karlfeldt och dalmålarna* (Karlfeldtsamfundets skriftserie, 28), Malung, Dalaförlaget, 1996, 128 pp., considers K.'s unique suite of poems 'Dalmålningar utlagda på rim' in his *Fridolins lustgård* (1901), and any possible connection with the naive folk art of the Dala painters in the previous century, at the time hardly known or appreciated outside the province of Dalarna. Fries concludes that there is an affinity in the general cultural inheritance, not least the language in the old Bible, but that K.'s poems are nevertheless independent creations linking provincial traditions with European symbolism. K., *I Dalarne och Lukt och doft*, ed. Jöran Mjöberg (Karlfeldtsamfundet), Uppsala, Hallgren & Fallgren, 1995, 48 pp., provides background to K.'s poetry between the years 1895 and 1927.

KEY, ELLEN. *Parnass*, no. 6, is a special issue on K.

LAGERLÖF, SELMA. *Selma Lagerlöf och kärleken*, ed. Karl Erik Lagerlöf (Lagerlöfstudier 1997), Hedemora, Selma Lagerlöf-sällskapet–Gidlunds, 176 pp., explores this key theme of L.'s in 11 articles, and includes: Y. Toijer-Nilsson, on the triangle drama involving L., Valborg Olander and Sophie Elkan, stressing the considerable literary importance of the correspondence with Olander; M. Rossholm Lagerlöf, on *Gösta Berlings saga*; K. Petherick, on the story *Dunungen*; L.-O. Franzén, on *En herrgårdssägen*; A. Pleijel and M. Nikolajeva, on *Jerusalem*; L. Vinge, on *Herr Arnes penningar* in a comparative study with *Hamlet*; P. O. Enquist, on L.'s relationship with her alcoholic father allegedly depicted in *Körkarlen* and *Kejsaren av Portugallien*; K. E. Lagerlöf, on the father's love in the latter novel; U. Torpe, on *Bannlyst*; V. Edström, on the cottage as the room of love. Sven Arne Bergmann, *Getabock och gravlilja. Selma Lagerlöfs En herrgårdssägen som konstnärlig text* (SLIGU, 30), 473 pp., is a doctoral dissertation, which explores L.'s qualities as a storyteller in her classic psychological novel from 1899. Bergmann shows convincingly how the artistry of her narrative method is present both in its manifest simplicity and latent complexity. The novel is a mixture, or rather a subtle blend of genres; some conclusions of the study point to close similarity with psychoanalytical, others to feminist theories, although gender impartiality is closer to the mark. Altogether, the study stresses L.'s unique narrative talent: it proposes a shift from biographic, genetic and folklore approaches to a focus on narratological, structural and thematic ones. M. Ehrenberg, 'Selma Lagerlöfs "Stor-Kerstin och Lill-Kerstin" och dess förbindelse med den muntliga traditionen', *Fest. Vinge*, 351–66. P. Graves, 'Narrator, theme and covert plot: a reading of Selma Lagerlöf's *Löwensköldska ringen*', *Scandinavica*, 36:7–21. B. T. Thomsen, 'Aspects of topography in Selma Lagerlöf's *Jerusalem*, Vol. I', *ib.*, 23–41. H. Forsås-Scott, 'Beyond the dead body: masculine representation and the feminine project in Selma Lagerlöf's *Herr Arnes penningar*', *ib.*, 217–38. H. Wivel, 'Distancens lidenskab. Den litterære

biografi: metode, mulighed og nogle idealforestillinger', *TsSk*,
18:9–31. Robinson, *Women*, II, 602–10.

SANDELL-BERG, LINA. Astri Valen-Sendstad, *Lina Sandell. Et dikter-
liv til Herrens aere*, Oslo, Lunde, 1995, 219 pp., is a monograph on the
hymnist S.

STRINDBERG, AUGUST. Harry G. Carlson, *Out of Inferno. Strindberg's
Reawakening as an Artist*, Seattle, Washington U.P., 1996, 390 pp.,
explores a story that has only been partly told hitherto. It investigates
how the coalescence of various forces in the *fin de siècle* climate
influenced S.'s own personal renewal as an artist and spurred him to
discoveries about art and the power of visual imagination both before
and after the Inferno period. It attempts to define the way he saw and
sensed things with his painter's eye and Romantic conscience. Hans-
Göran Ekman, *Villornas värld. Studier i Strindbergs kammarspel*, Hedemora, Gidlunds, 285 pp. + xxxii illus., explores S.'s four chamber
plays from the first half of 1907, namely *Oväder*, *Brända tomten*,
Spöksonaten, and *Pelikanen*. The plays are studied against the background of S.'s life-long interest in the physiology of the senses; from
being a firm believer in the five senses, he later rejects them in favour
of wisdom and an inner vision, leading to the gradual development of
his philosophy of 'the world of illusions'; the chamber plays express
in condensed form the quintessence of his experiences during and
after the Inferno crisis. Johannes F. Evelein, *August Strindberg und das
expressionistische Stationendrama. Eine Formstudie* (STML, 13), 1996,
xi + 218 pp., is a comparative study exploring S.'s station dramas
together with 35 Expressionist plays. Thelma Hanson, *Karl Kraus och
Strindberg* (Acta Regiae Societatis scientiarum et litterarum Gothobur-
gensis. Humaniora, 36), Gothenburg, Kungl. Vetenskaps- och vit-
terhetssamhället, 1996, 86 pp., examines the presence of S. in the
Kraus journal *Die Fackel*. Per-Anders Hellqvist, *En sjungande August.
Om Strindberg och musiken i hans liv*, Bromma, Edition Reimers, 296 pp.,
emphasizes S. the music lover, and the importance music had in his
works. It explores S.'s relationship with music from his early teens
and the family music-making, his ambition to be an opera singer, his
dream about unheard-of modern music during his Inferno crisis, and
his preference for Beethoven in his old age. S.'s detailed musical
instructions, not least in his dramas, are typical of his interest and
knowledge. Annette Kullenberg, *Strindberg — murveln. En bok om
journalisten August Strindberg*, Wahlström & Widstrand, 364 pp., examines journalistic techniques in a variety of texts from the whole range
of S.'s *œuvre*, pinpointing the devices that are characteristic of S.'s
striking style and language. Alice Rasmussen, *'Det går en oro genom
själen.' Strindbergs hem och vistelseorter i Norden*, Carlssons, 343 pp., gives
detailed information on S.'s many homes and their fundamental

importance for his works and inspiration. *Strindbergiana*, ed. Birgitta Steene (Strindbergssällskapet, 12), Atlantis, 176 pp., examines S. and film with reference to its centenary, and includes: B. Lagerkvist, on filming *Hemsöborna* and *Röda rummet* (11–23); M. V. Lagercrantz, on Anna Hoffmann Uddgren, the first Swedish female film director (24–45); B. Steene, on the Danish filmstar Asta Nielsen (46–61); M. Björkin, on filming *Brott och brott* (62–80); F. Rokem, on filmic traits in S.'s drama (81–99); E. Törnqvist, on the TV version of *Pelikanen* (100–21); R. Bark, on theatre productions in 1993–96 (122–45); B. Steene, on film and TV versions (146–75). *August Strindberg*, ed. Stig Sæterbakken (Marginal, 4), Oslo, Cappelen, 115 pp., is a collection of essays on S. after 1897, dedicated to the memory of Bertil Nolin whose contribution 'Det moderna, det faustiska och ondskans triumf. Om Strindberg efter Inferno' (7–16), was the last paper he wrote before his death in 1996. It includes further studies of *Inferno* and *Till Damaskus*, of *Dödsdansen*, *Ett drömspel*, *Ensam*, *Svarta fanor*, *Taklagsöl*, *Spöksonaten*, *Pelikanen*, and *En blå bok*. S. Runestam, 'Nathan Söderblom om August Strindberg. Känt och okänt. Några iakttagelser', *Samlaren*, 117.1, 1996 [1997]:84–93. L. Lingard, 'The daughter's double bind: the single-parent family as cultural analogue in two turn-of-the-century dramas', *ModD*, 40:123–38, on Henrik Ibsen's *Hedda Gabler* and S.'s *Miss Julie*. D. Davy, 'Strindberg's unknown comedy', *ib.*, 305–24, on *Brott och brott*. L. R. Wilkinson, 'Strindberg, Peter Szondi, and the origins of modern (tragic) drama', *ScSt*, 69:1–28.

6. THE TWENTIETH CENTURY

The large project on Nordic female writing is nearing its completion, with only the fifth and final bibliographical volume still to come: *Nordisk kvinnolitteraturhistoria*. IV. *På jorden 1960–1990*, ed. Elisabeth Møller Jensen, Lisbeth Larsson, et al., Höganäs, Bra Böcker, 597 pp., has now reached contemporary writing with this fourth, very attractively illustrated and beautifully produced volume. The earlier largely historical and sociological approach has changed into one that is more text-oriented. Women's experiences and perspectives as expressed in writing have now become more and more part of the common human condition in a context somewhat different from the predominantly male literary history of the past. The publication of this work and current research into the established literary canon will no doubt help to do away with what is still supposed to be the marginalization of women writers. More awareness of the problem is certainly welcome, but neither quality nor quantity should be overlooked when trying to achieve a kind of gender balance. The contributions by Kerstin Ekman and Sara Lidman in their series of novels about the development of Swedish industrialization are characteristic of the impact women writers achieved in the 1970s and 1980s. The modernism of the 1960s is explored under the telling chapter headings 'Förnyelser' and 'Förändra språket', while 'Världen i rörelse' reflects the variety of voices that were suddenly heard in the following decade, the experience of which is still aesthetically inspiring and innovative. The young writers of the 1980s are the daughters of the 1960s; in order to 'Bliva sig själv' they have to try to find new aesthetic form and language, at the risk of being sidelined as incomprehensible or failures. Paradoxically, there seems to be a need for a literary history of women writers as long as they are considered on the basis of their sex, rather than as individuals. Robinson, *Women*, includes entries on Karin Boye, Kerstin Ekman, Tove Jansson, Sara Lidman, Astrid Lindgren, Moa Martinson, Solveig von Schoultz, Edith Södergran, Märta Tikkanen, and Birgitta Trotzig. Magnus William-Olsson, *Obegränsningens ljus. Texter om poesi*, Gedins, 241 pp., looks at poetry criticism by Hans Ruin, Göran Printz-Påhlson, and Anders Olsson, but also analyses individual modern poets such as Gunnar Björling, Lars Forssell, Göran Sonnevi, Birgitta Trotzig, and Karl Vennberg, in addition to the Romantic Erik Johan Stagnelius. Staffan Bergsten, *Klang och åter. Tre röster i samtida svensk kvinnolyrik* (FIB:s lyrikklubbs bibliotek, 268), FIB:s lyrikklubb, 266 pp., discusses poetry published in the first half of the 1990s by Katarina Frostenson, Ann Jäderlund, and Birgitta Lillpers; several of the chapters are revised essays originally published in journals such as *Artes*, *BLM*, and *TidLit*. Margarethe Schmid-Hunziker, *Den stora sorgen. Schwedische Lyrik über den modernen Menschen zwischen Fortschrittsglaube und Umweltzerstörung*, Zurich U.P., 1996, 245 pp., is a doctoral dissertation on poetry from the 1950s to the 1990s with the emphasis on texts from the 1970s and 1980s that deal with different aspects of environmental problems. A. Olsson, 'Poesi och nihilism. En skiss, en typologi och fyra exempel (Stevens, Björling, Ekelöf och Celan)', *TidLit*, 26.3–4:3–18. P. E. Ljung, 'Att läsa poetik. Några anteckningar inför studiet av Hans Larssons *Poesiens logik* och Hans Ruins *Poesiens mystik*', *ib.*, 198–208. B. Green, 'The syntax revolt in Swedish poetry', *Procs* (BASS 10), 87–105, includes a number of modern poets. H. von Born, 'Nordic literature. Voyage into a landscape of moving light', *ib.*, 140–50, refers to several obvious names, including Werner Aspenström, Kjell Espmark, and Ragnar Thoursie. *Five Swedish Poets*, ed. and trans. Robin Fulton, Norwich, Norvik Press, 199 pp., includes introductions to Kjell Espmark, Lennart Sjögren, Eva Ström, Staffan Söderblom, and Werner Aspenström. Göran Lundstedt, *Till bords med de bästa. Om kritikern Knut Jaensson*, Lund, Ellerströms, 134 pp., is a study about the critic and essayist Knut Jaensson and his work from the 1930s to his death in 1958 in journals such as *Fönstret, Karavan, Tidevarvet*, and *BLM*, and the daily newspaper *Dagens Nyheter* where he was a permanent member of the staff from 1946. Both professionally and personally Jaensson was close to the avant-garde among the young writers of the 1930s. His essays on Harry Martinson and Jan Fridegård in 1946 were the first comprehensive studies of their work. The study lists a bibliography of Jaensson's essays and other writings, and is based partly on unpublished material. Per Rydén et al., *Litteraturens ställning*, Carlssons, 160 pp., takes up a problem that is being discussed in several quarters. The status of literature is considered from various angles by the contributors to this work, all of them connected with the Department of Literature at the University of Lund. Sven Ljungberg, *Minnesbilder. Med trägravyrer av författaren*, Bonnier Alba, 214 pp., provides glimpses of the artist's professional and personal dealings with a number of writers, giving interesting inside information about his woodcut illustrations in works by Fritiof Nilsson Piraten, Ivar Lo-Johansson, Pär Lagerkvist, Tage Aurell, and Bo Setterlind. Lars Gustafsson, *Vänner bland de döda. Essäer om litteratur*, Natur och Kultur, 122 pp., deals with a number of dead literary friends and their works, among them Carl Michael Bellman (9–25), Selma Lagerlöf's *Gösta Berlings saga* (43–64), Gunnar Mascoll Silfverstolpe's poem 'Finn Malmgren' (74–92), and Gunnar Ekelöf's prose text 'Diner' in *Non Serviam* (93–111). *Utsikter. Föreläsningar från Helgonabacken*, ed. Birthe Sjöberg (Absalon, 12), SLILU, 240 pp., is the third collection of public lectures in the series from the University of Lund. Apart from B. Romberg on the poet C. J. L. Almqvist (149–62), it deals exclusively with aspects of 20th-c. writers, such as Birgitta Trotzig, Ola Larsmo, Lars Jakobsson, Astrid Lindgren, Carola Hansson, Per Gunnar Evander, Göran Sonnevi, and Harriet Löwenhjelm, as well as love in contemporary poetry. Pär Wästberg, *En ung författares dagbok. Från sjutton till tjugo år 1951–1953*, Wahlström & Widstrand, 331 pp., gives snapshots of the literary life of Stockholm at the time, writer colleagues, books, journals, and publishers. Jan-Magnus Jansson, *Tidiga möten. Litteratur och politik från 30-tal till 60-tal*, Esbo, Schildts, 1996, 258 pp., is an essay collection that discusses the significance of lyrical modernism and political democracy. Among the modernistic writers assessed in individual chapters are Rabbe Enckell (17–37), Elmer Diktonius (38–48), Gunnar Björling (49–58), Karin Boye (59–71), and Harry Martinson (72–82), in addition to Jansson's own two collections of poetry, namely *Morgon och uppbrott* (1944), and *Enskild* (1952) (83–102). Cecilia Lengefeld, *Förlaget Albert Bonniers äventyr i Tyskland 1911–1913* (Litteratur och samhälle, 32/1), MLIUU, 103 pp., investigates the setting-up of a Bonnier publishing house in Germany, and why the expected success turned into a business failure. Lena Kåreland, *Traditionalist och smakdomare. Eva von Zweigbergks barnbokskritik under 1940-talet* (Litteratur och Samhälle, 32/2), MLIUU, 179 pp., discusses the impact on children's literature of the influential literary criticism by the *Dagens Nyheter* journalist Eva von Zweigbergk during the 1940s. The study is part of a more comprehensive current project, 'Children's literature and modernism'. It examines literary debates about both children's and adult literature, resulting in the breakthrough of modernism. Conny Svensson, *Tarzan i slukaråldern* (SSBI, 61), Rabén Prisma, 224 pp., considers the author's own boyhood reading in the 1940s and 1950s, with a summary in English. His list is strikingly similar to the books many a girl who did not like girls' books read at the same time! Strangely enough, there is no mention of any current Astrid Lindgren books. Apart from several internationally well-known writers of Anglo-Saxon or American origin, it includes comic papers such as *Karl-Alfred*, *Kalle Anka*, and *Serie-magasinet*, popular periodicals like *Alibi-magasinet*, and the weeklies *Rekord-magasinet*, *Lektyr*, and *Levande livet* as well as Gösta Knutsson's *Pelle Svanslös* books, the historical novels by Carl August Cederborg and Åke Holmberg's lisping detective Ture Sventon. *Barn och humor*, ed. Gunnar Berefelt (SCB, 27), 168 pp., is a sample of the lectures given at a symposium in May 1996, and investigates the subject children and humour. The detective novel genre is discussed by L. Thompson, 'Henning Mankell and Håkan Nesser', *SBR*, no.2:29–31; *ib.*, 42–59, assessess the crisis in the publishing industry. B. Widegren, 'Mästerverkens år. Den svenska litteraturen 1996', *NT*, 73:367–75. G. Widén, 'Drakarnas flykt över Helsingfors. Finlandssvensk litteratur 1996', *ib.*, 327–33. A.-C. Snickars, 'De definitiva uppbrottens tid. Några nedslag i fjolårsprosan', *FT*:69–80. B. Wallén, 'Chorus av röster. Lyrikåret 1996', *ib.*, 139–49. *Svenska samtidsförfattare*, 1, Lund, Bibliotekstjänst, 159 pp., presents 15 contemporary writers in one volume, previously introduced in individual folders in the series 'Författarporträtt' (1994–96).

AHLIN, LARS. Carin Röjdalen, *'Men jag ville hjälpa.' Studier i Lars Ahlins 1940-talsnovellistik* (SLIGU, 31), 230 pp., is the first doctoral dissertation on A. as a short-story writer, and explores the 'text strategies' of his three collections of stories in the 1940s, namely *Inga ögon väntar mig*, *Fångnas glädje*, and *Huset har ingen filial*. The study aims to describe 'the literary strategies that make the orientation of the text visible in terms of a certain method of reading'; it also deals with the reception of the stories at the time they were published.

ANDERSSON, PAUL. *'Sensitiv som en frostskadad mimosa.' Biografi över Paul Andersson, Metamorfosgruppen och femtitalets nyromantik* (MLIGU, 22), 132 pp., explores the life of this 1950s poet who was forgotten, but is now being reassessed in literary handbooks after the publication of his collected works in 1991.

BENGTSSON, FRANS G. *Frans G. Bengtsson i västerled. Frans G. Bengtsson-studier*, II, ed. Lennart Ploman (Frans G. Bengtsson-sällskapet, 7), Lund, 32 pp., includes M. Meyer, 'Frans G. Bengtsson to his translator' (5–15); G. R. Buckhorn, 'Frans G. Bengtsson och lärdomen i Lund ur skotsk synvinkel' (19–32). J. Ellerström, 'Inledning och kommentarer', [pp. 3–4 and 22–24] of *Rubaiyat om Lund* (Frans G. Bengtsson-sällskapet, 6), Lund, [24 pp.], a reprint of a joint venture by B., Hjalmar Gullberg, and Sigfrid Lindström in *Lundagård*, 1925, no. 6.

BERGMAN, INGMAR. M. B. Sandberg, 'Tracking out. "The Bergman film" in retrospect', *ScSt*, 69:357–75.

BOIJ, HANS. A.-M. Berglund, 'Poeten och hans fotspår. Ett samtal med Hans Boij', *Horisont*, 44.3–4:8–14.

BONDESTAM, ANNA. M. Antas, 'Klarsynthet och kollektivitet. Variationer på Anna Bondestams upplysningstema', *HLS*, 72:215–42 (SSLF, 608).

BOYE, KARIN. Camilla Hammarström, *Karin Boye* (Litterära profiler), Natur och Kultur, 269 pp., is an attempt to get away from the established and stereotyped myths contained in the biography by Margit Abenius. The prose writings are discussed extensively together with B. as a literary critic. The approach makes it a very worthwhile introduction to B.'s whole *œuvre*.

BRENNER, ARVID. Ingemar Hermansson, *Den fruktbara hemlösheten. Arvid Brenner och din nästas ansikte*, Carlssons, 258 pp., is an attempt to rediscover a forgotten writer whose warning about Nazism in the mid-1930s came too early to be heeded.

CARPELAN, BO. Jutta Voigtmann; '*Hon är det gåtfulla och underbara.' Kvinnobilden i Bo Carpelans romaner Axel och Urwind* (MLIÅA, 24), 110 pp., investigates the female characters in two of C.'s novels, concluding that they correspond to traditional and mythical ideas.

DAGERMAN, STIG. C. Ahlund, 'Stig Dagerman som lyriker i "Birgitta svit"', *Samlaren*, 117.1, 1996 [1997]:28–50.

DELBLANC, SVEN. L. Bäckström, 'Sven Delblanc och Hitlers barndom', *Horisont*, 44.1:38–45. C. Whittingham, 'Expressing the inexpressible: Sven Delblanc and the role of the artist', *Scandinavica*, 36:59–75.

DIKTONIUS, ELMER. C. Zilliacus, 'The roaring twenties of Elmer Diktonius: a centenarian as wonder boy', *ScSt*, 69:171–88. See also JOHNSON, EYVIND.

EKARV, MARGARETA. M. Wirmark, '*Nådasmulor, Drömmarnas barn och I Högom tid*. Om Margareta Ekarvs regionala dramatik', *Fest. Vinge*, 183–95.

EKELUND, VILHELM. N. G. Valdén, 'Kommentar', pp. i–xxi of Vilhelm Ekelund, *Sak och sken* and *På hafsstranden*, Lund, Vilhelm Ekelundsamfundet–Ellerströms, 179 + 248 + xxi pp., is a facsimile of the 1922 editions with an afterword and commentary by Nils Gösta Valdén; it is the latest volume of E.'s collected prose works in this annotated reprint series by the E. Society. A. Johansson, 'Form och modernitet i Vilhelm Ekelunds *Elpidi*', *Edda*:155–71, is an analysis on the basis of Theodor W. Adorno's *Ästhetische Theorie*, 1970.

EKELÖF, GUNNAR. Paul Berf, *Reisen durch Zeit und Raum. Eine thematische Analyse von Gunnar Ekelöfs 'En Mölna-Elegi'* (Artes et litterae septentrionales, 15), Morsbach, Norden, 1995, 227 pp., analyses the poem that E. himself considered his most important and even central work. Anders Olsson, *Gunnar Ekelöf* (Litterära profiler), Natur och Kultur, 160 pp., is a useful introduction, not least because of Olsson's detailed knowledge of E. and his *œuvre*. He shows convincingly that E.'s works are characterized by great uniformity, in spite of their apparent contradictions. E. Thygesen, 'Translator's introduction', pp. 13–79 of Gunnar Ekelöf, *Modus Vivendi. Selected Prose*, ed. and trans. Erik Thygesen, Norwich, Norvik Press, 1996, 253 pp., provides useful information on E.'s prose writings. E. Stenmark, 'Aktaions horn. Ett ledmotiv hos Gunnar Ekelöf', *HLS*, 72:185–214 (SSLF, 608). *Parnass*, no. 3, is a special issue on E.

EKMAN, KERSTIN. M. Schottenius, 'Så modern och så olycklig! Om tre kvinnliga nordiska författarskap', *Fest. Vinge*, 423–30, on E.'s tetralogy *Kvinnorna och staden* and similar series by Kirsten Thorup and Herbjörg Wassmo. L. Schenck, 'Translator's introduction', pp. 5–8 of Kerstin Ekman, *Witches' Rings*, trans. Linda Schenck, Norwich, Norvik Press, 358 pp., the first novel in E.'s tetralogy. E., 'My approach to literature', *Procs* (BASS 10), 196–205, discusses mainly her own writing.

ENCKELL, RABBE. Mikael Enckell, *Öppningen i taket. En biografisk studie över Rabbe Enckell 1950–1974*, Helsinki, Söderströms, 382 pp., is the third and final part of Enckell's biography of his father, the first being *Under beständighetens stjärna* (1986), and the second — *dess ljus lyse* (1991). One of the main reasons for writing this study is an attempt to rehabilitate E. and the Finland-Swedish modernism of the 1920s following the misunderstanding and aggressive depreciation it has been subjected to. Being a psychoanalyst, Enckell questions whether parricide is necessary for regeneration, and thus makes his study a late contribution to the discussion on modernism. This pioneering biography is a well-documented and dedicated depiction of the period.

EVANDER, PER GUNNAR. A. Ohlsson, 'Filmens funktion i Per Gunnar Evanders roman *Berättelsen om Josef*', *Fest. Vinge*, 317–31.

Literature

FOGELKLOU, EMILIA. Ingrid Meijling Bäckman, *Den resfärdiga. Studier i Emilia Fogelklous självbiografi*, Eslöv, Symposion, 287 pp., is the first doctoral dissertation about the first Swedish woman theologian on the basis of her autobiography in three parts. As a Christian humanist, teacher, and writer, she devoted her life to a number of causes; together with Elin Wägner she is the most influential personality in Swedish feminism in the generation after Ellen Key.

FROSTENSON, KATARINA. C. Franzén, 'Ur det negativa. Om ett motdrag i Katarina Frostensons poesi', *TidLit*, 26.2:41–59.

GARDELL, JONAS. N. Smith, 'Jonas Gardell', *SBR*, no.2:16–17.

GYLLENSTEN, LARS. Thure Stenström, *Gyllensten i hjärtats öken. Strövtåg i Lars Gyllenstens författarskap, särskilt Grottan i öknen* (Acta Universitatis Upsaliensis. Historia litterarum, 19), Uppsala U.P.– Almqvist & Wiksell International, 1996, 365 pp., is an impressive and eye-opening study, with a summary in German, of one of the most important contemporary Swedish writers, focusing on a central work in G.'s *œuvre*. The author has had access to G.'s private notes and been able to relate to G.'s comprehensive familiarity with a number of philosophers and theologians: G.'s 'treatment of man's fundamental powerlessness and captivity in the material world and his interpretation of the relationship between man and the cosmos carries echoes of Plato, St. Paul and St. Augustine and of Swedenborg, Linnæus and Strindberg'; a kind of synthesis is possible even nowadays for a despised, commonplace person who manages to find a code for living a practical life. The analysis of G.'s unconfessional thinking is accompanied by a running commentary on his narrative technique.

JOHNSON, EYVIND. *Och så vill jag prata med dig. Brevväxlingen mellan Eyvind Johnson och Elmer Diktonius*, ed. Örjan Lindberger, Bonniers, 280 pp., is a welcome complement to the volume of letters by Diktonius published in 1995, described by Lindberger in the preface as 'a selection' in which some of the letters to J. are missing. This personal contact from 1930 until a few years before the death of Diktonius in 1961 was initially important to both writers: as early as the 1920s Diktonius had noticed J. as a writer of outstanding promise and significant for the modern Swedish novel and his own equal; to J., Diktonius was an authority and one of the pioneers of lyrical modernism. Of particular interest are the letters exchanged during the Finnish winter war in 1939–40, which reflect the fervent concern of both for the cause of Finland. By the end of the correspondence, their roles have been reversed: Diktonius is fading away, while J., now a successful novelist, has been elected a member of the Swedish Academy. L.-Å. Skalin, 'I Berättelsernas famn — eller i Lögnens. Odysseus som berättare hos Homeros och Eyvind Johnson', *Samlaren*,

117.1, 1996 [1997]:5–16. A. Cullhed, '"Sova, kanske drömma."' Kring drömtemat i Eyvind Johnsons historiska romaner', *ib.*, 17–27. L. Dahlberg, 'På tröskeln till en romantisk berättelse. Musik och komposition hos Eyvind Johnson', *TidLit*, 26.1:3–25. M. Snygg, 'Budbäraren och budskapet i Eyvind Johnsons roman "Strändernas svall"', *Fenix*, 13.3:14–47, concludes that the main symbol for the message about the individual's responsibility is the presence of Hermes as god incarnate.

JÄDERLUND, ANN. L. Malmberg, 'Att höra en fjäril. Om tystnaden i Ann Jäderlunds lyrik', *Fest. Vinge*, 486–93.

KEY-ÅBERG, SANDRO. Sven Nyberg, *'Dikten finns överallt.' Sandro Key-Åbergs tidiga diktning från debuten fram till O. Scenprator*, Umeå U.P., 230 pp., is the first dissertation and book-length study to explore K.'s writing. Nyberg gives a detailed account of K.'s traumatic childhood, and discusses possible influences, such as Harry Martinson and Gunnar Ekelöf, on K.'s early poetry before focusing on his writing in the 1960s; he concludes by stressing the continuity that links the early poetry and the 1960s *O. Scenprator*. P. Bäckström, *'Poetisk lek —* en studie i Sandro Key-Åbergs litteraturpedagogik', *Fest. Vinge*, 448–62.

KYRKLUND, WILLY. *Skeptikerns dilemma. Texter om Willy Kyrklunds författarskap*, ed. Vasilis Papageorgiou, Eslöv, Symposion, 176 pp., is an informative collection of critical essays by ten contributors, exploring K.'s *œuvre* from his first collection of short stories in 1948 to *Om godheten* (1988); among them are: U. Olsson, 'Den rätta texten? En kommentar till Willy Kyrklunds slutledningskonst' (55–67); J. Dahlbäck, 'Blind oändlighet. Variationen som tema i *8 variationer*' (105–16); A. Florin, 'Om stilisering och reduktion i Willy Kyrklunds kortprosa' (87–103), the last two about K.'s short prose writings; P. E. Ljung, 'Pastisch and polemik i *Mästaren Ma*' (69–86); R. Lysell and V. Papageorgiou both write on the Greek presence in the dramas *Gudar och människor* and *Medea från Mbongo* respectively.

LAGERKVIST, PÄR. Bengt Larsson, *Pär Lagerkvist och det stora samhällsbygget. Kring ett motiv i en opublicerad berättelse från hösten 1917* (Pär Lagerkvist-Samfundets skriftserie, 5), Växjö, Pär Lagerkvist-Samfundets förlag, 1995, 28 pp., explores a MS fragment of an untitled nightmare story in the L. archive of the National Library, here called, from its opening words, *Hur länge han irrat kring i sin öken*. It attempts to place the MS within what Larsson calls *Sista mänskan-diktningen*, L.'s main motif in 1916 and 1917 about the extinction of mankind, often reminiscent of the poems in *Ångest* (1916), and a sign of a personal crisis at the time. The comments focus on the symbol of building, also present in the unfinished novel project *Det yttersta ödet* and other fragments from the same period. Tatiana Tjesnokova, *Pär Lagerkvist som teater- och litteraturkritiker* (Pär Lagerkvist-Samfundets skriftserie, 6), Växjö, Pär Lagerkvist-Samfundets förlag, 1996, 15 pp., focuses on L.'s early criticism.

LARSSON, STIG. A. Ohlsson, 'Synen av ett oavbrutet ingenting. Filmanknytning i Stig Larssons romaner *Autisterna* och *Nyår*', *TidLit*, 26.1:70–89.

LIDMAN, SARA. H. Forsås-Scott, 'Sara Lidman, colonialism and the environment', *SBR*, supplement:53–57.

LINDGREN, ARNE H. I. Selander, 'Lundaförfattaren Arne H. Lindgren som psalmdiktare', *Fest. Vinge*, 229–46.

LINDGREN, ASTRID. L.'s 90th birthday has produced a number of studies: Vivi Edström, *Astrid Lindgren och sagans makt* (SSBI, 62), Rabén & Sjögren, 243 pp., examines the great role that fairy-tales have played in L.'s *œuvre*, originally for the child that L. was, but also in her own collections of fairy-tales, preceding the works with a fairy-tale pattern, such as *Mio, min Mio, Bröderna Lejonhjärta,* and *Ronja rövardotter.* Kerstin Kvint, *Astrid i vida världen. Sannsagan om Astrid Lindgrens internationella succé,* Kvints, 168 pp., concentrates on L.'s international success, and is not simply, as it claims, an annotated bibliography by L.'s foreign-rights agent; however, the select bibliography 1946–97 (119–68) of original editions and their translations in various languages is a useful tool. Felizitas von Schönborn, *Astrid Lindgren. Das Paradies der Kinder,* Freiburg im Breisgau, Herder, 1995, 197 pp., includes an interview with L., a summary of her life, and a chapter about the impact she has had on children's literature since Pippi. *Bild och text i Astrid Lindgrens värld,* ed. Helene Ehriander and Birger Hedén (Absalon, 13), SLILU, 175 pp., is based on courses given in the Department of Literature at Lund, and concentrates on illustrations and illustrators of the works and their interplay with the text, and a more general approach to L. and her *œuvre,* among them A. Carlsson, on the Karlsson books (85–110), and T. Persson, on parental gender roles (141–74). S. Death, '*Pippi Långstrump* and *Anne of Green Gables*: tribute and subversion', *Procs* (BASS 10), 212–21. B. Thompson, 'Astrid Lindgren — the young ninety-year-old', *SBR*, no.2:2–6.

LUNDKVIST, ARTUR. *Parnass*, no. 1, is devoted to L.

MARTINSON, HARRY. J. Wrede, 'Föreställningens rymd', pp. 195–232 of Harry Martinson, *Aniara*, ed. Stefan Sandelin, Harry Martinson-sällskapet–Bonniers, 244 pp., is in certain respects a revision of Wrede's own 1965 monograph on the work. Together with M.'s preface to the 1963 paperback edition, it provides excellent background information about this first volume of a new ten-volume edition of M.'s collected works. J. Lundberg, 'En rörlighetens och hemlöshetens lyrik', pp. 285–319 of Harry Martinson, *Dikter 1929–1945*, ed. Stefan Sandelin, Harry Martinson-sällskapet–Bonniers, 348 pp., is both a guide to M.'s early poetry and a survey of research to date in the second volume of the collected works. B. Green, 'Foregrounding and prominence: finding patterns in Harry Martinson's poetry', *Scandinavica*, 36:43–57.

MARTINSON, MOA. *Parnass*, no. 2, is devoted to M.

MOBERG, VILHELM. Johan Norberg, *Motståndsmannen Vilhelm Moberg*, Timbro, 192 pp., is an essential companion to M., and examines an aspect that is intrinsic to the writer and his works by stressing his liberalism and his active commitment to the freedom of the individual. It investigates his critical views and his fight against bureaucracy and abuse of power, such as increasing state control even in democratic states, not least Sweden. P. Holmes, '*Soldat med brutet gevär* femtio år efteråt eller tjugofem år innan', *Procs* (BASS 10), 206–11, discusses various tendentious aspects of the novel.

NORÉN, LARS. Lars Nylander, *Den långa vägen hem. Lars Noréns författarskap från poesi till dramatik*, Bonniers, 372 pp., is the first comprehensive study of N., following in the wake of Sjöholm's book in 1996 on the unconscious in N.'s postmodern texts from the 1960s. Nylander concentrates on the psychodynamic dimension of his writing, and traces its development on six levels until the 'homecoming' in the early 1980s, i.e. N.'s dramatic breakthrough and intensive productivity as a playwright with dramas revolving around traumatic, Oedipal parent-child relationships. Nylander focuses on how the very process of writing has shaped and changed the identity and self of the writer. Mikael van Reis, *Det slutna rummet. Sex kapitel om Lars Noréns författarskap 1963–1983*, Eslöv, Symposion, 512 pp., is a doctoral dissertation that concentrates on how N. is conscious of the writing process as he creates his own works, and also assimilates works by other writers. Van Reis stresses, paradoxically perhaps when it comes to N., that his approach is not primarily psychoanalytical but literary, and based on close reading of the text. The closed room is seen as the main theme throughout N.'s writing, and is identified as fundamental to his *œuvre*. The aim of the study is to follow the inner thematic continuity which generates the changes in his writing, from his first published work in 1963 to the dramas 20 years later in *Två skådespel*, namely *Natten är dagens mor* and *Kaos är granne med Gud*.

PIRATEN, FRITIOF NILSSON. *Nya minnen av Piraten. Essäer och humoresker*, ed. Helmer Lång, Vollsjö, Piratensällskapet–Litteraturtjänst, 1996, 116 pp., celebrates the centenary of P.'s birth and includes: H. Lång, a short biography (10–24), comments on the novel *Bock i örtagård* (36–38), and a comparison between P. and Albert Engström; I. Holm, on P.'s friendship with Olle Holmberg and Jolo, i.e. Jan Olof Olsson (25–35); and M. Öhrn, on P.'s style (90–105). *Inte bara vänbrev*, ed. Helmer Lång, Vollsjö, Piratensällskapet–Litteraturtjänst, 125 pp., includes H. Lång, on the relations between P. and Olle

Holmberg, professor of literature at the University of Lund (7–18), and most of P.'s correspondence with Holmberg 1940–71 (19–105), edited and with comments by Lång. In spite of its slender size, this is a volume of biographical and documentary interest, providing further insight into the life and writings of P.

RINGELL, SUSANNE. A.-L. Keski-Nisula, 'Mannen i den gröna klänningen. Om transvestism och könsroller i Susanne Ringells pjäs *Edelweiss*', *HLS*: 243–75 (SSLF, 608).

RYDSTEDT, ANNA. A. Palm, 'Orden som ger stenen liv — från Pygmalion till en ovidiansk metamorfos i Lund', *Fest. Vinge*, 213–28.

RÖNBLOM, HANS-KRISTER. Lars Wendelius, *Deckarförfattaren H.-K. Rönblom. En profilteckning* (Litteratur och samhälle, 30/2), MLIUU, 1995, 103 pp., is the first comprehensive study of R., one of Sweden's most successful writers of detective novels in the tradition of the Anglo-Saxon 'whodunnit'. It explores R.'s descriptions of individuals and society, his plots and literary allusions.

SJÖBERG, BIRGER. *Samtal och sång*, ed. Eva Hættner Aurelius and Lars Helge Tunving, Vänersborg, Birger Sjöberg-sällskapet, 1995, 185 pp., concentrates on S.'s music, including the way music flavours his writing. In 1996, instead of a yearbook, the Society published two audiocassettes of old recordings of *Fridas visor. Skapande och kriser*, ed. Eva Hættner Aurelius, Johan Svedjedal, and Lars Helge Tunving, Vänersborg, Birger Sjöberg-sällskapet, 188 pp., includes: J. Svedjedal, on S.'s literary debut in the humorous periodical *Karbasen*, an extract from his current S. biography (31–59); E. Hættner Aurelius, 'Narcissus och det omedvetna — anteckningar om drivkrafter i och bakom Kriser och kransar' (60–82, see *Fest. Vinge*, 81–96); O. Larsmo, and L. H. Tunving, on *Kvartetten som sprängdes* (83–104, 105–86); the latter essay deals with S.'s difficulties with the first three chapters.

STIERNSTEDT, MARIKA. M. Fahlgren, 'Genus och modernitet i det litterära sekelskiftet', *TidLit*, 26.2 : 32–40.

SUNDMAN, PER OLOF. Per Olof Sundman och nazismen, ed. Lars Bäckström (*TLM*, 1996, no.2), Fören. Thélème, 1996, 89 pp., includes relevant articles and comments about the revelations of S.'s early Nazi inclinations, among them J. Fogelqvist, 'Per Olof Sundman, nazismen och myterna' (13–23), his original article in *Arbetaren*, 1995, no.34, which started the discussion; S.'s short story 'Lek' (25–32); L. Bäckström, 'Sanningen och Sundman' (35–66). T. Forslid, 'Nordpolens magi och andra icke-dokumentära drag i Per Olof Sundmans *Ingenjör Andrées luftfärd*', *Horisont*, 44.1 : 29–37.

SVENBRO, JESPER. J. Stenström, 'Öresund och Joniska havet — skånskt och antikt i Jesper Svenbros diktning', *Fest. Vinge*, 260–70.

SÖDERBERG, HJALMAR. Merete Mazzarella, *Otrohetens lockelse. En bok om äktenskapet*, Forum, 350 pp., deals intelligently and humorously with infidelity and marriage with reference to a number of classical love stories. There are brief mentions of, among others, Victoria Benedictsson and Alma Söderhjelm, in addition to a chapter on S.'s novel *Den allvarsamma leken*, 'Den andra kvinnan: den fatala kvinnan?' (183–204); it also includes a comparison with the defence of Lydia in Gun-Britt Sundström's novel *För Lydia* (1973). It explores the creation of a *femme fatale* after the girl Lydia is betrayed by Arvid, her first and only love. The study is proof of how exciting literary research can be in skilful hands. B. Holm, 'Det bortkomna brevet. En röst ur seklets början', *Samlaren*, 117.1, 1996 [1997]: 79–84, deals with S. and Maria von Platen, with John Landquist, Elin Wägner, and Ellen Key.

SÖDERGRAN, EDITH. Ebba Witt-Brattström, *Ediths jag. Edith Södergran och modernismens födelse*, Norstedts, 349 pp., is intended as a new approach to S. and her influence in the light of feministic theories, indeed as the beginning of new S. research. Particularly fruitful seems Witt-Brattström's emphasis on cultural, historical, and cosmopolitan influences at the time, not least that of St Petersburg at the turn of the century, the Russian cultural and political climate, German Expressionism, the wider perspective that Switzerland provided, and contemporary views of Nietzsche. A new approach to S. is certainly mapped out here. In short, what matters is more acute awareness than before of the general cultural climate of the period, and of the revolutionary and literary trends in Russia in particular, in order to enable a full appreciation of her poetry, and also to understand her creation of the New Woman, even in the face of her own death. A selection of S.'s early poems written when she was a schoolgirl has been published with a preface by Witt-Brattström: *Vaxdukshäftet. Ungdomsdikter i urval*, Norstedts, 64 pp. B. Hackman, 'Diktens rum. Kärlekstematik och estetisk förnyelse i Edith Södergrans ungdomsdiktning', *TidLit*, 26.2:18–31. H. Lillqvist, 'Att vara utom sig. Individualitet och sublimitet hos Södergran, Baudelaire och Nietzsche', *Fenix*, 13.1:46–97. W. Baumgartner, 'Das Geheimnis des Mondes — oder des Windes? Ein Gedicht von Edith Södergran', *Skandinavistik*, 27:1–14.

SÖDERHJELM, ALMA. B. Odén, 'Alma Söderhjelm — synliggjord', *NT*, 73:41–48.

SÖDERSTRÖM, OLE. G. Lundstedt and B. Magnusson, '2x Ole Söderström', *Horisont*, 44.2:40–43.

TAUBE, EVERT. *Parnass*, no. 3–4, is devoted to T.

THOURSIE, RAGNAR. Inger Ring, *Minnet regngardinen genombryter. En studie av Ragnar Thoursies lyrik till och med Emaljögat*, Eslöv, Symposion, 392 pp., is a doctoral dissertation on this avant-garde poet of the 1940s, based on close reading of his early poems and also his first book of poetry *Emaljögat*, which became an inspiration to others together with the second collection a few years later. The study explores the striking differences between early and late poems in *Emaljögat*, which in effect means it is two volumes of poetry in one. The impact of T. S. Eliot and the new direction of Swedish literature around the end of World War II are seen as decisive factors.

TRANSTRÖMER, TOMAS. N. Schiöler, 'Transcendensens tåg. Tranströmer tolkar Turner', *TidLit*, 26.1 : 59–69.

TYKESSON, ELISABETH. I. Larsson, 'Den vanskliga vandringen längs knivens egg: fragment till en berättelse om Elisabeth Tykesson', *Fest. Vinge*, 367–80.

VENNBERG, KARL. Sigvard Lindqvist, *Karl Vennbergs kluvenhet. Iakttagelser under studier och brevväxling*, Jönköping, Wettern, 39 pp., is an important contribution to the assessment of V.'s well-known divided loyalties as regards political views and ideological beliefs in general, to his life-long 'balancing-act' for survival. More specifically it is about his wavering in the 1930s and early 1940s between the two extremes, Nazism and Communism. Through his private correspondence with V. in the early 1990s, Lindqvist is able to shed new light on the issue and on V.'s poetry by pointing out facts that have not been noted before.

WEISS, PETER. Annie Bourguignon, *Der Schriftsteller Peter Weiss und Schweden* (SBL, 54), 314 pp., is a revised version of the author's doctoral dissertation presented at the Sorbonne. The main problem is whether the Swede W. is to be considered a German or a Swedish writer, since he wrote mainly in his native German. He spent his adult life in Sweden and was closely associated with and influenced by Swedish literature and cultural life. If, instead of general Swedish indifference to him, he had managed a real breakthrough in his adopted country in the 1950s, he might have developed into a Swedish writer or film-maker. The not-so-surprising conclusion is that he distinguished himself by enriching German literature with some Swedish characteristics. S. Sem-Sandberg, 'The exit door leads in. Utanförskap och exil hos Kafka och Weiss', *BLM*, 66.1 : 46–53. S. Packalén, 'Peter Weiss och den dialogiska principen', *Horisont*, 44.3–4 : 44–54.

WESTERMARCK, HELENA H. Westermarck, 'Kvinnokagalen. Ett återfunnet manuskript med förord och kommentarer av Alexandra Ramsay', *HLS*, 72 : 146–74 (SSLF, 608). G. Claesson Pipping, 'Helena Westermarck mellan två sekler', *FT*:88–93. Although often labelled a feminist writer of the 1880s, she also belongs firmly to the 20th c.

WÄGNER, ELIN. Gunnar Sundberg, *Väckarklockas återklang* (Elin Wägner-sällskapet, 7), Växjö, 1996, 18 pp., stresses the urgent importance for the present day of the message in W.'s work of 1941.

Elin och Bang. En livslång vänskap (Elin Wägner-sällskapet, 8), Växjö, 19 pp., contains a 60th birthday tribute to W. by B. Alving, and B. Dahlström, 'Elin in Bangs brev'. H. Forsås-Scott, 'Elin Wägner: feminism and the environment', *SBR*, supplement:40–44.
ÖSTERGREN, KLAS. J. Schiedermair, '"Alla var nu döda." Die Rache des toten Autors. Klas Östergrens Roman *Fantomerna* versus Julia Kristevas Intertextualitätsbegriff', *Skandinavistik*, 26:115–32.

5

SLAVONIC LANGUAGES*

I. CZECH STUDIES

LANGUAGE

By Marie Nováková and Jana Papcunová,
Ústav pro jazyk český Akademie věd České republiky, Prague

1. General and Bibliographies

A major work this year *Český jazyk na přelomu tisíciletí*, a collection of papers by a team of authors led by František Daneš, Prague, Academia, 292 pp., documents the present state of the Czech language at the turn of the millenium. The authors pay attention to the language situation and general state of present Czech (F. Daneš, 12–24); to various types of language communication (the language of politics, science, journalism, management, computers, literature, advertising, economic documents); J. Kraus (288–92) gives the results of a questionnaire survey of Czech of the 1990s; J. Kořenský (260–63) follows the development of the language law in the territory of the present Czech Republic in 1945–95. Another large section of the volume is devoted to colloquial speech and dialects. F. Čermák and P. Sgall, *SaS*, 58 : 15–25, comment on research into spoken Czech and emphasize the importance of this research for the need for systematic description of this sphere of language. J. Kořenský, *ib.*, 35–42, analyses three basic ways of the understanding and interpretation of the theory of Czech as a national language; O. Müllerová and J. Hoffmannová, *ib.*, 42–54, report on standard, colloquial, common, and specifically spoken Czech in present-day communication; F. Čermák, J. Králík, and K. Kučera, *ib.*, 117–24, discuss the reception of Czech against the background of the Czech National Corpus, concentrating on synchronic and written phenomena from the quantitative point of view.

Bibliographies. Lumír Klimeš, *Komentovaný přehled výzkumu slangu v Československu, v České republice a ve Slovenské republice v letech 1920–1996*, Plzeň, Západočeská Univ., 47 pp., has compiled an interesting

---

* For languages using the Cyrillic alphabet names are transliterated according to the Library of Congress system, omitting diacritics and ligatures.

bibliography of slang with basic information on Czech and Slovak slang research; J. Nekvapil, *Sociolinguistica*, Tübingen, 11:243–44, has prepared a selective bibliography of Czech sociolinguistics. A. Nejedlá and J. Papcunová, *Miloš Dokulil — 85 let*, Prague, Ústav pro jazyk český, 9–28, have produced a personal bibliography for M. Dokulil, covering the period 1938–96. J. Hladký has compiled 'Bibliography of Professor Josef Vachek's works' (for the years 1931–96), *SPFFBU, řada anglicistická*, S3: 15–42. Z. Tyl and M. Tylová, *Bibliographie linguistique de l'année 1994*, ed. M. Janse and S. Tol, Dordrecht, 792–813, present a selective bibliography of Czech linguistics.

2. History of the Language

History and especially the development of the language is the topic of a publication by Patrik Ouředník, *Hledání ztraceného jazyka*, Středokluky, Susa, 43 pp. Vladimír Kyas, *Česká bible v dějinách národního písemnictví*, Prague, Vyšehrad, 318 pp., focuses on the history of Czech translation of the Bible: its beginnings, four redactions of the Old Czech Bible, printed bibles of the 16th c., bibles of the Bohemian Brethren and Baroque bibles. P. Kosek, *SPFFBU, řada jazykovědná*, A45: 95–103, investigates the expression *sice* in Baroque Czech. The other two works discuss the development of Czech at the beginning of the National Revival. J. Kraus, *LPr*: 4–11, looks at the development of rhetoric and examines the literary and language style of Josef Jungmann; while L. Kusáková, *ČL*, 45:28–43, analyses J. L. Ziegler's 1814–15 translation of Fénélon's *Télemaque* (*Příběhy Telemacha, syna Ulysova*).

3. Phonetics and Phonology

F. Daneš, *Dialogue Analysis*, Tübingen, Niemeyer, pp. 65–74, analyses and interprets several working discussions in Czech with regard to specific pragmatic information which it is possible to obtain from the phonetic form of discourse.

4. Morphology and Word Formation

Otakar Mališ, Svatava Machová, and Jaroslav Suk, *Současný český jazyk: Lexikologie*, Prague, Karolinum, 87 pp., have completed their book on Czech word formation of rudiments of Czech lexicography and of an instruction about the gathering of slang material and its investigation. M. Homolková, *SaS*, 58:96–104, describes the word-formative process in all lexical units with the word-formative morpheme *proti-*

registered until 1500; O. Martincová, *ib.*, 161–64, examines the concurrence of word-formative elements in the most recent vocabulary and focuses on the concurrence of prefixes in neologisms; A. M. Perissutti, *SPFFBU, řada jazykovědná*, A45: 73–83, analyses the Czech indefinite determiner *-koli* (in comparison to the indefinite determiner *ně-*). The vogue feminist linguistics, concentrated on the questions of gender in the language, has also entered Czech linguistics. J. Valdrová, *NŘ*, 80 : 87–91, briefly sketches the origins of Czech gender linguistics, examines its specific features in Czech and puts forward a proposal for a gender reform in Czech, specifically in the lexicon. F. Daneš, *ib.*, 256–59, very critically comments on the previous article and sets right some ideas of the authoress. Finally, S. Čmejrková, *Český jazyk na přelomu tisíciletí*, 146–58, deals with the question of gender and with the formation of feminines from masculines in Czech.

5. SYNTAX AND TEXT

A work of great importance is Naďa Svozilová, Hana Prouzová, and Anna Jirsová, *Slovesa pro praxi. Valenční slovník nejčastějších českých sloves*, Prague, Academia, 359 pp. The authors follow the sentence-formative role of verbs and give sentence patterns and valency analysis for each verbal unit. K. Pala and P. Ševeček, *SPFFBU, řada jazykovědná*, A45: 41–54, also deal with the valency of Czech verbs (from the semantic point of view). J. Hrbáček, *NŘ*, 80 : 169–77, refers to syntactic correlations and their terminology. He points out that there are some defects in the description of sentence correlations in Czech analytical syntax, since there are confused sentence correlations (from the analytical syntax) and sentence-formative correlations (from the valency syntax). He uses a modified terminological system for the description of syntactic sentence-formative correlations. F. Štícha, *ib.*, 73–80, analyses less usual linking expressions in present-day Czech typical for journalism (*poté, co* and *bez toho, aby / že*), considering their suitability; E. Koktová, *SaS*, 58 : 8–14, is on classification of the Czech complex sentence from the communicative pragmatic point of view; L. Uhlířová, *ib.*, 174–84, examines the relationship between word length and word placement in the sentence; she also publishes an article entitled 'Length vs. order: word length and clause length from the perspective of word order', *Journal of Quantitative Linguistics*, 4 : 266–75. P. Karlík, *SPFFBU, řada jazykovědná*, A45: 63–71, discusses clauses with the conjunction *jestliže*; F. Esvan, *ib.*, 85–93, deals with correlations between word order and accentuation in Czech (presenting a typology of clitics, too).

6. Orthography

M. Černá, *Varia VI: Zborník zo VI. kolokvia mladých jazykovedcov*, Bratislava, Slovenská jazykovedná spoločnosť při SAV, 96–102, follows the development of Czech orthography; she points out that copies of Dalimil's chronicle from the 15th c. provide documentary evidence for the transition from the digraphic to the diacritic orthographic system. Alois Bauer, *Dělení slov*, Olomouc, Nakladatelství Olomouc, 349 pp., mentions both the mechanism of word formation and breaking of words in Czech, which is indicated in the dictionary section of the book. Another handbook by Vladimír Staněk, *Jak psát správně čárky*, Prague, Fortuna, 85 pp., summarizes the rules of punctuation in Czech simple and complex sentences.

7. Lexicology and Phraseology

The outstanding and popular dictionary by Václav Machek, *Etymologický slovník jazyka českého*, Prague, Lidové noviny, 866 pp., which has been inaccessible for years, has been published as a reprint of the 1971 edition. I. Němec, *NŘ*, 80:113–15, documents a shift in vocabulary in some collective designations. Originally, the expressions such as *husita, viklefista, psohlavci, legionář* have been uncomplimentary or even abusive; nevertheless, their development has come to have positive meaning and they have even become honorary titles. Id., *Občasník historických skupin ZB a R–3*, 27–31, examines the origin and the meaning of Czech words used in the Czechoslovak resistance movement. Other etymological articles to be noted here: E. Michálek, *NŘ*, 80:52–53, on the etymology of the word *háv* which has been mentioned in Klaret's *Glosář*; L. Švestková, *ib.*, 53–54, on the expression *perma*; and Z. Kavková, *ib.*, 55–56, on the expression *kulturistika*.

8. Semantics and Pragmatics

O. Müllerová submits a paper entitled 'Cooperation and conflict in dialogue. On material of Czech TV publicism', pp. 469–75 of *Dialoganalyse V.*, Tübingen, Niemeyer. She analyses dialogues in the journalistic programmes of Czech TV stations from the pragmatic point of view, in particular she is concerned with the types of form of address. M. Friš, *SaS*, 58:105–11, studies the distribution of semantic classes in a Czech novel using a classification of the two thousand most frequent Czech words into 40 semantic classes.

9. SOCIOLINGUISTICS AND DIALECTOLOGY

Czech linguists have turned their interest to the investigation of the spoken language, especially of colloquial speech and of other non-standard forms of speech. A great number of papers from the collection *Český jazyk na přelomu tisíciletí* deal with colloquial speech: M. Krčmová (160–72) defines the concept 'colloquial speech' and describes the spoken language in common situations using the scale of standard language — common Czech — dialects; she (225–30) also discusses changes of speech in the city of Brno; P. Jančák (200–11) refers to colloquial speech in Prague, looking at its development and its dialectal background; further, Id. (239–49) investigates colloquial speech in the North-West Bohemian border area; J. Jančáková (174–82) proves by an analysis of the dialect in the Central Bohemian village Dobrovíz that the regional markedness of the speech stays although the colloquial speech is levelled out; M. Šipková (212–18) who examines the adaptation of dialectal speakers to speech in the Moravian city of Prostějov, arrives at similar conclusions; S. Kloferová (250–57) refers to speech in the North Moravian border area, which is still under a strong dialect influence. Further papers in the collection concern Czech dialects: J. Bachmannová (183–92) follows the process of levelling of the traditional dialect in the region of Železný Brod (based on research of the speech of young people); M. Krčmová (219–24) treats the relationship between children's speech and dialects or idiolects in the present language situation in Moravia. Finally, two papers relate to the present development of dialects in South Bohemia (M. Janečková, 193–99) and in Silesia (R. Šrámek, 231–38). Dana Davidová, Irena Bogoczová, Karel Fic, Jaroslav Hubáček, Jan Chloupek, and Eva Jandová, *Mluvená čeština na Moravě*, Ostrava, Tilia, 171 pp., submit a treatise in which they describe and linguistically assess the used language code in language communication of Moravian and Silesian inhabitants. In this region, it is possible to follow the whole scale from pure dialects to the colloquial language. Similar topics: P. Jančák, *NŘ*, 80:248–55, on urban speech in Prague; J. Bachmannová, *ib.*, 184–89, on the speech of young people in the region of the Giant Mountains; D. Davidová, *ib*, 135–41, discusses the language code of unofficial speeches in the region of Czech Silesia: she follows the declension of standard elements at the transition to the unofficial speech for the benefit of common speech, interdialects, and dialects.

A. Jaklová, 'K současnému stavu chodského nářečí z hlediska sociolingvistického', *NŘ*, 80:64–72, 116–22, submits phonological, word-formative and lexical characterization of present Chodovian dialect; Z. Hladká, *SPFFBU, řada jazykovědná*, A45: 119–29, deals with dialectal names of plants with an animal name in attribute. Finally, the second volume of *Český jazykový atlas*, Prague, Academia, 507 pp., has been published. This volume presents dialectal material from these thematic spheres: garden and orchard, animal world, forest and flora, country, time and weather, village in the past and nowadays, entertainment and customs.

10. STYLISTICS

A fundamental work of this discipline is *Stylistika současné češtiny*, by Marie Čechová, Jan Chloupek, Marie Krčmová, and Eva Minářová, Prague, Institut sociálních vztahů, 282 pp., treating the theory of communication, the theory of standard language and the Czech language situation as well. Edvard Lotko, *Kapitoly ze současné rétoriky*, Olomouc, Vydavatelství Univ. Palackého, 166 pp., provides basic information on Czech rhetoric. S. Čmejrková, *NŘ*, 80: 225–47, focuses on the style of e-mail dialogues and on Czech computer communication.

ASPECTS OF THE LANGUAGE OF INDIVIDUAL WRITERS. M. Červenka and K. Sgallová, 'Verš a věta. Rytmické a větné členění v české poezii druhé poloviny 19. století', *SaS*, 58: 241–87, investigate the relationship between the structure of verse and of the sentence in Czech 19th-c. verse (iambic and trochaic tetrameter and pentameter, and alexandrine); A. Macurová and J. Janáčková, *ib.*, 86–95, examine multilingualism (especially the use of German) in the correspondence of Božena Němcová; J. Hoffmannová, *Od moderny k postmoderne*, Nitra, Univ. Konštantína Filozofa, 99–106, analyses the style and vocabulary in post-modern texts of Jáchym Topol and Vít Kremlička; M. Křístek, *SPFFBU, řada jazykovědná*, A45: 111–18, discusses narrative modes and types of narrator in four novels by Michal Viewegh; I. Nebeská, *NŘ*, 80: 19–25, examines the Czech feminist texts of Carola Biedermannová and presents a linguistic analysis of them; R. Jílek, *ČL*, 45: 16–27, is on metaphor in the symbolist work of Otokar Březina; L. Klimeš, *J. V. Sládek 1845–1995*, Zbiroh, Muzeum J. V. Sládka, 6–11, studies individual neologisms in Sládek's collection *Na prahu ráje*; V. Viktora, *ib.*, 23–25, investigates the verse of Sládek's poems; L. Tyllner, *Český lid*, 84: 265–74, analyses texts of Czech folk songs.

11. ONOMASTICS

M. Knappová and M. Harvalík, 'Zur Entwicklung der Zunamen in Böhmen', *Personennamen und Identität*, Graz, Akademische Druck- und

Verlagsanstalt, 333–44, elucidate the origin of Czech names and surnames including the sociolinguistic viewpoint. J. Malenínská, *NŘ*, 80:26–33, reconstructs the extinct common nouns *hrochot* and *kyta* occurring in toponyms; L. Hašová, *ib*, 195–201, treats the results of a questionnaire research on the use of the ethnonym *Rom, Cikán* in Czech; M. Grygerková, *ČDS*, 5:49–53, comments on the names of pubs and resturants in North Moravia; R. Šrámek, *Český jazyk na přelomu tisíciletí*, 280–86, deals with a topical subject — the incorporation of foreign names into Czech. The present practice does not tend to Czechicization of the names, which causes the disappearance of traditional exonyms in the border area.

Ivan Lutterer and Rudolf Šrámek, *Zeměpisná jména v Čechách, na Moravě a ve Slezsku*, Havlíčkův Brod, Tobiáš, 317 pp., have published a dictionary of geographic names explaining their origin and historical development. *Pražský uličník. Encyklopedie názvů pražských veřejných prostranství*, vol. 1, Prague, Libri, 604 pp., gives a survey of the origin, development, and changes of Prague street names.

12.   LANGUAGE IN CONTACT AND COMPARATIVE STUDIES

The contact of Czech with other languages in history and at present is still topical in Czech linguistics. J. Kořenský, *Český jazyk na přelomu tisíciletí*, 264–70, endeavours to submit a general view of the Czech language situation and the influence of foreign languages; I. Bozděchová, *ib.*, 271–79, tries to generalize the influence of English on Czech; E. Koktová, *JP*, 27:523–27, analyses pronouns in the sentence in English and Czech and concentrates on cases when it is possible to omit English expressions starting with *wh-* and corresponding Czech expressions with *kd-*; S. Čmejrková and F. Daneš, *Culture and Styles of Academic Discourse*, Berlin, de Gruyter, 41–62, compare the style of academic writing in English and Czech; they both, *Sprache, Wirtschaft, Kultur. Deutsche und Tschechen in Interaktion*, Munich, Iudicium, 163–87, compare functional types of Czech and German specialized (scientific) texts from the viewpoint of syntax; M. Nekula, *ib.*, 147–59, focuses on changes in the attitude to German after 1989, on code switching and Germanisms (based on material of Czech advertising); J. Chamonikolasová, *SPFFBU, řada anglicistická*, S3: 43–50, presents a contrastive study of Czech and English intonation. Edvard Lotko, *Synchronní konfrontace češtiny a polštiny*, Olomouc, Vydavatelství Univ. Palackého, 152 pp., submits 12 papers comparing Czech and Polish; M. Godlewski, *PFil*, 42:147–51, analyses the qualitative genitive in Czech, Slovak, Slovenian, and Polish; H. Běličová, *ČMF*, 79:81–87, studies the imperative in Russian and

Czech; J. Bartáková, *SPFFBU, řada jazykovědná,* A45: 131–35, compares expressive feminine appellations in Czech and Slovak.

The two following papers deal with a long-lasting influence of a foreign language on the language used by Czechs living abroad: J. Vojtová, *NŘ,* 80: 123–28, concentrates on the influence of German on the language of Czech newspapers published in Vienna; E. Eckert, *ib.,* 260–69, describes American Czech on tombstones in Texas, which document changes in language usage of Czech emigrants (transition from Czech to English in 1860–1960).

LITERATURE

POSTPONED

II. SLOVAK STUDIES

POSTPONED

III. POLISH STUDIES

LANGUAGE

By JOHN BATES, *University of Glasgow*

1. BIBLIOGRAPHIES, SURVEYS, AND APPRECIATIONS

Bibliographies include the invaluable K. Długosz-Kurczabowa et al., 'Przegląd polskich prac językoznawczych ogłoszonych drukiem w roku 1996', *PJ*, no. 4 (543):25–65, and its supplement, *ib.*, no. 6 (545):30–47.
**Język polski czasu drugiej wojny światowej (1939–1945)*, ed. I. Bajerowa, Wa, Wyd. Energeia, 1996, 507 pp., is a continuation of Z. Klemensiewicz's *Historia języka polskiego*. S. Dubisz, 'Rozwój współczesnej polszczyzny', *PrzH*, 1995, no. 5 (332):69–88; A. Markowski, 'Przemiany w strukturze normy współczesnej polszczyzny ogólnej', *ib.*, 89–99.

Appreciations include: M. Jurkowski, 'Wspomnienie o Profesorze Władysławie Kuraszkiewiczu', *PJ*, no. 3 (543):2–5; J. Kobylińska, 'Prof. dr hab. Maria Schabowska (1925–1995)', *JPol*, 77:50–51; K. Pisarkowa, 'Śp. Jolanta Rokoszowa (1944–1997)', *ib.*, 246–50; J. Porayski-Pomsta, 'Wspomnienie o Michale Jaworskim', *PJ*, 1996, no. 10 (539):1–3; B. Taras, 'Sylwetka naukowa Docent Roxany Sinielnikoff', *ib.*, 1996, no. 9 (538):2–4; and B. Walczak, 'Profesor Władysław Kuraszkiewicz (1905–1997)', *JPol*, 77:241–45.

2. PHONOLOGY, MORPHOLOGY, WORD FORMATION

Piotr Lobacz, *Polska fonologia dziecięca. Studia fonetyczno-akustyczne*, Wa, Wyd. Energeia, 1996, 200 pp.

J. Maćkiewicz, 'Potoczna fonetyka — składnik językowego obrazu świata', *JPol*, 77:266–75; J. Perlin, 'Czy zwarcie krtaniowe jest fonemem w języku polskim?', *PJ*, no. 6 (545):26–29; Id., 'O psychicznym obrazie dźwięku, czyli kiedy Polacy nie palatalizują *n* przed *i*', *ib.*, no. 5 (544):42–45; H. Sojka-Masztalerz, 'Zjawiska fonetyczne we współczesnej polszczyźnie lwowian', *ib.*, no. 1 (540):53–67.

Stanisław Mędak, *Słownik form koniugacyjnych czasowników polskich*, Kw, Universitas, xxvii + 1,046 pp., the largest undertaking of its kind, presents 17,000 verbs and 334 conjugation paradigms.

M. Majewska, 'Analiza morfologiczna przymiotnikowych homonimów całkowitych', *PFil*, 1996, 40:63–77; I. Masojć, 'Kształtowanie się rodzaju męskoosobowego w języku polskim na Wileńszczyźnie',

Janowska, *Język*, 1, 72–79; W. R. Rzepka and W. B. Twardzik, 'Archaizmy fleksyjne w *Rozmyślaniu przemyskim*', *JPol*, 77:41–46, 102–11, 298–302; H[alina] S[atkiewicz], 'Liczebnik *jeden* — niesforny element polskiej składni', *PJ*, no. 5 (544):79–80, continues her deliberations on the numbers 2, 3, 4 and the plural forms of 'jeden' in 'Kłopoty z liczebnikami ciąg dalszy', *ib.*, no. 4 (543): 79–80, and 'Ach, te liczebniki ... Zakres użycia, odmiana i składnia liczebników zbiorowych', *ib.*, no. 2 (541):74–75; M. Skarżyński, 'O pewnej dziewiętnastowiecznej próbie fleksyjnej klasyfikacji części mowy', *JPol*, 77:303–06; L. Stercz-Przebinda, 'Homonimiczność pewnych form czasownikowych i jej konsekwencje fleksyjne', *ib.*, 77:259–65.

Hanna Jadacka, *Rzeczownik polski jako baza derywacyjna*, Wa, PWN, 1995, 216 pp., a much extended version of her *Aktywność słowotwórcza polskich rzeczowników niemotywowanych (na materiale gniazdowym)* (1991), is a sophisticated analysis of the word-forming potential of substantives; *Słowotwórstwo języka doby staropolskiej. Przegląd formacji rzeczownikowych*, ed. Krystyna Kleszczowa, Katowice, Wyd. Uniwersytetu Śląskiego, 1996, 486 pp.; Bogusław Kreja, **Studia z polskiego słowotwórstwa*, Gd, Wyd. Uniwersytetu Gdańskiego, 1996, 271 pp., is a collection of previously published articles.

B. Kreja, 'Formacje na *-iniec* typu *babiniec, krowiniec* w języku polskim (na tle słowiańskim)', *PFil*, 1996, 40:7–27; Id., 'Rzeczownik *półgodzina* i historia złożeń z *pół-* (z sugestią ortograficzną)', *JPol*, 77:32–40; B. Nowowiejski, 'Z dziejów *ober*(-) w języku polskim', *PFil*, 1996, 40:175–87; J. Okoniowa, 'Przeciwstawienia leksykalne z przedrostkiem *bez-* w nauczaniu języka polskiego jako obcego', Janowska, *Język*, 2, 106–15. E. Wójcikowska, 'Zanegowane przymiotniki deadiektywne — formacje prefiksalne', *ib.*, vol. 1, 155–59.

3. SYNTAX

Maria Lesz-Duk, *Funkcje składniowe rzeczowników w dopełniaczu*, Wyd. WSP w Częstochowie, 1995, 171 pp., is a historically-based analysis of the non-prepositional (part I) and prepositional (part II) functions of the genitive case and the changes they have undergone. Alicja Nagórko, *Zarys gramatyki polskiej*, Wa, PWN, 1996, 235 pp., represents a fairly conventional approach to Polish grammar, while Jerzy Podracki, *Składnia polska*, Wa, WsiP, 248 pp., gives a more popular, general introduction to the subject. Marek Świdziński, *Własności składniowe wypowiedników polskich*, Wa, 1996, x + 163 pp., is a statistical analysis of syntactic utterances, the result of a three-year project at Warsaw University, whose data 'throw some light on [the] syntactic peculiarities of particular stylistic variants of contemporary Polish'.

M. Derwojedowa, 'Zdaniowe i niezdaniowe wypowiedniki polskie. Klasyfikacja i własności składniowe', *PJ*, no. 3 (542): 22–35, bases her analysis on the half-million word corpus of *Słownik frekwencyjny polszczyzny współczesnej*; M. Gębka-Wolak, 'Struktura grupy przymiotnikowej a jej szyk', *JPol*, 77:123–30; E. Łuczyński, 'Ukośnik — nowy znak interpunkcyjny?', *ib.*, 380–81; J. Mędelska, 'Osobliwe wykrzykniki w kulturalnej polszczyźnie wileńskiej (na podstawie języka prasy)', Janowska, *Język*, vol. 1, 80–90; M. Ruszkowski, 'Próba gramatycznej i stylistycznej charakterystyki tzw. zawiadomień', *JPol*, 77:117–22; E. Szkudlarek, 'Wskaźniki nawiązania międzyzdaniowego w pozycji pierwszego argumentu predykatu (na materiale współczesnej nowelistyki polskiej), *RKJŁ*, 41.1, 1996:157–65; H[alina] S[atkiewicz], 'Nowe tendencje w używaniu imiesłowów biernych', *PJ*, 1996, no. 8 (537):76–77, brands the past passive participle forms in such sentences as 'czekają na homilię Papieża wygłoszoną jutro w Central Park', which are encountered with increasing frequency in the Polish press, as 'not only linguistically, but logically, erroneous constructions'.

4. LEXICOLOGY AND PHRASEOLOGY

W. Kopaliński, *Słownik eponimów, czyli wyrazów odimiennych*, Wa, PWN, 290 pp., contains *c.* 1,100 eponyms derived from proper nouns. J. Biniewicz, 'Kryteria oceny językowej terminów (nauki ścisłe)', *PJ*, 1995, nos 9–10 (528–29):35–44, describes the criteria employed by the late 18th-c. 'Towarzystwo do Ksiąg Elementarnych' in their choice of scientific terminology. M. Górnicz, 'Nazwa nowotworu a stopień jego złośliwości', *PJ*, no. 3 (542):36–43, complements his 'Sposoby i granice kompresji terminów (Na podstawie terminologii medycznej — nazwy nowotworów)', *ib.*, no. 2 (541):25–32. Z. Kurzowa, 'Przeszłość i przyszłość słownika polskich synonimów', *ib.*, no. 5 (544):1–14, is partly a report of the new *Słownik synonimów* due to appear in PWN in 1998; J. Matusiak, 'Polskie słownictwo komputerowe', *ib.*, no. 1 (540):24–28; A. Michał, 'Słownictwo włókiennicze w *Ziemi obiecanej* Władysława Stanisława Reymonta i *Bawełnie* Wincentego Kosiakiewicza', *ib.*, 29–45; D. Ochmann, 'Prasowe kontaminacje leksykalne (Analiza strukturalna)', *JPol*, 77:131–44; Z. Saloni, 'Perspektywy polskiej leksykografii jednojęzycznej', *PJ*, 1996, no. 7 (536):1–18; Id., 'Słownik Doroszewskiego w wersji elektronicznej', *ib.*, no. 5 (544):64–65; Id., 'Drobiazgi słownikowe. Jeszcze o słowie *no* i jego opisie słownikowym', *PJ*, no. 1 (540):38–45. K. Sokólski, 'Uwagi o definicjach niektórych terminów prawniczych w *Słowniku języka polskiego* pod. red. W. Doroszewskiego', *PFil*, 40, 1996:189–99.

D. Adamiec, 'Wyraz *Bóg* i frazeologia z nim związana w XVII wieku', *ib.*, 137–48; S. Bąba, '*Co to, to nie*', *JPol*, 77:239–40; Id., '*Obiecywać gruszki na wierzbie — gruszki na wierzbie*', *ib.*, 376–77; Id., '*Przewracać się w grobie*', *ib.*, 235–39; Id., '*Przyprawić komuś rogi*', *ib.*, 372–74; Id., '*Puszka Pandory — otworzyć puszkę Pandory*', *ib.*, 374–76; Id., '*Wylewać, ronić krokodyle (krokodylowe) łzy*', 75–77; Id., '*Żywy trup*', *ib.*, 73–75; W. Chlebda, 'W stronę frazeologii pragmatycznej', *PJ*, no. 2 (541):1–10, contains several new proposals, including the need to take account in future analyses of the 'phonic, prosodic dimension' of the functioning of phraseology; A. Dąbrowska, 'Frazeologizmy biblijne z nazwami roślin w słownikach języka polskiego', *ib.*, 1996, no. 10 (539):25–32. S. Koziara, 'O frazeologizmach w polskich przekładach biblijnych. Od Biblii Wujka do Biblii Tysiąclecia', *JPol*, 77:89–96; B. Kreja, '684. *Módl się za nami*', *ib.*, 384, concludes that the use of the genitive is now standard, while the instrumental is archaic, preserved only in prayers; W. Kupiszewski, 'Wyraz *dzień* w nazwach pór dnia', *PJ*, 1996, no. 9 (538):48–51; J. Maćkiewicz, '*Partaczyć, pichcić, klecić* ...., czyli potocznie o twórczości', *JPol*, 77:10–16; T. Malec, '*Dowód wdzięczności i prywatyzacja*', *ib.*, 240; Id., '*Eschatyczny*', *ib.*, 77–78; Id., '*Kompresy gazowe*', *ib.*, 77; Id., '*Warsztaty NATO*', *ib.*, 377–78; J. Miodek, 'Co znaczy *onegdaj*?', *PJ*, 1996, no. 7 (536):80–81, notes that its 'new' meaning of 'fairly recently' is in fact an old, forgotten meaning, which is more commonly used than the more specific meaning of 'the day before yesterday'; J. Nalepa, '*Bresin* w *Słowniku staropolskim* to *mreża* (*merża), czyli mrzeża "rodzaj sieci" ', *JPol*, 77:47–49; M. Nowak, 'O *kamerowaniu, widele* i *widelcu* (z obserwacji polszczyzny mówionej)', *ib*, 378–79; W. Pisarek, '683. *Pismo Święte czy Pismo święte?*', *ib.*, 382–83. H[alina] S[atkiewicz], 'Czym można się cieszyć?', *PJ*, no. 1 (540):82–83; 'Kilka słów o *etosie*', *ib.*, 1995, no. 8 (527):82–83; her 'Kontaminacje a synonima we frazeologii', *ib.*, 1996, no. 9 (538):75–76, and 'Jeszcze o kontaminacjach frazeologicznych', *ib.*, 1996, no. 10 (539):82–83, conclude that abstract constructions are more prone to contamination from graphic constructions than vice versa, as in sports commentators' 'stoczyć mecz'. E. Sękowska, 'Domy sarmatów — słownictwo związane z urządzeniem wnętrz (XVII w.)', *PJ*, no. 3 (542):44–53, takes into interiors her 'Słownictwo związane z 'dworem' i 'budynkami gospodarczymi' na podstawie inwentarzy dóbr ziemskich (XVII w.)', *ib.*, 1996, no. 9 (538):13–19; W. Serafin, 'Kilka uwag o przenikaniu niektórych leksemów z subkodu rockowego do języka młodzieży', *JPol*, 77:17–21. R[oxana] S[inielnikoff], '*Charyzma* i *filozofia*', *ib.*, 1995, nos 9–10 (528–29):101–04; her '*Kuroniówka* i *falandyzacja*', *ib.*, 1995, no. 8 (527):74–81, surveys a number of nouns and verbs derived from the names of prominent public figures, e.g. 'wałęsówka', 'pawlakizm' and 'glempić'. M. Stachowski, '*Kaza(ch)ski i kecki*, czyli rozterki orientalisty', *ib.*, 379–80. J. Wawrzyńczyk, 'O niby-słowie *ostrzqs*', *ib.*, 72–73; K. Wojtczuk, '*Suchołuska, nieśmiertelnik, suchotnik* czyli wariantywne nazwy kwiatów ozdobnych we współczesnej polszczyźnie', *ib.*, 55–62.

5. SEMANTICS AND PRAGMATICS

Studia pragmalingwistyczne, ed. J. Porayski-Pomsta and H. Zgółkowa, Wa, Dom Wydawniczy ELIPSA, 151 pp. includes: D. Bartosiewicz, 'O znaczeniu akapitu. Na przykładzie tekstów uczniowskich' (9–24); K. Czarnecka, 'Pragmatyczne spojrzenie uczniów na współczesną polszczyznę' (25–32); and M. Święcicka, 'Pragmalingwistyczna charakterystyka wypowiedzi dziecięcych' (133–39).

W. Banyś, 'O reprezentacjach semantyczno-kognitywnych wyrażeń językowych. (Na przykładzie znaczenia spójnika *jeśli*)', *PJ*, no. 1 (540):12–23; H. Grochola-Szczepanek, 'Czy każda babka jest prawdziwa? (Przyczynek do semantyki wyrazów *babka* i *dziadek*)', *JPol*, 77:72–73; M. Grochowski, 'Functional and semantic equivalence of sequential exponents in Polish simple and complex sentences', *ScSl*, 43:134–46, considers the functional equivalence of the conjunctions 'jak', 'kiedy', 'gdy' and the preposition 'po'; R. Laskowski, 'Expressions désignant le changement d'état en polonais', *ib.*, 147–72, examines verbs and periphrastic expressions incorporating verbs which indicate changes of state; M. Witkowska-Gutkowska, 'Funkcje znaczeniowe prefiksu *wz*- i przyimka *wz* w staropolszczyźnie', *RKJŁ*, 41.1, 1996:67–76.

M. Łaziński and B. Wiemer, 'Terminatywność jako kategoria stopniowalna', *PFil*, 40, 1996:99–126; K. Mosiołek-Kłosińska, 'O zakłóceniach łączliwości systemowej wyrazów. Zakłócenie łączliwości a błąd semantyczny', *PJ*, no. 3 (542):6–21, and her 'Zakłócenie łączliwości normatywnej wyrazów jako przejaw działania tendencji do usuwania wyjątków', *ib.*, no. 6 (545):9–18; J. Puzynina, '*Naród, społeczeństwo, państwo, kraj*', *ib.*, 1996, no. 10 (539):4–13; I. Szczepankowska, 'O niektórych sposobach wskazywania tematu wypowiedzi w różnych odmianach polszczyzny', *ib.*, no. 4 (543):1–7, uses Szymborska's 'Terrorysta, on patrzy' as illustration; E. Walusiak, 'Metatekstowe wykładniki hierarchizacji wypowiedzi (Na przykładzie wyrażeń z segmentem *jak*)', *PJ*, 1996, no. 7 (536):19–31; E. Wierzbicka, '*To* jako wykładnik sytuacji', *PFil*, 40, 1996:127–34.

E. Awramiuk, 'Zagadnienia homonimii w kształceniu sprawności językowej', *PJ*, no. 6 (545):48–58; E. Kołodziejek, 'Kilka uwag o kryterium zwyczaju językowego', *PJ*, 1995, nos 9–10 (528–29):29–34, argues for the pre-eminence of cultural authority over use as the most important measure of the correctness of linguistic facts; M. Ruszkowski, 'Zastosowanie kryterium funkcjonalnego w normatywnym wartościowaniu pleonazmów i tautologii', *ib.*, 22–28; H. Satkiewicz, 'Zakres przydatności kryterium funkcjonalnego w ocenie zjawisk językowych', *ib.*, 17–21; H. K. Ulatowska et al., 'Przysłowia w badaniu neurolingwistycznym', *ib.*, 1996, no. 7 (536):32–41, considers their significance for aphasia sufferers; B. Walczak, 'Przegląd kryteriów poprawności językowej', *ib.*, 1995, nos 9–10 (528–29):1–16; K. Wojtczuk, 'Liczba i/lub cyfra jako ocena szkolna w języku nauczycieli i uczniów', *ib.*, 1996, no. 10 (539):68–73; M. Załęska, 'Językowe wykładniki kategoryzowania obiektów nietypowych', *ib.*, no. 2 (541):11–17.

6. Sociolinguistics and Dialectology

B. Dobek-Ostrowska et al., *Teoria i praktyka propagandy*, Ww, WUW, 132 pp., includes a survey chapter on the language of political propaganda with examples from the post-1989 period. The appearance of Michal Głowiński's *Mowa w stanie oblężenia 1982–1985*, Wa, Wyd. OPEN, 1996, 338 pp., means that his analysis of Polish Newspeak based on newspapers now covers almost a twenty-year period. Danuta Wesołowska's impressive *Słowa z piekieł rodem. Lagerszpracha*, Kw, Oficyna Wydawnicza "Impuls", 1996, 208 pp., details the linguistic dehumanization of concentration camp inmates and contains extensive materials about the etymology of such key terms as 'kapo' and 'muzułman'.

I. Borkowski, 'Wartościowanie etyczne jako źródło nacechowania emocjonalnego niektórych terminów z dziedziny języka polityki', *PJ*, 1995, nos 9–10 (528–29):45–53, considers such terms as 'propaganda', 'agitacja' and 'perswazja'; M. Danielewiczowa and D. Zdunkiewicz-Jedynak, 'Język jako narzędzie budowania i niszczenia wspólnoty', *ib.*, 1996, no. 8 (537):8–20; K. Dziedzioł-Zabierowska, 'Wyraz *elita* w świadomości współczesnych Polaków', *ib.*, no. 1 (540):1–11, sees a lack of clarity in current definitions; D. Grzywaczewski, 'Słowa sztandarowe i potępiane w wybranych tekstach publicystycznych', *ib.*, no. 5 (544):15–31; A. Janowska and M. Pastuchowa, 'Niebezpieczna kompetencja', *ib.*, 1995, no. 8 (527):11–19, argue that the term 'linguistic competence' is inappropriate in relation to Old Polish and favour the notion of 'a feeling for language' instead; K. Kozłowska, 'Język i jego poprawność jako wartości społeczne', *PJ*, no. 6 (545):59–64; B. Kudra, 'Sposoby powstawania prasowych okazjonalizmów politycznych', *ib.*, 1996, no. 8 (537):35–44; J. Kurowicki, 'Kulturowe konteksty narracji reporterskiej', *ib.*, 1995, nos 9–10 (528–29):54–63. J. Z. Lichański,

'Retoryczne aspekty reklamy (Przykład polski)', *PrzH*, 1996, no. 5 (338):57–64; A. Mamcarz, 'Metodologia badań nad językiem nakłaniania. Zarys problematyki', *PJ*, 1996, no. 10 (539):14–24. M. Przybysz-Piwkowa, 'Język elementem tworzenia lub rujnowania wspólnoty. Nastolatki we wspólnocie rodzinnej, szkolnej i środowisku pozaszkolnym', *ib.*, 1996, no. 8 (537):21–27; J. Puzynina, 'Problem kodyfikacji normy języka polskiego', *ib.*, no. 6 (545):1–8. E. Sękowska, 'Etykieta językowa osób polilingwalnych', Janowska, *Język*, vol. 1, 117–23. R[oxana] S[inielnikoff], 'Wulgaryzmy w literaturze', *PJ*, no. 6 (545):71–77, is complemented by her 'Wulgaryzmy', *ib.*, no. 5 (544):75–78. J. Winiarska, 'Retoryka tekstów użytkowych', *JPol*, 77:320–22. H. Zgółkowa, 'Szkic językowego obrazu świata', *Polonistyka*, no. 6:327–31, examines linguistic stereotypes such as 'cyganić'.

N. Ananiewa, 'Zjawisko interferencji w początkowym etapie nauczania języka polskiego w środowisku rosyjskojęzycznym', Miodunka, *Nauczanie*, 197–208. W. Decyk, 'O zmianach polskich antroponimów w zbiorowościach polonijnych', *PFil*, 1996, 40:203–13; W. Decyk and S. Dubisz, 'Zmiany polskich antroponimów w zbiorowościach polonijnych a procesy integracji kulturowej', *PrzH*, 1995, no. 2 (329):105–21; S. Dubisz, 'Język polski poza granicami kraju (1945–1995) — zagadnienia metodologii opisu', *PFil*, 40, 1996:215–27, and similarly, 'Typologia odmian polszczyzny poza granicami kraju', Janowska, *Język*, 1, 35–42; A. Furdal, 'Kultura współżycia języków', *PJ*, 1995, nos 9–10 (528–29):73–77; Z. Gałecki, 'Gdzie i jak po polsku śpiewają słowiki? Glosa do polszczyzny kijowskiej', *ib.*, 1996, no. 9 (538):52–62; H. Karaś, 'Społeczne uwarunkowania zapożyczeń rosyjskojęzycznych w polszczyźnie w okresie zaborów', *Studia pragmalingwistyczne*: 59–81, is an interesting survey of the linguistic consequences of Russification in 19th-c. Poland; her 'Uwagi o błędach fleksyjnych w języku studentów polonistyki wileńskiej', *PJ*, 1996, no. 9 (538):63–70, complements 'Uwagi o sytuacji języka polskiego na Łotwie', Janowska, *Język*, 1, 52–61; M. Krajewska, 'Uwagi o używaniu czasownika *posiadać* (na materiale gazety "Głos znad Niemna")', *PJ*, no. 5 (544):55–63; B. Krucka, 'Błędy frazeologiczne w języku Polonii ze Wschodu', Janowska, *Język*, vol. 1, 62–71; K. Kwapisiewicz, 'O świadomości językowej przedstawicieli Polonii w Chicago', *PJ*, no. 1 (540):46–52. M. Marszałek and J. Mędelska, 'O języku podręczników dla polskich szkół na radzieckiej Litwie', *ib.*, no. 4 (543):8–24. W. Morawski, 'O stronie semantycznej angielskich zapożyczeń leksykalnych w języku środowisk polonijnych usytuowanych w otoczeniu anglojęzycznym', Janowska, *Język*, vol. 1, 91–98. J. Porayski-Pomsta, 'Z badań nad mową polską w rodzinach etnicznie mieszanych w Wilnie. Postawa emocjonalna mówiącego a interferencja', *ib.*, 99–105; Z. Sawaniewska-Mochowa, 'Co wiemy o języku polskim szlachty litewskiej XIX wieku', *ib.*, 106–16; E. Sękowska, 'Sprawność językowa przedstawicieli Polonii w Republice Południowej Afryki (na podstawie nagrań idiolektów)', *PFil*, 40, 1996:229–36; B. Szydłowska-Ceglowa, 'Język polski w Rosji porewolucyjnej i ZSRR (do roku 1935)', *JPol*, 77:251–58. Barbara Dzilewicz, *Język mieszkańców wsi Bujwidze na Wileńszczyźnie*, Wa, Wyd. DiG, 139 pp. W. Decyk, 'Próba opisu polskiej gwary we wsi Wierszyna', *PJ*, 1995, no. 8 (527):20–31; W. Mańczak, 'Czy istniały języki lechickie?', *JPol*, 77:97–101; H. Pelcowa, 'Z kilku nadbużańskich wsi woj. chełmskiego', *ib.*, 190–97; H. Skoczylas-Stawska, 'Cechy gwar wieluńskich w dziele Oskara Kolberga', *PFil*, 40, 1996:385–95; I. Szczepankowska, 'Gwarowe nomina attributiva — struktura i funkcje compositów', *ib.*, 89–95.

7. INDIVIDUALS, WORKS, STYLISTICS

ABRAMOWICZ. J. Joachimiak, 'Regionalizmy północnokresowe w utworach Władysława Abramowicza (Przyczynek do badań nad kulturalną polszczyzną wileńską w dwudziestoleciu międzywojennym)', *PJ*, 1996, no. 10 (539):40–56.

BOTER. K. Zierhoffer and Z. Zierhofferowa, 'Zachodnioeuropejskie nazewnictwo w dziele Giovanniego Botera "Le Relationi universali" i w jego polskim przekładzie', *Onomastica*, 41, 1996:21–39.

CAROLS. M. Borejszo, 'O wariantywności tekstów polskich kolęd', *PJ*, 1995, no. 8 (527):1–10.

CHILDREN'S MAGAZINES. J. Lizak, 'O tematyczno-rematycznej strukturze tekstu w czasopismach dla dzieci', *JPol*, 77:145–49.

CHMIELEWSKI. E. Makowska, 'Swoiste sposoby tworzenia rzeczowników złożonych czyli o dowcipie językowym w "Tytusie, Romku i A'Tomku" H. J. Chmielewskiego', *JPol*, 77:22–26.

CINCIAŁA. H. Horodyska, 'Słownik dialektu Śląska Cieszyńskiego Andrzeja Cinciały', *PJ*, no. 5 (544):66–70.

DYGASIŃSKI. W. Kupiszewski, 'Z zagadnień frazeologii w powieści A. Dygasińskiego *W Kielcach*', *PFil*, 40, 1996:149–52.

DZIENNIK BERLIŃSKI. H. Burkhardt, 'Kilka uwag o słownictwie w "Dzienniku Berlińskim" (1916–1917)', *PFil*, 40, 1996:155–66.

GOSZCZYŃSKI. A. Kępińska, 'O rzeczownikach podzielnych słowotwórczo w "Dzienniku Sprawy Bożej" Seweryna Goszczyńskiego (nomina actionis)', *PFil*, 40, 1996:29–62.

INTERWAR PROSE. M. Ruszkowski, 'Wypowiedzenia luźnie połączone w prozie polskiej (1918–1939)', *PJ*, 1996, no. 7 (536):53–58.

IWASZKIEWICZ. D. Bartol-Jarosińska, 'Pola leksykalno-semantyczne śmierci, miłości i przyrody w "Brzezinie" Jarosława Iwaszkiewicza i jej tłumaczeniu', Janowska, *Język*, 1, 170–83.

KONOPNICKA. A. Rejter, 'Jednorodność stylistyczna tekstu a problem złożoności gatunku mowy (Na przykładzie "Listów z podróży" Marii Konopnickiej)', *PJ*, 1996, no. 7 (536): 59–67.

KONSTANTINOV. M. Kostowa, ' "Baj Ganiu" Aleko Konstantinowa w polskim tłumaczeniu', Janowska, *Język*, 1, 200–04.

LEM. I. Domaciuk, 'Nazwy osobowe w "Obłoku Magellana" Stanisława Lema', *Onomastica*, 41, 1996: 213–45.

LINDE. A. Nowakowska, 'Frazeologia w *Słowniku języka polskiego* S. B. Lindego', *PJ*, 1995, no. 8 (527): 32–39.

MALINOWSKI. I. Dzendzeliv'skii, 'Материали до истории польскої та слов'янської филологiї ИИ. листування Л. Малиновьского з В. Ягичем', *PFil*, 40, 1996: 309–84.

MOSTNIK. P. Fijałkowski, 'Michał Mostnik i najstarsze zabytki piśmiennictwa polskiego na Pomorzu', *JPol*, 77: 183–89.

MOTTY. U. Sokólska, 'Uwagi o języku *Listów Wojtusia z Zawad* Marcelego Motty'ego', *PFil*, 40, 1996: 239–97.

OGÓREK. M. Jochemczyk, 'O mechaniźmie ironii w felietonach Michała Ogórka', *PJ*, no. 5 (544): 32–41.

POETRY OF BAR. S. Dubisz, 'Modlitewno-religijne incipity utworów wierszowanych okresu konfederacji barskiej', *PJ*, 1996, no. 9 (538): 41–47.

PRZERWA-TETMAJER. I. Loewe, 'Konstrukcje analityczne wśród metafor (Struktura, semantyka, funkcja analityzmów w poezji K. Przerwy-Tetmajera)', *PJ*, 1996, no. 7 (536): 42–52.

PSAŁTERZ. M. Cybulski, *Staropolskie przekłady Psałterza*, *RKJŁ*, 41.2, 1996. E. Woźniak, 'Cechy charakterystyczne polskiego tłumaczenia *Psałterza krakowskiego*', *ib.*, 77–96.

RHETORICAL QUESTIONS. B. Taras, 'Pytania retoryczne w zabytkach języka polskiego', *PJ*, 1996, no. 9 (538): 31–40.

RZEWUSKI. B. Bartnicka, 'Dziewiętnastowieczne funkcje składniowe przypadków (na materiale z utworów Henryka Rzewuskiego)', *PJ*, 1996, no. 9 (538): 5–12.

SEBASTIAN PETRYCY Z PILZNA. I. Winiarska, '*Ekonomika, ekonomia, ekonom* w *Przydatku do dwojga ksiąg Ekonomiki Arystotelesowej* Sebastiana Petrycego z Pilzna', *PJ*, 1996, no. 9 (538): 20–30.

SERMONS. A. Sieradzka-Mruk, 'Zakończenie kazania jako struktura tekstowa o funkcji apelatywnej', *JPol*, 77: 287–91.

SŁOWACKI. P. Paziak, 'Uwagi o semantyce nazw kolorów — bieli i czerwieni — w *Balladynie*', *PJ*, no. 2 (541): 18–24.

SZOBER. T. Bronicka, 'Regionalizmy północnokresowe żywe w dwudziestoleciu międzywojennym (Na podstawie *Słownika orto-epicznego* Stanisława Szobera)', *PJ*, no. 2 (541): 33–47.

SZYMBORSKA. W. Śliwiński, 'O rybie w wierszu Wisławy Szymborskiej (analiza składniowa i poetycka)', *JPol*, 77: 6–9.

TROJAŃSKI. E. Worbs, 'Das "Ausführliche Polnisch-Deutsche Handwörterbuch" von Jan Kajetan Trojański — Ein Beitrag zur polnischen Lexikographie des 19. Jh.', *PFil*, 40, 1996: 397–413.

ULYSSES. T. Szczerbowski, 'Z problemów krytyki przekładu: *Ulisses* Jamesa Joyce'a', *PJ*, nos 9–10 (528–29): 64–72.

WOJTYŁA. A. Cegielska, 'Stylizacja biblijna w dramacie *Jeremiasz* Karola Wojtyły', *RKJŁ*, 41.1, 1996: 5–32.

8. POLISH AND OTHER LANGUAGES

Romuald Huszcza, *Honoryfikatywność. Gramatyka. Pragmatyka. Typologia*, Wa, Wyd. Akademickie DIALOG, 1996, 256 pp., a very interesting study of honorifics, compares Polish and other European languages with Oriental languages; *Modalność. Problemy teoretyczne*, vol. 6 (1). *Gramatyka konfrontatywna Bułgarsko-Polska*, ed. Violetta Koseska-Zoszewa et al., Wa, Slawistyczny Ośrodek Wydawniczy, 1996, 201 pp.; Bronisława Ligara, *Polskie czasowniki modalne i ich francuskie ekwiwalenty tłumaczeniowe*, Kw, Universitas, 296 pp.; Jerzy Rusch, *Dzieje nazw zawodów w językach słowiańskich*, Wa, Wyd. Energeia, 1996, 160 pp., includes sections on land cultivation, animal husbandry, fishing, and pottery; *Język wobec przemian kultury*, ed. Emil Tokarz, Katowice, Wyd. Uniwersytetu Śląskiego, 1997, 144 pp., includes Włodzimierz Pianka, 'Związki formalne między fleksyjną a słowo-twórczą kategorią liczby w językach słowiańskich' (26–39); *Studia Linguistica XVII. Heteronomie języka*, ed. Zdzisław Wąsik, Ww, WUW, 1996, 106 pp., includes M. Szymik-Gupczyk, 'Niegramatykalizowane wykładniki wysokiej intensywności w języku polskim i angielskim' (81–94).

W. Askoczeńska, 'Funkcje semantyczno-składniowe bezoko-licznika w językach słowiańskich', Janowska, *Język*, 1, 29–34, analyses parallel sentences in Polish, Russian, and Ukrainian; C. Bogacki, 'La traduction des adjectifs français en polonais', *SILTA*, 1996, no. 3: 585–96; J. Bubak, 'Francuskie imiona w historii języka polskiego', *Onomastica*, 41, 1996: 65–72; M. Gaszyńska-Magiera, 'Język a wizja świata (zdania czasowe hiszpańskie i polskie)', Miodunka, *Nauczanie*, 77–84; W. Gruszczyński, 'Na marginesie *Słownika polsko-szwedzkiego* Jacka Kubitsky'ego', *PJ*, 1995, no. 8 (527): 40–54; W. Gruszczyński and L. Larsson, 'Polsko-szwedzki słowniczek paronimów z początku XVIII wieku', *ib.*, no. 3

(542):54–68; R. Grzegorczykowa, 'O projekcie badań porównawczych w zakresie semantyki leksykalnej', Janowska, *Język*, vol. 1, 43–51; W. Kamiński, 'Фразеологические соотвествия русского и польского языков (на материале фразеологических единиц, обозначающих природные явления)', *SRP*, 26, 1995:191–97; S. Karolak, 'Sullo status dell'aggettivo nel systema della lingua', *SILTA*, 1996, no. 3:653–65, which contains material on Polish, Macedonian, Bulgarian, and French; A. Kiklewitsch, 'Über die Quantifikation von Situationen (am Material der russischen und der polnischen Sprache)', *ASP*, 23, 1995:35–44; M. Korytkowska, 'Kategoria imperceptywności a dopuszczalność kontekstu wyrażającego możliwość/konieczność (na materiale bułgarskim i polskim)', *RKJŁ*, 41.1, 1996:45–56; A. Kreisberg, 'A propos de certains adjectifs évaluatifs en italien et en polonais', *SILTA*, 1996, no. 3:571–84; compares 'ładny', 'piękny' and forms prefixed with 'nie-' and their French equivalents, A. Ławrinienko, 'O utraconym pokrewieństwie leksykalnym języka rosyjskiego i polskiego', *SRP*, 27, 1996:233–42; E. Mańczak-Wohlfeld, 'Czy rzeczywiście nadużywamy zapożyczeń angielskich w polszczyźnie pisanej?', *JPol*, 77:292–97, concludes that the influence of English on Polish is less than that of classical languages or German or French; in 'Najnowsze zapożyczenia angielskie w polskiej prasie', *PJ*, no. 3 (542):84–86, she attributes the use of such neologisms as 'spaming' and 'spamować' to journalists' snobbishness or laziness. M. Marcjanik, 'Czy istnieją uniwersalia grzecznościowe? Na marginesie książki R. Huszczy *Honoryfikatywność. Gramatyka, Pragmatyka, Typologia*', *PJ*, no. 6 (545):19–25, is inconclusive; B. Nowicka, 'O internacjonalizacji frazeologizmów', *SRP*, 27, 1996:153–60, considers such expressions as 'fifth wheel' in French, German, English, Russian, and Polish; A. Otwinowska, 'Uwagi o kilku anglicyzmach gramatycznych, semantycznych i frazeologicznych w polszczyźnie', *PJ*, no. 2 (541):48–53; A. Paciechina, 'Projekt dystrybutywnego słownika polsko-białoruskiego', Janowska, *Język*, vol. 2, 116–19; P. K. Paudey, 'Optionality, lexicality and sound change', *JL*, no. 1:91–130, includes material on Polish; L. Pisarek, 'Перформативное предложение как объект сопоставительного исследования', *SRP*, 26, 1995:199–205, contrasts Russian and Polish expressions of gratitude, apology, and congratulations; G. Sawicka, 'Norma a problem tak zwanych "zapożyczeń"', *PJ*, 1995, nos 9–10 (528–29):78–86, considers such anglo-americanisms as 'biznes plan'. A. Seretny, 'Analiza porównawcza słowników dydaktycznych języka polskiego i angielskiego', Miodunka, *Nauczanie*, 57–75, concludes that Polish learners' dictionaries are less well oriented towards their users' needs than their English equivalents. R[oxana] S[inielnikoff], 'Obce nazwy', *PJ*, 1996, no. 8 (537):71–75;

'Obce nazwiska w polskiej praktyce językowej', *ib.*, 1996, no. 10 (539):78–81, and no. 1 (540):78–81, and her 'Znów o kłopotach z wyrazami obcymi', *ib.*, 1995, nos 9–10 (528–29):105–07. B. Wiemer and O. Burenina-Pietrova, 'Jaki jest zasięg wpływów polskich w mowie rosyjskiej rodzin etnicznie mieszanych w Wilnie?', Janowska, *Język*, 1, 130–44; E. Wierzbicka, 'Indeksowanie cytatów z języka polskiego w tekstach angielskich i włoskich', *ib.*, 145–54; W. Zmarzer, 'Internacjonalizmy w nazwach typów socjalnych w języku rosyjskim, polskim i francuskim', *SRP*, 27, 1996:145–51; Id., 'Социальные стереотипы в русском и польском языках', *ib.*, 26, 1995:119–26.

9. Onomastics

Ewa Rzetelska-Feleszko and Jerzy Duma, *Językowa przeszłość Pomorza Zachodniego na podstawie nazw miejscowych*, Wa, Slawistyczny Ośrodek Wydawniczy, 1996, 341 + 2 pp. *Hydronomia słowiańskie II*, ed. Kazimierz Rymut, Kw, PAN IJP, no date, 171 pp., includes: J. Duma, 'Uwagi o niektórych hydronimach dorzecza Pilicy i Bzury' (25–31); H. Mól, 'Budowa słowotwórcza nazw wodnych dorzecza Wieprza' (33–46); E. Wolnicz-Pawłowska, 'Uwagi o fleksji nazw wodnych' (155–60); and E. Rzetelska-Feleszko, 'Wzajemne stosunki nazw rzecznych i nazw miejscowych' (161–66). *Rozprawy Slawistyczne 11. Systemy zoonomiczne w językach słowiańskich*, ed. Stefan Warchoł, Lublin, Wyd. Uniwersytetu MCS, 1996, 354 pp., includes: Z. Cygal-Krupa, 'Nazwy koni i krów w południowo-zachodniej Limanowszczyźnie' (37–47) and Cz. Kosyl, 'Nazwy krów w polskiej literaturze pięknej' (231–44). Witold Śmiech, *Przymiotnikowe nazwy terenowe Polski*, Łódź, ŁTN, 1996, 163 pp., presents adjectives derived from common expressions (part 1) and from proper nouns (part 2). G. Białuński, 'Nazwy osobowe na Mazurach w XV–XVIII w. (ze szczególnym uwzględnieniem Krainy Wielkich Jezior Mazurskich)', *Onomastica*, 41, 1996:83–95; T. Brajerski, 'Nazwiska z -*owicz* i -*ewicz* w lubelskiej książce telefonicznej', *JPol*, 77:163–68; A. Cieślikowa, 'Metody w onomastycznych badaniach różnych kategorii nazw własnych', *Onomastica*, 41, 1996:5–19; L. Dacewicz, 'Nazewnictwo osobowe regionu białostockiego w ujęciu historycznym', *ib.*, 73–81; W. Decyk, 'Motywacyjność zoonimów', *PJ*, 1996, no. 9 (538):52–56; E. Grzelakowa, 'Nazwy terenowe w formie wyrażeń terenowych', *Studia pragmalingwistyczne*: 33–37; C. Kosyl, 'Kynonimy literackie na tle zoonomii uzualnej (część I)', *Onomastica*, 41, 1996:153–211; B. Kreja, 'Pomorskie nazwiska odmiejscowe (Na przykładzie województwa gdańskiego)', *JPol*, 77:311–19; Id., 'Z księgi polskich nazwisk', *ib.*, 169–82; M. Król, 'O funkcjach imion osobowych we współczesnej polszczyźnie', *PJ*, 1996, no. 10 (539):57–67, examines the personal names given to chocolate, biscuits, dogs, and hamsters, among other things; W. Mańczak, 'W sprawie nazwy *Poprad*', *JPol*, 77:234–35;J. Nalepa, 'Polacy nie przejęli od Ukraincόw nazwy rzeki San. Ze studiόw nad najdawniejszym pograniczem polsko-ruskim', *ib.*, 150–62; G. Olszowska, 'Antyk jako wieczny powrόt?', *ib.*, 307–10, sees the continuing relevance of classical languages in the names of products and TV programmes;J. Parzniewska, 'Imiona nadawane w Krakowie w 1992 roku', *Onomastica*, 41, 1996:139–51; M. Rutkowski, 'Nazwy drόg wspinaczkowych jako kategoria onomastyczna', *ib.*, 41–50; E. Rzetulska-Feleszko, 'Imiona łużyckich katolikόw w latach 1945–1995', *ib.*, 247–75; G. Surma, 'Nazwy miejscowe z członem *Wola, Wόlka, Wolica* w procesie komunikacji językowej (na przykładzie Opoczyńskiego)', *ib.*, 51–56; T. Zduńczyk, 'O prawie zapomnianych polskich nazwach niedziel (na materiale XVI wieku)', *PJ*, no. 3 (542):69–77.

LITERATURE

POSTPONED

IV. RUSSIAN STUDIES*

LANGUAGE

By PETER MAYO, *Erstwhile Senior Lecturer in Russian and Slavonic Studies,
University of Sheffield*

(This survey covers the years 1996–97)

1. COLLECTIVE AND GENERAL

*Russische Umgangssprache. Phonetik, Morphologie, Syntax, Wortbildung,
Wortstellung, Lexik, Nomination, Sprachspiel,* ed. S. Koester-Thoma and
E. A. Zemskaia, Berlin, Dieter Lenz Vlg, 1995, 305 pp., is both a
scientific monograph and an informative manual on current Russian
colloquial speech. *Studies in Russian Linguistics* (SSGL, 19), ed.
R. Sprenger, Amsterdam–Atlanta, GA, Rodopi, 1992, 434 pp.,
comprises 13 articles covering, as the title would suggest, a wide range
of subject matter. David K. Hart, *Topics in the Structure of Russian: An
Introduction to Russian Linguistics,* Columbus, Ohio, Slavica, 1996,
x + 294 pp. L. N. Zybatow, *Russisch im Wandel. Die russische Sprache
seit der Perestrojka,* Wiesbaden, Harassowitz, 1995, 350 pp., is more
narrowly focused on the 1980s and 1990s (though with some
excursions back into the 1960s and 1970s). A. D. Dulichenko,
Русский язык конца XX столетия (SB, 317), (pref. Werner
Lehfeldt), Munich, Sagner, 1994, 347 pp., offers a diagnosis and a
prognosis for the language's further development. *Исследования по
славянскому языкознанию. Памяти профессора Г. А. Хабургаева,*
Moscow U.P., 1993, 207 pp., contains 17 tribute articles covering a
wide range of problems in Slavonic linguistics: history of the Slavonic
written tradition, linguistic-textological reconstruction of OCS translations, ethnic consciousness in the epoch of Kievan Rus′ as reflected
in *Повесть временных лет,* historical morphology and syntax of
Russian, dialectology and linguistic geography, history of the Russian
literary language. D. R. Andrews, *Slavianovedenie,* no. 2 : 18–30, offers
five approaches to the lingusitic analysis of Russian emigrants to the
USA.

2. HISTORY OF THE LANGUAGE

E. Pallasová, *ASP,* 23, 1995 : 9–18, analyses as to whether the verbs
iměti, chotěti/chъtěti in OCS are future-tense or modal auxiliaries.

---

* The place of publication of all books in the Russian section is Moscow, unless
otherwise stated.

E. I. Serebriakova, 'О новонайденном мартовском томе Софийского комплекта Великих Миней Четьих митрополита Макария (предварительные наблюдения)', *ib.*, 131–58. G. I. Tiraspol'skii, 'Из истории древнерусских фразеологизмов', *FilN*, 1996, no.6:54–61. A. Timberlake, *RLing*, 21:49–62, describes the distribution of old and innovative accusatives in the *Повесть временных лет* in terms of templates — conventionalized syntactic patterns composed of a verb and a noun. A. A. Zalizniak, **Древненовгородский диалект* Shkola 'Iazyki russkoi kul'tury', 1995, 720 pp. W. Vermeer, 'Notes on medieval Novgorod sociolinguistics', *RLing*, 21:23–47, bases his discussion on Zalizniak's book, taking issue with what he perceives as some flaws in the work: its speculativeness in certain areas, its reflection of a Stammbaum view of lingusitic differentiation, and the fact that it is cast in a terminology which suggests the presence of much more solid knowledge than is actually available. J. Nørgård-Sørensen, 'Tense, aspect and verbal derivation in the language of the Novgorod birch bark letters', *ib.*, 1–21, is a study of fundamental problems related to OR verbal categories, especially as they are reflected in the birch bark letters of Novgorod.

3. Phonetics and Phonology

R. Kuhn Plupp, 'Russian /i/ and /ɨ/ as underlying segments', *JSL*, 4, 1996:76–108, provides evidence that /i/ and /ɨ/ must be distinct underlying segments within a derivational analysis of modern Russian. Zheng-Min Dong, 'On phonologically null prepositions in Russian: a reply to Fowler and Yadroff', *ib.*, 3, 1995:378–86, argues against the hypothesis of Fowler and Yadroff that the accusative case in such expressions as всю неделю is assigned by a null preposition. H. S. Coats, 'On the phonemic status of Russian [š':]', *RLing*, 21:157–64, presents empirical evidence that non-alternating [š':] is the phonetic realization of two (or more) phonemes rather than just one.

4. Morphology and Word Formation

V. B. Krys'ko, **Развитие категории одушевленности в истории русского языка*, Lyceum, 1994, 224 pp., is a useful and interesting treatment of a classic problem. L. E. Feinberg, 'An automorphic approach to paradigm structure: towards a new model of Russian case morphology', *JSL*, 5:51–79, argues that an automorphic approach allows us to motivate both the direction of syncretism and the division into paradigms. Sung-ho Choi, 'Aspect and negated modality in Russian: their conceptual compatibility', *ib.*, 20–50, examines aspectual choice in the context of two negated modal predicates, не мочь and нельзя. K. E. Robblee, 'Effects of the lexicon and aspect on nominative/genitive case variation', *ib.*, 4, 1996:344–69, examines case marking in Russian negative intransitive constructions, focusing on the lexicon and aspect. R. Beard, 'The gender-animacy hypothesis', *ib.*, 3, 1995:59–96, maintains that if the categories of natural gender, agreement and declinsion class are properly described, animacy may be reduced to natural gender and removed from the grammatical description of Slavonic languages. (The article is based mainly — though not exclusively — on examples from Russian.) P. Durst-Andersen, 'Russian case as mood', *ib.*, 4, 1996:177–273, sets up specific requirements for a theory of Russian case and against this background a new theory is constructed which is based on the assumption that an isomorphic relationship exists between the structure of the nominal system and that of the verbal system; he argues that Russian case is the nominal equivalent to mood. M. Yadroff, 'Modern Russian vocatives: a case of subtractive morphology', *ib.*, 133–53. Iu. S. Kudriavtsev, 'Русский dualis как живая категория', *RLing*, 20, 1996:227–35, investigates how live a form the dual is. A. Hippisley, 'Russian expressive derivation: a network morphology account', *SEER*, 74, 1996:201–22, uses the lexical representation language DATR to show how Russian expressive derivation is similar to inflection in that it preserves the word-class of the base and morphosyntactic features such as gender and animacy. V. Beliakov and M. Guiraud-Weber, 'О некоторых свойствах вторичных глагольных приставок', *RLing*, 21:165–75. V. M. Glukhikh, 'Что это — слово или аффикс?', *FilN*, 1996, no. 5:65–73, deals with the status of кое-, не-, нн-, and -либо, -нибудь, -ся, -то. Tore Nesset, **Russian Stress: Stress as an Inflectional Formative in Russian Noun Paradigms and Bybee's Cognitive Morphology* (Oslo-Studier i Sprakvitenskap, 9), Oslo, Novus, 1994, 172 pp. F. Y. Gladney, 'The accent of Russian verbforms', *JSL*, 3, 1995:97–138, proposes a decription of verbal accent based not on stems (roots plus themes) but roots and endings. Also noted: D. Götz, 'Wortbildung und Wortfügung bei Neologismen der Wirtschafts- und Geschäftssprache im gegenwärtigen Russischen', *ASP*, 23, 1995:19–24; M. Dumitrescu, 'Образования с -ист/-ист- в лексике русского языка', *FilZ*, 20–21, 1992–93:75–78.

5. Syntax. Semantics and Pragmatics

V. B. Krys'ko, **Исторический синтаксис русского языка. Объект и переходность*, Izd. 'Indrik', 424 pp., is, according to a reviewer, 'a highly knowledgeable, sophisticated, and profound piece of research combining the best traditions of Russian syntactic studies with an original, innovative approach'. Edna Andrews, *The Semantics of Suffixation: Agentive Substantival Suffixes in Contemporary Standard Russian* (LINCOM Studies in Slavic Lingusitics, 5), Munich, Lincom Europa, 1996, 261 pp. Uwe Junghanns, *Syntaktische und semantische Eigenschaften russischer finaler Infinitiveinbettungen* (SB, 315), 1994, 227 pp. A. Shmelev, *Референциальные механизмы русского языка* (Slavica Tamperensia, 4), Tampere U.P., 1996, 281 pp. P. Schmidt and W. Lehfeldt, *Kongruenz. Rektion. Adjunktion: Systematische und historische Untersuchungen zur allgemeinen Morphosyntax und zu den Wortfügungen (словосочетания) im Russischen* (Specimina philologiae slavicae, Supplementband 37), Munich, Sagner, 1995, x + 360 pp. L. A. Biriulin, *Семантика и синтаксис русского имперсонала: verba meteorologica и их диатезмы* (Specimina philologiae slavicae, 102), Munich, Sagner, 1994, 164 pp.

J. S. Levine and C. Jones, 'Agent, purpose and Russian middles', *JSL*, 4, 1996: 50–75, argue against the notion that lexical assignment of some kind of agent thematic role to subject position is relative to the distribution of adjuncts and offer an account of their distribution in terms of a more formal property of the argument structure of certain verbs: the absence of lexically determined thematic content for the verb's characteristic external argument. A. Israeli, 'Discourse analysis of Russian aspect: accent on creativity', *ib.*, 8–49, sees the traditional definition 'general factual meaning' of certain imperfective usage in the past as inadequate and demonstrates that in verbs denoting creative acts a completely different set of parameters guides the usage of perfective vs imperfective. J. Rouhier-Willoughby, 'The effect of discourse functions of the voice on bidiathesis -*sja* verbs', *ib.*, 3, 1995: 357–77, re-examines the claim that verbs suffixed in -*sja* in CSR are distinguished by voice, i.e. imperfectives in -*sja* may be read as passives, while perfectives may not. She shows that passive readings of -*sja* are much more restricted than has been previously suggested, discourse analysis supporting the claim that these verbs are not distinguished by voice. S. Brown and S. Franks, 'Asymmetries in the scope of Russian negation', *ib.*, 239–87, propose a functional category analysis of sentential negation in Russian in order to accommodate a distributional asymmetry between negative polarity and the genitive of negation. They then develop an account of pleonastic negation in terms of the idea that this involves a negation phrase which lacks a negation operator, and demonstrate how this account effectively handles various phenomena associated with pleonastic negation. J. F. Bailyn, 'Underlying phrase structure and "short" verb movement in Russian', *ib.*, 13–58, makes two claims about the structure of the Russian sentence: firstly, it motivates an underlying phrase structure with three distinct argument positions; secondly, it demonstrates the existence of 'short' verb movement in Russian, i.e. overt raising of the verb to the next higher head position. G. Fowler, 'Oblique passivization in Russian', *SEEJ*, 40, 1996:519–45, addresses the question of the extent to which oblique-complement verbs permit the formation of passive constructions. V. A. Podlesskaia, 'Syntax and semantics of resumption: some evidence from Russian conditional conjuncts', *RLing*, 21:125–55, offers data which speak for the scalar approach which takes into consideration all possible semantic, pragmatic, suprasegmental and other criteria to formulate cross-linguistically relevant notions of co-ordination and the subordination in clause combining. G. Hentschel, 'О квантитативных препятствиях на пути к качеству', *ib.*, 20, 1996:265–81, offers some observations on, and criticism of, A. Mustajoki and H. Heino, *Case Selection for the Direct Object in Russian Negative Clauses* (Helsinki U.P., 1991). L. D. Chesnokova, 'Имена числительные и имена собственные', *FilN*, 1996, no. 1:104–13, discusses their semantic differences. Also noted: J.-P. Benoist, 'О некоторых метафорически пространственных ситуациях русского языка (на основе ролевой грамматики русского языка)', *RLing*, 20, 1996:201–26; R. Roudet, 'Un cas de concurrence entre accusatif et instrumental. Convient-il de postuler une nouvelle catégorie des verbes?', *RSl*, 68, 1996:91–101; M. Guiraud-Weber, 'La syntaxe du comparatif russe: quelques précisions', *ib.*, 487–96; I. A. Shirshov, 'Типы полисемии в производном слове', *FilN*, 1996, no. 1:55–66; T. V. Markelova, 'Взаимодействие оценочных и модальных значений в русском языке', *ib.*, 80–89; A. I. Ostanin, 'К основам анализа адресатиой соотносительности обращения и высказывания (на материале русской разговорной речи)', *ib.*, no. 3:64–71.

6. Lexicology and Phraseology

A. Rodimkina and J. Davie, 'Developments in the modern Russian lexis', *Rusistika*, 12, 1995:43–48. G. Kurokhtina, 'Новые слова и значения в современном русском языке', *ib.*, 13, 1996:21–25, discusses some of the most recent borrowings and changes in meaning, while the topic is further explored, in a more theoretical way, by M. A. Breiter, 'Современные лексические заимствования в русском языке: «чужеродные речения» или средство обогащения литературного языка?', *ib.*, 14, 1996:33–45, and by J. Russell and S. Carsten, 'The impact of Gorbachev's new thinking on the Russian language, 1985–1995', *ib.*, 13, 1996:26–33. A. A. Zalizniak and I. B. Levontina, *RLing*, 20, 1996:237–64, examine the expression of national character in Russian lexis. R. Comtet, 'L'adaptation accentuelle des emprunts anglo-américains en russe', *RSl*, 68,

1996:103–18, is an analysis of Russian word stress in Anglo-American borrowed words, based on the Russian *Contemporary Dictionary of Foreign Words* published in 1992. In about a third of the English loanwords mentioned there is a shift of word stress, mostly explicable by the Russian system of composition, affixation and stressing. J. Davie, '*Texno, trans* and *džank*: new waves of *anglicizmy* in Russian youth slang', *ASEES*, 11.1–2:1–17, brings us up to date on slang words which have recently entered Russian youth-speak, many of them from English, but some as a reinterpretation of the original meaning of native words (e.g. кислота = acid).

J. Rieger, 'The main stages of the development of Russian place names', *CanSP*, 37, 1995:455–66, maintains that, whilst the real revolution in Russian toponymy took place in the 16th and 17th cs, Russian Soviet place names continued the earlier 'church' and imperial traditions. On Greek borrowings into Russian see E. Zunis, 'К вопросу о греческих заимствованиях в русском языке', *Romanoslavica*, 33, 1995:81–89. Also noted: A. Levin-Steinmann, 'Antonymische und synonymische Beziehungen im phraseologischen System der russischen Sprache und Möglichkeiten ihrer lexikographischen Darstellung', *ASP*, 23, 1995:25–33; Zh. Zh. Varbot, 'К этимологии рус. диал. *пестерь*', *Slavianovedenie*, 1996, no. 1:3–6.

N. A. Es'kova, **Краткий словарь трудностей русского языка: Грамматические формы. Ударение*, RIa, 1994, 448 pp., is a valuable work which goes beyond the traditional 'correct', 'incorrect' labels. Jürgen Petermann, Renate Hansen-Kokuruš, and Tamara Bill, **Russisch-deutsches phraseologisches Wörterbuch*, ed. Josip Matešič, Leipzig–Berlin–Munich, Langenscheidt, 1994, xxviii + 946 pp. E. Sekaninová, **Vel'ki slovensko-ruski slovník*, SAV 'Veda', 1979–95, completes this six-volume work.

7. LANGUAGES IN CONTACT AND IN CONTRAST

J. E. M. Clarke, *ASEES*, 10.2, 1996:37–46, deals with what he calls the '+[n]' subconjugation in Russian and Ukrainian, while M. Popović and R. I. Trostkinska, 'Tvorba budućeg vremena u hrvatskom, ruskom i ukrajinskom kniževnom jeziku', *FilŽ*, 20–21, 1992–93:363–73, consider synthetic and analytic future-tense formations and debate whether the former in Ukrainian is only historically synthetic but now a simple form. R. Volos, 'Upotreba instrumentalnih prijedloga s prostornim značenjem u ruskom i hrvatskom jeziku', *ib.*, 517–27, demonstrate that, whilst used in the same function in both languages, their representation in translating from Russian into Serbo-Croat is sometimes equivalent, sometimes not. Ž. Fink, 'Frazemi sa značenjem "vrlo daleko" u ruskom i hrvatskom jeziku', *ib.*, 24–25, 1995:121–27, divides them into three groups according to submeanings — place, direction or a combination of the two; see also his 'Tipovi adjektivnih frazeologizama (na materijalu ruskog i hrvatskog jezika)', *ib.*, 20–21, 1992–93:91–101. Also noted: A. Dergana, 'Несколько заметок в связи с перформативными глаголами в русском и словенском языках', *ib.*, 67–74; R. Maroevic, 'К типологии русского и сербского языков', *Slavianovedenie*, 1995, no. 4:63–77; T. Stoeva, 'Функциональная нагрузка твердых-мягких согласных в слоговых структурах русского и болгарского языков', *BR*, 1994, no. 2:26–31; T. Chalykova, 'Акустические и перцептивные аспекты исследования неоднородных вокальных сегментов (на материале русского и болгарского языков)', *ib.*, 32–34; A. Kiklewitsch, 'Über die Quantifikation von Situationen (am Material der russischen und der polnischen Sprache)', *ASP*, 23, 1995:35–44.

P. Cubberley, 'The pressure of pattern in stress placement on transferred names in Russian and English', *ASEES*, 10.2, 1996:47–62, notes for English a larger proportion of initial stress than in common words and an unexpected preference for the initial syllable in two- and three-syllable words and for the penult in longer words. Also noted: Xu Gaoyu, 'Сопоставительный анализ образования сложных цветонаименований в русском и китайском языках', *FilZ*, 20–21, 1992–93:565–71.

LITERATURE, to 1700
POSTPONED

LITERATURE, 1700–1820
POSTPONED

LITERATURE, 1820–1880
POSTPONED

LITERATURE, 1880–1917
POSTPONED

LITERATURE, 1917 TO THE PRESENT DAY
POSTPONED

V. UKRAINIAN STUDIES
POSTPONED

VI. BELARUSIAN STUDIES
POSTPONED

VII. SERBO-CROAT STUDIES
POSTPONED

VIII. BULGARIAN STUDIES
POSTPONED

ABBREVIATIONS

I. ACTA, FESTSCHRIFTEN AND OTHER COLLECTIVE AND GENERAL WORKS

Actas (AHLM 6): *Actas del VI Congreso Internacional de la Asociación Hispánica de Literatura Medieval, Alcalá de Henares, 12–16 de septiembre de 1995*, ed. José Manuel Lucía Megías, 2 vols, Universidad de Alcalá, 1-787, 799-1618 pp.

Actas (AISO 1993): *Studia Aurea. Actas del III Congreso de la AISO (Toulouse 1993), I. Plenarios, General, Poesía, II. Teatro, III. Prosa*, ed. I. Arellano, M. C. Pinillos, F. Serralta, and M. Vitse, 3 vols, Pamplona, Grupo de Investigación Siglo de Oro y Literatura Española Medieval y del Siglo de Oro, 1996, 550, 442, 541 pp.

Actas (Alcalá): *La literatura en la época de Sancho IV (Actas del Congreso Internacional 'La literatura en la época de Sancho IV', Alcalá de Henares, 21–24 de febrero de 1994)*, ed. Carlos Alvar and José Manuel Lucia Megías, Alcalá U.P., 573 pp.

Actas (APL 1996): *Actas do XII° Encontro Nacional da Associação Portuguesa de Linguística (Braga-Guimarães, 30 de Setembro a 2 de Outubro de 1996), I. Linguística, II. Linguística Histórica e História da Linguística*, ed. Ivo Castro, 2 vols, Lisbon, Associação Portuguesa de Linguística, 355, 625 pp.

Actas (Granada) I–IV: *Medioevo y Literatura. Actas del V Congreso de la Asociación Hispánica de Literatura Medieval. Granada, 1993*, 4 vols, ed. Juan Paredes, Granada U.P., 1995, 545, 560, 551, 560 pp.

Actas (Lisbon) I: *Actas do IV Congresso da Associação Hispânica de Literatura Medieval. I, Sessões plenárias*, Lisbon, Cosmos, 1991, 135 pp.

Actas (Lisbon) II–IV: *Actas do IV Congresso da Associação Hispânica de Literatura Medieval (30 de setembro – 8 de outubro de 1991)*, ed. Aires do Nascimento and Cristina Almeida Ribeiro, Lisbon, Cosmos, 1993, 373, 359, 387 pp.

Actas (Salamanca): *Actas del III Congreso de la Asociación Hispánica de Literatura Medieval. Salamanca, 1989*, 2 vols, ed. Maria Isabel Toro Pascua, Salamanca, Departamento de Literatura Española e Hispanoamericana, 1994, 1181 pp.

Actas (Santiago de Compostela), I: *Actas do XIX Congreso Internacional de Lingüística e Filoloxía Románicas, Universidade de Santiago de Compostela, 1989. I. Sección I. Lingüística teórica e lingüística sincrónica*, ed. Ramón Lorenzo, Corunna, Fundación 'Pedro Barrié de la Maza, Conde de Fenosa', 1134 pp.

Actas (Santiago de Compostela), VII: *Actas do XIX Congreso Internacional de Lingüística e Filoloxía Románicas, Universidade de Santiago de Compostela, 1989. VII. Sección IX. Filoloxía medieval e renacentista*, ed. Ramón Lorenzo, Corunna, Fundación 'Pedro Barrié de la Maza, Conde de Fenosa', 1994, 997 pp.

Actas (Santiago de Compostela), VIII: *Actas do XIX Congreso Internacional de Lingüística e Filoloxía Románicas, Universidade de Santiago de Compostela, 1989. VIII. Sección X. Historia da lingüística e da filoloxía románicas. Sección XI. Traballos en curso e programas de investigación nacionais e internacionais*, ed. Ramón Lorenzo, Corunna, Fundación 'Pedro Barrié de la Maza, Conde de Fenosa', 1996, 866 pp.

Actes (AIEO 1995): *Le rayonnement des troubadours. Actes du Colloque de l'Association International d'Études Occitanes, Amsterdam, 16–18 octobre 1995*, ed. Anton Touber (Internationale Forschungen zur Allgemeinen und Vergleichenden Literaturwissenschaft, 27), Amsterdam–Atlanta, Rodopi, 312 pp.

Actes (Baltimore): *La Génération Marot: poètes français et néo-latins (1515–1550). Actes du Colloque International de Baltimore, 5–7 décembre 1996*, ed. G. Defaux (Colloques, congrès et conférences sur la Renaissance, 11), Paris, Champion, 558 pp.

Actes (Cahors): *Clément Marot, 'prince des poètes françois', 1496–1996: Actes du Colloque International de Cahors en Quercy*, ed. G. Defaux and M. Simonin (Colloques, congrès et conférences sur la Renaissance, 8), Paris, Champion, 868 pp.

Actes (Corte): *Bases de données linguistiques: conceptions, réalisations, exploitations. Actes du Colloque International de Corte, 11–14 octobre 1995*, ed. Georges Moracchini, Corte, Univ. de Corse, 1996, 328 pp.

Actes (Étaples): *Jacques Lefevre d'Étaples (1450?-1536). Actes du Colloque d'Étaples les 7 et 8 novembre 1992*, ed. J.-F. Pernot (Colloques, congrès et conférences sur la Renaissance, 5), Paris, Champion, 1995, 290 pp.

Actes (GREHAM 3): *Genèse médiévale de l'anthroponymie moderne* III. *Enquêtes généalogiques et données prosopographiques. (Études d'anthroponymie médiévale, Vᵉ et VIᵉ rencontres d'Azay-le-Ferron, 1991–1993)*, ed. Monique Bourin and Pascal Chareille, Tours, Université François-Rabelais, 1995, 241 pp.

Actes (Keio): *Les Animaux dans la littérature. Actes du Colloque de Tokyo de la Société Internationale Renardienne du 22 au 24 juillet 1996 à l'Université Keio*, ed. Hideichi Matsubara, Satoru Suzuki, Naoyuki Fukumoto, and Noboru Harano, Tokyo, Keio U.P., iv + 392 pp.

Actes (Monaco): *Actes du 9ᵉ Colloque des langues dialectales*, Monaco, Académie des Langues Dialectales, 1996.

Actes (Montpellier): *Conformité et déviances au moyen âge. Actes du deuxième colloque internationale de Montpellier, Université Paul-Valéry (25–27 Novembre 1993)*, Montpellier, C.R.I.S.I.M.A., 1995, 334 pp.

Actes (Nancy): *Le Moyen Français. Philologie et Linguistique. Approches du texte et du discours. Actes du VIIIᵉ Colloque international sur le moyen français (Nancy 5–6–7 septembre, 1994)*, ed. Bernard Combettes and Simone Monsonégo, Paris, Didier Érudition, 629 pp.

Actes (Nice): *Ordre et désordre dans la civilisation de la Renaissance: Actes du colloque Renaissance, Humanisme, Réforme, Nice-septembre 1993*, ed. G. A. Pérouse and F. Goyet, Saint-Étienne, Université de Saint-Étienne, 1996, 354 pp.

Actes (Pau): *L'Occitanie romantique: Actes du Colloque de Pau (22, 23 et 24 septembre 1994)*, ed. Claire Torreilles (Annales de la Littérature Occitane, 3), Bordes, Centre d'Étude de la Littérature Occitane, 1996[1997], 375 pp.

Actes (Rheims): *Le Mécénat et l'influence des Guises: Actes du colloque organisé par le Centre de Recherche sur la littérature de la Renaissance de l'Université de Reims et tenu à Joinville du 31 mai au 4 juin 1994 (et à Reims pour la journée du 2 juin)*, ed. Y. Bellenger (Colloques, congrès et conférences sur la Renaissance, 9) Paris, Champion, 755 pp.

Actes (SIEM 6): *Actes du VIᵉ Symposium International d'Études Morisques sur 'État des recherches en moriscologie durant les trente dernières années'*, ed. Abdeljelil Temimi, Zaghouan, FTERSI, 1995, 368 pp.

Actes (SIEM 7): *Actes du VIIᵉ Symposium International d'Études Morisques sur 'Famille morisque: femmes et enfants'*, ed. Abdeljelil Temimi, Zaghouan, FTERSI, 348 + 92 pp.

Actes (Thessalonica): *Montaigne: espace, voyage, écriture. Actes du Congrès international de Thessalonique du 23–25 septembre 1992*, Paris, Champion, 1995, 329 pp.

Actes (Trier), VI: *Actes du XVIIIᶜ Congrès International de Linguistique et Philologie Romanes*, vol. VI, ed. Dieter Kremer, Tübingen, Niemeyer, 1988, xi + 548 pp.

Actes (Zaghouan): *Actes du IIᵉ Congres international sur Chrétiens et Musulmans à l'époque de la Renaissance*, ed. Abdeljelil Temimi, Zaghouan, FTERSI, 258 + 16 pp.

Actes (Zurich), V: *Actes du XXᵉ Congrès International de Linguistique et Philologie Romanes. Université de Zurich (6–11 avril 1992), tome V, Section VII – La poésie lyrique romane (XIIᵉ et XIIIᵉ siècles). Section VIII – L'art narratif au XIIᵉ et XIIIᵉ siècles*, ed. Gerold Hilty et al., Tübingen–Basel, Francke, 1993, vi + 457 pp.

Adam, *Geselligkeit: Geselligkeit und Gesellschaft im Barockzeitalter*, ed. Wolfgang Adam, Knut Kiesant, Winfried Schulze, and Christoph Strosetzki (Wolfenbütteler Arbeiten zur Barockforschung, 28), Wiesbaden, Harrassowitz, xi + 884 pp.

Alvar, *Manual: Manual de dialectología hispánica. El español de España*, ed. Manuel Alvar, Barcelona, Ariel, 1996, 394 pp.

Antonini Vol.: Operosa Parva. Per Gianni Antonini, ed. Domenico De Robertis and Franco Gavazzeni, Verona, Edizioni Valdonega, 1996, xv + 403 pp.

Arnold, *History*, III: *A History of Literature in the Caribbean*, ed. A. James Arnold, vol. III, *Cross Cultural Studies*, Amsterdam, Benjamins, 381 pp.

Arnould, *Tourments: Tourments, doutes et ruptures dans l'Europe des XVIe et XVIIe siècles: Actes du colloque organisé par l'Université de Nancy II, 25–27 novembre 1993*, ed. J.-C. Arnould, Paris, Champion, 1995, 270 pp.

Atti (AISLLI 15): *Letteratura e industria. Atti del XV Congresso dell'Associazione Internazionale per gli Studi di Lingua e Letteratura Italiana (Torino, 15–19 maggio 1994)*, ed. Giorgio Bárberi Squarotti and Carlo Ossola, 2 vols, Florence, Olschki, xviii + 1288 pp. + 76 pls.

Atti (Ferrara), I–II: *Italia ed Europa nella linguistica del Rinascimento: confronti e relazioni. Atti del Convegno internazionale, Ferrara, Palazzo Paradiso, 20–24 marzo 1991*, ed. Mirko Tavoni et al., Modena, Panini, 1230 pp.

Atti (Naples): *Medioevo romanzo e orientale. Oralità, scrittura, modelli narrativi. Atti del II Colloquio Internazionale, Napoli 17–19 febbraio 1994*, ed. Antonio Pioletti and Francesca Rizzo Nervo, Soveria Mannelli, Rubbettino, 1995, x + 332 pp.

Atti (Perugia): *Atti del Terzo Convegno della Società Internazionale di Linguistica e Filologia Italiana (Perugia, 27–29 giugno 1994)*, ed. L. Agostiniani et al. (Università degli Studi di Perugia, Pubblicazioni dell'Istituto di Linguistica, 2), 2 vols, Naples, Edizioni Scientifiche Italiane, x + 736 pp.

Baum Vol.: Kunst und Kommunikation. Betrachungen zum medium Sprache in der Romania. Festschrift zum 60. Geburtstag von Richard Baum, ed. Maria Lieber and Willi Hirdt, Tübingen, Stauffenburg, xvi + 554 pp.

Beer, *Translation: Translation and the Transmission of Culture between 1300 and 1600*, ed. J. Beer and K. Lloyd-Jones (Studies in Medieval Culture, 35), Kalamazoo, Michigan, Medieval Institute, Western Michigan University, 1995, xii + 358 pp.

Beer, *Translation Theory: Translation Theory and Practice in the Middle Ages*, ed. Jeanette Beer (Studies in Medieval Culture, 38), Kalamazoo, Michigan, Medieval Institute, Western Michigan University, 282 pp.

Bell, *Aphorism:* Mark Bell, *Aphorism in the Francophone Novel of the Twentieth Century*, Liverpool U.P. – McGill-Queen's U.P., 154 pp.

Bellini Vol.: El Girador. Studi di letterature iberiche e ibero-americane offerti a Giuseppe Bellini, ed. G. B. De Cesare and S. Serafin, 2 vols, Rome, Bulzoni, 1993, 1051 pp.

Berriot-Salvadore, *Jerusalem: Le mythe de Jerusalem, du Moyen Age à la Renaissance*, ed. Evelyne Berriot-Salvadore, Saint-Étienne, Publications de l'Université de Saint-Étienne, 1995, 270 pp.

Besomi Vol.: 'Feconde venner le carte'. Studi in onore di Ottavio Besomi, ed. Tatiana Crivelli, 2 vols, Bellinzona, Casagrande, 849 pp.

Binebine, *Manuscrit arabe: Le Manuscrit arabe et la codicologie*, coord. Ahmed Shawqi Binebine, Rabat, Manshurat kulliat al-adab wa-l'ulum al-insaniyah, 1994, 129 + 124 pp.

Birkett, *French Literature:* Jennifer Birkett and James Kearns, *A Guide to French Literature from Early Modern to Postmodern*, London, Macmillan, x + 361 pp.

Bleznick Vol.: Studies in Honor of Donald W. Bleznick, ed. Delia V. Galván, Anita K. Stoll, and Philippa Brown Yin, Newark NJ, Juan de la Cuesta, 1995, 218 pp.

Bloch, *Medievalism: Medievalism and the Modernist Temper*, ed. R. Howard Bloch and Stephen G. Nichols, Baltimore, Johns Hopkins U.P., 1996, viii + 496 pp.

Blum, *Montaigne: Éditer les 'Essais' de Montaigne. Actes du colloque tenu à l'Université de Paris IV-Sorbonne les 27 et 28 janvier 1995*, ed. C. Blum and A. Tournon (Études Montaignistes, 28), Paris, Champion, 234 pp.

Bonn, *Littérature francophone: Littérature francophone.* I: *Le roman*, ed. C. Bonn, X. Garnier, and J. Lecarme, Paris, Hatier — Montreal, UREF/AUPELF, 351 pp.

Brenner, *Literaturgeschichte:* Peter J. Brenner, *Neue deutsche Literaturgeschichte. Von 'Ackermann' zu Günter Grass*, Tübingen, Niemeyer, 1996, viii + 379 pp.

Brown, *Celticism: Celticism*, ed. Terence Brown (Studia imagologica: Amsterdam Studies on Cultural Identity, 8), Amsterdam, Rodopi, 1996, viii + 299 pp.

Brucker, *Traduction: Traduction et adaptation en France à la fin du Moyen Age et à la Renaissance. Actes du colloque organisé à l'Université de Nancy II, 23–25 mars 1995*, ed. C. Brucker (Colloques, congrès et conférences sur la Renaissance, 10), Paris, Champion, 406 pp.

Brunel, *Transparences: Pierre Brunel, Transparences du roman. Le romancier et ses doubles au XXe siècle. Calvino, Cendrars, Cortázar, Echenoz, Joyce, Kundera, Thomas Mann, Proust, Yourcenar,* Paris, José Corti, 305 pp.

Buckl, *Krisenzeit: Das 14. Jahrhundert. Krisenzeit,* ed. Walter Buckl (Eichstätter Kolloquium, 1), Regensburg, Pustet, 1995, 240 pp.

Burns, *Emperor of Culture: Emperor of Culture: Alfonso X the Learned of Castile and his Thirteenth-Century Renaissance,* ed. R. I. Burns, Philadelphia, University of Pennsylvania Press, 1990, xii + 272 pp.

Carnero, *Teatro:* G. Carnero, *Estudios sobre el teatro español del siglo XVIII,* Zaragoza U.P., 310 pp.

Carozzi, *Peuples: Peuples au moyen âge: problèmes d'identification,* ed. Claude Carozzi and Huguette Taviani-Carozzi (Séminaires société, idéologies et croyances au moyen âge), Aix-en-Provence, Publications de l'Université de Provence, 1996, 211 pp.

Castilho, *Português falado* IV: *Gramática do Português falado.* IV. *Estudos descritivos,* ed. Ataliba Teixeira de Castilho and Margarida Basílio, Campinas, UNICAMP — São Paulo, FAPESP, 1996, 510 pp.

Catalán, *Balada y Lírica: De Balada y Lírica: 3er Coloquio Internacional del Romancero,* ed. Diego Catalán et al., 2 vols, Madrid, Fundación Ramón Menédez Pidal — Univ. Complutense, 1994.

Chance, *Gender: Gender and Text in the Later Middle Ages,* ed. Jane Chance, Gainesville–Tallahassee–Tampa–Boca Raton–Pensacola–Orlando–Miami–Jacksonville, Florida U.P., xv + 342 pp.

Chomarat Vol.: Centuriae latinae. Cent-une figures humanistes de la Renaissance aux Lumières offertes à J. Chomarat, ed. Colette Nativel (THR, 314), Geneva, Droz, 818 pp.

Colloque Manciet: Bernard Manciet: Le feu est dans la langue. Actes du 'Colloque Bernard Manciet: Le feu est dans la langue' (20–21 novembre 1992, Bordeaux - Musée d'Aquitaine), ed. Guy Latry (Annales de littérature occitane, 2), Bordes, Centre d'Étude de la Littérature Occitane, 1996, 241 pp.

Actes (Villeneuve-lès-Avignon): *Frédéric Mistral et 'Lou Pouème dóu Rose': Actes du Colloque de Villeneuve-lès-Avignon (10–11 mai 1996),* ed. Philippe Gardy and Claire Toreilles (Annales de la Littérature Occitane, 5), Bordes, Centre d'Étude de la Littérature Occitane, 1996 [1997], 295 pp.

Cortelazzo Vol.: I dialetti e il mare. Atti del congresso internazionale di studi in onore di Manlio Cortelazzo, Chioggia, 21–25 settembre 1996, ed. Gianna Marcato, Padua, Unipress, iv + 482 pp.

Croce Vol.: Studi di filologia e letteratura offerti a Franco Croce, pref. Vittorio Coletti, Rome, Bulzoni, xlix + 719 pp.

Cueto Vol.: Convivium: Celebratory Essays for Ronald Cueto, ed. John Macklin and Margaret A. Rees, Leeds, Cañada Blanch Foundation–University of Leeds–Trinity and All Saints College, xii + 369 pp.

Currie, *Object: The Sculpted Object 1400–1700,* ed. Stuart Currie and Peta Motture, Aldershot, Scolar, xxiii + 250 pp.

D'Agostino, *Aspetti: Aspetti della variabilità: ricerche linguistiche siciliane,* ed. M. D'Agostino, Palermo, CSFLS, 213 pp.

Dahmen, *Romanischen Sprachen: Die Bedeutung der romanischen Sprachen im Europea der Zukunft,* ed. Wolfgang Dahmen, Günter Holtus, Johannes Kramer, Michael Metzeltin, Wolfgang Schweickard, and Otto Winkelmann, Tübingen, Narr, 1996, xvi + 203 pp.

Dahmen, *Sprache und Geschlecht: Sprache und Geschlecht in der Romania. Romanistisches Kolloquium X* (TBL, 417), ed. Wolfgang Dahmen, Günter Holtus, Johannes Kramer, Michael Metzeltin, Wolfgang Schweickard, and Otto Winkelmann, Tübingen, Narr, viii + 399 pp.

D'Andrea Vol.: Da una riva all'altra. Studi in onore di Antonio D'Andrea, ed. Dante Della Terza, Fiesole, Cadmo, 1995, xxiii + 435 pp.

Dauphiné, *Marot: Clément Marot: à propos de 'L'Adolescence Clémentine'. Actes des quatrièmes journées du Centre Jacques de Laprade, tenues au Musée national du château de Pau les 29 et 30 novembre 1996,* ed. J. Dauphiné, Biarritz, J & D Éditeurs, 1996, 176 pp.

Dauphiné, *Tiers Livre: Rabelais: autour du 'Tiers Livre'. Actes des troisièmes journées du Centre Jacques de Laprade, tenues au Musée national du château de Pau, les 8 et 9 décembre 1995*, ed. J. Dauphiné (Cahiers du Centre Jacques de Laprade 3), Biarritz, J & D Éditeurs, 1995, 144 pp.

Debatin, *Metaphor: Metaphor and Rational Discourse*, ed. Bernhard Debatin, Timothy R. Jackson, and Daniel Steuer, Tübingen, Niemeyer, viii + 264 pp.

Della Casa Vol.: Bandhu. Scritti in onore di Carlo Della Casa in occasione del suo settantesimo compleanno, ed. Renato Arena, Maria Patrizia Bologna, Maria Luisa Mayer Modena, and Alessandro Passi, Alessandria, Edizioni dell'Orso, xix + 886 pp.

Della Terza, *Strutture poetiche:* Dante Della Terza, *Strutture poetiche, esperienze letterarie: percorsi culturali da Dante ai contemporanei*, Naples, Edizioni Scientifiche Italiane, 1995, 289 pp.

De Mulder, *Relations anaphoriques: Relations anaphoriques et (in)cohérence*, ed. Walter De Mulder, Liliane Tasmowski-De Rijk, and Carl Vetters, Amsterdam–Atlanta, Rodopi, x + 314 pp.

Deyermond Vol.: The Medieval Mind: Hispanic Studies in Honour of Alan Deyermond, ed. Ian Macpherson and Ralph J. Penny, Woodbridge, Suffolk, Támesis, xxiv + 552 pp.

Deyermond Vol. (QMW): *Quien hubiese tal ventura: Medieval Hispanic Studies in Honour of Alan Deyermond*, ed. Andrew M. Beresford, London, Department of Hispanic Studies, Queen Mary and Westfield College, 400 pp.

Duby Vol.: Georges Duby, L'Écriture de l'histoire, ed. Claudie Duhamel-Amado and Guy Lobrichon (Bibliothèque du Moyen Age, 6), Brussels, de Boeck, 1996, 492 pp.

Dvorak, *Création: La Création biographique / Biographical Creation*, ed. Marta Dvorak, Rennes U.P., 315 pp.

Engler, *Exempla: Exempla. Studien zur Bedeutung und Funktion exemplarischen Erzählens*, ed. Bernd Engler and Kurt Müller, Berlin, Duncker & Humblot, 1995, 520 pp.

Erfen, *Fremdheit: Fremdheit und Reisen im Mittelalter*, ed. Irene Erfen and Karl-Heinz Spiess, Stuttgart, Steiner, vii + 319 pp.

Ekrem, *Reformation: Reformation and Latin Literature in Northern Europe*, ed. Inger Ekrem, Minna Skafte Jensen, and Egil Kraggerud, Oslo, Scandinavian U.P., 1996, xiv + 254 pp.

Faria, *Portuguese: Studies in the Acquisition of Portuguese*, ed. Isabel Hub Faria and Maria João Freitas, Lisbon, Associação Portuguesa de Linguística-Colibri, 1995, 214 pp.

Fest. Arndt: Wie redet der Deudsche man jnn solchem fall? Studien zur deutschen Sprachgeschichte. Festschrift anläßlich des 65. Geburtstages von Erwin Arndt, ed. Gisela Brandt and Rainer Hünecke (Stuttgarter Arbeiten zur Germanistik, 318), Stuttgart, Heinz, 1995, 181 pp.

Fest. Bergmann: Grammatica ianua artium. Festschrift für Rolf Bergmann zum 60. Geburtstag, ed. Elvira Glaser, Michael Schlaefer, and Ludwig Rübekeil, Heidelberg, Winter, xiv + 525 pp.

Fest. Figge: Semiotische Prozesse und naturliche Sprache. Festschrift für Udo L. Figge zum 60. Geburtstag, ed. Andreas Gather and Heinz Werner, Stuttgart, Franz Steiner, xviii + 600 pp.

Fest. Fisiak: Language History and Language Modelling. A Festschrift for Jacek Fisiak on his 60th Birthday. I: Language History, II: Linguistic Modelling, ed. Raymond Hickey and Stanislaw Puppel, Berlin, Mouton de Gruyter, 2 vols, xxxciii + 1138, xvi + 1139–2121 pp.

Fest. Härd: Kleine Beiträge zur Germanistik. Festschrift für John Evert Härd, ed. Bo Andersson and Gernot Müller (Acta Universitatis Upsaliensis. Studia Germanistica Upsaliensia, 37), Uppsala U.P., 314 pp.

Fest. Iwasaki: Sprache, Literatur und Kommunikation im kulturellen Wandel. Festschrift für Eijiro Iwasaki anläßlich seines 75. Geburtstags, ed. Tozo Hayakawa, Tokyo, Dogakusha, 611 pp.

Fest. Kontzi: Romanica Arabica. Festschrift für Reinhold Kontzi zum 70 Geburtstag, ed. Jens Lüdtke, Tübingen, Narr, 1996, 508 pp.

Fest. Laufhütte: Methodisch reflektiertes Interpretieren. Festschrift für Hartmut Laufhütte zum 60. Geburtstag, ed. Hans-Peter Ecker, Passau, Rothe, 444 pp.

Fest. Möhn: Varietäten der deutschen Sprache. Festschrift für Dieter Möhn, ed. Jörg Hennig and Jürgen Meier (Sprache in der Gesellschaft, 23), Frankfurt, Lang, 1996, 381 pp.

Fest. Pfister: Italica et Romanica: Festschrift für Max Pfister zum 65. Geburtstag, ed. Günter Holtus, Johannes Kramer, and Wolfgang Schweickard, 3 vols, Tübingen, Niemeyer, xl + 487, vi + 367, vi + 513 pp.

Fest. Schwob: Durch aubenteuer muess man wagen vil. Festschrift für Anton Schwob zum 60. Geburtstag, ed. Wernfried Hofmeister and Bernd Steinbauer (Innsbrucker Beiträge zur Kulturwissenschaft. Germanistische Reihe, 57), Univ. Innsbruck, Institut für Germanistik, xvi + 598 pp.

Fest. Steinsdorff: Schnittpunkt Romantik. Text- und Quellenstudien zur Literatur des 19. Jahrhunderts. Festschrift für Sibylle von Steinsdorff, ed. Wolfgang Bunzel, Konrad Feilchenfeldt, and Walter Schmitz, Tübingen, Niemeyer, viii + 354 pp.

Fest. Stillfried: Viribus Unitis. Österreichs Wissenschaft und Kultur im Ausland. Impulse und Wechselwirkungen. Festschrift für Bernhard Stillfried aus Anlaß seines 70. Geburtstags, ed. Ilona Slawinski and Joseph P. Strelka, Berne, Lang, 1996, 570 pp.

Fest. Strelka: Ein Leben für Dichtung und Freiheit: Festschrift zum 70. Geburtstag von Joseph P. Strelka, ed. K. F. Auckenthaler, H. H. Rudnick, and K. Wessenberger, Tübingen, Stauffenburg, xx + 685 pp.

Fest. Tarot: Wahrheit und Wort. Festschrift für Rolf Tarot zum 65. Geburtstag, ed. Gabriela Scherer and Beatrice Wehrli, Berne, Lang, 1996, 570 pp.

Fest. Vinge: I lärdomens trädgård. Festskrift till Louise Vinge, ed. Christina Sjöblad et al., Lund U.P., 1996, 540 pp.

Fest. Werner: Vergleichende germanische Philologie und Skandinavistik. Festschrift für Otmar Werner, ed. Thomas Birkmann, Heinz Klingenberg, Damaris Nübling, and Elke Ronneberger-Sibold, Tübingen, Niemeyer, viii + 310 pp.

Fest. Worstbrock: Mediävistische Komparatistik. Festschrift für Franz Josef Worstbrock zum 60. Geburtstag, ed. Wolfgang Harms, Jan-Dirk Müller, Susanne Köbele, and Bruno Quast, Stuttgart, Hirzel, 361 pp.

Fisher, *Difference: Dominique D. Fisher and Lawrence R. Schehr, Articulations of Difference. Gender Studies and Writing in French*, Stanford, California, Stanford U.P., xi + 294 pp.

Fisiak, *Dialectology: Medieval Dialectology*, ed. Jacek Fisiak (Trends in Linguistics, Studies and Monographs, 79), Berlin–New York, Mouton de Gruyter, 1995, viii + 331 pp.

Fossier Vol.: Campagnes Médiévales: l'homme et son espace. Études offertes à Robert Fossier, ed. Elisabeth Mornet (Histoire ancienne et médiévale, 31), Publications de la Sorbonne, 1995, 736 pp.

Fragonard, *Transfert: Transfert de thèmes, transfert de textes. Mythes, légendes et langues entre Catalogne et Languedoc*, ed. M. M. Fragonard and C. Martínez, Barcelona U.P., 189 pp.

Freidman, *Brave New Words: Brave New Words. Studies in Spanish Golden Age Literature*, ed. Edward H. Friedman and Catherine Larson, New Orleans, University Press of the South, 1996, xvii + 279 pp.

Glessgen, *Philologie: Alte und neue Philologie*, ed. Martin-Dietrich Glessgen and Franz Lebsanft (*Editio*, Beihefte, 8), Tübingen, Niemeyer, x + 384 pp.

Godinho, *Imagem: A imagem do mundo na Idade Média: Actas do Colóquio Internacional*, ed. Helder Godinho et al., Lisbon, ICALP, 1992, 305 pp.

Gontard, *Francophonie: Regards sur la francophonie*, ed. Marc Gontard and Maryse Bray, Rennes U.P., 322 pp.

Guida, *Uc de Saint Circ:* Saverio Guida, *Primi approcci a Uc de Saint Circ*, Catanzaro, Rubbettino, 1996, 245 pp.

Günsberg, *Gender:* Maggie Günsberg, *Gender and the Italian Stage: from the Renaissance to the Present Day*, CUP, xi + 275 pp.

Gwara, *Studies: Studies on the Spanish Sentimental Romance (1440–1550)*, ed. Joseph G. Gwara and E. Michael Gerli, London, Támesis, xx + 219 pp.

Haferland, *Erzählungen: Erzählungen in Erzählungen: Phänomene der Narration in Mittelalter und Früher Neuzeit*, ed. Harald Haferland and Michael Mecklenburg (Forschungen zur Geschichte der älteren deutschen Literatur, 19), Munich, Fink, 454 pp.

Hajek, *Nasalization: John Hajek, Universals of Sound Change in Nasalization* (Publications of the Philological Society, 31), Oxford–Boston, Blackwell, xvi + 254 pp.

Harms, *Wahrnehmen: Fremdes wahrnehmen - fremdes Wahrnehmen. Studien zur Geschichte der Wahrnehmung und zur Begegnung von Kulturen in Mittelalter und früher Neuzeit*, ed. Wolfgang Harms, C. Stephen Jaeger, and Alexandra Stein, Stuttgart–Leipzig, Hirzel, 280 pp.

Herrero Vol.: *Negotiating Past and Present. Studies in Spanish Literature for Javier Herrero*, ed. David Thatcher Gies, Charlottesville, Rookwood, 272 pp.

Holler Vol.: *Würzburger Fachprosa-Studien. Beiträge zur mittelalterlichen Medizin-, Pharmazie- und Standesgeschichte aus dem Würzburger medizinhistorischen Institut. Michael Holler zum 60. Geburtstag*, ed. Gundolf Keil (Würzburger medizinhistorische Forschungen, 38), Würzburg, Königshausen & Neumann, 1995, xi + 362 pp.

Holtus, *Lexikon, II/2: Lexikon der Romanistischen Linguistik (LRL). II.2. Die einzelnen romanischen Sprachen und Sprachgebiete vom Mittelalter bis zur Renaissance*, ed. Günter Holtus, Michael Metzeltin, and Christian Schmitt, Tübingen, Niemeyer, 1995, xlii + 753 pp.

Holzner, *Literatur: Literatur und Sprachkultur in Tirol*, ed. Johann Holzner, Oskar Putzer, and Max Siller (Innsbrucker Beiträge zur Kulturwissenschaft. Germanistische Reihe, 55), Univ. Innsbruck, Inst. für Germanistik, 566 pp.

Homenagem Stegagno Picchio: *Estudos Portugueses. Homenagem a Luciana Stegagno Picchio*, ed. Eugenio Asensio et al., Lisbon, Difel, 1991, lviii + 1132 pp.

Homenaje Fórneas Besteiro: *Homenaje a José María Fórneas Besteiro*, 2 vols, Granada U.P., 1995, 1281 pp.

Homenaje Rubio García I: *Homenaje al profesor Rubio García* I. (*Estudios Romanicos*, 4), Granada U.P., 675 pp.

Homenaxe Garcia: *Homenaxe ó professor Constantino Garcia*, ed. Mercedes Brea and Francisco Fernandez Rei, 2 vols, Santiago de Compostela U.P., 1991, 539, 628 pp.

Hommage Baril: *Morales du XVIe siècle: hommage à Denis Baril*, ed. J.-F. Louette (Recherches et Travaux, 50), Grenoble, Univ. Stendhal, 1996, 287 pp.

Hommage Brunet: *Hommage à Jacqueline Brunet*, ed. Marcella Diaz-Rozzotto (Annales Littéraires de l'Université de Franche-Comté), 2 vols, 588, 388 pp.

Ijsewijn Vol.: *Ut granum sinapis. Essays on Neo-Latin Literature in Honour of Jozef Ijsewijn* (Supplementa Humanistica Lovaniensia, 12), Leuven U.P., x + 362 pp.

Ingold, *Autor: Der Autor im Dialog. Beiträge zu Autorität und Autorschaft*, ed. Felix Philipp Ingold and Werner Wunderlich, St Gall, UVK, 1995, 210 pp.

Janowska, *Język: Język polski w kraju i za granicą*, ed. Barbara Janowska and Józef Porayski-Pomsta, 2 vols, Warsaw, Dom Wydawniczy ELIPSA, 246, 270 pp.

Jones, *Francophonie: Francophonie: Mythes, masques et réalités*, ed B. Jones, A. Miguet, and P. Corcoran, Paris, Publisud, 1996, 319 pp.

Kagay, *Iberia: Medieval Iberia. Essays on the History and Literature of Medieval Spain*, ed. Donald J. Kagay and Joseph T. Snow (Iberica, 25), New York, Lang, xx + 268 pp.

Kemenade, *Parameters: Parameters of Morphosyntactic Change*, ed. Ans van Kemenade and Nigel Vincent, CUP, xii + 544 pp.

Kornbichler, *Liebe: Variationen der Liebe. Historische Psychologie der Geschlechterbeziehung*, ed. Thomas Kornbichler and Wolfgang Maaz (Forum Psychohistorie, 4), Tübingen, Diskord, 1995, 367 pp.

La Chispa '95: *La Chispa '95. Selected Proceedings of the Sixteenth Louisiana Conference on Hispanic Languages and Literatures*, ed. Claire J. Paolini, New Orleans, Tulane U.P.

La Chispa '97: *La Chispa '97. Selected Proceedings of the Seventeenth Louisiana Conference on Hispanic Languages and Literatures*, ed. Claire J. Paolini, New Orleans, Tulane U.P., 488 pp.

Lavallée, *Brasil-Canadá: Laços de Cooperação Cultural Brasil-Canadá*, ed. Denise Maria Gurgel Lavallée, Bahia, ABECAN/UNEB, 1995, 190 pp.

Le Calvez, *Texte(s) et Intertexte(s): Texte(s) et Intertexte(s)*, ed. E. Le Calvez, S. Alyn-Stacey, and M. C. Canova-Green (Faux Titre,139), Amsterdam–Atlanta, Rodopi, 294 pp.

Leube Vol.: *Text und Tradition: Gedenkschrift Eberhard Leube*, ed. Klaus Ley, Ludwig Schrader, and Winfried Wehle, Frankfurt, Lang, 1996, 463 pp.

Levy, *Italian Regionalism: Italian Regionalism: History, Identity and Politics*, ed. Carl Levy, Oxford–Washington D.C., Berg, 1996.

Lippi-Green, *Linguistics: Germanic Linguistics: Synchronic and Diachronic*, ed. Rosina L. Lippi-Green and Joseph C. Salmons (Current Issues in Linguistic Theory, 137), Amsterdam–Philadelphia, Benjamins, 1996, viii + 192 pp.

Little, *Black Accents: Black Accents: Writing in French from Africa, Mauritius and the Caribbean*, ed. J. P. Little and Roger Little, London, Grant and Cutler, 286 pp.

Luti Vol.: I segni e la storia. Studi e testimonianze in onore di Giorgio Luti, Florence, Le Lettere, 1996, viii + 518 pp.

Maiden, *Dialects: The Dialects of Italy*, ed. Martin Maiden and Mair Parry, London, Routledge, xvii + 472 pp.

Mańczak Vol.: Munus amicitiae. Studia linguistica in honorem Witoldi Mańczak septuagenarii, ed. Anna Bochnakowa and Stanislau Widlak, Cracow, Uniwersytet Jagielloński, 1995, xxx + 224 pp.

Márquez-Villanueva, *Alfonso X: Alfonso X of Castile, the Learned King (1221–1284)*, ed. F. Márquez-Villanueva and C. A. Vega (Harvard Studies in Romance Languages, 43), Department of Romance Languages and Literatures of Harvard University, 1990, 165 pp.

Martin Vol.: Les formes du sens. Études de linguistique française médiévale et générale offertes à Robert Martin à l'occasion de ses 60 ans, ed. Georges Kleiber and Martin Riegel, Paris, Duculot, 446 pp.

Martínez-Gil, *Issues: Issues in the Phonology and Morphology of the Major Iberian Languages*, ed. Fernando Martínez-Gil and Alfonso Morales-Front, Washington D.C., Georgetown U.P., xiv + 694 pp.

Mélanges Cardaillac: Mélanges Louis Cardaillac, ed. Abdeljelil Temimi, 2 vols, Zaghouan, FTERSI, 1995, 816, 220 pp.

Mélanges Devos: Chemins d'histoire alpine: mélanges dédiés à la mémoire de Roger Devos, ed. M. Fol, C. Sorrel, and H. Viallet, Annecy, Association des Amis de Roger Devos, 510 pp.

Mélanges Iehl: Les songes de la raison: mélanges offerts à Dominique Iehl (Contacts, Sér. 3, Études et documents, 26), Toulouse, Université de Toulouse–le–Mirail, Centre de recherche sur l'Allemagne moderne — Berne–New York, Lang, 1995, 508 pp.

Mélanges Roux: Mélanges dédiées à la memoire du prof. Paul Roux, ed. P. Fabre, Toulon–La Farlède, AVEP, 1995, 383 pp.

Meumann, *Angst: Ein Schauplatz herber Angst. Wahrnehmung und Darstellung von Gewalt im 17. Jahrhundert*, ed. Markus Meumann and Dirk Niefanger, Göttingen, Wallstein, 272 pp.

Mildonian, *Parodia: Parodia, pastiche, mimetismo. Atti del Convegno Internazionale di Letterature Comparate, Venezia 13–15 Ottobre 1993*, ed. Paola Mildonian, Venice, Bulzoni, 1996, 458 pp.

Minogue Vol.: Narrative Voices in Modern French Fiction. Studies in Honour of Valerie Minogue on the Occasion of her Retirement, ed. Michael Cardy, George Evans and Gabriel Jacobs, Cardiff, University of Wales Press, xvi + 260 pp.

Miodunka, *Nauczanie: Nauczanie języka polskiego jako obcego*, ed. Władysław T. Miodunka, Krakow, Księgarnia Akademicka, 274 pp.

Nisbet, *Criticism: The Cambridge History of Literary Criticism*, IV. *The Eighteenth Century*, ed. H. B. Nisbet and Claude Rawson, Cambridge University Press, xviii + 951 pp.

Obermayer, *Österreich: 1000 Jahre Österreich im Spiegel seiner Literatur*, ed. August Obermayer, Dunedin, University of Otago Department of German, 234 pp.

O Cantar dos Trobadores: O Cantar dos Trobadores. Actas do Congreso celebrado en Santiago de Compostela entre os dias 26 e 29 de abril de 1993, Santiago de Compostela, Xunta de Galicia, 1993, 567 pp.

O Hehir Vol.: A Celtic Florilegium. Studies in Memory of Brendan O Hehir, ed. Kathryn A. Klar, Eve E. Sweetser, and Claire Thomas, Lawrence–Andover, Massachusetts, Celtic Studies Publications, 1996, xxxvi + 226 pp.

Oliva, *L'operosa stagione:* Gianni Oliva, *L'operosa stagione. Verga, D'Annunzio e altri studi di letteratura postunitaria*, Rome, Bulzoni, 409 pp.

Omaggio Federico II: Il Paese di Cortesia. Omaggio a Federico II nell'VIII centenario della nascita, ed. Ida Li Vigni, Paolo Aldo Rosso, and Stefano Zuffi, Genoa, Erga, 1995, 212 pp.

Papers (ICHL 11): *Historical Linguistics 1993. Selected Papers from the 11th International Conference on Historical Linguistics, Los Angeles, 16–20 August 1993*, ed. Henning Andersen (Current Issues in Linguistic Theory, 124), Amsterdam, Benjamins, 1995, x + 460 pp.

Papers (ICLS 5): *Courtly Literature - Culture and Context: Selected Papers from the 5th Triennial Congress of the International Courtly Literature Society, Dalfsen, the Netherlands, 9–16 August, 1986*, ed. K. Busby and E. Kooper, Amsterdam, Benjamins, 1990, 621 pp.

Papers (ICLS 7): *Literary Aspects of Courtly Culture: Selected Papers from the Seventh Triennial Congress of the International Courtly Literature Society, University of Massachusetts, Amherst, USA, 27 July–1 Aug. 1992*, ed. D. Maddox and S. Storm-Maddox, Cambridge, Brewer, 1994, 360 pp.

Papers (ICLS 8): *The Court and Cultural Diversity. Selected Papers from the Eighth Triennial Congress of the International Courtly Literature Society, The Queen's University of Belfast, 26 July–1 August 1995*, ed. Evelyn Mullally and John Thompson, Cambridge, Brewer, x + 426 pp.

Papers (LSRL 24): *Aspects of Romance Linguistics: Selected Papers from the Linguistic Symposium on Romance Languages XXIV, March 10–13, 1994*, ed. Claudia Parodi, Carlos Quicoli, Mario Saltarelli, and María Luisa Zubizarreta, Washington DC, Georgetown U.P., 1996, xiv + 530 pp.

Papers (LSRL 25): *Grammatical Theory and Romance Languages: Selected Papers from the 25th Linguistic Symposium on Romance Languages (LSRL XXV), Seattle, 2–4 March 1995*, ed. Karen Zagona (Current Issues in Linguistic Theory, 133), Amsterdam, Benjamins, 1996, vi + 330 pp.

Peers Vol.: Spain and its Literature. Essays in Memory of E. Allison Peers, ed. Ann L. Mackenzie, Liverpool U.P., 379 pp.

Peron, *Strategie: Strategie del testo. Preliminari, partizioni, pause. Atti del XVI e del XVII Convegno Interuniversitario (Bressanone, 1988 e 1989)*, ed. Gianfelice Peron, pref. Gianfranco Folena, Padua, Esedra, 1995.

Piel Vol: Homenagem a Joseph M. Piel por ocasião do seu 85° aniversario, ed. Dieter Kremer, Tübingen, Niemeyer, 1988, xiv + 798 pp.

Pinchard, *Fine Folie: Fine Folie ou la catastrophe humaniste: études sur les transcendantaux à la Renaissance*, ed. B. Pinchard (Le Savoir de Mantice, 1), Paris, Champion, 1995, 268 pp.

Pisanti, *L'un lito e l'altro:* Tommaso Pisanti, *L'un lito e l'altro. Circolazione dantesca e altri saggi*, Naples, I.iguori, 1995, vi + 197 pp..

Piva, *L'ombra: L'ombra, il doppio, il riflesso*, ed. Franco Piva et al., Verona, Università degli Studi, 125 pp.

Poirion Vol.: L'Hostellerie de pensée. Études sur l'art littéraire au Moyen Age offertes à Daniel Poirion par ses anciens élèves, comp. Michel Zink and Danielle Bohler, ed. Eric Hicks and Manuela Python (Cultures et Civilisations Médiévales, 12), Presses de l'Université de Paris-Sorbonne, 1996, 510 pp.

Poppe, *Mary of Egypt: The Legend of Mary of Egypt in Medieval Insular Hagiography*, ed. Erich Poppe and Bianca Ross, Blackrock, Co. Dublin–Portland, Oregon, Four Courts Press, 1996, vii + 299 pp.

Portela, *Jornadas: Jornadas de la emigración gallega a Puerto Rico*, ed. C. Portela, Sada, Castro, 249 pp.

Pratt, *Roland and Charlemagne: Roland and Charlemagne in Europe: Essays on the Reception and Transformation of a Legend*, ed. Karen Pratt (King's College London Medieval Studies), London, King's College London Centre for Late Antique and Medieval Studies, 1996, 218 pp. + pls.

Procs (BASS 10): *Proceedings of the Tenth Biennial Conference of the British Association of Scandinavian Studies held at the University of Surrey, Department of Linguistic and International Studies, 9–12 April 1995*, ed. Gunilla Anderman and Christine Banér, Surrey U.P., 1996, 242 pp.

Procs (Brasília): *Language and Literature Today. Proceedings of the XIXth Triennial Congress of the International Federation for Modern Languages and Literatures / Actes du XIXᵉ Congrès de la Fédération Internationale des Langues et Littératures Modernes. Brasília 22–30 August 1993*, ed. Neide de Faria. I. *Modernity and Postmodernity. Technologies and Translation in the 'Global Village'. The Canon and Canonicity: Global Perspectives.* II. *Languages and Literatures in the*

'Global Village'. Interdisciplinary Approaches to Language and Literature. III. *The Literatures of Latin America*, 3 vols, Universidade de Brasília, 1996, xxxvi + 1–502, xviii + 503–1014, xviii + 1015–1391 pp.

Procs (Harvard), 14: *Proceedings of the Harvard Celtic Colloquium (April 29–May 1, 1994)*, ed. P. Hopkins, L. Maney, and D. Wong, vol. 14, 1994[1997], ix + 218 pp.

Procs (Madison): *The Medieval 'Opus': Imitation, Rewriting and Transmission in the French Tradition. Proceedings of the Colloquium of the Institute for Research in the Humanities, 5–7 October 1995, The University of Wisconsin-Madison*, ed. Douglas Kelly (Faux Titre, 166), Amsterdam–Atlanta, Rodopi, 1996, xv + 427 pp.

Procs (MHRS 8): *Proceedings of the Eighth Colloquium*, ed. Andrew M. Beresford and Alan Deyermond (Papers of the Medieval Hispanic Research Seminar, 5), London, Department of Hispanic Studies, Queen Mary and Westfield College, 162 pp.

Renzi, *Linguistica: La linguistica italiana fuori d'Italia. Studi, Istituzioni*, ed. Lorenzo Renzi and Michele A. Cortelazzo (Società di Linguistica Italiana, 38), Rome, Bulzoni, 290 pp.

Reynolds-Cornell, *Marguerite de Navarre: International Colloquium celebrating the 500th Anniversary of the Birth of Marguerite de Navarre*, ed. R. Reynolds-Cornell, Alabama, Summa, 1995, 133 pp.

Ribeiro, *Género: O género do texto medieval*, ed. Cristina Almeida Ribeiro and Margarida Madureira (Medievalia, 12), Lisbon, Cosmos, 281 pp.

Rinne, *Antilles: Elles écrivent des Antilles (Haïti, Guadeloupe, Martinique)*, ed. Susanne Rinne and Joelle Vitiello, Paris, L'Harmattan, 397 pp.

Robinson, *Women*, I–IV: *Modern Women Writers*, comp. and ed. Lillian S. Robinson, 4 vols, New York, Continuum, 1996, xxxiii + 838, ix + 819, ix + 830, viii + 904 pp.

Rossi, *Jongleurs: Les jongleurs en spectacle*, ed. Luciano Rossi (Versants, 28), Paris, Champion—Geneva, Slatkine, 1995, 189 pp.

Rothwell Vol.: De Mot en Mot: Aspects of Medieval Linguistics. Essays in Honour of William Rothwell, ed. Stewart Gregory and D. A. Trotter, Cardiff, Univ. of Wales Press–MHRA, xxii + 282 pp.

Schena, *Lingua del diritto:* Leo Schena, *La Lingua del diritto. Difficoltà traduttive, applicazioni didattiche. Atti del primo Convegno Internazionale. Milano, 5–6 ottobre 1995, Centro Linguistico dell'Università Bocconi*, Rome, CISU, 285 pp.

Schmidt-Dengler, *Komik: Komik in der österreichischen Literatur*, ed. W. Schmidt-Dengler et al. (Philologische Studien und Quellen, 142), Berlin, Schmidt, 1996, 308 pp.

Schwob, *Edition: Quelle—Text—Édition. Ergebnisse der österreichisch-deutschen Fachtagung der Arbeitsgemeinschaft für germanistische Edition in Graz vom 28. Februar bis 3. März 1996*, ed. Anton Schwob, Erwin Streitfeld, and Karin Kranich-Hofbauer (Editio, Beiheft 9), Tübingen, Niemeyer, viii + 386 pp.

Siganos, *Solitudes: Solitudes. Écriture et représentation*, ed. André Siganos, Grenoble, ELLUG, Université Stendhal, 1995, 242 pp.

Simonin, *Rabelais: Rabelais pour le XXIᵉ siècle. Actes du colloque du Centre d'Études Supérieures de la Renaissance (Chinon-Tours, 1994)*, ed. M. Simonin (Etudes Rabelaisiennes, 33), Geneva, Droz, 443 pp.

Smet, *Eros et Priapus: Eros et Priapus: Érotisme et obscénité dans la littérature néo-latine*, ed. I. de Smet and P. Ford (Cahiers d'Humanisme et Renaissance, 51), Geneva, Droz, xviii + 188 pp.

Sørensen, *Geschichte*, I–II: Steffen Arndal, Helge Nielsen, Annelise Ballegaard Petersen, Reinhold Schröder, and Bengt Algot Sørensen, *Geschichte der deutschen Literatur*. I. *Vom Mittelalter bis zur Romantik*. II. *Vom 19. Jahrhundert bis zur Gegenwart*, ed. Bengt Algot Sørensen, 2 vols, Munich, Beck, 352, 448 pp.

Studi Giacomelli: Studi linguistici offerti a Gabriella Giacomelli dagli amici e dagli allievi, ed. Amalia Catagnoti, Padua, Unipress, 420 pp.

Studi Aguzzi: Studi filologici e letterari in memoria di Danilo Aguzzi-Barbagli, ed. Daniela Boccassini (*Forum italicum*, Supplement 13), Stony Brook, NY, Forum Italicum, viii + 229 pp.

Tarugi, *Petrarca: Petrarca e la cultura europea*, ed. Luisa Rotondi Secchi Tarugi, Milan, Nuovi Orizzonti, 374 pp.

Taylor Torsello, *Grammatica: Grammatica. Studi interlinguistici*, ed. Carol Taylor Torsello, Padua, Unipress.

Tetel, *Montaigne: Montaigne et Marie de Gournay: Actes du Colloque international de Duke, 31 mars–1er avril 1995*, ed. M. Tetel (Études Montaignistes, 30), Paris, Champion, 298 pp.

Timpanaro, *Nuovi studi:* S. Timpanaro, *Nuovi studi sul nostro Ottocento*, Pisa, Nistri Lischi, 1995, xix + 246 pp.

Toscano, *Estudios alfonsinos: Estudios alfonsinos y otros escritos. En homenaje a John Esten Keller y a Anibal A. Biglieri*, ed. Nicolas Toscano Liria, New York, NEH, 1991, 270 pp.

Tristram, *Celtic Englishes: The Celtic Englishes*, ed. Hildegard L. C. Tristram, Heidelberg, Universitätsverlag C. Winter, xii + 441 pp.

Ungar, *Identity: Identity Papers. Contested Nationhood in Twentieth-Century France*, ed. Steven Ungar and Tom Conley, Minneapolis–London, University of Minnesota Press, 1996, ix + 299 pp.

Unwin, *French Novel: The Cambridge Companion to the French Novel from 1800 to the Present*, ed. Timothy Unwin, CUP, xxiii + 281 pp.

Vázquez Vol.: Homenaxe á profesora Pilar Vázquez Cuesta, ed. Ramón Lorenzo and Rosario Álvarez, Santiago de Compostela U.P., 829 pp.

Viaut, *Langues d'Aquitaine: Langues d'Aquitaine. Dynamiques institutionnelles et patrimoine linguistique*, ed. Alain Viaut and Jean-Jacques Cheval, Bordeaux, Maison des Sciences de l'Homme d'Aquitaine, 1996, 312 pp.

Villari Vol.: Sguardi sull'Italia. Miscellanea dedicata a Francesco Villari dalla Society for Italian Studies, ed. Gino Bedani, Zygmunt Barański, Anna Laura Lepschy, and Brian Richardson (The Society for Italian Studies Occasional Papers, 3), Leeds, Maney, 259 pp.

Watanabe, *History: The Cambridge History of German Literature*, ed. Helen Watanabe-O'Kelly, CUP, xiv + 613 pp.

Wenzel, *Gespräche: Gespräche-Boten-Briefe. Körpergedächtnis und Schriftgedächtnis im Mittelalter*, ed. Horst Wenzel, Peter Göhler, Werner Röcke, Andreas Klare, and Haiko Wandhoff (Philologische Studien und Quellen, 143), Berlin, Schmidt, 374 pp.

Wilcox, *Women Poets:* John C. Wilcox, *Women Poets of Spain, 1860–1990. Towards a Gynocentric Vision*, Urbana-Chicago, Illinois U.P., xix + 366 pp.

Willis Vol.: Portuguese, Brazilian and African Studies. Studies Presented to Clive Willis on his Retirement, ed. T. F. Earle and Nigel Griffin, Warminster, Aris & Phillips, 1995, xii + 440 pp.

Wing, *Belief: Belief and Unbelief in Hispanic Literature. Papers from a Conference at the University of Hull, 12–13 December 1994*, ed. Helen Wing and John Jones, Warminster, Aris & Phillips, 1995, vi + 185 pp.

Winkler, *Heine: Heinrich Heine und die Romantik. Heinrich Heine and Romanticism. Erträge eines Symposiums an der Pennsylvania State University (21.–23. September 1995)*, Tübingen, Niemeyer, xiii + 232 pp.

II. GENERAL

abbrev.	abbreviation, abbreviated to
Acad., Akad.	Academy, Academia, etc.
acc.	accusative
ann.	annotated (by)
anon.	anonymous
appx	appendix
Arg.	Argentinian (and foreign equivalents)
Assoc.	Association (and foreign equivalents)
Auv.	Auvergnat
Bel.	Belarusian
BL	British Library
BM	British Museum
BN	Bibliothèque Nationale, Biblioteka Narodowa, etc.
BPtg.	Brazilian Portuguese
bull.	bulletin
c.	century
c.	circa
Cat.	Catalan
ch.	chapter
col.	column
comm.	commentary (by)
comp.	compiler, compiled (by)
Cz.	Czech
diss.	dissertation
ed.	edited (by), editor (and foreign equivalents)
edn	edition
EPtg.	European Portuguese
fac.	facsimile
fasc.	fascicle
Fest.	Festschrift, Festskrift
Fin.	Finnish
Fr.	France, French, Français
Gal.-Ptg.	Galician-Portuguese (and equivalents)
Gasc.	Gascon
Ger.	German(y)
Gk	Greek
Gmc	Germanic
IE	Indo-European
illus.	illustrated, illustration(s)
impr.	impression
incl.	including, include(s)
Inst.	Institute (and foreign equivalents)
introd.	introduction, introduced by, introductory
It.	Italian
izd.	издание
izd-vo	издательство
Jb.	Jahrbuch
Jg	Jahrgang
Jh.	Jahrhundert
Lang.	Languedocien
Lat.	Latin
Lim.	Limousin

lit.	literature
med.	medieval
MHG	Middle High German
Mid. Ir.	Middle Irish
Mil.	Milanese
MS	manuscript
n.d.	no date
n.F.	neue Folge
no.	number (and foreign equivalents)
nom.	nominative
n.pl.	no place of publication
n.s.	new series
O Auv.	Old Auvergnat
Occ.	Occitan
OE	Old English
OF	Old French
O Gasc.	Old Gascon
OHG	Old High German
O Ir.	Old Irish
O Lim.	Old Limousin
O Occ.	Old Occitan
O Pr.	Old Provençal
O Ptg.	Old Portuguese
org.	organized (by), organizer (and foreign equivalents)
OS	Old Saxon
OW	Old Welsh
part.	participle
ped.	педагогический, etc.
PIE	Proto-Indo-European
Pied.	Piedmontese
PGmc	Primitive Germanic
pl.	plate
plur.	plural
Pol.	Polish
p.p.	privately published
Pr.	Provençal
pref.	preface (by)
Procs	Proceedings
Ptg.	Portuguese
publ.	publication, published (by)
Ren.	Renaissance
repr.	reprint(ed)
Rev.	Review, Revista, Revue
rev.	revised (by)
Russ.	Russian
s.	siècle
ser.	series
sg.	singular
Slg	Sammlung
Soc.	Society (and foreign equivalents)
Sp.	Spanish
supp.	supplement
Sw.	Swedish
Trans.	Transactions

trans.	translated (by), translation
Ukr.	Ukrainian
Univ.	University (and foreign equivalents)
unpubl.	unpublished
U.P.	University Press (and foreign equivalents)
Vlg	Verlag
vol.	volume
vs	versus
W.	Welsh
wyd.	wydawnictwo

* before a publication signifies that it has not been seen by the contributor.

III. PLACE NAMES

B	Barcelona	Na	Naples
BA	Buenos Aires	NY	New York
Be	Belgrade	O	Oporto
Bo	Bologna	Pń	Poznań
C	Coimbra	R	Rio de Janeiro
F	Florence	Ro	Rome
Gd	Gdańsk	SPo	São Paulo
Kw	Kraków, Cracow	StP	St Petersburg
L	Lisbon	T	Turin
Ld	Leningrad	V	Valencia
M	Madrid	Wa	Warsaw
Mi	Milan	Ww	Wrocław
Mw	Moscow	Z	Zagreb

IV. PERIODICALS, INSTITUTIONS, PUBLISHERS

AA, Antike und Abendland

AAA, Ardis Publishers, Ann Arbor, Michigan

AAA, Archivio per l'Alto Adige

AAASS, American Association for the Advancement of Slavic Studies

AABC, Anuari de l'Agrupació Borrianenca de Cultura

AAC, Atti dell'Accademia Clementina

AAL, Atti dell'Accademia dei Lincei

AALP, L'Arvista dl'Academia dla Lenga Piemontèisa

AAM, Association des Amis de Maynard

AAPH, Anais da Academia Portuguesa da História

AAPN, Atti dell'Accademia Pontaniana di Napoli

AAPP, Atti Accademia Peloritana dei Pericolanti. Classe di Lettere Filosofia e Belle Arti

AARA, Atti della Accademia Roveretana degli Agiati

AASB, Atti dell'Accademia delle Scienze dell'Istituto di Bologna

AASF, Annales Academiae Scientiarum Fennicae

AASLAP, Atti dell'Accademia di Scienze, Lettere ed Arti di Palermo

AASLAU, Atti dell'Accademia di Scienze, Lettere e Arti di Udine

AASN, Atti dell'Accademia di Scienze Morali e Politiche di Napoli

AAST, Atti dell'Accademia delle Scienze di Torino

AAVM, Atti e Memorie dell'Accademia Virgiliana di Mantova

AAWG, Abhandlungen der Akademie der Wissenschaften in Göttingen, phil.-hist. Kl., 3rd ser., Göttingen, Vandenhoeck & Ruprecht

AB, Analecta Bollandiana

ABa, L'Année Balzacienne

ABÄG, Amsterdamer Beiträge zur älteren Germanistik

ABB, Archives et Bibliothèques de Belgique — Archief– en Bibliotheekswezen in België

ABDB, Aus dem Antiquariat. Beiträge zum Börsenblatt für den deutschen Buchhandel

ABDO, Association Bourguignonne de Dialectologie et d'Onomastique, Fontaine lès Dijon

ABHL, Annual Bulletin of Historical Literature

ABI, Accademie e Biblioteche d'Italia

ABN, Anais da Biblioteca Nacional, Rio de Janeiro

ABNG, Amsterdamer Beiträge zur neueren Germanistik, Amsterdam, Rodopi

ABor, Acta Borussica

ABP, Arquivo de Bibliografia Portuguesa

ABR, American Benedictine Review

ABr, Annales de Bretagne et des Pays de l'Ouest

ABS, Acta Baltico-Slavica

AC, Analecta Cisterciensa, Rome

ACCT, Agence de Coopération Culturelle et Technique

ACer, Anales Cervantinos, Madrid

ACIS, Association for Contemporary Iberian Studies

ACo, Acta Comeniana, Prague

AColl, Actes et Colloques

Acme, Annali della Facoltà di Filosofia e Lettere dell'Università Statale di Milano

ACP, L'Amitié Charles Péguy

ACUA, Anales del Colegio Universitario de Almería

AD, Analysen und Dokumente. Beiträge zur Neueren Literatur, Berne, Lang

ADEVA, Akademische Druck- und Verlagsanstalt, Graz

AE, Artemis Einführungen, Munich, Artemis

AE, L'Autre Europe

AEA, Anuario de Estudios Atlánticos, Las Palmas

AECI, Agencia Española de Cooperación Internacional

AEd, Arbeiten zur Editionswissenschaft, Frankfurt, Lang

AEF, Anuario de Estudios Filológicos, Cáceres

AEL, Anuario de la Escuela de Letras, Mérida, Venezuela

AELG, Anuario de Estudios Literarios Galegos

AEM, Anuario de Estudios Medievales

AF, Anuario de Filología, Barcelona

AFA, Archivo de Filología Aragonesa

AfAf, African Affairs

AfC, Afrique Contemporaine

AFe, L'Armana di Felibre

AFF, Anali Filološkog fakulteta, Belgrade

AFH, Archivum Franciscanum Historicum

AFHis, Anales de Filología Hispánica

AfHR, Afro-Hispanic Review

AfL, L'Afrique Littéraire

AFLE, Annali della Fondazione Luigi Einaudi

AFLFUB, Annali della Facoltà di Lettere e Filosofia dell'Università di Bari

AFLFUC, Annali della Facoltà di Lettere e Filosofia dell'Università di Cagliari

AFLFUG, Annali della Facoltà di Lettere e Filosofia dell'Università degli Studi di Genova

AFLFUM, Annali della Facoltà di Lettere e Filosofia dell'Università di Macerata

AFLFUN, Annali della Facoltà di Lettere e Filosofia dell'Università di Napoli

AFLFUP(SF), Annali dellà Facoltà di Lettere e Filosofia dell'Università di Perugia. 1. Studi Filosofici

AFLFUP(SLL), Annali della Facoltà di Lettere e Filosofia dell'Università di Perugia. 3. Studi Linguistici-Letterari

AFLFUS, Annali della Facoltà di Lettere e Filosofia dell'Università di Siena

AFLLS, Annali della Facoltà di Lingua e Letterature Straniere di Ca' Foscari, Venice

AFLN, Annales de la Faculté des Lettres et Sciences Humaines de Nice

AFP, Archivum Fratrum Praedicatorum

AFrP, Athlone French Poets, London, The Athlone Press

AG, Anales Galdosianos

AGB, Archiv für Geschichte des Buchwesens

AGF, Anuario Galego de Filoloxía

AGI, Archivio Glottologico Italiano

AGJSG, Acta Germanica. Jahrbuch des Südafrikanischen Germanistenverbandes

AGP, Archiv für Geschichte der Philosophie

AH, Archivo Hispalense

AHAW, Abhandlungen der Heidelberger Akademie der Wissenschaften, phil-hist. Kl

AHCP, Arquivos de História de Cultura Portuguesa

AHDLMA, Archives d'Histoire Doctrinale et Littéraire du Moyen Âge

AHF, Archiwum Historii Filozofii i Myśli Społecznej

AHP, Archivum Historiae Pontificae

AHPr, Annales de Haute-Provence, Digne-les-Bains

AHR, American Historical Review

AHRF, Annales Historiques de la Révolution Française

AHRou, Archives historiques du Rouergue

AHSJ, Archivum Historicum Societatis Jesu

AHSS, Annales: Histoire — Sciences Sociales

AI, Almanacco Italiano

AIB, Annali dell'Istituto Banfi

AIBL, Académie des Inscriptions et Belles-Lettres, Comptes Rendus

AIEM, Anales del Instituto de Estudios Madrileños

AIEO, Association Internationale d'Études Occitanes

AIFMUR, Annali dell'Istituto di Filologia Moderna dell'Università di Roma

AIFUF, Annali dell'Istituto di Filosofia dell'Università di Firenze

AIHI, Archives Internationales d'Histoire des Idées, The Hague, Nijhoff

AIHS, Archives Internationales d'Histoire des Sciences

AIL, Associação Internacional de Lusitanistas

AILLC, Associació Internacional de Llengua i Literatura Catalanes

AISIGT, Annali dell'Istituto Storico Italo-Germanico di Trento

AION(FG), Annali dell'Istituto Universitario Orientale, Naples: Sezione Germanica. Filologia Germanica

AION(SF), Annali dell'Istituto Universitario Orientale, Naples: Studi Filosofici

AION(SL), Annali dell'Istituto Universitario Orientale, Naples: Sezione Linguistica

AION(SR), Annali dell'Istituto Universitario Orientale, Naples: Sezione Romanza

AION(SS), Annali dell'Istituto Universitario Orientale, Naples: Sezione Slava

AION(ST), Annali dell'Istituto Universitario Orientale, Naples: Sezione Germanica. Studi Tedeschi

AIPHS, Annuaire de l'Institut de Philologie et de l'Histoire Orientales et Slaves

AIPS, Annales Instituti Philologiae Slavica Universitatis Debreceniensis de Ludovico Kossuth Nominatae — Slavica

AIISS, Annali dell'Istituto Italiano per gli Studi Storici

AITCA, Arxiu informatizat de textos catalans antics

AIV, Atti dell'Istituto Veneto

AJ, Alemannisches Jahrbuch

AJCAI, Actas de las Jornadas de Cultura Arabe e Islámica

AJFS, Australian Journal of French Studies

AJGLL, American Journal of Germanic Linguistics and Literatures

AJL, Australian Journal of Linguistics

AJP, American Journal of Philology

AKG, Archiv für Kulturgeschichte

AKML, Abhandlungen zur Kunst-, Musik- und Literaturwissenschaft, Bonn, Bouvier

AL, Anuario de Letras, Mexico

AlAm, Alba de América

ALB, Annales de la Faculté des Lettres de Besançon

ALC, African Languages and Cultures

ALE, Anales de Literatura Española, Alicante

ALEC, Anales de Literatura Española Contemporánea

ALet, Armas y Letras, Universidad de Nuevo León

ALEUA, Anales de Literatura Española de la Universidad de Alicante

ALFL, Actes de Langue Française et de Linguistique

ALH, Acta Linguistica Hungaricae

ALHA, Anales de la Literatura Hispanoamericana

ALHa, Acta Linguistica Hafniensia

ALHisp, Anuario de Lingüística Hispánica

ALHist, Annales: Littérature et Histoire

ALit, Acta Literaria, Chile

ALitH, Acta Litteraria Hungarica

ALLI, Atlante Linguistico dei Laghi Italiani

ALM, Archives des Lettres Modernes

ALMA, Archivum Latinitatis Medii Aevi (Bulletin du Cange)

ALo, Armanac de Louzero

ALP, Atlas linguistique et ethnographique de Provence, CNRS, 1975–86

AlS, Almanac Setòri

ALT, African Literature Today

ALUB, Annales Littéraires de l'Université de Besançon

AM, Analecta Musicologica

AMAA, Atti e Memorie dell'Accademia d'Arcadia

AMAASLV, Atti e Memorie dell'Accademia di Agricultura, Scienze e Lettere di Verona

AMal, Analecta Malacitana

AMAP, Atti e Memorie dell'Accademia Patavina di Scienze, Lettere ed Arti

AMAPet, Atti e Memorie dell'Accademia Petrarca di Lettere, Arti e Scienze, Arezzo

AMAT, Atti e Memorie dell'Accademia Toscana di Scienze e Lettere, La Colombaria

AMDLS, Arbeiten zur Mittleren Deutschen Literatur und Sprache, Berne, Lang

AMDSPAPM, Atti e Memorie della Deputazione di Storia Patria per le Antiche Province Modenesi

AMGG, Abhandlungen der Marburger Gelehrten Gesellschaft, Munich, Fink

AmH, American Hispanist

AMid, Annales du Midi

AML, Main Monographien Literaturwissenschaft, Frankfurt, Main

AmIn, América Indígena, Mexico

AMSSSP, Atti e Memorie della Società Savonese di Storia Patria

AN, Академия наук

AN, Americana Norvegica

ANABA, Asociación Nacional de Bibliotecarios, Arquiveros y Arqueólogos

AnAlf, Annali Alfieriani

AnEA, Anaquel de Estudios Arabes

ANeo, Acta Neophilologica, Ljubljana

ANF, Arkiv för nordisk filologi

AnI, Annali d'Italianistica

AnL, Anthropological Linguistics

AnM, Anuario Medieval

AnN, Annales de Normandie

AnnM, Annuale Medievale

ANQ, American Notes and Queries

ANTS, Anglo-Norman Text Society

AnVi, Antologia Vieusseux

ANZSGLL, Australian and New Zealand Studies in German Language and Literature, Berne, Lang

AO, Almanac occitan, Foix

AÖAW, Anzeiger der Österreichischen Akademie der Wissenschaften

AP, Aurea Parma

APIFN, Актуальные проблемы истории философии народов СССР.

APK, Aufsätze zur portugiesischen Kulturgeschichte, Görres-Gesellschaft, Münster

ApL, Applied Linguistics

APL, Associação Portuguesa de Linguística

APPP, Abhandlungen zur Philosophie, Psychologie und Pädagogik, Bonn, Bouvier

APr, Analecta Praemonstratensia

AProu, Armana Prouvençau, Marseilles

APS, Acta Philologica Scandinavica

APSL, Amsterdamer Publikationen zur Sprache und Literatur, Amsterdam, Rodopi

APUCF, Association des Publications de la Faculté des Lettres et Sciences Humaines de l'Université de Clermont-Ferrand II, Nouvelle Série

AQ, Arizona Quarterly

AqAq, Aquò d'aquí, Gap

AR, Archiv für Reformationsgeschichte

ARAJ, American Romanian Academy Journal

ARAL, Australian Review of Applied Linguistics

ARCA, ARCA: Papers of the Liverpool Latin Seminar

ArCCP, Arquivos do Centro Cultural Português, Paris

ArEM, Aragón en la Edad Media

ArFil, Archivio di Filosofia

ArI, Arthurian Interpretations

ARI, Архив русской истории

ARL, Athlone Renaissance Library

ArL, Archivum Linguisticum

ArLit, Arthurian Literature

ArP, Археографски прилози

ArSP, Archivio Storico Pugliese

ArSPr, Archivio Storico Pratese

ArSt, Archivi per la Storia

ART, Atelier Reproduction des Thèses, Univ. de Lille III, Paris, Champion

AS, The American Scholar

ASAvS, Annuaire de la Société des Amis du vieux-Strasbourg

ASB, Archivio Storico Bergamasco

ASCALF, Association for the Study of Caribbean and African Literature in French

ASCALFB, ASCALF Bulletin

ASCALFY, ASCALF Yearbook

ASE, Annali di Storia dell'Esegesi

ASEES, Australian Slavonic and East European Studies

ASELGC, 1616. Anuario de la Sociedad Española de Literatura General y Comparada

ASGM, Atti del Sodalizio Glottologico Milanese

ASI, Archivio Storico Italiano

ASJ, Acta Slavonica Japonica

ASL, Archivio Storico Lombardo

ASMC, Annali di Storia Moderna e Contemporanea

ASNP, Annali della Scuola Normale Superiore di Pisa, Bologna

ASNS, Archiv für das Studium der Neueren Sprachen und Literaturen

ASocRous, Annales de la Société J.-J. Rousseau

ASolP, A Sol Post, Editorial Marfil, Alcoi

ASP, Anzeiger für slavische Philologie

AsP, L'Astrado prouvençalo. Revisto Bilengo de Prouvenço/Revue Bilingue de Provence, Berre L'Étang.

ASPN, Archivio Storico per le Province Napoletane

ASPP, Archivio Storico per le Province Parmensi

ASR, Annalas de la Società Retorumantscha

ASRSP, Archivio della Società Romana di Storia Patria

ASSO, Archivio Storico per la Sicilia Orientale

ASSUL, Annali del Dipartimento di Scienze Storiche e Sociali dell'Università di Lecce

AST, Analecta Sacra Tarraconensia

ASt, Austrian Studies

ASTic, Archivio Storico Ticinese

AŞUI, (e), (f), Analele Ştiinţifice ale Universităţii 'Al. I. Cuza' din Iaşi, secţ. e, Lingvistică, secţ. f, Literatură

AT, Athenäums Taschenbücher, Frankfurt, Athenäum

ATB, Altdeutsche Textbibliothek, Tübingen, Niemeyer

ATCA, Arxiu de Textos Catalans Antics, IEC, Barcelona

Ate, Nueva Atenea, Universidad de Concepción, Chile

ATO, A Trabe de Ouro

ATS, Arbeiten und Texte zur Slavistik, Munich, Sagner

ATV, Aufbau Taschenbuch Verlag, Berlin, Aufbau

AtV, Ateneo Veneto

AUBLLR, Analele Universităţii Bucureşti, Limba şi literatura română

AUBLLS, Analele Universităţii Bucureşti, Limbi şi literaturi străine

AUC, Anales de la Universidad de Cuenca

AUCP, Acta Universitatis Carolinae Pragensis

AUL, Acta Universitatis Lodziensis

AUL, Annali della Facoltà di Lettere e Filosofia dell'Università di Lecce

AUMCS, Annales Uniwersytetu Marii Curie-Skłodowskiej, Lublin

AUML, Anales de la Universidad de Murcia: Letras

AUMLA, Journal of the Australasian Universities Modern Language Association

AUN, Annali della Facoltà di Lettere e Filosofia dell'Università di Napoli

AUNCFP, Acta Universitatis Nicolai Copernici. Filologia Polska, Toruń

AUPO, Acta Universitatis Palackianae Olomucensis

AUS, American University Studies, Berne–New York, Lang

AUSP, Annali dell'Università per Stranieri di Perugia

AUSSR, Acta Universitatis Stockholmiensis. Stockholm Studies in Russian Literature

AUSSS, Acta Universitatis Stockholmiensis. Stockholm Slavic Studies

AUTŞF, Analele Universităţii din Timişoara, Ştiinţe Filologice

AUUSRU, Acta Universitatis Upsaliensis. Studia Romanica Upsaliensia

AUUUSH, Acta Universitatis Umensis, Umeå Studies in the Humanities, Umeå U.P.

AUW, Acta Universitatis Wratislaviensis

AVen, Archivio Veneto

AVEP, Assouciacien vareso pèr l'ensignamen dòu prouvençou, La Farlède

AVEPB, Bulletin AVEP, La Farlède

AvT, L'Avant-Scène Théâtre

AWR, Anglo-Welsh Review

BA, Bollettino d'Arte

BAAA, Bulletin de l'Association des Amis d'Alain

BAAG, Bulletin des Amis d'André Gide

BAAJG, Bulletin de l'Association des Amis de Jean Giono

BAAL, Boletín de la Academia Argentina de Letras

BaB, Bargfelder Bote

BAC, Biblioteca de Autores Cristianos

BACol, Boletín de la Academia Colombiana

BÄDL, Beiträge zur Älteren Deutschen Literaturgeschichte, Berne, Lang

BADLit, Bonner Arbeiten zur deutschen Literatur, Bonn, Bouvier

BAE, Biblioteca de Autores Españoles

BAEO, Boletín de la Asociación Española de Orientalistas

BAFJ, Bulletin de l'Association Francis Jammes

BAG, Boletín de la Academia Gallega

BAIEO, Bulletins de l'Association Internationale d'Études Occitanes

BAJR, Bulletin des Amis de Jules Romains

BAJRAF, Bulletin des Amis de Jacques Rivière et d'Alain-Fournier

BALI, Bollettino dell'Atlante Linguistico Italiano

BALM, Bollettino dell'Atlante Linguistico Mediterraneo

BalS, Balkan Studies, Institute for Balkan Studies, Thessaloniki

BAN, Българска Академия на Науките, София

BAO, Biblioteca Abat Oliva, Publicacions de l'Abadia de Montserrat, Barcelona

BAPC, Bulletin de l'Association Paul Claudel

BAPRLE, Boletín de la Academia Puertorrigueña de la Lengua Española

BAR, Biblioteca dell'Archivum Romanicum

BARLLF, Bulletin de l'Académie Royale de Langues et de Littératures Françaises de Bruxelles

BAWA, Bayerische Akademie der Wissenschaften. Phil.-hist. Kl. Abhandlungen, n.F.

BB, Biblioteca Breve, Lisbon

BB, Bulletin of Bibliography

BBAHLM, Boletín Bibliografico de la Asociación Hispánica de Literatura Medieval

BBB, Berner Beiträge zur Barockgermanistik, Berne, Lang

BBGN, Brünner Beiträge zur Germanistik und Nordistik

BBib, Bulletin du Bibliophile

BBL, Bayreuther Beiträge zur Literaturwissenschaft, Frankfurt, Lang

BBLI, Bremer Beiträge zur Literatur- und Ideengeschichte, Frankfurt, Lang

BBMP, Boletín de la Biblioteca de Menéndez Pelayo

BBN, Bibliotheca Bibliographica Neerlandica, Nieuwkoop, De Graaf

BBNDL, Berliner Beiträge zur neueren deutschen Literaturgeschichte, Berne, Lang

BBSANZ, Bulletin of the Bibliographical Society of Australia and New Zealand

BBSIA, Bulletin Bibliographique de la Société Internationale Arthurienne

BBSMES, Bulletin of the British Society for Middle Eastern Studies

BBUC, Boletim da Biblioteca da Universidade de Coimbra

BC, Bulletin of the 'Comediantes', University of Wisconsin

BCB, Boletín Cultural y Bibliográfico, Bogatá

BCEC, Bwletin Cymdeithas Emynwyr Cymru

BCél, Bulletin Célinien

BCh, Болдинские чтения

BCLSMP, Académie Royale de Belgique: Bulletin de la Classe des Lettres et des Sciences Morales et Politiques

BCMV, Bollettino Civici Musei Veneziani

BCRLT, Bulletin du Centre de Romanistique et de Latinité Tardive

BCS, Bulletin of Canadian Studies

BCSM, Bulletin of the Cantigueiros de Santa Maria

BCSS, Bollettino del Centro di Studi Filologici e Linguistici Siciliani

BCSV, Bollettino del Centro di Studi Vichiani

BCZG, Blätter der Carl Zuckmayer Gesellschaft

BD, Беларуская думка

BDADA, Bulletin de documentation des Archives départementales de l'Aveyron, Rodez

BDB, Börsenblatt für den deutschen Buchhandel

BDBA, Bien Dire et Bien Aprandre

BDP, Beiträge zur Deutschen Philologie, Giessen, Schmitz

BEA, Bulletin des Études Africaines

BEC, Bibliothèque de l'École des Chartes

BelE, Беларуская энцыклапедыя

BelL, Беларуская лінгвістыка

BelS, Беларускі сьвет

BEP, Bulletin des Études Portugaises

BEPar, Bulletin des Études Parnassiennes et Symbolistes

BEzLit, Български език и литература

BF, Boletim de Filologia

BFA, Bulletin of Francophone Africa

BFC, Boletín de Filología, Univ. de Chile

BFE, Boletín de Filología Española

BFF, Bulletin Francophone de Finlande

BFFGL, Boletín de la Fundación Federico García Lorca

BFi, Bollettino Filosofico

BFLS, Bulletin de la Faculté des Lettres de Strasbourg

BFo, Biuletyn Fonograficzny

BFPLUL, Bibliothèque de la Faculté de Philosophie et Lettres de l'Université de Liège

BFR, Bibliothèque Française et Romane, Paris, Klincksieck

BFR, Bulletin of the Fondation C.F. Ramuz

BFr, Börsenblatt Frankfurt

BG, Bibliotheca Germanica, Tübingen, Francke

BGB, Bulletin de l'Association Guillaume Budé

BGDSL, Beiträge zur Geschichte der deutschen Sprache und Literatur, Tübingen

BGKT, Беларускае грамадска-культуральнае таварыства

BGL, Boletin Galego de Literatura

BGLKAJ, Beiträge zur Geschichte der Literatur und Kunst des 18. Jahrhunderts, Heidelberg, Winter

BGP, Bristol German Publications, Bristol U.P

BGREC, Bulletin du Groupe de Recherches et d'Études du Clermontais, Clermont-l'Hérault

BGS, Beiträge zur Geschichte der Sprachwissenschaft

BGS, Beiträge zur germanistischen Sprachwissenschaft, Hamburg, Buske

BGT, Blackwell German Texts, Oxford, Blackwell

BH, Bulletin Hispanique

BHR, Bibliothèque d'Humanisme et Renaissance

BHS(G), Bulletin of Hispanic Studies (Glasgow)

BHS(L), Bulletin of Hispanic Studies (Liverpool)

BI, Bibliographisches Institut, Leipzig

BibAN, Библиотека Академии наук СССР

BIDS, Bulletin of the International Dostoevsky Society, Klagenfurt

BIEA, Boletín del Instituto de Estudios Asturianos

BIHBR, Bulletin de l'Institut Historique Belge de Rome

BIHR, Bulletin of the Institute of Historical Research

BJA, British Journal of Aesthetics

BJCS, British Journal for Canadian Studies

BJECS, The British Journal for Eighteenth-Century Studies

BJHP, British Journal of the History of Philosophy

BJHS, British Journal of the History of Science

BJL, Belgian Journal of Linguistics

BJR, Bulletin of the John Rylands University Library of Manchester

BKF, Beiträge zur Kleist-Forschung

BL, Brain and Language

BLAR, Bulletin of Latin American Research

BLBI, Bulletin des Leo Baeck Instituts

BLe, Börsenblatt Leipzig

BLFCUP, Bibliothèque de Littérature Française Contemporaine de l'Université Paris 7

BLI, Beiträge zur Linguistik und Informationsverarbeitung

BLi, Беларуская літаратура. Міжвузаўскі зборнік.

BLJ, British Library Journal

BLL, Beiträge zur Literatur und Literaturwissenschaft des 20. Jahrhunderts, Berne, Lang
BLM, Bonniers Litterära Magasin
BLR, Bibliothèque Littéraire de la Renaissance, Geneva, Slatkine — Paris, Champion
BLR, Bodleian Library Record
BLVS, Bibliothek des Literarischen Vereins, Stuttgart, Hiersemann
BM, Bibliothek Metzier, Stuttgart
BMBP, Bollettino del Museo Bodoniano di Parma
BMCP, Bollettino del Museo Civico di Padova
BML, Беларуская мова i літаратура ў школе
BMo, Беларуская мова. Міжвузаўкі зборнік
BNE, Beiträge zur neueren Epochenforschung, Berne, Lang
BNF, Beiträge zur Namenforschung
BNL, Beiträge zur neueren Literaturgeschichte, 3rd ser., Heidelberg, Winter
BNP, Beiträge zur nordischen Philologie, Basel, Helbing & Lichtenhahn
BO, Biblioteca Orientalis
BOCES, Boletín del Centro de Estudios del Siglo XVIII, Oviedo
BOP, Bradford Occasional Papers
ВР, Български писател
BP, Lo Bornat dau Perigòrd
BPTJ, Biuletyn Polskiego Towarzystwa Językoznawczego
BR, Болгарская русистика.
BRA, Bonner Romanistische Arbeiten, Berne, Lang
BRABLB, Boletín de la Real Academia de Buenas Letras de Barcelona
BRAC, Boletín de la Real Academia de Córdoba de Ciencias, Bellas Letras, y Nobles Artes
BRAE, Boletín de la Real Academia Española
BRAH, Boletín de la Real Academia de la Historia
BrC, Bruniana & Campanelliana
BRIES, Bibliothèque Russe de l'Institut d'Études Slaves, Paris, Institut d'Études Slaves

BRJL, Bulletin ruského jazyka a literatury
BrL La Bretagne Linguistique
BRP, Beiträge zur romanischen Philologie
BS, Biuletyn slawistyczny, Łódź
BSAHH, Bulletin de la Société Archéologique et Historique des Hauts Cantons de l'Hérault, Bédarieux
BSAHL, Bulletin de la Société Archéologique et Historique du Limousin, Limoges
BSAHLSG, Bulletin de la Société Archéologique, Historique, Littéraire et Scientifique du Gers
BSAM, Bulletin de la Société des Amis de Montaigne
BSAMPAC, Bulletin de la Société des Amis de Marcel Proust et des Amis de Combray
BSASLB, Bulletin de la Société Archéologique, Scientifique et Littéraire de Béziers
BSATG, Bulletin de la Société Archéologique de Tarn-et-Garonne
BSBS, Bollettino Storico-Bibliografico Subalpino
BSCC, Boletín de la Sociedad Castellonense de Cultura
BSD, Bithell Series of Dissertations — MHRA Texts and Dissertations, London, Modern Humanities Research Association
BSD, Bulletin de la Société de Borda, Dax
BSDL, Bochumer Schriften zur deutschen Literatur, Berne, Lang
BSDSL, Basler Studien zur deutschen Sprache und Literatur, Tübingen, Francke
BSE, Галоўная рэдакцыя Беларускай савеюкай энцыклапедыі
BSEHA, Bulletin de la Société d'Études des Hautes-Alpes, Gap
BSEHTD, Bulletin de la Société d'Études Historiques du Texte Dialectal
BSELSAL, Bulletin de la Société des Études Littéraires, Scientifiques et Artistiques du Lot

BSF, Bollettino di Storia della Filosofia

BSG, Berliner Studien zur Germanistik, Frankfurt, Lang

BSHAP, Bulletin de la Société Historique et Archéologique du Périgord, Périgueux

BSHPF, Bulletin de la Société de l'Histoire du Protestantisme Français

BSIH, Brill's Studies in Intellectual History, Leiden, Brill

BSIS, Bulletin of the Society for Italian Studies

BSLLW, Bulletin de la Société de Langue et Littérature Wallonnes

BSLP, Bulletin de la Société de Linguistique de Paris

BSLV, Bollettino della Società Letteraria di Verona

BSM, Birmingham Slavonic Monographs, University of Birmingham

BSOAS, Bulletin of the School of Oriental and African Studies

BSP, Bollettino Storico Pisano

BSPC, Bulletin de la Société Paul Claudel

BSPia, Bollettino Storico Piacentino

BSPN, Bollettino Storico per le Province di Novara

BSPSP, Bollettino della Società Pavese di Storia Patria

BsR, Beck'sche Reihe, Munich, Beck

BSRS, Bulletin of the Society for Renaissance Studies

BSSAAPC, Bollettino della Società per gli Studi Storici, Archeologici ed Artistici della Provincia di Cuneo

BSSCLE, Bulletin of the Society for the Study of the Crusades and the Latin East

BSSP, Bullettino Senese di Storia Patria

BSSPin, Bollettino della Società Storica Pinerolese, Pinerolo, Piedmont.

BSSPHS, Bulletin of the Society for Spanish and Portuguese Historical Studies

BSSV, Bollettino della Società Storica Valtellinese

BSZJPS, Bałtosłowiańskie związki językowe. Prace Slawistyczne

BT, Богословские труды, Moscow

BTe, Biblioteca Teatrale

BTH, Boletim de Trabalhos Historicos

BulEz, Български език

BW, Bibliothek und Wissenschaft

BySt, Byzantine Studies

CA, Cuadernos Americanos

CAAM, Cahiers de l'Association Les Amis de Milosz

CAB, Commentari dell'Ateneo di Brescia

CAC, Les Cahiers de l'Abbaye de Créteil

CadL, Cadernos da Lingua

CAG, Cahiers André Gide

CAIEF, Cahiers de l'Association Internationale des Études Françaises

CalLet, Calabria Letteraria

CAm, Casa de las Américas, Havana

CAm, Casa de las Américas, Havana

CanJL, Canadian Journal of Linguistics

CanL, Canadian Literature

CanSP, Canadian Slavonic Papers

CanSS, Canadian-American Slavic Studies

CARB, Cahiers des Amis de Robert Brasillach

CarQ, Caribbean Quarterly

CAT, Cahiers d'Analyse Textuelle, Liège, Les Belles Lettres

CatR, Catalan Review

CAVL, Cahiers des Amis de Valery Larbaud

CB, Cuadernos Bibliográficos

CC, Comparative Criticism

CCe, Cahiers du Cerf XX

CCend, Continent Cendrars

CCF, Cuadernos de la Cátedra Feijoo

CCMe, Cahiers de Civilisation Médiévale

CCol, Cahiers Colette

CCU, Cuadernos de la Cátedra M. de Unamuno

CD, Cuadernos para el Diálogo

CdA, Camp de l'Arpa

CDA, Christliche deutsche Autoren des 20. Jahrhunderts, Berne, Lang
CDB, Coleção Documentos Brasileiros
CDr, Comparative Drama
ČDS, Čeština doma a ve světě
CDs, Cahiers du Dix-septième, Athens, Georgia
CDU, Centre de Documentation Universitaire
CduC, Cahiers de CERES. Série littéraire, Tunis
CE, Cahiers Élisabéthains
CEA, Cahiers d'Études Africaines
CEAL, Centro Editor de América Latina
CEC, Cahiers d'Études Cathares, Narbonne
CEC, Conselho Estadual de Cultura, Comissão de Literatura, São Paulo
CECAES, Centre d'Études des Cultures d'Aquitaine et d'Europe du Sud, Université de Bordeaux III
CEcr, Corps Écrit
CEDAM, Casa Editrice Dott. A. Milani
CEG, Cuadernos de Estudios Gallegos
CEL, Cadernos de Estudos Lingüísticos, Campinas, Brazil
CELO, Centre d'Etude de la Littérature Occitane, Bordes.
CEM, Cahiers d'Études Médiévales, Univ. of Montreal
CEMa, Cahiers d'Études Maghrebines, Cologne
CEMed, Cuadernos de Estudios Medievales
CEPL, Centre d'Étude et de Promotion de la Lecture, Paris
CEPON, Centre per l'estudi e la promocion de l'Occitan normat.
CEPONB, CEPON Bulletin d'échange.
CER, Cahiers d'Études Romanes
CERCLiD, Cahiers d'Études Romanes, Centre de Linguistique et de Dialectologie, Toulouse
CERoum, Cahiers d'Études Roumaines
CeS, Cultura e Scuola

CESCM, Centre d'Études Supérieures de Civilisation Médiévale, Poitiers
CET, Centro Editoriale Toscano
CEtGer, Cahiers d'Études Germaniques
CF, Les Cahiers de Fontenay
CFC, Contemporary French Civilization
CFI, Cuadernos de Filologia Italiana
CFLA, Cuadernos de Filología. Literaturas: Análisis, Valencia
CFM, Cahiers François Mauriac
CFMA, Collection des Classiques Français du Moyen Age
CFol, Classical Folia
CFS, Cahiers Ferdinand de Saussure
CFSLH, Cuadernos de Filología: Studia Linguistica Hispanica
CFTM, Classiques Français des Temps Modernes, Paris, Champion
CG, Cahiers de Grammaire
CGD, Cahiers Georges Duhamel
CGFT, Critical Guides to French Texts, London, Grant & Cutler
CGGT, Critical Guides to German Texts, London, Grant & Cutler
CGP, Carleton Germanic Papers
CGS, Colloquia Germanica Stetinensia
CGST, Critical Guides to Spanish Texts, London, Támesis–Grant & Cutler
CH, Crítica Hispánica
CHA, Cuadernos Hispano-Americanos
CHAC, Cuadernos Hispano-Americanos. Los complementarios
CHB, Cahiers Henri Bosco
ChC, Chemins Critiques
ChR, The Chesterton Review
ChRev, Chaucer Review
ChrA, Chroniques Allemandes
ChrI, Chroniques Italiennes
ChrL, Christianity and Literature
ChrN, Chronica Nova
ChS, Champs du Signe
CHum, Computers and the Humanities
CHLR, Cahiers d'Histoire des Littératures Romanes

CHP, Cahiers Henri Pourrat
CI, Critical Inquiry
CiD, La Ciudad de Dios
CIDO, Centre International de Documentation Occitane, Béziers
CIEL, Centre International de l'Écrit en Langue d'Òc, Berre
CIEM, Comité International d'Études Morisques
CIF, Cuadernos de Investigación Filológica
CIH, Cuadernos de Investigación Historica
CILF, Conseil International de la Langue Française
CILH, Cuadernos para Investigación de la Literatura Hispanica
CILL, Cahiers de l'Institut de Linguistique de l'Université de Louvain
CIMAGL, Cahiers de l'Institut du Moyen Age Grec et Latin, Copenhagen
CIn, Cahiers Intersignes
CIRVI, Centro Interuniversitario di Ricerche sul 'Viaggio in Italia', Moncalieri
CISAM, Centro Italiano di Studi sull'Alto Medioevo
CIt, Carte Italiane
CIUS, Canadian Institute of Ukrainian Studies Edmonton
CivC, Civiltà Cattolica
CJ, Conditio Judaica, Tübingen, Niemeyer
CJb, Celan-Jahrbuch
CJC, Cahiers Jacques Chardonne
CJG, Cahiers Jean Giraudoux
CJIS, Canadian Journal of Italian Studies
ČJL, Český jazyk a literatura
CJNS, Canadian Journal of Netherlandic Studies
CJP, Cahiers Jean Paulhan
CJR, Cahiers Jules Romains
CL, Cuadernos de Leiden
CL, Comparative Literature
ČL, Česká literatura
CLA, Cahiers du LACITO
CLAJ, College Language Association Journal
CLCC, Cahiers de Littérature Canadienne Comparée

CLE, Comunicaciones de Literatura Española, Buenos Aires
CLe, Cahiers de Lexicologie
CLEAM, Coleción de Literatura Española Aljamiado–Morisca, Madrid, Gredos
CLESP, Cooperativa Libraria Editrice degli Studenti dell'Università di Padova, Padua
CLett, Critica Letteraria
CLF, Cahiers de Linguistique Française
CLHM, Cahiers de Linguistique Hispanique Médiévale
CLin, Cercetări de Lingvistica
CLit, Cadernos de Literatura, Coimbra
ClL, La Clau lemosina
CLO, Cahiers Linguistiques d'Ottawa
ClP, Classical Philology
CLS, Comparative Literature Studies
CLSl, Cahiers de Linguistique Slave
CLTA, Cahiers de Linguistique Théorique et Appliquée
CLTL, Cadernos de Lingüística e Teoria da Literatura
CLUEB, Cooperativa Libraria Universitaria Editrice Bologna
CLus, Convergência Lusíada, Rio de Janeiro
CM, Classica et Mediaevalia
CMA, Cahier Marcel Aymé
CMar, Cuadernos de Marcha
CMCS, Cambrian Medieval Celtic Studies
CMERSA, Center for Medieval and Early Renaissance Studies, State University of New York at Binghamton. Acta
ČMF (PhP), Časopis pro moderni filologii: Philologica Pragensia
CMHLB, Cahiers du Monde Hispanique et Luso-Brésilien
CMi, Cultura Milano
CML, Classical and Modern Literature
ČMM, Časopis Matice Moravské
CMon, Communication Monographs
CMP, Cahiers Marcel Proust
CMRS, Cahiers du Monde Russe et Soviétique
CN, Cultura Neolatina

CNat, Les Cahiers Naturalistes

CNCDP, Comissão Nacional para a Comemoração dos Descobrimentos Portugueses, Lisbon

CNor, Los Cuadernos del Norte

CNR, Consiglio Nazionale delle Ricerche

CNRS, Centre National de la Recherche Scientifique

CO, Camera Obscura

CoF, Collectanea Franciscana

COK, Centralny Ośrodek Kultury, Warsaw

CoL, Compás de Letras

ColA, Colóquio Artes

ColGer, Colloquia Germanica

ColH, Colloquium Helveticum

ColL, Colóquio Letras

ComB, Communications of the International Brecht Society

ComGer, Comunicaciones Germánicas

CompL, Computational Linguistics

ConL, Contrastive Linguistics

ConLet, Il Confronto Letterario

ConLit, Contemporary Literature

ConS, Condorcet Studies

CORDAE, Centre Occitan de Recèrca, de Documentacion e d'Animacion Etnografica, Cordes

CP, Castrum Peregrini

CPE, Cahiers Prévost d'Exiles, Grenoble

CPL, Cahiers Paul Léautand

CPr, Cahiers de Praxématique

CPR, Chroniques de Port-Royal

CPUC, Cadernos PUC, São Paulo

CQ, Critical Quarterly

CR, Contemporary Review

CRAC, Cahiers Roucher — André Chénier

CRCL, Canadian Review of Comparative Literature

CREL, Cahiers Roumains d'Études Littéraires

CRev, Centennial Review

CRI, Cuadernos de Ruedo Ibérico

CRIAR, Cahiers du Centre de Recherches Ibériques et Ibéro-Américaines de l'Université de Rouen

CRLN, Cahiers de Recherches des Instituts Néerlandais de Langue et Littérature Françaises

CRLN, Comparative Romance Linguistics Newsletter

CRQ, Cahiers Raymond Queneau

CRR, Cincinnati Romance Review

CRRI, Centre de Recherche sur la Renaissance Italienne, Paris

CS, Cornish Studies

ČSAV, Československá akademie věd

CSDI, Centro di Studio per la Dialettologia Italiana

CSem, Caiete de Semiotică

CSFLS, Centro di Studi Filologici e Linguistici Siciliani, Palermo

CSG, Cambridge Studies in German, Cambridge U.P.

CSGLL, Canadian Studies in German Language and Literature, Berne–New York–Frankfurt, Lang

CSH, Cahiers des Sciences Humaines

CSIC, Consejo Superior de Investigaciones Científicas, Madrid

CSJP, Cahiers Saint-John Perse

CSl, Critica Slovia, Florence

CSM, Les Cahiers de Saint-Martin

ČSp, Československý spisovatel

CSS, California Slavic Studies

CSSH, Comparative Studies in Society and History

CST, Cahiers de Sémiotique Textuelle

CSt, Critica Storica

CT, Christianity Today

CTC, Cuadernos de Teatro Clásico

CTE, Cuadernos de Traducción e Interpretación

CTe, Cuadernos de Teología

CTex, Cahiers Textuels

CTH, Cahiers Tristan l'Hermite

CTh, Ciencia Tomista

CTL, Current Trends in Linguistics

CTLin, Commissione per i Testi di Lingua, Bologna

CUECM, Cooperativa Universitaria Editrice Catanese Magistero

CUER MA, Centre Universitaire d'Études et de Recherches

Médiévales d'Aix, Université de Provence, Aix-en-Provence
CUP, Cambridge University Press
CUUCV, Cultura Universitaria de la Universidad Central de Venezuela
CWPL, Catalan Working Papers in Linguistics
CWPWL, Cardiff Working Papers in Welsh Linguistics

DAEM, Deutsches Archiv für Erforschung des Mittelalters
DaF, Deutsch als Fremdsprache
DAG, Dictionnaire onomasiologique de l'ancien gascon, Tübingen, Niemeyer
DalR, Dalhousie Review
DanU, Dansk Udsyn
DAO, Dictionnaire onomasiologique de l'ancien occitan, Tübingen, Niemeyer
DaSt, Dante Studies
DB, Дзяржаўная бібліятэка БССР
DB, Doitsu Bungaku
DBl, Driemaandelijkse Bladen
DBO, Deutsche Bibliothek des Ostens, Berlin, Nicolai
DBR, Les Dialectes Belgo-Romans
DBr, Doitsu Bungakoranko
DCFH, Dicenda. Cuadernos de Filología Hispánica
DD, Diskussion Deutsch
DDG, Deutsche Dialektgeographie, Marburg, Elwert
DDJ, Deutsches Dante-Jahrbuch
DegSec, Degré Second
DELTA, Revista de Documentação de Estudos em Lingüística Teórica e Aplicada, Šao Paulo
DESB, Delta Epsilon Sigma Bulletin, Dubuque, Iowa
DeutB, Deutsche Bücher
DeutUB, Deutschungarische Beiträge
DFC, Durham French Colloquies
DFS, Dalhousie French Studies
DGF, Dokumentation germanistischer Forschung, Frankfurt, Lang
DgF, Danmarks gamle Folkeviser

DHA, Diálogos Hispánicos de Amsterdam, Rodopi
DHR, Duquesne Hispanic Review
DhS, Dix-huitième Siècle
DI, Deutscher Idealismus, Stuttgart, Klett-Cotta Verlag
DI, Декоративное искусство
DIAS, Dublin Institute for Advanced Studies
DiL, Dictionnairique et Lexicographie
DiS, Dickinson Studies
DisA, Dissertation Abstracts
DisSlSHL, Dissertationes Slavicae: Sectio Historiae Litterarum
DisSlSL, Dissertationes Slavicae: Sectio Linguistica
DK, Duitse Kroniek
DkJb, Deutschkanadisches Jahrbuch
DKV, Deutscher Klassiker Verlag, Frankfurt
DL, Детская литература
DLA, Deutsche Literatur von den Anfängen bis 1700, Berne– Frankfurt–Paris– New York, Lang
DLit, Discurso Literario
DLM, Deutsche Literatur des Mittelalters (Wissenschaftliche Beiträge der Ernst-Moritz-Arndt-Universität Greifswald)
DLR, Deutsche Literatur in Reprints, Munich, Fink
DLRECL, Diálogo de la Lengua. Revista de Estudio y Creación Literaria, Cuenca
DM, Dirassat Masrahiyyat
DMRPH, De Montfort Research Papers in the Humanities, De Montfort University, Leicester
DMTS, Davis Medieval Texts and Studies, Leiden, Brill
DN, Дружба народов
DNT, De Nieuwe Taalgids
DOLMA, Documenta Onomastica Litteralia Medii Aevi, Hildesheim, Olms
DOM, Dictionnaire de l'occitan médiéval, Tübingen, Niemeyer, 1996–
DosS, Dostoevsky Studies
DoV, Дошкольное воспитание

DPA, Documents pour servir à
l'histoire du département des
Pyrénées-Atlantiques, Pau
DPL, De Proprietatibus Litterarum,
The Hague, Mouton
DpL, День поэзии, Leningrad
DpM, День поэзии, Moscow
DR, Drama Review
DRev, Downside Review
DRLAV, DRLAV, Revue de
Linguistique
DS, Diderot Studies
DSEÜ, Deutsche Sprache in
Europa und Übersee, Stuttgart,
Steiner
DSL, Det danske Sprog- og
Litteraturselskab
DSp, Deutsche Sprache
DSRPD, Documenta et Scripta.
Rubrica Paleographica et
Diplomatica, Barcelona
DSS, XVIIᵉ Siècle
DSt, Deutsche Studien,
Meisenheim, Hain
DSt, Danske Studier
DT, Deutsche Texte, Tübingen,
Niemeyer
DteolT, Dansk teologisk Tidsskrift
DtL, Die deutsche Literatur
DTM, Deutsche Texte des
Mittelalters, Berlin, Akademie
DTV, Deutscher Taschenbuch
Verlag, Munich
DUB, Deutschunterricht, East
Berlin
DUJ, Durham University Journal
(New Series)
DUS, Der Deutschunterricht,
Stuttgart
DUSA, Deutschunterricht in
Südafrika
DV, Дальний Восток
DVA, Deutsche Verlags-Anstalt,
Stuttgart
DVLG, Deutsche Vierteljahresschrift
für Literaturwissenschaft und
Geistesgeschichte

E, Verlag Enzyklopädie, Leipzig
EAL, Early American Literature
EALS, Europäische Aufklärung in
Literatur und Sprache, Frankfurt,
Lang

EAS, Europe-Asia Studies
EB, Estudos Brasileiros
EBal, Etudes Balkaniques
EBM, Era Bouts dera mountanho,
Aurignac
EBTch, Études Balkaniques
Tchécoslovaques
EC, El Escritor y la Crítica,
Colección Persiles, Madrid,
Taurus
EC, Études Celtiques
ECan, Études Canadiennes
ECar, Espace Caraïbe
ECent, The Eighteenth Century,
Lubbock, Texas
ECentF, Eighteenth-Century Fiction
ECF, Écrits du Canada Français
ECI, Eighteenth-Century Ireland
ECIG, Edizioni Culturali
Internazionali Genova
ECla, Les Études Classiques
ECon, España Contemporánea
EconH, Économie et Humanisme
ECr, Essays in Criticism
ECS, Eighteenth Century Studies
EDESA, Ediciones Españolas S.A.
EDHS, Études sur le XVIIIᵉ Siècle
EDL, Études de Lettres
EDT, Edizioni di Torino
EE, Erasmus in English
EEM, East European Monographs
EEQ, East European Quarterly
EF, Erträge der Forschung,
Darmstadt, Wissenschaftliche
Buchgesellschaft
EF, Études Françaises
EFAA, Échanges Franco-Allemands
sur l'Afrique
EFE, Estudios de Fonética
Experimental
EFF, Ergebnisse der
Frauenforschung, Stuttgart,
Metzler
EFil, Estudios Filológicos, Valdivia,
Chile
EFL, Essays in French Literature,
Univ. of Western Australia
EFR, Éditeurs Français Réunis
EG, Études Germaniques
EH, Europäische
Hochschulschriften, Berne–
Frankfurt, Lang
EH, Estudios Humanísticos

EHF, Estudios Humanísticos.
  Filología
EHN, Estudios de Historia
  Novohispana
EHQ, European History Quarterly
EHR, English Historical Review
EHS, Estudios de Historia Social
EHT, Exeter Hispanic Texts,
  Exeter
EIA, Estudos Ibero-Americanos
EIP, Estudos Italianos em Portugal
EL, Esperienze Letterarie
El, Elementa, Würzburg,
  Königshausen & Neumann —
  Amsterdam, Rodopi
ELA, Études de Linguistique
  Appliquée
ELF, Études Littéraires Françaises,
  Paris, J.-M. Place — Tübingen,
  Narr
ELH, English Literary History
El'H, Études sur l'Hérault, Pézenas
ELit, Essays in Literature
ELLC, Estudis de Llengua i
  Literatura Catalanes
ELLF, Études de Langue et
  Littérature Françaises, Tokyo
ELM, Études littéraires
  maghrébines
ELR, English Literary Renaissance
EM, English Miscellany, Rome
EMarg, Els Marges
EMus, Early Music
ENC, Els Nostres Clàssics,
  Barcelona, Barcino
ENSJF, École Nationale Supérieure
  de Jeunes Filles
EO, Edition Orpheus, Tübingen,
  Francke
EO, Europa Orientalis
EOc, Estudis Occitans
EP, Études Philosophiques
Ep, Epistemata, Würzburg,
  Königshausen & Neumann
EPESA, Ediciones y Publicaciones
  Españolas S.A.
EPoet, Essays in Poetics
ER, Estudis Romànics
ERab, Études Rabelaisiennes
ERB, Études Romanes de Brno
ER(BSRLR), Études Romanes
  (Bulletin de la Société Roumaine
  de Linguistique Romane)
ERL, Études Romanes de Lund

ErlF, Erlanger Forschungen
ERLIMA, Équipe de recherche sur
  la littérature d'imagination du
  moyen âge, Centre d'Études
  Supérieures de Civilisation
  Médiévale, Faculté des Lettres et
  des Langues, Université de
  Poitiers.
EROPD, Ежегодник рукописного
  отдела Пушкинского дома
ERR, European Romantic Review
ES, Erlanger Studien, Erlangen,
  Palm & Enke
ES, Estudios Segovianos
EsC, L'Esprit Créateur
ESGP, Early Studies in Germanic
  Philology, Amsterdam, Rodopi
ESI, Edizioni Scientifiche Italiane
ESk, Edition Suhrkamp, Frankfurt,
  Suhrkamp
ESor, Études Sorguaises
EspA, Español Actual
ESt, English Studies
EstE, Estudios Escénicos
EstG, Estudi General
EstH, Estudios Hispánicos
EstL, Estudios de Lingüística,
  Alicante
EstR, Estudios Románticos
EStud, Essays and Studies
ET, L'Écrit du Temps
EtCan, Études Canadiennes
ETF, Espacio, Tiempo y Forma,
  Revista de la Facultad de
  Geografía e Historia, UNED
EtF, Études francophones
EtH, Études sur l'Hérault, Pézenas
EthS, Ethnologia Slavica
ETJ, Educational Theatre Journal
ETL, Explicación de Textos
  Literarios
EtLitt, Études Littéraires, Quebec
EUDEBA, Editorial Universitaria
  de Buenos Aires
EUNSA, Ediciones Universidad de
  Navarra, Pamplona
EUS, European University Studies,
  Berne, Lang
ExP, Excerpta Philologica
EzLit, Език и литература

FAL, Forum Academicum
  Literaturwissenschaft,
  Königstein, Hain

FAPESP, Fundação de Amparo à Pesquisa do Estado de São Paulo
FAR, French-American Review
FAS, Frankfurter Abhandlungen zur Slavistik, Giessen, Schmitz
FBAN, Фундаментальная бібліятэка Акадэміі навук БССР
FBG, Frankfurter Beiträge zur Germanistik, Heidelberg, Winter
FBS, Franco-British Studies
FC, Filologia e Critica
FCE, Fondo de Cultura Económica, Mexico
FCG — CCP, Fondation Calouste Gulbenkian — Centre Culturel Portugais, Paris
FCS, Fifteenth Century Studies
FD, Fonetică şi Dialectologie
FDL, Facetten deutscher Literatur, Berne, Haupt
FEI, Faites entrer l'infini. Journal de la Société des Amis de Louis Aragon et Elsa Triolet
FEK, Forschungen zur europäischen Kultur, Berne, Lang
FemSt, Feministische Studien
FF, Forma y Función
FFM, French Forum Monographs, Lexington, Kentucky
FGÄDL, Forschungen zur Geschichte der älteren deutschen Literatur, Munich, Fink
FH, Fundamenta Historica, Stuttgart-Bad Cannstatt, Frommann-Holzboog
FH, Frankfurter Hefte
FHL, Forum Homosexualität und Literatur
FHS, French Historical Studies
FIDS, Forschungsberichte des Instituts für Deutsche Sprache, Tübingen, Narr
FilM, Filologia Mediolatina
FilMod, Filologia Moderna, Udine–Pisa
FilN, Филологические науки
FilR, Filologia Romanza
FilS, Filologické studie
FilZ, Filologija, Zagreb
FiM, Filologia Moderna, Facultad de Filosofía y Letras, Madrid
FinS, Fin de Siglo

FIRL, Forum at Iowa on Russian Literature
FL, La France Latine
FLa, Faits de Langues
FLG, Freiburger literaturpsychologische Gespräche
FLin, Folia Linguistica
FLinHist, Folia Linguistica Historica
FLK, Forschungen zur Literatur- und Kulturgeschichte. Beiträge zur Sprach- und Literaturwissenschaft, Berne, Lang
FLS, French Literature Series
FLV, Fontes Linguae Vasconum
FM, Le Français Moderne
FMADIUR, FM: Annali del Dipartimento di Italianistica, Università di Roma 'La Sapienza'
FMDA, Forschungen und Materialen zur deutschen Aufklärung, Stuttgart — Bad Cannstatt, Frommann-Holzboog
FMLS, Forum for Modern Language Studies
FmSt, Frühmittelalterliche Studien
FMT, Forum Modernes Theater
FN, Frühe Neuzeit, Tübingen, Niemeyer
FNDIR, Fédération nationale des déportés et internés résistants
FNS, Frühneuzeit-Studien, Frankfurt, Lang
FoH, Foro Hispánico, Amsterdam
FNT, Foilseacháin Náisiúnta Tta
FoI, Forum Italicum
FoS, Le Forme e la Storia
FP, Folia Phonetica
FPub, First Publications
FR, French Review
FrA, Le Français Aujourd'hui
FranS, Franciscan Studies
FrCS, French Cultural Studies
FrF, French Forum
FrH, Französisch Heute
FrP Le Français Préclassique
FS, Forum Slavicum, Munich, Fink
FS, French Studies
FSB, French Studies Bulletin
FSlav, Folia Slavica
FSSA, French Studies in Southern Africa

FT, Fischer Taschenbuch, Frankfurt, Fischer

FT, Finsk Tidskrift

FTCG, 'La Talanquere': Folklore, Tradition, Culture Gasconne, Nogano

FUE, Fundación Universitaria Española

FV, Fortuna Vitrea, Tübingen, Niemeyer

FZPT, Freiburger Zeitschrift für Philosophie und Theologie

GA, Germanistische Arbeitshefte, Tübingen, Niemeyer

GAB, Göppinger Akademische Beiträge, Lauterburg, Kümmerle

GAG, Göppinger Arbeiten zur Germanistik, Lauterburg, Kümmerle

GAKS, Gesammelte Aufsätze zur Kulturgeschichte Spaniens

GalR, Galician Review, Birmingham

GANDLL, Giessener Arbeiten zur neueren deutschen Literatur und Literaturwissenschaft, Berne, Lang

GAS, German-Australian Studies, Berne, Lang

GASK, Germanistische Arbeiten zu Sprache und Kulturgeschichte, Frankfurt, Lang

GBA, Gazette des Beaux-Arts

GBE, Germanistik in der Blauen Eule

GC, Generalitat de Catalunya

GCFI, Giornale Critico della Filosofia Italiana

GEMP, Groupement d'Ethnomusicologie en Midi-Pyrénées, La Talvèra

GerAb, Germanistische Abhandlungen, Stuttgart, Metzler

GerLux, Germanistik Luxembourg

GermL, Germanistische Linguistik

GeW, Germanica Wratislaviensia

GF, Giornale di Fisica

GFFNS, Godišnjak Filozofskog fakulteta u Novom Sadu

GG, Geschichte und Gesellschaft

GGF, Göteborger Germanistische Forschungen, University of Gothenburg

GGVD, Grundlagen und Gedanken zum Verständnis des Dramas, Frankfurt, Diesterweg

GGF, Greifswalder Germanistische Forschungen

GGVEL, Grundlagen und Gedanken zum Verständnis erzählender Literatur, Frankfurt, Diesterweg

GIDILOc, Grop d'Iniciativa per un Diccionari Informatizat de la Lenga Occitana, Montpellier

GIF, Giornale Italiano di Filologia

GIGFL, Glasgow Introductory Guides to French Literature

GIGGL, Glasgow Introductory Guides to German Literature

GJ, Gutenberg-Jahrbuch

GJb, Goethe Jahrbuch

GJLL, The Georgetown Journal of Language and Linguistics

GK, Goldmann Klassiker, Munich, Goldmann

GL, Germanistische Lehrbuchsammlung, Berne, Lang

GL, General Linguistics

GLC, German Life and Civilisation, Berne, Lang

GLL, German Life and Letters

GLML, The Garland Library of Medieval Literature, New York–London, Garland

GLR, García Lorca Review

GLS, Grazer Linguistische Studien

Glyph, Glyph: Johns Hopkins Textual Studies, Baltimore

GM, Germanistische Mitteilungen

GML, Gothenburg Monographs in Linguistics

GMon, German Monitor

GN, Germanic Notes and Reviews

GPB, Гос. публичная библиотека им. М. Е. Салтыкова-Щедрина

GPC, Geiriadur Prifysgol Cymru: A Dictionary of the Welsh Language, Cardiff, University of Wales Press

GPI, Государственный педагогический институт

GPSR, Glossaire des Patois de la Suisse Romande

GQ, German Quarterly
GR, Germanic Review
GREC, Groupe de Recherches et d'Études du Clermontais, Clermont-l'Hérault
GREHAM, Genèse médiévale de l'anthroponymie moderne, Tours, Université François-Rabelais
GRELCA, Groupe de Recherche sur les Littératures de la Caraïbe, Université Laval
GRLH, Garland Reference Library of the Humanities, New York–London, Garland
GRLM, Grundriss der romanischen Literaturen des Mittelalters
GRM, Germanisch-Romanische Monatsschrift
GrSt, Grundtvig Studier
GS, Lo Gai Saber, Toulouse
GSA, Germanic Studies in America, Berne–Frankfurt, Lang
GSC, German Studies in Canada, Frankfurt, Lang
GSI, German Studies in India
GSl, Germano-Slavica, Ontario
GSLI, Giornale Storico della Letteratura Italiana
GSR, German Studies Review
GSSL, Göttinger Schriften zur Sprach– und Literaturwissenschaft, Göttingen, Herodot
GTN, Gdańskie Towarzystwo Naukowe
GTS, Germanistische Texte und Studien, Hildesheim, Olms
GV, Generalitat Valenciana
GY, Goethe Yearbook

H, Hochschulschriften, Cologne, Pahl-Rugenstein
HAHR, Hispanic American Historical Review
HB, Horváth Blätter
HBA, Historiografía y Bibliografía Americanistas, Seville
HBG, Hamburger Beiträge zur Germanistik, Frankfurt, Lang
HDG, Huis aan de Drie Grachten, Amsterdam
HEI, History of European Ideas

HEL, Histoire, Epistemologie, Language
HES, Histoire, Économie et Société
HeyJ, Heythrop Journal
HF, Heidelberger Forschungen, Heidelberg, Winter
HHS, History of the Human Sciences
HI, Historica Ibérica
HIAR, Hamburger Ibero-Amerikanische Reihe
HICL, Histoire des Idées et Critique Littéraire, Geneva, Droz
HIGL, Holland Institute for Generative Linguistics, Leiden
HisJ, Hispanic Journal, Indiana–Pennsylvania
HisL, Hispanic Linguistics
HistL, Historiographia Linguistica
HistS, History of Science
His(US), Hispania, Los Angeles
HJ, Historical Journal
HJb, Heidelberger Jahrbücher
HJBS, Hispanic Journal of Behavioural Sciences
HKADL, Historisch-kritische Arbeiten zur deutschen Literatur, Frankfurt, Lang
HKZMTLG, Handelingen van de Koninklijke Zuidnederlandse Maatschappij voor Taalen, Letterkunde en Geschiedenis
HL, Hochschulschriften Literaturwissenschaft, Königstein, Hain
HL, Humanistica Lovaniensia
HLB, Harvard Library Bulletin
HLQ, Huntington Library Quarterly
HLS, Historiska och litteraturhistoriska studier
HM, Hommes et Migrations
HMJb, Heinrich Mann Jahrbuch
HP, History of Psychiatry
HPh, Historical Philology
HPos, Hispanica Posnaniensia
HPS, Hamburger Philologische Studien, Hamburg, Buske
HPSl, Heidelberger Publikationen zur Slavistik, Frankfurt, Lang
HPT, History of Political Thought
HR, Hispanic Review
HRel, History of Religions
HRev, Hrvatska revija

HRSHM, Heresis, revue semestrielle d'hérésiologie médiévale
HS, Helfant Studien, Stuttgart, Helfant
HS, Hispania Sacra
HSLA, Hebrew University Studies in Literature and the Arts
HSlav, Hungaro-Slavica
HSMS, Hispanic Seminary of Medieval Studies, Madison
HSp, Historische Sprachforschung (Historical Linguistics)
HSSL, Harvard Studies in Slavic Linguistics
HSt, Hispanische Studien
HSWSL, Hallesche Studien zur Wirkung von Sprache und Literatur
HT, Helfant Texte, Stuttgart, Helfant
HT, History Today
HTh, History and Theory
HTR, Harvard Theological Review
HUS, Harvard Ukrainian Studies
HY, Herder Yearbook
HZ, Historische Zeitschrift

IÅ, Ibsen-Årbok, Oslo
IAP, Ibero-Americana Pragensia
IAr, Iberoamerikanisches Archiv
IARB, Inter-American Review of Bibliography
IASL, Internationales Archiv für Sozialgeschichte der deutschen Literatur
IASLS, Internationales Archiv für Sozialgeschichte der deutschen Literatur: Sonderheft
IB, Insel-Bücherei, Frankfurt, Insel
IBKG, Innsbrucker Beiträge zur Kulturwissenschaft. Germanistische Reihe
IBL, Instytut Badań Literackich PAN, Warsaw
IBLA, Institut des Belles Lettres Arabes
IBLe, Insel-Bücherei, Leipzig, Insel
IBS, Innsbrücker Beiträge zur Sprachwissenschaft
IC, Index on Censorship
ICALP, Instituto de Cultura e Língua Portuguesa, Lisbon

ICALPR, Instituto de Cultura e Língua Portuguesa. Revista
ICC, Instituto Caro y Cuervo, Bogotà
ICMA, Instituto de Cooperación con el Mundo Árabe
ID, Italia Dialettale
IDF, Informationen Deutsch als Fremdsprache
IDL, Indices zur deutschen Literatur, Tübingen, Niemeyer
IdLit, Ideologies and Literature
IEC, Institut d'Estudis Catalans
IEI, Istituto dell'Enciclopedia Italiana
IEO, Institut d'Estudis Occitans
IES, Institut d'Études Slaves, Paris
IF, Impulse der Forschung, Darmstadt, Wissenschaftliche Buchgesellschaft
IF, Indogermanische Forschungen
IFC, Institutión Fernando el Católico
IFEE, Investigación Franco-Española. Estudios
IFiS, Instytut Filozofii i Socjologii PAN, Warsaw
IFOTT, Institut voor Functioneel Onderzoek naar Taal en Taalgebruik, Amsterdam
IFR, International Fiction Review
IG, Informations Grammaticales
IHC, Italian History and Culture
IHE, Índice Histórico Español
IHS, Irish Historical Studies
II, Information und Interpretation, Frankfurt, Lang
IIa, Институт языкознания
III, Институт истории искусств
IIFV, Institut Interuniversitari de Filologia Valenciana, Valencia
IJ, Italian Journal
IJAL, International Journal of American Linguistics
IJBAG, Internationales Jahrbuch der Bettina-von-Arnim Gesellschaft
IJCS, International Journal of Canadian Studies
IJFS, International Journal of Francophone Studies, Leeds
IJHL, Indiana Journal of Hispanic Literatures

IJL, International Journal of Lexicography

IJP, International Journal of Psycholinguistics

IJSL, International Journal for the Sociology of Language

IJSLP, International Journal of Slavic Linguistics and Poetics

IK, Искусство кино

IKU, Institut za književnost i umetnost, Belgrade

IL, L'Information Littéraire

ILASLR, Istituto Lombardo. Accademia di Scienze e Lettere. Rendiconti

ILen, Искусство Ленинграда

ILing, Incontri Linguistici

ILTEC, Instituto de Linguística Teórica e Computacional, Lisbon

IMN, Irisleabhar Mhá Nuad

IMR, International Migration Review

IMU, Italia Medioevale e Umanistica

INCM, Imprensa Nacional, Casa da Moeda, Lisbon

InfD, Informationen und Didaktik

INLF, Institut National de la Langue Française

INIC, Instituto Nacional de Investigação Científica

InL, Иностранная литература

INLE, Instituto Nacional del Libro Español

InstEB, Instituto de Estudos Brasileiros

InstNL, Instituto Nacional do Livro, Brasilia

IO, Italiano e Oltre

IPL, Istituto di Propaganda Libraria

IPZS, Istituto Poligrafico e Zecca dello Stato, Rome

IR, L'Immagine Riflessa

IRAL, International Review of Applied Linguistics

IRIa, Институт русского языка Российской Академии Наук

IrR, The Irish Review

IRSH, International Review of Social History

IRSL, International Review of Slavic Linguistics

ISC, Institut de Sociolingüística Catalana

ISLIa, Известия Академии наук СССР. Серия литературы и языка

ISOAN, Известия сибирского отделения АН СССР, Novosibirsk

ISP, International Studies in Philosophy

ISS, Irish Slavonic Studies

IsS, Islamic Studies, Islamabad

ISSA, Studi d'Italianistica nell'Africa Australe: Italian Studies in Southern Africa

ISt, Italian Studies

IT, Insel Taschenbuch, Frankfurt, Insel

ItC, Italian Culture

ITL, ITL. Review of Applied Linguistics, Instituut voor Toegepaste Linguistiek, Leuven

ItQ, Italian Quarterly

ItStudien, Italienische Studien

IUJF, Internationales Uwe-Johnson-Forum

IULA, Institut Universitari de Lingüística Aplicada, Universitat Pompeu Fabra, Barcelona

IUP, Irish University Press

IUR, Irish University Review

IV, Istituto Veneto di Scienze, Lettere ed Arti

IVAS, Indices Verborum zum altdeutschen Schrifttum, Amsterdam, Rodopi

IVN, Internationale Vereniging voor Nederlandistiek

JAAC, Journal of Aesthetics and Art Criticism

JACIS, Journal of the Association for Contemporary Iberian Studies

JAE, Journal of Aesthetic Education

JAMS, Journal of the American Musicological Society

JAOS, Journal of the American Oriental Society

JanL, Janua Linguarum, The Hague, Mouton

JAPLA, Journal of the Atlantic Provinces Linguistic Association

JARA, Journal of the American Romanian Academy of Arts and Sciences

JAS, The Journal of Algerian Studies

JASI, Jahrbuch des Adalbert-Stifter-Instituts

JATI, Association of Teachers of Italian Journal

JazA, Jazykovědné aktuality

JazŠ, Jazykovedné štúdie

JAZU, Jugoslavenska akademija znanosti i umjetnosti

JBSP, Journal of the British Society for Phenomenology

JČ, Jazykovedný časopis, Bratislava

JCanS, Journal of Canadian Studies

JCHAS, Journal of the Cork Historical and Archaeological Society

JCL, Journal of Child Language

JCLin, Journal of Celtic Linguistics

JCS, Journal of Celtic Studies

JDASD, Deutsche Akademie für Sprache und Dichtung: Jahrbuch

JDF, Jahrbuch Deutsch als Fremdsprache

JDSG, Jahrbuch der Deutschen Schiller-Gesellschaft

JEA, Lou Journalet de l'Escandihado Aubagnenco

JEGP, Journal of English and Germanic Philology

JEH, Journal of Ecclesiastical History

JEL, Journal of English Linguistics

JES, Journal of European Studies

JF, Južnoslovenski filolog

JFDH, Jahrbuch des Freien Deutschen Hochstifts

JFinL, Jahrbuch für finnisch-deutsche Literaturbeziehungen

JFL, Jahrbuch für fränkische Landesforschung

JFLS, Journal of French Language Studies

JFR, Journal of Folklore Research

JG, Jahrbuch für Geschichte, Berlin, Akademie

JGO, Jahrbücher für die Geschichte Osteuropas

JHA, Journal for the History of Astronomy

JHI, Journal of the History of Ideas

JHispP, Journal of Hispanic Philology

JHP, Journal of the History of Philosophy

JHR, Journal of Hispanic Research

JHS, Journal of the History of Sexuality

JIAS, Journal of Inter-American Studies

JIES, Journal of Indo-European Studies

JIG, Jahrbuch für Internationale Germanistik

JIL, Journal of Italian Linguistics

JILS, Journal of Interdisciplinary Literary Studies

JIPA, Journal of the International Phonetic Association

JIRS, Journal of the Institute of Romance Studies

JJQ, James Joyce Quarterly

JJS, Journal of Jewish Studies

JL, Journal of Linguistics

JLACS, Journal of Latin American Cultural Studies

JLAL, Journal of Latin American Lore

JLAS, Journal of Latin American Studies

JLH, Journal of Library History

JLS, Journal of Literary Semantics

JLSP, Journal of Language and Social Psychology

JMemL, Journal of Memory and Language

JMEMS, Journal of Medieval and Early Modern Studies

JMH, Journal of Medieval History

JML, Journal of Modern Literature

JMLat, Journal of Medieval Latin

JMMD, Journal of Multilingual and Multicultural Development

JMMLA, Journal of the Midwest Modern Language Association

JModH, Journal of Modern History

JMP, Journal of Medicine and Philosophy

JMRS, Journal of Medieval and Renaissance Studies

JMS, Journal of Maghrebi Studies

JNT, Journal of Narrative Technique

JO.NVL, Een Jaarboek: Overzicht van de Nederlandse en Vlaamse Literatuur
JOWG, Jahrbuch der Oswald von Wolkenstein Gesellschaft
JP, Journal of Pragmatics
JPC, Journal of Popular Culture
JPCL, Journal of Pidgin and Creole Languages
JPh, Journal of Phonetics
JPol, Język Polski
JPR, Journal of Psycholinguistic Research
JQ, Jacques e i suoi Quaderni
JRA, Journal of Religion in Africa
JRG, Jahrbücher der Reineke-Gesellschaft
JRH, Journal of Religious History
JRIC, Journal of the Royal Institution of Cornwall
JŘJR, Jazyk a řeč jihočeského regionu. České Budějovice, Pedagogická fakulta Jihočeské univerzity
JRMA, Journal of the Royal Musical Association
JRMMRA, Journal of the Rocky Mountain Medieval and Renaissance Association
JRS, Journal of Romance Studies
JRUL, Journal of the Rutgers University Libraries
JS, Journal des Savants
JSEES, Japanese Slavic and East European Studies
JSem, Journal of Semantics
JSFWUB, Jahrbuch der Schlesischen Friedrich-Wilhelms-Universität zu Breslau
JSH, Jihočeský sborník historický
JSHR, Journal of Speech and Hearing Research
JSL, Journal of Slavic Linguistics
JSS, Journal of Spanish Studies: Twentieth Century
JTS, Journal of Theological Studies
JU, Judentum und Umwelt, Berne, Lang.
JUS, Journal of Ukrainian Studies
JV, Jahrbuch für Volkskunde
JVF, Jahrbuch für Volksliedforschung
JVLVB, Journal of Verbal Learning and Verbal Behavior

JWBS, Journal of the Welsh Bibliographical Society
JWCI, Journal of the Warburg and Courtauld Institutes
JWGV, Jahrbuch des Wiener Goethe-Vereins, Neue Folge
JWH, Journal of World History
JWIL, Journal of West Indian Literature
JZ, Jazykovedný zborník

KANTL, Koninklijke Akademie voor Nederlandse Taal- en Letterkunde
KASL, Kasseler Arbeiten zur Sprache und Literatur, Frankfurt, Lang
KAW, Krajowa Agencja Wydawnicza
KAWLSK, Koninklijke Academie voor Wetenschappen, Letteren en Schone Kunsten van België, Brussels
KB, Književni barok
KBGL, Kopenhagener Beiträge zur germanistischen Linguistik
Kbl, Korrespondenzblatt des Vereins für niederdeutsche Sprachforschung
KDPM, Kleine deutsche Prosadenkmäler des Mittelalters, Munich, Fink
KGOS, Kultur- und geistesgeschichtliche Ostmitteleuropa-Studien, Marburg, Elwert
KGS, Kölner germanistische Studien, Cologne, Böhlau
KGS, Kairoer germanistische Studien
KH, Komparatistische Hefte
KhL, Художественная литература
KI, Književna istorija
KiW, Książka i Wiedza
KJ, Književnost i jezik
KK, Kirke og Kultur
KJb, Kleist-Jahrbuch
KLWL, Krieg und Literatur: War and Literature
Klage, Klage: Kölner linguistische Arbeiten. Germanistik, Hürth-Efferen, Gabel

KN, Kwartalnik Neofilologiczny
KnK, Kniževna kritika
KO, Университетско
 издателство
 'Климент Охридски'
KO, Книжное обозрение
KP, Книжная палата
KRA, Kölner Romanistische
 Arbeiten, Geneva, Droz
KS, Kúltura slova
KSDL, Kieler Studien zur
 deutschen Literaturgeschichte,
 Neumünster, Wachholtz
KSL, Kölner Studien zur
 Literaturwissenschaft, Frankfurt,
 Lang
KSt, Kant Studien
KTA, Kröners Taschenausgabe,
 Stuttgart, Kröner
KTRM, Klassische Texte des
 romanischen Mittelalters,
 Munich, Fink
KU, Konstanzer Universitäts-
 reden
KUL, Katolicki Uniwersytet
 Lubelski, Lublin
KuSDL, Kulturwissenschaftliche
 Studien zur deutschen Literatur,
 Opladen, Westdeutscher Verlag
KZG, Koreanische Zeitschrift für
 Germanistik
KZMTLG, Koninklijke
 Zuidnederlandse Maatschappij
 voor Taal- en Letterkunde en
 Geschiedenis, Brussels
KZMTLGH, Koninklijke
 Zuidnederlandse Maatschaapij
 voor Taal- en Letterkunde en
 Geschiedenis. Handelingen

LA, Linguistische Arbeiten,
 Tübingen, Niemeyer
LA, Linguistic Analysis
LaA, Language Acquisition
LAbs, Linguistics Abstracts
LaF, Langue Française
LAILJ, Latin American Indian
 Literatures Journal
LaLi, Langues et Linguistique
LALR, Latin-American Literary
 Review
LaM, Les Langues Modernes
LangH, Le Langage et l'Homme

LArb, Linguistische Arbeitsberichte
LARR, Latin-American Research
 Review
LaS, Langage et Société
LATR, Latin-American Theatre
 Review
LatT, Latin Teaching, Shrewsbury
LB, Leuvense Bijdragen
LBer, Linguistische Berichte
LBIYB, Leo Baeck Institute Year
 Book
LBR, Luso-Brazilian Review
LC, Letture Classensi
LCC, Léachtaí Cholm Cille
LCh, Literatura Chilena
LCP, Language and Cognitive
 Processes
LCrit, Lavoro Critico
LCUTA, Library Chronicle of the
 University of Texas at Austin
LD, Libri e Documenti
LDan, Lectura Dantis
LDanN, Lectura Dantis
 Newberryana
LDGM, Ligam-DiGaM. Quadèrn
 de lingüística e lexicografia
 gasconas, Fontenay aux Roses
LE, Language and Education
LEA, Lingüística Española Actual
LebS, Lebende Sprachen
LEMIR, Literatura Española
 Medieval y del Renacimiento,
 Valencia U.P.; http://
 www.uv.es/ ~lemir/Revista.html
LenP, Ленинградская панорама
LetA, Letterature d'America
LetD, Letras de Deusto
LETHB, Laboratoires d'Études
 Théâtrales de l'Université de
 Haute-Bretagne. Études et
 Documents, Rennes
LetL, Letras e Letras, Departmento
 de Línguas Estrangeiras
 Modernas, Universidade Federal
 de Uberlândia, Brazil
LetMS, Letopis Matice srpske, Novi
 Sad
LetP, Il Lettore di Provincia
LetS, Letras Soltas
LevT, Levende Talen
LF, Letras Femeninas
LFil, Listy filologické
LFQ, Literature and Film Quarterly

LGF, Lunder Germanistische Forschungen, Stockholm, Almqvist & Wiksell

LGGL, Literatur in der Geschichte, Geschichte in der Literatur, Cologne–Vienna, Böhlau

LGL, Langs Germanistische Lehrbuchsammlung, Berne, Lang

LGP, Leicester German Poets, Leicester U.P.

LGW, Literaturwissenschaft — Gesellschaftswissenschaft, Stuttgart, Klett

LH, Lingüística Hispánica

LHum, Litteraria Humanitas, Brno

LI, Linguistic Inquiry

LIÅA, Litteraturvetenskapliga institutionen vid Åbo Akademi, Åbo Akademi U.P.

LiB, Literatur in Bayern

LIC, Letteratura Italiana Contemporanea

LiCC, Lien des chercheurs cévenols

LIE, Lessico Intellettuale Europeo, Rome, Ateneo

LiL, Limbă şi Literatură

LiLi, Zeitschrift für Literaturwissenschaft und Linguistik

LingAk, Linguistik Aktuell, Amsterdam, Benjamins

LingBal, Галканско езикознание – Linguistique Balkanique

LingCon, Lingua e Contesto

LingFil, Linguistica e Filologia, Dipartimento di Linguistica e Letterature Comparate, Bergamo

LingLett, Linguistica e Letteratura

LíngLit, Língua e Literatura, São Paulo

LinLit, Lingüística y Literatura

LINQ, Linq [Literature in North Queensland]

LInv, Lingvisticae Investigationes

LiR, Limba Română

LIT, Literature Interpretation Theory

LIt, Lettera dall'Italia

LitAP, Literární archív Památníku národního pisemnictví

LItal, Lettere Italiane

LitB, Literatura, Budapest

LitC, Littératures Classiques

LitG, Литературная газета, Moscow

LitH, Literature and History

LItL, Letteratura Italiana Laterza, Bari, Laterza

LitL, Literatur für Leser

LitLing, Literatura y Lingüística

LitM, Literární měsíčník

LitMis, Литературна мисъл

LitP, Literature and Psychology

LitR, The Literary Review

LittB, Litteraria, Bratislava

LittK, Litterae, Lauterburg, Kümmerle

LittS, Litteratur og Samfund

LittW, Litteraria, Wrocław

LiU, Літературна Україна

LJb, Literaturwissenschaftliches Jahrbuch der Görres-Gesellschaft

LK, Literatur-Kommentare, Munich, Hanser

LK, Literatur und Kritik

LKol, Loccumer Kolloquium

LL, Langues et Littératures, Rabat

LlA, Lletres Asturianes

LLC, Literary and Linguistic Computing

LlC, Llên Cymru

LlLi, Llengua i Literatura

LLS, Lenguas, Literaturas, Sociedades. Cuadernos Hispánicos

LLSEE, Linguistic and Literary Studies in Eastern Europe, Amsterdam, Benjamins

LM, Le Lingue del Mondo

LN, Lingua Nostra

LNB, Leipziger namenkundliche Beiträge

LNL, Les Langues Néo-Latines

LNouv, Les Lettres Nouvelles

LoP, Loccumer Protokolle

LOS, Literary Onomastic Studies

LP, Le Livre de Poche, Librairie Générale Française

LP, Lingua Posnaniensis

LPen, Letras Peninsulares

LPh, Linguistics and Philosophy

LPLP, Language Problems and Language Planning

LPO, Lenga e Païs d'Oc, Montpellier

LPr, Linguistica Pragensia

LQ, Language Quarterly, University of S. Florida
LR, Linguistische Reihe, Munich, Hueber
LR, Les Lettres Romanes
LRev, Linguistic Review
LRI, Libri e Riviste d'Italia
LS, Literatur als Sprache, Münster, Aschendorff
LS, Lingua e Stile
LSa, Lusitania Sacra
LSc, Language Sciences
LSil, Linguistica Silesiana
LSNS, Lundastudier i Nordisk Språkvetenskap
LSo, Language in Society
LSp, Language and Speech
LSPS, Lou Sourgentin/La Petite Source. Revue culturelle bilingue nissart-français, Nice
LSty, Language and Style
LSW, Ludowa Spółdzielnia Wydawnicza
LTG, Literaturwissenschaft, Theorie und Geschichte, Frankfurt, Lang
ŁTN, Łódzkie Towarzystwo Naukowe
LTP, Laval Théologique et Philosophique
LU, Literarhistorische Untersuchungen, Berne, Lang
LVC, Language Variation and Change
LW, Literatur und Wirklichkeit, Bonn, Bouvier
LWU, Literatur in Wissenschaft und Unterricht
LY, Lessing Yearbook

MA, Moyen Âge
MAASC, Mémoires de l'Académie des Arts et des Sciences de Carcassonne
MACL, Memórias da Academia de Ciências de Lisboa, Classe de Letras
MAe, Medium Aevum
MAKDDR, Mitteilungen der Akademie der Künste der DDR
MAL, Modern Austrian Literature
MaL, Le Maghreb Littéraire – Revue Canadienne des Littératures Maghrébines, Toronto
MaM, Marbacher Magazin
MAPS, Medium Aevum. Philologische Studien, Munich, Fink
MAST, Memorie dell'Accademia delle Scienze di Torino
MatSl, Matica Slovenská
MBA, Mitteilungen aus dem Brenner-Archiv
MBAV, Miscellanea Bibliothecae Apostolicae Vaticanae
MBMRF, Münchener Beiträge zur Mediävistik und Renaissance-Forschung, Bachenhausen, Arbeo
MBRP, Münstersche Beiträge zur romanischen Philologie, Münster, Kleinheinrich
MBSL, Mannheimer Beiträge zur Sprach- und Literaturwissenschaft, Tübingen, Narr
MC, Misure Critiche
MCV, Mélanges de la Casa de Velázquez
MD, Musica Disciplina
MDan, Meddelser fra Dansklærerforeningen.
MDG, Mitteilungen des deutschen Germanistenverbandes
MDL, Mittlere Deutsche Literatur, in Neu- und Nachdrucken, Berne, Lang
MDr, Momentum Dramaticum
MDU, Monatshefte für den deutschen Unterricht
MEC, Ministerio de Educação e Cultura, Rio de Janeiro
MedC, La Méditerranée et ses Cultures
MedH, Medioevo e Umanesimo
MedLR, Mediterranean Language Review
MedRom, Medioevo Romanzo
MedS, Medieval Studies
MEFR, Mélanges de l'École Française de Rome, Moyen Age
MerP, Mercurio Peruano
MF, Mercure de France
MFDT, Mainzer Forschungen zu Drama und Theater, Tübingen, Francke
MFS, Modern Fiction Studies

MG, Молодая гвардия
MG, Молодая гвардия
MGB, Münchner Germanistische Beiträge, Munich, Fink
MGG, Mystik in Geschichte und Gegenwart, Stuttgart-Bad Cannstatt, Frommann-Holzboog
MGS, Marburger Germanistische Studien, Frankfurt, Lang
MGS, Michigan Germanic Studies
MGSL, Minas Gerais, Suplemento Literário
MH, Medievalia et Humanistica
MHLS, Mid-Hudson Language Studies
MHRA, Modern Humanities Research Association
MichRS, Michigan Romance Studies
MILUS, Meddelanden från Institutionen i Lingvistik vid Universitetet i Stockholm
MINS, Meddelanden från institutionen för nordiska språk vid Stockholms universitet, Stockholm U.P.
MiscBarc, Miscellanea Barcinonensia
MiscEB, Miscel·lània d'Estudis Bagencs
MiscP, Miscel·lània Penedesenca
MJ, Mittellateinisches Jahrbuch
MK, Maske und Kothurn
MKH, Deutsche Forschungsgemeinschaft: Mitteilung der Kommission für Humanismusforschung, Weinheim, Acta Humaniora
MKNAWL, Mededelingen der Koninklijke Nederlandse Akademie van Wetenschappen, Afd. Letterkunde, Amsterdam
ML, Mediaevalia Lovaniensia, Leuven U.P.
ML, Modern Languages
MLAIntBibl, Modern Language Association International Bibliography
MLIÅA, Meddelanden utgivna av Litteraturvetenskapliga institutionen vid Åbo Akademi, Åbo Akademi U.P.
MLIGU, Meddelanden utgivna av Litteraturvetenskapliga

institutionen vid Göteborgs universitet, Gothenburg U.P.
MLit, Мастацкая літаратура
MLit, Miesięcznik Literacki
MLIUU, Meddelanden utgivna av Litteraturvetenskapliga institutionen vid Uppsala universitet, Uppsala U.P.
MLJ, Modern Language Journal
MLN, Modern Language Notes
MLQ, Modern Language Quarterly
MLR, Modern Language Review
MLS, Modern Language Studies
MM, Maal og Minne
MMS, Münstersche Mittelalter-Schriften, Munich, Fink
MN, Man and Nature. L'Homme et la Nature
MNGT, Manchester New German Texts, Manchester U.P.
ModD, Modern Drama
ModS, Modern Schoolman
MoL, Modellanalysen: Literatur, Paderborn, Schöningh–Munich, Fink
MON, Ministerstwo Obrony Narodowej, Warsaw
MosR, Московский рабочий
MoyFr, Le Moyen Français
MP, Modern Philology
MQ, Mississippi Quarterly
MQR, Michigan Quarterly Review
MR, Die Mainzer Reihe, Mainz, Hase & Koehler
MR, Medioevo e Rinascimento
MRev, Maghreb Review
MRo, Marche Romane
MRS, Medieval and Renaissance Studies
MRTS, Medieval and Renaissance Texts and Studies, Tempe, Arizona, Arizona State University
MS, Marbacher Schriften, Stuttgart, Cotta
MS, Moderna Språk
MSC, Medjunarodni slavistički centar, Belgrade
MSG, Marburger Studien zur Germanistik, Marburg, Hitzeroth
MSISS, Materiali della Società Italiana di Studi sul Secolo XVIII
MSL, Marburger Studien zur Literatur, Marburg, Hitzeroth

MSLKD, Münchener Studien zur
literarischen Kultur in
Deutschland, Frankfurt, Lang
MSMS, Middeleeuse Studies —
Medieval Studies, Johannesburg
MSNH, Mémoires de la Société
Néophilologique de Helsinki
MSp, Moderne Sprachen
(Zeitschrift des Verbandes der
österreichischen Neuphilologen)
MSSp, Münchener Studien zur
Sprachwissenschaft, Munich
MTCGT, Methuen's Twentieth-
Century German Texts, London,
Methuen
MTG, Mitteilungen zur
Theatergeschichte der
Goethezeit, Bonn, Bouvier
MTNF, Monographien und Texte
zur Nietzsche-Forschung,
Berlin–New York, de Gruyter
MTU, Münchener Texte und
Untersuchungen zur deutschen
Literatur des Mittelalters,
Tübingen, Niemeyer
MTUB, Mitteilungen der T. U.
Braunschweig
MUP, Manchester University Press
MusL, Music and Letters
MusP, Museum Patavinum
MyQ, Mystics Quarterly

NA, Nuova Antologia
NAFMUM, Nuovi Annali della
Facoltà di Magistero
dell'Università di Messina
NArg, Nuovi Argomenti
NAS, Nouveaux Actes Sémiotiques,
PULIM, Université de Limoges
NASNCGL, North American
Studies in Nineteenth-Century
German Literature, Berne, Lang
NASSAB, Nuovi Annali della Scuola
Speciale per Archivisti e
Bibliotecari
NAWG, Nachrichten der Akademie
der Wissenschaften zu Göttingen,
phil.-hist. Kl., Göttingen,
Vandenhoeck & Ruprecht
NBGF, Neue Beiträge zur George-
Forschung
NC, New Criterion

NCA, Nouveaux Cahiers
d'Allemand
NCEFRW, Nouvelles du Centre
d'études francoprovençales 'René
Willien'
NCF, Nineteenth-Century Fiction
NCFS, Nineteenth-Century French
Studies
NCo, New Comparison
NCSRLL, North Carolina Studies
in the Romance Languages and
Literatures, Chapel Hill
ND, Наукова думка
NDH, Neue deutsche Hefte
NdJb, Niederdeutsches Jahrbuch
NDL, Nachdrucke deutscher
Literatur des 17. Jahrhunderts,
Berne, Lang
NDL, Neue deutsche Literatur
NdS, Niederdeutsche Studien,
Cologne, Böhlau
NDSK, Nydanske Studier og almen
kommunikationsteori
NdW, Niederdeutsches Wort
NE, Nueva Estafeta
NEL, Nouvelles Éditions Latines,
Paris
NFF, Novel: A Forum in Fiction
NFS, Nottingham French Studies
NFT, Német Filológiai
Tanulmányok. Arbeiten zur
deutschen Philologie
NG, Nordistica Gothoburgensia
NGC, New German Critique
NGFH, Die Neue Gesellschaft/
Frankfurter Hefte
NGR, New German Review
NGS, New German Studies, Hull
NH, Nuevo Hispanismo
NHi, Nice Historique
NHLS, North Holland Linguistic
Series, Amsterdam
NHVKSG, Neujahrsblatt des
Historischen Vereins des Kantons
St Gallen
NI, Наука и изкуство
NIMLA, NIMLA. Journal of the
Modern Language Association of
Northern Ireland
NJ, Naš jezik
NJL, Nordic Journal of Linguistics
NKT, Norske klassiker-tekster,
Bergen, Eide
NL, Nouvelles Littéraires

NLÅ, Norsk Litterær Årbok
NLD, Nuove Letture Dantesche
NLe, Nuove Lettere
NLH, New Literary History
NLi, Notre Librairie
NLLT, Natural Language and
  Linguistic Theory
NLN, Neo-Latin News
NLT, Norsk Lingvistisk Tidsskrift
NLWJ, National Library of Wales
  Journal
NM, Народна младеж
NMi, Neuphilologische
  Mitteilungen
NMS, Nottingham Medieval Studies
NN, Наше наследие
NNH, Nueva Narrativa Hispano-
  americana
NNR, New Novel Review
NOR, New Orleans Review
NORNA, Nordiska
  samarbetskommittén för
  namnforskning, Uppsala
NovE, Novos Estudos (CEBRAP)
NovM, Новый мир
NovR, Nova Renascenza
NOWELE, North-Western
  European Language Evolution.
  Nowele
NP, Народна просвета
NP, Nouvello de Prouvènço (Li),
  Avignon, Parlaren Païs
  d'Avignoun
NQ, Notes and Queries
NR, New Review
NŘ, Naše řeč
NRE, Nuova Rivista Europea
NRF, Nouvelle Revue Française
NRFH, Nueva Revista de Filología
  Hispánica
NRL, Neue russische Literatur.
  Almanach, Salzburg
NRLett, Nouvelles de la République
  des Lettres
NRMI, Nuova Rivista Musicale
  Italiana
NRO, Nouvelle Revue
  d'Onomastique
NRP, Nouvelle Revue de
  Psychanalyse
NRS, Nuova Rivista Storica
NRSS, Nouvelle Revue du Seizième
  Siècle
NRu, Die Neue Rundschau

NS, Die Neueren Sprachen
NSc, New Scholar
NSh, Начальная школа
NSL, Det Norske Språk- og
  Litteraturselskap
NSlg, Neue Sammlung
NSo, Наш современник . . .
  Альманах
NSP, Nuovi Studi Politici
NSS, Nysvenska Studier
NSt, Naše stvaranje
NT, Навука і тэхніка
NT, Nordisk Tidskrift
NTBB, Nordisk Tidskrift för Bok-
  och Biblioteksväsen
NTC, Nuevo Texto Crítico
NTE, Народна творчість та
  етнографія
NTg, Nieuwe Taalgids
NTQ, New Theatre Quarterly
NTSh, Наукове товариство ім.
  Шевченка
NTW, News from the Top of the
  World: Norwegian Literature
  Today
NU, Narodna umjetnost
NV, Новое время
NVS, New Vico Studies
NWIG, Niewe West-Indische Gids
NyS, Nydanske Studier/Almen
  Kommunikationsteori
NYSNDL, New Yorker Studien zur
  neueren deutschen
  Literaturgeschichte, Berne,
  Lang
NYUOS, New York University
  Ottendorfer Series, Berne,
  Lang
NZh, Новый журнал
NZh (StP), Новый журнал, St
  Petersburg
NZJFS, New Zealand Journal of
  French Studies
NZSJ, New Zealand Slavonic
  Journal

OA, Отечественные архивы
OB, Ord och Bild
OBS, Osnabrücker Beiträge zur
  Sprachtheorie, Oldenbourg,
  OBST
OBTUP, Universitetsforlaget
  Oslo–Bergen–Tromsø

ÖBV, Österreichischer Bundesverlag, Vienna
OC, Œuvres et Critiques
OcL, Oceanic Linguistics
OCP, Orientalia Christiana Periodica, Rome
OCS, Occitan/Catalan Studies
ÖGL, Österreich in Geschichte und Literatur
OGS, Oxford German Studies
OH, Ottawa Hispánica
OIU, Oldenbourg Interpretationen mit Unterrichtshilfen, Munich, Oldenbourg
OL, Orbis Litterarum
OLR, Oxford Literary Review
OLSI, Osservatorio Linguistico della Svizzera Italiana
OM, L'Oc Médiéval
ON, Otto/Novecento
OPBS, Occasional Papers in Belarusian Studies
OPEN, Oficyna Polska Encyklopedia Nezależna
OPI, Overseas Publications Interchange, London
OPL, Osservatore Politico Letterario
OPM, 'Ou Païs Mentounasc': Bulletin de la Société d'Art et d'Histoire du Mentonnais, Menton
OPRPNZ, Общество по распространению политических и научных знаний
OPSLL, Occasional Papers in Slavic Languages and Literatures
OR, Odrodzenie i Reformacja w Polsce
ORP, Oriental Research Partners, Cambridge
OS, 'Oc Sulpic': Bulletin de l'Association Occitane du Québec, Montreal
OSP, Oxford Slavonic Papers
OT, Oral Tradition
OTS, Onderzoeksinstituut voor Taal en Spraak, Utrecht
OUP, Oxford University Press
OUSL, Odense University Studies in Literature
OUSSLL, Odense University Studies in Scandinavian Languages and Literatures, Odense U.P.

OWPLC, Odense Working Papers in Language and Communication
OZ, Onomastický zpravodaj

PA, Présence Africaine
PAf, Politique Africaine
PAGS, Proceedings of the Australian Goethe Society
Pal, Palaeobulgarica — Старобългаристика
PAM, Publicacions de l'Abadia de Montserrat, Barcelona
PAN, Polska Akademia Nauk, Warsaw
PaP, Past and Present
PapBSA, Papers of the Bibliographical Society of America
PAPhS, Proceedings of the American Philosophical Society
PapL, Papiere zur Linguistik
ParL, Paragone Letteratura
PartR, Partisan Review
PaS, Pamiętnik Słowiański
PASJ, Pictish Arts Society Journal
PAX, Instytut Wydawniczy PAX, Warsaw
РВ, Д-р Петър Берон
PBA, Proceedings of the British Academy
PBib, Philosophische Bibliothek, Hamburg, Meiner
PBLS, Proceedings of the Annual Meeting of the Berkeley Linguistic Society
PBML, Prague Bulletin of Mathematical Linguistics
PBSA, Publications of the Bibliographical Society of America
PC, Problems of Communism
PCLS, Proceedings of the Chicago Linguistic Society
PCP, Pacific Coast Philology
PD, Probleme der Dichtung, Heidelberg, Winter
PDA, Pagine della Dante
PdO, Paraula d'oc, Centre International de Recerca i Documentació d'Oc, Valencia
PE, Poesía Española

PEGS(NS), Publications of the English Goethe Society (New Series)
PenP, Il Pensiero Politico
PerM, Perspectives Médiévales
PEs, Lou Prouvençau à l'Escolo
PF, Présences Francophones
PFil, Prace Filologiczne
PFPS, Z problemów frazeologii polskiej i słowiańskiej, ZNiO
PFSCL, Papers on French Seventeenth Century Literature
PG, Païs gascons
PGA, Lo pais gascon/Lou pais gascoun, Anglet
PGIG, Publikationen der Gesellschaft für interkulturelle Germanistik, Munich, Iudicium
PH, La Palabra y el Hombre
PhilosQ, Philosophical Quarterly
PhilP, Philological Papers, West Virginia University
PhilR, Philosophy and Rhetoric
PhilRev, Philosophical Review
PhLC, Phréatique, Langage et Création
PHol, Le Pauvre Holterling
PhonPr, Phonetica Pragensia
PhP, Philologica Pragensia
PhR, Phoenix Review
PHSL, Proceedings of the Huguenot Society of London
PI, педагогическиб институт
PId, Le Parole e le Idee
PIGS, Publications of the Institute of Germanic Studies, University of London
PiH, Il Piccolo Hans
PIMA, Proceedings of the Illinois Medieval Association
PIMS, Publications of the Institute for Medieval Studies, Toronto
PIW, Państwowy Instytut Wydawniczy, Warsaw
PJ, Poradnik Językowy
PLing, Papers in Linguistics
PLit, Philosophy and Literature
PLL, Papers on Language and Literature
PL(L), Pamiętnik Literacki, London
PLRL, Patio de Letras/La Rosa als Llavis
PLS, Přednášky z běhu Letní školy slovanských studií

PL(W), Pamiętnik Literacki, Warsaw
PM, Pleine Marge
PMH, Portugaliae Monumenta Historica
PMHRS, Papers of the Medieval Hispanic Research Seminar, London, Department of Hispanic Studies, Queen Mary and Westfield College
PMLA, Publications of the Modern Language Association of America
PMPA, Publications of the Missouri Philological Association
PN, Paraulas de novelum, Périgueux
PNCIP, Plurilinguismo. Notizario del Centro Internazionale sul Plurilinguismo
PNR, Poetry and Nation Review
PNUS, Prace Naukowe Uniwersytetu Śląskiego, Katowice
PoetT, Poetics Today
PolR, Polish Review
PortSt, Portuguese Studies
PP, Prace Polonistyczne
PPNCFL, Proceedings of the Pacific Northwest Conference on Foreign Languages
PPr, Papers in Pragmatics
PPU, Promociones y Publicaciones Universitarias, S.A., Barcelona
PQ, The Philological Quarterly
PR, Podravska Revija
PrA, Prouvenço aro, Marseilles
PraRu, Prace Rusycystyczne
PRF, Publications Romanes et Françaises, Geneva, Droz
PRH, Pahl-Rugenstein Hochschulschriften, Cologne, Pahl–Rugenstein
PrH, Provence Historique
PrHlit, Prace Historycznoliterackie
PrHum, Prace Humanistyczne
PRIA, Proceedings of the Royal Irish Academy
PrIJP, Prace Instytutu Języka Polskiego
Prilozi, Prilozi za književnost, jezik, istoriju i folklor, Belgrade
PrilPJ, Prilozi proučavanju jezika
PRIS-MA, Bulletin de liaison de l'ERLIMA, Université de Poitiers
PrLit, Prace Literackie

PRom, Papers in Romance
PrRu, Przegląd Rusycystyczny
PrzH, Przegląd Humanistyczny
PrzW, Przegląd Wschodni
PS, Проблеми слов'янознавства
PSCL, Papers and Studies in
  Contrastive Linguistics
PSE, Prague Studies in English
PSGAS, Politics and Society in
  Germany, Austria and
  Switzerland
PSLu, Pagine Storiche Luganesi
PSML, Prague Studies in
  Mathematical Linguistics
PSQ, Philologische Studien und
  Quellen, Berlin, Schmidt
PSR, Portuguese Studies Review
PSRL, Полное собрание русских
  летописей
PSS, Z polskich studiów
  slawistycznych, Warsaw, PWN
PSSLSAA, Procès-verbaux des
  séances de la Société des Lettres,
  Sciences et Arts de l'Aveyron
PSV, Polono-Slavica Varsoviensia
PT, Pamiętnik Teatralny
PUC, Pontifícia Universidade
  Católica, São Paulo
PUE, Publications Universitaires,
  Européennes, New York–
  Berne–Frankfurt, Lang
PUF, Presses Universitaires de
  France, Paris
PUMRL, Purdue University
  Monographs in Romance
  Languages, Amsterdam —
  Philadelphia, Benjamins
PUStE, Publications de l'Université
  de Saint-Étienne
PW, Poetry Wales
PWN, Państwowe Wydawnictwo
  Naukowe, Warsaw, etc.

QALT, Quaderni dell'Atlante
  Lessicale Toscano
QASIS, Quaderni di lavoro
  dell'ASIS (Atlante Sintattico
  dell'Italia Settentrionale), Centro
  di Studio per la Dialettologia
  Italiana 'O. Parlangèli',
  Università degli Studi di Padova
QCFLP, Quaderni del Circolo
  Filologico Linguistico Padovano

QDLC, Quaderni del Dipartimento
  di Linguistica, Università della
  Calabria
QDLF, Quaderni del Dipartimento
  di Linguistica, Università degli
  Studi, Firenze
QDLLSMG, Quaderni del
  Dipartimento di Lingue e
  Letterature Straniere Moderne,
  Università di Genova
QDSL, Quellen zur deutschen
  Sprach- und Literaturgeschichte,
  Heidelberg, Winter
QFCC, Quaderni della Fondazione
  Camillo Caetani, Rome
QFESM, Quellen und Forschungen
  zur Erbauungsliteratur des späten
  Mittelalters und der frühen
  Neuzeit, Amsterdam, Rodopi
QFGB, Quaderni di Filologia
  Germanica della Facoltà di
  Lettere e Filosofia dell'Università
  di Bologna
QFIAB, Quellen und Forschungen
  aus italienischen Archiven und
  Bibliotheken
QFLK, Quellen und Forschungen
  zur Literatur- und
  Kulturgeschichte, Berlin, de
  Gruyter
QFLR, Quaderni di Filologia e
  Lingua Romanze, Università di
  Macerata
QFSK, Quellen und Forschungen
  zur Sprach- und Kulturge-
  schichte der germanischen
  Völker, Berlin, de Gruyter
QI, Quaderni d'Italianistica
QIA, Quaderni Ibero-Americani
QIGC, Quaderni dell'Istituto di
  Glottologia, Università degli
  Studi 'G. D'Annunzio' di Chieti,
  Facoltà di Lettere e Filosofia
QIICM, Quaderni dell'Istituto
  Italiano di Cultura, Melbourne
QILLSB, Quaderni dell'Istituto di
  Lingue e Letterature Straniere
  della Facoltà di Magistero
  dell'Università degli Studi di Bari
QILUU, Quaderni dell'Istituto di
  Linguistica dell'Università di
  Urbino

QINSRM, Quaderni dell'Istituto Nazionale di Studi sul Rinascimento Meridionale
QJMFL, A Quarterly Journal in Modern Foreign Literatures
QJS, Quarterly Journal of Speech, Speech Association of America
QLII, Quaderni di Letterature Iberiche e Iberoamericane
QLL, Quaderni di Lingue e Letterature, Verona
QLLSP, Quaderni di Lingua e Letteratura Straniere, Facoltà di Magistero, Università degli Studi di Palermo
QLO, Quasèrns de Lingüistica Occitana
QM, Quaderni Milanesi
QMed, Quaderni Medievali
QP, Quaderns de Ponent
QPet, Quaderni Petrarcheschi
QPL, Quaderni Patavini di Linguistica
QQ, Queen's Quarterly, Kingston, Ontario
QR, Quercy Recherche, Cahors
QRCDLIM, Quaderni di Ricerca, Centro di Dialettologia e Linguistica Italiana di Manchester
QRP, Quaderni di Retorica e Poetica
QS, Quaderni di Semantica
QSF, Quaderni del Seicento Francese
QSGLL, Queensland Studies in German Language and Literature, Berne, Francke
QSt, Quaderni Storici
QStef, Quaderni Stefaniani
QSUP, Quaderni per la Storia dell'Università di Padova
QT, Quaderni di Teatro
QuF, Québec français
QuS, Quebec Studies
QV, Quaderni del Vittoriale
QVen, Quaderni Veneti
QVer, Quaderni Veronesi di Filologia, Lingua e Letteratura Italiana

RA, Romanistische Arbeitshefte, Tübingen, Niemeyer

RA, Revista Agustiniana
RAA, Rendiconti dell'Accademia di Archeologia, Lettere e Belle Arti
RABM, Revista de Archivos, Bibliotecas y Museos
RAct, Regards sur l'Actualité
Rad, Rad Jugoslavenske akademije znanosti i umjetnosti
RAE, Real Academia Española
RAfL, Research in African Literatures
RAL, Revista Argentina de Lingüística
RAN, Regards sur l'Afrique du Nord
RANL, Rendiconti dell'Accademia Nazionale dei Lincei, Classe di scienze morali, storiche e filologiche, serie IX
RAPL, Revista da Academia Paulista de Letras, São Paulo
RAR, Renaissance and Reformation
RAS, Rassegna degli Archivi di Stato
RB, Revue Bénédictine
RBC, Research Bibliographies and Checklists, London, Grant & Cutler
RBDSL, Regensburger Beiträge zur deutschen Sprach- und Literaturwissenschaft, Frankfurt–Berne, Lang
RBG, Reclams de Bearn et Gasconha
RBGd, Rocznik Biblioteki Gdańskiej PAN (Libri Gedanenses)
RBKr, Rocznik Biblioteki PAN w Krakowie
RBL, Revista Brasileira de Lingüística
RBLL, Revista Brasileira de Lingua e Literatura
RBN, Revista da Biblioteca Nacional
RBPH, Revue Belge de Philologie et d'Histoire
RC, Le Ragioni Critiche
RCat, Revista de Catalunya
RČAV, Rozpravy Československé akademie věd, Prague, ČSAV
RCB, Revista de Cultura Brasileña
RCCM, Rivista di Cultura Classica e Medioevale
RCEH, Revista Canadiense de Estudios Hispánicos

RCEN, Revue Canadienne d'Études Néerlandaises

RCF, Review of Contemporary Fiction

RCL, Revista Chilena de Literatura

RCLL, Revista de Crítica Literaria Latino-Americana

RCo, Revue de Comminges

RCSF, Rivista Critica di Storia della Filosofia

RCVS, Rassegna di Cultura e Vita Scolastica

RD, Revue Drômoise: archéologie, histoire, géographie

RDE, Recherches sur Diderot et sur l'"Encyclopédie'

RDM, Revue des Deux Mondes

RDsS, Recherches sur le XVIIe Siècle

RDTP, Revista de Dialectología y Tradiciones Populares

RE, Revista de Espiritualidad

REC, Revista de Estudios del Caribe

RedLet, Red Letters

REE, Revista de Estudios Extremeños

REEI, Revista del Instituto Egipcio de Estudios Islámicos, Madrid

REH, Revista de Estudios Hispánicos, Washington University, St Louis

REHisp, Revista de Estudios Hispánicos, Puerto Rico

REI, Revue des Études Italiennes

REJ, Revista de Estudios de Juventud

REL, Revue des Études Latines

RELA, Revista Española de Lingüística Aplicada

RelCL, Religion in Communist Lands

RELI, Rassegna Europea di Letteratura Italiana

RELing, Revista Española de Lingüística, Madrid

RelLit, Religious Literature

ReMS, Renaissance and Modern Studies

RenD, Renaissance Drama

RenP, Renaissance Papers

RenR, Renaissance and Reformation

RenS, Renaissance Studies

RES, Review of English Studies

RESEE, Revue des Études Sud-Est Européennes

RESS, Revue Européenne des Sciences Sociales et Cahiers Vilfredo Pareto

RevA, Revue d'Allemagne

RevAl, Revista de l'Alguer

RevAR, Revue des Amis de Ronsard

RevAuv, Revue d'Auvergne, Clermont-Ferrand

RevEL, Revista de Estudos da Linguagem, Faculdade de Letras, Universidade Federal de Minas Gerais

RevF, Revista de Filología

RevHA, Revue de la Haute-Auvergne

RevG, Revista de Girona

RevIb, Revista Iberoamericana

RevL, Revista Lusitana

RevLM, Revista de Literatura Medieval

RevLR, Revista do Livro

RevO, La Revista Occitana, Montpellier

RevP, Revue PArole, Université de Mons-Hainault

RevPF, Revista Portuguesa de Filosofia

RevR, Revue Romane

RF, Romanische Forschungen

RFe, Razón y Fe

RFE, Revista de Filología Española

RFHL, Revue Française d'Histoire du Livre

RFLSJ, Revista de Filosofía y Lingüística de San José, Costa Rica

RFLUL, Revista da Faculdade de Letras da Universidade de Lisboa

RFLUP, Revista da Faculdade de Letras da Universidade do Porto

RFN, Rivisti di Filosofia Neoscolastica

RFo, Ricerca Folklorica

RFP, Recherches sur le Français Parlé

RFR, Revista de Filología Románica

RFr, Revue Frontenac

RG, Recherches Germaniques

RGand, Romanica Gandensia

RGCC, Revue du Gévaudan, des Causses et des Cévennes

RGG, Rivista di Grammatica
　　Generativa
RGI, Revue Germanique
　　Internationale
RGL, Reihe Germanistische
　　Linguistik, Tübingen, Niemeyer
RGo, Romanica Gothoburgensia
RGT, Revista Galega de Teatro
RH, Reihe Hanser, Munich,
　　Hanser
RH, Revue Hebdomadaire
RHA, Revista de Historia de
　　America
RHAM, Revue Historique et
　　Archéologique du Maine
RHCS, Rocznik Historii
　　Czasopiśmiennictwa Polskiego
RHDFE, Revue Historique de Droit
　　Français et Étranger
RHE, Revue d'Histoire
　　Ecclésiastique
RHEF, Revue d'Histoire de l'Église
　　de France
RHel, Romanica Helvetica,
　　Tübingen and Basle, Francke
RHFB, Rapports — Het Franse
　　Boek
RHI, Revista da Historia das Ideias
RHis, Revue Historique
RHL, Reihe Hanser
　　Literaturkommentare, Munich,
　　Hanser
RHLF, Revue d'Histoire Littéraire
　　de la France
RHLP, Revista de História Literária
　　de Portugal
RHM, Revista Hispánica Moderna
RHMag, Revue d'Histoire
　　Maghrébine
RHMC, Revue d'Histoire Moderne
　　et Contemporaine
RHPR, Revue d'Histoire et de
　　Philosophie Religieuses
RHR, Réforme, Humanisme,
　　Renaissance
RHRel, Revue de l'Histoire des
　　Religions
RHS, Revue Historique de la
　　Spiritualité
RHSc, Revue d'Histoire des
　　Sciences
RHSt, Ricarda Huch. Studien zu
　　ihrem Leben und Werk
RHT, Revue d'Histoire du Théâtre

RHTe, Revue d'Histoire des Textes
RI, Rassegna Iberistica
RIA, Rivista Italiana di Acustica
RIa, Русский язык
RIAB, Revista Interamericana de
　　Bibliografía
RIaR, Русский язык за рубежом
RICC, Revue Itinéraires et Contacts
　　de Culture
RICP, Revista del Instituto de
　　Cultura Puertorriqueña
RicSl, Ricerche Slavistiche
RID, Rivista Italiana di
　　Dialettologia
RIE, Revista de Ideas Estéticas
RIEB, Revista do Instituto de
　　Estudos Brasileiros
RIL, Rendiconti dell'Istituto
　　Lombardo
RILA, Rassegna Italiana di
　　Linguistica Applicata
RILCE, Revista del Instituto de
　　Lengua y Cultura Españoles
RILP, Revista Internacional da
　　Língua Portuguesa
RIM, Rivista Italiana di Musicologia
RIndM, Revista de Indias
RInv, Revista de Investigación
RIO, Revue Internationale
　　d'Onomastique
RIOn, Rivista Italiana di
　　Onomastica
RIP, Revue Internationale de
　　Philosophie
RIS, Revue de l'Institut de
　　Sociologie, Université Libre,
　　Brussels
RiS, Ricerche Storiche
RITL, Revista de Istorie şi Teorie
　　Literară, Bucharest
RivF, Rivista di Filosofia
RivL, Rivista di Linguistica
RJ, Romanistisches Jahrbuch
RKHlit, Rocznik Komisji
　　Historycznoliterackiej PAN
RKJŁ, Rozprawy Komisji Językowej
　　Łódzkiego Towarzystwa
　　Naukowego
RKJW, Rozprawy Komisji
　　Językowej Wrocławskiego
　　Towarzystwa Naukowego
RLA, Romance Languages Annual
RLaR, Revue des Langues Romanes

RLB, Recueil Linguistique de Bratislava

RLC, Revue de Littérature Comparée

RLD, Revista de Llengua i Dret

RLet, Revista de Letras

RLettI, Rivista di Letteratura Italiana

RLF, Revista de Literatura Fantástica

RLFRU, Recherches de Linguistique Française et Romane d'Utrecht

RLH, Revista de Literatura Hispanoamericana

RLI, Rassegna della Letteratura Italiana

RLib, Rivista dei Libri

RLing, Russian Linguistics

RLiR, Revue de Linguistique Romane

RLit, Revista de Literatura

RLJ, Russian Language Journal

RLLCGV, Revista de Lengua y Literatura Catalana, Gallega y Vasca, Madrid

RLLR, Romance Literature and Linguistics Review

RLM, Revista de Literaturas Modernas, Cuyo

RLMC, Rivista di Letterature Moderne e Comparate

RLMed, Revista de Literatura Medieval

RLMod, Revue des Lettres Modernes

RLModCB, Revue des Lettres Modernes. Carnets Bibliographiques

RLSer, Revista de Literatura Ser, Puerto Rico

RLSL, Revista de Lingvisticǎ şi Ştiinţǎ Literarǎ

RLT, Russian Literature Triquarterly

RLTA, Revista de Lingüística Teórica y Aplicada

RLV, Revue des Langues Vivantes

RLVin, Recherches Linguistiques de Vincennes

RM, Romance Monograph Series, University, Mississippi

RM, Remate de Males

RMAL, Revue du Moyen Age Latin

RMar, Revue Marivaux

RMEH, Revista Marroquí de Estudios Hispánicos

RMH, Recherches sur le Monde Hispanique au XIXᵉ Siècle

RMM, Revue de Métaphysique et de Morale

RMRLL, Rocky Mountain Review of Language and Literature

RMS, Reading Medieval Studies

RNC, Revista Nacional de Cultura, Carácas

RNDWSPK, Rocznik Naukowo-Dydaktyczny WSP w Krakowie

RO, Revista de Occidente

RoczH, Roczniki Humanistyczne Katolickiego Uniw. Lubelskiego

RoczSl, Rocznik Slawistyczny

ROl, Rossica Olomucensia

RoM, Rowohlts Monographien, Reinbek, Rowohlt

RomGG, Romanistik in Geschichte und Gegenwart

ROMM, Revue de L'Occident Musulman et de la Méditerranée

RoN, Romance Notes

RoQ, Romance Quarterly

RORD, Research Opportunities in Renaissance Drama

RoS, Romance Studies

RoSl, Роднае слова

RP, Радянський письменник

RP, Revista de Portugal

RPA, Revue de Phonétique Appliquée

RPac, Revue du Pacifique

RPC, Revue Pédagogique et Culturelle de l'AVEP

RPF, Revista Portuguesa de Filologia

RPFE, Revue Philosophique de la France et de l'Étranger

RPh, Romance Philology

RPL, Revue Philosophique de Louvain

RPl, Río de la Plata

RPLit, Res Publica Litterarum

RPP, Romanticism Past and Present

RPr, Raison Présente

RPS, Revista Paraguaya de Sociologia

RPyr, Recherches pyrénéennes, Toulouse

RQ, Renaissance Quarterly

RQL, Revue Québécoise de Linguistique
RR, Romanic Review
RRe, Русская речь
RRL, Revue Roumaine de Linguistique
RRou, Revue du Rouergue
RS, Reihe Siegen, Heidelberg, Winter
RS, Revue de Synthèse
RSC, Rivista di Studi Canadesi
RSCI, Rivista di Storia della Chiesa in Italia
RSEAV, Revue de la Société des enfants et amis de Villeneuve-de-Berg
RSF, Rivista di Storia della Filosofia
RSH, Revue des Sciences Humaines
RSh, Радянська школа
RSI, Rivista Storica Italiana
RSJb, Reinhold Schneider Jahrbuch
RSL, Rusycystyczne Studia Literaturoznawcze
RSl, Revue des Études Slaves
RSLR, Rivista di Storia e Letteratura Religiose
RSPT, Revue des Sciences Philosophiques et Théologiques
RSR, Rassegna Storica del Risorgimento
RSSR, Rivista di Storia Sociale e Religiosa
RST, Rassegna Storica Toscana
RSt, Research Studies
RStI, Rivista di Studi Italiani
RT, Revue du Tarn
RTAM, Recherches de Théologie Ancienne et Médiévale
RTLiM, Rocznik Towarzystwa Literackiego im. Adama Mickiewicza
RTr, Recherches et Travaux, Université de Grenoble
RTUG, Recherches et Travaux de l'Université de Grenoble III
RUB, Revue de l'Université de Bruxelles
RUC, Revista de la Universidad Complutense
RuLit, Ruch Literacki
RUM, Revista de la Universidad de Madrid
RUMex, Revista de la Universidad de México

RUOt, Revue de l'Université d'Ottawa
RUS, Rice University Studies
RusH, Russian History
RusL, Русская литература, ПД, Leningrad
RusM, Русская мысль
RusMed, Russia Medievalis
RusR, Russian Review
RUW, Rozprawy Uniwersytetu Warsawskiego, Warsaw
RVB, Rheinische Vierteljahrsblätter
RVF, Revista Valenciana de Filología
RVi, Revue du Vivarais
RVQ, Romanica Vulgaria Quaderni
RVV, Romanische Versuche und Vorarbeiten, Bonn U.P.
RVVig, Reihe der Villa Vigoni, Tübingen, Niemeyer
RyF, Razón y Fe
RZLG, Romanistische Zeitschrift für Literaturgeschichte
RZSF, Radovi Zavoda za slavensku filologiju

SA, Studien zum Althochdeutschen, Göttingen, Vandenhoeck & Ruprecht
SAB, South Atlantic Bulletin
Sac, Sacris Erudiri
SAG, Stuttgarter Arbeiten zur Germanistik, Stuttgart, Heinz
SAH, Studies in American Humour
SANU, Srpska akademija nauka i umetnosti
SAOB, Svenska Akademiens Ordbok
SAQ, South Atlantic Quarterly
SAR, South Atlantic Review
SAS, Studia Academica Slovaca
SaS, Slovo a slovesnost
SASc, Studia Anthroponymica Scandinavica
SATF, Société des Anciens Textes Français
SAV, Slovenská akadémia vied
SAVL, Studien zur allgemeinen und vergleichenden Literaturwissenschaft, Stuttgart, Metzler
SB, Slavistische Beiträge, Munich, Sagner
SB, Studies in Bibliography

SBAW, Sitzungsberichte der Bayerischen Akad. der Wissenschaften, phil-hist. Kl., Munich, Beck

SBL, Saarbrücker Beiträge zur Literaturwissenschaft, St. Ingbert, Röhrig

SBL, Старобългарска литература

SBR, Swedish Book Review

SBVS, Saga-Book of the Viking Society

SC, Studia Celtica, The Bulletin of the Board of Celtic Studies

SCB, Skrifter utgivna av Centrum för barnkulturforskning, Stockholm U.P.

SCC, Studies in Comparative Communism

SCen, The Seventeenth Century

SCES, Sixteenth Century Essays and Studies, Kirksville, Missouri, Sixteenth Century Journal

SCFS, Seventeenth-Century French Studies

SchG, Schriftsteller der Gegenwart, Berlin, Volk & Wissen

SchSch, Schlern-Schriften, Innsbruck, Wagner

SchwM, Schweizer Monatshefte

SCJ, Sixteenth Century Journal

SCL, Studii şi Cercetări Lingvistice

SCl, Stendhal Club

ScL, Scottish Language

ScM, Scripta Mediterranea

SCN, Seventeenth Century News

SCO, Studii şi Cercetări de Onomastică

ScO, Scriptoralia, Tübingen, Narr

SCR, Studies in Comparative Religion

ScRev, Scandinavian Review

ScSl, Scando-Slavica

ScSt, Scandinavian Studies

SD, Sprache und Dichtung, n.F., Berne, Haupt

SD, Современная драматургия.

SdA, Storia dell'Arte

SDFU, Skrifter utgivna genom Dialekt- och folkminnesarkivet i Uppsala

SDG, Studien zur deutschen Grammatik, Tübingen, Narr

SDL, Studien zur deutschen Literatur, Tübingen, Niemeyer

SDLNZ, Studien zur deutschen Literatur des 19. und 20. Jahrhunderts, Berne, Lang

SdO, Serra d'Or

SDOFU, Skrifter utgivna av Dialekt-, ortnamns- och folkminnesarkivet i Umeå

SDS, Studien zur Dialektologie in Südwestdeutschland, Marburg, Elwert

SDSp, Studien zur deutschen Sprache, Tübingen, Narr

SDv, Sprache und Datenverarbeitung

SE, Série Esludos Uberaba

SeC, Scrittura e Civiltà

SECC, Studies in Eighteenth-Century Culture

SEDES, Société d'Éditions d'Enseignement Supérieur

SEEA, Slavic and East European Arts

SEEJ, The Slavic and East European Journal

SEER, Slavonic and East European Review

SEES, Slavic and East European Studies

SEI, Società Editrice Internazionale, Turin

SELA, South Eastern Latin Americanist

SemL, Seminarios de Linguística, Universidade do Algarve, Faro

SEN, Società Editrice Napoletana, Naples

SEP, Secretaría de Educación Pública, Mexico

SeS, Serbian Studies

SEz, Съпоставително езикознание

SF, Slavistische Forschungen, Cologne — Vienna, Böhlau

SFAIEO, Section Française de l'Association Internationale d'Études Occitanes, Montpellier

SFI, Studi di Filologia Italiana

SFIS, Stanford French and Italian Studies

SFKG, Schriftenreihe der Franz–Kafka–Gesellschaft, Vienna, Braumüller

SFL, Studies in French Literature, London, Arnold

SFL, Studi di Filologia e Letteratura
SFPS, Studia z Filologii Polskiej i
 Słowiańskiej PAN
SFR, Stanford French Review
SFr, Studi Francesi
SFRS, Studia z Filologii Rosyjskiej i
 Slowiańskiej, Warsaw
SFS, Swiss-French Studies
SFUŠ, Sborník Filozofickej Fakulty
 Univerzity P. J. Šafárika, Prešov
SG, Sprache der Gegenwart,
 Düsseldorf, Schwann
SGAK, Studien zu Germanistik,
 Anglistik und Komparatistik,
 Bonn, Bouvier
SGECRN, Study Group on
 Eighteenth-Century Russia
 Newsletter
SGEL, Sociedad General Española
 de Librería
SGesch, Sprache und Geschichte,
 Stuttgart, Klett-Cotta
SGF, Stockholmer Germanistische
 Forschungen, Stockholm,
 Almqvist & Wiksell
SGG, Studia Germanica Gandensia
SGI, Studi di Grammatica Italiana
SGLL, Studies in German
 Language and Literature,
 Lewiston-Queenston-Lampeter
SGLLC, Studies in German
 Literature, Linguistics, and
 Culture, Columbia, S.C.,
 Camden House, Woodbridge,
 Boydell & Brewer
SGP, Studia Germanica
 Posnaniensia
SGS, Stanford German Studies,
 Berne, Lang
SGS, Scottish Gaelic Studies
SGU, Studia Germanistica
 Upsaliensia, Stockholm, Almqvist
 & Wiksell
SH, Slavica Helvetica, Berne, Lang
SH, Studia Hibernica
ShAn, Sharq al-Andalus
SHAW, Sitzungsberichte der
 Heidelberger Akademie der
 Wissenschaften, phil.-hist. Klasse,
 Heidelberg, Winter
SHCT, Studies in the History of
 Christian Thought, Leiden, Brill
SHPF, Société de l'Histoire du
 Protestantisme Français

SHPS, Studies in History and
 Philosophy of Science
SHR, The Scottish Historical
 Review
SI, Sprache und Information,
 Tübingen, Niemeyer
SIAA, Studi di Italianistica
 nell'Africa Australe
SiCh, Слово i час
SIDES, Société Internationale de
 Diffusion et d'Édition
 Scientifiques, Antony
SIDS, Schriften des Instituts für
 deutsche Sprache, Berlin, de
 Gruyter
Siglo XX, Siglo XX/20th Century
SILTA, Studi Italiani di Linguistica
 Teorica ed Applicata
SiN, Sin Nombre
SINSU, Skrifter utgivna av
 institutionen för nordiska språk
 vid Uppsala universitet, Uppsala
 U.P.
SIR, Stanford Italian Review
SIsp, Studi Ispanici
SISSD, Società Italiana di Studi sul
 Secolo XVIII
SJLŠ, Slovenský jazyk a literatúra v
 škole
SkSt, Skandinavistische Studien
SKZ, Srpska Književna Zadruga,
 Belgrade
SL, Sammlung Luchterhand,
 Darmstadt, Luchterhand
SL, Studia Linguistica
SLÅ, Svensk Lärarföreningens
 Årsskrift
SlaG, Slavica Gandensia
SlaH, Slavica Helsingensia
SlaL, Slavica Lundensia
SlavFil, Славянска филология,
 Sofia
SlavH, Slavica Hierosolymitana
SlavLit, Славянските литератури
 в България
SlavRev, Slavistična revija
SlaW, Slavica Wratislaviensia
SLeg, Studium Legionense
SLeI, Studi di Lessicografia Italiana
SLESPO, Suplemento Literário do
 Estado de São Paulo
SLF, Studi di Letteratura Francese
SLG, Studia Linguistica
 Germanica, Berlin, de Gruyter

SLI, Società di Linguistica Italiana

SLI, Studi Linguistici Italiani

SLIGU, Skrifter utgivna av
Litteraturvetenskapliga
institutionen vid Göteborgs
universitet, Gothenburg U.P.

SLILU, Skrifter utgivna av
Litteraturvetenskapliga
institutionen vid Lunds
universitet, Lund U.P.

SLit, Schriften zur
Literaturwissenschaft, Berlin,
Duncker & Humblot

SLit, Slovenská literatúra

SLitR, Stanford Literature Review

SLIUU, Skrifter utgivna av
Litteraturvetenskapliga
institutionen vid Uppsala
universitet, Uppsala U.P.

SLK, Schwerpunkte Linguistik und
Kommunikationswissenschaft

SLL, Skrifter utg. genom
Landsmålsarkivet i Lund

SLM, Studien zur Literatur der
Moderne, Bonn, Bouvier

SlN, Slovenský národopis

SLO, Slavica Lublinensia et
Olomucensia

SlO, Slavia Orientalis

SlOc, Slavia Occidentalis

SlOth, Slavica Othinensia

SlPN, Slovenské pedagogické
nakladateľstvo

SlPoh, Slovenské pohľady

SlPr, Slavica Pragensia

SLPS, Studia Linguistica Polono-
Slovaca

SLR, Second Language Research

SLS, Studies in the Linguistic
Sciences

SlSb, Slezský sborník

SlSl, Slavica Slovaca

SlSp, Slovenský spisovateľ

SLRev, Southern Literary Review

SLu, Studia Lulliana

SLWU, Sprach und Literatur in
Wissenschaft und Unterricht

SM, Sammlung Metzler, Stuttgart,
Metzler

SM, Studi Medievali

SMC, Studies in Medieval Culture

SME, Schöninghs mediävistische
Editionen, Paderborn, Schöningh

SMer, Студенческий меридиан

SMGL, Studies in Modern German
Literature, Berne – Frankfurt –
New York, Lang

SMLS, Strathclyde Modern
Language Studies

SMRT, Studies in Medieval and
Reformation Thought, Leiden,
Brill

SMS, Sewanee Medieval Studies

SMu, Советский музей

SMV, Studi Mediolatini e Volgari

SN, Studia Neophilologica

SNL, Sveučilišna naklada Liber,
Zagreb

SNM, Sborník Národního muzea

SNov, Seara Nova

SNTL, Státní nakladatelství
technické literatury

SÖAW, Sitzungsberichte der
Österreichischen Akademie der
Wissenschaften, phil.-hist. Klasse

SoCR, South Central Review

SOH, Studia Onomastica
Helvetica, Arbon, Eurotext:
Historisch-Archäologischer
Verlag

SoK, Sprog og Kultur

SopL, Sophia Linguistica, Tokyo

SoRA, Southern Review, Adelaide

SoRL, Southern Review, Louisiana

SOU, Skrifter utgivna genom
Ortnamnsarkivet i Uppsala

SP, Sammlung Profile, Bonn,
Bouvier

SP, Studies in Philology

SPat, Studi Patavini

SpC, Speech Communication

SPCT, Studi e Problemi di Critica
Testuale

SPES, Studio per Edizioni Scelte,
Florence

SPFB, Sborník Pedagogické fakulty
v Brně

SPFFBU, Sborník prací Filosofické
fakulty Brněnské Univerzity

SPFHK, Sborník Pedagogické
fakulty, Hradec Králové

SPFO, Sborník Pedagogické fakulty,
Ostrava

SPFOl, Sborník Pedagogické fakulty,
Olomouc

SPFUK, Sborník Pedagogické
fakulty Univerzity Karlovy,
Prague

SPGS, Scottish Papers in Germanic Studies, Glasgow
SPh, Studia philologica, Olomouc
SPi, Serie Piper, Munich, Piper
SPIEL, Siegener Periodicum zur Internationalen Empirischen Literaturwissenschaft
SPK, Studia nad polszczyzną kresową, Wrocław
SpLit, Sprache und Literatur
SpMod, Spicilegio Moderno, Pisa
SPN, Státní pedagogické nakladatelství
SPol, Studia Polonistyczne
SPR, Slavistic Printings and Reprintings, The Hague, Mouton
SpR, Spunti e Ricerche
SPRF, Société de Publications Romanes et Françaises, Geneva, Droz
SPS, Specimina Philologiae Slavicae, Munich, Otto Sagner
SPS, Studia Philologica Salmanticensia
SPSO, Studia Polono–Slavica–Orientalia. Acta Litteraria
SpSt, Spanish Studies
SPUAM, Studia Polonistyczna Uniwersytetu Adama Mickiewicza, Poznań
SR, Slovenská reč
SRAZ, Studia Romanica et Anglica Zagrabiensia
SRev, Slavic Review
SRF, Studi e Ricerche Francescane
SRL, Studia Romanica et Linguistica, Frankfurt, Lang
SRLF, Saggi e Ricerche di Letteratura Francese
SRo, Studi Romanzi
SRom, Studi Romeni
SRoP, Studia Romanica Posnaniensia
SRP, Studia Rossica Posnaniensia
SRU, Studia Romanica Upsaliensia
SS, Symbolae Slavicae, Frankfurt–Berne–Cirencester, Lang
SS, Syn og Segn
SSBI, Skrifter utgivna av Svenska barnboksinstitutet
SSB, Strenna Storica Bolognese
SSCJ, Southern Speech Communication Journal

SSDSP, Società Savonese di Storia Patria
SSE, Studi di Storia dell'Educazione
SSF, Studies in Short Fiction
SSFin, Studia Slavica Finlandensia
SSGL, Studies in Slavic and General Linguistics, Amsterdam, Rodopi
SSH, Studia Slavica Academiae Scientiarum Hungaricae
SSL, Studi e Saggi Linguistici
SSLF, Skrifter utgivna av Svenska Litteratursällskapet i Finland
SSLP, Studies in Slavic Literature and Poetics, Amsterdam, Rodopi
SSLS, Studi Storici Luigi Simeoni
SSMP, Stockholm Studies in Modern Philology
SSPHS, Society for Spanish and Portuguese Historical Studies, Millersville
SSS, Stanford Slavic Studies
SSSAS, Society of Spanish and Spanish-American Studies, Boulder, Colorado
SSSlg, Sagners Slavistische Sammlung, Munich, Sagner
SSSN, Skrifter utgivna av Svenska språknämnden
SSSP, Stockholm Studies in Scandinavian Philology
SST, Sprache — System und Tätigkeit, Frankfurt, Lang
SSt, Slavic Studies, Hokkaido
ST, Suhrkamp Taschenbuch, Frankfurt, Suhrkamp
ST, Studi Testuali, Alessandria, Edizioni dell'Orso
StB, Studi sul Boccaccio
STC, Studies in the Twentieth Century
StCJ, Studia Celtica Japonica
STCL, Studies in Twentieth Century Literature
StCL, Studies in Canadian Literature
StCrit, Strumenti Critici
StD, Studi Danteschi
StF, Studie Francescani
StFil, Studia Filozoficzne
STFM, Société des Textes Français Modernes
StG, Studi Germanici
StGol, Studi Goldoniani

StH, Studies in the Humanities
StI, Studi Italici, Kyoto
StIt, Studi Italiani
StL, Studium Linguistik
StLa, Studies in Language, Amsterdam
StLI, Studi di Letteratura Ispano-Americana
StLIt, Studi Latini e Italiani
StLM, Studies in the Literary Imagination
StLo, Studia Logica
StM, Studies in Medievalism
STM, Suhrkamp Taschenbuch Materialien, Frankfurt, Suhrkamp
STML, Studies on Themes and Motifs in Literature, New York, Lang
StMon, Studia Monastica
StMus, Studie Musicali
StMy, Studia Mystica
StN, Studi Novecenteschi
StNF, Studier i Nordisk Filologi
StO, Studium Ovetense
StP, Studi Piemontesi
StPet, Studi Petrarcheschi
StR, Studie o rukopisech
StRLLF, Studi e Ricerche di Letteratura e Linguistica Francese
StRo, Studi Romani
StRom, Studies in Romanticism
StRu, Studia Russica, Budapest
StS, Studi Storici
StSec, Studi Secenteschi
StSk, Studia Skandinavica
StSet, Studi Settecenteschi
STSL, Studien und Texte zur Sozialgeschichte der Literatur, Tübingen, Niemeyer
StT, Studi Tassiani
STUF, Sprachtypologie und Universalienforschung
StV, Studies on Voltaire and the 18th Century
STW, Suhrkamp Taschenbücher Wissenschaft, Frankfurt, Suhrkamp
StZ, Sprache im technischen Zeitalter
SU, Studi Urbinati
SUBBP, Studia Universitatis Babeş-Bolyai, Philologia, Cluj

SUDAM, Editorial Sudamericana, Buenos Aires
SuF, Sinn und Form
SUP, Spisy University J. E. Purkyně, Brno
SupEz, Съпоставително езикознание, Sofia
SV, Studi Veneziani
SZ, Studia Zamorensia

TAL, Travaux d'Archéologie Limousine, Limoges
TAm, The Americas, Bethesda
TAPS, Transactions of the American Philosophical Society
TB, Tempo Brasileiro
TBL, Tübinger Beiträge zur Linguistik, Tübingen, Narr
TC, Texto Crítico
TCBS, Transactions of the Cambridge Bibliographical Society
TCERFM, Travaux du Centre d'Études et de Recherches sur François Mauriac, Bordeaux
TCL, Twentieth-Century Literature
TCLN, Travaux du Cercle Linguistique de Nice
TCWAAS, Transactions of the Cumberland and Westmorland Antiquarian and Archaeological Society
TD, Teksty Drugie
TDC, Textes et Documents pour la Classe
TEC, Teresianum Ephemerides Carmeliticae
TECC, Textos i Estudis de Cultura Catalana, Curial — Publicacions de l'Abadia de Montserrat, Barcelona
TeK, Text und Kontext
TELK, Trouvaillen — Editionen zur Literatur- und Kulturgeschichte, Berne, Lang
TeN, Terminologies Nouvelles
TeSt, Teatro e Storia
TE(XVIII), Textos y Estudios del Siglo XVIII
TF, Texte zur Forschung, Darmstadt, Wissenschaftliche Buchgesellschaft
TFN, Texte der Frühen Neuzeit, Frankfurt am Main, Keip

TGLSK, Theorie und Geschichte der Literatur und der Schönen Künste, Munich, Fink

TGSI, Transactions of the Gaelic Society of Inverness

THL, Theory and History of Literature, Manchester U.P.

THM, Textos Hispánicos Modernos, Barcelona, Labor

THR, Travaux d'Humanisme et Renaissance, Geneva, Droz

THSC, Transactions of the Honourable Society of Cymmrodorion

TI, Le Texte et l'Idée

TidLit, Tidskrift för Litteraturvetenskap

TILAS, Travaux de l'Institut d'Études Latino-Américaines de l'Université de Strasbourg

TILL, Travaux de l'Institut de Linguistique de Lund

TJ, Theatre Journal

TK, Text und Kritik, Munich

TKS, Търновска книжевна школа, Sofia

TL, Theoretical Linguistics

TLF, Textes Littéraires Français, Geneva, Droz

TLit, Travaux de Littérature

TLP, Travaux de Linguistique et de Philologie

TLQ, Travaux de Linguistique Québécoise

TLTL, Teaching Language Through Literature

TM, Les Temps Modernes

TMJb, Thomas Mann-Jahrbuch

TMo, O Tempo e o Modo

TMS, Thomas Mann–Studien, Berne, Francke

TN, Theatre Notebook

TNA, Tijdschrift voor Nederlands en Afrikaans

TNT, Towarzystwo Naukowe w Toruniu

TODL, Труды Отдела древнерусской литературы Института русской литературы АН СССР

TP, Textual Practice

TPa, Torre de Papel

TPS, Transactions of the Philological Society

TQ, Theatre Quarterly

TR, Телевидение и радиовещание

TravL, Travaux de Linguistique, Luxembourg

TRCTL, Texte-Revue de Critique et de Théorie Littéraire

TRI, Theatre Research International

TrK, Трезвость и культура

TrL, Travaux de Linguistique

TrLit, Translation and Literature

TRS, The Transactions of the Radnorshire Society

TS, Theatre Survey

TSC, Treballs de Sociolingüística Catalana

TSDL, Tübinger Studien zur deutschen Literatur, Frankfurt, Lang

TSJ, Tolstoy Studies Journal

TSL, Trierer Studien zur Literatur, Frankfurt, Lang

TSLL, Texas Studies in Literature and Language

TSM, Texte des späten Mittelalters und der frühen Neuzeit, Berlin, Schmidt

TsNTL, Tijdschrift voor Nederlandse Taal- en Letterkunde

TSRLL, Tulane Studies in Romance Languages and Literature

TsSk, Tijdschrift voor Skandinavistiek

TsSV, Tijdschrift voor de Studie van de Verlichting

TSWL, Tulsa Studies in Women's Literature

TT, Tekst en Tijd, Nijmegen, Alfa

TT, Travail Théâtral

TTAS, Twayne Theatrical Arts Series, Boston–New York

TTG, Texte und Textgeschichte, Tübingen, Niemeyer

TTr, Terminologie et Traduction

TUGS, Texte und Untersuchungen zur Germanistik und Skandinavistik, Frankfurt, Lang

TVS, Theorie und Vermittlung der Sprache, Frankfurt, Lang

TWAS, Twayne's World Authors Series, Boston–New York

TWQ, Third World Quarterly

UAB, Universitat Autònoma de Barcelona
UAC, Universidad de Antioquia, Colombia
UAM, Uniwersytet Adama Mickiewicza, Poznań
UB, Universal-Bibliothek, Stuttgart, Reclam
UBL, Universal-Bibliothek, Leipzig, Reclam
UCPL, University of California Publications in Linguistics
UCPMP, University of California Publications in Modern Philology
UDL, Untersuchungen zur deutschen Literaturgeschichte, Tübingen, Niemeyer
UDR, University of Dayton Review
UFPB, Universidade Federal da Paraiba
UFRGS, Universidade Federal do Rio Grande do Sul (Brazil)
UFRJ, Universidade Federal do Rio de Janeiro
UFSC, Universidade Federal de Santa Catarina
UGE, Union Générale d'Éditions
UGFGP, University of Glasgow French and German Publications
UL, Українське літературознавство, Lvov U.P.
UM, Українська мова і література в школі
UMCS, Uniwersytet Marii Curie-Skłodowskiej, Lublin
UMov, Українське мовазнавство
UNAM, Universidad Nacional Autónoma de Mexico
UNC, Univ. of North Carolina
UNCSGL, University of North Carolina Studies in Germanic Languages and Literatures, Chapel Hill
UNED, Universidad Nacional de Enseñanza a Distancia
UNESP, Universidade Estadual de São Paulo
UNMH, University of Nottingham Monographs in the Humanities
UPP, University of Pennsylvania Press, Philadelphia

UQ, Ukrainian Quarterly
UR, Umjetnost riječi
USCFLS, University of South Carolina French Literature Series
USFLQ, University of South Florida Language Quarterly
USH, Umeå Studies in the Humanities, Stockholm, Almqvist & Wiksell International
USLL, Utah Studies in Literature and Linguistics, Berne, Lang
USP, Universidade de São Paulo
UTB, Uni-Taschenbücher
UTET, Unione Tipografico-Editrice Torinese
UTPLF, Università di Torino, Pubblicazioni della Facoltà di Lettere e Filosofia
UTQ, University of Toronto Quarterly
UVAN, Українська Вільна Академія Наук, Winnipeg
UVWPL, University of Venice Working Papers in Linguistics
UWCASWC, The University of Wales Centre for Advanced Studies in Welsh and Celtic
UZLU, Ученые записки Ленинградского университета

VAM, Vergessene Autoren der Moderne, Siegen U.P.
VAS, Vorträge und Abhandlungen zur Slavistik, Giessen, Schmitz
VASSLOI, Veröffentlichungen der Abteilung für Slavische Sprachen und Literaturen des Osteuropa–Instituts (Slavistiches Seminar) an der Freien Universität Berlin
VB, Vestigia Bibliae
VBDU, Веснік Беларускага дзяржаўнага ўніверсітэта імя У. І. Леніна. Серыя IV
VCT, Les Voies de la Création Théâtrale
VDASD, Veröffentlichungen der Deutschen Akademie für Sprache und Dichtung, Darmstadt, Luchterhand
VF, Вопросы философии
VGBIL, Всесоюзная государственная библиотека иностранной литературы

VH, Vida Hispánica,
  Wolverhampton
VHis, Verba Hispanica
VI, Военно издателство
VI, Voix et Images
VIa, Вопросы языкознания
VIN, Veröffentlichungen des
  Instituts für niederländische
  Philologie, Erftstadt, Lukassen
ViSH, Вища школа
VIst, Вопросы истории
Vit, Вітчизна
VKP, Всесоюзная книжная
  палата
VL, Вопросы литературы
VLet, Voz y Letras
VM, Время и мы, New York —
  Paris — Jerusalem
VMKA, Verslagen en Mededelingen,
  Koninklijke Academie voor
  Nederlandse Taal- en
  Letterkunde
VMUF, Вестник Московского
  университета. Серия IX,
  филология
VMUFil, Вестник Московского
  университета. Серия VII,
  философия
Voz, Возрождение
VP, Встречи с прошлым, Moscow
VPen, Vita e Pensiero
VR, Vox Romanica
VRKhD, Вестник Русского
  христианского движения
VRL, Вопросы русской
  литературы
VRM, Volkskultur am Rhein und
  Maas
VS, Вопросы семантики
VSAV, Vydavateľstvo Slovenskej
  akadémie vied
VSh, Вышэйшая школа
VSh, Визвольний шлях
VSPU, Вестник Санкт-
  Петербургского университета
VSSH, Вечерняя средняя школа
VV, Византийский временник
VVM, Vlastivědný věstník moravský
VVSh, Вестник высшей школы
VWGÖ, Verband der
  wissenschaftlichen Gesellschaften
  Österreichs
VySh, Вища школа
VysSh, Высшая школа

VyV, Verdad y Vida
VZ, Vukova zadužbina, Belgrade

WAB, Wolfenbütteler Arbeiten zur
  Barockforschung, Wiesbaden,
  Harrassowitz
WADL, Wiener Arbeiten zur
  deutschen Literatur, Vienna,
  Braumüller
WAGAPH, Wiener Arbeiten zur
  germanischen Altertumskunde
  und Philologie, Vienna, Halosar
WAiF, Wydawnictwa Artystyczne i
  Filmowe, Warsaw
WaT, Wagenbachs
  Taschenbücherei, Berlin,
  Wagenbach
WB, Weimarer Beiträge
WBDP, Würzburger Beiträge zur
  deutschen Philologie, Würzburg,
  Königshausen & Neumann
WBG, Wissenschaftliche
  Buchgesellschaft, Darmstadt
WBN, Wolfenbütteler Barock-
  Nachrichten
WF, Wege der Forschung,
  Darmstadt, Wissenschaftliche
  Buchgesellschaft
WGCR, West Georgia College
  Review
WGY, Women in German Yearbook
WHNDL, Würzburger
  Hochschulschriften zur neueren
  Deutschen Literaturgeschichte,
  Frankfurt, Lang
WHR, The Welsh History Review
WIFS, Women in French Studies
WKJb, Wissenschaftskolleg.
  Institute for Advanced Study,
  Berlin. Jahrbuch
WL, Wydawnictwo Literackie,
  Cracow
WŁ, Wydawnictwo Łódzkie
WLub, Wydawnictwo Lubelskie
WLT, World Literature Today
WM, Wissensliteratur im
  Mittelalter, Wiesbaden, Reichert
WNB, Wolfenbütteler Notizen zur
  Buchgeschichte
WNT, Wydawnictwa Naukowo-
  Techniczne
WoB, Wolfenbütteler Beiträge
WP, Wiedza Powszechna, Warsaw

WPEL, Working Papers in
Educational Linguistics
WPFG, Working Papers in
Functional Grammar,
Amsterdam U.P.
WRM, Wolfenbütteler Renaissance
Mitteilungen
WS, Wort und Sinn
WSA, Wolfenbütteler Studien zur
Aufklärung, Tübingen, Niemeyer
WSiP, Wydawnictwa Szkolne i
Pedagogiczne, Warsaw
WSJ, Wiener Slavistisches Jahrbuch
WSl, Die Welt der Slaven
WSlA, Wiener Slawistischer
Almanach
WSP, Wyższa Szkoła Pedagogiczna
WSp, Word and Spirit
WSPRRNDFP, Wyższa Szkoła
Pedagogiczna w Rzeszowie.
Rocznik Naukowo-Dydaktyczny.
Filologia Polska
WuW, Welt und Wort
WUW, Wydawnictwo Uniwersytetu
Wrocławskiego
WW, Wirkendes Wort
WWAG, Woman Writers in the Age
of Goethe
WWE, Welsh Writing in English. A
Yearbook of Critical Essays
WZHUB, Wissenschaftliche
Zeitschrift der Humboldt-
Universität, Berlin: gesellschafts-
und sprachwissenschaftliche
Reihe
WZPHP, Wissenschaftliche
Zeitschrift der pädagogischen
Hochschule Potsdam.
Gesellschafts- und
sprachwissenschaftliche Reihe
WZUG, Wissenschaftliche
Zeitschrift der Ernst-Moritz-
Arndt- Universität Greifswald
WZUH, Wissenschaftliche
Zeitschrift der Martin-Luther-
Universität Halle-Wittenberg:
gesellschafts- und
sprachwissenschaftliche Reihe
WZUJ, Wissenschaftliche
Zeitschrift der Friedrich-Schiller-
Universität Jena/Thüringen:
gesellschafts-und
sprachwissenschaftliche Reihe

WZUL, Wissenschaftliche
Zeitschrift der Karl Marx
Universität Leipzig: gesellschafts-
und sprachwissenschaftliche
Reihe
WZUR, Wissenschaftliche
Zeitschrift der Universität
Rostock: gesellschafts- und
sprachwissenschaftliche Reihe

YaIS, Yale Italian Studies
YB, Ysgrifau Beirniadol
YCC, Yearbook of Comparative
Criticism
YCGL, Yearbook of Comparative
and General Literature
YDAMEIS, Yearbook of the Dutch
Association for Middle Eastern
and Islamic Studies
YEEP, Yale Russian and East
European Publications, New
Haven, Yale Center for
International and Area Studies
YES, Yearbook of English Studies
YFS, Yale French Studies
YIS, Yearbook of Italian Studies
YJC, Yale Journal of Criticism
YM, Yearbook of Morphology
YPL, York Papers in Linguistics
YR, Yale Review
YSGP, Yearbook. Seminar for
Germanic Philology
YSPS, The Yearbook of the Society
of Pirandello Studies
YWMLS, The Year's Work in
Modern Language Studies

ZÄAK, Zeitschrift für Ästhetik und
allgemeine Kunstwissenschaft
ZB, Zeitschrift für Balkanologie
ZBL, Zeitschrift für bayerische
Landesgeschichte
ZbS, Zbornik za slavistiku
ZCP, Zeitschrift für celtische
Philologie
ZD, Zielsprache Deutsch
ZDA, Zeitschrift für deutsches
Altertum und deutsche Literatur
ZDL, Zeitschrift für Dialektologie
und Linguistik

ZDNÖL, Zirkular.
Dokumentationsstelle für neuere österreichische Literatur
ZDP, Zeitschrift für deutsche Philologie
ZFKPhil, Zborník Filozofickej fakulty Univerzity Komenského. Philologica
ZFL, Zbornik za filologiju i lingvistiku
ZFSL, Zeitschrift für französische Sprache und Literatur
ZGB, Zagreber germanistische Beiträge
ZGer, Zeitschrift für Germanistik
ZGKS, Zeitschrift der Gesellschaft für Kanada-Studien
ZGL, Zeitschrift für germanistische Linguistik
ZGS, Zürcher germanistische Studien, Berne, Lang
ZK, Zeitschrift für Katalanistik
ZL, Zeszyty Literackie, Paris
ZMS(FL), Zbornik Matice srpske za filologiju i lingvistiku
ZMS(KJ), Zbornik Matice srpske za književnost i jezik
ZMS(Sl), Zbornik Matice srpske za slavistiku
ZNiO, Zakład Narodowy im. Ossolińskich, Wrocław
ZnS, Знание — сила
ZNTSh, Записки Наукового товариства ім. Шевченка
ZNUG, Zeszyty Naukowe Uniw. Gdańskiego, Gdańsk
ZNUJ, Zeszyty Naukowe Uniw. Jagiellońskiego, Cracow

ZNWHFR, Zeszyty Naukowe Wydziału Humanistycznego. Filologia Rosyjska
ZNWSPO, Zeszyty Naukowe Wyższej Szkoły Pedagogicznej w Opolu
ZO, Zeitschrift für Ostforschung
ZPSSlav, Zborník Pedagogickej fakulty v Prešove Univerzity Pavla Jozefa Šafárika v Košiciach-Slavistika, Bratislava
ZR, Zadarska revija
ZRAG, Записки русской академической группы в США
ZRBI, Зборник радова бизантолошког института, Belgrade
ZRL, Zagadnienia Rodzajów Literackich
ZRP, Zeitschrift für romanische Philologie
ZS, Zeitschrift für Sprachwissenschaft
ZSJ, Zápisnik slovenského jazykovedca
ZSK, Ze Skarbca Kultury
ZSL, Zeitschrift für siebenbürgische Landeskunde
ZSl, Zeitschrift für Slawistik
ZSP, Zeitschrift für slavische Philologie
ZSVS, Zborník Spolku vojvodinských slovakistov, Novi Sad
ZT, Здесь и теперь
ZV, Zeitschrift für Volkskunde
ZvV, Звезда востока
ZWL, Zeitschrift für württembergische Landesgeschichte

NAME INDEX